Jason Jeong

International POLITICS

International POLITICS

Classic and Contemporary Readings

SCOTT P. HANDLER, EDITOR
United States Military Academy

SAGE | CQPRESS
Los Angeles | London | New Delhi
Singapore | Washington DC

Los Angeles | London | New Delhi
Singapore | Washington DC

FOR INFORMATION:

CQ Press
An Imprint of SAGE Publications, Inc.
2455 Teller Road
Thousand Oaks, California 91320
E-mail: order@sagepub.com

SAGE Publications Ltd.
1 Oliver's Yard
55 City Road
London EC1Y 1SP
United Kingdom

SAGE Publications India Pvt. Ltd.
B 1/I 1 Mohan Cooperative Industrial Area
Mathura Road, New Delhi 110 044
India

SAGE Publications Asia-Pacific Pte. Ltd.
3 Church Street
#10-04 Samsung Hub
Singapore 049483

Acquisitions Editor: Elise Frasier
Production Editor: Laura Barrett
Copy Editor: Megan Granger
Typesetter: C&M Digitals (P) Ltd.
Proofreader: Laura Webb
Cover Designer: Michael Dubowe
Marketing Manager: Jonathan Mason
Permissions Editor: Sheri Gilbert

Printed in the United States of America

Library of Congress Cataloging-in-Publication Data

Handler, Scott P.

International politics : classic and contemporary readings / editor, Scott P. Handler, United States Military Academy.—First Edition.

pages cm

Includes bibliographical references and index.

ISBN 978-1-4522-6799-9 (pbk. : alk. paper) 1. International relations. I. Title.

JZ1242.H365 2013

327—dc23 2012036926

This book is printed on acid-free paper.

18 10 9 8 7 6 5 4 3

Contents

Preface

Teaching and Learning at the United States Military Academy

The mission of the United States Military Academy at West Point is

> to educate, train, and inspire the Corps of Cadets so that each graduate is a commissioned leader of character committed to the values of Duty, Honor, Country and prepared for a career of professional excellence and service to the Nation as an officer in the United States Army.

To accomplish the education component of this mission, West Point offers a classical liberal arts education. Every cadet must take 30 core courses, as well as courses required for their individual majors. Of the core courses, 16 are in the humanities and social sciences and 14 are in science, technology, engineering, and mathematics. West Point maintains this broad curriculum to teach cadets how, rather than what, to think. Upon graduation, cadets must be prepared to deal with uncertainty and be able to "anticipate and respond effectively to the uncertainties of a changing technological, social, political, and economic world."

The Department of Social Sciences at West Point, which houses the political science and economics programs, maintains responsibility for the core courses on international relations, American politics, and economics. Cadets take the American politics and economics courses their sophomore year and the international relations core course their junior year. Although the international relations course from which this book emerged is taught during the junior year at West Point, largely due to scheduling associated with the broad core curriculum requirements, this book is equally appropriate for freshmen, sophomores, and seniors at any college or university.

In designing this reader, principally for introductory courses, we sought to improve each student's critical reading and thinking ability through the use of leading classic and contemporary scholarship. That goal supports the Department of Social Sciences' long-standing commitment to stay at the cutting edge of teaching pedagogy and its pride in keeping the curriculum up-to-date with current developments in each discipline. As a teaching college, the Academy limits classes to 18 students to provide a focused and interactive learning environment, requiring faculty members to teach the core curriculum, major courses, and electives. Each of the core courses is conducted by a teaching team that instructs from a common syllabus.

Each semester, between 12 and 14 instructors teach the core international relations course to about 550 cadets at West Point. Instructors at West Point lead their lessons more as seminars than as lectures, but the design of this reader also supports international relations courses taught in a lecture format with discussion sections led by a professor or teaching assistant. While the first part of the course at West Point, theoretical traditions in international relations, generally requires more guided discussions to build the foundation for the rest of the course, professors expect cadets to come to class prepared to discuss the readings. Focusing on a seminar discussion helps transition cadets to future leaders who are agile in responding to uncertainty and anticipating changes to the political, social, and economic environments in which they will operate.

The father of the U.S. Military Academy, Sylvanus Thayer, established the teaching method used today at West Point, where students are expected to have done their reading and homework in advance of class and are instructed to apply that knowledge to different problems or issues. This method encourages cadets to engage the material and think for themselves, and it allows the faculty to serve as what General Martin Dempsey, chairman of the Joint Chiefs of Staff, calls the "guide on the side rather than the sage on the stage."

This desire at West Point to help students take ownership of their learning and thinking is no different from the goal of any other college or university that seeks to develop future contributors to, innovators within, and leaders of society, industry, and government. Students at any college or university will face the same changes to the political, social, and economic environments and will have to adapt to and anticipate them in order to succeed in their chosen professions. The "guide on the side" advice, achieved through discussions in seminar-style classes or discussion sessions led by a professor or teaching assistant, is equally appropriate in helping students at any college or university learn to think for themselves and become innovative contributors to and leaders in society and various professions.

The international relations faculty members are subject-matter experts who serve as experienced and trusted guides and are capable of becoming sages when necessary. The faculty remains focused on six course goals and makes cadets responsible for their own learning, helping them find answers and think for themselves. The faculty at West Point is made up of a combination of military and civilian professors and instructors: About 19% are senior military officers with doctorate degrees, about 28% are civilians with doctorates, and the remaining 53% are rotating midgrade military officers with master's or doctorate degrees. West Point selects the finest officers and helps bring their practical experience to the classroom. West Point and the Army also invest in each of these officers by sending them to the nation's leading graduate programs in their respective fields of study. The international relations faculty has earned degrees from Stanford, Harvard, Princeton, Chicago, Columbia, Johns Hopkins, Tufts, and Oxford. After finishing their teaching tours, the rotating military faculty members return to the Army as West Point's "second graduating class," where they apply the knowledge gained in graduate school and in teaching cadets to their decision making in positions of greater responsibility within the U.S. Army.

About International Politics

International Politics: Classic and Contemporary Readings came into being during a reevaluation of the international relations core course at West Point. While professors at the Academy update courses before each semester, we find it valuable to conduct a complete reevaluation of our courses every few years. The purpose of this reassessment process is to ensure that the course objectives still help our students achieve what we want them to through the course, the materials help our students achieve those objectives, our courses remain current with the state of our disciplines, and the course maintains its intended coherence after several updates. During the latest reevaluation of the international relations core course, six principal course objectives were established.

Cadets must emerge from the course fully prepared

1. to think critically about international affairs, appreciating the value of "intellectual pluralism";
2. to read critically to distinguish arguments, scrutinize the internal logic of those arguments, and assess the validity of empirical evidence;
3. to anticipate international behavior through the synthesis of theoretical arguments and evidence;
4. to develop policy recommendations grounded in critical thought and empirical analysis;
5. to consider and understand the ethical implications of foreign policy decisions or recommendations; and
6. to communicate analysis and arguments verbally and in writing clearly and effectively.

In an effort to meet these objectives and stay current with the state of the field, the teaching team surveyed international relations courses taught at more than 30 universities and reviewed currently available teaching materials. We decided that a broad survey course that combined classic works and contemporary literature in the field would best help us achieve our course objectives. Using classic and contemporary book sections and articles by leading scholars, rather than a textbook that merely synthesized those statements, allowed us to challenge our students to engage original scholarship to develop their critical reading, conceptual thinking, and critical thinking skills.

We have tested three draft versions of this book on more than 1,100 students, making modifications after each semester based on student and instructor feedback. This book consists of four parts that seek to bridge the theoretical traditions of international relations to contemporary challenges the field is trying to understand. Part I focuses on social scientific analysis and familiarizes the reader with the major theoretical traditions of international relations. The remaining parts emphasize the application of theories derived from the traditions to different contemporary challenges in international relations. In Part II, readers learn about and evaluate theories of war and peace. Part III exposes readers to issues within international political economy. Finally, Part IV focuses on emerging issues in international relations, including poverty and inequality, state failure, state-building, international law, and climate change. Readers should evaluate all the theories throughout this book using social scientific analysis. At the end of each part, readers consider the ethical implications of the explanations of conflict and cooperation (i.e., war and peace, protectionism and free trade, state failure and development assistance, etc.) surveyed in this book.

We built the book around these four parts because we have collectively found that initially establishing a foundation in the fundamentals of social scientific thinking and the theoretical roots and evolution of international relations theory allows students to engage in deeper critical analysis, application of the theories, and assessment of ethical implications of foreign policy when studying the more specific topics contained in Parts II through IV. And since this book was designed for introductory courses on international relations, we chose to provide a broad survey of the field. We have found that exposing our students to several articles on each topic helps develop their critical reading skills and improves their ability to communicate analyses and arguments by seeing how top scholars, as well as well-known public intellectuals, conduct their analyses and make their arguments.

Throughout the book, in each part and within each section, we selected readings that are foundational works in the field, trace the intellectual and social scientific development of different theories, provide debates within and between the international relations traditions, demonstrate applications of the theories through foreign policy, and debate the ethical implications of such applications. Each part of the book includes head notes and discussion questions. The purpose of the head notes is to help the student understand why each reading selection was chosen and how the different readings relate to one another. The headers do not summarize the selections for the students but, rather, help the students focus their reading efforts. The discussion questions raise broader concepts and issues that also help students focus their reading efforts, developing their ability to think critically and synthesize arguments.

While 90-plus articles may seem like a lot of material, the articles were carefully edited, focusing on retaining each author's development of the argument, presentation of general evidence to support the argument, and the conclusion or findings. We have found in our collective teaching experiences with this book that these editorial decisions have exposed students to a broad, but not overwhelming, series of important and concise readings. Conscious choices were made in the editing to ensure that the selections help students engage with the material to develop their critical reading skills, rather than merely summarizing the authors' arguments.

As this book was principally designed for introductory international relations courses based on the six principal course objectives stated above—although it could be used for more advanced students as well—data analysis findings have remained, while detailed explanations of quantitative and formal analysis have been removed in the editing process. Instructors who want to use any regression tables, data descriptions, or formal games for specific teaching points can assign students the full original readings for discussion.

As students progress through the book, we have found that the choice to include 90-plus articles allows students continually to improve their ability to distinguish arguments, scrutinize the internal logic of these arguments, and assess the validity of empirical findings presented by the authors.

ACKNOWLEDGMENTS

I received excellent advice and guidance from many people in developing this reader. COL Suzanne Nielsen, director of the International Relations Program at West Point, provided the strategic guidance and direction that made this book possible. She provided me with the challenge to update the core course and the latitude and support to redesign the syllabus and materials used to teach the course. COL Mike Meese and COL Cindy Jebb, the head and deputy head of the Department of Social Sciences, have created an environment that encourages the faculty to be the best teachers possible and to pursue research and writing opportunities. Professors Stephen Krasner and Mike Tomz allowed me to serve as the head teaching assistant for their Introduction to International Relations courses at Stanford University while I was a doctoral candidate. While both use very different teaching styles and structures for their courses, I am grateful for how much I learned about international relations, teaching, and course design from both of them, as well as the standards they each set and inspired me to try to achieve.

My colleagues in the International Relations Program at West Point offered tremendous support throughout the course redesign and the testing of the materials in the classroom, providing constructive feedback and making this book a better teaching and learning tool. Thank you to MAJ Brian Babcock-Lumish, MAJ Jordan Becker, MAJ Keith Benedict, Mr. Joe Blady, LTC Liam Collins, MAJ Jeanne Godfroy, LTC John Hagen, LTC Paul Larson, MAJ Irv Oliver, MAJ Melissa Ringhiesen, MAJ Mike Rosol, MAJ Bill Parsons, Dr. Rob Person, MAJ Bryan Price, MAJ Tony Posey, MAJ Dev Purewal, MAJ Abby Mower, Mr. Phil Salter, and Mr. Tom Walsh.

The book's many external reviewers provided critical and encouraging feedback for which we are grateful. Our thanks to Erica Chenoweth, Wesleyan University; John Doces, Bucknell University; Dennis Foster, Virginia Military Institute; Douglas Foyle, Wesleyan University; Claus Hofhansel, Rhode Island College; Gregory Koblentz, George Mason University; Jason Morrissette, Marshall University; Rita Peters, University of Massachusetts-Boston; Sarah Tenney, The Citadel; Steven Ward, Georgetown University; Dov Waxman, Baruch College; Eric Wiebelhaus-Brahm, Florida State University; Matt Zierler, Michigan State University; and three other anonymous reviewers.

Additionally, I have to thank the cadets who took SS307—International Relations during Academic Years 11-3 (summer), 12-1 (fall), 12-2 (spring), and 12-3 (summer) for their feedback and for challenging us to provide them with the best education possible. Elise Frasier and the team at CQ Press have also been a tremendous help in bringing this book to fruition, and I am thankful to Elise and the editorial board for the value they saw in this project. Finally, I want to thank my wife, Stephenie, for her patience and encouragement as I took on this project, which grew beyond either of our expectations.

This work was privately produced and is not the product of an official of the U.S. Army acting in an official capacity. The contents of this work, including words, images, and opinions, are unofficial and are not to be considered as the official views of the United States Military Academy, U.S. Army, or Department of Defense. Neither this work nor its contents are endorsed by the United States Military Academy, U.S. Army, or Department of Defense.

Part I

Theoretical Traditions in International Relations

The field of **international relations** studies interactions that take place within the **international system**. While many actors exist in the international system, international relations scholarship has largely focused on the **state** as the principal actor. The state takes on the role of the central unit of analysis since there is no higher governing authority above it in the international system—in other words, no "world government" has authority over sovereign states. In international relations, this absence of a higher authority is known as **anarchy**. Readers should be careful not to confuse anarchy with chaos, as order does exist in the anarchic structure of states. Since 9/11, many scholars have tried to understand the impact that **non-state actors** have on the system and their role in shaping state action. Some of those works will be examined in later parts of this book, but the purpose of Part I is to explore the social scientific method and the primary traditions of international relations in order to build the foundation for exploring two driving questions in international relations: "Why do states do what they do?" and "What causes conflict and cooperation in the international system?" While Part I breaks the traditions into distinct components, many of the theories discussed in later parts of this book consciously combine elements from the different traditions to develop richer theories with greater explanatory value. This self-conscious effort to use multiple and competing perspectives to test and improve understanding is known as **intellectual pluralism.** This approach proceeds from the understanding that due to the complexity of the modern world, no single tradition, theory, or model can adequately address the central questions in international relations. Instead, the variety of viewpoints stemming from debates taking place in the field helps more fully illuminate the causes of state behavior.[1]

Introduction

The introductory reading by political scientist Joseph S. Nye traces the evolution of international politics through three general forms, focusing on the emergence of the modern anarchic state system that arose following the **Peace of Westphalia** in 1648. This selection also provides a brief overview of three principal traditions through which scholars seek to understand and explain international relations: **realism**, **liberalism**, and **constructivism**.

The second article, "Good Writing in Political Science," does not address questions that drive the development of the traditions in international relations, but this article helps students understand how to read and write more effectively. Political scientist Henry Farrell's article is in the introduction in order to help students focus from the outset on how to write effectively in their courses and how to read critically the materials in this book. One should read each of the selections in this book critically in order to analyze the strength and validity of the arguments made by the authors, and also to learn how to write better. Examine each selection to see how well the authors follow Farrell's advice about answering the question, cutting to the chase, avoiding data dumps, organizing structures, and exercising style.

Social Scientific and Theoretical Analysis

The field of international relations has become largely dominated by the **positivist tradition**—seeking facts through the use of the scientific method to gather and test data against logically derived hypotheses. In actuality, scientific analysis in the "soft" sciences, such as political science, can be more challenging than in the "hard" sciences due to the volume of uncontrollable variables that exist in the real world and because, for practical and ethical reasons, political scientists cannot conduct controlled experiments with countries or societies the way lab scientists can with medicines or engineering designs. Political scientists Kenneth R. Hoover and Todd Donovan debunk myths about science and explain why using the **scientific method** is as important in the social sciences as in the physical sciences. They describe the importance of being systematic in research, differentiating reasoned judgment from opinion, and defining the elements of science: concepts, variables, hypotheses, measurements, and theories.

While many actors exist in the international system, the state is usually the principal actor of concern within the traditions of realism and liberalism. In his classic work, political scientist Kenneth N. Waltz describes three general **levels of analysis**, or what he calls images, that help one understand what drives state behavior in the international system. We can conceive of these levels of analysis as different places where observers can look for the answers to the foundational questions of why states do what they do and what causes conflict and cooperation in the international system. Is state behavior driven by human nature, the internal structure of a state, or the anarchic structure of the state system? This question lies at the core of Waltz's work, and his levels-of-analysis framework helps researchers compare like units when seeking answers to these research questions.

Realism

Realism is the tradition in international relations that holds **power** and **security** as its key values. While the **human nature** variant of realism (sometimes referred to as **classical or modern realism**) sees power as an end in itself, the **structural realism** (or **neorealism**) variant views power as a means to an end (security). However, both share the assumption that states are **rational**, self-interested, power-seeking actors that live in a condition of nature defined by anarchy.

While not an international relations theorist, Thomas Hobbes provided many of the philosophical roots for the realist tradition. Living during the English Civil War (1642–1651) and having translated ancient historian Thucydides' *History of the Peloponnesian War*, Hobbes held a generally pessimistic view of the nature of man, famously stating that when men live in an ungoverned situation, their lives are likely to be "solitary, poor, nasty, brutish, and short."[2] He explained how equality among men leads to conflict. They fight due to competition for resources, out of fear and the need to find safety, or to seek glory for reputation. Hans Morgenthau, a leading 20th century international relations theorist, projected the Hobbesian view of human nature onto the state as the principal actor of concern, suggesting that state behavior is driven by the same motives. Morgenthau presents a theory to describe international politics based on power.

The story of the outbreak of the Peloponnesian War, summarized by Joseph S. Nye, provides a classic example of the power dynamics that took place in an earlier form of the anarchic state system—one based on city-states. Where Thucydides provides an historical account of the war between the Greek city-states driven by Athens and Sparta, Niccolo Machiavelli provides policy advice to a Medici prince. Machiavelli wrote *The Prince* during the period of the Great Italian Wars (1494–1559) between the city-states of Italy, as well as the Papal States and many other Western European states. He advised the Medici prince on how—through accumulation of power and renown—to rule over his people, enter into alliances, and absorb the population of conquered territories.

In the latter part of the 20th century, neorealism emerged as an alternative to the traditional realist explanation of state behavior based on human nature. Kenneth N. Waltz helped lead this movement to a more positivist approach to explain why states do what they do. Waltz focused on the structure of the international system—rather than the strategies or motivations of national leaders—as the driver of state action, ultimately explaining the conditions under which war is likely between states. He explained that anarchy creates a **self-help world** in which states must provide for their own security, and that threats to security abound. Just as neorealism, or structural realism, is a variant within the realist tradition, different theories exist within neorealism.

As opposed to Waltz's "**defensive realist**" view that expects states to focus on maintaining the status quo of power distribution to maintain their security, political scientist John Mearsheimer provides an "**offensive realist**" perspective, arguing that anarchy forces states, particularly great powers, to maximize power. While not an international relations theorist, historian Robert Kagan makes an argument, based on his interpretation of current world politics, for why the United States must remain the predominant power in the international system. This reading shows how international relations theory still influences and shapes U.S. foreign policy. Readers should analyze Kagan's arguments carefully to identify the underlying theoretical logic, specifically looking for the elements of realism.

Liberalism

Liberalism is a major international relations tradition—sometimes referred to as **idealism**—that holds a more optimistic view about the possibility for cooperation in the international system than does realism. The key values for liberals are **freedom**, **equality**, and **prosperity**. Readers should not confuse *liberalism*, as defined in international relations, with the partisan use of the word in American political discourse today.

One can find the philosophical roots of the liberal tradition in the **Enlightenment**. Philosopher John Locke, while not describing the interaction among states, does explain that it is not a given that the state of nature will become a state of war between men. Locke describes men as equally endowed with natural rights and the ability to pursue life, liberty, and property but says that pursuit of these rights is not a license to deprive others of those same rights. To ensure that all men maintain these rights, Locke argues that men must behave reciprocally and society must have known rules derived from common consent, an indifferent judge, and an impartial enforcer.

Philosopher Immanuel Kant provides a philosophical sketch for how to achieve lasting peace among states. His first definitive article is closely tied to Locke's description of **civil law** and what the internal composition of states should look like: States must have a republican constitution. The second definitive article focuses on **international law**, arguing that the law of nations must be based in a federation of free states that seek collective security. Finally, Kant argues for **cosmopolitan law**, or respecting foreigners under one's own civil law, to promote commerce and, ultimately, interdependence between states.

Political scientist Michael W. Doyle describes a theory of **liberal peace**, explaining how Kant's thoughts have influenced the development of the ideas and institutions (or rules) that have shaped the liberal view of international relations. But Doyle also cautions against the misperception that liberals are inherently "peace-loving" or even peaceful in intent. Rather, liberalism as a social scientific theory describes and explains the conditions under which cooperation and peace are more likely from a liberal perspective. Conversely, liberalism suggests that the absence of these conditions may lead to conflict among states.

Kant and Doyle combine multiple elements of liberalism that others have broken into their constituent parts to explain state behavior. Joseph S. Nye describes these three strands of liberal thinking as **economic**, **social**, and **political liberalism**, further dividing the political into two parts: one focused on democracy and the other on institutions.

Economic historian Richard Rosecrance explains why trade develops interdependence between states based on equality, and that the pursuit of improved national welfare by one state does not prevent the same pursuit by another state. Using intellectual pluralism, political scientist Dale C. Copeland provides an argument that exemplifies intellectual pluralism, consciously drawing on realist and liberal insights, including ideas from Rosecrance, to explain how future expectations about trade determine when interdependence is more likely to contribute to cooperation or conflict.

While Doyle helped explain the democratic component of the political strand of liberalism, political scientist Robert O. Keohane emphasizes the role of institutions in reducing the effects of anarchy and contributing to cooperation between states. This strand is also known as **neoliberalism** or **institutionalism**, and it explains how **institutions** (or **regimes**) provide principles, norms, rules, and procedures for sharing information and establishing expectations about the future.

Before the development of neoliberalism, President Woodrow Wilson, a political scientist himself, wrote his "Fourteen Points" address at the end of World War I to call for a new international order based on liberal principles to avoid the calamities of the realist, balance-of-power system that led to WWI. One can see elements of all the strands of liberalism throughout the speech, and the legacy Wilson established in this speech remains a component of contemporary U.S. foreign policy. Readers should be able to distinguish the key tenets of liberalism from those of realism and should return to the reading by Robert Kagan to determine which aspects of liberalism, in addition to realism, underlie his argument about why the world needs America.

CONSTRUCTIVISM

These two sections of readings introduce the reader to the developing tradition of constructivism. Where realism and liberalism have much more developed research programs, constructivist scholars have been working to build this emerging tradition that focuses on the importance of **beliefs, norms**, and **identities** in shaping state behavior. Constructivism I focuses on "conventional" variants of this tradition, while Constructivism II introduces "critical" variants.

The selection from political scientist Ted Hopf provides an overview of conventional (or positivist) constructivist efforts to develop a research program that provides alternative explanations of mainstream theories developed under the realist and liberal traditions. He discusses the constructivist critique of the fundamentality of anarchy in international relations, reexamines the conceptualization of power, and describes how norms shape identities, which in turn shape interests that ultimately shape state behavior.

Political scientists Martha Finnemore and Kathryn Sikkink provide a theory to explain the connection between domestic and international norms. The theory describes a "life cycle" for how norms emerge, spread between states, and are ultimately internalized due to different actors, motivations, and mechanisms. Political scientist Nina Tannenwald focuses on explaining the emergence of a specific type of norm: **taboos**. Tannenwald defines a taboo as something that is abhorrent or held in widespread revulsion and is considered completely unacceptable. Using historical evidence, Tannenwald traces the origins, development, and endurance of the taboo against use of nuclear weapons.

International relations scholar J. Ann Tickner introduces critical variants of constructivism, addressing concerns about U.S.-centric perspectives and positivist methods dominating the field of international relations, and summarizes current debates among critical theory scholars. She argues that international relations needs a more pluralistic understanding of what shapes behavior in the international system in terms of perspectives and methods. Tickner argues that international relations should treat the **normative tradition**—utilizing values and judgments about the way things ought to be rather than the way they are—as an equal to the positivist tradition. Tickner draws on **postcolonial** and **feminist** literatures and argues that ideas from these areas must be brought into the mainstream of international relations studies and be treated with equal credibility.

Although an economist and not an international relations scholar, Nobel Laureate Amartya Sen examines the impact competing identities can have on international relations. In this writing, he draws on his experiences growing up in postcolonial India and observing different ethnic and religious conflicts today to understand why identity conflicts persist seemingly unabated. Sen recognizes the power of competing identities, examines how views about others shape individual and community behavior, and discusses how identity can contribute positively and negatively to the relations between people and communities.

Readers should seek to frame how constructivism views the international system differently than do realism and liberalism, as well as trying to find commonalities.

Decision-Making Models

Political scientist Graham T. Allison's classic work on the Cuban Missile Crisis provides three different models for understanding how states make the decisions that lead to state action. Allison explains that the common model for explaining state behavior views the state as a black box where decisions are made based on a **Rational Policy Model** that treats states as unified actors. Allison provides two alternative models that look inside the black box: (1) the **Organizational Process Model** and (2) the **Bureaucratic Politics Model**. He then tests each model against historical evidence surrounding the Cuban Missile Crisis and information from within the Kennedy administration. One should be able to follow Allison's example when examining contemporary decisions of governments to better understand why states do what they do.

Ethical Traditions in International Relations

Some argue that ethics have no role in international relations. Others argue that ethics are important but have a lesser role in international politics than in domestic politics. Still others argue that international relations should shape how the world ought to be, so it is not possible to divorce ethics from international relations. **Ethics**, or moral philosophy, is a field that tries to understand and explain concepts of right and wrong behavior.

Philosopher James Fieser describes the general categories of **normative ethics**: **virtue ethics**, **duty ethics**, and **consequentialism**. These are not international relations theories, but these underlying concepts are used in discussing the ethics of state behavior in the international system. While Joseph S. Nye does not refer to the ethical theory terms used by Fieser, those moral philosophical concepts are inherent in Nye's discussion of the three views of morality in international relations. Readers should try to identify the underlying ethical traditions in Nye's views of morality.

Just as intellectual pluralism is found throughout many theories in international relations, it also exists in the application of the ethical traditions. In "The Melian Dialogue," Thucydides captures the realist belief that morality has no place in international relations. During this dialogue, the Melians' arguments to dissuade Athens from attacking Melos parallel the different normative ethical traditions. Again, the reader should try to recognize the modern ethical traditions that emerge from the classic arguments made by the Melians. Ultimately, the Athenians respond by explaining that morality is not a luxury statesmen have, because the world is not as people hope it to be.

Discussion Questions for Part I: Theoretical Traditions in International Relations

1. What is the social scientific method? How are theories developed and tested in international relations? Why does the field try to use the scientific method?

2. Explain the general tenets (worldview) of realism, liberalism, and constructivism. How does each tradition view the state of nature? How does each tradition view human nature? What are the key values for each tradition, and how are they defined? What are the expectations of state behavior for each tradition (i.e., under what conditions does each tradition expect conflict, and under what conditions does each tradition expect cooperation)? What are the foreign policy implications for each tradition?

3. What is interdependence? What does each tradition expect of state behavior when states are interdependent? Does interdependence promote conflict or cooperation? Explain why and under what conditions.

4. Compare and contrast structural realism with neoliberal institutionalism. Explain which level of analysis these two theories fall under and why. Identify the independent (causal) variables, dependent (outcome) variables, and the underlying causal logic for these structural theories.

5. What distinguishes "conventional" from "critical" variants of constructivism? Do these distinctions of variants matter? Why or why not? Explain what value constructivism adds to the field of international relations.

6. What is intellectual pluralism? Why is it an important concept?

7. Differentiate the main ethical traditions that influence international relations. Explain how these ethical traditions are reflected in the traditions of international relations.

Key Concepts

anarchy	**identities**	**Peace of Westphalia**
beliefs	**institutionalism**	**political liberalism**
Bureaucratic Politics Model	**institutions (regimes)**	**positivist tradition**
civil law	**intellectual pluralism**	**postcolonial**
classical (or modern) realism	**international law**	**power**
consequentialism	**international relations**	**prosperity**
constructivism	**international system**	**rational**
cosmopolitan law	**levels of analysis**	**Rational Policy Model**
defensive realist	**liberal peace**	**realism**
duty ethics	**liberalism**	**scientific method**
economic liberalism	**neoliberalism**	**security**
Enlightenment	**neorealism**	**self-help world**
equality	**non-state actors**	**social liberalism**
ethics	**normative ethics**	**state**
feminist	**normative tradition**	**structural realism**
freedom	**norms**	**taboos**
human nature	**offensive realist**	**virtue ethics**
idealism	**Organizational Process Model**	

Notes

1. Daniel J. Kaufman, Jay M. Parker, and Kimberly C. Field, *Understanding International Relations: The Value of Alternative Lenses,* 4th ed. (New York: McGraw Hill, 1999), 1.
2. Thomas Hobbes, "Of Natural Condition of Mankind as Concerning Their Felicity and Misery." *Leviathan* Chapter XIII, p. 33.

1 Introduction

1.1

What is International Politics?

Joseph S. Nye

The world has not always been divided into a system of separate states. Over the centuries there have been three basic forms of world politics. In a *world imperial system*, one government controls most of the world with which it has contact. The greatest example in the Western world was the Roman Empire. Spain in the sixteenth century and France in the late seventeenth century tried to gain similar supremacy, but they failed. In the nineteenth century, the British Empire spanned the globe, but even the British had to share the world with other strong states. Ancient world empires—the Sumerian, the Persian, the Chinese—were actually regional empires. They thought they ruled the world, but they were protected from conflict with other empires by lack of communication. Their fights with barbarians on the peripheries of the empire were not the same as wars among roughly equal states.

A second basic form of international politics is a *feudal system*, in which human loyalties and political obligations are not fixed primarily by territorial boundaries. Feudalism was common in Europe after the collapse of the Roman Empire. An individual had obligations to a local lord, but might also owe duties to some distant noble or bishop as well as to the pope in Rome. Political obligations were determined to a large extent by what happened to one's superiors. If a ruler married, an area and its people might find their obligations rearranged as part of a wedding dowry. Townspeople born French might suddenly find themselves made Flemish or even English. Cities and leagues of cities sometimes had a special semi-independent status. The crazy quilt of wars that accompanied the feudal situation were not what we think of as modern territorial wars. They could occur within as well as across territories and were related to these crosscutting, non-territorial loyalties and conflicts.

A third form of world politics is an *anarchic system of states*, composed of states that are relatively cohesive but with no higher government above them. Examples include the city-states of ancient Greece or Machiavelli's fifteenth-century Italy. Another example of an anarchic state system is the dynastic territorial state whose coherence comes from control by a ruling family. Examples can be found in India or China in the fifth century B.C. Large territorial dynasties reemerged in Europe about 1500, and other forms of international polities such as city-states or loose leagues of territories began to vanish. In 1648, the Peace of Westphalia ended Europe's Thirty Years' War, sometimes called the last of the great wars of religion and the first of the wars of modern states. In retrospect, that treaty enshrined the sovereign territorial state as the dominant form of international organization.

Thus today when we speak of international politics, we usually mean this territorial state system,

---

and we define *international politics* as politics in the absence of a common sovereign, politics among entities with no ruler above them. International politics is a self-help system. Thomas Hobbes, the seventeenth-century English philosopher, called such anarchic systems a "state of nature." For some, the words *state of nature* may conjure up images of a herd of cows grazing peacefully on a farm, but that is not what Hobbes meant. Think of a Texas town without a sheriff in the days of the Old West, or Lebanon after its government broke down in the 1970s, or Somalia in the 1990s. Hobbes's state of nature is not benign; it is a war of all against all because there is no higher ruler to enforce order. As Hobbes famously declared, life in such a world tends to be nasty, brutish, and short.

The result is that legal, political, and social differences exist between domestic and international politics. Domestic law is generally obeyed and if not, the police and courts enforce sanctions against lawbreakers. International law, on the other hand, rests on competing legal systems, and there is no common enforcement; no international police to enforce International law.

Force plays a different role in domestic and international politics. In a well-ordered domestic political system, the government has a monopoly on the legitimate use of force. In international politics, no one has a monopoly on the use of force. Because international politics is the realm of self-help, and some states are stronger than others, there is always a danger that they may resort to force. When force cannot be ruled out, the result is mistrust and suspicion.

Domestic and international politics also differ in their underlying sense of community. In a well-ordered domestic society, a widespread sense of community gives rise to common loyalties, standards of justice, and views of what is legitimate authority. In international politics, divided peoples do not share the same loyalties. Any sense of global community is weak. People often disagree about what seems just and legitimate. The result is a great gap between two basic political values: order and justice. In such a world, most people place national concerns before international justice. Law and ethics play a role in international politics, but in the absence of a sense of community norms, they are not as binding as they are in domestic politics.

Of the three basic systems—*world imperial, feudal,* and *anarchic system of states*—some people speculate that the twenty-first century may see the gradual evolution of a new feudalism, or less plausibly, an American world empire.

Two Views of Anarchic Politics

International politics is anarchic in the sense that there is no higher government. But even political philosophy offers two different views of how harsh a state of nature need be. Hobbes, who wrote in a seventeenth-century England wracked by civil war, emphasized insecurity, force, and survival. He described humanity as being in a constant state of war. A half century later, John Locke, writing in a more stable England, argued that although a state of nature lacked a common sovereign, people could develop ties and make contracts, and therefore anarchy was less threatening. Those two views of a state of nature are the philosophical precursors of two current views of international politics, one more pessimistic and one more optimistic: the *realist* and *liberal* approaches to international politics.

Realism has been the dominant tradition in thinking about international politics. For the realist, the central problem of international politics is war and the use of force, and the central actors are states. Among modern Americans, realism is exemplified by the writings and policies of President Richard Nixon and his secretary of state, Henry Kissinger. The realist starts from the assumption of the anarchic system of states. Kissinger and Nixon, for example, sought to maximize the power of the United States and to minimize the ability of other states to jeopardize U.S. security. According to the realist, the beginning and the end of international politics is the individual state in interaction with other states.

The other tradition, *liberalism*, can be traced back in Western political philosophy to Baron de Montesquieu and Immanuel Kant in eighteenth-century France and Germany, respectively, and such nineteenth-century British philosophers as Jeremy Bentham and John Stuart Mill. A modern American example can be found in the writings and policies of political scientist and President Woodrow Wilson.

Liberals see a global society that functions alongside the states and sets part of the context for states. Trade crosses borders, people have contacts with each other (such as students studying in foreign countries), and international institutions such as the United Nations create a context in which the realist view of pure anarchy is insufficient. Liberals complain that realists portray states as hard billiard balls careening off one another in the attempt to balance power, but that is not enough because people do have contacts across borders and because there is an international society. Realists, claim liberals, overstate the difference between domestic and international politics. Because the realist picture of anarchy as a Hobbesian "state of war" focuses only on extreme situations, in the liberals' view it misses the growth of economic interdependence and the evolution of a transnational global society.

Realists respond by quoting Hobbes: "Just as stormy weather does not mean perpetual rain, so a state of war does not mean constant war."[1] Just as Londoners carry umbrellas on sunny April days, the prospect of war in an anarchic system makes states keep armies even in times of peace. Realists point to previous liberal predictions that went awry. For example, in 1910 the president of Stanford University said future war was no longer possible because the nations could not afford it. Books proclaimed war to be obsolete; civilization had gone beyond war. Economic interdependence, ties between labor unions and intellectuals, and the flow of capital all made war impossible. Of course, these predictions failed catastrophically in 1914, and the realists were vindicated.

1910: The "Unseen Vampire" of War

If there were no other reason for making an end of war, the financial ruin it involves must sooner or later bring the civilized nations of the world to their senses. As President David Starr Jordan of Leland Stanford University said at Tufts College, "Future war is impossible because the nations cannot afford it." In Europe, he says, the war debt is $26 billion, "all owed to the unseen vampire, and which the nations will never pay and which taxes poor people $95 million a year." The burdens of militarism in time of peace are exhausting the strength of the leading nations, already overloaded with debts. The certain result of a great war would be overwhelming bankruptcy.

—*The New York World*[2]

Neither history nor the argument stopped in 1914. The 1970s saw a resurgence of liberal claims that rising economic and social interdependence was changing the nature of international politics. In the 1980s, Richard Rosecrance, a California professor, wrote that states can increase their power in two ways, either aggressively by territorial conquest or peacefully through trade. He used the experience of Japan as an example: In the 1930s, Japan tried territorial conquest and suffered the disaster of World War II. But since then, Japan has used trade and investment to become the second largest economy in the world (measured by official exchange rates), and a significant power in East Asia. Japan succeeded without a major military force. Thus Rosecrance and modern liberals argue that the nature of international politics is changing.

Some new liberals look even further to the future and believe that dramatic growth in ecological interdependence will so blur the differences between domestic and international politics that humanity will evolve toward a world without borders. For example, everyone will be affected without regard to boundaries if the depletion of ozone in the upper atmosphere causes skin cancer. If carbon dioxide accumulation warms the climate and causes the polar ice caps to melt, rising seas will affect all coastal states. Some problems such as AIDS and drugs cross borders with such ease that we may be on our way to a different world. Professor Richard Falk of Princeton argues that these transnational problems and values will alter the state-centric orientation of the international system that has dominated for the last 400 years. Transnational forces are undoing the Peace of Westphalia, and humanity is evolving toward a new form of international politics.

In 1990, realists replied, "Tell that to Saddam Hussein!" Iraq showed that force and war are ever-present dangers when it invaded its small neighbor Kuwait. Liberals responded by arguing that politics in the Middle East is the exception. Over time, they say, the world is moving beyond the anarchy of the sovereign state system. These divergent views on the nature of international politics and how it is changing will not soon be reconciled. Realists stress continuity; liberals stress change. Both claim the high ground of realism with a small *r*. Liberals tend to see realists as cynics whose fascination with the past blinds them to change. Realists, in turn, call the liberals utopian dreamers and label their thought "globaloney."

Who's right? Both are right and both are wrong. A clear-cut answer might be nice, but it would also be less accurate and less interesting. The mix of continuity and change that characterizes today's world makes it impossible to arrive at one simple synthetic explanation.

Because it involves changeable human behaviors, international politics will never be like physics: it has no strong determinist theory. What is more, realism and liberalism are not the only approaches. For much of the past century *Marxism*, with its predictions of class conflict and warfare caused by problems among capitalist states, was a credible alternative for many people. Even before the 1991 collapse of the Soviet Union, however, the failure of Marxist theory to account for peace among major capitalist states and warfare among some communist states left it lagging in the explanatory competition. In the 1960s and 1970s, *dependency theory* was popular. It predicted that the wealthy countries in the "center" of the global marketplace would control and hold back poorer countries on the "periphery." While dependency theory helped illuminate some structural causes of economic inequality, it lost credibility when it could not explain why, in the 1980s and 1990s, peripheral countries in East Asia such as South Korea, Singapore, and Malaysia grew more rapidly than "central" countries such as the United States and Europe. This loss of credibility was underlined when Fernando Henrique Cardoso, an academic leader among dependency theorists in the 1970s, turned to liberal policies of increasing dependence on global markets after he was elected president of Brazil in the 1990s.

In the 1980s, analysts on both sides of the realist-liberal divide attempted to devise more deductive theories similar to those of microeconomics. "Neorealists" such as Kenneth Waltz and "neoliberals" such as Robert Keohane developed structural models of states as rational actors constrained by the international system. Neorealists and neoliberals increased the simplicity and elegance of theory, but they did so at the cost of discarding much of the rich complexity of classical realist and liberal theories. "By the end of the 1980s, the theoretical contest that might have been was reduced to relatively narrow disagreements within one state-centric rationalist model of international relations."[3]

More recently, a diverse group of theorists labeled *constructivists* has argued that realism and liberalism fail to adequately explain long-term change in world politics. Constructivists emphasize the importance of ideas and culture in shaping both the reality and the discourse of international politics. They stress the ultimate subjectivity of interests and their links to changing identities. There are many types of constructivists, but they all tend to agree that the two major theories are far from being true pictures of the world, and that we need not just explanations of how things are, but explanations of how they become what they are. Constructivists have focused on important questions about identities, norms, culture, national interests, and international governance.[4] They believe that leaders and other people are motivated not only by material interests, but also by their sense of identity, morality, and what a society or culture considers appropriate. And such norms change over time.

Neorealists and neoliberals take for granted how the goals that states sought changed over time. Constructivists draw on different fields and disciplines to examine the processes by which leaders, peoples, and cultures alter their preferences, shape their identities, and learn new behavior. For example, both slavery in the nineteenth century and racial apartheid in South Africa were once accepted by most states, but later were widely opposed. Constructivists ask, why the change? What role did ideas play? Will the practice of war go the same way someday? What about the concept of the sovereign nation-state? The world is full of political entities such as tribes, nations, and nongovernmental organizations. Only in recent centuries has the sovereign state been a dominant concept. Constructivists suggest that concepts such as nation and sovereignty that give meaning to our lives as well as to our theories are socially constructed, not just "out there" as permanent reality. Feminist constructivists add that the language and imageries of war as a central instrument of world politics have been heavily influenced by gender.

Constructivism is an approach rather than a theory, but it provides both a useful critique and an important supplement to the main theories of realism and liberalism. Though sometimes loosely formulated and lacking in predictive power, constructivist approaches remind us of what the two main theories often miss. As [one] shall see . . . , it is important to look beyond the instrumental rationality of pursuing current goals and to ask how changing identities and interests can sometimes lead to subtle shifts in states' policies, and sometimes to profound changes in international affairs. Constructivists help us understand how preferences are formed and knowledge is generated prior to the exercise of instrumental rationality. In that sense, constructivist thought complements rather than opposes the two main theories.

When I was working in Washington and helping formulate American foreign policies as an assistant secretary in the State Department and the Pentagon, I found myself borrowing elements from all three types of thinking: realism, liberalism, and constructivism. I found all of them helpful, though in different ways and in different circumstances. Sometimes practical men and women wonder why we should bother with theories at all. The answer is that theories are the road maps that allow us to make sense of unfamiliar terrain. We are lost without them. Even when we think we are just using common sense, there is usually an implicit theory guiding our actions. We simply do not know or have forgotten what it is. If we are more conscious of the theories that are guiding us, we are better able to understand their strengths and weaknesses and when best to apply them. As the British economist John Maynard Keynes once put it, practical men who consider themselves above theory are usually listening to some dead scribbler from the past whose name they have long forgotten.[5]

Notes

1. Thomas Hobbes, *Leviathan*, ed. C. B. MacPherson (London: Penguin, 1981), p. 186.

2. *The New York World*, "From Our Dec. 13 Pages, 75 Years Ago," *International Herald Tribune*, December 13, 1985.

3. Miles Kahler, "Inventing International Relations: International Relations Theory After 1945," in Michael W. Doyle and G. John Ikenberry, eds., *New Thinking in International Relations Theory* (Boulder, CO: Westview, 1977), p. 38.

4. Emanuel Adler, "Constructivism in International Relations: Sources, Contributions, Debates and Future Directions," in Walter Carlsnaes, Thomas Risse, and Beth Simmons, eds., *Handbook of International Relations* (Thousand Oaks, CA: Sage, 2003).

5. John Maynard Keynes, *The General Theory of Employment, Interest and Money* (London: Macmillan, 1936), p. 383.

Further Readings

Axelrod, Robert M., *The Evolution of Cooperation* (New York: Basic, 1984).

Bagby, Laurie, "The Use and Abuse of Thucydides," *International Organization* 48:1 (Winter 1994), pp. 131–153.

Baldwin, David, *Neorealism and Neoliberalism: The Contemporary Debate* (New York: Columbia University Press, 1993).

Beitz, Charles R., *Political Theory and International Politics* (Princeton, NJ: Princeton University Press, 1979).

Betts, Richard, "Should Strategic Studies Survive?" *World Politics* 50:1 (October 1997), pp. 7–54.

Brown, Michael, et al., *Theories of War and Peace* (Cambridge, MA: MIT Press, 1998).

Bull, Hedley, *The Anarchical Society: A Study of Order in World Politics* (New York: Columbia University Press, 1977).

Caporaso, James A., ed., "Dependence and Dependency in the Global System," special issue, *International Organization* 32:1 (Winter 1978).

Dessler, David, "Constructivism Within a Positivist Social Science," *Review of International Studies* 25 (1999).

Doyle, Michael W., *Ways of War and Peace* (New York: Norton, 1997).

Doyle, Michael W., and G. John Ikenberry, eds., *New Thinking in International Relations Theory* (Boulder, CO: Westview, 1997).

Elshtain, Jean Bethke, *Women and War*, 2nd ed., (Chicago: University of Chicago Press, 1994).

Finnemore, Martha, and Kathryn Sikkink, "Taking Stock: The Constructivist Research Program in Interna tional Relations and World Politics," *Annual Review of Political Science* 4 (June 2001), pp. 391–416.

Gaddis, John Lewis, *The Landscape of History: How Historians Map the Past* (New York: Oxford University Press, 2002).

Gilpin, Robert, *War and Change in World Politics* (Cambridge: Cambridge University Press, 1981).

Goldstein, Joshua S., *War and Gender* (Cambridge: Cambridge University Press, 2001).

Hinsley, F. H., *Power and the Pursuit of Peace* (London: Cambridge University Press, 1967).

Hoffmann, Stanley, *Duties Beyond Borders: On the Limits and Possibilities of Ethical International Politics* (Syracuse, NY: Syracuse University Press, 1981).

Jervis, Robert, "Realism, Game Theory, and Cooperation," *World Politics* 40:3 (April 1988), pp. 317–349.

Katzenstein, Peter J., ed., *The Culture of National Security* (New York: Columbia University Press, 1996).

Katzenstein, Peter J., Robert Keohane, and Stephen Krasner, "International Organization and the Study of World Politics," International Organization 52:4 (Fall 1998).

Keohane, Robert O., ed., Neo-Realism and Its Critics (New York: Columbia University Press, 1986).

Kissinger, Henry, *Diplomacy* (New York: Simon & Schuster, 1994).

Lapid, Yosef, and Friedrich Kratochwil, eds., *The Return of Culture and Identity in International Relations Theory* (Boulder, CO: Lynne Rienner, 1996).

Levy, Jack S., *War in the Modern Great Power System, 1495–1975* (Lexington: University Press of Kentucky, 1983).

Mercer, Jonathan, "Anarchy and Identity," International Organization 49:2 (Spring 1995), pp. 229–252.

Oneal, John, and Bruce Russett, "The Classical Liberals Were Right: Democracy, Interdependence, and Conflict, 1950–1985," International Studies Quarterly 41 (1997), pp. 267–293.

Rawls, John, *The Law of Peoples* (Cambridge, MA: Harvard University Press, 1999).

Rosecrance, Richard N., *The Rise of the Trading State: Commerce and Conquest in the Modern World* (New York: Basic, 1986).

Rosenau, James N., *Turbulence in World Politics: A Theory of Change and Continuity* (Princeton, NJ: Princeton University Press, 1990).

Ruggie, John G., "What Makes the World Hang Together: Neo-Utilitarianism and the Social Constructivist Challenge," *International Organization* 52:4 (1998), pp. 855–885.

1.2

Good Writing in Political Science

An Undergraduate Student's Short Illustrated Primer V.1.01

Henry Farrell

Introduction

Leo Tolstoy famously observed that "happy families are all alike; every unhappy family is unhappy in its own way."[1] Tolstoy, happily for all of us, was not a teaching political scientist. Had he been, he might have observed that undergraduate political science papers are subject to a different logic. Really good papers are unique—each has its own particular thesis, style of argumentation, body of empirical evidence and set of conclusions. Really bad papers, in contrast, tend toward a dismal uniformity. They draw on the same evidence (garbled versions of what the professor has presented in class), are organized according to similar principles of incoherence, and all wend their eventual ways towards banal conclusions that strenuously avoid making any claims or positive arguments whatsoever.

This short set of guidelines cannot make you into a really good essayist. For that you need time, practice, and native genius. What it can do, however, is help you avoid some of the most common pitfalls of undergraduate essay writers. You can surely avoid being a very bad essayist, and you can very likely become a better essayist than you are already. What follows is a short set of suggestions, accompanied, where available, with cautionary examples drawn from online essay mills.

Read the Requirements for the Assignment

This suggestion may be taken as insulting because it is so obvious; still, it is commonly ignored in practice. The professor usually drops some very strong hints about what she is looking for when she assigns a piece of writing. It is best to pay attention to those hints. For example, if you are asked to write a term paper on a problem of international cooperation, you should ensure that your term paper explicitly focuses on a topic that (a) involves cooperation, (b) has, at the least, some international aspect, and (c) is potentially problematic.

Sometimes, assignments are ambiguous. Professors too may err. The assignment may be inexactly worded or involve contradictory requirements. In these cases it is obviously best to ask the professor what she is looking for (it is often better to ask via email, to ensure that you have a written explanation of what the professor wants that you can refer to later). Where this is not possible (e.g. if you are trying to write an exam answer), you may want to be quite clear in saying how you are interpreting the question. For example, you might want to start by saying "In this answer, I interpret the phrase 'international cooperation' to mean . . ." If your interpretation is a reasonable one, this places the onus on the professor to either read the essay according to your interpretation or to justify (at least to herself) why not.

Avoid Data Dumps

Poor essays very often ignore the question asked in a quite specific way. The student spots some topic in the assignment that seems familiar, and immediately sets about writing an essay which tells the professor everything they know about that topic, in no particular order. For obvious reasons, such essays rarely receive high grades. Universities encourage (or, at least, they *should* encourage) students in the social sciences and liberal humanities to criticize, to analyze, and, ideally, to think. Mere demonstration that one possesses a disorganized body of knowledge on a topic, and is prepared to inflict this jumble upon the professor in printed or (worse) handwritten form, suggests that this encouragement has fallen on untilled ground.

Source: Reprinted by permission of Harry Farrell.

Cut to the Chase

Undergraduate essays frequently begin with an extended session of throat-clearing irrelevances and vague generalities. They talk about everything *except* the question that has been asked. Take this example (drawn from a free term paper).

> The onset of computers on the general population has given a boost to the Economy in the world's market. People who weren't much aware of the world became drawn to computers, which in turn brought about the Internet, connecting the world all over. The Internet has played a major role in the lives of people all over the world. Now, it is not limited to just important organizations or governments. Everyone who owns a computer is logged on to the Internet; and this has made the world seem smaller. No one has to wait for the postman to deliver the mail, but instead one can just connect to the Internet and right away, you got mail.

This, like many other essays that I have corrected on the political consequences of the Internet (I sometimes teach a course on this topic) begins with a paragraph that has nothing whatsoever to say about the politics of the Internet. Instead, the paper's author sees the word 'Internet' and grabs desperately for banalities that he associates with this word.

Alternatively, students sometimes state and re-state the question in a manner intended to suggest that they understand it, without ever providing anything so provocative as an actual answer.

> Should the internet be censored? The internet is a wonderful place for entertainment and education, but, like all places used by millions of people, it has some peculiarities that lead to a lot of talking and arguing over, should the internet be censored? Most of people who use the internet are furious about the censorship on the internet. The issue of whether is it necessary to censor the internet is being argued all over the world.

This essay starts off well. It sets out a short, pithy question that the reader might hope will be answered in the paper. But then it goes horribly, *horribly* wrong. The second sentence restates the first, garnished with a couple of irrelevant commonplaces. The third sentence suggests that there is controversy surrounding the topic of Internet censorship (a safe guess, given that the writer has been asked to write a paper about this controversy). The fourth sentence repeats the third. And so on. The writer evidently knows little or nothing about the essay topic, and is trying to conceal that fact. Unfortunately, he or she is failing.

These are the beginning sections of very bad essays. Most undergraduate essays are not nearly as bad as that. Still, many essays do begin with weak and meandering introductions that do not address the topic of their paper. This is a shame. It is important that you get the introduction right. This is your best opportunity to grab the reader's attention and to persuade her that you have something interesting to say. Don't waste it.

By the time the reader has finished reading the first two sentences, she should know which question the essay addresses. By the time the reader has finished reading the first five or six, she should have a pretty good idea of how the author is going to tackle the question. The following provides one example of a punchy beginning ([note]: this is not taken from an essay mill):

> Should the Internet be censored? While many Americans would say no, there is in fact a very good case for limited Internet censorship. Pedophiles can use the Internet to find each other and to swap child pornography. Terrorists can use the Internet to propagandize for their beliefs, and to recruit for their causes. Neo-Nazis and others can spread disinformation to the gullible, and persuade them that the Holocaust never occurred. In this essay, I argue that some kinds of Internet speech (child pornography, terrorist recruitment and hate speech) should be banned. I acknowledge that this may hurt legitimate forms of free speech if they become confused with the harmful kinds, but show that the beneficial consequences of banning bad speech outweigh the harmful consequences of accidentally banning (some) good speech.

This is, in my opinion, a good opening paragraph (since I wrote it myself as an illustration, it is perhaps unsurprising that I like it). It immediately states the question that the essay will try to answer. Shortly afterwards, it provides the reader with the proposed answer, and briefly describes the kind of evidence that it will use to support this answer. The introduction also acknowledges that there is a strong opposing case (that banning 'harmful' speech will hurt other kinds of speech), and promises that it will try to answer that case. The essay will not necessarily convince its readers (it takes a quite controversial stand), but it does signal to the reader that it has a clear question, a clear answer to that question, and a willingness to address the best arguments against the case it is making. That is all that any professor may reasonably ask for; not that she *agree* with the writer's argument and conclusions, but that she recognizes them as well written, well structured, and well supported by the evidence.

Organize, Organize, Organize

Many student papers are badly organized. They wander from point to point. They tack an introduction and conclusion onto a main body that does not have any internal system of order. Or they do not have a distinguishable introduction, body, and conclusion at all.

Some excellent essayists can get away with apparently disorganized writing. It is usually a very bad idea to try to emulate them. Very often, apparently disorganized work is in fact highly organized. The author has merely kicked away the essay's supports and scaffolding (e.g. an explicit introductory section and so on) as soon as it was strong enough to stand on its own. Sometimes, apparent disorganization is instead the product of a highly subtle mind, or of an elliptical writing style that approaches its topics indirectly rather than directly. Unless you are *very confident indeed* (and have evidence in the form of past work, print publications, etc. to justify this confidence) I strongly recommend that you avoid overly clever and non-linear approaches to writing. They require a lot of practice (usually at the more traditional sorts of writing) before they can be carried off well, and when they are carried off badly, they are very bad indeed. Genius may do as it will; mere intelligence and talent should be appropriately modest in their ambitions.

Thus, the need for *structure*. You should structure your essay at three levels.

Macro-structure

This is the broad structure of the essay itself. Unless you feel very comfortable that you are an excellent writer, it is usually best to stick to the traditional frame of an introductory section, a main body, and a conclusion. The introduction tells the reader what you are going to say. The main body tells the reader what you are saying. The conclusions tell the reader what she has just read (perhaps adding some thoughts as to its broader implications if you are feeling adventurous).

This not only helps the reader understand your argument, but disciplines your thought and prose. It forces you to begin your essay with a clear, concise account of your major claims. When you write the main section of the essay (or re-write it, as needs be) the introduction will provide you with a roadmap of what you need to do. Your conclusions, in contrast, should draw the threads together, showing how the facts and arguments you have laid out in the main body actually speak to the broad themes discussed in the introduction, and drawing the threads of your narrative together into a proper whole. Of course, for this to work it is necessary that the main body of your essay actually speak to the arguments laid out in your introduction, that your conclusions relate to the main body, and so on.

Meso-structure

This is perhaps the most commonly neglected element of structured writing. It concerns the paragraphs into which your prose is organized. Each paragraph should focus on one main point. The point of each paragraph should build on that in the previous paragraph, and create the foundations of the next. Each paragraph should be a necessary part of the overall structure of your essay.

I find that a useful mental exercise is to boil down the arguments of each paragraph, one after the other, into single sentences. Then, put all these sentences together into a consecutive narrative, looking to see whether each sentence can be made to flow naturally from the sentence previous to it, and into the sentence following. This will highlight any major structural problems. If you are not able to boil down each of the paragraphs into a single sentence summary (however simplistic), then the offending paragraphs most likely need to be rewritten more clearly. If there are gaps or non-sequiturs when you put the one sentence summaries together, then the meso-structure of your essay needs to be re-organized, by cutting and pasting paragraphs, or by introducing new paragraphs to fill the gaps, or deleting old paragraphs that detract from the flow of your argument.

Micro-structure

What is true of the paragraph is also true of the sentence. Each individual sentence should flow in a logical and obvious way from the sentence before, and into the sentence after. Consider the following paragraph, taken from a term paper on global warming which is available for free online.

> Weather these days has become very unpredictable. The increase in the world's temperatures, believed to be caused in part by the greenhouse effect which is known as

global warming has and will have a serious effect on the future. Global warming creates massive concerns for the entire earth. If the heat continues to increase several species may struggle to survive. There are numerous political, environmental, economic, and social issues when it comes to global warming. Global warming is an inevitable issue and by no stretch of the imagination can be slowed down easily. There is an inconceivable amount of causes that connect to global warming.

This is quite wretched writing. The first sentence is a vague generality that does not mean very much. The second sentence does not flow in any obvious way from the first. What does the greenhouse effect have to do with unpredictable weather? No explanation is provided for the reader. The third sentence merely repeats the argument of the second, with greater rhetorical alarm. The fourth does a little better, but loses force because it is so badly written (the claim that 'several species' may struggle to survive suggests that only five or six species are in danger, which sits awkwardly with the previous sentence's suggestion that global warming causes "massive concerns" for the entire earth). The fifth sentence seems to build a new set of claims, and should be at the beginning of a new paragraph. However, it never goes anywhere. Instead, the sixth sentence warns that global warming is "an inevitable issue" (whatever that means), while the seventh sentence wrings its hands in despair over yet another new claim—that there is an "inconceivable amount" (sic) of causes "that connect" to global warming. These sentences are not only bad in themselves—they are not connected in any logical or orderly way. The result is that they do not add up to a coherent argument.

Exercises in Style

Political science is not a discipline notable for lovely prose. The best historians often write beautifully; the best political scientists rarely do. Good political science writing does not require striking metaphors or clever verbal constructions (while these are not precisely discouraged, they are not commonly regarded as necessary). Instead, it requires simple, direct writing, which communicates its arguments and evidence as clearly and unambiguously as possible.

The implications for prose style are straightforward. First, use direct language when at all possible. This not only reads better; it communicates clearly who is responsible for what. For example, the sentence

The Iranian government censors newspapers and political websites.

not only reads much better than

Newspapers and political websites are subject to a censorship regime in Iran.

but it conveys more information in fewer words. It tells the reader who is responsible for censoring information (the government). The alternative version provides less information (the reader may guess that the government is responsible for censorship, but she cannot be sure). It also sounds cumbersome and laborious. Students sometimes use indirect constructions or the passive voice rather than direct language and active verbs because they think this will make their writing more sophisticated and 'academic.' They are wrong. Even worse, they sometimes prefer indirect language because they believe that it allows them get away with knowing less, by fudging their argument so that it can be interpreted in more than one way. Neither are good reasons. Indirect language often sounds weak, uncertain, and bureaucratic, and experienced readers will recognize when it is being used to bamboozle them. Sometimes, passive and indirect writing is appropriate, but it should be used with caution.

Second, prefer simple words to complex words, and plain language to jargon. Sometimes it will be impossible to avoid jargon or obscure terms. However, it will usually be possible to use simple terms to convey your meaning. When you can do so, do so. Plain language makes life easier for the reader. It also makes it harder for the writer to get away with nonsense. If you use flowery language, you can sometimes persuade yourself that you understand topics and debates which you really do not. If you use plain language you will be forced to confront your areas of weak understanding and to rectify them.

Third, prefer straightforward sentence structures to complex ones. Again, simple sentences usually read better. Some writers (the historian Edward Gibbon is a fine example) can use complex sentence structure to convey irony and secondary meaning. You—unless you have grown up conversant with a prose tradition like Gibbon's, in which case you have *no need whatsoever* to read primers like this—probably cannot. You should typically prefer simple sentences with the bare minimum of sub-clauses needed to convey your argument. Formless and incoherent sentences usually suggest formless and incoherent thought, and indeed they may plausibly *cause* intellectual incoherence. If you reduce your language down to plain, simple sentences with clear structure then you will again be less likely to hide any lack of understanding from the reader and yourself.

Conclusion

Writing good political science essays is not as hard as it seems. It does not require verbal creativity so much as an ordered and disciplined mind. Most obviously and simply, you should read and understand the essay assignment. You should begin by grabbing the attention of the reader with a clear statement of the question that you wish to answer, and how you wish to answer it. You should ensure that your essay is structured and well organized, so that each part does its part, and fits together well with the other parts. Finally, you should ensure that your prose style does not get in the way of clear thinking and clear exposition. If you adhere to these simple rules, you are not guaranteed to write a good essay. *No* set of mechanical rules can provide such a guarantee. You will, however, avoid the basic mistakes that have plagued 80% of the bad political science essays that I have read over my nine years of teaching.

Notes

1. I am grateful to Marty Finnemore and the readers of Crooked Timber and the Monkey Cage for comments on this essay.

2 Social Scientific and Theoretical Analysis

2.1

The Elements of Social Scientific Thinking

Kenneth R. Hoover and Todd Donovan

Thinking Scientifically

"Social science" in cold print gives rise to images of some robot in a statistics laboratory reducing human activity to bloodless digits and simplified formulas. Research reports filled with mechanical-sounding words such as *empirical, quantitative, operational, inverse,* and *correlation* aren't very poetic. Yet the stereotypes of social science created by these images are, as we will try to show, wrong.

Like any other mode of knowing, social science can be used for perverse ends; however, it can also be used for humane personal understanding. By testing thoughts against observations of reality, science helps liberate inquiry from bias, prejudice, and just plain muddle-headedness. So it is unwise to be put off by simple stereotypes—too many people accept these stereotypes and deny themselves the power of social scientific understanding.

The word **science** stands for a very great deal in our culture—some even see science as the rival of religion in the modern age. Our objective here is not to examine the whole tangle of issues associated with science; it is to find a path into the scientific way of thinking about things. In order to find that path, we will begin by allowing some descriptions of science to emerge out of contrasts with other forms of knowledge. . . .

Just as science is not technology, neither is it some specific body of knowledge. The popular phrase "Science tells us [for example] that smoking can kill you" really misleads. "Science" doesn't tell us anything; people tell us things—in this case, people who have used scientific strategies to investigate the relationship of smoking to cancer. Science as a way of thought and investigation is best conceived of as existing not in books, machinery, or reports containing numbers but rather in that invisible world of the mind. Science has to do with the way questions are formulated and answered; it is a set of rules and forms for inquiry and observation created by people who want verifiable answers. . . .

In becoming more conscious of your own habits of thought, you will find that there is a bit of the scientist in each of us. We measure, compare, modify beliefs, and acquire a kind of savvy about evidence in the daily business of figuring out what to do next and how to relate to others. The simplest of games involves the testing of tactics and strategies against the data of performance, and that is crudely scientific.

The scientific way of thought is one of a number of strategies by which we try to cope with a vital reality: the uncertainty of life. . . .

Science is a process of thinking and asking questions, not a body of knowledge. It is one of several ways of claiming that we know something. In one sense, the scientific method is a set of criteria for deciding how conflicts about differing views of reality can be resolved. It offers a strategy that researchers can use when approaching a question. It offers consumers of research the ability to critically assess how evidence has been developed and used in reaching a conclusion.

The scientific approach has many competitors in the search for understanding. For many people throughout most of history, the competitors have prevailed. Analysis of reality has usually been much less popular than myths, conspiracy theories, superstitions, and hunches, which have the reassuring feel of certainty *before* the event they try to predict or control, though seldom afterward. Sometimes unverified belief sponsors an inspired action or sustains the doubtful until a better day. Certainly personal beliefs are a vital part of our lives. The point is that the refusal to analyze is crippling, and the skilled analyst is in a position of strength.

Why Bother to be Systematic?

. . . The need to understand what is happening around us and to share experiences with others makes systematic thought and inquiry essential.

Because society is interesting for the drama it contains, there is a tendency to dispense with systematic understanding and get on with the descriptions, stories, and personal judgments. Although these can be illuminating, they often have limited usefulness because highly subjective accounts of life form a poor basis for the development of common understanding and common action.

The intricate task of getting people to bridge the differences that arise from the singularity of their experience requires a disciplined approach to knowledge. Knowledge is socially powerful only if it is knowledge that can be put to use. Social knowledge, if it is to be useful, must be communicable, valid, and compelling.

In order to be **communicable**, knowledge must be expressed in clear form. And if the knowledge is intended to be used as a spur to action, it must be **valid** in light of the appropriate evidence and **compelling** in the way that it fits the question raised. A personal opinion such as "I think that capitalism exploits the poor" may influence your friends and even your relatives to think that there is some injustice in our society. But it probably won't make any waves with others. If, however, you can cite evidence that nearly one in five American children lives in poverty, a more compelling argument results, because you relate a judgment to a measurement of reality.[1] People who don't even like you but who favor some kind of fairness in wealth distribution might find such a statement a powerful cue to examine our economic system critically. Knowledge built on evidence, and captured in clear transmissible form, makes for power over the environment.

Accumulating knowledge so that past mistakes can be avoided has always intrigued civilized humanity. One can record the sayings of wise people, and that does contribute greatly to cultural enrichment. Yet there is surely room for another kind of cumulative effort: the building up of statements evidenced in a manner that can be double-checked by others. To double-check a statement requires that one know precisely what was claimed and how the claim was tested. This is a major part of the enterprise of science.

The Role of Reasoned Judgment and Opinion

All this vaguely ominous talk about systematic thinking is not meant to cast out reasoned judgment, opinion, and imagination. After all, there is no particular sense in limiting the facilities of the mind in any inquiry.

Reasoned judgment is a staple of human understanding. A reasoned judgment bears a respectable relationship to evidence. Because people inevitably have to act in the absence of complete evidence for decision-making, the term *judgment* is important. Judgment connotes decision-making in which all the powers of the mind are activated to make the best use of available knowledge.

Social science does not eliminate the role of judgment from the research process. Indeed, judgment plays a crucial role in how scientific evidence is gathered and evaluated. We can observe that the highest-earning 1 percent of Americans collect over 16 percent of all income—double their share in 1980. Since 2000, the income of the typical American has remained stagnant despite American workers becoming more productive than ever. It is another matter, however, to link this evidence to broad social questions about capitalism, inequality, poverty, wealth, exploitation, productivity, economic development, and other issues. Logic and good judgment are required to interpret the evidence.[2] . . .

Opinion, likewise, plays an inescapable role in scientific analysis, because all efforts at inquiry proceed from some personal interest or other. No one asks a question unless there is an interest in what the conclusion might be. Furthermore, each person's angle of vision on reality is necessarily slightly different from the angle of another. Opinion can't be eliminated from inquiry, but it can be controlled so that it does not fly off into complete fantasy. One practice that assists in reducing the role of opinion is for the researcher to be conscious of his or her values and opinions.

Plato's famous aphorism "Know thyself" applies here. Much damage has been done to the cause of good social science by those who pretend **objectivity** to the point at which their research conceals opinions that covertly structure their conclusions. No one is truly objective, certainly not about the nature of society—there are too many personal stakes involved for that.

Ultimately, good science provides its own check on the influence of values in an inquiry. If the method by which the study has been done and the evidence for conclusions are clearly and fully stated, the study can be examined by anyone for the fit of conclusions to evidence. If there is doubt about the validity of what has been done, the study itself can be double-checked, or "replicated," to use the technical term. This feature distinguishes science from personal judgment and protects against personal bias.

No one can double-check everything that goes on, as the mind deals with inner feelings, perceptions of experience, and thought processes. Science brings the steps of inquiry out of the mind and into public view so that they can be shared as part of the process of accumulating knowledge.

The Elements of Science

To see scientific thought in the context of other kinds of thinking, as we have tried to do, tells us why we should be interested in science. Now it is time to see what science is made of.

The elements of a scientific strategy are, in themselves, simple to understand. They are concepts, variables, hypotheses, measurements, and theories. The way in which these are combined constitutes the scientific method. It is the function of theory to give meaning and motivation to this method by enabling us to interpret what is observed. First, we will try to put each element in place.

The Origin and Utility of Concepts

If you had to purge all words and other symbols from your mind and confront the world with a virgin mind, what would you do? Without a body to sustain, you might do nothing. The necessities of survival, however, start closing in, and the first act of the mind might be to sort out the edible objects from the inedible, then the warm from the cold, the friendly from the hostile. From there it isn't very far to forming concepts like food, shelter, and warmth, and symbolizing these concepts in the form of words or utterances. Thus, humbly, emerges the instrument called language. The search for truly usable concepts and categories is under way. Languages are nothing more than huge collections of **concepts**—names for things, feelings, and ideas generated or acquired by people in the course of relating to each other and to their environment. . .

Notice that reality testing is built right into the process of naming things, one of the most elementary transactions of existence. That back and forth between the stimuli of the environment and the reflections of the mind makes up the kind of thought we will be trying to capture for analysis.

After several thousand years of human history, we still have to face the fact that the process of naming things is difficult. Language emerges essentially by agreement. You and I and the other members of the family (or tribe, state, nation, world) agree, for example, to call things that twinkle in the sky *stars*. Unfortunately, these agreements may not be very precise. In common usage, the term *star* covers a multitude of objects, big and small, hot and cold, solid and gaseous.

To call a thing by a precise name is the beginning of understanding, because it is the key to the procedure that allows the mind to grasp reality and its many relationships. . . .

To capture meaning in language is a profound and subtle process, even if it is a little sloppy. . . .

Naming is a process that can give the namer great power. Properties of the concept *race* are not easily named. Names of races, moreover, confer different identities on different people. In your own expression of social scientific thinking, although you are invited to be precise about concepts, you are not invited to be arrogant about the utility of your new knowledge for reworking lives, societies, and civilizations.

The importance of having the right name for a thing can hardly be overestimated. Thomas Hobbes, a 17th-century English political theorist, thought the proper naming of things so important to the establishment of political order that he made it a central function of the sovereign. King James understood the message and ordered an authoritative translation of the Bible as a way of overcoming violent squabbles about the precise meanings of words in the Scriptures.

More germane to the modern scene, George Orwell, in his anti-utopian novel *1984,* gave us a vision of a whole bureaucracy devoted to reconstructing language concepts to enhance the power of a totalitarian society. In recent U.S. political history, American presidents have attempted to defuse controversy about unpopular wars they conducted by redefining the concept of military success. These examples are intended to make you aware that, by tinkering with the meanings of concepts, one can play with the foundations of human understanding and social control.

But it will be a while before you master the scientific method sufficiently to pull off anything very grand. For now, the point is that, for scientific purposes, concepts are (1) tentative, (2) based on agreement, and (3) useful only to the degree that they capture or isolate some significant and definable item in reality. . . .

Thought and theory develop through the linking of concepts. Consider, as an example, Pierre Proudhon's famous proposition "Property is theft!" *Property*, as a concept, stands for the notion that a person can claim exclusive ownership of land or other resources. *Theft*, of course, means the act of taking something without justification. By linking these two concepts through the verb "is," Proudhon meant to equate the institution of private property with the denial of humankind's common ownership of nature's resources. The concept of privately owned property was, he thought, unjustifiable thievery. While Proudhon's declaration illustrates the linkage of concepts at the lofty philosophical level, the humblest sentence performs the same operation.

Science is a way of checking on the formulation of concepts and of testing the possible linkages between them through references to observable phenomena. The next step is to see how scientists turn concepts into something that can be observed. When concepts are defined as variables, they can be used to form a special kind of sentence, the hypothesis.

What is a Variable?

A **variable** is a name for something that is thought to influence (or be influenced by) a particular state of being in something else. Heat is one variable in making water boil, and so is pressure. Age has been established as a modestly important variable in voting; however, there are many other more significant variables: socioeconomic standing, parental influence, race, gender, region of residence, and so on.

A variable is, in addition, a special kind of concept that contains within it a notion of degree or differentiation. Temperature is an easily understood example of a variable. It includes the notion of more or less heat—that is, of degree. As the name suggests, variables are things that vary. Interesting questions in social science center on concepts that involve variation and how changes in one phenomenon help to explain variation in another.

Consider, as an example, the relationship between religion and voting. In the first place, religion is a different kind of variable than, say, temperature. Although there may be such a thing as degrees of "religiosity,"[3] it is likely we would discuss variation in the concept *religion* in terms of religious denominations such as Buddhist, Christian, and Muslim. There is substantial variation in the religions with which people identify. For example, exit poll date were used to assess the importance of religion in the 2008 election when Democratic presidential candidate Barack Obama challenged Republican candidate John McCain. Data collected by a consortium of media firms found that fully 78 percent of Jewish voters supported Obama (compared to 21 percent for McCain), whereas 65 percent of white Protestants voted for McCain (compared to 34 percent for Obama). Fifty-four percent of Catholics voted for Obama, while 45 percent voted for McCain. Obama won three-quarters of the votes from those reporting no religious affiliation and 73 percent among those with "other" religions.[4] Data such as these permit us to say something meaningful about the relationship between the variable *religion* and the variable *voting behavior*.

Although most variables deal with differences of degree, as in temperature, or differences of variety, as in religion, some variables are even simpler. These deal with the most elementary kind of variation: present or absent, there or not there, existent or nonexistent. Take pregnancy, for example. There is no such thing as a little bit of it. Either the condition exists or it doesn't.

Turning concepts into variables, dull as it may seem, is a very creative process and often raises intriguing questions. Consider, as an illustration, such an ordinary variable as *time.* The early Greeks puzzled a good deal over how to conceptualize this variable. It seems obvious that time has to be thought of as having a beginning—so philosophers went about trying to figure out when the beginning was. Yet the nagging question always popped up: What happened before that? . . .

The social science done by introductory students seldom involves such mind-boggling conceptual problems, yet it wouldn't do to pretend that these problems don't exist. The variable *personality*, for example, is reputed to have more than 400 definitions in the professional literature, partly because personality is a compound of a huge range of other variables: class, status, self-concept, race, socialization, and so forth. The complexity of personality as a variable has driven social scientists to such awkward definitions as "One's acquired, relatively enduring, yet dynamic, unique system of predispositions to psychological and social behavior."[5]

Even when social scientists agree on the description of a variable, that doesn't mean the definition possesses the qualities of eternal truth—it just means that some people who have thought about it carefully agree that a given definition seems to help answer some questions. Moreover, researchers often settle on a definition of a variable for reasons of convenience. Party identification in the United States is conventionally measured by survey question responses that place voters on a continuum reflecting their identification with the two major political parties. The continuum is represented by this seven-point scale:

←strong Dem—weak Dem—Ind leaning Dem—Ind—Ind leaning Rep—Weak Rep—strong Rep→

Political independents are assumed to be in the center of the political spectrum. Yet the truth of the matter might be that many "independents" think of themselves as radicals who are outside the center. Some might be so nonpartisan or apolitical that they just don't think of themselves in terms of political parties at all. Furthermore, some "leaning" independents are nearly as partisan in their voting as "weak" partisans.[6] Although this definition of the variable might not perfectly reflect the underlying truth of the concept partisanship, it continues to have predictive power. The question has been asked on surveys for decades, so it allows researchers to evaluate trends in partisanship over time. As the difficulties of categorizing independents on this spectrum become apparent, new definitions of partisanship will emerge. Ignoring the problem of specifying how concepts should be turned into variables doesn't make the problem go away; it just gets you further into the linguistic soup. . . .

Unfortunately for social science, we have barely figured out how to lay the foundation for a structure of theory to explain social behavior. Many new students of social science do not see—especially when confronted by thick texts in introductory courses—the context of struggle and accomplishment, tentativeness and probability, behind what has been achieved in social understanding.

Social science currently contains many subdivisions (including political science, sociology, economics, psychology, and education), all of which are working on defining, observing, and linking specific variables within subsystems of behavior. Social scientists are in the process of chasing a good many possible connections between variables. The bits of tested knowledge that do emerge await integration across the lines of these inquiries. Relatively few have been attempted, though these efforts are bound to increase in view of the dramatic need for comprehensive social understanding.

The Hypothesis

Although much of the preceding discussion may have seemed like a serial review of bits and pieces of scientific thinking, a discussion of hypotheses will bring these matters together.

A **hypothesis** is a sentence of a particularly well-cultivated breed. The purpose of a hypothesis is to organize a study. If the hypothesis is carefully formed, all the steps of the scientific method follow, as does an outline for the project, a bibliography, a list of resources needed, and a specification of the measures appropriate to the study. The hypothesis provides the structure.

A hypothesis proposes a relationship between two or more variables. For example: Political participation *increases* with education. This simple assertion can be seen as a hypothesis. It has a subject (the variable *political participation*), a connective verb (a relationship, *increases*), and an object (the variable *education*). . . .

It is crucial to realize that a hypothesis is a supposition, as the Oxford English Dictionary points out, "which serves as a starting point for further investigation by which it may be proved or disproved . . . " A hypothesis stands at the beginning, not the end, of a study, although good studies may suggest new paths of fruitful inquiry and new hypotheses.

So far, . . . our examples . . . have been quite simple. But to go from the straightforward to the bizarre, let us cite an experience in teaching scientific thinking.

A student came to one of us with the following proposal for research:

> The fragile psycho-pathological type of double helical existence issuing from the precarious relationship of the colonizer and the colonized (which figuratively is similar to the relationship of Siamese twins) and their respective interaction within the colonial situation is psychologically effective, which ramifications lead to psychological maladjustments, i.e., neuroses which subsequently define the nature of the political particulars therein.

That was just the beginning of the proposal! In all that confusing language, there are lots of variables and many relationships. Sorting it out, however, yields two hypotheses:

> Colonialism is *associated with* neurotic behavior by colonizer and colonial.

> This neurotic behavior *influences* the political structure of colonialism.

These two hypotheses, large as they are, are somewhat manageable. The concept *colonialism* describes a well-established political situation. The relationship is *associated with* was a retreat from saying *causes*—a precaution taken in view of the limited research resources available to the student. Neurotic behavior is a tricky concept, but it has parentage in the literature of psychoanalytic theory; there are behaviors that can respectably be labeled neurotic. From there it becomes a matter of showing the links between the kinds of neurotic, self-destructive behavior that occur in colonial situations and the repressive and authoritarian patterns of colonial politics.

Had the student accomplished all that these hypotheses imply by way of evidence gathering, measurement, and evaluation, he would have been in line for a Ph.D. As long as we both knew that he was just scratching the surface, his paper (bravely entitled "Colonialism: A Game for Neurotics") was good enough for undergraduate requirements.

One of the things this example illustrates is that there is often a prior step to hypothesis formation. The step is called **problem reformulation**. In the preceding example, we began with a generalized concern about colonialism and neurosis. The student elaborated that concern into a complex description of the problem. We narrowed it down by specifying variables and relationships into something that could be dealt with, at least in a general way. With a workable reformulation, defining the ways that variables are represented becomes easier.

One of the arts of social science is skillful problem reformulation. Reformulation requires, in addition to some analytic common sense, the ability to see the variables in a situation and the possible relationships between them. A good first step is to break the problem into its component variables and relationships. Writing down lists of hypotheses associated with a problem enables you to select the ones that answer two questions: Which hypotheses are crucial to the solution of the whole problem? For which hypotheses is there information within the range of your resources? Sometimes these questions force some unpleasant choices, but they help prevent arriving at the end of a research effort with nothing substantial on which to hang a conclusion. The preceding example on colonialism and neurosis illustrates the point.

The importance of establishing a hypothesis correctly before starting off on a research task can hardly be overstated. The following rules will help:

1. The variables must be clearly specified and measurable by some technique you know how to use.
2. The relationship between the variables must be precisely stated and measurable.
3. The hypothesis should be testable, so that evidence of the relationship can be observed, demonstrated, or falsified.

If these rules are not followed, the hypothesis may be unwieldy, ridiculous, or just too hard to research in view of available resources. Precise definitions and thoughtful specification of measurements are, in short, the keys. The struggle to form a hypothesis carefully may not be enjoyable, but the questions raised in the process have to be answered sooner or later.

The hypothesis, then, provides the structure for your entire research effort, whether it involves interviews and surveys, analysis of previously collected data, library research, or all three. It will direct you to relevant information so you do not waste time and effort. The relationships proposed between the variables suggest the measurement tools and standards for evaluation that you will need to use. The results of the hypothesis test are the substance of your conclusions.

Once relationships between variables have been established through hypothesis formation and testing, these relationships can be expressed as **generalizations**.

Generalizations based on tested relationships are the object of science. A generalization is a hypothesis affirmed by testing. As generalizations in a field of study accumulate, they form the raw stuff of theories. But this gets us ahead of the story. For now, we need to see how the scientific method sets the procedure for research into a logical sequence.

The Scientific Method

The technique known as the **scientific method** is quite commonsensical. The model inquiry proceeds by steps that include the following:

1. The identification of the variables to be studied
2. A hypothesis about the relation of one variable to another or to a situation
3. A reality test whereby changes in the variables are measured to see if the hypothesized relationship is evidenced
4. An evaluation in which the measured relationship between the variables is compared with the original hypothesis and generalizations about the findings are developed
5. Suggestions about the theoretical significance of the findings, factors involved in the test that may have distorted the results, and other hypotheses that the inquiry brings to mind

Although we have sketched here the bare bones of the scientific method, the actual procedure of research does not always start directly with hypothesis formation. As a preliminary to stating hypotheses, social scientists often examine the data collected in a subject area to see if there are connections between the variables. The relationships brought to light by various statistical processes frequently suggest the hypotheses it would be fruitful to explore. Occasionally, simply getting involved with a set of data triggers an interesting thought, a chance insight, or a new idea. A great quantity of data has been generated over the past few decades, so researchers can usually avoid having to begin at the beginning with every inquiry. The analysis of existing data can be extremely helpful in identifying new data needed to test a crucial relationship. . . .

The point is that the scientific method seeks to test thoughts against observable evidence in a disciplined manner, with each step in the process made explicit.

Consider the differences between two kinds of studies: (1) an empirical scientific study in which the author states his or her values, forms hypotheses, lays out a testing procedure, carefully selects and discusses measurements, produces a specific result, and relates this to the hypotheses; and (2) a nonscientific study in which the author expresses values, develops a general thesis, examines relevant examples, and states the conclusions.

Notice that the tension between thought and investigation is present in both studies. But one important difference is the feasibility of checking the validity of the conclusions in the first example as opposed to the second, by repeating the study. **Replication** is the word social scientists use to indicate the ability to repeat a study as a way of checking on its validity. Replication constitutes a very strong test of a good study because it can reveal errors that might have crept in through the procedures and evaluative judgments contained in the principal study.

A second difficulty with a nonscientific study lies in the problem of relating one study to another. Have you ever been annoyed in a discussion when someone asks you to define your terms? Have you ever gotten into arguments that end with "How do you know that is true?"

A good scientific study presents all the information needed to see what took place. For example, if standard variable definitions are used, a study of voters' assessments of candidates can be added to studies of how voters view issues, parties, or whatever. As scientists try to build cumulative bodies of knowledge, different studies of the same variables using different measures can be compared to see if measurement techniques create alternative results. The point, once again, is that science regulates and specifies the relationship between thought and investigation in such a way that others may know exactly what has been done.

The Many Roles of Theory

Science rests its claim to authority upon its firm basis in observable evidence about something called "reality." We have occasionally described science as, simply, reality testing. Since everybody thinks he or she knows what reality is, science acquires a fundamental appeal. Yet the necessary partner of realism in science is that wholly imaginary phenomenon, **theory.** Without the many roles that theory plays, there would be no science (and, some would argue, there would be no understandable "reality," either).

Just as language arises out of the experience of coming to grips with human needs, so also does theory arise from tasks that people face. The hardest task is to explain what's really going on out there. Volumes have been written about what theory is and isn't. For our purposes, a theory is a set of related propositions that suggest why events occur in the manner that they do.

The propositions that make up theories are of the same form as hypotheses. They consist of concepts and the linkages or relationships between them. Theories are built up as hypotheses are tested and new relationships emerge.

Theory abounds in the most ordinary transactions of life. There are theories of everything from the payoff of slot machines to the inner meaning of Dilbert cartoons. The grandest theories of all are religious and philosophical, embracing huge orders of questions about the origin of the physical universe, the history of the species, the purposes of life, and the norms of behavior that lead to virtue and, possibly, happiness. To the faithful, such theories are made true by a belief in supernatural phenomena. These kinds of theories are presented as if they were embedded in the larger cosmos of our existence, awaiting our arrival at understanding.

Social science, by contrast, generally operates from a different perspective on theory. The most conventional posture of a social scientist is one of pragmatism: A theory is only as good as its present and potential uses in explaining observations. The point of any science is to develop a set of theories to explain the events within their range of observation. . . .

Social science theory is often derived from fundamental assumptions about human behavior. Rational actor theories suggest that individuals, organizations, and nation-states are motivated by a desire to maximize their material interests. Based on this type of theory, we might hypothesize that voters select candidates that further their own economic interest. Alternatively, psychological theories assume that voting actions are determined by people's long-term feelings of attachment for political parties. Voters are thought to be socialized, via the family, to be loyal to a particular party. From this theory, we might hypothesize that voters act like their parents, or that they select candidates of the same party year after year. The origins of wars have been explained by rational actor theories and psychological theories, as well as by Marxian theories and other forms of social theory.

We have been discussing what theory is and is not. The next question is: What does it do? The answer is: many things. We list four particular uses of theory in social scientific thinking:

1. Theory provides patterns for the interpretation of data.
2. Theory links one study with another.
3. Theory supplies frameworks within which concepts and variables acquire substantive significance.
4. Theory allows us to interpret the larger meaning of our finding for ourselves and others.

Let's illustrate these four uses of theory by looking at the question of voter participation. The rate of voter participation is an important indicator of democracy. It is reasonable to expect that different types of election rules will affect how many people think it is worth their time and effort to vote. We will show how theory influences the way we look at questions of political participation under contrasting sets of election rules. The patterns observed in the data, the links established between studies, the substantive significance of the findings, and their larger meaning are all shaped by the theories the researcher uses.

In this illustration, we will focus on how election rules translate people's votes into seats for parties in a legislature. In the United States, nearly all elections are for single-member districts. These rules award a single seat to the candidate who wins the most votes in each district. Where the rules allow a wider variety of parties to win seats [as in proportional representation (PR) systems], presumably more people will vote.[7] In PR systems, each party wins a proportion of the total number of seats based on its percentage of the vote. Thus, if 10 legislative seats are to be allocated in an election, most of the seats would likely go to candidates from large parties, but smaller parties can elect candidates to one or two seats by winning 10 or 20 percent of the vote.

Some theorize that winner-take-all rules in single-member districts might reduce participation. In the United States, the rules mean that nearly all seats are won by candidates from the Democratic and Republican parties. The hypothesis would be that citizens who are not oriented toward candidates from the major parties might be discouraged from voting.[8] Since a large slice of the electorate see themselves as "independents," this becomes an important factor in assessing the effectiveness of U.S. democracy.

Consider the data presented in Table 2.1. The table shows the average level of turnout for elections held in various countries under three types of election rules. Winner-take-all rules award seats only to candidates that finish first in a single district. Proportional systems typically allow voters to select a party's slate of candidates, then allocate multiple seats roughly proportionate to each party's vote share. Some nations elect part of their legislature with winner take-all rules and the rest with proportional rules. These nations have mixed systems.

What is the message of these data? Looking at the top row of data, we find that election rules might affect participation in national elections. Countries that use PR averaged 73 percent turnout, compared with a 54 percent turnout rate for the nations that used winner-take-all rules. These data are averages based on elections in different countries. The data suggest but do not prove conclusively that proportional representation influences more citizens to vote. However, rival explanations and intervening variables, such as cultural differences, might explain these patterns as well.[9]

Where does the theory enter in? What theories fit this pattern of data? One theory is that people are more likely to act—in this case, to vote—when they think their action will have tangible consequences. In other words, they're more likely to vote if they think their most preferred party might win, or if they think their vote might make a difference in a close election. Thus PR systems might attract followers of smaller parties to vote because of the greater likelihood that their vote could have the effect of electing a representative. Since PR allows more parties in a legislature, the data in Table 2.1 seem to support the theory that PR mobilizes a wider range of citizens because their vote is more likely to have a tangible result.

Another theory proposes that people vote out of a sense of civic duty. Under this theory, they vote regardless of perceptions about their preferred party's chances of winning seats.[10] Since we have no data about how the public's sense of civic duty varies across these nations, the fact that our data are consistent with one theory does not mean that we can reject the rival theory.

Being aware of different theories allows social scientists to link their studies with previous research. It also provides a means to generate additional tests that might allow us to reject rival theories that offer alternative explanations for patterns seen in the data. If we found, for example, that there were no differences in perceived civic duty among the places reflected in the data in Table 2.1, a stronger case could be made that PR motivates more people to vote than winner-take-all elections.

PR might cause the perceived benefits of voting (greater chances of representation) to outweigh the costs. It might be that non-voters in the United States are those who feel politically marginalized by electoral institutions that prevent their preferred candidates from winning office. Through these links in reasoning, social scientists can accumulate knowledge of relationships between different theoretical constructs. So far we have seen two uses of theory in relation to the example in Table 2.1: the patterns theory provides and the ways that theory links one study to another.

Table 2.1 Turnout at National Elections, 2000-2009

	Type of Election Rules for National Legislature		
	Winner-take-all[a]	Proportional[b]	Mixed[c]
Average turnout	54.5%	73.4%	70.3%
Standard deviation	3.0%	12.8%	7.7%
Number of nations	4	12	3

[a] Canada, Great Britain, France, and the United States
[b] Denmark, Finland, Greece, Iceland, Ireland, Israel, Netherlands, Norway, Portugal, Spain, Sweden, and Switzerland
[c] Germany, Japan, and New Zealand

Note: Average turnout for national elections held in 19 advanced industrialized democracies where voting is largely noncompulsory.

Source: Authors' calculations from data posted at the Institute for Democracy and Electoral Assistance, http://www.idea.int/

The third use of theory is now apparent. We need to assess the substantive significance of what is observed here.[11] That is, we need to ask if the observations have implications that are interesting or important. This result could be important for testing the usefulness of rational actor theories in explaining political behavior. In this case, we might infer that a switch to PR rules could boost turnout substantially in a nation using winner-take-all elections.[12]

It would seem that giving people more choices in elections might lead to greater citizen participation. This raises a host of interesting substantive questions: How would the participation of these voters change a political system? What new parties might succeed? How would institutions such as Congress function with several parties?

The larger meaning of these findings for theories relating political institutions to human behavior lies beyond these specific substantive questions. Participation in a representative democracy is not just a matter of having the formal right to vote. People are also sensitive to the results of the process and to the constraints that institutions create. Clearly, other factors are involved, but it would seem that election systems that lead to the representation of more social groups also encourage more people to vote. Proportional rules that produce representation for a wider variety of people are also likely to have broader effects on citizens' attitudes about politics and government generally.[13]

In discussing theory, we have presented an illustration of its uses in social scientific research. Most researchers are intent on proving their theory to be "right." However, Karl Popper, an influential analyst of the social sciences, shows us that the best use of science is often to refute theories rather than to "prove" them:

> Of nearly every theory it may be said that it agrees with many facts: this is one of the reasons why a theory can be said to be corroborated only if we are unable to find refuting facts, rather than if we are able to find supporting facts.[14]

In other words, data may be more impressive as evidence for the theories they refute than for the theories they support.

What we have not captured in this discussion of theory is the subtlety and creativity with which people think about what they are observing. Theory illuminates observations. Yet, like a beam of light playing on an object, every theory leaves shadows that challenge our imaginations.

On one hand, we can only say that without theory, social science would be an incoherent and meaningless pile of observations, data, and statistics. On the other hand, not all social science can be tied to rigorous and specific theoretical formulations. However, it is absolutely clear that complex social problems need all the well-informed study we can develop. The organization and evaluation of that knowledge in theoretical form is almost as important as gathering it in the first place. History is littered with the wreckage of poorly conceived social theories—sometimes with tragic results—though the power of theoretical imagination has been responsible for some of civilization's greatest advances.

Notes

1. See Ayama Douglas-Hall and Heather Koball, "The New Poor: Regional Trends in Poverty Since 2000," Mailman School of Public Health, Columbia University. National Center for Children in Poverty, 2006. This report used U.S. Census Bureau Data from March 1976 to March 2004, and noted that 18 percent of children lived in poverty. This was a dramatic increase since 2000.

2. "The Rich, the Poor and the Growing Gap Between Them: Rich Are Big Gainers in America's New Prosperity," *Economist* (June 15, 2006). Thomas Piketty and Emmanuel Saez, "The Evolution of Top Income Groups: A Historical and International Perspective." *NBER working paper 11955* (January 2006). These studies showed that the income gap between rich and poor was the largest since 1921, and was growing.

3. Various attempts have been made to measure degrees of individual "religiosity" in terms of attitudinal and behavioral traits such as regularity of church atten dance. For an example, see Lyman A. Kellstedt and Mark A. Noll, "Religion, Voting for President and Party Identification, 1948–1984," in *Religion and American Politics: From the Colonial Period to the 1980s*, ed. Mark A. Noll (Oxford, England: Oxford University Press, 1990), p. 347.

4. CNN.com Election 2008 Results. U.S. President Exit Poll. At www.cnn.com/ELECTIONI2008/results/polls.main/

5. Gordon DiRenzo, *Personality and Politics* (Garden City, N.Y.: Anchor Books, 1974), p. 16.

6. William Flanigan and' Nancy Zingale, *Political Behavior of the American Electorate*, 11th ed. (Washington, D.C.: Congressional Quarterly Press, 2006), pp. 89–91. These authors note that the American electorate is becoming "more nonpartisan overall, but not invariably more independent" as more nonpartisans fail even to call themselves independent.

7. See, for example, G. Bingham Powell, "American Voter Turnout in Comparative Perspective," *American Political Science Review* 80, no. 1 (1986), pp. 1743.

8. One study attempted to hold cultural differences constant by comparing turnout in U.S. local elections that used winner-take-all to those using "semiproportional" elections. It found that "semi-PR" systems increased turnout by about 5 percent. See Shaun Bowler, David Brockington, and Todd Donovan, "Election Systems and Voter Turnout: Experiments in the United States," *Journal of Politics*, 63, no. 3, (2001), pp. 902–915,

9. Douglas Amy, *Real Choices, New Voices* (Cambridge, UK: Cambridge University Press, 1993), pp. 140–153; Arend Lijphart, "Unequal Participation: Democracy's Unresolved Dilemma," *American Political Science Review* 91, no. 1 (1997), pp. 1–14.

10. For a discussion of these rival theories, see Donald Green and Ian Shapiro, *Pathologies of Rational Choice Theory* (New Haven, Conn.: Yale University Press, 1994). Cf. Kristen Monroe, *The Heart of Altrusim: Perceptions if a Common Humanity* (Princeton, NJ.: Princeton University Press, 1996).

11. This should not be confused with statistical significance (see Chapter Five), which tells whether the difference between winner-take-all and PR elections may have occurred by chance. Substantive significance relates to theory rather than to statistical probability.

12. Comparative studies that account for additional variables suggest that the independent effect of PR on turnout varies between 3 and 7 percent. See Andre Blais and Agnieszka Dobrzyniska, "Turnout in Electoral Democracies," *European Journal of Political Research* 18 (1998), pp. 167–181; Andres Lander and Henry Milner, "Do Voters Turn Out More Under Proportional Than Majoritarian Systems?," *Electoral Studies*, 18 (1999), pp. 235–250.

13. C. Anderson and C. Guilloty, "Political Institutions and Satisfaction with Democracy: A Cross-National Analysis of Consensus and Majoritarian System," *American Political Science Review* 91, no 1 (1997), pp. 68–81.

14. In *Popper Selections*, ed. David Miller (Princeton, N.J.: Princeton University Press, 1985), p. 437.

2.2

Man, the State, and War

A Theoretical Analysis

Kenneth N.Waltz

International Conflict and Human Behavior

The First Image

> *There is deceit and cunning and from these wars arise.*
>
> —Confucius

According to the first image of international relations, the locus of the important causes of war is found in the nature and behavior of man. Wars result from selfishness, from misdirected aggressive impulses, from stupidity. Other causes are secondary and have to be interpreted in the light of these factors. If these are the primary causes of war, then the elimination of war must come through uplifting and enlightening men or securing their psychic-social readjustment. This estimate of causes and cures has been dominant in the writings of many serious students of human affairs from Confucius to present-day pacifists. It is the leitmotif of many modern behavioral scientists as well.[1]

Prescriptions associated with first-image analyses need not be identical in content, as a few examples will indicate. Henry Wadsworth Longfellow, moved to poetic expression by a visit to the arsenal at Springfield, set down the following thoughts:

> Were half the power that fills the world with terror,
> Were half the wealth bestowed on camps and courts,
> Given to redeem the human mind from error,
> There were no need of arsenals or forts.

Implicit in these lines is the idea that the people will insist that the right policies be adopted if only they know what the right policies are. Their instincts are good, though their present gullibility may prompt them to follow false leaders. By attributing present difficulties to a defect in knowledge, education becomes the remedy for war. The idea is widespread. . . . By others, increasing the chances of peace has been said to require not so much a change in "instincts" as a channeling of energies that are presently expended in the destructive folly of war. If there were something that men would rather do than fight, they would cease to fight altogether. Aristophanes saw the point. If the women of Athens would deny themselves to husbands and lovers, their men would have to choose between the pleasures of the couch and the exhilarating experiences of the battlefield. Aristophanes thought he knew the men, and women, of Athens well enough to make the outcome a foregone conclusion. William James was in the same tradition. War, in his view, is rooted in man's bellicose nature, which is the product of centuries-old tradition. His nature cannot be changed or his drives suppressed, but they can be diverted. . . .

The prescriptions vary, but common to them all is the thought that in order to achieve a more peaceful world men must be changed, whether in their moral-intellectual outlook or in their psychic-social behavior. One may, however, agree with the first-image analysis of causes without admitting the possibility of practicable prescriptions for their removal. Among those who accept a first-image explanation of war there are both optimists and pessimists, those who think the possibilities of progress so great that wars will end before the next generation is dead and those who think that wars will continue to occur though by them we may all die. . . .

***

The evilness of men, or their improper behavior, leads to war; individual goodness, if it could be universalized,

---

Source: Kenneth Waltz. *Man, the State, and War: A Theoretical Analysis.* New York: Columbia University Press, 1959 (2001). Reprinted with permission.

would mean peace: this is a summary statement of the first image. For the pessimists peace is at once a goal and a utopian dream, but others have taken seriously the presumption that a reform of individuals sufficient to bring lasting peace to the world is possible. Men are good; therefore no social or political problems—is this a true statement? Would the reform of individuals, if realized, cure social and political ills? The difficulty obviously lies in the word "good." How is "good" to be defined? "Those people are good who spontaneously act in perfect harmony with one another." This is a tautological definition, but nevertheless a revealing one. What first-image analysts, optimists and pessimists alike, have done is: (1) to notice conflict, (2) to ask themselves why conflict occurs, and (3) to pin the blame on one or a small number of behavior traits. First-image optimists betray a naïveté in politics that vitiates their efforts to construct a new and better world. Their lack of success is directly related to a view of man that is simple and pleasing, but wrong. First-image pessimists have expertly dismantled the air castles of the optimists but have had less success in their endeavors to build the serviceable but necessarily uninspiring dwellings that must take their place. They have countered a theory of politics built on an optimistic definition of man's capabilities by pointing out that men are not what most pacifists and many liberals think them.

International Conflict and the Internal Structure of States

The Second Image

> *However conceived in an image of the world, foreign policy is a phase of domestic policy, an inescapable phase.*
>
> —Charles Beard, A Foreign Policy for America

The first image did not exclude the influence of the state, but the role of the state was introduced as a consideration less important than, and to be explained in terms of, human behavior. According to the first image, to say that the state acts is to speak metonymically. We say that the state acts when we mean that the people in it act, just as we say that the pot boils when we mean that the water in it boils. The preceding [section] concentrated on the contents rather than the container; the present [section] alters the balance of emphasis in favor of the latter. To continue the figure: Water running out of a faucet is chemically the same as water in a container, but once the water is in a container, it can be made to "behave" in different ways. It can be turned into steam and used to power an engine, or, if the water is sealed in and heated to extreme temperatures, it can become the instrument of a destructive explosion. Wars would not exist were human nature not what it is, but neither would Sunday schools and brothels, philanthropic organizations and criminal gangs. Since everything is related to human nature, to explain anything one must consider more than human nature. The events to be explained are so many and so varied that human nature cannot possibly be the single determinant. . . .

To understand war and peace political analysis must be used to supplement and order the findings of psychology and sociology. What kind of political analysis is needed? For possible explanations of the occurrence or nonoccurrence of war, one can look to international politics (since war occurs among states), or one can look to the states themselves (since it is in the name of the state that the fighting is actually done). The former approach is postponed; according to the second image, the internal organization of states is the key to understanding war and peace.

One explanation of the second-image type is illustrated as follows. War most often promotes the internal unity of each state involved. The state plagued by internal strife may then, instead of waiting for the accidental attack, seek the war that will bring internal peace. Bodin saw this clearly, for he concludes that "the best way of preserving a state, and guaranteeing it against sedition, rebellion, and civil war is to keep the subjects in amity one with another, and to this end, to find an enemy against whom they can make common cause." . . .

The use of internal defects to explain those external acts of the state that bring war can take many forms. Such explanation may be related to a type of government that is thought to be generically bad. For example, it is often thought that the deprivations imposed by despots upon their subjects produce tensions that may find expression in foreign adventure. Or the explanation may be given in terms of defects in a government not itself considered bad. Thus it has been argued that the restrictions placed upon a government in order to protect the prescribed rights of its citizens act as impediments to the making and executing of foreign policy. These restrictions, laudable in original purpose, may have the unfortunate effect of making difficult or impossible the effective action of that government for the maintenance of peace in the world.[2] And, as a final example, explanation may be made in terms of geographic or economic deprivations or in terms of deprivations too vaguely defined to be labeled at all. Thus a nation may argue that it has not attained its "natural" frontiers, that such frontiers are necessary to its security, that war to extend the state to its deserved compass is justified or even necessary.[3] The possible variations on this theme have been made familiar by the "have-not" arguments so popular in this century. Such arguments have been used both to explain why "deprived" countries undertake war and to urge the satiated to make the compensatory adjustments thought necessary if peace is to be perpetuated.[4] . . .

International Conflict and International Anarchy

The Third Image

With many sovereign states, with no system of law enforceable among them, with each state judging its grievances and ambitions according to the dictates of its own reason or desire—conflict, sometimes leading to war, is bound to occur. To achieve a favorable outcome from such conflict a state has to rely on its own devices, the relative efficiency of which must be its constant concern. This, the idea of the third image, is to be examined in the present [section]. It is not an esoteric idea; it is not a new idea. Thucydides implied it when he wrote that it was "the growth of the Athenian power, which terrified the Lacedaemonians and forced them into war."[5] John Adams implied it when he wrote to the citizens of Petersburg, Virginia, that "a war with France, if just and necessary, might wean us from fond and blind affections, which no Nation ought ever to feel towards another, as our experience in more than one instance abundantly testifies."[6] There is an obvious relation between the concern over relative power position expressed by Thucydides and the admonition of John Adams that love affairs between states are inappropriate and dangerous. This relation is made explicit in Frederick Dunn's statement that "so long as the notion of self-help persists, the aim of maintaining the power position of the nation is paramount to all other considerations."[7]

In anarchy there is no automatic harmony. The three preceding statements reflect this fact. A state will use force to attain its goals if, after assessing the prospects for success, it values those goals more than it values the pleasures of peace. Because each state is the final judge of its own cause, any state may at any time use force to implement its policies. Because any state may at any time use force, all states must constantly be ready either to counter force with force or to pay the cost of weakness. The requirements of state action are, in this view, imposed by the circumstances in which all states exist.

In a manner of speaking, all three images are a part of nature. So fundamental are man, the state, and the state system in any attempt to understand international relations that seldom does an analyst, however wedded to one image, entirely overlook the other two. Still, emphasis on one image may distort one's interpretation of the others. It is, for example, not uncommon to find those inclined to see the world in terms of either the first or the second image countering the oft-made argument that arms breed not war but security, and possibly even peace, by pointing out that the argument is a compound of dishonest myth, to cover the interests of politicians, armament makers, and others, and honest illusion entertained by patriots sincerely interested in the safety of their states. To dispel the illusion, Cobden, to recall one of the many who have argued this way, once pointed out that doubling armaments, if everyone does it, makes no state more secure and, similarly, that none would be endangered if all military establishments were simultaneously reduced by, say, 50 percent.[8] Putting aside the thought that the arithmetic is not necessarily an accurate reflection of what the situation would be, this argument illustrates a supposedly practical application of the first and second images. Whether by educating citizens and leaders of the separate states or by improving the organization of each of them, a condition is sought in which the lesson here adumbrated becomes the basis for the policies of states. The result?—disarmament, and thus economy, together with peace, and thus security, for all states. If some states display a willingness to pare down their military establishments, other states will be able to pursue similar policies. In emphasizing the interdependence of the policies of all states, the argument pays heed to the third image. The optimism is, however, the result of ignoring some inherent difficulties. . . .

***

The present [section] provides a basic explanation of the third image of international relations. That there is still important ground to cover is made clear by two points. First, there is no obvious logical relation between the proposition that "in anarchy there is no automatic harmony" and the proposition that "among autonomous states *war* is inevitable," both of which were put forth in this [reading]. Second, although it has by now become apparent that there is a considerable interdependence among the three images, we have not systematically considered the problem of interrelating them.

Notes

1. They are discussed at length in ch. iii, below.
2. Cf. Sherwood, *Roosevelt and Hopkins*, pp. 67–68, 102, 126, 133–36, 272, and especially 931; and Secretary of State Hay's statement in Adams, *The Education of Henry Adams*, p. 374. Note that in this case the fault is one that is thought to decrease the ability of a country to implement a peaceful policy. In the other examples, the defect is thought to increase the propensity of a country to go to war.
3. Cf. Bertrand Russell, who in 1917 wrote: "There can be no good international system until the boundaries of states coincide as nearly as possible with the boundaries of nations." *Political Ideals*, p. 146.
4. Cf. Simonds and Emeny, The Great Powers in World Politics, passim; Thompson, Danger Spots in World Population, especially Preface, chs. i, xiii.
5. Thucydides, *History of the Peloponnesian War*, tr. Jowett, Book I, par. 23.
6. Letter of John Adams to the citizens of the town of Petersburg, dated June 6, 1798, and reprinted in the program for the visit of William Howard Taft, Petersburg, Va., May 19, 1909.
7. Dunn, Peaceful Change, p. 13.
8. Cobden, especially his Speeches on Peace, Financial Reform, Colonial Reform, and Other Subjects Delivered during 1849, p. 135.

3 Realism I

3.1

Of the Natural Condition of Mankind as Concerning Their Felicity and Misery

Thomas Hobbes

Nature hath made men so equal in the faculties of body and mind as that, though there be found one man sometimes manifestly stronger in body or of quicker mind than another, yet when all is reckoned together the difference between man and man is not so considerable as that one man can thereupon claim to himself any benefit to which another may not pretend as well as he. For as to the strength of body, the weakest has strength enough to kill the strongest, either by secret machination or by confederacy with others that are in the same danger with himself.

And as to the faculties of the mind, setting aside the arts grounded upon words, and especially that skill of proceeding upon general and infallible rules, called science, which very few have and but in few things, as being not a native faculty born with us, nor attained, as prudence, while we look after somewhat else, I find yet a greater equality amongst men than that of strength. For prudence is but experience, which equal time equally bestows on all men in those things they equally apply themselves unto. That which may perhaps make such equality incredible is but a vain conceit of one's own wisdom, which almost all men think they have in a greater degree than the vulgar; that is, than all men but themselves, and a few others, whom by fame, or for concurring with themselves, they approve. For such is the nature of men that howsoever they may acknowledge many others to be more witty, or more eloquent or more learned, yet they will hardly believe there be many so wise as themselves; for they see their own wit at hand, and other men's at a distance. But this proveth rather that men are in that point equal, than unequal. For there is not ordinarily a greater sign of the equal distribution of anything than that every man is contented with his share.

From this equality of ability ariseth equality of hope in the attaining of our ends. And therefore if any two men desire the same thing, which nevertheless they cannot both enjoy, they become enemies; and in the way to their end (which is principally their own conservation, and sometimes their delectation only) endeavour to destroy or subdue one another. And from hence it comes to pass that where an invader hath no more to fear than another man's single power, if one plant, sow, build, or possess a convenient seat, others may probably be expected to come prepared with forces united to dispossess and deprive him, not only of the fruit of his labour, but also of his life or liberty. And the invader again is in the like danger of another.

And from this diffidence of one another, there is no way for any man to secure himself so reasonable as anticipation; that is, by force, or wiles, to master the persons of all men he can so long till he see no other power great enough to endanger him: and this is no more than his own conservation requireth, and is

Source: Thomas Hobbes (1651), "On the Nature and Condition of Man," in *Leviathan* Chapter XIII.

generally allowed. Also, because there be some that, taking pleasure in contemplating their own power in the acts of conquest, which they pursue farther than their security requires, if others, that otherwise would be glad to be at ease within modest bounds, should not by invasion increase their power, they would not be able, long time, by standing only on their defence, to subsist. And by consequence, such augmentation of dominion over men being necessary to a man's conservation, it ought to be allowed him.

Again, men have no pleasure (but on the contrary a great deal of grief) in keeping company where there is no power able to overawe them all. For every man looketh that his companion should value him at the same rate he sets upon himself, and upon all signs of contempt or undervaluing naturally endeavours, as far as he dares (which amongst them that have no common power to keep them in quiet is far enough to make them destroy each other), to extort a greater value from his contemners, by damage; and from others, by the example.

So that in the nature of man, we find three principal causes of quarrel. First, competition; secondly, diffidence; thirdly, glory.

The first maketh men invade for gain; the second, for safety; and the third, for reputation. The first use violence, to make themselves masters of other men's persons, wives, children, and cattle; the second, to defend them; the third, for trifles, as a word, a smile, a different opinion, and any other sign of undervalue, either direct in their persons or by reflection in their kindred, their friends, their nation, their profession, or their name.

Hereby it is manifest that during the time men live without a common power to keep them all in awe, they are in that condition which is called war; and such a war as is of every man against every man. For war consisteth not in battle only, or the act of fighting, but in a tract of time, wherein the will to contend by battle is sufficiently known: and therefore the notion of time is to be considered in the nature of war, as it is in the nature of weather. For as the nature of foul weather lieth not in a shower or two of rain, but in an inclination thereto of many days together: so the nature of war consisteth not in actual fighting, but in the known disposition thereto during all the time there is no assurance to the contrary. All other time is peace.

Whatsoever therefore is consequent to a time of war, where every man is enemy to every man, the same consequent to the time wherein men live without other security than what their own strength and their own invention shall furnish them withal. In such condition there is no place for industry, because the fruit thereof is uncertain: and consequently no culture of the earth; no navigation, nor use of the commodities that may be imported by sea; no commodious building; no instruments of moving and removing such things as require much force; no knowledge of the face of the earth; no account of time; no arts; no letters; no society; and which is worst of all, continual fear, and danger of violent death; and the life of man, solitary, poor, nasty, brutish, and short.

It may seem strange to some man that has not well weighed these things that Nature should thus dissociate and render men apt to invade and destroy one another: and he may therefore, not trusting to this inference, made from the passions, desire perhaps to have the same confirmed by experience. Let him therefore consider with himself: when taking a journey, he arms himself and seeks to go well accompanied; when going to sleep, he locks his doors; when even in his house he locks his chests; and this when he knows there be laws and public officers, armed, to revenge all injuries shall be done him; what opinion he has of his fellow subjects, when he rides armed; of his fellow citizens, when he locks his doors; and of his children, and servants, when he locks his chests. Does he not there as much accuse mankind by his actions as I do by my words? But neither of us accuse man's nature in it. The desires, and other passions of man, are in themselves no sin. No more are the actions that proceed from those passions till they know a law that forbids them; which till laws be made they cannot know, nor can any law be made till they have agreed upon the person that shall make it.

It may peradventure be thought there was never such a time nor condition of war as this; and I believe it was never generally so, over all the world: but there are many places where they live so now. For the savage people in many places of America, except the government of small families, the concord whereof dependeth on natural lust, have no government at all, and live at this day in that brutish manner, as I said before. Howsoever, it may be perceived what manner of life there would be, where there were no common power to fear, by the manner of life which men that have formerly lived under a peaceful government use to degenerate into a civil war.

But though there had never been any time wherein particular men were in a condition of war one against another, yet in all times kings and persons of sovereign authority, because of their independency, are in continual jealousies, and in the state and posture of gladiators, having their weapons pointing, and their eyes fixed on one another; that is, their forts, garrisons, and guns upon the frontiers of their kingdoms, and continual spies upon their neighbours, which is a posture of war. But because they uphold thereby the industry of their subjects, there does not follow from it that misery which accompanies the liberty of particular men.

To this war of every man against every man, this also is consequent; that nothing can be unjust. The notions of right and wrong, justice and injustice, have there no place. Where there is no common power, there is no law; where no law, no injustice. Force and fraud are in war the two cardinal virtues. Justice and injustice are none of the faculties neither of the body nor mind. If they were, they might be in a man that were alone in the world, as well as his senses and passions. They are qualities that relate to men in society, not in solitude. It is consequent also to the same condition that there be no propriety, no dominion, no mine and thine distinct; but only that to be every man's that he can get, and for so long as he can keep it. And thus much for the ill condition which man by mere nature is actually placed in; though with a possibility to come out of it, consisting partly in the passions, partly in his reason.

The passions that incline men to peace are: fear of death; desire of such things as are necessary to commodious living; and a hope by their industry to obtain them. And reason suggesteth convenient articles of peace upon which men may be drawn to agreement. These articles are they which otherwise are called the laws of nature.

3.2

The Prince

Niccolo Machiavelli

Concerning Cruelty and Clemency, and Whether it is Better to be Loved than Feared

Coming now to the other qualities mentioned above, I say that every prince ought to desire to be considered clement and not cruel. Nevertheless he ought to take care not to misuse this clemency. Cesare Borgia was considered cruel; notwithstanding, his cruelty reconciled the Romagna, unified it, and restored it to peace and loyalty. And if this be rightly considered, he will be seen to have been much more merciful than the Florentine people, who, to avoid a reputation for cruelty, permitted Pistoia to be destroyed. Therefore a prince, so long as he keeps his subjects united and loyal, ought not to mind the reproach of cruelty; because with a few examples he will be more merciful than those who, through too much mercy, allow disorders to arise, from which follow murders or robberies; for these are wont to injure the whole people, whilst those executions which originate with a prince offend the individual only.

And of all princes, it is impossible for the new prince to avoid the imputation of cruelty, owing to new states being full of dangers. Hence Virgil, through the mouth of Dido, excuses the inhumanity of her reign owing to its being new, saying:

> Res dura, et regni novitas me talia cogunt
>
> Moliri, et late fines custode tueri.[1]

Nevertheless he ought to be slow to believe and to act, nor should he himself show fear, but proceed in a temperate manner with prudence and humanity, so that too much confidence may not make him incautious and too much distrust render him intolerable.

Upon this a question arises: whether it be better to be loved than feared or feared than loved? It may be answered that one should wish to be both, but, because it is difficult to unite them in one person, is much safer to be feared than loved, when, of the two, either must be dispensed with. Because this is to be asserted in general of men, that they are ungrateful, fickle, false, cowardly, covetous, and as long as you succeed they are yours entirely; they will offer you their blood, property, life and children, as is said above, when the need is far distant; but when it approaches they turn against you. And that prince who, relying entirely on their promises, has neglected other precautions, is ruined; because friendships that are obtained by payments, and not by greatness or nobility of mind, may indeed be earned, but they are not secured, and in time of need cannot be relied upon; and men have less scruple in offending one who is beloved than one who is feared, for love is preserved by the link of obligation which, owing to the baseness of men, is broken at every opportunity for their advantage; but fear preserves you by a dread of punishment which never fails.

Nevertheless a prince ought to inspire fear in such a way that, if he does not win love, he avoids hatred; because he can endure very well being feared whilst he is not hated, which will always be as long as he abstains from the property of his citizens and subjects and from their women. But when it is necessary for him to proceed against the life of someone, he must do it on proper justification and for manifest cause, but above all things he must keep his hands off the property of others, because men more quickly forget the death of their father than the loss of their patrimony. Besides, pretexts for taking away the property are never wanting; for he who has once begun to live by robbery will always find pretexts for seizing what belongs to others; but reasons for taking life, on the contrary, are more difficult to find and sooner lapse. But when a prince is with his army, and has under control a multitude of soldiers, then it is quite necessary for him to disregard the reputation of cruelty, for without it he would never hold his army united or disposed to its duties.

Source: Niccolo Machiavelli, *The Prince*, 1532, Chapters XVII, XVIII, and XXI.

Among the wonderful deeds of Hannibal this one is enumerated: that having led an enormous army, composed of many various races of men, to fight in foreign lands, no dissensions arose either among them or against the prince, whether in his bad or in his good fortune. This arose from nothing else than his inhuman cruelty, which, with his boundless valour, made him revered and terrible in the sight of his soldiers, but without that cruelty, his other virtues were not sufficient to produce this effect. And shortsighted writers admire his deeds from one point of view and from another condemn the principal cause of them. That it is true his other virtues would not have been sufficient for him may be proved by the case of Scipio, that most excellent man, not of his own times but within the memory of man, against whom, nevertheless, his army rebelled in Spain; this arose from nothing but his too great forbearance, which gave his soldiers more licence than is consistent with military discipline. For this he was upbraided in the Senate by Fabius Maximus, and called the corrupter of the Roman soldiery. The Locrians were laid waste by a legate of Scipio, yet they were not avenged by him, nor was the insolence of the legate punished, owing entirely to his easy nature. Insomuch that someone in the Senate, wishing to excuse him, said there were many men who knew much better how not to err than to correct the errors of others. This disposition, if he had been continued in the command, would have destroyed in time the fame and glory of Scipio; but, he being under the control of the Senate, this injurious characteristic not only concealed itself, but contributed to his glory.

Returning to the question of being feared or loved, I come to the conclusion that, men loving according to their own will and fearing according to that of the prince, a wise prince should establish himself on that which is in his own control and not in that of others; he must endeavour only to avoid hatred, as is noted.

Concerning the Way in which Princes Should Keep Faith

Every one admits how praiseworthy it is in a prince to keep faith, and to live with integrity and not with craft. Nevertheless our experience has been that those princes who have done great things have held good faith of little account, and have known how to circumvent the intellect of men by craft, and in the end have overcome those who have relied on their word. You must know there are two ways of contesting, the one by the law, the other by force; the first method is proper to men, the second to beasts; but because the first is frequently not sufficient, it is necessary to have recourse to the second. Therefore it is necessary for a prince to understand how to avail himself of the beast and the man. This has been figuratively taught to princes by ancient writers, who describe how Achilles and many other princes of old were given to the Centaur Chiron to nurse, who brought them up in his discipline; which means solely that, as they had for a teacher one who was half beast and half man, so it is necessary for a prince to know how to make use of both natures, and that one without the other is not durable. A prince, therefore, being compelled knowingly to adopt the beast, ought to choose the fox and the lion; because the lion cannot defend himself against snares and the fox cannot defend himself against wolves. Therefore, it is necessary to be a fox to discover the snares and a lion to terrify the wolves. Those who rely simply on the lion do not understand what they are about. Therefore a wise lord cannot, nor ought he to, keep faith when such observance may be turned against him, and when the reasons that caused him to pledge it exist no longer. If men were entirely good this precept would not hold, but because they are bad, and will not keep faith with you, you too are not bound to observe it with them. Nor will there ever be wanting to a prince legitimate reasons to excuse this nonobservance. Of this endless modern examples could be given, showing how many treaties and engagements have been made void and of no effect through the faithlessness of princes; and he who has known best how to employ the fox has succeeded best.

But it is necessary to know well how to disguise this characteristic, and to be a great pretender and dissembler; and men are so simple, and so subject to present necessities, that he who seeks to deceive will always find someone who will allow himself to be deceived. One recent example I cannot pass over in silence. Alexander VI did nothing else but deceive men, nor ever thought of doing otherwise, and he always found victims; for there never was a man who had greater power in asserting, or who with greater oaths would affirm a thing, yet would observe it less; nevertheless his deceits always succeeded according to his wishes, because he well understood this side of mankind.

Therefore it is unnecessary for a prince to have all the good qualities I have enumerated, but it is very necessary to appear to have them. And I shall dare to say this also, that to have them and always to observe them is injurious, and that to appear to have them is useful; to appear merciful, faithful, humane, religious, upright, and to be so, but with a mind so framed that should you require not to be so, you may be able and know how to change to the opposite.

And you have to understand this, that a prince, especially a new one, cannot observe all those things for which men are esteemed, being often forced, in order to maintain the state, to act contrary to faith, friendship, humanity, and religion. Therefore it is necessary for him to have a mind ready to turn itself accordingly as the winds and variations of fortune force it, yet, as I have said above, not to diverge from the good if he can avoid doing so, but, if compelled, then to know how to set about it.

For this reason a prince ought to take care that he never lets anything slip from his lips that is not replete with the above-named five qualities, that he may appear to him who sees and hears him altogether merciful, faithful, humane, upright, and religious. There is nothing more necessary to appear to have than this last quality, inasmuch as men judge generally more by the eye than by the hand, because it belongs to everybody to see you, to few to come in touch with you. Everyone sees what you appear to be, few really know what you are, and those few dare not oppose themselves to the opinion of the many, who have the majesty of the state to defend them; and in the actions of all men, and especially of princes, which it is not prudent to challenge, one judges by the result.

For that reason, let a prince have the credit of conquering and holding his state, the means will always be considered honest, and he will be praised by everybody because the vulgar are always taken by what a thing seems to be and by what comes of it; and in the world there are only the vulgar, for the few find a place there only when the many have no ground to rest on.

One prince[2] of the present time, whom it is not well to name, never preaches anything else but peace and good faith, and to both he is most hostile, and either, if he had kept it, would have deprived him of reputation and kingdom many a time.

How a Prince Should Conduct Himself as to Gain Renown

Nothing makes a prince so much esteemed as great enterprises and setting a fine example. We have in our time Ferdinand of Aragon, the present King of Spain. He can almost be called a new prince, because he has risen, by fame and glory, from being an insignificant king to be the foremost king in Christendom; and if you will consider his deeds you will find them all great and some of them extraordinary. In the beginning of his reign he attacked Granada, and this enterprise was the foundation of his dominions. He did this quietly at first and without any fear of hindrance, for he held the minds of the barons of Castile occupied in thinking of the war and not anticipating any innovations; thus they did not perceive that by these means he was acquiring power and authority over them. He was able with the money of the Church and of the people to sustain his armies, and by that long war to lay the foundation for the military skill which has since distinguished him. Further, always using religion as a plea, so as to undertake greater schemes, he devoted himself with a pious cruelty to driving out and clearing his kingdom of the Moors; nor could there be a more admirable example, nor one more rare. Under this same cloak he assailed Africa, he came down on Italy, he has finally attacked France; and thus his achievements and designs have always been great, and have kept the minds of his people in suspense and admiration and occupied with the issue of them. And his actions have arisen in such a way, one out of the other, that men have never been given time to work steadily against him.

Again, it much assists a prince to set unusual examples in internal affairs, similar to those which are related of Messer Bernabo da Milano, who, when he had the opportunity, by any one in civil life doing some extraordinary thing, either good or bad, would take some method of rewarding or punishing him, which would be much spoken about. And a prince ought, above all things, always to endeavour in every action to gain for himself the reputation of being a great and remarkable man.

A prince is also respected when he is either a true friend or a downright enemy, that to say, when, without any reservation, he declares himself in favour of one party against the other; which course will always be more advantageous than standing neutral; because if two of your powerful neighbours come to blows, they are of such a character that, if one of them conquers, you have either to fear him or not. In either case it will always be more advantageous for you to declare yourself and to make war strenuously; because, in the first case, if you do not declare yourself, you will invariably fall a prey to the conqueror, to the pleasure and satisfaction of him who has been conquered, and you will have no reasons to offer, nor anything to protect or to shelter you. Because he who conquers does not want doubtful friends who will not aid him in the time of trial; and he who loses will not harbour you because you did not willingly, sword in hand, court his fate.

Antiochus went into Greece, being sent for by the Aetolians to drive out the Romans. He sent envoys to the Achaeans, who were friends of the Romans, exhorting them to remain neutral; and on the other hand the Romans urged them to take up arms. This question came to be discussed in the council of the Achaeans, where the legate of Antiochus urged them to stand neutral. To this the Roman legate answered: "As for that which has been said, that it is better and more advantageous for your state not to interfere in our war, nothing can be more erroneous; because by not interfering you will be left, without favour or consideration, the guerdon of the conqueror." Thus it will always happen that he who is not your friend will demand your neutrality, whilst he who is your friend will entreat you to declare yourself with arms. And irresolute princes, to avoid present dangers, generally follow the neutral path, and are generally ruined. But when a prince declares himself gallantly in favour of one side, if the party with whom he allies himself conquers, although the victor may be powerful and may have him at his mercy, yet he is indebted to him, and there is established a bond of amity; and men are never so shameless as to become a monument of ingratitude by oppressing you. Victories after all are never so complete that the victor must not show some regard, especially to justice. But if he with whom you ally yourself loses, you may be sheltered by him, and whilst he is able he may aid you, and you become companions in a fortune that may rise again.

In the second case, when those who fight are of such a character that you have no anxiety as to who may conquer, so much the more is it greater prudence to be allied, because you assist at the destruction of one by the aid of another who, if he had been wise, would have saved him; and conquering, as it is impossible that he should not with your assistance, he remains at your discretion. And here it is to be noted that a prince ought to take care never to make an alliance with one more powerful than himself for the purpose of attacking others, unless necessity compels him, as is said above; because if he conquers you are at his discretion, and princes ought to avoid as much as possible being at the discretion of any one. The Venetians joined with France against the Duke of Milan, and this alliance, which caused their ruin, could have been avoided. But when it cannot be avoided, as happened to the Florentines when the Pope and Spain sent armies to attack Lombardy, then in such a case, for the above reasons, the prince ought to favour one of the parties.

Never let any Government imagine that it can choose perfectly safe courses; rather let it expect to have to take very doubtful ones, because it is found in ordinary affairs that one never seeks to avoid one trouble without running into another; but prudence consists in knowing how to distinguish the character of troubles, and for choice to take the lesser evil.

A prince ought also to show himself a patron of ability, and to honour the proficient in every art. At the same time he should encourage his citizens to practise their callings peaceably, both in commerce and agriculture, and in every other following, so that the one should not be deterred from improving his possessions for fear lest they be taken away from him or another from opening up trade for fear of taxes; but the prince ought to offer rewards to whoever wishes to do these things and designs in any way to honour his city or state.

Further, he ought to entertain the people with festivals and spectacles at convenient seasons of the year; and as every city is divided into guilds or into societies, he ought to hold such bodies in esteem, and associate with them sometimes, and show himself an example of courtesy and liberality; nevertheless, always maintaining the majesty of his rank, for this he must never consent to abate in anything.

Notes

1. . . . against my will, my fate, A throne unsettled, and an infant state, Bid me defend my realms with all my pow'rs, And guard with these severities my shores.
2. Maximilian I, Holy Roman Emperor.

3.3

A Realist Theory of International Politics

Hans Morgenthau

This [reading] purports to present a theory of international politics. The test by which such a theory must be judged is not a priori and abstract but empirical and pragmatic. The theory, in other words, must be judged not by some preconceived abstract principle or concept unrelated to reality, but by its purpose: to bring order and meaning to a mass of phenomena that without it would remain disconnected and unintelligible. It must meet a dual test, an empirical and a logical one: do the facts as they actually are lend themselves to the interpretation the theory has put upon them, and do the conclusions at which the theory arrives follow with logical necessity from its premises? In short, is the theory consistent with the facts and within itself?

The issue this theory raises concerns the nature of all politics. The history of modern political thought is the story of a contest between two schools that differ fundamentally in their conceptions of the nature of man, society, and politics. One believes that a rational and moral political order, derived from universally valid abstract principles, can be achieved here and now. It assumes the essential goodness and infinite malleability of human nature, and blames the failure of the social order to measure up to the rational standards on lack of knowledge and understanding, obsolescent social institutions, or the depravity of certain isolated individuals or groups. It trusts in education, reform, and the sporadic use of force to remedy these defects.

The other school believes that the world, imperfect as it is from the rational point of view, is the result of forces inherent in human nature. To improve the world one must work with those forces, not against them. This being inherently a world of opposing interests and of conflict among them, moral principles can never be fully realized but must at best be approximated through the ever temporary balancing of interests and the ever precarious settlement of conflicts. This school, then, sees in a system of checks and balances a universal principle for all pluralist societies. It appeals to historical precedent rather than to abstract principles and aims at the realization of the lesser evil rather than of the absolute good.

This theoretical concern with human nature as it actually is, and with the historical processes as they actually take place, has earned for the theory presented here the name of *realism*. What are the tenets of political realism? No systematic exposition of the philosophy of political realism can be attempted here; it will suffice to single out six fundamental principles, which have frequently been misunderstood.

Six Principles of Political Realism

1. Political realism believes that politics, like society in general, is governed by objective laws that have their roots in human nature. In order to improve society it is first necessary to understand the laws by which society lives. The operation of these laws being impervious to our preferences, men will challenge them only at the risk of failure.

Realism, believing as it does in the objectivity of the laws of politics, must also believe in the possibility of developing a rational theory that reflects, however imperfectly and one-sidedly, these objective laws. It believes also, then, in the possibility of distinguishing in politics between truth and opinion—between what is true objectively and rationally, supported by evidence and illuminated by reason, and what is only a subjective judgment, divorced from the facts as they are and informed by prejudice and wishful thinking. . . .

For realism, theory consists in ascertaining facts and giving them meaning through reason. It assumes that the character of a foreign policy can be ascertained only through the examination of the political acts performed and of the foreseeable consequences of these acts. Thus we can find out what statesmen have actually

---

done, and from the foreseeable consequences of their acts we can surmise what their objectives might have been.

Yet examination of the facts is not enough. To give meaning to the factual raw material of foreign policy, we must approach political reality with a kind of rational outline, a map that suggests to us the possible meanings of foreign policy. In other words, we put ourselves in the position of a statesman who must meet a certain problem of foreign policy under certain circumstances, and we ask ourselves what the rational alternatives are from which a statesman may choose who must meet this problem under these circumstances (presuming always that he acts in a rational manner), and which of these rational alternatives this particular statesman, acting under these circumstances, is likely to choose. It is the testing of this rational hypothesis against the actual facts and their consequences that gives theoretical meaning to the facts of international politics.

2. The main signpost that helps political realism to find its way through the landscape of international politics is the concept of interest defined in terms of power. This concept provides the link between reason trying to understand international politics and the facts to be understood. . . .

We assume that statesmen think and act in terms of interest defined as power, and the evidence of history bears that assumption out. That assumption allows us to retrace and anticipate, as it were, the steps a statesman—past, present, or future—has taken or will take on the political scene. We look over his shoulder when he writes his dispatches; we listen in on his conversations with other statesmen; we read and anticipate his very thoughts. Thinking in terms of interest defined as power, we think as he does, and as disinterested observers we understand his thoughts and actions perhaps better than he, the actor on the political scene, does himself.

The concept of interest defined as power imposes intellectual discipline upon the observer, infuses rational order into the subject matter of politics, and thus makes the theoretical understanding of politics possible. . . . A realist theory of international politics, then, will guard against two popular fallacies: the concern with motives and the concern with ideological preferences. . . .

Yet even if we had access to the real motives of statesmen, that knowledge would help us little in understanding foreign policies and might well lead us astray. It is true that the knowledge of the statesman's motives may give us one among many clues as to what the direction of his foreign policy might be. It cannot give us, however, the one clue by which to predict his foreign policies. History shows no exact and necessary correlation between the quality of motives and the quality of foreign policy. This is true in both moral and political terms.

We cannot conclude from the good intentions of a statesman that his foreign policies will be either morally praiseworthy or politically successful. Judging his motives, we can say that he will not intentionally pursue policies that are morally wrong, but we can say nothing about the probability of their success. If we want to know the moral and political qualities of his actions, we must know them, not his motives. How often have statesmen been motivated by the desire to improve the world and ended by making it worse? And how often have they sought one goal, and ended by achieving something they neither expected nor desired?

Neville Chamberlain's politics of appeasement were, as far as we can judge, inspired by good motives; he was probably less motivated by considerations of personal power than were many other British prime ministers, and he sought to preserve peace and to assure the happiness of all concerned. Yet his policies helped to make the Second World War inevitable and to bring untold miseries to millions of people. Sir Winston Churchill's motives, on the other hand, were much less universal in scope and much more narrowly directed toward personal and national power, yet the foreign policies that sprang from these inferior motives were certainly superior in moral and political quality to those pursued by his predecessor. Judged by his motives, Robespierre was one of the most virtuous men who ever lived. Yet it was the utopian radicalism of that very virtue that made him kill those less virtuous than himself, brought him to the scaffold, and destroyed the revolution of which he was a leader.

Good motives give assurance against deliberately bad policies; they do not guarantee the moral goodness and political success of the policies they inspire. What is important to know, if one wants to understand foreign policy, is not primarily the motives of a statesman but his intellectual ability to comprehend the essentials of foreign policy, as well as his political ability to translate what he has comprehended into successful political action. It follows that, while ethics in the abstract judges the moral qualities of motives, political theory must judge the political qualities of intellect, will, and action.

A realist theory of international politics will also avoid the other popular fallacy of equating the foreign policies of a statesman with his philosophic or political sympathies, and of deducing the former from the latter. Statesmen, especially under contemporary conditions, may well make a habit of presenting their foreign policies in terms of their philosophic and political sympathies in order to gain popular support for them. Yet they will distinguish with Lincoln between their "*official* duty," which is to think and act in terms of the national interest, and their "*personal* wish," which is to see their own moral values and political principles realized throughout the world. Political realism does not require, nor does it condone, indifference to political ideals and moral principles, but it requires indeed a sharp distinction between the desirable and the possible—between what is desirable everywhere and at all times and what is possible under the concrete circumstances of time and place. . . .

On the international plane it is no exaggeration to say that the very structure of international relations—as reflected in political institutions, diplomatic procedures, and legal arrangements has tended to become at variance with, and in large measure irrelevant to, the reality of international politics. While the former assumes the "sovereign equality" of all nations, the latter is dominated by an extreme inequality of nations, two of which are called superpowers because they hold in their hands the unprecedented power of total destruction, and many of which are called "ministates" because their power is minuscule even compared with that of the traditional nation-states. It is this contrast and incompatibility between the reality of international politics and the concepts, institutions, and procedures designed to make intelligible and control the former that have caused, at least below the great-power level, the unmanageability of international relations, which borders on anarchy. International terrorism and the different government reactions to it, the involvement of foreign governments in the Lebanese civil war, the military operations of the United States in Southeast Asia, and the military intervention of the Soviet Union in Eastern Europe cannot be explained or justified by reference to traditional concepts, institutions, and procedures. . . .

The difference between international politics as it actually is and a rational theory derived from it is like the difference between a photograph and a painted portrait. The photograph shows everything that can be seen by the naked eye; the painted portrait does not show everything that can be seen by the naked eye, but it shows, or at least seeks to show, one thing that the naked eye cannot see: the human essence of the person portrayed.

Political realism contains not only a theoretical but also a normative element. It knows that political reality is replete with contingencies and systemic irrationalities, and points to the typical influences they exert upon foreign policy. Yet it shares with all social theory the need, for the sake of theoretical understanding, to stress the rational elements of political reality; for it is these rational elements that make reality intelligible for theory. Political realism presents the theoretical construct of a rational foreign policy that experience can never completely achieve.

At the same time political realism considers a rational foreign policy to be good foreign policy; for only a rational foreign policy minimizes risks and maximizes benefits and, hence, complies with both the moral precept of prudence and the political requirement of success. Political realism wants the photographic picture of the political world to resemble as much as possible its painted portrait. Aware of the inevitable gap between good—that is, rational—foreign policy and foreign policy as it actually is, political realism maintains not only that theory must focus upon the rational elements of political reality but also that foreign policy ought to be rational in view of its own moral and practical purposes.

Hence, it is no argument against the theory here presented that actual foreign policy does not or cannot live up to it. That argument misunderstands the intention of this book, which is to present not an indiscriminate description of political reality but a rational theory of international politics. Far from being invalidated by the fact that, for instance, a perfect balance of power policy will scarcely be found in reality, it assumes that reality, being deficient in this respect, must be understood and evaluated as an approximation to an ideal system of balance of power.

3. Realism assumes that its key concept of interest defined as power is an objective category that is universally valid, but it does not endow that concept with a meaning that is fixed once and for all. The idea of interest is indeed of the essence of politics and is unaffected by the circumstances of time and place. . . .

Yet the kind of interest determining political action in a particular period of history depends upon the political and cultural context within which foreign policy is formulated. The goals that might be pursued by nations in their foreign policy can run the whole gamut of objectives any nation has ever pursued or might possibly pursue.

The same observations apply to the concept of power. Its content and the manner of its use are determined by the political and cultural environment. Power may comprise anything that establishes and maintains the control of man over man. Thus power covers all social relationships that serve that end, from physical violence to the most subtle psychological ties by which one mind controls another. Power covers the domination of man by man, both when it is disciplined by moral ends and controlled by constitutional safeguards, as in Western democracies, and when it is that untamed and barbaric force that finds its laws in nothing but its own strength and its sole justification in its aggrandizement. . . .

The realist parts company with other schools of thought before the all-important question of how the contemporary world is to be transformed. The realist is persuaded that this transformation can be achieved only through the workmanlike manipulation of the perennial forces that have shaped the past as they will the future. The realist cannot be persuaded that we can bring about that transformation by confronting a political reality that has its own laws with an abstract ideal that refuses to take those laws into account.

4. Political realism is aware of the moral significance of political action. It is also aware of the ineluctable tension between the moral command and the requirements of successful political action. And it is unwilling to gloss over and obliterate that tension and thus to obfuscate both the moral and the political issues by making it appear as though the stark facts of politics were morally more satisfying than they actually are, and the moral law less exacting than it actually is.

Realism maintains that universal moral principles cannot be applied to the actions of states in their abstract universal formulation but that they must be filtered through the concrete circumstances of time and place. The individual may say for himself, "*Fiat justitia, pereat mundus* (Let justice be done, even if the world perish)," but the state has no right to say so in the name of those who are in its care. Both individual and state must judge political action by universal moral principles, such as that of liberty. Yet while the individual has a moral right to sacrifice himself in defense of such a moral principle, the state has no right to let its moral disapprobation of the infringement of liberty get in the way of successful political action, itself inspired by the moral principle of national survival. There can be no political morality without prudence, that is, without consideration of the political consequences of seemingly moral action. Realism, then, considers prudence—the weighing of the consequences of alternative political actions—to be the supreme virtue in politics. Ethics in the abstract judges action by its conformity with the moral law; political ethics judges action by its political consequences. . . .

5. Political realism refuses to identify the moral aspirations of a particular nation with the moral laws that govern the universe. As it distinguishes between truth and opinion, so it distinguishes between truth and idolatry. All nations are tempted—and few have been able to resist the temptation for long—to clothe their own particular aspirations and actions in the moral purposes of the universe. To know that nations are subject to the moral law is one thing, while to pretend to know with certainty what is good and evil in the relations among nations is quite another. There is a world of difference between the belief that all nations stand under the judgment of God, inscrutable to the human mind, and the blasphemous conviction that God is always on one's side and that what one wills oneself cannot fail to be willed by God also.

The lighthearted equation between a particular nationalism and the counsels of Providence is morally indefensible, for it is that very sin of pride against which the Greek tragedians and the biblical prophets have warned rulers and ruled. That equation is also politically pernicious, for it is liable to engender the distortion in judgment that, in the blindness of crusading frenzy, destroys nations and civilizations—in the name of moral principle, ideal, or God himself.

On the other hand, it is exactly the concept of interest defined in terms of power that saves us from both that moral excess and that political folly. For if we look at all nations, our own included, as political entities pursuing their respective interests defined in terms of power, we are able to do justice to all of them. And we are able to do justice to all of them in a dual sense: we are able to judge other nations as we judge our own and, having judged them in this fashion, we are then capable of pursuing policies that respect the interests of other nations while protecting and promoting those of our own. Moderation in policy cannot fail to reflect the moderation of moral judgment.

6. . . . Intellectually, the political realist maintains the autonomy of the political sphere, as the economist, the lawyer, the moralist maintain theirs. He thinks in terms of interest defined as power, as the economist thinks in terms of interest defined as wealth; the lawyer, of the conformity of action with legal rules; the moralist, of the conformity of action with moral principles. The economist asks: "How does this policy affect the wealth of society, or a segment of it?" The lawyer asks: "Is this policy in accord with the rules of law?" The moralist asks: "Is this policy in accord with moral principles?" And the political realist asks: "How does this policy affect the power of the nation?" (Or of the federal government, of Congress, of the party, of agriculture, as the case may be.)

The political realist is not unaware of the existence and the relevance of standards of thought other than political ones. As political realist he cannot but subordinate these other standards to those of politics. And he parts company with other schools when they impose standards of thought appropriate to other spheres upon the political spheres. It is here that political realism takes issue with the "legalistic-moralistic approach" to international politics. . . .

This realist defense of the autonomy of the political sphere against its subversion by other modes of thought does not imply disregard for the existence and importance of these other modes of thought. It rather implies that each should be assigned its proper sphere and function. Political realism is based upon a pluralistic conception of human nature. Real man is a composite of "economic man," "political man," "moral man," "religious man," etc. A man who was nothing but "political man" would be a beast, for he would be completely lacking in moral restraints. A man who was nothing but "moral man" would be a fool, for he would be completely lacking in prudence.

A man who was nothing but "religious man" would be a saint, for he would be completely lacking in worldly desires.

Recognizing that these different facets of human nature exist, political realism also recognizes that in order to understand one of them one has to deal with it on its own terms. That is to say, if I want to understand "religious man," I must for the time being abstract from the other aspects of human nature and deal with its religious aspect as if it were the only one. Furthermore, I must apply to the religious sphere the standards of thought appropriate to it, always remaining aware of the existence of other standards and their actual influence upon the religious qualities of man. What is true of this facet of human nature is true of all the others. No modern economist, for instance, would conceive of his science and its relations to other sciences of man in any other way. It is exactly through such a process of emancipation from other standards of thought, and the development of one appropriate to its subject matter, that economics has developed as an autonomous theory of the economic activities of man. To contribute to a similar development in the field of politics is indeed the purpose of political realism.

3.4

The Peloponnesian War

Joseph S. Nye

Thucydides is [considered by some to be] the father of realism, the theory most people use when thinking about international politics even when they do not know they are using a theory. Theories are the indispensable tools we use to organize facts. Many of today's leaders and editorial writers use realist theories even if they have not heard of Thucydides. A member of the Athenian elite who lived during Athens's greatest age, he participated in some of the events described in his *History of the Peloponnesian War*. Robert Gilpin, a realist, asserted, "In honesty, one must inquire whether or not twentieth-century students of international relations know anything that Thucydides and his fifth-century B.C. compatriots did not know about the behavior of states." He then answered his own query: "Ultimately international politics can still be characterized as it was by Thucydides."[1] Gilpin's proposition is debatable, but to debate it, we must know Thucydides's argument. And what better introduction to realist theory is there than one of history's great stories? However, like many great stories, it has its limits. One of the things we learn from the Peloponnesian War is how to avoid too simplistic a reading of history.

A Short Version of a Long Story

Early in the fifth century, Athens and Sparta (Figure 3.1) were allies that had cooperated to defeat the Persian Empire (480 B.C.). Sparta was a conservative land-oriented state that turned inward after the victory over Persia; Athens was a commercial and sea-oriented state that turned outward. In the middle of the century, Athens had 50 years of growth that led to the development of an Athenian empire. Athens formed the Delian League, an alliance of states around the Aegean Sea, for mutual protection against the Persians. Sparta, in turn, organized its neighbors on the Peloponnesian peninsula into a defensive alliance. States that had joined Athens freely for protection against the Persians soon had to pay taxes to the Athenians. Because of the growing strength of Athens and the resistance of some to its growing empire, a war broke out in 461 B.C., about 20 years after the Greek defeat of the Persians. By 445 B.C., the first Peloponnesian War ended and was followed by a treaty that promised peace for 30 years. Thus Greece enjoyed a period of stable peace before the second, more significant, Peloponnesian War.

In 434 B.C., a civil war broke out in the small peripheral city-state of Epidamnus. Like a pebble that begins an avalanche, this event triggered a series of reactions that led ultimately to the Peloponnesian War. Large conflicts are often precipitated by relatively insignificant crises in out-of-the-way places, [another example being] World War I.

In Epidamnus, the democrats fought with oligarchs over how the country would be ruled. The democrats appealed to the city-state of Corcyra, which had helped establish Epidamnus, but were turned down. They then turned to another city-state, Corinth, and the Corinthians decided to help. This angered the Corcyraeans, who sent a fleet to recapture Epidamnus, their former colony. In the process, the Corcyraeans defeated the Corinthian fleet. Corinth was outraged and declared war on Corcyra. Corcyra, fearing the attack from Corinth, turned to Athens for help. Both Corcyra and Corinth sent representatives to Athens.

The Athenians, after listening to both sides, were in a dilemma. They did not want to break the truce that had lasted for a decade, but if the Corinthians (who were close to the Peloponnesians) conquered Corcyra and took control of its large navy, the balance of power among the Greek states would be tipped against Athens. The Athenians felt they could not risk letting the Corcyraean navy fall into the hands of the Corinthians, so they decided to become "a little bit involved." They launched a small endeavor to scare the Corinthians, sending ten ships with instructions not to fight unless attacked. But deterrence failed; Corinth attacked, and when the Corcyraeans began to lose the battle, the Athenian ships were drawn into the fray more than intended. The Athenian involvement infuriated Corinth,

Figure 3.1 Classical Greece

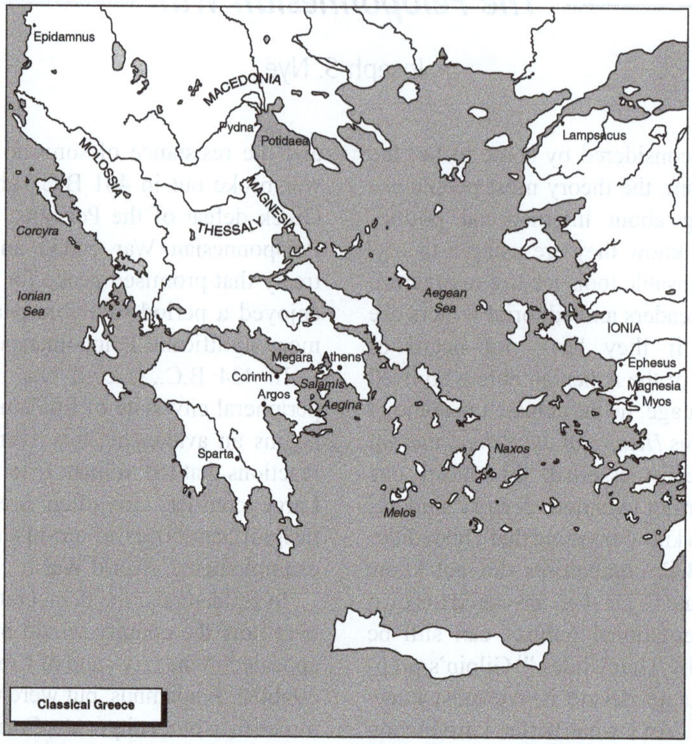

which in turn worried the Athenians. In particular, Athens worried that Corinth would stir up problems in Potidaea, which, although an Athenian ally, had historic ties to Corinth. Sparta promised to help Corinth if Athens attacked Potidaea. When a revolt did occur in Potidaea, Athens sent forces to put it down.

At that point there was a great debate in Sparta. The Athenians appealed to the Spartans to stay neutral. The Corinthians urged the Spartans to go to war and warned them against failing to check the rising power of Athens. Megara, another important city, agreed with Corinth because contrary to the treaty, the Athenians had banned Megara's trade. Sparta was torn, but the Spartans voted in favor of war because they were afraid that if Athenian power was not checked, Athens might control the whole of Greece. Sparta went to war to maintain the balance of power among the Greek city-states.

Athens rejected Sparta's ultimatum, and war broke out in 431 B.C. The Athenian mood was one of imperial greatness, with pride and patriotism about their city and their social system, and optimism that they would prevail in the war. The early phase of the war came to a stalemate. A truce was declared after ten years (421 B.C.), but the truce was fragile and war broke out again. In 413 B.C., Athens undertook a very risky venture. It sent two fleets and infantry to conquer Sicily, the great island off the south of Italy, which had a number of Greek colonies allied to Sparta. The result was a terrible defeat for the Athenians. At the same time Sparta received additional money from the Persians, who were only too happy to see Athens trounced. After the defeat in Sicily, Athens was internally divided. In 411 B.C. the oligarchs overthrew the democrats, and 400 oligarchs attempted to rule Athens. These events were not the end, but Athens never really recovered. An Athenian naval victory in 410 B.C. was followed five years later by a Spartan naval victory, and by 404 B.C. Athens was compelled to sue for peace. Sparta demanded that Athens pull down the long walls that protected it from attack by land-based powers. Athens's power was broken.

Note

1. Robert Gilpin, *War and Change in World Politics* (Cambridge: Cambridge University Press, 1981), pp. 227–228.

4 Realism II

4.1

The Origins of War in Neorealist Theory

Kenneth N. Waltz

Like most historians, many students of international politics have been skeptical about the possibility of creating a theory that might help one to understand and explain the international events that interest us. Thus Morgenthau, foremost among traditional realists, was fond of repeating Blaise Pascal's remark that "the history of the world would have been different had Cleopatra's nose been a bit shorter" and then asking "How do you systemize that?"[1] His appreciation of the role of the accidental and the occurrence of the unexpected in politics dampened his theoretical ambition.

The response of neorealists is that, although difficulties abound, some of the obstacles that seem most daunting lie in misapprehensions about theory. Theory obviously cannot explain the accidental or account for unexpected events; it deals in regularities and repetitions and is possible only if these can be identified. A further difficulty is found in the failure of realists to conceive of international politics as a distinct domain about which theories can be fashioned. Morgenthau, for example, insisted on "the autonomy of politics," but he failed to apply the concept to international politics. A theory is a depiction of the organization of a domain and of the connections among its parts. A theory indicates that some factors are more important than others and specifies relations among them. In reality, everything is related to everything else, and one domain cannot be separated from others. But theory isolates one realm from all others in order to deal with it intellectually. By defining the structure of international political systems, neorealism establishes the autonomy of international politics and thus makes a theory about it possible.[2]

In developing a theory of international politics, neorealism retains the main tenets of *realpolitik*, but means and ends are viewed differently, as are causes and effects. Morgenthau, for example, thought of the "rational" statesman as ever striving to accumulate more and more power. He viewed power as an end in itself. Although he acknowledged that nations at times act out of considerations other than power, Morgenthau insisted that, when they do so, their actions are not "of a political nature."[3] In contrast, neorealism sees power as a possibly useful means, with states running risks if they have either too little or too much of it. Excessive weakness may invite an attack that greater strength would have dissuaded an adversary from launching. Excessive strength may prompt other states to increase their arms and pool their efforts against the dominant state. Because power is a possibly useful means, sensible statesmen try to have an appropriate amount of it. In crucial situations, however, the ultimate concern of states is not for power but for security. This revision is an important one.

An even more important revision is found in a shift of causal relations. The infinite materials of any realm

Source: Kenneth Waltz. "The Origins of War in Neorealist Theory," reprinted from *The Journal of Interdisciplinary History* XVIII (1988): 615–620 and 627–628 with permission of the editors of *The Journal of Interdisciplinary History* and The MIT Press, Cambridge, Massachusetts.

can be organized in endlessly different ways. Realism thinks of causes as moving in only one direction, from the interactions of individuals and states to the outcomes that their acts and interactions produce. Morgenthau recognized that, when there is competition for scarce goods and no one to serve as arbiter, a struggle for power will ensue among the competitors and that consequently the struggle for power can be explained without reference to the evil born in men. The struggle for power arises simply because men want things, not because of the evil in their desires. He labeled man's desire for scarce goods as one of the two roots of conflict, but, even while discussing it, he seemed to pull toward the "other root of conflict and concomitant evil"— "the *animus dominandi*, the desire for power." He often considered that man's drive for power is more basic than the chance conditions under which struggles for power occur. This attitude is seen in his statement that "in a world where power counts, no nation pursuing a rational policy has a choice between renouncing and wanting power; *and, if it could*, the lust for power for the individual's sake would still confront us with its less spectacular yet no less pressing moral defects."[4]

Students of international politics have typically inferred outcomes from salient attributes of the actors producing them. Thus Marxists, like liberals, have linked the outbreak of war or the prevalence of peace to the internal qualities of states. Governmental forms, economic systems, social institutions, political ideologies—these are but a few examples of where the causes of war have been found. Yet, although causes are specifically assigned, we know that states with widely divergent economic institutions, social customs, and political ideologies have all fought wars. More striking still, many different sorts of organizations fight wars, whether those organizations be tribes, petty principalities, empires, nations, or street gangs. If an identified condition seems to have caused a given war, one must wonder why wars occur repeatedly even though their causes vary. Variations in the characteristics of the states are not linked directly to the outcomes that their behaviors produce, nor are variations in their patterns of interaction. Many historians, for example, have claimed that World War I was caused by the interaction of two opposed and closely balanced coalitions. But then many have claimed that World War II was caused by the failure of some states to combine forces in an effort to right an imbalance of power created by an existing alliance.

Neorealism contends that international politics can be understood only if the effects of structure are added to the unit-level explanations of traditional realism. By emphasizing how structures affect actions and outcomes, neorealism rejects the assumption that man's innate lust for power constitutes a sufficient cause of war in the absence of any other. It reconceives the causal link between interacting units and international outcomes. According to the logic of international politics, one must believe that some causes of international outcomes are the result of interactions at the unit level, and, since variations in presumed causes do not correspond very closely to variations in observed outcomes, one must also assume that others are located at the structural level. Causes at the level of units interact with those at the level of structure, and, because they do so, explanation at the unit level alone is bound to be misleading. If an approach allows the consideration of both unit-level and structural-level causes, then it can cope with both the changes and the continuities that occur in a system.

Structural realism presents a systemic portrait of international politics depicting component units according to the manner of their arrangement. For the purpose of developing a theory, states are cast as unitary actors wanting at least to survive, and are taken to be the system's constituent units. The essential structural quality of the system is anarchy—the absence of a central monopoly of legitimate force. Changes of structure and hence of system occur with variations in the number of great powers. The range of expected outcomes is inferred from the assumed motivation of the units and the structure of the system in which they act.

A systems theory of international politics deals with forces at the international, and not at the national, level. With both systems-level and unit-level forces in play, how can one construct a theory of international politics without simultaneously constructing a theory of foreign policy? An international-political theory does not imply or require a theory of foreign policy any more than a market theory implies or requires a theory of the firm. Systems theories, whether political or economic, are theories that explain how the organization of a realm acts as a constraining and disposing force on the interacting units within it. Such theories tell us about the forces to which the units are subjected. From them, we can draw some inferences about the expected behavior and fate of the units: namely, how they will have to compete with and adjust to one another if they are to survive and flourish. To the extent that the dynamics of a system limit the freedom of its units, their behavior and the outcomes of their behavior become predictable. How do we expect firms to respond to differently structured markets, and states to differently structured international-political systems? These theoretical questions require us to take firms as firms, and states as states, without paying attention to differences among them. The questions are then answered by reference to the placement of the units in their system and not by reference to the internal qualities of the units. Systems theories explain why different units behave similarly and, despite their variations, produce outcomes that fall within expected ranges. Conversely, theories at the unit level tell us why different units behave differently despite their similar placement in a system. A theory about foreign policy is a theory at the national level. It leads to expectations about the responses that dissimilar polities will make to external pressures. A theory of international politics bears on the foreign policies of nations although it claims to explain only certain aspects of them. It can tell us what international conditions national policies have to cope with.

From the vantage point of neorealist theory, competition and conflict among states stem directly from the twin facts of life under conditions of anarchy: States in an anarchic order must provide for their own security, and threats or seeming threats to their security abound. Preoccupation with identifying dangers and counteracting them become a way of life. Relations remain tense; the actors are usually suspicious and often hostile even though by nature they may not be given to suspicion and hostility. Individually, states may only be doing what they can to bolster their security. Their individual intentions aside, collectively their actions yield arms races and alliances. The uneasy state of affairs is exacerbated by the familiar "security dilemma," wherein measures that enhance one state's security typically diminish that of others.[5] In an anarchic domain, the source of one's own comfort is the source of another's worry. Hence a state that is amassing instruments of war, even for its own defensive, is cast by others as a threat requiring response. The response itself then serves to confirm the first state's belief that it had reason to worry. Similarly an alliance that in the interest of defense moves to increase cohesion among its members and add to its ranks inadvertently imperils an opposing alliance and provokes countermeasures.

Some states may hunger for power for power's sake. Neorealist theory, however, shows that it is not necessary to assume an innate lust for power in order to account for the sometimes fierce competition that marks the international arena. In an anarchic domain, a state of war exists if all parties lust for power. But so too will a state of war exist if all states seek only to ensure their own safety.

Although neorealist theory does not explain why particular wars are fought, it does explain war's dismal recurrence through the millennia. Neorealists point not to the ambitions or the intrigues that punctuate the outbreak of individual conflicts but instead to the existing structure within which events, whether by design or accident, can precipitate open clashes of arms. The origins of hot wars lie in cold wars, and the origins of cold wars are found in the anarchic ordering of the international arena.

The recurrence of war is explained by the structure of the international system. Theorists explain what historians know: War is normal. Any given war is explained not by looking at the structure of the international-political system but by looking at the particularities within it: the situations, the characters, and the interactions of states. Although particular explanations are found at the unit level, general explanations are also needed. Wars vary in frequency, and in other ways as well. A central question for a structural theory is this: How do changes of the system affect the expected frequency of war?

***

Wars, hot and cold, originate in the structure of the international political system. Most Americans blame the Soviet Union for creating the Cold War, by the actions that follow necessarily from the nature of its society and government. Revisionist historians, attacking the dominant view, assign blame to the United States. Some American error, or sinister interest, or faulty assumption about Soviet aims, they argue, is what started the Cold War. Either way, the main point is lost. In a bipolar world, each of the two great powers is bound to focus its fears on the other, to distrust its motives, and to impute offensive intentions to defensive measures. The proper question is what, not who, started the Cold War. Although its content and virulence vary as unit-level forces change and interact, the Cold War continues. It is firmly rooted in the structure of postwar international politics, and will last as long as that structure endures.

In any closely competitive system, it may seem that one is either paranoid or a loser. The many Americans who ascribe paranoia to the Soviet Union are saying little about its political elite and much about the international-political system. Yet, in the presence of nuclear weapons, the Cold War has not become a hot one, a raging war among major states. Constraints on fighting big wars have bound the major nuclear states into a system of uneasy peace. Hot wars originate in the structure of international politics. So does the Cold War, with its temperature kept low by the presence of nuclear weapons.

Notes

1. Hans J. Morgenthau, "International Relations: Quantitative and Qualitative Approaches," in Norman D. Palmer (ed.), *A Design for International Relations Research: Scope, Theory, Methods, and Relevance* (Philadelphia, 1970), 78.

2. Morgenthau, *Politics among Nations* (New York, 1973; 5th ed.), 11. Ludwig Boltzman (trans. Rudolf Weingartner), "Theories as Representations," excerpted in Arthur Danto and Sidney Morgenbesser (eds.), *Philosophy of Science* (Cleveland, 1960), 245–252. Neorealism is sometimes dubbed structural realism. I use the terms interchangeably and, throughout this article, refer to my own formulation of neorealist theory. See Waltz, *Theory of International Politics* (Reading, Mass., 1979); Robert Keohane (ed.), *Neorealism and its Critics* (New York, 1986).

3. Morgenthau, Politics among Nations, 27.

4. *Idem, Scientific Man vs. Power Politics* (Chicago, 1946), 192, 200. Italics added.

5. See John H. Herz, "Idealist Internationalism and the Security Dilemma," *World Politics*, II (1950), 157–180.

4.2

Anarchy and the Struggle for Power

John Mearsheimer

Great powers, I argue, are always searching for opportunities to gain power over their rivals, with hegemony as their final goal. This perspective does not allow for status quo powers, except for the unusual state that achieves preponderance. Instead, the system is populated with great powers that have revisionist intentions at their core.[1] This [reading] presents a theory that explains this competition for power. Specifically, I attempt to show that there is a compelling logic behind my claim that great powers seek to maximize their share of world power. I do not, however, test offensive realism against the historical record in this [reading].

Why States Pursue Power

My explanation for why great powers vie with each other for power and strive for hegemony is derived from five assumptions about the international system. None of these assumptions alone mandates that states behave competitively. Taken together, however, they depict a world in which states have considerable reason to think and sometimes behave aggressively. In particular, the system encourages states to look for opportunities to maximize their power vis-à-vis other states. . . .

Bedrock Assumptions

The first assumption is that the international system is anarchic, which does not mean that it is chaotic or riven by disorder. It is easy to draw that conclusion, since realism depicts a world characterized by security competition and war. By itself, however, the realist notion of anarchy has nothing to do with conflict; it is an ordering principle, which says that the system comprises independent states that have no central authority above them.[2] Sovereignty, in other words, inheres in states because there is no higher ruling body in the international system.[3] There is no "government over governments."[4]

The second assumption is that great powers inherently possess some offensive military capability, which gives them the wherewithal to hurt and possibly destroy each other. States are potentially dangerous to each other, although some states have more military might than others and are therefore more dangerous. A state's military power is usually identified with the particular weaponry at its disposal, although even if there were no weapons, the individuals in those states could still use their feet and hands to attack the population of another state. After all, for every neck, there are two hands to choke it.

The third assumption is that states can never be certain about other states' intentions. Specifically, no state can be sure that another state will not use its offensive military capability to attack the first state. This is not to say that states necessarily have hostile intentions. Indeed, all of the states in the system may be reliably benign, but it is impossible to be sure of that judgment because intentions are impossible to divine with 100 percent certainty.[5] There are many possible causes of aggression, and no state can be sure that another state is not motivated by one of them.[6] Furthermore, intentions can change quickly, so a state's intentions can be benign one day and hostile the next. Uncertainty about intentions is unavoidable, which means that states can never be sure that other states do not have offensive intentions to go along with their offensive capabilities.

The fourth assumption is that survival is the primary goal of great powers. Specifically, states seek to maintain their territorial integrity and the autonomy of their domestic political order. Survival dominates other motives because, once a state is conquered, it is unlikely to be in a position to pursue other aims. Soviet leader Josef Stalin put the point well during a war scare in 1927: "We can and must build socialism in the [Soviet Union]. But in order to do so we first of all have to exist."[7] States can and do pursue other goals, of course, but security is their most important objective.

Source: "Anarchy and the Struggle for Power" from *The Tragedy of Great Power Politics* by John Mearsheimer.

The fifth assumption is that great powers are rational actors. They are aware of their external environment and they think strategically about how to survive in it. In particular, they consider the preferences of other states and how their own behavior is likely to affect the behavior of those other states, and how the behavior of those other states is likely to affect their own strategy for survival. Moreover, states pay attention to the long term as well as the immediate consequences of their actions.

As emphasized, none of these assumptions alone dictates that great powers as a general rule *should* behave aggressively toward each other. There is surely the possibility that some state might have hostile intentions, but the only assumption dealing with a specific motive that is common to all states says that their principal objective is to survive, which by itself is a rather harmless goal. Nevertheless, when the five assumptions are married together, they create powerful incentives for great powers to think and act offensively with regard to each other. In particular, three general patterns of behavior result: fear, self-help, and power maximization.

State Behavior

Great powers fear each other. They regard each other with suspicion, and they worry that war might be in the offing. They anticipate danger. There is little room for trust among states. For sure, the level of fear varies across time and space, but it cannot be reduced to a trivial level. From the perspective of any one great power, all other great powers are potential enemies. This point is illustrated by the reaction of the United Kingdom and France to German reunification at the end of the Cold War. Despite the fact that these three states had been close allies for almost forty-five years, both the United Kingdom and France immediately began worrying about the potential dangers of a united Germany.[8]

The basis of this fear is that in a world where great powers have the capability to attack each other and might have the motive to do so, any state bent on survival must be at least suspicious of other states and reluctant to trust them. Add to this the "911" problem—the absence of a central authority to which a threatened state can turn for help—and states have even greater incentive to fear each other. Moreover, there is no mechanism, other than the possible self-interest of third parties, for punishing an aggressor. Because it is sometimes difficult to deter potential aggressors, states have ample reason not to trust other states and to be prepared for war with them.

The possible consequences of falling victim to aggression further amplify the importance of fear as a motivating force in world politics. Great powers do not compete with each other as if international politics were merely an economic marketplace. Political competition among states is a much more dangerous business than mere economic intercourse; the former can lead to war, and war often means mass killing on the battlefield as well as mass murder of civilians. In extreme cases, war can even lead to the destruction of states. The horrible consequences of war sometimes cause states to view each other not just as competitors, but as potentially deadly enemies. Political antagonism, in short, tends to be intense, because the stakes are great.

States in the international system also aim to guarantee their own survival. Because other states are potential threats, and because there is no higher authority to come to their rescue when they dial 911, states cannot depend on others for their own security. Each state tends to see itself as vulnerable and alone, and therefore it aims to provide for its own survival. In international politics, God helps those who help themselves. This emphasis on self-help does not preclude states from forming alliances.[9] But alliances are only temporary marriages of convenience: today's alliance partner might be tomorrow's enemy, and today's enemy might be tomorrow's alliance partner. For example, the United States fought with China and the Soviet Union against Germany and Japan in World War II, but soon thereafter flip-flopped enemies and partners and allied with West Germany and Japan against China and the Soviet Union during the Cold War.

States operating in a self-help world almost always act according to their own self-interest and do not subordinate their interests to the interests of other states, or to the interests of the so-called international community. The reason is simple: it pays to be selfish in a self-help world. This is true in the short term as well as in the long term, because if a state loses in the short run, it might not be around for the long haul.

Apprehensive about the ultimate intentions of other states, and aware that they operate in a self-help system, states quickly understand that the best way to ensure their survival is to be the most powerful state in the system. The stronger a state is relative to its potential rivals, the less likely it is that any of those rivals will attack it and threaten its survival. Weaker states will be reluctant to pick fights with more powerful states because the weaker states are likely to suffer military defeat. Indeed, the bigger the gap in power between any two states, the less likely it is that the weaker will attack the stronger. Neither Canada nor Mexico, for example, would countenance attacking the United States, which is far more powerful than its neighbors. The ideal situation is to be the hegemon in the system. As Immanuel Kant said. "It is the desire of every state, or of its ruler, to arrive at a condition of perpetual peace by conquering the whole world, if that were possible."[10] Survival would then be almost guaranteed.[11]

Consequently, states pay close attention to how power is distributed among them, and they make a special effort to maximize their share of world power. Specifically, they look for opportunities to alter the balance of power by acquiring additional increments of power at the expense of potential rivals. States employ a variety of means—economic, diplomatic, and military—to shift the balance of power in their favor, even if doing so makes other states suspicious or even hostile. Because one state's gain in power is another state's loss, great powers tend to have a zero-sum mentality when dealing with each other. The trick, of course, is to be the winner in this competition and to dominate the other states in the system. Thus, the claim that states maximize relative power is tantamount to arguing that states are disposed to think offensively toward other states, even though their ultimate motive is simply to survive. In short, great powers have aggressive intentions.[12]

Even when a great power achieves a distinct military advantage over its rivals, it continues looking for chances to gain more power. The pursuit of power stops only when hegemony is achieved. The idea that a great power might feel secure without dominating the system, provided it has an "appropriate amount" of power, is not persuasive, for two reasons.[13] First, it is difficult to assess how much relative power one state must have over its rivals before it is secure. Is twice as much power an appropriate threshold? Or is three times as much power the magic number? The root of the problem is that power calculations alone do not determine which side wins a war. Clever strategies, for example, sometimes allow less powerful states to defeat more powerful foes.

Second, determining how much power is enough becomes even more complicated when great powers contemplate how power will be distributed among them ten or twenty years down the road. The capabilities of individual states vary over time, sometimes markedly, and it is often difficult to predict the direction and scope of change in the balance of power. Remember, few in the West anticipated the collapse of the Soviet Union before it happened. In fact, during the first half of the Cold War, many in the West feared that the Soviet economy would eventually generate greater wealth than the American economy, which would cause a marked power shift against the United States and its allies. What the future holds for China and Russia and what the balance of power will look like in 2020 is difficult to foresee.

Given the difficulty of determining how much power is enough for today and tomorrow, great powers recognize that the best way to ensure their security is to achieve hegemony now, thus eliminating any possibility of a challenge by another great power. Only a misguided state would pass up an opportunity to be the hegemon in the system because it thought it already had sufficient power to survive.[14] But even if a great power does not have the wherewithal to achieve hegemony (and that is usually the case), it will still act offensively to amass as much power as it can, because states are almost always better off with more rather than less power. In short, states do not become status quo powers until they completely dominate the system.

All states are influenced by this logic, which means that not only do they look for opportunities to take advantage of one another, they also work to ensure that other states do not take advantage of them. After all, rival states are driven by the same logic, and most states are likely to recognize their own motives at play in the actions of other states. In short, states ultimately pay attention to defense as well as offense. They think about conquest themselves, and they work to check aggressor states from gaining power at their expense. This inexorably leads to a world of constant security competition, where states are willing to lie, cheat, and use brute force if it helps them gain advantage over their rivals. Peace, if one defines that concept as a state of tranquility or mutual concord, is not likely to break out in this world.

The "security dilemma," which is one of the most well-known concepts in the international relations literature, reflects the basic logic of offensive realism. The essence of the dilemma is that the measures a state takes to increase its own security usually decrease the security of other states. Thus, it is difficult for a state to increase its own chances of survival without threatening the survival of other states. John Herz first introduced the security dilemma in a 1950 article in the journal *World Politics*.[15] After discussing the anarchic nature of international politics, he writes, "Striving to attain security from . . . attack, [states] are driven to acquire more and more power in order to escape the impact of the power of others. This, in turn, renders the others more insecure and compels them to prepare for the worst. Since none can ever feel entirely secure in such a world of competing units, power competition ensues, and the vicious circle of security and power accumulation is on."[16] The implication of Herz's analysis is clear: the best way for a state to survive in anarchy is to take advantage of other states and gain power at their expense. The best defense is a good offense. Since this message is widely understood, ceaseless security competition ensues. Unfortunately, little can be done to ameliorate the security dilemma as long as states operate in anarchy.

It should be apparent from this discussion that saying that states are power maximizers is tantamount to saying that they care about relative power, not absolute power. There is an important distinction here, because states concerned about relative power behave differently than do states interested in absolute power.[17] States that maximize relative power are concerned primarily with the distribution of material capabilities. In particular, they try to gain as large a power advantage as possible over potential rivals, because power is the best means to survival in a dangerous world. Thus, states motivated by relative power concerns are likely to forgo large gains in their own power, if such gains give rival states even greater power, for smaller national gains that nevertheless provide them with a power advantage over their rivals.[18] States that maximize absolute power, on the other hand, care only about the size of their own gains, not those of other states. They are not motivated by balance-of-power logic but instead are concerned with amassing power without regard to how much power other states control. They would jump at the opportunity for large gains, even if a rival gained more in the deal. Power, according to this logic, is not a means to an end (survival), but an end in itself.[19]

Calculated Aggression

There is obviously little room for status quo powers in a world where states are inclined to look for opportunities to gain more power. Nevertheless, great powers cannot always act on their offensive intentions, because behavior is influenced not only by what states want, but also by their capacity to realize these desires. Every state might want to be king of the hill, but not every state has the wherewithal to compete for that lofty position, much less achieve it. Much depends on how military might is distributed among the great powers. A great power that has a marked power advantage over its rivals is likely to behave more aggressively, because it has the capability as well as the incentive to do so.

By contrast, great powers facing powerful opponents will be less inclined to consider offensive action and more concerned with defending the existing balance of power from threats by their more powerful opponents. Let there be an opportunity for those weaker states to revise the balance in their own favor, however, and they will take advantage of it. Stalin put the point well at the end of World War II: "Everyone imposes his own system as far as his army can reach. It cannot be otherwise."[20] States might also have the capability to gain advantage over a rival power but nevertheless decide that the perceived costs of offense are too high and do not justify the expected benefits.

In short, great powers are not mindless aggressors so bent on gaining power that they charge headlong into losing wars or pursue Pyrrhic victories. On the contrary, before great powers take offensive actions, they think carefully about the balance of power and about how other states will react to their moves. They weigh the costs and risks of offense against the likely benefits. If the benefits do not outweigh the risks, they sit tight and wait for a more propitious moment. Nor do states start arms races that are unlikely to improve their overall position. . . . States sometimes limit defense spending either because spending more would bring no strategic advantage or because spending more would weaken the economy and undermine the state's power in the long run.[21] To paraphrase Clint Eastwood, a state has to know its limitations to survive in the international system.

Nevertheless, great powers miscalculate from time to time because they invariably make important decisions on the basis of imperfect information. States hardly ever have complete information about any situation they confront. There are two dimensions to this problem. Potential adversaries have incentives to misrepresent their own strength or weakness, and to conceal their true aims.[22] For example, a weaker state trying to deter a stronger state is likely to exaggerate its own power to discourage the potential aggressor from attacking. On the other hand, a state bent on aggression is likely to emphasize its peaceful goals while exaggerating its military weakness, so that the potential victim does not build up its own arms and thus leaves itself vulnerable to attack. Probably no national leader was better at practicing this kind of deception than Adolf Hitler.

But even if disinformation was not a problem, great powers are often unsure about how their own military forces, as well as the adversary's, will perform on the battlefield. For example, it is sometimes difficult to determine in advance how new weapons and untested combat units will perform in the face of enemy fire. Peacetime maneuvers and war games are helpful but imperfect indicators of what is likely to happen in actual combat. Fighting wars is a complicated business in which it is often difficult to predict outcomes. Remember that although the United States and its allies scored a stunning and remarkably easy victory against Iraq in early 1991, most experts at the time believed that Iraq's military would be a formidable foe and put up stubborn resistance before finally succumbing to American military might.[23]

Great powers are also sometimes unsure about the resolve of opposing states as well as allies. For example, Germany believed that if it went to war against France and Russia in the summer of 1914, the United Kingdom would probably stay out of the fight. Saddam Hussein expected the United States to stand aside when he invaded Kuwait in August 1990. Both aggressors guessed wrong, but each had good reason to think that its initial judgment was correct. In the 1930s, Adolf Hitler believed that his great-power rivals would be easy to exploit and isolate because each had little interest in fighting Germany and instead was determined to get someone else to assume that burden. He guessed right. In short, great powers constantly find themselves confronting situations in which they have to make important decisions with incomplete information. Not surprisingly, they sometimes make faulty judgments and end up doing themselves serious harm.

Some defensive realists go so far as to suggest that the constraints of the international system are so powerful that offense rarely succeeds, and that aggressive great powers invariably end up being punished.[24] As noted, they emphasize that 1) threatened states balance against aggressors and ultimately crush them, and 2) there is an offense-defense balance that is usually heavily tilted toward the defense, thus making conquest especially difficult. Great powers, therefore, should be content with the existing balance of power and not try to change it by force. After all, it makes little sense for a state to initiate a war that it is likely to lose; that would be self-defeating behavior. It is better to concentrate instead on preserving the balance of power.[25] Moreover, because aggressors seldom succeed, states should understand that security is abundant, and thus there is no good strategic reason for wanting more power in the first place. In a world where conquest seldom pays, states should have relatively benign intentions toward each other. If they do not, these defensive realists argue, the reason is probably poisonous domestic politics, not smart calculations about how to guarantee one's security in an anarchic world. . . .

The Hierarchy of State Goals

Survival is the number one goal of great powers, according to my theory. In practice, however, states pursue non-security goals as well. For example, great powers invariably seek greater economic prosperity to enhance the welfare of their citizenry. They sometimes seek to promote a particular ideology abroad, as happened during the Cold War when the United States tried to spread democracy around the world and the Soviet Union tried to sell communism. National unification is another goal that sometimes motivates states, as it did with Prussia and Italy in the nineteenth century and Germany after the Cold War. Great powers also occasionally try to foster human rights around the globe. States might pursue any of these, as well as a number of other non-security goals.

Offensive realism certainly recognizes that great powers might pursue these non-security goals, but it has little to say about them, save for one important point: states can pursue them as long as the requisite behavior does not conflict with balance-of-power logic, which is often the case.[26] Indeed, the pursuit of these non-security goals sometimes complements the hunt for relative power. For example, Nazi Germany expanded into eastern Europe for both ideological and realist reasons, and the superpowers competed with each other during the Cold War for similar reasons. Furthermore, greater economic prosperity invariably means greater wealth, which has significant implications for security, because wealth is the foundation of military power. Wealthy states can afford powerful military forces, which enhance a state's prospects for survival. As the political economist Jacob Viner noted more than fifty years ago, "there is a long-run harmony" between wealth and power.[27] National unification is another goal that usually complements the pursuit of power. For example, the unified German state that emerged in 1871 was more powerful than the Prussian state it replaced.

Sometimes the pursuit of non-security goals has hardly any effect on the balance of power, one way or the other. Human rights interventions usually fit this description, because they tend to be small-scale operations that cost little and do not detract from a great power's prospects for survival. For better or for worse, states are rarely willing to expend blood and treasure to protect foreign populations from gross abuses, including genocide. For instance, despite claims that American foreign policy is infused with moralism, Somalia (1992–93) is the only instance during the past one hundred years in which U.S. soldiers were killed in action on a humanitarian mission. And in that case, the loss of a mere eighteen soldiers in an infamous firefight in October 1993 so traumatized American policymakers that they immediately pulled all U.S. troops out of Somalia and then refused to intervene in Rwanda in the spring of 1994, when ethnic Hutu went on a genocidal rampage against their Tutsi neighbors.[28] Stopping that genocide would have been relatively easy and it would have had virtually no effect on the position of the United States in the balance of power.[29] Yet nothing was done. In short, although realism does not prescribe human rights interventions, it does not necessarily proscribe them.

But sometimes the pursuit of non-security goals conflicts with balance-of-power logic, in which case states usually act according to the dictates of realism. For example, despite the U.S. commitment to spreading democracy across the globe, it helped overthrow democratically elected governments and embraced a number of authoritarian regimes during the Cold War, when American policymakers felt that these actions would help contain the Soviet Union.[30] In World War II, the liberal democracies put aside their antipathy for communism and formed an alliance with the Soviet Union against Nazi Germany. "I can't take communism," Franklin Roosevelt emphasized, but to defeat Hitler "I would hold hands with the Devil."[31] In the same way, Stalin repeatedly demonstrated that when his ideological preferences clashed with power considerations, the latter won out. To lake the most blatant example of his realism, the Soviet Union formed a non-aggression pact with Nazi Germany in August 1939—the infamous Molotov-Ribbentrop Pact—in hopes that the agreement would at least temporarily satisfy Hitler's territorial ambitions in eastern Europe and turn the Wehrmacht toward France and the United Kingdom.[32] When great powers confront a serious threat, in short, they pay little attention to ideology as they search for alliance partners.[33]

Security also trumps wealth when those two goals conflict, because "defence," as Adam Smith wrote in *The Wealth of Nations*, "is of much more importance than opulence."[34] Smith provides a good illustration of how states behave when forced to choose between wealth and relative power. In 1651, England put into effect the famous Navigation Act, protectionist legislation designed to damage Holland's commerce and ultimately cripple the Dutch economy. The legislation mandated that all goods imported into England be carried either in English ships or ships owned by the country that originally produced the goods. Since the Dutch produced few goods themselves, this measure would badly damage their shipping, the central ingredient in their economic success. Of course, the Navigation Act would hurt England's economy as well, mainly because it would rob England of the benefits of free trade. "The act of navigation," Smith wrote, "is not favorable to foreign commerce, or to the growth of that opulence that can arise from it." Nevertheless, Smith considered the legislation "the wisest of all the commercial regulations of England" because it did more damage to the Dutch economy than to the English economy, and in the mid-seventeenth century Holland was "the only naval power which could endanger the security of England."[35]

Creating World Order

The claim is sometimes made that great powers can transcend realist logic by working together to build an international order that fosters peace and justice. World peace, it would appear, can only enhance a state's prosperity and security. America's political leaders paid considerable lip service to this line of argument over the course of the twentieth century. President Clinton, for example, told an audience at the United Nations in September 1993 that "at the birth of this organization 48 years ago . . . a generation of gifted leaders from many nations stepped forward to organize the world's efforts on behalf of security and prosperity. . . . Now history has granted to us a moment of even greater opportunity. . . . Let us resolve that we will dream larger. . . . Let us ensure that the world we pass to our children is healthier, safer and more abundant than the one we inhabit today."[36]

This rhetoric notwithstanding, great powers do not work together to promote world order for its own sake. Instead, each seeks to maximize its own share of world power, which is likely to clash with the goal of creating and sustaining stable international orders.[37] This is not to say that great powers never aim to prevent wars and keep the peace. On the contrary, they work hard to deter wars in which they would be the likely victim. In such cases, however, state behavior is driven largely by narrow calculations about relative power, not by a commitment to build a world order independent of a state's own interests. The United States, for example, devoted enormous resources to deterring the Soviet Union from starting a war in Europe during the Cold War, not because of some deep-seated commitment to promoting peace around the world, but because American leaders feared that a Soviet victory would lead to a dangerous shift in the balance of power[38].

The particular international order that obtains at any time is mainly a by-product of the self-interested behavior of the system's great powers. The configuration of the system, in other words, is the unintended consequence of great-power security competition, not the result of states acting together to organize peace. The establishment of the Cold War order in Europe illustrates this point. Neither the Soviet Union nor the United States intended to establish it, nor did they work together to create it. In fact, each superpower worked hard in the early years of the Cold War to gain power at the expense of the other, while preventing the other from doing likewise.[39] The system that emerged in Europe in the aftermath of World War II was the unplanned consequence of intense security competition between the superpowers. . . .

Cooperation Among States

One might conclude from the preceding discussion that my theory does not allow for any cooperation among the great powers. But this conclusion would be wrong. States can cooperate, although cooperation is sometimes difficult to achieve and always difficult to sustain. Two factors inhibit cooperation: considerations about relative gains and concern about cheating.[40] Ultimately, great powers live in a fundamentally competitive world where they view each other as real, or at least potential, enemies, and they therefore look to gain power at each other's expense.

Any two states contemplating cooperation must consider how profits or gains will be distributed between them. They can think about the division in terms of either absolute or relative gains (recall the distinction made earlier between pursuing either absolute power or relative power; the concept here is the same). With absolute gains, each side is concerned with maximizing its own profits and cares little about how much the other side gains or loses in the deal. Each side cares about the other only to the extent that the other side's behavior affects its own prospects for achieving maximum profits. With relative gains, on the other hand, each side considers not only its own individual gain, but also how well it fares compared to the other side.

Because great powers care deeply about the balance of power, their thinking focuses on relative gains when they consider cooperating with other states. For sure, each state tries to maximize its absolute gains; still, it is more important for a state to make sure that it does no worse, and perhaps better, than the other state in any agreement. Cooperation is more difficult to achieve, however, when states are attuned to relative gains rather than absolute gains.[41] This is because states concerned about absolute gains have to make sure that if the pie is expanding, they are getting at least some portion of the increase, whereas states that worry about relative gains must pay careful attention to how the pie is divided, which complicates cooperative efforts.

Concerns about cheating also hinder cooperation. Great powers are often reluctant to enter into cooperative agreements for fear that the other side will cheat on the agreement and gain a significant advantage. This concern is especially acute in the military realm, causing a "special peril of defection," because the nature of military weaponry allows for rapid shifts in the balance of power.[42] Such a development could create a window of opportunity for the state that cheats to inflict a decisive defeat on its victim.

These barriers to cooperation notwithstanding, great powers do cooperate in a realist world. Balance-of-power logic often causes great powers to form alliances and cooperate against common enemies. The United Kingdom, France, and Russia, for example, were allies against Germany before and during World War I. States sometimes cooperate to gang up on a third state, as Germany and the Soviet Union did against Poland in 1939.[43] More recently, Serbia and Croatia agreed to conquer and divide Bosnia between them, although the United States and its European allies prevented them from executing their agreement.[44]

Rivals as well as allies cooperate. After all, deals can be struck that roughly reflect the distribution of power and satisfy concerns about cheating. The various arms control agreements signed by the superpowers during the Cold War illustrate this point.

The bottom line, however, is that cooperation takes place in a world that is competitive at its core—one where states have powerful incentives to take advantage of other states. This point is graphically highlighted by the state of European politics in the forty years before World War I. The great powers cooperated frequently during this period, but that did not stop them from going to war on August 1, 1914.[45] The United States and the Soviet Union also cooperated considerably during World War II, but that cooperation did not prevent the outbreak of the Cold War shortly after Germany and Japan were defeated. Perhaps most amazingly, there was significant economic and military cooperation between Nazi Germany and the Soviet Union during the two years before the Wehrmacht attacked the Red Army.[46] No amount of cooperation can eliminate the dominating logic of security competition. Genuine peace, or a world in which states do not compete for power, is not likely as long as the state system remains anarchic.

Conclusion

In sum, my argument is that the structure of the international system, not the particular characteristics of individual great powers, causes them to think and act offensively and to seek hegemony.[47] I do not adopt Morgenthau's claim that states invariably behave aggressively because they have a will to power hardwired into them. Instead, I assume that the principal motive behind great-power behavior is survival. In anarchy, however, the desire to survive encourages states to behave aggressively. Nor does my theory classify states as more or less aggressive on the basis of their economic or political systems. Offensive realism makes only a handful of assumptions about great powers, and these assumptions apply equally to all great powers. Except for differences in how much power each state controls, the theory treats all states alike.

Notes

1. Most realist scholars allow in their theories for status quo powers that are not hegemons. At least some states, they argue, are likely to be satisfied with the balance of power and thus have no incentive to change it. See Randall L. Schweller, "Neorealism's Status-Quo Bias: What Security Dilemma?" *Security Studies* 5, No. 3 (Spring 1996, special issue on "Realism: Restatements and Renewal," ed. Benjamin Frankel), pp. 98–101; and Arnold Wolfers, *Discord and Collaboration: Essays on International Politics* (Baltimore, MD: Johns Hopkins University Press, 1962), pp. 84–86, 91–92, 125–26.

2. The concept of anarchy and its consequences for international politics was first articulated by G. Lowes Dickinson, *The European Anarchy* (New York: Macmillan, 1916). For a more recent and more elaborate discussion of anarchy, see Waltz, *Theory of International Politics*, pp. 88–93. Also see Robert J. Art and Robert Jervis, eds., *International Politics: Anarchy, Force, Imperialism* (Boston: Little, Brown, 1973), pt. 1; and Helen Milner, "The Assumption of Anarchy in International Relations Theory: A Critique," *Review of International Studies* 17, No. 1 (January 1991), pp. 67–85.

3. Although the focus in this study is on the state system, realist logic can be applied to other kinds of anarchic systems. After all, it is the absence of central authority, not any special characteristic of states, that causes them to compete for power. Markus Fischer, for example, applies the theory to Europe in the Middle Ages, before the state system emerged in 1648. See Fischer, "Feudal Europe, 800–1300: Communal Discourse and Conflictual Practices," *International Organization* 46, No. 2 (Spring 1992), pp. 427–66. The theory can also be used to explain the behavior of individuals. The most important work in this regard is Thomas Hobbes, *Leviathan*, ed. C. B. Macpherson (Harmondsworth, UK: Penguin, 1986). Also see Elijah Anderson, "The Code of the Streets," *Atlantic Monthly*, May 1994, pp. 80–94; Barry R. Posen, "The Security Dilemma and Ethnic Conflict," *Survival* 35, No. 1 (Spring 1993), pp. 27–47; and Robert J. Spitzer, *The Politics of Gun Control* (Chatham, NJ: Chatham House, 1995), chap. 6.

4. Inis L. Claude, Jr., *Swords into Plowshares: The Problems and Progress of International Organization*. 4th ed. (New York: Random House, 1971), p. 14.

5. The claim that states might have benign intentions is simply a starting assumption. I argue subsequently that when you combine the theory's five assumptions, states are put in a position in which they are strongly disposed to having hostile intentions toward each other.

6. My theory ultimately argues that great powers behave offensively toward each other because that is the best way for them to guarantee their security in an anarchic world. The assumption here, however, is that there are many reasons besides security for why a state might behave aggressively toward another state. In fact, it is uncertainty about whether those non-security causes of war are at play or might come into play, that pushes great powers to worry about their survival and thus act offensively. Security concerns alone cannot cause great powers to act aggressively. The possibility

that at least one state might be motivated by non-security calculations is a necessary condition for offensive realism, as well as for any other structural theory of international politics that predicts security competition. Schweller puts the point well: "If states are assumed to seek nothing more than their own survival, why would they feel threatened? Why would they engage in balancing behavior? In a hypothetical world that has never experienced crime, the concept of security is meaningless." Schweller, "Neorealism's Status-Quo Bias," p. 91. Herbert Butterfield makes essentially the same point when he writes, "Wars would hardly be likely to occur if all men were Christian saints, competing with one another in nothing, perhaps, save self-renunciation." C. T. McIntire, ed., *Herbert Butterfield: Writings on Christianity and History* (Oxford: Oxford University Press, 1979), p. 73. Also see Jack Donnelly, *Realism and International Relations* (Cambridge: Cambridge University Press, 2000), chap. 2.

7. Quoted in Jon Jacobson, *When the Soviet Union Entered World Politics* (Berkeley: University of California Press, 1994), p. 271.

8. See Elizabeth Pond, *Beyond the Wall: Germany's Road to Unification* (Washington, DC: Brookings Institution Press, 1993), chap. 12; Margaret Thatcher, *The Downing Street Years* (New York: HarperCollins, 1993), chaps. 25–26; and Philip Zelikow and Condoleezza Rice, *Germany Unified and Europe Transformed: A Study in Statecraft* (Cambridge, MA: Harvard University Press, 1995), chap. 4.

9. Frederick Schuman introduced the concept of self-help in *International Politics: An Introduction to the Western State System* (New York: McGraw-Hill, 1933), pp. 199–202, 514, although Waltz made the concept famous in *Theory of International Politics*, chap. 6. On realism and alliances, see Stephen M. Walt, *The Origins of Alliances* (Ithaca, NY: Cornell University Press, 1987).

10. Quoted in Martin Wight, *Power Politics* (London: Royal Institute of International Affairs, 1946), p. 40.

11. If one state achieves hegemony, the system ceases to be anarchic and becomes hierarchic. Offensive realism, which assumes international anarchy, has little to say about politics under hierarchy. But as discussed later, it is highly unlikely that any state will become a global hegemon, although regional hegemony is feasible. Thus, realism is likely to provide important insights about world politics for the foreseeable future, save for what goes on inside in a region that is dominated by a hegemon.

12. Although great powers always have aggressive intentions, they are not always *aggressors*, mainly because sometimes they do not have the capability to behave aggressively. I use the term "aggressor" throughout this book to denote great powers that have the material wherewithal to act on their aggressive intentions.

13. Kenneth Waltz maintains that great powers should not pursue hegemony but instead should aim to control an "appropriate" amount of world power. See Waltz, "The Origins of War in Neorealist Theory," in Robert I. Rotberg and Theodore K. Rabb, eds., *The Origin and Prevention of Major Wars* (Cambridge: Cambridge University Press, 1989), p. 40.

14. The following hypothetical example illustrates this point. Assume that American policymakers were forced to choose between two different power balances in the Western Hemisphere. The first is the present distribution of power, whereby the United States is a hegemon that no state in the region would dare challenge militarily. In the second scenario, China replaces Canada and Germany takes the place of Mexico. Even though the United States would have a significant military advantage over both China and Germany, it is difficult to imagine any American strategist opting for this scenario over U.S. hegemony in the Western Hemisphere.

15. John H. Herz, "Idealist Internationalism and the Security Dilemma," *World Politics* 2, No. 2 (January 1950), pp. 157–80. Although Dickinson did not use the term "security dilemma," its logic is clearly articulated in *European Anarchy*, pp. 20, 88.

16. Herz, "Idealist Internationalism," p. 157.

17. See Joseph M. Grieco, "Anarchy and the Limits of Cooperation: A Realist Critique of the Newest Liberal Institutionalism," *International Organization* 42, No. 3 (Summer 1988), pp. 485–507; Stephen D. Krasner, "Global Communications and National Power: Life on the Pareto Frontier," *World Politics* 43, No. 3 (April 1991), pp. 336–66; and Robert Powell, "Absolute and Relative Gains in International Relations Theory," *American Political Science Review* 85, No. 4 (December 1991), pp. 1303–20.

18. See Michael Mastanduno, "Do Relative Gains Matter? America's Response to Japanese Industrial Policy," *International Security* 16, No. 1 (Summer 1991), pp. 73–113.

19. Waltz maintains that in Hans Morgenthau's theory, states seek power as an end in itself; thus, they are concerned with absolute power, not relative power. See Waltz, "Origins of War," pp. 40–41; and Waltz, *Theory of International Politics*, pp. 126–27. Although Morgenthau occasionally makes statements that appear to support Waltz's charge, there is abundant evidence in Morgenthau, Politics among Nations: The Struggle for Power and Peace, 5th ed. (New York: Knopf, 1973) that states are concerned mainly with the pursuit of relative power.

20. Quoted in Marc Trachtenberg, *A Constructed Peace: The Making of the European Settlement, 1945–1963* (Princeton, NJ: Princeton University Press, 1999), p. 36.

21. In short, the key issue for evaluating offensive realism is not whether a state is constantly trying to conquer other countries or going all out in terms of defense spending, but whether or not great powers routinely pass up promising opportunities to gain power over rivals.

22. See Richard K. Betts, *Surprise Attack: Lessons for Defense Planning* (Washington, DC: Brookings Institution Press, 1982); James D. Fearon, "Rationalist Explanations for War," *International Organization* 49, No. 3 (Summer 1995), pp. 390–401; Robert Jervis, *The Logic of Images in*

International Relations (Princeton, NJ: Princeton University Press, 1970); and Stephen Van Evera, *Causes of War: Power and the Roots of Conflict* (Ithaca, NY: Cornell University Press, 1999), pp. 45–51, 83, 137–42.

23. See Joel Achenbach, "The Experts in Retreat: After-the-Fact Explanations for the Gloomy Predictions," *Washington Post*, February 28, 1991; and Jacob Weisberg, "Gulfballs: How the Experts Blew It, Big-Time," *New Republic*, March 25, 1991.

24. Jack Snyder and Stephen Van Evera make this argument in its boldest form. See Jack Snyder, *Myths of Empire: Domestic Politics and International Ambition* (Ithaca, NY: Cornell University Press, 1991), esp. pp. 1, 307–8; and Van Evera, *Causes of War*, esp. pp. 6, 9.

25. Relatedly, some defensive realists interpret the security dilemma to say that the offensive measures a state takes to enhance its own security force rival states to respond in kind, leaving all states no better off than if they had done nothing, and possibly even worse off. See Charles L. Glaser, "The Security Dilemma Revisited," *World Politics* 50, No. 1 (October 1997), pp. 171–201. Given this understanding of the security dilemma, hardly any security competition should ensue among rational states, because it would be fruitless, maybe even counterproductive, to try to gain advantage over rival powers. Indeed, it is difficult to see why states operating in a world where aggressive behavior equals self-defeating behavior would face a "security dilemma." It would seem to make good sense for all states to forsake war and live in peace. Of course, Herz did not describe the security dilemma this way when he introduced it in 1950. As noted, his original rendition of the concept is a synoptic statement of offensive realism.

26. See note 6 in this chapter.

27. Jacob Viner, "Power versus Plenty as Objectives of Foreign Policy in the Seventeenth and Eighteenth Centuries," *World Politics* 1, No. 1 (October 1948), p. 10.

28. See Mark Bowden, *Black Hawk Dawn: A Story of Modern War* (London: Penguin, 1999); Alison Des Forges, *"Leave None to Tell the Story": Genocide in Rwanda* (New York: Human Rights Watch, 1999), pp. 623–25; and Gerard Prunier, *The Rwanda Crisis: History of a Genocide* (New York: Columbia University Press, 1995), pp. 274–75.

29. See Scott R. Feil, *Preventing Genocide: How the Early Use of Force Might Have Succeeded in Rwanda* (New York: Carnegie Corporation, 1998); and John Mueller, "The Banality of 'Ethnic War,'" International Security 25, No. 1 (Summer 2000), pp. 58–62. For a less sanguine view of how many lives would have been saved had the United States intervened in Rwanda, see Alan J. Kuperman, "Rwanda in Retrospect," Foreign Affairs 79, No. 1 (January–February 2000), pp. 94–118.

30. See David F. Schmitz, *Thank God They're on Our Side: The United States and Right-Wing Dictatorships, 1921–1965* (Chapel Hill: University of North Carolina Press, 1999), chaps. 4–6; Gaddis Smith, *The Last Years of the Monroe Doctrine, 1945–1993* (New York: Hill and Wang, 1994); Tony Smith, *America's Mission: The United States and the Worldwide Struggle for Democracy in the Twentieth Century* (Princeton, NJ: Princeton University Press, 1994); and Stephen Van Evera, "Why Europe Matters, Why the Third World Doesn't: American Grand Strategy after the Cold War," *Journal of Strategic Studies* 13, No. 2 (June 1990), pp. 25–30.

31. Quoted in John M. Carroll and George C. Herring, eds., *Modern American Diplomacy*, rev. ed. (Wilmington, DE: Scholarly Resources, 1996), p. 122.

32. Nikita Khrushchev makes a similar point about Stalin's policy toward Chinese nationalist leader Chiang Kai-shek during World War II: "Despite his conflict with the Chinese Communist Party, Chiang Kai-shek was fighting against Japanese imperialism. Therefore, Stalin—and consequently the Soviet government—considered Chiang a progressive force. Japan was our number one enemy in the East, so it was in the interests of the Soviet Union to support Chiang. Of course, we supported him only insofar as we didn't want to see him defeated by the Japanese—in much the same way that Churchill, who had been our enemy since the first days of the Soviet Union, was sensible enough to support us in the war against Hitler." *Khrushchev Remembers: The Last Testament*, trans. and ed. Strobe Talbott (Boston: Little, Brown, 1974), pp. 237–38.

33. See Walt, *Origins of Alliances*, pp. 5, 266–68.

34. Adam Smith, *An Inquiry into the Nature and Causes of the Wealth of Nations*, ed. Edwin Cannan (Chicago: University of Chicago Press, 1976), Vol. 1, p. 487. All the quotes in this paragraph are from pp. 484–87 of that book.

35. For an overview of the Anglo-Dutch rivalry, see Jack S. Levy, "The Rise and Decline of the Anglo-Dutch Rivalry, 1609–1689," in William R. Thompson, ed., *Great Power Rivalries* (Columbia: University of South Carolina Press, 1999), pp. 172–200; and Paul M. Kennedy, *The Rise and Fall of British Naval Mastery* (London: Allen Lane, 1976), chap. 2. This example has direct bearing on the earlier discussion of relative versus absolute power. Specifically, without the Navigation Act, both England and Holland probably would have made greater absolute gains, because their economies would have benefited from open trade. England, however, probably would not have gained much of a relative advantage over Holland. With the Navigation Act, England gained a significant relative advantage over Holland, but both sides suffered in terms of absolute gains. The bottom line is that relative power considerations drive great-power behavior.

36. William J. Clinton, "Address by the President to the 48th Session of the United Nations General Assembly," United Nations, New York, September 27, 1993. Also see George Bush, "Toward a New World Order: Address by the President to a Joint Session of Congress," September 11, 1990.

37. Bradley Thayer examined whether the victorious powers were able to create and maintain stable security orders in the aftermath of the Napoleonic Wars, World War I,

and World War II, or whether they competed among themselves for power, as realism would predict. In particular, he looked at the workings of the Concert of Europe, the League of Nations, and the United Nations, which were purportedly designed to limit, if not eliminate, realist behavior by the great powers. Thayer concludes that the rhetoric of the triumphant powers notwithstanding, they remained firmly committed to gaining power at each other's expense. See Bradley A. Thayer, "Creating Stability in New World Orders," Ph.D. diss., University of Chicago, August 1996. Also see Korina Kagan, "The Myth of the European Concert," *Security Studies* 7, No. 2 (Winter 1997–98), pp. 1–57. She concludes that the Concert of Europe "was a weak and ineffective institution that was largely irrelevant to great power behavior" (p. 3).

38. See Melvyn P. Leffler, *A Preponderance of Power: National Security, the Truman Administration, and the Cold War* (Stanford, CA: Stanford University Press, 1992).

39. For a discussion of American efforts to undermine Soviet control of Eastern Europe, see Peter Grose, *Operation Rollback: America's Secret War behind the Iron Curtain* (Boston: Houghton Mifflin, 2000); Walter L. Hixson, *Parting the Curtain: Propaganda, Culture, and the Cold War, 1945–1961* (New York: St. Martin's, 1997); and Gregory Mitrovich. *Undermining the Kremlin: America's Strategy to Subvert the Soviet Bloc*, 1947–1956 (Ithaca, NY: Cornell University Press, 2000).

40. See Grieco, "Anarchy and the Limits of Cooperation," pp. 498, 500.

41. For evidence of relative gains considerations thwarting cooperation among states, see Paul W. Schroeder, *The Transformation of European Politics, 1763–1848* (Oxford: Clarendon, 1994), chap. 3.

42. Charles Lipson, "International Cooperation in Economic and Security Affairs," *World Politics* 37, No. 1 (October 1984), p. 14.

43. See Randall L. Schweller, "Bandwagoning for Profit: Bringing the Revisionist State Back In," *International Security* 19, No. 1 (Summer 1994), pp. 72–107. See also the works cited in note 59 in this chapter.

44. See Misha Glenny, *The Fall of Yugoslavia: The Third Balkan War*, 3d rev. ed. (New York: Penguin, 1996), p. 149; Philip Sherwell and Alina Petric, "Tudjman Tapes Reveal Plans to Divide Bosnia and Hide War Crimes," *Sunday Telegraph* (London), June 18, 2000; Laura Silber and Allan Little, *Yugoslavia: Death of a Nation*, rev. ed. (New York: Penguin, 1997), pp. 131–32, 213; and Warren Zimmerman, *Origins of a Catastrophe: Yugoslavia and Its Destroyers—America's Last Ambassador Tells What Happened and Why* (New York: Times Books, 1996), pp. 116–17.

45. See John Maynard Keynes, *The Economic Consequences of the Peace* (New York: Penguin, 1988), chap. 2; and J. M. Roberts, *Europe, 1880–1945* (London: Longman, 1970), pp. 239–41.

46. For information on the Molotov-Ribbentrop Pact of August 1939 and the ensuing cooperation between those states, see Alan Bullock, *Hitler and Stalin: Parallel Lives* (London: HarperCollins, 1991), chaps. 14–15; I.C.B. Dear, ed., *The Oxford Companion to World War II* (Oxford: Oxford University Press, 1995), pp. 780–82; Anthony Read and David Fisher, *The Deadly Embrace: Hitler, Stalin, and the Nazi-Soviet Pact, 1939–1941* (New York: Norton, 1988); Geoffrey Roberts. *The Unholy Alliance: Stalin's Pact with Hitler* (Bloomington: Indiana University Press, 1989), chaps. 8–10; and Adam B. *Ulam, Expansion and Coexistence: Soviet Foreign Policy*, 1917–1973, 2d ed. (New York: Holt, Rinehart, and Winston, 1974), chap. 6.

47. Waltz maintains that structural theories can explain international outcomes—i.e., whether war is more likely in bipolar or multipolar systems—but that they cannot explain the foreign policy behavior of particular states. A separate theory of foreign policy, he argues, is needed for that task. See *Theory of International Politics*, pp. 71–72, 121–23. Colin Elman challenges Waltz on this point, arguing that there is no logical reason why systemic theories cannot be used as a theory of foreign policy. The key issue, as Elman notes, is whether the particular structural theory helps us understand the foreign policy decisions that states make. I will attempt to show that offensive realism can be used to explain both the foreign policy of individual states and international outcomes. See Colin Elman, "Horses for Courses: Why Not Neorealist Theories of Foreign Policy?"; Kenneth N. Waltz, "International Politics Is Not Foreign Policy"; and Colin Elman, "Cause, Effect, and Consistency: A Response to Kenneth Waltz," in *Security Studies* 6, No. 1 (Autumn 1996), pp. 7–61.

4.3

Why the World Needs America

Robert Kagan

History shows that world orders, including our own, are transient. They rise and fall, and the institutions they erect, the beliefs and "norms" that guide them, the economic systems they support—they rise and fall, too. The downfall of the Roman Empire brought an end not just to Roman rule but to Roman government and law and to an entire economic system stretching from Northern Europe to North Africa. Culture, the arts, even progress in science and technology, were set back for centuries.

Modern history has followed a similar pattern. After the Napoleonic Wars of the early 19th century, British control of the seas and the balance of great powers on the European continent provided relative security and stability. Prosperity grew, personal freedoms expanded, and the world was knit more closely together by revolutions in commerce and communication.

With the outbreak of World War I, the age of settled peace and advancing liberalism—of European civilization approaching its pinnacle—collapsed into an age of hyper-nationalism, despotism and economic calamity. The once-promising spread of democracy and liberalism halted and then reversed course, leaving a handful of outnumbered and besieged democracies living nervously in the shadow of fascist and totalitarian neighbors. The collapse of the British and European orders in the 20th century did not produce a new dark age—though if Nazi Germany and imperial Japan had prevailed, it might have—but the horrific conflict that it produced was, in its own way, just as devastating.

Would the end of the present American-dominated order have less dire consequences? A surprising number of American intellectuals, politicians and policy makers greet the prospect with equanimity. There is a general sense that the end of the era of American pre-eminence, if and when it comes, need not mean the end of the present international order, with its widespread freedom, unprecedented global prosperity (even amid the current economic crisis) and absence of war among the great powers.

American power may diminish, the political scientist G. John Ikenberry argues, but "the underlying foundations of the liberal international order will survive and thrive." The commentator Fareed Zakaria believes that even as the balance shifts against the U.S., rising powers like China "will continue to live within the framework of the current international system." And there are elements across the political spectrum—Republicans who call for retrenchment, Democrats who put their faith in international law and institutions—who don't imagine that a "post-American world" would look very different from the American world.

If all of this sounds too good to be true, it is. The present world order was largely shaped by American power and reflects American interests and preferences. If the balance of power shifts in the direction of other nations, the world order will change to suit their interests and preferences. Nor can we assume that all the great powers in a post-American world would agree on the benefits of preserving the present order, or have the capacity to preserve it, even if they wanted to.

Take the issue of democracy. For several decades, the balance of power in the world has favored democratic governments. In a genuinely post-American world, the balance would shift toward the great-power autocracies. Both Beijing and Moscow already protect dictators like Syria's Bashar al-Assad. If they gain greater relative influence in the future, we will see fewer democratic transitions and more autocrats hanging on to power. The balance in a new, multipolar world might be more favorable to democracy if some of the rising democracies—Brazil, India, Turkey, South Africa—picked up the slack from a declining U.S. Yet not all of them have the desire or the capacity to do it.

What about the economic order of free markets and free trade? People assume that China and other rising powers that have benefited so much from the present

Source: Robert Kagan. "Why the World Needs America," in *The Wall Street Journal*, February 11, 2012: C1.

system would have a stake in preserving it. They wouldn't kill the goose that lays the golden eggs.

Unfortunately, they might not be able to help themselves. The creation and survival of a liberal economic order has depended, historically, on great powers that are both willing and able to support open trade and free markets, often with naval power. If a declining America is unable to maintain its long-standing hegemony on the high seas, would other nations take on the burdens and the expense of sustaining navies to fill in the gaps?

Even if they did, would this produce an open global commons—or rising tension? China and India are building bigger navies, but the result so far has been greater competition, not greater security. As Mohan Malik has noted in this newspaper, their "maritime rivalry could spill into the open in a decade or two," when India deploys an aircraft carrier in the Pacific Ocean and China deploys one in the Indian Ocean. The move from American-dominated oceans to collective policing by several great powers could be a recipe for competition and conflict rather than for a liberal economic order.

And do the Chinese really value an open economic system? The Chinese economy soon may become the largest in the world, but it will be far from the richest. Its size is a product of the country's enormous population, but in per capita terms, China remains relatively poor. The U.S., Germany and Japan have a per capita GDP of over $40,000. China's is a little over $4,000, putting it at the same level as Angola, Algeria and Belize. Even if optimistic forecasts are correct, China's per capita GDP by 2030 would still only be half that of the U.S., putting it roughly where Slovenia and Greece are today.

As Arvind Subramanian and other economists have pointed out, this will make for a historically unique situation. In the past, the largest and most dominant economies in the world have also been the richest. Nations whose peoples are such obvious winners in a relatively unfettered economic system have less temptation to pursue protectionist measures and have more of an incentive to keep the system open.

China's leaders, presiding over a poorer and still developing country, may prove less willing to open their economy. They have already begun closing some sectors to foreign competition and are likely to close others in the future. Even optimists like Mr. Subramanian believe that the liberal economic order will require "some insurance" against a scenario in which "China exercises its dominance by either reversing its previous policies or failing to open areas of the economy that are now highly protected." American economic dominance has been welcomed by much of the world because, like the mobster Hyman Roth in "The Godfather," the U.S. has always made money for its partners. Chinese economic dominance may get a different reception.

Another problem is that China's form of capitalism is heavily dominated by the state, with the ultimate goal of preserving the rule of the Communist Party. Unlike the eras of British and American pre-eminence, when the leading economic powers were dominated largely by private individuals or companies, China's system is more like the mercantilist arrangements of previous centuries. The government amasses wealth in order to secure its continued rule and to pay for armies and navies to compete with other great powers.

Although the Chinese have been beneficiaries of an open international economic order, they could end up undermining it simply because, as an autocratic society, their priority is to preserve the state's control of wealth and the power that it brings. They might kill the goose that lays the golden eggs because they can't figure out how to keep both it and themselves alive.

Finally, what about the long peace that has held among the great powers for the better part of six decades? Would it survive in a post-American world?

Most commentators who welcome this scenario imagine that American predominance would be replaced by some kind of multipolar harmony. But multipolar systems have historically been neither particularly stable nor particularly peaceful. Rough parity among powerful nations is a source of uncertainty that leads to miscalculation. Conflicts erupt as a result of fluctuations in the delicate power equation.

War among the great powers was a common, if not constant, occurrence in the long periods of multipolarity from the 16th to the 18th centuries, culminating in the series of enormously destructive Europe-wide wars that followed the French Revolution and ended with Napoleon's defeat in 1815.

The 19th century was notable for two stretches of great-power peace of roughly four decades each, punctuated by major conflicts. The Crimean War (1853–1856) was a mini-world war involving well over a million Russian, French, British and Turkish troops, as well as forces from nine other nations; it produced almost a half-million dead combatants and many more wounded. In the Franco-Prussian War (1870–1871), the two nations together fielded close to two million troops, of whom nearly a half-million were killed or wounded.

The peace that followed these conflicts was characterized by increasing tension and competition, numerous war scares and massive increases in armaments on both land and sea. Its climax was World War I, the most destructive and deadly conflict that mankind had known up to that point. As the political scientist Robert W. Tucker has observed, "Such stability and moderation as the balance brought rested ultimately on the threat or use of force. War remained the essential means for maintaining the balance of power."

There is little reason to believe that a return to multipolarity in the 21st century would bring greater peace and stability than it has in the past. The era of American predominance has shown that there is no better recipe for great-power peace than certainty about who holds the upper hand.

President Bill Clinton left office believing that the key task for America was to "create the world we would like to live in when we are no longer the world's only superpower," to prepare for "a time when we would have to share the stage." It is an eminently sensible-sounding proposal. But can it be done? For particularly in matters of security, the rules and institutions of international order rarely survive the decline of the nations that erected them. They are like scaffolding around a building: They don't hold the building up; the building holds them up.

Many foreign-policy experts see the present international order as the inevitable result of human progress, a combination of advancing science and technology, an increasingly global economy, strengthening international institutions, evolving "norms" of international behavior and the gradual but inevitable triumph of liberal democracy over other forms of government—forces of change that transcend the actions of men and nations.

Americans certainly like to believe that our preferred order survives because it is right and just—not only for us but for everyone. We assume that the triumph of democracy is the triumph of a better idea, and the victory of market capitalism is the victory of a better system, and that both are irreversible. That is why Francis Fukuyama's thesis about "the end of history" was so attractive at the end of the Cold War and retains its appeal even now, after it has been discredited by events. The idea of inevitable evolution means that there is no requirement to impose a decent order. It will merely happen.

But international order is not an evolution; it is an imposition. It is the domination of one vision over others—in America's case, the domination of free-market and democratic principles, together with an international system that supports them. The present order will last only as long as those who favor it and benefit from it retain the will and capacity to defend it.

There was nothing inevitable about the world that was created after World War II. No divine providence or unfolding Hegelian dialectic required the triumph of democracy and capitalism, and there is no guarantee that their success will outlast the powerful nations that have fought for them. Democratic progress and liberal economics have been and can be reversed and undone. The ancient democracies of Greece and the republics of Rome and Venice all fell to more powerful forces or through their own failings. The evolving liberal economic order of Europe collapsed in the 1920s and 1930s. The better idea doesn't have to win just because it is a better idea. It requires great powers to champion it.

If and when American power declines, the institutions and norms that American power has supported will decline, too. Or more likely, if history is a guide, they may collapse altogether as we make a transition to another kind of world order, or to disorder. We may discover then that the U.S. was essential to keeping the present world order together and that the alternative to American power was not peace and harmony but chaos and catastrophe—which is what the world looked like right before the American order came into being.

5 Liberalism I

5.1

Of the State of Nature, Of the State of War, and Of the Ends of Political Society and Government

John Locke

Of the State of Nature

Sec. 4. To understand political power right, and derive it from its original, we must consider, what state all men are naturally in, and that is, a state of perfect freedom to order their actions, and dispose of their possessions and persons, as they think fit, within the bounds of the law of nature, without asking leave, or depending upon the will of any other man.

A state also of equality, wherein all the power and jurisdiction is reciprocal, no one having more than another; there being nothing more evident, than that creatures of the same species and rank, promiscuously born to all the same advantages of nature, and the use of the same faculties, should also be equal one amongst another without subordination or subjection, unless the lord and master of them all should, by any manifest declaration of his will, set one above another, and confer on him, by an evident and clear appointment, an undoubted right to dominion and sovereignty.

Sec. 5. This equality of men by nature, the judicious Hooker looks upon as so evident in itself, and beyond all question, that he makes it the foundation of that obligation to mutual love amongst men, on which he builds the duties they owe one another, and from whence he derives the great maxims of justice and charity. . . .

Sec. 6. But though this be a state of liberty, yet it is not a state of licence: though man in that state have an uncontroulable liberty to dispose of his person or possessions, yet he has not liberty to destroy himself, or so much as any creature in his possession, but where some nobler use than its bare preservation calls for it. The state of nature has a law of nature to govern it, which obliges every one: and reason, which is that law, teaches all mankind, who will but consult it, that being all equal and independent, no one ought to harm another in his life, health, liberty, or possessions: for men being all the workmanship of one omnipotent, and infinitely wise maker; all the servants of one sovereign master, sent into the world by his order, and about his business; they are his property, whose workmanship they are, made to last during his, not one another's pleasure: and being furnished with like faculties, sharing all in one community of nature, there cannot be supposed any such subordination among us, that may authorize us to destroy one another, as if we were made for one another's uses, as the inferior ranks of creatures are for our's. Every one, as he is bound to preserve himself, and not to quit his station wilfully, so by the like reason, when his own preservation comes not in competition, ought he, as much as he can, to preserve the rest of mankind, and may not, unless it be to do justice on an offender, take away, or impair the life, or

Source: John Locke (1690), "Of the State of Nature, Of the State of War, and Of the Ends of Political Society and Government," in *The Second Treatise of Government*.

what tends to the preservation of the life, the liberty, health, limb, or goods of another.

Sec. 7. And that all men may be restrained from invading others rights, and from doing hurt to one another, and the law of nature be observed, which willeth the peace and preservation of all mankind, the execution of the law of nature is, in that state, put into every man's hands, whereby every one has a right to punish the transgressors of that law to such a degree, as may hinder its violation: for the law of nature would, as all other laws that concern men in this world be in vain, if there were no body that in the state of nature had a power to execute that law, and thereby preserve the innocent and restrain offenders. And if any one in the state of nature may punish another for any evil he has done, every one may do so: for in that state of perfect equality, where naturally there is no superiority or jurisdiction of one over another, what any may do in prosecution of that law, every one must needs have a right to do.

Sec. 8. And thus, in the state of nature, one man comes by a power over another; but yet no absolute or arbitrary power, to use a criminal, when he has got him in his hands, according to the passionate heats, or boundless extravagancy of his own will; but only to retribute to him, so far as calm reason and conscience dictate, what is proportionate to his transgression, which is so much as may serve for reparation and restraint: for these two are the only reasons, why one man may lawfully do harm to another, which is that we call punishment. In transgressing the law of nature, the offender declares himself to live by another rule than that of reason and common equity, which is that measure God has set to the actions of men, for their mutual security; and so he becomes dangerous to mankind, the tye, which is to secure them from injury and violence, being slighted and broken by him. Which being a trespass against the whole species, and the peace and safety of it, provided for by the law of nature, every man upon this score, by the right he hath to preserve mankind in general, may restrain, or where it is necessary, destroy things noxious to them, and so may bring such evil on any one, who hath transgressed that law, as may make him repent the doing of it, and thereby deter him, and by his example others, from doing the like mischief. And in the case, and upon this ground, every man hath a right to punish the offender, and be executioner of the law of nature.

Sec. 9. I doubt not but this will seem a very strange doctrine to some men: but before they condemn it, I desire them to resolve me, by what right any prince or state can put to death, or punish an alien, for any crime he commits in their country. It is certain their laws, by virtue of any sanction they receive from the promulgated will of the legislative, reach not a stranger: they speak not to him, nor, if they did, is he bound to hearken to them. The legislative authority, by which they are in force over the subjects of that commonwealth, hath no power over him. Those who have the supreme power of making laws in England, France or Holland, are to an Indian, but like the rest of the world, men without authority: and therefore, if by the law of nature every man hath not a power to punish offences against it, as he soberly judges the case to require, I see not how the magistrates of any community can punish an alien of another country; since, in reference to him, they can have no more power than what every man naturally may have over another.

Sec. 10. Besides the crime which consists in violating the law, and varying from the right rule of reason, whereby a man so far becomes degenerate, and declares himself to quit the principles of human nature, and to be a noxious creature, there is commonly injury done to some person or other, and some other man receives damage by his transgression: in which case he who hath received any damage, has, besides the right of punishment common to him with other men, a particular right to seek reparation from him that has done it: and any other person, who finds it just, may also join with him that is injured, and assist him in recovering from the offender so much as may make satisfaction for the harm he has suffered.

Sec. 11. From these two distinct rights, the one of punishing the crime for restraint, and preventing the like offence, which right of punishing is in every body; the other of taking reparation, which belongs only to the injured party, comes it to pass that the magistrate, who by being magistrate hath the common right of punishing put into his hands, can often, where the public good demands not the execution of the law, remit the punishment of criminal offences by his own authority, but yet cannot remit the satisfaction due to any private man for the damage he has received. That, he who has suffered the damage has a right to demand in his own name, and he alone can remit: the damnified person has this power of appropriating to himself the goods or service of the offender, by right of self-preservation, as every man has a power to punish the crime, to prevent its being committed again, by the right he has of preserving all mankind, and doing all reasonable things he can in order to that end: and thus it is, that every man, in the state of nature, has a power to kill a murderer, both to deter others from doing the like injury, which no reparation can compensate, by the example of the punishment that attends it from every body, and also to secure men from the attempts of a criminal, who having renounced reason, the common rule and measure God hath given to mankind, hath, by the unjust violence and slaughter he hath committed upon one, declared war against all mankind, and therefore may be destroyed as a lion or a tiger, one of those wild savage beasts, with whom men can have no society nor security: and upon this is grounded that great law of nature, Whoso sheddeth man's blood, by man shall his blood be shed. And Cain was so fully convinced, that every one had a right to destroy such a criminal, that after the murder of his brother, he cries out, Every one that findeth me, shall slay me; so plain was it writ in the hearts of all mankind.

Sec. 12. By the same reason may a man in the state of nature punish the lesser breaches of that law. It will perhaps be demanded, with death? I answer, each transgression may be punished to that degree, and with so much severity, as will suffice to make it an ill bargain to the offender, give him cause to repent, and terrify others from doing the like. Every offence, that can be committed in the state of nature, may in the state of nature be also punished equally, and as far forth as it may, in a commonwealth: for though it would be besides my present purpose, to enter here into the particulars of the law of nature, or its measures of punishment; yet, it is certain there is such a law, and that too, as intelligible and plain to a rational creature, and a studier of that law, as the positive laws of commonwealths; nay, possibly plainer; as much as reason is easier to be understood, than the fancies and intricate contrivances of men, following contrary and hidden interests put into words; for so truly are a great part of the municipal laws of countries, which are only so far right, as they are founded on the law of nature, by which they are to be regulated and interpreted.

Sec. 13. To this strange doctrine, viz. That in the state of nature every one has the executive power of the law of nature, I doubt not but it will be objected, that it is unreasonable for men to be judges in their own cases, that selflove will make men partial to themselves and their friends: and on the other side, that ill nature, passion and revenge will carry them too far in punishing others; and hence nothing but confusion and disorder will follow, and that therefore God hath certainly appointed government to restrain the partiality and violence of men. I easily grant, that civil government is the proper remedy for the inconveniencies of the state of nature, which must certainly be great, where men may be judges in their own case, since it is easy to be imagined, that he who was so unjust as to do his brother an injury, will scarce be so just as to condemn himself for it: but I shall desire those who make this objection, to remember, that absolute monarchs are but men; and if government is to be the remedy of those evils, which necessarily follow from men's being judges in their own cases, and the state of nature is therefore not to be endured, I desire to know what kind of government that is, and how much better it is than the state of nature, where one man, commanding a multitude, has the liberty to be judge in his own case, and may do to all his subjects whatever he pleases, without the least liberty to any one to question or controul those who execute his pleasure and in whatsoever he doth, whether led by reason, mistake or passion, must be submitted to. Much better it is in the state of nature, wherein men are not bound to submit to the unjust will of another. And if he that judges, judges amiss in his own, or any other case, he is answerable for it to the rest of mankind.

Sec. 14. It is often asked as a mighty objection, where are, or ever were there any men in such a state of nature? To which it may suffice as an answer at present, that since all princes and rulers of independent governments all through the world, are in a state of nature, it is plain the world never was, nor ever will be, without numbers of men in that state. I have named all governors of independent communities, whether they are, or are not, in league with others: for it is not every compact that puts an end to the state of nature between men, but only this one of agreeing together mutually to enter into one community, and make one body politic; other promises, and compacts, men may make one with another, and yet still be in the state of nature. The promises and bargains for truck, &c. between the two men in the desert island, mentioned by Garcilasso de la Vega, in his history of Peru; or between a Swiss and an Indian, in the woods of America, are binding to them, though they are perfectly in a state of nature, in reference to one another: for truth and keeping of faith belongs to men, as men, and not as members of society.

Sec. 15. To those that say, there were never any men in the state of nature, I will not only oppose the authority of the judicious Hooker, Eccl. Pol. lib. i. sect. 10, where he says, "The laws which have been hitherto mentioned, i.e. the laws of nature, do bind men absolutely, even as they are men, although they have never any settled fellowship, never any solemn agreement amongst themselves what to do, or not to do: but forasmuch as we are not by ourselves sufficient to furnish ourselves with competent store of things, needful for such a life as our nature doth desire, a life fit for the dignity of man; therefore to supply those defects and imperfections which are in us, as living single and solely by ourselves, we are naturally induced to seek communion and fellowship with others: this was the cause of men's uniting themselves at first in politic societies." But I moreover affirm, that all men are naturally in that state, and remain so, till by their own consents they make themselves members of some politic society; and I doubt not in the sequel of this discourse, to make it very clear.

Of the State of War

Sec. 16. THE state of war is a state of enmity and destruction: and therefore declaring by word or action, not a passionate and hasty, but a sedate settled design upon another man's life, puts him in a state of war with him against whom he has declared such an intention, and so has exposed his life to the other's power to be taken away by him, or any one that joins with him in his defence, and espouses his quarrel; it being reasonable and just, I should have a right to destroy that which threatens me with destruction: for, by the fundamental law of nature, man being to be preserved as much as possible, when all cannot be preserved, the safety of the innocent is to be preferred: and one may destroy a man who makes war upon him, or has discovered an enmity to his being, for the same reason that he may kill a wolf or a lion; because such men are not under the ties of the common law of reason, have no other rule, but that of force and violence, and so may be treated as beasts of prey, those dangerous and noxious creatures, that will be sure to destroy him whenever he falls into their power.

Sec. 17. And hence it is, that he who attempts to get another man into his absolute power, does thereby put himself into a state of war with him; it being to be understood as a declaration of a design upon his life: for I have reason to conclude, that he who would get me into his power without my consent, would use me as he pleased when he had got me there, and destroy me too when he had a fancy to it; for no body can desire to have me in his absolute power, unless it be to compel me by force to that which is against the right of my freedom, i.e. make me a slave. To be free from such force is the only security of my preservation; and reason bids me look on him, as an enemy to my preservation, who would take away that freedom which is the fence to it; so that he who makes an attempt to enslave me, thereby puts himself into a state of war with me. He that, in the state of nature, would take away the freedom that belongs to any one in that state, must necessarily be supposed to have a foundation of all the rest; as he that in the state of society, would take away the freedom belonging to those of that society or commonwealth, must be supposed to design to take away from them every thing else, and so be looked on as in a state of war.

Sec. 18. This makes it lawful for a man to kill a thief, who has not in the least hurt him, nor declared any design upon his life, any farther than, by the use of force, so to get him in his power, as to take away his money, or what he pleases, from him; because using force, where he has no right, to get me into his power, let his pretence be what it will, I have no reason to suppose, that he, who would take away my liberty, would not, when he had me in his power, take away every thing else. And therefore it is lawful for me to treat him as one who has put himself into a state of war with me, i.e. kill him if I can; for to that hazard does he justly expose himself, whoever introduces a state of war, and is aggressor in it.

Sec. 19. And here we have the plain difference between the state of nature and the state of war, which however some men have confounded, are as far distant, as a state of peace, good will, mutual assistance and preservation, and a state of enmity, malice, violence and mutual destruction, are one from another. Men living together according to reason, without a common superior on earth, with authority to judge between them, is properly the state of nature. But force, or a declared design of force, upon the person of another, where there is no common superior on earth to appeal to for relief, is the state of war: and it is the want of such an appeal gives a man the right of war even against an aggressor, tho' he be in society and a fellow subject. Thus a thief, whom I cannot harm, but by appeal to the law, for having stolen all that I am worth, I may kill, when he sets on me to rob me but of my horse or coat; because the law, which was made for my preservation, where it cannot interpose to secure my life from present force, which, if lost, is capable of no reparation, permits me my own defence, and the right of war, a liberty to kill the aggressor, because the aggressor allows not time to appeal to our common judge, nor the decision of the law, for remedy in a case where the mischief may be irreparable. Want of a common judge with authority, puts all men in a state of nature: force without right, upon a man's person, makes a state of war, both where there is, and is not, a common judge.

Sec. 20. But when the actual force is over, the state of war ceases between those that are in society, and are equally on both sides subjected to the fair determination of the law; because then there lies open the remedy of appeal for the past injury, and to prevent future harm: but where no such appeal is, as in the state of nature, for want of positive laws, and judges with authority to appeal to, the state of war once begun, continues, with a right to the innocent party to destroy the other whenever he can, until the aggressor offers peace, and desires reconciliation on such terms as may repair any wrongs he has already done, and secure the innocent for the future; nay, where an appeal to the law, and constituted judges, lies open, but the remedy is denied by a manifest perverting of justice, and a barefaced wresting of the laws to protect or indemnify the violence or injuries of some men, or party of men, there it is hard to imagine any thing but a state of war: for wherever violence is used, and injury done, though by hands appointed to administer justice, it is still violence and injury, however coloured with the name, pretences, or forms of law, the end whereof being to protect and redress the innocent, by an unbiassed application of it, to all who are under it; wherever that is not bona fide done, war is made upon the sufferers, who having no appeal on earth to right them, they are left to the only remedy in such cases, an appeal to heaven.

Sec. 21. To avoid this state of war (wherein there is no appeal but to heaven, and wherein even the least difference is apt to end, where there is no authority to decide between the contenders) is one great reason of men's putting themselves into society, and quitting the state of nature: for where there is an authority, a power on earth, from which relief can be had by appeal, there the continuance of the state of war is excluded, and the controversy is decided by that power. Had there been any such court, any superior jurisdiction on earth, to determine the right between Jephtha and the Ammonites, they had never come to a state of war: but we see he was forced to appeal to heaven. The Lord the Judge (says he) be judge this day between the children of Israel and the children of Ammon, Judg. xi. 27. and then prosecuting, and relying on his appeal, he leads out his army to battle: and therefore in such controversies, where the question is put, who shall be judge? It cannot be meant, who shall decide the controversy; every one knows what Jephtha here tells us, that the Lord the Judge shall judge. Where there is no judge on earth, the appeal lies to God in heaven. That question then cannot mean, who shall judge, whether another hath put himself in a state of war with me, and whether I may, as Jephtha did, appeal to heaven in it? of that I myself can only be judge in my own conscience, as I will answer it, at the great day, to the supreme judge of all men.

Of the Ends of Political Society and Government

Sec. 123. IF man in the state of nature be so free, as has been said; if he be absolute lord of his own person and possessions, equal to the greatest, and subject to no body, why will he part with his freedom? Why will he give up this empire, and subject himself to the dominion and controul of any other power? To which it is obvious to answer, that though in the state of nature he hath such a right, yet the enjoyment of it is very uncertain, and constantly exposed to the invasion of others: for all being kings as much as he, every man his equal, and the greater part no strict observers of equity and justice, the enjoyment of the property he has in this state is very unsafe, very unsecure. This makes him willing to quit a condition, which, however free, is full of fears and continual dangers: and it is not without reason, that he seeks out, and is willing to join in society with others, who are already united, or have a mind to unite, for the mutual preservation of their lives, liberties and estates, which I call by the general name, property.

Sec. 124. The great and chief end, therefore, of men's uniting into commonwealths, and putting themselves under government, is the preservation of their property. To which in the state of nature there are many things wanting.

First, There wants an established, settled, known law, received and allowed by common consent to be the standard of right and wrong, and the common measure to decide all controversies between them: for though the law of nature be plain and intelligible to all rational creatures; yet men being biased by their interest, as well as ignorant for want of study of it, are not apt to allow of it as a law binding to them in the application of it to their particular cases.

Sec. 125. Secondly, In the state of nature there wants a known and indifferent judge, with authority to determine all differences according to the established law: for every one in that state being both judge and executioner of the law of nature, men being partial to themselves, passion and revenge is very apt to carry them too far, and with too much heat, in their own cases; as well as negligence, and unconcernedness, to make them too remiss in other men's.

Sec. 126. Thirdly, In the state of nature there often wants power to back and support the sentence when right, and to give it due execution, They who by any injustice offended, will seldom fail, where they are able, by force to make good their injustice; such resistance many times makes the punishment dangerous, and frequently destructive, to those who attempt it.

Sec. 127. Thus mankind, notwithstanding all the privileges of the state of nature, being but in an ill condition, while they remain in it, are quickly driven into society. Hence it comes to pass, that we seldom find any number of men live any time together in this state. The inconveniencies that they are therein exposed to, by the irregular and uncertain exercise of the power every man has of punishing the transgressions of others, make them take sanctuary under the established laws of government, and therein seek the preservation of their property. It is this makes them so willingly give up every one his single power of punishing, to be exercised by such alone, as shall be appointed to it amongst them; and by such rules as the community, or those authorized by them to that purpose, shall agree on. And in this we have the original right and rise of both the legislative and executive power, as well as of the governments and societies themselves.

Sec. 128. For in the state of nature, to omit the liberty he has of innocent delights, a man has two powers.

The first is to do whatsoever he thinks fit for the preservation of himself, and others within the permission of the law of nature: by which law, common to them all, he and all the rest of mankind are one community, make up one society, distinct from all other creatures. And were it not for the corruption and vitiousness of degenerate men, there would be no need of any other; no necessity that men should separate from this great and natural community, and by positive agreements combine into smaller and divided associations.

The other power a man has in the state of nature, is the power to punish the crimes committed against that law. Both these he gives up, when he joins in a private, if I may so call it, or particular politic society, and incorporates into any commonwealth, separate from the rest of mankind.

Sec. 129. The first power, viz. of doing whatsoever he thought for the preservation of himself, and the rest of mankind, he gives up to be regulated by laws made by the society, so far forth as the preservation of himself, and the rest of that society shall require; which laws of the society in many things confine the liberty he had by the law of nature.

Sec. 130. Secondly, The power of punishing he wholly gives up, and engages his natural force, (which he might before employ in the execution of the law of nature, by his own single authority, as he thought fit) to assist the executive power of the society, as the law thereof shall require: for being now in a new state, wherein he is to enjoy many conveniencies, from the labour, assistance, and society of others in the same community, as well as protection from its whole strength; he is to part also with as much of his natural liberty, in providing for himself, as the good, prosperity, and safety of the society shall require; which is not only necessary, but just, since the other members of the society do the like.

Sec. 131. But though men, when they enter into society, give up the equality, liberty, and executive power they had in the state of nature, into the hands of the society, to be so far disposed of by the legislative, as the good of the society shall require; yet it being only with an intention in every one the better to preserve himself, his liberty and property; (for no rational creature can be supposed to change his condition with an intention to be worse) the power of the society, or legislative constituted by them, can never be supposed to extend farther, than the common good; but is obliged to secure every one's property, by providing against those three defects above mentioned, that made the state of nature so unsafe and uneasy. And so whoever has the legislative or supreme power of any commonwealth, is bound to govern by established standing laws, promulgated and known to the people, and not by extemporary decrees; by indifferent and upright judges, who are to decide controversies by those laws; and to employ the force of the community at home, only in the execution of such laws, or abroad to prevent or redress foreign injuries, and secure the community from inroads and invasion. And all this to be directed to no other end, but the peace, safety, and public good of the people.

5.2

Perpetual Peace

A Philosophical Sketch

Immanuel Kant

Containing the Definitive Articles for Perpetual Peace Among States

The state of peace among men living side by side is not the natural state *(status naturalis)*; the natural state is one of war. This does not always mean open hostilities, but at least an unceasing threat of war. A state of peace, therefore, must be established, for in order to be secured against hostility it is not sufficient that hostilities simply be not committed; and, unless this security is pledged to each by his neighbor (a thing that can occur only in a civil state), each may treat his neighbor, from whom he demands this security, as an enemy.

First Definitive Article for Perpetual Peace

"The Civil Constitution of Every State Should Be Republican"

The only constitution which derives from the idea of the original compact, and on which all juridical legislation of a people must be based, is the republican. This constitution is established, firstly, by principles of the freedom of the members of a society (as men); secondly, by principles of dependence of all upon a single common legislation (as subjects); and, thirdly, by the law of their equality (as citizens). The republican constitution, therefore, is, with respect to law, the one which is the original basis of every form of civil constitution. The only question now is: Is it also the one which can lead to perpetual peace?

The republican constitution, besides the purity of its origin (having sprung from the pure source of the concept of law), also gives a favorable prospect for the desired consequence, i.e., perpetual peace. The reason is this: if the consent of the citizens is required in order to decide that war should be declared (and in this constitution it cannot but be the case), nothing is more natural than that they would be very cautious in commencing such a poor game, decreeing for themselves all the calamities of war. Among the latter would be: having to fight, having to pay the costs of war from their own resources, having painfully to repair the devastation war leaves behind, and, to fill up the measure of evils, load themselves with a heavy national debt that would embitter peace itself and that can never be liquidated on account of constant wars in the future. But, on the other hand, in a constitution which is not republican, and under which the subjects are not citizens, a declaration of war is the easiest thing in the world to decide upon, because war does not require of the ruler, who is the proprietor and not a member of the state, the least sacrifice of the pleasures of his table, the chase, his country houses, his court functions, and the like. He may, therefore, resolve on war as on a pleasure party for the most trivial reasons, and with perfect indifference leave the justification which decency requires to the diplomatic corps who are ever ready to provide it.

In order not to confuse the republican constitution with the democratic (as is commonly done), the following should be noted. The forms of a state *(civitas)* can be divided either according to the persons who possess the sovereign power or according to the mode of administration exercised over the people by the chief, whoever he may be. The first is properly called the form of sovereignty *(forma imperii)*, and there are only three possible forms of it: autocracy, in which one, aristocracy, in which some associated together, or democracy, in which all those who constitute society, possess sovereign power. They may be characterized, respectively, as the power of a monarch, of the nobility, or of the people. The second division is that by the form of government (*forma regiminis*) and is based on

Source: Immanuel Kant (1798), "Eternal Peace: Section II. The Definitive Articles of Perpetual Peace Among States," in *Essays and Treaties on Moral, Political, and Various Philosophical Subjects.*

the way in which the state makes use of its power; this way is based on the constitution, which is the act of the general will through which the many persons become one nation. In this respect government is either republican or despotic. Republicanism is the political principle of the separation of the executive power (the administration) from the legislative; despotism is that of the autonomous execution by the state of laws which it has itself decreed. Thus in a despotism the public will is administered by the ruler as his own will. Of the three forms of the state, that of democracy is, properly speaking, necessarily a despotism, because it establishes an executive power in which "all" decide for or even against one who does not agree; that is, "all," who are not quite all, decide, and this is a contradiction of the general will with itself and with freedom.

Every form of government which is not representative is, properly speaking, *without form*. The legislator can unite in one and the same person his function as legislative and as executor of his will just as little as the universal of the major premise in a syllogism can also be the subsumption of the particular under the universal in the minor. And even though the other two constitutions are always defective to the extent that they do leave room for this mode of administration, it is at least possible for them to assume a mode of government conforming to the spirit of a representative system (as when Frederick II at least said he was merely the first servant of the state). On the other hand, the democratic mode of government makes this impossible, since everyone wishes to be master. Therefore, we can say: the smaller the personnel of the government (the smaller the number of rulers), the greater is their representation and the more nearly the constitution approaches to the possibility of republicanism; thus the constitution may be expected by gradual reform finally to raise itself to republicanism. For these reasons it is more difficult for an aristocracy than for a monarchy to achieve the one completely juridical constitution, and it is impossible for a democracy to do so except by violent revolution.

The mode of governments, however, is incomparably more important to the people than the form of sovereignty, although much depends on the greater or lesser suitability of the latter to the end of [good] government. To conform to the concept of law, however, government must have a representative form, and in this system only a republican mode of government is possible; without it, government is despotic and arbitrary, whatever the constitution may be. None of the ancient so-called "republics" knew this system, and they all finally and inevitably degenerated into despotism under the sovereignty of one, which is the most bearable of all forms of despotism.

Second Definitive Article for A Perpetual Peace

"The Law of Nations Shall be Founded on a Federation of Free States"

Peoples, as states, like individuals, may be judged to injure one another merely by their coexistence in the state of nature (i.e., while independent of external laws). Each of them, may and should for the sake of its own security demand that the others enter with it into a constitution similar to the civil constitution, for under such a constitution each can be secure in his right. This would be a league of nations, but it would not have to be a state consisting of nations. That would be contradictory, since a state implies the relation of a superior (legislating) to an inferior (obeying), i.e., the people, and many nations in one state would then constitute only one nation. This contradicts the presupposition, for here we have to weigh the rights of nations against each other so far as they are distinct states and not amalgamated into one.

When we see the attachment of savages to their lawless freedom, preferring ceaseless combat to subjection to a lawful constraint which they might establish, and thus preferring senseless freedom to rational freedom, we regard it with deep contempt as barbarity, rudeness, and a brutish degradation of humanity. Accordingly, one would think that civilized people (each united in a state) would hasten all the more to escape, the sooner the better, from such a depraved condition. But, instead, each state places its majesty (for it is absurd to speak of the majesty of the people) in being subject to no external juridical restraint, and the splendor of its sovereign consists in the fact that many thousands stand at his command to sacrifice themselves for something that does not concern them and without his needing to place himself in the least danger. The chief difference between European and American savages lies in the fact that many tribes of the latter have been eaten by their enemies, while the former know how to make better use of their conquered enemies than to dine off them; they know better how to use them to increase the number of their subjects and thus the quantity of instruments for even more extensive wars.

When we consider the perverseness of human nature which is nakedly revealed in the uncontrolled relations between nations (this perverseness being veiled in the state of civil law by the constraint exercised by government), we may well be astonished that the word "law" has not yet been banished from war politics as pedantic, and that no state has yet been bold enough to advocate this point of view. Up to the present, Hugo Grotius, Pufendorf, Vattel, and many other irritating comforters have been cited in justification of war, though their code, philosophically or diplomatically formulated, has not and cannot have the least legal force, because states as such do not stand under a common external power. There is no instance on record that a state has ever been moved to desist from its purpose because of arguments backed up by the testimony of such great men. But the homage which each state pays (at least in words) to the concept of law proves that there is slumbering in man an even greater moral disposition to become master of the evil principle in himself (which he cannot disclaim) and to hope for the same from others. Otherwise the word "law" would never be pronounced by states which wish to war upon one another; it would be used only ironically, as a Gallic prince interpreted it when he said, "It is the prerogative which nature has given the stronger that the weaker should obey him."

States do not plead their cause before a tribunal; war alone is their way of bringing suit. But by war and its favorable issue, in victory, right is not decided, and though by a treaty of peace this particular war is brought to an end, the state of war, of always finding a new pretext to hostilities, is not terminated. Nor can this be declared wrong, considering the fact that in this state each is the judge of his own case. Notwithstanding, the obligation which men in a lawless condition have under the natural law, and which requires them to abandon the state of nature, does not quite apply to states under the law of nations, for as states they already have an internal juridical constitution and have thus outgrown compulsion from others to submit to a more extended lawful constitution according to their ideas of right. This is true in spite of the fact that reason, from its throne of supreme moral legislating authority, absolutely condemns war as a legal recourse and makes a state of peace a direct duty, even though peace cannot be established or secured except by a compact among nations.

For these reasons there must be a league of a particular kind, which can be called a league of peace *(foedus pacificum)*, and which would be distinguished from a treaty of peace *(pactum pacis)* by the fact that the latter terminates only one war, while the former seeks to make an end of all wars forever. This league does not tend to any dominion over the power of the state but only to the maintenance and security of the freedom of the state itself and of other states in league with it, without there being any need for them to submit to civil laws and their compulsion, as men in a state of nature must submit.

The practicability (objective reality) of this idea of federation, which should gradually spread to all states and thus lead to perpetual peace, can be proved. For if fortune directs that a powerful and enlightened people can make itself a republic, which by its nature must be inclined to perpetual peace, this gives a fulcrum to the federation with other states so that they may adhere to it and thus secure freedom under the idea of the law of nations. By more and more such associations, the federation may be gradually extended.

We may readily conceive that a people should say, "There ought to be no war among us, for we want to make ourselves into a state; that is, we want to establish a supreme legislative, executive, and judiciary power which will reconcile our differences peaceably." But when this state says, "There ought to be no war between myself and other states, even though I acknowledge no supreme legislative power by which our rights are mutually guaranteed," it is not at all clear on what I can base my confidence in my own rights unless it is the free federation, the surrogate of the civil social order, which reason necessarily associates with the concept of the law of nations— assuming that something is really meant by the latter.

The concept of a law of nations as a right to make war does not really mean anything, because it is then a law of deciding what is right by unilateral maxims through force and not by universally valid public laws which restrict the freedom of each one. The only conceivable meaning of such a law of nations might be that it serves men right who are so inclined that they should destroy each other and thus find perpetual peace in the vast grave that swallows both the atrocities and their perpetrators. For states in their relation to each other, there cannot be any reasonable way out of the lawless condition which entails only war except that they, like individual men, should give up their savage (lawless) freedom, adjust themselves to the constraints of public law, and thus establish a continuously growing state consisting of various nations *(civitas gentium)*, which will ultimately include all the nations of the world. But under the idea of the law of nations they do not wish this, and reject in practice what is correct in theory. If all is not to be lost, there can be, then, in place of the positive idea of a world republic, only the negative surrogate of an alliance which averts war, endures, spreads, and holds back the stream of those hostile passions which fear the law, though such an alliance is in constant peril of their breaking loose again. . . .

Third Definitive Article for a Perpetual Peace

"The Law of World Citizenship Shall Be Limited to Conditions of Universal Hospitality"

Here, as in the preceding articles, it is not a question of philanthropy but of right. Hospitality means the right of a stranger not to be treated as an enemy when he arrives in the land of another. One may refuse to receive him when this can be done without causing his destruction; but, so long as he peacefully occupies his place, one may not treat him with hostility. It is not the right to be a permanent visitor that one may demand. A special beneficent agreement would be needed in order to give an outsider a right to become a fellow inhabitant for a certain length of time. It is only a right of temporary sojourn, a right to associate, which all men have. They have it by virtue of their common possession of the surface of the earth, where, as a globe, they cannot infinitely disperse and hence must finally tolerate the presence of each other. Originally, no one had more right than another to a particular part of the earth.

Uninhabitable parts of the earth—the sea and the deserts—divide this community of all men, but the ship and the camel (the desert ship) enable them to approach each other across these unruled regions and to establish communication by using the common right to the face of the earth, which belongs to human beings generally. The inhospitality of the inhabitants of coasts (for instance, of the Barbary Coast) in robbing ships in neighboring seas or enslaving stranded travelers, or the inhospitality of the inhabitants of the deserts (for instance, the Bedouin Arabs) who view contact with nomadic tribes as conferring the right to plunder them, is thus opposed to natural law, even though it extends the right of hospitality, i.e., the privilege of foreign arrivals, no further than to conditions of the possibility of seeking to communicate with the prior inhabitants. In this way distant parts of the world can come into peaceable relations with each other, and these are finally publicly established by law. Thus the human race can gradually be brought closer and closer to a constitution establishing world citizenship.

But to this perfection compare the inhospitable actions of the civilized and especially of the commercial states of our part of the world.

The injustice which they show to lands and peoples they visit (which is equivalent to conquering them) is carried by them to terrifying lengths. America, the lands inhabited by the Negro, the Spice Islands, the Cape, etc., were at the time of their discovery considered by these civilized intruders as lands without owners, for they counted the inhabitants as nothing. In East India (Hindustan), under the pretense of establishing economic undertakings, they brought in foreign soldiers and used them to oppress the natives, excited widespread wars among the various states, spread famine, rebellion, perfidy, and the whole litany of evils which afflict mankind.

China and Japan (Nippon), who have had experience with such guests, have wisely refused them entry, the former permitting their approach to their shores but not their entry, while the latter permit this approach to only one European people, the Dutch, but treat them like prisoners, not allowing them any communication with the inhabitants. The worst of this (or, to speak with the moralist, the best) is that all these outrages profit them nothing, since all these commercial ventures stand on the verge of collapse, and the Sugar Islands, that place of the most refined and cruel slavery, produces no real revenue except indirectly, only serving a not very praiseworthy purpose of furnishing sailors for war fleets and thus for the conduct of war in Europe. This service is rendered to powers which make a great show of their piety, and, while they drink injustice like water, they regard themselves as the elect in point of orthodoxy.

Since the narrower or wider community of the peoples of the earth has developed so far that a violation of rights in one place is felt throughout the world, the idea of a law of world citizenship is no high-flown or exaggerated notion. It is a supplement to the unwritten code of the civil and international law, indispensable for the maintenance of the public human rights and hence also of perpetual peace. One cannot flatter oneself into believing one can approach this peace except under the condition outlined here.

5.3

Kant, Liberal Legacies, and Foreign Affairs

Michael W. Doyle

I

What difference do liberal principles and institutions make to the conduct of the foreign affairs of liberal states? A thicket of conflicting judgments suggests that the legacies of liberalism have not been clearly appreciated. For many citizens of liberal states, liberal principles and institutions have so fully absorbed domestic politics that their influence on foreign affairs tends to be either overlooked altogether or, when perceived, exaggerated. Liberalism becomes either unselfconsciously patriotic or inherently " peace-loving." For many scholars and diplomats, the relations among independent states appear to differ so significantly from domestic politics that influences of liberal principles and domestic liberal institutions are denied or denigrated. They judge that international relations are governed by perceptions of national security and the balance of power; liberal principles and institutions, when they do intrude, confuse and disrupt the pursuit of balance-of-power politics.[1]

Although liberalism is misinterpreted from both these points of view, a crucial aspect of the liberal legacy is captured by each. Liberalism is a distinct ideology and set of institutions that has shaped the perceptions of and capacities for foreign relations of political societies that range from social welfare or social democratic to laissez faire. It defines much of the content of the liberal patriot's nationalism. Liberalism does appear to disrupt the pursuit of balance-of-power politics. Thus its foreign relations cannot be adequately explained (or prescribed) by a sole reliance on the balance-of-power. But liberalism is not inherently "peace-loving"; nor is it consistently restrained or peaceful in intent. Furthermore, liberal practice may reduce the probability that states will successfully exercise the consistent restraint and peaceful intentions that a world peace may well require in the nuclear age. Yet the peaceful intent and restraint that liberalism does manifest in limited aspects of its foreign affairs announces the possibility of a world peace this side of the grave or of world conquest. It has strengthened the prospects for a world peace established by the steady expansion of a separate peace among liberal societies.

Putting together these apparently contradictory (but, in fact, compatible) pieces of the liberal legacy begins with a discussion of the range of liberal principle and practice. This article highlights the differences between liberal practice toward other liberal societies and liberal practice toward nonliberal societies. It argues that liberalism has achieved extraordinary success in the first and has contributed to exceptional confusion in the second. Appreciating these liberal legacies calls for another look at one of the greatest of liberal philosophers, Immanuel Kant, for he is a source of insight, policy, and hope.

II

Liberalism has been identified with an essential principle—the importance of the freedom of the individual. Above all, this is a belief in the importance of moral freedom, of the right to be treated and a duty to treat others as ethical subjects, and not as objects or means only. This principle has generated rights and institutions.

A commitment to a threefold set of rights forms the foundation of liberalism. Liberalism calls for freedom from arbitrary authority, often called "negative freedom," which includes freedom of conscience, a free press and free speech, equality under the law, and the right to hold, and therefore to exchange, property without fear of arbitrary seizure. Liberalism also calls for those rights necessary to protect and promote the capacity and opportunity for freedom, the "positive freedoms." Such social and economic rights as equality of opportunity in education and rights to health care

Source: Michael W. Doyle, "Kant, Liberal Legacies, and Foreign Policy," *Philosophy and Public Affairs* 12(3): 205–208; 213; 215; 217; 225–232.

and employment, necessary for effective self-expression and participation, are thus among liberal rights. A third liberal right, democratic participation or representation, is necessary to guarantee the other two. To ensure that morally autonomous individuals remain free in those areas of social action where public authority is needed, public legislation has to express the will of the citizens making laws for their own community. . . .

But the dilemma within liberalism is how to reconcile the three sets of liberal rights. The right to private property, for example, can conflict with equality of opportunity and both rights can be violated by democratic legislation. During the 180 years since Kant wrote, the liberal tradition has evolved two high roads to individual freedom and social order; one is laissez-faire or "conservative" liberalism and the other is social welfare, or social democratic, or "liberal" liberalism. Both reconcile these conflicting rights (though in differing ways) by successfully organizing free individuals into a political order. . . .

In order to protect the opportunity of the citizen to exercise freedom, laissez-faire liberalism has leaned toward a highly constrained role for the state and a much wider role for private property and the market. In order to promote the opportunity of the citizen to exercise freedom, welfare liberalism has expanded the role of the state and constricted the role of the market.[2] . . .

III

In foreign affairs liberalism has shown, as it has in the domestic realm, serious weaknesses. But unlike liberalism's domestic realm, its foreign affairs have experienced startling but less than fully appreciated successes. Together they shape an unrecognized dilemma, for both these successes and weaknesses in large part spring from the same cause: the international implications of liberal principles and institutions.

The basic postulate of liberal international theory holds that states have the right to be free from foreign intervention. Since morally autonomous citizens hold rights to liberty, the states that democratically represent them have the right to exercise political independence. Mutual respect for these rights then becomes the touchstone of international liberal theory.[3] When states respect each other's rights, individuals are free to establish private international ties without state interference. Profitable exchanges between merchants and educational exchanges among scholars then create a web of mutual advantages and commitments that bolsters sentiments of public respect.

These conventions of mutual respect have formed a cooperative foundation for relations among liberal democracies of a remarkably effective kind. *Even though liberal states have become involved in numerous wars with nonliberal states, constitutionally secure liberal states have yet to engage in war with one another.*[4] No one should argue that such wars are impossible; but preliminary evidence does appear to indicate that there exists a significant predisposition against warfare between liberal states. Indeed, threats of war also have been regarded as illegitimate. A liberal zone of peace, a pacific union, has been maintained and has expanded despite numerous particular conflicts of economic and strategic interest. . . .

Statistically, war between any two states (in any single year or other: short period of time) is a low probability event. War between any two adjacent states, considered over a long period of time, may be somewhat more probable. The apparent absence of war among the more clearly liberal states, whether adjacent or not, for almost two hundred years, thus has some significance. Politically more significant, perhaps, is that when states are forced to decide, by the pressure of an impinging world war, on which side of a world contest they will fight, liberal states wind up all on the same side, despite the real complexity of the historical economic and political factors that affect their foreign policies. . . .

IV

Most liberal theorists have offered inadequate guidance in understanding the exceptional nature of liberal pacification. Some have argued that democratic states would be inherently peaceful simply and solely because in these states citizens rule the polity and bear the costs of wars. Unlike monarchs, citizens are not able to indulge their aggressive passions and have the consequences suffered by someone else. Other liberals have argued that laissez-faire capitalism contains an inherent tendency toward rationalism, and that, since war is irrational, liberal capitalisms will be pacifistic. Others still, such as Montesquieu, claim that "commerce is the cure for the most destructive prejudices," and "Peace is the natural effect of trade."[5] While these developments can help account for the liberal peace, they do not explain the fact that liberal states are peaceful only in relations with other liberal states. France and England fought expansionist, colonial wars throughout the nineteenth century (in the 1830s and 1840s against Algeria and China); the United States fought a similar war with Mexico in 1848 and intervened again in 1914 under President Wilson. Liberal states are as aggressive and war prone as any other form of government or society in their relations with nonliberal states.

Immanuel Kant offers the best guidance. "Perpetual Peace," written in 1795, predicts the ever-widening pacification of the liberal pacific union, explains that pacification, and at the same time suggests why liberal states are not pacific in their relations with nonliberal states. Kant argues that Perpetual Peace will be guaranteed by the ever-widening acceptance of three "definitive articles" of peace. When all nations have accepted the definitive articles in a metaphorical "treaty" of perpetual peace he asks them to sign, perpetual peace will have been established.

The First Definitive Article holds that the civil constitution of the state must be republican. By republican Kant means a political society that has solved the problem of combining moral autonomy, individualism, and social order. A basically private property and market-oriented economy partially addressed that dilemma in the private sphere. The public, or political, sphere was more troubling. His answer was a republic that preserved juridical freedom—the legal equality of citizens as subjects on the basis of a representative government with a separation of powers. Juridical freedom is preserved because the morally autonomous individual is by means of representation a self-legislator making laws that apply to all citizens equally including himself. And tyranny is avoided because the individual is subject to laws he does not also administer.[6]

Liberal republics will progressively establish peace among themselves by means of the "pacific union" described in the Second Definitive Article of the Eternal Peace. The pacific union is limited to "a treaty of the nations among themselves" which "maintains itself, prevents wars, and steadily expands." The world will not have achieved the "perpetual peace" that provides the ultimate guarantor of republican freedom until "very late and after many unsuccessful attempts." Then right conceptions of the appropriate constitution, great and sad experience, and good will will have taught all the nations the lessons of peace. Not until then will individuals enjoy perfect republican rights or the full guarantee of a global and just peace. But in the meantime, the "pacific union" of liberal republics "*steadily expands* [my emphasis]" bringing within it more and more republics (despite republican collapses, backsliding, and war disasters) and creating an ever expanding separate peace.[7] The pacific union is neither a single peace treaty ending one war nor a world state or state of nations. The first is insufficient; the second and third are impossible or potentially tyrannical. Kant develops no organizational embodiment of this treaty, and presumably he does not find institutionalization necessary. He appears to have in mind a mutual nonaggression pact, perhaps a collective security agreement, and the cosmopolitan law set forth in the Third Definitive Article.[8]

The Third Definitive Article of the Eternal Peace establishes a cosmopolitan law to operate in conjunction with the pacific union. The cosmopolitan law "shall be limited to conditions of universal hospitality." In this he calls for the recognition of the "right of a foreigner not to be treated with hostility when he arrives upon the soil of another [country]," which "does not extend further than to the conditions which enable them [the foreigners] to attempt the developing of intercourse [commerce] with the old inhabitants." Hospitality does not require extending either the right to citizenship to foreigners or the right to settlement, unless the foreign visitors would perish if they were expelled. Foreign conquest and plunder also find no justification under this right. Hospitality does appear to include the right of access and the obligation of maintaining the opportunity for citizens to exchange goods and ideas, without imposing the obligation to trade (a voluntary act in all cases under liberal constitutions).[9]

Kant then explains each of the three definitive articles for a liberal peace. In doing so he develops both an account of why liberal states do maintain peace among themselves and of how it will (by implication, has) come about that the pacific union will expand. His central claim is that a natural evolution will produce "a harmony from the very disharmony of men against their will."[10]

The first source derives from a political evolution, from a *constitutional law*. Nature (providence) has seen to it that human beings can live in all the regions where they have been driven to settle by wars. (Kant, who once taught geography, reports on the Lapps, the Samoyeds, the Pescheras.) "Asocial sociability" draws men together to fulfill needs for security and material welfare as it drives them into conflicts over the distribution and control of social products. This violent natural evolution tends toward the liberal peace because "asocial sociability" inevitably leads toward republican governments and republican governments are a source of the liberal peace.

Republican representation and separation of powers are produced because they are the means by which the state is "organized well" to prepare for and meet foreign threats (by unity) and to tame the ambitions of selfish and aggressive individuals (by authority derived from representation, by general laws, and by nondespotic administration). States which are not organized in this fashion fail. Monarchs thus cede rights of representation to their subjects in order to strengthen their political support or to obtain tax revenue. This argument provides a plausible, logical connection between conflict, internal and external, and republicanism; and it highlights interesting associations between the rising incidence of international war and the increasing number of republics.

Nevertheless, constant preparation for war can enhance the role of military institutions in a society to the point that they become the society's rulers. Civil conflict can lead to praetorian coups. Conversely, an environment of security can provide a political climate for weakening the state by constitutional restraints.[11] Significantly, the most war-affected states have not been liberal republics.[12] More importantly, the argument is so indistinct as to serve only as a very general hypothesis that mobilizing self-interested individuals into the political life of states in an insecure world will eventually engender pressures for republican participation. Kant needs no more than this to suggest that republicanism and a liberal peace are possible (and thus a moral obligation). If it is possible, then sometime over the course of history it may be inevitable. But attempting to make its date of achievement predictable—projecting a steady trend he suggests, may be asking too much. He anticipates backsliding and destructive wars, though these will serve to educate the nations to the importance of peace.[13]

Kant shows how republics, once established, lead to peaceful relations. He argues that once the aggressive interests of absolutist monarchies are tamed and once the habit of respect for individual rights is engrained by republican government, wars would appear as the disaster to the people's welfare that he and the other liberals thought them to be. The fundamental reason is this:

> If the consent of the citizens is required in order to decide that war should be declared (and in this constitution it cannot but be the case), nothing is more natural than that they would be very cautious in commencing such a poor game, decreeing for themselves all the calamities of war. Among the latter would be: having to fight, having to pay the costs of war from their own resources, having painfully to repair the devastation war leaves behind, and, to fill up the measure of evils, load themselves with a heavy national debt that would embitter peace itself and that can never be liquidated on account of constant wars in the future. But, on the other hand, in a constitution which is not republican, and under which the subjects are not citizens, a declaration of war is the easiest thing in the world to decide upon, because war does not require of the ruler, who is the proprietor and not a member of the state, the least sacrifice of the pleasure of his table, the chase, his country houses, his court functions, and the like. He may, therefore, resolve on war as on a pleasure party for the most trivial reasons, and with perfect indifference leave the justification which decency requires to the diplomatic corps who are ever ready to provide it.[14]

One could add to Kant's list another source of pacification specific to liberal constitutions. The regular rotation of office in liberal democratic polities is a nontrivial device that helps ensure that personal animosities among heads of government provide no lasting, escalating source of tension.

These domestic republican restraints do not end war. If they did, liberal states would not be warlike, which is far from the case. They do introduce Kant's "caution" in place of monarchical caprice. Liberal wars are only fought for popular, liberal purposes. To see how this removes the occasion of wars among liberal states and not wars between liberal and nonliberal states, we need to shift our attention from constitutional law to international law, Kant's second source.

Complementing the constitutional guarantee of caution, *international law* adds a second source—a guarantee of respect. The separation of nations that asocial sociability encourages is reinforced by the development of separate languages and religions. These further guarantee a world of separate states—an essential condition needed to avoid a "global, soul-less despotism." Yet, at the same time, they also morally integrate liberal states "as culture progresses and men gradually come closer together toward a greater agreement on principles for peace and understanding."[15] As republics emerge (the first source) and as culture progresses, an understanding of the legitimate rights of all citizens and of all republics comes into play; and this, now that caution characterizes policy, sets up the moral foundations for the liberal peace. Correspondingly, international law highlights the importance of Kantian publicity. Domestically, publicity helps ensure that the officials of republics act according to the principles they profess to hold just and according to the interests of the electors they claim to represent. Internationally, free speech and the effective communication of accurate conceptions of the political life of foreign peoples is essential to establish and preserve the understanding on which the guarantee of respect depends. In short, domestically just republics, which rest on consent, presume foreign republics to be also consensual, just, and therefore deserving of accommodation. The experience of cooperation helps engender further cooperative behavior when the consequences of state policy are unclear but (potentially) mutually beneficial.[16]

Lastly, *cosmopolitan law* adds material incentives to moral commitments. The cosmopolitan right to hospitality permits the "spirit of commerce" sooner or later to take hold of every nation, thus impelling states to promote peace and to try to avert war.

Liberal economic theory holds that these cosmopolitan ties derive from a cooperative international division of labor and free trade according to comparative advantage. Each economy is said to be better off than it would have been under autarky; each thus acquires an incentive to avoid policies that would lead the other to break these economic ties. Since keeping open markets rests upon the assumption that the next set of transactions will also be determined by prices rather than coercion, a sense of mutual security is vital to avoid security-motivated searches for economic autarky. Thus avoiding a challenge to another liberal state's security or even enhancing each other's security by means of alliance naturally follows economic interdependence.

A further cosmopolitan source of liberal peace is that the international market removes difficult decisions of production and distribution from the direct sphere of state policy.

A foreign state thus does not appear directly responsible for these outcomes; states can stand aside from, and to some degree above, these contentious market rivalries and be ready to step in to resolve crises. Furthermore, the interdependence of commerce and the connections of state officials help create crosscutting transnational ties that serve as lobbies for mutual accommodation. According to modem liberal scholars, international financiers and transnational, bureaucratic, and domestic organizations create interests in favor of accommodation and have ensured by their variety that no single conflict sours an entire relationship.[17]

No one of these constitutional, international or cosmopolitan sources is alone sufficient, but together (and only where together) they plausibly connect the characteristics of liberal polities and economies with sustained liberal peace. Liberal states have not escaped from the Realists' "security dilemma," the insecurity caused by anarchy in the world political system considered as a whole. But the effects of international anarchy have been tamed in the relations among states of a similarly liberal character. Alliances of purely mutual strategic interest among liberal and nonliberal states have been broken, economic ties between liberal and non-liberal states have proven fragile, but the political bond of liberal rights and interests have proven a remarkably firm foundation for mutual nonaggression. A separate peace exists among liberal states. . . .

Notes

1. The liberal-patriotic view was reiterated by President Reagan in a speech before the British Parliament on 8 June 1982. There he proclaimed "a global campaign for democratic development." This "crusade for freedom" will be the latest campaign in a tradition that, he claimed, began with the Magna Carta and stretched in this century through two world wars and a cold war. He added that liberal foreign policies have shown "restraint" and "peaceful intentions" and that this crusade will strengthen the prospects for a world at peace (*New York Times*, 9 June 1982). The skeptical scholars and diplomats represent the predominant Realist interpretation of international relations. See ns. 4 and 12 for references.

2. The sources of classic, laissez-faire liberalism can be found in Locke, *the Federalist Papers*, Kant, and Robert Nozick, *Anarchy, State and Utopia* (New York: Basic Books, 1974). Expositions of welfare liberalism are in the work of the Fabians and John Rawls, *A Theory of Justice* (Cambridge, MA: Harvard University Press, 1971). Amy Gutmann, *Liberal Equality* (Cambridge: Cambridge University Press, 1980), discusses variants of liberal thought.

Uncomfortably paralleling each of the high roads are "low roads" that, while achieving certain liberal values, fail to reconcile freedom and order. An over whelming terror of anarchy and a speculation on preserving property can drive laissez-faire liberals to support a law-and-order authoritarian rule that sacrifices democracy. Authoritarianism to preserve order is the argument of Hobbes's *Leviathan*. It also shapes the argument of right wing liberals who seek to draw a distinction between "authoritarian" and "totalitarian" and dictatorships. The justification sometimes advanced by liberals for the former is that they can be temporary and educate the population into an acceptance of property individual rights, and, eventually, representative government. See Jeane Kirkpatrick", Dictatorships and Double Standards," *Commentary* 68 (November I979): 34–45. Complementarily when social inequalities are judged to be extreme, the welfare liberal can argue that establishing (or reestablishing) the foundations of liberal society requires a nonliberal method of reform, a second low road of redistributing authoritarianism Aristide Zolberg reports a "liberal left" sensibility among.

3. Charles Beitz, *Political Theory and International Relations* (Princeton: Princeton University Press, 1979) offers a clear and insightful discussion of liberal ideas on intervention and nonintervention.

4. There appear to be some exceptions to the tendency for liberal states not to engage in a war with each other. Peru and Ecuador, for example, entered into conflict. But for each, the war came within one to three years after the establishment of a liberal regime, that is, before the pacifying effects of liberalism could become deeply ingrained. The Palestinians and the Israelis clashed frequently along the Lebanese border, which Lebanon could not hold secure from either belligerent. But at the beginning of the 1967 War, Lebanon seems to have sent a flight of its own jets into Israel. The jets were repulsed. Alone among Israel's Arab neighbors, Lebanon engaged in no further hostilities with Israel. Israel's recent attack on the territory of Lebanon was an attack on a country that had already been occupied by Syria (and the P.L.O.). Whether Israel actually will withdraw (if Syria withdraws) and restore an independent Lebanon is yet to be determined.

5. The incompatibility of democracy and war is forcefully asserted by Paine in *The Rights of Man*. The connection between liberal capitalism, democracy, and peace is argued by, among others, Joseph Schumpeter in *Imperialism and Social Classes* (New York: Meridian, 1955); and Montesquieu, *Spirit of the Laws* I, bk. 20, chap. 1. This literature is surveyed and analyzed by Albert Hirschman, "Rival Interpretations of Market Society: Civilizing, Destructive, or Feeble?" *Journal of Economic Literature* 20 (December 1982).

6. Two classic sources that examine Kant's international theory from a Realist perspective are Stanley Hoffmann, "Rousseau on War and Peace" in the *State of War* (New York: Praeger, 1965) and Kenneth Waltz, "Kant, Liberalism, and War, "*American Political Science Review* 56, no. 2 (June 1962). I have benefited from their analysis and from those of Karl Friedrich, *Inevitable Peace* (Cambridge, MA: Harvard University Press, 1948); F. H. Hinsley, *Power and the Pursuit of Peace* (Cambridge: Cambridge University Press, 1967), chap. 4; W. B. Gallie, *Philosophers of Peace and War* (Cambridge: Cambridge University Press, 1978), chap. 1; and particularly Patrick Riley, *Kant's Political Philosophy* (Totowa, NJ: Rowman and Littlefield, 1983). But some of the conclusions of this article differ markedly from theirs.

Kant's republican constitution is described in Kant, "Perpetual Peace," *The Philosophy of Kant*, p. 437 and analyzed by Riley, *Kant's Political Philosophy*, chap. 5.

7. Kant, "Universal History, "*The Philosophy of Kant*, p. 123. The pacific union follows a process of "federalization" such that it "can be realized by a gradual extension to all states, leading to eternal peace." This interpretation contrasts with those cited in n. 24. I think Kant meant that the peace would be established among liberal regimes and would expand as new liberal regimes appeared. By a process of gradual extension the peace would become global and then perpetual; the occasion for wars with nonliberals would disappear as nonliberal regimes disappeared.

8. Kant's "Pacific Union," the *foedus pacificum*, is thus neither a *pactum pacis* (a single peace treaty) nor a *civitas gentium* (a world state). He appears to have anticipated something like a less formally institutionalized League of Nations or United Nations. One could argue that these two institutions in practice worked for liberal states and only for liberal states. But no specifically liberal "pacific union" was institutionalized. Instead liberal states have behaved for the past 180 years as if such a Kantian pacific union and treaty of Perpetual Peace had been signed. This follows Riley's views of the legal, not the organizational, character of the *foedus pacificum*.

9. Kant, "Perpetual Peace," pp. 444–47.

10. Kant, the fourth principle of "The Idea for a Universal History" in *The Philosophy of Kant*, p. 120. Interestingly, Kant's three sources of peace (republicanism, respect, and commerce) parallel quite closely Aristotle's three sources of friendship (goodness, pleasure or appreciation, and utility). See *Nicomachean Ethics*, bk. 8, chap. 3, trans. J.A. K. Thomson (Baltimore, MD: Penguin, 1955).

11. The "Prussian Model" suggests the connection between insecurity, war, and authoritarianism. See *The Anglo-American Tradition* in *Foreign Affairs*, ed. Arnold Wolfers and Laurence Martin (New Haven: Yale University Press, I956), "Introduction," for an argument linking security and liberalism.

12. Small and Singer, *Resort to Arms*, pp. 176–79.

13. Kant, "The Idea for a Universal History," p. 124.

14. Immanuel Kant, "Perpetual Peace" in *The Enlightenment*, ed. Peter Gay (New York: Simon & Schuster, 1974), pp. 790–92.

Gallie in *Philosophers of Peace and War* criticizes Kant for neglecting economic, religious, nationalistic drives toward war and for failing to appreciate that "regimes" make war in order to enhance their domestic political support. But Kant holds that these drives should be subordinated to justice in a liberal society (he specifically criticizes colonial wars stimulated by rapaciousness). He also argues that *republics* derive their legitimacy from their accordance with law and representation, thereby freeing them from crises of domestic political support. Kant thus acknowledges both Gallie's sets of motives for war but argues that they would not apply within the pacific union.

15. Kant, *The Philosophy of Kant*, p. 454. These factors also have a bearing on Karl Deutsch's "compatibility of values" and "predictability of behavior" (see n. 20).

16. A highly stylized version of this effect can be found in the Realist's "Prisoner's Dilemma" game. There is a failure of mutual trust and the incentives to enhance one's own position produce a non-cooperative solution that makes both parties worse off. Contrarily, cooperation, a commitment to avoid exploiting the other party, produces joint gains. The significance of the game in this context is the character of its participants. The "prisoners" are presumed to be felonious, unrelated apart from their partnership in crime, and lacking in mutual trust—competitive nation states in an anarchic world. A similar game between fraternal or sororal twins—Kant's republics—would be likely to lead to different results. See Robert Jervis, "Hypotheses on Misperception," *World Politics* 20, no. 3 (April 1968), for an exposition of the role of presumptions; and "Cooperation Under the Security Dilemma," *World Politics* 30, no. 2 (January 1978), for the factors Realists see as mitigating the security dilemma caused by anarchy.

Also, expectations (including theory and history) can influence behavior, making liberal states expect (and fulfill) pacific policies toward each other. These effects are explored at a theoretical level in R. Dacey, "Some Implications of 'Theory Absorption' for Economic Theory and the Economics of Information" in *Philosophical Dimensions of Economics*, ed. J. Pitt (Dordrecht, Holland: D. Reidel, 1980).

17. Karl Polanyi, *The Great Transformation* (Boston: Beacon Press, 1944), chaps. 1–2, and Samuel Huntington and Z. Brzezinski, *Political Power*: *USA/USSR* (New York: Viking Press, 1963, 1964), chap. 9. And see Richard Neustadt, *Alliance Politics* (New York: Columbia University Press, 1970) for a detailed case study of interliberal politics.

6 LIBERALISM II

6.1

Liberalism Revived

Joseph S. Nye

The two world wars and the failure of collective security in the interwar period discredited liberal theories. Most writing about international politics in the United States after World War II was strongly realist in flavor. However, as transnational economic interdependence increased, the late 1960s and 1970s saw a revival of interest in liberal theories. There are three strands of this liberal thinking: economic, social, and political. The political strand has two parts, one relating to institutions and the other to democracy.

The economic strand focuses heavily on trade. Liberals argue that trade is important, not because it prevents states from going to war, but because it may lead states to define their interests in a way that makes war less important to them. Trade offers states a way to transform their position through economic growth rather than through military conquest. Richard Rosecrance points to the example of Japan. In the 1930s, Japan thought the only way to gain access to markets was to create a "Greater East Asia Co-Prosperity Sphere," which in turn required conquering its neighbors and requiring them to trade. Already in 1939, Eugene Staley, a Chicago economist, argued that part of Japan's behavior in the 1930s could be explained by economic protectionism at the time. Staley believed that when economic walls are erected along political boundaries, possession of territory is made to coincide with economic opportunity. A better solution for avoiding war is to pursue economic growth in an open trading system without military conquest. In contrast to the 1930s, Japan today has successfully transformed its position in the world through trade. Japan's share of the world product went from about 5 percent in 1960 to about 12 percent today, making it the second largest national economy in the world (measured by official exchange rates).

Realists reply that Japan was able to accomplish this amazing economic growth because somebody else was providing for its security. Specifically, Japan relied on the United States for security against its large nuclear neighbors, the Soviet Union and China. Some realists predicted that, with the Soviet Union gone, the United States would withdraw its security presence in East Asia and raise barriers against Japanese trade. Japan would remilitarize, and eventually there would be conflict between Japan and the United States as predicted by theories of hegemonic transition.

On the other hand, liberals replied that modem Japan is a very different domestic society from the Japan of the 1930s. It is nonmilitarist, partly because of economic opportunities. The most attractive career opportunities in Japan are in business, not in the military. Liberals argue that the realists are not paying

Source: Joseph S. Nye, *Understanding International Conflicts,* 6th Edition.

enough attention to domestic politics and the way that Japan has changed as a result of economic opportunities. Whatever the outcome, the liberal economic argument says trade may not prevent war, but it does lead to changes in how states see their opportunities, which in turn may lead to a social structure that is less inclined to war.

The second form of liberalism is social. It argues that person-to-person contacts reduce conflict by promoting understanding. Such transnational contacts occur at many levels, including through students, businesspeople, and tourists. Such contacts make others seem less foreign and less hateful. That, in turn, leads to a lower likelihood of conflict. The evidence for this view is mixed. After all, bankers, aristocrats, and labor union officials had broad contacts in 1914, but that did not stop them from killing one another once they put on khaki uniforms. Obviously, the idea that social contact breeds understanding and prevents war is far too simple. Nonetheless, it may make a modest contribution to understanding. Western Europe today is very different from 1914. There are constant contacts across international borders in Europe, and textbook editors try to treat other nationalities fairly. The images of the other peoples of Europe are very different from the images of 1914. Public-opinion polls show that a sense of European identity coexists with a sense of national identity. Transnational society affects what people in a democracy want from their foreign policy. It is worth noting how France responded to the reunification of Germany in 1990. A residue of uncertainty and anxiety remained among the foreign policy experts, but public-opinion polls showed that most French people welcomed German unification. Such attitudes were a sharp contrast to those of August 1914.

The third form of liberalism emphasizes the role of institutions; this strand is often labeled "neoliberalism." Why do international institutions matter? According to the Princeton political scientist Robert O. Keohane, they provide information and a framework that shapes expectations. They allow people to believe there is not going to be a conflict. They lengthen the shadow of the future and reduce the acuteness of the security dilemma. Institutions reduce the effect of the anarchy that the realists assume. Hobbes saw international politics as a state of war. He was careful to say that a state of war does not mean constant fighting, but a propensity to war, just as cloudy weather means a likelihood of rain. In the same sense, a state of peace means a propensity toward peace, and that people can develop peaceful expectations when anarchy is limited and stabilized by international institutions.

Institutions stabilize expectations in four ways. First, they provide a sense of continuity; for example, most Western Europeans expect the European Union to last. It is likely to be there tomorrow. At the end of the Cold War, many Eastern European governments agreed and made plans to join the European Union. That affected their behavior even before they eventually joined in 2004. Second, institutions provide an opportunity for reciprocity. If the French get a little bit more today, the Italians might get a little more tomorrow. There is less need to worry about each transaction because over time it will likely balance out. Third, institutions provide a flow of information. Who is doing what? Are the Italians actually obeying the rules passed by the European Union? Is the flow of trade roughly equal? The institutions of the union provide information on how it is all working out. Finally, institutions provide ways to resolve conflicts. In the European Union, bargaining goes on within the Council of Ministers and in the European Commission, and there is also a European court of justice. Thus institutions create a climate in which expectations of stable peace develop.

Classical liberals expect "peace breaking out all over"; today's liberals look for *islands* of peace where institutions and stable expectations have developed. The political scientist Karl Deutsch called such areas "pluralistic security communities" in which war between countries became so unthinkable that stable expectations of peace developed. Institutions helped reinforce such expectations. The Scandinavian countries, for example, once fought each other bitterly, and the United States fought Britain, Canada, and Mexico. Today such actions are unthinkable. The advanced industrial countries seem to have a propensity for peace, and institutions such as the European Union, the North American Free Trade Agreement (NAFTA), and the Organization of American States create a culture in which peace is expected and provide forums for negotiation. Expectations of stability can provide a way to escape the Prisoner's Dilemma situations that realists assume. They lengthen and strengthen the shadow of the future.

Some realists expect the security dilemma to reemerge in Europe despite the liberal institutions of the European Union (EU). After the high hopes that greeted European integration in 1992, some opposition arose to further unity, particularly in disputes over the single European currency, the euro, which came into use in 2002. Countries such as Great Britain feared that ceding further power to the government of the European Union would jeopardize the autonomy and prosperity of the individual nations. Efforts in 2003 and 2004 to develop a new European constitution proved difficult, and in 2005 voters in France and the Netherlands refused to ratify it. At the same time, Britain and others worried that if they opted out of the European Union entirely, countries such as Germany, France, and Italy that opted in would gain a competitive edge. Despite such obstacles to further integration, the former communist countries of central Europe were attracted to join. While the European Union was not becoming a superstate, its institutions helped transform relations between European states.

6.2

The Worlds of International Relations

The Military-Political World, the Trading World

Richard Rosecrance

The choice between territorial and trading means to national advancement has always lain before states. Most often, however, nations have selected a point between extremes though nearer the territorial end. In the early years of the modern period in the sixteenth and seventeenth centuries, that point was close to the territorial and military pole; at mid-nineteenth century it briefly moved toward the trading pole. In World Wars I and II the military and territorial orientation was chosen once again. Only after 1945 did a group of trading nations emerge in world politics. Over time this group has grown and its success, at least in economic terms, has been greater than that of either the United States or the Soviet Union. Before we look at the hybrid forms that have been attempted, it may be desirable to sketch the polar or pure types: the military-political and the trading worlds.

The Military-Political World

In a military-political world nations are ranged in terms of power and territory from the greatest to the weakest. States in such a world are homogeneous in form; that is, they do not have differentiated objectives or perform a variety of functions. They all seek the same territorial objectives and each, at least among the major powers, strives to be the leading power in the system. None of the contenders wishes to depend upon any other for any vital function, from the provision of defense to economic resources. Such a world might be stable in the sense of avoiding war if one single state achieved hegemony over the others.

If one power attained total mastery, the other members of the system would finally cease resisting because no advantage could be gained. Instead, they could compete for favors from the hegemonic overlord, who would reward them from his seemingly inexhaustible political and military surplus. Recognizing that opposition served no purpose, the members would return allegiance and support. Historically, only the Roman Empire attained such mastery in the Western tradition: Charlemagne, Louis XIV, Napoleon, and Hitler never achieved it. Since the decline of the Roman Empire in the third to the fifth century A.D., contending feudal or state units have been the order of the day, and anarchy has been the principle of interstate relations.

The military-political world involves a continual recourse to war because the units within it compete for primacy. None is content to accept the hegemony of one of their number if it can be prevented; each is afraid that the dominance of one power will undermine its domestic autonomy and perhaps its very existence. Hence the balance of power becomes a means of resistance to threatened hegemony. The means of constructing a balance ultimately involves a resort to force to discipline an ambitious pretender. Warfare may be stabilizing if it succeeds in restraining challenge, but it cannot be acceptable if the destruction it causes more than outweighs the evil it seeks to prevent. In addition, since every state in a political-military order seeks to be self-sufficient, each strives to grow larger in order to achieve full independence. This drive itself is a cause of war.

The Trading World

In contrast, the trading world is not composed of states ranked in order of their power and territory, all seeking preponderance. Instead, it is composed of nations differentiated in terms of function. Each may seek to improve its position, but because nations supply different services and products, in defense as well as

Source: Richard Rosecrance. "The Worlds of International Relations: the Military-Political World, the Trading World," in *The Rise of the Trading State.*

economics, they come to depend upon each other. While some will be stronger than others, their functions give them a kind of equality of status. They may specialize in terms of particular defense functions: conventional or nuclear forces. They may offer raw materials or primary products to the international trading system as opposed to manufactured goods. Within the category of manufacturers, there may be intra-industry specialization in terms of technology. Certain industrial countries may concentrate, like Switzerland and Italy, on producing goods of very high quality and craftsmanship. Others, like Korea or Taiwan, may produce shoes, watches, textiles, steel, or ships on an efficient low-cost basis. Trading states will also normally form alliances as a precaution against sudden intrusion by military-political nations.

While trading states try to improve their position and their own domestic allocation of resources, they do so within a context of accepted interdependence. They recognize that the attempt to provide every service and fulfill every function of statehood on an independent and autonomous basis is extremely inefficient, and they prefer a situation which provides for specialization and division of labor among nations. One nation's attempt to improve its own access to products and resources, therefore, does not conflict with another state's attempt to do the same. The incentive to wage war is absent in such a system for war disrupts trade and the interdependence on which trade is based. Trading states recognize that they can do better through internal economic development sustained by a worldwide market for their goods and services than by trying to conquer and assimilate large tracts of land.

In general terms, the competition for power emerges in social relations wherever needs are provided for independently and without reciprocity and where resources are limited. If needs do not have to be met independently, a reciprocal division of labor may give rise to stable cooperation. If resources are in unlimited supply, self-sufficient persons or nations may gain all they need without encroaching on the wants of others. Hence in a bountiful state of nature, primitive people could have an idyllic existence free from competition and conflict. Alternatively, in a social order characterized by a degree of scarcity, conflict could still be limited by interdependence, exchange, and sharing. But where scarcity and the urge to full independence exist, government and law are needed to restrain a competition over power leading to social conflict.

In international society where government does not exist, nations will have power conflicts unless they can work out a system of interdependence to satisfy their needs. Only the reciprocal exchange and division of labor represented by the trading world can prevent conflict in such an anarchic environment. Industrial and population growth strengthen interdependence and make it harder to achieve national objectives autonomously. When technology was rudimentary and population sparse, states had little contact with one another and did not generally get in each other's way. With the commercial and industrial revolutions, however, they were brought into closer proximity. As the Industrial Revolution demanded energy resources—great quantities of food, coal, iron, water, power, and petroleum—the number of states which could be fully independent declined. Those which sought complete autonomy and even autarchy had to conquer the lands which contained the materials they needed. The military-political and territorial system, then, required more war. Only a shift in direction toward an interdependent trading system, giving up autonomy in return for greater access to world resources and markets, could produce greater cooperation among nations.

The trading system does not require large, self-sufficient units. As the national objective is exchange and trade with other states, trading countries do not need large territories and populations. Like Singapore and Hong Kong, they may be small countries, little more than cities, which manufacture the raw materials of other nations into finished commodities, gaining a high return in foreign trade.

Military technology also influences the trend toward one system or the other. One theory of historical development charts an increase in the size of the state as developments in military technology make smaller predecessors vulnerable to attack. Thus the medieval castle became vulnerable to gunpowder loaded in the siege gun. Large territorial states achieved a hard-shell character for a time, but even they become permeable when economic blockade, airpower, and the intercontinental missile allowed one country to strike at the very heart of another's population. Now the largest territorial state is no longer immune to attack and depends upon its opponent's decisions. Such trends make the goals of the military-political and territorial system harder and harder to achieve.

Shifts in domestic cohesion also affect the choice between trading and military-political worlds. The ramshackle feudal monarchies were hardly integrated enough to fight purposeful and continuous war against each other. They did not enjoy the loyalty of their citizens and were hard pressed to find the finances for military campaigns. As greater resources were tapped by the new administrative systems of the centralizing monarchies emerging from the Reformation, the conquest of adjacent territories became easier. Sixteenth-century Spain and eighteenth-century England proved that states with relatively efficient administrative structures could create large navies and conquer empires. The French Revolution and the Napoleonic reforms lent even greater authority to the revolutionary leader or his imperial successor. With greater discipline existing in citizen armies, soldiers fighting for their country would be more effective than the hired mercenaries of eighteenth-century monarchies. New vistas of territorial expansion beckoned. Finally, in the late nineteenth and first half of the twentieth centuries, further increases in nationalism and support for the policies of the government produced the final gusher of massive violence in World Wars I and II. The greater the obedience of an unquestioning citizenry, the more acceptable were the demands of the military-political and territorial world.

Conversely, the trading system depended on setting free the productive and trading energies of peoples and merchants who, without guidance and direction from the administrative capital of the state, would find markets for their goods overseas. Governments had to loosen control of their populace in order to generate the opportunities required to establish the trading system. They had to revoke mercantilist requirements and controls, abolish monopolies and chartered companies to enlist the efforts of capitalists and bring forth the necessary investment to finance productive enterprise. In certain cases trading cities with a wide range of independence grew up inside territorial states. They served the economic and financial interests of merchants and investors in other countries as well as their own. The nineteenth-century age of laissez faire in which government moved out of domestic economic activity fostered their aims better than the old official sponsorship and control. By liberating groups engaged in commerce on the high seas, governments in fact created classes of persons who were not exclusively loyal to the national state but catered to a wider constituency. In the American Civil War, New York merchants and financiers were close to the trading cities of the Confederacy and were initially tempted to secede as well. In the late nineteenth century, Hamburg traders were closer to their English markets and suppliers than they were to the administrative and imperial center in Berlin. The development of such trading relations stimulated the revival of connections like those uniting the trading city-states of the Renaissance. Free from imperial supervision and control these early-modern city-states banded together, as in the Hanseatic League, to further mutual relations, protection, and trade, enforcing contracts between them. In the nineteenth century although no such formal organization was established, the connections of centers of commerce were much the same. They transcended exclusive loyalties to a single political jurisdiction.

To sum up: military-political and territorial states are homogeneous competing countries. Each seeks to secure hegemony or at a minimum to gain independence and self-sufficiency from foreign control. They do not generally cooperate except when the balance of power requires opposition to a hegemonic aspirant. In the territorial system in the past, wars were continually fought to safeguard independence and prevent preponderance by any single power. Trading states, in contrast, are interdependent nations which accept equality of status on the basis of differentiation of function. Their objectives—to improve national welfare and the allocation of resources through internal development and trade—do not require preventing other states from achieving similar goals. As long as states were generally out of contact with one another and the waging of war was relatively easy, the military-political and territorial world would predominate over the trading world. When interdependence grew with large populations, industrialization, and need for resources, the military-political world faced greater difficulties. Rulers in that tradition sought to compensate by drawing more support from their people for imperial policies and war, but this solution only went so far.

6.3

Economic Interdependence and War

A Theory of Trade Expectations

Dale C. Copeland

Does economic interdependence increase or decrease the probability of war among states? With the Cold War over, this question is taking on importance as trade levels between established powers such as the United States and Russia and emerging powers such as Japan, China, and Western Europe grow to new heights. In this [reading], I provide a new dynamic theory to help overcome some of the theoretical and empirical problems with current liberal and realist views on the question.

The prolonged debate between realists and liberals on the causes of war has been largely a debate about the relative salience of different causal variables. Realists stress such factors as relative power, while liberals focus on the absence or presence of collective security regimes and the pervasiveness of democratic communities.[1] Economic interdependence is the only factor that plays an important causal role in the thinking of both camps, and their perspectives are diametrically opposed.

Liberals argue that economic interdependence lowers the likelihood of war by increasing the value of trading over the alternative of aggression: interdependent states would rather trade than invade. As long as high levels of interdependence can be maintained, liberals assert, we have reason for optimism. Realists dismiss the liberal argument, arguing that high interdependence increases rather than decreases the probability of war. In anarchy, states must constantly worry about their security. Accordingly, interdependence—meaning mutual dependence and thus vulnerability—gives states an incentive to initiate war, if only to ensure continued access to necessary materials and goods.

The unsatisfactory nature of both liberal and realist theories is shown by their difficulties in explaining the run-ups to the two World Wars. The period up to World War I exposes a glaring anomaly for liberal theory: the European powers had reached unprecedented levels of trade, yet that did not prevent them from going to war. Realists certainly have the correlation right—the war was preceded by high interdependence—but trade levels had been high for the previous thirty years; hence, even if interdependence was a necessary condition for the war, it was not sufficient.

At first glance, the period from 1920 to 1940 seems to support liberalism over realism. In the 1920s, interdependence was high, and the world was essentially peaceful; in the 1930s, as entrenched protectionism caused interdependence to fall, international tension rose to the point of world war. Yet the two most aggressive states in the system during the 1930s, Germany and Japan, were also the most highly dependent despite their efforts towards autarchy, relying on other states, including other great powers, for critical raw materials. Realism thus seems correct in arguing that high dependence may lead to conflict, as states use war to ensure access to vital goods. Realism's problem with the interwar era, however, is that Germany and Japan had been even more dependent in the 1920s, yet they sought war only in the late 1930s when their dependence, although still significant, had fallen.

The theory presented in this article—the theory of trade expectations—helps to resolve these problems. The theory starts by clarifying the notion of economic interdependence, fusing the liberal insight that the benefits of trade give states an incentive to avoid war with the realist view that the potential costs of being cut off can push states to war to secure vital goods. The total of the benefits and potential costs of trade versus autarchy reveals the true level of dependence a state faces, for if trade is completely severed, the state not only loses the gains from trade but also suffers the costs of adjusting its economy to the new situation.

Trade expectations theory introduces a new causal variable, the expectations of future trade, examining its impact on the overall expected value of the trading option

---

Source: Dale C. Copeland, "Economic Interdependence and War: A Theory of Trade Expectations," *International Security* 20:4 (Spring, 1996), pp. 5–11.

if a state decides to forgo war. This supplements the static consideration in liberalism and realism of the levels of interdependence at any point in time, with the importance of leaders' dynamic expectations into the future.

Levels of interdependence and expectations of future trade, considered simultaneously, lead to new predictions. Interdependence can foster peace, as liberals argue, but this will only be so when states expect that trade levels will be high into the foreseeable future. If highly interdependent states expect that trade will be severely restricted—that is, if their expectations for future trade are low—realists are likely to be right: the most highly dependent states will be the ones most likely to initiate war, for fear of losing the economic wealth that supports their long-term security. In short, high interdependence can be either peace-inducing or war-inducing, depending on the expectations of future trade.

This dynamic perspective helps bridge the gaps within and between current approaches. Separating levels of interdependence from expectations of future trade indicates that states may be pushed into war even if current trade levels are high, if leaders have good reason to suspect that others will cut them off in the future. In such a situation, the expected value of trade will likely be negative, and hence the value of continued peace is also negative, making war an attractive alternative. This insight helps resolve the liberal problem with World War I: despite high trade levels in 1913–14, declining expectations for future trade pushed German leaders to attack, to ensure long-term access to markets and raw materials.

Even when current trade is low or non-existent, positive expectations for future trade will produce a positive expected value for trade, and therefore an incentive for continued peace. This helps explain the two main periods of detente between the Cold War superpowers, from 1971 to 1973 and in the late 1980s: positive signs from U.S. leaders that trade would soon be significantly increased coaxed the Soviets into a more cooperative relationship, reducing the probability of war. But in situations of low trade where there is no prospect that high trade levels will be restored in the future, highly dependent states may be pushed into conflict. This was the German and Japanese dilemma before World War II.

The Liberal and Realist Debate on Economic Interdependence and War

The core liberal position is straightforward.[2] Trade provides valuable benefits, or "gains from trade," to any particular state. A dependent state should therefore seek to avoid war, since peaceful trading gives it all the benefits of close ties without any of the costs and risks of war. Trade pays more than war, so dependent states should prefer to trade not invade. This argument is often supported by the auxiliary proposition that modern technology greatly increases the costs and risks of aggression, making the trading option even more rational.

The argument was first made popular in the 1850s by Richard Cobden, who asserted that free trade "unites" states, "making each equally anxious for the prosperity and happiness of both."[3] This view was restated in *The Great Illusion* by Norman Angell just prior to World War I and again in 1933. Angell saw states having to choose between new ways of thinking, namely peaceful trade, and the "old method" of power politics. Even if war was once profitable, modernization now makes it impossible to "enrich" oneself through force; indeed, by destroying trading bonds, war is "commercially suicidal."[4]

Why do wars nevertheless occur? While the start of World War I just after *The Great Illusion's* initial publication might seem to refute his thesis, Angell in the 1933 edition argued that the debacle simply confirmed the unprofitability of modern wars. He thus upheld the common liberal view that wars, especially major wars, result from the misperceptions of leaders caught up in the outmoded belief that war still pays. Accordingly, his is "not a plea for the impossibility of war . . . but for its futility," since "our ignorance on this matter makes war not only possible, but extremely likely."[5] In short, if leaders fail to see how unprofitable war is compared to the benefits of trade, they may still erroneously choose the former.

Richard Rosecrance provides the most extensive update of the Cobden-Angell thesis to the nuclear era. States must choose between being "trading states," concerned with promoting wealth through commerce, and "territorial states," obsessed with military expansion. Modern conditions push states towards a predominantly trading mode: wars are not only too costly, but with the peaceful trading option, "the benefits that one nation gains from trade can also be realized by others." When the system is highly interdependent, therefore, the "incentive to wage war is absent," since "trading states recognize that they can do *better* through internal economic development sustained by a worldwide market for their goods and services than by trying to conquer and assimilate large tracts of land."[6]

Rosecrance thus neatly summarizes the liberal view that high interdependence fosters peace by making trading more profitable than invading.[7]

Realists turn the liberal argument on its head, arguing that economic interdependence not only fails to promote peace, but in fact heightens the likelihood of war.[8] States concerned about security will dislike dependence, since it means that crucial imported goods could be cut off during a crisis. This problem is particularly acute for imports like oil and raw materials; while they may be only a small percentage of the total import bill, without them most modern economies would collapse. Consequently, states dependent on others for vital goods have an increased incentive to go to war to assure themselves of continued access of supply.

Neorealist Kenneth Waltz puts the argument as follows: actors within a domestic polity have little reason to fear the dependence that goes with specialization. The anarchic structure of international politics, however, makes states worry about their vulnerability, thus compelling them "to control what they depend on or to lessen the extent of their dependency." For Waltz, it is this "simple thought" that explains, among other things, "their imperial thrusts to widen the scope of their control."[9] For John Mearsheimer, nations that "depend on others for critical economic supplies will fear cutoff or blackmail in time of crisis or war." Consequently, "they may try to extend political control to the source of supply, giving rise to conflict with the source or with its other customers." Interdependence, therefore, "will probably lead to greater security competition."[10]

This modern realist understanding of economic interdependence and war finds its roots in mercantilist writings dating from the seventeenth century. Mercantilists saw states as locked in a competition for relative power and for the wealth that underpins that power.[11] For mercantilists, imperial expansion—the acquisition of colonies—is driven by the state's need to secure greater control over sources of supply and markets for its goods, and to build relative power in the process. By allowing the metropole and the colonies to specialize in production and trade of complementary products (particularly manufactured goods for raw materials), while ensuring political control over the process, colonies "opened up the possibility of providing a system of supply within a self-contained empire."[12]

In this, we see the underpinning for the neorealist view that interdependence leads to war. Mercantilist imperialism represents a reaction to a state's dependence; states reduce their fears of external specialization by increasing *internal* specialization within a now larger political realm. The imperial state as it expands thus acquires more and more of the characteristics of Waltz's domestic polity, with its hierarchy of specialized functions secure from the unpredictable policies of others.

In sum, realists seek to emphasize one main point: political concerns driven by anarchy must be injected into the liberal calculus. Since states must be primarily concerned with security and therefore with control over resources and markets, one must discount the liberal optimism that great trading partners will always continue to be great trading partners simply because both states benefit absolutely. Accordingly, a state vulnerable to another's policies because of dependence will tend to use force to overcome that vulnerability.

Notes

1. For a summary of the causal variables in the two schools, see John J. Mearsheimer, "Back to the Future: Instability in Europe After the Cold War," *International Security*, Vol. 15, No. 1 (Summer 1990), pp. 5–56; Robert O. Keohane, "International Liberalism Reconsidered," in John Dunn, ed., *The Economic Limits to Modern Politics* (Cambridge: Cambridge University Press, 1990), pp. 165–194.

2. Four other subsidiary liberal arguments, employing intervening variables, are not sufficiently compelling to discuss here. The first suggests that high trade levels promote domestic prosperity, thereby lessening the internal problems that push leaders into war. The second argues that interdependence helps to foster increased understanding between peoples, which reduces the misunderstandings that lead to war. The third asserts that trade alters the domestic structure of states, heightening the influence of groups with a vested interest in peaceful trade. The final argument contends that trade has the "spill–over" effect of increasing political ties between trading partners, thus improving the prospects for long–term cooperation. For an critical analysis of these views, see Dale Copeland, "Economic Interdependence and the Outbreak of War," paper presented to University of Virginia Department of Government's faculty workshop, March 1995.

3. Richard Cobden, *The Political Writings of Richard Cobden* (London: T. Fischer Unwin, 1903), p. 225.

4. Norman Angell, *The Great Illusion*, 2d ed. (New York: G. P Putnam's Sons, 1933), pp. 33, 59–60, 87–89.

5. Ibid., pp. 59–62, 256.

6. Richard Rosecrance, *The Rise of the Trading State: Commerce and Conquest in the Modern World* (New York: Basic Books, 1986), pp. 13–14; 24–25 (emphasis added); see also Rosecrance, "War, Trade and Interdependence," in James N. Rosenau and Hylke Tromp, eds., *Interdependence*

and Conflict in World Politics (Aldershot, U.K.: Avebury, 1989), pp. 48–57; Rosecrance, "A New Concert of Powers," *Foreign Affairs*, Vol. 71, No. 2 (Spring 1992), pp. 64–82.

7. A book often seen as a statement on the peace—inducing effects of interdependence—Robert O. Keohane and Joseph S. Nye, *Power and Interdependence* (Boston: Little, Brown, 1977)—actually contains no such causal argument. For Keohane and Nye, "complex interdependence" is more peaceful by definition: it is "a valuable concept for analyzing the political process" only when military force is "unthinkable" (pp. 29, 24). In the second edition: "since we *define* complex interdependence in terms of [policy] goals and instruments," arguments "about how goals and instruments are affected by the degree to which a situation approximates complex interdependence or realism will be tautological." Thus, "we are left essentially with two dependent variables: changes in agendas and changes in the roles of international organizations." Keohane and Nye, *Power and Interdependence*, 2d ed. (Glenview, Ill.: Scott, Foresman, 1989), p. 255; emphasis in original. The dependent variable of this article—the likelihood of war—is nowhere to be found, which is not surprising, since it is assumed away. Other works on interdependence from the 1970s, which largely examined dependent variables other than war, are discussed in Copeland, "Economic Interdependence and the Outbreak of War."

8. One might contend that realists doubt the causal importance of economic interdependence, since relative gains concerns convince great powers to avoid becoming dependent in the first place. Aside from arguments showing why states may cooperate despite concerns for relative gains (see essays by Powell, Snidal, and Keohane in David A. Baldwin, ed., *Neorealism and Neoliberalism: The Contemporary Debate* [New York: Columbia University Press, 1993]; Dale Copeland, "Why Relative Gains Concerns May *Promote* Economic Cooperation: A Realist Explanation for Great Power Interdependence," presented at the annual meeting of the International Studies Association, San Diego, April 1996), the argument is empirically false. Periods of high interdependence have arisen even when the security competition between great powers was particularly intense, such as from 1880 to 1914, as Waltz acknowledges. Kenneth Waltz, "The Myth of Interdependence," in Ray Maghoori and Bennett Ramberg, *Globalism versus Realism* (Boulder, Colo.: Westview Press, 1982), p. 83. Since the reality of high interdependence cannot be argued or assumed away, I focus here on the core realist claim that whenever high levels of interdependence are reached, for whatever reason, war is more likely.

9. Kenneth Waltz, *Theory of International Politics* (New York: Random House, 1979), p. 106.

10. John J. Mearsheimer, "Disorder Restored," in Graham Allison and Gregory F. Treverton, eds., *Rethinking America's Security* (New York: W. W. Norton, 1992), p. 223; Mearsheimer, "Back to the Future," p. 45. See also Robert Gilpin, "Economic Interdependence and National Security in Historical Perspective," in Klaus Knorr and Frank N. Trager, eds., *Economic Issues and National Security* (Lawrence, Kan.: Allen, 1977), p. 29. Adopting the realist argument, but emphasizing how dependence leads states to adopt destabilizing offensive strategies, is Anne Uchitel, "Interdependence and Instability," in Jack Snyder and Robert Jervis, eds., *Coping with Complexity in the International System* (Boulder, Colo.: Westview Press, 1993), pp. 243–264. For Barry Buzan, since liberal free–trading systems are dependent on a hegemon which invariably declines, such systems are destined to fall into "malevolent" mercantilist practices, as states scramble to control access to goods formerly safeguarded by the hegemon. Avoiding the liberal system altogether, through a "benign" mercantilist system of self—sufficient trading blocs, will be therefore preferred. Buzan, "Economic Structure and International Security: The Limits of the Liberal Case," *International Organization*, Vol. 38, No. 4 (Autumn 1984), esp. pp. 597, 609–623. For a similar argument, see Robert Gilpin, *U.S. Power and the Multinational Corporation* (New York: Basic Books), 1975, p. 259.

11. See Eli F. Heckscher, *Mercantilism*, vol. 2, trans. Mendel Shapiro (London: George Allen, 1931), p. 15; Jacob Viner, "Power Versus Plenty as Objectives of Foreign Policy in the Seventeenth and Eighteenth Centuries," *World Politics*, Vol. 1, No. 1 (October 1948), p. 10; David A. Baldwin, *Economic Statecraft* (Princeton, N.J.: Princeton University Press, 1985), chap. 5.

12. Heckscher, *Mercantilism*, vol. 2, p. 40.

6.4

Harmony, Cooperation, and Discord

Robert O. Keohane

Cooperation must be distinguished from harmony. Harmony refers to a situation in which actors' policies (pursued in their own self-interest without regard for others) *automatically* facilitate the attainment of others' goals. The classic example of harmony is the hypothetical competitive-market world of the classical economists, in which the Invisible Hand ensures that the pursuit of self-interest by each contributes to the interest of all. In this idealized, unreal world, no one's actions damage anyone else; there are no "negative externalities," in the economists' jargon. Where harmony reigns, cooperation is unnecessary. It may even be injurious, if it means that certain individuals conspire to exploit others. Adam Smith, for one, was very critical of guilds and other conspiracies against freedom of trade (1776/1976). Cooperation and harmony are by no means identical and ought not to be confused with one another.

Cooperation requires that the actions of separate individuals or organizations—which are not in pre-existent harmony—be brought into conformity with one another through a process of negotiation, which is often referred to as "policy coordination." Charles E. Lindblom has defined policy coordination as follows (1965, p. 227):

> A set of decisions is coordinated if adjustments have been made in them, such that the adverse consequences of any one decision for other decisions are to a degree and in some frequency avoided, reduced, or counterbalanced or overweighed.

Cooperation occurs when actors adjust their behavior to the actual or anticipated preferences of others, through a process of policy coordination. To summarize more formally, *intergovernmental cooperation takes place when the policies actually followed by one government are regarded by its partners as facilitating realization of their own objectives, as the result of a process of policy coordination.*

With this definition in mind, we can differentiate among cooperation, harmony, and discord, as illustrated by Figure 6.1. First, we ask whether actors' policies automatically facilitate the attainment of others' goals. If so, there is harmony: no adjustments need to take place. Yet harmony is rare in world politics. Rousseau sought to account for this rarity when he declared that even two countries guided by the General Will in their internal affairs would come into conflict if they had extensive contact with one another, since the General Will of each would not be general for both. Each would have a partial, self-interested perspective on their mutual interactions. Even for Adam Smith, efforts to ensure state security took precedence over measures to increase national prosperity. In defending the Navigation Acts, Smith declared: "As defence is of much more importance than opulence, the act of navigation is, perhaps, the wisest of all the commercial regulations of England" (1776/1976, p. 487). Waltz summarizes the point by saying that "in anarchy there is no automatic harmony" (1959, p. 182).

Yet this insight tells us nothing definitive about the prospects for cooperation. For this we need to ask a further question about situations in which harmony does not exist. Are attempts made by actors (governmental or nongovernmental) to adjust their policies to each others' objectives? If no such attempts are made, the result is discord: a situation in which governments regard each others' policies as hindering the attainment of their goals, and hold each other responsible for these constraints.

Discord often leads to efforts to induce others to change their policies; when these attempts meet resistance, policy conflict results. Insofar as these attempts at policy adjustment succeed in making policies more compatible, however, cooperation ensues. The policy coordination that leads to cooperation need not involve bargaining or negotiation at all. What Lindblom calls "adaptive" as opposed to "manipulative" adjustment can take place: one country may shift its policy in the direction of another's preferences without regard for the effect of its action on the other state, defer to the

Source: Robert O. Keohane, *After Hegemony: Cooperation and Discord in the World Political Economy.* Copyright 1984 Princeton: Princeton University Press. Reprinted by permission of Princeton University Press.

Figure 6.1 Harmony, Cooperation, and Discord

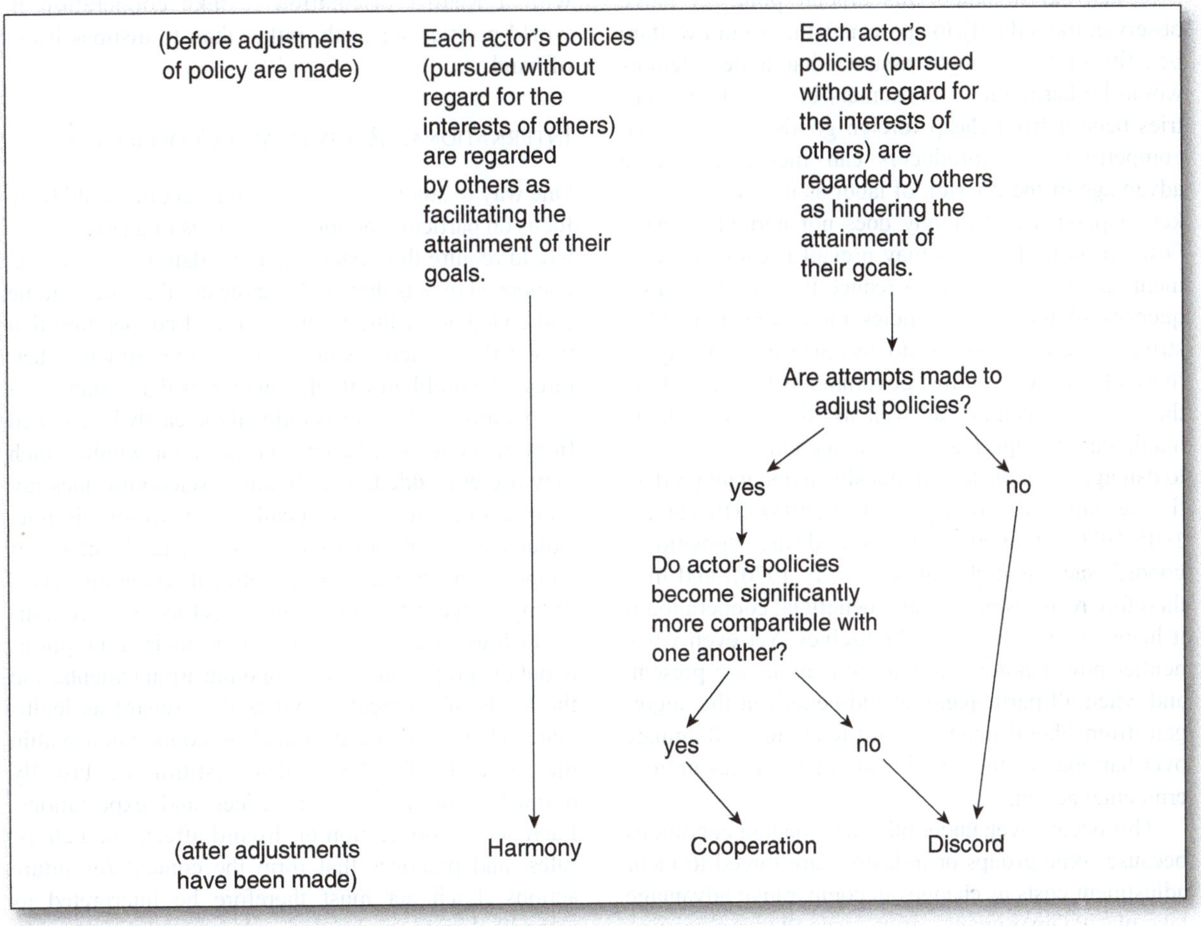

other country, or partially shift its policy in order to avoid adverse consequences for its partner. Or non-bargained manipulation—such as one actor confronting another with a *fait accompli*—may occur (Lindblom, 1965, pp. 33–34 and ch. 4). Frequently, of course, negotiation and bargaining indeed take place, often accompanied by other actions that are designed to induce others to adjust their policies to one's own. Each government pursues what it perceives as its self-interest, but looks for bargains that can benefit all parties to the deal, though not necessarily equally.

Harmony and cooperation are not usually distinguished from one another so clearly. Yet, in the study of world politics, they should be. Harmony is apolitical. No communication is necessary, and no influence need be exercised. Cooperation, by contrast, is highly political: somehow, patterns of behavior must be altered. This change may be accomplished through negative as well as positive inducements. Indeed, studies of international crises, as well as game-theoretic experiments and simulations, have shown that under a variety of conditions strategies that involve threats and punishments as well as promises and rewards are more effective in attaining cooperative outcomes than those that rely entirely on persuasion and the force of good example (Axelrod, 1981, 1984; Lebow, 1981; Snyder and Diesing, 1977).

Cooperation therefore does not imply an absence of conflict. On the contrary, it is typically mixed with conflict and reflects partially successful efforts to overcome conflict, real or potential. Cooperation takes place only in situations in which actors perceive that their policies are actually or potentially in conflict, not where there is harmony. Cooperation should not be viewed as the absence of conflict, but rather as a reaction to conflict or potential conflict. Without the specter of conflict, there is no need to cooperate.

The example of trade relations among friendly countries in a liberal international political economy may help to illustrate this crucial point. A naive observer, trained only to appreciate the overall welfare benefits of trade, might assume that trade relations would be harmonious; consumers in importing countries benefit from cheap foreign goods and increased competition, and producers can increasingly take advantage of the division of labor as their export markets expand. But harmony does not normally ensue. Discord on trade issues may prevail because governments do not even seek to reduce the adverse consequences of their own policies for others, but rather strive in certain respects to increase the severity of those effects. Mercantilist governments have sought in the twentieth century as well as the seventeenth to manipulate foreign trade, in conjunction with warfare, to damage each other economically and to gain productive resources themselves (Wilson, 1957; Hirschman, 1945/1980). Governments may desire "positional goods," such as high status (Hirsch, 1976), and may therefore resist even mutually beneficial cooperation if it helps others more than themselves. Yet even when neither power nor positional motivations are present, and when all participants would benefit in the aggregate from liberal trade, discord tends to predominate over harmony as the initial result of independent governmental action.

This occurs even under otherwise benign conditions because some groups or industries are forced to incur adjustment costs as changes in comparative advantage take place. Governments often respond to the ensuing demands for protection by attempting, more or less effectively, to cushion the burdens of adjustment for groups and industries that are politically influential at home. Yet unilateral measures to this effect almost always impose adjustment costs abroad, and discord continually threatens. Governments enter into international negotiations in order to reduce the conflict that would otherwise result. Even substantial potential common benefits do not create harmony when state power can be exercised on behalf of certain interests and against others. In world politics, harmony tends to vanish: attainment of the gains from pursuing complementary policies depends on cooperation.

Observers of world politics who take power and conflict seriously should be attracted to this way of defining cooperation, since my definition does not relegate cooperation to the mythological world of relations among equals in power. Hegemonic cooperation is not a contradiction in terms. Defining cooperation in contrast to harmony should, I hope, lead readers with a Realist orientation to take cooperation in world politics seriously rather than to dismiss it out of hand. . . .

International Regimes and Cooperation

One way to study cooperation and discord would be to focus on particular actions as the units of analysis. This would require the systematic compilation of a data set composed of acts that could be regarded as comparable and coded according to the degree of cooperation that they reflect. Such a strategy has some attractive features. The problem with it, however, is that instances of cooperation and discord could all too easily be isolated from the context of beliefs and behavior within which they are embedded. This [reading selection] does not view cooperation atomistically as a set of discrete, isolated acts, but rather seeks to understand patterns of cooperation in the world political economy. Accordingly, we need to examine actors' expectations about future patterns of interaction, their assumptions about the proper nature of economic arrangements, and the kinds of political activities they regard as legitimate. That is, we need to analyze cooperation within the context of international institutions, broadly defined, . . . in terms of practices and expectations. Each act of cooperation or discord affects the beliefs, rules, and practices that form the context for future actions. Each act must therefore be interpreted as embedded within a chain of such acts and their successive cognitive and institutional residues.

This argument parallels Clifford Geertz's discussion of how anthropologists should use the concept of culture to interpret the societies they investigate. Geertz sees culture as the "webs of significance" that people have created for themselves. On their surface, they are enigmatical; the observer has to interpret them so that they make sense. Culture, for Geertz, "is a context, something within which [social events] can be intelligibly described" (1973, p. 14). It makes little sense to describe naturalistically what goes on at a Balinese cock-fight unless one understands the meaning of the event for Balinese culture. There is not a world culture in the fullest sense, but even in world politics, human beings spin webs of significance. They develop implicit standards for behavior, some of which emphasize the principle of sovereignty and legitimize the pursuit of self-interest, while others rely on quite different principles. Any act of cooperation or apparent cooperation needs to be interpreted within the context of related actions, and of prevailing expectations and shared beliefs, before its meaning can be properly understood. Fragments of political behavior become comprehensible when viewed as part of a larger mosaic.

The concept of international regimes not only enables us to describe patterns of cooperation; it also helps to account for both cooperation and discord. Although regimes themselves depend on conditions that are conducive to interstate agreements, they may also facilitate further efforts to coordinate policies.

Defining and Identifying Regimes

When John Ruggie introduced the concept of international regimes into the international politics literature in 1975, he defined a regime as "a set of mutual expectations, rules and regulations, plans, organizational energies and financial commitments, which have been accepted by a group of states" (p. 570). More recently, a collective definition, worked out at a conference on the subject, defined international regimes as "sets of implicit or explicit principles, norms, rules and decision-making procedures around which actors' expectations converge in a given area of international relations. Principles are beliefs of fact, causation, and rectitude. Norms are standards of behavior defined in terms of rights and obligations. Rules are specific prescriptions or proscriptions for action. Decision-making procedures are prevailing practices for making and implementing collective choice" (Krasner, 1983, p. 2).

This definition provides a useful starting-point for analysis, since it begins with the general conception of regimes as social institutions and explicates it further. The concept of norms, however, is ambiguous. It is important that we understand norms in this definition simply as standards of behavior defined in terms of rights and obligations. Another usage would distinguish norms from rules and principles by stipulating that participants in a social system regard norms, but not rules and principles, as morally binding regardless of considerations of narrowly defined self-interest. But to include norms, thus defined, in a definition of necessary regime characteristics would be to make the conception of regimes based strictly on self-interest a contradiction in terms. Since this book regards regimes as largely based on self-interest, I will maintain a definition of norms simply as standards of behavior, whether adopted on grounds of self-interest or otherwise.

The principles of regimes define, in general, the purposes that their members are expected to pursue. For instance, the principles of the postwar trade and monetary regimes have emphasized the value of open, nondiscriminatory patterns of international economic transactions; the fundamental principle of the nonproliferation regime is that the spread of nuclear weapons is dangerous. Norms contain somewhat clearer injunctions to members about legitimate and illegitimate behavior, still defining responsibilities and obligations in relatively general terms. For instance, the norms of the General Agreement on Tariffs and Trade (GATT) do not require that members resort to free trade immediately, but incorporate injunctions to members to practice non-discrimination and reciprocity and to move toward increased liberalization. Fundamental to the nonproliferation regime is the norm that members of the regime should not act in ways that facilitate nuclear proliferation.

The rules of a regime are difficult to distinguish from its norms; at the margin, they merge into one another. Rules are, however, more specific: they indicate in more detail the specific rights and obligations of members. Rules can be altered more easily than principles or norms, since there may be more than one set of rules that can attain a given set of purposes. Finally, at the same level of specificity as rules, but referring to procedures rather than substances, the decision-making procedures of regimes provide ways of implementing their principles and altering their rules.

An example from the field of international monetary relations may be helpful. The most important principle of the international balance-of-payments regime since the end of World War II has been that of liberalization of trade and payments. A key norm of the regime has been the injunction to states not to manipulate their exchange rates unilaterally for national advantage. Between 1958 and 1971 this norm was realized through pegged exchange rates and procedures for consultation in the event of change, supplemented with a variety of devices to help governments avoid exchange-rate changes through a combination of borrowing and internal adjustment. After 1973 governments have subscribed to the same norm, although it has been implemented more informally and probably less effectively under a system of floating exchange rates. Ruggie (1983b) has argued that the abstract principle of liberalization, subject to constraints imposed by the acceptance of the welfare state, has been maintained throughout the postwar period: "embedded liberalism" continues, reflecting a fundamental element of continuity in the international balance-of-payments regime. The norm of non-manipulation has also been maintained, even though the specific rules of the 1958-71 system having to do with adjustment have been swept away.

The concept of international regime is complex because it is defined in terms of four distinct components: principles, norms, rules, and decision-making procedures. It is tempting to select one of these levels of specificity—particularly, principles and norms or rules and procedures—as *the* defining characteristic of regimes (Krasner, 1983; Ruggie, 1983b). Such an approach, however, creates a false dichotomy between principles on the one hand and rules and procedures on the other. As we have noted, at the margin norms and rules cannot be sharply distinguished from each other. It is difficult if not impossible to tell the difference between an "implicit rule" of broad significance and a well-understood, relatively specific operating principle. Both rules and principles may affect expectations and even values. In a strong international regime, the linkages between principles and rules are likely to be tight. Indeed, it is precisely the linkages among principles, norms, and rules that give regimes their legitimacy. Since rules, norms, and principles are so closely inter-wined, judgments about whether changes in rules constitute changes of regime or merely changes *within* regimes necessarily contain arbitrary elements.

Principles, norms, rules, and procedures all contain injunctions about behavior: they prescribe certain actions and proscribe others. They imply obligations, even though these obligations are not enforceable through a hierarchical legal system. It clarifies the definition of regime, therefore, to think of it in terms of injunctions of greater or lesser specificity. Some are far-reaching and extremely important. They may change only rarely. At the other extreme, injunctions may be merely technical, matters of convenience that can be altered without great political or economic impact. In-between are injunctions that are both specific enough that violations of them are in principle identifiable and that changes in them can be observed, and sufficiently significant that changes in them make a difference for the behavior of actors and the nature of the international political economy. It is these intermediate injunctions—politically consequential but specific enough that violations and changes can be identified—that I take as the essence of international regimes.[1] . . .

[W]e regard the scope of international regimes as corresponding, in general, to the boundaries of issue-areas, since governments establish regimes to deal with problems that they regard as so closely linked that they should be dealt with together. Issue-areas are best defined as sets of issues that are in fact dealt with in common negotiations and by the same, or closely coordinated, bureaucracies, as opposed to issues that are dealt with separately and in uncoordinated fashion. Since issue-areas depend on actors' perceptions and behavior rather than on inherent qualities of the subject-matters, their boundaries change gradually over time. . . . Issue-areas are defined and redefined by changing patterns of human intervention; so are international regimes. . . .

Compliance with International Regimes

International regimes are decentralized institutions. Decentralization does not imply an absence of mechanisms for compliance, but it does mean that any sanctions for violation of regime principles or rules have to be enacted by the individual members (Young, 1979, p. 35). The regime provides procedures and rules through which such sanctions can be coordinated. Decentralized enforcement of regime rules and principles is neither swift nor certain. Yet, in many instances, rules are obeyed. Indeed, Louis Henkin goes so far as to say that "almost all nations observe almost all principles of international law and almost all of their obligations almost all of the time" (1979, p. 47). In the world political economy, we observe a good deal of compliance even when governments have incentives, on the basis of myopic self-interest, to violate the rules. . . .

The extent of international compliance should not be overstated. As we will see, the trade and monetary regimes both became weaker during the 1970s. American and European policies became more protectionist in textiles, steel, and other threatened sectors (Aggarwal, 1983; Verreydt and Waelbroeck, 1982; Woolcock, 1982). Nevertheless, despite the economic disruptions of the 1970s and 1980s, there has been no headlong rush to reduce trade drastically. . . . The form that protectionism takes, furthermore, is, like hypocrisy, "the tribute that vice pays to virtue": much contemporary protectionism is designed to avoid running directly afoul of international agreements. For instance, American protectionism in manufactured goods consists largely of "voluntary export restraints" rather than unilaterally imposed import quotas, despite the fact that import quotas do not require laborious international negotiations and capture more rents for the government or private firms in the importing country (Bergsten, 1975b). Voluntary export restraints are often chosen because they bypass GATT restrictions without directly violating explicit GATT prohibitions; yet this advantage is gained at the expense of frequently building in loopholes permitting imports to continue to increase rapidly (Yoffie, 1983). . . .

The puzzle of compliance is why governments, seeking to promote their own interests, ever comply with the rules of international regimes when they view these rules as in conflict with what I will call their "myopic self-interest." Myopic self-interest refers to governments' perception of the relative costs and benefits to them of alternative courses of action with regard to a particular issue, *when that issue is considered in isolation from others.* An action is in a government's myopic self-interest if it has the highest expected value of any alternative, apart from the indirect effects that actions on the specific issue in question would have on other issues. That governments often comply with rules that conflict with their myopic self-interest poses a potential anomaly for theories . . . that assume rational, egoistic action in world politics. Why should an egoistic actor behave, on a given issue, in a way that is inconsistent with its self-interest on that issue? If we observe compliance with the rules of international regimes, is this not inconsistent with the assumption of egoism?

The murky language of national interests allows some Realists, such as Hans J. Morgenthau, to avoid this issue. Morgenthau notes the existence of functional organizations such as the specialized agencies of the United Nations system, but contents himself with the observation that when there is a conflict between the national interest and the operation of such agencies, "the national interest wins out over the international objective" (1948/1966, p. 509). This begs the question of whether the national interest is defined myopically, without regard to the effects of one's actions on other issues or other values, or in a more farsighted way, taking into account the impact of violating international rules and norms on other state objectives. Yet the crucial issues are precisely those of how interests are defined, and how institutions affect states' definitions of their own interests. An understanding of the puzzle of compliance requires an examination of how international regimes affect the calculations of self-interest in which rational, egoistic governments engage. . . .

The Value of Existing Regimes

We have seen that it is difficult even for perfectly rational individuals to make agreements with one another in the absence of provisions for central enforcement of contracts. In world politics, international regimes help to facilitate the making of agreements by reducing barriers created by high transaction costs and uncertainty. But these very difficulties make it hard to create the regimes themselves in the first place.

The importance of transaction costs and uncertainty means that regimes are easier to maintain than they are to create. Complementary interests are necessary but not sufficient conditions for their emergence. The construction of international regimes may require active efforts by a hegemonic state, as the IMF and GATT did after World War II; or regime-creation in the absence of hegemony may be spurred on by the pressures of a sudden and severe crisis, such that which led to the IEA. Even with complementary interests, it is difficult to overcome problems of transaction costs and uncertainty.

Once an international regime has been established, however, it begins to benefit from the relatively high and symmetrical level of information that it generates, and from the ways in which it makes regime-supporting bargains easier to consummate. We will see in chapter 9 that the international organizations at the center of the international monetary and trade regimes have outlived the period of U.S. hegemony that brought them into being. Viewing international regimes as information-providing and transaction cost-reducing entities rather than as quasi-governmental rule-makers helps us to understand such persistence. Effective international regimes facilitate informal contact and communication among officials. Indeed, they may lead to "transgovernmental" networks of acquaintance and friendship: supposedly confidential documents of one government may be seen by officials of another; informal coalitions of like-minded officials develop to achieve common purposes; and critical discussions by professionals probe the assumptions and assertions of state policies (Neustadt, 1970; Keohane and Nye, 1974; Keohane, 1978). These transgovernmental relationships may increase opportunities for cooperation in world politics by providing policymakers with high-quality information about what their counterparts are likely to do.[2] . . .

International regimes embody sunk costs, and we can understand why they persist even when all members would prefer somewhat different mixtures of principles, rules, and institutions.

It is precisely the costliness of agreements, and of regimes themselves, that make them important. The high costs of regime-building help existing regimes to persist.

Networks of Issues and Regimes

In thinking about compliance, we should recall the previous discussion of how regimes facilitate the making of agreements. To some extent, it is governments' anticipation that international regimes will increase compliance that accounts for their willingness to enter into these arrangements in the first place. Insofar as regimes create incentives for compliance, they also make it more attractive for conscientious potential members to join them. We saw that, by linking issues to one another, regimes create situations that are more like iterated, open-ended Prisoners' Dilemma, in which cooperation may be rational, than like single-play Prisoners' Dilemma, in which it is not. Violation of one's commitments on a given issue, in pursuit of myopic self-interest, will affect others' actions on other questions. Pursuit of its farsighted self-interest may therefore lead a government to eschew its myopic self-interest.

As the Prisoners' Dilemma example suggests, social pressure, exercised through linkages among issues, provides the most compelling set of reasons for governments to comply with their commitments. That is, egoistic governments may comply with rules because if they fail to do so, other governments will observe their behavior, evaluate it negatively, and perhaps take retaliatory action. Sometimes retaliation will be specific and authorized under the rules of a regime; sometimes it will be more general and diffuse.

Suppose, for example, that a member of GATT is under pressure from domestic manufacturers of nuts and bolts to enact import quotas on these products. Even if the government perceives that it has a myopic self-interest in doing so, it knows that such an action in violation of the rules would have negative implications for it on other trade questions—let us say, in opening markets for its semiconductors abroad. The principles and rules of the regime, since they facilitate linkage among issues, will in such circumstances render pursuit of myopic self-interest less attractive. Indeed, the prospect of discord as a result of its rule-violation may lead the government to continue to engage in cooperation, whereas if it could have gotten away with the violation without risking discord, it would have gone ahead. . . .

In the absence of specific retaliation, governments may still have incentives to comply with regime rules and principles if they are concerned about precedent or believe that their reputations are at stake. Governments worry about establishing bad precedents because they fear that their own rule-violations will promote rule-violations by others, even if no specific penalty is imposed on themselves. That is, breaking rules may create an individual benefit, but it produces a "collective bad." The effect of the collective bad on the utility of the individual government may under certain circumstances outweigh the benefit. . . .

Our analysis of uncertainty earlier in this [reading] suggests how important reputation can be even to governments not concerned with personal honor and self-respect. Under conditions of uncertainty and decentralization, governments will decide whom to make agreements with, and on what terms, largely on the basis of their expectations about their partners' willingness and ability to keep their commitments. A good reputation makes it easier for a government to enter into advantageous international agreements; tarnishing that reputation imposes costs by making agreements more difficult to reach.[3] . . .

For reasons of reputation, as well as fear of retaliation and concern about the effects of precedents, egoistic governments may follow the rules and principles of international regimes even when myopic self-interest counsels them not to. As we have seen in this section, they could do so strictly on the basis of calculations of costs and benefits. Each time that they seem to have incentives to violate the provisions of regimes, they could calculate whether the benefits of doing so outweigh the costs, taking into account the effects on their reputations as well as the probability of retaliation and the effects of rule-violation on the system as a whole. They might often decide, in light of this cost-benefit calculation, to conform to the rules. Rational egoism can lead governments not only to make agreements, but to keep them even when they turn out poorly.

Notes

1. Some authors have defined "regime" as equivalent to the conventional concept of international system. For instance, Puchala and Hopkins (1983) claim that "a regime exists in every substantive issue-area in international relations where there is discernibly patterned behavior" (p. 63). To adopt this definition would be to make either "system" or "regime" a redundant term. At the opposite extreme, the concept of regime could be limited to situations with genuine normative content, in which governments followed regime rules *instead of* pursuing their own self-interests when the two conflicted. If this course were chosen, the concept of regime would be just another way of expressing ancient "idealist" sentiments in international relations. The category of regime would become virtually empty. This dichotomy poses a false choice between using "regime" as a new label for old patterns and defining regimes as utopias. Either strategy would make the term irrelevant.

2. At the very highest levels of government, however, these transgovernmental interactions are often quite limited (Russell, 1973; Putnam and Bayne, 1984).

3. Heymann makes this point succinctly for the general case: "Since coordinated actions to obtain outcomes of benefit to all parties often depend upon trust, each actor who wants to be a participant in, and thus beneficiary of, such cooperative schemes in the long run and on a number of separable occasions has an important stake in creating and preserving a reputation as a trustworthy party" (1973, p. 822). He also points out that the incentive to obey agreed-upon rules for the sake of one's reputation only operates when one's actions are not secret and others retain the capability to retaliate effectively against one's infractions.

6.5

Fourteen Points

Woodrow Wilson

8 January, 1918: President Woodrow Wilson's Fourteen Points

It will be our wish and purpose that the processes of peace, when they are begun, shall be absolutely open and that they shall involve and permit henceforth no secret understandings of any kind. The day of conquest and aggrandizement is gone by; so is also the day of secret covenants entered into in the interest of particular governments and likely at some unlooked-for moment to upset the peace of the world. It is this happy fact, now clear to the view of every public man whose thoughts do not still linger in an age that is dead and gone, which makes it possible for every nation whose purposes are consistent with justice and the peace of the world to avow now or at any other time the objects it has in view.

We entered this war because violations of right had occurred which touched us to the quick and made the life of our own people impossible unless they were corrected and the world secure once for all against their recurrence. What we demand in this war, therefore, is nothing peculiar to ourselves. It is that the world be made fit and safe to live in; and particularly that it be made safe for every peace-loving nation which, like our own, wishes to live its own life, determine its own institutions, be assured of justice and fair dealing by the other peoples of the world as against force and selfish aggression. All the peoples of the world are in effect partners in this interest, and for our own part we see very clearly that unless justice be done to others it will not be done to us. The program of the world's peace, therefore, is our program; and that program, the only possible program, as we see it, is this:

I. Open covenants of peace, openly arrived at, after which there shall be no private international understandings of any kind but diplomacy shall proceed always frankly and in the public view.

II. Absolute freedom of navigation upon the seas, outside territorial waters, alike in peace and in war, except as the seas may be closed in whole or in part by international action for the enforcement of international covenants.

III. The removal, so far as possible, of all economic barriers and the establishment of an equality of trade conditions among all the nations consenting to the peace and associating themselves for its maintenance.

IV. Adequate guarantees given and taken that national armaments will be reduced to the lowest point consistent with domestic safety.

V. A free, open-minded, and absolutely impartial adjustment of all colonial claims, based upon a strict observance of the principle that in determining all such questions of sovereignty the interests of the populations concerned must have equal weight with the equitable claims of the government whose title is to be determined.

VI. The evacuation of all Russian territory and such a settlement of all questions affecting Russia as will secure the best and freest cooperation of the other nations of the world in obtaining for her an unhampered and unembarrassed opportunity for the independent determination of her own political development and national policy and assure her of a sincere welcome into the society of free nations under institutions of her own choosing; and, more than a welcome, assistance also of every kind that she may need and may herself desire. The treatment accorded Russia by her sister nations in the months to come will be the acid test of their good will, of their comprehension of her needs as distinguished from their own

Source: Woodrow Wilson, "The Fourteen Points" from his 8 January 1918 Address to the U.S. Congress.

interests, and of their intelligent and unselfish sympathy.

VII. Belgium, the whole world will agree, must be evacuated and restored, without any attempt to limit the sovereignty which she enjoys in common with all other free nations. No other single act will serve as this will serve to restore confidence among the nations in the laws which they have themselves set and determined for the government of their relations with one another. Without this healing act the whole structure and validity of international law is forever impaired.

VIII. All French territory should be freed and the invaded portions restored, and the wrong done to France by Prussia in 1871 in the matter of Alsace-Lorraine, which has unsettled the peace of the world for nearly fifty years, should be righted, in order that peace may once more be made secure in the interest of all.

IX. A readjustment of the frontiers of Italy should be effected along clearly recognizable lines of nationality.

X. The peoples of Austria-Hungary, whose place among the nations we wish to see safeguarded and assured, should be accorded the freest opportunity to autonomous development.

XI. Rumania, Serbia, and Montenegro should be evacuated; occupied territories restored; Serbia accorded free and secure access to the sea; and the relations of the several Balkan states to one another determined by friendly counsel along historically established lines of allegiance and nationality; and international guarantees of the political and economic independence and territorial integrity of the several Balkan states should be entered into.

XII. The Turkish portion of the present Ottoman Empire should be assured a secure sovereignty, but the other nationalities which are now under Turkish rule should be assured an undoubted security of life and an absolutely unmolested opportunity of autonomous development, and the Dardanelles should be permanently opened as a free passage to the ships and commerce of all nations under international guarantees.

XIII. An independent Polish state should be erected which should include the territories inhabited by indisputably Polish populations, which should be assured a free and secure access to the sea, and whose political and economic independence and territorial integrity should be guaranteed by international covenant.

XIV. A general association of nations must be formed under specific covenants for the purpose of affording mutual guarantees of political independence and territorial integrity to great and small states alike.

In regard to these essential rectifications of wrong and assertions of right we feel ourselves to be intimate partners of all the governments and peoples associated together against the Imperialists. We cannot be separated in interest or divided in purpose. We stand together until the end.

For such arrangements and covenants we are willing to fight and to continue to fight until they are achieved; but only because we wish the right to prevail and desire a just and stable peace such as can be secured only by removing the chief provocations to war, which this program does remove. We have no jealousy of German greatness, and there is nothing in this program that impairs it. We grudge her no achievement or distinction of learning or of pacific enterprise such as have made her record very bright and very enviable. We do not wish to injure her or to block in any way her legitimate influence or power. We do not wish to fight her either with arms or with hostile arrangements of trade if she is willing to associate herself with us and other peace-loving nations of the world in covenants of justice and law and fair dealing. We wish her only to accept a place of equality among the peoples of the world—the new world in which we now live. . . .

7 Constructivism I

7.1

The Promise of Constructivism in International Relations Theory

Ted Hopf

A challenger to the continuing dominance of neorealism and neoliberal institutionalism in the study of international relations in the United States, constructivism is regarded with a great deal of skepticism by mainstream scholars.[1] While the reasons for this reception are many, three central ones are the mainstream's miscasting of constructivism as necessarily postmodern and anti-positivist; constructivism's own ambivalence about whether it can buy into mainstream social science methods without sacrificing its theoretical distinctiveness; and, related to this ambivalence, constructivism's failure to advance an alternative research program. In this [reading], I clarify constructivism's claims, outline the differences between "conventional" and "critical" constructivism, and suggest a research agenda that both provides alternative understandings of mainstream international relations puzzles and offers a few examples of what constructivism can uniquely bring to an understanding of world politics.

Constructivism offers alternative understandings of a number of the central themes in international relations theory, including: the meaning of anarchy and balance of power, the relationship between state identity and interest, an elaboration of power, and the prospects for change in world politics. Constructivism itself should be understood in its *conventional* and *critical* variants, the latter being more closely tied to critical social theory. The conventional constructivist desire to present an alternative to mainstream international relations theory requires a research program. Such a program includes constructivist reconceptualizations of balance-of-threat theory, the security dilemma, neoliberal cooperation theory, and the democratic peace. The constructivist research program has its own puzzles that concentrate on issues of identity in world politics and the theorization of domestic politics and culture in international relations theory.

Conventional Constructivism and Issues in Mainstream International Relations Theory

Since constructivism is best defined in relation to the issues it claims to apprehend, I present its position on several of the most significant themes in international relations theory today.

Actors and Structures are Mutually Constituted

How much do structures constrain and enable the actions of actors, and how much can actors deviate from the constraints of structure? In world politics, a

Source: Ted Hopf, "The Promise of Constructivism in International Relations Theory" *International Security* 23:1 (Summer, 1998), 171–200.

structure is a set of relatively unchangeable constraints on the behavior of states.[2] Although these constraints can take the form of systems of material dis/incentives, such as a balance of power or a market, as important from a constructivist perspective is how an action does or does not reproduce both the actor and the structure.[3] For example, to the extent that U.S. appeasement in Vietnam was unimaginable because of U.S. identity as a great power, military intervention constituted the United States as a great power. Appeasement was an unimaginable act. By engaging in the "enabled" action of intervention, the United States reproduced its own identity of great power, as well as the structure that gave meaning to its action. So, U.S. intervention in Vietnam perpetuated the international intersubjective understanding of great powers as those states that use military power against others.

Meaningful behavior, or action,[4] is possible only within an intersubjective social context. Actors develop their relations with, and understandings of, others through the media of norms and practices. In the absence of norms, exercises of power, or actions, would be devoid of meaning. Constitutive norms define an identity by specifying the actions that will cause Others to recognize that identity and respond to it appropriately.[5] Since structure is meaningless without some intersubjective set of norms and practices, anarchy, mainstream international relations theory's most crucial structural component, is meaningless. Neither anarchy, that is, the absence of any authority above the state, nor the distribution of capabilities, can "socialize" states to the desiderata of the international system's structure absent some set of meaningful norms and practices.[6]

A story many use in first-year international relations courses to demonstrate the structural extreme, that is, a situation where no agency is imaginable, illustrates the point. The scenario is a fire in a theater where all run for the exits.[7] But absent knowledge of social practices or constitutive norms, structure, even in this seemingly overdetermined circumstance, is still indeterminate. Even in a theater with just one door, while all run for that exit, who goes first? Are they the strongest or the disabled, the women or the children, the aged or the infirm, or is it just a mad dash? Determining the outcome will require knowing more about the situation than about the distribution of material power or the structure of authority. One will need to know about the culture, norms, institutions, procedures, rules, and social practices that constitute the actors and the structure alike.

Anarchy as an Imagined Community

Given that anarchy is structural, it must be mutually constituted by actors employing constitutive rules and social practices, implying that anarchy is as indeterminate as Arnold Wolfers's fire. Alexander Wendt has offered a constructivist critique of this fundamental structural pillar of mainstream international relations theory.[8] But still more fundamentally, this move opens the possibility of thinking of anarchy as having multiple meanings for different actors based on their own communities of intersubjective understandings and practices. And if multiple understandings of anarchy are possible, then one can begin to theorize about different domains and issue areas of international politics that are understood by actors as more, or less, anarchic.

Self-help, the neorealist inference that all states should prefer security independence whenever possible, is a structurally determined behavior of an actor only to the extent that a single particular understanding of anarchy prevails.[9] If the implications of anarchy are not constant across all relationships and issue areas of international politics, then a continuum of anarchies is possible. Where there are catastrophic consequences for not being able to rely on one's own capacity to enforce an agreement, such as arms control in a world of offensive military advantage, neorealist conceptualizations of anarchy are most apt. But where actors do not worry much about the potential costs of ceding control over outcomes to other states or institutions, such as in the enforcement of trade agreements, this is a realm of world politics where neorealist ideas of anarchy are just imaginary.

Identities and Interests in World Politics

Identities are necessary, in international politics and domestic society alike, in order to ensure at least some minimal level of predictability and order.[10] Durable expectations between states require intersubjective identities that are sufficiently stable to ensure predictable patterns of behavior. A world without identities is a world of chaos, a world of pervasive and irremediable uncertainty, a world much more dangerous than anarchy. Identities perform three necessary functions in a society: they tell you and others who you are and they tell you who others are.[11] In telling you who you are, identities strongly imply a particular set of interests or preferences with respect to choices of action in particular domains, and with respect to particular actors.

The identity of a state implies its preferences and consequent actions.[12] A state understands others according to the identity it attributes to them, while simultaneously reproducing its own identity through daily social practice. The crucial observation here is that the producer of the identity is not in control of what it ultimately means to others; the intersubjective structure is the final arbiter of meaning. For example, during the Cold War, Yugoslavia and other East European countries often understood the Soviet Union as Russia, despite the fact that the Soviet Union was trying hard not to have that identity. Soviet control over its own identity was structurally constrained not only by East European understanding, but also by daily Soviet practice, which of course included conversing with East Europeans in Russian.

Whereas constructivism treats identity as an empirical question to be theorized within a historical context, neorealism assumes that all units in global politics have only one meaningful identity, that of self-interested states. Constructivism stresses that this proposition exempts from theorization the very fundamentals of international political life, the nature and definition of the actors. The neorealist assumption of self-interest presumes to know, *a priori*, just what is the self being identified. In other words, the state in international politics, across time and space, is assumed to have a single eternal meaning. Constructivism instead assumes that the selves, or identities, of states are a variable; they likely depend on historical, cultural, political, and social context.

Constructivism and neorealism share the assumption that interests imply choices, but neorealism further assumes that states have the same *a priori* interests. Such a homogenizing assumption is possible only if one denies that interests are the products of the social practices that mutually constitute actors and structures.[13] Given that interests are the product of identity, that is, having the identity "great power" implies a particular set of interests different from those implied by the identity "European Union member," and that identities are multiple, constructivist logic precludes acceptance of pregiven interests.[14]

By making interests a central variable, constructivism explores not only how particular interests come to be, but also why many interests do not. The tautological, and therefore also true, most common, and unsatisfying explanation is that interests are absent where there is no reason for them, where promised gains are too meager. Constructivism, instead, theorizes about the meaning of absent interests. Just as identities and interests are produced through social practices, missing interests are understood by constructivists as produced absences, omissions that are the understandable product of social practices and structure. The social practices that constitute an identity cannot imply interests that are not consistent with the practices and structure that constitute that identity. At the extreme, an actor would not be able to imagine an absent interest, even if presented with it.[15]

The consequences of this treatment of interests and identities work in the same direction as constructivism's account of structure, agency, and anarchy: states are expected to have (1) a far wider array of potential choices of action before them than is assumed by neorealism, and (2) these choices will be constrained by social structures that are mutually created by states and structures via social practices. In other words, states have more agency under constructivism, but that agency is not in any sense unconstrained. To the contrary, choices are rigorously constrained by the webs of understanding of the practices, identities, and interests of other actors that prevail in particular historical contexts.

The Power of Practice

Power is a central theoretical element for both mainstream and constructivist approaches to international relations theory, but their conceptualizations of power are vastly different. Neorealism and neoliberal institutionalism assume that material power, whether military or economic or both, is the single most important source of influence and authority in global politics.[16] Constructivism argues that both material and discursive power are necessary for any understanding of world affairs. I emphasize both because often constructivists are dismissed as unRealistic for believing in the power of knowledge, ideas, culture, ideology, and language, that is, discourse.[17] The notion that ideas are a form of power, that power is more than brute force, and that material and discursive power are related is not new. Michel Foucault's articulation of the power/knowledge nexus, Antonio Gramsci's theory of ideological hegemony, and Max Weber's differentiation of coercion from authority are all precursors to constructivism's position on power in political life.[18] Empirical work exists in both international relations theory and security studies that demonstrates the need to appreciate both the material and the discursive aspects of power.[19] Given that the operation of the material side of power is familiar from the mainstream literature, here I concentrate on the discursive side, the power of practice in constructivism.

The power of social practices lies in their capacity to reproduce the intersubjective meanings that constitute social structures and actors alike. The U.S. military intervention in Vietnam was consistent with a number of U.S. identities: great power, imperialist, enemy, ally, and so on. Others observing the United States not only inferred U.S. identity from its actions in Vietnam, but also reproduced the intersubjective web of meaning about what precisely constituted that identity. To the extent, for example, that a group of countries attributed an imperialist identity to the United States, the meaning of being an imperialist state was reproduced by the U.S. military intervention. In this way, social practices not only reproduce actors through identity, but also reproduce an intersubjective social structure through social practice. A most important power of practice is its capacity to produce predictability and so, order. Social practices greatly reduce uncertainty among actors within a socially structured community, thereby increasing confidence that what actions one takes will be followed by certain consequences and responses from others.[20]

An actor is not even able to act as its identity until the relevant community of meaning, to paraphrase Karl Deutsch,[21] acknowledges the legitimacy of that action, by that actor, in that social context. The power of practice is the power to produce intersubjective meaning within a social structure. It is a short step from this authorizing power of practice to an understanding of practice as a way of bounding, or disciplining interpretation, making some interpretations of reality less likely to occur or prevail within a particular community.[22] The meanings of actions of members of the community, as well as the actions of Others, become fixed through practice; boundaries of understanding become well known. In this way, the ultimate power of practice is to reproduce and police an intersubjective reality.[23] Social practices, to the extent that they authorize, discipline, and police, have the power to reproduce entire communities, including the international community, as well as the many communities of identity found therein.[24]

State actions in the foreign policy realm are constrained and empowered by prevailing social practices at home and abroad. Richard Ashley, for example, writes of a foreign policy choice as being a kind of social practice that at once constitutes and empowers the state, defines its socially recognized competence, and secures the boundaries that differentiate the domestic and international economic and political spheres of practice and, with them, the appropriate domains in which specific actors may secure recognition and act competently. Finally, Ashley concludes, foreign policy practice depends on the existence of intersubjective "precedents and shared symbolic materials—in order to impose interpretations upon events, silence alternative interpretations, structure practices, and orchestrate the collective making of history."[25]

Although I have necessarily concentrated on articulating how discursive power works in this section, the power to control intersubjective understanding is not the only form of power relevant to a constructivist approach to world politics. Having resources that allow oneself to deploy discursive power—the economic and military wherewithal to sustain institutions necessary for the formalized reproduction of social practices—is almost always part of the story as well.

Change In World Politics

Constructivism is agnostic about change in world politics.[26] It restores much variety and difference to world affairs and points out the practices by which intersubjective order is maintained, but it does not offer any more hope for change in world politics than neorealism. Constructivism's insight that anarchy is what states make of it, for example, implies that there are many different understandings of anarchy in the world, and so state actions should be more varied than only self-help. But this is an observation of already-existing reality, or, more precisely, a set of hypotheses about the same. These different understandings of anarchy are still rooted in social structures, maintained by the power of practice, and quite impervious to change. What constructivism does offer is an account of how and where change may occur.

One aspect of constructivist power is the power to reproduce, discipline, and police. When such power is realized, change in world politics is very hard indeed. These intersubjective structures, however, although difficult to challenge, are not impregnable. Alternative actors with alternative identities, practices, and sufficient material resources are theoretically capable of effecting change. Robert Cox's account of British and American supremacy, for example, perhaps best illustrates the extraordinary staying power of a well-articulated ideological hegemony, but also its possible demise. And Walker rightly observes that constructivism, to the extent that it surfaces diversity, difference, and particularity, opens up at least potential alternatives to the current prevailing structures.[27] Constructivism conceives of the politics of identity as a continual contest for control over the power necessary to produce meaning in a social group. So long as there is difference, there is a potential for change.

Thus, contrary to some critics[28] who assert that constructivism believes that change in world politics is easy, that "bad" neorealist structures need only be thought away, in fact constructivism appreciates the power of structure, if for no other reason then it assumes that actors reproduce daily their own constraints through ordinary practice. Constructivism's conceptualization of the relationship between agency and structure grounds its view that social change is both possible and difficult. Neorealism's position that all states are meaningfully identical denies a fair amount of possible change to its theoretical structure.

In sum, neorealism and constructivism share fundamental concerns with the role of structure in world politics, the effects of anarchy on state behavior, the definition of state interests, the nature of power, and the prospects for change. They disagree fundamentally, however, on each concern. Contra neorealism, constructivism assumes that actors and structures mutually constitute each other; anarchy must be interpreted to have meaning; state interests are part of the process of identity construction; power is both material and discursive; and change in world politics is both possible and difficult.

Notes

1. The canonical neorealist work remains Kenneth N. Waltz, *Theory of International Politics* (Reading, Mass.: Addison-Wesley, 1979). The debate between neorealism and neoliberal institutionalism is presented and summarized in David A. Baldwin, ed., *Neorealism and Neoliberalism* (New York: Columbia University Press, 1993). Constructivist challenges can be found in Nicholas Greenwood Onuf, *World of Our Making: Rules and Rule in Social Theory and International Relations* (Columbia: University of South Carolina Press, 1989); Peter J. Katzenstein, ed., *The Culture of National Security: Norms and Identity in World Politics* (New York: Columbia University Press, 1996); and Yosef Lapid and Friedrich V. Kratochwil, eds., *The Return of Culture and Identity in IR Theory* (Boulder, Colo.: Lynne Rienner, 1996).

2. Most important for this article, this is the neorealist conceptualization of international structure. All references to neorealism, unless otherwise noted, are from Waltz, *Theory of International Politics*.

3. Friedrich Kratochwil suggests that this difference in the understanding of structure is because structuralism entered international relations theory not through sociolinguistics, but through microeconomics. Friedrich V. Kratochwil, "Is the Ship of Culture at Sea or Returning?" in Lapid and Kratochwil, *The Return of Culture and Identity*, p. 211.

4. The critical distinction between action and behavior is made by Charles Taylor," Interpretation and the Sciences of Man," in Paul Rabinow and William M. Sullivan, eds., *Interpretive Social Science: A Second Look* (Berkeley: University of California Press, 1987), pp. 33–81.

5. Ronald L. Jepperson, Alexander Wendt, and Peter J.Katzenstein, "Norms, Identity, and Culture in National Security" in Katzenstein, *The Culture of National Security*, p. 54

6. David Dessler, "What's At Stake in the Agent-Structure Debate?" *International Organization*, Vol. 43, No. 3 (summer 1989), pp. 459–460.

7. Arnold Wolfers, *Discord and Collaboration* (Baltimore, Md.: Johns Hopkins University Press, 1962).

8. Alexander Wendt, "Anarchy Is What States Make of It: The Social Construction of Power Politics," *International Organization*, Vol. 46, No. 2 (Spring 1992), 391–425.

9. Elizabeth Kier, for example, shows how the same "objective" external structural arrangement of power cannot account for French military strategy between the two world wars. Elizabeth Kier, "Culture and French Military Doctrine before World War II," in Katzenstein, *The Culture of National Security*, pp. 186–215.

10. The focus on identity does not reflect a lack of appreciation for other elements in the constructivist approach, such as norms, culture, and institutions. Insofar as identities are the most proximate causes of choices, preferences, and action, I concentrate on them, but with the full recognition that identities cannot be understood without a simultaneous account of normative, cultural, and institutional context.

11. Henri Tajfel, *Human Groups and Social Categories: Studies in Social Psychology* (Cambridge, U.K.: Cambridge University Press, 1981), p. 255. Although there are many accounts of the origin of identity, I offer a cognitive explanation because it has minimal a priori expectations, assuming only that identities are needed to reduce complexity to some manageable level.

12. Dana Eyre and Mark Suchman, for example, find that, controlling for rational strategic need, domestic coalition politics, and superpower manipulation, countries in the third world prefer certain weapons systems over others because of their understanding of what it means to be "modern" in the twentieth century. Dana P. Eyre and Mark C. Suchman, "Status, Norms, and the Proliferation of Conventional Weapons: An Institutional Theory Approach," in Katzenstein, *The Culture of National Security*, pp. 73–113. Other examples of empirical research that have linked particular identities to particular sets of preferences are "civilized" identities driving attitudes toward weapons of mass destruction; notions of what constitutes "humanitarian" shaping decisions to intervene in other states; the identity of a "normal" state implying particular Soviet foreign policies; and "antimilitarist" identities in Japan and German shaping their post-World War II foreign policies. These arguments can be found in Richard Price and Nina Tannenwald, "Norms and Deterrence: The Nuclear and Chemical Weapons

Taboos," pp. 114–152; Martha Finnemore, "Constructing Norms of Humanitarian Intervention," pp. 153–185; Robert Herman, "Identity, Norms, and National Security: The Soviet Foreign Policy Revolution and the End of the Cold War," pp. 271–316; and Thomas U. Berger, "Norms, Identity, and National Security in Germany and Japan," pp. 317–356. All of the above are in Katzenstein, *The Culture of National Security*. On identity and mutual intelligibility, see Roxanne Lynn Doty, "The Bounds of 'Race' in International Relations," *Millennium: Journal of International Studies*, Vol. 22, No. 3 (Winter 1993), p. 454.

13. Robert Keohane calls the failure to contextualize interests one of the major weaknesses of mainstream international relations theory. Robert O. Keohane, "International Institutions: Two Approaches," *International Studies Quarterly*, Vol. 32, No. 4 (December 1988), pp. 390–391.

14. Jeffrey Legro, for example, has shown how the preferences of great powers before and during World War II with respect to the use and nonuse of strategic bombing, and chemical and submarine warfare, are unfathomable without first understanding the identities of the military organizations responsible for shaping those preferences. Jeffrey W. Legro, "Culture and Preferences in the International Cooperation Two-Step," *American Political Science Review*, Vol. 90, No. 1 (March 1996), pp. 118–137.

15. See, for example, Tannenwald, "Norms and Deterrence," and Kier, "Culture and French Military Doctrine before World War II," p. 203. for a brilliant account of how social structure enables and impedes the construction of identity and interest, see Jane K. Cowan, "Going Out for Coffee? Contesting the Grounds of Gendered Pleasures in Everyday Sociability," in Peter Loizos and Evthymios Papataxiarchis, eds., *Contested Identities: Gender and Kinship in Modern Greece* (Princeton, N.J.: Princeton University Press, 1991), pp. 196–197.

16. A rare effort in the mainstream literature to break away from this focus on material power is Judith Goldstein and Robert O. Keohane, eds., *Ideas and Foreign Policy* (Ithaca, N.Y.: Cornell University Press, 1993).

17. As R.B.J. Walker has clarified, "To suggest that culture and ideology are crucial for the analysis of world politics is not necessarily to take an idealist position. . . . On the contrary, it is important to recognize that ideas, consciousness, culture, and ideology are bound up with more immediately visible kinds of political, military, and economic power." In R.B.J. Walker, "East Wind, West Wind: Civilizations, Hegemonies, and World Orders," in Walker, ed., *Culture, Ideology, and World Order* (Boulder, Colo.: Westview Press, 1984), p. 3. See also Onuf, *World of Our Making*, p. 64. Joseph Nye's conceptualization of "soft" power could be usefully read through a constructivist interpretation. See Joseph S. Nye, Jr., *Bound to Lead: The Changing Nature of American Power* (New York: Basic Books, 1991), esp. pp. 173–201.

18. Colin Gordon, ed., Power/Knowledge: Selected Interviews and Other Writings, 1972–1997, by Michel *Foucault* (Brighton, Sussex, U.K.: Harvester Press, 1980); Antonio Gramsci, *Selections from the Prison Notebooks*, trans. and ed., Quinton Hoare and Geoffrey Nowell Smith (New York: International Publishers, 1992); and Max Weber, *From Max Weber,* ed., Hans Gerth and C. Wright Mills (New York: Oxford University Press, 1946).

19. Price and Tannenwald show that even power as material as nuclear missiles and chemical artillery had to be understood and interpreted before it had any meaning. In Price and Tannenwald, "Norms and Deterrence." Robert Cox has provided an account of the rise, reproduction, and demise of nineteenth-century British supremacy, and the rise and reproduction of U.S. dominance in the twentieth century through a close reading of the interaction between material and discursive power. Robert W. Cox, "Social Forces, States, and World Orders: Beyond International Relations Theory," *Millennium: Journal of International Studies*, Vol. 10, No. 1 (Spring 1981), pp. 126–155.

20. Onuf sees these reproducible patterns of action as the product of "reflexive self-regulation," whereby agents refer to their own and other's past and anticipated actions in deciding how to act. Onuf, *World of Our Making*, p. 62.

21. Karl W. Deutsch, *Nationalism and Social Communication*: *An Inquiry into the Foundations of Nationality* (New York: MIT Press, 1953), pp. 60–80. Deutsch was a constructivist long ahead of his time to the extent that he argued that individuals could not engage in meaningful action absent some community-wide intersubjectivity. Another work constructivist in essence is Robert Jervis's *The Logic of Images in International Relations* (Princeton, N.J.: Princeton University Press, 1970). Applying Erving Goffmann's self-presentation theory to international politics, Jervis pointed out that state actions, such as gunboat diplomacy, were meaningless unless situated in a larger intersubjective community of diplomatic practice.

22. See Doty, "The Bounds of Race," p. 454; and Carol Cohn, "Sex and Death in the Rational World of Defense Intellectuals," *Signs: Journal of Women in Culture and Society*, Vol. 12, No. 32 (Summer 1987), pp. 687–718.

23. See Richard K. Ashley, "Untying the Sovereign State: A Double Reading of the Anarchy Proble'matique," *Millennium: Journal of International Studies*, Vol. 17, No. 2 (Summer 1988), p. 243, for a discussion of this process.

24. Richard K. Ashley, "The Geopolitics of Geopolitical Space: Toward a Critical Social Theory of International Politics," *Alternatives*, Vol. 12, No. 4 (October–December 1987), p. 409.

25. Richard K. Ashley, "Foreign Policy as Political Performance," *International Studies Notes* (1988), p. 53.

26. Critical constructivism denies this vigorously.

27. R.B.J. Walker, "Realism, Change, and International Political Theory," *International Studies Quarterly*, Vol. 31, No. 1 (March 1987), pp. 76–77.

28. See, for example, John J. Mearsheimer, "The False Promise of International Institutions," *International Security,* Vol. 19, No. 1 (Winter 1994/1995), pp. 5–49, esp. 37–47.

7.2

International Norm Dynamics and Political Change

Martha Finnemore and Kathryn Sikkink

Definitions

There is general agreement on the definition of a norm as a standard of appropriate behavior for actors with a given identity,[1] but a number of related conceptual issues still cause confusion and debate. First, whereas constructivists in political science talk a language of norms, sociologists talk a language of "institutions" to refer to these same behavioral rules. Thus, elsewhere, . . . March and Olsen define "institution" as "a relatively stable collection of practices and rules defining appropriate behavior for specific groups of actors in specific situations."[2] One difference between "norm" and "institution" (in the sociological sense) is aggregation: the norm definition isolates single standards of behavior, whereas institutions emphasize the way in which behavioral rules are structured together and interrelate (a "collection of practices and rules"). The danger in using the norm language is that it can obscure distinct and interrelated elements of social institutions if not used carefully. For example, political scientists tend to slip into discussions of "sovereignty" or "slavery" as if they were norms, when in fact they are (or were) collections of norms and the mix of rules and practices that structure these institutions has varied significantly over time.[3] Used carefully, however, norm language can help to steer scholars toward looking inside social institutions and considering the components of social institutions as well as the way these elements are renegotiated into new arrangements over time to create new patterns of politics.[4]

Scholars across disciplines have recognized different types or categories of norms. The most common distinction is between regulative norms, which order and constrain behavior, and constitutive norms, which create new actors, interests, or categories of action.[5] Some scholars have also discussed a category of norms called evaluative or prescriptive norms, but these have received much less attention and, indeed, are often explicitly omitted from analysis.[6] This lack of attention is puzzling, since it is precisely the prescriptive (or evaluative) quality of "oughtness" that sets norms apart from other kinds of rules. Because norms involve standards of "appropriate" or "proper" behavior, both the intersubjective and the evaluative dimensions are inescapable when discussing norms. We only know what is appropriate by reference to the judgments of a community or a society. We recognize norm-breaking behavior because it generates disapproval or stigma and norm conforming behavior either because it produces praise, or, in the case of a highly internalized norm, because it is so taken for granted that it provokes no reaction whatsoever.[7] Thus, James Fearon argues that social norms take the generic form "Good people do (or do not do) X in situations A, B, C . . . " because "we typically do not consider a rule of conduct to be a social norm unless a shared moral assessment is attached to its observance or non-observance."[8]

One logical corollary to the prescriptive quality of norms is that, by definition, there are no bad norms from the vantage point of those who promote the norm. Norms most of us would consider "bad"—norms about racial superiority, divine right, imperialism—were once powerful because some groups believed in the appropriateness (that is, the "goodness") of the norm, and others either accepted it as obvious or inevitable or had no choice but to accept it. Slaveholders and many non-slaveholders believed that slavery was appropriate behavior; without that belief, the institution of slavery would not have been possible.

Given this discussion, we can begin to answer the essential research question: how do we know a norm when we see one? We can only have indirect evidence of norms just as we can only have indirect evidence of most other motivations for political action (interests or threats, for example). However, because norms by definition embody a quality of "oughtness" and shared moral assessment, norms prompt justifications for

Source: Martha Finnemore and Kathryn Sikkink "International Norm Dynamics and Political Change," *International Organization* 52(4): (Autumn, 1998), 887–917 © 1998 by the IO Foundation and the Massachusetts Institute of Technology.

action and leave an extensive trail of communication among actors that we can study. For example, the United States' explanations about why it feels compelled to continue using land mines in South Korea reveal that it recognizes the emerging norm against the use of such mines. If not for the norm, there would be no need to mention, explain, or justify the use of mines in Korea at all. Note that we separate norm existence or strength from actual behavioral change in our operationalization. Because one central question of norms research is the effect of norms on state behavior, it is important to operationalize a norm in a way that is distinct from the state or nonstate behavior it is designed to explain.[9]

Norms as shared assessments raise the question of how many actors must share the assessment before we call it a norm. In part this is a question of empirical domain. Norms may be regional, for example, but not global. Even within a community, norms are "continuous, rather than dichotomous, entities. . . . [They] come in varying strengths" with different norms commanding different levels of agreement.[10] We argue that one way to understand the dynamics of this agreement process is by examining what we call the "life cycle" of norms. We show how agreement among a critical mass of actors on some emergent norm can create a tipping point after which agreement becomes widespread in many empirical cases, and we provide some suggestions about common features of "critical mass."

Connecting Domestic and International Norms

In this [reading] we are concerned with international or regional norms that set standards for the appropriate behavior of states.[11] Domestic norms, however, are deeply entwined with the workings of international norms. Many international norms began as domestic norms and become international through the efforts of entrepreneurs of various kinds. Women's suffrage, for example, began as a demand for domestic change within a handful of countries and eventually became an international norm.[12] In addition, international norms must always work their influence through the filter of domestic structures and domestic norms, which can produce important variations in compliance and interpretation of these norms.[13] Even in situations where it might appear at first glance that international norms simply trump domestic norms, what we often see is a process by which domestic "norm entrepreneurs" advocating a minority position use international norms to strengthen their position in domestic debates. In other words, there is a two-level norm game occurring in which the domestic and the international norm tables are increasingly linked.[14] We argue later, however, that all these domestic influences are strongest at the early stage of a norm's life cycle, and domestic influences lessen significantly once a norm has become institutionalized in the international system.

Recent work in U.S. legal circles also suggests that there is more similarity in the way norms and law work domestically and internationally than IR scholars have thought. IR scholars have generally assumed that the existence of a coercive state able to enforce laws made domestic order very different from international order. A prominent group of legal scholars at the University of Chicago, however, now argue that, even within a domestic setting, making successful law and policy requires an understanding of the pervasive influence of social norms of behavior. This is a particularly compelling insight for IR scholars, since the international system is characterized by law and norms operating without direct punitive capacity. The processes through which these legal scholars claim that norms work domestically—involving norm entrepreneurs, imitation, "norm cascades," and "norm bandwagons"—are entirely consistent with the research done on norms by scholars in IR and suggest that IR norms research might also learn from domestic analogies. For example, the normative and legal process through which Southern gentlemen in the United States stopped dueling, examined by Lawrence Lessig, may be relevant for thinking about what kinds of norms and rules could lead to a decrease in conflict in the international system.[15]

Stability Versus Change

Macro-level theorizing has provided good explanations of the way norms produce social order and stability. Norms channel and regularize behavior; they often limit the range of choice and constrain actions.[16] From a constructivist perspective, international structure is determined by the international distribution of ideas.[17] Shared ideas, expectations, and beliefs about appropriate behavior are what give the world structure, order, and stability. The problem for constructivists thus becomes the same problem facing realists—explaining change. In an ideational international structure, idea shifts and norm shifts are the main vehicles for system transformation. Norm shifts are to the ideational theorist what changes in the balance of power are to the realist.

John Ruggie argues in this issue that "having identified the possibility of system transformation in the macro level, corresponding micro practices that may have transformative effects must be identified and inventoried." The following section is an attempt to identify these practices.

Evolution and Influence of Norms

In this section we advance some propositions about (1) the origins or emergence of international norms, (2) the processes through which norms influence state and non state behavior, and (3) which norms will matter and under what conditions. We illustrate the arguments with material drawn from two major issue areas: women's rights, especially suffrage, and laws of war. International norms about women's rights often came into direct competition with strongly held domestic norms, and, typically, there was no self-evident state "interest" in the promotion of such norms. Although topics related to gender and women have been absent from the pages of *International Organization*,[18] the suffrage campaign led to the formal political participation of half of the world's population and therefore seems worthy of study. Laws of war allow us to discuss the impact of norms where we might least expect it—the traditional security field, where such norms limit state discretion in an area perceived as essential to national sovereignty and security field, where such norms limit state discretion in an area perceived as essential to national sovereignty and security.

The Norm "Life Cycle"

Norm influence may be understood as a three-stage process. As shown in Figure 7.1, the first stage is "norm emergence"; the second stage involves broad norm acceptance, which we term, following Cass Sunstein,[19] a "norm cascade"; and the third stage involves internalization. The first two stages are divided by a threshold or "tipping" point, at which a critical mass of relevant state actors adopt the norm. This pattern of norm influence has been found independently in work on social norms in U.S. legal theory, quantitative research by sociology's institutionalists or "world polity" theorists, and various scholars of norms in IR.[20] The pattern is important for researchers to understand because different social processes and logics of action may be involved at different stages in a norm's "life cycle." Thus, theoretical debates about the degree to which norm-based behavior is driven by choice or habit, specification issues about the costs of norm-violation or benefits from norm adherence, and related research issues often turn out to hinge on the stage of the norm's evolution one examines. Change at each stage, we argue, is characterized by different actors, motives, and mechanisms of influence.

The characteristic mechanism of the first stage, norm emergence, is persuasion by norm entrepreneurs. Norm entrepreneurs attempt to convince a critical mass of states (norm leaders) to embrace new norms. The second stage is characterized more by a dynamic of imitation as the norm leaders attempt to socialize other states to become norm followers. The exact motivation for this second stage where the norm "cascades" through the rest of the population (in this case, of states) may vary, but we argue that a combination of pressure for conformity, desire to enhance international legitimation, and the desire of state leaders to enhance their self-esteem facilitate norm cascades. At the far end of the norm cascade, norm internalization occurs; norms acquire a taken-for-granted quality and are no longer a matter of broad public debate. For example, few people today discuss whether women should be allowed to vote, whether slavery is useful, or whether medical personnel should be granted immunity during war. Completion of the "life cycle" is not an inevitable process. Many emergent norms fail to reach a tipping point, and later we offer arguments about which norms are more likely to succeed. Internalized or cascading

Figure 7.1 Norm life cycle

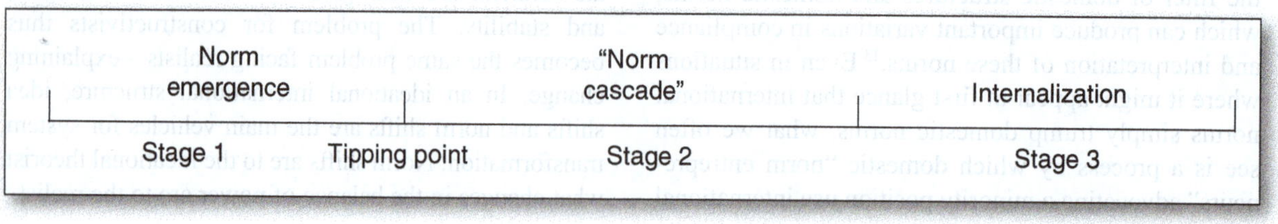

norms may eventually become the prevailing standard of appropriateness against which new norms emerge and compete for support. . . .

Stage 1: Origins or emergence of norms. Although little theoretical work has focused exclusively on the process of "norm building," the accounts of norm origins in most studies stress human agency, indeterminacy, chance occurrences, and favorable events, using process tracing or genealogy as a method.[21] Generalizing from these accounts, two elements seem common in the successful creation of most new norms: norm entrepreneurs and organizational platforms from which entrepreneurs act.

NORM ENTREPRENEURS. Norms do not appear out of thin air; they are actively built by agents having strong notions about appropriate or desirable behavior in their community. Prevailing norms that medical personnel and those wounded in war be treated as neutrals and noncombatants are clearly traceable to the efforts of one man, a Genevese Swiss banker named Henry Dunant. Dunant had a transformative personal experience at the battle of Solferino in 1859 and helped found an organization to promote this cause (what became the International Committee of the Red Cross) through an international treaty (the first Geneva Convention). The international campaign for women's suffrage was similarly indebted to the initial leadership of such norm entrepreneurs as Elizabeth Cady Stanton and Susan B. Anthony in the United States and Millicent Garrett Fawcett and Emmeline Pankhurst in England. Both of these cases are consistent with the description Ethan Nadelmann gives of "transnational moral entrepreneurs" who engage in "moral proselytism."[22] Legal theorist Lessig uses the term "meaning managers" or "meaning architects" to describe the same kind of agency in the process of creating norms and larger contexts of social meaning.[23]

Norm entrepreneurs are critical for norm emergence because they call attention to issues or even "create" issues by using language that names, interprets, and dramatizes them. Social movement theorists refer to this reinterpretation or renaming process as "framing."[24] The construction of cognitive frames is an essential component of norm entrepreneurs' political strategies, since, when they are successful, the new frames resonate with broader public understandings and are adopted as new ways of talking about and understanding issues. In constructing their frames, norm entrepreneurs face firmly embedded alternative norms and frames that create alternative perceptions of both appropriateness and interest. In the case of the Red Cross, Dunant and his colleagues had to persuade military commanders not to treat valuable medical personnel and resources they captured as spoils of war, to be treated as they saw fit. In the case of women's suffrage and later women's rights, norm entrepreneurs encountered alternative norms about women's interests and the appropriate role for women. In other words, new norms never enter a normative vacuum but instead emerge in a highly contested normative space where they must compete with other norms and perceptions of interest.

This normative contestation has important implications for our understandings of the ways in which a "logic of appropriateness" relates to norms.[25] Efforts to promote a new norm take place within the standards of "appropriateness" defined by prior norms. To challenge existing logics of appropriateness, activists may need to be explicitly "inappropriate." Suffragettes chained themselves to fences, went on hunger strikes, broke windows of government buildings, and refused to pay taxes as ways of protesting their exclusion from political participation. Deliberately inappropriate acts (such as organized civil disobedience), especially those entailing social ostracism or legal punishment, can be powerful tools for norm entrepreneurs seeking to send a message and frame an issue. Thus, at this emergent stage of a norm's life cycle, invoking a logic of appropriateness to explain behavior is complicated by the fact that standards of appropriateness are precisely what is being contested.

Given the costs of inappropriate action and many of the persuasive tools they use, one has to wonder what could possibly motivate norm entrepreneurs (see Table 7.1). Obviously the answer varies with the norm and the entrepreneur, but for many of the social norms of interest to political scientists, it is very difficult to explain the motivations of norm entrepreneurs without reference to empathy, altruism, and ideational commitment. Empathy exists when actors have the capacity for participating in another's feelings or ideas. Such empathy may lead to empathetic interdependence, where actors "are interested in the welfare of others for its own sake, even if this has no effect on their own material well-being or security."[26] Altruism exists when actors actually take "action designed to benefit another even at the risk of significant harm to the actor's own well-being."[27] Kristen Monroe argues that the essence or "heart" of altruism is a "shared perception of common humanity. . . . A very simple but deeply felt recognition that we all share certain characteristics and are entitled to certain rights, merely by virtue of our common humanity."[28] Ideational

Table 7.1 Stages of norms

	Stage 1 Norm emergence	Stage 2 Norm cascade	Stage 3 Internationalization
Actors	Norm entrepreneurs with organization platforms	States, international organization networks	Law, professions bureaucracy
Motives	Altruism, empathy, ideational, commitment	Legitimacy, reputation, esteem	Conformity
Dominant Mechanisms	Persuasion	Socialization, institutionalization, demonstration	Habit, institutionalization

commitment is the main motivation when entrepreneurs promote norms or ideas because they believe in the ideals and values embodied in the norms, even though the pursuit of the norms may have no effect on their well-being.

Of course, many norm entrepreneurs do not so much act against their interests as they act in accordance with a redefined understanding of their interests. Suffragists, for example, were working on behalf of a coherent conception of women's political interests, but it was not an understanding initially shared by the great majority of women in the world. Women had to be persuaded that it was indeed in their interests to pursue suffrage. Similarly, the Red Cross had to persuade military leaders that protecting the wounded was compatible with their war aims.

ORGANIZATIONAL PLATFORMS. All norm promoters at the international level need some kind of organizational platform from and through which they promote their norms. Sometimes these platforms are constructed specifically for the purpose of promoting the norm, as are many nongovernmental organizations (NGOs) (such as Greenpeace, the Red Cross, and Transafrica) and the larger transnational advocacy networks of which these NGOs become a part (such as those promoting human rights, environmental norms, and a ban on land mines or those that opposed apartheid in South Africa).[29] Often, however, entrepreneurs work from standing international organizations that have purposes and agendas other than simply promoting one specific norm. Those other agendas may shape the content of norms promoted by the organization significantly.[30] The structure of the World Bank has been amply documented to effect the kinds of development norms promulgated from that institution; its organizational structure, the professions from which it recruits, and its relationship with member states and private finance all filter the kinds of norms emerging from it.[31] The UN, similarly, has distinctive structural features that influence the kinds of norms it promulgates about such matters as decolonization, sovereignty, and humanitarian relief.[32] The tripartite structure of the International Labor Organization, which includes labor and business as well as states, strongly influences the kinds of norms it promotes and the ways it promotes them.[33]

One prominent feature of modern organizations and an important source of influence for international organizations in particular is their use of expertise and information to change the behavior of other actors. Expertise, in turn, usually resides in professionals, and a number of empirical studies document the ways that professional training of bureaucrats in these organizations helps or blocks the promotion of new norms within standing organizations. Peter Haas's study of the cleanup of the Mediterranean shows how ecologists were successful in promoting their norms over others' in part because they were able to persuade governments to create new agencies to deal with the cleanup and to staff those posts with like-minded ecologists. Studies of the World Bank similarly document a strong role for professional training in filtering the norms that the bank promotes. In this case, the inability to quantify many costs and benefits associated with antipoverty and basic human needs norms created resistance among the many economists staffing the bank, because projects promoting these norms could not be justified on the basis of "good economics."[34]

Whatever their platform, norm entrepreneurs and the organizations they inhabit usually need to secure the support of state actors to endorse their norms and make norm socialization a part of their agenda, and different organizational platforms provide different kinds of tools for entrepreneurs to do this.[35] International organizations like the UN and the World Bank, though not tailored to norm promotion, may have the advantage of resources and leverage over weak or developing states they seek to convert to their normative convictions. Networks of NGOs and intergovernmental organizations (IGOs) dealing with powerful states, however, are rarely able to "coerce" agreement to a norm—they must persuade. They must take what is seen as natural or appropriate and convert it into something perceived as wrong or inappropriate. This process is not necessarily or entirely in the realm of reason, though facts and information may be marshaled to support claims. Affect, empathy, and principled or moral beliefs may also be deeply involved, since the ultimate goal is not to challenge the "truth" of something, but to challenge whether it is good, appropriate, and deserving of praise.[36] In these cases, what the organizational network provides is information and access to important audiences for that information, especially media and decision maker.

In most cases, for an emergent norm to reach a threshold and move toward the second stage, it must become institutionalized in specific sets of international rules and organizations.[37] Since 1948, emergent norms have increasingly become institutionalized in international law, in the rules of multilateral organizations, and in bilateral foreign policies. Such institutionalization contributes strongly to the possibility for a norm cascade both by clarifying what, exactly, the norm is and what constitutes violation (often a matter of some disagreement among actors) and by spelling out specific procedures by which norm leaders coordinate disapproval and sanctions for norm breaking. Institutionalization of norms about biological and chemical weapons, for example, has been essential to coordinating the near universal sanctions on Iraq following the Gulf War and has enabled states to coordinate an invasive inspections regime aimed at securing compliance with those norms. Institutionalization is not a necessary condition for a norm cascade, however, and institutionalization may follow, rather than precede, the initiation of a norm cascade. Women's suffrage was not institutionalized in international rules or organizations prior to the beginning of the norm cascade. The first intergovernmental agency created to deal with women's issues was a regional organization, the Inter-American Commission of Women (CIM), established in 1928. Although scholars locate the tipping point on women's suffrage around 1930, the norm cascaded in similar ways both in Latin America (where it was institutionalized) and in other places around the world where women's rights were not similarly institutionalized.

TIPPING OR THRESHOLD POINTS. After norm entrepreneurs have persuaded a critical mass of states to become norm leaders and adopt new norms, we can say the norm reaches a threshold or tipping point. Although scholars have provided convincing quantitative empirical support for the idea of a norm tipping point and norm cascades, they have not yet provided a theoretical account for why norm tipping occurs, nor criteria for specifying *a priori* where, when, and how we would expect it. We propose two tentative hypotheses about what constitutes a "critical mass" and when and where to expect norm tipping. First, although it is not possible to predict exactly how many states must accept a norm to "tip" the process, because states are not equal when it comes to normative weight, empirical studies suggest that norm tipping rarely occurs before one-third of the total states in the system adopt the norm.[38] In the case of women's suffrage, Francisco Ramirez, Yasemin Soysal, and Suzanne Shanahan place the threshold point in 1930, when twenty states (or approximately one-third of the total states in the system at that time) had accepted women's suffrage.[39] In case of land mines, by May 1997 the number of states supporting the ban on anti-personnel land mines reached 60, or approximately one-third of the total states in the system. After that point, a norm cascade occurred, and 124 states ratified the Ottawa land mine treaty in December 1997.

It also matters which states adopt the norm. Some states are critical to a norm's adoption; others are less so. What constitutes a "critical state" will vary from issue to issue, but one criterion is that critical states are those without which the achievement of the substantive norm goal is compromised. Thus, in the case of land mines, a state that did not produce or use land mines would not have been a critical state. By contrast, the decision in mid-1997 by France and Great Britain, both land mines producers, to support the treaty could well have contributed to the norm cascade that happened in late 1997.[40] Securing support of those same two states was simply essential to producing the norm cascade and near universal acceptance of the first Geneva Convention in Europe 130 years earlier. States may also be "critical" because they have a certain moral stature. For example, the decision of South Africa under Nelson Mandela to support the land mine treaty was very influential, especially with other states in Africa but also globally.[41] Although cascades require support from some critical states, unanimity among them is not essential. For example, after initially supporting the norm of banning land mines, the United States refused to support the treaty, but the norm cascaded nevertheless.

Stage 2: Norm cascades. Up to the tipping point, little normative change occurs without significant domestic movements supporting such change. After the tipping point has been reached, however, a different dynamic begins. More countries begin to adopt new norms more rapidly even without domestic pressure for such change. Empirical studies suggest that, at this point, often an international or regional demonstration effect or "contagion" occurs in which international and transnational norm influences become more important than domestic politics for effecting norm change.[42] Contagion, however, is too passive a metaphor; we argue that the primary mechanism for promoting norm cascades is an active process of international socialization intended to induce norm breakers to become norm followers.[43] Kenneth Waltz suggested some of the ways socialization in occurs: emulation (of heroes), praise (for behavior that conforms to group norms), and ridicule (for deviation).[44] In the context of international politics, socialization involves diplomatic praise or censure, either bilateral or multilateral, which is reinforced by material sanctions and incentives. States, however, are not the only agents of socialization. Networks of norm entrepreneurs and international organizations also act as agents of socialization by pressuring targeted actors to adopt new policies and laws and to ratify treaties and by monitoring compliance with international standards. The International Committee of the Red Cross (ICRC) certainly did not disappear with the signing of the first Geneva Convention. Instead, the ICRC became its chief socializing agent, helping states to teach the new rules of war to their soldiers, collecting information about violations, and publicizing them to pressure violators to conform.

Socialization is thus the dominant mechanism of a norm cascade—the mechanism through which norm leaders persuade others to adhere—but what makes socialization work? What are the motives that induce states opposed to the norm to adhere and adhere quickly? We argue that states comply with norms in stage 2 for reasons that relate to their identities as members of an international society. Recognition that state identity fundamentally shapes state behavior, and that state identity is, in turn, shaped by the cultural-institutional context within which states act, has been an important contribution of recent norms research.[45] James Fearon similarly argues that one's identity is as a member of a particular social category, and part of the definition of that category is that all members follow certain norms.[46] What happens at the tipping point is that enough states and enough critical states endorse the new norm to redefine appropriate behavior for the identity called "state" or some relevant subset of states (such as a "liberal" state or a European state).

To the degree that states and state elites fashion a political self or identity in relation to the international community, the concept of socialization suggests that the cumulative effect of many countries in a region adopting new norms "may be analogous to 'peer pressure' among countries."[47] Three possible motivations for responding to such "peer pressure" are legitimation, conformity, and esteem.

Scholars have long understood that legitimation is important for states and have recognized the role of international sources of legitimation in shaping state behavior. Claude, for example, described international organizations as "custodians of the seals of international approval and disapproval," and emphasized their crucial role in establishing and assuring adherence to international norms.[48] Certainly there are costs that come with being labeled a "rogue state" in international interactions, since this entails loss of reputation, trust, and credibility, the presence of which have been amply documented to contribute to Pareto-improving effects from interstate interaction. We argue, though, that states also care about international legitimation because it has become an essential contributor to perceptions of domestic legitimacy held by a state's own citizens. Domestic legitimacy is the belief that existing political institutions are better than other alternatives and therefore deserve obedience.[49] Increasingly, citizens make judgments about whether their government is better than alternatives by looking at those alternatives (in the international and regional arena) and by seeing what other people and countries say about their country. Domestic legitimation is obviously important because it promotes compliance with government rules and laws; ruling by force alone is almost impossible. Thus, international legitimation is important insofar as it reflects back on a government's domestic basis of legitimation and consent and thus ultimately on its ability to stay in power. This dynamic was part of the explanation for regime transitions in South Africa, Latin America, and southern Europe.[50]

Conformity and esteem similarly involve evaluative relationships between states and their state "peers." Conformity involves what Robert Axelrod refers to as "social proof"—states comply with norms to demonstrate that they have adapted to the social environment—that they "belong." "By conforming to the actions of those around us, we fulfill a psychological need to be part of a group."[51] Esteem is related to both conformity and legitimacy, but it goes deeper, since it suggests that leaders of states sometimes follow norms because they want others to think well of them, and they want to think well of themselves.[52] Social norms are sustained, in part, by "feelings of embarrassment, anxiety, guilt, and shame that a person suffers at the prospect of violating them."[53] Fearon has argued that identity is based on those aspects of the self in which an individual has special pride or from which an individual gains self-esteem.[54] Thus, the desire to gain or defend one's pride or esteem can explain norm following. In this sense, states care about following norms associated with liberalism because being "liberal states" is part of their identity in the sense of something they take pride in or from which they gain self-esteem. . . .

Stage 3: Internalization. At the extreme of a norm cascade, norms may become so widely accepted that they are internalized by actors and achieve a "taken-for-granted" quality that makes conformance with the norm almost automatic. For this reason, internalized norms can be both extremely powerful (because behavior according to the norm is not questioned) and hard to discern (because actors do not seriously consider or discuss whether to conform). Precisely because they are not controversial, however, these norms are often not the centerpiece of political debate and for that reason tend to be ignored by political scientists. Institutionalists in sociology, however, have made many of these most internalized norms the centerpiece of their research program and have done us the service of problematizing and "denaturalizing" many of the most prominent Western norms that we take for granted—such as those about market exchange, sovereignty, and individualism. Instead of trying to explain variation in state behavior, these scholars are puzzled by the degree of similarity or "isomorphism" among states and societies and how those similarities have increased in recent years. Their explanations for these similarities point to past norm cascades leading to states taking up new responsibilities or endowing individuals with new rights as a matter of course.[55]

Professions often serve as powerful and pervasive agents working to internalize norms among their members. Professional training does more than simply transfer technical knowledge; it actively socializes people to value certain things above others. Doctors are trained to value life above all else. Soldiers are trained to sacrifice life for certain strategic goals. Economists, ecologists, and lawyers all carry different normative biases systematically instilled by their professional training. As state bureaucracies and international organizations have become more and more professionalized over the twentieth century, we should expect to see policy increasingly reflecting the normative biases of the professions that staff decision-making agencies.[56] A number of empirical studies have already documented a role for highly internalized norms held by professionals determining policy. In addition to the role of economists at the World Bank mentioned earlier, Anne-Marie Burley's work shows a crucial role for legal professional norms in creating the post-World War II political order, and her work with Walter Mattli shows their importance in the European Union.[57]

Another powerful and related mechanism contributing to the consolidation and universalization of norms after a norm cascade may be iterated behavior and habit. Political scientists have understood the power of these mechanisms for years but have not connected them theoretically to norms and social construction debates. The core of the neofunctionalist argument about integration in Europe, after all, was that frequent interactions among people involving joint work on technical tasks would ultimately create predictability, stability, and habits of trust. As trust became habitual, it would become internalized and internalized trust would, in turn, change affect among the participants. Changed affect meant changed identity and changed norms as empathy and identification with others shifted. Thus, the engine of integration was indirect and evolutionary. Diplomatic tools such as confidence-building measures and track 2 diplomacy may follow a similar logic. Generalized, this argument suggests that routes to normative change may be similarly indirect and evolutionary: procedural changes that create new political processes can lead to gradual and inadvertent normative, ideational, and political convergence.[58]

Notes

1. See Katzenstein 1996b, 5; Finnemore 1996a, 22; and Klotz 1995b.
2. March and Olsen, this issue.
3. Krasner 1984, 1988, 1993; Thomson 1994; Strang 1991; Ruggie 1993; and Spruyt 1994.
4. For an excellent discussion of these issues, see Jepperson 1991.
5. Ruggie, this issue; Searle 1995; Katzenstein 1996b; and Wendt forthcoming.
6. Gelpi 1997. See, for example, the treatment in Katzenstein 1996b, 5, fnl2.
7. For a particularly good discussion of the way in which conventions produce judgments of social "oughtness" and morality, see Sugden 1989. See also Elster 1989a,c; and Sunstein 1997.

8. Fearon 1997, 25, fnl8.
9. Legro 1997.
10. Ibid., 33.
11. For analyses of domestic norms and their influence on domestic politics, see Kier 1997; Johnston 1995a; Katzenstein 1996a, 1993; and Berger 1998. For a critique of this emphasis on international as opposed to domestic norms, see Checkel 1998.
12. Dubois 1994.
13. See Risse-Kappen 1995b; and Risse, Ropp, and Sikkink forthcoming.
14. See Putnam 1988; and Evans, Jacobson, and Putnam 1993.
15. See Sunstein 1997; and Lessig 1995. For an interesting journalist's overview, see Rosen 1997.
16. See Katzenstein 1996a, 3; and Sunstein 1997, 40. Even Waltz, in his discussion of socialization, says that norms encourage conformity and that "socialization reduces variety." Waltz 1979, 76.
17. Wendt 1992 and forthcoming.
18. In its first fifty years *International Organization* has published only one article on any issue related to gender or women, Craig Murphy's review essay on gender and international relations; Murphy 1996. We suggest that there may have been a well-internalized norm (with a taken-for-granted quality) that research on gender and women did not constitute an appropriate topic for international relations scholarship. Note that as with any well-internalized norm, this does not imply that the editors self-consciously rejected articles on gender-related topics. To the contrary, we know a strong norm is in effect when it does not occur to authors to write on the topic or submit articles because it is not generally understood as an appropriate topic.
19. Sunstein 1997.
20. See Sunstein 1997; Meyer and Hannan 1979; Bergesen 1980; Thomas et al. 1987; and Finnemore 1993.
21. See Kowert and Legro 1996; and Price 1995.
22. Nadelmann 1990.
23. Lessig 1995.
24. David Snow has called this strategic activity *frame alignment*—"by rendering events or occurrences meaningful, frames function to organize experience and guide action, whether individual or collective." Snow et al. 1986, 464.
25. March and Olsen 1989, and this issue.
26. See Keohane 1984, chap. 7; Keohane 1990a; and Mansbridge 1990.
27. Monroe 1996. See also Oliner and Oliner 1988.
28. Monroe 1996, 206.
29. See Sikkink 1993a; Keck and Sikkink 1998; Klotz 1995a,b; and Price 1997.
30. See Strang and Chang 1993; Finnemore 1996a; Adler 1992; and Ikenberry and Kupchan 1990.
31. See Ascher 1983; Miller-Adams 1997; Wade 1996b; and Finnemore 1996a.
32. See Barnett 1995, 1997; McNeely 1995; and Weiss and Pasic 1997.
33. Strang and Chang 1993.
34. See Ascher 1983; Miller-Adams 1997; and Finnemore 1996a.
35. Paul Wapner points out that there are exceptions to the centrality of the state in these processes in environmental politics where activists lobby polluting corporations directly to bring about change (for example, the campaign against McDonald's clamshell containers for its sandwiches). Wapner 1996.
36. Fearon 1997.
37. See Goldstein and Keohane 1993b; and Katzenstein 1996b.
38. International law has had to wrestle with this problem repeatedly, since many modern international norms are embodied in treaties. Treaties implicitly recognize this concept of critical mass by specifying that a particular number of countries must ratify for the treaty to enter into force. Where treaties exist, the entry into force of the treaty may be a useful proxy for the critical mass necessary to say that a norm exists.
39. Ramirez, Soysal, and Shanahan 1997.
40. Price 1998.
41. Ibid.
42. See Ramirez, Soysal, and Shanahan 1997; and Whitehead 1996.
43. Socialization involves the "induction of new members . . . into the ways of behavior that are preferred in a society." Barnes, Carter, and Skidmore 1980, 35. Socialization can thus be seen as a mechanism through which new states are induced to change their behavior by adopting those norms preferred by an international society of states. See also Risse, Ropp, and Sikkink, forthcoming.
44. Waltz 1979, 75–76.
45. Katzenstein 1996b.
46. Fearon 1997.
47. Ramirez, Soysal, and Shanahan 1997.
48. Claude 1966. For more contemporary arguments that international organizations continue to play this role, see Barnett 1997, 1995; and Barnett and Finnemore 1997.
49. Linz 1978.
50. See Klotz 1995a,b; and Whitehead 1996.
51. Axelrod 1986, 1105.
52. Fearon 1997.
53. Elster 1989c.
54. Fearon 1997, 23.
55. See Bergesen 1980; Thomas et al. 1987; Scott and Meyer 1994; McNeely 1995; Meyer et al. 1997; and Finnemore 1996b.
56. See Haas 1989; Ascher 1983; Adler 1992; Miller-Adams 1997; Finnemore 1995; and Bamett and Finnemore 1997.
57. See Burley 1993; and Burley and Mattli 1993. These empirical findings are consistent with theoretical arguments made by DiMaggio and Powell 1983.
58. See also Rosenau 1986.

7.3

Stigmatizing the Bomb

Origins of the Nuclear Taboo

Nina Tannenwald

In 1958 Lt. Gen. James Gavin, a principal promoter in the U.S. military of the development of tactical nuclear weapons, wrote, "Nuclear weapons will become conventional for several reasons, among them cost, effectiveness against enemy weapons, and ease of handling."[1] Indeed, during the 1950s numerous U.S. leaders fully expected that a nuclear weapon would become "just another weapon." . . .

These leaders were articulating a view with a long tradition in the history of weapons and warfare: a weapon once introduced inevitably comes to be widely accepted as legitimate. In reality, however, nuclear weapons have come to be defined as abhorrent and unacceptable weapons of mass destruction, with a taboo on their use. This taboo is associated with a widespread revulsion toward nuclear weapons and broadly held inhibitions on their use. . . .

Evidence suggests that the taboo has helped to constrain resort to the use of nuclear weapons since 1945 both by reinforcing deterrence and by inducing restraint even in cases where deterrence did not operate.[2]

What gave rise to this taboo? . . . Within the field of international relations, there has been little systematic analysis of the nuclear taboo. Traditional realists, of course, would be skeptical of the existence of a taboo, tending to see it as largely indistinguishable from prudential behavior. To the extent that a tradition of nonuse existed, it would reflect the interests of the most powerful (nuclear) states.[3] Rationalist approaches, which are often sympathetic to norms, could easily incorporate the existence of a taboo.[4] They would emphasize the uniquely destructive nature of nuclear weapons, the impossibility of defense, and therefore the (obvious) rationality of having a social convention on their use.[5]

As I show in this [reading], although there is some truth to these explanations, they are inadequate. The nuclear taboo was pursued in part against the preferences of the United States, which, for the first part of the nuclear era, opposed creation of a taboo because it would deny the self-proclaimed right of the United States to rely on nuclear weapons for its security. I argue for a broader explanation that emphasizes the role of a global antinuclear weapons movement and nonnuclear states, as well as Cold War power politics, in the development of the taboo.[6] The model of norm creation here highlights the role of antinuclear discourse and politics in the creation of the taboo. Although rationalist variables are important, the taboo cannot be explained simply as the straightforward result of rational adaptation to strategic circumstances.

The larger questions are: where do global norms come from? How and why do they develop? And how are they maintained, disseminated, and strengthened? The case of the nuclear taboo is important theoretically because it challenges conventional views that international norms, especially in the security area, are created mainly by and for the powerful. The case is important practically because it illuminates an important source of restraint on the use of nuclear weapons.

In this [reading] I locate the origins of the nuclear taboo after 1945 in a set of domestic and international factors and trace its subsequent development. . . . Ideally, a full account would require an examination of how the taboo came to be accepted and internalized in the decisionmaking of other countries as well. The central role of the United States in the development of the taboo, however, makes it a particularly significant case.

The [reading] proceeds in [three] parts. First, I lay out the main characteristics of the nuclear taboo and the core of my argument. Second, taking a process-tracing approach, I analyze the evolution of the nuclear taboo and identify the main factors and mechanisms that account for this development. . . . In conclusion, I summarize some implications of the argument for theory and policy.

Source: Nina Tannewald. "Stigmatizing the Bomb: Origins of the Nuclear Taboo," in *International Security* 29(4): 5–14, 33–34, and 46–48.

The Nuclear Taboo: A De Facto Normative Prohibition

In this section I define the nuclear taboo, describe its main features, and outline the process by which it arose.

Characteristics of the Nuclear Taboo

The nuclear taboo refers to a de facto prohibition against the first use of nuclear weapons. The taboo is not the behavior (of nonuse) itself but rather the normative belief about the behavior. By "norm," I mean a standard of right or wrong, a prescription or proscription for behavior "for a given identity,"[7] A taboo is a particularly forceful kind of normative prohibition that is concerned with the protection of individuals and societies from behavior that is defined or perceived to be dangerous. It typically refers to something that is not done, not said, or not touched.[8]

What makes the prohibition against using nuclear weapons a taboo rather than simply a norm? There are two elements to a taboo: its objective characteristics and its intersubjective, phenomenological aspect, that is, the meaning it has for people. Objectively, the nuclear taboo exhibits many, although not all, of the characteristics associated with taboos: it is a prohibition, it refers to danger, and it involves expectations of awful or uncertain consequences or sanctions if violated. Further, it is also a "bright line" norm: once the threshold between use and nonuse is crossed, one is immediately in a new world with all the unimaginable consequences that could follow.[9] Finally, the nuclear taboo counteracts the deep attraction that nuclear weapons present to national leaders as the "ultimate weapon" and reminds them of the danger that lurks behind such weapons.[10]

Several aspects of the nuclear prohibition, however, are decidedly unlike those of other taboos: it is not legalized (many taboos in modern society are), and it does not entirely prohibit the acquisition of taboo objects or overt preparations for their use (unlike, say, the Hindu taboo on eating beef). Under the 1968 Nuclear Nonproliferation Treaty (NPT), the vast majority of states are prohibited from acquiring or possessing nuclear weapons. The five declared nuclear states (Britain, China, France, Russia, and the United States), however, are allowed by the treaty to possess nuclear weapons temporarily pending complete disarmament and to prepare to use them.[11] Thus the nuclear prohibition departs in some ways from the objective characteristics of a taboo.

The nuclear taboo, however, also has an intersubjective or a phenomenological aspect: it is a taboo because people believe it to be. Political and military leaders themselves began using the term to refer to this normative perception starting in the early 1950s, even when, objectively, a tradition of nonuse hardly existed. If actors see the use of nuclear weapons as if it were a taboo, as their rhetoric suggests, then this could affect their choices and behavior. In the words of sociologists William and Dorothy Thomas, "If men define situations as real, they are real in their consequences."[12] This subjective (and intersubjective) sense of "taboo-ness" is one of the factors that makes the tradition of nuclear nonuse a taboo rather than simply a norm. . . .

As noted earlier, the taboo is a de facto, not a legal, norm. There is no explicit international legal prohibition on the use of nuclear weapons such as exists for, say, chemical weapons. . . .

Nevertheless, legal use has been gradually chipped away through incremental restrictions—an array of treaties and regimes that together circumscribe the realm of legitimate nuclear use and restrict freedom of action with respect to nuclear weapons. These agreements include nuclear weapons-free zones, bilateral and multilateral arms control agreements, and negative security assurances (i.e., political declarations by the nuclear powers that they will not use nuclear weapons against nonnuclear states that are members of the NPT). Together, these agreements enhance the normative presumption against nuclear use. By multiplying the number of forums where a decision to use nuclear weapons would have to be defended, they substantially increase the burden of proof for any such decision.[13] . . .

Explanation of the Nuclear Taboo

Realist and rationalist explanations would emphasize the role of material power and interest in the creation of the taboo, but several anomalies exist for these explanations. First, the rise of the taboo historically has not been a simple function of the interests of the nuclear powers. Although Cold War power politics played a role, the rise of the taboo has been driven significantly by a grass-roots global antinuclear weapons movement, the UN, and nonnuclear states. The taboo developed in the face of consistent, vociferous, and long-standing official resistance by the U.S. government and the other democratic nuclear powers to any efforts to ban the use of nuclear weapons. In the critical first fifteen years of the nuclear era, when important precedents of nonuse were set, and continuing in some fashion through to the present, less powerful states and nonstate actors have sought to stigmatize nuclear weapons, exerting pressure in favor of nuclear arms control and calling for a ban on their use. The eventual strategic stalemate between the superpowers also contributed to the development of the taboo, but this factor entered into account only in the 1960s, after a tentative taboo had already begun to emerge.

Further, the taboo possesses an important moral component, for which power and interest explanations cannot fully account. At its core is the belief that nuclear weapons, because of their immense destructive power, flagrantly violate long-standing moral principles of discrimination and proportionality in the use of force. These principles, in turn, have at their core the moral intuition that it is wrong to kill noncombatants, or more generally, the innocent, and to cause excessive destruction.

The particular shape the taboo took, however, was a matter of politics and history.[14] In fact, the evolution of the taboo has been shaped by the ongoing competition of two approaches to the moral interpretation of nuclear weapons. The first is grounded in the traditional military argument that technology itself is value-neutral and that the moral nature of the weapon depends on how it is used. The second view, which ultimately prevailed, though not without struggle, is that any use of the weapons is prohibited; that is, the weapons themselves are proscribed. Rationalists might explain the success of the second view as providing the clearest and most easily agreed-upon threshold against further escalation, and thus as an example of a "focal point" solution.[15] Focal points, however, are not natural or intrinsic. They depend on the cultural, political, and social context, and on the identities of the actors.[16] The line between conventional and nuclear weapons did not always exist but had to be created. Then it had to be maintained—sometimes precariously—in the face of repeated challenges made possible by advancing technology and the development of smaller, less destructive nuclear weapons.

Thus a straightforward rationalist account is inadequate. A full explanation must deal with the origins of moral categories and interpretations, and these cannot simply be deduced from the nature of the technology. Rather, they develop in the context of particular political and institutional structures: the emerging Cold War, the preexisting normative tradition of the laws of war and its disregard in World War II, domestic institutions and values, and more taken-for-granted norms such as "civilization."

While preserving realist and rationalist insights about how norms can arise out of power and self-interest, I also draw on constructivist perspectives, which focus on the origins of interests and the historically constructed nature of both rationality and morality.[17] Thomas Risse, Stephen Ropp, and Kathryn Sikkink have identified three processes by which international norms develop and become implemented domestically: instrumental adaptation and strategic bargaining, moral consciousness-raising, and institutionalization and habitualization.[18] I draw on these to construct four pathways by which the taboo developed.

The first pathway, societal pressure, is a bottom-up process of normative change in which domestic and transnational social groups—such as the anti-nuclear weapons movement—along with international organizations politicize issues and put pressure on decision-makers to change state policy or practices.[19] Such groups act especially through moral consciousness-raising—identifying problems, providing information, framing issues, and shaping discourse.[20]

A second pathway is normative power politics, in which states seek, through rhetoric and diplomacy, to publicly delegitimize weapons that are perceived to give the adversary a power advantage. The adversary, in turn, seeks to defend the legitimacy of its weapons. Here, actors can be viewed as engaging in processes of "strategic social construction," a realist notion wherein the construction of norms is part of the game of power.[21]

A third pathway is the role of individual state decisionmakers whose actions in crucial ways foster nuclear restraint. Individual leaders may act for reasons of moral conscience (e.g., they believe that using nuclear weapons would simply be wrong) or on the basis of cognitive assumptions (e.g., they come to believe that the weapons lack military utility).[22]

The fourth pathway of normative development, iterated behavior over time, is similar to the notion of custom in international law, where obligation arises out of convention. The iteration of nonuse over time, for whatever reasons—deterrence, lack of readiness, scarcity of bombs, moral inhibitions, or contingency—becomes a convention, and a convention eventually gives rise to a normative obligation.[23] This pathway emphasizes the role of precedent, habit, and pattern in the development of a norm.

Together these mechanisms contribute to changing the discourse regarding nuclear weapons. As the taboo develops, it becomes increasingly internalized in the belief systems of decisionmakers and institutionalized within governments. As evidence of this, one should expect to see identity and self-interest defined in ways that increasingly take the taboo for granted. That is, the process of norm creation does not simply change the incentives for behavior (the rationalist view); it transforms the identity and interests of the actors themselves (the constructivist view).

I divide the history of the taboo into two stages: an initial period of emergence and a second period, following the 1962 Cuban missile crisis, when the taboo began to become institutionalized and internalized. In the first stage, the taboo is tentative and competes with other possible nuclear norms that were being promoted (such as "conventionalization"); in the second stage, the taboo has begun to prevail over competing discourses. . . .

Emergence and Evolution of the Nuclear Taboo

Analysis of the Taboo

How and why did the nuclear taboo emerge and prevail? First, it was actively promoted by a grassroots and state-level antinuclear weapons movement, which successfully used the UN and other international forums in a discursive strategy both to maintain a categorical distinction between conventional and nuclear weapons and to stigmatize the latter as unacceptable weapons of mass destruction. Soviet antinuclear propaganda contributed to and reinforced this movement. As democracies, the United States and its allies, for both strategic and legitimacy reasons, could not wholly ignore broad public fear and opprobrium toward nuclear weapons. The antinuclear movement promoted both causal knowledge and principled beliefs and fostered alternative discourses of nuclear weapons. Additionally, the UN and other international organizations played a key role in disseminating antinuclear weapons norms. UN disarmament conferences, for example, such as the special sessions on disarmament in 1978 and 1982, helped greatly to stimulate popular interest in disarmament, further contributing to antinuclear public sentiment.[24]

Second, the actual practice of nonuse by the superpowers (in contrast to the official nuclear doctrines emphasizing use) in the face of repeated Cold War crises bolstered the formation of a convention on nonuse as a total, rather than selective, prohibition on use of nuclear weapons. Third, a taboo was more consistent with escalation concerns than were the competing norms, which it in turn helped to reinforce. Fourth, the slow spread of nuclear weapons to other states, inhibited initially by the difficulty of nuclear weapons technology and later by nonproliferation policies and norms, created time for the taboo to take root.

Finally, the role of historical contingency in the development of the taboo must be taken into account. For example, if Eisenhower had been president before Truman, the development of the taboo might have proceeded quite differently—or not at all.

Conclusion

This analysis shows that the rise of a nuclear taboo in world politics and in U.S. policy cannot simply be attributed straightforwardly to superpower self-interest, but instead is the result of a much broader set of factors, including importantly, a significant role for nonstate actors and antinuclear public opinion. Once a situation of mutual capacity to inflict unacceptable damage developed in the late 1950s, a primary factor driving the strengthening of the taboo was superpower self-interest. But in the critical early period of the nuclear era, when important precedents of nonuse were set, and continuing in some fashion through to the present, a global grassroots antinuclear weapons movement and nonnuclear states have played a critical role in subjecting nuclear weapons to criticism and castigating them as unacceptable for use. Given that use was what was institutionalized in the U.S. military, the development of the taboo is all the more remarkable.

This case thus adds to a growing body of research that finds that transnational movements and less powerful states have played an important role in global norm creation.[25] They are often greatly facilitated in this endeavor by the platform—or bullhorn—provided by international organizations. The case also suggests that norms do not need to be formalized to have an effect, and that there may be some virtues in a de facto norm. The "demands" for a stronger taboo, however, have always been greater than what the nuclear powers have been willing to deliver. Here, the taboo runs up against realism. The absence of a formal legal prohibition on nuclear weapons stems primarily from the fact that the great powers do not want it. But having a de facto norm has helped to stabilize and legitimize deterrence between the nuclear states, even as it has undermined deterrence between nuclear and nonnuclear states. . . .

One of the policy implications of this argument is that it will be easier to ban the use of nuclear weapons than to ban the weapons themselves. The negotiations on nuclear disarmament that have been going on under the auspices of the United Nations since the 1950s have been far more effective in contributing to the normative opprobrium against nuclear weapons than in reducing their numbers. Although complete nuclear disarmament will undoubtedly continue to be the goal of many nonnuclear states, it is probably unlikely to happen, in part because of fears of "breakout" (secret rearming) by the nuclear power.[26] It will be politically easier to pursue strong restrictions and prohibitions on use. . . .

Notes

1. James M. Gavin, *War and Peace in the Space Age* (New York: Harper and Brothers, 1958), p. 265.
2. See Nina Tannenwald, "The Nuclear Taboo: The United States and Normative Basis of Nuclear Nonuse," *International Organization,* Vol. 53, No. 3 (Summer 1999), p. 433–468.
3. For realist arguments on norms, see Stephen Krasner, *Sovereignty: Organized Hypocrisy* (Princeton, N.J.: Princeton University Press, 1999); and Scott D. Sagan, "Realist Perspectives on Ethical Norms and Weapons of Mass Destruction," in Sohail H. Hashmi and Steven P. Lee, eds., *Ethics and Weapons of Mass Destruction: Religious and Secular Perspectives* (Cambridge: Cambridge University Press, 2004), pp. 73–95.
4. For rationalist arguments on norms, see James D. Morrow, "The Laws of War, Common Conjectures, and Legal Systems in International Politics," *Journal of Legal Studies,* Vol. 31, Pt. 2 (January 2002), pp. S41-S60; Jon Elster, "Social Norms and Economic Theory," *Journal of Economic Perspectives,* Vol. 3, No. 4 (Fall 1989), pp. 99–117; Russell Hardin, *One for All: The Logic of Group Conflict* (Princeton, N.J.: Princeton University Press, 1995), chaps. 4, 5; and Edna Ullman-Margalit, *The Emergence of Norms* (Oxford: Oxford University Press, 1977).
5. Nuclear weapons are uniquely destructive per pound or per weapon, but of course need not be more destructive than bombardment by conventional weapons in the aggregate.
6. For a defense of analytical eclecticism, see Peter J. Katzensein and Nobuo Okawara, "Japan, Asian-Pacific Security, and the Case for Analytical Eclecticism," *International Security*, Vol. 26, No. 3 (Winter 2001/02), pp. 153–185.
7. Peter J. Katzenstein, Alexander Wendt, and Ronald Jepperson, "Norms, Identity, and Culture in National Security," in Katzenstein, ed., *The Culture of National Security: Norms and Identity in World Politics* (New York: Columbia University Press, 1996), p. 54.
8. Franz Steiner, *Taboo* (London: Cohen and West, 1956), p. 21; and Mary Douglas, *Purity and Danger: An Analysis of the Concepts of Pollution and Taboo* (London: Routledge, 1966).
9. Deterrence analysts commonly refer to the "nuclear threshold." For an analogous nonnuclear example of such a threshold, one might consider the terrorist attacks of September 11, 2001, on the United States. They produced this sense of crossing a bright line and creating a newworld from which it is impossible to return.
10. The dual nature of the bomb as both an awesome and awful temptation to leaders is evident in the internal deliberations of almost every country that has thought about acquiring (or has acquired) nuclear weapons.
11. Under article 6 of the Nuclear Nonproliferation Treaty, the declared nuclear states are obligated to pursue complete nuclear disarmament.
12. William I. Thomas and Dorothy Swaine Thomas, *The Child in America: Behavior Problems and Programs* (New York: Alfred A. Knopf, 1928), p. 572.
13. Harald Mueller, "The Internalization of Principles, Norms, and Rules by Governments: The Case of Security Regimes," in Volker Rittberger, ed., *Regime Theory and International Relations* (Oxford: Clarendon, 1993), pp. 361–388.
14. For a useful distinction between abstract moral norms and ethical norms of international politics, see Ward Thomas, *The Ethics of Destruction: Norms and Force in International Relations* (Ithaca, N.Y.: Cornell University Press, 2001).
15. Thomas C. Schelling, *The Strategy of Conflict* (Cambridge, Mass: Harvard University Press, 1960); and Schelling, "The Role of Nuclear Weapons."
16. Albert Yee, "Thick Rationality and the Missing 'Brute Fact': The Limits of Rationalist Incorporation of Norms and Ideas," *Journal of Politics,* Vol. 59, No. 4 (November 1997), p. 1026.
17. Alexander Wendt, *Social Theory of International Politics* (Cambridge: Cambridge University Press, 1999); Emanuel Adler, "Seizing the Middle Ground: Constructivism and World Politics," *European Journal of International Relations,* Vol. 3, No. 3 (September 1997), pp. 319–363; and Richard Price, *The Chemical Weapons Taboo* (Ithaca, N.Y.; Cornell University Press, 1997).
18. Thomas Risse, Stephen C. Ropp, and Kathryn Sikkink, eds., *The Power of Human Rights: International Norms and Domestic Change* (Cambridge: Cambridge University Press, 1999), p. 5.
19. Jeffrey Checkel, "Norms, Institutions, and National Identity in Contemporary Europe," *International Studies Quarterly*, Vol. 43, No. 1 (March 1999), p. 88.

20. Margaret E. Keck and Kathryn Sikkink, *Activists beyond Borders: Advocacy Networks in International Politics* (Ithaca, N.Y.: Cornell University Press, 1998), pp. 17–19. See also Sanjeev Khagram, James V. Riker, and Kathryn Sikkink, eds., *Restructuring World Politics: Transnational Social Movements, Networks, and Norms* (Minneapolis: University of Minnesota Press, 2002); and Jackie Smith, Charles Chatfield, and Ron Pagnucco, *Transnational Social Movements and Global Politics: Solidarity beyond the State* (Syracuse, N.Y.: Syracuse University Press, 1997).

21. Krasner, *Sovereignty*.

22. On the role of the moral conscience of individuals, see Robert W. McElroy, *Morality and American Foreign Policy* (Princeton, N.J.: Princeton University Press, 1992).

23. George I. Mavrodes, "Conventions and Morality of War," in Charles R. Beitz, Marshall Cohen, Thomas Scanlon and A. John Simmons, eds., *International Ethics* (Princeton, N.J.: Princeton University Press, 1985), pp. 75–89.

24. Wittner, *Toward Nuclear Abolition*, pp. 28–29.

25. See, for example, Matthew Evangelista, *Unarmed Forces: The Transnational Movement to End the Cold War* (Ithaca, N.Y.: Cornell University Press, 1999); and Richard Price, "Reversing the Gun Sights: Transnational Civil Society Targets Landmines," *International Organization*, Vol. 52, No. 3 (Summer 1998), pp. 613–644.

26. Charles L. Glaser, "The Flawed Case for Nuclear Disarmament," *Survival*, Vol. 40, No. 4 (Spring 1998), pp. 112–128.

8 Constructivism II

8.1

Dealing with Difference

Problems and Possibilities for Dialogue in International Relations

J. Ann Tickner

. . . In the introduction to their recent book *International Scholarship around the World*, Ole Waever and Arlene Tickner describe an IR that still speaks from the centre about the whole, an IR where there is scant dialogue among competing perspectives; they see a discipline that is neither international nor reflexive about its own practices.[1] . . . As they argue, true dialogue can only begin when there is more than one voice and, I would add, when there is mutual respect across geographical and methodological boundaries and when communication is among equal conversational partners. . . . Although I cannot claim to speak from a non-Western perspective, I shall offer some thoughts on how those of us in the West, who speak from a critical perspective, might contribute to this post-Western vision.

Drawing on the observations of scholars who have reflected on the origins and development of what many claim is still a US-dominated field, I shall begin by briefly revisiting IR's great debates since they represent the way the discipline has traditionally defined itself historically. Disciplinary history is rarely a neutral or impartial undertaking. Rather, it is tied to the intellectual struggles to legitimate the contemporary identity of the field.[2] For the most part, these debates have been about challenging the predominance of a US-centred discipline and its commitment to neo-positivist methodologies. Drawing on postcolonial and feminist literatures, I shall then offer some suggestions as to how we might envisage an IR that is built on more global foundations and on a more pluralist understanding of what we define as scientific knowledge. Since women, and marginalised people more generally, have rarely been the creators or subjects of knowledge, postcolonial and feminist scholars have been on the forefront of critical disciplinary self-reflection.[3] . . . In conclusion, I shall offer some thoughts on possible paths towards placing different scientific traditions on a more equal and mutually respectful footing.

Revisiting the Great Debates

As Ole Waever claimed in his 1998 article, 'The Sociology of a Not So International Discipline', IR scholars have tended to write about the history of the discipline as a series of methodological debates about who is right and who is wrong, about how we construct knowledge.[4] As he points out, issues of power and privilege are at stake; the winners, many of them located in the mainstream of what he describes as a US-dominated social science, have rarely been willing to engage the losers—not a very promising path to dialogue.

Source: J. Ann Tickner. "Dealing with Difference: Problems and Possibilities for Dialogue in International Relations," in *Millenium – Journal of International Studies* 39(3): 607–618.

The first debate, between realists and idealists, traditionally portrayed as the founding moment of the discipline, was well suited to the emergence of realism as the dominant paradigm, and the United States as the dominant site, for IR in the post-World War II era. The second debate, between traditionalists, whose main protagonist was English School founder, Hedley Bull,[5] and (mostly) US-based social scientists, seemed, in the United States at least, to signal victory for the scientists where quantification, formal modelling and rational choice have become methodologies of choice. Early self-identified 'scientists', such as J. David Singer and Marion Levy, made reference to physics and economics, expressing the hope that IR could enjoy similar success by becoming equally scientific.[6] While this shift was less evident in Europe, it did grant American IR a 'scientific' legitimacy.

Naming Hans Morgenthau as the founding father of the discipline, Stanley Hoffmann, in his much-cited 1977 article, asked why it was in the United States that *Politics Among Nations* received such widespread attention and why henceforward IR became what he, somewhat ironically, termed 'an American social science'.[7] According to Hoffmann, the realist view of the world was well suited to America's new role as emerging global superpower. Although Morgenthau himself was ambivalent about a 'science' of international politics,[8] the post-war United States provided a favourable institutional climate for the receptivity of the scientific tradition, as well as a peculiarly American conviction that all problems can be resolved and that the way to solve them is to apply the scientific method—assumed to be value-free—combining empirical investigation, hypothesis formation and testing.[9] The aura around this very limited and narrow definition of science has placed an enormous burden on other approaches to demonstrate their scientific credibility and has, in my view, been the greatest barrier to constructive dialogue across paradigms.

Hoffmann did note that the popularity of scientific methodologies in the United States did not travel well to other parts of the world. What he saw as the failure of IR to become a truly international discipline has remained a dominant theme among those who have reflected subsequently on the evolution of the field. In 1998, almost 10 years after the third, or what some have termed the fourth, debate variously described as one between positivists and post-positivists, or rationalists and reflectivists, Ole Waever noted a continuation of US hegemony and its continued bias towards rational choice theory.[10] . . .

While I recognise that there is a much more methodologically pluralist IR scholarship outside the US—in Europe and elsewhere—it is the case that US theoretical traditions and American foreign policy concerns have shaped, and continue to shape, to a disproportionate degree, the agenda of IR as well as its methods of analysis. Following Hoffmann, Thomas Biersteker . . . suggests that the insularity of American IR prevents US scholars from recognising the extent to which IR's theoretical constructs, frameworks and debates are driven by American foreign policy concerns.[11] . . . I will next offer some thoughts as to how we might get beyond these unproductive debates that I have outlined and move towards a more international and pluralist discipline that is built on less West-centric foundations and is more respectful of multiple ways of understanding our complex world.

Building More Inclusive Foundational Stories

As Sandra Halperin has claimed, the historical accounts on which much of mainstream IR theory depends are shaped by a profound mythology about modern European history, one that wrongly places Europe at the centre of modernity and transforms Europe's imperial expansion into a story of enlightenment and progress.[12] IR dates the beginnings of modern international politics to the treaty of Westphalia in 1648 and the rise of the modern nation-state in Europe. This Eurocentric account portrays a linear progression towards modernity whereby values of liberty and democracy and economic development were spread around the world through the power, knowledge and agency of European states. After the collapse of the colonial empires during the 20th century, the European state system became universalised.

As Halperin reminds us, missing from this story is Europe's brutal expansion that began in 1492 with the so-called 'voyages of discovery'. Although IR has focused on relations between the great powers in a world of nation-states, it is European colonisation and imperialism that have shaped the present and future of more than two-thirds of the world's population. Curiously missing, both from the progressive Eurocentric Westphalian narrative and from the contemporary discipline which describes and analyses it, are issues of imperialism and race, subjects which were of vital concern to IR scholars at the discipline's founding moments in the early 20th century. A discipline that claims to be international, of relevance to all peoples and states, traces its modern origins to a time at which imperialism was at its height; yet most recent surveys of IR have little to say about the history of four hundred years of European colonisation or of decolonisation, one of the most important historical processes of the 20th century.[13]

Any attempt to construct a global IR must recognise this historical legacy of imperialism. . . . Races as well as states were the early discipline's two most important units of analysis. The first IR journal in the United States, founded in 1910, was called the *Journal of Race Development*; in 1919 it was renamed the *Journal of International Relations* and, three years later in 1922, it became *Foreign Affairs*, the official journal of the Council on Foreign Relations. The lead article of the first issue made the case for a research agenda focused on the progress of backward races and states. As the journal's original title makes clear, boundaries that we draw today between what is inside and outside the national space, were not made in the same way in 1910. The question as to who was inside and who was outside the national space was not so much a territorial question as a biological one. An imperialist world order produced administrative problems for the colonisers that begged for scientific study and solutions—an important motivator for the young discipline of International Relations.[14] In other words, the importance of the scientific study of global issues was recognised well before post-World War II realism.

Postcolonial historians and philosophers of science have long recognised the intimate relationship between Western science more generally and the imperial project. Philosopher Sandra Harding claims that, traditionally, science has typically asked questions about nature and social life that certain men (usually privileged men) want answered. She traces the relationship between the development of modern Western science and the history of European expansion. Challenging the claims to value-neutrality that modern science makes with respect to the questions it asks, she argues that the voyages of discovery . . . went hand in hand with the development of modern science and technology. . . . Such questions became intellectually interesting in order to solve colonialism s everyday problems.[15]

. . . The Cartesian revolution of the 17th century shifted knowledge based on resemblances to knowledge based on difference—such as the differences between mind and body, men and women, West and East, and colonisers and colonised. Studying, classifying and ordering humanity within an imperial context gave rise to peculiar and powerful ideas about race, culture and nation that were conceptual instruments that the West used to divide up and to educate the world.[16] . . .

Agreeing that one can be Eurocentric at the same time as being critical of the West, John Hobson has observed that many critical IR theorists end up reiterating the conventional Western narrative.[17] . . . He suggests using the term *hybridity*, a co-constitutive process that recognises that histories of different civilisations are mutually constitutive of each from other. Instead of a clash of civilisations he suggests a dialogue that demonstrates the multiple non-conflictual ways that each civilisation borrows and emanates from others. This happens at what he calls the edges of civilisations, conceptualised as *imperial dialectical frontiers* where a bottom-up logic of emancipation/resistance is intertwined with a top-down logic of imperial domination.[18] Hobson talks of the pressing need for the creation of political dialogue between West and East, which he defines as all parts of the world outside the West. This would be accomplished by an empathetic approach where all peoples of the world can communicate together as equal partners, where Self and Other are not separate and exclusive, but intimately intertwined.[19]

Of course there are major stumbling blocks to Hobson's call for a mutually respectful dialogue among equal partners who respect each other's foundational stories and knowledge traditions. First and foremost is whose knowledge is considered legitimate and whose gets ignored when we decide what counts as knowledge about global politics? Also there are enormous inequalities in material resources that determine where, and by whom, that knowledge gets produced. Forgetting the imperial roots of one's disciplinary history only reinforces IR's ability to protect the status of the detached neutral observer with layers of distance-enhancing effects.[20] The problems of creating mutual dialogue in the face of these hierarchies of power and lack of disciplinary self-reflection, even within the West, have been of central concern to feminist theory. Drawing on some recent feminist contributions to IR, I shall now suggest some ways that we might envisage a more pluralist discipline that is open to different knowledge traditions.

Building a More Methodologically Inclusive IR

As Brooke Ackerly, Maria Stern and Jacqui True remind us, developing feminist methodologies and conducting feminist research have presented major challenges in a state-centric discipline that is notorious for its lack of self-reflection on its own origins.[21] Yet I believe that the ways feminists have gone about meeting these challenges are instructive for thinking about possibilities for constructing a more genuinely pluralist discipline of International Relations. IR feminist scholarship has built on a variety of methodologies and methods, both mainstream and critical, and both from inside and outside the discipline. What makes feminist methodologies distinctive is their commitment to constructing knowledge from multiple locations, and from the perspective of both marginalised and non-marginalised subjects. Emerging in the 1970s as a critical theory sensitive to the relationship between the production of knowledge and the privileges of power, feminist standpoint theory has suggested that if we start thinking from marginalised lives, we are likely to get less partial and distorted accounts, not only of their lives, but of the whole social order as well.[22] Since it offers us a more complex picture of reality, knowledge from below has the potential to extend the boundaries and even transform the discipline in ways that are beneficial to everyone.

Feminists have long held a deep scepticism about the claims to universality of knowledge that, in reality, is based largely on certain privileged men's lives and men's experiences. Unlike the 'view from nowhere' to which empirical social science aspires, most feminists insist that the inquirer be placed in the same critical plane as the subject matter. Most IR feminists claim the that, as social scientists, we are part of the world we are trying to understand and that the world is always changing and affected by the way we study it.[23] Sandra Harding suggests that acknowledging the subjective element in one's analysis that, in reality, exists in all social science research, actually increases the objectivity of one's research.[24] Acknowledging that all human beliefs are socially situated, it requires critical evaluation to determine which social situations tend to generate the most objective knowledge claims. Harding argues for what she calls 'strong objectivity' which extends the task of scientific research to include a systematic examination of powerful background beliefs and making strange what has hitherto appeared as familiar.[25]

Feminism alerts us to the importance of studying silences and absences, as well as studying marginalised peoples' experiences, in order to better understand our local and global world.[26] Ackerly and True conceive of feminist methodologies as involving self-conscious reflection on the purpose of one's research, one's conceptual frameworks, one's ethical responsibilities, one's methods choices and one's assumptions about what it means to know rather than just believe something.[27] They describe this set of practices as a feminist research ethic—'a methodological commitment to any set of practices that reflect on the power of epistemology, boundaries, dimensions of the researcher's own location and to a normative commitment to transforming the social order in order to promote gender justice'.[28] A feminist research ethic alerts us to the power of disciplinary boundaries that operate in the way that researchers construct boundaries about what is acceptable and not acceptable in a discipline. IR's frequent dismissal of scholarship deemed unscientific is an example of such disciplining.

Patrick Jackson acknowledges the importance of feminism in introducing reflexivity into IR and also cites Tickner and Waever's call for a global sociology of IR as an example of reflexive scholarship.[29] Reflexivity has a long history in the social sciences more generally. The capacity of human beings to reflect on their own situations has served as the foundation for arguments for separating the social from the natural sciences. Human beings, unlike inanimate objects, have cultures and identities and volition and, therefore, cannot be studied in the same way as inanimate objects. The knowing subject is located in a variety of hierarchical social structures, such as race, class and gender, and knowledge of the world begins with the socially situated self, not with a world that can ever be independent of the researcher. Reflexivists are committed to the proposition that a systematic effort to analyse their own role as knowledge producers and to locate themselves within their broader social contexts will yield knowledge, not merely of things experienced, but valid knowledge of the social arrangements that order and give rise to those experiences. Knowledge of the social world begins not with that world, but with the self, a claim with which many feminists would agree.[30] Reflexivity then is deeper than reflection or what mainstream scholars mean when they use the term reflectivist.

Possibilities for a Pluralist 'Science' of IR

Jackson offers one possible way out of these methodological disputes that have inhibited a genuinely international dialogical IR and contributed to the dominance of an 'American discipline'. Like Steve Smith, Jackson claims that science has been a powerful resource among IR scholars, since accusing work of being 'non-scientific' carries very negative connotations.[31] Frequently, it is used as a disciplining function that renders the approach in question unworthy of serious consideration.[32] Although it is lauded in the discipline, there is considerable ambiguity as to what 'science' actually means, although, in IR, it has come to be identified with positivism's goal of formulating testable hypotheses. Jackson argues for a broader Weberian definition that equates science with any empirical inquiry designed to produce systematic and valid knowledge about the world, a definition that allows for a variety of 'scientific' approaches.[33] Rather than the usual dualistic divide between 'scientific' and 'non-scientific' approaches that has characterised the great debates, Jackson suggests a fourfold ideal type classificatory scheme for IR scholarship that he labels neo-positivist, critical realist, analyticist and reflexivist. An important distinction between these four traditions, all of which he calls 'scientific', is the relationship between the knower and the known or how their practitioners are hooked up to the world—whether as outsiders or insiders. Positivism and critical realism both accept the Cartesian mind-world dualism while analyticism and reflexivity, typical of some of the literature I have discussed, assume a mind-world monism where the researcher is part of the world that she or he is studying. Whatever approach scholars choose to take is up to them; no one approach should be labelled 'correct' methodologically, but, importantly, all are granted the status of science. This means that we must all accept that it is not permissible to judge one methodology by standards of evaluation suitable for another; for example, neo-positivists would judge success by their research programme's ability to generate testable hypotheses about a mind-independent world that exists outside the researcher. For reflectivists, however, such a mind-independent world does not exist; they claim that, since all knowledge is contingent and contextual, it is not possible to evaluate reflectivist scholarship in these terms. For example, one of the goals of reflexive knowledge is emancipation; therefore, for reflectivists, one measure of success would be that their knowledge claims contribute in some way to transforming the social conditions they highlight.[34]

Such very different standards of evaluation for IR scholarship cause a good deal of misperception and misunderstanding. Nevertheless, as I have argued elsewhere, dialogues about different ways of knowing will never be productive until methodologies that are labelled 'unscientific' by the mainstream are accorded their scientific legitimacy and those who work outside positivist scientific traditions are not asked to redefine their research in positivist terms.[35] Labelling research as 'non-scientific' is a disciplining function and serves as a reason for not engaging claims at odds with one's own 'scientific' tradition. While still speaking from a Western scientific tradition—albeit one that is more broadly defined—Jackson's wider definition of science offers a useful path to more productive dialogues. However, it is difficult to have productive conversations when power differentials are so great. In the United States at least, inequalities between the mainstream and critical approaches, broadly defined, allow for greater ignorance by the mainstream about other approaches than is possible for critical scholars if they are to be taken seriously. Academic placement, resources and access to publication in top journals are often awarded on the basis of one's methodological preferences rather than strictly on merit.

As I stated earlier, we also need to think about how we could construct an IR that is more conducive to dialogue across geographical as well as methodological boundaries.[36] We live in a world in which the majority of the world's population does not live in the West. Yet most of us do not feel any responsibility for reading and assigning texts that are not authored in the West or by non-English-speaking scholars. For IR to become a more truly international discipline, it will need to acknowledge the importance of the non-West in contributing to the knowledge that we call International Relations. IR continues to rely on a highly idealised account of Western political history. I have suggested some ways in which revisionist histories and feminist and postcolonial scholarship are beginning to critically explore the assumptions that have shaped this Western self-understanding. While we in the West have the responsibility to be reflective about our own knowledge and the power implications of our choices in how to conduct our research, in Abraham Heschel's words, we must also seek out ways for mutual enrichment and dialogue, and show respect for a variety of knowledge traditions, outside our own, each of which can illuminate paths to less conflictual and more just futures.

Notes

1. Ole Waever and Arlene B. Tickner, 'Introduction: Geocultural Epistemologies', in *International Relations Scholarship around the World*, ed. Arlene B. Tickner and Ole

Waever (New York: Routledge, 2009), 3–4. Waever and Tickner claim that, the extent to which there is reflection about IR's practices, it is mostly limited to the context of comparisons between the United States and Europe.

2. David Long and Brian C. Schmidt, 'Introduction', in *Imperialism and Internationalism in the Discipline of International Relations*, eds Long and Schmidt (Albany, NY: State University of New York Press, 2005), 5.

3. For some examples, see A.M. Agathangelou and L. H. M. Ling, 'The House of IR: From Family Power Politics to the Poisies of Worldism', *International Studies Review* 6 (2004): 21–49; Branwen Gruffydd Jones, ed., *Decolonizing International Relations* (London: Rowman and Littlefield, 2006); Sandra Harding, *Is Science Multicultural? Postcolonialisms, Feminisms, and Epistemologies* (Bloomington, IN: Indiana University Press, 1998); Naeem Inayatullah and David Blaney, *International Relations and the Problem of Difference* (London: Routledge, 2004).

4. Ole Waever, 'The Sociology of a Not So International Discipline: American and European Developments in International Relations', *International Organization* 52 (1998): 687–727.

5. See Hedley Bull, 'International Theory: The Case for a Classical Approach', in *Contending Approaches to International Politics*, eds Klaus Knorr and James N. Rosenau (Princeton, NJ: Princeton University Press, 1969), 20–38.

6. Jackson, *The Conduct of Inquiry*, 6.

7. Stanley Hoffman, 'An American Social Science: International Relations', *Daedalus* 106, no. 3 (1977): 41–60.

8. Hans J. Morgenthau articulated this ambivalence most forcefully in *Scientific Man vs. Power Politics* (Chicago: Chicago University Press, 1945).

9. Hoffman, 'An American Social Science', 45.

10. Waever, 'The Sociology of a Not So International Discipline'.

11. Thomas J. Biersteker, 'The Parochialism of Hegemony: Challenges for "American" International Relations', in *International Relations Scholarship*, eds Tickner and Waever, 321.

12. Sandra Halperin, 'International Relations Theory and the Hegemony of Western Conceptions of Modernity', in *Decolonizing International Relations*, ed. Gruffydd Jones, 57–8. Halperin notes the differences between Western historical stories and those of Islamic scholarship. She claims that Western thinkers have promoted the view that Europe's rise to modernity was a radical disjuncture with all that had happened previously, whereas Islamic scholars have been more ready to embrace a view of history as transcending the history of a particular culture or period.

13. Branwen Gruffydd Jones, 'Introduction: International Relations, Eurocentricism, and Imperialism', in *Decolonizing International Relations*, ed. Gruffydd Jones, 2.

14. Robert Vitalis, 'Birth of a Discipline', in *Imperialism and Internationalism*, eds Long and Schmidt, 162.

15. Harding, Is *Science Multicultural*?, 39–54.

16. John Willinsky, *Learning to Divide the World: Education at Empires End* (Minneapolis: University of Minnesota Press, 1998), 27.

17. John M. Hobson, 'Is Critical Theory Always for the White West and for Western Imperialism? Beyond Westphalian to a Post-Racist Critical IR', *Review of International Studies* 33 (2007): 91–116 at 93.

18. Ibid., 107–8.

19. Ibid., 115.

20. Vitalis, 'Birth of a Discipline', 162.

21. Brooke Ackerly, Maria Stern and Jacqui True, eds, *Feminist Methodologies for International Relations* (New York: Cambridge University Press, 2006), 1.

22. Sandra Harding, ed., *The Feminist Standpoint Theory Reader* (New York: Routledge, 2004), 128.

23. Brooke Ackerly and Jacqui True, *Doing Feminist Research in Political and Social Science* (New York: Palgrave Macmillan, 2010), 3.

24. Harding, *The Feminist Standpoint Theory Reader*, 136.

25. Sandra Harding, *Whose Science? Whose Knowledge? Thinking from Women's Lives* (Ithaca, NY: Cornell University Press, 1991), 142, 149.

26. Ackerly and *Doing Feminist Research*, 7.

27. Ibid., 6.

28. Ibid., 2.

29. Jackson, *The Conduct of Inquiry*, 185.

30. Ibid., 157–60.

31. Ibid., ch. 1.

32. Ibid., 18.

33. Ibid., 193.

34. Ibid., 173.

35. An example of this evaluation problem can be found in my article 'You Just Don't Understand: Troubled Engagements between Feminist and IR Theorists', *International Studies Quarterly* 41 (1997): 611–32 and my subsequent exchange in *International Studies Quarterly* with Robert Keohane. See 'Beyond Dichotomy: Conversations between International Relations and Feminist Theory', *International Studies Quarterly* 42 (1998): 193–8 and Tickner, 'Continuing the Conversation *International Studies Quarterly* 42 (1998): 205–10.

36. As Waever and Tickner claim, little work has been done on combining what they call two increasingly dynamic areas of research—critical disciplinary self-reflection in the core and the periphery's revolt against core concepts. See Waever and Tickner, 'Introduction: Geocultural Epistemologies', 3.

8.2

The Violence of Illusion

Amartya Sen

Langston Hughes, the African-American writer, describes in his 1940 autobiography, *The Big Sea*, the exhilaration that seized him as he left New York for Africa. He threw his American books into the sea: "[I]t was like throwing a million bricks out of my heart." He was on his way to his "Africa, Motherland of the negro people!" Soon he would experience "the real thing, to be touched and seen, not merely read about in a book." A sense of identity can be a source not merely of pride and joy, but also of strength and confidence. It is not surprising that the idea of identity receives such widespread admiration, from popular advocacy of loving your neighbor to high theories of social capital and of communitarian self-definition.

And yet identity can also kill—and kill with abandon. A strong—and exclusive—sense of belonging to one group can in many cases carry with it the perception of distance and divergence from other groups. Within-group solidarity can help to feed between-group discord. We may suddenly be informed that we are not just Rwandans but specifically Hutus ("we hate Tutsis"), or that we are not really mere Yugoslavs but actually Serbs ("we absolutely don't like Muslims"). From my own childhood memory of Hindu-Muslim riots in the 1940s, linked with the politics of partition, I recollect the speed with which the broad human beings of January were suddenly transformed into the ruthless Hindus and fierce Muslims of July. Hundreds of thousands perished at the hands of people who, led by the commanders of carnage, killed others on behalf of their "own people." Violence is fomented by the imposition of singular and belligerent identities on gullible people, championed by proficient artisans of terror.

The sense of identity can make an important contribution to the strength and the warmth of our relations with others, such as neighbors, or members of the same community, or fellow citizens, or followers of the same religion. Our focus on particular identities can enrich our bonds and make us do many things for each other and can help to take us beyond our self-centered lives. The recent literature on "social capital," powerfully explored by Robert Putnam and others, has brought out clearly enough how an identity with others in the same social community can make the lives of all go much better in that community; a sense of belonging to a community is thus seen as a resource—like capital. That understanding is important, but it has to be supplemented by a further recognition that a sense of identity can firmly exclude many people even as it warmly embraces others. The well-integrated community in which residents instinctively do absolutely wonderful things for each other with great immediacy and solidarity can be the very same community in which bricks are thrown through the windows of immigrants who move into the region from elsewhere. The adversity of exclusion can be made to go hand in hand with the gifts of inclusion.

The cultivated violence associated with identity conflicts seems to repeat itself around the world with increasing persistence. Even though the balance of power in Rwanda and Congo may have changed, the targeting of one group by another continues with much force. The marshaling of an aggressive Sudanese Islamic identity along with exploitation of racial divisions has led to the raping and killing of overpowered victims in the south of that appallingly militarized polity. Israel and Palestine continue to experience the fury of dichotomized identities ready to inflict hateful penalties on the other side. Al Qaeda relies heavily on cultivating and exploiting a militant Islamic identity specifically aimed against Western people.

And reports keep coming in, from Abu Ghraib and elsewhere, that the activities of some American or British soldiers sent out to fight for the cause of freedom and democracy included what is called a "softening-up" of prisoners in utterly inhuman ways. Unrestrained power over the lives of suspected enemy combatants, or presumed miscreants, sharply bifurcates the prisoners and the custodians across a hardened line of divisive identities ("they are a separate breed from us"). It seems to crowd out, often enough, any consideration of other, less confrontational features of the people on the opposite side of the breach, including, among other things, their shared membership of the human race.

Recognition of Competing Affiliations

If identity-based thinking can be amenable to such brutal manipulation, where can the remedy be found? It can hardly be sought in trying to suppress or stifle the invoking of identity in general. For one thing, identity can be a source of richness and warmth as well as of violence and terror, and it would make little sense to treat identity as a general evil. Rather, we have to draw on the understanding that the force of a bellicose identity can be challenged by the power of *competing* identities. These can, of course, include the broad commonality of our shared humanity, but also many other identities that everyone simultaneously has. This leads to other ways of classifying people, which can restrain the exploitation of a specifically aggressive use of one particular categorization.

A Hutu laborer from Kigali may be pressured to see himself only as a Hutu and incited to kill Tutsis, and yet he is not only a Hutu, but also a Kigalian, a Rwandan, an African, a laborer, and a human being. Along with the recognition of the plurality of our identities and their diverse implications, there is a critically important need to see the role of *choice* in determining the cogency and relevance of particular identities which arc inescapably diverse.

That may be plain enough, but it is important to see that this illusion receives well-intentioned but rather disastrous support from practitioners of a variety of respected—and indeed highly respectable—schools of intellectual thought. They include, among others, dedicated communitarians who take the community identity to be peerless and paramount in a predetermined way, as if by nature, without any need for human volition (just "recognition"—to use a much-loved concept), and also unswerving cultural theorists who partition the people of the world into little boxes of disparate civilizations.

In our normal lives, we see ourselves as members of a variety of groups—we belong to all of them. A person's citizenship, residence, geographic origin, gender, class, politics, profession, employment, food habits, sports interests, taste in music, social commitments, etc., make us members of a variety of groups. Each of these collectivities, to all of which this person simultaneously belongs, gives her a particular identity. None of them can be taken to be the person's only identity or singular membership category.

Constraints and Freedoms

Many communitarian thinkers tend to argue that a dominant communal identity is only a matter of self-realization, not of choice. It is, however, hard to believe that a person really has no choice in deciding what relative importance to attach to the various groups to which he or she belongs, and that she must just "discover" her identities, as if it were a purely natural phenomenon (like determining whether it is day or night). In fact, we are all constantly making choices, if only implicitly, about the priorities to be attached to our different affiliations and associations. The freedom to determine our loyalties and priorities between the different groups to all of which we may belong is a peculiarly important liberty which we have reason to recognize, value, and defend.

The existence of choice does not, of course, indicate that there are no constraints restricting choice. Indeed, choices are always made within the limits of what are seen as feasible. The feasibilities in the case of identities will depend on individual characteristics and circumstances that determine the alternative possibilities open to us. This, however, is *not* a remarkable fact. It is just the way every choice in any field is actually faced. Indeed, nothing can be more elementary and universal than the fact that choices of all kinds in every area are always made within particular limits. For example, when we decide what to buy at the market, we can hardly ignore the fact that there are limits on how much we can spend. The "budget constraint," as economists call it, is omnipresent. The fact that every buyer has to make choices does not indicate that there is no budget constraint, but only that choices have to be made *within* the budget constraint the person faces.

What is true in elementary economics is also true in complex political and social decisions. Even when one is inescapably seen—by oneself as well as by others—as French, or Jewish, or Brazilian, or African-American, or (particularly in the context of the present-day turmoil) as an Arab or as a Muslim, one still has to decide what exact importance to attach to that identity over the relevance of other categories to which one also belongs.

Convincing Others

However, even when we are clear about how we want to see ourselves, we may still have difficulty in being able to persuade *others* to see us in just that way. A nonwhite person in apartheid-dominated South Africa could not insist that she be treated just as a human being, irrespective of her racial characteristics. She would typically have been placed in the category that the state and the dominant members of the society reserved for her. Our freedom to assert our personal identities can sometimes be extraordinarily limited in the eyes of others, no matter how we see ourselves.

Indeed, sometimes we may not even be fully aware how others identify us, which may differ from self-perception. There is an interesting lesson in an old Italian story—from the 1920s when support for fascist politics was spreading rapidly across Italy—concerning a political recruiter from the Fascist Party arguing with a rural socialist that he should join the Fascist Party instead. "How can I," said the potential recruit, "join your party? My father was a socialist. My grandfather was a socialist. I cannot really join the Fascist Party." "What kind of an argument is this?" said the Fascist recruiter, reasonably enough. "What would you have done," he asked the rural socialist, "if your father had been a murderer and your grandfather had also been a murderer? What would you have done then?" "Ah, then," said the potential recruit, "then, of course, I would have joined the Fascist Party."

This may be a case of fairly reasonable, even benign, attribution, but quite often ascription goes with denigration, which is used to incite violence against the vilified person. "The Jew is a man," Jean-Paul Sartre argued in *Portrait of the Anti-Semite*, "whom other men look upon as a Jew; . . . it is the anti-Semite who *makes* the Jew." Charged attributions can incorporate two distinct but interrelated distortions: misdescription of people belonging to a targeted category, and an insistence that the misdescribed characteristics are the only relevant features of the targeted person's identity. In opposing external imposition, a person can both try to resist the ascription of particular characteristics and point to other identities a person has, much as Shylock attempted to do in Shakespeare's brilliantly cluttered story: "Hath not a Jew eyes? hath not a Jew hands, organs, dimensions, senses, affections, passions? fed with the same food, hurt with the same weapons, subject to the same diseases, healed by the same means, warmed and cooled by the same winter and summer, as a Christian is?"

The assertion of human commonality has been a part of resistance to degrading attributions in different cultures at different points in time. In the Indian epic *Mahabharata*, dating from around two thousand years ago, Bharadvaja, an argumentative interlocutor, responds to the defense of the caste system by Bhrigu (a pillar of the establishment) by asking: "We all seem to be affected by desire, anger, fear, sorrow, worry, hunger, and labor; how do we have caste differences then?"

The foundations of degradation include not only descriptive misrepresentation, but also the illusion of a singular identity that others must attribute to the person to be demeaned. "There used to be a me," Peter Sellers, the English actor, said in a famous interview, "but I had it surgically removed." That removal is challenging enough, but no less radical is the surgical implantation of a "real me" by others who are determined to make us different from what we think we are. Organized attribution can prepare the ground for persecution and burial.

Furthermore, even if in particular circumstances people have difficulty in convincing others to acknowledge the relevance of identities other than what is marshaled for the purpose of denigration (along with descriptive distortions of the ascribed identity), that is not reason enough to ignore those other identities when circumstances are different. This applies, for example, to Jewish people in Israel today, rather than in Germany in the 1930s. It would be a long-run victory of Nazism if the barbarities of the 1930s eliminated forever a Jewish person's freedom and ability to invoke any identity other than his or her Jewishness.

Similarly, the role of reasoned choice needs emphasis in resisting the ascription of singular identities and the recruitment of foot soldiers in the bloody campaign to terrorize targeted victims. Campaigns to switch perceived self-identities have been responsible for many atrocities in the world, making old friends into new enemies and odious sectarians into suddenly powerful political leaders. The need to recognize the role of reasoning and choice in identity-based thinking is thus both exacting and extremely important.

Denial of Choice and Responsibility

If choices do exist and yet it is assumed that they are not there, the use of reasoning may well be replaced by uncritical acceptance of conformist behavior, no matter how rejectable it may be. Typically, such conformism tends to have conservative implications, and works in the direction of shielding old customs and practices from intelligent scrutiny. Indeed, traditional inequalities, such as unequal treatment of women in sexist societies (and even violence against them), or discrimination against members of other racial groups, survive by the unquestioning acceptance of received beliefs (including the subservient roles of the traditional underdog). Many past practices and assumed identities have crumbled in response to questioning and scrutiny. Traditions can shift even within a particular country and culture. It is perhaps worth recollecting that John Stuart Mill's *The Subjection of Women*, published in 1874, was taken by many of his British readers to be the ultimate proof of his eccentricity, and as a matter of fact, interest in the subject was so minimal that this is the only book of Mill's on which his publisher lost money.

However, the unquestioning acceptance of a social identity may not always have traditionalist implications. It can also involve a radical reorientation in identity which could then be sold as a piece of alleged "discovery" without reasoned choice. This can play an awesome role in the fomenting of violence. My disturbing memories of Hindu-Muslim riots in India in the 1940s, to which I referred earlier, include seeing—with the bewildered eyes of a child—the massive identity shifts that followed divisive politics. A great many persons' identities as Indians, as subcontinentals, as Asians, or as members of the human race, seemed to give way—quite suddenly—to sectarian identification with Hindu, Muslim, or Sikh communities. The carnage that followed had much to do with elementary herd behavior by which people were made to "discover" their newly detected belligerent identities, without subjecting the process to critical examination. The same people were suddenly different.

Civilizational Incarceration

A remarkable use of imagined singularity can be found in the basic classificatory idea that serves as the intellectual background to the much-discussed thesis of "the clash of civilizations," which has been championed recently, particularly following the publication of Samuel Huntington's influential book, *The Clash of Civilizations and the Remaking of the World Order*. The difficulty with this approach begins with unique categorization, well before the issue of a clash—or not—is even raised. Indeed, the thesis of a civilizational *clash* is conceptually parasitic on the commanding power of a unique *categorization* along so-called civilizational lines, which as it happens closely follows religious divisions to which singular attention is paid. Huntington contrasts Western civilization with "Islamic civilization," "Hindu civilization," "Buddhist civilization," and so on. The alleged confrontations of religious differences are incorporated into a sharply carpentered vision of one of dominant and hardened divisiveness.

In fact, of course, the people of the world can be classified according to many other systems of partitioning, each of which has some—often far-reaching—relevance in our lives: such as nationalities, locations, classes, occupations, social status, languages, politics, and many others. While religious categories have received much airing in recent years, they cannot be presumed to obliterate other distinctions, and even less can they be seen as the only relevant system of classifying people across the globe. In partitioning the population of the world into those belonging to "the Islamic world," "the Western world," "the Hindu world," "the Buddhist world," the divisive power of classificatory priority is implicitly used to place people firmly inside a unique set of rigid boxes. Other divisions (say, between the rich and the poor, between members of different classes and occupations, between people of different politics, between distinct nationalities and residential locations, between language groups, etc.) are all submerged by this allegedly primal way of seeing the differences between people.

The difficulty with the thesis of the clash of civilizations begins well before we come to the issue of an inevitable clash; it begins with the presumption of the unique relevance of a singular classification. Indeed, the question "do civilizations clash?" is founded on the presumption that humanity can be preeminently classified into distinct and discrete civilizations, and that the relations *between different human beings* can somehow be seen, without serious loss of understanding, in terms of relations *between different civilizations*. The basic flaw of the thesis much precedes the point where it is asked whether civilizations must *clash*.

This reductionist view is typically combined, I am afraid, with a rather foggy perception of world history which overlooks, first, the extent of *internal* diversities within these civilizational categories, and second, the reach and influence of *interactions*—intellectual as well as material—that go right across the regional borders of so-called civilizations. And its power to befuddle can trap not only those who would like to support the thesis of a clash (varying from Western chauvinists to Islamic fundamentalists), but also those who would like to *dispute* it and yet try to respond within the strait-jacket of its pre-specified terms of reference.

The limitations of such civilization-based thinking can prove to be just as treacherous for programs of "dialogue among civilizations" (something that seems to be much sought after these days) as they are for theories of a clash of civilizations. The noble and elevating search for amity among people seen as amity between civilizations speedily reduces many-sided human beings into one dimension each and muzzles the variety of involvements that have provided rich and diverse grounds for cross-border interactions over many centuries, including the arts, literature, science, mathematics, games, trade, politics, and other arenas of shared human interest. Well-meaning attempts at pursuing global peace can have very counterproductive consequences when these attempts are founded on a fundamentally illusory understanding of the world of human beings.

More than a Federation of Religions

Increasing reliance on religion-based classification of the people of the world also tends to make the Western response to global terrorism and conflict peculiarly ham-handed. Respect for "other people" is shown by praising their religious books, rather than by taking note of the many-sided involvements and achievements, in nonreligious as well as religious fields, of different people in a globally interactive world. In confronting what is called "Islamic terrorism," in the muddled vocabulary of contemporary global politics, the intellectual force of Western policy is aimed quite substantially at trying to define—or redefine—Islam.

However, to focus just on the grand religious classification is not only to miss other significant concerns and ideas that move people, it also has the effect of generally magnifying the voice of religious authority. The Muslim clerics, for example, are then treated as the ex-officio spokesmen for the so-called Islamic world, even though a great many people who happen to be Muslim by religion have profound differences with what is proposed by one mullah or another. Despite our *diverse diversities*, the world is suddenly seen not as a collection of people, but as a federation of religions and civilizations. In Britain a confounded view of what a multiethnic society must do has led to encouraging the development of state-financed Muslim schools, Hindu schools, Sikh schools, etc., to supplement preexisting state-supported Christian schools, and young children are powerfully placed in the domain of singular affiliations well before they have the ability to reason about different systems of identification that may compete for their attention. Earlier on, state-run denominational schools in Northern Ireland had fed the political distancing of Catholics and Protestants along one line of divisive categorization assigned at infancy, and the same predetermination of "discovered" identities is now being allowed and, in effect, encouraged to sow even more alienation among a different part of the British population.

Religious or civilizational classification can, of course, be a source of belligerent distortion as well. It can, for example, take the form of crude beliefs well exemplified by U.S. Lieutenant General William Boykin's blaring—and by now well-known—remark describing his battle against Muslims with disarming coarseness: "I knew that my God was bigger than his," and that the Christian God "was a real God, and [the Muslim's] was an idol." The idiocy of such dense bigotry is, of course, easy to diagnose, and for this reason there is, I believe, comparatively limited danger in the uncouth hurling of such unguided missiles. There is, in contrast, a much more serious problem in the use in Western public policy of intellectual "guided missiles" that present a superficially nobler vision to woo Muslim activists away from opposition through the apparently benign strategy of defining Islam appropriately. They try to wrench Islamic terrorists from violence by insisting that Islam is a religion of peace, and that a "true Muslim" must be a tolerant individual ("so come off it and be peaceful"). The rejection of a confrontational view of Islam is certainly appropriate and extremely important at this time, but we must also ask whether it is at all necessary or useful, or even possible, to try to define in largely political terms what a "true Muslim" must be like.

Muslims and Intellectual Diversity

A person's religion need not be his or her all-encompassing and exclusive identity. In particular, Islam, as a religion, does not obliterate responsible choice for Muslims in many spheres of life. Indeed, it is possible for one Muslim to take a confrontational view and another to be thoroughly tolerant of heterodoxy without either of them ceasing to be a Muslim for that reason alone.

The response to Islamic fundamentalism and to the terrorism linked with it also becomes particularly confused when there is a general failure to distinguish between Islamic history and the history of Muslim people. Muslims, like all other people, in the world, have many different pursuits, and not all of their priorities and values need be placed within their singular identity of being Islamic. It is, of course, not surprising at all that the champions of Islamic fundamentalism would like to suppress all other identities of Muslims in favor of being only Islamic. But it is extremely odd that those who want to overcome the tensions and conflicts linked with Islamic fundamentalism also seem unable to see Muslim people in any form other than their being just Islamic, which is combined with attempts to redefine Islam, rather than seeing the many-dimensional nature of diverse human beings who happen to be Muslim.

People see themselves—and have reason to see themselves—in many different ways. For example, a Bangladeshi Muslim is not only a Muslim but also a Bengali and a Bangladeshi, typically quite proud of the Bengali language, literature, and music, not to mention the other identities he or she may have connected with class, gender, occupation, politics, aesthetic taste, and so on. Bangladesh's separation from Pakistan was not based on religion at all, since a Muslim identity was shared by the bulk of the population in the two wings of undivided Pakistan. The separatist issues related to language, literature, and politics.

Similarly, there is no empirical reason at all why champions of the Muslim past, or for that matter of the Arab heritage, have to concentrate specifically on religious beliefs only, and not also on science and mathematics, to which Arab and Muslim societies have contributed so much, and which can also be part of a Muslim or an Arab identity. Despite the importance of this heritage, crude classifications have tended to put science and mathematics in the basket of "Western science," leaving other people to mine their pride in religious depths. If the disaffected Arab activist today can take pride only in the purity of Islam, rather than in the many-sided richness of Arab history, the unique prioritization of religion, shared by warriors on both sides, plays a major part in incarcerating people within the enclosure of a singular identity.

Even the frantic Western search for "the moderate Muslim" confounds moderation in political beliefs with moderateness of religious faith. A person can have strong religious faith—Islamic or any other—along with tolerant politics. Emperor Saladin, who fought valiantly for Islam in the Crusades in the twelfth century, could offer, without any contradiction, an honored place in his Egyptian royal court to Maimonides as that distinguished Jewish philosopher fled an intolerant Europe. When, at the turn of the sixteenth century, the heretic Giordano Bruno was burned at the stake in Campo dei Fiori in Rome, the Great Mughal emperor Akbar (who was born a Muslim and died a Muslim) had just finished, in Agra, his large project of legally codifying minority rights, including religious freedom for all.

The point that needs particular attention is that while Akbar was free to pursue his liberal politics without ceasing to be a Muslim, that liberality was in no way ordained—nor of course prohibited—by Islam. Another Mughal emperor, Aurangzeb, could deny minority rights and persecute non-Muslims without, for that reason, failing to be a Muslim, in exactly the same way that Akbar did not terminate being a Muslim because of his tolerantly pluralist politics.

The Flames of Confusion

The insistence, if only implicitly, on a choiceless singularity of human identity not only diminishes us all, it also makes the world much more flammable. The alternative to the divisiveness of one preeminent categorization is not any unreal claim that we are all much the same. That we are not. Rather, the main hope of harmony in our troubled world lies in the plurality of our identities, which cut across each other and work against sharp divisions around one single hardened line of vehement division that allegedly cannot be resisted. Our shared humanity gets savagely challenged when our differences are narrowed into one devised system of uniquely powerful categorization.

Perhaps the worst impairment comes from the neglect—and denial—of the role of reasoning and choice, which follows from the recognition of our plural identities. The illusion of unique identity is much more divisive than the universe of plural and diverse classifications that characterize the world in which we actually live. The descriptive weakness of choiceless singularity has the effect of momentously impoverishing the power and reach of our social and political reasoning. The illusion of destiny exacts a remarkably heavy price.

9 Decision-Making Models

9.1

Conceptual Models and the Cuban Missile Crisis

Graham T. Allison

The Cuban missile crisis is a seminal event. For thirteen days of October 1962, there was a higher probability that more human lives would end suddenly than ever before in history. Had the worst occurred, the death of 100 million Americans, over 100 million Russians, and millions of Europeans as well would make previous natural calamities and inhumanities appear insignificant. Given the probability of disaster—which President Kennedy estimated as between 1 out of 3 and even "—our escape seems awesome."[1] This event symbolizes a central, if only partially thinkable, fact about our existence. That such consequences could follow from the choices and actions of national governments obliges students of government as well as participants in governance to think hard about these problems.

Improved understanding of this crisis depends in part on more information and more probing analyses of available evidence. To contribute to these efforts is part of the purpose of this study. But here the missile crisis serves primarily as grist for a more general investigation.

This study proceeds from the premise that marked improvement in our understanding of such events depends critically on more self-consciousness about what observers bring to the analysis. What each analyst sees and judges to be important is a function not only of the evidence about what happened but also of the "conceptual lenses" through which he looks at the evidence. The principal purpose of this essay is to explore some of the fundamental assumptions and categories employed by analysts in thinking about problems of governmental behavior, especially in foreign and military affairs.

The general argument can be summarized in three propositions:

1. Analysts think about problems of foreign and military policy in terms of largely implicit conceptual models that have significant consequences for the content of their thought.[2]

Though the present product of foreign policy analysis is neither systematic nor powerful, if one carefully examines explanations produced by analysts, a number of fundamental similarities emerge. Explanations produced by particular analysts display quite regular, predictable features. This predictability suggests a substructure. These regularities reflect an analyst's assumptions about the character of puzzles, the categories in which problems should be considered, the types of evidence that are relevant, and the determinants of occurrences. The first proposition is that clusters of such related assumptions constitute basic frames of reference or conceptual models in terms of which analysts both ask and answer the questions: What happened? Why did the event happen? What will happen?[3] Such assumptions are central to the activities of

Source: Graham Allison. "Conceptual Models and the Cuban Missile Crisis," *American Political Science Review* 63(3): 689–695, 698–703, and 707–718.

explanation and prediction, for in attempting to explain a particular event, the analyst cannot simply describe the full state of the world leading up to that event. The logic of explanation requires that he single out the relevant, important determinants of the occurrence.[4] Moreover, as the logic of prediction underscores, the analyst must summarize the various determinants as they bear on the event in question. Conceptual models both fix the mesh of the nets that the analyst drags through the material in order to explain a particular action or decision and direct him to cast his net in select ponds, at certain depths, in order to catch the fish he is after.

2. Most analysts explain (and predict) the behavior of national governments in terms of various forms of one basic conceptual model, here entitled the Rational Policy Model (Model I).[5]

In terms of this conceptual model, analysts attempt to understand happenings as the more or less purposive acts of unified national governments. For these analysts, the point of an explanation is to show how the nation or government could have chosen the action in question, given the strategic problem that it faced. For example, in confronting the problem posed by the Soviet installation of missiles in Cuba, rational policy model analysts attempt to show how this was a reasonable act from the point of view of the Soviet Union, given Soviet strategic objectives.

3. Two "alternative" conceptual models, here labeled an Organizational Process Model (Model II) and a Bureaucratic Politics Model (Model III) provide a base for improved explanation and prediction.

Although the standard frame of reference has proved useful for many purposes, there is powerful evidence that it must be supplemented, if not supplanted, by frames of reference which focus upon the large organizations and political actors involved in the policy process. Model I's implication that important events have important causes, i.e., that monoliths perform large actions for big reasons, must be balanced by an appreciation of the facts (a) that monoliths are black boxes covering various gears and levers in a highly differentiated decision-making structure, and (b) that large acts are the consequences of innumerable and often conflicting smaller actions by individuals at various levels of bureaucratic organizations in the service of a variety of only partially compatible conceptions of national goals, organizational goals, and political objectives. Recent developments in the field of organization theory provide the foundation for the second model. According to this organizational process model, what Model I categorizes as "acts" and "choices" are instead outputs of large organizations functioning according to certain regular patterns of behavior. Faced with the problem of Soviet missiles in Cuba, a Model II analyst identifies the relevant organizations and displays the patterns of organizational behavior from which this action emerged. The third model focuses on the internal politics of a government. Happenings in foreign affairs are understood, according to the bureaucratic politics model, neither as choices nor as outputs. Instead, what happens is categorized as outcomes of various overlapping bargaining games among players arranged hierarchically in the national government. In confronting the problem posed by Soviet missiles in Cuba, a Model III analyst displays the perceptions, motivations, positions, power, and maneuvers of principal players from which the outcome emerged.[6]

A central metaphor illuminates differences among these models. Foreign policy has often been compared to moves, sequences of moves, and games of chess. If one were limited to observations on a screen upon which moves in the chess game were projected without information as to how the pieces came to be moved, he would assume—as Model I does—that an individual chess player was moving the pieces with reference to plans and maneuvers toward the goal of winning the game. But a pattern of moves can be imagined that would lead the serious observer, after watching several games, to consider the hypothesis that the chess player was not a single individual but rather a loose alliance of semi-independent organizations, each of which moved its set of pieces according to standard operating procedures. For example, movement of separate sets of pieces might proceed in turn, each according to a routine, the king's rook, bishop, and their pawns repeatedly attacking the opponent according to a fixed plan. Furthermore, it is conceivable that the pattern of play would suggest to an observer that a number of distinct players, with distinct objectives but shared power over the pieces, were determining the moves as the resultant of collegial bargaining. For example, the black rook's move might contribute to the loss of a black knight with no comparable gain for the black team, but with the black rook becoming the principal guardian of the "palace" on that side of the board.

The space available does not permit full development and support of such a general argument.[7] Rather, the sections that follow simply sketch each conceptual model, articulate it as an analytic paradigm, and apply it to produce an explanation. But each model is applied to the same event: the U.S. blockade of Cuba during the missile crisis. These "alternative explanations" of the same happening illustrate differences among the models—*at work*.[8] A crisis decision, by a small group of men in the context of ultimate threat, this is a case of the rational policy model *par excellence.* The dimensions and factors that Models II and III uncover in this case are therefore particularly suggestive. The concluding section of this paper suggests how the three models may be related and how they can be extended to generate predictions.

Model I: Rational Policy

Rational Policy Model Illustrated

Where is the pinch of the puzzle raised by the *New York Times* over Soviet deployment of an antiballistic missile system?[9] The question, as the *Times* states it, concerns the Soviet Union's objective in allocating such large sums of money for this weapon system while at the same time seeming to pursue a policy of increasing détente. In former President Johnson's words, "the paradox is that this [Soviet deployment of an antiballistic missile system] should be happening at a time when there is abundant evidence that our mutual antagonism is beginning to ease."[10] This question troubles people primarily because Soviet antiballistic missile deployment, and evidence of Soviet actions towards détente, when juxtaposed in our implicit model, produce a question. With reference to what objective could the Soviet government have rationally chosen the simultaneous pursuit of these two courses of actions? This question arises only when the analyst attempts to structure events as purposive choices of consistent actors.

How do analysts attempt to explain the Soviet emplacement of missiles in Cuba? The most widely cited explanation of this occurrence has been produced by two RAND Sovietologists, Arnold Horelick and Myron Rush.[11] They conclude that "the introduction of strategic missiles into Cuba was motivated chiefly by the Soviet leaders' desire to overcome . . . the existing large margin of U.S. strategic superiority."[12] How do they reach this conclusion? In Sherlock Holmes style, they seize several salient characteristics of this action and use these features as criteria against which to test alternative hypotheses about Soviet objectives. For example, the size of the Soviet deployment, and the simultaneous emplacement of more expensive, more visible intermediate range missiles as well as medium range missiles, it is argued, exclude an explanation of the action in terms of Cuban defense—since that objective could have been secured with a much smaller number of medium range missiles alone. Their explanation presents an argument for one objective that permits interpretation of the details of Soviet behavior as a value maximizing choice.

How do analysts account for the coming of the First World War? According to Hans Morgenthau, "the First World War had its origin exclusively in the fear of a disturbance of the European balance of power."[13] In the period preceding World War I, the Triple Alliance precariously balanced the Triple Entente. If either power combination could gain a decisive advantage in the Balkans, it would achieve a decisive advantage in the balance of power. "It was this fear," Morgenthau asserts, "that motivated Austria in July 1914 to settle its accounts with Serbia once and for all, and that induced Germany to support Austria unconditionally. It was the same fear that brought Russia to the support of Serbia, and France to the support of Russia."[14] How is Morgenthau able to resolve this problem so confidently? By imposing on the data a "rational outline."[15] The value of this method, according to Morgenthau, is that "it provides for rational discipline in action and creates astounding continuity in foreign policy which makes American, British, or Russian foreign policy appear as an intelligent, rational continuum . . . regardless of the different motives, preferences, and intellectual and moral qualities of successive statesmen."[16] . . .

What is striking about these examples from the literature of foreign policy and international relations are the similarities among analysts of various styles when they are called upon to produce explanations. Each assumes that what must be explained is an action, i.e., the realization of some purpose or intention. Each assumes that the actor is the national government. Each assumes that the action is chosen as a calculated response to a strategic problem. For each, explanation consists of showing what goal the government was pursuing in committing the act and how this action was a reasonable choice, given the nation's objectives. This set of assumptions characterizes the rational policy model. The assertion that Model I is the standard frame of reference implies no denial of highly visible differences among the interests of Sovietologists, diplomatic historians, international relations theorists, and strategists. . . .

Most contemporary analysts (as well as laymen) proceed predominantly—albeit most often implicitly—in terms of this model when attempting to explain happenings in foreign affairs. Indeed, that occurrences in foreign affairs are the *acts* of *nations* seems so fundamental to thinking about such problems that this underlying model has rarely been recognized: to explain an occurrence in foreign policy simply means to show how the government could have rationally chosen that action.[17] These brief examples illustrate five uses of the model. To prove that most analysts think largely in terms of the rational policy model is not possible. In this limited space it is not even possible to illustrate the range of employment of the framework. Rather, my purpose is to convey to the reader a grasp of the model and a challenge: let the reader examine the literature with which he is most familiar and make his judgment.

The general characterization can be sharpened by articulating the rational policy model as an "analytic paradigm" in the technical sense developed by Robert K. Merton for sociological analyses.[18] Systematic statement of basic assumptions, concepts, and propositions employed by Model I analysts highlights the distinctive thrust of this style of analysis. To articulate a largely implicit framework is of necessity to caricature. But caricature can be instructive.

Rational Policy Paradigm

I. Basic Unit of Analysis: Policy as National Choice

Happenings in foreign affairs are conceived as actions chosen by the nation or national government.[19] Governments select the action that will maximize strategic goals and objectives. These "solutions" to strategic problems are the fundamental categories in terms of which the analyst perceives what is to be explained.

II. Organizing Concepts

A. *National Actor.* The nation or government, conceived as a rational, unitary decision-maker, is the agent. This actor has one set of specified goals (the equivalent of a consistent utility function), one set of perceived options, and a single estimate of the consequences that follow from each alternative.

B. *The Problem.* Action is chosen in response to the strategic problem which the nation faces. Threats and opportunities arising in the "international strategic market place" move the nation to act.

C. *Static Selection.* The sum of activity of representatives of the government relevant to a problem constitutes what the nation has chosen as its "solution." Thus the action is conceived as a steady-state choice among alternative outcomes (rather than, for example, a large number of partial choices in a dynamic stream).

D. Action as Rational Choice. The components include:

1. *Goals and Objectives.* National security and national interests are the principal categories in which strategic goals are conceived. Nations seek security and a range of further objectives. (Analysts rarely translate strategic goals and objectives into an explicit utility function; nevertheless, analysts do focus on major goals and objectives and trade off side effects in an intuitive fashion.)
2. *Options.* Various courses of action relevant to a strategic problem provide the spectrum of options.
3. *Consequences.* Enactment of each alternative course of action will produce a series of consequences. The relevant consequences constitute benefits and costs in terms of strategic goals and objectives.
4. *Choice.* Rational choice is value-maximizing. The rational agent selects the alternative whose consequences rank highest in terms of his goals and objectives.

III. Dominant Inference Pattern

This paradigm leads analysts to rely on the following pattern of inference: if a nation performed a particular action, that nation must have had ends towards which the action constituted an optimal means. The rational policy model's explanatory power stems from this inference pattern. Puzzlement is relieved by revealing the purposive pattern within which the occurrence can be located as a value-maximizing means.

IV. General Propositions

The disgrace of political science is the infrequency with which propositions of any generality are formulated and tested. "Paradigmatic analysis" argues for explicitness about the terms in which analysis proceeds, and seriousness about the logic of explanation. Simply to illustrate the kind of propositions on which analysts who employ this model rely, the formulation includes several.

The basic assumption of value-maximizing behavior produces propositions central to most explanations. The general principle can be formulated as follows: the likelihood of any particular action results from a combination of the nation's (1) relevant values and objectives, (2) perceived alternative courses of action, (3) estimates of various sets of consequences (which will follow from each alternative), and (4) net valuation of each set of consequences. This yields two propositions.

A. An increase in the cost of an alternative, i.e., a reduction in the value of the set of consequences which will follow from that action, or a reduction in the probability of attaining fixed consequences, reduces the likelihood of that alternative being chosen.

B. A decrease in the costs of an alternative, i.e., an increase in the value of the set of consequences which will follow from that alternative, or an increase in the probability of attaining fixed consequences, increases the likelihood of that action being chosen.[20]

V. Specific Propositions

A. *Deterrence.* The likelihood of any particular attack results from the factors specified in the general proposition. Combined with factual assertions, this general proposition yields the propositions of the sub-theory of deterrence.

1. A stable nuclear balance reduces the likelihood of nuclear attack. This proposition is derived from the general proposition plus the asserted fact that a second-strike capability affects the potential attacker's calculations by increasing the likelihood and the costs of one particular set of consequences which might follow from attack—namely, retaliation.

2. A stable nuclear balance increases the probability of limited war. This proposition is derived from the general proposition plus the asserted fact that though increasing the costs of a nuclear exchange, a stable nuclear balance nevertheless produces a more significant reduction in the probability that such consequences would be chosen in response to a limited war. Thus this set of consequences weighs less heavily in the calculus.

B. *Soviet Force Posture.* The Soviet Union chooses its force posture (i.e., its weapons and their deployment) as a value-maximizing means of implementing Soviet strategic objectives and military doctrine. A proposition of this sort underlies Secretary of Defense Laird's inference from the fact of 200 SS-9s (large intercontinental missiles) to the assertion that, "the Soviets are going for a first-strike capability, and there's no question about it."[21] . . .

Model II: Organizational Process

For some purposes, governmental behavior can be usefully summarized as action chosen by a unitary, rational decisionmaker: centrally controlled, completely informed, and value maximizing. But this simplification must not be allowed to conceal the fact that a "government" consists of a conglomerate of semi-feudal, loosely allied organizations, each with a substantial life of its own. Government leaders do sit formally, and to some extent in fact, on top of this conglomerate. But governments perceive problems through organizational sensors. Governments define alternatives and estimate consequences as organizations process information. Governments act as these organizations enact routines. Government behavior can therefore be understood according to a second conceptual model, less as deliberate choices of leaders and more as *outputs* of large organizations functioning according to standard patterns of behavior.

To be responsive to a broad spectrum of problems, governments consist of large organizations among which primary responsibility for particular areas is divided. Each organization attends to a special set of problems and acts in quasi-independence on these problems. But few important problems fall exclusively within the domain of a single organization. Thus government behavior relevant to any important problem reflects the independent output of several organizations, partially coordinated by government leaders. Government leaders can substantially disturb, but not substantially control, the behavior of these organizations.

To perform complex routines, the behavior of large numbers of individuals must be coordinated. Coordination requires standard operating procedures: rules according to which things are done. Assured capability for reliable performance of action that depends upon the behavior of hundreds of persons requires established "programs." Indeed, if the eleven members of a football team are to perform adequately on any particular down, each player must not "do what he thinks needs to be done" or "do what the quarterback tells him to do." Rather, each player must perform the maneuvers specified by a previously established play which the quarterback has simply called in this situation.

At any given time, a government consists of *existing* organizations, each with a *fixed* set of standard operating procedures and programs. The behavior of these organizations—and consequently of the government—relevant to an issue in any particular instance is, therefore, determined primarily by routines established in these organizations prior to that instance. But organizations do change. Learning occurs gradually, over time. Dramatic organizational change occurs in response to major crises. Both learning and change are influenced by existing organizational capabilities.

Borrowed from studies of organizations, these loosely formulated propositions amount simply to *tendencies*. Each must be hedged by modifiers like "other things being equal" and "under certain conditions." In particular instances, tendencies hold—more or less. In specific situations, the relevant question is: more or less? But this is as it should be. For, on the one hand, "organizations" are no more homogeneous a class than "solids." When scientists tried to generalize about "solids," they achieved similar results. Solids tend to expand when heated, but some do and some don't. More adequate categorization of the various elements now lumped under the rubric "organizations" is thus required. On the other hand, the behavior of particular organizations seems considerably more complex than the behavior of solids. Additional information about a particular organization is required for further specification of the tendency statements. In spite of these two caveats, the characterization of government action as organizational output differs distinctly from Model I. Attempts to understand problems of foreign affairs in terms of this frame of reference should produce quite different explanations.[22]

Organizational Process Paradigm[23]

I. Basic Unit of Analysis: Policy as Organizational Output

The happenings of international politics are, in three critical senses, outputs of organizational processes. First, the actual occurrences are organizational outputs. For example, Chinese entry into the Korean War—that is, the fact that Chinese soldiers were firing at U.N. soldiers south of the Yalu in 1950—is an organizational action: the action of men who are soldiers in platoons which are in companies, which in turn are in armies, responding as privates to lieutenants who are responsible to captains and so on to the commander, moving into Korea, advancing against enemy troops, and firing according to fixed routines of the Chinese Army. Government leaders' decisions trigger organizational routines. Government leaders can trim the edges of this output and exercise some choice in combining outputs. But the mass of behavior is determined by previously established procedures. Second, existing organizational routines for employing present physical capabilities constitute the effective options open to government leaders confronted with any problem. Only the existence of men, equipped and trained as armies and capable of being transported to North Korea, made entry into the Korean War a live option for the Chinese leaders. The fact that fixed programs (equipment, men, and routines which exist at the particular time) exhaust the range of buttons that leaders can push is not always perceived by these leaders. But in every case it is critical for an understanding of what is actually done. Third, organizational outputs structure the situation within the narrow constraints of which leaders must contribute their "decision" concerning an issue. Outputs raise the problem, provide the information, and make the initial moves that color the face of the issue that is turned to the leaders. As Theodore Sorensen has observed: "Presidents rarely, if ever, make decisions—particularly in foreign affairs—in the sense of writing their conclusions on a clean slate . . . The basic decisions, which confine their choices, have all too often been previously made."[24] If one understands the structure of the situation and the face of the issue—which are determined by the organizational outputs—the formal choice of the leaders is frequently anti-climactic.

II. Organizing Concepts

A. *Organizational Actors.* The actor is not a monolithic "nation" or "government" but rather a constellation of loosely allied organizations on top of which government leaders sit. This constellation acts only as component organizations perform routines.[25]

B. *Factored Problems and Fractionated Power.* Surveillance of the multiple facets of foreign affairs requires that problems be cut up and parceled out to various organizations. To avoid paralysis, primary power must accompany primary responsibility. But if organizations are permitted to do anything, a large part of what they do will be determined within the organization. Thus each organization perceives problems, processes information, and performs a range of actions in quasi-independence (within broad guidelines of national policy). Factored problems and fractionated power are two edges of the same sword. Factoring permits more specialized attention to particular facets of problems than would be possible if government leaders tried to cope with these problems by themselves. But this additional attention must be paid for in the coin of discretion for *what* an organization attends to, and *how* organizational responses are programmed.

C. *Parochial Priorities, Perceptions, and Issues.* Primary responsibility for a narrow set of problems encourages organizational parochialism. These tendencies are enhanced by a number of additional factors: (1) selective information available to the organization, (2) recruitment of personnel into the organization, (3) tenure of individuals in the organization, (4) small group pressures within the organization, and (5) distribution of rewards by the organization. Clients (e.g., interest groups), government allies (e.g., Congressional committees), and extra-national counterparts (e.g., the British Ministry of Defense for the Department of Defense . . . or the British Foreign Office for the Department of State . . .) galvanize this parochialism. Thus organizations develop relatively stable propensities concerning operational priorities, perceptions, and issues.

D. *Action as Organizational Output.* The preeminent feature of organizational activity is its programmed character: the extent to which behavior in any particular case is an enactment of preestablished routines. In producing outputs, the activity of each organization is characterized by:

1. *Goals: Constraints Defining Acceptable Performance.* The operational goals of an organization are seldom revealed by formal mandates. Rather, each organization's operational goals emerge as a set of constraints defining acceptable performance. Central among these constraints is organizational health, defined usually in terms of bodies assigned and dollars appropriated. The set of constraints emerges from a mix of expectations and demands of other organizations in the government, statutory authority, demands from citizens and special interest groups, and bargaining within the organization. These constraints represent a quasi-resolution of conflict—the constraints are relatively stable, so there is some resolution. But conflict among alternative goals is always latent; hence, it is a quasi-resolution. Typically, the constraints are formulated as imperatives to avoid roughly specified discomforts and disasters.[26]

2. *Sequential Attention to Goals.* The existence of conflict among operational constraints is resolved by the device of sequential attention. As a problem arises, the subunits of the organization most concerned with that problem deal with it in terms of the constraints they take to be most important. When the next problem arises, another cluster of subunits deals with it, focusing on a different set of constraints.

3. *Standard Operating Procedures.* Organizations perform their "higher" functions, such as attending to problem areas, monitoring information, and preparing relevant responses for likely contingencies, by doing "lower" tasks, for example, preparing budgets, producing reports, and developing hardware. Reliable performance of these tasks requires standard operating procedures (hereafter SOPs). Since procedures are "standard" they do not change quickly

or easily. Without these standard procedures, it would not be possible to perform certain concerted tasks. But because of standard procedures, organizational behavior in particular instances often appears unduly formalized, sluggish, or inappropriate.

4. *Programs and Repertoires.* Organizations must be capable of performing actions in which the behavior of large numbers of individuals is carefully coordinated. Assured performance requires clusters of rehearsed SOPs for producing specific actions, e.g., fighting enemy units or answering an embassy's cable. Each cluster comprises a "program" (in the terms both of drama and computers) which the organization has available for dealing with a situation. The list of programs relevant to a type of activity, e.g., fighting, constitutes an organizational repertoire. The number of programs in a repertoire is always quite limited. When properly triggered, organizations execute programs; programs cannot be substantially changed in a particular situation. The more complex the action and the greater the number of individuals involved, the more important are programs and repertoires as determinants of organizational behavior.

5. *Uncertainty Avoidance.* Organizations do not attempt to estimate the probability distribution of future occurrences. Rather, organizations avoid uncertainty. By arranging a *negotiated environment,* organizations regularize the reactions of other actors with whom they have to deal. The primary environment, relations with other organizations that comprise the government, is stabilized by such arrangements as agreed budgetary splits, accepted areas of responsibility, and established conventional practices. The secondary environment, relations with the international world, is stabilized between allies by the establishment of contracts (alliances) and "club relations" (U.S. State and U.K. Foreign Office or U.S. Treasury and U.K. Treasury). Between enemies, contracts and accepted conventional practices perform a similar function, for example, the rules of the "precarious status quo" which President Kennedy referred to in the missile crisis. Where the international environment cannot be negotiated, organizations deal with remaining uncertainties by establishing a set of *standard scenarios* that constitute the contingencies for which they prepare. For example, the standard scenario for Tactical Air Command of the U.S. Air Force involves combat with enemy aircraft. Planes are designed and pilots trained to meet this problem. That these preparations are less relevant to more probable contingencies, e.g., provision of close-in ground support in limited wars like Vietnam, has had little impact on the scenario.

6. *Problem-directed Search.* Where situations cannot be construed as standard, organizations engage in search. The style of search and the solution are largely determined by existing routines. Organizational search for alternative courses of action is problem-oriented: it focuses on the atypical discomfort that must be avoided. It is simple-minded: the neighborhood of the symptom is searched first; then, the neighborhood of the current alternative. Patterns of search reveal biases which in turn reflect such factors as specialized training or experience and patterns of communication.

7. *Organizational Learning and Change.* The parameters of organizational behavior mostly persist. In response to non-standard problems, organizations search and routines evolve, assimilating new situations. Thus learning and change follow in large part from existing procedures. But marked changes in organizations do sometimes occur. Conditions in which dramatic changes are more likely include: (1) Periods of budgetary feast. Typically, organizations devour budgetary feasts by purchasing additional items on the existing shopping list. Nevertheless, if committed to change, leaders who control the budget can use extra funds to effect changes. (2) Periods of prolonged budgetary famine. Though a single year's famine typically results in few changes in organizational structure but a loss of effectiveness in performing some programs, prolonged famine forces major retrenchment. (3) Dramatic performance

failures. Dramatic change occurs (mostly) in response to major disasters. Confronted with an undeniable failure of procedures and repertoires, authorities outside the organization demand change, existing personnel are less resistant to change, and critical members of the organization are replaced by individuals committed to change.

E. *Central Coordination and Control.* Action requires decentralization of responsibility and power. But problems lap over the jurisdictions of several organizations. Thus the necessity for decentralization runs headlong into the requirement for coordination. (Advocates of one horn or the other of this dilemma—responsive action entails decentralized power vs. coordinated action requires central control—account for a considerable part of the persistent demand for government reorganization.) Both the necessity for coordination and the centrality of foreign policy to national welfare guarantee the involvement of government leaders in the procedures of the organizations among which problems are divided and power shared. Each organization's propensities and routines can be disturbed by government leaders' intervention. Central direction and persistent control of organizational activity, however, is not possible. The relation among organizations, and between organizations and the government leaders depends critically on a number of structural variables including: (1) the nature of the job, (2) the measures and information available to government leaders, (3) the system of rewards and punishments for organizational members, and (4) the procedures by which human and material resources get committed. For example, to the extent that rewards and punishments for the members of an organization are distributed by higher authorities, these authorities can exercise some control by specifying criteria in terms of which organizational output is to be evaluated. These criteria become constraints within which organizational activity proceeds. But constraint is a crude instrument of control.

Intervention by government leaders does sometimes change the activity of an organization in an intended direction. But instances are fewer than might be expected. As Franklin Roosevelt, the master manipulator of government organizations, remarked:

> The Treasury is so large and far-flung and ingrained in its practices that I find it is almost impossible to get the action and results I want. . . . But the Treasury is not to be compared with the State Department. You should go through the experience of trying to get any changes in the thinking, policy, and action of the career diplomats and then you'd know what a real problem was. But the Treasury and the State Department put together are nothing compared with the Navy . . . To change anything in the Navy is like punching a feather bed. You punch it with your right and you punch it with your left until you are finally exhausted, and then you find the damn bed just as it was before you started punching.[27]

John Kennedy's experience seems to have been similar: "The State Department," he asserted, "is a bowl full of jelly."[28] And lest the McNamara revolution in the Defense Department seem too striking a counterexample, the Navy's recent rejection of McNamara's major intervention in Naval weapons procurement, the F-111B, should be studied as an antidote.

F. *Decisions of Government Leaders.* Organizational persistence does not exclude shifts in governmental behavior. For government leaders sit atop the conglomerate of organizations. Many important issues of governmental action require that these leaders decide what organizations will play out which programs where. Thus stability in the parochialisms and SOPs of individual organizations is consistent with some important shifts in the behavior of governments. The range of these shifts is defined by existing organizational programs.

III. Dominant Inference Pattern

If a nation performs an action of this type today, its organizational components must yesterday have been performing (or have had established routines for performing) an action only marginally different from this action. At any specific point in time, a government consists of an established conglomerate of organizations, each with existing goals, programs, and repertoires. The characteristics of a government's action in any instance follows from those established routines, and from the choice of government leaders—on the basis of information and estimates provided by existing routines—among existing programs. The best explanation of an organization's behavior at t is $t - 1$; the prediction of $t + 1$ is t. Model II's explanatory power is achieved by uncovering the organizational routines and repertoires that produced the outputs that comprise the puzzling occurrence.

IV. General Propositions

A number of general propositions have been stated above. In order to illustrate clearly the type of proposition employed by Model II analysts, this section formulates several more precisely.

A. *Organizational Action.* Activity according to SOPs and programs does not constitute far-sighted, flexible adaptation to "the issue" (as it is conceived by the analyst). Detail and nuance of actions by organizations are determined predominantly by organizational routines, not government leaders' directions.

1. SOPs constitute routines for dealing with *standard* situations. Routines allow large numbers of ordinary individuals to deal with numerous instances, day after day, without considerable thought, by responding to basic stimuli. But this regularized capability for adequate performance is purchased at the price of standardization. If the SOPs are appropriate, average performance, i.e., performance averaged over the range of cases, is better than it would be if each instance were approached individually (given fixed talent, timing, and resource constraints). But specific instances, particularly critical instances that typically do not have "standard" characteristics, are often handled sluggishly or inappropriately.

2. A program, i.e., a complex action chosen from a short list of programs in a repertoire, is rarely tailored to the specific situation in which it is executed. Rather, the program is (at best) the most appropriate of the programs in a previously developed repertoire.

3. Since repertoires are developed by parochial organizations for standard scenarios defined by that organization, programs available for dealing with a particular situation are often ill-suited.

B. *Limited Flexibility and Incremental Change.* Major lines of organizational action are straight, i.e., behavior at one time is marginally different from that behavior at $t - 1$. Simple-minded predictions work best: Behavior at $t + 1$ will be marginally different from behavior at the present time.

1. Organizational budgets change incrementally—both with respect to totals and with respect to intra-organizational splits. Though organizations could divide the money available each year by carving up the pie anew (in the light of changes in objectives or environment), in practice, organizations take last year's budget as a base and adjust incrementally. Predictions that require large budgetary shifts in a single year between organizations or between units within an organization should be hedged.

2. Once undertaken, an organizational investment is not dropped at the point where "objective" costs outweigh benefits. Organizational stakes in adopted projects carry them quite beyond the loss point.

C. *Administrative Feasibility.* Adequate explanation, analysis, and prediction must include administrative feasibility as a major dimension. A considerable gap separates what leaders choose (or might rationally have chosen) and what organizations implement.

1. Organizations are blunt instruments. Projects that require several organizations to act with high degrees of precision and coordination are not likely to succeed.

2. Projects that demand that existing organizational units depart from their accustomed functions and perform previously unprogrammed tasks are rarely accomplished in their designed form.

3. Government leaders can expect that each organization will do its "part" in terms of what the organization knows how to do.

4. Government leaders can expect incomplete and distorted information from each organization concerning its part of the problem.

5. Where an assigned piece of a problem is contrary to the existing goals of an organization, resistance to implementation of that piece will be encountered.

V. Specific Propositions.

1. *Deterrence.* The probability of nuclear attack is less sensitive to balance and imbalance, or stability and instability (as these concepts are employed by Model I strategists) than it is to a number of organizational factors. Except for the special case in which the Soviet Union acquires a credible capability to destroy the U.S. with a disarming blow, U.S. superiority or inferiority affects the probability of a nuclear attack less than do a number of organizational factors.

First, if a nuclear attack occurs, it will result from organizational activity: the firing of rockets by members of a missile group. The enemy's *control system,* i.e., physical mechanisms and standard procedures which determine who can launch rockets when, is critical. Second, the enemy's programs for bringing his strategic forces to *alert status* determine probabilities of accidental firing and momentum. At the outbreak of World War I, if the Russian Tsar had understood the organizational processes which his order of full mobilization triggered, he would have realized that he had chosen war. Third, organizational repertoires fix the range of effective choice open to enemy leaders. The menu available to Tsar Nicholas in 1914 has two entrees: full mobilization and no mobilization. Partial mobilization was not an organizational option.

Fourth, since organizational routines set the chessboard, the training and deployment of troops and nuclear weapons is crucial. Given that the outbreak of hostilities in Berlin is more probable than most scenarios for nuclear war, facts about deployment, training, and tactical nuclear equipment of Soviet troops stationed in East Germany—which will influence the face of the issue seen by Soviet leaders at the outbreak of hostilities and the manner in which choice is implemented—are as critical as the question of "balance."

2. *Soviet Force Posture.* Soviet force posture, i.e., the fact that certain weapons rather than others are procured and deployed, is determined by organizational factors such as the goals and procedures of existing military services and the goals and processes of research and design labs, within budgetary constraints that emerge from the government leader's choices. The frailty of the Soviet Air Force within the Soviet military establishment seems to have been a crucial element in the Soviet failure to acquire a large bomber force in the 1950s (thereby faulting American intelligence predictions of a "bomber gap"). The fact that missiles were controlled until 1960 in the Soviet Union by the Soviet Ground Forces, whose goals and procedures reflected no interest in an intercontinental mission, was not irrelevant to the slow Soviet buildup of ICBMs (thereby faulting U.S. intelligence predictions of a "missile gap"). These organizational factors (Soviet Ground Forces' control of missiles and that service's fixation with European scenarios) make the Soviet deployment of so many MRBMs that European targets could be destroyed three times over, more understandable. Recent weapon developments, e.g., the testing of a Fractional Orbital Bombardment System (FOBS) and multiple warheads for the SS-9, very likely reflect the activity and interests of a cluster of Soviet research and development organizations, rather than a decision by Soviet leaders to acquire a first strike weapon system. Careful attention to the organizational components of the Soviet military establishment (Strategic Rocket Forces, Navy, Air Force, Ground Forces, and National Air Defense), the missions and weapons systems to which each component is wedded (an independent weapon system assists survival as an independent service), and existing budgetary splits (which probably are relatively stable in the Soviet Union as they tend to be everywhere) offer potential improvements in medium and longer term predictions. . . .

Model III: Bureaucratic Politics

The leaders who sit on top of organizations are not a monolithic group. Rather, each is, in his own right, a player in a central, competitive game. The name of the game is bureaucratic politics: bargaining along regularized channels among players positioned hierarchically within the government. Government behavior can thus be understood according to a third conceptual model not as organizational outputs, but as outcomes of bargaining games. In contrast with Model I, the bureaucratic politics model sees no unitary actor but rather many actors as players, who focus not on a single strategic issue but on many diverse intra-national problems as well, in terms of no consistent set of strategic objectives but rather according to various conceptions of national, organizational, and personal goals, making government decisions not by rational choice but by the pulling and hauling that is politics.

The apparatus of each national government constitutes a complex arena for the intra-national game. Political leaders at the top of this apparatus plus the men who occupy positions on top of the critical organizations form the circle of central players. Ascendancy to this circle assures some independent standing. The necessary decentralization of decisions required for action on the broad range of foreign policy problems guarantees that each player has considerable discretion. Thus power is shared.

The nature of problems of foreign policy permits fundamental disagreement among reasonable men concerning what ought to be done. Analyses yield conflicting recommendations. Separate responsibilities laid on the shoulders of individual personalities encourage differences in perceptions and priorities. But the issues are of first order importance. What the nation does really matters. A wrong choice could mean irreparable damage. Thus responsible men are obliged to fight for what they are convinced is right.

Men share power. Men differ concerning what must be done. The differences matter. This milieu necessitates that policy be resolved by politics. What the nation does is sometimes the result of the triumph of one group over others. More often, however, different groups pulling in different directions yield a resultant distinct from what anyone intended. What moves the chess pieces is not simply the reasons which support a course of action, nor the routines of organizations which enact an alternative, but the power and skill of proponents and opponents of the action in question.

This characterization captures the thrust of the bureaucratic politics orientation. If problems of foreign policy arose as discreet issues, and decisions were determined one game at a time, this account would suffice. But most "issues," e.g., Vietnam or the proliferation of nuclear weapons, emerge piecemeal, over time, one lump in one context, a second in another. Hundreds of issues compete for players' attention every day. Each player is forced to fix upon his issues for that day, fight them on their own terms, and rush on to the next. Thus the character of emerging issues and the pace at which the game is played converge to yield government "decisions" and "actions" as collages. Choices by one player, outcomes of minor games, outcomes of central games, and "foul-ups"—these pieces, when stuck to the same canvas, constitute government behavior relevant to an issue.

The concept of national security policy as political outcome contradicts both public imagery and academic orthodoxy. Issues vital to national security, it is said, are too important to be settled by political games. They must be "above" politics. To accuse someone of "playing politics with national security" is a most serious charge. What public conviction demands, the academic penchant for intellectual elegance reinforces. Internal politics is messy; moreover, according to prevailing doctrine, politicking lacks intellectual content. As such, it constitutes gossip for journalists rather than a subject for serious investigation. Occasional memoirs, anecdotes in historical accounts, and several detailed case studies to the contrary, most of the literature of foreign policy avoids bureaucratic politics. The gap between academic literature and the experience of participants in government is nowhere wider than at this point.

Bureaucratic Politics Paradigm[29]

I. Basic Unit of Analysis: Policy as Political Outcome

The decisions and actions of governments are essentially intra-national political outcomes: outcomes in the sense that what happens is not chosen as a solution to a problem but rather results from compromise, coalition, competition, and confusion among government officials who see different faces of an issue; political in the sense that the activity from which the outcomes emerge is best characterized as bargaining. Following Wittgenstein's use of the concept of a "game," national behavior in international affairs can be conceived as outcomes of intricate and subtle, simultaneous, overlapping games among players located in positions, the hierarchical arrangement of which constitutes the government.[30] These games proceed neither at random nor at leisure. Regular channels structure the game. Deadlines force issues to the attention of busy players. The moves in the chess game are thus to be explained in terms of the bargaining among players with separate and unequal power over particular pieces and with separable objectives in distinguishable subgames.

II. Organizing Concepts

A. *Players in Positions*. The actor is neither a unitary nation, nor a conglomerate of organizations, but rather a number of individual players.

> Groups of these players constitute the agent for particular government decisions and actions. Players are men in jobs.

Individuals become players in the national security policy game by occupying a critical position in an administration. For example, in the U.S. government the players include "Chiefs": the President, Secretaries of State, Defense, and Treasury, Director of the CIA, Joint Chiefs of Staff, and, since 1961, the Special Assistant for National Security Affair;[31] "Staffers": the immediate staff of each Chief; "Indians": the political appointees and permanent government officials within each of the departments and agencies; and "*Ad Hoc* Players": actors in the wider government game (especially "Congressional Influentials"), members of the press, spokesmen for important interest groups (especially the "bipartisan foreign policy establishment" in and out of Congress), and surrogates for each of these groups. Other members of the Congress, press, interest groups, and public form concentric circles around the central arena—circles which demarcate the permissive limits within which the game is played.

Positions define what players both may and must do. The advantages and handicaps with which each player can enter and play in various games stems from his position. So does a cluster of obligations for the performance of certain tasks. The two sides of this coin are illustrated by the position of the modern Secretary of State. First, in form and usually in fact, he is the primary repository of political judgment on the political-military issues that are the stuff of contemporary foreign policy; consequently, he is a senior personal advisor to the President. Second, he is the colleague of the President's other senior advisers on the problems of foreign policy, the Secretaries of Defense and Treasury, and the Special Assistant for National Security Affairs. Third, he is the ranking U.S. diplomat for serious negotiation. Fourth, he serves as an Administration voice to Congress, the country, and the world. Finally, he is "Mr. State Department" or "Mr. Foreign Office," "leader of Officials, spokesman for their causes, guardian of their interests, judge of their disputes, superintendent of their work, master of their careers."[32] But he is not first one, and then the other. All of these obligations are his simultaneously. His performance in one affects his credit and power in the others. The perspective stemming from the daily work which he must over-see—the cable traffic by which his department maintains relations with other foreign offices—conflicts with the President's requirement that he serve as a generalist and coordinator of contrasting perspectives. The necessity that he be close to the President restricts the extent to which, and the force with which, he can front for his department. When he defers to the Secretary of Defense rather than fighting for his department's position—as he often must—he strains the loyalty of his officialdom. The Secretary's resolution of these conflicts depends not only upon the position, but also upon the player who occupies the position.

For players are also people. Men's metabolisms differ. The core of the bureaucratic politics mix is personality. How each man manages to stand the heat in his kitchen, each player's basic operating style, and the complementarity or contradiction among personalities and styles in the inner circles are irreducible pieces of the policy blend. Moreover, each person comes to his position with baggage in tow, including sensitivities to certain issues, commitments to various programs, and personal standing and debts with groups in the society.

B. *Parochial Priorities, Perceptions and Issues.* Answers to the questions: "What is the issue?" and "What must be done?" are colored by the position from which the questions are considered. For the factors which encourage organizational parochialism also influence the players who occupy positions on top of (or within) these organizations. To motivate members of his organization, a player must be sensitive to the organization's orientation. The games into which the player can enter and the advantages with which he plays enhance these pressures. Thus propensities of perception stemming from position permit reliable prediction about a player's stances in many cases. But these propensities are filtered through the baggage which players bring to positions. Sensitivity to both the pressures and the baggage is thus required for many predictions.

C. *Interests, Stakes, and Power.* Games are played to determine outcomes. But outcomes advance and impede each player's conception of the national interest, specific programs to which he is committed, the welfare of his friends, and his personal interests. These overlapping interests constitute the stakes for which games are played. Each player's ability to play successfully depends upon his power. Power, i.e., effective influence on policy outcomes, is an elusive blend of at least three elements: bargaining advantages (drawn from formal authority and obligations, institutional backing, constituents, expertise, and status), skill and will in using bargaining advantages, and other players' perceptions of the first two ingredients. Power wisely invested yields an enhanced reputation for effectiveness. Unsuccessful investment depletes both the stock of capital and the reputation. Thus each player must pick the issues on which he can play with a reasonable probability of success. But no player's power is sufficient to guarantee satisfactory outcomes. Each player's needs and fears run to many other players. What ensues is the most intricate and subtle of games known to man.

D. *The Problem and the Problems*. "Solutions" to strategic problems are not derived by detached analysts focusing coolly on *the* problem. Instead, deadlines and events raise issues in games, and demand decisions of busy players in contexts that influence the face the issue wears. The problems for the players are both narrower and broader than *the* strategic problem. For each player focuses not on the total strategic problem but rather on the decision that must be made now. But each decision has critical consequences not only for the strategic problem but for each player's organizational, reputational, and personal stakes. Thus the gap between the problems the player was solving and the problem upon which the analyst focuses is often very wide.

E. *Action-Channels*. Bargaining games do not proceed randomly. Action-channels, i.e., regularized ways of producing action concerning types of issues, structure the game by preselecting the major players, determining their points of entrance into the game, and distributing particular advantages and disadvantages for each game. Most critically, channels determine "who's got the action," that is, which department's Indians actually do whatever is chosen. Weapon procurement decisions are made within the annual budgeting process; embassies' demands for action cables are answered according to routines of consultation and clearance from State to Defense and White House; requests for instructions from military groups (concerning assistance all the time, concerning operations during war) are composed by the military in consultation with the Office of the Secretary of Defense, State, and White House; crisis responses are debated among White House, State, Defense, CIA, and Ad Hoc players; major political speeches, especially by the President but also by other Chiefs, are cleared through established channels.

F. *Action as Politics*. Government decisions are made and government actions emerge neither as the calculated choice of a unified group, nor as a formal summary of leaders' preferences. Rather the context of shared power but separate judgments concerning important choices, determines that politics is the mechanism of choice. Note the *environment* in which the game is played: inordinate uncertainty about what must be done, the necessity that something be done, and crucial consequences of whatever is done. These features force responsible men to become active players. The *pace of the game*—hundreds of issues, numerous games, and multiple channels—compels players to fight to "get other's attention," to make them "see the facts," to assure that they "take the time to think seriously about the broader issue." The *structure of the game*—power shared by individuals with separate responsibilities— validates each player's feeling that "others don't see my problem," and "others must be persuaded to look at the issue from a less parochial perspective." The *rules of the game*— he who hesitates loses his chance to play at that point, and he who is uncertain about his recommendation is overpowered by others who are sure—pressures players to come down on one side of a 51–49 issue and play. The *rewards of the game*—effectiveness, i.e., impact on outcomes, as the immediate measure of performance—encourages hard play. Thus, most players come to fight to "make the government do what is right." The strategies and tactics employed are quite similar to those formalized by theorists of international relations.

G. *Streams of Outcomes*. Important government decisions or actions emerge as collages composed of individual acts, outcomes of minor and major games, and foul-ups. Outcomes which could never have been chosen by an actor and would never have emerged from bargaining in a single game over the issue are fabricated piece by piece. Understanding of the outcome requires that it be disaggregated.

III. Dominant Inference Pattern

If a nation performed an action, that action was the *outcome* of bargaining among individuals and groups within the government. That outcome included *results* achieved by groups committed to a decision or action, *resultants* which emerged from bargaining among groups with quite different positions and *foul-ups*. Model III's explanatory power is achieved by revealing the pulling and hauling of various players, with different perceptions and priorities, focusing on separate problems, which yielded the outcomes that constitute the action in question.

IV. General Propositions

1. *Action and Intention*. Action does not presuppose intention. The sum of behavior of representatives of a government relevant to an issue was rarely intended by any individual or group. Rather separate individuals with different intentions contributed pieces which compose an outcome distinct from what anyone would have chosen.

2. *Where you stand depends on where you sit.*[33] Horizontally, the diverse demands upon each player shape his priorities, perceptions, and issues. For large classes of issues, e.g., budgets and procurement decisions, the stance of a particular player can be predicted with high reliability from information concerning his seat. In the notorious B-36 controversy, no one was surprised by Admiral Radford's testimony that "the B-36 under any theory of war, is a bad gamble with national security," as opposed to Air Force Secretary Symington's claim that "a B-36 with an A-bomb can destroy distant objectives which might require ground armies years to take."[34]

3. *Chiefs and Indians*. The aphorism "where you stand depends on where you sit" has vertical as well as horizontal application. Vertically, the demands upon the President, Chiefs, Staffers, and Indians are quite distinct.

The foreign policy issues with which the President can deal are limited primarily by his crowded schedule: the necessity of dealing first with what comes next. His problem is to probe the special face worn by issues that come to his attention, to preserve his leeway until time has clarified the uncertainties, and to assess the relevant risks.

Foreign policy Chiefs deal most often with the hottest issue *de jour*, though they can get the attention of the President and other members of the government for other issues which they judge important. What they cannot guarantee is that "the President will pay the price" or that "the others will get on board." They must build a coalition of the relevant powers that be. They must "give the President confidence" in the right course of action.

Most problems are framed, alternatives specified, and proposals pushed, however, by Indians. Indians fight with Indians of other departments; for example, struggles between International Security Affairs of the Department of Defense and Political-Military of the State Department are a microcosm of the action at higher levels. But the Indian's major problem is how to get the *attention* of Chiefs, how to get an issue decided, how to get the government "to do what is right."

In policy making then, the issue looking *down* is options: how to preserve my leeway until time clarifies uncertainties. The issue looking *sideways* is commitment: how to get others committed to my coalition. The issue looking *upwards* is confidence: how to give the boss confidence in doing what must be done. To paraphrase one of Neustadt's assertions which can be applied down the length of the ladder, the essence of a responsible official's task is to induce others to see that what needs to be done is what their own appraisal of their own responsibilities requires them to do in their own interests.

V. Specific Propositions

1. *Deterrence*. The probability of nuclear attack depends primarily on the probability of attack emerging as an outcome of the bureaucratic politics of the attacking government. First, which players can decide to launch an attack? Whether the effective power over action is controlled by an individual, a minor game or the central game, is critical. Second, though Model I's confidence in nuclear deterrence stems from an assertion that, in the end, governments will not commit suicide, Model III recalls historical precedents.

Admiral Yamamoto, who designed the Japanese attack on Pearl Harbor, estimated accurately: "In the first six months to a year of war against the U.S. and England I will run wild, and I will show you an uninterrupted succession of victories; I must also tell you that, should the war be prolonged for two or three years, I have no confidence in our ultimate victory."[35] But Japan attacked. Thus, three questions might be considered. One: could any member of the government solve his problem by attack? What patterns of bargaining could yield attack as an outcome? The major difference between a stable balance of terror and a questionable balance may simply be that in the first case most members of the government appreciate fully the consequences of attack and are thus on guard against the emergence of this outcome. Two: what stream of outcomes might lead to an attack? At what point in that stream is the potential attacker's politics? If members of the U.S. government had been sensitive to the stream of decisions from which the Japanese attack on Pearl Harbor emerged, they would have been aware of a considerable probability of that attack. Three: how might miscalculation and confusion generate foul-ups that yield attack as an outcome? For example, in a crisis or after the beginning of conventional war, what happens to the information available to, and the effective power of, members of the central game?

The U.S. Blockade Of Cuba: A Third Cut

The Politics of Discovery. A series of overlapping bargaining games determined both the *date* of the discovery of the Soviet missiles and the *impact* of this discovery on the Administration. An explanation of the politics of the discovery is consequently a considerable piece of the explanation of the U.S. blockade.

Cuba was the Kennedy Administration's "political Achilles' heel."[36] The months preceding the crisis were also months before the Congressional elections, and the Republican Senatorial and Congressional Campaign Committee had announced that Cuba would be "the dominant issue of the 1962 campaign."[37] What the administration billed as a "more positive and indirect approach of isolating Castro from developing, democratic Latin America," Senators Keating, Goldwater, Capehart, Thurmond, and others attacked as a "do-nothing" policy.[38] In statements on the floor of the House and Senate, campaign speeches across the country, and interviews and articles carried by national news media, Cuba—particularly the Soviet program of increased arms aid—served as a stick for stirring the domestic political scene.[39]

These attacks drew blood. Prudence demanded a vigorous reaction. The President decided to meet the issue head-on. The Administration mounted a forceful campaign of denial designed to discredit critics' claims. The President himself manned the front line of this offensive, though almost all Administration officials participated. In his news conference on August 19, President Kennedy attacked as "irresponsible" calls for an invasion of Cuba, stressing rather "the totality of our obligations" and promising to "watch what happens in Cuba with the closest attention."[40] On September 4, he issued a strong statement denying any provocative Soviet action in Cuba.[41] On September 13, he lashed out at "loose talk" calling for an invasion of Cuba.[42] The day before the flight of the U-2 which discovered the missiles, he campaigned in Capehart's Indiana against those "self-appointed generals and admirals who want to send someone else's sons to war."[43]

On Sunday, October 14, just as a U-2 was taking the first pictures of Soviet missiles, McGeorge Bundy was asserting:

> I *know* that there is no present evidence, and I think that there is no present likelihood that the Cuban government and the Soviet government would, in combination, attempt to install a major offensive capability.[44]

In this campaign to puncture the critics' charges, the Administration discovered that the public needed positive slogans. Thus, Kennedy fell into a tenuous semantic distinction between "offensive" and "defensive" weapons. This distinction originated in his September 4 statement that there was no evidence of "offensive ground to ground missiles" and warned "were it to be otherwise, the gravest issues would arise."[45] His September 13 statement turned on this distinction between "defensive" and "offensive" weapons and announced a firm commitment to action if the Soviet Union attempted to introduce the latter into Cuba.[46] Congressional committees elicited from administration officials' testimony which read this distinction and the President's commitment into the *Congressional Record*.[47]

What the President least wanted to hear, the CIA was most hesitant to say plainly. On August 22, John

McCone met privately with the President and voiced suspicions that the Soviets were preparing to introduce offensive missiles into Cuba.[48] Kennedy heard this as what it was: the suspicion of a hawk. McCone left Washington for a month's honeymoon on the Riviera. Fretting at Cap Ferrat, he bombarded his deputy, General Marshall Carter, with telegrams, but Carter, knowing that McCone had informed the President of his suspicions and received a cold reception, was reluctant to distribute these telegrams outside the CIA.[49] On September 9 a U-2 "on loan" to the Chinese Nationalists was downed over mainland China.[50] The Committee on Overhead Reconnaissance (COMOR) convened on September 10 with a sense of urgency.[51] Loss of another U-2 might incite world opinion to demand cancellation of U-2 flights. The President's campaign against those who asserted that the Soviets were acting provocatively in Cuba had begun. To risk downing a U-2 over Cuba was to risk chopping off the limb on which the President was sitting. That meeting decided to shy away from the western end of Cuba (where SAMs were becoming operational) and modify the flight pattern of the U-2s in order to reduce the probability that a U-2 would be lost.[52] USIB's unanimous approval of the September estimate reflects similar sensitivities. On September 13 the President had asserted that there were no Soviet offensive missiles in Cuba and committed his Administration to act if offensive missiles were discovered. Before Congressional committees, Administration officials were denying that there was any evidence whatever of offensive missiles in Cuba. The implications of a National Intelligence estimate which concluded that the Soviets were introducing offensive missiles into Cuba were not lost on the men who constituted America's highest intelligence assembly.

The October 4 COMOR decision to direct a flight over the western end of Cuba in effect "overturned" the September estimate, but without officially raising that issue. The decision represented McCone's victory for which he had lobbied with the President before the September 10 decision, in telegrams before the September 19 estimate, and in person after his return to Washington. Though the politics of the intelligence community is closely guarded, several pieces of the story can be told.[53] By September 27, Colonel Wright and others in DIA believed that the Soviet Union was placing missiles in the San Cristobal area.[54] This area was marked suspicious by the CIA on September 29 and certified top priority on October 3. By October 4, McCone had the evidence required to raise the issue officially. The members of COMOR heard McCone's argument, but were reluctant to make the hard decision he demanded. The significant probability that a U-2 would be downed made overflight of western Cuba a matter of real concern.[55]

The Politics of Issues. The U-2 photographs presented incontrovertible evidence of Soviet offensive missiles in Cuba. This revelation fell upon politicized players in a complex context. As one high official recalled, Khrushchev had caught us "with our pants down." What each of the central participants saw, and what each did to cover both his own and the Administration's nakedness, created the spectrum of issues and answers.

At approximately 9:00 A.M., Tuesday morning, October 16, McGeorge Bundy went to the President's living quarters with the message: "Mr. President, there is now hard photographic evidence that the Russians have offensive missiles in Cuba."[56] Much has been made of Kennedy's "expression of surprise,"[57] but "surprise" fails to capture the character of his initial reaction. Rather, it was one of startled anger, most adequately conveyed by the exclamation: "He can't do that to *me!*"[58] In terms of the President's attention and priorities at that moment, Khrushchev had chosen the most unhelpful act of all. Kennedy had staked his full Presidential authority on the assertion that the Soviets would not place offensive weapons in Cuba. Moreover, Khrushchev had assured the President through the most direct and personal channels that he was aware of the President's domestic political problem and that nothing would be done to exacerbate this problem. The Chairman had *lied* to the President. Kennedy's initial reaction entailed action. The missiles must be removed.[59] The alternatives of "doing nothing" or "taking a diplomatic approach" could not have been less relevant to *his* problem.

These two tracks—doing nothing and taking a diplomatic approach—were the solutions advocated by two of his principal advisors. For Secretary of Defense McNamara, the missiles raised the specter of nuclear war. He first framed the issue as a straightforward strategic problem. To understand the issue, one had to grasp two obvious but difficult points. First, the missiles represented an inevitable occurrence: narrowing of the missile gap. It simply happened sooner rather than later. Second, the United States could accept this occurrence since its consequences were minor: "seven-to-one missile 'superiority,' one-to-one missile 'equality,' one-to-seven missile 'inferiority'—the three postures are identical." McNamara's statement of this argument at the first meeting of the ExCom was summed up in the phrase, "a missile is a missile."[60] "It makes no great difference," he maintained, "whether you are killed by a missile from the Soviet Union or Cuba."[61] The implication was clear. The United States should not initiate a crisis with the Soviet Union, risking a significant probability of nuclear war over an occurrence which had such small strategic implications.

The perceptions of McGeorge Bundy, the President's Assistant for National Security Affairs, are the most difficult of all to reconstruct. There is no question that he initially argued for a diplomatic track.[62] But was Bundy laboring under his acknowledged burden of responsibility in Cuba I [the Bay of Pigs]? Or was he playing the role of devil's advocate in order to make the President probe his own initial reaction and consider other options?

The President's brother, Robert Kennedy, saw most clearly the political wall against which Khrushchev had backed the President. But he, like McNamara, saw the prospect of nuclear doom. Was Khrushchev going to force the President to an insane act? At the first meeting of the ExCom, he scribbled a note, "Now I know how Tojo felt when he was planning Pearl Harbor."[63] From the outset he searched for an alternative that would prevent the air strike.

The initial reaction of Theodore Sorensen, the President's Special Counsel and "alter ego," fell somewhere between that of the President and his brother. Like the President, Sorensen felt the poignancy of betrayal. If the President had been the architect of the policy which the missiles punctured, Sorensen was the draftsman. Khrushchev's deceitful move demanded a strong counter-move. But like Robert Kennedy, Sorensen feared lest the shock and disgrace lead to disaster.

To the Joint Chiefs of Staff the issue was clear. *Now* was the time to do the job for which they had prepared contingency plans. Cuba I had been badly done; Cuba II would not be. The missiles provided the *occasion* to deal with the issue: cleansing the Western Hemisphere of Castro's Communism. As the President recalled on the day the crisis ended, "An invasion would have been a mistake—a wrong use of our power. But the military are mad. They wanted to do this. It's lucky for us that we have McNamara over there."[64]

McCone's perceptions flowed from his confirmed prediction. As the Cassandra of the incident, he argued forcefully that the Soviets had installed the missiles in a daring political probe which the United States must meet with force. The time for an air strike was now.[65]

The Politics of Choice. The process by which the blockade emerged is a story of the most subtle and intricate probing, pulling, and hauling; leading, guiding, and spurring. Reconstruction of this process can only be tentative. Initially the President and most of his advisers wanted the clean, surgical air strike. On the first day of the crisis, when informing Stevenson of the missiles, the President mentioned only two alternatives: "I suppose the alternatives are to go in by air and wipe them out, or to take other steps to render them inoperable."[66] At the end of the week a sizeable minority still favored an air strike. As Robert Kennedy recalled: "The fourteen people involved were very significant. . . . If six of them had been President of the U.S., I think that the world might have been blown up."[67] What prevented the air strike was a fortuitous coincidence of a number of factors—the absence of any one of which might have permitted that option to prevail.

First, McNamara's vision of holocaust set him firmly against the air strike. His initial attempt to frame the issue in strategic terms struck Kennedy as particularly inappropriate. Once McNamara realized that the name of the game was a strong response, however, he and his deputy Gilpatric chose the blockade as a fallback. When the Secretary of Defense—whose department had the action, whose reputation in the Cabinet was unequaled, in whom the President demonstrated full confidence—marshaled the arguments for the blockade and refused to be moved, the blockade became a formidable alternative.

Second, Robert Kennedy—the President's closest confidant—was unwilling to see his brother become a "Tojo." His arguments against the air strike on moral grounds struck a chord in the President. Moreover, once his brother had stated these arguments so forcefully, the President could not have chosen his initially preferred course without, in effect, agreeing to become what RFK had condemned.

The President learned of the missiles on Tuesday morning. On Wednesday morning, in order to mask our discovery from the Russians, the President flew to Connecticut to keep a campaign commitment, leaving RFK as the unofficial chairman of the group. By the time the President returned on Wednesday evening, a critical third piece had been added to the picture. McNamara had presented his argument for the blockade.

Robert Kennedy and Sorensen had joined McNamara. A powerful coalition of the advisers in whom the President had the greatest confidence, and with whom his style was most compatible, had emerged.

Fourth, the coalition that had formed behind the President's initial preference gave him reason to pause. *Who* supported the air strike—the Chiefs, McCone, Rusk, Nitze, and Acheson—as much as *how* they supported it, counted. Fifth, a piece of inaccurate information, which no one probed, permitted the blockade advocates to fuel (potential) uncertainties in the President's mind. When the President returned to Washington Wednesday evening, RFK and Sorensen met him at the airport. Sorensen gave the President a four-page memorandum outlining the areas of agreement and disagreement. The strongest argument was that the air strike simply could not be surgical.[68] After a day of prodding and questioning, the Air Force had asserted that it could not guarantee the success of a surgical air strike limited to the missiles alone.

Thursday evening, the President convened the ExCom at the White House. He declared his tentative choice of the blockade and directed that preparations be made to put it into effect by Monday morning.[69] Though he raised a question about the possibility of a surgical air strike subsequently, he seems to have accepted the experts' opinion that this was no live option.[70] (Acceptance of this estimate suggests that he may have learned the lesson of the Bay of Pigs—"Never rely on experts"—less well than he supposed.)[71] But this information was incorrect. That no one probed this estimate during the first week of the crisis poses an interesting question for further investigation.

A coalition, including the President, thus emerged from the President's initial decision that something had to be done; McNamara, Robert Kennedy, and Sorensen's resistance to the air strike; incompatibility between the President and the air strike advocates; and an inaccurate piece of information.[72]

Conclusion

This essay has obviously bitten off more than it has chewed. For further developments and synthesis of these arguments the reader is referred to the larger study.[73] In spite of the limits of space, however, it would be inappropriate to stop without spelling out several implications of the argument and addressing the question of relations among the models and extensions of them to activity beyond explanation.

At a minimum, the intended implications of the argument presented here are four. First, formulation of alternative frames of reference and demonstration that different analysts, relying predominantly on different models, produce quite different explanations should encourage the analyst's self-consciousness about the nets he employs. The effect of these "spectacles" in sensitizing him to particular aspects of what is going on—framing the puzzle in one way rather than another, encouraging him to examine the problem in terms of certain categories rather than others, directing him to particular kinds of evidence, and relieving puzzlement by one procedure rather than another—must be recognized and explored.

Second, the argument implies a position on the problem of "the state of the art." While accepting the commonplace characterization of the present condition of foreign policy analysis—personalistic, non-cumulative, and sometimes insightful—this essay rejects both the counsel of despair's justification of this condition as a consequence of the character of the enterprise, and the "new frontiersmen's" demand for *a priori* theorizing on the frontiers and *ad hoc* appropriation of "new techniques."[74] What is required as a first step is non-casual examination of the present product: inspection of existing explanations, articulation of the conceptual models employed in producing them, formulation of the propositions relied upon, specification of the logic of the various intellectual enterprises, and reflection on the questions being asked. Though it is difficult to overemphasize the need for more systematic processing of more data, these preliminary matters of formulating questions with clarity and sensitivity to categories and assumptions so that fruitful acquisition of large quantities of data is possible are still a major hurdle in considering most important problems.

Third, the preliminary, partial paradigms presented here provide a basis for serious reexamination of many problems of foreign and military policy. Model II and Model III cuts at problems typically treated in Model I terms can permit significant improvements in explanation and prediction.[75] Full Model II and III analyses require large amounts of information. But even in cases where the information base is severely limited, improvements are possible. Consider the problem of predicting Soviet strategic forces. In the mid-1950s, Model I style calculations led to predictions that the Soviets would rapidly deploy large numbers of long-range bombers. From a Model II perspective, both the frailty of the Air Force within the Soviet military establishment and the budgetary implications of such a buildup, would have led analysts to hedge this prediction. Moreover, Model II would have pointed to a sure, visible indicator of such a buildup: noisy struggles among the Services over major budgetary shifts. In the late 1950s and early 1960s, Model I calculations led to the prediction of immediate, massive Soviet deployment of ICBMs. Again, a Model II cut would have reduced this number because, in the earlier period, strategic rockets were controlled by the Soviet Ground Forces rather than an independent Service, and in the later period, this would have necessitated massive shifts in budgetary splits. Today, Model I considerations lead many analysts both to recommend that an agreement not to deploy ABMs be a major American objective in upcoming strategic negotiations with the USSR, and to predict success. From a Model II vantage point, the existence of an ongoing Soviet ABM program, the strength of the organization (National Air Defense) that controls ABMs, and the fact that an agreement to stop ABM deployment would force the virtual dismantling of this organization, make a viable agreement of this sort much less likely. A Model III cut suggests that (a) there must be significant differences among perceptions and priorities of Soviet leaders over strategic negotiations, (b) any agreement will affect some players' power bases, and (c) agreements that do not require extensive cuts in the sources of some major players' power will prove easier to negotiate and more viable.

Fourth, the present formulation of paradigms is simply an initial step. As such it leaves a long list of critical questions unanswered. Given any action, an imaginative analyst should always be able to construct some rationale for the government's choice. By imposing, and relaxing, constraints on the parameters of rational choice (as in variants of Model I) analysts can construct a large number of accounts of any act as a rational choice. But does a statement of reasons why a rational actor would choose an action constitute an explanation of the *occurrence* of that action? How can Model I analysis be forced to make more systematic contributions to the question of the determinants of occurrences? Model II's explanation of t in terms of $t - 1$ is explanation. The world is contiguous. But governments sometimes make sharp departures. Can an organizational process model be modified to suggest where change is likely? Attention to organizational change should afford greater understanding of why particular programs and SOPs are maintained by identifiable types of organizations and also how a manager can improve organizational performance. Model III tells a fascinating "story." But its complexity is enormous, the information requirements are often overwhelming, and many of the details of the bargaining may be superfluous. How can such a model be made parsimonious? The three models are obviously not exclusive alternatives. Indeed, the paradigms highlight the partial emphasis of the framework—what each emphasizes and what it leaves out. Each concentrates on one class of variables, in effect, relegating other important factors to a *ceteris parabus* clause. Model I concentrates on "market factors:" pressures and incentives created by the "international strategic marketplace." Models II and III focus on the internal mechanism of the government that chooses in this environment. But can these relations be more fully specified? Adequate synthesis would require a typology of decisions and actions, some of which are more amenable to treatment in terms of one model and some to another. Government behavior is but one cluster of factors relevant to occurrences in foreign affairs. Most students of foreign policy adopt this focus (at least when explaining and predicting). Nevertheless, the dimensions of the chess board, the character of the pieces, and the rules of the game—factors considered by international systems theorists—constitute the context in which the pieces are moved. Can the major variables in the full function of determinants of foreign policy outcomes be identified?

Both the outline of a partial, *ad hoc* working synthesis of the models, and a sketch of their uses in activities other than explanation can be suggested by generating predictions in terms of each. Strategic surrender is an important problem of international relations and diplomatic history. War termination is a new, developing area of the strategic literature. Both of these interests lead scholars to address a central question: *Why* do nations surrender *when*? Whether implicit in explanations or more explicit in analysis, diplomatic historians and strategists rely upon propositions which can be turned forward to produce predictions. Thus at the risk of being timely—and in error—the present situation (August, 1968) offers an interesting test case: Why will North Vietnam surrender when?[76]

In a nutshell, analysis according to Model I asserts: nations quit when costs outweigh the benefits. North Vietnam will surrender when she realizes "that continued fighting can only generate additional costs without hope of compensating gains, this expectation being largely the consequence of the previous application of force by the dominant side."[77] U.S. actions can increase or decrease Hanoi's strategic costs. Bombing North Vietnam increases the pain and thus increases the probability of surrender. This proposition and prediction are not without meaning. That—"other things being equal"—nations are more likely to surrender when the strategic cost-benefit balance is negative, is true. Nations rarely surrender when they are winning. The proposition specifies a range within which nations surrender. But over this broad range, the relevant question is: why do nations surrender?

Models II and III focus upon the government machine through which this fact about the international strategic marketplace must be filtered to produce a surrender. These analysts are considerably less sanguine about the possibility of surrender *at the point* that the cost-benefit calculus turns negative. Never in history (i.e., in none of the five cases I have examined) have nations surrendered at that point. Surrender occurs sometime thereafter. *When* depends on process of organizations and politics of players within these governments—as they are affected by the opposing government. Moreover, the effects of the victorious power's action upon the surrendering nation cannot be adequately summarized as increasing or decreasing strategic costs. Imposing additional costs by bombing a nation may increase the probability of surrender. But it also may reduce it. An appreciation of the impact of the acts of one nation upon another thus requires some understanding of the machine which is being influenced. For more precise prediction, Models II and III require considerably more information about the organizations and politics of North Vietnam than is publicly available. On the basis of the limited public information, however, these models can be suggestive.

Model II examines two sub-problems. First, to have lost is not sufficient. The government must know that the strategic cost-benefit calculus is negative. But neither the categories, nor the indicators, of strategic costs and benefits are clear. And the sources of information about both are organizations whose parochial priorities and perceptions do not facilitate accurate information or estimation. Military evaluation of military performance, military estimates of factors like "enemy morale," and military predictions concerning when "the tide will turn" or "the corner will have been turned" are typically distorted. In cases of highly decentralized guerrilla operations, like Vietnam, these problems are exacerbated. Thus strategic costs will be underestimated. Only highly *visible* costs can have direct impact on leaders without being filtered through organizational channels. Second, since organizations define the details of options and execute actions, surrender (and negotiation) is likely to entail considerable bungling in the early stages. No organization can define options or prepare programs for this treasonous act. Thus, early overtures will be uncoordinated with the acts of other organizations, e.g., the fighting forces, creating contradictory "signals" to the victor.

Model III suggests that surrender will not come at the point that strategic costs outweigh benefits, but that it will not wait until the leadership group concludes that the war is lost. Rather the problem is better understood in terms of four additional propositions. First, strong advocates of the war effort, whose careers are closely identified with the war, rarely come to the conclusion that costs outweigh benefits. Second, quite often from the outset of a war, a number of members of the government (particularly those whose responsibilities sensitize them to problems other than war, e.g., economic planners or intelligence experts) are convinced that the war effort is futile. Third, surrender is likely to come as the result of a political shift that enhances the effective power of the latter group (and adds swing members to it). Fourth, the course of the war, particularly actions of the victor, can influence the advantages and disadvantages of players in the loser's government. Thus, North Vietnam will surrender not when its leaders have a change of heart, but when Hanoi has a change of leaders (or a change of effective power within the central circle). How U.S. bombing (or pause), threats, promises, or action in the South affect the game in Hanoi is subtle but nonetheless crucial.

That these three models could be applied to the surrender of governments other than North Vietnam should be obvious. But that exercise is left for the reader.

Notes

- A longer version of this paper was presented at the Annual Meeting of the American Political Science Association, September, 1968 (reproduced by the Rand Corporation, P-3919). The paper is part of a larger study, scheduled for publication in 1969 under the title *Bureaucracy and Policy: Conceptual Models and the Cuban Missile Crisis*. For support in various stages of this work I am indebted to the Institute of Politics in the John F. Kennedy School of Government and the Center for

International Affairs, both at Harvard University, the Rand Corporation, and the Council on Foreign Relations. For critical stimulation and advice I am especially grateful to Richard E. Neustadt, Thomas C. Schelling, Andrew W. Marshall, and Elisabeth K. Allison.

1. Theodore Sorensen, *Kennedy* (New York, 1965), p. 705.

2. In attempting to understand problems of foreign affairs, analysts engage in a number of related, but logically separable enterprises: (a) description, (b) explanation, (c) prediction, (d) evaluation, and (e) recommendation. This essay focuses primarily on explanation (and by implication, prediction).

3. In arguing that explanations proceed in terms of implicit conceptual models, this essay makes no claim that foreign policy analysts have developed any satisfactory, empirically tested theory. In this essay, the use of the term "model" without qualifiers should be read "conceptual scheme."

4. For the purpose of this argument we shall accept Carl G. Hempel's characterization of the logic of explanation: an explanation "answers the question, '*Why* did the explanadum-phenomenon occur?' by showing that the phenomenon resulted from particular circumstances, specified in C1, C2, . . . Ck, in accordance with laws L1, L2, . . . Lr. By pointing this out, the argument shows that, given the particular circumstances and the laws in question, the occurrence of the phenomenon was to be *expected;* and it is in this sense that the explanation enables us to understand why the phenomenon occurred." *Aspects of Scientific Explanation* (New York, 1965), p. 337. While various patterns of explanation can be distinguished, *viz.*, Ernest Nagel, *The Structure of Science: Problems in the Logic of Scientific Explanation,* New York, 1961), satisfactory scientific explanations exhibit this basic logic. Consequently prediction is the converse of explanation.

5. Earlier drafts of this argument have aroused heated arguments concerning proper names for these models. To choose names from ordinary language is to court confusion, as well as familiarity. Perhaps it is best to think of these models as I, II, and III.

6. In strict terms, the "outcomes" which these three models attempt to explain are essentially actions of national governments, i.e., the sum of activities of all individuals employed by a government relevant to an issue. These models focus not on a state of affairs, i.e., a full description of the world, but upon national decision and implementation. This distinction is stated clearly by Harold and Margaret Sprout, "Environmental Factors on the Study of International Politics," in James Rosenau (ed.), *International Politics and Foreign Policy* (Glencoe, Illinois, 1961), p. 116. This restriction excludes explanations offered principally in terms of international systems theories. Nevertheless, this restriction is not severe, since few interesting explanations of occurrences in foreign policy have been produced at that level of analysis. According to David Singer, "The nation state—our primary actor in international relations . . . is clearly the traditional focus among Western students and is the one which dominates all of the texts employed in English-speaking colleges and universities." David Singer, "The Level-of-Analysis Problem in International Relations," Klaus Knorr and Sidney Verba (eds.), *The International System* (Princeton, 1961). Similarly, Richard Brody's review of contemporary trends in the study of international relations finds that "scholars have come increasingly to focus on acts of nations. That is, they all focus on the behavior of nations in some respect. Having an interest in accounting for the behavior of nations in common, the prospects for a common frame of reference are enhanced."

7. For further development and support of these arguments see the author's larger study, *Bureaucracy and Policy: Conceptual Models and the Cuban Missile Crisis* (forthcoming). In its abbreviated form, the argument must, at some points, appear overly stark. The limits of space have forced the omission of many reservations and refinements.

8. Each of the three "case snapshots" displays the work of a conceptual model as it is applied to explain the U.S. blockade of Cuba. But these three cuts are primarily exercises in hypothesis generation rather than hypothesis testing. Especially when separated from the larger study, these accounts may be misleading. The sources for these accounts include the full public record plus a large number of interviews with participants in the crisis.

9. *New York Times*, February 18, 1967.

10. *Ibid.*

11. Arnold Horelick and Myron Rush, *Strategic Power and Soviet Foreign Policy* (Chicago, 1965). Based on A. Horelick, "The Cuban Missile Crisis: An Analysis of Soviet Calculations and Behavior," *World Politics* (April, 1964).

12. Horelick and Rush, Strategic Power and Soviet Foreign Policy, p. 154.

13. Hans Morgenthau, *Politics Among Nations* (3rd ed.; New York, 1960), p. 191.

14. *Ibid.*, p. 192.

15. Ibid., p. 5.

16. *Ibid.*, pp. 5–6.

17. The larger study examines several exceptions to this generalization. Sidney Verba's excellent essay "Assumptions of Rationality and Non-Rationality in Models of the International System" is less an exception than it is an approach to a some what different problem. Verba focuses upon models of rationality and irrationality of *individual* statesmen: in Knorr and Verba, *The International System.*

18. Robert K. Merton, *Social Theory and Social Structures* (Revised and Enlarged Edition; New York, 1957), pp. 12-16. Considerably weaker than a satisfactory theoretical model, paradigms nevertheless represent a short step in that direction from looser, implicit conceptual models. Neither the concepts nor the relations among the variables are sufficiently specified to yield propositions deductively.

"Paradigmatic Analysis" nevertheless has considerable promise for clarifying and codifying styles of analysis in political science. Each of the paradigms stated here can be represented rigorously in mathematical terms. For example, Model I lends itself to mathematical formulation along the lines of Herbert Simon's "Behavioral Theory of Rationality," *Models of Man* (New York, 1957). But this does not solve the most difficult problem of "measurement and estimation."

19. Though a variant of this model could easily be stochastic, this paradigm is stated in non-probabilistic terms. In contemporary strategy, a stochastic version of this model is sometimes used for predictions; but it is almost impossible to find an explanation of an occurrence in foreign affairs that is consistently probabilistic. Analogies between Model I and the concept of explanation developed by R. G. Collingwood, William Dray, and other "revisionists" among philosophers concerned with the critical philosophy of history are not accidental. For a summary of the "revisionist position" see Maurice Mandelbaum, "Historical Explanation: The Problem of Covering Laws," *History and Theory* (1960).

20. This model is an analogue of the theory of the rational entrepreneur which has been developed extensively in economic theories of the firm and the consumer. These two propositions specify the "substitution effect." Refinement of this model and specification of additional general propositions by translating from the economic theory is straightforward.

21. *New York Times*, March 22, 1969.

22. The influence of organizational studies upon the present literature of foreign affairs is minimal. Specialists in international politics are not students of organization theory. Organization theory has only recently begun to study organizations as decision-makers and has not yet produced behavioral studies of national security organizations from a decision-making perspective. It seems unlikely, however, that these gaps will remain unfilled much longer. Considerable progress has been made in the study of the business firm as an organization. Scholars have begun applying these insights to government organizations, and interest in an organizational perspective is spreading among institutions and individuals concerned with actual government operations. The "decisionmaking" approach represented by Richard Snyder, R. Bruck, and B. Sapin, *Foreign Policy Decision-Making* (Glencoe, Illinois, 1962), incorporates a number of insights from organization theory.

23. The formulation of this paradigm is indebted both to the orientation and insights of Herbert Simon and to the behavioral model of the firm stated by Richard Cyert and James March, *A Behavioral Theory of the Firm* (Englewood Cliffs, 1963). Here, however, one is forced to grapple with the less routine, less quantified functions of the less differentiated elements in government organizations.

24. Theodore Sorensen, "You Get to Walk to Work," *New York Times Magazine,* March 19, 1967.

25. Organizations are not monolithic. The proper level of disaggregation depends upon the objectives of a piece of analysis. This paradigm is formulated with reference to the major organizations that constitute the U.S. government. Generalization to the major components of each department and agency should be relatively straightforward.

26. The stability of these constraints is dependent on such factors as rules for promotion and reward, budgeting and accounting procedures, and mundane operating procedures.

27. Marriner Eccles, *Beckoning Frontiers* (New York, 1951), p. 336.

28. Arthur Schlesinger, *A Thousand Days* (Boston, 1965), p. 406.

29. This paradigm relies upon the small group of analysts who have begun to fill the gap. My primary source is the model implicit in the work of Richard E. Neustadt, though his concentration on presidential action has been generalized to a concern with policy as the outcome of political bargaining among a number of independent players, the President amounting to no more than a "superpower" among many lesser but considerable powers. As Warner Schilling argues, the substantive problems are of such inordinate difficulty that uncertainties and differences with regard to goals, alternatives, and consequences are inevitable. This necessitates what Roger Hilsman describes as the process of conflict and consensus building. The techniques employed in this process often resemble those used in legislative assemblies, though Samuel Huntington's characterization of the process as "legislative" overemphasizes the equality of participants as opposed to the hierarchy which structures the game. Moreover, whereas for Huntington, foreign policy (in contrast to military policy) is set by the executive, this paradigm maintains that the activities which he describes as legislative are characteristic of the process by which foreign policy is made.

30. The theatrical metaphor of stage, roles, and actors is more common than this metaphor of games, positions, and players. Nevertheless, the rigidity connoted by the concept of "role" both in the theatrical sense of actors reciting fixed lines and in the sociological sense of fixed responses to specified social situations makes the concept of games, positions, and players more useful for this analysis of active participants in the determination of national policy. Objections to the terminology on the grounds that "game" connotes non-serious play overlook the concept's application to most serious problems both in Wittgenstein's philosophy and in contemporary game theory. Game theory typically treats more precisely structured games, but Wittgenstein's examination of the "language game" wherein men use words to communicate is quite analogous to this analysis of the less specified game of bureaucratic politics. See Ludwig Wittgenstein, *Philosophical Investigations,* and Thomas Schelling, "What is Game Theory?" in James Charlesworth, *Contemporary Political Analysis.*

31. Inclusion of the President's Special Assistant for National Security Affairs in the tier of "Chiefs" rather than

among the "Staffers" involves a debatable choice. In fact he is both super-staffer and near-chief. His position has no statutory authority. He is especially dependent upon good relations with the President and the Secretaries of Defense and State. Nevertheless, he stands astride a genuine action-channel. The decision to include this position among the Chiefs reflects my judgment that the Bundy function is becoming institutionalized.

32. Richard E. Neustadt, Testimony, United States Senate, Committee on Government Operations, Subcommittee on National Security Staffing, *Administration of National Security*, March 26, 1963, pp. 82–83.

33. This aphorism was stated first, I think, by Don K. Price.

34. Paul Y. Hammond, "Super Carriers and B-36 Bombers," in Harold Stein (ed.), *American Civil-Military Decisions* (Birmingham, 1963).

35. Roberta Wohlstetter, *Pearl Harbor* (Stanford, 1962), p. 350.

36. Sorensen, *Kennedy*, p. 670.

37. *Ibid*.

38. *Ibid*., pp. 670ff.

39. *New york Times*, August, September, 1962.

40. *New York Times*, August 20, 1962.

41. *New York Times*, September 5, 1962.

42. *New York Times*, September 14, 1962.

43. *New york Times* October14, 1962.

44. Cited by Abel, *op. cit*., p. 13.

45. *New York Times*, September 5, 1962.

46. *New York Times*, September 14, 1962.

47. Senate Foreign Relations Committee; Senate Armed Services Committee; House Committee on Appropriation; House Select Committee on Export Control.

48. Abel, *op. cit*., pp. 17–18. According to McCone, he told Kennedy, "The only construction I can put on the material going into Cuba is that the Russians are preparing to introduce offensive missiles." See also Weintal and Bartlett, *op. cit*., pp. 60–61.

49. Abel, *op. cit*., p. 23.

50. *New York Times*, September 10, 1962.

51. See Abel, *op. cit*., pp. 25–26; and Hilsman, *op. cit*., p. 174.

52. Department of Defense Appropriation, *Hearings*, 69.

53. A basic, but somewhat contradictory, account of parts of this story emerges in the Department of Defense Appropriations, *Hearings*. 1–70.

54. Department of Defense Appropriations, *Hearings*, 71.

55. The details of the 10 days between the October 4 decision and the October 14 flight must be held in abeyance.

56. Abel, *op. cit*., p. 44.

57. *Ibid*., pp. 44ff.

58. See Richard Neustadt, "Afterword," *Presidential Power* (New York, 1964).

59. Sorensen, *Kennedy*, p. 676; Schlesinger, *op. cit*., p. 801.

60. Hilsman, *op. cit*., p. 195.

61. *Ibid*.

62. Weintal and Bartlett, *op. cit*., p. 67; Abel, *op. cit*., p. 53.

63. Schlesinger, *op. cit*., p. 803.

64. *Ibid*., p. 831.

65. Abel, *op. cit*., p. 186.

66. *Ibid*., p. 49.

67. Interview, quoted by Ronald Steel, *New York Review of Books*, March 13, 1969, p. 22.

68. Sorensen, *Kennedy*, p. 686.

69. *Ibid*., p. 691.

70. *Ibid*., pp. 691–692.

71. Schlesinger, *op. cit*., p. 296.

72. Space will not permit an account of the path from this coalition to the formal government decision on Saturday and action on Monday.

73. *Bureaucracy and Policy* (forthcoming, 1969).

74. Thus my position is quite distinct from both poles in the recent "great debate" about international relations. While many "traditionalists" of the sort Kaplan attacks adopt the first posture and many "scientists" of the sort attacked by Bull adopt the second, this third posture is relatively neutral with respect to whatever is in substantive dispute. See Hedly Bull, "International Theory: The Case for a Classical Approach," *World Politics* (April, 1966); and Morton Kaplan, "The New Great Debate: Traditionalism vs. Science in International Relations," *World Politics* (October, 1966).

75. A number of problems are now being examined in these terms both in the Bureaucracy Study Group on Bureaucracy and Policy of the Institute of Politics at Harvard University and at the Rand Corporation.

76. In response to several readers' recommendations, what follows is reproduced *verbatim* from the paper delivered at the September, 1968 Association meetings (Rand P-3919). The discussion is heavily indebted to Ernest R. May.

77. Richard Snyder, *Deterrence and Defense* (Princeton, 1961), p. 11. For a more general presentation of this position see Paul Kecskemeti, *Strategic Surrender* (New York, 1964).

10 Ethical Traditions in International Relations

10.1

The Melian Dialogue

Thucydides

Sixteenth Year of the War—The Melian Conference—Fate of Melos

The next summer Alcibiades sailed with twenty ships to Argos and seized the suspected persons still left of the Lacedaemonian faction to the number of three hundred, whom the Athenians forthwith lodged in the neighbouring islands of their empire. The Athenians also made an expedition against the isle of Melos with thirty ships of their own, six Chian, and two Lesbian vessels, sixteen hundred heavy infantry, three hundred archers, and twenty mounted archers from Athens, and about fifteen hundred heavy infantry from the allies and the islanders. The Melians are a colony of Lacedaemon that would not submit to the Athenians like the other islanders, and at first remained neutral and took no part in the struggle, but afterwards upon the Athenians using violence and plundering their territory, assumed an attitude of open hostility. Cleomedes, son of Lycomedes, and Tisias, son of Tisimachus, the generals, encamping in their territory with the above armament, before doing any harm to their land, sent envoys to negotiate. These the Melians did not bring before the people, but bade them state the object of their mission to the magistrates and the few; upon which the Athenian envoys spoke as follows:

ATHENIANS. Since the negotiations are not to go on before the people, in order that we may not be able to speak straight on without interruption, and deceive the ears of the multitude by seductive arguments which would pass without refutation (for we know that this is the meaning of our being brought before the few), what if you who sit there were to pursue a method more cautious still? Make no set speech yourselves, but take us up at whatever you do not like, and settle that before going any farther. And first tell us if this proposition of ours suits you.

The Melian commissioners answered:

MELIANS. To the fairness of quietly instructing each other as you propose there is nothing to object; but your military preparations are too far advanced to agree with what you say, as we see you are come to be judges in your own cause, and that all we can reasonably expect from this negotiation is war, if we prove to have right on our side and refuse to submit, and in the contrary case, slavery.

ATHENIANS. If you have met to reason about presentiments of the future, or for anything else than to consult for the safety of your state upon the facts that you see before you, we will give over; otherwise we will go on.

Source: Excerpts from Thucydides (431 BCE), "The Melian Dialogue," in *The History of the Peloponnesian War*, Book V, Chapters 84–116.

MELIANS. It is natural and excusable for men in our position to turn more ways than one both in thought and utterance. However, the question in this conference is, as you say, the safety of our country; and the discussion, if you please, can proceed in the way which you propose.

ATHENIANS. For ourselves, we shall not trouble you with specious pretences—either of how we have a right to our empire because we overthrew the Mede, or are now attacking you because of wrong that you have done us—and make a long speech which would not be believed; and in return we hope that you, instead of thinking to influence us by saying that you did not join the Lacedaemonians, although their colonists, or that you have done us no wrong, will aim at what is feasible, holding in view the real sentiments of us both; since you know as well as we do that right, as the world goes, is only in question between equals in power, while the strong do what they can and the weak suffer what they must.

MELIANS. As we think, at any rate, it is expedient—we speak as we are obliged, since you enjoin us to let right alone and talk only of interest—that you should not destroy what is our common protection, the privilege of being allowed in danger to invoke what is fair and right, and even to profit by arguments not strictly valid if they can be got to pass current. And you are as much interested in this as any, as your fall would be a signal for the heaviest vengeance and an example for the world to meditate upon.

ATHENIANS. The end of our empire, if end it should, does not frighten us: a rival empire like Lacedaemon, even if Lacedaemon was our real antagonist, is not so terrible to the vanquished as subjects who by themselves attack and overpower their rulers. This, however, is a risk that we are content to take. We will now proceed to show you that we come here in the interest of our empire, and that we shall say what we are now going to say, for the preservation of your country; as we would fain exercise that empire over you without trouble, and see you preserved for the good of us both.

MELIANS. And how, pray, could it turn out as good for us to serve as for you to rule?

ATHENIANS. Because you would have the advantage of submitting before suffering the worst, and we should gain by not destroying you.

MELIANS. So that you would not consent to our being neutral, friends instead of enemies, but allies of neither side.

ATHENIANS. No; for your hostility cannot so much hurt us as your friendship will be an argument to our subjects of our weakness, and your enmity of our power.

MELIANS. Is that your subjects' idea of equity, to put those who have nothing to do with you in the same category with peoples that are most of them your own colonists, and some conquered rebels?

ATHENIANS. As far as right goes they think one has as much of it as the other, and that if any maintain their independence it is because they are strong, and that if we do not molest them it is because we are afraid; so that besides extending our empire we should gain in security by your subjection; the fact that you are islanders and weaker than others rendering it all the more important that you should not succeed in baffling the masters of the sea.

MELIANS. But do you consider that there is no security in the policy which we indicate? For here again if you debar us from talking about justice and invite us to obey your interest, we also must explain ours, and try to persuade you, if the two happen to coincide. How can you avoid making enemies of all existing neutrals who shall look at case from it that one day or another you will attack them? And what is this but to make greater the enemies that you have already, and to force others to become so who would otherwise have never thought of it?

ATHENIANS. Why, the fact is that continentals generally give us but little alarm; the liberty which they enjoy will long prevent their taking precautions against us; it is rather islanders like yourselves, outside our empire, and subjects smarting under the yoke, who would be the most likely to take a rash step and lead themselves and us into obvious danger.

MELIANS. Well then, if you risk so much to retain your empire, and your subjects to get rid of it, it were surely great baseness and cowardice in us who are still free not to try everything that can be tried, before submitting to your yoke.

ATHENIANS. Not if you are well advised, the contest not being an equal one, with honour as the prize and shame as the penalty, but a question of self-preservation and of not resisting those who are far stronger than you are.

MELIANS. But we know that the fortune of war is sometimes more impartial than the disproportion of numbers might lead one to suppose; to submit is to give ourselves over to despair, while action still preserves for us a hope that we may stand erect.

ATHENIANS. Hope, danger's comforter, may be indulged in by those who have abundant resources, if not without loss at all events without ruin; but its nature is to be extravagant, and those who go so far as to put their all upon the venture see it in its true colours only when they are ruined; but so long as the discovery would enable them to guard against it, it is never found wanting. Let not this be the case with you, who are weak and hang on a single turn of the scale; nor be like the vulgar, who, abandoning such security as human means may still afford, when visible hopes fail them in extremity, turn to invisible, to prophecies and oracles, and other such inventions that delude men with hopes to their destruction.

MELIANS. You may be sure that we are as well aware as you of the difficulty of contending against your power and fortune, unless the terms be equal. But we trust that the gods may grant us fortune as good as yours, since we are just men fighting against unjust, and that what we want in power will be made up by the alliance of the Lacedaemonians, who are bound, if only for very shame, to come to the aid of their kindred. Our confidence, therefore, after all is not so utterly irrational.

ATHENIANS. When you speak of the favour of the gods, we may as fairly hope for that as yourselves; neither our pretensions nor our conduct being in any way contrary to what men believe of the gods, or practise among themselves. Of the gods we believe, and of men we know, that by a necessary law of their nature they rule wherever they can. And it is not as if we were the first to make this law, or to act upon it when made: we found it existing before us, and shall leave it to exist for ever after us; all we do is to make use of it, knowing that you and everybody else, having the same power as we have, would do the same as we do. Thus, as far as the gods are concerned, we have no fear and no reason to fear that we shall be at a disadvantage. But when we come to your notion about the Lacedaemonians, which leads you to believe that shame will make them help you, here we bless your simplicity but do not envy your folly. The Lacedaemonians, when their own interests or their country's laws are in question, are the worthiest men alive; of their conduct towards others much might be said, but no clearer idea of it could be given than by shortly saying that of all the men we know they are most conspicuous in considering what is agreeable honourable, and what is expedient just. Such a way of thinking does not promise much for the safety which you now unreasonably count upon.

MELIANS. But it is for this very reason that we now trust to their respect for expediency to prevent them from betraying the Melians, their colonists, and thereby losing the confidence of their friends in Hellas and helping their enemies.

ATHENIANS. Then you do not adopt the view that expediency goes with security, while justice and honour cannot be followed without danger; and danger the Lacedaemonians generally court as little as possible.

MELIANS. But we believe that they would be more likely to face even danger for our sake, and with more confidence than for others, as our nearness to Peloponnese makes it easier for them to act, and our common blood ensures our fidelity.

ATHENIANS. Yes, but what an intending ally trusts to is not the goodwill of those who ask his aid, but a decided superiority of power for action; and the Lacedaemonians look to this even more than others. At least, such is their distrust of their home resources that it is only with numerous allies that they attack a neighbour; now is it likely that while we are masters of the sea they will cross over to an island?

MELIANS. But they would have others to send. The Cretan Sea is a wide one, and it is more difficult for those who command it to intercept others, than for those who wish to elude them to do so safely. And should the Lacedaemonians miscarry in this, they would fall upon your land, and upon those left of your allies whom Brasidas did not reach; and instead of places which are not yours, you will have to fight for your own country and your own confederacy.

ATHENIANS. Some diversion of the kind you speak of you may one day experience, only to learn, as others have done, that the Athenians never once yet withdrew from a siege for fear of any. But we are struck by the fact that, after saying you would consult for the safety of your country, in all this discussion you have mentioned nothing which men might trust in and think to be saved by. Your strongest arguments depend upon hope and the future, and your actual resources are too scanty, as compared with those arrayed against you, for you to come out victorious. You will therefore show great blindness of judgment, unless, after allowing us to retire, you can find some counsel more prudent than this. You will surely not be caught by that idea of disgrace, which in dangers that are disgraceful, and at the same time too plain to be mistaken, proves so fatal to mankind; since in too many cases the very men that have their eyes perfectly open to what they are rushing into, let the thing called disgrace, by the mere influence of a seductive name, lead them on to a point at which they become so enslaved by the phrase as in fact to fall wilfully into hopeless disaster, and incur disgrace more disgraceful as the companion of error, than when it comes as the result of misfortune. This, if you are well advised, you will guard against; and you will not think it dishonourable to submit to the greatest city in Hellas, when it makes you the moderate offer of becoming its tributary ally, without ceasing to enjoy the country that belongs to you; nor when you have the choice given you between war and security, will you be so blinded as to choose the worse. And it is certain that those who do not yield to their equals, who keep terms with their superiors, and are moderate towards their inferiors, on the whole succeed best. Think over the matter, therefore, after our withdrawal, and reflect once and again that it is for your country that you are consulting, that you have not more than one, and that upon this one deliberation depends its prosperity or ruin.

The Athenians now withdrew from the conference; and the Melians, left to themselves, came to a decision corresponding with what they had maintained in the discussion, and answered:

> "Our resolution, Athenians, is the same as it was at first. We will not in a moment deprive of freedom a city that has been inhabited these seven hundred years; but we put our trust in the fortune by which the gods have preserved it until now, and in the help of men, that is, of the Lacedaemonians; and so we will try and save ourselves. Meanwhile we invite you to allow us to be friends to you and foes to neither party, and to retire from our country after making such a treaty as shall seem fit to us both."

Such was the answer of the Melians. The Athenians now departing from the conference said:

> "Well, you alone, as it seems to us, judging from these resolutions, regard what is future as more certain than what is before your eyes, and what is out of sight, in your eagerness, as already coming to pass; and as you have staked most on, and trusted most in, the Lacedaemonians, your fortune, and your hopes, so will you be most completely deceived."

The Athenian envoys now returned to the army; and the Melians showing no signs of yielding, the generals at once betook themselves to hostilities, and drew a line of circumvallation round the Melians, dividing the work among the different states. Subsequently the Athenians returned with most of their army, leaving behind them a certain number of their own citizens and of the allies to keep guard by land and sea. The force thus left stayed on and besieged the place.

About the same time the Argives invaded the territory of Phlius and lost eighty men cut off in an ambush by the Phliasians and Argive exiles. Meanwhile the Athenians at Pylos took so much plunder from the Lacedaemonians that the latter, although they still refrained from breaking off the treaty and going to war with Athens, yet proclaimed that any of their people that chose might plunder the Athenians. The Corinthians also commenced hostilities with the Athenians for private quarrels of their own; but the rest of the Peloponnesians stayed quiet. Meanwhile the Melians attacked by night and took the part of the Athenian lines over against the market, and killed some of the men, and brought in corn and all else that they could find useful to them, and so returned and kept quiet, while the Athenians took measures to keep better guard in future.

Summer was now over. The next winter the Lacedaemonians intended to invade the Argive territory, but arriving at the frontier found the sacrifices for crossing unfavourable, and went back again. This intention of theirs gave the Argives suspicions of certain of their fellow citizens, some of whom they arrested; others, however, escaped them. About the same time the Melians again took another part of the Athenian lines which were but feebly garrisoned. Reinforcements afterwards arriving from Athens in consequence, under the command of Philocrates, son of Demeas, the siege was now pressed vigorously; and some treachery taking place inside, the Melians surrendered at discretion to the Athenians, who put to death all the grown men whom they took, and sold the women and children for slaves, and subsequently sent out five hundred colonists and inhabited the place themselves.

10.2

Normative Ethics

James Fieser

Normative ethics involves arriving at moral standards that regulate right and wrong conduct. In a sense, it is a search for an ideal litmus test of proper behavior. The Golden Rule is a classic example of a normative principle: We should do to others what we would want others to do to us. Since I do not want my neighbor to steal my car, then it is wrong for me to steal her car. Since I would want people to feed me if I was starving, then I should help feed starving people. Using this same reasoning, I can theoretically determine whether any possible action is right or wrong. So, based on the Golden Rule, it would also be wrong for me to lie to, harass, victimize, assault, or kill others. The Golden Rule is an example of a normative theory that establishes a *single principle* against which we judge all actions. Other normative theories focus on a *set* of foundational principles, or a set of good character traits.

The key assumption in normative ethics is that there is only *one* ultimate criterion of moral conduct, whether it is a single rule or a set of principles. Three strategies will be noted here: (1) virtue theories, (2) duty theories, and (3) consequentialist theories.

Virtue Theories

Many philosophers believe that morality consists of following precisely defined rules of conduct, such as "don't kill," or "don't steal." Presumably, I must learn these rules, and then make sure each of my actions live up to the rules. Virtue ethics, however, places less emphasis on learning rules, and instead stresses the importance of developing *good habits of character*, such as benevolence. Once I've acquired benevolence, for example, I will then habitually act in a benevolent manner. Historically, virtue theory is one of the oldest normative traditions in Western philosophy, having its roots in ancient Greek civilization. Plato emphasized four virtues in particular, which were later called *cardinal virtues*: wisdom, courage, temperance and justice. Other important virtues are fortitude, generosity, self-respect, good temper, and sincerity. In addition to advocating good habits of character, virtue theorists hold that we should avoid acquiring bad character traits, or *vices*, such as cowardice, insensibility, injustice, and vanity. Virtue theory emphasizes moral education since virtuous character traits are developed in one's youth. Adults, therefore, are responsible for instilling virtues in the young.

Aristotle argued that virtues are good habits that we acquire, which regulate our emotions. For example, in response to my natural feelings of fear, I should develop the virtue of courage, which allows me to be firm when facing danger. Analyzing 11 specific virtues, Aristotle argued that most virtues fall at a mean between more extreme character traits. With courage, for example, if I do not have enough courage, I develop the disposition of cowardice, which is a vice. If I have too much courage I develop the disposition of rashness, which is also a vice. According to Aristotle, it is not an easy task to find the perfect mean between extreme character traits. In fact, we need assistance from our reason to do this. After Aristotle, medieval theologians supplemented Greek lists of virtues with three Christian ones, or *theological virtues*: faith, hope, and charity. Interest in virtue theory continued through the middle ages and declined in the 19th century with the rise of alternative moral theories below. In the mid 20th century virtue theory received special attention from philosophers who believed that more recent approaches ethical theories were misguided for focusing too heavily on rules and actions, rather than on virtuous character traits. Alasdaire MacIntyre (1984) defended the central role of virtues in moral theory and argued that virtues are grounded in and emerge from within social traditions.

Duty Theories

Many of us feel that there are clear obligations we have as human beings, such as to care for our children, and

Source: Reprinted by permission of James Fieser.

to not commit murder. Duty theories base morality on specific, foundational principles of obligation. These theories are sometimes called *deontological*, from the Greek word *deon*, or duty, in view of the foundational nature of our duty or obligation. They are also sometimes called *nonconsequentialist* since these principles are obligatory, irrespective of the consequences that might follow from our actions. For example, it is wrong to not care for our children even if it results in some great benefit, such as financial savings. There are four central duty theories.

The *first* is that championed by 17th century German philosopher Samuel Pufendorf, who classified dozens of duties under three headings: duties to God, duties to oneself, and duties to others. Concerning our duties towards God, he argued that there are two kinds:

- a theoretical duty to know the existence and nature of God, and
- a practical duty to both inwardly and outwardly worship God.

Concerning our duties towards oneself, these are also of two sorts:

- duties of the soul, which involve developing one's skills and talents, and
- duties of the body, which involve not harming our bodies, as we might through gluttony or drunkenness, and not killing oneself.

Concerning our duties towards others, Pufendorf divides these between absolute duties, which are universally binding on people, and conditional duties, which are the result of contracts between people. Absolute duties are of three sorts:

- avoid wronging others,
- treat people as equals, and
- promote the good of others.

Conditional duties involve various types of agreements; the principal one of which is the duty is to keep one's promises.

A *second* duty-based approach to ethics is *rights theory*. Most generally, a "right" is a justified claim against another person's behavior—such as my right to not be harmed by you. Rights and duties are related in such a way that the rights of one person implies the duties of another person. For example, if I have a right to payment of $10 by Smith, then Smith has a duty to pay me $10. This is called the correlativity of rights and duties. The most influential early account of rights theory is that of 17th century British philosopher John Locke, who argued that the laws of nature mandate that we should not harm anyone's life, health, liberty or possessions. For Locke, these are our natural rights, given to us by God. Following Locke, the United States Declaration of Independence authored by Thomas Jefferson recognizes three foundational rights: life, liberty, and the pursuit of happiness. Jefferson and other rights theorists maintained that we deduce other more specific rights from these, including the rights of property, movement, speech, and religious expression. There are four features traditionally associated with moral rights. First, rights are *natural* insofar as they are not invented or created by governments. Second, they are *universal* insofar as they do not change from country to country. Third, they are *equal* in the sense that rights are the same for all people, irrespective of gender, race, or handicap. Fourth, they are *inalienable* which means that I cannot hand over my rights to another person, such as by selling myself into slavery.

A *third* duty-based theory is that by Kant, which emphasizes a single principle of duty. Influenced by Pufendorf, Kant agreed that we have moral duties to oneself and others, such as developing one's talents, and keeping our promises to others. However, Kant argued that there is a more foundational principle of duty that encompasses our particular duties. It is a single, self-evident principle of reason that he calls the "categorical imperative." A categorical imperative, he argued, is fundamentally different from hypothetical imperatives that hinge on some personal desire that we have, for example, "If you want to get a good job, then you ought to go to college." By contrast, a categorical imperative simply mandates an action, irrespective of one's personal desires, such as "You ought to do X." Kant gives at least four versions of the categorical imperative, but one is especially direct: Treat people as an end, and never as a means to an end. That is, we should always treat people with dignity, and never use them as mere instruments. For Kant, we treat people as an end whenever our actions toward someone reflect the inherent value of that person. Donating to charity, for example, is morally correct since this acknowledges the inherent value of the recipient. By contrast, we treat someone as a means to an end whenever we treat that person as a tool to achieve something else. It is wrong, for example, to steal my neighbor's car since I would be treating her as a means to my own happiness. The categorical imperative also regulates the morality of actions that affect us individually. Suicide, for example, would be wrong since I would be treating my life as a means to the alleviation of my misery. Kant believes that the morality of all actions can be determined by appealing to this single principle of duty.

A *fourth* and more recent duty-based theory is that by British philosopher W.D. Ross, which emphasizes *prima facie* duties. Like his 17th and 18th century counterparts, Ross argues that our duties are "part of the fundamental nature of the universe." However, Ross's list of duties is much shorter, which he believes reflects our actual moral convictions:

- *Fidelity*: the duty to keep promises
- *Reparation*: the duty to compensate others when we harm them
- *Gratitude*: the duty to thank those who help us
- *Justice*: the duty to recognize merit
- *Beneficence*: the duty to improve the conditions of others
- *Self-improvement*: the duty to improve our virtue and intelligence
- *Nonmaleficence*: the duty to not injure others

Ross recognizes that situations will arise when we must choose between two conflicting duties. In a classic example, suppose I borrow my neighbor's gun and promise to return it when he asks for it. One day, in a fit of rage, my neighbor pounds on my door and asks for the gun so that he can take vengeance on someone. On the one hand, the duty of fidelity obligates me to return the gun; on the other hand, the duty of nonmaleficence obligates me to avoid injuring others and thus not return the gun. According to Ross, I will intuitively know which of these duties is my *actual* duty, and which is my apparent or *prima facie* duty. In this case, my duty of nonmaleficence emerges as my actual duty and I should not return the gun.

Consequentialist Theories

It is common for us to determine our moral responsibility by weighing the consequences of our actions. According to consequentialism, correct moral conduct is determined *solely* by a cost-benefit analysis of an action's consequences:

> *Consequentialism*: An action is morally right if the consequences of that action are more favorable than unfavorable.

Consequentialist normative principles require that we first tally both the good and bad consequences of an action. Second, we then determine whether the total good consequences outweigh the total bad consequences. If the good consequences are greater, then the action is morally proper. If the bad consequences are greater, then the action is morally improper. Consequentialist theories are sometimes called *teleological* theories, from the Greek word *telos*, or end, since the end result of the action is the sole determining factor of its morality.

Consequentialist theories became popular in the 18th century by philosophers who wanted a quick way to morally assess an action by appealing to experience, rather than by appealing to gut intuitions or long lists of questionable duties. In fact, the most attractive feature of consequentialism is that it appeals to publicly observable consequences of actions. Most versions of consequentialism are more precisely formulated than the general principle above. In particular, competing consequentialist theories specify which consequences for affected groups of people are relevant. Three subdivisions of consequentialism emerge:

- *Ethical Egoism*: an action is morally right if the consequences of that action are more favorable than unfavorable *only to the agent* performing the action.
- *Ethical Altruism*: an action is morally right if the consequences of that action are more favorable than unfavorable *to everyone except the agent*.
- *Utilitarianism*: an action is morally right if the consequences of that action are more favorable than unfavorable *to everyone*.

All three of these theories focus on the consequences of actions for different groups of people. But, like all normative theories, the above three theories are rivals of each other. They also yield different conclusions. Consider the following example. A woman was traveling through a developing country when she witnessed a car in front of her run off the road and roll over several times. She asked the hired driver to pull over to assist, but, to her surprise, the driver accelerated nervously past the scene. A few miles down the road the driver explained that in his country if someone assists an accident victim, then the police often hold the assisting person responsible for the accident itself. If the victim dies, then the assisting person could be held responsible for the death. The driver continued explaining that road accident victims are therefore usually left unattended and often die from exposure to the country's harsh desert conditions. On the principle of ethical egoism, the woman in this illustration would only be concerned with the consequences of her attempted assistance as *she* would be affected. Clearly, the decision to drive on would be the morally proper choice. On the principle of ethical altruism, she would be concerned only with the consequences of her action as *others* are affected, particularly the accident victim. Tallying only those consequences reveals that assisting the victim would be the morally correct choice, irrespective of the negative consequences that result for her. On the principle of utilitarianism, she must consider the consequences for both herself and the victim. The outcome here is less clear, and the woman would need to precisely calculate the overall benefit versus disbenefit of her action.

Types of Utilitarianism

Jeremy Bentham presented one of the earliest fully developed systems of utilitarianism. Two features of his theory are noteworthy. First, Bentham proposed that we tally the consequences of each action we perform and thereby determine on a case-by-case basis whether an action is morally right or wrong. This aspect of Bentham's theory is known as *act-utilitarianism*. Second, Bentham also proposed that we tally the pleasure and pain, which results from our actions. For Bentham, pleasure and pain are the only consequences that matter in determining whether our conduct is moral. This aspect of Bentham's theory is known as *hedonistic utilitarianism*. Critics point out limitations in both of these aspects.

First, according to act-utilitarianism, it would be morally wrong to waste time on leisure activities such as watching television, since our time could be spent in ways that produced a greater social benefit, such as charity work. But prohibiting leisure activities doesn't seem reasonable. More significantly, according to act-utilitarianism, specific acts of torture or slavery would be morally permissible if the social benefit of these actions outweighed the disbenefit. A revised version of utilitarianism called *rule-utilitarianism* addresses these problems. According to rule-utilitarianism, a behavioral code or rule is morally right if the consequences of adopting that rule are more favorable than unfavorable to everyone. Unlike act utilitarianism, which weighs the consequences of each particular action, rule-utilitarianism offers a litmus test only for the morality of moral rules, such as "stealing is wrong." Adopting a rule against theft clearly has more favorable consequences than unfavorable consequences for everyone. The same is true for moral rules against lying or murdering. Rule-utilitarianism, then, offers a three-tiered method for judging conduct. A particular action, such as stealing my neighbor's car, is judged wrong since it violates a moral rule against theft. In turn, the rule against theft is morally binding because adopting this rule produces favorable consequences for everyone. John Stuart Mill's version of utilitarianism is rule-oriented.

Second, according to hedonistic utilitarianism, pleasurable consequences are the only factors that matter, morally speaking. This, though, seems too restrictive since it ignores other morally significant consequences that are not necessarily pleasing or painful. For example, acts which foster loyalty and friendship are valued, yet they are not always pleasing. In response to this problem, G. E. Moore proposed *ideal utilitarianism*, which involves tallying any consequence that we intuitively recognize as good or bad (and not simply as pleasurable or painful). Also, R. M. Hare proposed *preference utilitarianism*, which involves tallying any consequence that fulfills our preferences.

Ethical Egoism and Social Contract Theory

Hobbes was an advocate of the meta-ethical theory of psychological egoism—the view that all of our actions are selfishly motivated. Upon that foundation, Hobbes developed a normative theory known as *social contract theory*, which is a type of rule-ethical-egoism. According to Hobbes, for purely selfish reasons, the agent is better off living in a world with moral rules than one without moral rules. For without moral rules, we are subject to the whims of other people's selfish interests. Our property, our families, and even our lives are at continual risk. Selfishness alone will therefore motivate each agent to adopt a basic set of rules which will allow for a civilized community. Not surprisingly, these rules would include prohibitions against lying, stealing, and killing. However, these rules will ensure safety for each agent only if the rules are enforced. As selfish creatures, each of us would plunder our neighbors' property once their guards were down. Each agent would then be at risk from his neighbor. Therefore, for selfish reasons alone, we devise a means of enforcing these rules: we create a policing agency which punishes us if we violate these rules.

References

Anscombe, Elizabeth "Modern Moral Philosophy," *Philosophy*, 1958, Vol. 33, reprinted in her *Ethics, Religion and Politics* (Oxford: Blackwell, 1981).

Aristotle, *Nichomachean Ethics*, in Barnes, Jonathan, ed., *The Complete Works of Aristotle* (Princeton, N.J.: Princeton University Press, 1984).

Ayer, A. J., *Language, Truth and Logic* (New York: Dover Publications, 1946).

Baier, Kurt, *The Moral Point of View: A Rational Basis of Ethics* (Cornell University Press, 1958).

Bentham, Jeremy, Introduction to the *Principles of Morals and Legislation (1789), in The Works of Jeremy Bentham*, edited by John Bowring (London: 1838–1843).

Hare, R. M., *Moral Thinking*, (Oxford: Clarendon Press, 1981).

Hare, R. M., *The Language of Morals* (Oxford: Oxford University Press, 1952).

Hobbes, Thomas, *Leviathan*, ed., E. Curley, (Chicago, IL: Hackett Publishing Company, 1994).

Hume, David, *A Treatise of Human Nature* (1739–1740), eds. David Fate Norton, Mary J. Norton (Oxford; New York: Oxford University Press, 2000).

Kant, Immanuel, *Grounding for the Metaphysics of Morals*, tr., James W. Ellington (Indianapolis: Hackett Publishing Company, 1985).

Locke, John, *Two Treatises*, ed., Peter Laslett (Cambridge: Cambridge University Press, 1963).

MacIntyre, Alasdair, *After Virtue*, second edition, (Notre Dame: Notre Dame University Press, 1984).

Mackie, John L., *Ethics: Inventing Right and Wrong*, (New York: Penguin Books, 1977).

Mill, John Stuart, "Utilitarianism," in *Collected Works of John Stuart Mill*, ed., J. M. Robson (London: Routledge and Toronto, Ont.: University of Toronto Press, 1991).

Moore, G. E., *Principia Ethica*, (Cambridge: Cambridge University Press, 1903).

Noddings, Nel, "Ethics from the Stand Point Of Women," in Deborah L. Rhode, ed., *Theoretical Perspectives on Sexual Difference* (New Haven, CT: Yale University Press, 1990).

Ockham, William of, *Fourth Book of the Sentences*, tr. Lucan Freppert, *The Basis of Morality According to William* Ockham (Chicago: Franciscan Herald Press, 1988).

Plato, *Republic*, 6:510–511, in Cooper, John M., ed., *Plato: Complete Works* (Indianapolis: Hackett Publishing Company, 1997).

Samuel Pufendorf, *De Jure Naturae et Gentium (1762), tr. Of the Law of Nature and Nations.*

Samuel Pufendorf, *De officio hominis et civis juxta legem naturalem (1673), tr., The Whole Duty of Man according to the Law of Nature* (London, 1691).

Sextus Empiricus, *Outlines of Pyrrhonism*, trs. J. Annas and J. Barnes, *Outlines of Scepticism* (Cambridge: Cambridge University Press, 1994).

Stevenson, Charles L., *The Ethics of Language*, (New Haven: Yale University Press, 1944).

Sumner, William Graham, *Folkways* (Boston: Guinn, 1906).

10.3

Ethical Questions and International Politics

Joseph S. Nye

Given the nature of the security dilemma, some realists believe that moral concerns play no role in international conflicts. However, ethics do play a role in international relations, although not the same role as in domestic politics. Moral arguments have been used since the days of Thucydides. When Corcyra went to Athens to plead for help against Corinth, it used the language of ethics: "First of all, you will not be helping aggressors, but people who are the victims of aggression. Secondly, you will win our undying gratitude."[1] Substitute *Bosnia* for *Corcyra* and *Serbia* for *Corinth*, and those words could be uttered in modern times.

Moral arguments move and constrain people. In that sense morality is a powerful reality. However, moral arguments can also be used rhetorically as propaganda to disguise less elevated motives, and those with more power are often able to ignore moral considerations. During the Peloponnesian War, the Athenians sailed to the island of Melos to suppress a revolt. In 416 B.C., the Athenian spokesmen told the Melians that they could fight and die or they could surrender. When the Melians protested that they were fighting for their freedom, the Athenians responded that "the strong do what they have the power to do and the weak accept what they have to accept."[2] In essence, the Athenians stated that in a realist world, morality has little place. Might makes right. When Iraq invades Kuwait, or the United States invades Grenada or Panama, or the Indonesians suppress a revolt in East Timor, they all to some degree employ similar logic. But, in the modern world, it is increasingly less acceptable to state one's motives as plainly as Thucydides suggests the Athenians did in Melos. Does this mean that morality has come to occupy a more prominent place in international relations, or simply that states have become more adept at propaganda? Has international politics changed dramatically, with states more attuned to ethical concerns, or is there a clear continuity between the actions of the Athenians 2,500 years ago and the actions of Iraq or Serbia in the late twentieth century?

Moral arguments are not all the same. Some are more compelling than others. We ask whether they are logical and consistent. For instance, when the activist Phyllis Schlafly argued that nuclear weapons are a good thing because God gave them to the free world, we should wonder why God also gave them to Stalin's Soviet Union and Mao's China. Moral arguments are not all equal.

The basic touchstone for moral arguments is impartiality—the view that all interests are judged by the same criteria. Your interests deserve the same attention as mine. Within this framework of impartiality, however, there are two different traditions in Western political culture about how to judge moral arguments. One descends from Immanuel Kant, the eighteenth-century German philosopher, the other from British utilitarians of the early nineteenth century such as Jeremy Bentham. As an illustration of the two approaches, imagine walking into a poor village and finding that a military officer is about to shoot three people lined up against the wall. You ask, "Why are you shooting these peasants? They look quite harmless." The officer says, "Last night somebody in this village shot one of my men. I know somebody in this village is guilty, so I am going to shoot these three to set an example." You say, "You can't do that! You're going to kill an innocent person. If only one shot was fired, then at least two of these people are innocent, perhaps all three. You just can't do that." The officer takes a rifle from one of his men and hands it to you saying, "You shoot one of them for me and I'll let the other two go. You can save two lives if you will shoot one of them. I'm going to teach you that in civil war you can't have these holier-than-thou attitudes." What are you going to do?

You could try to mow down all the troops in a Rambo-like move, but the officer has a soldier aiming his gun at you. So your choice is to kill one innocent

Source: Joseph S. Nye, *Understanding International Conflicts*, 6th Edition.

person in order to save two or to drop the gun and have clean hands. The Kantian tradition that you do things only when they are right would require that you refuse to perpetrate the evil deed. The utilitarian tradition might suggest that if you can save two lives, you should do it. If you choose the Kantian solution, imagine the numbers were increased. Suppose there were 100 people against the wall. Or imagine you could save a city full of people from a terrorist's bomb. Should you refuse to save a million people in order to keep your hands and conscience clean? At some point, consequences matter. Moral arguments can be judged in three ways: by the motives or intentions involved, by the means used, and by their consequences or net effects. Although these dimensions are not always easily reconciled, good moral argument tries to take all three into account.

Limits on Ethics in International Relations

Ethics plays less of a role in international politics than in domestic politics for four reasons. One is the weak international consensus on values. There are cultural and religious differences over the justice of some acts. Second, states are not like individuals. States are abstractions, and although their leaders are individuals, statesmen are judged differently than when they act as individuals. For instance, when picking a roommate, most people want a person who believes "thou shalt not kill." But the same people might vote against a presidential candidate who said, "Under no circumstances will I ever take an action that will lead to a death." A president is entrusted by citizens to protect their interests, and under some circumstances this may require the use of force. Presidents who saved their own souls but failed to protect their people would not be good trustees.

In private morality, sacrifice may be the highest proof of a moral action, but should leaders sacrifice their whole people? During the Peloponnesian War, the Athenians told the leaders of the island of Melos that if they resisted, Athens would kill everyone. The Melian leaders resisted and their people were slaughtered. Should they have come to terms? In 1962, should President Kennedy have run a risk of nuclear war to force the Soviets to remove missiles from Cuba when the United States had similar missiles in Turkey? Different people may answer these questions differently. The point is when individuals act as leaders of states, their actions are judged somewhat differently.

A third reason ethics plays a lesser role in international politics is the complexity of causation. It is hard enough to know the consequences of actions in domestic affairs, but international relations has another layer of complexity: the interaction of states. That extra dimension makes it harder to accurately predict consequences. A famous example is the 1933 debate among students at the Oxford Union, the debating society of Oxford University. Mindful of the 20 million people killed in World War I, the majority of students voted for a resolution that they would never again fight for king and country. But someone else was listening: Adolf Hitler. He concluded that democracies were soft and that he could press them as hard as he wanted because they would not fight back. In the end, he pressed too far and the result was World War II, a consequence not desired or expected by those students who voted never to fight for king and country. Many later did, and many died.

A more trivial example is the "hamburger argument" of the early 1970s when people were worried about shortages of food in the world. A number of students in American colleges said, "When we go to the dining hall, refuse to eat meat because a pound of beef equals eight pounds of grain that could be used to feed poor people around the world." Many students stopped eating hamburger and felt good about themselves, but they did not help starving people in Africa or Bangladesh one bit. Why not? The grain freed up by not eating hamburgers in America did not reach the starving people in Bangladesh because those starving had no money to buy the grain. The grain was simply a surplus on the American market, which meant American prices went down and farmers produced less. To help peasants in Bangladesh required getting money to them so they could buy some of the excess grain. By launching a campaign against eating hamburger and failing to look at the complexity of the causal chain that would relate their well-intended act to its consequences, the students failed.

Finally, there is the argument that the institutions of international society are particularly weak and that the disjunction between order and justice is greater in international than in domestic politics. Order and justice are both important. In a domestic polity, we tend to take order for granted. In fact, sometimes protesters purposefully disrupt order for the sake of promoting their view of justice. But if there is total disorder, it is very hard to have any justice; witness the bombing, kidnapping, and killing by all sides in Lebanon in the 1980s or in Somalia in the 1990s. Some degree of order is a prior condition for justice. In international politics, the absence of a common legislature, central executive, or strong judiciary makes it much harder to preserve the order that precedes justice.

Three Views of the Role of Morality

At least three different views of ethics exist in international relations: those of the *skeptics*, the *state moralists*, and the *cosmopolitans*. Although there is no logical connection, people who are realists in their descriptive analysis of world politics often tend to be either skeptics or state moralists in their evaluative approach, whereas those who emphasize a liberal analysis tend toward either the state moralist or cosmopolitan moral viewpoints.

Skeptics. The *skeptic* says that moral categories have no *meaning* in international relations because no institutions exist to provide order. In addition, there is no sense of community, and therefore no moral rights and duties. For the skeptics, the classic statement about ethics in international politics was the Athenians' response to the Melians' plea for mercy: "The strong do what they have the power to do and the weak accept what they have to accept." Might makes right. And that, for the skeptics, is all there is to say.

Philosophers often say that *ought* (moral obligation) implies *can* (the capacity to do something). Morality requires choice. If something is impossible, we cannot have an obligation to do it. If international relations are simply the realm of "kill or be killed," then presumably there is no choice, and that would justify the skeptics' position. But international politics consists of more than mere survival. If choices exist in international relations, pretending choices do not exist is merely a disguised form of choice. To think only in terms of narrow national interests is simply smuggling in values without admitting it. The French diplomat who once told me, "What is moral is whatever is good for France," was ducking hard choices about why only French interests should be considered. The leader who says, "I had no choice," often did have a choice, albeit not a pleasant one. If there is some degree of order and of community in international relations—if it is not constantly "kill or be killed"—then there is room for choices. Anarchy means without government, but it does not necessarily mean chaos or total disorder. There are rudimentary practices and institutions that provide enough order to allow some important choices: balance of power, international law, and international organizations. Each is critical to understanding why the skeptical argument is not sufficient.

Thomas Hobbes argued that to escape from "the state of nature" in which anyone might kill anyone else, individuals give up their freedom to a leviathan, or government, for protection because life in the state of nature is nasty, brutish, and short. Why then don't governments form a superleviathan? Why isn't there a world government? The reason, Hobbes said, is that insecurity is not so great at the international level as at the individual level. Governments provide some degree of protection against the brutality of the biggest individuals taking whatever they want, and the balance of power among states provides some degree of order. Even though states are in a hostile posture of potential war, "they still uphold the daily industry of their subjects." The international state of nature does not create the day-to-day misery that would accompany a state of nature among individuals. In other words, Hobbes believed that the existence of states in a balance of power alleviates the condition of international anarchy enough to allow some degree of order.

Liberals point further to the existence of international law and customs. Even if rudimentary, such rules put a burden of proof on those who break them. Consider the Persian Gulf crisis in 1990. Saddam Hussein claimed that he annexed Kuwait to recover a province stolen from Iraq in colonial times. But because international law forbids crossing borders for such reasons, an overwhelming majority of states viewed his action as a violation of the UN charter. The 12 resolutions passed by the UN Security Council showed clearly that Saddam's view of the situation ran against international norms. Law and norms did not stop Saddam from invading Kuwait, but they did make it more difficult for him to recruit support, and they contributed to the creation of the coalition that expelled him from Kuwait.

International institutions, even if rudimentary, also provide a degree of order by facilitating and encouraging communication and some degree of reciprocity in bargaining. Given this situation of nearly constant communication, international politics is not always, as the skeptics claim, "kill or be killed." The energies and attention of leaders are not focused on security and survival all the time. Cooperation (as well as conflict) occurs in large areas of economic, social, and military interaction. And even though cultural differences exist about the notion of justice, moral arguments take place in international politics and principles are enshrined in international law.

Even in the extreme circumstances of war, law and morality may sometimes play a role. The *just war doctrine*, which originated in the early Christian church and became secularized after the seventeenth century, prohibits the killing of innocent civilians. The prohibition on killing innocents starts from the premise "thou shalt not kill." But if that is a basic moral premise, how is any killing ever justified? Absolute pacifists say that no one should kill anyone else for any reason. Usually this is asserted on Kantian grounds, but some pacifists add a consequentialist argument that "violence only begets more violence." Sometimes, however, the failure to respond to violence can also beget more violence. For example, it is unlikely that Osama bin Laden would have left the United States alone if President Bush had turned the other cheek after September 11.

In contrast to pacifism, the just war tradition combines a concern for the intentions, means, and consequences of actions. It argues that if someone is about to kill you and you refuse to act in self-defense, the result is that evil will prevail. By refusing to defend themselves, the good die. If one is in imminent peril of being killed, it can be moral to kill in self-defense. But we must distinguish between those who can be killed and those who cannot be killed. For example, if a soldier rushes at me with a rifle, I can kill him in self-defense, but the minute the soldier drops the rifle, puts up his hands, and says, "I surrender," he is a prisoner of war and I have no right to take his life. In fact, this is enshrined in international law, and also in the U.S. military code. An American soldier who shoots an enemy soldier after he surrenders can be tried for murder in an American court. Some American officers in the Vietnam War were sent to prison for violating such laws. The prohibition against intentionally killing people who pose no harm also helps explain why terrorism is wrong. Some skeptics argue that "one man's terrorist is just another man's freedom fighter." However, under just war doctrine, you can fight for freedom, but you cannot target innocent civilians. Though they are often violated, some norms exist even under the harshest international circumstances. The rudimentary sense of justice enshrined in an imperfectly obeyed international law belies the skeptics' argument that no choices exist in a situation of war.

We can therefore reject complete skepticism because some room exists for morality in international politics. Morality is about choice, and meaningful choice varies with the conditions of survival. The greater the threats to survival, the less room for moral choice. At the start of the Peloponnesian War, the Athenians argued, "Those who really deserve praise are the people who, while human enough to enjoy power, nevertheless pay more attention to justice than they are compelled to do by their situation."[3] Unfortunately, the Athenians lost sight of that wisdom later in their war, but it reminds us that situations with absolutely no choice are rare and that national security and degrees of threat are often ambiguous. Skeptics avoid hard moral choices by pretending to the contrary. To sum up in an aphorism: Humans may not live wholly by the word, but neither do they live solely by the sword.

Many writers and leaders who are realists in their descriptive analysis are also skeptics in their views about values in world politics. But not all realists are complete skeptics. Some recognize that moral obligations exist, but say that order has to come first. Peace is a moral priority, even if it is an unjust peace. The disorder of war makes justice difficult, especially in the nuclear age. The best way to preserve order is to preserve a balance of power among states. Moral crusades disrupt balances of power. For example, if the United States becomes too concerned about spreading democracy or human rights throughout the world, it may create disorder that will actually do more damage than good in the long run.

The realists have a valid argument, up to a point. International order is important, but it is a matter of degrees, and there are trade-offs between justice and order. How much order is necessary before we start worrying about justice? For example, after the 1990 Soviet crackdown in the Baltic republics in which a number of people were killed, some Americans urged a break in relations with the Soviet Union. In their view, Americans should express their values of democracy and human rights in foreign policy, even if that meant instability and the end of arms control talks. Others argued that while concerns for peace and for human rights were important, it was more important to control nuclear weapons and negotiate an arms reduction treaty. In the end, the American government went ahead with the arms negotiations, but linked the provision of economic aid to respect for human rights. Over and over in international politics, the question is not absolute order versus justice, but how to trade off choices in particular situations. The realists have a valid point of view, but they overstate it when they argue that it has to be all order before any justice.

State Moralists. State moralists argue that international politics rests on a society of states with certain rules, although those rules are not always perfectly obeyed. The most important rule is state sovereignty, which prohibits states from intervening across borders into each others' jurisdiction. The political scientist Michael Walzer, for example, argues that national boundaries have a moral significance because states represent the pooled rights of individuals who have come together for a common life. Thus respect for the sovereignty and territorial integrity of states is related to respect for individuals. Others argue more simply that respect for sovereignty is the best way to preserve order. "Good fences make good neighbors," in the words of the poet Robert Frost.

In practice, these rules of state behavior are frequently violated. In the last few decades, Vietnam invaded Cambodia, China invaded Vietnam, Tanzania invaded Uganda, Israel invaded Lebanon, the Soviet Union invaded Afghanistan, the United States invaded Grenada and Panama, Iraq invaded Iran and Kuwait, the United States and Britain invaded Iraq, and NATO bombed Serbia because of its mistreatment of ethnic Albanians in the province of Kosovo—to name just a few examples. Determining when it is appropriate to respect another state's sovereignty is a long-standing challenge. In 1979, Americans condemned the Soviet invasion of Afghanistan in strong moral terms. The Soviets responded by pointing to the Dominican Republic, where in 1965 the United States sent 25,000 troops to prevent the formation of a communist government. The intention behind the American intervention in the Dominican Republic, preventing a hostile regime from coming to power in the Caribbean, and the intention of the Soviet intervention in Afghanistan, preventing the formation of a hostile government on their border, were quite similar.

To find differences, we have to look further than intentions. In terms of the means used, very few people were killed by the U.S. intervention in the Dominican Republic, and the Americans soon withdrew. In the Afghan case, many people were killed, and the Soviet forces remained for nearly a decade. In the 1990s, some critics compared the Iraqi invasion of Kuwait with the American invasion of Panama. In December 1989, the United States sent troops to overthrow the Panamanian dictator Manuel Noriega, and in August 1990, Iraq sent troops into Kuwait to overthrow the emir. Both the United States and Iraq violated the rule of nonintervention. But again there were differences in means and consequences. In Panama, the Americans put into office a government that had been duly elected but that Noriega had not permitted to take office. The Americans did not try to annex Panama. In Kuwait, the Iraqi government tried to annex the country and caused much bloodshed in the process. Such considerations do not mean that the Panama case was all right or all wrong, problems often arise when applying simple rules of nonintervention and sovereignty.

Intervention

Imagine the following scene in Afghanistan in December 1979:

An Afghan communist leader came to power promoting a platform of greater independence from the Soviet Union. This worried Soviet leaders because an independent regime on their border might foment trouble throughout Central Asia (including Soviet Central Asia) and would create a dangerous precedent of a small communist neighbor escaping the Soviet Empire. Imagine the Russian general in charge of the Soviet invasion force confronting the renegade Afghan leader, whom he is about to kill, explaining why he is doing these things against the international rules of sovereignty and nonintervention. "So far as right and wrong are concerned, China and others think there is no difference between the two and if we fail to attack you, it is because we are afraid. So by conquering you, we shall increase not only the size but the security of our empire. We rule the Central Asian landmass and you are a border state, and weaker than the others. It is therefore particularly important that you should not escape."

Those words are Thucydides's Melian dialogue with the word *China* added and *Central Asia* substituted for *sea* and *border state* for *islands*. Intervention is not a new problem!

Cosmopolitans. Cosmopolitans such as the political theorist Charles Beitz see international politics not just as a society of states, but as a society of individuals. When we speak about justice, say the cosmopolitans, we should speak about justice for individuals. They argue that realists focus too much on issues of war and peace. If realists focused on issues of distributive justice—that is, who gets what—cosmopolitans contend that realists would notice the interdependence of the global economy. Constant economic intervention across borders can sometimes have life-or-death effects. For example, it is a life-and-death matter if you are a peasant in the Philippines and your child dies of a curable disease because the local boy who went to medical school is now working in the United States for a much higher salary.

Cosmopolitans argue that national boundaries have no moral standing; they simply defend an inequality that should be abolished if we think in terms of distributive justice. Realists (who include both moral skeptics and some state moralists) reply that the danger in the cosmopolitans' approach is that it may lead to enormous disorder. Taken literally, efforts at radical redistribution of resources are likely to lead to violent conflict because people do not give up their wealth easily. A more limited cosmopolitan argument rests on the fact that people often have multiple loyalties—to families, friends, neighborhoods, and nations; perhaps to some transnational religious groups; and to the concept of common humanity. Most people are moved by pictures of starving Sudanese children or Kosovar refugees, for some common community exists beyond the national level, albeit a weaker one. We are all humans.

Cosmopolitans remind us of the distributive dimensions to international relations in which morality matters as much in peace as in war. Policies can be designed to assist basic human needs and basic human rights without destroying order. And in cases of gross abuse of human rights, cosmopolitan views have been written into international laws such as the international convention against genocide. As a result, policy makers are more conscious of moral concerns. For example, President Clinton has said that one of his worst mistakes was not to have done more to stop genocide in Rwanda in 1994, and the United States and other countries have supported African peacekeeping troops in efforts to suppress genocidal violence in the Sudanese province of Darfur.

Of the approaches to international morality, the skeptic makes a valid point about order being necessary for justice but misses the trade-offs between order and justice. The state moralist who sees a society of states with rules against intervention illustrates an institutional approach to order but does not provide enough answers regarding when some interventions may be justified. Finally, the cosmopolitan who focuses on a society of individuals has a profound insight about common humanity but runs the risk of fomenting enormous disorder by pursuing massive redistributive policies. Most people develop a hybrid position; labels are less important than the central point that trade-offs exist among these approaches.

Because of the differences between domestic and international politics, morality is harder to apply in international politics. But just because there is a plurality of principles, it does not follow there are no principles at all. How far should we go in applying morality to international politics? The answer is to be careful, for when moral judgments determine everything, morality can lead to a sense of outrage, and outrage can lead to heightened risk. Prudence can be a virtue, particularly when the alternative is disastrous unintended consequences. After all, there are no moral questions among the incinerated. But we cannot honestly ignore morality in international politics. Each person must study events and make his or her own decisions about judgments and trade-offs. The enduring logic of international conflict does not remove the responsibility for moral choices, although it does require an understanding of the special setting that makes those choices difficult.

While the specific moral and security dilemmas of the Peloponnesian War are unique, many of the issues recur over history. As we trace the evolution of international relations, we will see again and again the tension between realism and liberalism, between skeptics and cosmopolitans, between an anarchic system of states and international organizations. We will revisit the Prisoner's Dilemma and continue to grapple with the ethical conundrums of war. We will see how different actors on the world stage have approached the crises of their time and how their goals and instruments vary. As mentioned at the outset, certain variables that characterize international politics today simply did not exist in Thucydides's day: no nuclear weapons, no United Nations, no Internet, no transnational corporations, no cartels. The study of international conflict is an inexact science combining history and theory. In weaving our way through theories and examples, we try to keep in mind both what has changed and what has remained constant so we may better understand our past and our present and better navigate the unknown shoals of the future.

Notes

1. Thucydides, *History of the Peloponnesian War*, p. 55.
2. Ibid., p. 402.
3. Ibid., p. 80.

Selected Reading

1. Thucydides, *History of the Peloponnesian War*, trans. Rex Warner, ed. M. K. Finley (London: Penguin, 1972), pp. 35–87, 400–408.

Part II

War and Peace

One of the major subdisciplines within international relations is security studies. Part II focuses on the questions, "Why do states do what they do?" and "What causes conflict and cooperation in the international system?"—with conflict being war and cooperation being peace, or at least the absence of war. In order to understand some of the concepts and theories the readings focus on in this section, the reader will need to draw on the foundation built in Part I: Theoretical Traditions in International Relations. Some of the concepts in this section contribute to the development of theories rooted in different traditions, while some of the theories draw on multiple traditions and demonstrate the value of intellectual pluralism.

The Security Dilemma

The seemingly simple concept of the **security dilemma** arises from the condition of anarchy in the international system: One state's effort to improve its security can lead other states to perceive that their own security has decreased. Readers should recall from Part I that *anarchy* means the absence of a higher authority above the state and should not be confused with chaos, as order does exist in the anarchic structure of states. With the security dilemma's implicit focus on **relative power**, different theories explain state behavior in response to this dilemma. Part I introduced the defensive and offensive variants of **structural realism** that explain why states do what they do in response to the security dilemma. This section, however, explores the security dilemma in more depth.

In political scientist Robert Jervis's classic work, he develops a theory to determine the intensity of the security dilemma and the conditions under which conflict or cooperation is more likely to occur. Jervis uses two basic **game theory** models, the Prisoner's Dilemma and the Stag Hunt, to explain the underlying logic behind his theory, which is based on an **offense-defense balance** measurement—that is, a combination of offense-defense distinguishability and the favorability to the offense or defense. Game theory is simply the science of strategic thinking. It is a methodology, not a specific theory, used in international relations that uses mathematical analysis to understand strategic interactions (i.e., the interaction between two states).

Another theoretical implication that arises from the security dilemma is that as fear grows in a state due to perceived hostile actions by another state, this will cause an escalation in hostile behavior and fear among the states, leading to preemptive war—a theory known as the **spiral model**. Political scientist Dan Reiter explains the logic behind both the spiral model and the offense-defense balance theory, since both predict **preemptive war**. Testing these hypotheses against data on interstate wars, Reiter shows that preemptive war rarely occurs. This leads one to consider if preventive war is more likely than preemptive or if deterrence helps avoid preemption. Political scientist Jack S. Levy explains the logic of **preventive war**, arguing that the motivation for war and the fear of power shifts is how prevention should be understood, rather than as a discrete event.

BALANCE OF POWER

In response to the above security concerns that lead states to seek relative gains, cooperation becomes difficult based on fear or mistrust and competition over the scarce resource of power or security. Arising out of this understanding, **balance of power** (and its variants) has emerged as the workhorse theory of realism to explain under what conditions cooperation or conflict is most likely to occur.

Balance of power systems consist of **status quo** and **revisionist states**, which seek to maintain or alter the power distribution among states through changing alliances. Hans Morgenthau explains the traditional realist understanding of balance of power as a direct opposition between two states or a pattern of competition between two major powers to influence weaker states, with the goal of changing the distribution of power between the two greater states.

Political scientist Stephen M. Walt provides the neorealist explanation of balance of power, explaining that the structure of the international system drives states to seek power as a means to an end—security—rather than as an end in itself, as it is for Morgenthau. Walt then modifies the theory by changing the causal variable that explains alliance behavior, focusing on threat rather than power and developing **balance of threat** theory. Walt describes the logic behind the alliance behaviors of **balancing** and **bandwagoning**, and when one can expect a state to respond to a threat with either of these behaviors.

Structurally, the balancing system can take one of three forms: a **multipolar**, **bipolar**, or **unipolar system**. Each of these different structures of power distribution comes with different expectations about the stability of the system and state behavior under it. Political scientist Robert A. Pape distinguishes unipolarity from **hegemony** and explains the conditions under which states may attempt to balance against a unipole and the methods states can use to achieve that goal.

DETERRENCE

Diplomacy, as economist Thomas C. Schelling states, is a form of bargaining in which two adversaries seek outcomes that may not be ideal for either party but are better than the alternatives. Rather than using **brute force**, which is taking what you want, most states seek through threats to influence others to take a desired action. Under **coercive diplomacy**, states can either attempt to prevent another state from taking a proscribed action (**deterrence**) and, thus, maintain the status quo, or encourage another state to take a prescribed action (**compellence**) and, thus, alter the status quo. In his classic work, Schelling explains the strategic logic of deterrence and how the nuclear age has impacted that logic.

A great contemporary debate rages about the ability to deter Iran. Two principle subquestions within this debate are, "Is it possible to deter Iran from acquiring a nuclear weapon?" and "Is it possible to deter Iran from using a nuclear weapon if it obtains one?" Political scientist Barry R. Posen prefers that Iran not acquire a nuclear weapon but argues that if it does, a policy of deterrence and **containment** will reduce proliferation and usage risks. International affairs professor Robert J. Lieber and Middle East scholar Amatzia Baram, however, argue that the historical analogies and arguments used to explain how deterrence worked in the past do not apply to Iran and that a nuclear-armed Iran will lead to greater instability in the Middle East.

Bargaining and War

The logic of the **bargaining model** of war is quite intuitive: War is seen as a continuation, rather than a failure, of the bargaining process. This logic is seen in military strategist Carl Von Clausewitz's maxim that war is an extension of politics by other means and in Thomas C. Schelling's discussion of violence as vicious diplomacy.

In this section, Dan Reiter explains the theoretical evolution of the bargaining model in order to understand the underlying logic of the model more formally. This model covers all **phases of war**—pre-war, war, war termination, and peace duration—but focuses on three conditions under which the outbreak of war may occur. Reiter also explains how to apply the bargaining model to the other phases of war and discusses how the model relates to other theories of conflict—compatible as well as contradictory theories.

With the current debate about whether or not to negotiate with the Taliban in Afghanistan and Pakistan, understanding the bargaining model allows the reader to think about the purpose behind bargaining and the conditions under which a cooperative outcome is possible. The selections by former Assistant Secretary of Defense James Shinn and former Ambassador James Dobbins and by journalist David Rohde allow the reader to apply the model and engage in the current debate about whether or not the United States and NATO should negotiate with the Taliban.

Theories of Democracy and War

Just as balance of power is the workhorse theory for realists, the **democratic peace** theory is the workhorse theory used by liberals to explain the conditions under which conflict and cooperation occur between states. One can trace the roots of the theory back to Immanuel Kant's philosophical sketch of perpetual peace.

Political scientist Bruce Russett examines the phenomenon of interstate war not taking place between two democracies by carefully defining the causal variable—**regime type**—and the dependent variable—war—and explaining the underlying causal logic for two models of the democratic peace: cultural/normative and structural/institutional. Russett further explains that democracies are not inherently peaceful toward all other types of states and that, under certain conditions, democracies are as likely to go to war as are non-democracies.

Political scientists Edward D. Mansfield and Jack Snyder reexamine the conditions under which democratic peace theory holds, differentiating mature democracies from emerging democracies and arguing that wars do occur between democracies. Economist Henry S. Farber and political scientist Joanne Gowa provide a critique of the theory, using quantitative data to test the expectations of the theory, and argue that common interests rather than a common regime type explain the absence of conflict between democracies since 1945.

Civil Conflict

Intrastate (or civil) conflict has become a major concern for international security since the end of the Cold War, as **interstate conflict** has declined while intrastate conflict has increased. States have become concerned that those states mired in internal conflict can become safe havens for non-state actors who want to harm other states, and about the contagion effects of intrastate conflict, the impact on human security within these states, and the effects on economic growth and poverty. Before examining the implications of civil conflict, which the sections in Part IV will cover, it is important to understand some of its causes.

Political scientists Macartan Humphreys and Jeremy M. Weinstein examine and test the prevailing rival theories that explain the determinants of participation in civil war. Through their empirical analysis, they challenge the standard interpretation that grievances cause participation, and they find that other competing theories may actually be complementary, further demonstrating the importance of intellectual pluralism.

Just as the bargaining model describes four phases of war for interstate conflict, civil conflict encompasses the same phases. Political scientist Barbara F. Walter applies elements of different theories examined in previous sections of this book to develop a theory about civil conflict resolution, focusing on problems during the phase of peace implementation. Strategist and historian Edward N. Luttwak provides an alternative, and controversial, perspective on how to achieve a lasting peace: avoid intervention and allow wars to run their course and determine a victor.

Terrorism

In the wake of 9/11, terrorism has become a renewed area of academic interest. Scholars have tried to search for answers to what motivates terrorists and what distinguishes **terrorism** as a tactic from terrorism as a strategy. Political scientist David C. Rapoport provides a historical description of the evolution of terror that has occurred in four life-cycle waves and the level of success in achieving the goals of each wave.

Political scientist Martha Crenshaw uses historical analysis to differentiate common causes of terrorism. She distinguishes between preconditions and precipitants that set the conditions that enable or allow terrorism and the sparks that directly lead to a terrorist act. Understanding the origins and causes of terrorism is important, but it is also important to understand the strategic logic behind the use of terrorism. Political scientists Andrew H. Kydd and Barbara F. Walter focus on understanding the strategies employed by terrorist organizations and the conditions under which they are most likely to succeed or fail.

The Ethics of War

While a debate over the importance of morality in state action exists in international relations, religious traditions and international law have made ethics a consideration in the decision-making process that leads to war, how to conduct a war, and what to do in the aftermath of war, whether for rhetorical or humanistic purposes. One could hear the ethical arguments made before the decisions to invade Afghanistan and Iraq—during the presidential debates in 2008—about which was the "right" or "just" war, about the role of detentions and "torture" or "enhanced interrogation techniques" in the conduct of the wars, and about interveners needing to "fix what they broke" in the aftermath of the wars.

Just war theory—and the principles of *jus in bello, jus ad bellum,* and *jus post bellum*—is what most people turn to when debating the ethics of going to war, how to fight a war, and what to do after a war ends. This theory combines elements of the deontological and consequentialist traditions discussed at the end of Part I. Philosopher and ethicist Thomas Nagel applies just war theory, particularly the principles of *jus in bello*, to the conduct of the war in Vietnam. The reader should see parallels in this discussion to arguments about contemporary wars.

Political and moral philosopher John Rawls also focuses on the principles of *jus in bello* but thinks through the ethics in war from a perspective that emphasizes democratic justice and rights. Through an examination of the bombings of Hiroshima and Nagasaki, Rawls argues that an ethically coherent way of fighting a war must also consider how that conduct of war will bring about justice after war—*jus post bellum*. As part of a 50th anniversary retrospective of the dropping of the atomic bombs, columnist Jim Holt also analyzes the action through a consequentialist lens and critiques how such decisions are made.

Discussion Questions for Part II: War and Peace

1. Analyze the differences between balance of power and balance of threat. Which is more compelling, and why?

2. Analyze the arguments for and against deterrence working with respect to Iran's suspected pursuit of nuclear weapons. Which argument is more compelling? What theory (or theories) helps explain why Iran may want to gain a nuclear weapon? What theory (or theories) helps explain why Israel does not want Iran to obtain a nuclear weapon? Do the same or different theories explain the U.S. opposition to Iran obtaining a nuclear weapon? Explain your answer to each of these questions.

3. Why cannot opposing sides in a conflict find a solution that would allow them to reach a less costly, peaceful bargain when the costs of war are staggering for all sides, as evidenced by the Iraq and/or Afghanistan Wars?

4. Discuss the implications for international relations if states in the Middle East, such as Egypt and Iraq, complete their transitions to democracy. What are the implications for relations between states within the region as well as beyond?

5. Compare and contrast the possible causes, preconditions, and precipitants of civil conflict and terrorism, as well as the strategies for each and possible solutions. Explain the commonalities and distinctions between these two phenomena that raise national security concerns.

6. Apply the just war ethical arguments made by Thomas Nagel, the justice arguments made by John Rawls, and the consequentialist arguments made by Jim Holt to the policy of using unmanned drone strikes to conduct the targeted killing of individuals. Do you find such strikes ethical? Why or why not?

Key Concepts

balance of power
balance of threat
balancing
bandwagoning
bargaining model
bipolar system
brute force
coercive diplomacy
compellence
containment
democratic peace
deterrence
game theory
hegemony
interstate conflict
intrastate (or civil) conflict
just war theory
multipolar system
offense-defense balance
phases of war
preemptive war
preventive war
regime type
relative power
revisionist states
security dilemma
spiral model
status quo states
structural realism
terrorism
unipolar system

11 The Security Dilemma

11.1

Cooperation Under the Security Dilemma

Robert Jervis

Anarchy and the Security Dilemma

The lack of an international sovereign not only permits wars to occur, but also makes it difficult for states that are satisfied with the status quo to arrive at goals that they recognize as being in their common interest. Because there are no institutions or authorities that can make and enforce international laws, the policies of cooperation that will bring mutual rewards if others cooperate may bring disaster if they do not. Because states are aware of this, anarchy encourages behavior that leaves all concerned worse off than they could be, even in the extreme case in which all states would like to freeze the status quo. This is true of the men in Rousseau's "Stag Hunt." If they cooperate to trap the stag, they will all eat well. But if one person defects to chase a rabbit—which he likes less than stag—none of the others will get anything. Thus, all actors have the same preference order, and there is a solution that gives each his first choice: (1) cooperate and trap the stag (the international analogue being cooperation and disarmament); (2) chase a rabbit while others remain at their posts (maintain a high level of arms while others are disarmed); (3) all chase rabbits (arms competition and high risk of war); and (4) stay at the original position while another chases a rabbit (being disarmed while others are armed).[1]

Unless each person thinks that the others will cooperate, he himself will not. And why might he fear that any other person would do something that would sacrifice his own first choice? The other might not understand the situation, or might not be able to control his impulses if he saw a rabbit, or might fear that some other member of the group is unreliable. If the person voices any of these suspicions, others are more likely to fear that he will defect, thus making them more likely to defect, thus making it more rational for him to defect. Of course in this simple case—and in many that are more realistic—there are a number of arrangements that could permit cooperation. But the main point remains: although actors may know that they seek a common goal, they may not be able to reach it.

Even when there is a solution that is everyone's first choice, the international case is characterized by three difficulties not present in the Stag Hunt. First, to the incentives to defect given above must be added the potent fear that even if the other state now supports the status quo, it may become dissatisfied later. No matter how much decision makers are committed to the status quo, they cannot bind themselves and their successors to the same path. Minds can be changed, new leaders can come to power, values can shift, new opportunities and dangers can arise.

Source: Robert Jervis. "Cooperation Under the Security Dilemma," in *World Politics* 30(2): 167–171 and 211–214.

The second problem arises from a possible solution. In order to protect their possessions, states often seek to control resources or land outside their own territory. Countries that are not self-sufficient must try to assure that the necessary supplies will continue to flow in wartime. This was part of the explanation for Japan's drive into China and Southeast Asia before World War II. If there were an international authority that could guarantee access, this motive for control would disappear. But since there is not, even a state that would prefer the status quo to increasing its area of control may pursue the latter policy.

When there are believed to be tight linkages between domestic and foreign policy or between the domestic politics of two states, the quest for security may drive states to interfere preemptively in the domestic politics of others in order to provide an ideological buffer zone. Thus, Metternich's justification for supervising the politics of the Italian states has been summarized as follows:

> Every state is absolutely sovereign in its internal affairs. But this implies that every state must do nothing to interfere in the internal affairs of any other. However, any false or pernicious step taken by any state in its internal affairs may disturb the repose of another state, and this consequent disturbance of another state's repose constitutes an interference in that state's internal affairs. Therefore, every state—or rather, every sovereign of a great power—has the duty, in the name of the sacred right of independence of every state, to supervise the governments of smaller states and to prevent them from taking false and pernicious steps in their internal affairs.[2]

More frequently, the concern is with direct attack. In order to protect themselves, states seek to control, or at least to neutralize, areas on their borders. But attempts to establish buffer zones can alarm others who have stakes there, who fear that undesirable precedents will be set, or who believe that their own vulnerability will be increased. When buffers are sought in areas empty of great powers, expansion tends to feed on itself in order to protect what is acquired, as was often noted by those who opposed colonial expansion. Balfour's complaint was typical: "Every time I come to a discussion—at intervals of, say, five years—I find there is a new sphere which we have got to guard, which is supposed to protect the gateways of India. Those gateways are getting further and further away from India, and I do not know how far west they are going to be brought by the General Staff."[3]

Though this process is most clearly visible when it involves territorial expansion, it often operates with the increase of less tangible power and influence. The expansion of power usually brings with it an expansion of responsibilities and commitments; to meet them, still greater power is required. The state will take many positions that are subject to challenge. It will be involved with a wide range of controversial issues unrelated to its core values. And retreats that would be seen as normal if made by a small power would be taken as an index of weakness inviting predation if made by a large one.

The third problem present in international politics but not in the Stag Hunt is the security dilemma: many of the means by which a state tries to increase its security decrease the security of others. In domestic society, there are several ways to increase the safety of one's person and property without endangering others. One can move to a safer neighborhood, put bars on the windows, avoid dark streets, and keep a distance from suspicious-looking characters. Of course these measures are not convenient, cheap, or certain of success. But no one save criminals need be alarmed if a person takes them. In international politics, however, one state's gain in security often inadvertently threatens others. In explaining British policy on naval disarmament in the interwar period to the Japanese, Ramsey MacDonald said that "Nobody wanted Japan to be insecure."[4] But the problem was not with British desires, but with the consequences of her policy. In earlier periods, too, Britain had needed a navy large enough to keep the shipping lanes open. But such a navy could not avoid being a menace to any other state with a coast that could be raided, trade that could be interdicted, or colonies that could be isolated. When Germany started building a powerful navy before World War I, Britain objected that it could only be an offensive weapon aimed at her. As Sir Edward Grey, the Foreign Secretary, put it to King Edward VII: "If the German Fleet ever becomes superior to ours, the German Army can conquer this country. There is no corresponding risk of this kind to Germany; for however superior our Fleet was, no naval victory could bring us any nearer to Berlin." The English position was half correct: Germany's navy was an anti-British instrument. But the British often overlooked what the Germans knew full well: "in every quarrel with England, German colonies and trade were . . hostages for England to take." Thus, whether she intended it or not, the British Navy constituted an important instrument of coercion.[5]

What Makes Cooperation More Likely?

Given this gloomy picture, the obvious question is, why are we not all dead? Or, to put it less starkly, what kinds of variables ameliorate the impact of anarchy and the security dilemma? The workings of several can be seen in terms of the Stag Hunt or repeated plays of the Prisoner's Dilemma. The Prisoner's Dilemma differs from the Stag Hunt in that there is no solution that is in the best interests of all the participants; there are offensive as well as defensive incentives to defect from the coalition with the others; and, if the game is to be played only once, the only rational response is to defect. But if the game is repeated indefinitely, the latter characteristic no longer holds and we can analyze the game in terms similar to those applied to the Stag Hunt. It would be in the interest of each actor to have others deprived of the power to defect; each would be willing to sacrifice this ability if others were similarly restrained. But if the others are not, then it is in the actor's interest to retain the power to defect.[6] The game theory matrices for these two situations are given below, with the numbers in the boxes being the order of the actors' preferences.

STAG HUNT

B \ A	COOPERATE	DEFECT
COOPERATE	1 / 1	2 / 4
DEFECT	4 / 2	3 / 3

PRISONER'S DILEMMA

B \ A	COOPERATE	DEFECT
COOPERATE	2 / 2	1 / 4
DEFECT	4 / 1	3 / 3

We can see the logical possibilities by rephrasing our question: "Given either of the above situations, what makes it more or less likely that the players will cooperate and arrive at CC?" The chances of achieving this outcome will be increased by: (1) anything that increases incentives to cooperate by increasing the gains of mutual cooperation (CC) and/or decreasing the costs the actor will pay if he cooperates and the other does not (CD); (2) anything that decreases the incentives for defecting by decreasing the gains of taking advantage of the other (DC) and/or increasing the costs of mutual noncooperation (DD); (3) anything that increases each side's expectation that the other will cooperate.[7] . . .

Four Worlds

The two variables we have been discussing—whether the offense or the defense has the advantage, and whether offensive postures can be distinguished from defensive ones—can be combined to yield four possible worlds.

The first world is the worst for status-quo states. There is no way to get security without menacing others, and security through defense is terribly difficult to obtain. Because offensive and defensive postures are the same, status-quo states acquire the same kind of arms that are sought by aggressors. And because the offense has the advantage over the defense, attacking is the best route to protecting what you have; status-quo states will therefore behave like aggressors. The situation will be unstable. Arms races are likely. Incentives to strike first will turn crises into wars. Decisive victories and conquests will be common. States will grow and shrink rapidly, and it will be hard for any state to maintain its size and influence without trying to increase them. Cooperation among status-quo powers will be extremely hard to achieve.

	OFFENSE HAS THE ADVANTAGE	DEFENSE HAS THE ADVANTAGE
OFFENSIVE POSTURE NOT DISTINGUISHABLE FROM DEFENSIVE ONE	1 Doubly dangerous	2 Security dilemma, but security requirements may be compatible
OFFENSIVE POSTURE DISTINGUISHABLE FROM DEFENSIVE ONE	3 No security dilemma, but aggression possible. Status-quo states can follow different policy than aggressors. Warning given	4 Doubly stable

There are no cases that totally fit this picture, but it bears more than a passing resemblance to Europe before World War I. Britain and Germany, although in many respects natural allies, ended up as enemies. Of course much of the explanation lies in Germany's ill-chosen policy. And from the perspective of our theory, the powers' ability to avoid war in a series of earlier crises cannot be easily explained. Nevertheless, much of the behavior in this period was the product of technology and beliefs that magnified the security dilemma. Decision makers thought that the offense had a big advantage and saw little difference between offensive and defensive military postures. The era was characterized by arms races. And once war seemed likely, mobilization races created powerful incentives to strike first.

In the nuclear era, the first world would be one in which each side relied on vulnerable weapons that were aimed at similar forces and each side understood the situation. In this case, the incentives to strike first would be very high—so high that status-quo powers as well as aggressors would be sorely tempted to pre-empt. And since the forces could be used to change the status quo as well as to preserve it, there would be no way for both sides to increase their security simultaneously. Now the familiar logic of deterrence leads both sides to see the dangers in this world. Indeed, the new understanding of this situation was one reason why vulnerable bombers and missiles were replaced. Ironically, the 1950's would have been more hazardous if the decision makers had been aware of the dangers of their posture and had therefore felt greater pressure to strike first. This situation could be recreated if both sides were to rely on MIRVed ICBMs [intercontinental ballistic missiles].

In the second world, the security dilemma operates because offensive and defensive postures cannot be distinguished; but it does not operate as strongly as in the first world because the defense has the advantage, and so an increment in one side's strength increases its security more than it decreases the other's. So, if both sides have reasonable subjective security requirements, are of roughly equal power, and the variables discussed earlier are favorable, it is quite likely that status-quo states can adopt compatible security policies. Although a state will not be able to judge the other's intentions from the kinds of weapons it procures, the level of arms spending will give important evidence. Of course a state that seeks a high level of arms might be not an aggressor but merely an insecure state, which if conciliated will reduce its arms, and if confronted will reply in kind. To assume that the apparently excessive level of arms indicates aggressiveness could therefore lead to a response that would deepen the dilemma and create needless conflict. But empathy and skillful statesmanship can reduce this danger. Furthermore, the advantageous position of the defense means that a status-quo state can often maintain a high degree of security with a level of arms lower than that of its expected adversary. Such a state demonstrates that it lacks the ability or desire to alter the status quo, at least at the present time. The strength of the defense also allows states to react slowly and with restraint when they fear that others are menacing them. So, although status-quo powers will to some extent be threatening to others, that extent will be limited.

This world is the one that comes closest to matching most periods in history. Attacking is usually harder than defending because of the strength of fortifications and obstacles. But purely defensive postures are rarely possible because fortifications are usually supplemented by armies and mobile guns which can support an attack. In the nuclear era, this world would be one in which both sides relied on relatively invulnerable ICBMs and believed that limited nuclear war was impossible. Assuming no MIRVs [multiple independently targetable reentry vehicles], it would take more than one attacking missile to destroy one of the adversary's. Pre-emption is therefore unattractive. If both sides have large inventories, they can ignore all but drastic increases on the other side. A world of either ICBMs or SLBMs [submarine launched ballistic missiles] in which both sides adopted the "Schlesinger Doctrine" would probably fit in this category too. The means of preserving the status quo would also be the means of changing it, as we discussed earlier. And the defense usually would have the advantage, because compellence is more difficult than deterrence. Although a state might succeed in changing the status quo on issues that matter much more to it than to others, status-quo powers could deter major provocations under most circumstances.

In the third world there may be no security dilemma, but there are security problems. Because states can procure defensive systems that do not threaten others, the dilemma need not operate. But because the offense has the advantage, aggression is possible, and perhaps easy. If the offense has enough of an advantage, even a status-quo state may take the initiative rather than risk being attacked and defeated. If the offense has less of an advantage, stability and cooperation are likely, because the status-quo states will procure defensive forces. They need not react to others who are similarly armed, but can wait for the warning they would receive if others started to deploy offensive weapons. But each state will have to watch the others carefully, and there is room for false suspicions. The costliness of the defense and the allure of the offense can lead to unnecessary mistrust, hostility, and war, unless some of the variables discussed earlier are operating to restrain defection.

A hypothetical nuclear world that would fit this description would be one in which both sides relied on SLBMs, but in which ASW [anti-submarine warfare] techniques were very effective. Offense and defense would be different, but the former would have the advantage. This situation is not likely to occur; but if it did, a status-quo state could show its lack of desire to exploit the other by refraining from threatening its submarines. The desire to have more protecting you than merely the other side's fear of retaliation is a strong one, however, and a state that knows that it would not expand even if its cities were safe is likely to believe that the other would not feel threatened by its ASW program. It is easy to see how such a world could become unstable, and how spirals of tensions and conflict could develop.

The fourth world is doubly safe. The differentiation between offensive and defensive systems permits a way out of the security dilemma; the advantage of the defense disposes of the problems discussed in the previous paragraphs. There is no reason for a status-quo power to be tempted to procure offensive forces, and aggressors give notice of their intentions by the posture they adopt. Indeed, if the advantage of the defense is great enough, there are no security problems. The loss of the ultimate form of the power to alter the status quo would allow greater scope for the exercise of nonmilitary means and probably would tend to freeze the distribution of values.

This world would have existed in the first decade of the 20th century if the decision makers had understood the available technology. In that case, the European powers would have followed different policies both in the long run and in the summer of 1914. Even Germany, facing powerful enemies on both sides, could have made herself secure by developing strong defenses. France could also have made her frontier almost impregnable. Furthermore, when crises arose, no one would have had incentives to strike first. There would have been no competitive mobilization races reducing the time available for negotiations.

In the nuclear era, this world would be one in which the superpowers relied on SLBMs, ASW technology was not up to its task, and limited nuclear options were not taken seriously. We have discussed this situation earlier; here we need only add that, even if our analysis is correct and even if the policies and postures of both sides were to move in this direction, the problem of violence below the nuclear threshold would remain. On issues other than defense of the homeland, there would still be security dilemmas and security problems. But the world would nevertheless be safer than it has usually been.

Notes

* I am grateful to Robert Art, Bernard Brodie, and Glenn Snyder for comments, and to the Committee on Research of the UCLA Academic Senate for financial support. An earlier version of this essay appeared as Working Paper No. 5, UCLA Program in Arms Control and International Security.

1. This kind of rank-ordering is not entirely an analyst's invention, as is shown by the following section of a British army memo of 1903 dealing with British and Russian railroad construction near the Persia-Afghanistan border:

The conditions of the problem may . . . be briefly summarized as follows:

a) If we make a railway to Seistan while Russia remains inactive, we gain a considerable defensive advantage at considerable financial cost;

b) If Russia makes a railway to Seistan, while we remain inactive, she gains a considerable offensive advantage at considerable financial cost;

c) If both we and Russia make railways to Seistan, the defensive and offensive advantages may be held to neutralize each other; in other words, we shall have spent a good deal of money and be no better off than we are at present. On the other hand, we shall be no worse off, whereas under alternative (b) we shall be much worse off. Consequently, the theoretical balance of advantage lies with the proposed railway extension from Quetta to Seistan.

W. G. Nicholson, "Memorandum on Seistan and Other Points Raised in the Discussion on the Defence of India," (Committee of Imperial Defence, March 20, 1903). It should be noted that the possibility of neither side building railways was not mentioned, thus strongly biasing the analysis.

2. Paul Schroeder, *Metternich's Diplomacy at Its Zenith, 1820–1823* (Westport, Conn.: Greenwood Press 1969), 126.

3. Quoted in Michael Howard, *The Continental Commitment* (Harmondsworth, England: Penguin 1974), 67.

4. Quoted in Gerald Wheeler, *Prelude to Pearl Harbor* (Columbia: University of Missouri Press 1963), 167.

5. Quoted in Leonard Wainstein, "The Dreadnought Gap," in Robert Art and Kenneth Waltz, eds., *The Use of Force* (Boston: Little, Brown 1971), 155; Raymond Sontag, *European Diplomatic History*, 1871–1932 (New York: Appleton-Century-Crorts 1933), 147. The French had made a similar argument 50 years earlier; see James Phinney Baxter III, *The Introduction of the Ironclad Warship* (Cambridge: Harvard University Press 1933), 149. For a more detailed discussion of the security dilemma, see Jervis, *Perception and Misperception in International Politics* (Princeton: Princeton University Press 1976), 62–76.

6. Experimental evidence for this proposition is summarized in James Tedeschi, Barry Schlenker, and Thomas Bonoma, *Conflict, Power, and Games* (Chicago: Aldine 1973), 135–41.

7. The results of Prisoner's Dilemma games played in the laboratory support this argument. See Anatol Rapoport and Albert Chammah, *Prisoner's Dilemma* (Ann Arbor: University of Michigan Press 1965), 33–50. Also see Robert Axelrod, *Conflict of Interest* (Chicago: Markham 1970), 60–70.

11.2

Exploding the Powder Keg Myth

Preemptive Wars Almost Never Happen

Dan Reiter

Concerns with preemptive war—war in which one side attacks to forestall what it sees as an impending attack on itself—have in recent years played a dominant role in discourse on the causes of war. In academic circles, preemption ties together two important theories of war, the spiral model and the offense-defense balance. In policy discussions, fears of preemptive war ran through the Cold War debate on U.S. strategy toward the Soviet Union, and continue to frame debates on a number of post-Cold War issues. Both academics and policy analysts have argued that preemption is in many environments the most likely path to armed conflict; they see the international system as a primed powder keg, waiting for a single spark to explode into war.

However, the deep theoretical and policy interest in preemptive war has not been matched by extensive empirical scholarship. There have been no quantitative studies testing preemptive war hypotheses, and most case studies of preemption focus on the same small number of cases. As a result, our hunches about the dangers of preemption remain largely just that—hunches.

This article fills this empirical gap to expand our understanding of preemptive war by focusing on the important question of how many preemptive wars have happened in the modern era. In other words, which modern wars have begun primarily because the attacking state feared it was about to be a target? In one sense, this is a rather limited ambition, as only the frequency of the event is measured, while hypotheses that predict its occurrence are not tested. However, providing a systematic account of the occurrence of preemptive war is an important first step toward understanding its role in international relations. In particular, assessing the frequency of preemptive war sheds light on more general theories of international conflict.

The main empirical finding of this article is that preemptive wars almost never happen. Of all interstate wars since 1816, only three are preemptive: World War I, Chinese intervention in the Korean War, and the 1967 Arab-Israeli War. Moreover, these cases indicate that the conditions hypothesized to lead to preemptive war, especially beliefs in the military advantages of attacking first and hostile images of the adversary, are associated with the occurrence of preemptive war only when they are present to a very high degree and when the attacker also has other motives for war. This suggests that these factors are relatively insubstantial causal forces, and that the importance of preemption as a path to war has been exaggerated.

The first part of this article defines preemptive war, frames its place in academic theories on the causes of war, and explains the role preemption has had in policy debates. The last section discusses theoretical and policy implications of these findings.

Preemptive War in Theory and Policy

Preemption is not a theory of war, but rather a path to or scenario for war predicted by some theories. A war is preemptive if it breaks out primarily because the attacker feels that it will itself be the target of a military attack in the short term. The essence of preemption, then, is that it is motivated by fear, not by greed.[1]

This definition is limited to perceptions of short-term threats to national security: in contrast, the term preventive war is used for a war that begins when a state attacks because it feels that in the longer term (usually the next few years) it will be attacked or will suffer relatively increasing strategic inferiority Most scholars emphasize the dimension of time as a crucial distinction between preemptive and preventive wars.[2]

Source: Dan Reiter, "Exploding the Powder Keg Myth: Preemptive Wars Almost Never Happen," *International Security* 20: 2 (Fall, 1995), pp. 5–12 and 32–34.

A preemptive attack is not the same thing as a surprise attack, the latter implying only that the target had little or no warning. Preemptive attacks are often surprise attacks, but not all surprise attacks are preemptive, as a state may make a surprise attack for reasons other than fear of immediate attack, such as the pursuit of expansionist goals. Examples of non-preemptive surprise attacks include Nazi Germany's attack on Poland in 1939 and Japan's attack on Pearl Harbor in 1941.[3] Preemptive attacks are also distinguished from wars that erupt from unauthorized actions taken by military commanders or mechanical error.[4] Finally, mobilizations in anticipation of imminent strikes may be preemptive mobilizations, but they are not preemptive attacks. One might hypothesize that preemptive mobilizations increase the chances of war, but they remain conceptually distinct from preemptive attacks.

Two leading theories about the causes of war predict preemption as a central path to war. The first is the spiral model, which argues that relations between states are often characterized by escalating spirals of hostility and fear. The spiral model is often used as an explanation of the dynamics of international crises, and the predicted outcome of a spiral in a crisis is preemptive war. The basic scenario is that tensions between two states escalate to the point where one state believes that its adversary is about to attack, leading the state to strike first, preemptively. Scholars argue that spirals are driven by two underlying forces: the ineluctable anarchy of the international order, which forces states to make worst-case assumptions about the intentions of others, and the tendency of decision-makers to exaggerate the hostility of other states as a result of cognitive misperceptions. An important hypothesis of the spiral model is that preemptive wars become more likely when states believe that other states are hostile and pose imminent military threats.[5]

The spiral model predicts other outcomes, such as arms races and colonial competitions, but the preemption prediction is especially important, as it taps into a central theoretical dispute in the study of the causes of war. Robert Jervis contrasts the spiral model, which warns of the dangers of displays of military capability and hostility, with the deterrence model of war, which argues that the best way to prevent war is to demonstrate capability and resolve when facing a potential aggressor. This is also a dispute about who goes to war, as the spiral model contends that even a state interested in protecting the status quo can go to war (out of fear), whereas the deterrence model posits that there are status quo states and revisionist states and that only the latter are attackers. Assessing the frequency of preemption, therefore, helps us answer the fundamental question of whether belligerent diplomacy keeps the peace or threatens war—of whether we should be worried about repeating the mistakes of Sarajevo or the mistakes of Munich.[6]

A second theory predicting preemption is based on the offense-defense balance. This theory argues that wars are more likely when the offense is perceived to have a relative advantage on the battlefield.[7] Such advantages are usually believed to emerge from military technology, strategy, and terrain. When states believe that the offense is dominant, the chances of war are thought to increase in a number of ways. First, wars fought for expansionist or revisionist motives become more likely because aggression is cheaper. Second, preventive wars become more likely because when offense is easy, future shifts in the strategic balance will have worse consequences. Third, preemptive wars become more likely, both because states fear that an adversary's attack in a crisis is more likely, hence are more motivated to preempt, and because actually executing the preemption looks more attractive because of the military advantage of striking first.[8]

Though preemptive war is only one path to war predicted by offense-defense theory, it is an important one. It is the central argument scholars make when discussing how perceived offense dominance can cause crises to escalate to war.[9] Thomas Schelling argued that offensive advantages could encourage preemption in a crisis:

> The worst military confrontation is one in which each side thinks it can win if it gets the jump on the other and will lose if it is slow. . . . Both sides are trapped by an unstable technology, a technology that can convert a likelihood of war into certainty. Military technology that puts a premium on haste in a crisis puts a premium on war itself. A vulnerable military force is one that cannot wait, especially if it faces an enemy force that is vulnerable if the enemy waits.[10]

Preemption is an especially interesting prediction of offense-defense theory, as it is an explanation of how states with essentially defensive foreign policy aims can stumble into war with each other. Offense dominance might make wars of aggression more likely, but this amounts to the relatively unsurprising statement that if a state thinks war is cheaper, it is more likely to attack.[11] Beliefs about offense dominance are a lesser component of the decision calculus regarding preventive wars than are beliefs about the dynamics of the balance of power relationship and the hostility of the adversary.

In sum, preemptive war is a central prediction of the spiral model of war and an important component of offense-defense theory, two leading theories of the causes of war. Academic debate about preemptive war shows no signs of abating. For example, recent scholarship exploring links between revolution and war views preemption as a leading scenario. Further, some works on the democratic peace propose that democracies do not fight each other because increased confidence in negotiations decreases preemptive incentives, and that otherwise pacific democracies may preemptively attack autocracies.[12]

Concerns with preemption have been even more important to some policy debates than they have been in academic discourse. In thinking about how war might break out between the superpowers, a number of observers during the Cold War stressed the possibility that one side might preempt during a high-stakes political crisis, and that the best way to protect superpower peace was to improve crisis stability. This argument received a strong boost following the Cuban Missile Crisis in 1962, and dominated one side of the ongoing debate on U.S. foreign policy and nuclear strategy right through the end of the Cold War.[13] As illustration of the dominance of the vision of preemption, consider this 1987 description of how war could have broken out in Europe during the Cold War. It is worth quoting both because of the evident dominance of preemptive war logic, and because the authors include leading policy analysts and academics, among them Desmond Ball, Hans Bethe, Bruce Blair, Paul Bracken, Ashton Carter, Richard Garwin, David Holloway, Henry Kendall, Richard Ned Lebow, Condoleezza Rice, and John Steinbruner:

> The scenarios that seek to flesh out these speculations largely hang from a common thread: Loss of full political control by the Soviet Union in Poland or East Germany; infusion of Soviet reinforcements that aggravates the upheaval, and simultaneously threatens NATO, thereby triggering a chain reaction of escalating military preparations, viewed as defensive by each side but threatening to the other; culminating in the outbreak of fighting, either by a preemptive attack on NATO, or through a process resembling spontaneous combustion.[14]

Robert Jervis, a leading academic proponent of the significance of mutual assured destruction and critic of the countervailing nuclear strategy, declared unequivocally: "A wide variety of issues and chains of events could lead to all-out nuclear war, but the last step in almost all of them would be preemption. Total war could not occur in the absence of the belief that war is imminent and inevitable and that, as terrible as striking first would be, receiving the first blow would be even worse."[15]

More specifically, a number of analysts have argued that certain weapons and strategies could increase the chances of preemption during a crisis, including counterforce weapons and targeting strategies, the forward-based maritime strategy, strategic defenses, anti-satellite weapons, battlefield nuclear weapons, intermediate-range nuclear forces, counter-political and counter-command targeting, and conventional deep strike strategies.[16] Though debate on these topics has cooled considerably since the end of the Cold War, fears of preemption crop up in discourse on issues such as new security structures in Europe and the proliferation of nuclear weapons and ballistic missile technologies.[17] . . .

Conclusions

There were only three examples of preemption among the 67 interstate wars between 1816 and 1980. When preemptive wars have broken out, the conditions hypothesized to stimulate preemption—specifically hostile images of the enemy and the belief in the importance of attacking first—were present to very high degrees, and non-preemptive motivations for war were also present. These findings suggest that preemption is rare, and only happens when its occurrence is overdetermined. They indicate that the significance of preemption has been exaggerated as a path to war, and ought to play a relatively minor role in our understanding of how wars break out.

What are the implications for theories of the causes of war? For offense-defense theory, this is evidence against only one of the three scenarios for war envisioned by the theory (the other two being aggressive and preventive wars). However, preemptive war is an important prediction of offense-defense theory, as it is the most counterintuitive prediction of the theory. The rarity of preemption, then, undercuts the utility of offense-defense theory for helping us understand why wars break out.

The damage done to the spiral model is greater. Spirals of hostility may lead to competitions for influence or arms races, but war via preemption is the model's central prediction. The finding here that preemption almost never happens, then, is a significant blow to the spiral model as an explanation of the causes of war. The evidence here is not adequate to make the further claim that the deterrence model is a better predictor of outcomes, but the data do indicate that there are important constraints on preemption, namely political costs and leaders' willingness to dampen spirals of hostility before they escalate. The latter factor confirms the persuasive power of the spiral model, as it indicates that preemption can be a self-denying prophecy because decision-makers believe that the spiral model is accurate. Paradoxically, precisely because the spiral model seems to be a powerful insight into how decision-makers think about international crises, its power to predict actual outcomes turns out to be quite limited.

More broadly, these findings point to the importance of ideas in international relations. Both types of constraints on preemption are driven by ideas rather than by material structure: preemption can be politically costly because the idea that preemption is undesirable is enforced by third parties through threats of withholding aid, and preemption can be a self-denying prophecy because leaders believe in the spiral model of war. The rarity of preemption supports the argument, then, that purely structural factors are often insufficient to predict outcomes in international relations.

These theoretical conclusions beg an important policy-related question: was the emphasis on the dangers of preemption during the Cold War misplaced? One interpretation would be that the United States could have been more aggressive in its crisis behavior, given that preemptive war was so unlikely.

This is a position with which I disagree, for several reasons. First, the findings in this article do not exclude completely the possibility of preemption. Given that a superpower nuclear war would have been an unparalleled catastrophe, there is a good argument that actions to avoid even a small risk of such a preemptive war are justified. Second, the Cold War provided conditions that made the probability of a preemptive war relatively high. For much of the Cold War, the United States and the Soviet Union believed in the military benefits of a nuclear first strike, or thought that its adversary believed in the military benefits of a nuclear first strike. Also, both sides at times believed in the implacable hostility and militarism of the other side. These are the conditions that raise the probability of preemptive war. Third, one would be hard-pressed to find any instances in which a U.S. fear of preemption led to an important sacrifice of foreign policy goals. In both Berlin crises and in the Taiwanese islands crises, the United States made no serious concessions and maintained its deterrent credibility. In the Cuban Missile Crisis, the Soviet missiles were removed at the costs, acceptable to the United States, of the removal of unimportant missiles in Turkey and the promise not to invade Cuba. Israel was not destroyed and did not make any major territorial concessions after the 1973 Yom Kippur War, and the outcome of the war led eventually to one of America's greatest foreign policy victories of the Cold War, the defection of Egypt from the Soviet camp.

These empirical findings have important implications for current policy questions. They indicate that it takes a lot to provoke a state to preempt, meaning that states can probably get away with more in the way of military mobilization during a crisis without sparking preemption. If the traditional dilemma in crisis management is between doing too little militarily, risking war from deterrence breakdown, and too much, risking war via preemption, these results would prescribe making more military preparations to avoid deterrence breakdown, because the risks of preemption via an escalation spiral are quite low. Further, these results indicate that fears of preemptive strikes against nuclear forces of new nuclear states in international crises might be exaggerated. Lastly, peace can be protected by stressing to crisis participants the unacceptability of striking first, especially if real costs (such as withholding military aid) are imposed on surprise attackers. Further, emphasizing the dangers of preemption might reinforce the self-denying prophecy effect. Though genuinely aggressive states willing to accept international censure may be immune to such efforts, such actions could help preserve peace in some crises, especially when the adversaries prefer a peaceful solution or are vulnerable to outside pressure.

Notes

1. See Thomas C. Schelling, *The Strategy of Conflict* (Cambridge: Harvard University Press, 1960); Thomas C. Schelling, *Arms and Influence* (New Haven: Yale University Press, 1966); and Glenn H. Snyder, *Deterrence and Defense: Toward a Theory of National Security* (Princeton: Princeton University Press, 1961). Wars caused by reciprocal fear of surprise attack are a subset of preemptive wars.

2. Stephen Van Evera distinguishes them differently, defining a war as preemptive if a state is motivated to attack

because there is an advantage in making the first move whether the war happens now or later, and preventive if the attacker prefers war now to later regardless of who moves first. For Van Evera, a war is preventive if the attacker prefers to attack now rather than be attacked in the near future if the additional time would afford the adversary a relative advantage. Stephen Van Evera, *Causes of War*, Volume I: *The Structure of Power and the Roots of War* (Ithaca, N.Y.: Cornell University Press, forthcoming). I find the time distinction more useful, as it enables the separation of wars that emerge from concerns with long-term shifts in power (preventive wars) from wars emerging out of crisis dynamics (preemptive wars). Works that distinguish between preemptive and preventive wars on the basis of time include Jack S. Levy, "Declining Power and the Preventive Motivation for War," *World Politics*, Vol. 40, No. 1 (October 1987), pp. 90–92; Alfred Vagts, *Defense and Diplomacy: The Soldier and the Conduct of Foreign Relations* (New York: King's Crown Press, 1956), p. 263; and Robert Jervis, "Cooperation under the Security Dilemma," *World Politics*, Vol. 30, No. 2 (January 1978), pp. 188–189. Fritz Fischer (and Bismarck, for that matter) used the time distinction. Fritz Fischer, *War of Illusions: German Policies from 1911 to 1914*, trans. Marian Jackson (London: Chatto & Windus, 1975), p. 461.

3. On surprise attacks, see Richard K. Betts, *Surprise Attack: Lessons for Defense Planning* (Washington, D.C.: Brookings, 1982); Robert Axelrod, "The Rational Timing of Surprise," *World Politics*, Vol. 31, No. 2 (January 1979), pp. 228–246; and Klaus Knorr and Patrick Morgan, eds., *Strategic Military Surprise: Incentives and Opportunities* (New Brunswick: Transaction Books, 1983). New research reveals that surprise attack does not necessarily increase the chances of a quick victory. See D. Scott Bennett and Allan C. Stam III, "How Long (Has This Been Going On)? The Duration of Interstate Wars, 1816–1985," presented at the Annual Meeting of the Peace Science Society, Champaign, Illinois, November 4–6, 1994.

4. Several scholars have argued that accidental wars are either rare or non-occurring events in modern history. See Michael Howard, *The Causes of War and Other Essays*, 2nd ed. (London: Temple Smith, 1983), p. 12; Geoffrey Blainey, *The Causes of War*, 3rd ed. (London: Macmillan, 1988), pp. 127–145; and Scott D. Sagan, *The Limits of Safety: Organizations, Accidents and Nuclear Weapons* (Princeton, N.J.: Princeton University Press, 1993), pp. 262–264.

5. Robert Jervis, *Perception and Misperception in International Politics* (Princeton, N.J.: Princeton University Press, 1976), pp. 58–113. For expansion and refinement of the spiral model, see Charles L. Glaser, "Political Consequences of Military Strategy: Expanding and Refining the Spiral and Deterrence Models," *World Politics*, Vol. 44, No. 4 (July 1992), pp. 497–538; Charles L. Glaser and Ted Hopf, "Models of Soviet-American Relations and Their Implications for Future Russian-American Relations," in William Zimmerman, ed., *Beyond the Soviet Threat: Rethinking American Security Policy in a New Era* (Ann Arbor: University of Michigan Press, 1992); and James D. Fearon, "Deterrence and the Spiral Model: The Role of Costly Signals in Crisis Bargaining," paper presented at the annual meeting of the American Political Science Association, 1990. The logic of the spiral model is closely related to that of the security dilemma.

6. Jervis, *Perception and Misperception.*

7. On the dangers of beliefs in the advantages of striking first, see Schelling, *Arms and Influence*; Jervis, "Cooperation under the Security Dilemma"; Jack Snyder, "Civil-Military Relations and the Cult of the Offensive, 1914 and 1984," *International Security*, Vol. 9, No. 1 (Summer 1984), pp. 108–146; George H. Quester, *Offense and Defense in the International System* (New York: John Wiley & Sons, 1977); Stephen Van Evera, "The Cult of the Offensive and the Origins of the First World War," *International Security*, Vol. 9, No. 1 (Summer 1984), pp. 58–107; Thomas J. Christensen and Jack Snyder, "Chain Gangs and Passed Bucks: Predicting Alliance Patterns in Multipolarity," *International Organization*, Vol. 44, No. 2 (Spring 1990), pp. 137–168; and Ted Hopf, "Polarity, the Offense-Defense Balance, and War," *American Political Science Review*, Vol. 85, No. 2 (June 1991), pp. 475–493. For theoretical and empirical critiques of offense-defense theory, see Jack S. Levy, "The Offensive/ Defensive Balance of Military Technology: A Theoretical and Historical Analysis," *International Studies Quarterly*, Vol. 28, No. 2 (June 1984), pp. 219–238; Jonathan Shimshoni, "Technology, Military Advantage, and World War I: A Case for Military Entrepreneurship," *International Security*, Vol. 15, No. 3 (Winter 1990/91), pp. 187–215; and James D. Fearon, "The Offense-Defense Balance and War Since 1648," paper presented at the Annual Convention of the International Studies Association, Chicago, Illinois, February 1995. For a response to the critiques and a discussion of the nature of the offense-defense balance, see Sean M. Lynn-Jones, "Offense-Defense Theory and its Critics," *Security Studies*, Vol. 4, No. 4 (Summer 1995), pp. 660–691.

8. Van Evera, "Cult of the Offensive." Van Evera actually lists five "major dangers," but for the purposes of this paper they can be folded into the three scenarios discussed here. One might also argue that the offense-defense balance affects international relations in other ways, for example, by making states more belligerent in their peacetime diplomacy, but the phenomenon under examination here is the outbreak of war.

9. For example, Jervis, "Cooperation under the Security Dilemma," pp. 188–189.

10. Schelling, *Arms and Influence*, pp. 224–225.

11. Some might argue that offense-defense theory is interesting because it predicts when war is cheap. Here the theory offers little predictive punch, however, as most proponents concede that it is the perception of the offense-defense balance, rather than the objective balance, that matters. So the theory does not make a useful prediction such as, 'Wars

of aggression are more likely when technology tends to favor mobility," but rather it says, "Wars of aggression are more likely if aggressive decision-makers think victory is easier"; this prediction may be valid, but it is not very counterintuitive and less interesting.

12. Stephen M. Walt, "Revolution and War," *World Politics*, Vol. 44, No. 3 (April 1992), pp. 321–368; Bruce Bueno de Mesquita and David Lalman, *War and Reason: Domestic and International Imperatives* (New Haven: Yale University Press, 1992), pp. 35, 158–159; and Bruce Russett, *Grasping the Democratic Peace: Principles for a Post-Cold War World* (Princeton, N.J.: Princeton University Press, 1993), pp. 39–40.

13. See, for example, Richard Ned Lebow, *Between Peace and War* (Baltimore: Johns Hopkins University Press, 1981); Richard Ned Lebow, *Nuclear Crisis Management: A Dangerous Illusion* (Ithaca, N.Y.: Cornell University Press, 1987); and Daniel Frei, *Risks of Unintentional Nuclear War* (Totowa, N.J.: Rowman & Allanheld, 1983).

14. Desmond Ball, et al., *Crisis Stability and Nuclear War*, Cornell University Peace Studies Program Report (Ithaca, N.Y.: Peace Studies Program, Cornell University, January 1987), p. 28.

15. Robert Jervis, *The Meaning of the Nuclear Revolution: Statecraft and the Prospect of Armageddon* (Ithaca, N.Y.: Cornell University Press, 1989), p. 136.

16. See, for example, Ashton B. Carter, John D. Steinbruner, and Charles A. Zraket, eds., *Managing Nuclear Operations* (Washington, D.C.: Brookings, 1987); Charles L. Glaser, *Analyzing Strategic Nuclear Policy* (Princeton, N.J.: Princeton University Press, 1990); Office of Technology Assessment, *New Technology for NATO: Implementing Follow-on Forces Attack* (Washington, D.C.: National Technical Information Service, 1987); Richard K. Betts, "Conventional Deterrence: Predictive Uncertainty and Policy Confidence," *World Politics*, Vol. 37, No. 2 (January 1985), pp. 153–179; John J. Mearsheimer, "A Strategic Misstep: The Maritime Strategy and Deterrence in Europe," *International Security*, Vol. 11, No. 1 (Summer 1986); Robert Jervis, *The Illogic of American Nuclear Strategy* (Ithaca, N.Y: Cornell University Press, 1984); Bruce G. Blair, *Strategic Command and Control: Redefining the Nuclear Threat* (Washington, D.C.: Brookings, 1985); and Paul Bracken, *The Command and Control of Nuclear Forces* (New Haven: Yale University Press, 1983).

17. See, for example, Steven E. Miller, "The Case Against a Ukrainian Nuclear Deterrent," *Foreign Affairs*, Vol. 72, No. 5 (Summer 1993), pp. 67–80; Steve Fetter, "Ballistic Missiles and Weapons of Mass Destruction," *International Security*, Vol. 16, No. 1 (Summer 1991), pp. 5–42; Peter D. Feaver, "Command and Control in Emerging Nuclear Nations," *International Security*, Vol. 17, No. 3 (Winter 1992/93), pp. 160–187; and Charles A. Kupchan and Clifford A. Kupchan, "Concerts, Collective Security, and the Future of Europe," *International Security*, Vol. 16, No. 1 (Summer 1991), pp. 136–137.

11.3

Preventive War and Democratic Politics

Jack S. Levy

Preventive war is a strategy designed to forestall an adverse shift in the balance of power and driven by better-now-than-later logic. Faced with a rising and potentially hostile adversary, it is better to fight now rather than risk the likely consequences of inaction—a decline in relative power, diminishing bargaining leverage, and the risk of war under less favorable circumstances later.

The concept of preventive war is a familiar one to diplomatic historians, political leaders, international relations theorists, and international legal scholars and just-war theorists. Historians have used the term to characterize the causes of numerous wars and limited military strikes, ranging from the Peloponnesian War to the Israeli strike against the Iraqi nuclear reactor in 1981.[1] Political leaders from Frederick the Great to George W. Bush have explicitly invoked the concept, sometimes to justify a policy they regarded as imperative and sometimes to criticize a policy they saw as unnecessarily risky. Preventive logic has long been central to realist theories of international conflict, including Morgenthau's (1948) balance-of-power theory, Gilpin's (1981) hegemonic-transition theory, and Copeland's (2000) dynamic-differentials theory.[2] Prevention is one of several possible causal mechanisms intervening between power shifts and war in power-transition theory (Kugler and Lemke 1996) and in long-cycle theory (Rasler and Thompson 1994), and its logic underlies the commitment problem in the bargaining model of war (Fearon 1995; Powell 2006). Questions of the moral and legal status of prevention and preemption have also been a key focus of theories of anticipatory self-defense and the law of war (Walzer 1977).

Despite a long history of preventive behavior, only a limited theoretical literature had emerged by the end of the Cold War (Levy 1987; Vagts 1956; Van Evera 1999). That all changed with the Bush Administration's emphasis on the logic of prevention in its National Security Strategy and in its initial rationalization for the 2003 Iraq War. Public intellectuals debated the causal role of preventive logic in U.S. decision-making leading up to the Iraq War and the appropriateness of U.S. preventive strikes against other aspiring nuclear powers. Historians and political scientists began to examine the role of preemption and prevention in the history of American foreign policy, in part to assess the extent to which this aspect of the Bush Doctrine constituted a new departure in American foreign policy (Gaddis 2004; Trachtenberg 2007). Scholars examined other historical cases in an attempt to understand the conditions under which states are most likely to adopt strategies of prevention (Copeland 2000; Renshon 2006; Ripsman and Levy 2007), and to examine the possible constraining effects of democratic institutions and political cultures (Schweller 1992; Silverstone 2007). Philosophers and international legal theorists began to rethink conventional theories of anticipated self-defense in a changing technological and political environment (Doyle 2008; Luban 2004; Shue and Rodin 2007).[3]

This surge of research has enhanced our understanding of preventive war, but still left us short of a satisfactory theory. Conceptual problems remain, as many scholars continue to confuse prevention and preemption or to define the concept so broadly that it loses its analytic utility. We lack a set of conditional generalizations that specify which kinds of states, facing which kinds of rising adversaries, adopt preventive military strategies instead of other strategies, and under what conditions. This is a serious omission, because narrowing power differentials do not usually lead to preventive attacks (Lemke 2003). The unconditional argument that democracies do not fight preventive wars, once widely accepted, is no longer credible; yet there is hardly any empirical research on this question (Schweller 1992). Scholars have given almost no attention to the consequences of preventive strategies—for the preventer, for the target, and for the international system.

I cannot deal with all of these issues in this essay, but I can move things forward on a number of fronts. First, I define the concept of prevention, distinguish it

Source: Jack S. Levy. "Preventive War and Democratic Politics," in *International Studies Quarterly* 52(1):1–8. Copyright 2008 International Studies Association. Reprinted with permission.

from preemption and other sources of better-now-than-later logic, and deal with a number of conceptual issues that impede theoretical development and empirical research on preventive war. I then turn to the question of whether democracies are significantly inhibited in their preventive use of military force. I specify the theoretical arguments advanced on behalf of the democracies-do-not-fight-preventive-wars proposition, and assess the validity of those causal mechanisms in a number of historical cases. I give only passing attention to moral and legal aspects of prevention and preemption, or to the consequences of preventively-motivated wars or limited strikes.

The Concept of Preventive War

Scholars have applied the concept of prevention not only to such relatively straightforward cases as the 1981 Israeli attack against the Iraqi nuclear reactor (Nakdimon 1987; Perlmutter, Handel, and Bar-Joseph 2003), German policy in 1914 (Fischer 1967), and to the Bush Doctrine, but also to U.S. military interventions on its western frontier in the 19th century, in Central America in the early 20th century (Gaddis 2004), and in Grenada in 1983 (Mueller et al. 2006, 182–187). The expansive view of prevention by some reflects continued ambiguity regarding the meaning of the term and threatens to strip the concept of analytic utility. Admittedly, no single definition is optimal for all theoretical purposes, and different theoretical aims might call for different definitions. My primary aim is to understand the causes of war, which requires an assessment of the relative weights of different causal variables and of their interaction effects, and I proceed with that objective in mind.[4]

We can talk about a state's strategy of preventive war, driven by better-now-than-later logic (as further refined below). We can also talk about the preventive motivation for war, or preventive logic, as a variable that intervenes between power shifts and war and that provides one possible causal mechanism through which the former can lead to the latter. The concept of "a preventive war," though widely used, is problematic. It implies that preventive war is a type of war, as defined by its causes. Like any categorization of outcomes in terms of their causes, this confounds cause and effect in a single concept and complicates efforts to explain outcomes. Most wars have multiple causes, and to identify a war as "a preventive war" privileges one cause over others. It also emphasizes the motivations of one state while neglecting those of the other.

Referring to a particular war as preventive would not be a problem if the preventive motivation was a sufficient condition for the war—if current issues, conflicts of interest, and perceptions of adversary intentions played no role, and if the only issue was future power and the bargaining leverage it provided. Yet I have not been able to find a single case that qualifies.[5]

One can find numerous cases for which the preventive motivation was a necessary condition for war. Many of these cases involved other necessary conditions, however, and labeling the war as preventive privileges one necessary condition over others and downgrades the causal impact of other causal variables.[6]

Preventive logic can also influence the timing of a war sought for other reasons, and it would be misleading to characterize the war as "a preventive war." An important motivation for the German invasion of the Soviet Union in 1941 was the perception that Soviet economic power and military potential were growing while Germany's was reaching its peak, leaving a window of opportunity for war in the east that would close by 1943 (Copeland 2000, 137–144; Tooze 2007). Given Hitler's well-established plans for a war in the east (Mawdsley 2005; Weinberg 1994), however, it would be misleading to explain the war itself primarily in terms of preventive logic—unless, perhaps, one were to argue that adverse demographic trends in the east were the primary motivation for Hitler's expansionist policies (Weisiger 2008).

A similar argument applies to preemption, which by definition causally preempts something that the initiator believes is about to happen for other reasons.[7] The concept of "a preemptive war" may help to describe the proximate path to war, but it fails to capture the underlying causes of the war.[8]

For these reasons, it is better to avoid the concept of "a preventive war" and focus instead on the preventive motivation for war as a causal variable that intervenes between power shifts and war. Given my emphasis on the anticipation of a power shift and the fear of its consequences, I treat the preventive motivation as a perceptual variable, the strength of which varies with psychological as well as structural factors. An alternative approach would be to treat the preventive motivation as an "objective" variable, equivalent to changes in relative capabilities. This is useful for the important task of assessing the aggregate relationship between power shifts and war,[9] but in my view it does not fully capture the nuances of preventive logic.[10] Perceptions of the magnitude and even the direction of a power shift may vary across states and across leaders, and these perceptions are critical in assessing behavior.[11]

Another conceptual problem is the persistent tendency, despite ample clarification in the literature for at least two decades, for scholars to confuse prevention with preemption, or to deliberately treat the two concepts as interchangeable.[12] This is not helpful. Prevention and preemption are each forms of better-now-than-latter logic, but they are responses to different threats involving different time horizons and calling for different strategic responses. Preemption involves striking now in the anticipation of an imminent adversary attack, with the aim of securing first-mover advantages. Prevention is a response to a future threat rather than an immediate threat. It is driven by the anticipation of an adverse power shift and the fear of the consequences, including the deterioration of one's relative military position and bargaining power and the risk of war—or of extensive concessions necessary to avoid war—under less favorable circumstances later. The incentive is to forestall the power shift by blocking the rise of the adversary while the opportunity is still available.[13]

Most preemptors do not want war but believe it is imminent and unavoidable. Preventers want war in the short-term to avoid the risk of a worse war in the future. Preventers often initiate war, but they sometimes attempt to provoke the adversary into initiating a war so as to secure for themselves the diplomatic and domestic political advantages of appearing as the defender.[14] The classic example of preemption is the Israeli initiation of the 1967 war (Oren 2002). The classic example of prevention is the Israeli strike against the Iraqi nuclear reactor in 1981.[15] Thus the Bush Doctrine of preemption is based on the logic of prevention, though the causal role of preventive logic in the complex processes leading to the 2003 Iraq war has yet to be established.[16]

The distinction between preemption and prevention is important for many reasons. Historically, prevention is far more common than preemption.[17] Theoretically, the conditions under which states adopt each strategy are quite different.[18] Legally, preemption is far easier to justify than is prevention because imminent threats, unlike temporally distant threats, preclude alternative strategic responses that take time to implement (Doyle 2008; Walzer 1977). In terms of policy, optimal strategic responses to threats of prevention differ from those for preemption. As Betts (1982, 144–145) argues, "Countermobilization is the best way to deter an enemy contemplating preventive attack and the worst way to deter one considering preemption."

Even if we limit the concept of prevention to forestalling future threats, we need to specify what kinds of threats qualify. How broadly prevention is defined helps to shape assessments of both the historical frequency and the effectiveness of preventive war strategies, which in turn can have an enormous impact on policy debates that invoke history for support. Many critics of the Bush Doctrine implicitly adopt a narrow definition of prevention and argue that the emphasis on preventive logic marks a new departure in American foreign policy, while the administration's supporters adopt a broader definition and often emphasize continuity with a deeply rooted historical tradition. This raises the concern that policy arguments that seek justification from history are often shaped more by definition than by history, and that definitions themselves are shaped by policy preferences rather than by their analytic utility (Levy 2007).

Turning to more serious scholarly analyses, Renshon (2006, chapter 1) defines prevention as "an action . . . fought to forestall a grave national security threat," which he defines to include the loss of status or prestige as well as a decline in relative military power.[19] Gaddis (2004, 16–22), while less explicit, also uses an expansive conception of "preemption," which he uses interchangeably with prevention. He describes as preemptive John Adams' response to cross-border incursions from Spanish Florida and Andrew Jackson's policy of using military force on the vulnerable western frontier before specific threats materialized. He also refers to a "succession of preemptive interventions" by the United States to contain political instability in Central and South America in the early 20th century. He argues that "even the prospect of power vacuums invited preemption," and that "concerns about 'failed' or 'derelict' states, then, are nothing new in the history of United States foreign relations, nor are strategies of preemption in dealing with them."

Gaddis's (2004) argument, with its emphasis on defensively motivated expansion driven by the security dilemma and a worst-case analysis of potential threats, provides a useful counter to interpretations that emphasize a more offensively oriented expansionism, though more extensive testing of these rival interpretations is warranted. It is not useful, however, to classify such actions as preventive. That would lump U.S. interventions on the Western frontier in the 19th century and in Central and South America early in the 20th century in the same category as Israel's 1981 strike against Iraq's nuclear reactor or Germany's strategy for a war in 1914 before Russia grew too strong. Similarly, Mueller et al. (2006, 182–187) go too far in classifying the 1983 U.S. invasion of Grenada as preventive (to forestall the establishment of a Soviet military base).

Some define prevention even more broadly to include any development that might leave the state worse off in the future. Taylor (1954, 166), for example, argues that each great power war in the 1848–1918 period "started as a preventive war." The problem with expansive conceptions of prevention is that they incorporate too many different things under a single category and, in the extreme, result in nearly all wars being classified as preventive. This is a classic case of "conceptual stretching" (Sartori 1970). It weakens the discriminatory power of our analytic concepts and complicates efforts to construct an explanatory theory that applies to all cases within a given category.[20]

It makes a difference, for explanatory theory, whether the use of military force is driven by a fear of imminent attack, fear of a deteriorating power position that might leave one vulnerable in several years, fear of political instability on one's borders, or a fear of a loss of prestige or status in the international system. Thus we need different concepts to describe these behaviors. With regard to Renshon's (2006) inclusion of an anticipated loss of both prestige and of relative power in his definition of prevention, I agree that prestige can reinforce power, but would argue that it is only by analytically distinguishing between these two variables that we can assess their separate causal effects.[21]

For these reasons I focus narrowly on the perception of threat deriving from changing power differentials and on a military response to the threat, and exclude other sources of better-now-than-later logic from the category of prevention.[22] I am not necessarily suggesting that these other factors have a smaller causal impact than do negative power shifts and preventive logic. That is an empirical question, and one that can be answered only by first analytically distinguishing among various causal variables.

Preventive logic can lead to a limited military strike as well as to an all-out war.[23] Whether a limited strike remains limited or escalates to war depends not only on the actions of the preventer, but also on those of the target. Presumably the initiator anticipates the target's likely response and incorporates it into its initial decision calculus. It might launch a limited military strike if it expects no military response and refrain from military action if it expects a major military response. Israel's anticipation that Iraq would not respond to a limited Israeli strike contributed to its decision to launch a surgical strike against the Iraqi nuclear reactor in 1981 (Nakdimon 1987; Perlmutter et al. 2003). In contrast, the U.S. anticipation that North Korea would probably respond to a limited strike against its nuclear facilities in 1994 with an all-out attack on South Korea was a major factor in the U.S. decision against military action (Sigal 1997; Wit, Poneman, and Gallucci 2004). Similarly, India was deterred from launching a surgical strike against Pakistan's nuclear facilities by its belief that Pakistan would respond in kind and that the radioactive fallout from an attack on India's nuclear reactors would be enormously costly (Ganguly and Hagerty 2005, 55–57; Perkovich 1999).

The preventive motivation for war, usually associated with power transitions involving the overtaking of a declining leader by a rising challenger, can also arise in response to more limited power shifts. One example is a "rapid approach" that levels off short of a power transition (Wayman 1996). Another is the challenger's crossing a particular threshold of military power, leading to a step-level power shift. While such limited power shifts are presumably less threatening than those leading to a reversal of power relations, they can still trigger military responses, even in a non-nuclear context. The Czech/Russian arms sale to Egypt was a major factor leading to Israel's preventive motivation for war in the 1956 Sinai Campaign (Levy and Gochal 2001–2002). The anticipated completion of Russia's trans-Siberian railroad and its expected enhancement of Russia's power projection capabilities in East Asia contributed to Japan's decision for war in 1904 (Patrikeeff and Shukman 2007).

The crossing of the nuclear threshold is the most consequential manifestation of a step-level power shift. In addition to their role in triggering Israel's attack against the Iraqi nuclear reactor in 1981 and possibly the American war in Iraq in 2003, fears that an adversary was about to acquire nuclear weapons led to serious considerations of a preventively motivated military strike by India against Pakistan in the early 1980s (Ganguly and Hagerty 2005; Perkovich 1999), by the United States against North Korea in 1994 (Wit, Pone-man, and Gallucci 2004), and, to a lesser extent, by the United States against the Soviet Union and then against China in the 1950s and 1960s (Silverstone 2007; Trachtenberg 2007).

The preventive logic associated with an anticipated power shift that falls short of a complete power transition is the same that underlies any power shift—the expectation that a decline in relative military capabilities will lead to a commensurate decline in its bargaining leverage, leaving the state less able to defend its interests, less able to defend its allies, and compelled to make unwanted concessions in the future. This, and not the fear of a power transition per se, was what motivated the

United States in the 1994 North Korean nuclear crisis, and was a major factor for some (but not all) U.S. decision-makers in their support of the 2003 Iraq war.

While the literature on prevention focuses primarily on dyadic power shifts, third states can also play an important role. First, the target of the threat posed by the rising power may be one's allies rather than oneself, as suggested by the U.S.-Iraqi case in 2003. Second, the source of the threat may not be the primary adversary alone, but instead a coalition of states. Frederick the Great, anticipating the formation of a hostile coalition of Austria, Russia, and France, attacked Austria in 1756.[24] In 1914, German leaders never doubted their ability to defeat their rising Russian adversary in a bilateral war, but they feared the implications of Russia's rise for Germany's ability to defeat Russia and France together in a two-front war by 1917.

In elaborating on the concept of prevention, I have focused more on the perceptions and decisions of the preventer than on the behavior of the target. This reflects my working assumption—which needs to be explored empirically—that power shifts often involve relatively little bargaining between the declining and rising state, precisely because it is difficult to reach a negotiated settlement under conditions of shifting power. As I argued before (Levy 1987, 96), the declining state hesitates to accept a settlement, even one involving substantial concessions, knowing that the rising state can repudiate any agreement once it becomes dominant. Each knows there is nothing the rising state can do to assure its adversary that it will refrain from using its new power to overturn a settlement, so that current agreements are not enforceable. The only concessions the declining state would be likely to accept are those that place limits on growth of the rising state's power, which the latter is unlikely to grant. This argument has been stated more formally and rigorously in the bargaining model of war, and is now well known as the "commitment problem" (Fearon 1995; Powell 2006; Wagner 2000).

Let me end this section by emphasizing that I do not attach any particular normative evaluation to this definition of preventive war strategies. "Preventive" does not necessarily mean "defensive" or normatively justifiable. If state *A* embarks on an aggressive war and conquers territory from *B*, *B* then gradually begins to build up its arms, and *A* then strikes at *B* to forestall *B*'s further rise in power and any potential threat to *A*'s new territories, I would label the motivation preventive but not necessarily as defensive.[25]

Perceptions of an impending power shift might also lead through preventive logic to shape the timing of a fundamentally aggressive war. The German invasion of the Soviet Union in 1941 is one example. German policy in World War I is another, regardless of whether one views Germany as seeking a war to maintain a favorable status quo in Europe (Albertini 1952–1957) or to overturn the status quo and achieve hegemony over Europe (Fischer 1967, 1975, 470; Lieber 2007; Mombauer 2001). In either case, the rise of Russian power in combination with the threat of a two-front war in Europe made it a "now or never" situation for Germany. German leaders hoped that a local war in the Balkans would break up the Franco-Russian alliance and precipitate a diplomatic realignment in Europe, but they were willing to fight a continental war if necessary to block the rise of Russia while the opportunity was still available. Mombauer (2001, 108) describes German policy as preventive "not in the sense of preempting an attack from one of Germany's possible future enemies, but of preventing a situation in which Germany would no longer herself be able to launch an attack successfully" (in pursuit of its revisionist aims).[26] . . .

Notes

1. Thucydides (1996, 16) argued that the underlying cause of the Peloponnesian War was "Sparta's fear of the rising power of Athens."

2. Preventive war strategies fit nicely into offensive realist theory, and it is odd that Mearsheimer (2001) never mentions them.

3. Most modern theories of anticipatory self-defense begin with the criteria proposed by U.S. Secretary of State Daniel Webster in the 1837 *Caroline* case. Webster argued that the use of force in self-defense is justified only if the "necessity of self-defence is instant, overwhelming, and leaving no choice of means, and no moment for deliberation," and if force is not "unreasonable or excessive." Daniel Webster, letters to British Foreign Minister Lord Ashbutton, August 6, 1842, and to Mr. Fox, April 24, 1841. Cited in Henkin, Pugh, Schachter, and Smit (1980, 890–891). These basic criteria of necessity, imminency, and proportionality are widely accepted in customary international law and in theories of just war. Walzer (1977, 80–85) argued for "the moral necessity of rejecting any attack that is merely preventive in character that does not wait upon and respond to the willful acts of an adversary."

4. This section draws on Levy (2007).

5. As Kydd (1997, 148) argues, "preventive wars sparked by fears about the future motivations of currently benign states almost never happen." The Israeli attack on the

Iraqi nuclear reactor in 1981 come close to a "pure" case of prevention, but as I show later even that falls short.

6. On possible criteria for evaluating the relative causal weights of multiple necessary conditions, see Goertz and Levy (2007, 39–43).

7. This raises some interesting issues in the philosophical analysis of causation, including "causal preemption" and "preemptive prevention" (Collins 2000).

8. If the initiator's perception of an imminent attack is mistaken, the sources of the misperception and the strategy of preemption that followed take on greater causal weight.

9. Lemke (2003) finds no relationship between power shifts and the onset of war. Weisiger (2008) concurs, but finds that wars involving power shifts on the eve of war are longer and more intense than wars that do not involve such power shifts.

10. Aggregate studies of power shifts and war need to give greater attention to the relative weight of different dimensions of power. The Correlates of War Project's summary measure (Bremer 1980)—which gives equal weight to military, economic, and demographic indicators of power—may not be appropriate for testing propositions on preventive war. My hypothesis is that in decisions regarding the resort to a preventive war strategy in response to an adverse power shift, leaders are most frequently concerned with the military dimension, occasionally concerned with the economic dimension, and rarely concerned with the demographic dimension. One advantage of case study approaches is that they can investigate how various political leaders evaluated different elements of shifting power.

11. Prior to Munich, for example, French and British leaders had diametrically opposed perceptions of the relative balance of power and how it was changing. French leaders believed that Germany was weaker than France and Britain, but growing stronger, while British leaders believed that Germany was already stronger but that its lead would not last, particularly if Britain began to rearm. The French were driven by better-now-than-later logic to prefer a strong stand against Germany at Munich, but only with British support, while the British were led by better-later-than-now logic to prefer a strategy of appeasement to buy time for rearmament (Ripsman and Levy 2007).

12. The distinguished scholars Gaddis (2004), Quester (2000), Schroeder (2002), and Trachtenberg (2007) each use preemption and prevention interchangeably. A useful RAND study (Mueller et al. 2006, xii) argues that prevention and preemption are driven by "similar logic," and subsumes them both under the larger category of "anticipatory attack."

13. For similar conceptualizations see Betts (1982, 145), Freedman (2004, 85–89), Huntington (1957, 360), Levy (1987), Renshon (2006, chapter 1), and Silverstone (2007, chapter 1), Van Evera (1999, 76), Walter (1977, 76).

14. Lebow (1981) captures this in his concept of a "justification of hostility" crisis. In 1914, for example, German leaders feared the rising power of Russia and wanted a war before power shifted further, but they did not want to mobilize first, for fear of appearing as the aggressor. Once Russia mobilized Germany then struck first to gain first-mover military advantages. See Albertini (1952–1957) and Fischer (1967).

15. Other wars commonly attributed to preventive logic include Prussia in the Seven Years War (1756–1763), Japan in the Russo-Japanese War (1904–1905), Germany in World War I, and Japan in the 1941–1945 Pacific War (Copeland 2000; Mueller et al. 2006; Vagts 1956; Van Evera 1999).

16. The Bush Administration's rhetorical emphasis on preemption is probably explained by its recognition of the problematic legal basis of prevention, though it is also conceivable that they (like many scholars) did not appreciate the analytic distinction.

17. As Reiter (1995) notes, "preemptive wars almost never happen."

18. States in relative decline are most likely to adopt preventive strategies when they expect that a power transition is virtually certain, that the adversary will have a substantial advantage, that the adversary is hostile and revisionist, and that a future war is likely. For these and other hypotheses see Copeland (2000), Ripsman and Levy (2007), and Van Evera (1999).

19. Buchanan and Keohane (2004), whose aims are more normative, define the preventive use of force as "the initiation of military action in anticipation of harmful actions that are neither presently occurring nor immediately impending."

20. Excessively narrow definitions, which are less common, also strip the concept of much of its discriminating power by reducing it to a null set. Wolfers (1962, 153), for example, concluded that "there seems to be no case in history in which a country started a preventive war on the grounds of security."

21. Press (2005) demonstrates the utility of distinguishing between power and reputation by showing that states are influenced more by adversary capabilities and interests than by its credibility in responding to past threats.

22. My concept of the preventive motivation for war excludes "preventive diplomacy," "preventive deployment," and "preventive intervention," which generally aim to avert humanitarian disasters. I also exclude nonmilitary actions to forestall economic or military decline, such as economic restructuring. Covert actions to degrade adversary military capabilities are preventively motivated, but I prefer to distinguish them from preventively motivated strikes and wars undertaken by a state's organized military forces, which is a defining element of war (Vasquez 1993, chapter 2).

23. Limited preventive strikes and the importance of relative power were key themes in Levy (1987), but Renshon (2006, 148–151) mischaracterizes that discussion.

24. Anderson (1966, 34) calls this "the most famous preventive war in history."

25. Thus I dissent from Mueller et al.'s (2006, xii) statement that prevention and preemption are "offensive strategies carried out for defensive reasons."

26. I thank Keir Lieber for his guidance on the new historiography of World War I.

12 Balance of Power

12.1

The Balance of Power

Hans Morgenthau

The aspiration for power on the part of several nations, each trying either to maintain or overthrow the status quo, leads of necessity to a configuration that is called the balance of power[1] and to policies that aim at preserving it. We say "of necessity" advisedly. For here again we are confronted with the basic misconception that has impeded the understanding of international politics and has made us the prey of illusions. This misconception asserts that men have a choice between power politics and its necessary outgrowth, the balance of power, on the one hand, and a different, better kind of international relations, on the other. It insists that a foreign policy based on the balance of power is one among several possible foreign policies and that only stupid and evil men will choose the former and reject the latter.

It will be shown in the following pages that the international balance of power is only a particular manifestation of a general social principle to which all societies composed of a number of autonomous units owe the autonomy of their component parts; that the balance of power and policies aiming at its preservation are not only inevitable but are an essential stabilizing factor in a society of sovereign nations; and that the instability of the international balance of power is due not to the faultiness of the principle but to the particular conditions under which the principle must operate in a society of sovereign nations. . . .

Nowhere have the mechanics of social equilibrium been described more brilliantly and at the same time more simply than in *The Federalist*. Concerning the system of checks and balances of the American government, No. 51 of *The Federalist* says:

> This policy of supplying, by opposite and rival interests, the defect of better motives, might be traced to the whole system of human affairs, private as well as public. We see it particularly displayed in all the subordinate distributions of power, where the constant aim is to divide and arrange the several offices in such a manner as that each may be a check on the other—that the private interests of every individual may be a sentinel over the public rights. These inventions of prudence cannot be less requisite in the distribution of the supreme powers of the state.

In the words of John Randolph, "You may cover whole skins of parchment with limitations, but power alone can limit power."[2]

Two Main Patterns of the Balance of Power

Two factors are at the basis of international society: one is the multiplicity and the other is the antagonism of its elements, the individual nations. The aspirations for power of the individual nations can come into

Source: Hans Morgenthau, "The Balance of Power" and "The Structure of the Balance of Power," in *Politics among Nations: The Struggle for Power and Peace*, 7th ed.

conflict with one another—and some, if not most of them, do at any particular moment in history—in two different ways. In other words, the struggle for power on the international scene can be carried on in two typical patterns.

The Pattern of Direct Opposition

Nation A may embark upon an imperialistic policy with regard to Nation B, and Nation B may counter that policy with a policy of the status quo or with an imperialistic policy of its own. France and its allies opposing Russia in 1812, Japan opposing China from 1931 to 1941, and the Allied nations versus the Axis from 1941 on correspond to that pattern. The pattern is one of direct opposition between the nation that wants to establish its power over another nation and the latter, which refuses to yield.

Nation A may also pursue an imperialistic policy toward Nation C, which may either resist or acquiesce in that policy, while Nation B follows with regard to Nation C either a policy of imperialism or one of the status quo. In this case the domination of C is a goal of A's policy. B, on the other hand, is opposed to A's policy because it either wants to preserve the status quo with respect to C or wants the domination of C for itself. The pattern of the struggle for power between A and B is here not one of direct opposition but of competition, the object of which is the domination of C, and it is only through the intermediary of that competition that the contest for power between A and B takes place. This pattern is visible, for instance, in the competition between Great Britain and Russia for the domination of Iran, in which the struggle for power between the two countries has repeatedly manifested itself during the last hundred years. It is also clear in the competition for dominant influence in Germany that in the aftermath of the Second World War has marked the relations between France, Great Britain, the Soviet Union, and the United States. The competition between the United States and China or between the Soviet Union and China for control of the countries of Southeast Asia offers another example of the same pattern.

It is in situations such as these that the balance of power operates and fulfills its typical functions. In the pattern of direct opposition, the balance of power results directly from the desire of either nation to see its policies prevail over the policies of the other. A tries to increase its power in relation to B to such an extent that it can control the decisions of B and thus lead its imperialistic policy to success. B, on the other hand, will try to increase its power to such an extent that it can resist A's pressure and thus frustrate A's policy or else embark upon an imperialistic policy of its own with a chance for success. In the latter case, A must, in turn, increase its power in order to be able to resist B's imperialistic policy and to pursue its own with a chance for success. This balancing of opposing forces will go on, the increase in the power of one nation calling forth an at least proportionate increase in the power of the other, until the nations concerned change the objectives of their imperialistic policies—if they do not give them up altogether—or until one nation gains or believes it has gained a decisive advantage over the other. Then either the weaker yields to the stronger or war decides the issue.

So long as the balance of power operates successfully in such a situation, it fulfills two functions. It creates a precarious stability in the relations between the respective nations, a stability that is always in danger of being disturbed and, therefore, is always in need of being restored. This is, however, the only stability obtainable under the assumed conditions of the power pattern. For we are here in the presence of an inevitable inner contradiction of the balance of power. One of the two functions the balance of power is supposed to fulfill is stability in the power relations among nations; yet these relations are, as we have seen, by their very nature subject to continuous change. They are essentially unstable. Since the weights that determine the relative position of the scales have a tendency to change continuously by growing either heavier or lighter, whatever stability the balance of power may achieve must be precarious and subject to perpetual adjustments in conformity with intervening changes. The other function that a successful balance of power fulfills under these conditions is to insure the freedom of one nation from domination by the other.

Owing to the essentially unstable and dynamic character of the balance, which is not unstable and dynamic by accident or only part of the time, but by nature and always, the independence of the nations concerned is also essentially precarious and in danger. Here again, however, it must be said that, given the conditions of the power pattern, the independence of the respective nations can rest on no other foundation than the power of each individual nation to prevent the power of the other nations from encroaching upon its freedom. The following diagram illustrates this situation:

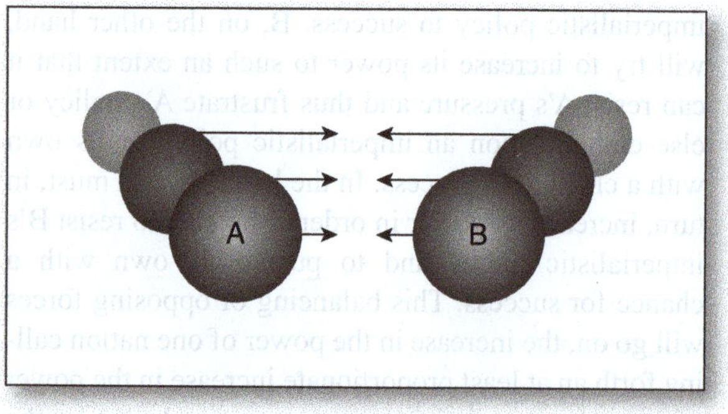

The Pattern of Competition

In the other pattern, the pattern of competition, the mechanics of the balance of power are identical with those discussed. The power of A necessary to dominate C in the face of B's opposition is balanced, if not outweighed, by B's power, while, in turn, B's power to gain dominion over C is balanced, if not outweighed, by the power of A. The additional function, however, that the balance fulfills here, aside from creating a precarious stability and security in the relations between A and B, consists in safeguarding the independence of C against encroachments by A or B. The independence of C is a mere function of the power relations existing between A and B:

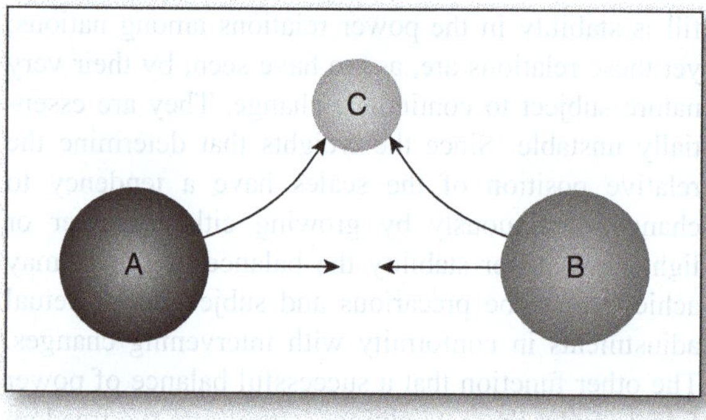

If these relations take a decisive turn in favor of the imperialistic nation—that is, A—the independence of C will at once be in jeopardy:

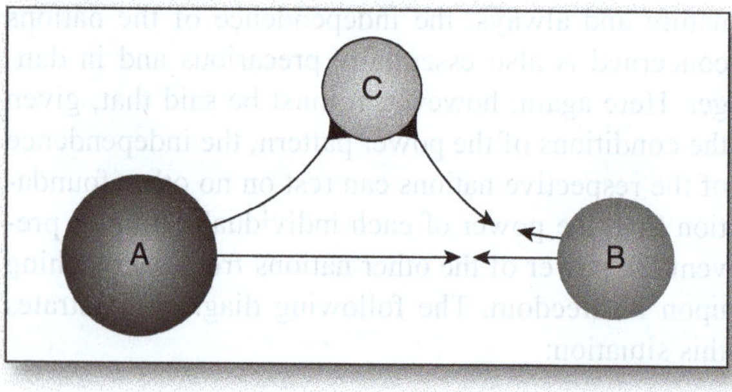

If the status quo nation—that is, B—should gain a decisive and permanent advantage, C's freedom will be more secure in the measure of that advantage:

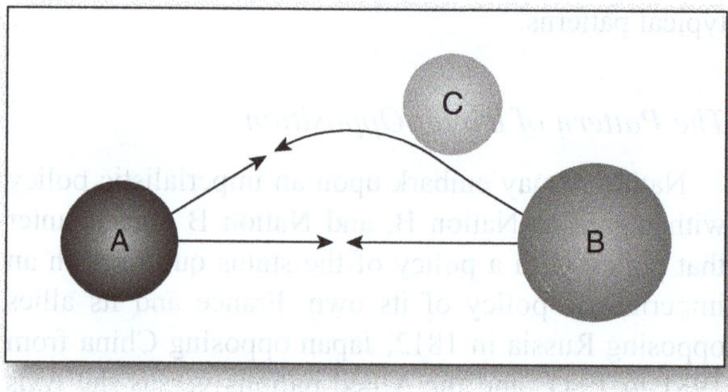

If, finally, the imperialistic nation—A—should give up its imperialistic policies altogether or shift them permanently from C to another objective—that is, D—the freedom of C would be permanently secured:

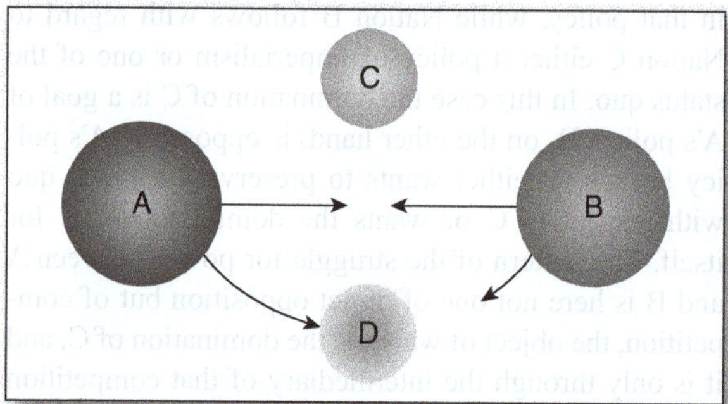

No one has recognized this function of the balance of power to preserve the independence of weak nations more clearly than Edmund Burke. He said in 1791 in his "Thoughts on French Affairs":

> As long as those two princes [the king of Prussia and the German emperor], are at variance, so long the liberties of Germany are safe. But if ever they should so far understand one another as to be persuaded that they have a more direct and more certainly defined interest in a proportioned mutual aggrandizement than in a reciprocal reduction, that is, if they come to think that they are more likely to be enriched by a division of spoil than to be rendered secure by keeping to the old policy of preventing others from being spoiled by either of them, from that moment the liberties of Germany are no more.[3]

Small nations have always owed their independence either to the balance of power (Belgium and the Balkan countries until the Second World War), or to the preponderance of one protecting power (the small nations of Central and South America, and Portugal), or to their lack of attractiveness for imperialistic aspirations (Switzerland and Spain). The ability of such small nations to maintain their neutrality has always been due to one or the other or all of these factors, for instance, the Netherlands, Denmark, and Norway in the First, in contrast to the Second, World War, and Switzerland and Sweden in both world wars.

The same factors are responsible for the existence of so-called buffer states—weak states located close to powerful ones and serving their military security. The outstanding example of a buffer state owing its existence to the balance of power is Belgium from the beginning of its history as an independent state in 1831 to the Second World War. The nations belonging to the so-called Russian security belt, which stretches along the western and southwestern frontiers of the Soviet Union from Finland to Bulgaria, exist by leave of their preponderant neighbor, whose military and economic interests they serve.

Korea and the Balance of Power

All these different factors have brought to bear successively upon the fate of Korea. Because of its geographic location in the proximity of China, it has existed as an autonomous state for most of its long history by virtue of the control or intervention of its powerful neighbor. Whenever the power of China was not sufficient to protect the autonomy of Korea, another nation, generally Japan, would try to gain a foothold on the Korean peninsula. Since the first century B.C.E., the international status of Korea has by and large been determined either by Chinese supremacy or by rivalry between China and Japan.

The very unification of Korea in the seventh century was a result of Chinese intervention. From the thirteenth century to the decline of Chinese power in the nineteenth century, Korea stood in a relationship of subservience to China as its suzerain and accepted Chinese leadership in politics and culture. From the end of the sixteenth century, Japan, after it had invaded Korea without lasting success, opposed to the claim of China its own claim to control of the country. Japan was able to make good that claim as a result of its victory in the Sino-Japanese War of 1894–95. Then Japan was challenged in its control of Korea by Russia, and from 1896 on the influence of Russia became dominant. The rivalry between Japan and Russia for control of Korea ended with the defeat of Russia in the Russo-Japanese War of 1904–05. Japanese control of Korea, thus firmly established, was terminated with the defeat of Japan in the Second World War. From then on, the United States replaced Japan as a check upon Russian ambitions in Korea. China, by intervening in the Korean War, resumed its traditional interest in the control of Korea. Thus for more than two thousand years the fate of Korea has been a function either of the predominance of one nation controlling Korea or of a balance of power between two nations competing for that control.

NOTES

1. The term "balance of power" is used in the text with four different meanings: (1) as a policy aimed at a certain state of affairs, (2) as an actual state of affairs, (3) as an approximately equal distribution of power, or (4) as any distribution of power. Whenever the term is used without qualification, it refers to an actual state of affairs in which power is distributed among several nations with approximately equal distribution of power.
2. Quoted after William Cabell Bruce, *John Randolph of Roanoke* (New York and London: G. P. Putnam's Sons, 1922), Vol. II, p. 211.
3. *Works* (Boston: Little, Brown, 1889), Vol. IV, p. 331.

12.2

Alliance Formation and the Balance of World Power

Stephen M. Walt

The question "what causes alignment?" is a central issue in debates on American foreign policy, and the choices that are made often turn on which hypotheses of alliance formation are endorsed. In general, those who believe that American security is fragile most often assume that Soviet allies are reliable and America's are prone to defect, while those who believe it is robust tend to view American allies as stronger and more reliable than those of the U.S.S.R. These divergent beliefs clash over a variety of specific issues. For example, should the U.S. increase its commitment to NATO to prevent the growth of Soviet military power from leading to the "Finlandization" of Europe? Alternatively, should the U.S. do less in the expectation that its allies will do more? Should the U.S. oppose leftist regimes in the developing world because their domestic ideology will lead them to ally with the Soviet Union, or can a policy of accommodating radical nationalist regimes lead to good relations with them? Can Soviet or American military aid create reliable proxies in the Third World? Is it worth the effort and expense? Each of these questions carries important implications for American national security policy, and the answers ultimately turn upon which hypotheses of alliance formation are believed to be most valid.

Despite the obvious importance of understanding how states select their partners, most scholarly research on alliances has ignored or obscured these questions.[1] This article is intended to correct these omissions by outlining some of the most important hypotheses of alliance formation, and by exploring the policy implications of each. The first section explores the competing propositions that states either balance against strong or threatening states or, alternatively, that they "bandwagon" with them. I shall also consider the sharply different foreign and defense policies that each proposition implies. . . .

Balancing Versus Bandwagoning: Alliances as a Response to Threat

Alliances are most commonly viewed as a response to threats, yet there is sharp disagreement as to what that response will be. When entering an alliance, states may either *balance* (ally in opposition to the principal source of danger) or *bandwagon* (ally with the state that poses the major threat).[2] These contrasting hypotheses depict very different worlds, and the policies that follow from each are equally distinct. In the simplest terms, if balancing is more common than bandwagoning, then states are more secure because aggressors will face combined opposition. Status quo states should therefore avoid provoking countervailing coalitions by eschewing threatening foreign and defense policies. But if bandwagoning is the dominant tendency, then security is scarce because aggression is rewarded. A more belligerent foreign policy and a more capable military establishment are the logical policy choices.

Although both of these hypotheses have been examined by scholars and embraced by statesmen, important details have been neglected. Accordingly, I shall first present each hypothesis in its simplest (and most common) form, and then indicate how they should be revised. That task accomplished, I shall then consider which hypothesis describes the dominant tendency in international politics.

Balancing Behavior

The proposition that states will join alliances in order to avoid domination by stronger powers lies at the heart of traditional balance of power theory.[3] According to this hypothesis, states join alliances to protect themselves from states or coalitions whose superior resources could pose a threat. States will choose to balance for two main reasons.

Source: Stephen M. Walt, "Alliance Formation and the Balance of World Power", *International Security* 9: 4 (Spring, 1985), pp. 3–18.

First, states risk their own survival if they fail to curb a potential hegemon before it becomes too strong. To ally *with* the dominant power means placing one's trust in its continued benevolence. The safer strategy is to join with those who cannot readily dominate their allies, in order to avoid being dominated by those who can.[4] As Winston Churchill explained Britain's traditional alliance policy:

> For four hundred years the foreign policy of England has been to oppose the strongest, most aggressive, most dominating power on the Continent. . . . it would have been easy . . . and tempting to join with the stronger and share the fruits of his conquest. However, we always took the harder course, joined with the less strong Powers, . . . and thus defeated the Continental military tyrant whoever he was. . . . [5]

In the same way, Henry Kissinger advocated *rapprochement* with China rather than the Soviet Union because he believed that, in a triangular relationship, it was better to align with the weaker side.[6]

Second, joining the more vulnerable side increases the new member's influence, because the weaker side has greater need for assistance. Joining the stronger side, by contrast, reduces the new member's influence (because it adds relatively less to the coalition) *and* leaves it vulnerable to the whims of its new partners. Alignment with the weaker side is thus the preferred choice.[7]

The appeal of balance of power theory as an explanation for alliance formation is unsurprising, given the numerous examples of states joining together to resist a threatening state or coalition.[8] Yet despite the powerful evidence that history provides in support of this hypothesis, it is often suggested that the opposite response is more likely, that states will prefer to ally with the strongest power. Who argues that bandwagoning is the dominant tendency in international politics, and why do they think so?

Bandwagoning Behavior

The belief that states will tend to ally *with* rather than against the dominant side is surprisingly common. According to one scholar,

> [In international politics] momentum accrues to the gainer and accelerates his movement. The appearance of irreversibility in his gains enfeebles one side and stimulates the other all the more. The bandwagon collects those on the sidelines.[9]

Scholars are not alone in this conception. For example, the German Admiral Alfred von Tirpitz's famous "risk theory" implied such a view. By building a great battle fleet, Tirpitz argued, Germany could force England into neutrality or alliance with it by posing a threat to England's vital maritime supremacy.[10] More recently, American officials have repeatedly embraced the bandwagoning hypothesis in justifying American foreign policy commitments. John F. Kennedy claimed that, "if the United States were to falter, the whole world . . . would inevitably begin to move toward the Communist bloc."[11] Although the *rapprochement* with China showed his own willingness to balance, Henry Kissinger also revealed his belief that most states tend to bandwagon by suggesting that "if leaders around the world . . . assume that the U.S. lacked either the forces or the will . . . they will accommodate themselves to the dominant trend."[12] And Ronald Reagan has endorsed the same beliefs in his claim that "if we cannot defend ourselves [in Central America] . . . then we cannot expect to prevail elsewhere . . . our credibility will collapse and our alliances will crumble."[13]

Statements like these reveal a common theme: states are attracted to strength. The more powerful you are and the more clearly this is demonstrated, the more likely others are to ally with you. By contrast, a decline in relative position will lead one's allies to opt for neutrality at best or to defect to the other side at worst.

What is the logic behind the bandwagoning hypothesis? Two distinct motives can be identified. First, bandwagoning may be adopted as a form of appeasement. By aligning with the threatening state or coalition, the bandwagoner may hope to avoid an attack on himself by diverting it elsewhere. Second, a state may align with the dominant side in war in order to share the spoils of victory. Mussolini's declaration of war on France and Russia's entry into the war against Japan in 1945 illustrate this type of bandwagoning, as do Italian and Rumanian alliance choices in World War I.[14] By joining what they believed was the stronger side, each hoped to make territorial gains at the end of the fighting.

Stalin's decision to ally with Hitler in 1939 illustrates *both* motives nicely. The Nazi-Soviet Pact led to the dismemberment of Poland and may have deflected Hitler's ambitions westward. Stalin was thus able to gain both time and territory by bandwagoning with Hitler.[15] In general, however, these two motives for bandwagoning are quite different. In the first, bandwagoning is chosen for *defensive* reasons, as a means of maintaining independence in the face of a potential threat. In the second, a bandwagoning state chooses the leading side for *offensive* reasons, in order to acquire territory. Regardless of the specific motive, however, bandwagoning behavior stands in sharp contrast to the predictions of balance of power theory. The two hypotheses thus offer mutually exclusive explanations for how states will make their alliance choices.

Different Sources of Threat

Balancing and bandwagoning are usually framed solely in terms of power. Balancing is alignment with the weaker side; bandwagoning means to choose the stronger.[16] This view is seriously flawed, however, because it ignores the other factors that statesmen will consider when identifying potential threats and prospective allies. Although power is an important factor in their calculations, it is not the only one. Rather than allying in response to power alone, it is more accurate to say that states will ally with or against the most *threatening* power. For example, states may *balance* by allying with other strong states, if a weaker power is more dangerous for other reasons. Thus the coalitions that defeated Germany in World Wars I and II were vastly superior in total resources, but united by their common recognition that German expansionism posed the greater danger.[17] Because balancing and bandwagoning are more accurately viewed as a response to threats, it is important to consider all the factors that will affect the level of threat that states may pose. I shall therefore discuss the impact of: 1) aggregate power; 2) proximity; 3) offensive capability; and 4) offensive intentions.

Aggregate Power. The greater a state's total resources (i.e., population, industrial and military capability, technological prowess, etc.), the greater a potential threat it can pose to others. Recognizing this, Walter Lippmann and George Kennan defined the aim of American grand strategy to be preventing any single state from controlling the combined resources of industrial Eurasia, and they advocated U.S. intervention on whichever side was weaker when this prospect emerged.[18] Similarly, Lord Grey, British Foreign Secretary in 1914, justified British intervention against the Dual Alliance by saying:

> To stand aside would mean the domination of Germany; the subordination of France and Russia; the isolation of Britain, . . . and ultimately Germany would wield the whole power of the continent.[19]

In the same way, Castlereagh's aim to create a "just distribution of the forces in Europe" reveals his own concern for the distribution of aggregate power, as does Bismarck's dictum that "in a system of five great powers, the goal must always be to be in a group of three or more."[20] The overall power that states can wield is thus an important component of the threat they can pose to others.

If power can be threatening, however, it can also be prized. States with great power have the capacity either to punish enemies or reward friends. By itself, therefore, another state's aggregate power may be a motive for either balancing or bandwagoning.

Proximate Power. States will also align in response to threats from proximate power. Because the ability to project power declines with distance, states that are nearby pose a greater threat than those that are far away.[21] For example, the British Foreign Office explained why Britain was especially sensitive to German naval expansion by saying:

> If the British press pays more attention to the increase of Germany's naval power than to a similar movement in Brazil . . . this is no doubt due to the proximity of the German coasts and the remoteness of Brazil.[22]

As with aggregate power, proximate threats can produce either a balancing or a bandwagoning response. When proximate threats trigger a balancing response, alliance networks that resemble checkerboards are the likely result. Students of diplomatic history have long been told that "neighbors of neighbors are friends," and the tendency for encircling states to align against a central power has been known since Kautilya's writings in the 4th century.[23] Examples include: France and Russia against Wilhelmine Germany; France and the "Little Entente" in the 1930s; the Soviet Union and Vietnam against China and Cambodia in the 1970s; the U.S.S.R. and India against the U.S. and Pakistan presently; and the tacit alignment between Iran and Syria against Iraq and its various Arab supporters. When a threat from proximate power leads to bandwagoning, by contrast, the familiar phenomenon of a "sphere of influence" is created. Small states bordering a great power may be so vulnerable that they choose to bandwagon rather than balance, especially if their powerful neighbor has demonstrated its ability to compel obedience. Thus Finland, whose name has become synonymous with bandwagoning, chose to do so only after losing two major wars against the Soviet Union within a five-year period.

Offensive Power. All else being equal, states with large offensive capabilities are more likely to provoke an alliance than those who are either militarily weak or capable only of defending.[24] Once again, the effects of this factor vary. On the one hand, the immediate threat that such capabilities pose may lead states to balance by allying with others.[25] Tirpitz's "risk strategy" backfired for precisely this reason. England viewed the German battle fleet as a potent offensive threat, and redoubled its own naval efforts while reinforcing its ties with France and Russia.[26] On the other hand, when offensive power permits rapid conquest, vulnerable states may see little hope in resisting. Balancing may seem unwise because one's allies may not be able to provide assistance quickly enough. This is another reason why "spheres of influence" may form: states bordering those with large offensive capabilities (and who are far from potential allies) may be forced to bandwagon because balancing alliances are simply not viable.[27]

Offensive Intentions. Finally, states that appear aggressive are likely to provoke others to balance against them. As I noted earlier, Nazi Germany provoked an overwhelming coalition against itself because it combined substantial power with extremely offensive ambitions. Indeed, even states with rather modest capabilities may trigger a balancing response if they are perceived as especially aggressive. Thus Libya under Colonel Qaddafi has prompted Egypt, Israel, France, the U.S., Chad, and the Sudan to coordinate political and military responses in order to defend against Libyan activities.[28]

Perceptions of intent play an especially crucial role in alliance choices. In addition to the factors already mentioned, for example, changing perceptions of German aims helped create the Triple Entente. Whereas Bismarck had followed a careful policy of defending the status quo after 1870, the expansionist ambitions of his successors provoked steadily increasing alarm among the other European powers.[29] Although the growth of German power played a major role, the importance of German intentions should not be ignored. This is nicely revealed by Eyre Crowe's famous 1907 memorandum defining British policy towards Germany. The analysis is all the more striking because Crowe obviously has few objections to the growth of German power *per se:*

> It cannot for a moment be questioned that the mere existence and healthy activity of a powerful Germany is an undoubted blessing for all. . . . *So long, then, as Germany competes for an intellectual and moral leadership of the world in reliance on its own natural advantages and energies* England cannot but admire. . . . [So] *long as Germany's action does not overstep the line of legitimate protection of existing rights it can always count upon the sympathy and good will*, and even the moral support of England. . . . It would be of real advantage if the determination not to bar Germany's *legitimate and peaceful expansion* were made as patent and pronounced as authoritatively as possible, provided that care was taken at the same time to make it quite clear that *this benevolent attitude will give way to determined opposition at the first sign of* British or allied interests being adversely affected.[30]

In short, Britain will oppose Germany only if Germany seeks to expand through conquest. Intentions, not power, are crucial.

When a state is believed to be unalterably aggressive, others are unlikely to bandwagon. After all, if an aggressor's intentions are impossible to change, then balancing with others is the best way to avoid becoming a victim. Thus Prime Minister de Broqueville of Belgium rejected the German ultimatum of August 2, 1914 by saying:

> If die we must, better death with honor. We have no other choice. Our submission would serve no end . . . if Germany is victorious, Belgium, *whatever her attitude*, will be annexed to the Reich.[31]

In short, the more aggressive or expansionist a state appears, the more likely it is to trigger an opposing coalition.

By refining the basic hypotheses to consider several sources of threat, we gain a more complete picture of the factors that statesmen will consider when making alliance choices. However, one cannot say *a priori* which sources of threat will be most important in any given case, only that all of them are likely to play a role. The next step is to consider which—balancing or bandwagoning—is the dominant tendency in international affairs.

The Implications of Balancing and Bandwagoning

The two hypotheses I have just elaborated paint starkly contrasting pictures of international politics. Resolving the question of which picture is more accurate is especially important because the two hypotheses imply very different policy prescriptions. What are the worlds that each depicts, and what policies are implied?

If balancing is the dominant tendency, then threatening states will provoke others to align against them. Because those who seek to dominate others will attract widespread opposition, status quo states can take a relatively sanguine view of threats. Credibility is less important in a balancing world because one's allies will resist threatening states out of their own self-interest, not because they expect others to do it for them. Thus the fear that allies will defect declines. Moreover, if balancing is the norm *and* if statesmen understand this tendency, aggression is discouraged because those who contemplate it will anticipate resistance.

In a balancing world, policies that demonstrate restraint and benevolence are best. Strong states may be valued as allies because they have much to offer their partners, but they must take particular care to avoid appearing aggressive. Foreign and defense policies that minimize the threat one poses to others make the most sense in such a world.

By contrast, a bandwagoning world is much more competitive. If states tend to ally with the strongest and most threatening state, then great powers will be rewarded if they appear both strong and potentially dangerous. International rivalries will be more intense, because a single defeat may signal the decline of one side and the ascendancy of the other. This is especially alarming in a bandwagoning world, because additional defections and a further decline in the loser's position are to be expected. Moreover, if statesmen believe that bandwagoning is widespread, they will be more inclined to use force to resolve international disputes. This is because they will both fear the gains that others may make by demonstrating *their* power or resolve, and because they will assume that others will be unlikely to balance against them.[32]

Finally, misperceiving the relative propensity to balance or bandwagon is dangerous, because the policies that are appropriate for one situation will backfire *completely* in the other. If statesmen follow the balancing prescription in a bandwagoning world, their moderate responses and relaxed view of threats will encourage their allies to defect, leaving them isolated against an overwhelming coalition. Conversely, following the bandwagoning prescription (employing power and threats frequently) in a world of balancers will merely lead others to oppose you more and more vigorously.[33]

These concerns are not just theoretical. In the 1930s, France failed to recognize that its allies in the "Little Entente" were prone to bandwagon, a tendency that French military and diplomatic policies reinforced. By contrast, Soviet attempts to intimidate Turkey after World War II backfired by provoking a greater U.S. commitment in the area and by cementing Turkey's interest in a formal alliance with the West.[34] Likewise, the self-encircling bellicosity of Wilhelmine Germany and Imperial Japan reflected the assumption, prevalent in both states, that bandwagoning was the dominant tendency in international affairs.

Why Balancing is More Common than Bandwagoning

Which of these two worlds most resembles reality? Which hypothesis describes the dominant tendency in international politics? Although statesmen frequently justify their actions by invoking the bandwagoning hypothesis, history provides little evidence for this assertion. On the contrary, balance of power theorists from Ranke forward have persistently and persuasively shown that states facing an external threat overwhelmingly prefer to balance against the threat rather than bandwagon with it. This is primarily because an alignment that preserves most of a state's freedom of action is preferable to accepting subordination under a potential hegemon. Because intentions can change and perceptions are unreliable, it is safer to balance against potential threats than to hope that strong states will remain benevolent.

The overwhelming tendency for states to balance rather than bandwagon defeated the hegemonic aspirations of Spain under Philip II, France under Louis XIV and Napoleon, and Germany under Wilhelm II and Hitler. Where the bandwagoning hypothesis predicts that these potential hegemons should have attracted more and more support as they expanded, the actual response of the powers that they threatened was precisely the opposite. The more clearly any one state sought to dominate the rest, the more reliably the others combined to counter the threat.[35]

Nor is this tendency confined to Europe, as a few examples will illustrate. The American defeat in Indochina, rather than inviting bandwagoning throughout Southeast Asia, brought renewed cooperation among the ASEAN states and permitted the traditional animosity between China and Vietnam to burst forth anew. In the 1950s, the long-standing rivalry between the House of Saud in Saudi Arabia and the Hashemite dynasties in Iraq and Jordan gave way to the "King's

Alliance" when Nasser's Egypt emerged as the dominant power in the region. The desire to balance against regional threats has also inspired most Middle Eastern states to align with one or the other superpower, just as the superpower rivalry itself made the Soviet Union and the United States willing to support these regional clients.[36] In the same way, the threat from revolutionary Iran has provoked the formation of the Gulf Cooperation Council, led by Saudi Arabia. Whatever one may think of the *efficacy* of these various arrangements, the *tendency* that they illustrate is striking.[37] Even in widely different contexts, the strong tendency for states to balance when making alliance choices is confirmed.

Scholars or statesmen who argue the opposite view—whether in the guise of "Finlandization," the "domino theory," or other variations on bandwagoning logic—are placing themselves in direct opposition to the most widely accepted theory in the field of international relations. Just as clearly, their predictions about expected state behavior are contrary to most of international history. The effects of this disregard for evidence are severe: 1) such views exaggerate American insecurity by portraying U.S. allies as excessively prone to defect; 2) they distort American security priorities by inflating the perceived benefits of large military forces and "get-tough" policies; and 3) they make it easier for allies to "free-ride," by encouraging the U.S. to do too much. Thus the U.S. pays a high price for its failure to appreciate the dominant tendency for others to balance. Indeed, the erroneous fear that bandwagoning was likely has probably been the principal intellectual error underlying the most counterproductive excesses in post-war American foreign policy.

This is not to say that bandwagoning never occurs. Three conditions may increase somewhat the generally low tendency for states to bandwagon. First, especially weak states will be more likely to bandwagon, both because they are more vulnerable to pressure and because the capabilities they can add to either side are unlikely to make much difference. Because they can do little to affect the outcome, they are more likely to opt for the winning side.[38] Thus King Leopold of Belgium and Urho Kekkonen of Finland justified their own alliance policies with reference to the special vulnerabilities of small states bordering upon great powers.[39] A further deduction is that weak states may balance against other weak states, but may be relatively more likely to bandwagon when confronted by a great power.

Second, weak states are more likely to bandwagon when allies are simply unavailable. Even weak states may be persuaded to balance when they are confident of allied support; in its absence, however, accommodation with the threatening power may be the only viable alternative. Thus a further prerequisite for effective balancing behavior is an active system of diplomatic communication, permitting potential allies to recognize their shared interests and coordinate their responses.[40] If weak states see no possibility of external assistance, accommodation through alignment with the threatening power may be chosen as a last resort. Thus the first Shah of Iran took the British withdrawal from Kandahar in 1881 as a signal to bandwagon with Russia. As he told the British representative, all he had received from Britain was "good advice and honeyed words—nothing else."[41] Finland's foreign policy suggests the same lesson. Finland's bandwagoning alliance with the Soviet Union after World War II was encouraged by the fact that Finland's *balancing* alliance with Nazi Germany during the war had alienated the potential allies it might have sought against Soviet pressure.[42]

This means that a concern for credibility is not entirely mistaken. Those who argue for American isolation ignore the possibility that weak states might be forced to bandwagon with other powers, were the prospect of American support eliminated entirely. Yet the opposite error is more common: the exaggerated fear that bandwagoning is likely leads the U.S. to squander resources in strategically meaningless conflicts (e.g., Vietnam) in order to reassure allies who are likely to remain loyal in any event.

Taken together, these two factors help explain why great powers are occasionally able to create spheres of influence. Although strong neighbors will balance, small and weak states in close proximity to a great power are the most likely candidates for bandwagoning. Because they will be the first victims of an attack, because potential allies may be scarce or distant, and because they lack the capabilities to stand alone or alter the balance significantly, accommodating a neighboring great power may occasionally make more sense.

Such circumstances, however, are rare; and such alliances will decay when the disparities that produce them erode.[43] Moreover, even if weak states do bandwagon on occasion, their decisions will have little impact on the global balance of power. For the states that matter, balancing is the rule: they will join forces against the threats posed by the power, proximity, offensive capabilities, and intentions of others. . . .

NOTES

1. For representative examples of typical scholarly efforts, consult: Robert Rood and Patrick McGowan, "Alliance Behavior in Balance of Power Systems," *American Political Science Review*, Vol. 69, No. 3 (September 1975); George T. Duncan and Randolph Siverson, "Flexibility of Alliance Partner Choice in Multipolar Systems," *International Studies Quarterly*, Vol. 26, No. 4 (December 1982); R. P. Y. Li and W. R. Thompson, "The Stochastic Process of Alliance Formation Behavior," *American Political Science Review*, Vol. 72, No. 3 (December 1978). More traditional works on alliances are: George Liska, *Nations in Alliance* (Baltimore: Johns Hopkins University Press, 1962), and Robert L. Rothstein, *Alliances and Small Powers* (New York: Columbia University Press, 1968). Useful summaries of the literature on alliances may be found in: Ole Holsti, P. Terrence Hopmann, and John D. Sullivan, *Unity and Disintegration in International Alliances* (New York: Wiley— Interscience, 1973), Chapter 1 and Appendix C; Bruce Bueno de Mesquita and J. David Singer, "Alliance, Capabilities, and War," *Political Science Annual*, Vol. 4 (1974); Philip Burgess and David Moore, "Inter-nation Alliances: An Inventory and Appraisal of Propositions," *Political Science Annual*, Vol. 3 (1973); and Michael Don Ward, "Research Gaps in Alliance Dynamics," *Monograph Series in International Affairs*, Vol. 19, No. 1 (Denver: University of Denver, Graduate School of International Studies, 1982).

2. My use of the terms "balancing" and "bandwagoning" follows that of Kenneth Waltz in his *Theory of International Politics* (Reading, Mass.: Addison-Wesley, 1979). Arnold Wolfers uses a similar terminology in his essay "The Balance of Power in Theory and Practice," in *Discord and Collaboration* (Baltimore: Johns Hopkins University Press, 1962), pp. 122–124.

3. For impressive analyses of the classical writings on the balance of power, see: Edward V. Gulick, *Europe's Classical Balance of Power* (New York: W.W. Norton, 1955), Part I; F. H. Hinsley, *Power and the Pursuit of Peace: Theory and Practice in the History of Relations between States* (Cambridge: Cambridge University Press, 1963), Part I; Inis L. Claude, *Power and International Relations* (New York: Random House, 1962), Chapters 2 and 3; Robert Osgood and Robert Tucker, *Force, Order, and Justice* (Baltimore: Johns Hopkins University Press, 1967), pp. 96–104 and *passim;* and Martin Wight, "The Balance of Power," in Martin Wight and Herbert Butterfield, eds., *Diplomatic Investigations* (London: Allen and Unwin, 1966). For modern versions of the theory, see Waltz, *Theory of International Politics*, Chapter 6; Morton Kaplan, *System and Process in International Politics* (New York: John Wiley, 1957); and Hans J. Morgenthau, *Politics Among Nations*, 5th ed. (New York: Alfred A. Knopf, 1978), Part IV.

4. As Vattel wrote several centuries ago: "The surest means of preserving this balance of power would be to bring it about that no State should be much superior to the others . . . but this could not be realized without injustice and violence. . . . [It] is simpler, easier, and more just . . . to form alliances in order to make a stand against a very powerful sovereign and prevent him from dominating." Quoted in Gulick, *Europe's Classical Balance of Power*, pp. 61–62.

5. Winston S. Churchill, *The Second World War: Volume I, The Gathering Storm* (Boston: Houghton Mifflin, 1948), pp. 207–208.

6. Henry A. Kissinger, *White House Years* (Boston: Little, Brown, 1979), p. 178.

7. In the words of Kenneth Waltz: "Secondary states, if they are free to choose, flock to the weaker side; for it is the stronger side that threatens them. On the weaker side, they are both more appreciated and safer, provided, of course, that the coalition they join achieves enough defensive or deterrent strength to dissuade adversaries from attacking." See his *Theory of International Politics*, p. 127.

8. This theme is explored in Ludwig Dehio, *The Precarious Balance* (New York: Vintage, 1965); Hinsley, *Power and the Pursuit of Peace*; and Gulick, *Europe's Classical Balance of Power*.

9. W. Scott Thompson, "The Communist International System," *Orbis*, Vol. 20, No. 4 (Winter 1977), p. 843.

10. See William L. Langer, *The Diplomacy of Imperialism* (New York: Alfred A. Knopf, 1953), pp. 434–435; and Gordon L. Craig, *Germany: 1866–1945* (London: Oxford University Press, 1978), pp. 303–314. This view was not confined to military circles in Germany. In February 1914, Secretary of State Jagow predicted that Britain would remain neutral in the event of a Continental war, expressing the widespread view that drove German policy prior to World War I. As he told the German Ambassador in London: "We have not built our fleet in vain, and in my opinion, people in England will seriously ask themselves whether it will be just that simple and without danger to play the role of France's guardian angel against us." Quoted in Imanuel Geiss, *July 1914* (New York: W.W. Norton, 1967), pp. 24–25.

11. Quoted in Seyom Brown, *The Faces of Power* (New York: Columbia University Press, 1968), p. 217.

12. Quoted in Committee on International Relations, "The Soviet Union and the Third World: Watershed in Great Power Policy?," U.S. House of Representatives, 97th Congress, 1st session (Washington, D.C.: U.S. Government Printing Office, 1977), pp. 157–158.

13. "President Reagan's Address to a Joint Session of Congress on Central America," *The New York Times*, April 28, 1983, p. A–12. In the same speech, Reagan also said, "if Central America were to fall, what would the consequences be for our position in Asia and Europe and for alliances such as NATO. . . . Which ally, which friend would trust us then?"

14. See Denis Mack Smith, *Mussolini* (New York: AlfredKnopf, 1982), pp. 234–235, 246–250; Adam B. Ulam, *Expansion and Coexistence* (New York: Praeger, 1972), pp. 394–398; and A.J.P. Taylor, *The First World War* (New York: Perigee Books, 1980), pp. 88–90, 153.

15. See Ulam, *Expansion and Coexistence*, pp. 276–277; Isaac Deutscher, *Stalin: A Political Biography* (London: Pelican Books, 1966), pp. 437–443; and Joachim Fest, *Hitler* (New York: Vintage, 1974), pp. 583–584, 592–593.

16. The preeminent example of balance of power theory focusing exclusively on the distribution of capabilities is Waltz, *Theory of International Politics*, Chapter 6. For examples of theorists who acknowledge that other factors can be important, see Gulick, *Europe's Classical Balance of Power*, pp. 25, 45–47, 60–62.

17. In World War I, the alliance of Great Britain, France, and Russia controlled 27.9 percent of world industrial production, while Germany and Austria together controlled only 19.2 percent. With Russia out of the war but the United States joining Britain and France, the percentage opposing the Dual Alliance reached 51.7 percent, an advantage of more than 2 to 1. In World War II, the defense expenditures of the U.S., Great Britain, and the Soviet Union exceeded those of Germany by roughly 4.5 to 1. Even allowing for Germany's control of Europe and the need to fight Japan, the Grand Alliance possessed an enormous advantage in latent capabilities. Thus balancing against *power* was not the sole explanation for these alliances. For these and other statistics on the relative power in these two wars, see: Paul M. Kennedy, "The First World War and the International Power System," *International Security*, Vol. 9, No. 1 (Summer 1984), pp. 7–40; and *The Rise and Fall of British Naval Mastery* (London: Macmillan, 1983), pp. 309–315.

18. For a summary of these ideas, see John Lewis Gaddis, *Strategies of Containment* (New York: Oxford University Press, 1982), pp. 25–88. Kennan's own thoughts are found in his *Realities of American Foreign Policy* (New York: New American Library, 1951), p. 10. Lippmann's still compelling analysis is found in his *The Cold War: A Study of U.S. Foreign Policy* (New York: Harper Brothers, 1947).

19. Quoted in Bernadotte Schmitt, *The Coming of the War in 1914* (New York: Howard Fertig, 1968), Vol. 2, p. 115.

20. Castlereagh's policy is described in Harold Nicolson, *The Congress of Vienna* (New York: Harcourt, Brace, Jovanovich, 1946), pp. 205–206. Bismarck's statement is quoted in William L. Langer, *European Alliances and Alignments*, 2nd ed. (New York: Random House, 1950), p. 197.

21. See Harvey Starr and Benjamin A. Most, "The Substance and Study of Borders in International Relations Research," *International Studies Quarterly*, Vol. 20 (1976). For a discussion of the relationship between power and distance, see Kenneth A. Boulding, *Conflict and Defense: A General Theory* (New York: Harper Torchbooks, 1962), pp. 229–230, 245–247. For an interesting practical critique, see Albert Wohlstetter, "Illusions of Distance," *Foreign Affairs*, Vol. 46, No. 2 (Fall 1968).

22. Quoted in Paul M. Kennedy, *The Rise of the Anglo—German Antagonism* (London: Allen and Unwin, 1980), p. 421.

23. Kautilya's analysis ran as follows: "The king who is situated anywhere immediately on the circumference of the conqueror's territory is termed the enemy. The king who is likewise situated close to the enemy, but separated from the conqueror only by the enemy is termed the friend (of the conqueror). . . . In front of the conqueror and close to the enemy, there happened to be situated kings such as the conqueror's friend, next to him the enemy's friend, and next to the last the conqueror's friend's friend, and next, the enemy's friend's friend." See "Arthasastra" (Science of Politics), in Paul A. Seabury, ed., *Balance of Power* (San Francisco: Chandler, 1965), p. 8.

24. The best discussions of the implications of offense and defense are: Robert Jervis, "Cooperation Under the Security Dilemma," *World Politics*, Vol. 30, No. 2 (January 1978); Stephen W. Van Evera, "Causes of War" (Ph.D. dissertation, University of California, Berkeley, 1984); and George H. Quester, *Offense and Defense in the International System* (New York: Wiley, 1977).

25. See Langer, *European Alliances and Alignments*, pp. 3–5; Raymond J. Sontag, *European Diplomatic History, 1871–1932* (New York: Appleton-Century Crofts, 1933), pp. 4–5; Jervis, "Cooperation Under the Security Dilemma," p. 189; and Quester, *Offense and Defense in the International System*, pp. 105–106.

26. As Imanuel Geiss notes: "Finding an agreement with Britain along German lines without a substantial naval agreement thus amounted to squaring the circle." See his *German Foreign Policy* (London: Routledge and Kegan Paul, 1977), p. 131. See also Kennedy, *The Rise of the Anglo—German Antagonism*, pp. 416–423.

27. Thus alliance formation becomes more frenetic when the offense is believed to have the advantage: great powers will balance more vigorously while weak states seek protection by bandwagoning more frequently. A world of tight alliances and few neutral states is the likely result.

28. For a discussion of Libya's international position, see Claudia Wright, "Libya and the West: Headlong Into Confrontation?," *International Affairs* (London), Vol. 58, No. 1 (Winter 1981–82), pp. 13–41.

29. See Craig, *Germany: 1866–1945*, pp. 101, 242–247, and Chapter 10; Geiss, *German Foreign Policy*, pp. 66–68; and Kennedy, *The Rise of the Anglo—German Antagonism*, Chapters 14 and 20.

30. "Memorandum by Sir Eyre Crowe on the Present State of British Relations with France and Germany, January 1, 1907," in G.P. Gooch and Harold Temperley, eds., *British Documents on the Origins of the War, 1898–1914* (London: British Foreign Office, 1928), Volume 3, pp. 403 and *passim* (emphasis added). See also G.W. Monger, *The End of Isolation: British Foreign Policy 1900–1907* (London: Thomas Nelson, 1963), pp. 313–315.

31. Quoted in Luigi Albertini, *The Origins of the War* Volume 3, p. 458 (emphasis added).

32. Thus both Napoleon and Hitler underestimated the costs of aggression by assuming their potential enemies would bandwagon. After Munich, for example, Hitler dismissed the likelihood he would be opposed by claiming that the leaders of France and Britain were "little worms," Napoleon apparently believed that "England cannot reasonably make war on us unaided," and assumed that England would remain pacified after the Peace of Amiens. On these points, see Fest, *Hitler*, pp. 594–595; Liska, *Nations in Alliance*, p. 45; and Geoffrey Bruun, *Europe and the French Imperium* (New York: Harper Torchbooks, 1938), p. 118. Because Hitler and Napoleon believed in a bandwagoning world, they were unwisely eager to go to war.

33. This situation is analogous to Robert Jervis's distinction between the spiral model and the deterrence model. The former calls for appeasement, the latter for opposition to a suspected aggressor. Balancing and bandwagoning are the alliance equivalents of deterring and appeasing. See Jervis, *Perception and Misperception in International Politics* (Princeton: Princeton University Press, 1976), Chapter 3.

34. The French attempt to contain Germany after World War I was undermined both by the Locarno Treaty (which guaranteed the French border with Germany but failed to provide similar guarantees for its allies) and by the French adoption of a defensive military doctrine, which made it impossible for it come to the aid of its allies. See Telford Taylor, *Munich: The Price of Peace* (New York: Vintage, 1980), pp. 111–112; and Richard D. Challener, *The French Theory of the Nation in Arms* (New York: Columbia University Press, 1969), pp. 264–265. For the effects of Soviet pressure on Turkey, see: George Lenczowski, *The Middle East in World Affairs* (Ithaca: Cornell University Press, 1980), pp. 134–138; and Bruce R. Kuniholm, *The Origins of the Cold War in the Near East* (Princeton: Princeton University Press, 1980), pp. 355–378.

35. See Jack S. Levy, "Theories of General War," unpublished ms., 1984. (An extensively revised version of this paper will be published in *World Politics*, April 1985.)

36. For evidence and analysis on this point, see Stephen M. Walt, "The Origins of Alliances" (Ph.D. dissertation, University of California, Berkeley, 1983), especially Chapter 6.

37. See Mahnaz Zehra Ispahani, "Alone Together: Regional Security Arrangements in Southern Africa and the Arabian Gulf," *International Security*, Vol. 8, *1914* (London: Oxford University Press, 1952), No. 4 (Spring 1984), pp. 152–175.

38. See Rothstein, Alliances and Small Powers, p. 11.

39. As King Leopold explained Belgian neutrality after World War I, "an alliance, even if purely defensive, does not lead to the goal [of security], for no matter how prompt the help of an ally might be, it would not come until after the invader's attack which will be overwhelming. . . . " Quoted in Rothstein, *Alliances and Small Powers*, pp. 111–112. Kekkonen of Finland argued for accommodation with the U.S.S.R. by saying: "A small state cannot stand forever armed to the teeth . . . the first to be overrun by the enemy, and devoid of political importance to lend any significance to its word when decisions over war and peace are being taken. . . . " See Urho Kekkonen, *A President's View*, trans. Gregory Coogan (London: Heinemann, 1982), pp. 42–43.

40. One reason for Rome's durable hegemony in the ancient world was the fact that its various opponents lacked the diplomatic means to coordinate opposition against Rome effectively. See Edward N. Luttwak, *The Grand Strategy of the Roman Empire* (Baltimore: Johns Hopkins University Press, 1976), pp. 192, 199–200. When a workable diplomatic system was established in the Renaissance, prospects for European hegemony declined drastically. On this point, see Gulick, *Europe's Classical Balance of Power*, p. 16; Hedley Bull, *The Anarchical Society* (New York: Columbia University Press, 1977), p. 106 and Chapter 7; Garrett Mattingly, *Renaissance Diplomacy* (Boston: Houghton Mifflin, 1971), Chapters 13–16; and Harold Nicolson, *Diplomacy* (London: Oxford University Press, 1963), Chapter 1.

41. Quoted in C.J. Lowe, *The Reluctant Imperialists* (New York: Macmillan, 1967), p. 85.

42. See Fred Singleton, "The Myth of Finlandisation," *International Affairs* (London), Vol. 57, No. 2 (Spring 1981), especially pp. 276–278. Singleton points out that the Western allies approved the 1944 armistice between Finland and the U.S.S.R. (which established Soviet predominance there) in 1947.

43. This seems to be true both in Latin America and Eastern Europe. As the relative power of both superpowers has declined, the ability of states in their respective spheres to defy the hegemonic power has increased. Obviously, this tendency is more pronounced in the Western Hemisphere than Eastern Europe, because geography makes it easier for the Soviets to enforce their control.

12.3

Soft Balancing Against the United States

Robert A. Pape

A Theory of Security in a Unipolar World

Although the United States is commonly described as "a unipolar superpower," a clear definition of the meaning of unipolarity remains elusive. To determine how today's structure of the international system affects the incentives and behavior of both the unipolar leader and the world's other important powers, it is important to clarify the conceptual boundary that separates unipolarity from either a multipolar or bipolar system, on the one hand, and a hegemonic or imperial system, on the other.

Definition of Unipolarity

The distinct quality of a system with only one superpower is that no other single state is powerful enough to balance against it. As a unipolar leader, the United States is also more secure than any other state in the world, able to determine the outcome of most international disputes, and has significant opportunities to control the internal and external behavior of virtually any small state in the system.

A unipolar world, however, is a balance of power system, not a hegemonic one. Powerful as it may be, a unipolar leader is still not altogether immune to the possibility of balancing by most or all of the second-ranked powers acting in concert. To escape balancing altogether, the leading state in the system would need to be stronger than all second-ranked powers acting as members of a counterbalancing coalition seeking to contain the unipolar leader. The term "global hegemon" is appropriate for a state that enjoys this further increase in power, because it could act virtually without constraint by any collection of other states anywhere in the world (see Figure 12.1).

In a unipolar world, the extraordinary power of the leading state is a serious barrier to attempts to form a counterbalancing coalition for two reasons. First, the coalition would have to include most or possibly even all of the lesser major powers. Second, assembling such a coalition is especially difficult to coordinate. As a result, forming a balancing coalition requires the sudden solution of a difficult collective action problem in which several powers must trust one another where buck-passing by any could doom them all.

In multipolar systems, too, the strongest power may enjoy such a wide margin of superiority over all others that containing it may require a coalition of several states. This situation of "unbalanced" multipolarity, however, is distinguishable from a unipolar world by the existence of at least one state that can mount a reasonable defense, at least for a time, even against the multipolar leader. In doing so, the state can provide the public good of serving as an "anchor" for a counterbalancing coalition by shouldering the risk of containing the leading state when others are unable, unwilling, or undecided. The most famous example is Britain's role in sparking the several coalitions against Napoleonic France from 1793 to 1815. Similarly, in Europe in 1940–41, both Britain and the Soviet Union showed themselves capable of serving as an anchor against Nazi

Figure 12.1 International Systems with One Strong State

Balance of Power Systems	Hegemonic Systems
multipolarity ⟷ unipolarity	hegemony ⟶ empire

Germany until an even larger coalition could be formed.[1] Today, however, no possible rival of the United States could reasonably assume this role. The absence of such an anchor marks the critical break between today's world and the past several centuries of major power politics.

Degrees of hegemony are also distinguishable. The difference between a global hegemon and an imperial hegemon is the level of control that the most powerful state exercises over subordinate states. A global hegemon is unchallengeably powerful. An imperial hegemon exercises a measure of control over second-ranked powers, regulating their external behavior according to the established hierarchy, even to the point of enforcing acceptable forms of internal behavior within the subordinate states.[2] Further, an imperial hegemon can create and enforce rules over the use of force, norms that apply to subordinate states but not to the hegemon itself. As a result, it can take steps to establish a monopoly on the use of force, and even second-ranked powers can lose important aspects of their sovereignty even if they are not formally occupied.[3]

Although differences in specific systems are important, from the standpoint of a theory of unipolar politics, the key boundary is between a balance of power system and a hegemonic one. This line separates a world in which the second-ranked powers can still act to preserve their security independent of the leading state from a world in which they cannot. Once the relative power of the leading state reaches this threshold, second-ranked powers may begin to worry about the consequences this might have for their security, but they can do little about it. As a result, second-ranked powers have tremendous incentives to contain the unipolar superpower's further expansion, or even to seek a shift in the distribution of power back toward multipolarity, depending on the perceived intentions of the leading state.

Conditions that Threaten Second-Ranked Powers

In a balance of power system, states must guard against three security problems: (1) the threat of direct attack by another major power; (2) the threat of indirect harm, in which the military actions of a major power undermine the security of another, even if unintentionally; and (3) the possibility that one major power will become a global hegemon and thus capable of many harmful actions, such as rewriting the rules of international conduct to its long-term advantage, exploiting world economic resources for relative gain, imposing imperial rule on second-ranked powers, and even conquering any state in the system.

In general, major powers have commonly balanced against indirect as well as direct threats to their security. For instance, the United States acted to balance Germany before both world wars, even though it did not pose a direct threat to the United States in either case. Although historians debate whether the United States entered World War I in 1917 in response to the spillover effects of Germany's submarine campaign against Great Britain or the general fear that a victorious Germany would become a global hegemon, no major scholar contends that Germany posed an imminent threat to the United States. In World War II, the leading realist analysis calling for U.S. intervention to balance Germany explicitly ruled out a direct threat to invade or bombard the United States, and instead justified intervention on the basis of the indirect harm to U.S. security that might occur if a victorious Germany went on to establish exclusive control over economic resources and markets in Europe, Asia, and South America.[4] The experience of the United States before both world wars was not unique, because the European balancing coalitions against Germany began to form long before the aspiring hegemon actually attacked a major power.[5]

Concerns over indirect threats are likely to be greater in unipolar systems than in other balance of power systems. A unipolar leader is so strong that it may engage in military actions in distant regions of the world that are often likely to have real, if inadvertent, consequences for the security of major powers that are geographically close or have important economic ties to the region. For instance, how the unipolar leader wages a war on transnational terrorism can reduce or improve the security of other major powers, giving them a powerful security interest in how such a war is waged. Further, there is less ambiguity in a unipolar than a multipolar world about which state can make a bid for global hegemony, and even minor steps in this direction by a unipolar leader can create a common fear among second-ranked powers. Hence, other states may have reason to oppose military action by a unipolar leader, even if it has no intention of harming them directly.

This logic implies that perceptions of the most powerful state's intentions are more important in unipolar than in multipolar worlds. Because a unipolar leader is already stronger than all individual second-ranked powers, additional increments of power are unlikely to significantly increase its ability to become a global hegemon. For this reason, although the leading state's relative power gains are viewed with suspicion, they are ultimately of secondary importance in the politics of unipolarity.

More important is how others perceive the unipolar leader's motives. The overwhelming power of the unipolar leader means that even a modest change in how others perceive the aggressiveness of its intentions can significantly increase the fear that it would make a bid for global hegemony. In fact, the threshold for what counts as an "aggressive" intention by a unipolar leader is lower than for major powers in a multipolar world because its capability to become a global hegemon is given. Thus, even a unipolar leader that adopts unilateral policies that merely expand its control over small states or that make only modest relative power gains can be viewed as aggressive, because these unilateral acts signal a willingness to make gains independently, and possibly at the expense of others.

The Logic of Balancing Against A Sole Superpower

Major states have at least as much incentive to balance against a unipolar leader that poses a direct or indirect threat to their security as they would against strong states in a multipolar world. The main question is whether they can do so, and how.

Balancing against a unipolar leader is possible, but it does not operate according to the rules of other balance of power systems. In general, states may cope with an expansionist state through either "internal" balancing (i.e., rearmament or accelerated economic growth to support eventual rearmament) or "external" balancing (i.e., organization of counterbalancing alliances). In most multipolar systems, both forms of balancing are possible.[6]

Against a unipolar leader, however, internal balancing is not a viable option because no increase in standing military forces or economic strength by just one state is adequate to the task. This follows from the definition of a unipolar world and not from specific details about individual states' capabilities. Attempts at internal balancing by any one state are also likely to lead to a prompt, harsh response by the unipolar leader; this possibility is sufficiently obvious that individual states would rarely try such efforts on their own.[7]

States concerned about a unipolar leader, thus, have only the option of external balancing, but they face serious difficulties in coordinating their efforts. As developed below, soft balancing is a viable strategy for second-ranked powers to solve the coordination problems they encounter in coping with an expansionist unipolar leader. So long as the unipolar leader has not already become a global hegemon, the lesser major powers can band together to contain its predominate military power. The key question is not whether these states have the collective power to do so, but whether they can solve their collective action problem and work together to form a balancing coalition.

Scholars of international politics are used to thinking about the problem of collective action in the context of a multipolar system, where buck-passing is the main obstacle to the formation of a counterbalancing coalition. Balancing is risky business. Strong states rarely welcome others standing in their way and can impose harsh penalties on those that do. In a multipolar system, major powers have a reasonable chance of defending themselves individually against even the strongest state in the system, and so each can try to make others pay the price for confronting the revisionist state. For this reason, states in a mulitpolar system are often slow to balance against powerful rivals, and the formation of a balancing coalition is generally an incremental process in which new members are added over time.[8]

The dynamics of balancing are different in a unipolar system. Balancing against a unipolar leader cannot be done by any one state alone; it can only be done by several second-ranked states acting collectively. This means that buck-passing is not an option. Because no one state—by definition—is powerful enough to balance a sole superpower, no state is available to catch the buck. Instead, the main problem of states wanting to balance against the unipolar leader is fear of collective failure. An individual state may fear that there are not enough states to form an effective counter-coalition, that it will take too long for a sufficient number to organize, or that the unipolar leader will single it out for harsh treatment before the balancing coalition has coalesced.

Thus, the logic of balancing against a sole superpower is a game of coordination in which assuring timely cooperation is the principal obstacle. In this situation, each member of a potential balancing coalition is best off cooperating with others to balance the unipolar leader.

At the same time, each member's decision to balance depends on the expectation that others will also balance, which in turn depends on the others' expectations of its balancing behavior. As Thomas Schelling articulated, the outcome of coordination games depends on the process of converging expectations[9]—a process that is especially likely to delay hard balancing. Directly confronting the preponderant military capability of a sole superpower before the full coalition has assembled would likely lead to a quick defeat and the loss of valuable members of an effective balancing coalition. Hence, the formation of a hard-balancing coalition against a unipolar leader is likely to occur abruptly, or not at all, rather than by incrementally adding members to a balancing coalition over time.

Although a sole superpower's preponderance of strength increases the incentive for second-ranked powers to delay hard balancing until they can coordinate collective action, it does not weaken the common interest that these states have in balancing against an aggressive unipolar leader. In a unipolar system, states balance against threats, defined by the power and aggressive intentions of the revisionist state. The power of a unipolar leader may keep other states from forming a balancing coalition, but it is still a key reason why these states may wish to do so. As a result, second-ranked states that cannot solve their coordination problem by traditional means may turn to soft-balancing measures to achieve this aim.

Soft-balancing measures do not directly challenge a unipolar leader's military preponderance, but they can delay, complicate, or increase the costs of using that extraordinary power. Non-military tools, such as international institutions, economic statecraft, and strict interpretations of neutrality, can have a real, if indirect, effect on the military prospects of a unipolar leader.[10]

Most important, soft balancing can establish a basis of cooperation for more forceful, hard-balancing measures in the future. The logic of balancing against a sole superpower is about coordinating expectations of collective action among a number of second-ranked states. In the short term, this encourages states to pursue balancing strategies that are more effective at developing a convergence of expectations than in opposing the military power of the leading state. Building cooperation with non-military tools is an effective means for this end.

The logic of unipolarity would suggest that the more aggressive the intentions of the unipolar hegemon, the more intense the balancing by second-ranked states, to the extent balancing is possible at all. If the unipolar leader does not pursue aggressively unilateral military policies, there should be little balancing of any kind against it. If, however, the unipolar leader pursues aggressive unilateral military policies that change how most of the world's major powers view its intentions, one should expect, first, soft balancing and, if the unipolar leader's aggressive policies do not abate, increasingly intense balancing efforts that could evolve into hard balancing.

Why the United States has been Exempt— Until Now

Thus far, the long ascendancy of the United States has been a remarkable exception to the general rule that states balance against superior power.[11] The United States was the world's strongest state throughout the twentieth century and, since the end of the Cold War, has been the leader of a unipolar international system. The most reliable long-run measure of a state's power is the size of its gross national product, because economic strength ultimately determines the limit of a state's military potential. For the past century, the U.S. share of gross world product was often double (or more) the share of any other state: 32 percent in 1913, 31 percent in 1938, 26 percent in 1960, 22 percent in 1980, and 27 percent in 2000.[12] During this period, the United States fought numerous major wars, determining the outcomes of World Wars I and II and, more recently, fighting against Iraq in 1991, Bosnia in 1995, and Serbia in 1999. Yet aside from the Soviet Union, no major power has sought to balance against the United States.[13] Why not?

Scholars of international politics have given three answers. The first is that states balance against superior power,[14] but the process is uneven and slow.[15] As Kenneth Waltz argues, the weak have a common interest in balancing against the strong, and there is little that the dominant state can do to arrest this tendency: "A dominant power may behave with moderation, restraint, and forbearance. Even if it does, however, weaker states will worry about its future behavior."[16] Yet balancing poses risks. Superior powers do not take kindly to states that oppose their will. Weak states recognize these risks and are often content to pass the buck on to others. Buck-passing explains why balancing was slow to develop against Germany before both world wars and why balancing has been slow to emerge against the United States since the end of the Cold War.

The second answer stresses the U.S. reputation for benign intentions. Stephen Walt contends that states balance not so much against power alone, as against threat—the combination of raw power and perceived aggressive intent. In his view, states may have good or bad intentions, and only states with aggressive intentions provoke others to balance against it.[17] The United States has had fairly moderate foreign policy intentions compared with those of most other great powers throughout the past two centuries, never seeking to conquer a major country that was not already at war with it or one of its allies and never seeking to build an empire or to establish a sphere of influence beyond its own region of the world.[18] Thus, during the Cold War, Western Europe and Japan sided with the stronger United States against the weaker, but more aggressive Soviet Union. Despite the enormous potential threat posed by U.S. power, no one has balanced against the United States because it has generally manifested nonaggressive intentions.

The third answer focuses on U.S. grand strategy. Mearsheimer argues that the United States pursued a strategy of "offshore balancing" throughout the twentieth century, focusing on preventing strong states from dominating important regions of the world rather than dominating those regions itself.[19] It was this strategy that called the United States to the defense of its European allies in World Wars I and II, of South Korea and Vietnam during the Cold War, and of Kuwait in 1991. As a result, U.S. grand strategy has effectively reassured major powers such as Europe, Russia, Japan, and China that the United States, even as a sole superpower, poses little threat to them.[20] At least until the Bush Doctrine, U.S. grand strategy avoided giving others much reason to balance against the United States.

Scholars may argue over which of these answers is the most convincing. Each, however, has an element of truth and together explain more than any one alone. No other great power in history has been so dominant, has had such a high reputation for nonaggressive intentions, and has limited itself to offshore balancing—all at the same time. This triple combination is probably the best explanation for why the United States has gotten a pass from balance of power politics so far.

To the extent that one factor has been especially important since the United States became the sole superpower, it is probably the U.S. reputation for benign intent. Consider the evidence that would be needed to support each of the above three positions. If, as Waltz suggests, the structure of the unipolar system encourages balancing but that buck-passing will make the process slow and uneven, then evidence of either balancing or buck-passing among the major powers should exist, especially during periods when the United States used its considerable military power. If, however, Walt and Mearsheimer are correct that the United States' reputation for good intentions, bolstered by a grand strategy of offshore balancing, effectively reassures major powers, then there should be little evidence of either balancing or buck-passing.

Strikingly, from 1990 to 2000 no significant instances of balancing occurred against the United States; nor was there notable buck-passing among the world's major powers in which one encouraged another to balance U.S. power. In the 1990s, resentment of U.S. preponderance led some major powers to complain of U.S. "arrogance" and to call for a new "counterweight" to American strength. Counterbalancing was limited to rhetoric, however, and it did not involve changes in military spending or opposition to U.S. uses of force, either directly or indirectly.[21] Starting in the mid-1990s, the United States began to increase its defense spending, while Europe, Japan, and China did not and Russia's military spending rapidly declined.[22] At the start of the 1990s, U.S. defense spending exceeded the next seven countries combined. By the decade's end, it exceeded the next eight.

Similarly, major powers did not act to restrain the use of U.S. military power in three extended conflicts during the period: Iraq in 1991, Bosnia in 1995, and Kovoso in 1999. Although major powers were often reluctant to join these military campaigns, in no case did they take action to impede, frustrate, or delay U.S. war plans; or actively oppose the use of U.S. military power; or discourage other states from supporting America's wars. In Iraq in 1991 and Kosovo in 1999, the United States ended with more military allies than it began. As in the Vietnam War in the 1960s and 1970s, some major states grumbled, but none took measures to contain the use of U.S. military power.

Overall, the record of the 1990s does not reflect a balancing process that was slow or erratic. The politics of unipolarity changed, however, once the United States began to act in ways that would undermine its reputation for benign intent. . . .

Notes

1. Strictly speaking, the Soviet Union was not fighting alone in 1941. In practice, however, Britain and the United States provided so little assistance or distraction until late 1942 that Moscow had to shoulder most of the burden of

confronting German military power during this period. For a discussion of unbalanced multipolarity, see John J. Mearsheimer, *The Tragedy of Great Power Politics* (New York: W. W. Norton, 2001).

2. On the definition of empire, see Stephen Peter Rosen, "An Empire, If You Can Keep It," *National Interest*, No. 71 (Spring 2003), pp. 51–62.

3. A unipolar superpower, like great powers in general, could create and maintain one or several regional empires that regulate the behavior of weak states according to the established hierarchy. Arguably, the United States has done just this in Central America and may be doing this in the Persian Gulf.

4. On the decision of the United States to balance Germany before both world wars, see Ernest R. May, *The World War and American Isolationism, 1914–1917* (Cambridge, Mass.: Harvard University Press, 1959); George F. Kennan, *American Diplomacy, 1900–1950* (New York: New American Library, 1951); Richard Ned Lebow, *Between Peace and War: The Nature of International Crisis* (Baltimore, Md.: Johns Hopkins University Press, 1981), pp. 41–56; and Nicholas John Spykman, *America's Strategy in World Politics: The United States and the Balance of Power* (New York: Harcourt, Brace, and Company, 1942).

5. V. R. Berghahn, *Germany and the Approach to War in 1914* (London: Macmillan, 1973); and Williamson Murray, *The Change in the European Balance of Power, 1938–1939* (Princeton, N.J.: Princeton University Press, 1984).

6. In bipolar systems, only internal balancing is relevant because no third state is strong enough to matter. On internal and external balancing and the logic of bipolarity, see Kenneth N. Waltz, *Theory of International Politics* (Reading, Mass.: Addison-Wesley, 1979), chap. 8.

7. The futility of internal balancing has another important implication. Although one might think that a major power's attempts to balance a unipolar leader through internal efforts would spark local counterbalancing against the major power by other major powers, the obvious weakness of individual internal balancing against a unipolar leader means that this scenario is not likely to emerge in the first place.

8. In cases of hegemonic challengers in multipolar international systems, buck-passing was a problem. Before both world wars, Great Britain, France, and Russia were slow to cooperate against the German challenge and paid stiff penalties for their foot-dragging. Members of the final coalition, however, were able to solve their buck-passing problems, with the result that balancing was late but did eventually occur.

9. Thomas C. Schelling, *The Strategy of Conflict* (Cambridge, Mass.: Harvard University Press, 1960).

10. Soft balancing differs from "soft power," which refers to the ability of (some) states to use the attractiveness of their social, cultural, economic, or political resources to encourage other governments and publics to accept policies favorable toward their state, society, and policies. Although uses of soft power are not limited to security issues, in principle a state with excellent soft-power resources might be in a better than average position to organize a balancing coalition (or to prevent the formation of one against it). Favorable perceptions of a unipolar leader's intentions are thus an important soft-power asset. If a unipolar leader's aggressive unilateralism undermines favorable perceptions of its intentions, this also has the effect of reducing its soft power to block the formation of a counterbalancing coalition. In general, however, soft power is an attribute of a state, whereas soft balancing involves the non-military policies that states can use to limit and offset the leading state in the international system. On soft power, see Joseph S. Nye Jr., *Bound to Lead: The Changing Nature of American Power* (New York: Basic Books, 1990).

11. On the tendency for an international balance of power to emerge and for this tendency to increase with the relative power of the leading state, see Hans J. Morgenthau, *Politics among Nations,* 4th ed. (New York: Alfred A. Knopf, 1967); Waltz, *Theory of International Politics;* and Mearsheimer, *The Tragedy of Great Power Politics.*

12. Paul Kennedy, *The Rise and Fall of the Great Powers* (New York: Random House, 1987), pp. 202, 436; and *World Development Indicators* (Washington, D.C.: World Bank, 2000).

13. Other important exceptions include mid-nineteenth-century Britain and Germany. Moreover, many scholars have doubted the universal applicability of balance of power theory. For historical exceptions, see Brian Healy and Arthur Stein, "The Balance of Power in International History: Theory and Reality," *Journal of Conflict Resolution,* Vol. 17, No. 1 (March 1973), pp. 33–61; and Paul Schroeder, "Alliances, 1815–1945: Weapons of Power and Tools of Management," in Klaus Knorr, ed., *Historical Dimensions of National Security Problems* (Lawrence: University Press of Kansas, 1976), pp. 173–225. For a broad challenge that argues that balance of threat rather than balance of power better explains the causes of alliances, see Stephen M. Walt, *The Origins of Alliances* (Ithaca, N.Y.: Cornell University Press, 1987).

14. Why do states not bandwagon with a threat rather than balance against it? Although there are important qualifications, international relations scholarship has found that major powers have a strong preference for balancing, because bandwagoning—even for profit—still leaves them vulnerable to an expansionist power. Bandwagoning is favored overwhelmingly by small states too weak to defend themselves without a major power patron. See Walt, *The Origins of Alliances;* and Randall L. Schweller, "Bandwagoning for Profit: Bringing the Revisionist State Back In,"

International Security, Vol. 19, No. 1 (Summer 1994), pp. 72–107.

15. Waltz, *Theory of International Politics,* chap. 8.

16. Waltz, "Evaluating Theories," p. 915.

17. To be clear, a state that is seen as aggressive, even if it is not the most powerful in the system, can provoke others to balance against it. Conversely, even the most powerful state may avoid becoming the target of balancing, provided that other powerful states are seen as much more aggressive. Walt, *The Origins of Alliances.*

18. For instance, in the late 1930s when U.S.-Japanese relations deteriorated, none of the main powers in the region—Britain, the Soviet Union, the Netherlands, and China—sided with the weaker, but expansionist Japan. Similarly, during the Cold War, Western Europe and Japan sided with the stronger United States against the weaker, but more aggressive Soviet Union.

19. Mearsheimer, *The Tragedy of Great Power Politics.*

20. Mearsheimer believes that the U.S. strategy of off-shore balancing is dictated more by limits in U.S. capabilities than by benign intentions. He agrees with Walt, however, on the effect of the United States pursuing a limited-aims grand strategy.

21. In 1991 French Foreign Minister Roland Dumas warned that "[U.S.] might reigns without balancing weight," while Chinese leaders warned that "unipolarity was a far worse state of affairs than bipolarity." Quoted in Layne, "The Unipolar Illusion," p. 36.

22. International Institute of Strategic Studies, *The Military Balance, 1998/99* (London: IISS, 2000).

13 Deterrence

13.1

The Diplomacy of Violence

Thomas C. Schelling

The usual distinction between diplomacy and force is not merely in the instruments, words or bullets, but in the relation between adversaries—in the interplay of motives and the role of communication, understandings, compromise, and restraint. Diplomacy is bargaining; it seeks outcomes that, though not ideal for either party, are better for both than some of the alternatives. In diplomacy each party somewhat controls what the other wants, and can get more by compromise, exchange, or collaboration than by taking things in his own hands and ignoring the other's wishes. The bargaining can be polite or rude, entail threats as well as offers, assume a status quo or ignore all rights and privileges, and assume mistrust rather than trust. But whether polite or impolite, constructive or aggressive, respectful or vicious, whether it occurs among friends or antagonists and whether or not there is a basis for trust and goodwill, there must be some common interest, if only in the avoidance of mutual damage, and an awareness of the need to make the other party prefer an outcome acceptable to oneself.

With enough military force a country may not need to bargain. Some things a country wants it can take, and some things it has it can keep, by sheer strength, skill and ingenuity. It can do this *forcibly*, accommodating only to opposing strength, skill, and ingenuity and without trying to appeal to an enemy's wishes. Forcibly a country can repel and expel, penetrate and occupy, seize, exterminate, disarm and disable, confine, deny access, and directly frustrate intrusion or attack. It can, that is, if it has enough strength. "Enough" depends on how much an opponent has.

There is something else, though, that force can do. It is less military, less heroic, less impersonal, and less unilateral; it is uglier, and has received less attention in Western military strategy. In addition to seizing and holding, disarming and confining, penetrating and obstructing, and all that, military force can be used *to hurt*. In addition to taking and protecting things of value it can *destroy* value. In addition to weakening an enemy militarily it can cause an enemy plain suffering.

Pain and shock, loss and grief, privation and horror are always in some degree, sometimes in terrible degree, among the results of warfare; but in traditional military science they are incidental, they are not the object. If violence can be done incidentally, though, it can also be done purposely. The power to hurt can be counted among the most impressive attributes of military force.

Hurting, unlike forcible seizure or self-defense, is not unconcerned with the interest of others. It is measured in the suffering it can cause and the victims' motivation to avoid it. Forcible action will work against weeds or floods as well as against armies, but suffering requires a victim that can feel pain or has something to lose. To inflict suffering gains nothing

---

and saves nothing directly; it can only make people behave to avoid it. The only purpose, unless sport or revenge, must be to influence somebody's behavior, to coerce his decision or choice. To be coercive, violence has to be anticipated. And it has to be avoidable by accommodation. The power to hurt is bargaining power. To exploit it is diplomacy—vicious diplomacy, but diplomacy.

The Contrast of Brute Force with Coercion

There is a difference between taking what you want and making someone give it to you, between fending off assault and making someone afraid to assault you, between holding what people are trying to take and making them afraid to take it, between losing what someone can forcibly take and giving it up to avoid risk or damage. It is the difference between defense and deterrence, between brute force and intimidation, between conquest and blackmail, between action and threats. It is the difference between the unilateral, "undiplomatic" recourse to strength, and coercive diplomacy based on the power to hurt.

The contrasts are several. The purely "military" or "undiplomatic" recourse to forcible action is concerned with enemy strength, not enemy interests; the coercive use of the power to hurt, though, is the very exploitation of enemy wants and fears. And brute strength is usually measured relative to enemy strength, the one directly opposing the other, while the power to hurt is typically not reduced by the enemy's power to hurt in return. Opposing strengths may cancel each other, pain and grief do not. The willingness to hurt, the credibility of a threat, and the ability to exploit the power to hurt will indeed depend on how much the adversary can hurt in return; but there is little or nothing about an adversary's pain or grief that directly reduces one's own. Two sides cannot both overcome each other with superior strength; they may both be able to hurt each other. With strength they can dispute objects of value; with sheer violence they can destroy them.

And brute force succeeds when it is used, whereas the power to hurt is most successful when held in reserve. It is the *threat* of damage, or of more damage to come, that can make someone yield or comply. It is *latent* violence that can influence someone's choice—violence that can still be withheld or inflicted, or that a victim believes can be withheld or inflicted. The threat of pain tries to structure someone's motives, while brute force tries to overcome his strength. Unhappily, the power to hurt is often communicated by some performance of it. Whether it is sheer terroristic violence to induce an irrational response, or cool premeditated violence to persuade somebody that you mean it and may do it again, it is not the pain and damage itself but its influence on somebody's behavior that matters. It is the expectation of *more* violence that gets the wanted behavior, if the power to hurt can get it at all.

To exploit a capacity for hurting and inflicting damage one needs to know what an adversary treasures and what scares him and one needs the adversary to understand what behavior of his will cause the violence to be inflicted and what will cause it to be withheld. The victim has to know what is wanted, and he may have to be assured of what is not wanted. The pain and suffering have to appear *contingent* on his behavior; it is not alone the threat that is effective—the threat of pain or loss if he fails to comply—but the corresponding assurance, possibly an implicit one, that he can avoid the pain or loss if he does comply. The prospect of certain death may stun him, but it gives him no choice.

Coercion by threat of damage also requires that our interests and our opponent's not be absolutely opposed. If his pain were our greatest delight and our satisfaction his greatest woe, we would just proceed to hurt and to frustrate each other. It is when his pain gives us little or no satisfaction compared with what he can do for us, and the action or inaction that satisfies us costs him less than the pain we can cause, that there is room for coercion. Coercion requires finding a bargain, arranging for him to be better off doing what we want—worse off not doing what we want—when he takes the threatened penalty into account.

It is this capacity for pure damage, pure violence, that is usually associated with the most vicious labor disputes, with racial disorders, with civil uprisings and their suppression, with racketeering. It is also the power to hurt rather than brute force that we use in dealing with criminals; we hurt them afterward, or threaten to, for their misdeeds rather than protect ourselves with cordons of electric wires, masonry walls, and armed guards. . . .

This difference between coercion and brute force is as often in the intent as in the instrument. To hunt down Comanches and to exterminate them was brute force; to raid their villages to make them behave was coercive diplomacy, based on the power to hurt. The pain and loss to the Indians might have looked much the same one way as the other; the difference was one of purpose and effect. If Indians were killed because they were in the way, or somebody wanted their land, or the authorities despaired of making them behave and could not confine them and decided to exterminate them, that was pure unilateral force. If *some* Indians were killed to make *other* Indians behave, that was coercive violence—or intended to be, whether or not it was effective. . . . And of course, since any use of force tends to be brutal, thoughtless, vengeful, or plain obstinate, the motives themselves can be mixed and confused. The fact that heroism and brutality can be either coercive diplomacy or a contest in pure strength does not promise that the distinction will be made, and the strategies enlightened by the distinction, every time some vicious enterprise gets launched. . . .

Coercive Violence in Warfare

This distinction between the power to hurt and the power to seize or hold forcibly is important in modern war, both big war and little war, hypothetical war and real war. For many years the Greeks and the Turks on Cyprus could hurt each other indefinitely but neither could quite take or hold forcibly what they wanted or protect themselves from violence by physical means. The Jews in Palestine could not expel the British in the late 1940s but they could cause pain and fear and frustration through terrorism, and eventually influence somebody's decision. The brutal war in Algeria was more a contest in pure violence than in military strength; the question was who would first find the pain and degradation unendurable. The French troops preferred— indeed they continually tried—to make it a contest of strength, to pit military force against the nationalists' capacity for terror, to exterminate or disable the nationalists and to screen off the nationalists from the victims of their violence. But because in civil war terrorists commonly have access to victims by sheer physical propinquity, the victims and their properties could not be forcibly defended and in the end the French troops themselves resorted, unsuccessfully, to a war of pain.

Nobody believes that the Russians can take Hawaii from us, or New York, or Chicago, but nobody doubts that they might destroy people and buildings in Hawaii, Chicago, or New York. Whether the Russians can conquer West Germany in any meaningful sense is questionable; whether they can hurt it terribly is not doubted. That the United States can destroy a large part of Russia is universally taken for granted; that the United States can keep from being badly hurt, even devastated, in return, or can keep Western Europe from being devastated while itself destroying Russia, is at best arguable; and it is virtually out of the question that we could conquer Russia territorially and use its economic assets unless it were by threatening disaster and inducing compliance. It is the power to hurt, not military strength in the traditional sense, that inheres in our most impressive military capabilities at the present time. We have a Department of *Defense* but emphasize *retaliation*—"to return evil for evil" (synonyms: requital, reprisal, revenge, vengeance, retribution). And it is pain and violence, not force in the traditional sense, that inheres also in some of the least impressive military capabilities of the present time—the plastic bomb, the terrorist's bullet, the burnt crops, and the tortured farmer.

War appears to be, or threatens to be, not so much a contest of strength as one of endurance, nerve, obstinacy, and pain. It appears to be, and threatens to be, not so much a contest of military strength as a bargaining process—dirty, extortionate, and often quite reluctant bargaining on one side or both—nevertheless a bargaining process.

The difference cannot quite be expressed as one between the *use* of force and the *threat* of force. The actions involved in forcible accomplishment, on the one hand, and in fulfilling a threat, on the other, can be quite different. Sometimes the most effective direct action inflicts enough cost or pain on the enemy to serve as a threat, sometimes not. The United States threatens the Soviet Union with virtual destruction of its society in the event of a surprise attack on the United States; a hundred million deaths are awesome as pure damage, but they are useless in stopping the Soviet attack—especially if the threat is to do it all afterward anyway. So it is worthwhile to keep the concepts distinct—to distinguish forcible action from the threat of pain—recognizing that some actions serve as both a means of forcible accomplishment and a means of inflicting pure damage, some do not. Hostages tend to entail almost pure pain and damage, as do all forms of reprisal after the fact. Some modes of self-defense may exact so little in blood or treasure as to entail negligible violence; and some forcible actions entail so much violence that their threat can be effective by itself.

The power to hurt, though it can usually accomplish nothing directly, is potentially more versatile than a straightforward capacity for forcible accomplishment. By force alone we cannot even lead a horse to water—we have to drag him—much less make him drink. Any affirmative action, any collaboration, almost anything but physical exclusion, expulsion, or extermination, requires that an opponent or a victim *do* something, even if only to stop or get out. The threat of pain and damage may make him want to do it, and anything he can do is potentially susceptible to inducement. Brute force can only accomplish what requires no collaboration. The principle is illustrated by a technique of unarmed combat: one can disable a man by various stunning, fracturing, or killing blows, but to take him to jail one has to exploit the man's own efforts. "Come-along" holds are those that threaten pain or disablement, giving relief as long as the victim complies, giving him the option of using his own legs to get to jail. . . .

The fact that violence—pure pain and damage—can be used or threatened to coerce and to deter, to intimidate and to blackmail, to demoralize and to paralyze, in a conscious process of dirty bargaining, does not by any means imply that violence is not often wanton and meaningless or, even when purposive, in danger of getting out of hand. Ancient wars were often quite "total" for the loser, the men being put to death, the women sold as slaves, the boys castrated, the cattle slaughtered, and the buildings leveled, for the sake of revenge, justice, personal gain, or merely custom. If an enemy bombs a city, by design or by carelessness, we usually bomb his if we can. In the excitement and fatigue of warfare, revenge is one of the few satisfactions that can be savored; and justice can often be construed to demand the enemy's punishment, even if it is delivered with more enthusiasm than justice requires. . . .

But if the occurrence of violence does not always bespeak a shrewd purpose, the absence of pain and destruction is no sign that violence was idle. Violence is most purposive and most successful when it is threatened and not used. Successful threats are those that do not have to be carried out. By European standards, Denmark was virtually unharmed in the Second World War; it was violence that made the Danes submit. Withheld violence—successfully threatened violence—can look clean, even merciful. The fact that a kidnap victim is returned unharmed, against receipt of ample ransom, does not make kidnapping a nonviolent enterprise. . . .

The Strategic Role of Pain and Damage

Pure violence, non-military violence, appears most conspicuously in relations between unequal countries, where there is no substantial military challenge and the outcome of military engagement is not in question. Hitler could make his threats contemptuously and brutally against Austria; he could make them, if he wished, in a more refined way against Denmark. It is noteworthy that it was Hitler, not his generals, who used this kind of language; proud military establishments do not like to think of themselves as extortionists. Their favorite job is to deliver victory, to dispose of opposing military force and to leave most of the civilian violence to politics and diplomacy. But if there is no room for doubt how a contest in strength will come out, it may be possible to bypass the military stage altogether and to proceed at once to the coercive bargaining.

A typical confrontation of unequal forces occurs at the *end* of a war, between victor and vanquished. Where Austria was vulnerable before a shot was fired, France was vulnerable after its military shield had collapsed in 1940. Surrender negotiations are the place where the threat of civil violence can come to the fore. Surrender negotiations are often so one-sided, or the potential violence so unmistakable, that bargaining succeeds and the violence remains in reserve. But the fact that most of the actual damage was done during the military stage of the war, prior to victory and defeat, does not mean that violence was idle in the aftermath, only that it was latent and the threat of it successful.

Indeed, victory is often but a prerequisite to the exploitation of the power to hurt. When Xenophon was fighting in Asia Minor under Persian leadership, it took military strength to disperse enemy soldiers and occupy their lands; but land was not what the victor wanted, nor was victory for its own sake.

> Next day the Persian leader burned the villages to the ground, not leaving a single house standing, so as to strike terror into the other tribes to show them what would happen if they did not give in. . . . He sent some of the prisoners into the hills and told them to say that if the inhabitants did not come down and settle in their houses to submit to him, he would burn up their villages too and destroy their crops, and they would die of hunger.[1]

Military victory was but the *price of admission*. The payoff depended upon the successful threat of violence.

Like the Persian leader, the Russians crushed Budapest in 1956 and cowed Poland and other neighboring countries. There was a lag of ten years between military victory and this show of violence, but the principle was the one explained by Xenophon. Military victory is often the prelude to violence, not the end of it, and the fact that successful violence is usually held in reserve should not deceive us about the role it plays. . . .

The Nuclear Contribution to Terror and Violence

Man has, it is said, for the first time in history enough military power to eliminate his species from the earth, weapons against which there is no conceivable defense. War has become, it is said, so destructive and terrible that it ceases to be an instrument of national power. "For the first time in human history," says Max Lerner in a book whose title, *The Age of Overkill*, conveys the point, "men have bottled up a power . . . which they have thus far not dared to use."[2] And Soviet military authorities, whose party dislikes having to accommodate an entire theory of history to a single technological event, have had to reexamine a set of principles that had been given the embarrassing name of "permanently operating factors" in warfare. Indeed, our era is epitomized by words like "the first time in human history," and by the abdication of what was "permanent."

For dramatic impact these statements are splendid. Some of them display a tendency, not at all necessary, to belittle the catastrophe of earlier wars. They may exaggerate the historical novelty of deterrence and the balance of terror.[3] More important, they do not help to identify just what is new about war when so much destructive energy can be packed in warheads at a price that permits advanced countries to have them in large numbers. Nuclear warheads are incomparably more devastating than anything packaged before. What does that imply about war?

It is not true that for the first time in history man has the capability to destroy a large fraction, even the major part, of the human race. Japan was defenseless by August 1945. With a combination of bombing and blockade, eventually invasion, and if necessary the deliberate spread of disease, the United States could probably have exterminated the population of the Japanese islands without nuclear weapons. It would have been a gruesome, expensive, and mortifying campaign; it would have taken time and demanded persistence. But we had the economic and technical capacity to do it; and, together with the Russians or without them, we could have done the same in many populous parts of the world. Against defenseless people there is not much that nuclear weapons can do that cannot be done with an ice pick. And it would not have strained our Gross National Product to do it with ice picks.

It is a grisly thing to talk about. We did not do it and it is not imaginable that we would have done it. We had no reason; if we had had a reason, we would not have the persistence of purpose, once the fury of war had been dissipated in victory and we had taken on the task of executioner. If we and our enemies might do such a thing to each other now, and to others as well, it is not because nuclear weapons have for the first time made it feasible.

Nuclear weapons can do it quickly. That makes a difference. . . .

That nuclear weapons make it *possible* to compress the fury of global war into a few hours does not mean that they make it *inevitable*. . . .

There is no guarantee, of course, that a slower war would not persist. . . .

In the past it has usually been the victors who could do what they pleased to the enemy. War has often been "total war" for the loser. With deadly monotony the Persians, Greeks, or Romans "put to death all men of military age, and sold the women and children into slavery," leaving the defeated territory nothing but its name until new settlers arrived sometime later. But the defeated could not do the same to their victors. . . .

Nuclear weapons make it possible to do monstrous violence to the enemy without first achieving victory. With nuclear weapons and today's means of delivery, one expects to penetrate an enemy homeland without first collapsing his military force. What nuclear weapons have done, or appear to do, is to promote this kind of warfare to first place. Nuclear weapons threaten to make war less military, and are responsible for the lowered status of "military victory" at the present time. *Victory is no longer a prerequisite for hurting the enemy*. And it is no assurance against being terribly hurt. One need not wait until he has won the war before inflicting "unendurable" damages on his enemy. One need not wait until he has lost the war. There was a time when the assurance of victory—false or genuine assurance—could make national leaders not just willing but sometimes enthusiastic about war. Not now.

Not only *can* nuclear weapons hurt the enemy before the war has been won, and perhaps hurt decisively enough to make the military engagement academic, but it is widely assumed that in a major war that is *all* they can do. Major war is often discussed as though it would be only a contest in national destruction. If this is indeed the case—if the destruction of cities and their populations has become, with nuclear weapons, the primary object in an all-out war—the sequence of war has been reversed. Instead of destroying enemy forces as a prelude to imposing one's will on the enemy nation, one would have to destroy the nation as a means or a prelude to destroying the enemy forces. If one cannot disable enemy forces without virtually destroying the country, the victor does not even have the option of sparing the conquered nation. He has already destroyed it. Even with blockade and strategic bombing it could be supposed that a country would be defeated before it was destroyed, or would elect surrender before annihilation had gone far. In the Civil War it could be hoped that the South would become too weak to fight before it became too weak to survive. For "all-out" war, nuclear weapons threaten to reverse this sequence.

So nuclear weapons do make a difference, marking an epoch in warfare. The difference is not just in the amount of destruction that can be accomplished but in the role of destruction and in the decision process. Nuclear weapons can change the speed of events, the control of events, the sequence of events, the relation of victor to vanquished, and the relation of homeland to fighting front. Deterrence rests today on the threat of pain and extinction, not just on the threat of military defeat. We may argue about the wisdom of announcing "unconditional surrender" as an aim in the last major war, but seem to expect "unconditional destruction" as a matter of course in another one.

Something like the same destruction always *could* be done. With nuclear weapons there is an expectation that it *would* be done. It is not "overkill" that is new; the American army surely had enough 30-caliber bullets to kill everybody in the world in 1945, or if it did not it could have bought them without any strain. What is new is plain "kill"—the idea that major war might be just contest in the killing of countries, or not even a contest but just two parallel exercises in devastation.

That is the difference nuclear weapons make. At least they *may* make that difference. They also may not. If the weapons themselves are vulnerable to attack, or the machines that carry them, a successful surprise might eliminate the opponent's means of retribution. That an enormous explosion can be packaged in a single bomb does not by itself guarantee that the victor will receive deadly punishment. Two gunfighters facing each other in a Western town had an unquestioned capacity to kill one another; that did not guarantee that both would die in a gunfight—only the slower of the two. Less deadly weapons, permitting an injured one to shoot back before he died, might have been more conducive to a restraining balance of terror, or of caution. The very efficiency of nuclear weapons could make them ideal for starting war, if they can suddenly eliminate the enemy's capability to shoot back.

And there is a contrary possibility: that nuclear weapons are not vulnerable to attack and prove not to be terribly effective against each other, posing no need to shoot them quickly for fear they will be destroyed before they are launched, and with no task available but the systematic destruction of the enemy country and no necessary reason to do it fast rather than slowly. Imagine that nuclear destruction *had* to go slowly—that the bombs could be dropped only one per day. The prospect would look very different, something like the most terroristic guerilla warfare on a massive scale. It happens that nuclear war does not have to go slowly; but it may also not have to go speedily. The mere existence of nuclear weapons does not itself determine that everything must go off in a blinding flash, any more than that it must go slowly. Nuclear weapons do not simplify things quite that much. . . .

War no longer looks like just a contest of strength. War and the brink of war are more a contest of nerve and risk-taking, of pain and endurance. Small wars embody the threat of a larger war; they are not just military engagements but "crisis diplomacy." The threat of war has always been somewhere underneath international diplomacy, but for Americans it is now much nearer the surface. Like the threat of a strike in industrial relations, the threat of divorce in a family dispute, or the threat of bolting the party at a political convention, the threat of violence continuously circumscribes international politics. Neither strength nor goodwill procures immunity.

Military strategy can no longer be thought of, as it could for some countries in some eras, as the science of military victory. It is now equally, if not more, the art of coercion, of intimidation and deterrence. The instruments of war are more punitive than acquisitive. Military strategy, whether we like it or not, has become the diplomacy of violence.

Notes

1. Xenophon, *The Persian Expedition*, Rex Warner, transl. (Baltimore, Penguin Books, 1949), p. 272. "The 'rational' goal of the threat of violence," says H. L. Nieburg, "is an accommodation of interests, not the provocation of actual violence. Similarly the 'rational' goal of actual violence is demonstration of the will and capability of action, establishing a measure of the credibility of future threats, not the exhaustion of that capability in unlimited conflict." "Uses of Violence," *Journal of Conflict Resolution, 7* (1963), 44.

2. New York, Simon and Schuster, 1962, p. 47.

3. Winston Churchill is often credited with the term, "balance of terror," and the following quotation succinctly expresses the familiar notion of nuclear mutual deterrence. This, though, is from a speech in Commons in November 1934. "The fact remains that when all is said and done as regards defensive methods, pending some new discovery the only direct measure of defense upon a great scale is the certainty of being able to inflict simultaneously upon the enemy as great damage as he can inflict upon ourselves. Do not let us undervalue the efficacy of this procedure. It may well prove in practice—I admit I cannot prove it in theory—capable of giving complete immunity. If two Powers show themselves equally capable of inflicting damage upon each other by some particular process of war, so that neither gains an advantage from its adoption and both suffer the most hideous reciprocal injuries, it is not only possible but it seems probable that neither will employ that means." A fascinating reexamination of concepts like deterrence, preemptive attack, counterforce and counter-city warfare, retaliation, reprisal, and limited war, in the strategic literature of the air age from the turn of the century to the close of World War II, is in Quester's book, cited above.

13.2

A Nuclear-Armed Iran

A Difficult but Not Impossible Policy Problem

Barry R. Posen

INTRODUCTION

Iran's nuclear energy research and development efforts seem on course to achieve an ability to produce highly enriched uranium, the key element of a nuclear weapon. While the capability itself would not be a violation of the Nuclear Non-Proliferation Treaty (NPT) if it were under the full scope safeguards of the International Atomic Energy Agency (IAEA), Iran's deceptive behavior in the development of this technology, as well as the flimsy economic arguments Iran has used to justify this capability, have produced broad international opposition to the program. Many reasonably fear that Iran's actual purpose is to produce nuclear weapons, though there is no definite proof that it has decided to do so. It should be acknowledged that Iran could insist on its right to enrich uranium for power reactors, but refrain from producing nuclear weapons. France, Germany, and the United Kingdom, acting under the auspices of the European Union, and with the support of the United States, have negotiated intensively with Iran since 2003 to discourage further Iranian nuclear enrichment progress; the United Nations Security Council demanded that Iran suspend enrichment and implement other important arms control measures with Resolution 1696 in July 2006. Nevertheless diplomacy has thus far been unsuccessful, and there is no guarantee of future success.

If negotiations fail, interested powers such as the United States, the European Union, and Iran's neighbors will face three alternatives: (1) they could move from diplomacy to economic and political coercion; (2) one or more states (most probably the United States or Israel) could launch a preventive attack to erode or destroy the Iranian nuclear program; or (3) these powers could develop strategies of containment and deterrence to coexist with a nuclear-armed Iran—if Iran achieves weapons capability.

The primary purpose of this paper is to address the third option—to spell out a strategy of containment and deterrence and show how it could work. I systematically review the standard objections to this strategy, and explain why they are misplaced. Summarizing the other options, I then argue that a containment and deterrence strategy is more likely to achieve U.S. strategic goals, and do so at lower risks and costs. Finally, I briefly review the proliferation risks that would arise from an Iranian nuclear program, and argue that these risks can be reduced by a deterrence and containment strategy. That said, containment of a nuclear-armed Iran is not the preferred outcome. It would be better if diplomacy were to succeed. Thus, one implication of this analysis is that the United States and its allies should review their current diplomatic approach to Iran and try to devise a more promising political strategy.

For many reasons, it would be better if Iran had neither nuclear weapons, nor the enabling technologies that would permit it to build nuclear weapons:

- Neither nuclear energy nor nuclear weapons are risk-free technologies—new civil and military nuclear powers run the risks of any novice. These include environmental problems, equipment failures, and unsafe or insecure weapons storage.
- It is natural for the nonnuclear states in the region to fear a nuclear Iran. These fears may cause countermeasures that are fraught with danger—including national nuclear energy or weapons programs of their own—which also would run "novice" risks.
- As other states try to acquire nuclear weapons, they may inadvertently threaten each other, setting off new security competitions.
- Iran and any of its neighbors that chose to deploy nuclear weapons may have problems developing a secure basing method, which could tempt them

Source: Excerpts from Barry R. Posen (2006), "A Nuclear-Armed Iran: A Difficult but Not Impossible Policy Problem," (New York: Century Foundation). Reprinted by permission of The Century Foundation.

to adopt "hair trigger," day-to-day alert postures, which in turn could raise the risks of accidental war or preemptive war.

- Iran may be emboldened by its possession of nuclear weapons, and could threaten the security of regional or distant powers.

These are all valid concerns, which should make even Iran wary of nuclear weaponry. These risks have prompted the international diplomatic efforts to induce Iran to refrain from the enrichment of uranium (or the reprocessing of plutonium). If these efforts fail, however, concerned states will need to choose from the three remaining alternative policies—non-military coercion mainly through sanctions, preventive military strikes, or containment and deterrence.

Economic Coercion

Though economic coercion should be attempted if the current round of diplomacy fails, this seems unlikely to work unless it is combined with a new set of incentives. First, it is improbable that a particularly strong international sanctions regime can be organized against Iran. Russia, China, and even many European states fear that the initiation of a strong sanctions policy, blessed by the UN, is the first step on the road to war. Sanctions may not change Iranian behavior, but they will have further committed the international community to do something about Iran's program. Some states also will oppose a strong sanctions policy because they profit from their relationships with Iran, due to its energy resources, or expect to profit even more if they help shield Iran from stern measures. Finally, given tight oil markets and high prices, most states would not support a sanctions regime that embargoed the export of Iranian oil.[1]

Second, though Iran is not a wealthy country, it has a relatively well-rounded economy. Aside from its obvious strengths in oil and gas production, Iran is endowed with abundant raw materials and agricultural land, and has a moderately well developed industrial sector. If a sanctions regime did not close off Iran's oil exports, it seems very likely that, with its own endowments and the cash it raises from energy exports, it could weather any plausible sanctions regime.[2]

If the threat of international economic sanctions were accompanied by more focused diplomacy, it might find more support and be more credible. In particular, the United States would need to assure Iran that it has abandoned any hopes to overthrow the current regime. Some have suggested a "grand bargain" in which the United States would offer Iran a security guarantee, an end to sanctions, and the normalization of diplomatic relations, in exchange for major concessions on Iran's nuclear program and an end to support for terrorism.[3] Such a negotiating offer might reduce the concerns of fence sitters such as Russia and China, who fear that the ultimate U.S. objective is regime change, and that the United States intends to leverage ineffective sanctions into an argument for war. The offer of a grand bargain also would put Iran in a difficult position, insofar as declining the offer would be tantamount to admitting its ambitions to produce a nuclear weapon. Moreover, if such a negotiating gambit fails, and the United States turns to a strategy of containment, states in the region will be even more likely to want U.S. assistance, and will more easily be able to portray a strengthened relationship with the United States as an essential counter to Iranian ambitions.

Preventive Military Action

A military attack on Iran's nuclear infrastructure could set back the program, but probably not prevent its recovery, unless the attack were somehow to topple the Iranian government and bring a very different ruling group to power. A military strike carries significant political and military risks. If time bought by setting back the Iranian program through military strikes would be used to good effect—that is, if in the interim other disputes in which Iran is directly or indirectly involved were solved, or if Iran became a liberal-democratic mirror-image of a Western democracy—a preventive attack might look attractive. But there is no reason to believe that this will be the case, and the reverse is more probable. Small or large attacks on Iran will inject energy into Persian nationalism, strengthen the regime's argument that the West is a threat, and leave Iran with a grudge that it may express by deepening or initiating relationships with other states and groups hostile to U.S. purposes. Even regional states with something to fear from a nuclear armed Iran probably would not welcome a preventive attack, simply because the region is already so roiled with violence, much of it attributed to mistaken U.S. policies.

Published assessments of possible attacks on Iran's nuclear infrastructure necessarily involve some speculation. There are nuclear facilities that we have good public information about, but there is likely a great deal of information that is known by western intelligence agencies that has not leaked into the public domain, and more information in Iran that has not leaked to anyone. Poor intelligence alone is one factor that might hinder the success of these operations. That said, three types of attack, of increasing strength, have been suggested.

First, some have considered very limited attacks on what seem to be critical nodes in a nuclear weapons production chain—especially Iran's plants at Isfahan to produce uranium hexafluoride gas and its facilities at Natanz to process this gas through centrifuges in order to enrich its fissionable material content. One careful analysis suggests that even Israeli fighter-bombers, armed with precision guided weapons Israel is known to possess, could destroy these facilities, presuming that they could refuel from aerial tankers en route, and fly over Jordan and Iraq, or Saudi Arabia, or Turkey.[4] For the United States, destroying these facilities would be a trivial matter. That said, the rest of the Iranian nuclear research and development effort would survive, and it seems likely that failing a change of government, Iran would persevere, and do so in a way that leaves the program less vulnerable. One might believe that a limited attack, however, would produce a relatively modest Iranian military response.

Second, some have suggested that one should try for maximum damage to the entire Iranian nuclear program. A recent analysis suggests that an attack on the Iranian nuclear infrastructure would involve four hundred aim points. The Pentagon's own intelligence would produce an even bigger target set. The United States easily could strike four hundred aim points with precision guided munitions in a single night.[5] Though no one could guarantee that this would be the end of Iran's program, it seems likely that the setback would be far greater than the limited attack on two critical nodes. An Iranian regime might determine that an attack of this size needed to be answered with a forceful response. The regime would look weak regionally, and domestically, if it simply accepted such an attack without a response. The regime reasonably could fear that failure to respond simply would invite further attacks, because the United States would doubt Iran's capability and will. Insofar as the United States has made plain that it wants to overthrow the Iranian regime, it is unlikely that Iran would view such a large attack as the final move.

Finally, precisely because civilian and military strategists in the Bush administration seem to have accepted the preceding logic, rumors have surfaced of even larger attack plans. To the target list associated with Iran's nuclear infrastructure, would be added an array of conventional targets—including naval bases, airfields, surface-to-air missile sites, surface-to-surface missiles sites, and so on. During the first three nights of the 1991 Gulf War, coalition aircraft struck nearly three thousand targets of this kind.[6] Such attacks would have the purpose of forestalling an Iranian military retaliation against countries as close as Kuwait and as distant as Israel, U.S. forces in the region including those in Iraq, and oil tanker routes. Attacks of this size may also have the purpose of weakening the Iranian regime, though the precise mechanism is unclear, insofar as attacks of this kind have typically strengthened rather than weakened national cohesion and public support of governments, at least in the first instance. Though such an attack may succeed in reducing Iran's retaliatory options, it is implausible that it can reduce them to zero. U.S. forces in Iraq, and their line of communication, which runs through Shia populated areas where Iran has considerable influence, are quite vulnerable to tactical rocket and commando attacks that U.S. air strikes probably cannot prevent.[7] Beyond these significant immediate local costs, the United States attack will become a significant factor in future Iranian politics, discrediting any political faction that seems remotely associated with the United States or its purposes, and providing a potent political/ideological rationale for violence against the United States and its friends for many years to come.

Given that the odds of non-military coercion achieving a success seem low, and the possible costs of a significant, if partly successful, large military operation seem high, it is reasonable to consider the remaining alternative systematically—containment and deterrence of a nuclear-armed Iran.

"Grand Strategy"—Iran and the United States

Before considering the consequences of a nuclear-armed Iran for both the stability of the Middle East and Persian Gulf region and the security interests of the United States, one ought to consider the objectives that an Iranian nuclear force might be meant to serve. This requires some speculation about Iran's own "grand strategy."

Given that Iran is the most populous and economically developed state in the Persian Gulf area, a realist expects it to have ambitions to expand its power and influence in the region. Indeed, it is reasonable to expect that revolutionary Iran, like Iran under the Shah, has pretensions to regional hegemony. This is a general prediction, however, and much depends on what this means to Iran. For example, though many analysts do believe Iran has hegemonic ambitions, they usually couch this in cultural and political terms, not military terms.[8] Iran is active in expanding its influence, especially among Shia Arab populations in Iraq, in the Gulf region, and in Lebanon. Though Iran does have some disputes about islands, water rights, waterways, and coastal zones, according to the Central Intelligence Agency it has no major territorial claims beyond its borders.[9] The United States is no doubt perceived as an obstacle to Iran's regional ambitions. Iran surely would like to reduce the United States' presence in the Gulf region, especially since the Bush administration adopted regime change in Iran as an objective.

Iran uses military force with some calculation, to increase the costs to others who might obstruct its goals, rather than to remove obstacles directly. Iran is not shy about using military assistance to non-state actors as a way to discomfit those it defines as enemies, such as the United States and Israel. Iran sees some interest in maintaining a plausible capability to disrupt the flow of oil from the Persian Gulf, by leveraging its own limited naval capacity and its geographic control of one side of the narrow Strait of Hormuz to create a threat to Western economies. This threat is probably dissuasive—a retaliatory capability, as Iran cannot disrupt the flow of oil out of the Gulf without losing its own ability to export, which is vital to its economy. On the whole, Iran seems deliberate, unafraid to use violence in limited ways, but cautious as it tries to increase its influence and reduce that of others. The main exception to this description is its inflammatory rhetoric about Israel. I hypothesize, however, that much of this rhetoric is instrumental. Iran faces a major obstacle in expanding its influence—it is a Persian state amidst Arabs, and a Shia state amidst Sunnis. These differences are important and cause most Arab regimes to mistrust Iran. Iran may be using the struggle with Israel to submerge these differences in the face of a common enemy, and so legitimate itself among those not affectively inclined to follow its leadership, and weak enough to fear its power.

The United States pursues an ambitious interrelated complex of economic, security, and political objectives in the Persian Gulf. At this moment, political and security goals loom largest. President Bush wishes to transform the politics of the region and bring liberal democracy to the regional states, including Iran. The president identifies the absence of democracy in the region as a cause of terrorism, and terrorism as a danger to the United States. Hence political transformation is a security goal. The president also believes that the West cannot wait for transformation to end terror, so he pursues terrorists, and real and suspected state sponsors, with conventional military power—and is waging two wars to do so. Finally, the president believes that the United States must ensure that hostile powers, which Iran is deemed to be, do not get their hands on weapons of mass destruction, because the president and his allies do not agree with the analysis I advance below.

The United States also has more traditional economic interests in the Gulf, which also are connected to security interests. Much of the world's internationally traded oil comes from the Gulf, so the United States is interested in the free flow of oil from the region. It also wishes to ensure that the oil resources not come under the control of hostile powers that might use it as a coercive lever. And finally, the United States wants to assure that the earnings from oil exports not end up in mischievous hands. These concerns generate a broad security agenda—including the defense of oil routes, the prevention of the conquest of any oil state by another, and watchful oversight of the internal politics of certain countries to ensure that dangerous elements not come to power. U.S. strategists may also believe that U.S. hegemony in the Gulf region gives them some leverage over oil exports, and thus increases U.S. power in other parts of the world. For all these reasons, the United States must maintain a very large military presence, and remain the predominant military power in the Gulf region.

This brief assessment of Iranian and U.S. goals suggests that these two powers are destined to be in an intensely competitive relationship. Each has cards to play in this competition. Iran knows the region well, has an excellent geographic position, and may be able to find support in Shiite Arab populations in neighboring countries. Though economically and militarily weak compared to the United States, it is the strongest power in the Gulf, and has proven itself capable of mobilizing very large ground forces. The United States has a giant economy and the world's most advanced military. The United States also has two potential political advantages. Historically, most states consider large proximate land powers such as Iran to be more dangerous to them than distant sea powers such as the United States. And, Iran—an Islamic country, with potential Shia domestic allies in many Gulf states—poses a more credible threat of domestic destabilization than does the U.S. rhetoric of democratization. However powerful and assertive the United States may be, neighboring Iran poses at least as great a threat—and perhaps a greater threat. Hence, despite the present diplomatic ill effects of its mistakes in Iraq, over time the United States is likely to prove the more attractive ally to most states in the region.

Nuclear weapons would make Iran a somewhat more powerful state, which could allow it to pursue certain interests with greater vigor. Fear of Iranian nuclear weapons may cause other states in the region to want their own nuclear weapons, which may in turn cause still others to want nuclear weapons. This would not only be a problem in its own terms, it could further damage the Nuclear Non-Proliferation Treaty and the institutions that sustain it. The ability of the United States and its allies and friends outside and inside the region to contain and deter Iran will affect whether or not significant nuclear proliferation occurs in the region, so I turn first to the likely U.S. and regional responses to a nuclear Iran.

Nuclear-Armed Iran's Four Threats

Reviewing the debate over Iranian nuclear weapons, one can find four different strategic fears of a nuclear-armed Iran: (1) Iran could be emboldened by the possession of a deterrent force and its foreign policy thus would become more adventurous and more violent; (2) Iran could directly threaten others with nuclear attack unless certain demands were met; (3) Iran could give nuclear weapons to non-state actors; and (4) Iran simply could attack Israel with nuclear weapons—heedless of the inevitable Israeli nuclear retaliation.

A More Adventurous Iran

During the recent fighting between Israel and Hezbollah, President Bush averred that the event would have been much more dangerous had Iran possessed nuclear weapons, but he did not explain why. His implication was that Iran would have been more inclined to involve itself directly in the crisis. The argument would be that Iran's leadership would shelter behind its nuclear deterrent. Great powers would be afraid to attack Iran directly, especially to invade Iran, if they faced the risk of nuclear escalation. So Iran would be free to do anything from meddling in the internal affairs of other countries to invading them with conventional forces, because it could control its costs.

This concern is quite reasonable; Iran's leaders might have this idea, but how much different would the situation be than it is today?

Iran already dabbles in subversion and terror. Its leaders do not seem too concerned about invasion, and overthrow, and with good reason. Iran's population is some 70 million, and its land area is roughly three times the size of France. The United States, with the most capable army in the world, is having a difficult time controlling five of Iraq's eighteen provinces, and perhaps 12 million of its 26.8 million people. Iran is surely concerned about other retaliatory responses, including air attacks and even embargos. This is why Iran is somewhat careful to limit its activities and cover its tracks. It might perceive itself to be more secure from retaliatory air attack with a nuclear deterrent, but Israel's nuclear deterrent did not save it from rocket attack in the recent fighting in Lebanon. And from what is known about U.S. Cold War military planning for war against the Soviet Union, and for that matter possible conflict with China today, large nuclear retaliatory forces do not deter the United States from planning large scale conventional air operations against nuclear-armed countries.

Direct Threats from Iran

A second possible use of Iran's nuclear weapons is bald nuclear coercion—especially against nonnuclear neighbors. Nuclear coercion, even against the weak, has certain risks, so it is hard to guess what Iranian interest would be worth such a gambit. In a drive for Gulf hegemony, Iran might demand that those of its neighbors who are close to the United States should weaken these ties—throw out U.S. forces, deny them ports of call and landing rights, destroy prepositioned equipment sites, and cease importing U.S. weapons. Less plausibly, Iran might demand that other oil producing states agree with its own views at any given time about how much oil to pump, or what to charge for it, though this does not seem worth a nuclear crisis. It is worth noting that, since the end of World War II, no nuclear power has found a way to use nuclear threats to achieve offensive strategic objectives.

These gambits are unlikely to work, and the United States and its allies can act to forestall them. During the Cold War, the United States offered the protection of its nuclear deterrent forces to many allies who did not possess nuclear weapons—every NATO member state except Britain and France. The United States promised that if NATO were to be attacked by the Soviet Union with nuclear weapons, it would respond. Indeed, NATO strategy called for the employment of nuclear weapons in the event of a successful Soviet conventional invasion of NATO states. The United States made this commitment in spite of virtual nuclear parity with the Soviet Union. The United States risked annihilation to secure its interests in Europe. . . .

Iran and Non-state Actors

Since the September 11, 2001, attacks on the United States, many have been concerned that nuclear weapons could fall into the hands of terrorists. One way this could occur, it is feared, would be for a state with a weapons program to give or sell one to a terrorist group. Such action seems unlikely in the case of Iran, or any state, because it serves no strategic purpose, invites retaliation, and cannot be controlled. It is perhaps the most self-destructive thing that any nation state can do.

What strategic purpose, other than pure destruction, could such an action serve? A single nuclear weapon exploded in the United States, or any other state, would be a truly horrible event. But it would not destroy the existence of that state, or destroy its political power. And it would enrage that state, and no doubt cause extraordinary efforts to discover, and punish, the source of the attack.

If the weapon is tracked back to the source, the source country will be blamed. It will be blamed not only by the victim, but by other states, terrified by the implications of the action. The victim surely will try to punish the supplier, and it is likely that this punishment would involve nuclear strikes. Iran or any other nuclear weapons provider might hope to avoid detection, but they could only hope—they could not count on it. The characteristics of the explosion may provide some indications of the origin of the weapon.[10] Moreover, once the explosion occurs, intelligence collected and either ignored or misunderstood prior to the event will be reviewed in light of the event, and may have new meaning. Additionally, there are not all that many potential sources of a nuclear weapon—wherever an explosion occurs one can be sure that intelligence would quickly focus on nuclear problem states such as North Korea, Iran, and Pakistan. Indeed, these states are so likely to end up in the spotlight for a terrorist use of a nuclear weapon, they probably have an interest in stopping *any* conspiracies of this kind that they discover. . . .

Iran and Israel

It is occasionally suggested that Iran in particular, because of its leaders' undisguised hatred for the state of Israel, and quite open assertions that the Middle East would be better off if Israel disappeared, might act to make their fantasies a reality. Iran could use its future nuclear weapons to annihilate the state of Israel, unconcerned about Israeli nuclear retaliation because Iran is a large country that would somehow survive a nuclear exchange with Israel, while Israel is a small country that would be entirely destroyed.

A few fission weapons would horribly damage the state of Israel, and a few fusion weapons would surely destroy it. But neither kind of attack could reliably shield Iran from a devastating response. Israel has had years to work on developing and shielding its nuclear deterrent. It is generally attributed with as many as 200 fission warheads, deliverable by several different methods, including Intermediate Range Ballistic Missile.[11] Were Iran to proceed with a weapons program, Israel would surely improve its own capabilities. Though Iran's population is large, and much of it is dispersed, about a quarter of Iranians (over fifteen million people) live in eight cities conservatively within range of Israel's Jericho II missile.[12] Much of Iran's economic capacity is also concentrated in these cities.[13] Nuclear attacks on these cities, plus some oil industry targets, would destroy Iran as a functioning society and prevent its recovery. There is little in the behavior of the leaders of revolutionary Iran that suggests they would see this as a good trade.

A premise of the foregoing fears is that Iran is led by religious fanatics, who might be more interested in the next world than this one. The current president of Iran, Mahmoud Ahmadinejad, has made statements that have caused observers to doubt his risk aversion and his grasp on reality. It is important to note, however, that in Iran's governing structure, the president does not have much influence over security policy. . . .

Other Issues Resulting from a Nuclear-Armed Iran

A final set of concerns about a nuclear-armed Iran arise not from what Iran would or would not do from the point of view of considered strategy, but from a mixed bag of concerns about inadequate Iranian resources, organizational incompetence, and political decentralization. These concerns are not trivial, but even those who raise them do not advocate preventive war to avoid them, which helps put the risks in context.[14]

The first problem is the risk that, due to their relative poverty and inexperience, new nuclear states, such as Iran, will be unable or unwilling to develop the secure retaliatory forces necessary for a stable deterrent relationship. Iran's nuclear force could be small, vulnerable to attack, and lacking secure command and control. Such a force could attract preemption by a neighbor. Or, fearing preemption by a neighbor, Iran could adopt "hair-trigger" alert postures, or due to poor command and control, a fearful Iran might in a crisis inadvertently launch a nuclear weapon. These are all valid concerns, but many of these problems would be in Iran's hands to solve. . . .

Iran's most reasonable strategy is to disperse and hide its small force as best it can, and keep it quiet so that foreign intelligence means cannot attack it. This means eschewing dangerous alert postures, first strike doctrines, and the like. Dispersal, secrecy, stealth, and communications security are the means to survival, though they may present some command and control issues, and some nuclear security issues. There is no reason in principle, however, why a state such as Iran cannot use multiple-key arrangements to ensure against the unauthorized launch of its weapons.

Analysts of nuclear weapons organizations, however, fairly point to the fact that states do not always base their nuclear weapons in reasonable ways. And they do not necessarily confine their objectives to basic deterrence. Iran may decide that it wants a first-strike capability versus its neighbors, such as Israel. . . .

On the other hand, it is virtually impossible for Iran to achieve a first-strike capability versus the United States. Any risks that Iran took in its basing mode and alert posture to get ready for a first strike against Israel could easily make it more vulnerable to a first strike from the United States. Spending its nuclear forces on Israel would leave Iran politically and militarily vulnerable to a huge U.S. retaliation. By striking first, it would have legitimated a U.S. nuclear attack, while simultaneously weakening its own deterrent with the weapons it had expended. The United States is the greater threat to Iran because it is much more powerful than Israel, and has actual strategic objectives in the Gulf. It is strategically reasonable for Iran to focus its deterrent energies on the United States, which it can only influence with a secure retaliatory force, capable of threatening U.S. forces and interests in the region.

A final potential problem in Iran is the apparent decentralization of power in the country. Iran essentially has two military organizations: the "professional" military, and the Revolutionary Guard Corps. The latter is ideologically motivated, secretive, and involved in assisting armed groups abroad in Iraq and Lebanon. Many fear that the latter would end up in control of the weapons, or at least with considerable access to them. Given the nature of this organization, some of its members might be willing to do things that the higher political authorities in the state would not choose to do. . . .

Regional Nuclear Proliferation and Risks to the Non-Proliferation Treaty

States in range of Iran's nuclear weapons will reasonably wish to take measures to protect themselves against nuclear coercion and nuclear attack. Iran's neighbors have three policy options to ensure themselves against a nuclear-armed Iran. They can choose to appease Iran comprehensively; they can find a nuclear guarantor; they can build their own nuclear weapons. Though elements of these three policies could be combined, one will tend to dominate.

Most countries will decline to appease Iran, if they have another plausible option, because most nation-states enjoy their autonomy and do not wish to give it up. Comprehensive appeasement is the road to ruin; one set of concessions to a demanding Iran could easily lead to another, until the state in question loses the ability to recover any shred of sovereignty. Comprehensive appeasement will likely only prove preferable to states facing a disastrous war, or disastrous defeat, with no hope of survival. Historically, this sort of behavior is generally only found among the very weak, and typically when they lack any other option.

The most important choice is whether states will seek their own nuclear weapons, or seek the protection of another nuclear power, if that protection is offered. That said, only a few states in the Middle East and

Persian Gulf have the resources to attempt their own autonomous nuclear weapons programs. I have argued above that the United States likely would offer protection to regional states in order to protect its interests in the Persian Gulf from Iran. It also may offer such protection in order to forestall a spasm of nuclear proliferation in the region. The policies of the United States, and to a lesser extent the principal European states and the European Union, will be the most decisive determinant of whether or not Iran's nuclear programs are emulated.

At this time, and for the foreseeable future, four regional powers can be considered candidate nuclear competitors with Iran: Israel (already a nuclear-armed state), Egypt, Saudi Arabia, and Turkey. . . .

Though Iran is quite vulnerable to nuclear attack today, Israel might intensify its preparations to ensure that Iran understands just how dangerous nuclear threats toward Israel would be. Not many Israeli nuclear weapons would need to survive an attempted Iranian first strike to ruin Iran forever. Open improvements in Israeli nuclear capabilities, especially if accompanied by extensive public rhetoric, would likely raise security and prestige concerns among its neighbors. The United States would be wise to urge Israel to refrain from strong nuclear declarations, unless Iran's own public declarations about its nuclear capability demand a response.

Egypt would be concerned for reasons of both prestige and security if Iran was to become a nuclear weapons state, and Israel was to become an open nuclear power. Egypt at one time had an active nuclear energy research program, and there was concern that it could become a nuclear weapons program. It has the technological and scientific expertise and has recently announced a new civilian nuclear energy program.[15] Absent active U.S. diplomacy, and strategic guarantees, Egypt probably would follow suit in developing nuclear weapons. Egypt faces a number of barriers, however. First, it is highly dependent on the United States for conventional weaponry. The United States surely would suspend this relationship if Egypt decided to pursue nuclear weapons. This would be quite unsettling to Egypt's internal politics. Second, Egypt is a poor country; foreign economic assistance would also dry up if Egypt decided to go nuclear. Third, given that Israel is already a nuclear weapons state, and Iran is well ahead of Egypt, Egypt would go through a period of both conventional and nuclear vulnerability as it attempted to produce nuclear weapons. Egypt could choose to accept all these risks and costs, but it seems more plausible that the United States and the European Union could find a package of assurances and incentives that would be acceptable to Egypt.

Saudi Arabia would face similar, though stronger temptations, than Egypt. Saudi Arabia is arguably the other "great power" of the Persian Gulf region, and thus a natural competitor with Iran. With the demise of Iraq, it is the undisputed leader of the Arab states in the Gulf, and thus a rival to an Iran trying to expand its sphere of influence. Due to their proximity, Iran and Saudi Arabia are vulnerable to one another's conventional military power. Saudi Arabia likely views itself as the protector of Sunni Arabs from Shia Arabs, and from Shia Iran. . . .

Saudi Arabia does have good reason to believe that outsiders are committed to its security. The United States and other great powers have extensive economic and military interests in maintaining Saudi security. The United States has demonstrated its commitment in many ways, including war. The Saudis are accustomed to security cooperation with the United States. A U.S. guarantee likely would prove the most attractive option for Saudi Arabia.

Turkey also will be concerned, for security and prestige reasons, about a nuclear weapons capability in neighboring Iran. Turkey's economic, scientific, and engineering capabilities probably make it more capable of going nuclear than either Egypt or Saudi Arabia. Turkey's calculation will be affected by other political interests, however. Turkey is a member of NATO, a nuclear alliance, and thus already enjoys a nuclear guarantee by the United States. Dozens of tactical nuclear weapons are based in Turkey, and some of Turkey's aircraft are wired to deliver these weapons, which could be turned over to them under circumstances determined by the United States, and based on long-standing procedures agreed within NATO. This relationship would be jeopardized were Turkey to embark on its own independent nuclear weapons program. Turkey also aspires to membership in the European Union. Though the Europeans have been only moderately encouraging, it seems likely that the EU would discourage an independent Turkish nuclear effort. Conversely, it seems possible that the EU might become more accommodating of Turkey's effort to join the EU if that helped discourage a Turkish nuclear program.

In sum, a nuclear Iran creates risks of additional nuclear proliferation in the Persian Gulf and Middle

East regions. At the same time, these risks will be affected by the U.S. response. If the United States behaves consistent with its past interpretation of its regional interests and global interests, then it can mute the incentives of three of the four states in question to acquire nuclear weapons. This is not a sure thing, of course, and the United States will need to show leadership and sagacity. That said, it looks as if the kinds of policies recommended in this paper in the event of an Iranian nuclear weapons capability are similar to what the United States, its allies, and other Asian powers are doing in response to the North Korean nuclear weapons test. The United States and its allies have demonstrated their solidarity; North Korea has been warned not to export its nuclear weapons; and the United Nations has instituted a sanctions regime, which effectively legalizes searches of North Korean ships, planes, trucks, and railroad cars for nuclear contraband. . . .

Conclusion

A nuclear-armed Iran is not a trivial problem—for its neighbors or the United States. Indeed, Iran itself would be entering a difficult new period in its history. It would be better by far for Iran to forgo those technology development initiatives that would allow it to make a decision to become a nuclear weapons state. But current diplomatic efforts may fail, and the question arises as to whether preventive war dominates a strategy of containment and deterrence. This choice can only be considered if a strategy of containment is elucidated, and its odds of success assessed. Should Iran become a nuclear power, both the immediate strategic risks and the proliferation risks can be addressed with a reinvigorated commitment of U.S. power to stability and security in the Persian Gulf and the Middle East. Such a commitment is reasonable given U.S. strategic interests in the region. The United States should seek the help of outside partners in Europe and elsewhere in making this commitment. The United States can and should make it clear to Iran that the overt or covert use of its nuclear weapons, for blackmail or for war, would put Iran in the gravest danger of nuclear retaliation. The United States should similarly explain to regional actors why it is willing to make this commitment. Both the United States and regional actors may wish to reinforce this commitment with security agreements and some visible military preparations. At the same time, it will be necessary for the United States to forgo any future efforts to replace the Iranian regime. This would run nuclear risks that neither the United States, nor other great powers, nor regional powers will wish to run.

The strategy of deterrence and containment has worked for the United States before; there is no reason why it cannot work again. Relative to Iran, the United States and its likely allies have vastly superior material capabilities, a far more favorable situation than the in Cold War. In a confrontation with the United States, Iran would run risks of complete destruction, and it cannot threaten the United States with comparable damage.

Bismarck said of preventive war that it was like committing suicide out of fear of death. A preventive war versus Iran might not be suicidal, but it will definitely hurt. The United States and its allies have many military and diplomatic cards to play to manage the dangers posed by a nuclear-armed Iran. That said, a replay of the Cold War competition in the Persian Gulf is not a happy outcome. Though I think it is preferable to preventive war, far better would be a diplomatic solution. Since it is unlikely that economic pressure alone will bring diplomatic success, it would be wise to offer Iran a package of incentives more consistent with its apparent concerns than has been offered thus far. If Iran were to decline such an offer, this clarification of its purposes would assist the ultimate diplomacy of containment and deterrence.

Notes

1. Jeffrey J. Schott, Institute for International Economics, "Economic Sanctions, Oil, and Iran," Testimony before the Joint Economic Committee, U.S. Congress, Hearing on "Energy and the Iranian Economy," July 25, 2006, available online at http://www.iie.com/ publications/papers/paper.cfm?ResearchID=649.

2. Lionel Beehner, "What Sanctions Mean for Iran's Economy," Council on Foreign Relations Background Paper, May 2006, available online at http://www.cfr.org/publication/10590/what_ sanctions_mean_for_irans_economy.html?

3. Flynt Leverett, "The Race for Iran," *New York Times*, June 20, 2006.

4. Austin Long and Whitney Raas, "Osirak Redux? Assessing Israeli Capabilities to Destroy Iranian Nuclear Facilities," April 2006, SSP Working Paper, available online at http://web.mit.edu/ssp/Publications/working_papers/wp_06-1.pdf.

5. For example, two hundred fighter bombers could easily deliver four hundred precision-guided weapons against

four hundred aim points. Given the U.S. naval and air presence in the Persian Gulf, this rather limited attack could probably be launched with little reinforcement.

6. Thomas A. Keaney and Eliot A. Cohen, *Gulf War Air Power Survey Summary Report* (Washington D.C.: Government Printing Office, 1993), Figure 5, "Coalition Air Strikes by Day Against Iraqi Target Sets," p. 13 (numbers estimated from graph).

7. The recent Israeli experience in Lebanon is relevant. Neither the Israeli Air Force nor the powerful counterbattery attacks of the Israeli Army's artillery could prevent Hezbollah from launching a hundred or more artillery rockets into northern Israel almost every night. Given the length of the Iran/Iraq border, it seems likely that Iran could infiltrate small units into Iraq to raid bases and truck convoys. At this moment, Iran likely has agents in Southern Iraq, and has sufficiently strong relationships with Shiite militias that some of these militias might assist Iran. Finally, Iran's intelligence on the location and strength of coalition forces is likely very good. It would not be surprising if Iran had precise coordinates for many of these potential targets, and spotters close to these targets, both of which would improve the performance of its otherwise inaccurate long range artillery rockets.

8. Robert Lowe and Claire Spencer, eds., *Iran, Its Neighbors and the Regional Crises, A Middle East Programme Report* (London: Royal Institute of International Affairs, 2006), pp. 6, 8–12; See also Vali Nasr, "When the Shiites Rise," *Foreign Affairs* 85 (July/August 2006): 58–74, esp. 66–68. Ray Takeyh, "A Profile in Defiance, Being Mahmoud Admadinejad," *National Interest*, no. 83 (Spring 2006): pp. 16–21 makes the point that the new Iranian president and his coterie of Iraq war veterans seem more religious, more nationalistic, and more confrontational than others in the Iranian political elite, but that they are only one faction.

9. *The World Factbook*, U.S. Central Intelligence Agency, available online at https://www.cia.gov/cia/publications/factbook/geos/ir.html, accessed Sept. 25, 2006.

10. William Dunlop and Harold Smith, "Who Did It? Using International Forensics to Detect and Deter Nuclear Terrorism," *Arms Control Today*, October 2006, available online at http://www.armscontrol.org/act/2006_10/CVRForensics.asp, accessed October 29, 2006.

11. *The Military Balance 2006* (London: International Institute for Strategic Studies, and Routledge, 2006), pp. 18, 187.

12. For population concentrations see, "World Urbanization Prospects: The 2005 Revision Population Database," "Iran," U.N. Population Division, available online at http://esa.un.org/unup, accessed 23 September 2006. Jericho II range estimates by Austin Long.

13. Perhaps a third of Iranian manufacturing industry is concentrated in or near Tehran, Karaj, and Isfahan alone. See "Table 7.9, Manufacturing Establishments by Legal Status and Ostan: 1381," Statistical Centre of Iran, available online at http://www.sci.org.ir/portal/faces/public/sci_en/sci_en.selecteddata/sci_en.yearbookdata, accessed September 29, 2006.

14. Scott D. Sagan, "How to Keep the Bomb From Iran," *Foreign Affairs* 85 (September/October 2006): 45–59. Sagan raises many of the concerns outlined here. These concerns lead him to advise a focused diplomatic effort to discourage Iran from proceeding with its enrichment program. He explicitly concludes, however, that preventive war is not an appropriate answer to the Iranian program. Implicitly, therefore, he accepts that however problematical a nuclear Iran might be, these risks do not exceed those associated with a preventive war.

15. For an excellent review of the nuclear potential of Egypt, Turkey, and Saudi Arabia, see Wyn Q. Bowen and Joanna Kidd, "The Nuclear Capabilities and Ambitions of Iran's Neighbors," in *Getting Ready for a Nuclear-Ready Iran*, Henry Sokolski and Patrick Clawson, eds. (Carlyle Barracks, Penn.: U.S. Army War College, Strategic Studies Institute, 2005), pp. 51–88, available online at www.strategicstudiesinstitute.army.mil/. See also William Wallis and Roula Khalaf, "Speculation after Egypt Revives Nuclear Plans," *Financial Times*, September 25, 2006, available online at http://www.ft.com/cms/s/6e01b312-4cba-11dbb03c-0000779e2340. html, accessed October 29, 2006.

13.3

Containment Breach

Robert J. Lieber and Amatzia Baram

A number of influential policymakers and foreign policy analysts appear much too complacent regarding the prospects of a nuclear-armed Iran. Former CENTCOM Commander Gen. John Abizaid has argued that "[d]eterrence will work with Iran," and former Deputy Director of National Intelligence Thomas Fingar, one of the authors of the 2007 National Intelligence Estimate on Iran's nuclear capabilities, has voiced similar opinions. Deterrence in the Middle East, they argue, could be just as stable as it was between the United States and the USSR during the Cold War. "Israel's massive nuclear force will deter Iran from ever contemplating using or giving away its own (hypothetical) weapon," wrote Fareed Zakaria in the Oct. 12 edition of Newsweek. "Deterrence worked with madmen like Mao, and with thugs like Stalin, and it will work with the calculating autocrats of Tehran."

But this historical analogy is dangerously misconceived. In reality, defusing an Israeli-Iranian nuclear standoff will be far more difficult than averting nuclear war during the Cuban Missile Crisis. This is true even if those Iranians with their fingers on the nuclear trigger are not given to messianic doomsday thinking. Here are five factors that will make an Israeli-Iranian nuclear confrontation potentially explosive.

Communication and trust

The October 1962 negotiations that settled the Cuban missile crisis were conducted through a fairly effective, though imperfect, communication system between the United States and Russia. There was also a limited degree of mutual trust between the two superpowers. This did not prevent confusion and suspicion, but it did facilitate the rivals' ability to understand the other's side and eventually resolve the crisis.

Israel and Iran, however, have no such avenues for communication. They don't even have embassies or fast and effective back-channel contacts—and, what's more, they mistrust each other completely. Israel has heard Iranian leaders—and not just President Mahmoud Ahmadinejad—call for its destruction. Meanwhile, Iranian leaders remain prone to paranoid and conspiratorial views of the outside world, especially Israel and the United States. In any future Iranian-Israeli crisis, each side could easily misinterpret the other's moves, leading to disaster. A proxy war conducted by Iran through Hezbollah or Hamas against Israel could quickly lead to a series of escalating threats.

Goals

The Soviets wanted to extend their power and spread Communism—they never pledged the annihilation of America. Iranian leaders, however, have called for Israel to be "wiped off the map of the Middle East." After the street protests that followed the June presidential election, Iran has entered into chronic instability. In a moment of heightened tension and urgent need for popular support, an Iranian leader could escalate not only rhetoric but action.

There is a strong precedent in the Middle East of such escalation leading to war. Arab threats to destroy any Jewish state preceded a massive invasion of the new Israeli state in May 1948. In May and June 1967, Egypt's President Gamal Abd al-Nasser loudly proclaimed his intent to "liberate Palestine" (i.e. Israel in its 1949 borders), and moved his panzer divisions to Israel's border. The result was the Six Day War.

Command and control

In 1962, the two superpowers possessed sophisticated command-and-control systems securing their nuclear weapons. Both also employed effective centralized decision-making systems. Neither may be the case with Iran: Its control technology will be rudimentary

Source: Robert J. Lieber and Amatzia Baram, "Containment Breach," *Foreign Policy*, December 22, 2009.

at first, and Tehran's decision-making process is relatively chaotic. Within Iran's byzantine power structure, the Islamic Revolutionary Guard Corps (IRGC) mounts an army and navy of its own alongside the regular army and navy, and internal differences within the regime over nuclear diplomacy are evidence of conflicting lines of authority. Recent events suggest that the IRGC, allied with Ahmadinejad, has increasingly infringed on the authority of the supreme leader, Ayatollah Ali Khamenei. As a result, no one can be certain how decisions are made and who makes them.

Mutual deterrence

Both the United States and USSR had second-strike capability made credible by huge land masses. They possessed hardened missile silos scattered throughout the countryside, large air forces equipped with nuclear bombs, and missile-launching submarines. In the Middle East, Iran stretches across a vast 636,000 square miles, against Israel's (pre-1967) 8,500 square miles of territory. This point was made by ex-president Hashemi Rafsanjani in 2001, who noted, "Israel is much smaller than Iran in land mass, and therefore far more vulnerable to nuclear attack." If this is the way an Iranian pragmatist thinks, how are the hard-liners thinking?

In contrast, by 1962, the two superpowers implicitly recognized the logic of mutually assured destruction. And yet, they still came relatively close to war—in John F. Kennedy's words, the risk of a nuclear conflict was "between one out of three and even." When Iran goes nuclear, the huge disparity in size will pose a psychological obstacle for its recognition of mutual deterrence. Even assuming the United States promises Israel a retaliatory nuclear umbrella, Iran will doubt U.S. resolve. The mullahs will be tempted to conclude that with Israel gone, the United States would see no point in destroying Iran. Given the criticism leveled today against President Harry Truman for using the bomb against Japanese civilians in World War II, what are the chances of American retaliation against Iran, especially if the Islamic Republic has not attacked the United States?

Crisis instability

In view of the above dangers, if and when a grave crisis does erupt, Israel would be tempted to strike first in order to prevent an Iranian nuclear attack, which would devastate its urban core. Iran will be well aware of Israel's calculations and, in the early years of becoming a nuclear power, will have a smaller and probably more vulnerable nuclear arsenal. This will give it, in turn, strong incentives to launch its own preemptive strike.

The implications of a nuclear-armed Iran go well beyond the risks of an Iranian-Israeli war. Once Iran is a nuclear power, the Middle East is likely to enter a fast-moving process of nuclear proliferation. Until now, most Arab governments have not made an effort to match Israel's nuclear arsenal. However, they perceive Iran's nuclear weapons as a real strategic threat. A Middle East where more and more states have nuclear arms, known to experts as a saturated multiplayer environment, will present an almost insurmountable challenge for deterrence calculations by regional or external powers, and a still greater risk of serious instability. Contrary to the wishful thinking of some analysts that the possession of nuclear weapons could make Iran more cautious, a nuclear Iran will likely be emboldened. It could press Hezbollah to be more aggressive in Lebanon, flex its muscles in the Persian Gulf, and step up its challenges against U.S. forces in the region.

If diplomacy and sanctions fail to prevent Iran from going nuclear, Israel will be caught on the horns of an acute existential dilemma not of its own making. If Israel does not act, it will face a future in which it will live under a nuclear sword of Damocles wielded by a state that has called for its destruction. If it does act in the face of what are, after all, probabilities rather than certainties, Israel must expect a serious conventional war that would include attacks from Iran's proxies, Hamas and Hezbollah, and an escalation in international terrorism, all in exchange for an uncertain degree of success. Contrary to the assessments of those who foresee a best case scenario of stable deterrence, a nuclear-armed Iran will usher in a new era of instability in the Middle East—with consequences that nobody can accurately predict, much less contain.

14 Bargaining and War

14.1

Exploring the Bargaining Model of War

Dan Reiter

What is the relationship between politics and war? Are they separate phenomena, in which war represents the failure of politics? Or as Carl von Clausewitz famously suggested, should war be considered as part of politics—that is, politics by other means?

The bargaining model of war sees war as politics all the way down. It views international politics as disputes over scarce goods, such as the placement of a border, the composition of a national government, or control over natural resources. States use both war and words as bargaining tools to help them achieve optimal allocations of goods. Critically, the bargaining model does not see war as the breakdown of diplomacy but rather as a continuation of bargaining, as negotiations occur during war, and war ends when a deal is struck. . . .

The Bargaining Model of War

Although many political scientists naturally resist the imperial tendencies of economists, it must be recognized that the generally accepted purview of economics, "the allocation of scarce resources among unlimited and competing uses," also describes a critical component of political life.[1] In particular, much of international politics can be accurately described as the allocation of resources under scarcity. Actors cannot all achieve their most desired goals simultaneously. Pakistan and India cannot each control all of Kashmir; Japanese nontariff barriers come at the expense of American economic welfare; the vetoes allocated to the permanent members of the United Nations Security Council diminish the institutional powers of other UN members; ameliorating global warming requires reducing the consumption of fossil fuels. At the limit of this perspective, if everyone could enjoy his or her most preferred set of policies and goods, then politics and economics would in some sense be unnecessary.

The bargaining model sees the essence of conflict, violent or otherwise, as disagreement over resource allocation and/or policy choice. Bargaining models have long been used to explain the resolution of conflict among actors. When some good or resource must be divided among at least two actors, bargaining is "the process of arriving at mutual agreement on the provisions of a contract."[2] In economics, bargaining illuminates the process by which a buyer and a seller agree on a price. Bargaining has also been used to describe the resolution of legal disputes.[3]

The bargaining perspective quite naturally offers an understanding of political-conflict resolution. The very stuff of politics is frequently bargaining: different wings of a party choosing a common platform, legislators making agreements to hold ruling coalitions together, congressmen assembling budgets to satisfy the needs of a number of constituencies, and so forth. Bargaining models have been constructively applied to

Source: Dan Reiter. "Exploring the Bargaining Model of War," in *Perspectives on Politics* 1(1): 27–36. Copyright 2003 Cambridge University Press. Reprinted with permission.

parliamentary dynamics, government formation, legislative rulemaking, and logrolling.[4]

International politics lends itself well to the bargaining perspective. Usually, international politics occurs among a small enough group of actors to make models of pure free markets inappropriate; notably, oligopoly models have been applied to international relations.[5] Further, international politics often concerns scarce goods, such as money. A state's decision to impose tariffs translates directly into lower sales for foreign producers.

Some scholars see security as a scarce good, as one side's efforts to increase security may impinge on the security of a neighbor.[6]

Bargaining plays an important role in a number of central areas in international politics. Interstate cooperation can be framed as a bargaining problem, in that states negotiate an agreed-upon course of action to advance the goals of all under conditions of scarcity.[7] International institutions facilitate bargaining by providing information and linking different issues. Importantly, the very design of institutions can be understood as bargaining, as the skeleton of an institution represents the distribution of finite resources (veto power, committee structure, voting rules, and so forth).[8]

Carl von Clausewitz's view of war fits into a bargaining perspective. Clausewitz noted centuries ago that war is a means of accomplishing political goals and not an end in itself, remarking that "[t]he political object is the goal, war is the means of reaching it, and means can never be considered in isolation from their purpose."[9] In other words, war for its own sake has no value, so one would never pursue it without hoping to accomplish some larger political aim. In modern bargaining model scholarship, discussed in greater detail below, this logic gets translated into the critical assumption that war itself—the actual fighting, aside from the political issues at stake—is always costly. Although this idea may seem truistic, some scholars (also discussed below) see fighting itself as serving a function: as an expression of cultural or gendered tendencies to aggression, as an affirmation of identity, or as a means of quelling domestic dissent.

Clausewitz also proposed that most "real" wars are limited rather than total. This insight re-emerged during the 1950s, when the Korean War demonstrated to American observers that the impending Cold War would probably take the form of limited conflicts rather than a third world war; it called for the development of ideas about how to fight, terminate, and win such smaller-scale conflicts.[10] The premise that wars are frequently limited laid the groundwork for developing a modern bargaining model of war: if wars are rarely total, then they usually end with a war-terminating bargain rather than with one side's decisive military defeat. Economist Thomas Schelling was one of the first modern social scientists to frame conflict as bargaining, using mostly informal discussion and early noncooperative game theory. He famously noted in 1960, that "most conflict situations are essentially *bargaining* situations."[11] Relatedly, some scholars during this period thought not just about how wars started but also about how they ended. Paul Kecskemeti framed the question of war-ending surrender in bargaining terms, examining four World War II surrenders. Some 13 years later, the "agonizing search for an exit" to the Vietnam War pushed Fred Iklé to think about how wars end, also within an informal bargaining framework.[12] As that war ended, Geoffrey Blainey and Steven Rosen separately made the important bargaining model observation that wars may occur because of disagreements about levels of strength or resolve.[13]

By the 1980s, the bargaining model of war was increasingly expressed in formal terms, as part of the burgeoning literature on rational-choice models of politics and war. At this stage, rational-choice models claimed that war is a deliberate political act, a view at odds with many psychology-based theories, which argued that war emerges from perceptual biases and miscalculations. Bruce Bueno de Mesquita developed this point in 1981, providing more theoretical and empirical support for the central point that war occurs when states prefer war to peace.[14] Throughout the 1980s and into the 1990s, a number of important papers fleshed out the view that international relations is composed of political choices to advance national aims; these papers developed models in which states bargained over issues. Some models allowed for at least one state to choose war as an alternative to accepting the status quo or continuing to bargain. James Fearon prominently contributed to this scholarship with his 1995 paper "Rationalist Explanations for War." He usefully highlighted the point that if states agreed on the outcome of a possible war, they could probably avoid war. Central to Fearon's paper is the importance of focusing on states' disagreement over their capabilities and/or resolve.[15]

The shift to more formal approaches during this period constituted both a step forward and a step back from earlier work by scholars such as Kecskemeti, Iklé, and Pillar. The introduction of formal models—applying rigorous, mathematized logic—was progress. However, these models incorporated an important simplification: although they considered the causes of war within a bargaining framework, they saw war itself not as part of the bargaining process but as an apolitical, two-outcome, costly lottery.[16] They assumed that once war starts, a random draw determines its outcome. War is costly because both sides must pay the costs of fighting, regardless of who wins, so there are fewer goods to distribute between the two sides after war than before. The only two possible outcomes are one side winning decisively or the other side winning decisively. Lastly, it is apolitical in that the models allow for no bargaining within war, interpreting the war-fighting process as fundamentally mechanical rather than strategic or instrumental. In contrast, the earlier, non-formal work generally did not employ the costly-lottery assumption and viewed the fighting and, especially, the termination of war as bargaining.

A second, roughly post-1995 wave of formal bargaining work has made important improvements over the earlier formal work. This newer scholarship views both the causes and the termination of wars as part of the bargaining process, explicitly relaxing the assumption that war is a costly lottery. Specifically, rather than seeing bargaining and war as exclusive but complementary phenomena, it has returned to the outlook of the earlier, non-formal work, which asserted that bargaining takes place during as well as before and after war.

I term this general perspective, which sees war as part of international bargaining, to be the bargaining model of war, although I recognize that it encompasses a number of different perspectives and theories. The bargaining model of war is similar to the common understanding of labor strikes. Labor and management bargain over contracts and exchange offers, and labor has the option of calling a strike to impose costs on management and thereby extracting more concessions. The strike itself is thus part of the bargaining process. Bargaining continues during the strike, as both sides exchange offers in negotiations and learn about each other's willingness to absorb costs until they arrive at a contract that each prefers over having the strike continue.

Importantly, the latest wave of research on the bargaining model covers all phases of war. Each phase is part of the bargaining process. Fighting breaks out when two sides cannot reach a bargain that both prefer to war. Each side fights to improve its chances of getting a desirable settlement of the disputed issue. The war ends when the two sides strike a bargain that both prefer to continuing the war, and the outcome is literally the bargain struck. Finally, the duration of peace following the war reflects the willingness of both sides not to break the war-ending bargain.

The Causes of War

The essence of the bargaining model as applied to the causes of war is that states experience disputes over the settlement of some issue, and war is one means by which states can achieve (or maintain) a better settlement. I structure my discussion around Fearon's seminal paper, in which he shows how a bargaining (or "rationalist") model explains the outbreak of war. Fearon uses a bargaining model to argue that if two states in dispute know the outcome of a possible war, they should in general prefer to reach a deal that would reflect the hypothetical post-war political settlement, rather than fight, reach that same settlement, and also suffer the costs of war. This view assumes that fighting itself is costly—that the belligerent always suffers some negative utility, no matter how the issue at stake is settled.

In fact, this assumption becomes necessary when one asserts that two states would *always* prefer to reach a bargain without fighting rather than fight and then reach the same bargain.[17]

Within his bargaining model, Fearon develops three conditions under which war is possible. First, there may be disagreement between the two sides as to the likely outcome of a war. If at least one side overestimates its chances of winning or underestimates the opponent's resolve, it may not raise its settlement offer enough to make the other side choose the offer over war. This lack of bargaining space stops a war-avoiding compromise.[18] In the months following Germany's June 1941 invasion of the U.S.S.R., for example, Hitler recognized that he had underestimated Soviet capabilities; he remarked that if he had believed the more pessimistic reports about Soviet strength he might not have ordered the attack.[19] This focus on uncertainty may explain the empirical finding that states of equal power are more war-prone than are states of unequal power: uncertainty under parity may make states optimistic enough to prefer war to peaceful settlement, whereas uncertainty under imbalance is usually not great enough to cast doubt on a war's ultimate outcome.[20]

This proposition immediately presents a puzzle. If complete information can help states avoid fighting, and states prefer to avoid fighting, then why don't states completely reveal their capabilities and resolve to one another? States have an incentive to exaggerate their capabilities and resolve in an attempt to extract better offers. Costly, more-credible signals of resolve, such as the mobilization of troops, may help states better reveal capabilities to one another, albeit at the expense of raising the risk of accidental war.[21] Additionally, there may be a military advantage to keeping secret a particular strategy, force, or capability if openness would undermine military effectiveness. For example, a crucial part of Israel's huge military advantage in the Six Day War was its plan to surprise attack Egyptian aircraft on the ground. Revelation of this strategy would have nullified its effectiveness, as Egypt could then have taken countermeasures. Hence, keeping information about capabilities secret may make war more likely by preventing the convergence of expectations, but doing so may also make the expected utility of war itself higher by raising a state's chances of winning.[22]

Fearon's second condition: war may occur because of an inability to commit not to fight in the future. If there are advantages to be had from striking first, then the outcome of the war differs depending on who attacks first, and the inability in anarchy for two sides to credibly commit not to attack may preclude a settlement. Additionally, if one side grows in power, then the outcome of war may change in the future, meaning that a bargain that is sufficiently war-avoiding now may not be when the balance changes. The inability of the growing side to commit not to attack in the future may undermine the ability of the two states to reach an accommodation.[23]

Fearon's third condition: bargaining may not avoid war if the item under dispute is indivisible. The all-or-nothing status[24] of the good might prevent the two states from reaching a mutually acceptable pre-war bargain if the projected outcome of the war is something other than a decisive victory for either side. Though Fearon downplays the likely incidence of indivisible issues, scholars have begun to explore the conditions under which an issue may be practicably if not literally indivisible. In particular, issue indivisibility may explain why some intranational ethnic disputes descend into war. A central government may be unwilling to strike a bargain with a minority group seeking autonomy, because doing so would create a precedent and encourage other groups to seek a bargain. This fear of establishing a precedent effectively makes the issue at stake indivisible.[25]

The Conduct and Termination of War

Here, I lay out how the bargaining model views the conduct and termination of war. A preliminary task to understanding the conduct of war and its relation to bargaining is to define combat, the actual activity of war. Combat is a violent clash between at least two politically distinct groups organized to wield force. War consists of sustained and substantial episodes of combat. Clausewitz saw episodes of combat as the building blocks of war, pointing out that "[c]ountless duels go to make up a war," and even more tersely that "[e]ssentially war is fighting."[26]

An armed force engaged in combat tries to accomplish one or more of three immediate tasks: the destruction of military forces, the occupation of territory, and the destruction of civilian assets. Destruction of military forces means just that: the killing, disabling, or capture of military personnel, and the destruction, disabling, or capture of military equipment. Territory is occupied when one can control movement into, out of, and through it. Destruction of civilian assets includes killing and injuring noncombatants and/or destroying and damaging material items, such as the means of production. Importantly, capturing territory and destroying forces can be both means and ends. An army might destroy a defending force in order to capture a piece of territory.

Alternatively, capturing territory might allow the destruction of enemy forces—for example, if seizing high ground provides fire control of an area.

The bargaining model proposes that military means are used as part of the bargaining process, to advance political ends. There are a variety of ideas about exactly what role combat plays within war (specifically, how it relates to bargaining). A common theme within the newer bargaining model scholarship is acceptance of Clausewitz's general distinction between limited (or "real") and absolute war.[27] The central difference is as follows: at the end of absolute war, the military capacity of the defeated state has been completely exhausted, whereas at the end of limited war, both sides retain at least some ability to fight.[28] Notably, though absolute war is a useful theoretical construct, it rarely occurs; states almost never fight to the last man and/or surrender unconditionally (the principal exceptions being perhaps Germany's surrender in 1945 and the 2001 defeat of the Taliban). Even Japan in 1945 extracted from the Allies the important concession that the emperor remain the spiritual (though not political) leader without facing prosecution as a war criminal. The terms of Germany's surrender in 1918 and the Confederacy's surrender in 1865 also were harsh but not unconditional.[29]

I identify here two separate means by which combat can accomplish political goals within the bargaining model of war. First, combat can seek total conquest, or the utter destruction of the enemy's means to resist, in order to achieve victory in a Clausewitzian absolute war. Second, combat can reduce uncertainty about the capabilities or resolve of the combatants. . . .

In short, this is an apolitical notion of combat's role in advancing national aims: brute force is used to crush the enemy's means of resistance. Some have argued that this conception of combat as brute force can also be applied to the accomplishment of limited aims. According to this perspective, war occurs when one side has completely lost faith in the chances of striking a bargain to settle the dispute and thus resorts to violence to impose a change. Brute force is used to destroy part of the adversary's military assets or to seize a piece of territory. Schelling discussed the possibility of accomplishing limited aims through physical force in his distinction between using violence as brute force and using it as coercion.[30] The bargaining model proposes that exercising brute force to accomplish limited aims is generally misguided. If both sides knew that the attacker could conquer a small piece of territory, then they would peacefully exchange the territory rather than fight. The failure of negotiations to facilitate territorial exchange probably indicates some other problem, such as disagreement over capabilities or the perceived indivisibility of the territory. One might imagine an environment in which the land is more easily defended once seized by the revisionist than it is in the hands of the original status quo power, although this view requires assumptions about asymmetrical surprise attack advantages or peculiar distributions of terrain that make one border easier to defend than another.

A more central role of combat in the bargaining model of war is the reduction of uncertainty. As discussed, a common bargaining model explanation of the outbreak of war is uncertainty about the outcome of a hypothetical war. Combat can reduce uncertainty by providing information about the actual balance of power. Or as some have put it, combat in a limited (or "real") war reveals information about what the outcome of an absolute war would be.[31] The outcome of combat is observed by both sides and should cause their expectations to converge regarding the likely outcomes of future combat. This increases the likelihood of reaching an agreement that both sides prefer over continued fighting. Rosen draws an analogy to "two men fighting in a darkened room. If the lights were turned on and some of the combatants had a clearer picture of the hopelessly superior size of their opponents, much of the fighting would end."[32] This finding deviates from an earlier proposition that fighting battles does not facilitate war termination, as a battle outcome would not bring two sides closer to reaching a deal, since the battle winner would raise its demands as the battle loser lowered its own, creating no bargaining space.[33] Note that this view holds even if a great victory convinces a battle winner that its capabilities are even greater than originally hoped and hence causes the victor to raise its war aims, as following such a battle the loser should, roughly speaking, lower its war aims more than the winner's were raised, bringing the sides' aims closer together.[34]

Combat might also reduce uncertainty about resolve and about military effectiveness. A defender that takes casualties in a battle may convey resolve to the other side. For example, Japanese troops inflicted heavy losses on invading American forces during the 1945 Iwo Jima and Okinawa campaigns. This caused the United States to update its beliefs and increase its casualty estimates for an invasion of Japan, which in turn strengthened the case for dropping the atomic bomb as a means of making such an invasion unnecessary.[35]

Some bargaining models allow for states to update their beliefs about each side's ability to absorb and/or inflict costs.[36] Note that this perspective contrasts with some older models that envision wars as games of attrition, in which each side inflicts costs on the other, and in which one side sues for peace if its threshold of acceptable costs is crossed.[37] The newer bargaining models propose that if the two sides could agree that the imposition of costs would cross at least one side's acceptability threshold, then they would reach a war-avoiding or war-terminating bargain reflecting what the outcome would have been if war had proceeded. For example, after invading the Netherlands in 1940,

Germany threatened to destroy Rotterdam and Utrecht unless all resistance ceased. Since the Germans had demonstrated a willingness and ability to destroy cities, the Dutch surrendered to spare their cities.[38] War happens because the sides disagree about their abilities to inflict and/or absorb costs, and combat helps end war by reducing disagreement between the two sides over these two factors and by creating bargaining space. . . .

The Consequences of War

Lastly, the bargaining model helps explain the consequences of war, specifically the stability of a post-war peace. Two important hypotheses have emerged from different versions of the bargaining model. Werner lays out the bargaining-model claim that wars are about the revelation of information about power and capabilities, and that the end of war creates a readjustment of goods consistent with a new understanding of the distribution of power. Her proposition is that the more the power balance between two former belligerents changes in the years following war, the more likely war becomes, as the two states will resort to war to realign the distribution of goods to match the changing balance of power.[39]

Smith and Stam produce a second argument. They propose that the more battles are fought, the more information is revealed, causing the expectations of the two sides to converge. Additionally, they posit that the greater the convergence of expectations about capabilities, the more stable will be the post-war peace. This argument provides a stronger theoretical basis for the long-standing war-weariness hypothesis, the speculation that peace lasts longer after long wars than after short wars.[40] . . .

Other Theoretical Perspectives

How does the bargaining model relate to other theories of war? Does it strike new ground, putting itself at odds with other leading theories of conflict and international relations? Here, I will work through a number of leading theories of war, drawing comparisons with the bargaining model. A central point is that the bargaining model is not necessarily a competitor with many leading theories, but rather these theories can be connected with the bargaining model—specifically if the other theories flesh out the basic conceptual structure of the bargaining model. A few theoretical perspectives, however, should be thought of as clashing directly with the bargaining model.

Deterrence, The Spiral Model, and Cognitive Psychological Biases

The bargaining model overlaps with deterrence theory. In deterrence theory, an actor (a defender) attempts to deter another state (a potential attacker) by promising to make a specific response if the second state takes some action. Deterrence succeeds when the potential attacker does not attack. Though there are many variations on deterrence theory, a basic proposition is that "[d]eterrence is predicted to succeed when the expected utility of using force is less than the expected utility of not using force."[41] This formulation fits into the bargaining model well, as both models make similar assumptions (states seek to advance their national interests, weigh costs and benefits, and sometimes see war as a useful tool of foreign policy) and some similar predictions (e.g., war becomes more likely as the perceived costs of war go down).

The bargaining model does make one important, different prediction. Classic deterrence theory predicts that as an imbalance of power between two states grows, war becomes more probable. The bargaining model, on the other hand, argues that it is not an imbalance of power that causes war, but rather disagreement over the balance of power (and over the likely outcome of war). From this emerges the prediction that balances of power might be more significantly associated with war than are imbalances of power, because there is more uncertainty about the outcome of an eventual war between two evenly matched states than about two unevenly matched states.[42]

Another major theory of war is the spiral model. In contrast to the deterrence model, which argues that war occurs out of greed, the spiral model predicts that war occurs out of fear. Anarchy makes the state prepare military forces, which threaten its neighbors and push them to arm; the resultant arms race makes all sides less secure, a dynamic known as the security dilemma. The spiral model forecasts two principal paths to war. Preventive war occurs when one state perceives the balance of power shifting against it and attacks sooner rather than later, when conditions would be less favorable. Preemptive war occurs when one state attacks in order to forestall a perceived imminent attack.[43]

Both types of war fit into the bargaining model. A changing balance of power may introduce commitment problems that make a war-avoiding bargain difficult to attain, leading to preventive war. Or incomplete information about preferences in the context of a shifting balance of power may make a preventive war more likely.[44] Conversely, growing perceptions of the advantages of attacking first can make preemption more probable, or at least can reduce bargaining space.[45]

The versions of the deterrence and spiral models laid out thus far have retained rationalist assumptions. Many scholars have built versions of these theories that incorporate non-rationalist assumptions and look instead to cognitive psychology. Some have argued that cognitive biases affect leaders' perceptions, so that leaders make attribution errors or maintain images of a hostile enemy even in the face of disconfirming evidence. Such biases may reinforce spirals of hostility by making defensively oriented moves look offensive and conflict more likely. Attribution errors cause states not to update their beliefs about the intentions of other states in patterns predicted by rationalist deterrence theory. Others have argued that motivated biases affect leaders' perceptions. For example, a leader may feel he faces domestic political pressures that demand an international victory in order for him or her to maintain power at home. The leader is then motivated to perceive that an international adversary can be defeated, and may then believe that victory is possible, even as the adversary becomes more powerful. In other words, the standard deterrence proposition that a more powerful defender makes deterrence success more likely does not hold.[46]

The cognitive-psychological school would level at least one general critique of the bargaining model: that revelation of information about the opponent during peacetime ought not significantly reduce the likelihood of war breaking out, and that revelation of information about the opponent during wartime ought not significantly reduce the likelihood of war ending. In the prewar case, the bargaining model would propose that, ceteris paribus, as two sides reveal information about their capabilities and intentions, bargaining space will open up to permit a war-avoiding bargain. Such revelations might come through increased transparency of societies (through democratization, for example), costly mobilization during international crises, the performance of armies in wars with third parties, and so forth. The cognitive-psychological school would doubt the ability of such revelations to preserve peace. Leaders' images of other countries as hostile or weak will likely persevere even in the face of credible evidence to the contrary. Further, if external factors such as domestic developments create an environment conducive to motivated bias, then leaders may develop beliefs that make war seem more appealing despite unfavorable military conditions. During wartime, similar dynamics may operate, precluding battle outcomes from causing leaders to update their beliefs about the resolve or capacity of the enemy. This is the view of some of the older war-termination literature, that cognitive and motivated biases are likely to swamp clear-headed thinking during war.[47]

Conducting decisive, competitive tests of these two perspectives may be difficult, as the difference is one of degree rather than kind. That is, the bargaining model says that the revelations that emerge from mobilization or battles are more likely to cause war avoidance and war termination, whereas the psychological perspective argues that such revelations will probably be less effective, though not completely useless.[48] The best approach would likely be to isolate specific factors—leaders' experience of formative events, for instance, or variation in the form of received information among leaders—that are hypothesized to cause some of these biases, such as the perseverance of beliefs in the face of disconfirming evidence.[49]

Organization Theory and The Conduct of War

Like cognitive psychology, organization theory is built on a set of assumptions that might be inconsistent with the unitary, rationalist assumptions of some versions of the bargaining model. Beliefs about preferences and capabilities in particular are filtered through organizations, frequently militaries. This might introduce systematic biases into the formation and evolution of beliefs. Some have argued, for example, that militaries tend to view adversaries as intractably hostile, implying perhaps that military intelligence might not recognize actions intended to signal benign intent.[50] Intelligence failures and poor collaboration between civilian and military leadership might distort pre-war assessment of capabilities, in turn precluding the emergence of a war-avoiding bargain.[51] Further, the rigidities of their organizational culture and beliefs might prevent militaries from recognizing that a particular strategy is not working; failures on the battlefield might not cause militaries to help open bargaining space by downgrading their estimates of their own abilities.[52]

The question of organizational rigidity is something of a double-edged sword for the bargaining model, however. Too-rigid militaries may not recognize that they have overestimated their own capabilities and underestimated those of their adversary, so again, information may not be taken from battle outcomes to provide war-terminating bargaining space. Yet more-flexible militaries that recognize the underperformance of troops in the field may not be content to accept it; such militaries may be entrepreneurial, changing strategy and the application of technology so as to minimize disadvantages and maximize advantages as they appear.[53] The bargaining model seems to envision militaries as rather odd institutions: completely clear-sighted in terms of using information to recognize strengths and weaknesses, but too rigid to address revealed weaknesses or emphasize emerging strengths. . . .

How might variation in military entrepreneurship affect war outcomes? The straightforward argument is that entrepreneurship is positively correlated with victory. More adaptive militaries are more effective, maximizing their own strengths and their enemies' weaknesses. The bargaining model, however, would make two different predictions. First, *militaries with higher levels of entrepreneurship should fight longer wars*. If the capability of militaries changes from battle to battle, then this will slow the convergence of expectations necessary for war termination. Second, *states confident in the high levels of entrepreneurship of their militaries may find it more difficult to avoid war through bargaining*. Entrepreneurship makes militaries more effective, but this is relatively difficult to convey to adversaries (as opposed to the obvious advantage of possessing fleets of combat aircraft, for example). More generally, the bargaining model might simply incorporate entrepreneurship into its assumptions, accepting the simple premise that if states update their beliefs and settlement offers they ought also to update their military strategies—since, after all, strategy is strategic.

Organization theory might offer other critiques of the bargaining model beyond issues of the rigidity/entrepreneurship of militaries. Organizations use quantitative indicators to demonstrate success or failure: firms use profit statements, graduate programs use job placement rates, and so on. Existing versions of the bargaining model assume that two opposing militaries use the same metric to determine success and failure. For example, success might be measured by the acquisition of forts (as in the Smith/Stam model), so as one side gains forts from the other, the former experiences success and the latter experiences failure. However, in some conflicts, militaries may have different measures of success; two opposing sides could conceivably observe the same battle outcome with both concluding that they were successful, coming no closer to agreement on the eventual outcome of the war. This is one interpretation of the Vietnam War, as the United States sought to inflict North Vietnamese casualties (the infamous body count) and North Vietnam sought to inflict American casualties. The occurrence of combat and casualties on both sides caused each to conclude that it was doing well, perhaps delaying the termination of the war. Similarly, in 1812 Napoleon viewed the French capture of Moscow as a step toward victory, whereas Russian General Mikhail Kutuzov saw it as hastening French overextension and defeat, commenting when he ordered the retreat from Moscow that "Napoleon is a torrent which we are as yet unable to stem. Moscow will be the sponge that will suck him dry." Note that the bargaining model is not completely incapable of accounting for organizations drawing inferences. The Smith/Stam relaxation of the non-common priors assumption permits two sides to draw different inferences from the same event.[54]

A more common problem is when all actors within a single side do not agree on the actual metric of success—that is, no indicator is dominant. The army might focus on territory captured, the navy on enemy tonnage sunk, the air force on bombing sorties carried out, the foreign service on allies lined up, and so on.[55] Optimally, a clearheaded civilian leader will stay focused enough on the political stakes to identify which military means best advance political goals; but such a view may be overly optimistic.

Domestic Politics and The Formation of Preferences

The role of domestic politics in world affairs has dominated the past decade of international-relations research. How can domestic political factors fit into the bargaining model? Most applications of the bargaining model have treated states as unitary actors. One model has incorporated domestic politics by distinguishing among regime types, generating an array of theoretical predictions that account for a variety of apparently contradictory empirical findings—for instance, that democracies win wars but are especially prone to being challenged militarily.[56]

The bargaining model lends itself well to other applications of domestic politics. Within war, variations in regime type may encourage different bargaining strategies. If a belligerent perceives its democratic opponent as particularly vulnerable to costs, it may be encouraged to initiate a battle as a means of demonstrating its capacity to inflict costs—as was perhaps Iraq's intention when it launched a ground attack against coalition forces at Khafji in late January 1991, or as was probably North Vietnam's intention when it launched the Tet offensive in January 1968.[57] The timing of elections may also play a role, because when a nation suffers a battlefield defeat, its leader (especially if elected) may be pushed from office. This was Hitler's hope in March 1944, when he argued that a failure of the coming Allied invasion of France "would prevent Roosevelt from being reelected—with any luck he'd finish up in jail somewhere!"[58] Relatedly, change in leadership may be necessary to permit a war-ending convergence of expectations.[59]

Another cut on domestic politics and the bargaining model concerns the "gamble for resurrection." A state losing a war may adopt a new strategy—a gamble for resurrection—that might increase the chances of winning at the expense of also increasing the chances of decisive defeat. In and of itself, the gamble is a useful conceptual step forward for the bargaining model, as it to some extent endogenizes military strategy by allowing states to choose between a strategy with higher mean and lower variance of outcomes and one with lower mean and higher variance. In terms of domestic politics, one might expect that leaders more fearful of suffering moderate defeat—such as those in semi-repressive regimes, who might be executed or imprisoned as a result—to be more likely to gamble for resurrection than are other kinds of leaders, such as democratic or dictatorial leaders. Goemans describes the German offensives on the Western Front in the spring of 1918 as a gamble by the German leadership staking the captured conquests in the East to defeat France in the West and maintain its hold on power.[60]

Domestic-politics theories can produce a deeper critique of the bargaining model. A fundamental assumption of the bargaining model is that fighting itself, divorced from the political issues at stake, is intrinsically costly. That is why the model sees war as a puzzle: both sides are better off striking a political settlement instead of fighting to reach that same political settlement, as each side's net utility must reflect the political benefit of the deal minus the costs of fighting.

But some domestic-politics theories have posited that leaders may prefer fighting over reaching a settlement peacefully. They may engage in conflict to divert public concern from internal problems, rallying citizens around the flag to increase support of the leadership. The evidence of such dynamics in the United States is generally weak.[61] However, there is some evidence (although it is not entirely supportive) that other kinds of states, especially semi-democratic regimes and states undergoing partial democratization, may view fighting as intrinsically valuable. Leaders of newly emerging democracies may wish to solidify their hold on power through scapegoating and calls to nationalism. If one assumes that the actual experience of conflict with another nation—as opposed to the favorable resolution of a disputed issue—serves a leader's goals, a war-avoiding bargain may be impossible to reach. If internal political change is a principal path to war because it makes leaders prefer fighting, this undermines the contribution of the bargaining model, as it would be more important to think about the sources of preferences for war than to think about how disagreement about capabilities or resolve contribute to war.[62]

Constructivism

Constructivism, a theory that emphasizes the importance of intersubjective social factors in determining critical phenomena such as identity and interests, claims that war is best understood as a social convention determined and shaped by norms and culture, not as a rationalist choice reflecting costs and benefits. The fundamental causes of war, then, are best explored in light of factors like the nature of international culture (i.e., whether it fosters Hobbesian anarchy or Rousseauian cooperation) and more specific cultural factors, such as taboos on the use of nuclear weapons.[63]

Constructivism's hypothesis that practice generates interests may also be outside the bargaining model. The bargaining model proposes that a state's preferences, especially regarding what constitutes acceptable terms of peace in relation to expectations about the course of future costs and battle outcomes, are stable across the war. Constructivism might propose that the practice of violence could polarize these preferences, pushing states to make more extreme demands as the war proceeds and an image of the enemy as an intractably hostile barbarian becomes solidified. One hypothesis might be that particularly bloody wars are more likely to have extreme terms of settlement, because states hold out longer for better terms. Arguably, the intensity of combat during World War II in the Pacific may have pushed the United States to demand unconditional surrender.[64]

Constructivism also poses a deeper challenge to the bargaining model, again returning to the assumption that fighting is costly. Some strains of constructivism posit that fighting serves important social functions, principally the formation of group identity. The definition of self requires the definition of other, and, some argue, the essential nature of the relationship between self and other is competitive and ultimately conflictual.[65] Hence, states may seek war not just to acquire goods, but as an end in itself to generate and reinforce national identity. Not coincidentally, there is overlap between this perspective and diversionary logic.[66] Some argue that war defines gender roles by sharpening the social distinctions and functions of men and women.[67]

Interestingly, some constructivist propositions may fit into the bargaining-model framework. The bargaining model predicts that war may become more likely if the issue at stake is indivisible. Some items in international politics may be physically divisible, but discourse and culture may make them practically indivisible. By describing the city of Jerusalem as practically if not literally indivisible, constructivism may help explain why the Arab-Israeli conflict seems intractable. It may similarly shed light on the Indo-Pakistani conflict, describing Kashmir as having characteristics of indivisibility.[68]

References

Ambrose, Stephen E. 1994. *D-Day, June 6, 1944: The Climactic Battle of World War II.* New York: Simon and Schuster.

——— 1997. *Citizen Soldiers: The U.S. Army from the Normandy Beaches to the Bulge to the Surrender of Germany, June 7, 1944–May 7, 1945.* New York: Simon and Schuster.

Analysis of Factors That Have Influenced Outcomes of Battles and Wars. 1983. Dunn Loring, Va.: Historical Evaluation and Research Organization.

Baron, David P. 1991. "A spatial bargaining theory of government formation in parliamentary systems." *American Political Science Review* 85:1, 137–64.

Baum, Matthew A. 2002. "The constituent foundations of the rally-round-the-flag phenomenon." *International Studies Quarterly* 46:2, 263–98.

Bearce, David H., and Eric O'N. Fisher. 2002. "Economic geography, trade, and war." *Journal of Conflict Resolution* 46:3, 365–93.

Bennett, D. Scott, and Allan C. Stam III. 1996. "The duration of interstate wars, 1816–1985." *American Political Science Review* 90:2, 239–57.

Biddle, Stephen, and Robert Zirkle. 1996. "Technology, civil-military relations, and warfare in the developing world." *Journal of Strategic Studies* 19:2, 194–5.

Blainey, Geoffrey. 1973. *The Causes of War.* New York: Free Press.

Box-Steffensmeier, Janet M., Dan Reiter, and Christopher J.W. Zorn. 2002. Repeated events and international conflict. Presented at the annual meeting of the Midwest Political Science Association, Chicago, 25–27 April.

——— 2003. "Nonproportional hazards and event history analysis in international relations." *Journal of Conflict Resolution* 47:1, 33–53.

Brooks, Risa. 2000. "Institutions at the domestic and international nexus: The political-military origins of strategic integration, military effectiveness and war." Ph.D. diss., University of California, San Diego.

——— 2002. "Information, military institutions, and war." Unpublished paper, Northwestern University.

Bueno de Mesquita, Bruce. 1981. *The War Trap.* New Haven: Yale University Press.

Bueno de Mesquita, Bruce, James D. Morrow, Randolph M. Siverson, and Alastair Smith. 1999. "An institutional explanation of the democratic peace." *American Political Science Review* 93:4, 791–807.

Carrubba, Clifford J., and Craig Volden. 2000. "Coalitional politics and logrolling in legislative institutions." *American Journal of Political Science* 44:2, 261–77.

Cetinyan, Rupen. 2002. "Ethnic bargaining in the shadow of third-party intervention." *International Organization* 56:3, 645–77.

Clausewitz, Carl von. 1976. *On War.* Michael Howard and Peter Paret, eds. and trans. Princeton: Princeton University Press.

Colaresi, Michael, and William R. Thompson. 2002. "Hot spots or hot hands?: Serial crisis behavior, escalating risks, and rivalry." *Journal of Politics* 64:4, 1,175–98.

Cooter, Robert D., and Daniel L. Rubinfeld. 1989. "Economic analysis of legal disputes and their resolution." *Journal of Economic Literature* 27:3, 1,067–97.

Dassell, Kurt, and Eric Reinhardt. 1999. "Domestic strife and the initiation of violence at home and abroad." *American Journal of Political Science* 43:1, 56–85.

De Marchi, Scott, and Hein Goemans. 2001. "Bargaining and complex preferences: Examining the case of the Israeli electorate." Presented at the annual meeting of the American Political Science Association, San Francisco, 29 August– 2 September.

Dower, John W. 1986. *War without Mercy: Race and Power in the Pacific War.* New York: Pantheon.

Fearon, James D. 1995. "Rationalist explanations for war." *International Organization* 49:3, 379–414.

——— 1996. "Bargaining over objects that influence future bargaining power." Unpublished manuscript, Department of Political Science, University of Chicago.

——— 1998. "Bargaining, enforcement, and international cooperation." *International Organization* 52:2, 269–305.

Filson, Darren, and Suzanne Werner. 2002a. "Bargaining and fighting: The impact of regime type on war onset, duration, and outcomes." Unpublished manuscript, Emory University, Atlanta, Ga.

——— 2002b. "A bargaining model of war and peace: Anticipating the onset, duration, and outcome of war." *American Journal of Political Science* 46:4, 819–38.

Fischer, Fritz. 1967. *Germany's Aims in the First World War.* New York: Norton.

Fordham, Benjamin O. 2002. Another look at "Parties, Voters and the Use of Force Abroad." *Journal of Conflict Resolution* 46:4, 572–96.

Fortna, Page. "Scraps of paper?: Agreements and the durability of peace." *International Organization.* Forthcoming.

Frank, Richard B. 1999. *Downfall: The End of the Imperial Japanese Empire.* New York: Random House.

Garfinkel, Michelle R., and Stergios Skaperdas. 2000. "Conflict without misperceptions or incomplete information: How the future matters." *Journal of Conflict Resolution* 44:6, 793–807.

Garofano, John. 2002. "Tragedy or choice in Vietnam? Learning to think outside the archival box." *International Security* 26:4, 143–65.

Gartner, Scott Sigmund. 1992. "Strategic assessment in war: A bounded rationality model of how organizations evaluate policy effectiveness." Ph.D. diss., University of Michigan.

——— 1997. *Strategic Assessment in War.* New Haven: Yale University Press.

Gartner, Scott Sigmund, and Gary Segura. 1998. "War, casualties, and public opinion." *Journal of Conflict Resolution* 42:3, 278–300.

Gartzke, Erik. 1999. "War is in the error term." *International Organization* 52:3, 567–87.

Giangreco, D.M. 1997. "Casualty projections for the U.S. invasions of Japan, 1945–1946: Planning and policy implications." *Journal of Military History* 61:3, 521–81.

Gleditsch, Kristian S., and Michael D. Ward. 2000. "War and peace in space and time: The role of democratization." *International Studies Quarterly* 44:1, 1–29.

Goddard, Stacie E. 2002. "A hard bargain: The dynamics of indivisible issues." Presented at the annual meeting of the International Studies Association, New Orleans, 24–27 March.

Goemans, H.E. 2000. *War and Punishment: The Causes of War Termination and the First World War.* Princeton: Princeton University Press.

Goldstein, Joshua S. 2001. *War and Gender: How Gender Shapes the War System and Vice Versa.* Cambridge: Cambridge University Press.

Gordon, Michael R., and Bernard E. Trainor. 1995. *The Generals' War: The Inside Story of the Conflict in the Gulf.* Boston: Little Brown.

Gowa, Joanne. 1998. "Politics at the water's edge: Parties, voters, and the use of force abroad." *International Organization* 52:2, 307–24.

Grieco, Joseph M. 2001. "Repetitive military challenges and recurrent international conflicts, 1918–1994." *International Studies Quarterly* 45:2, 295–316.

Guderian, Heinz. 1952. *Panzer Leader.* Constantine Fitzgibbon, trans. New York: E. P. Dutton.

Harrison, Mark. 1985. *Soviet Planning in Peace and War, 1938–1945.* Cambridge: Cambridge University Press.

Hopf, Ted. 1994. *Peripheral Visions: Deterrence Theory and American Foreign Policy in the Third World, 1965–1990.* Ann Arbor: University of Michigan Press.

——— 2002. *Social Construction of International Politics: Identities and Foreign Policies, Moscow, 1955 and 1999.* Ithaca: Cornell University Press.

Horowitz, Michael, and Dan Reiter. 2001. "When does aerial bombing work?: Quantitative empirical tests, 1917–1999." *Journal of Conflict Resolution* 45:2, 147–73.

Howard, Michael. 1983. *Clausewitz.* Oxford: Oxford University Press.

Huth, Paul, and Bruce Russett. 1990. "Testing deterrence theory: Rigor makes a difference." *World Politics* 42:4, 466–501.

Iklé, Fred Charles. 1991. *Every War Must End.* Revised ed. New York: Columbia University Press.

Jervis, Robert. 1976. *Perception and Misperception in International Politics.* Princeton: Princeton University Press.

——— 1978. "Cooperation under the security dilemma." *World Politics* 30:2, 167–214.

——— 1988. "Realism, game theory, and cooperation." *World Politics* 40:3, 317–49.

Jervis, Robert, Richard Ned Lebow, and Janice Gross Stein. 1985. *Psychology and Deterrence.* Baltimore: Johns Hopkins University Press.

John Endicott and Roy W. Stafford, Jr. Baltimore: Johns Hopkins University Press.

Karnow, Stanley. 1984. *Vietnam: A History.* New York: Penguin.

Katzenbach, Edward L., Jr. 1977. "The horse cavalry in the twentieth century." In *American Defense Policy.* 4th ed., eds. Katzenstein, Peter J., ed. 1996. *The Culture of National Security: Norms and Identity in World Politics.* New York: Columbia University Press.

Kaufmann, Chaim D. 1994. "Out of the lab and into the archives: A method for testing psychological explanations of political decision making." *International Studies Quarterly* 38:4, 557–86.

Kecskemeti, Paul. 1958. *Strategic Surrender: The Politics of Victory and Defeat.* Stanford: Stanford University Press.

Keegan, John. 1999. *The First World War.* New York: Knopf.

Kennan, John, and Robert Wilson. 1993. "Bargaining with private information." *Journal of Economic Literature* 31:1, 45–104.

Keohane, Robert O. 1984. *After Hegemony: Cooperation and Discord in the World Political Economy.* Princeton: Princeton University Press.

Khong, Yuen Foong. 1992. *Analogies at War: Korea, Munich, Dien Bien Phu, and the Vietnam Decisions of 1965.* Princeton: Princeton University Press.

Kier, Elizabeth. 1997. *Imagining War: French and British Military Doctrine Between the Wars.* Princeton: Princeton University Press.

Kinsella, David, and Bruce Russett. 2002. "Conflict emergence and escalation in interactive international dyads." *Journal of Politics* 64:4, 1,045–68.

Kirshner, Jonathan. 2000. "Rationalist explanations for wars?" *Security Studies* 10:1, 143–50.

Koremenos, Barbara, Charles Lipson, and Duncan Snidal. 2001. "The rational design of international institutions." *International Organization* 55:4, 761–99.

Labs, Eric J. 1997. "Beyond victory: Offensive realism and the expansion of war aims." *Security Studies* 6:4, 1–49.

Lai, Brian. 2001. "Military mobilization and the escalation and outcome of international crises." Ph.D. diss., Emory University.

Larson, Deborah Welch. 1985. *Origins of Containment: A Psychological Explanation.* Princeton: Princeton University Press, 1985.

Lebow, Richard Ned. 1981. *Between Peace and War: The Nature of International Crisis.* Baltimore: Johns Hopkins University Press.

Legro, Jeffrey. 1995. *Cooperation Under Fire: Anglo-German Restraint During World War II.* Ithaca: Cornell University Press.

Lepgold, Joseph, and Brent L. Sterling. 2000. "When do states fight limited wars?: Political risk, policy risk, and policy choice." *Security Studies* 9:4, 127–66.

Levy, Jack S. 1989. "The diversionary theory of war: A critique." In *Handbook of War Studies,* ed. Manus I. Midlarsky. Boston: Unwin Hyman, 259–88.

Liberman, Peter. 1996. *Does Conquest Pay?: The Exploitation of Occupied Industrial Societies.* Princeton: Princeton University Press.

Long, Ngo Vinh. 1996. "The Tet offensive and its aftermath." In *The Tet Offensive,* eds. Marc Jason Gilbert and William Head. Westport, Conn.: Praeger, 89–123.

MacEachin, Douglas J. 1998. *The Final Months of the War with Japan: Signals Intelligence, U.S. Invasion Planning, and the A-Bomb Decision.* Washington, D.C.: Center for the Study of Intelligence.

Mansfield, Edward D., and Jack Snyder. 2002. "Democratic transitions, institutional strength, and war." *International Organization* 56:2, 297–337.

May, Ernest R. 2000. *Strange Victory: Hitler's Conquest of France.* New York: Hill and Wang.

McPherson, James M. 1988. *Battle Cry of Freedom: The Civil War Era.* Oxford: Oxford University Press.

Meernik, James. 2001. "Domestic politics and the political use of military force by the United States." *Political Research Quarterly* 54:4, 889–904.

Mercer, Jonathan. 1995. "Anarchy and identity." *International Organization* 49:2, 229–52.

——— 1996. *Reputation and International Politics.* Ithaca: Cornell University Press.

Mitchell, Sara McLaughlin, and Will H. Moore. 2002. "Presidential uses of force during the Cold War: Aggregation, truncation, and temporal dynamics." *American Political Science Review* 46:2, 438–52.

Morgan, Patrick M. 1977. *Deterrence: A Conceptual Analysis.* Beverly Hills, Calif.: Sage.

Morgan, T. Clifton. 1984. "A spatial model of crisis bargaining." *International Studies Quarterly* 28:4, 407–26.

Morrow, James D. 1986. "A spatial model of international conflict." *American Political Science Review* 80:4, 1,131–50.

——— 1989. "Capabilities, uncertainty, and resolve: A limited information model of crisis bargaining." *American Journal of Political Science* 33:4, 941–72.

Mueller, John E. 1980. "The search for the "breaking point" in Vietnam: The statistics of a deadly quarrel." *International Studies Quarterly* 24:4, 497–519.

Murray, Williamson. 1981. "The German response to victory in Poland: A case study in professionalism." *Armed Forces and Society* 7:2, 285–98.

Nicolson, Nigel. 1985. *Napoleon 1812.* New York: Harper and Row.

Oren, Michael B. 2002. *Six Days of War: June 1967 and the Making of the Modern Middle East.* Oxford: Oxford University Press.

Osgood, Robert. 1957. *Limited War: The Challenge to American Strategy.* Chicago: University of Chicago Press.

Pape, Robert A. 1996. *Bombing to Win: Air Power and Coercion in War.* Ithaca: Cornell University Press.

Perkins, Bradford. 1993. *The Cambridge History of American Foreign Relations, Volume 1: The Creation of a Republican Empire, 1776–1865.* Cambridge: Cambridge University Press.

Pillar, Paul R. 1983. *Negotiating Peace: War Termination as a Bargaining Process.* Princeton: Princeton University Press.

Posen, Barry. 1984. *The Sources of Military Doctrine: France, Britain, and Germany between the World Wars.* Ithaca: Cornell University Press.

Powell, Robert. 1990. *Nuclear Deterrence Theory: The Search for Credibility.* New York: Cambridge University Press.

——— 1999. *In the Shadow of Power: States and Strategies in International Politics.* Princeton: Princeton University Press.

——— 2002a. "Bargaining and learning while fighting over the distribution of power." Unpublished manuscript, Berkeley, Calif.

——— 2002b. "Bargaining theory and international conflict." *Annual Review of Political Science* 5, 1–30.

Reed, William. 2002. "Power, information, and militarized conflict." Unpublished manuscript, Houston, Tex.

——— 2003. "Information and economic interdependence." *Journal of Conflict Resolution* 47:1.

Reed, William, and Wonjae Hwang. 2002. "Endogenous demands and militarized conflict." Unpublished manuscript, Houston, Tex.

Reiter, Dan. 1995. "Exploding the powder keg myth: Preemptive wars almost never happen." *International Security* 20:2, 5–34.

——— 1996. *Crucible of Beliefs: Learning, Alliances, and World Wars.* Ithaca: Cornell University Press.

Reiter, Dan, and Allan C. Stam. 2002. *Democracies at War.* Princeton: Princeton University Press.

Rhodes, Richard. 1986. *The Making of the Atomic Bomb.* New York: Simon and Schuster.

Rosen, Steven. 1972. "War power and the willingness to suffer." In *Peace, War, and Numbers,* ed. Bruce Russett. Beverly Hills, Calif.: Sage, 167–83.

Russett, Bruce, and John R. Oneal. 2001. *Triangulating Peace: Democracy, Interdependence, and International Organizations.* New York: Norton.

Schelling, Thomas C. 1960. *The Strategy of Conflict.* Cambridge: Harvard University Press.

——— 1966. *Arms and Influence.* New Haven: Yale University Press.

Schultz, Kenneth A. 2001. *Democracy and Coercive Diplomacy.* Cambridge: Cambridge University Press.

Shimshoni, Jonathan. 1990–91. "Technology, military advantage, and World War I: A case for military entrepreneurship." *International Security* 15:3, 187–215.

Sills, David L., ed. 1968. *International Encyclopedia of the Social Sciences.* New York: MacMillan.

Slantchev, Branislav. 2001. "The power to hurt: Costly conflict with completely informed states." Presented at the annual meeting of the Peace Science Society, 26–28 October, Atlanta, Ga.

Smith, Alastair. 1998. "Fighting battles, winning wars." *Journal of Conflict Resolution* 42:3, 301–20.

Smith, Alastair, and Allan C. Stam. 2002. "Bargaining and the nature of war." Unpublished manuscript, New York University.

Smith, J. Maynard. 1974. "The theory of games and the evolution of animal conflicts." *Journal of Theoretical Biology* 47:1, 209–21.

Snyder, Glenn. 1961. *Deterrence and Defense: Toward a Theory of National Security.* Princeton: Princeton University Press.

Snyder, Jack. 1984. *The Ideology of the Offensive: Military Decision Making and the Disasters of 1914.* Ithaca: Cornell University Press.

——— 2000. *From Voting to Violence: Democratization and Nationalist Conflict.* New York: Norton.

——— 2002. "Anarchy and culture: Insights from the anthropology of war." *International Organization* 56:1, 7–45.

Stam, Allan C., III. 1996. *Win, Lose, or Draw: Domestic Politics and the Crucible of War.* Ann Arbor: University of Michigan Press.

Stanley-Mitchell, Elizabeth. 2002. "Working out the inevitable: Chinese, Soviet, and U.S. decisions to end the Korean War." Unpublished manuscript, Washington, D.C.

Toft, Monica Duffy. 2002. "Indivisible territory and ethnic war." *Security Studies.* Forthcoming.

Van Evera, Stephen. 1999. *Causes of War: Power and the Roots of Conflict.* Ithaca: Cornell University Press.

Wagner, R. Harrison. 2000. "Bargaining and war." *American Journal of Political Science* 44:3, 469–84.

Walt, Stephen M. 1999. "Rigor or rigor mortis?: Rational choice and security studies." *International Security* 25:4, 5–48.

Walter, Barbara F. 2002. "Reputation and war: Explaining the intractability of territorial conflict." Presented at the annual meeting of the International Studies Association, New Orleans, 24–27 March.

Waltz, Kenneth N. 1979. *Theory of International Politics.* New York: Random House.

Wendt, Alexander. 1999. *Social Theory of International Politics.* Cambridge: Cambridge University Press.

Werner, Suzanne. 1998. "Negotiating the terms of settlement: War aims and bargaining leverage." *Journal of Conflict Resolution* 42:2, 321–43.

——— 1999a. "Choosing demands strategically: The distribution of power, the distribution of benefits, and the risk of conflict." *Journal of Conflict Resolution* 43:6, 705–26.

——— 1999b. "The precarious nature of peace: Resolving the issues, enforcing the settlement, and renegotiating the terms." *American Journal of Political Science* 43:3, 912–34.

——— 2000. "Deterring intervention: The stakes of war and third-party involvement." *American Journal of Political Science* 44:4, 720–32.

Wittman, Donald. 1979. "How a war ends: A rational model approach." *Journal of Conflict Resolution* 23:4, 743–63.

——— 2001. "War or peace?" Unpublished manuscript, University of California, Santa Cruz, Calif.

Zartman, I. William. 1989. *Ripe for Resolution: Conflict and Intervention in Africa.* New York: Oxford University Press.

Notes

1. Sills 1968, 472.
2. Kennan and Wilson 1993, 45.
3. Cooter and Rubinfeld 1989.

4. See Baron 1991; Carrubba and Volden 2000.
5. Waltz 1979.
6. This is known as the security dilemma. Jervis 1978.
7. Fearon 1998.
8. See Koremenos, Lipson, and Snidal 2001.
9. Clausewitz 1976, 87.
10. See Kaufmann 1994; Osgood 1957.
11. Schelling 1960, 5.
12. Kecskemeti 1958; Iklé 1991 (revised edition), vii for "agonizing search" quotation. Pillar 1983 informally applied a bargaining framework to war termination.
13. Blainey 1973; Rosen 1972.
14. Bueno de Mesquita 1981.
15. Bueno de Mesquita 1981; Morgan 1984; Morrow 1986; Morrow 1989; Powell 1990; Fearon 1995. A review of this literature is Powell 2002b.
16. See the discussion in Wagner 2000. For other examples of costly lottery models, see Bueno de Mesquita et al. 1999; Garfinkel and Skaperdas 2000; Bearce and Fisher 2002. Of course, not everyone before 1995 conceptualized war as a costly lottery. Three exceptions are Rosen 1972, Pillar 1983, and Wittman 1979.
17. Fearon 1995.
18. Gartzke 1999; Powell 2002b.
19. Guderian 1952, 190.
20. Wittman 2001; Reed 2002; Reed 2003.
21. Powell 1990; Fearon 1995.
22. Oren 2002; Lai 2001; Van Evera 1999.
23. Powell 1999; Fearon 1995.
24. In some models, the good need only be discretely divisible (as opposed to being continuously divisible) to prevent a bargain from being struck.
25. Goddard 2002; Walter 2002; Toft 2002; de Marchi and Goemans 2001.
26. Clausewitz 1976, 75, 127.
27. Clausewitz 1976; Wagner 2000; Howard 1983.
28. See also Osgood 1957, 1–2.
29. Kecskemeti 1958; Frank 1999; Keegan 1999, 418; McPherson 1988, 849.
30. Schelling 1966, 2–6; see also Snyder 1961.
31. Wagner 2000.
32. Rosen 1972, 183. See also Goemans 2000; Lepgold and Sterling 2000.
33. Wittman 1979.
34. Filson and Werner 2002b; Smith and Stam 2002. Realism proposes that militarily successful belligerents will expand their war aims. Labs 1997, esp. 19.
35. MacEachin 1998; Giangreco 1997.
36. See Powell 1990; Powell 2002a; Slantchev 2001.
37. Zartman 1989; Stam 1996; Smith 1974. There is a small amount of empirical evidence on this point, and it is mixed. Gartner and Segura 1998, for example, found that American opposition to war during the Korean and Vietnam Wars was driven both by the cumulative casualties suffered and by casualties recently suffered, the latter of which might be an indicator of expectations of likely future costs.
38. Pape 1996, 342–3.
39. Werner 1999b.
40. Smith and Stam 2002.
41. Huth and Russett 1990, 469–70. See also Morgan 1977; Jervis 1976.
42. Wittman 2001; Reed 2002.
43. Jervis 1976.
44. Powell 1999.
45. Fearon 1995. However, preemptive wars almost never happen; see Reiter 1995.
46. Lebow 1981; Jervis et al. 1985; Jervis 1976; Larson 1985; Mercer 1996; Hopf 1994.
47. See Kecskemeti 1958, 19–20; Iklé 1991, 96–7.
48. Some have argued, though, that deterrence essentially never succeeds. See Lebow 1981.
49. See Jervis 1976; Reiter 1996; Khong 1992; Kaufmann 1994.
50. Snyder 1984; Posen 1984.
51. Brooks 2002.
52. Legro 1995; Katzenbach 1977; Kier 1997; Gartner 1997.
53. Shimshoni 1990/91.
54. Gartner 1992; Kutuzov quoted in Nicolson 1985, 88; Smith and Stam 2002.
55. Iklé 1991, 96–7.
56. Filson and Werner 2002a.
57. Gordon and Trainor 1995, 267–88; Long 1996.
58. Quoted in Ambrose 1994, 29.
59. Stanley-Mitchell 2002.
60. Goemans 2000; Fischer 1967, 609.
61. See Gowa 1998; Fordham 2002; Baum 2002; Meernik 2001; Mitchell and Moore 2002; Levy 1989.
62. Dassell and Reinhardt 1999; Snyder 2000; Mansfield and Snyder 2002; Russett and Oneal 2001, chapter 3; Gleditsch and Ward 2000.
63. Wendt 1999; Katzenstein 1996; Hopf 2002. Note that there are important differences among constructivists.
64. Dower 1986. Settlements become more extreme as battle deaths increase; see Werner 1998.
65. Mercer 1995; Wendt 1999, 274–78; Snyder 2002.
66. A point recognized in Wendt 1999, 275.
67. Goldstein 2001.
68. Goddard 2002.

14.2

Afghan Peace Talks

A Primer

James Shinn and James Dobbins

The overarching American objective in Afghanistan should not simply be to prevent that country from becoming a haven for transnational terrorists but also to prevent it from becoming a terrorist ally. Prior to the attacks of September 11, 2001, Afghanistan was both a haven for and an ally of terrorists, and it would be so again if the Taliban returned to power with Al Qaeda backing. The United States can prevent this indefinitely as long as it is willing to commit significant military and economic resources to a counterinsurgency effort. It cannot eliminate the threat, however, as long as the Afghan insurgents enjoy sanctuary in and support from Pakistan. The United States could also achieve its objective if the Taliban could be persuaded to cut ties with Al Qaeda and end its insurgency in exchange for some role in Afghan governance short of total control.

Peace negotiations would obviously be desirable if they could succeed in achieving this objective, but they are also worth pursuing even if they fail, as the risks associated with entering such a process may be greater for the insurgents than for the Afghan government and its allies. The Taliban leadership is fighting a jihad [holy war] with a view to reimposing a religiously based form of government rooted in an extreme interpretation of Islam. Engaging in negotiations for something short of that goal undercuts the purity of that message. The Kabul regime, in contrast, is fighting for representative government (as well as its own survival and hold on power), and it is prepared to accept insurgent participation in government in some capacity if the insurgents lay down their arms. Opinion polling shows both overwhelming support within Afghan society for a negotiated settlement and a willingness to bring the Taliban back into the fold in something short of a dominant position. So, negotiating the terms of that entry with the Taliban is in no way inconsistent with the cause that the Kabul government espouses.

These considerations help explain why President Hamid Karzai, President Barack Obama, and leaders of other North Atlantic Treaty Organization (NATO) member countries have, in principle, endorsed peace negotiations while the insurgent leadership has remained much more circumspect. Nevertheless, conversations between a number of independent observers (including the authors) on one hand and Taliban representatives and those close to them on the other indicate serious insurgent interest in the possibility of a negotiated settlement. The recent death of Osama Bin Laden may help motivate Taliban leaders in two respects: first, making them more anxious about their own security and, second, perhaps removing whatever personal link there may have been between those leaders and Bin Laden. The latter may make it easier for the Taliban leaders to cut their remaining ties to Al Qaeda, a key American and NATO demand.

Getting the Afghan parties together is a necessary but not sufficient condition for a meaningful peace process. Afghanistan is a weak country surrounded by stronger neighbors. Historically, it has been at peace when its neighbors perceive a common interest in keeping that peace but at war—civil war—when one or more of those neighbors sees some advantage therein. Over the past 30 years, India, Iran, Pakistan, Russia, Saudi Arabia, and the United States have successfully supported insurgencies designed to overthrow the regime in Kabul. At present, it is Pakistan (and, to a much lesser degree, Iran) that is affording shelter and support to such an insurgency. Afghanistan will not be at peace until the governments of all of these countries see a common interest in that peace. To succeed, any

Source: James Shinn and James Dobbins. "Summary," in *Afghan Peace Talks: A Primer*, ix–xvi.

peace process must therefore include these countries in some fashion.

Close examination reveals that the priorities of all the potential parties to an Afghan peace process overlap to a considerable degree. For instance, each desires a withdrawal of Western armed forces—a situation especially desired by the publics in all of the Western countries. All Afghans want foreigners to stop interfering in their affairs. All foreign governments want assurances that Afghan territory will not be used to their disadvantage, whether by third parties or the Afghans themselves, and thus want to ensure that terrorists hostile to their countries cannot use Afghanistan as a sanctuary. Interests diverge less in the area of outcomes than in the area of timing. Western governments, under pressure from voters, want to withdraw NATO forces from Afghanistan (or at least from combat there) sooner rather than later, a preference shared by the Taliban leadership. Most other potential participants, including the Kabul government, are not in such a rush. Indeed, continuation of the current conflict, with the United States tied down and neither side able to prevail, is acceptable to most regional governments and, for Iran, probably optimal.

Negotiation among the Afghans will focus on the nature of any power-sharing arrangement, on possible modifications to the existing constitution, on social norms, and on the role of sharia law. Given the excessively centralized nature of the current Afghan government, it is not impossible that negotiations might actually lead to some improvement, via devolution, in subnational governance, although this would require both the Taliban leadership and the Kabul regime to alter their historical preference for a unitary, Kabul-centric system.

The American objective in these negotiations should be a stable and peaceful Afghanistan that neither hosts nor collaborates with international terrorists. Only to the extent that other issues impinge on this objective should American negotiators be drawn into a discussion of Afghanistan's social or constitutional issues. That qualification is significant, however, because constitutional issues will certainly affect Afghanistan's stability, as may social provisions if they are likely to antagonize influential elements of the population. In the end, however, the country's form of government and codes of behavior are preeminently of interest to the Afghans. Americans and other international actors should have some confidence that a reasonably representative Afghan government delegation will not stray far from the desires of its population, the overwhelming majority of whom are strongly opposed to a return of an Islamic emirate and desirous of retaining the many social and material gains most of them have made since 2001.

American and European opinion is, nevertheless, likely to be particularly sensitive to the issues of civil society and the role of women. However, the elements of Western society most concerned about such issues are also, in general, those least supportive of continued military engagement and thus the most likely to support unilateral steps that will reduce the negotiating leverage of both Washington and Kabul. This will lead to considerable dissonance in Western attitudes toward an enfolding peace process.

Other actors are likely to experience even greater dissonance. Neither the Kabul regime nor the Taliban is a well-integrated polity with a clear and reasonably unified sense of its respective interests and goals, Pakistani society may be even more divided than Afghan society, and the government in Islamabad often seems even less coherent than the one in Kabul, since the Pakistani political leadership and military establishment are autonomous actors with quite divergent priorities regarding domestic and foreign militancy and an Afghan settlement. Historically, the Pakistani military has employed militant groups and terrorism as instruments of policy. The country's civilian leadership seems convinced that this distinction between "good" and "bad" militants cannot be sustained now that the latter threaten the viability of the country's democracy. In contrast, the Pakistani military does not yet seem ready to cut ties with the terrorist groups with which it has long been associated. One of the main obstacles to any negotiated settlement will be getting the respective parties in Islamabad (and elsewhere) to decide what they really want and what they are willing to trade for it.

Herding such cats will strain the capacity of even the most skilled statesmen. As by far the most powerful and influential participant, the United States will have to play a leading role in this effort. But the United States is also one of the main protagonists in this conflict and therefore not in the best position to mediate. We thus recommend that Washington work to secure the appointment of a figure of international repute with the requisite impartiality, knowledge, contacts, and diplomatic skills to take charge of putting together and then orchestrating a multitiered negotiation process, one with the Afghans at its core as well as several concentric rings of regional and other interested governments actively but quietly engaged on the periphery.

Signaling and timing obviously matter a great deal in any peace process. The United States is due to begin withdrawing troops in mid-2011, and, with this withdrawal, its leverage in any negotiation will slowly diminish. Of all the possible major participants, therefore, the United States is likely to feel the greatest sense of urgency. Yet, its prospects of getting an acceptable agreement depend heavily on it not *needing* one. Only if Washington has an acceptable non-negotiated outcome in prospect will American diplomats have much chance of securing their negotiating objectives. This uncomfortable paradox accounts for much of the dissent and confusion in the American domestic debate on strategy in Afghanistan.

American policymakers must prepare for two futures: one negotiated, one not. Both must meet its bottom-line need to prevent Afghanistan from falling into the hands of an Al Qaeda—linked regime. This means preparing both to stay indefinitely and to go definitively. If negotiations fail, some level of American military engagement will probably be necessary well beyond the 2014 date by which President Obama has promised to remove all American combat forces. On the other hand, the full withdrawal of American troops from the country by some not-so-distant date is probably a necessary component of any peace deal. In bargaining terms, promising to leave is the American counterpart to the Taliban's commitment to cut its ties with Al Qaeda. Troubling as Americans may find this symmetry, these potential concessions represent each side's highest cards and are thus likely to be played only at the culmination of any negotiation process. Indeed, they will probably be essential to closing any deal.

It is thus perfectly reasonable for Washington and Kabul to be negotiating, as they are, the text of a long-term strategic partnership that involves an enduring military component. Without the prospect of such an enduring American presence, the Taliban would have little incentive to negotiate rather than just wait the United States and NATO out. On the other hand, American and Afghan officials should also be making clear, at least privately and perhaps publicly, that any such accord between Kabul and Washington is subject to amendment, depending on the outcome of a peace process and its successful implementation.

Just as the United States is poorly placed to broker a peace settlement, it will also require third-party assistance in overseeing the implementation of an accord, particularly one that calls for the withdrawal of American forces. The disarmament, demobilization, and reintegration of Afghan forces will be an essential element of any peace agreement. Given that there are between 25,000 and 35,000 insurgents but more than 250,000 Afghan army and police—a number far in excess of what the country will be able to afford or that donors will fund once the fighting ceases—the demobilization of government forces is likely to be even more demanding and certainly more expensive than the demobilization of the insurgents.[1] Indeed, some of the insurgents will probably have to be integrated into the government forces even as the total number of government forces is brought down. This will make it all the more important that those being marshaled out receive generous severance packages and some prospect of subsequent employment.

Of course, the United States will want to phase the implementation of any accord so that the removal of American forces occurs at the end of the process, by which time much of this local demobilization should be in train. The United States will also, as will be appropriate, insist that, before a full American departure, the Taliban completely break with Al Qaeda and other terrorist networks, evidence of which will be both (1) the Taliban's surrender of all its non-Afghan terrorist leaders still enjoying its hospitality and (2) its agreement to suitable means of verifying that these leaders are not invited back.

Even assuming such sequencing, the implementation of a peace accord will require a level of mutual trust likely to be absent on both sides. Additionally, whenever American and NATO troops do ultimately depart, they will leave behind something of a power vacuum. It will be important, therefore, to identify during the negotiating process some follow-on international presence, military as well as political, that can oversee the process of implementation. This presence need not be powerful enough to compel adherence (something even the United States and NATO have not been strong enough to do), but it should be sufficiently robust to deal with marginal spoilers and to set a high threshold for evasion by any party of its undertakings. This is a role that United Nations peacekeeping forces have successfully played in many other such circumstances, so that organization is the logical candidate to deploy a post-peace agreement force into Afghanistan.

Iraq is an inexact parallel to Afghanistan, but several components of any peaceful solution in the latter are likely to be similar to those employed in the former. First, the United States will have to tolerate—indeed, seek to broker—the inclusion of former insurgents in an enlarged coalition government. Second, the United States will have to promise to "go home," withdrawing its remaining combat forces on a fixed, mutually agreed schedule. Third, Washington will need to remain heavily engaged in the implementation of whatever accord is reached. . . .

Note

1. Number of insurgents according to an Afghan Defense Ministry spokesman ("Up to 35,000 Insurgents Active in Afghanistan: Officials," *Peoples Daily Online,* February 9, 2011); number of Afghan army and police according to a NATO news release (North Atlantic Treaty Organization, "Afghan National Security Forces (ANSF)," media backgrounder, March 2011).

14.3

It's Time for America to Negotiate With the Taliban

David Rohde

As American officials scramble to contain the fallout from an appalling video showing Marines urinating on dead Taliban fighters, news that the Obama administration is carrying out secret negotiations with the Taliban has barely registered on the American political landscape. The lack of interest in the talks—and public outrage at the video—reflects how little Americans apparently care about the conflict, despite its staggering human and fiscal cost.

Since 2001, the war in Afghanistan has killed at least 8,000 Afghan civilians, 5,500 Afghan police and soldiers, 1,800 American soldiers and 900 soldiers from other nations.

Thousands of Taliban fighters have died as well, according to American military estimates, but no reliable figure exists. While suffering heavy casualties in set-piece battles, the Taliban have excelled at suicide attacks, roadside bombs and propaganda that portrays American forces as abusive occupiers. The video showing Marines urinating on Taliban corpses—a hugely offensive act to Muslims and a potential war crime—will only reinforce that image. . . .

The United States, meanwhile, has spent $345 billion in Afghanistan over the last decade, with the overwhelming majority funding U.S. military operations, not imperative but largely overlooked civilian aid efforts. The war in Iraq, by comparison, cost almost twice as much, $673 billion, and featured the same sweeping focus on military efforts.

Across the political spectrum in Washington, there is little interest in engaging with the difficult but vital questions of the post-Arab spring. How can the U.S. devise ways to more consistently, quietly and effectively back moderate Muslims? Calls from the far left and far right for completely disengaging from the Greater Middle East are a fantasy. For decades to come, the American and world economies will rely on the region's oil.

And when it comes to Afghanistan, few are bothered by how America leaves. They just want it to happen quickly.

Opposition to the Iraq war made it chic for Democrats to be isolationist. Liberals who defend human rights glibly dismiss Afghanistan as nothing more than a quagmire. There is little acknowledgement of the gains Afghan moderates and women have made over the past decade, or the brutal payback a triumphant Taliban could mete out against them.

On the usually martial right, the Republican Party is split. John Huntsman and Ron Paul want an immediate pullout. Newt Gingrich has flip-flopped. And front-runner Mitt Romney opposes talks of any kind.

Romney is wrong. The chances of success are low, but given tepid American public support for the war, talking to the Taliban is the right step.

By any measure, many Taliban are reprehensible. They brutally ruled Afghanistan in the 1990s and sheltered Osama bin Laden and Al Qaeda members as they planned the 9/11 attacks. According to the latest United Nations figures, Taliban attacks—primarily suicide and roadside bombings—caused 80 percent of the 1,462 civilian deaths in Afghanistan in the first half of 2011.

Over the past decade, they have assassinated hundreds of moderate Afghans who were trying to stabilize the country. They have also kidnapped scores of Afghans and foreigners, including myself and two Afghan colleagues held captive for seven months in 2008 and 2009.

I despised the Taliban faction that kidnapped us—the Haqqani network—and saw them as criminals masquerading as a pious religious movement. Nonetheless, I believe negotiations represent a chance to split more moderate Taliban from hard-core supporters of Al Qaeda. If the Taliban refuse to compromise, exposing that grim truth will be valuable as well.

Obama administration officials emphasize that their goal is not a Treaty of Versailles-like agreement that will bring full-blown peace to Afghanistan. Instead, it is to begin a series of talks that might gradually reduce the overall level of violence in the country.

Source: David Rohde. "Talk to the Taliban" from reuters.com, January 12, 2012 Issue.

The latest opinion polls show that the American public has largely given up on the war. The central question, of course, is whether the Taliban have tired of the conflict as well. Despite claims that it had little effect, the Obama military surge weakened the Taliban and drove them from their strongholds in southern Afghanistan.

. . . The key remains the Pakistani military. As long as Pakistan's generals continue their foolhardy policy of backing the Afghan Taliban as proxies to counter Indian encroachment in Afghanistan, no American military victory is possible. Today, the Afghan Taliban are waiting out the Obama surge in their safe havens in Pakistan. Involving the Pakistani military in the talks is critical.

"I waited for the surge, I waited to see what would happen," Fariba Nawa, an Afghan American journalist and the author of the book "Opium Nation," told me last week. "But now Pakistan has won the war."

Nawa voiced the fear, anguish and despair of many Afghan moderates, who find themselves trapped between brutal Taliban, the erratic government of Afghan president Hamid Karzai, disingenuous Pakistani generals and shortsighted American political jockeying. Obama's promise to withdraw most American forces by the end of 2014, while popular in the U.S., signaled to the Taliban and their Pakistani military patrons that America is desperate for a way out.

Completing negotiations with Karzai on the level of American forces post-2014 would improve the chances of successful talks. Showing that the United States will train and fund Afghan security forces for years to come could help bring the Taliban seriously to the table. It will also show that Afghans must lead the fight now, not Americans.

At the same time, it is vital for understandably frustrated Americans not to see the mercurial Karzai as all of Afghanistan. The end of Karzai's second term in 2014—and promised departure from office—presents an opportunity. After a disjointed Bush administration effort and hugely expensive but brief Obama administration effort, the U.S. should try to do less over a longer period in Afghanistan. Throwing up our hands and completely walking away will haunt us for years.

Protecting Afghan moderates should be the bottom line of American negotiators. If the Taliban refuse to make concessions, the talks should be allowed to fail.

Across the region, the negotiations will be viewed as a measure of American reliability, practicality and respect for the enormous price moderate Muslims are paying in the struggle against extremism. Americans may no longer care, but our present and future Muslim allies are watching.

15 Theories of Democracy and War

15.1

The Fact of Democratic Peace

Bruce Russett

We have no quarrel with the German people. . . . It was not upon their impulse that their government acted in entering this war. It was not with their previous knowledge or approval. It was a war determined upon as wars used to be determined upon in the old unhappy days when peoples were nowhere consulted by their rulers and wars were provoked and waged in the interest of dynasties or of little groups of ambitious men who were accustomed to use their fellow men as pawns and tools. Self-governed nations do not fill their neighbor states with spies or set the course of intrigue to bring about some critical posture of affairs which will give them an opportunity to strike and make conquest. . . . Cunningly contrived plans of deception or aggression, carried, it may be from generation to generation, can be worked out and kept from the light only within the privacy of courts or behind the carefully guarded confidences of a narrow and privileged class.

—Woodrow Wilson's war message to Congress, April 2, 1917

Scholars and leaders now commonly say, "Democracies almost never fight each other." What does that mean? Is it true? If so, what does it imply for the future of international politics? Would the continued advance of democracy introduce an era of relative world peace? Can policymakers act so as to make that kind of peaceful world more likely, and, if so, how? Does the post—Cold War era represent merely the passing of a particular adversarial relationship, or does it offer a chance for fundamentally changed relations among nations? . . .

To the degree that countries once ruled by autocratic systems become democratic, a striking fact about the world comes to bear on any discussion of the future of international relations: in the modern international system, democracies have almost never fought each other. This statement represents a complex phenomenon: (a) Democracies rarely fight each other (an empirical statement) because (b) they have other means of resolving conflicts between them and therefore do not need to fight each other (a prudential statement), and (c) they believe that democracies should not fight each other (a normative statement about principles of right behavior), which reinforces the empirical statement. By this reasoning, the more democracies there are in the world, the fewer potential adversaries we and other democracies will have and the wider the zone of peace.

The vision of a peace among democratically governed states has long been invoked as part of a larger structure of institutions and practices to promote peace among nation-states. Immanuel Kant (1970) spoke of

Source: Bruce Russett. "The Fact of the Democratic Peace" and "Why the Democratic Peace?" in *Grasping the Democratic Peace* Copyright 1993 Princeton: Princeton University Press. Reprinted by permission of Princeton University Press.

perpetual peace based partially upon states sharing "republican constitutions." His meaning was compatible with basic contemporary understandings of democracy. As the elements of such a constitution he identified freedom (with legal equality of subjects), representative government, and separation of powers. The other key elements of his perpetual peace were "cosmopolitan law" embodying ties of international commerce and free trade, and a "pacific union" established by treaty in international law among republics.

Woodrow Wilson expressed the same vision for the twentieth century. This normative political basis of Wilson's vision of world order, evident as early as 1894, grew naturally from his progressive inclinations in domestic politics (Knock 1992, 9ff.); and his Fourteen Points sound almost as though Kant were guiding Wilson's writing hand. They included Kant's cosmopolitan law and pacific union. The third point demanded "the removal, so far as possible, of all economic barriers and the establishment of an equality of trade conditions among all the nations consenting to the peace and associating themselves for its maintenance"; and the fourteenth point called for "a general association of nations . . . formed under specific covenants for the purpose of affording mutual guarantees of political dependence and territorial integrity to great and small states alike." He did not so clearly invoke the need for universal democracy, since at that time not all of America's war allies were democracies. But the suggestion of this principle is clear enough if one thinks about the domestic political conditions necessary for his first point: "Open covenants of peace, openly arrived at, after which there shall be no private international understandings of any kind but diplomacy shall proceed always frankly and in the public view." Moreover, his 1917 war message openly asserted that "a steadfast concert of peace can never be maintained except by a partnership of democratic nations." . . .

Democracy, War, and Other Ambiguous Terms

This [reading] will establish the following:

1. Democratically organized political systems in general operate under restraints that make them more peaceful in their relations with other democracies. Democracies are not necessarily peaceful, however, in their relations with other kinds of political systems.
2. In the modern international system, democracies are less likely to use lethal violence toward other democracies than toward autocratically governed states or than autocratically governed states are toward each other. Furthermore, there are no clearcut cases of sovereign stable democracies waging war with each other in the modern international system.
3. The relationship of relative peace among democracies is importantly a result of some features of democracy, rather than being caused exclusively by economic or geopolitical characteristics correlated with democracy.

Exactly what those features are is a matter of theoretical debate, which we shall explore.

At the risk of boring the reader, further discussion requires some conceptual precision. Without it everyone can—and often does—endlessly debate counterexamples while bypassing the phenomenon itself. We need to define what we mean by democracy and war, so as to be able to say just how rare an occasion it is for two democracies to go to war with each other. When we do so it will be evident that those occasions virtually never arise. We then shall spend the rest of the [reading] trying to understand the reasons for that rarity. . . .

Interstate war. War here means large-scale institutionally organized lethal violence, and to define "large-scale" we shall use the threshold commonly used in the social scientific literature on war: one thousand battle fatalities (Small and Singer 1982). The figure of one thousand deaths is arbitrary but reasonable. It is meant to eliminate from the category of wars those violent events that might plausibly be ascribed to:

1. "Accident" (e.g., planes that may have strayed across a national boundary by mistake, and been downed).
2. Deliberate actions by local commanders, but not properly authorized by central authorities, as in many border incidents.
3. Limited, local authorized military actions not necessarily intended to progress to large-scale violent conflict but undertaken more as bargaining moves in a crisis, such as military probes intended to demonstrate one's own commitment and to test the resolve of the adversary.

4. Deliberate military actions larger than mere probes, but not substantially resisted by a usually much weaker adversary. The Soviet invasion of Czechoslovakia in 1968, which was met with substantial nonviolent resistance but not force of arms and resulted in less than a score of immediate deaths, is such an example, and contrasts with the Soviet invasion of Hungary in 1956 which produced roughly seventeen thousand Hungarian and Soviet dead.

A threshold of one thousand battle deaths rather neatly cuts off the above kinds of events while leaving largely intact the category of most conflicts that intuitively satisfy the commonsense meaning of war. . . .

For purposes of theoretical precision in argument yet another qualification is required, and that is a definition of "interstate" war. Here that term means war between sovereign "states" internationally recognized as such by other states, including by major powers whose recognition of a government typically confers *de facto* statehood. Some such definition focusing on organized independent states is common in the social science literature, and is important for the analysis of this book. It is meant to exclude those "colonial" wars fought for the acquisition of territory inhabited by "primitive" people without recognized states, as practiced by nineteenth-century imperialism, or for the twentieth-century liberation of those people. War it may certainly be, but interstate it is not unless or until both sides are generally recognized as having the attributes of statehood. Applying this definition may well display a Western cultural bias, but it is appropriate to the behavior of states which, in the period, also are defined as "democratic" by the admittedly Western standards spelled out below. Non-state participants would not meet those standards.

Wars of liberation—with one or both parties not yet recognized as a state—are in this respect similar to those civil wars in which one or both parties to the conflict fights precisely so as to be free of sharing statehood with the other. Such wars are fought to escape from the coercive institutions of a common state, and to include them would confuse rather than clarify the generalization that democracies rarely go to war with each other. A crucial element in that generalization often depends upon the role of democratic institutions and practices in promoting peaceful conflict resolution within states. Intrastate conflicts that become so fierce that lethal violence is common often indicate that the institutions of the state have become the problem rather than the solution. For example, the United Kingdom and the Republic of Ireland have lived in peace with each other, as separate states, since 1922; the conflict in Northern Ireland arises precisely because many people there emphatically do not wish to be governed as part of the existing common political structure. Democracies are only slightly less likely than other kinds of states to experience civil war (Bremer 1992b).

Democracy. For modern states, democracy (or polyarchy, following Dahl 1971) is usually identified with a voting franchise for a substantial fraction of citizens, a government brought to power in contested elections, and an executive either popularly elected or responsible to an elected legislature, often also with requirements for civil liberties such as free speech. Huntington (1991, 7, 9) uses very similar criteria of "a twentieth-century political system as democratic to the extent that its most powerful collective decision makers are selected through fair, honest, and periodic elections in which candidates freely compete for votes and in which virtually all the adult population is eligible to vote." In addition, he identifies a free election for transfer of power from a nondemocratic government as "the critical point in the process of democratization." Ray (1993) similarly requires that the possibility for the leaders of the government to be defeated in an election and replaced has been demonstrated by historical precedent.

A simple dichotomy between democracy and autocracy of course hides real shades of difference, and mixed systems that share features of both. Moreover, the precise application of these terms is to some degree culturally and temporally dependent. As we shall see, democracy did not mean quite the same to the ancient Greeks as it does to people of the late twentieth century. Even in the modern era the yardstick has been rubbery. Nineteenth century democracies often had property qualifications for the vote and typically excluded women, while the United States—democratic by virtually any standard of the day—disenfranchised blacks. Britain, with its royal prerogatives, rotten boroughs, and very restricted franchise before the Reform Act of 1832, hardly could be counted as a democracy. Even that reform brought voting rights to less than one-fifth of adult males, so one might reasonably withhold the "democracy" designation until after the Second Reform Act of 1867, or even until the secret ballot was introduced in 1872. By then, at the latest,

Britain took its place with the relatively few other states commonly characterized as democratic in the parlance of the era. But if, before the late nineteenth century, we admit countries with as few as 10 per cent of all adults eligible to vote as democratic (a criterion used by Small and Singer 1976; Doyle 1983a uses a cut-off of 30 percent of all males), by the middle to late twentieth century nothing less than a substantially universal franchise will suffice.

The term "contested elections" admits similar ambiguities, but in practice it has come to require two or more legally recognized parties. States with significant prerogatives in military and foreign affairs for non-elected agents (e.g., monarchs) should be excluded as having non-responsible executives, even in the nineteenth century.

By the middle to late twentieth century the matter of guaranteed and respected civil rights, including rights to political organization and political expression, also become a key element in any commonsense definition of democracy (Dahl 1989). The exercise of such civil rights tends to be highly correlated with the existence of democratic institutions as just elaborated, but not perfectly so. The institutions may be found without the regular widespread exercise of the rights; the opposite (civil liberties assured, but not democratic institutions) is rarer. For purposes of the discussion here we will nevertheless not use civil liberties per se as a defining quality, and we shall also ignore the matter of free-market economic liberties. While there is very likely a causal nexus between economic liberties and secure political freedom, the relationship is complex and, unlike some authors (Rummel 1983, Doyle 1983a) I will not build it into the definition.

In not including civil rights and economic liberty as defining qualities of democracy we are lowering the standards by which a country can be labeled a democracy. That is highly relevant to our next topic, an examination of conflicts alleged by some scholars to be wars between democracies. By lowering the standards we are making it more likely that some events will be labeled wars between democracies—events that I and many other writers contend are, at most, exceedingly rare.

Theoretical precision, however, requires one further qualification: some rather minimal stability or longevity. Huntington (1991, 11) emphasizes stability or institutionalization as "a central dimension in the analysis of any political system." To count a war as one waged by a democracy, Doyle (1983a) requires that representative government be in existence for at least three years prior to the war. Perhaps that is a bit too long, yet some period must have elapsed during which democratic processes and institutions could become established, so that both the citizens of the "democratic" state and its adversary could regard it as one governed by democratic principles. Most of the doubtful cases arise within a single year of the establishment of democratic government.

By application of these criteria it is impossible to identify unambiguously *any* wars between democratic states in the period since 1815. A few close calls exist, in which some relaxation of the criteria could produce such a case. But to have no clearcut cases, out of approximately 71 interstate wars involving a total of nearly 270 participants, is impressive. Even these numbers are deceptively low as representing total possibilities. For example, as listed by Small and Singer (1982), 21 states count as participating on the Allied side in World War II, with 8 on the Axis side. Thus in that war alone there were 168 pairs of warring states. Allowing for other multilateral wars, approximately 500 pairs of states went to war against each other in the period. Of these, fewer than a handful can with any plausibility at all be considered candidates for exceptions to a generalization that democracies do not fight each other. . . .

Why the Democratic Peace

Democratic Norms and Culture?

We should begin with the common assertion that democracies are *inherently* more peaceful or "dovish" internationally because of the political culture favoring the peaceful resolution of disputes, or because democratic processes produce restraint by the general populace which will have to pay the price of war in blood and money (Schumpeter 1955; Snyder 1991). Individual examples of the operation of these factors can easily be found. Over the course of a long war democratic governments may experience seriously eroding domestic support for the war effort, and may feel constrained, if they do go to war, to pursue strategies designed to minimize their own costs, especially in casualties. (U.S. strategy against Iraq in 1991 immediately comes to mind.)

This is a strong assertion, however, and, overall, the evidence for it as a generalization is not very compelling. It ignores the evidence for the familiar "rally round the flag effect" typically induced by the threat or use of force by democracies against other countries. Hostility especially to certain kinds of foreigners—those seen as governed autocratically—can often be mobilized to support military actions by democracies (Geva, DeRouen, and Mintz 1993; Mintz and Geva 1993). Elites can even feel impelled by popular pressures to act militarily (Russett 1990, chap. 2). Also, so long as this explanation focuses on the characteristics of single states, it cannot explain the consistent evidence that democracies are about as war-prone and disputatious in general (not toward other democracies) as are other kinds of states (recently, Maoz and Abdollali 1989; Bremer 1992a). Nor can it explain the pattern of nineteenth- and twentieth-century imperialism by democracies. (On Snyder's 1991 effort see Zakaria 1992.) And it would have us believe that the United States was regularly on the defensive, rarely on the offensive, during the Cold War. Though there are elements of plausibility in the argument that democracies are inherently peaceful, it contains too many holes, and is accompanied by too many exceptions, to be usable as a major theoretical building block.

A more plausible theoretical strain, however, yields a more limited assumption. It focuses on powerful norms within democratic states against the use of lethal force under certain conditions—namely, "dovishness" in relations between democracies, though not necessarily in their relations with other kinds of states. Several authors offer a perspective emphasizing social diversity, perceptions of individual rights, overlapping group memberships, cross-pressures, shifting coalitions, expectations of limited government, and toleration of dissent by a presumably loyal opposition. The basic norm of democratic theory is that disputes can be resolved without force through democratic political processes that in some balance ensure both majority rule and minority rights. A norm of equality operates both as voting equality and certain egalitarian rights to human dignity. Democratic government rests on the consent of the governed, but justice demands that consent not be abused. Resort to organized lethal violence, or the threat of it, is considered illegitimate, and unnecessary to secure one's "legitimate" rights. Dissent within broad limits by a loyal opposition is expected and even needed for enlightened policy-making, and the opposition's basic loyalty to the system is to be assumed in the absence of evidence to the contrary.

All participants in the political process are expected to share these norms. Even though all these images may be founded to a large extent on myth as well as on reality, they may operate as powerful restraints on violence between such systems. In practice the norms do sometimes break down, but the normative restraints on violent behavior—by state and citizens—are fully as important as the state's monopoly on the legitimate use of force in keeping incidents of the organized use of force rare. The norms themselves may be more important than any particular institutional structure (two-party/multiparty, republican/parliamentary) or formal constitutional provision. If institutions precede the development of norms in the polity, the basis for restraint is likely to be less secure.

By this hypothesis, the *culture, perceptions, and practices* that permit compromise and the peaceful resolution of conflicts without the threat of violence within countries come to apply across national boundaries toward other democratic countries. In short, if people in a democracy perceive themselves as autonomous, self-governing people who share norms of live-and-let-live, they will respect the rights of others to self-determination if those others are also perceived as self-governing and hence not easily led into aggressive foreign policies by a self-serving elite. The same structures and behaviors that "we" assume will limit our aggression, both internally and externally, may be expected similarly to limit similarly governed people in other polities. Those who claim the principle of self-determination for themselves are expected to extend it to others. Within a transnational democratic culture, as within a democratic nation, others are seen as possessing rights and exercising those rights in a spirit of enlightened self-interest. Acknowledgment of those rights allows us to mitigate our fears that they will try to dominate us. That acknowledgement also prevents us from wishing to dominate them; a norm that it would be wrong to do so in effect raises the "costs" to us of doing so.

By contrast, these restraints do not apply toward a country governed by very different and nondemocratic principles. According to democratic norms, authoritarian states do not rest on the proper consent of the governed, and thus they cannot properly represent the will of their peoples—if they did, they would not need to rule through undemocratic, authoritarian institutions. Rulers who control their own people by such means, who do not behave in a just way that respects, their own people's rights to self-determination, cannot be expected to behave better toward peoples outside their states. "Because non-liberal governments are in a state of aggression with their own people, their foreign relations become for liberal governments deeply suspect. In short, fellow liberals benefit from a presumption of amity; non-liberals suffer from a presumption of enmity" (Doyle 1986, 1161). The essence of America's Cold War ideology was that it had no quarrel with the Russian people, but only with the atheistic communist elites who repressed them. A vision of the other people as not in self-governing control of their own destiny justified a hostile policy. Authoritarian states are expected to aggress against others if given the power and the opportunity. By this reasoning, democracies must be eternally vigilant and may even need to engage in defensively motivated war or preemptive action anticipating an immediate attack.

Whereas wars against other democratic states are neither expected nor considered legitimate, wars against authoritarian states may often be both. Thus an international system composed of both democratic and authoritarian states will include both zones of peace (actual and expected, among the democracies) and zones of war or at best deterrence between democratic and authoritarian states. And by this reasoning democracies may fight wars and other lethal conflicts as often as authoritarian states do—which is what most of the systematic empirical evidence indicates. They just will not fight each other.

The presumption of enmity from and toward non-democracies was exemplified by American determination to root out aggressive fascism and Nazism in Japan and Germany after World War II, and to establish the basis for democratic government there. It took more dubious forms in many Cold War interventions (including convert operations . . .) and in the 1989 invasion of Panama. Elihu Root's (1917) wartime rhetoric, in his presidential address to the American Society of International Law, expressed the tradition vividly:

> So long as military autocracy continues, democracy is not safe from attacks, which are certain to come, and certain to find it unprepared. The conflict is inevitable and universal; and it is *à l'outrance*. To be safe democracy must kill its enemy when it can and where it can. The world can not be half democratic and half autocratic. It must be all democratic or all Prussian. There can be no compromise. If it is all Prussian, there can be no real international law. If it is all democratic, international law honored and observed may well be expected as a natural development of the principles which make democratic self-government possible.

These assumptions lead to the following propositions about democracies' external relations. The norms of regulated political competition, compromise solutions to political conflicts, and peaceful transfer of power are externalized by democracies in their dealing with other national actors in world politics. On the other hand, non-democracies may not externalize these norms. Hence, when two democracies come into a conflict of interest, they are able to apply democratic norms in their interaction, and these norms prevent most conflicts from mounting to the threat or use of military force. If they do go that far, at least they will not go to all-out war. By contrast, when a democracy comes into conflict with a non-democracy, it will not expect the non-democratic state to be restrained by those norms. It may feel obliged to adapt to the harsher norms of international conduct of the latter, lest it be exploited or eliminated by the non-democratic state that takes advantage of the inherent moderation of democracies. Similarly, conflict between non-democracies may be dominated by the norm of forceful conduct and search for decisive (non-compromise) outcome or elimination of the adversary. . . .

Governments and political institutions can change rapidly after a revolution, but norms take time to develop. Laws can change faster than the practices in which norms are embedded. Formal norms such as one of nonrecourse to war can be written into a constitution, but become effective only with the repeated practice of bargaining and conciliation (Kratochwil 1991). Thus if violent conflicts between democracies do occur, we would expect them to take place between democratic states that are relatively young in terms of the tenure of the democratic regime. That is, they would occur between states in at least one of which democratic norms have not matured to a degree that is expressed in moderate and dependable strategies of peaceful conflict management. Democratic governments in which democratic norms are not yet fully developed are likely to be unstable, or to be perceived by other states as unstable, so they may be unable to practice norms of democratic conflict resolution internationally. Equally important, the democratic states with whom they develop conflicts of interest may not perceive them as dependable in their practices. Newness and instability cloud others' perceptions.

Of course, democracies have not fought wars only out of motivations of self-defense, however broadly one may define self-defense, to include anticipation of others' aggression or to include "extended deterrence" for the defense of allies and other interests. Many of them have also fought imperialist wars to acquire or hold colonies, or to retain control of states formally independent but within their spheres of influence. Here is another aspect of perception and misperception, of cases where democracies have fought against people who on one ground or another could be characterized as not self-governing.

The nineteenth-century objects of colonial expansion were peoples who in most instances were outside the European state system. They were in most instances not people with white skins, and whose institutions of government did not conform to the Western democratic institutional forms of their colonizers. Europeans' ethnocentric views of those peoples carried the *assumption* that they did not have institutions of self-government. Not only were they available for imperial aggrandizement, they could be considered candidates for betterment and even "liberation"—the white man's burden, or *mission civilatrice*. They could be brought the benefits not only of modern material civilization, but of Western principles of self-government. If they did not have such institutions already, then by definition they were already being exploited and repressed. Their governments or tribal leaders could not, in this ethnocentric view, be just or consensual, and thus one need have few compunctions about conquering these legitimate candidates for "liberal" imperialism. Later, when Western forms of self-government did begin to take root on a local basis in many of the colonies, the extremes of pseudo-Darwinian racism lost their legitimacy. Decolonization came not only because the colonial governments lost the power to retain their colonies, but because in many cases they lost confidence in their normative right to rule.

We can now summarize all this discussion about restraints on violent conflict among democracies in a set of propositions as follows.

The Cultural/Normative Model

1. In relations with other states, decision-makers (whether they be few or many) will try to follow the same norms of conflict resolution as have been developed within and characterize their domestic political processes.
2. They will expect decision-makers in other states likewise to follow the same norms of conflict resolution as have been developed within and characterize those other states' domestic political processes.

A. Violent conflicts between democracies will be rare because:

3. In democracies, the relevant decision-makers expect to be able to resolve conflicts by compromise and nonviolence, respecting the rights and continued existence of opponents.
4. Therefore democracies will follow norms of peaceful conflict resolution with other democracies, and will expect other democracies to do so with them.
5. The more stable the democracy, the more will democratic norms govern its behavior with other democracies, and the more will other democracies expect democratic norms to govern its international behavior.
6. If violent conflicts between democracies do occur, at least one of the democracies is likely to be politically unstable.

B. Violent conflicts between non-democracies, and between democracies and non-democracies, will be more frequent because:

7. In non-democracies, decision-makers use, and may expect their opponents to use, violence and the threat of violence to resolve conflict as part of their domestic political processes.
8. Therefore non-democracies may use violence and the threat of violence in conflicts with other states, and other states may expect them to use violence and the threat of violence in such conflicts.
9. Democratic norms can be more easily exploited to force concessions than can non-democratic ones; to avoid exploitation democracies may adopt non-democratic norms in dealing with non-democracies.

The numbered propositions are part of the deductive structure, and whereas it will be useful further to illustrate their application and plausibility, we will not subject most of them to rigorous empirical testing. The basic empirical statements A and B, however, will be so tested, in the form that *violent conflicts between democracies should be observed much less frequently than between democracies and non-democracies. . . .*

Structural and Institutional Constraints?

As with the normative and cultural argument, it is best to avoid assuming that democracies are dovish or peaceful in all their relations. Rather, a plausible argument can be constructed on the strategic principles of rational action; that is, about how states, in interactions of threat and bargaining, behave in anticipation of how their bargaining adversaries will behave. Decision-makers develop images of the government and public opinion of other countries. They regard some governments or peoples as slow to fight, or as ready and eager to do so. In forming these images leaders look for various cues: in other leaders' and countries' past behavior in diplomatic or military disputes, and in other countries' form of government. Perhaps other governments will see a democracy as culturally (normatively) dovish on the above grounds, but Kant's own view argued that *institutional constraints*—a structure of division of powers, checks and balances—would make it difficult for democratic leaders to move their countries into war.

Democracies are constrained in going to war by the need to ensure broad popular support, manifested in various institutions of government. Leaders must mobilize public opinion to obtain legitimacy for their actions. Bureaucracies, the legislature, and private interest groups often incorporated in conceptualizations of the "state" must acquiesce. The nature and mix of institutions varies in different kinds of states (for example, "strong" states and "weak" states, parliamentary and presidential systems) but it is complex. Popular support in a democracy can be built by rhetoric and exhortation, but not readily compelled.

The complexity of the mobilization process means that leaders will not readily embark on an effort to prepare the country for war unless they are confident they can demonstrate a favorable ratio of costs and benefits to be achieved, at acceptable risk. Moreover, the complexity of the process requires time for mobilization, as the leaders of various institutions are convinced and formal approval is obtained. Not only may it take longer for democracies to gear up for war, the process is immensely more public than in an authoritarian state. Democratic governments can respond to sudden attack by using emergency powers, and by the same powers can even strike preemptively in crisis. But in normal times they are ill suited to launching surprise attacks. Apparently for these reasons, major-power democracies seem never to have launched preventive war (a deliberate attack not under immediate provocation) against another major power (Schweller 1992). The greater the scale, cost, and risk of using violence, the more effort must be devoted to preparations in public, and of the public.

Even if two states were totally ignorant of each other's form of government, structural delays in the process of mobilization for war in both states would provide time to elapse for negotiation and other means of peaceful conflict resolution. Yet perceptions matter here too. If another nation's leaders regard a state as democratic, they will anticipate a difficult and lengthy process before the democracy is likely to use significant military force against them. They will expect an opportunity to reach a negotiated settlement if they wish to achieve such a settlement. Perhaps most importantly, a democracy will not fear a surprise attack by another democracy, and thus need not cut short the negotiating process or launch a preemptive strike in anticipation of surprise attack.

If democratic leaders generally consider other democracies to be reluctant and slow to fight because of institutional constraints (and possibly because of a general aversion of the people to war), they will not fear being attacked by another democracy. Two democratic states—each constrained from going to war and anticipating the other to be so inhibited—likely will settle their conflicts short of war. Bueno de Mesquita and Allan (1992, chap. 4) provide a deductive argument that two such states, each with perfect information about the other's constraints, will always settle their conflicts by negotiation or by retaining the status quo. In the real world perfect information is lacking, but the presence of democratic institutions provides a visible and generally correct signal of "practical dovishness"—restraints on war in the form of institutional constraint if not of inherent disposition. Reading that sign, democracies will rarely if ever go to war with each other.

Leaders of nondemocratic states may also anticipate that a democratic country will be slow to go to war. But if they are themselves aggressive, they may be more likely to threaten or bully a democracy to make concessions. In turn, that would raise the threshold of provocation facing the democracy, and perhaps overcome its initial inhibition against fighting. That would explain why the overall frequency of war fighting by democracies is no different from that of nondemocratic states. But leaders of two nondemocratic states, neither encumbered by powerful structural constraints, are more likely than two democratic states to escalate to war.

This argument can be summarized as follows.

The Structural/Institutional Model

A. Violent conflicts between democracies will be infrequent because:

1. In democracies, the constraints of checks and balances, division of power, and need for public debate to enlist widespread support will slow decisions to use large-scale violence and reduce the likelihood that such decisions will be made.
2. Leaders of other states will perceive leaders of democracies as so constrained.
3. Thus leaders of democracies will expect, in conflicts with other democracies, time for processes of international conflict resolution to operate, and they will not fear surprise attack.

B. Violent conflicts between non-democracies, and between democracies and non-democracies, will be frequent because:

4. Leaders of non-democracies are not constrained as leaders of democracies are, so they can more easily, rapidly, and secretly initiate large-scale violence.
5. Leaders of states (democracies and non-democracies) in conflict with non-democracies may initiate violence rather than risk surprise attack.
6. Perceiving that leaders of democracies will be constrained, leaders of non-democracies may press democracies to make greater concessions over issues in conflict.
7. Democracies may initiate large-scale violence with non-democracies rather than make the greater concessions demanded.

Distinguishing The Explanations

The cultural/normative and institutional/structural explanations are not neatly separable. Institutions depend on norms and procedures. For example, stability, which we treated as a measure of normative acceptance of democratic processes, is also an institutional constraint if political structures are not subject to overthrow. States may also consider the dominant norms in other states, as well as their institutions, as signals; thus both explanations also depend in part on perceptions. Great emphasis on reading signals of the other's intention, however, slights the importance of self-constraint. Institutions may slow or obstruct one's own ability to fight. Perhaps more importantly, a norm that it is somehow not "right" to fight another democracy raises the moral and political cost, and thus limits one's own willingness to do so. Bueno de Mesquita and Lalman (1992) neglect this, as well as the opposition a democratic government might find among its own population against fighting another *democratic government* (Geva, DeRouen, and Mintz 1993). Within democracies, structural impediments to using force are less strong than within autocracies; normative restraints must bear the load. So we should not assume that normative constraints are unimportant in relations between democracies. Both norms and institutions may contribute to the phenomenon of peace between democracies; they are somewhat complementary and overlapping. But they are also in some degree distinctive and competing explanations, allowing us to look for greater impact of one or another in various contexts.

Other influences, such as trade and the network of international law and organizations as suggested by Kant, likely also play a role in directly supplementing and strengthening that of democracy. Further elaboration of the theoretical arguments is probably needed. Certainly, detailed empirical work is necessary on how institutions operate, and on how perceptions toward other countries evolve, so as to make it possible to weight the relative power of institutional and normative explanations. So too is the creation and application of systematic empirical tests to differentiate between the two kinds of explanations for violence in the modern interstate system. One such test, distinguishing between measures of democracy as stability (normative) and of democracy as the adoption of particular institutions, will be performed later in this book. The prediction about stable democracies being less likely than unstable ones to use military force against each other is embedded in the normative model, and more tenuously so in the structural one. . . .

Another test can be derived from the patterns of strategic interaction as discussed in the model of structural constraints. By that argument, two democracies engaged in a conflictual bargaining process with each other can reasonably expect each other not to escalate the dispute to the point of war or serious violence. Therefore, many bargaining models predict there would be few strategic restraints on escalating the conflict up to, but not beyond, the point of an exchange of lethal violence. In fact, each state might have strong incentives to go that far for the purpose of showing resolve; perhaps even escalating to the first (limited) use of force in confidence that the other would be unlikely to replay in any substantial military manner. Such behavior is implicit in the bargaining "game" of chicken, which is widely applied to crisis negotiation (Brams and Kilgore 1988; Brams 1990; Poundstone 1992). This reasoning, therefore, leads to the prediction that disputes between democracies should commonly escalate to the display and even limited use of force, though not to war. But, that is not the case. Democracy/democracy pairs are less likely to enter into militarized disputes at all than are other pairs of states, and less likely to escalate them at any level up the escalation ladder—not just at the top to war.

Rather, this suggests that to *use or threaten to use force is not usually normatively acceptable behavior in disputes between democracies*, even in the form of symbolic, ritualized bargaining behavior. Relations between democracies therefore fit into the category of "stable peace" (Boulding 1979) or a "security community" (Deutsch et al: 1957) in which states not only do not fight each other, they do not expect to fight each other, or significantly prepare to fight each other. In such relationships disputes are routinely settled without recourse to threat and military deterrence. Dependent as the definition of security community has been on expectations, it has been a difficult phenomenon to observe reliably; here, in the relative absence of militarized dispute and escalation, is a reasonably objective measure.

15.2

Democratization and War

Edward D. Mansfield and Jack Snyder

Dangers of Transition

The idea that democracies never fight wars against each other has become an axiom for many scholars. It is, as one scholar puts it, "as close as anything we have to an empirical law in international relations." This "law" is invoked by American statesmen to justify a foreign policy that encourages democratization abroad. In his 1994 State of the Union address, President Clinton asserted that no two democracies had ever gone to war with each other, thus explaining why promoting democracy abroad was a pillar of his foreign policy.

It is probably true that a world in which more countries were mature, stable democracies would be safer and preferable for the United States. But countries do not become mature democracies overnight. They usually go through a rocky transition, where mass politics mixes with authoritarian elite politics in a volatile way. Statistical evidence covering the past two centuries shows that in this transitional phase of democratization, countries become more aggressive and war-prone, not less, and they do fight wars with democratic states. In fact, formerly authoritarian states where democratic participation is on the rise are more likely to fight wars than are stable democracies or autocracies. States that make the biggest leap, from total autocracy to extensive mass democracy—like contemporary Russia—are about twice as likely to fight wars in the decade after democratization as are states that remain autocracies.

This historical pattern of democratization, belligerent nationalism, and war is already emerging in some of today's new or partial democracies, especially some formerly communist states. Two pairs of states—Serbia and Croatia, and Armenia and Azerbaijan—have found themselves at war while experimenting with varying degrees of electoral democracy. The electorate of Russia's partial democracy cast nearly a quarter of its votes for the party of radical nationalist Vladimir Zhirinovsky. Even mainstream Russian politicians have adopted an imperial tone in their dealings with neighboring former Soviet republics, and military force has been used ruthlessly in Chechnya.

The following evidence should raise questions about the Clinton administration's policy of promoting peace by promoting democratization. The expectation that the spread of democracy will probably contribute to peace in the long run, once new democracies mature, provides little comfort to those who might face a heightened risk of war in the short run. Pushing nuclear-armed great powers like Russia or China toward democratization is like spinning a roulette wheel: many of the outcomes are undesirable. Of course, in most cases the initial steps on the road to democratization will not be produced by any conscious policy of the United States. The roulette wheel is already spinning for Russia and perhaps will be soon for China. Washington and the international community need to think not so much about encouraging or discouraging democratization as about helping to smooth the transition in ways that minimize its risks. . . .

Nationalism and Democratization

The connection between democratization and nationalism is striking in both the historical record and today's headlines. We did not measure nationalism directly in our statistical tests. Nonetheless, historical and contemporary evidence strongly suggests that rising nationalism often goes hand in hand with rising democracy. It is no accident that the end of the Cold War brought both a wave of democratization and a revival of nationalist sentiment in the former communist states.

In eighteenth-century Britain and France, when nationalism first emerged as an explicit political doctrine, it meant self-rule by the people. It was the rallying cry of commoners and rising commercial classes against rule by aristocratic elites, who were charged with the sin of ruling in their own interests, rather than those of the nation. Indeed, dynastic rulers and imperial courts had hardly been interested in promoting

Source: Edward D. Mansfield and Jack Snyder, "Democratization and War." Reprinted by permission of *Foreign Affairs*.

nationalism as a banner of solidarity in their realms. They typically ruled over a linguistically and culturally diverse conglomeration of subjects and claimed to govern by divine right, not in the interest of the nation. Often, these rulers were more closely tied by kinship, language, or culture to elites in other states than to their own subjects. The position of the communist ruling class was strikingly similar: a transnational elite that ruled over an amalgamation of peoples and claimed legitimacy from the communist party's role as the vanguard of history, not from the consent of the governed. Popular forces challenging either traditional dynastic rulers or communist elites naturally tended to combine demands for national self-determination and democratic rule.

This concoction of nationalism and incipient democratization has been an intoxicating brew, leading in case after case to ill-conceived wars of expansion. The earliest instance remains one of the most dramatic. In the French Revolution, the radical Brissotin parliamentary faction polarized politics by harping on the king's slow response to the threat of war with other dynastic states. In the ensuing wars of the French Revolution, citizens flocked to join the revolutionary armies to defend popular self-rule and the French nation. Even after the revolution turned profoundly antidemocratic, Napoleon was able to harness this popular nationalism to the task of conquering Europe, substituting the popularity of empire for the substance of democratic rule.

After this experience, Europe's ruling elites decided to band together in 1815 in the Concert of Europe to contain the twin evils of nationalism and democratization. In this scheme, Europe's crowned heads tried to unite in squelching demands for constitutions, electoral and social democracy, and national self-determination. For a time nationalism and democratization were both held back, and Europe enjoyed a period of relative peace.

But in the long run, the strategy failed in the face of the economic changes strengthening popular forces in Western and Central Europe. British and French politicians soon saw that they would have to rule by co-opting nationalist and democratic demands, rather than suppressing them. Once the specter of revolution returned to Europe in 1848, this reversal of political tactics was complete, and it led quickly to the Crimean War. British Foreign Secretary Palmerston and French Emperor Napoleon III both tried to manage the clamor for a broader political arena by giving democrats what they wanted in foreign affairs— a "liberal" war to free imprisoned nations from autocratic rule and, incidentally, to expand commerce.

But this was just the dress rehearsal for history's most potent combination of mass politics and rising nationalism, which occurred in Germany around the turn of the twentieth century. Chancellor Otto von Bismarck, counting on the conservative votes of a docile peasantry, granted universal suffrage in the newly unified Reich after 1870, but in foreign and military affairs, he kept the elected Reichstag subordinate to the cabinet appointed by the kaiser. Like the sorcerer's apprentice, however, Bismarck underestimated the forces he was unleashing. With the rise of an industrial society, Bismarck's successors could not control this truncated democracy, where over 90 percent of the population voted.

Everyone was highly politicized, yet nobody could achieve their aims through the limited powers of the Reichstag. As a result, people organized direct pressure groups outside of electoral party politics. Some of these clamored for economic benefits, but many of them found it tactically useful to cloak their narrow interests in a broader vision of the nation's interests. This mass nationalist sentiment exerted constant pressure on German diplomacy in the Wilhelmine years before 1914 and pushed its vacillating elites toward war. . . .

The interconnection among nationalism, democratization, and war is even clearer in new states. In today's "Weimar Russia," voters disgruntled by economic distress backed belligerent nationalists like Zhirinovsky, put ostensible liberals like President Boris Yeltsin and Foreign Minister Andrei Kozyrev on the defensive on ethnic and foreign policy issues, and contributed to the climate that led to war in Chechnya. In "Wilhelmine Serbia," the political and military elites of the old regime, facing inexorable pressure for democratization, cynically but successfully created a new basis for legitimacy through nationalist propaganda and military action, and they recently won elections that were only partially manipulated. Until its recent decree suspending the activities of the main opposition party, Armenia had moved quite far toward full democracy while at the same time supporting an invasion of its ethnic foes in Azerbaijan. The Azeris have been less successful in sustaining momentum toward democracy. However, in Azerbaijan's one relatively free and fair presidential election, the winner, Abulfaz Ali Elchibey, attacked the incumbent for being insufficiently nationalist and populist. Elchibey's platform emphasized Turkic identity and the strengthening of the Azeri nation-state to try to mount a counteroffensive against the Armenians. In other ethnically divided societies, where holding an election is like taking a census, democratization has often become an opportunity to exercise the tyranny of the majority. . . .

The Causes of Democratic Wars

Democratization typically creates a syndrome of weak central authority, unstable domestic coalitions, and high-energy mass politics. It brings new social groups and classes onto the political stage. Political leaders, finding no way to reconcile incompatible interests, resort to shortsighted bargains or reckless gambles in order to maintain their governing coalitions. Elites need to gain mass allies to defend their weakened positions. Both the newly ambitious elites and the embattled old ruling groups often use appeals to nationalism to stay astride their unmanageable political coalitions.

Needing public support, they rouse the masses with nationalist propaganda but find that their mass allies, once mobilized by passionate appeals, are difficult to control. So are the powerful remnants of the old order—the military, for example—which promote militarism because it strengthens them institutionally. This is particularly true because democratization weakens the central government's ability to keep policy coherent and consistent. Governing a society that is democratizing is like driving a car while throwing away the steering wheel, stepping on the gas, and fighting over which passenger will be in the driver's seat. The result, often, is war.

Political stalemate and imperialist coalitions

Democratization creates a wider spectrum of politically significant groups with diverse and incompatible interests. In the period when the great powers were first democratizing, kings, aristocrats, peasants, and artisans shared the historical stage with industrialists, an urban working class, and a middle-class intelligentsia. Similarly, in the post-communist world, former party apparatchiks, atavistic heavy industrialists, and downwardly mobile military officers share the stage with populist demagogues, free-market entrepreneurs, disgruntled workers, and newly mobilized ethnic groups. In principle, mature democratic institutions can integrate even the widest spectrum of interests through competition for the favor of the average voter. But where political parties and representative institutions are still in their infancy, the diversity of interests may make political coalitions difficult to maintain. Often the solution is a belligerent nationalist coalition. . . .

In more recent times, incipient democratization has likewise caused political impasses by widening the political spectrum to include too many irreconcilable political forces. In the final days of Yugoslavia, efforts by moderates like former Prime Minister Ante Markovic´ to promote a federalist, democratic, economic reformist platform were hindered not only by ethnic divisions but also by the cleavage between market-oriented business interests on the one hand and party bosses and military officers on the other. Similarly, in Russia, the difficulty of reconciling liberal, neo-communist, and nationalist political platforms and the social interests behind them has led to parliamentary stalemate, attempts to break the stalemate by presidential decree, tanks in the streets, and the resort to freelancing by breakaway regions, the military, and spontaneous privatizers of state property. One interpretation of Yeltsin's decision to use force in Chechnya is that he felt it necessary to show that he could act decisively to prevent the unraveling of central authority, with respect not only to ethnic separatists but also to other ungovernable groups in a democratizing society. Chechnya, it was hoped, would allow Yeltsin to demonstrate his ability to coerce Russian society while at the same time exploiting a potentially popular nationalist issue.

Inflexible interests and short time horizons

Groups threatened by social change and democratization, including still-powerful elites, are often compelled to take an inflexible view of their interests, especially when their assets cannot be readily adapted to changing political and economic conditions. In extreme cases, there may be only one solution that will maintain the social position of the group. For Prussian landowners, it was agricultural protection in a nondemocratic state; for the Japanese military, it was organizational autonomy in an autarkic empire; for the Serbian military and party elites, it was a Serbian nationalist state. Since military bureaucracies and imperial interest groups occupied key positions in many authoritarian great powers, whether monarchal or communist, most interests threatened by democratization have been bound up with military programs and the state's international mission. Compromises that may lead down the slippery slope to social extinction or irrelevance have little appeal to such groups. This adds to the difficulty of finding an exit from the domestic political impasse and may make powerful domestic groups impervious to the international risks of their strategies.

Competing for popular support

The trouble intensifies when elites in a democratizing society try to recruit mass allies to their cause. Threatened elite groups have an overwhelming incentive to mobilize mass backers on the elites' terms, using whatever special resources they might retain. These resources have included monopolies of information (the Wilhelmine navy's unique "expertise" in making strategic assessments), propaganda assets (the Japanese army's public relations blitz justifying the invasion of Manchuria), patronage (Lord Palmerston's gifts of foreign service postings to the sons of cooperative journalists), wealth (the Krupp steel company's bankrolling of mass nationalist and militarist leagues), organizational skills and networks (the Japanese army's exploitation of rural reservist organizations to build a social base), and the ability to use the control of traditional political institutions to shape the political agenda and structure the terms of political bargains (the Wilhelmine ruling elite's agreement to eliminate anti-Catholic legislation in exchange for Catholic support in the Reichstag on the naval budget).

This elite mobilization of mass groups takes place in a highly competitive setting. Elite groups mobilize mass support to neutralize mass threats (for instance, creating patriotic leagues to counter workers' movements) and counter other elite groups' successful efforts at mass mobilization (such as the German Navy League, a political counterweight to the Junker-backed Agrarian League). The elites' resources allow them to influence the direction of mass political participation, but the imperative to compete for mass favor makes it difficult for a single elite group to control the outcome of this process. For example, mass groups that gain access to politics through elite-supported nationalist organizations often try to outbid their erstwhile sponsors. By 1911, German popular nationalist lobbies were in a position to claim that if Germany's foreign foes were really as threatening as the ruling elites had portrayed them, then the government had sold out German interests in reaching a compromise with France over the Moroccan dispute. In this way, elite mobilization of the masses adds to the ungovernability and political impasse of democratizing states.

Ideology takes on particular significance in the competition for mass support. New entrants to the political process, lacking established habits and good information, may be uncertain where their political interests lie. Ideology can yield big payoffs, particularly when there is no efficient free marketplace of ideas to counter false claims with reliable facts. Elites try out all sorts of ideological appeals depending on the social position they are defending, the nature of the mass group they want to recruit, and the kinds of appeals that seem politically plausible. A nearly universal element of these ideological appeals, however, is nationalism, which has the advantage of positing a community of interest uniting elites and masses. This distracts attention from class cleavages that divide elites from the masses they are trying to recruit.

The weakening of central authority

The political impasse and recklessness of democratizing states is deepened by the weakening of the state's authority. The autocrat can no longer dictate to elite interest groups or mass groups. Meanwhile, democratic institutions lack the strength to integrate these contending interests and views. Parties are weak and lack mass loyalty. Elections are rigged or intermittent. Institutions of public political participation are distrusted because they are subject to manipulation by elites and arbitrary constraints imposed by the state, which fears the outcome of unfettered competition. . . .

In each of these cases, the weak central leadership resorts to the same strategies as do the more parochial elite interests, using nationalist ideological appeals and special-interest payoffs to maintain their short-run viability, despite the long-run risks that these strategies may unleash.

Prestige strategies

One of the simplest but riskiest strategies for a hard-pressed regime in a democratizing country is to shore up its prestige at home by seeking victories abroad. During the Chechen intervention, newspaper commentators in Moscow and the West were reminded of Russian Interior Minister Viacheslav Plehve's fateful remark in 1904, on the eve of the disastrous

Russo-Japanese War, that what the tsar needed was "a short, victorious war" to boost his prestige. Though this strategy often backfires, it is a perennial temptation as a means for coping with the political strains of democratization. . . .

Managing the Dangers

Though mature democratic states have virtually never fought wars against each other, promoting democracy may not promote peace because states are especially war-prone during the transition toward democracy. This does not mean, however, that democratization should be squelched in the interests of peace. Many states are now democratizing or on the verge of it, and stemming that turbulent tide, even if it were desirable, may not be possible. Our statistical tests show that movements toward autocracy, including reversals of democratization, are only somewhat less likely to result in war than democratization itself. Consequently, the task is to draw on an understanding of the process of democratization to keep its unwanted side effects to a minimum.

Of course, democratization does not always lead to extreme forms of aggressive nationalism, just as it does not always lead to war. But it makes those outcomes more likely. Cases where states democratized without triggering a nationalist mobilization are particularly interesting, since they may hold clues about how to prevent such unwanted side effects. Among the great powers, the obvious successes were the democratization of Germany and Japan after 1945, due to occupation by liberal democracies and the favorable international setting provided by the Marshall Plan, the Bretton Woods economic system, and the democratic military alliance against the Soviet threat. More recently, numerous Latin American states have democratized without nationalism or war. The recent border skirmishes between Peru and Ecuador, however, coincide with democratizing trends in both states and a nationalist turn in Ecuadorian political discourse. Moreover, all three previous wars between that pair over the past two centuries occurred in periods of partial democratization.

In such cases, however, the cure is probably more democracy, not less. In "Wilhelmine Argentina," the Falkland Islands/Malvinas War came when the military junta needed a nationalist victory to stave off pressure for the return of democracy; the arrival of full democracy has produced more pacific policies. Among the East European states, nationalist politics has been unsuccessful in the most fully democratic ones—Poland, the Czech Republic, and Hungary—as protest votes have gone to former communists. Nationalism has figured more prominently in the politics of the less democratic formerly communist states that are nonetheless partially democratizing. States like Turkmenistan that remain outright autocracies have no nationalist mobilization—indeed no political mobilization of any kind. In those recent cases, in contrast to some of our statistical results, the rule seems to be: go fully democratic, or don't go at all. . . .

One of the major findings of scholarship on democratization in Latin America is that the process goes most smoothly when elites threatened by the transition—especially the military— are given a golden parachute. Above all, they need a guarantee that they will not wind up in jail if they relinquish power. The history of the democratizing great powers broadens this insight. Democratization was least likely to lead to war when the old elites saw a reasonably bright future for themselves in the new social order. British aristocrats, for example, had more of their wealth invested in commerce and industry than in agriculture, so they had many interests in common with the rising middle classes. They could face democratization with relative equanimity. In contrast, Prussia's capital-starved, small-scale Junker landholders had no choice but to rely on agricultural protection and military careers.

In today's context, finding benign, productive employment for the erstwhile communist nomenklatura, military officer corps, nuclear scientists, and smokestack industrialists ought to rank high on the list of priorities. Policies aimed at giving them a stake in the privatization process and subsidizing the conversion of their skills to new, peaceful tasks in a market economy seem like a step in the right direction. According to some interpretations, Russian Defense Minister Pavel Grachev was eager to use force to solve the Chechen confrontation in order to show that Russian military power was still useful and that increased investment in the Russian army would pay big dividends. Instead of pursuing this reckless path, the Russian military elite needs to be convinced that its prestige, housing, pensions, and technical competence will improve if and only if it transforms itself into a Western-style military, subordinate to civilian authority and resorting to force only in accordance with prevailing international norms. Not only do old elites need to be kept happy, they also need to be kept weak. Pacts should not prop up the remnants of the authoritarian system, but rather create a niche for them in the new system.

Another top priority must be creating a free, competitive, and responsible marketplace of ideas in the newly democratizing states. Most of the war-prone democratizing great powers had pluralistic public debates, but the debates were skewed to favor groups with money, privileged access to the media, and proprietary control over information ranging from archives to intelligence about the military balance. Pluralism is not enough. Without a level playing field, pluralism simply creates the incentive and opportunity for privileged groups to propound self-serving myths, which historically have often taken a nationalist turn. One of the rays of hope in the Chechen affair was the alacrity with which Russian journalists exposed the costs of the fighting and the lies of the government and the military. Though elites should get a golden parachute regarding their pecuniary interests, they should be given no quarter on the battlefield of ideas. Mythmaking should be held up to the utmost scrutiny by aggressive journalists who maintain their credibility by scrupulously distinguishing fact from opinion and tirelessly verifying their sources. Promoting this kind of journalistic infrastructure is probably the most highly leveraged investment the West can make in a peaceful democratic transition.

Finally, the kind of ruling coalition that emerges in the course of democratization depends a great deal on the incentives created by the international environment. Both Germany and Japan started on the path toward liberal, stable democratization in the mid-1920s, encouraged by abundant opportunities for trade with and investment by the advanced democracies and by credible security treaties that defused nationalist scaremongering in domestic politics. When the international supports for free trade and democracy were yanked out in the late 1920s, their liberal coalitions collapsed. For China, whose democratization may occur in the context of expanding economic ties with the West, a steady Western commercial partnership and security presence is likely to play a major role in shaping the incentives of proto-democratic coalition politics.

In the long run, the enlargement of the zone of stable democracy will probably enhance prospects for peace. In the short run, much work remains to be done to minimize the dangers of the turbulent transition.

15.3

Polities and Peace

Henry S. Farber and Joanne Gowa

In recent months, the Clinton administration has begun to advocate a replacement for the doctrine of containment that drove U.S. foreign policy during the Cold War. According to Anthony Lake, the Assistant to the President for National Security Affairs, the leading candidate to succeed containment is "a strategy of enlargement—enlargement of the world's . . . community of market democracies."[1] President Clinton concurs, noting that a strategy of enlargement serves U.S. interests because "democracies rarely wage war on one another."[2]

Several empirical analyses suggest that the Clinton administration's advocacy of enlargement is well-grounded. They conclude that democratic states do pursue distinctive foreign policies. Perhaps the most intriguing among their findings is that democratic states rarely, if ever, wage war against other democratic states. Indeed, some observers consider this finding to be "as close as anything we have to an empirical law in international relations."[3]

Yet doubts remain about whether the observed association reflects a causal relationship.[4] In this paper, we attempt to resolve these doubts. In order to do so, we reexamine both the logic and the empirical basis of the claim central to the "democratic peace" literature: that is, that members of pairs of democratic states are far less likely to wage war against or engage in serious disputes with each other than are members of other pairs of states.[5]

We first review the analytic foundations of the democratic peace literature. We conclude that these foundations are tenuous. Then we examine the evidence. We analyze the period before World War I and the period after World War II separately. The results that emerge differ markedly from those of previous studies.

First, we find that there is *no* statistically significant relationship between democracy and war before 1914. In the case of disputes short of war, we find that the probability that these disputes will occur is significantly higher between members of pairs of democratic states than between members of other pairs of states in the same period. Our analysis shows that it is only after 1945 that the probability of war or serious disputes is significantly lower between democratic states than between members of other pairs of states.

This pattern of cross-temporal variation contradicts the central claim of the democratic peace literature that dispute rates are consistently lower between democracies than between members of other pairs of states. It also suggests that the Cold War results may be a product of common interests, rather than of common polities.

Although extrapolating the results of any analysis is often problematic, our findings suggest that whether or not democratic polities become more common may not affect U.S. security interests strongly. Thus, although the evolution of democracy in the former Soviet bloc countries may be desirable on other grounds, the analysis presented here suggests that it will not affect an issue of central importance to the United States: the probability of serious interstate disputes.

Analytic Foundations

The democratic peace literature advances two explanations for the distinctive behavior of democracies. One is based on norms, the other on checks and balances. In this section, we argue that neither provides a compelling explanation of the peace that is said to prevail between democracies.[6]

Norms

Norms are "rules for conduct that provide standards by which behavior is approved or disapproved."[7] The democratic peace literature assigns the principal explanatory role to the norm that defines acceptable methods of conflict resolution. In democratic states, acceptable methods include "adjudication and bargaining,"

Source: Henry S. Farber and Joanne Gowa, "Polities and Peace," *International Security 20*(2) (Fall, 1995), pp. 123–128 and 145–146.

whereas the "use of force is disdained."[8] This norm is said to explain peace not only within but also between democracies because states "externalize . . . the norms of behavior that are developed within and characterize their domestic political processes and institutions."[9] Thus, if a norm regulates conflict resolution within two states, it will also regulate the process of conflict resolution between them.

In the extensive literature on norms, norms are defined in two ways. Norms may be regarded as "*ex ante* sources of action." As such, they are not "merely *ex post* rationalizations of self interests," but reflect the internalization of values.[10] Norms have also been interpreted, however, as reflections of interests.[11]

Contributors to the democratic peace literature define norms as sources of action independent of interests. Thus, they regard adherence to peaceful methods of conflict resolution as the product of internalized values. Yet adherence to this norm is of enormous instrumental value: it secures the social order that is the basis of any organized society. It therefore serves the private interest of leaders and the collective interests of those they rule. This implies that norms regulating conflict resolution can be very difficult to distinguish from interests.

This suggests, in turn, that whether the parties to an interstate dispute resort to violence also may depend upon interests rather than norms. In the context of international disputes, it does not seem logical to impute to democracies alone an interest in non-violent means of conflict resolution. Because war is more costly than bargaining, it seems more reasonable to impute a preference for negotiation over war to *all* potential belligerents.[12] As a result, the value added by describing a preference for peaceful methods of conflict resolution as a norm rather than an interest is not obvious.

The empirical foundations of the norms argument are no more compelling. The central problem is that there are no measures of norms or their effectiveness that are independent of interests. For example, Maoz and Russett use both the incidence of violent domestic disputes and the duration of regimes as proxies for the effectiveness of domestic norms.[13] As noted above, peaceful resolution of domestic disputes is quite likely to serve the interests of both leaders and the general populace. Thus, a low incidence of violent disputes domestically might well reflect interests rather than norms.

Using regime duration suffers from much the same flaw. Compliance with a norm of peaceful dispute resolution may be directly related to the tenure of a regime in office. The causal relationship, however, may be due to an increase in the efficacy of sanctions; presumably, the longer regimes endure, the better they learn to cope with violent opposition. In this case, again, increases in compliance may reflect interests induced by the stronger deterrent effect of more effective sanctions.

In the end, any explanation of the distinctiveness of democratic foreign policies based on the distinctiveness of the norms underlying them is not testable. This is because no direct measures of norms related to interstate disputes exist. Proxy measures are not adequate substitutes because their use requires the assumption that they are, in fact, linked to norms governing interstate disputes, rather than merely reflecting underlying interests.

Checks and Balances

The premise of the checks-and-balances argument is that constraints on would-be renegade leaders are much more effective in democratic than in autocratic polities.[14] This is at odds, however, with the conventional finding that, while democracies seem to fight with each other less frequently than do other country pairs, they are just as likely to wage war as are other polities.[15]

In addition, the checks and balances characteristic of democratic polities do not seem to protect the public from politicians maximizing their own interests rather than social welfare in widely varied policy areas. For example, tariffs exist in most democracies despite their negative effects on real income. Their existence is partly the product of the concentrated benefits and diffuse costs of a tariff. As a result of this distribution of cost and benefits, welfare-maximizing politicians gain some freedom to maneuver, at a cost to aggregate social welfare.[16]

The question raised by the case of tariffs is whether a fundamentally different policy process prevails in the case of war. As is true of tariffs, the benefits from war are concentrated, while its costs are diffuse. As a result, defense contractors are likely to be more effective political actors than is the population at large. Moreover, evidence from the United States suggests that the costs of war tend to fall disproportionately on low-income constituents, whose rates of political participation are relatively low.[17] The net effect, again, is to endow political officials with some freedom to maximize their own interests rather than social welfare.

We do not mean to suggest that there are no differences between the policy processes that produce tariffs and those that produce wars. For example, these processes are much more likely to resemble each other in the case of small than of large wars. However, we do want to suggest that there is no *a priori* reason to believe that checks and balances work as intended in the case of wars, since it is clear that they do not do so in other policy areas.

This implies that there may be a smaller gap between democratic and other polities with respect to the autonomy of would-be renegade leaders than is conventionally assumed. Other factors point in the same direction. For example, informal checks and balances are in effect in nondemocratic polities,[18] such as the dependence of their leaders of non-democratic societies on the coalition of interests that supports them.[19]

More generally, the most potent deterrent to war may not be the existence of *ex ante* formal or informal checks and balances, but the *ex post* ability of constituents to sanction their leaders.[20] The resort to war creates a risk to incumbency that can tightly constrain heads of states of autocracies as well as democracies.[21]

In summary, neither the norm-based argument nor the one based on checks and balances is completely convincing. . . .

Conclusion

The evidence we analyzed suggests that the democratic peace is of relatively recent origin. Indeed, it coincides with the Cold War. Whether the post-1945 result is the product of common polities is, at best, unclear. The onset of the Cold War precipitated strong common interests among a relatively large number of democratic states. Alliance patterns reflect this: after 1945, democratic states were more likely to join defense pacts with each other than were non-democracies. That this is far from typical is clear from the pre-World War I pattern: During the century before 1914, members of democratic dyads were less likely to join defense pacts with each other than were members of other dyads.[22] Thus, it is difficult to conclude that it is common polities, rather than common interests, that explain the relatively low incidence of disputes between democracies during the Cold War.

This finding is central to a long-standing debate in international relations about the relative importance of "Second Image" (domestic political) and "Third Image" (systemic) variables. The existing democratic peace literature suggests that Second Image variables play an essential role in explaining the incidence of war and disputes short of war, but our analysis does not support this conclusion.

Our analysis also suggests that the Clinton administration's foreign-policy strategy of "enlargement" may be misguided. On the basis of the historical record, it is not clear that the spread of democracy in and of itself will exert much influence on the incidence of serious interstate conflict. Although a policy of supporting the emergence of democratic regimes may be desirable on other grounds, there does not seem to be convincing evidence that enlarging the world's community of democracies will reduce the danger of international conflict. Instead, the analysis here suggests that the Clinton administration foreign policy will be more successful if it focuses on encouraging the emergence of common interests.

Notes

1. Anthony Lake, "From Containment to Enlargement," U.S. Department of State, Bureau of Public Affairs, *Dispatch*, Vol. 4, No. 39 (September 1993), p. 3.
2. William Clinton, "Confronting the Challenges of a Broader World," U.S. Department of State, Bureau of Public Affairs, *Dispatch*, Vol. 4, No. 39 (September 1993), p. 3.
3. Jack S. Levy, "Domestic Politics and War," *Journal of Interdisciplinary History*, Vol. 18, No. 4 (Spring 1988), pp. 653–673.
4. T. Clifton Morgan notes, for example, that he and many others "have long had nagging suspicions that the conclusions we have drawn from the empirical tests are spurious. It may well be that alliance patterns, power distributions, contiguity, or any of a number of other variables could be confounding our observed relationship." T. Clifton Morgan, "Democracy and War: Reflections on the Literature," *International Interactions*, Vol. 18, No. 3 (1993), p. 200.
5. See, e.g., Stuart Bremer, "Dangerous Dyads: Conditions Affecting the Likelihood of Interstate War," *Journal of Conflict Resolution*, Vol. 36, No. 2 (June 1992), pp. 309–341; Stuart Bremer, "Democracy and Militarized Interstate Conflict," *International Interactions*, Vol. 18, No. 3 (1993), pp. 231–249; Steve Chan, "Mirror, Mirror on the Wall . . . Are the Freer Countries More Pacific?" *Journal of Conflict Resolution*, Vol. 28, No. 4 (December 1984), pp. 616–648; Steve Chan, "Democracy and War: Some Thoughts on Future Research Agenda," *International Interactions*, Vol. 18, No. 3 (1993), pp. 205–214; William Dixon, "Democracy and the Peaceful Settlement of International Conflict," *American Political Science Review*,

Vol. 88, No. 1 (March 1994), pp. 14–32; Michael Doyle, "Liberalism and World Politics," *American Political Science Review*, Vol. 80, No. 4 (December 1986), pp. 1151–1169; Zeev Maoz and Nasrin Abdolali, "Regime Types and International Conflict," *Journal of Conflict Resolution*, Vol. 33, No. 1 (March 1989), pp. 3–35; Zeev Maoz and Bruce M. Russett, "Normative and Structural Causes of Democratic Peace, 1946–86," *American Political Science Review*, Vol. 87, No. 3 (September 1993), pp. 624–638; Bruce M. Russett, *Grasping the Democratic Peace: Principles for a Post-Cold War World* (Princeton: Princeton University Press, 1993); Melvin Small and J. David Singer, "The War-Proneness of Democratic Regimes," *Jerusalem Journal of International Relations*, Vol. 1, No. 4 (Summer 1976), pp. 50–68.

6. Part of this section draws on material developed in further detail in Joanne Gowa, "Democratic States and International Disputes," *International Organization*, Vol. 49, No. 3 (Summer 1995).

7. Michael Hechter, *Principles of Group Solidarity* (Berkeley: University of California Press, 1987), p. 62.

8. Morgan, "Democracy and War," p. 198.

9. Maoz and Russett, "Normative and Structural Causes."

10. Jon Elster, *The Cement of Society: A Study of Social Order* (Cambridge: Cambridge University Press, 1989), p. 125.

11. See, e.g., John Finley Scott, *The Internationalization of Norms: A Sociological Theory of Moral Commitment* (Englewood Cliffs, N.J.: Prentice Hall, 1971).

12. James D. Fearon, "Threats to Use Force: Costly Signals and Bargaining in International Crises," (Ph.D. dissertation, University of California, Berkeley, 1992).

13. Maoz and Russett, "Normative and Structural Causes."

14. T. Clifton Morgan and Sally Howard Campbell, "Domestic Structure, Decisional Constraints, and War: So Why Kant Democracies Fight?" *Journal of Conflict Resolution*, Vol. 35, No. 2 (June 1991), pp. 187–211. For a somewhat different argument that reaches the same conclusion, see David A. Lake, "Powerful Pacifists: Democratic States and War," *American Political Science Review*, Vol. 86, No. 1 (March 1992), pp. 24–37.

15. Bruce Bueno de Mesquita and David Lalman, *War and Reason: Domestic and International Imperatives* (New Haven: Yale University Press, 1992); Chan, "Mirror, Mirror on the Wall"; Doyle, "Liberalism and World Politics"; Levy, "Domestic Politics and War"; T. Clifton Morgan and Valerie L. Schwebach, "Take Two Democracies and Call Me In the Morning: A Prescription for Peace?" *International Interactions*, Vol. 17, No. 4 (1992), pp. 305–320; R. J. Rummel, "The Relationship between National Attributes and Foreign Conflict Behavior," in J. David Singer, ed., *Quantitative International Politics: Insights and Evidence* (Englewood Cliffs, N.J.: Prentice Hall, 1968).

16. For a more complete analysis of the political processes that lead to the adoption of tariffs, see, e.g., Susanne Lohmann and Sharyn O'Halloran, "Divided Government and U.S. Trade Policy: Theory and Evidence," *International Organization*, Vol. 48, No. 4 (Autumn 1994), pp. 595–632.

17. Richard V. L. Cooper, "Military Manpower Procurement: Equity, Efficiency, and National Security," in Martin Anderson, ed., *Registration and the Draft* (Stanford, Calif.: The Hoover Institution, 1982), pp. 343–376.

18. This also suggests one reason why empirical analyses of the relationship between formal constraints and dispute involvement have not found any statistically significant effects (see, e.g., Morgan and Campbell, "Domestic Structure"). Whether or not *de jure* constraints exist may not matter as much as the presence or absence of *de facto* constraints.

19. Bueno de Mesquita and Lalman argue that "the mean ratio of expected political costs from using force to the expected benefits from a negotiated resolution of a dispute" is higher for democracies than for other states. Bueno de Mesquita and Lalman, *War and Reason*, p. 153. This would imply that checks and balances are more effective in democracies than in non-democracies. The empirical basis of this claim is not clear, however.

20. Bruce Bueno de Mesquita, Randolph Siverson, and Gary Woller, "War and the Fate of Regimes: A Comparative Analysis," *American Political Science Review*, Vol. 86, No. 3 (1992), pp. 638–646.

21. Morgan and Campbell, "Domestic Structure," p. 191. Those to whom leaders are accountable differ: democratic leaders are accountable to voters at large; autocrats are not. But this difference may not matter: any war fought in the private interest of the leader will, by definition, arouse opposition among those to whom he is accountable, whether that group is small or large.

16 Civil Conflict

16.1

Who Fights? The Determinants of Participation in Civil War

Macartan Humphreys and Jeremy M. Weinstein

Why do some individuals take enormous risks to participate as fighters in civil war? What differentiates those who are mobilized from those who remain on the sidelines? What distinguishes those who rebel from those who fight to defend the status quo? In spite of a large literature on the topic, scholars continue to debate the conditions under which men and women take up arms to participate in deadly combat. In this article, we examine the evidence for prominent, competing arguments in the context of Sierra Leone's civil war, drawing on a unique dataset that records the attitudes and behavior of 1,043 excombatants alongside a sample of 184 noncombatants.

Participation in violence is not simply a question of academic concern. Since 1945, civil wars have engulfed 73 countries and caused the deaths of more than 16 million people (Fearon and Laitin 2003). Understanding the motivations of fighters can shed light on the origins and evolution of these conflicts. But it can also help in the evaluation of strategies of conflict resolution and post conflict reconstruction. If insurgent armies have been forged through the promise of resource rents from the extraction of minerals, peacemaking may depend on the ability of external actors to purchase the support of potential spoilers. If such armies have motivated participation instead by mobilizing popular discontent with government policies, postconflict arrangements may need to focus more on the establishment of institutional arrangements that address discrimination, oppression, and inequality. Data on individual participation in civil war offer insight into the formation and cohesion of armed factions, something that cannot be assessed using country-level data.

In this article, we revisit the literature and make existing theories operational and testable with micro-level survey data. In advancing a set of hypotheses, we focus attention on rebellion against the state and the organization of civilian resistance to insurgent movements. A rich theoretical literature exists that focuses primarily on the decision to rebel. Here we contend, however, that this work has insights to help us understand both why some choose to challenge the government and why others rise in defense of the status quo.

Our empirical analysis raises questions about critical, yet untested assumptions that shape existing theoretical debates about mobilization. Prominent accounts of why people join are not necessarily rival; indeed, our analysis suggests that different logics of participation may coexist in a single civil war. Moreover, previous theoretical work on participation has too radically separated the decision to rebel from the decision to participate in violence more generally. The proxies for grievance that we (and other scholars) employ do predict rebellion, *but they also predict participation in defense of the state*. The most immediate interpretation

Source: Macartan Humphreys and Jeremy M. Weinstein. "Who Fights? The Determinants of Participation in Civil War," in *American Journal of Political Science* 52(2): 436–437, 439–443, and 452–455. Copyright 2008 Midwest Political Science Association. Reprinted by permission of John Wiley and Sons.

of this finding is that marginalization produces a greater disposition to participate in violence, but not through the logic of protest underpinning classic arguments of rebellion. Our evidence suggests also that the widespread assumption that individuals have agency in making choices about participation is empirically suspect. Theoretical accounts have too rarely conceptualized abduction as a tool in a faction's menu of recruitment strategies, yet it appears essential in practice. . . .

But to properly assess competing explanations, we need a research design that permits a comparison of the characteristics of participants and nonparticipants. . . .

We begin our analysis with a brief discussion of the . . . previous work on mobilization for civil war and specify testable hypotheses about the conditions under which individuals join armed factions.

We conclude with a discussion of our results and their relevance for theoretical debates about high-risk collective action. . . .

Motivating Participation

At least three major schools of thought aim to explain patterns of participation (and nonparticipation) in civil war.[1] The first comes largely from scholars of revolution and pinpoints a range of expressive motivations, emphasizing the grievances that underlie participation. These approaches do not depend on rationalist foundations; instead, they highlight motivations rooted in individual frustration or a desire to act in the broader interest of one's social or economic group. Such arguments have been advanced largely to explain resistance to the state, yet they generate equally clear predictions about who will decide to defend the status quo.

Mancur Olson's (1965) analysis of collective action has given rise to two more approaches that accept, as a starting point, the idea that individuals weigh the costs and benefits of participation. The first emphasizes the importance of selective incentives—participation must be beneficial not only to groups but also to individuals. This in turn requires that private benefits be made available in exchange for participation. Critics that claim this reading of Olson is overly narrow or materialist focus instead on the importance of social sanctions. Strong communities can bring social pressures to bear that change how individuals evaluate the costs and benefits of joining a movement. The logic of both these approaches applies equally to insurgent and counterinsurgent mobilization. . . .

Grievance and Participation

Scholars of social revolution argue that the depth of an individual's discontent with his or her economic position in society is a major causal factor that differentiates participants in rebellion from nonparticipants. Discontent, when aggregated across individuals in a particular social class or ethnic group, provides the foundation for mobilization and the onset of violence against the state.[2] There are many variants of this basic argument, each emphasizing different elements of individual motivation.

The first identifies *social class* as the critical variable differentiating those who rebel from those who remain on the sidelines or, indeed, choose to defend the status quo.[3] Karl Marx, for example, proposed that the industrial proletariat would be the main engine of revolution against capitalist systems, owing to individuals' shared experiences of exploitation ([1848] 1968). However, the locus of participation in actual revolutions—poor, rural people rather than the urban working class—shifted the debate in the literature toward making distinctions among the mass of undifferentiated rural dwellers. . . .

Others have challenged this focus on land, suggesting that income inequality is the prime source of discontent and motivator of participation (Muller and Seligson 1987).

A second approach focuses on ethnic and political grievances rather than class differences as the factor shaping an individual's decision to join a military faction. For some, the logic of ethnic mobilization begins and ends with long-standing cultural practices that distinguish ethnic groups. Differences between groups, sometimes reflected in a history of animosity between them, are believed to make conflict more likely (Horowitz 1985). . . .

A third variant focuses on personal dislocation and the frustrations that arise from an individual's inability to express her concerns through "normal" nonviolent channels. . . .

Together, these three variants imply that an individual's social position determines his or her propensity to participate in violence. Individuals are more likely to join a rebellion if:

H1: They are economically deprived.

H2: They are marginalized from political decision making.

H3: They are alienated from mainstream political processes.

Stories about the expressive motivations that drive participation in revolutionary collective action also generate clear predictions about the characteristics of those who will mobilize in *opposition* to rebellion. Class-based accounts imply that those in a relatively better economic position will have a stake in defending the status quo.

Theories constructed around the importance of ethnic and political marginalization suggest that members of ethnic groups that benefit from political power have stronger incentives to prevent a successful rebellion. Approaches that emphasize social or political alienation as a driver of participation imply that individuals active and engaged in mainstream political processes will mobilize to defend the existing political system. In accounting for participation in counterinsurgent mobilization, then, a grievances approach generates predictions opposite to those enumerated above. . . .

Selective Incentives

Critiquing decades of scholarship that highlighted the centrality of grievance (or other shared interests) in explaining collective action, Mancur Olson (1965) observed that common interests are not sufficient to motivate participation. When successful, revolutionary mobilization produces public goods. If enjoyment of these benefits is not contingent on participation, he argues, rational, self-interested individuals will not bear the costs of acting and will instead free ride on the willingness of others to participate. Olson's formulation turned the literature on participation on its head: instead of assessing the depth of grievances held by particular classes and ethnic groups, the question became why anyone chooses to rebel at all.

Recognizing that collective action is often observed in practice, Olson offered an explanation for why some individuals choose to participate and take on unnecessary costs. He introduced the idea of selective incentives—inducements to participation that are private and can be made available on a selective basis. . . .

While much of this literature emphasizes the positive incentives that can be given to individuals who participate ("pull" factors), the theory only requires that the private benefits of joining outweigh the private benefits of not joining. . . .

In an environment of conflict, a key determinant of welfare for nonparticipants is the level of violence they will have to endure. Thus protection from violence (a "push" factor) may be a key private benefit that fighting groups offer. Indeed, joining a military faction may be the most important strategy individuals use to avoid the violence perpetrated by the opposing side(s) (Goodwin 2001; Kalyvas and Kocher 2007; Mason and Krane 1989).

Although a number of the determinants of the efficacy of selective incentives (for example, poverty which may indicate a relatively high marginal return to benefits) are consistent with rival explanations for participation, some distinct hypotheses can be identified. In particular, individuals are more likely to participate in rebellion if:

H4: They expect to receive selective incentives from the fighting group.

H5: They believe they would be safer inside a fighting faction than outside of it.

A selective incentives story is equally plausible as an explanation for participation in counterinsurgent mobilization. To the extent that rebel groups attack villages or threaten the status quo, all villagers would benefit from locally organized resistance that protects against rebel attacks. But participation in such activities is risky and costly. Selective incentives—whether positive or negative—potentially play an important role in helping leaders to mobilize individuals for high-risk collective action to fight *against* insurgent movements.

It is worth noting that Olson offered a second explanation for the extent of observed participation in collective action—one that has received far less exploration in the literature on mobilization for war. *Coercion,* he argued, could resolve the free-rider problem that undermines the capacity for collective action. This argument is especially germane in the context of civil wars (Gates 2002), a point we return to in the discussion of our results. . . .

Social Sanctions

A third school of thought links an individual's decision to participate to the characteristics of the community in which he or she is embedded. According to this approach an analysis that focuses only on private gains from membership without accounting for community-level features is incomplete. Strong communities that can monitor individual behavior and bring to bear a variety of social sanctions are essential for overcoming the free-rider problem that can limit participation in rebellion. . . .

The importance of preexisting social networks and shared collective identities was not lost on earlier scholars of revolution. . . . The community perspective suggests a number of additional hypotheses. Individuals are more likely to participate in rebellion if:

H6: Members of their community are active in the movement.

H7: Their community is characterized by strong social structures.

As with selective incentives, arguments about the efficacy of social sanctions for motivating high-risk collective action apply as concretely to situations of counterinsurgent mobilization as to rebellion itself. Leaders who wish to mobilize individuals to take enormous risks to prevent the rebellion from succeeding benefit also from the existence of dense communities with shared values and beliefs, as norms of generalized reciprocity are powerful inducements to individual participation. Of course, the ultimate impact of community cohesion likely depends on whether participation is in some sense in the community's interest—a point we return to below. . . .

Discussion and Conclusion

Statistical evidence from Sierra Leone's civil war offers support to three major literatures that seek to account for revolutionary mobilization. While political motivations, as proxied by support for opposition parties and membership of the Mende ethnic group, do not appear as prominent motivations, participation in a military faction does depend on an individual's relative social and economic position, the costs and benefits of joining, and the social pressures that emanate from friends and community members. While these arguments are often presented as rival, multiple logics of participation do coexist within the same conflict.

At the same time, our empirical results challenge conventional accounts of participation that emphasize grievances. While proxies for standard grievance explanations receive support in our study of those who rebel, we find that the same indicators—poverty, a lack of access to education, and political alienation—also predict the decision to *defend* the status quo. Moreover, these factors also distinguish those who are abducted into a fighting force from those who remain on the sidelines. Conventional interpretations of welfare measures which emphasize the individual and group frustrations that drive participation in violence are thus called into question. Individual characteristics that observers may readily take to be indicators of frustration with the state may instead proxy for features such as a greater vulnerability to political manipulation by political and military elites, a greater frustration with more peaceful forms of protest, or most simply, a lack of other options.

Our work suggests as well that involuntary participation is a fundamental part of revolutionary mobilization and political violence. Although this fact is already well appreciated by scholars of the Sierra Leone conflict, traditional theories of mobilization within political science make little mention of coerced participation. Understanding why groups abduct recruits and the implications of such a strategy for the dynamics of the war is an open research question, but one that can no longer be ignored in traditional debates about why people join.

Admittedly, these empirical observations emerge from an analysis of a single case. Yet in terms of its duration, the scale of its combatant organizations, and the scope of violence, the war in Sierra Leone is not unlike other recent conflicts that have engulfed countries in the developing world. Whether the specific membership patterns we highlight here are evident in other cases is an empirical question; nonetheless, the distinct mobilization processes we describe, and attempt to parse, are general.

Given the powerful evidence for multiple paths to participation in Sierra Leone, we believe that the debate now needs to shift from battles over the supremacy of particular theories to a concerted analysis of the conditions under which distinct strategies of recruitment are pursued by different groups at different times. . . .

Our empirical results suggest that both the supply side and the demand side of the labor market for fighters depend on strategic concerns. Needed is a theory not just of when collective action succeeds but a more complete model of the market for the supply and demand of fighters in a context where employers have both wages and violence at their disposal. . . .

Notes

1. Wood (2003) provides an example of a fourth approach not tested in this article. She argues that participation in the insurgency in El Salvador was motivated by a set of moral and emotional considerations; in particular, she argues that recruits took "pleasure in agency" and that, in El Salvador, these process-oriented motivations are superior to conventional explanations.

2. While this article focuses on individual-level determinants of participation, much of the literature emphasizing grievances seeks to explain why some countries experience revolution while others do not. Claims are made implicitly about what motivates individual participation; it is those claims that we seek to test in this article.

3. Although we do not have the data needed to test the argument, a variant on standard class accounts suggests that what matters most is a psychological mechanism—relative deprivation. Rather than assessing one's position as compared to others in society, individuals may judge their situation relative to their own expectations and past experiences. Individual frustration with a gap between expectations and actual achievement, it is hypothesized, may be a sufficient condition for participation. James Davies (1962) first identified this mechanism in his study of revolutionary mobilization in the United States, Russia, and Egypt. Ted Robert Gurr (1970) offered a more general theory of deprivation, arguing that gaps between expectations and capabilities determined the degree of relative deprivation and the potential for violence

References

Davies, James. 1962. "Toward a Theory of Revolution." *American Sociological Review 6* (February): 5–19.

Fearon, James, and David Laitin. 2003. "Ethnicity, Insurgency, and Civil War." *American Political Science Review* 97(February): 75–90.

Gates, Scott. 2002. "Recruitment and Allegiance*:* The Micro foundations of Rebellion*." Journal of Conflict Resolution* 26 (February): 111–30.

Goodwin, Jeffrey. *No other Way Out: States and Revolutionary Movements, 1945–1991.* New York: Cambridge University Press.

Gurr, Ted. 1970. *Why Men Rebel. Princeton,* NJ: Princeton University Press.

Horowitz, Donald. 1985. *Ethnic Groups in Conflict.* Berkeley: University of California Press.

Kalyvas, Stathis, and Matthew Kocher. 2007. "How 'Free' Is Free Riding in Civil Wars? Violence, Insurgency and the Collective Action Problem.*" World Politics* 59(January): 177–216.

Marx, Karl, and Friedrich Engels. 1968 [1848]. *The Communist Manifesto.* Middlesex: Penguin.

Mason, T. David, and Dale Krane. 1989. "The Political Economy of Death Squads: Toward a Theory of the Impact of State- Sanctioned Terror.*" International Studies Quarterly* 33(June): 175–98.

Muller, Edward, and Mitchell Seligson. 1987. "Inequality and Insurgency.*" American Political Science Review* 81(June): 425–52.

Olson, Mancur. 1965. *The Logic of Collective Action: Public Goods and the Theory of Groups*. Cambridge, MA: Harvard University Press

Wood, Elisabeth. 2003. *Insurgent Collective Action and Civil War in El Salvador.* Cambridge: Cambridge University Press.

16.2

Committing to Peace

Barbara F. Walter

The Puzzle

A close examination of all civil war negotiations between 1940 and 1992 shows that getting combatants to the bargaining table and resolving their grievances does not guarantee peace.[1] As Figure 16.1 shows, 62 percent of all negotiations during this period led to a signed bargain.[2] Yet as Figure 16.2 reveals, almost half of these treaties were never implemented. Contrary to common expectations, combatants do not have the greatest difficulty resolving underlying conflicts of interest and reaching bargains. They have the greatest difficulty implementing the resulting terms. In short, the conditions that encourage groups to initiate negotiations and sign settlements do not appear sufficient to bring peace.

Figure 16.1 Percentage of civil war negotiations that led to signed bargains, 1940–1992.

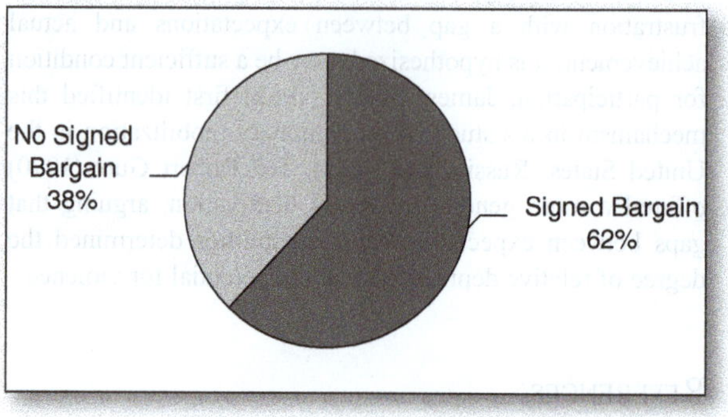

Figure 16.2 Percentage of signed bargains that were successfully implemented, 1940–1992.

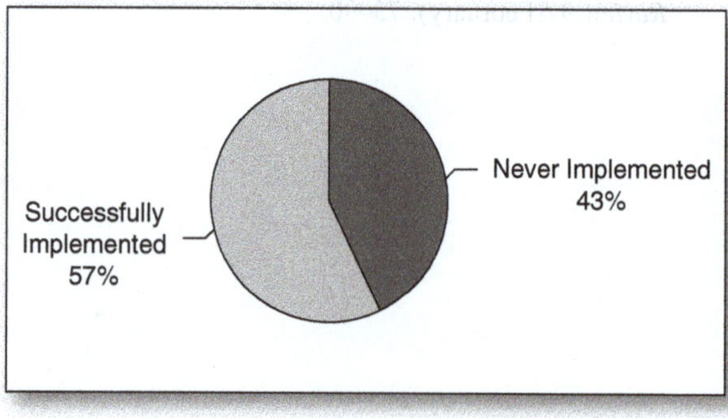

The Argument

An important and frequent reason why civil war negotiations fail is because it is almost impossible for the combatants themselves to arrange credible guarantees on the terms of the settlement. Negotiations frequently do not fail because the conditions on the ground are not "ripe for resolution," as many have argued. Combatants in most civil wars seek a negotiated settlement at some point during the conflict. Nor do negotiations frequently fail because bargains cannot be struck, as many others have argued. Adversaries often compromise on the basic issues underlying their conflict, and they often find mutually acceptable solutions to their problems. Negotiations fail because combatants cannot credibly promise to abide by terms that create numerous opportunities for exploitation after the treaty is signed and implementation begins. Only if a third party is willing to enforce or verify demobilization, and only if the combatants are willing to extend power-sharing guarantees, will promises to abide by the original terms be credible and negotiations succeed. I call this theory the *credible commitment theory* of civil war resolution.

In what follows, I show that resolving a civil war requires much more than negotiating a bargain and establishing a cease-fire. A successful peace settlement must integrate the previously warring fractions into a single state, create a new government capable of accommodating their interests, and build a national, nonpartisan military force. This process of integration, however, creates a transition period during which combatants become less and less able to survive a surprise attack and enforce subsequent terms. Thus, even under the very best conditions—when combatants have initiated negotiations and signed a mutually agreeable treaty—the desire for peace clashes with the realities of implementation, and groups frequently choose the safer, more certain option of war.

The fact that combatants have such difficulty enforcing and credibly committing to the terms of their own peace settlements, however, does not mean that the resolution of civil wars can be traced to a single cause, outside security guarantees. Combatants have no chance to settle their wars unless they are willing, first, to meet at the negotiating table and, second, to resolve their underlying grievances and strike a deal. Both of these steps are likely to be driven by a variety of factors that come into play long before third parties arrive on the scene. Although the credible commitment theory says almost nothing about these additional conditions for peace, the focus here on enforcement and commitment does serve a purpose. By emphasizing the structural problems of implementation I hope to show that in important ways, issues of post-treaty security are likely to pervade all decisions leading to settlement and play a critical role in the final outcome of civil wars. In the end, enforcement will matter a great deal.

Current Theories of Civil War Resolution

Six additional theories of civil war resolution can be found in the literature, and I present them for several reasons. The first is to give skeptical readers a better sense of the many variables purported to take combatants from war to peace and allow these readers to come to their own conclusions about the efficacy of my argument. My second purpose is to begin to identify the full range of factors that are likely to play a role in each of the three stages of the peace process. This tactic is designed to impose greater conceptual rigor on the study of civil war resolution and enable me to determine what factors are doing what work at each step along the way. My final aim is to determine whether third-party security guarantees and power-sharing pacts really do play critical, independent roles in the peaceful resolution of civil wars, or are only the end result of these other, more important, conditions.

Current theories of civil war termination can be roughly grouped into one of two camps. The first views negotiated settlements primarily as a function of the economic, military, or political conditions that exist on the ground and are likely to encourage combatants to initiate negotiations. This set of theories tends to assume that once these conditions favor negotiation, successful settlement is likely.[3] The second set of theories views negotiated settlements primarily as a function of combatants' ability to resolve underlying conflicts of interest. This camp assumes that once a bargain has been reached, successful settlement should follow. Both camps stand in contrast to the credible commitment theory, which argues that even if combatants reach a mutually agreeable bargain they will not implement its terms unless credible guarantees on the terms of the treaty are included.

Conditions that Affect "Ripeness for Resolution"

The most popular explanation for the success or failure of negotiations focuses on the importance of situational factors, conditions that make civil wars "ripe for resolution."[4] Three conditions in particular are believed to make war less attractive and encourage combatants to pursue compromise solutions: high costs of war, military stalemate, and certain domestic political institutions.

Costs of War

Expected utility choice theorists have long assumed that the decision to fight or negotiate is determined by the relative costs and benefits of a unilateral victory or a compromise settlement.[5] Proponents of this view argue that combatants carefully estimate their chances of winning a civil war, the amount of time it will take to achieve this victory, how much it will cost, and their relative payoffs from winning versus accepting a settlement. Settlement occurs when combatants believe they can do no better by continuing to fight than by bargaining.

There are good theoretical reasons to believe the costs of war have a significant effect on the process by which civil wars end. First, incumbent governments and rebels have a finite base of resources on which to draw and are forced to pursue alternate solutions to violence as war coffers dry up. Second, a full military victory becomes less attractive as the costs of achieving it increase. Third, leaders are likely to come under increasing domestic pressure to end violence as civilian suffering increases and war fatigue sets in. Peter De Vos, former U.S. ambassador to Liberia, Guinea-Bissau, Mozambique, Tanzanian, and Costa Rica, points out that "the participants are not ready to settle until they're just too weary. If you look at Mozambique, if you look at Angola, that's what's happened."[6] The costs of continuing a war, therefore, should be directly related to combatants' willingness to pursue a negotiated settlement.

Balance of Power

Theorists of international relations have long argued that the decision to go to war (or remain at peace) is strongly affected by the relative balance of power between adversaries.[7] A. F. K. Organski, for example, has argued that a balance of power produces peace because "no one side can achieve a great enough superiority to be sure that aggressive action would be crowned with success."[8] This logic should apply equally well to the resolution of civil wars. Combatants who are fairly equal on the civil war battlefield should be more likely to negotiate a settlement for at least two reasons. First, military stalemates often, although not always, indicate a determined opponent who promises a costly war of attrition. Second, military stalemates produce uncertainty as to the eventual winner, making each side less willing to risk a decisive loss.[9] "Stalemate," according to George Modelski, "is easily the most important condition of a settlement. Without it, one or both of the parties may hold justified hopes of an outright win and therefore have the incentive to go on fighting."[10] This theory, therefore, predicts that the more equally matched combatants are on the battlefield, the more likely they are to pursue negotiations.

Domestic Political Institutions

A third explanation for negotiated settlements can be drawn from institutional explanations for war and peace. One could argue that the decision to negotiate depends on the domestic political constraints placed on individual leaders. According to this view, civil wars that occur in democratic countries should be more likely to end in compromise settlements, for one of three reasons.[11] First, leaders of democracies face higher domestic constraints in their use of force than leaders of authoritarian governments and are, therefore, less likely to be allowed to pursue unpopular wars.[12] Presidents Johnson and Nixon were forced to respond to a public that increasingly demanded U.S. withdrawal from Vietnam. This stands in stark contrast to Russia's pursuit of its war with Chechnya. As one noted Russian scholar has observed:

> Russia's war with Chechnya most likely would not have occurred if Russia had been a consolidated democracy. From the very beginning, roughly two-thirds of all Russians opposed the war, a figure that grew steadily over the next two years. Had their interests been represented in the state through the usual pluralist institutions found in stable, liberal democracies, the decision to attack may not have been made.[13]

Second, democratic leaders are likely to find it easier to credibly commit to peace agreements since they are more likely to be held accountable by their voting publics for promises made.[14] Abraham Lincoln's signature on a peace agreement between the North and the South was a credible signal of the North's intent because of the full force of the democratic institutions that accorded him his power to sign. It was improbable that he would try to renege on a treaty. By contrast, General Anastasio Somoza's word to the Sandinistas during Nicaragua's war in 1978–79 was less credible because public penalties would not have followed any renouncement of peace.

Finally, democratic leaders accustomed to sharing political power have less to lose by opening the government than authoritarian leaders who stand to forfeit monopoly control of government.[15] The Conservative Party in Colombia, for example, gave up far less when it signed a peace treaty with the Liberal Party than did the absolutist government of Chiang Kai-shek when it agreed to a coalition government with the Chinese Communist Party. A focus on democratic political institutions, therefore, leads to the prediction that the more democratic a state, the more likely the government will be to negotiate a settlement to war.

Conditions that Encourage Combatants to Strike a Bargain

Scholars in the second camp shift the focus of attention away from the conditions that encourage combatants to initiate negotiations toward the conditions that encourage combatants to make real concessions to their enemy.[16] These scholars do not ignore the importance of preexisting military, economic, or political conditions that favor settlement. They simply stress that negotiations have no chance to succeed unless combatants are able to resolve the issues *driving* the war and reach a mutually agreeable deal. Three factors in particular are likely to affect the chances of a settlement: the identity of the combatants, the divisibility of the stakes over which they are fighting, and the presence of an outside mediator. If identities are malleable, if stakes are easy to divide, or if mediators are present, negotiations are more likely to succeed. If not, combatants are unlikely to resolve their differences, and war is likely to resume.

Ethnic Identity

It is widely assumed in both journalistic and scholarly accounts of civil wars that the identity of the combatants plays a large role in their willingness to compromise.[17] Civil wars between different ethnic groups are frequently depicted as intense value conflicts fought over issues close to the heart. Such wars are thus thought to be less amenable to rational calculations of costs and benefits than conflicts between combatants drawn from similar identity groups. Ethnic conflicts are viewed as the result of kinship turned bad, of "feuds" and "bitter rivalries," not power politics. "I have six sons," a Bosnian Croat farmer told a reporter when asked whether he would implement the Dayton peace accords of 1994, "and if we are told to share our government with Muslims, all of them will join me in the war that will come."[18] By this theory, once violence erupts, identities become cemented in ways that keep combatants from working together. This theory predicts that combatants fighting over issues tied to their identities will have greater difficulty reaching a compromise settlement than those fighting over more negotiable political or economic issues.[19]

The Divisibility of Stakes

Others argue that the success or failure of peace negotiations depends on how easy it is for the combatants to divide the stakes over which they are fighting. "If," Paul Pillar has written, "the stakes are chiefly indivisible, so that neither side can get most of what it wants without depriving the other of most of what it wants, negotiations are less apt to be successful."[20] Many civil wars may end in decisive military victories precisely because the goals combatants are pursuing tend to be absolute, "with nothing in between to contribute to the give and take of negotiation and bargaining."[21]

Two arguments regarding divisibility can be made. One could argue that rebels fighting for total goals such as the complete control of a country, the elimination of a rival, or the revolutionary overthrow of a hated political, economic, or social system are less likely to reach a negotiated settlement than rebels fighting for limited aims such as land reform or democratic adjustment.[22] In these cases, it is possible that a middle ground exists in which to draw a compromise settlement. This theory predicts that total wars are less likely to end in negotiated settlement than limited wars.

One could also argue, however, that rebels fighting over territory may make it easier for the central government to accommodate their demands because incumbent elites can part with territory and still retain power. If this is true, one would predict that secessionist conflicts and conflicts fought for greater territorial autonomy are more likely to find negotiated settlements because these conflicts do not threaten the very existence (or livelihood) of the incumbent elite.[23] This theory predicts that territorial wars will be more likely to reach negotiated settlement than nonterritorial conflicts.

Mediation

Finally, many scholars and practitioners champion the ability of a mediator to surmount difficult bargaining problems and help combatants reach an agreement.[24] Mediators serve at least three important roles. The first is informational. Mediators can supply missing information, transmit messages, highlight common interests, and encourage meaningful communication so

Table 16.1 The Competing Hypotheses

Theory	Associated Hypothesis	
Costs of war	Hypothesis 1	The more costly a war, the more likely combatants are to negotiate a settlement.
Balance of power	Hypothesis 2	The more equally matched combatants are on the battlefield, the more likely they are to end their war in a negotiated settlement.
Domestic political institutions	Hypothesis 3	The more democratic a state, the more likely its government is to negotiate a settlement.
Ethnic identity	Hypothesis 4	Combatants fighting over issues tied to their identity are less likely to end their war in a negotiated settlement than combatants whose identity is the same.
Divisibility of stakes	Hypothesis 5	The more divisible the stakes over which the combatants are fighting, the more likely the war is to end in a negotiated settlement.
Mediation	Hypothesis 6	The success of civil war negotiations varies directly with the presence or absence of an outside mediator.

that combatants can better locate a common middle ground. They can also play an important procedural role. Mediators can arrange for interactions between the parties, control the pace and formality of the meetings, and structure the agenda in order to keep the process focused on the issues. The third role is in some ways more coercive. Mediators can reward concessions made by the parties and punish intransigence in order to make disagreement costly.[25] Each of these functions is likely to help the combatants to break through bargaining impasses and locate terms agreeable to both parties. "The ability of the would-be mediator," Stephen Stedman argues, "is an independent variable that affects the success or failure of negotiation."[26] Given this theory, one expects the success of civil war negotiations to vary directly with the presence or absence of an outside mediator.

The preceding discussion reveals a range of alternative explanations for why some civil wars end peacefully while others do not. Table 16.1 lists these competing hypotheses.

What is Missing

Current theories of the resolution of civil wars tell us much about the conditions likely to bring combatants to the negotiating table and about the conditions then likely to encourage them to reach and sign compromise bargains. The theories do not explain, however, why even signed bargains fail to bring peace, and thus do not provide a comprehensive explanation for why some negotiations end in peace while others do not. As Figure 16.2 showed, a signed peace settlement does not guarantee that a civil war will end. Almost half of all combatants who signed comprehensive peace agreements during the period from 1940 to 1992 chose to return to war rather than implement the terms of the agreement. To understand why some civil wars end by negotiated settlement and others do not, we must understand how the parties' expectations about compliance with the terms of the agreement affect decisions to negotiate or fight at each step on the road to peace.

NOTES

1. Fifty-one percent of all civil wars that started between 1940 and 1992 experienced formal peace negotiations at some point during the conflict. See appendix 1 for the list of cases.

2. Only those agreements that included a political as well as a military solution to the conflict were defined as comprehensive peace agreements. See chapter 3 for a discussion of how peace agreements were defined and coded.

3. See especially I. William Zartman, *Ripe for Resolution: Conflict and Intervention in Africa* (New York: Oxford University Press, 1989); and Stephen John Stedman, *Peacemaking in Civil War: International Mediation in Zimbabwe, 1974–1980* (Boulder: Lynne Rienner Publishers, 1991).

4. The term "ripe for resolution" was coined by I. William Zartman in his book by that title.

5. See, for example, Donald Wittman, "How a War Ends: A Rational Model Approach," *Journal of Conflict Resolution* 23, no. 4 (1979): 743–63; Bruce Bueno de Mesquita and David Lalman, *War and Reason: Domestic and International Imperatives* (New Haven: Yale University Press, 1992); T. David Mason and Patrick J. Fett, "How Civil Wars End: A Rational Choice Approach," *Journal of Conflict Resolution* 40, no. 4 (1996): 546–68; and T. David Mason, Joseph P. Weingarten, Jr., and Patrick J. Fett, "Win, Lose, or Draw: Predicting the Outcome of Civil Wars," *Political Research Quarterly* 52, no. 2 (1999): 239–68.

6. From Dana Francis, ed., *Mediating Deadly Conflict* (Cambridge, Mass.: World Peace Foundation, 1998), 34–35.

7. See A. F. K. Organski, *World Politics*, 2d ed. (New York: Random House, 1968); Inis L. Claude, *Power and International Relations* (New York: Random House, 1962); Geoffrey Blainey, *The Causes of War* (New York: Free Press, 1973); Michael Howard, *The Causes of Wars* (Cambridge: Harvard University Press, 1983); Arthur Stein, *Why Nations Cooperate: Circumstances and Choice in International Relations* (Ithaca, N.Y.: Cornell University Press, 1990).

8. Organski, *World Politics*.

9. The power preponderance school would make the opposite prediction, arguing that combatants should be less likely to negotiate settlement when a balance of power exists since both groups can still hold onto the hope that they will eventually win the war. I do not include a discussion of this theory in the text because it has never been offered as an explanation for the resolution of civil wars. Nonetheless, the same hypothesis regarding the importance of a military stalemate could be used to test this prediction.

10. George Modelski, "International Settlement of Internal War," in *International Aspects of Civil Strife*, ed. James Rosenau (Princeton: Princeton University Press, 1964), 143. See also I. William Zartman, "The Unfinished Agenda: Negotiating Internal Conflicts," in *Stopping the Killing: How Civil Wars End*, ed. Roy Licklider (New York: New York University Press, 1993), 24; Zartman, *Ripe for Resolution;* Zartman, "Dynamics and Constraints in Negotiations in Internal Conflicts," in *Elusive Peace: Negotiating an End to Civil Wars*, ed. Zartman (Washington, D.C.: Brookings Institute, 1995), 11; and Robert Harrison Wagner, "The Causes of Peace," in Licklider, *Stopping the Killing*, 260.

11. Ted Gurr, however, has found that most democratic regimes have been able to avoid communal conflicts through various types of reform. Nonetheless, we should still observe a relationship between the degree of democracy in a country and the likelihood of settlement if this theory holds. See Ted Robert Gurr, *Minorities at Risk: A Global View of Ethnopolitical Conflicts* (Washington D.C.: United States Institute of Peace Press, 1993).

12. Bueno de Mesquita and Lalman, *War and Reason;* T. Clifton Morgan and Sally H. Campbell, "Domestic Structure, Decisional Constraints, and War: So Why Can't Democracies Fight?" *Journal of Conflict Resolution* 35, no. 2 (1991): 187–211. For a related argument see H. E. Goemans, *War and Punishment: The Causes of War Termination and the First World War* (Princeton: Princeton University Press, 2000).

13. Michael McFaul, "A Precarious Peace: Domestic Politics in the Making of Russian Foreign Policy," *International Security* 22, no 3 (1997–98): 5–35.

14. For discussions of how democratic institutions can help leaders reveal information about their intentions and thus overcome informational asymmetries see James D. Fearon, "Domestic Political Audiences and the Escalation of International Disputes," *American Political Science Review* 88 (1994): 577–92; and Kenneth A. Schultz, "Domestic Opposition and Signaling in International Crises," *American Political Science Review* 92 (1998): 829–44.

15. Although this depends on the goals of the rebels. Governments who are accustomed to power sharing are likely to be equally intransigent if rebels aim to overthrow their leader or secede. In these cases, even the most democratic leaders would have equally much to lose.

16. See especially Robert Randle, "The Domestic Origins of Peace," *Annals of the Academy of Political and Social Science* 392 (November 1970): 76–85; Fred C. Ikle, *Every War Must End* (New York Columbia University Press, 1971); Glenn Snyder and Paul Diesing, *Conflict among Nations* (Princeton: Princeton University Press, 1977); and James D. Fearon, "Rationalist Explanations for War," *International Organization* 49, no. 3 (1995): 379–414.

17. See Chaim Kaufmann, "Possible and Impossible Solutions to Ethnic Civil Wars," *International Security* 20, no. 4 (1996): 136–75; Patrick M. Regan, *Civil Wars and Foreign Powers: Outside Intervention in Intrastate Conflict* (Ann Arbor: University of Michigan Press, 2000); Ibrahim A. Elbadawi and Nicholas Sambanis, "External Interventions and the Duration of Civil Wars," World Bank Policy Research Paper, July 25, 2000; Francis, *Mediating Deadly Conflict*; John W. Burton, *Resolving Deep-Rooted Conflict: A Handbook* (Lanham, Md.: University Press of America, 1987); Cvijeto Job, "Yugoslavia's Ethnic Furies," *Foreign Policy* 92 (fall 1993): 52–74; Anthony D. Smith, "The Ethnic Sources of Nationalism," in *Ethnic Conflict and International Security*, ed. Michael E. Brown (Princeton: Princeton University Press, 1993), 27–41.

18. Mike O'Connor, "Bosnia Croats Resist Peace Accord," *New York Times*, February 13, 1996, A8.

19. See Robert Randle, *The Origins of Peace: A Study of Peacemaking and the Structure of Peace Settlements* (New York: Free Press, 1973), especially p. 430; Donald Horowitz, *Ethnic Groups in Conflict* (Berkeley and Los Angeles: University of California Press, 1985), especially chap. 14; and Burton, *Resolving Deep-Rooted Conflict*.

20. Paul Pillar, *Negotiating Peace: War Termination as a Bargaining Process* (Princeton: Princeton University Press, 1983), 24. For similar arguments see Ikle, *Every War Must End*, 95; Modelski, "International Settlement"; and Wagner, "The Causes of Peace."

21. Zartman, "The Unfinished Agenda," 25–26.

22. See Stephen John Stedman, "Negotiation and Mediation in Internal Conflict," in *The International Dimensions of Internal Conflict*, ed. Michael E. Brown (Cambridge: MIT Press, 1996); and Charles King, "Devolution of Power and Negotiated Settlements in Civil Wars," paper presented at the Second Annual Convention of the Association for the Study of Nationalities, New York, April 1997.

23. See especially, Stephen Stedman, "Spoiler Problems in Peace Processes," *International Security* 22, no. 2 (1997): 5–53.

24. See Jacob Bercovitch and Jeffrey Z. Rubin, eds., *Mediation in International Relations: Multiple Approaches to Conflict Management* (New York: St. Martin's Press, 1992); Jacob Bercovitch, *Social Conflicts and Third Parties: Strategies of Conflict Resolution* (Boulder: Westview Press, 1984); Francis, *Mediating Deadly Conflict*; C. R. Mitchell and K. Webb, eds., *New Approaches to International Mediation* (Westport, Conn.: Greenwood Press, 1988); Cyrus Vance, *Hard Choices: Critical Years in America's Foreign Policy* (New York: Simon and Schuster, 1983); David Owen, *Balkan Odyssey* (New York: Harcourt, Brace, 1995); and Chester A. Crocker, *High Noon in Southern Africa: Making Peace in a Rough Neighborhood* (New York: W. W. Norton, 1992).

25. This typology was developed by Saadia Touval and I. William Zartman, eds., *International Mediation in Theory and Practice* (Boulder: Westview Press, 1985). For a good overview see Jacob Bercovitch, "Mediation in International Conflict: An Overview of Theory, a Review of Practice," in *Peacemaking in International Conflict: Methods and Techniques*, ed. I. William Zartman and J. Lewis Rasmussen (Washington, D.C.: U.S. Institute of Peace, 1997).

26. Stedman, *Peacemaking in Civil War*, 23.

16.3

Give War a Chance

Edward N. Luttwak

Premature Peacemaking

An unpleasant truth often overlooked is that although war is a great evil, it does have a great virtue: it can resolve political conflicts and lead to peace. This can happen when all belligerents become exhausted or when one wins decisively. Either way the key is that the fighting must continue until a resolution is reached. War brings peace only after passing a culminating phase of violence. Hopes of military success must fade for accommodation to become more attractive than further combat.

Since the establishment of the United Nations and the enshrinement of great-power politics in its Security Council, however, wars among lesser powers have rarely been allowed to run their natural course. Instead, they have typically been interrupted early on, before they could burn themselves out and establish the preconditions for a lasting settlement. Cease-fires and armistices have frequently been imposed under the aegis of the Security Council in order to halt fighting. NATO's intervention in the Kosovo crisis follows this pattern.

But a cease-fire tends to arrest war-induced exhaustion and lets belligerents reconstitute and rearm their forces. It intensifies and prolongs the struggle once the cease-fire ends—and it does usually end. This was true of the Arab-Israeli war of 1948–49, which might have come to closure in a matter of weeks if two cease-fires ordained by the Security Council had not let the combatants recuperate. It has recently been true in the Balkans. Imposed cease-fires frequently interrupted the fighting between Serbs and Croats in Krajina, between the forces of the rump Yugoslav federation and the Croat army, and between the Serbs, Croats, and Muslims in Bosnia. Each time, the opponents used the pause to recruit, train, and equip additional forces for further combat, prolonging the war and widening the scope of its killing and destruction. Imposed armistices, meanwhile—again, unless followed by negotiated peace accords—artificially freeze conflict and perpetuate a state of war indefinitely by shielding the weaker side from the consequences of refusing to make concessions for peace.

The Cold War provided compelling justification for such behavior by the two superpowers, which sometimes collaborated in coercing less-powerful belligerents to avoid being drawn into their conflicts and clashing directly. Although imposed cease-fires ultimately did increase the total quantity of warfare among the lesser powers, and armistices did perpetuate states of war, both outcomes were clearly lesser evils (from a global point of view) than the possibility of nuclear war. But today, neither Americans nor Russians are inclined to intervene *competitively* in the wars of lesser powers, so the unfortunate consequences of interrupting war persist while no greater danger is averted. It might be best for all parties to let minor wars burn themselves out.

The Problems of Peacekeepers

Today cease-fires and armistices are imposed on lesser powers by multilateral agreement—not to avoid great-power competition but for essentially disinterested and indeed frivolous motives, such as television audiences' revulsion at harrowing scenes of war. But this, perversely, can *systematically* prevent the transformation of war into peace. The Dayton Accords are typical of the genre: they have condemned Bosnia to remain divided into three rival armed camps, with combat suspended momentarily but a state of hostility prolonged indefinitely. Since no side is threatened by defeat and loss, none has a sufficient incentive to negotiate a lasting settlement; because no path to peace is even visible, the dominant priority is to prepare for future war rather than to reconstruct devastated economies and ravaged societies. Uninterrupted war would

Source: Edward N. Luttwak, "Give War a Chance." Reprinted by permission of *Foreign Affairs*.

certainly have caused further suffering and led to an unjust outcome from one perspective or another, but it would also have led to a more stable situation that would have let the postwar era truly begin. Peace takes hold only when war is truly over.

A variety of multilateral organizations now make it their business to intervene in other peoples' wars. The defining characteristic of these entities is that they insert themselves in war situations while refusing to engage in combat. In the long run this only adds to the damage. If the United Nations helped the strong defeat the weak faster and more decisively, it would actually enhance the peacemaking potential of war. But the first priority of U.N. peacekeeping contingents is to avoid casualties among their own personnel. Unit commanders therefore habitually appease the *locally* stronger force, accepting its dictates and tolerating its abuses. This appeasement is not strategically purposeful, as siding with the stronger power overall would be; rather, it merely reflects the determination of each U.N. unit to avoid confrontation. The final result is to prevent the emergence of a coherent outcome, which requires an imbalance of strength sufficient to end the fighting.

Peacekeepers chary of violence are also unable to effectively protect civilians who are caught up in the fighting or deliberately attacked. At best, U.N. peacekeeping forces have been passive spectators to outrages and massacres, as in Bosnia and Rwanda; at worst, they collaborate with it, as Dutch U.N. troops did in the fall of Srebenica by helping the Bosnian Serbs separate the men of military age from the rest of the population.

The very presence of U.N. forces, meanwhile, inhibits the normal remedy of endangered civilians, which is to escape from the combat zone. Deluded into thinking that they will be protected, civilians in danger remain in place until it is too late to flee. During the 1992–94 siege of Sarajevo, appeasement interacted with the pretense of protection in an especially perverse manner: U.N. personnel inspected outgoing flights to prevent the escape of Sarajevo civilians in obedience to a cease-fire agreement negotiated with the locally dominant Bosnian Serbs—who habitually violated that deal. The more sensible, realistic response to a raging war would have been for the Muslims to either flee the city or drive the Serbs out.

Institutions such as the European Union, the Western European Union, and the Organization for Security and Cooperation in Europe lack even the U.N.'s rudimentary command structure and personnel, yet they too now seek to intervene in warlike situations, with predictable consequences. Bereft of forces even theoretically capable of combat, they satisfy the interventionist urges of member states (or their own institutional ambitions) by sending unarmed or lightly armed "observer" missions, which have the same problems as U.N. peacekeeping missions, only more so.

Military organizations such as NATO or the West African Peacekeeping Force (ECOMOG, recently at work in Sierra Leone) are capable of stopping warfare. Their interventions still have the destructive consequence of prolonging the state of war, but they can at least protect civilians from its consequences. Even that often fails to happen, however, because multinational military commands engaged in disinterested interventions tend to avoid any risk of combat, thereby limiting their effectiveness. U.S. troops in Bosnia, for example, repeatedly failed to arrest known war criminals passing through their checkpoints lest this provoke confrontation.

Multinational commands, moreover, find it difficult to control the quality and conduct of member states' troops, which can reduce the performance of all forces involved to the lowest common denominator. This was true of otherwise fine British troops in Bosnia and of the Nigerian marines in Sierra Leone. The phenomenon of troop degradation can rarely be detected by external observers, although its consequences are abundantly visible in the litter of dead, mutilated, raped, and tortured victims that attends such interventions. The true state of affairs is illuminated by the rare exception, such as the vigorous Danish tank battalion in Bosnia that replied to any attack on it by firing back in full force, quickly stopping the fighting. . . .

Refugee Nations

The most disinterested of all interventions in war—and the most destructive—are humanitarian relief activities. The largest and most protracted is the United Nations Relief and Works Agency (UNRWA). It was built on the model of its predecessor, the United Nations Relief and Rehabilitation Agency (UNRRA), which operated displaced persons' camps in Europe immediately after World War II. The UNRWA was established immediately after the 1948–49 Arab-Israeli war to feed, shelter, educate, and provide health services for Arab refugees who had fled Israeli zones in the former territory of Palestine.

By keeping refugees alive in spartan conditions that encouraged their rapid emigration or local resettlement, the UNRRA's camps in Europe had assuaged postwar resentments and helped disperse revanchist concentrations of national groups. But UNRWA camps in Lebanon, Syria, Jordan, the West Bank, and the Gaza Strip provided on the whole a higher standard of living than most Arab villagers had previously enjoyed, with a more varied diet, organized schooling, superior medical care, and no backbreaking labor in stony fields. They had, therefore, the opposite effect, becoming desirable homes rather than eagerly abandoned transit camps. With the encouragement of several Arab countries, the UNRWA turned escaping civilians into lifelong refugees who gave birth to refugee children, who have in turn had refugee children of their own.

During its half-century of operation, the UNRWA has thus perpetuated a Palestinian refugee nation, preserving its resentments in as fresh a condition as they were in 1948 and keeping the first bloom of revanchist emotion intact. By its very existence, the UNRWA dissuades integration into local society and inhibits emigration. The concentration of Palestinians in the camps, moreover, has facilitated the voluntary or forced enlistment of refugee youths by armed organizations that fight both Israel and each other. The UNRWA has contributed to a half-century of Arab-Israeli violence and still retards the advent of peace. . . .

The UNRWA has counterparts elsewhere, such as the Cambodian camps along the Thai border, which incidentally provided safe havens for the mass-murdering Khmer Rouge. But because the United Nations is limited by stingy national contributions, these camps' sabotage of peace is at least localized.

That is not true of the proliferating, feverishly competitive nongovernmental organizations (NGOs) that now aid war refugees. Like any other institution, these NGOS are interested in perpetuating themselves, which means that their first priority is to attract charitable contributions by being seen to be active in high-visibility situations. Only the most dramatic natural disasters attract any significant mass media attention, and then only briefly; soon after an earthquake or flood, the cameras depart. War refugees, by contrast, can win sustained press coverage if kept concentrated in reasonably accessible camps. Regular warfare among well-developed countries is rare and offers few opportunities for such NGOS, so they focus their efforts on aiding refugees in the poorest parts of the world. This ensures that the food, shelter, and health care offered—although abysmal by Western standards—exceeds what is locally available to non-refugees. The consequences are entirely predictable. Among many examples, the huge refugee camps along the Democratic Republic of Congo's border with Rwanda stand out. They sustain a Hutu nation that would otherwise have been dispersed, making the consolidation of Rwanda impossible and providing a base for radicals to launch more Tutsi-killing raids across the border. Humanitarian intervention has worsened the chances of a stable, long-term resolution of the tensions in Rwanda.

To keep refugee nations intact and preserve their resentments forever is bad enough, but inserting material aid into ongoing conflicts is even worse. Many NGOS that operate in an odor of sanctity routinely supply active combatants. Defenseless, they cannot exclude armed warriors from their feeding stations, clinics, and shelters. Since refugees are presumptively on the losing side, the warriors among them are usually in retreat. By intervening to help, NGOs systematically impede the progress of their enemies toward a decisive victory that could end the war. Sometimes NGOs, impartial to a fault, even help both sides, thus preventing mutual exhaustion and a resulting settlement. And in some extreme cases, such as Somalia, NGOs even pay protection money to local war bands, which use those funds to buy arms. Those NGOs are therefore helping prolong the warfare whose consequences they ostensibly seek to mitigate.

Make War to Make Peace

Too many wars nowadays become endemic conflicts that never end because the transformative effects of both decisive victory and exhaustion are blocked by outside intervention. Unlike the ancient problem of war, however, the compounding of its evils by disinterested interventions is a new malpractice that could be curtailed. Policy elites should actively resist the emotional impulse to intervene in other peoples' wars—not because they are indifferent to human suffering but precisely because they care about it and want to facilitate the advent of peace. The United States should dissuade multilateral interventions instead of leading them. New rules should be established for U.N. refugee relief activities to ensure that immediate succor is swiftly followed by repatriation, local absorption, or emigration, ruling out the establishment of permanent refugee camps. And although it may not be possible to constrain interventionist NGOs, they should at least be neither officially encouraged nor funded. Underlying these seemingly perverse measures would be a true appreciation of war's paradoxical logic and a commitment to let it serve its sole useful function: to bring peace.

17 Terrorism

17.1

The Four Waves of Rebel Terror and September 11[1]

David C. Rapoport

September 11, 2001 is the most destructive day in the long bloody history of rebel terrorism. The casualties and the economic damage were unprecedented. It could be the most important day too. President Bush declared a "war" to eliminate terror,[2] galvanizing a response that could reshape the international world.

Exactly 100 years ago, we heard a similar appeal. An Anarchist assassinated President William McKinley in September 1901, moving the new president Theodore Roosevelt to summon a worldwide crusade to exterminate terrorism everywhere.[3]

Will we succeed this time? No one knows, but even a brief acquaintance with the history of terrorism should make us more sensitive to the difficulties ahead. To this end, I will briefly describe rebel terrorism in the last 135 years to show how deeply implanted it has become in modern culture. . . .

Every state affected in the first wave, for example, radically transformed its police organizations. Plain-clothes police forces were created as indispensable tools to penetrate underground groups. The Russian *Okhrana*, Scotland Yard, and the FBI are conspicuous examples.[4] The new organizational form remains a permanent, perhaps indispensable, feature of modern life.

Terrorist tactics invariably produce rage and frustration, often driving governments to respond in unanticipated, extraordinary, illegal, and destructive ways. . . .

Democratic states over-react too. . . .

The Waves

In the 1880s, an initial "Anarchist Wave"[5] appeared which continued for some 40 years. Its successor, the "Anti-Colonial Wave" began in the 1920s, and by the 1960s had largely disappeared. The late 1960s witnessed the birth of the "New Left Wave," which dissipated largely in the 90s leaving a few groups still active in Sri Lanka, Spain, France, Peru, and Columbia. The fourth or "Religious Wave" began in 1979, and, if it follows the pattern of its predecessors, it still has twenty to twenty-five years to run.

Revolution was the overriding aim in every wave, but revolution was understood differently in each. Most terrorist organizations have understood revolution as secession or national self-determination. This principle, that a people should govern itself, was bequeathed by the American and French Revolutions. (The French Revolution also introduced the term "terror" to our vocabulary.[6]) In leaving open the question of what constitutes a "people," the principle is very ambiguous and can lead to endless conflict. . . .

The first three waves lasted approximately 40 to 45 years, but the "New Left Wave" was somewhat abbreviated. The pattern suggests a human life cycle pattern, where dreams that inspire fathers lose their attractiveness for the sons. Clearly, the life cycle of the waves does not correspond to that of organizations. Organizations normally dissipate before the wave does, though sometimes an organization survives its associated wave.

Source: David C. Rapoport (2002), "The Four Waves of Rebel Terror and September 11," *Anthropoetics* 8(1).

The Russian experience in the 1880s spread rapidly to other parts of Europe, the Americas, and Asia before reaching its peak and receding. Despite this extraordinary spread of activities, *no* first wave group achieved its goal. The three subsequent waves show similar, though not identical, patterns. Each begins in a different locale and the participating rebel groups often share purposes and tactics that distinguish them from participants in other waves. Local aims are common in all waves, but the crucial fact is that other states are simultaneously experiencing similar activities. The "Anti-Colonial Wave" produces the most successes, but they are few in number and, in every example, the achievement falls short of the stated aim, as we shall elaborate below.

Why does the first wave begin in the late 19th century? There may be many reasons, but two stand out: doctrine and technology. Russian writers, particularly Nechaev, Bakunin, and Kropotkin, created a doctrine or strategy for terror, an inheritance for successors to use, improve, and transmit. Participants, even those with different ultimate objectives, were now able to learn from each other. The distinctiveness of this pattern is brought home by comparing it with those of the ancient religious terrorists, who always stayed within their own religious traditions. Each religious tradition produced its own kind of terrorist, and sometimes their tactics were so uniform that they appear to be a form of ritual. But if one compares Nechaev's *Revolutionary Catechism* with the *Training Manual* Bin Laden wrote for Al-Qaeda, the paramount desire to learn from the experiences of both friends and enemies is clear.[7] The greatest tactical difference between them is that Nechaev understands women to be priceless assets, while Bin Laden defers to the Islamic tradition and employs men only.[8]

The transformation in communication and transportation patterns is the second reason that explains the timing and spread of the first wave. The telegraph, daily mass newspapers, and railroads flourished in this period; and subsequently throughout the 20th century, technology continued to shrink time and space. . . .

Narodnaya Volya ("The People's Will"), the first terrorist group in the first wave, inherited a world where traditional revolutionaries seemed obsolete or irrelevant. No longer could pamphlets, books, meetings, demonstrations produce mass uprisings, and even revolutionaries described themselves as "idle word spillers"! A "new form of communication" was needed, one that would be heard and command respect. Terror filled that need; no one could ignore it, and repeated acts of terror would generate the polarization necessary for revolution.

The Anarchist doctrine has four major points: 1) Modern society contains huge reservoirs of latent ambivalence and hostility.[9] 2) Society muffles and diffuses them by devising moral conventions to generate guilt and provide channels for settling some grievances and securing personal amenities. 3) However, conventions can be explained historically, and therefore acts we deem to be immoral, our children will hail as noble efforts to liberate humanity. 4) Terror is the quickest and most effective means to destroy conventions. The perpetrator frees himself from the paralyzing grip of convention to become a different sort of person, and society's defenders will respond in ways that undermine the rules they claim are sacred.[10]

An incident, often identified as the inspiration for the turbulent decades to follow, illustrates the process envisaged. Vera Zasulich wounded a Russian police commander who abused prisoners taken in a demonstration. Throwing her weapon to the floor, she proclaimed that she was a terrorist, not a killer.[11] In effect, the ensuing trial quickly became that of the police chief. When the court freed her, crowds greeted the verdict with thunderous applause.

A successful campaign entailed learning how to fight and how to die, and the most admirable death occurred as a result of a court trial where one accepted responsibility, using the occasion to indict the regime. The Russian writer Stepniak described the terrorist as "noble, terrible, irresistibly fascinating, uniting the two sublimities of human grandeur, the martyr and the hero." Dynamite, a recent invention, was the weapon of choice for the male terrorist, because it usually killed the person who threw the bomb also, demonstrating that he was not an ordinary criminal.[12]

Terror was extra-normal violence or violence beyond the moral conventions regulating violence. Most specifically, the conventions violated were the rules of war designed to distinguish combatants from non-combatants. Invariably, most onlookers would label the acts atrocities or outrages.

The rebels described themselves as terrorists, not guerrillas, tracing their lineage back to the French Revolution, and sometimes to the Order of Assassins in medieval Islam. They sought political targets with the potentiality to shake up public attitudes.[13]

Terrorism was a strategy, not an end. The specific tactics used depended upon both on the context and the rebel's political objectives. Judging a context so often in flux was both an art and a science.

What gave the creators of this strategy confidence that it would work? In this case, as in the later waves, the moving forces were major political events, which unexpectedly exposed new vulnerabilities of government. Hope was excited, and hope is always an indispensable lubricant of rebel activity. The turn of events that gave rebels evidence of Russian vulnerability was the dazzling effort of the young Czar Alexander II to transform the system virtually overnight. In one stroke of the pen (1861), he freed the serfs (one-third of the population) and gave them funds to buy land. Three years later he established limited local self-government, "westernized" the judicial system, relaxed censorship powers and control over education. Hopes were aroused but could not be fulfilled quickly enough—for example, the funds to subsidize the peasants to buy land proved to be insufficient—and in the wake of inevitable disappointment, systematic assassination campaigns largely against prominent officials began, culminating in the death of Alexander II himself. . . .

The Versailles Peace Treaty concluding World War I sparked the hope for the second or "Anti-Colonial Wave." The empires of the defeated states (which were mostly in Europe) were broken up by applying the principle of self-determination. Where independence was not immediately feasible, territories were understood to be "mandates" ultimately destined for independence. But the victors could not articulate the principle without also raising questions about the legitimacy of their own empires. The IRA emerged in the 1920s, and terrorist groups developed in all imperial domains except the Soviet Union after World War II. A variety of new states—Ireland, Israel, Cyprus, Yemen, Algeria . . . —emerged, and the wave receded as the empires it swept over dissolved.

Second wave tactics differed in some respects from those of first. Bank robberies were less common, partly because diaspora sources this time contributed more money. Most conspicuous was the lesson learned that assassinating prominent political figures was often counterproductive, and few attacks on the prominent occurred. . . . Martyrdom so often linked to assassinating the prominent seemed less significant too. The new strategy was first to eliminate via systematic assassinations the police, a government's eyes and ears. . . . Military units would replace them and would prove too clumsy to cope without producing counter-atrocities, increasing social support for the terrorists. If the process of atrocities and counter-atrocities was well planned, it worked nearly always to favor those perceived to be weak and without alternatives.[14]

Major energies went into guerrilla-like (hit and run) actions against troops, attacks that went beyond the rules of war, however, because weapons were concealed and the assailants had no identifying insignia.[15] Some groups (*e.g.*, Irgun and IRA) made efforts to give warnings in order to limit civilian casualties. In some cases (*e.g.*, Algeria) terror was one aspect of a more comprehensive rebellion dependent on guerrilla forces. Although an important ingredient in colonial dissolution, terrorist groups rarely achieved their original purposes. . . .

Anti-colonial causes were legitimate to many more parties than the causes articulated in the first wave, and that created a definition problem. The term "terrorist" had accumulated so many abusive connotations that those identified as terrorists found that they had enormous political liabilities. Rebels stopped calling themselves terrorists. Menachem Begin, leader of the Irgun (Lehi's contemporary and rival), concentrating on purpose rather than means, described his people as "freedom fighters" struggling against government terror. So appealing did this self-description prove to be that all subsequent terrorist groups followed suit. Governments appreciated the political value of "appropriate" language too, and began to describe all violent rebels as terrorists. The media corrupted language further, refusing to use terms consistently in the hope of avoiding being seen by the public as blatantly partisan.

The agonizing Vietnam War produced the psychological requisites for the third or "New Left Wave."

Many groups in the "developed world" (*e.g.*, American Weather Underground, West German RAF, Italian Red Brigades, Japanese Red Army, and the French Action Direct) saw themselves as vanguards for the masses of the Third World where much hostility to the West already existed. The Soviets encouraged these groups in many different ways. In Latin America, revolutionary groups repeated a pattern visible in the first wave; they abandoned the countryside and came to the city where they would be noticed.

In the third wave, radicalism was often combined with nationalism, as in the Basque Nation and Liberty (ETA), the Armenian Secret Army for the Liberation of Armenia (ASALA), the Corsican National Liberation Front (FNLC), and the IRA. The pattern reminds us of the first wave, where Anarchists sometimes linked themselves to nationalist aspirations, notably in Indian, Armenian, and Macedonian groups. Although every early effort failed, the linkage was renewed for the obvious reason that self-determination always appeals to a larger constituency than radical aspirations, and over time self-determination obscured the radical programs initially embraced. Nonetheless, most failed quickly. The survivors did not make much headway, because the countries concerned (Turkey, Spain, and France) did not understand themselves to be colonial powers nor did they display the ambivalence necessary for the separatists to succeed.

When the Vietnam War ended in 1975, the Palestine Liberation Organization (PLO) became the heroic model. Originating after three Arab armies collapsed, its very existence was a statement that terror offered more hope than conventional military forces. The central position of the PLO was augmented by three powerful circumstances; Israel, its chief enemy, was an integral part of the West, it got strong Soviet support, and it was able to provide facilities in Lebanon to train terrorists from many countries.

The term "international terrorism" (commonly used during the "Anarchist Wave") was revived to describe "New Left Wave" activities.[16] The revolutionary ethos created significant bonds between separate national groups. The PLO had provided extensive training facilities for other groups. The targets chosen reflected international dimensions. Some groups conducted more assaults abroad than on their home territories; the PLO, for example, was more active in Europe than on the West Bank, and sometimes more active in Europe than many European groups themselves. On their own soil, groups often struck targets with special international significance, especially Americans and their installations. Teams composed of different national groups cooperated in attacks. Libya, Iraq, and Syria employed terrorists in other countries as foreign policy instruments.

Airline hijacking was the most novel tactic in this wave, and over a hundred occurred during the 1970s. Hijacking had an international character because foreign rather than domestic landing fields were more available to hijacked planes. Hijacking also reflected an impulse for spectacular acts, a first wave theme abandoned in the second for more effective military-like strikes.

Planes were taken to get hostages, and hostage crises of various sorts dominated the era. . . .

Strikes on foreign embassies began in the third wave, when the PLO attacked the Saudi Embassy in Khartoum (1973). . . .

Initially, hostages were taken to gain political leverage. But it was soon apparent that hostages (especially company executives) could provide much cash. Companies insured their executives, and the unintended consequence was that it made kidnapping more lucrative and easier to consummate on the kidnappers' terms. . . .

The third wave began to ebb in the 1980s. Revolutionary terrorists were defeated in one country after another. Israel's invasion of Lebanon (1982) eliminated PLO facilities to train terrorist groups, and international counter-terrorist cooperation became increasingly effective.

The "religious wave" began in the same decade. In the three earlier waves, religious identity was always important; religious and ethnic identities often overlap, as the Armenian, Macedonian, Irish, Cypriot, Israeli, and Palestinian struggles illustrate. But the aim earlier was to create secular sovereign states, in principle no different from those present in the international world. Religion has a vastly different significance in the fourth wave, supplying justifications and organizing principles for the New World to be established.

Islam is the most important religion in this wave and will get special attention below. But we should remember that other religious communities produced terrorists too. . . .

Three events in the Islamic world provided the dramatic political turning point, or necessary condition, for a new wave. The Iranian Revolution was the first. Street demonstrations disintegrated the Shah's armies and provided proof that religion now had more political appeal than the prevailing revolutionary ethos. Significantly, Iranian Marxists also active against the Shah could muster only meager support.

The Iranians inspired and helped Shi'ite terror movements elsewhere, in Iraq, Saudi Arabia, Kuwait, and Lebanon. Most important were the events in Lebanon where Shi'ites, influenced by the self-martyrdom tactic of the early Assassins, introduced suicide bombing. The result was surprising, perhaps even to the Lebanese themselves. American and other foreign troops who had entered the country after the 1982 Israeli invasion quickly left and never returned.

Later, in Afghanistan, Muslim resistance (partly due to US aid in bringing Sunni volunteers to the battlefield[17]) forced the Soviets out, an event which became a crucial step in the stunning, unimaginable disintegration of the Soviet Union itself. Religion now manifested the ability to eliminate a secular super-power.

Iranian and Afghan events were unexpected, but a third ingredient to give religion its special significance was fully anticipated by believing Muslims. 1979 was the beginning of a new century according to the Muslim calendar, and the tradition is that a redeemer would come at that time, a tradition that had regularly sparked uprisings at the turn of Muslim centuries earlier. This tradition influenced the Iranian Revolution itself, which occurred in the crucial expected year and may even have intensified Afghan resistance. Certainly, it affected other events. Sunni Muslims stormed the Grand Mosque in Mecca in the first minutes of the new century and 10,000 casualties resulted. Whatever the specific local causes, Sunni terrorism soon appeared in many states with large Islamic populations. . . .

Assassinations and hostage taking, common features of the third wave, persisted, but "suicide bombing" was the most striking and deadly tactical innovation. It reasserted the martyrdom theme of the first wave, neglected by its two successors. . . .

Fourth wave groups, much more than their counterparts in the third wave, have made massive attacks against military and government installations. Americans, in particular, became frequent targets. . . .

The fourth wave produced an organization with a purpose and recruitment pattern unique in the history of terrorism; namely, Al Qaeda, led and financed by the Saudi Osama Bin Laden.

Notes

1. An earlier version of this essay was published in *Current History*, Dec. 2001, 419–25.

2. On September 20, the President told Congress that "any nation that continues to harbor or support terrorism will be regarded as a hostile regime . . . [The war] will not end until every terrorist group of *global reach* has been found, stopped, and defeated." (My emphasis).

3. See Richard B. Jensen, "The United States, International Policing the War against Anarchist Terrorism," *Terrorism and Political Violence* 13, 1 (Spring 2001): 15–46.

4. The Russian police prior to the rise of rebel terror also were not armed; they carried ceremonial sabers only.

5. Anarchists were the most dominant element in the first wave. But in the Balkans, Poland, the Ottoman Empire, India, those influenced by Anarchist strategy largely had separatist ends.

6. The term "terror" originally referred to actions of the Revolutionary government that went beyond the rules regulating punishment to make a people fit to govern itself.

7. See Jerry Post's edited versions of the Bin Laden work in *Terrorism and Political Violence* 14:2 (Summer 2002) forthcoming. It took time for this attitude to develop in Islam. If one compares Bin Laden's work with Faraj's *Neglected Duty,* a work used to justify the assassination of Egyptian President Sadat (1981), the two authors seem to be in two different worlds. Faraj cites *no* experience outside the Islamic tradition, and his most recent historical reference is to Napoleon's invasion of Europe! See my "Sacred Terror: A Case from Contemporary Islam" in Walter Reich ed. *Origins of Terrorism* (Cambridge: Cambridge University Press, 1990) pp. 103–130.

8. The traditional still binding Islamic view is that women may participate in fighting only when no men are available.

9. The French Revolution, in making us aware of the potentialities for perfection, was for the Anarchists the functional equivalent of the unredeemed divine promise for religious groups.

10. An equivalent for this argument in religious millennial thought is that that the world must become impossibly bad before it could become unimaginably good.

11. Adam B. Ulam, *In the Name of the People* (New York: Viking Press, 1977) p. 269. (my emphasis)

12. The bomb was most significant in Russia. While Russian women were crucial in the organization, they were not allowed to throw the bomb, presumably because most bombers did not escape from the scene. Other terrorists used the bomb extensively, but chose other weapons as well.

13. A guerrilla force has political objectives, as any army does, but it aims to weaken or destroy the enemy's military forces first. The terrorist strikes directly at the political sentiments that sustain his enemies.

14. The strategy is superbly described in the film "Battle of Algiers," which is based on the memoirs of Saadi, who organized the battle. Attacks against the police occur whose responses are limited by rules governing criminal procedure. In desperation, the police set a bomb off in the Casbah, inadvertently exploding an ammunition dump killing Algerian women and children. A mob emerges screaming for revenge, and at this point the FLN has the moral warrant to attack civilians.

There is another underlying element which makes rebel terrorism in a democratic world often have special weight. The atrocities of the strong always seem worse than that of the weak because it is believed the latter have no alternatives.

15. Guerrillas carry weapons openly and wear an identifying emblem, and we are obliged therefore to treat them as soldiers.

16. Most people using the term "international terrorism" thought that it was a product of the 60s and 70s.

17. This was not the first time secular forces would help launch the careers of those who would become religious terrorists. Israel helped Hamas to get started, thinking that it would compete to weaken the PLO, and to check left-wing opposition, President Sadat released religious elements from prison who later assassinated him.

17.2

The Causes of Terrorism

Martha Crenshaw

Terrorism occurs both in the context of violent resistance to the state as well as in the service of state interests. If we focus on terrorism directed against governments for purposes of political change, we are considering the premeditated use or threat of symbolic, low-level violence by conspiratorial organizations. Terrorist violence communicates a political message; its ends go beyond damaging an enemy's material resources.[1] The victims or objects of terrorist attack have little intrinsic value to the terrorist group but represent a larger human audience whose reaction the terrorists seek. Violence characterized by spontaneity, mass participation, or a primary intent of physical destruction can therefore be excluded from our investigation.

The study of terrorism can be organized around three questions: why terrorism occurs, how the process of terrorism works, and what its social and political effects are. Here the objective is to outline an approach to the analysis of the causes of terrorism, based on comparison of different cases of terrorism, in order to distinguish a common pattern of causation from the historically unique.

The subject of terrorism has inspired a voluminous literature in recent years. However, nowhere among the highly varied treatments does one find a general theoretical analysis of the causes of terrorism. This may be because terrorism has often been approached from historical perspectives, which, if we take Laqueur's work as an example, dismiss explanations that try to take into account more than a single case as "exceedingly vague or altogether wrong."[2] Certainly existing general accounts are often based on assumptions that are neither explicit nor factually demonstrable. . . .

Even the most persuasive of statements about terrorism are not cast in the form of testable propositions, nor are they broadly comparative in origin or intent. Many are partial analyses, limited in scope to revolutionary terrorism from the Left, not terrorism that is a form of protest or a reaction to political or social change. . . . In general, propositions about terrorism lack logical comparability, specification of the relationship of variables to each other, and a rank-ordering of variables in terms of explanatory power.

We would not wish to claim that a general explanation of the sources of terrorism is a simple task, but it is possible to make a useful beginning by establishing a theoretical order for different types and levels of causes. We approach terrorism as a form of political behavior resulting from the deliberate choice of a basically rational actor, the terrorist organization. A comprehensive explanation, however, must also take into account the environment in which terrorism occurs and address the question of whether broad political, social, and economic conditions make terrorism more likely in some contexts than in others. What sort of circumstances lead to the formation of a terrorist group? On the other hand, only a few of the people who experience a given situation practice terrorism. Not even all individuals who share the goals of a terrorist organization agree that terrorism is the best means. It is essential to consider the psychological variables that may encourage or inhibit individual participation in terrorist actions. The analysis of these three levels of causation will center first on situational variables, then on the strategy of the terrorist organization, and last on the problem of individual participation.

This paper represents only a preliminary set of ideas about the problem of causation; historical cases of terrorism are used as illustrations, not as demonstrations of hypotheses. . . . The term *terrorism* was coined to describe the systematic inducement of fear and anxiety to control and direct a civilian population, and the phenomenon of terrorism as a challenge to the authority of the state grew from the difficulties revolutionaries experienced in trying to recreate the mass uprisings of the French Revolution. . . .

Source: Martha Crenshaw (1981), "The Causes of Terrorism," *Comparative Politics* 13(4): 379–386 and 396–399. Reprinted by permission of Comparative Politics, City University of New York.

The Setting for Terrorism

To develop a framework for the analysis of likely settings for terrorism, we must establish conceptual distinctions among different types of factors. First, a significant difference exists between *preconditions*, factors that set the stage for terrorism over the long run, and *precipitants*, specific events that immediately precede the occurrence of terrorism. Second, a further classification divides preconditions into enabling or permissive factors, which provide opportunities for terrorism to happen, and situations that directly inspire and motivate terrorist campaigns. Precipitants are similar to the direct causes of terrorism.[3] Furthermore, no factor is neatly compartmentalized in a single nation-state; each has a transnational dimension that complicates the analysis.

First, modernization produces an interrelated set of factors that is a significant permissive cause of terrorism, as increased complexity on all levels of society and economy creates opportunities and vulnerabilities. Sophisticated networks of transportation and communication offer mobility and the means of publicity for terrorists. The terrorists of *Narodnaya Volya* would have been unable to operate without Russia's newly established rail system, and the Popular Front for the Liberation of Palestine could not indulge in hijacking without the jet aircraft. In Algeria, the FLN only adopted a strategy of urban bombings when they were able to acquire plastic explosives. . . .

Urbanization is part of the modern trend toward aggregation and complexity, which increases the number and accessibility of targets and methods. . . .

Social "facilitation," which Gurr found to be extremely powerful in bringing about civil strife in general, is also an important permissive factor. This concept refers to social habits and historical traditions that sanction the use of violence against the government, making it morally and politically justifiable, and even dictating an appropriate form, such as demonstrations, coups, or terrorism. Social myths, traditions, and habits permit the development of terrorism as an established political custom. . . .

Moreover, broad attitudes and beliefs that condone terrorism are communicated transnationally. Revolutionary ideologies have always crossed borders with ease. . . .

The most salient political factor in the category of permissive causes is a government's inability or unwillingness to prevent terrorism. The absence of adequate prevention by police and intelligence services permits the spread of conspiracy. . . . For many governments, however, the cost of disallowing terrorism is too high.

Turning now to a consideration of the direct causes of terrorism, we focus on background conditions that positively encourage resistance to the state. These instigating circumstances go beyond merely creating an environment in which terrorism is possible; they provide motivation and direction for the terrorist movement. We are dealing here with reasons rather than opportunities.

The first condition that can be considered a direct cause of terrorism is the existence of concrete grievances among an identifiable subgroup of a larger population, such as an ethnic minority discriminated against by the majority. A social movement develops in order to redress these grievances and to gain either equal rights or a separate state; terrorism is then the resort of an extremist faction of this broader movement. . . .

This is not to say, however, that the existence of a dissatisfied minority or majority is a necessary or a sufficient cause of terrorism. Not all those who are discriminated against turn to terrorism, nor does terrorism always reflect objective social or economic deprivation. In West Germany, Japan, and Italy, for example, terrorism has been the chosen method of the privileged, not the downtrodden. Some theoretical studies have suggested that the essential ingredient that must be added to real deprivation is the perception on the part of the deprived that this condition is not what they deserve or expect, in short, that discrimination is unjust. An attitude study, for example, found that "the idea of justice or fairness may be more centrally related to attitudes toward violence than are feelings of deprivation. It is the perceived injustice underlying the deprivation that gives rise to anger or frustration."[4] The intervening variables, as we have argued, lie in the terrorists' perceptions. Moreover, it seems likely that for terrorism to occur the government must be singled out to blame for popular suffering.

The second condition that creates motivations for terrorism is the lack of opportunity for political participation. Regimes that deny access to power and persecute dissenters create dissatisfaction. In this case, grievances are primarily political, without social or economic overtones. . . . The terrorist organization is not necessarily part of a broader social movement; indeed, the population may be largely apathetic. In situations where paths to the legal expression of opposition are blocked, but where the regime's repression is inefficient, revolutionary terrorism is doubly likely, as permissive and direct causes coincide. . . .

Context is especially significant as a direct cause of terrorism when it affects an elite, not the mass population. Terrorism is essentially the result of elite disaffection; it represents the strategy of a minority, who may act on behalf of a wider popular constituency who have not been consulted about, and do not necessarily approve of, the terrorists' aims or methods. There is remarkable relevance in E. J. Hobsbawn's comments on the political conspirators of post-Napoleonic Europe: "All revolutionaries regarded themselves, with some justification, as small elites of the emancipated and progressive operating among, and for the eventual benefit of, a vast and inert mass of the ignorant and misled common people, which would no doubt welcome liberation when it came, but could not be expected to take much part in preparing it."[5] Many terrorists today are young, well-educated, and middle class in background. Such students or young professionals, with prior political experience, are disillusioned with the prospects of changing society and see little chance of access to the system despite their privileged status. . . .

Perhaps terrorism is most likely to occur precisely where mass passivity and elite dissatisfaction coincide. Discontent is not generalized or severe enough to provoke the majority of the populace to action against the regime, yet a small minority, without access to the bases of power that would permit overthrow of the government through coup d'etat or subversion, seeks radical change. Terrorism may thus be a sign of a stable society rather than a symptom of fragility and impending collapse. Terrorism is the resort of an elite when conditions are not revolutionary. . . .

The last category of situational factors involves the concept of a precipitating event that immediately precedes outbreaks of terrorism. Although it is generally thought that precipitants are the most unpredictable of causes, there does seem to be a common pattern of government actions that act as catalysts for terrorism. Government use of unexpected and unusual force in response to protest or reform attempts often compels terrorist retaliation. The development of such an action-reaction syndrome then establishes the structure of the conflict between the regime and its challengers. . . .

This analysis of the background conditions for terrorism indicates that we must look at the terrorist organization's perception and interpretation of the situation. Terrorists view the context as permissive, making terrorism a viable option. In a material sense, the means are placed at their disposal by the environment. Circumstances also provide the terrorists with compelling reasons for seeking political change. Finally, an event occurs that snaps the terrorists' patience with the regime. Government action is now seen as intolerably unjust, and terrorism becomes not only a possible decision but a morally acceptable one. The regime has forfeited its status as the standard of legitimacy. For the terrorist, the end may now excuse the means.

The Reasons for Terrorism

Significant campaigns of terrorism depend on rational political choice. As purposeful activity, terrorism is the result of an organization's decision that it is a politically useful means to oppose a government. The argument that terrorist behavior should be analyzed as "rational" is based on the assumption that terrorist organizations possess internally consistent sets of values, beliefs, and images of the environment. Terrorism is seen collectively as a logical means to advance desired ends. The terrorist organization engages in decision-making calculations that an analyst can approximate. In short, the terrorist group's reasons for resorting to terrorism constitute an important factor in the process of causation.[6] . . .

Saying that extremist groups resort to terrorism in order to acquire political influence does not mean that all groups have equally precise objectives or that the relationship between means and ends is perfectly clear to an outside observer. Some groups are less realistic about the logic of means and ends than others. The leaders of *Narodnaya Volya*, for example, lacked a detailed conception of how the assassination of the tsar would force his successor to permit the liberalization they sought. Other terrorist groups are more pragmatic: the IRA of 1919–21 and the *Irgun*, for instance, shrewdly foresaw the utility of a war of attrition against the British. . . .

However diverse the long-run goals of terrorist groups, there is a common pattern of proximate or short-run objectives of a terrorist strategy. Proximate objectives are defined in terms of the reactions that terrorists want to achieve in their different audiences.[7] . . .

Conclusions

Terrorism per se is not usually a reflection of mass discontent or deep cleavages in society. More often it represents the disaffection of a fragment of the elite, who may take it upon themselves to act on the behalf of a majority unaware of its plight, unwilling to take action to remedy grievances, or unable to express dissent. This discontent, however subjective in origin or minor in scope, is blamed on the government and its supporters. Since the sources of terrorism are manifold, any society or polity that permits opportunities for terrorism is vulnerable. Government reactions that are inconsistent, wavering between tolerance and repression, seem most likely to encourage terrorism.

Given some source of disaffection—and in the centralized modern state with its faceless bureaucracies, lack of responsiveness to demands is ubiquitous—terrorism is an attractive strategy for small organizations of diverse ideological persuasions who want to attract attention for their cause, provoke the government, intimidate opponents, appeal for sympathy, impress an audience, or promote the adherence of the faithful. Terrorists perceive an absence of choice. Whether unable or unwilling to perceive a choice between terrorist and non-terrorist action, whether unpopular or prohibited by the government, the terrorist group reasons that there is no alternative. The ease, simplicity, and rapidity with which terrorism can be implemented and the prominence of models of terrorism strengthen its appeal, especially since terrorist groups are impatient to act. Long-standing social traditions that sanction terrorism against the state, as in Ireland, further enhance its attractiveness.

There are two fundamental questions about the psychological basis of terrorism. The first is why the individual takes the first step and chooses to engage in terrorism: why join? Does the terrorist possess specific psychological predispositions, identifiable in advance, that suit him or her for terrorism? That terrorists are people capable of intense commitment tells us little, and the motivations for terrorism vary immensely. Many individuals are potential terrorists, but few actually make that commitment. To explain why terrorism happens, another question is more appropriate: Why does involvement continue? What are the psychological mechanisms of group interaction? We are not dealing with a situation in which certain types of personalities suddenly turn to terrorism in answer to some inner call. Terrorism is the result of a gradual growth of commitment and opposition, a group development that furthermore depends on government action. The psychological relationships within the terrorist group—the interplay of commitment, risk, solidarity, loyalty, guilt, revenge, and isolation—discourage terrorists from changing the direction they have taken. This may explain why—even if objective circumstances change when, for example, grievances are satisfied, or if the logic of the situation changes when, for example, the terrorists are offered other alternatives for the expression of opposition—terrorism may endure until the terrorist group is physically destroyed.

NOTES

1. For discussions of the meaning of the concept of terrorism, see Thomas P. Thornton, "Terror as a Weapon of Political Agitation," in Harry Eckstein, ed. *Internal War* (New York, 1964), pp. 71–99; Martha Crenshaw Hutchinson, "The Concept of Revolutionary Terrorism," *Revolutionary Terrorism: The FLN in Algeria, 1954–1962* (Stanford: The Hoover Institution Press, 1978) chap. 2; and E. Victor Walter, *Terror and Resistance* (New York, 1969).

2. Walter Laqueur, "Interpretations of Terrorism— Fact, Fiction and Political Science," *Journal of Contemporary History*, 12 (January 1977), 1–42. See also his major work *Terrorism* (London: Weidenfeld and Nicolson, 1977).

3. A distinction between preconditions and precipitants is found in Eckstein, "On the Etiology of Internal Wars," *History and Theory*, 4 (1965), 133–62. Kenneth Waltz also differentiates between the framework for action as a permissive or underlying cause and special reasons as immediate or efficient causes. In some cases we can say of terrorism, as he says of war, that it occurs because there is nothing to prevent it. See *Man, the State and War* (New York, 1959), p. 232.

4. Monica D. Blumenthal, et al., *More About Justifying Violence: Methodological Studies of Attitudes and Behavior* (Ann Arbor: Survey Research Center, Institute for Social Research, University of Michigan, 1975), p. 108. Similarly, Peter Lupsha, "Explanation of Political Violence: Some Psychological Theories Versus Indignation," *Politics and Society*, 2 (1971), 89–104, contrasts the concept of "indignation" with Gurr's theory of relative deprivation, which holds that expectations exceed rewards (see *Why Men Rebel*, esp. pp. 24–30).

5. Hobsbawm, *Revolutionaries*, p. 143.

6. See Barbara Salert's critique of the rational choice model of revolutionary participation in *Revolutions and Revolutionaries* (New York, 1976). In addition, Abraham Kaplan discusses the distinction between reasons and causes in "The Psychodynamics of Terrorism," *Terrorism—An International Journal*, 1, 3 and 4 (1978), 237–54.

7. See Thornton's analysis of proximate goals in "Terror as a Weapon of Political Agitation," in Eckstein, ed. pp. 82–88.

17.3

The Strategies of Terrorism

Andrew H. Kydd and Barbara F. Walter

Terrorism often works. Extremist organizations such as al-Qaida, Hamas, and the Tamil Tigers engage in terrorism because it frequently delivers the desired response. The October 1983 suicide attack against the U.S. Marine barracks in Beirut, for example, convinced the United States to withdraw its soldiers from Lebanon.[1] The United States pulled its soldiers out of Saudi Arabia two years after the terrorist attacks of September 11, 2001, even though the U.S. military had been building up its forces in that country for more than a decade.[2] The Philippines recalled its troops from Iraq nearly a month early after a Filipino truck driver was kidnapped by Iraqi extremists.[3] In fact, terrorism has been so successful that between 1980 and 2003, half of all suicide terrorist campaigns were closely followed by substantial concessions by the target governments.[4] Hijacking planes, blowing up buses, and kidnapping individuals may seem irrational and incoherent to outside observers, but these tactics can be surprisingly effective in achieving a terrorist group's political aims.

Despite the salience of terrorism today, scholars and policymakers are only beginning to understand how and why it works. Much has been written on the origins of terror, the motivations of terrorists, and counterterror responses, but little has appeared on the strategies terrorist organizations employ and the conditions under which these strategies succeed or fail. Alan Krueger, David Laitin, Jitka Maleckova, and Alberto Abadie, for example, have traced the effects of poverty, education, and political freedom on terrorist recruitment.[5]

Jessica Stern has examined the grievances that give rise to terrorism and the networks, money, and operations that allow terrorist organizations to thrive.[6] What is lacking, however, is a clear understanding of the larger strategic games terrorists are playing and the ways in which state responses help or hinder them.

Effective counterstrategies cannot be designed without first understanding the strategic logic that drives terrorist violence. Terrorism works not simply because it instills fear in target populations, but because it causes governments and individuals to respond in ways that aid the terrorists' cause. The Irish Republican Army (IRA) bombed pubs, parks, and shopping districts in London because its leadership believed that such acts would convince Britain to relinquish Northern Ireland. In targeting the World Trade Center and the Pentagon on September 11, al-Qaida hoped to raise the costs for the United States of supporting Israel, Saudi Arabia, and other Arab regimes, and to provoke the United States into a military response designed to mobilize Muslims around the world. That so many targeted governments respond in the way that terrorist organizations intend underscores the need for understanding the reasoning behind this type of violence.

In this article we seek answers to four questions. First, what types of goals do terrorists seek to achieve? Second, what strategies do they pursue to achieve these goals? Third, why do these strategies work in some cases but not in others? And fourth, given these strategies, what are the targeted governments' best responses to prevent terrorism and protect their countries from future attacks?

The core of our argument is that terrorist violence is a form of costly signaling. Terrorists are too weak to impose their will directly by force of arms. They are sometimes strong enough, however, to persuade audiences to do as they wish by altering the audience's beliefs about such matters as the terrorist's ability to impose costs and their degree of commitment to their cause. Given the conflict of interest between terrorists and their targets, ordinary communication or "cheap talk" is insufficient to change minds or influence behavior. If al-Qaida had informed the United States

---

Source: Andrew H. Kydd and Barbara F. Walter. "The Strategies of Terrorism," in *International Security* 31(1): 49–53, 56–60, 64–66, 68–70, 72–76, and 78.

on September 10, 2001, that it would kill 3,000 Americans unless the United States withdrew from Saudi Arabia, the threat might have sparked concern, but it would not have had the same impact as the attacks that followed. Because it is hard for weak actors to make credible threats, terrorists are forced to display publicly just how far they are willing to go to obtain their desired results.

There are five principal strategic logics of costly signaling at work in terrorist campaigns: (1) attrition, (2) intimidation, (3) provocation, (4) spoiling, and (5) outbidding. In an attrition strategy, terrorists seek to persuade the enemy that the terrorists are strong enough to impose considerable costs if the enemy continues a particular policy. Terrorists using intimidation try to convince the population that the terrorists are strong enough to punish disobedience and that the government is too weak to stop them, so that people behave as the terrorists wish. A provocation strategy is an attempt to induce the enemy to respond to terrorism with indiscriminate violence, which radicalizes the population and moves them to support the terrorists. Spoilers attack in an effort to persuade the enemy that moderates on the terrorists' side are weak and untrustworthy, thus undermining attempts to reach a peace settlement. Groups engaged in outbidding use violence to convince the public that the terrorists have greater resolve to fight the enemy than rival groups, and therefore are worthy of support. Understanding these five distinct strategic logics is crucial not only for understanding terrorism but also for designing effective antiterror policies.[7]

The article is divided into two main sections. The first discusses the goals terrorists pursue and examines the forty-two groups currently on the U.S. State Department's list of foreign terrorist organizations (FTOs).[8] The second section develops the costly signaling approach to terrorism, analyzes the five strategies that terrorists use to achieve their goals, discusses the conditions in which each of these strategies is likely to be successful, and draws out the implications for the best counterterror responses.

The Goals of Terrorism

For years the press has portrayed terrorists as crazy extremists who commit indiscriminate acts of violence, without any larger goal beyond revenge or a desire to produce fear in an enemy population. This characterization derives some support from statements made by terrorists themselves. For example, a young Hamas suicide bomber whose bomb failed to detonate said, "I know that there are other ways to do jihad. But this one is sweet—the sweetest. All martyrdom operations, if done for Allah's sake, hurt less than a gnat's bite!"[9] Volunteers for a suicide mission may have a variety of motives—obtaining rewards in the afterlife, avenging a family member killed by the enemy, or simply collecting financial rewards for their descendants. By contrast, the goals driving terrorist organizations are usually political objectives, and it is these goals that determine whether and how terrorist campaigns will be launched.

We define "terrorism" as the use of violence against civilians by non-state actors to attain political goals.[10] These goals can be conceptualized in a variety of ways. Individuals and groups often have hierarchies of objectives, where broader goals lead to more proximate objectives, which then become specific goals in more tactical analyses.[11] For the sake of simplicity, we adopt the common distinction between goals (or ultimate desires) and strategies (or plans of action to attain the goals).

Although the ultimate goals of terrorists have varied over time, five have had enduring importance: regime change, territorial change, policy change, social control, and status quo maintenance. Regime change is the overthrow of a government and its replacement with one led by the terrorists or at least one more to their liking.[12] Most Marxist groups, including the Shining Path (*Sendero Luminoso*) in Peru have sought this goal. Territorial change is taking territory away from a state either to establish a new state (as the Tamil Tigers seek to do in Tamil areas of Sri Lanka) or to join another state (as *Lashkar-e Tayyiba* would like to do by incorporating Indian Kashmir into Pakistan).

Policy change is a broader category of lesser demands, such as al-Qaida's demand that the United States drop its support for Israel and corrupt Arab regimes such as Saudi Arabia. Social control constrains the behavior of individuals, rather than the state. In the United States, the Ku Klux Klan sought the continued oppression of African Americans after the Civil War. More recently, anti-abortion groups have sought to kill doctors who perform abortions to deter other doctors from providing this service. Finally, status quo maintenance is the support of an existing regime or a territorial arrangement against political groups that seek to change it. Many right-wing paramilitary organizations in Latin America, such as the United Self-Defense Force of Colombia, have sought this goal.[13] Protestant paramilitary groups in Northern Ireland supported maintenance of the territorial status quo (Northern Ireland as British territory) against IRA demands that the territory be transferred to Ireland.[14]

Some organizations hold multiple goals and may view one as facilitating another. For instance, by seeking to weaken U.S. support for Arab regimes (which would represent a policy change by the United States), al-Qaida is working toward the overthrow of those regimes (or regime change). As another example, Hamas aims to drive Israel out of the occupied territories (territorial change) and then to overthrow it (regime change). . . .

The Strategies of Terrorist Violence

To achieve their long-term objectives, terrorists pursue a variety of strategies. Scholars have suggested a number of typologies of terrorist strategies and tactics over the years. . . . Although these analyses are helpful in identifying strategies of terrorism, they fail to derive them from a coherent framework, spell out their logic in detail, and consider best responses to them.

A fruitful starting point for a theory of terrorist strategies is the literature on uncertainty, conflict, and costly signaling. Uncertainty has long been understood to be a cause of conflict. Geoffrey Blainey argued that wars begin when states disagree about their relative power, and they end when states agree again.[15] James Fearon and other theorists built upon this insight and showed that uncertainty about a state's willingness to fight can cause conflict.[16] If states are unsure what other states will fight for, they may demand too much in negotiations and end up in conflict. This uncertainty could reflect a disagreement about power, as Blainey understood, or a disagreement over resolve, willpower, or the intensity of preferences over the issue.

Uncertainty about trustworthiness or moderation of preferences can also cause conflict. Thomas Hobbes argued that if individuals mistrust each other, they have an incentive to initiate an attack rather than risk being attacked by surprise.[17] John Herz, Robert Jervis, and others have developed this concept in the international relations context under the heading of the security dilemma and the spiral model.[18] States are often uncertain about each other's ultimate ambitions, intentions, and preferences. Because of this, anything that increases one side's belief that the other is deceitful, expansionist, risk acceptant, or hostile increases incentives to fight rather than cooperate.

If uncertainty about power, resolve, and trustworthiness can lead to violence, then communication on these topics is the key to preventing (or instigating) conflict. The problem is that simple verbal statements are often not credible, because actors frequently have incentives to lie and bluff. . . . When Mikhail Gorbachev wanted to reassure the West and end the Cold War, verbal declarations of innocent intentions were insufficient, because previous Soviet leaders had made similar statements. Instead, real arms reductions, such as the 1987 Intermediate-Range Nuclear Forces Treaty, were necessary for Western opinion to change.

Because talk is cheap, states and terrorists who wish to influence the behavior of an adversary must resort to costly signals.[19] Costly signals are actions so costly that bluffers and liars are unwilling to take them.[20] In international crises, mobilizing forces or drawing a very public line in the sand are examples of strategies that less resolved actors might find too costly to take.[21] War itself, or the willingness to endure it, can serve as a forceful signal of resolve and provide believable information about power and capabilities.[22] Costly signals separate the wheat from the chaff and allow honest communication, although sometimes at a terrible price.

To obtain their political goals, terrorists need provide credible information to the audiences whose behavior they hope to influence. Terrorists play to two key audiences: governments whose policies they wish to influence and individuals on the terrorists' own side whose support or obedience they seek to gain.[23] The targeted governments are central because they can grant concessions over policy or territory that the terrorists are seeking. The terrorists' domestic audience is also important, because they can provide resources to the terrorist group and must obey its edicts on social or political issues.

Figure 17.1 shows how the three subjects of uncertainty (power, resolve, and trustworthiness) combine with the two targets of persuasion (the enemy government and the domestic population) to yield a family of five signalling strategies. These strategies form a theoretically cohesive set that we believe represents most of the commonly used strategies in important terrorist campaigns around the world today.[24] A terrorist organization can of course pursue more than one strategy at a time. The September 11 terrorist attacks, for example, were probably part of both an attrition strategy and a provocation strategy. By targeting the heart of the United States' financial district, al-Qaida may have been attempting to increase the cost of the U.S. policy of stationing soldiers in Saudi Arabia. But by targeting prominent symbols of American economic and military power, al-Qaida may also have been trying to goad the United States into an extreme military response that would serve al-Qaida's larger goal of radicalizing the world's Muslim population. The challenge for policymakers in targeted countries is to calibrate their responses in ways that do not further any of the terrorists' goals. . . .

Attrition: A Battle of Wills

The most important task for any terrorist group is to persuade the enemy that the group is strong and resolute enough to inflict serious costs, so that the enemy yields to the terrorists' demands.[25] The attrition strategy is designed to accomplish this task.[26] In an attrition campaign, the greater the costs a terrorist organization is able to inflict, the more credible its threat to inflict future costs, and the more likely the target is to grant concessions. During the last years of the British Empire, the Greeks in Cyprus, Jews in Palestine, and Arabs in Aden used a war of attrition strategy against their colonizer. By targeting Britain with terrorist attacks, they eventually convinced the political leadership that maintaining control over these territories would not be worth the cost in British lives.[27] Attacks by Hezbollah and Hamas against Israel, particularly during the second intifada, also appear to be guided by this strategy. In a letter written in the early 1990s to the leadership of Hamas, the organization's master bomb maker, Yahya Ayyash, said, "We paid a high price when we used only sling-shots and stones. We need to exert more pressure, make the cost of the occupation that much more expensive in human lives, that much more unbearable."[28] . . .

Best Responses to Attrition

There are at least five counterstrategies available to a state engaged in a war of attrition. First, the targeted government can concede inessential issues in exchange for peace, a strategy that we believe is frequently pursued though rarely admitted.[29]

Second, where the issue under dispute is important enough to the targeted state that it does not want to grant any concessions, the government may engage in targeted retaliation. Retaliation can target the leadership of the terrorist group, its followers, their assets, and other objects of value. Care must be taken, however, that the retaliation is precisely targeted, because the terrorist organization could simultaneously be pursuing a strategy of provocation. . . .

Third, a state can harden likely targets to minimize the costs the terrorist organization can inflict. If targeted governments can prevent most attacks from being executed, a war of attrition strategy will not be able to inflict the costs necessary to convince the target to concede. . . .

Fourth, states should seek to deny terrorists access to the most destructive weapons, especially nuclear and biological ones. Any weapon that can inflict enormous costs will be particularly attractive to terrorists pursuing a war of attrition. The greater the destruction, the higher the likelihood that the target will concede increasingly consequential issues. . . .

Finally, states can strive to minimize the psychological costs of terrorism and the tendency people have

Figure 17.1 Strategies of Terrorist Violence

		Target of Persuasion	
		Enemy	Own Population
Subject of Uncertainty	Power	attrition	intimidation
	Resolve		outbidding
	Trustworthiness	spoiling	provocation

to overreact. John Mueller has noted that the risks associated with terrorism are actually quite small; for the average U.S. citizen, the likelihood of being a victim of a terrorist attack is about the same as that of being struck by lighting.[30] Government public education programs should therefore be careful not to overstate the threat, for this plays into the hands of the terrorists. If Americans become convinced that terrorism, while a deadly problem, is no more of a health risk than drunk driving, smoking, or obesity, then al-Qaida's attrition strategy will be undercut. . . .

Intimidation: The Reign of Terror

Intimidation is akin to the strategy of deterrence, preventing some undesired behavior by means of threats and costly signals.[31] It is most frequently used when terrorist organizations wish to overthrow a government in power or gain social control over a given population. It works by demonstrating that the terrorists have the power to punish whoever disobeys them, and that the government is powerless to stop them.

Terrorists are often in competition with the government for the support of the population. Terrorists who wish to bring down a government must somehow convince the government's defenders that continued backing of the government will be costly. One way to do this is to provide clear evidence that the terrorist organization can kill those individuals who continue to sustain the regime. By targeting the government's more visible agents and supporters, such as mayors, police, prosecutors, and pro-regime citizens, terrorist organizations demonstrate that they have the ability to hurt their opponents and that the government is too weak to punish the terrorists or protect future victims.

Terrorists can also use an intimidation strategy to gain greater social control over a population. Terrorists may turn to this strategy in situations where a government has consistently refused to implement a policy a terrorist group favors and where efforts to change the state's policy appear futile. In this case, terrorists use intimidation to impose the desired policy directly on the population, gaining compliance through selective violence and the threat of future reprisals. . . .

Best Responses to Intimidation

When the terrorist goal is regime change, the best response to intimidation is to retake territory from the rebels in discrete chunks and in a decisive fashion. Ambiguity about who is in charge should be minimized, even if this means temporarily ceding some areas to the rebels to concentrate resources on selected sections of territory. This response is embodied in the "clear-and-hold strategy" that U.S. forces are employing in Iraq. The 2005 National Strategy for Victory in Iraq specifically identifies intimidation as the "strategy of our enemies."[32] The proper response, as Secretary of State Condoleezza Rice stated in October 2005, "is to clear, hold, and build: clear areas from insurgent control, hold them securely, and build durable national Iraqi institutions."[33] If rebels control their own zone and have no access to the government zone, they will have no incentive to kill the civilians they control and no ability to kill the civilians the government controls. In this situation, there is no uncertainty about who is in control; the information that would be provided by intimidation is already known. . . .

Provocation: Lighting the Fuse

A provocation strategy is often used in pursuit of regime change and territorial change, the most popular goals of the FTOs listed by the State Department. It is designed to persuade the domestic audience that the target of attacks is evil and untrustworthy and must be vigorously resisted.

Terrorist organizations seeking to replace a regime face a significant challenge: they are usually much more hostile to the regime than a majority of the state's citizens. Al-Qaida may wish to topple the House of Saud, but if a majority of citizens do not support this goal, al-Qaida is unlikely to achieve it. Similarly, if most Tamils are satisfied living in a united Sri Lanka, the Tamil Tigers' drive for independence will fail. To succeed, therefore, a terrorist organization must first convince moderate citizens that their government needs to be replaced or that independence from the central government is the only acceptable outcome.

Provocation helps shift citizen support away from the incumbent regime. In a provocation strategy, terrorists seek to goad the target government into a military response that harms civilians within the terrorist organization's home territory.[34] The aim is to convince them that the government is so evil that the radical goals of the terrorists are justified and support for their organization is warranted.[35] As one expert on this conflict writes, "Nothing radicalizes a people faster than the unleashing of undisciplined security forces on its towns and villages."[36] . . .

Best Responses to Provocation

The best response to provocation is a discriminating strategy that inflicts as little collateral damage as possible. Countries should seek out and destroy the terrorists and their immediate backers to reduce the likelihood of future terror attacks, but they must carefully isolate these targets from the general population, which may or may not be sympathetic to the terrorists.[37] This type of discriminating response will require superior intelligence capabilities. . . .

Spoiling: Sabotaging the Peace

The goal of a spoiling strategy is to ensure that peace overtures between moderate leaders on the terrorists' side and the target government do not succeed.[38] It works by playing on the mistrust between these two groups and succeeds when one or both parties fail to sign or implement a settlement. It is often employed when the ultimate objective is territorial change.

Terrorists resort to a spoiling strategy when relations between two enemies are improving and a peace agreement threatens the terrorists' more far-reaching goals. Peace agreements alarm terrorists because they understand that moderate citizens are less likely to support ongoing violence once a compromise agreement between more moderate groups has been reached. . . .

Terrorist acts are particularly effective during peace negotiations because opposing parties are naturally distrustful of each other's motives and have limited sources of information about each other's intentions. Thus, even if moderate leaders are willing to aggressively suppress extremists on their side, terrorists know that isolated violence might still convince the target to reject the deal. A reason for this is that the targeted group may not be able to readily observe the extent of the crackdown and must base its judgments primarily on whether terrorism occurs or not. Even a sincere effort at self-policing, therefore, will not necessarily convince the targeted group to proceed with a settlement if a terrorist attack occurs. . . .

Best Responses to Spoiling

When mutual trust is high, a peace settlement can be implemented despite ongoing terrorist acts and the potential vulnerabilities the agreement can create. Trust, however, is rarely high after long conflicts, which is why spoilers can strike with a reasonable chance that their attack will be successful. Strategies that build trust and reduce vulnerability are, therefore, the best response to spoiling. . . .

Outbidding: Zealots Versus Sellouts

Outbidding arises when two key conditions hold: two or more domestic parties are competing for leadership of their side, and the general population is uncertain about which of the groups best represents their interests.[39] The competition between Hamas and Fatah is a classic case where two groups vie for the support of the Palestinian citizens and where the average Palestinian is uncertain about which side he or she ought to back.

If citizens had full information about the preferences of the competing groups, an outbidding strategy would be unnecessary and ineffective; citizens would simply support the group that best aligned with their own interests. In reality, however, citizens cannot be sure if the group competing for power truly represents their preferences. The group could be a strong and resolute defender of the cause (zealots) or weak and ineffective stooges of the enemy (sellouts). If citizens support zealots, they get a strong champion but with some risk that they will be dragged into a confrontation with the enemy that they end up losing. If citizens support sellouts, they get peace but at the price of accepting a worse outcome than might have been achieved with additional armed struggle. Groups competing for power have an incentive to signal that they are zealots rather than sellouts. Terrorist attacks can serve this function by signaling that a group has the will to continue the armed struggle despite its costs. . . .

Best Responses to Outbidding

One solution to the problem of outbidding would be to eliminate the struggle for power by encouraging competing groups to consolidate into a unified opposition. If competition among resistance groups is eliminated, the incentive for outbidding also disappears. The downside of this counterstrategy is that a unified opposition may be stronger than a divided one. United oppositions, however, can make peace and deliver, whereas divided ones may face greater structural disincentives to do so.

An alternative strategy for the government to pursue in the face of outbidding is to validate the strategy chosen by nonviolent groups by granting them concessions and attempting to satisfy the demands of their constituents. If outbidding can be shown to yield poor results in comparison to playing within the system, groups may be persuaded to abandon the strategy. . . .

Notes

1. Thomas L. Friedman, "Marines Complete Beirut Pullback: Moslems Move In," *New York Times*, February 27, 2004.

2. Don Van Natta Jr., "The Struggle for Iraq: Last American Combat Troops Quit Saudi Arabia," *New York Times*, September 22, 2003.

3. James Glanz, "Hostage Is Freed after Philippine Troops Are Withdrawn from Iraq," *New York Times*, July 21, 2004.

4. Robert A. Pape, *Dying to Win: The Strategic Logic of Suicide Terrorism* (New York: Random House, 2005), p. 65.

5. Alan B. Krueger and David D. Laitin, "Kto Kogo? A Cross-Country Study of the Origins and Targets of Terrorism," Princeton University and Stanford University, 2003; Alan B. Krueger and Jitka Maleckova, "Education, Poverty, and Terrorism: Is There a Causal Connection?" *Journal of Economic Perspectives*, Vol. 17, No. 4 (November 2003), pp. 119–144; and Alberto Abadie, "Poverty, Political Freedom, and the Roots of Terrorism," Faculty Research Working Papers Series, RWP04043 (Cambridge, Mass.: John F. Kennedy School of Government, Harvard University, 2004).

6. Jessica Stern, *Terror in the Name of God: Why Religious Militants Kill* (New York: Ecco- HarperCollins, 2003).

7. Of course, terrorists will also be seeking best responses to government responses. A pair of strategies that are best responses to each other constitutes a Nash equilibrium, the fundamental prediction tool of game theory.

8. Office of Counterterrorism, U.S. Department of State, "Foreign Terrorist Organizations," Fact Sheet, October 11, 2005, http://www.state.gov/s/ct/rls/fs/3719.htm.

9. Quoted in Nasra Hassan, "An Arsenal of Believers: Talking to the 'Human Bombs,'" *New Yorker*, November 19, 2001, p. 37.

10. For discussion of differing definitions of terrorism, see Alex P. Schmid and Albert J. Jongman, *Political Terrorism: A New Guide to Actors, Authors, Concepts, Data Bases, Theories, and Literature* (New Brunswick, N.J.: Transaction, 1988), pp. 1–38. We do not focus on state terrorism because states face very different opportunities and constraints in their use of violence, and we do not believe the two cases are similar enough to be profitably analyzed together.

11. For the distinction between goals and strategies, see David A. Lake and Robert Powell, eds., *Strategic Choice and International Relations* (Princeton, N.J.: Princeton University Press, 1999), especially chap. 1.

12. On revolutionary terrorism, see Martha Crenshaw Hutchinson, "The Concept of Revolutionary Terrorism," *Journal of Conflict Resolution*, Vol. 16, No. 3 (September 1972), pp. 383–396; Martha Crenshaw Hutchinson, *Revolutionary Terrorism: The FLN in Algeria, 1954–1962* (Stanford, Calif.: Hoover Institution Press, 1978); and H. Edward Price Jr., "The Strategy and Tactics of Revolutionary Terrorism," *Comparative Studies in Society and History*, Vol. 19, No. 1 (January 1977), pp. 52–66.

13. This group has recently surrendered its weapons.

14. Some analysts argue that many terrorist organizations have degenerated into little more than self-perpetuating businesses that primarily seek to enhance their own power and wealth, and only articulate political goals for rhetorical purposes. See, for example, Stern, *Terror in the Name of God*, pp. 235–236. This suggests that power and wealth should be considered goals in their own right. All organizations, however, seek power and wealth to further their political objectives, and these are better viewed as instrumental in nature.

15. Geoffrey Blainey, *The Causes of War*, 3d ed. (New York: Free Press, 1988), p. 122.

16. James D. Fearon, "Rationalist Explanations for War," *International Organization*, Vol. 49, No. 3 (Summer 1995), pp. 379–414; and Robert Powell, "Bargaining Theory and International Conflict," *Annual Review of Political Science*, Vol. 5 (June 2002), pp. 1–30.

17. Thomas Hobbes, *Leviathan* (New York: Penguin, [1651] 1968), pp. 184.

18. John H. Herz, "Idealist Internationalism and the Security Dilemma," *World Politics*, Vol. 2, No. 2 (January 1950), pp. 157–180; Robert Jervis, *Perception and Misperception in International Politics* (Princeton, N.J.: Princeton University Press, 1976); Robert Jervis, "Cooperation under the Security Dilemma," *World Politics*, Vol. 30, No. 2 (January 1978), pp. 167–214; and Charles L. Glaser, "The Security Dilemma Revisited," *World Politics*, Vol. 50, No. 1 (October 1997), pp. 171–202.

19. Andrew H. Kydd, *Trust and Mistrust in International Relations* (Princeton, N.J.: Princeton University Press, 2005).

20. John G. Riley, "Silver Signals: Twenty-five Years of Screening and Signaling," *Journal of Economic Literature*, Vol. 39, No. 2 (June 2001), pp. 432–478.

21. James D. Fearon, "Signaling Foreign Policy Interests: Tying Hands vs. Sunk Costs," *Journal of Conflict Resolution*, Vol. 41, No. 1 (February 1977), pp. 68–90.

22. Dan Reiter, "Exploring the Bargaining Model of War," *Perspectives on Politics*, Vol. 1, No. 1 (March 2003), pp. 27–43; and Robert Powell, "Bargaining and Learning While Fighting," *American Journal of Political Science*, Vol. 48, No. 2 (April 2004), pp. 344–361.

23. Rival terrorist or moderate groups are also important, but terrorism is not often used to signal such groups. Sometimes rival groups are targeted in an effort to eliminate them, but this violence is usually thought of as internecine

warfare rather than terrorism. The targeted government may also be divided into multiple actors, but these divisions are not crucial for a broad understanding of terrorist strategies.

24. This list is not exhaustive. In particular, it omits two strategies that have received attention in the literature: advertising and retaliation. Advertising may play a role in the beginning of some conflicts, but it does not sustain long-term campaigns of terrorist violence. Retaliation is a motivation for some terrorists, but terrorism would continue even if the state did not strike at terrorists, because terrorism is designed to achieve some goal, not just avenge counterterrorist attacks.

25. Per Baltzer Overgaard, "The Scale of Terrorist Attacks as a Signal of Resources," *Journal of Conflict Resolution,* Vol. 38, No. 3 (September 1994), pp. 452–478; and Harvey E. Lapan and Todd Sandler, "Terrorism and Signaling," *European Journal of Political Economy,* Vol. 9, No. 3 (August 1993), pp. 383–398.

26. J. Maynard Smith, "The Theory of Games and Evolution in Animal Conflicts," *Journal of Theoretical Biology,* Vol. 47 (1974), pp. 209–211; John J. Mearsheimer, *Conventional Deterrence* (Ithaca, N.Y.: Cornell University Press, 1983), pp. 33–35; and James D. Fearon, "Bargaining, Enforcement, and International Cooperation," *International Organization,* Vol. 52, No. 2 (Spring 1998), pp. 269– 305.

27. Bernard Lewis, "The Revolt of Islam," *New Yorker,* November 19, 2001, p. 61.

28. Quoted in Hassan, "An Arsenal of Believers," p. 38.

29. Peter C. Sederberg, "Conciliation as Counterterrorist Strategy," *Journal of Peace Research,* Vol. 32, No. 3 (August 1995), pp. 295–312.

30. John Mueller, "Six Rather Unusual Propositions about Terrorism," *Terrorism and Political Violence,* Vol. 17, No. 4 (Winter 2005), pp. 487–505.

31. The literature on deterrence is vast. See, for example, Thomas C. Schelling, *Arms and Influence* (New Haven, Conn.: Yale University Press, 1966); and Christopher H. Achen and Duncan Snidal, "Rational Deterrence Theory and Comparative Case Studies," *World Politics,* Vol. 41, No. 2 (January 1989), pp. 143–169.

32. United States National Security Council, *National Strategy for Victory in Iraq* (Washington, D.C.: White House, November 2005), p. 7.

33. Secretary of State Condoleezza Rice, "Iraq and U.S. Policy," testimony before the U.S. Senate Committee on Foreign Relations, October 19, 2005, 109th Cong., 1st sess., http://www.foreign.senate.gov/testimony/2005/RiceTestimony051019.pdf.

34. Fromkin, "The Strategy of Terrorism."

35. Crenshaw, "The Causes of Terrorism," p. 387; and Price, "The Strategy and Tactics of Revolutionary Terrorism," p. 58.

36. Paddy Woodworth, "Why Do They Kill? The Basque Conflict in Spain," *World Policy Journal*, Vol. 18, No.1 (Spring 2001), p. 7.

37. A program of economic and social assistance to these more moderate elements would provide counterevidence that the target is not malicious or evil as the terrorist organizations had claimed.

38. Stephen John Stedman, "Spoiler Problems in Peace Processes," *International Security,* Vol. 22, No. 2 (Fall 1997), pp. 5–53.

39. For the most extensive treatment of terrorism and outbidding, see Mia Bloom, *Dying to Kill: The Allure of Suicide Terrorism* (New York: Columbia University Press, 2005). See also Stuart J. Kaufman, "Spiraling to Ethnic War: Elites, Masses, and Moscow in Moldova's Civil War," *International Security,* Vol. 21, No. 2 (Fall 1996), pp. 108–138.

18 THE ETHICS OF WAR

18.1

War and Massacre

Thomas Nagel

From the apathetic reaction to atrocities committed in Vietnam by the United States and its allies, one may conclude that moral restrictions on the conduct of war command almost as little sympathy among the general public as they do among those charged with the formation of U.S. military policy. Even when restrictions on the conduct of warfare are defended, it is usually on legal grounds alone: their moral basis is often poorly understood. I wish to argue that certain restrictions are neither arbitrary nor merely conventional, and that their validity does not depend simply on their usefulness. There is, in other words, a moral basis for the rules of war, even though the conventions now officially in force are far from giving it perfect expression.

I

No elaborate moral theory is required to account for what is wrong in cases like the *My Lai* massacre, since it did not serve, and was not intended to serve, any strategic purpose. Moreover, if the participation of the United States in the Indo-Chinese war is entirely wrong to begin with, then that engagement is incapable of providing a justification for *any* measures taken in its pursuit—not only for the measures which are atrocities in every war, however just its aims.

But this war has revealed attitudes of a more general kind that influenced the conduct of earlier wars as well. After it has ended, we shall still be faced with the problem of how warfare may be conducted, and the attitudes that have resulted in the specific conduct of this war will not have disappeared. Moreover, similar problems can arise in wars or rebellions fought for very different reasons, and against very different opponents. It is not easy to keep a firm grip on the idea of what is not permissible in warfare, because while some military actions are obvious atrocities, other cases are more difficult to assess, and the general principles underlying these judgments remain obscure. Such obscurity can lead to the abandonment of sound intuitions in favor of criteria whose rationale may be more obvious. If such a tendency is to be resisted, it will require a better understanding of the restrictions than we now have.

I propose to discuss the most general moral problem raised by the conduct of warfare: the problem of means and ends. In one view, there are limits on what may be done even in the service of an end worth pursuing—and even when adherence to the restriction may be very costly. A person who acknowledges the force of such restrictions can find himself in acute moral dilemmas. He may believe, for example, that by torturing a prisoner he can obtain information necessary to prevent a disaster, or that by obliterating one village with bombs he can halt a campaign of terrorism. If he believes that

Source: Thomas Nagel. "War and Massacre," *Philosophy and Public Affairs* 1(2): 123–142. Copyright 1972. Reproduced with permission of Blackwell Publishing Ltd.

the gains from a certain measure will clearly outweigh its costs, yet still suspects that he ought not to adopt it, then he is in a dilemma produced by the conflict between two disparate categories of moral reason: categories that may be called *utilitarian* and *absolutist*.

Utilitarianism gives primacy to a concern with what will *happen*. Absolutism gives primacy to a concern with what one is *doing*. The conflict between them arises because the alternatives we face are rarely just choices between *total outcomes*: they are also choices between alternative pathways or measures to be taken. When one of the choices is to do terrible things to another person, the problem is altered fundamentally; it is no longer merely a question of which outcome would be worse.

Few of us are completely immune to either of these types of moral intuition, though in some people, either naturally or for doctrinal reasons, one type will be dominant and the other suppressed or weak. But it is perfectly possible to feel the force of both types of reason very strongly; in that case the moral dilemma in certain situations of crisis will be acute, and it may appear that every possible course of action or inaction is unacceptable for one reason or another. . . .

III

One absolutist position that creates no problems of interpretation is pacifism: the view that one may not kill another person under any circumstances, no matter what good would be achieved or evil averted thereby. The type of absolutist position that I am going to discuss is different. Pacifism draws the conflict with utilitarian considerations very starkly. But there are other views according to which violence may be undertaken, even on a large scale, in a clearly just cause, so long as certain absolute restrictions on the character and direction of that violence are observed. The line is drawn somewhat closer to the bone, but it exists. . . .

The policy of attacking the civilian population in order to induce an enemy to surrender, or to damage his morale, seems to have been widely accepted in the civilized world, and seems to be accepted still, at least if the stakes are high enough. It gives evidence of a moral conviction that the deliberate killing of noncombatants—women, children, old people—is permissible if enough can be gained by it. This follows from the more general position that any means can in principle be justified if it leads to a sufficiently worthy end. Such an attitude is evident not only in the more spectacular current weapons systems but also in the day-to-day conduct of the non-global war in Indochina: the indiscriminate destructiveness of anti-personnel weapons, napalm, and aerial bombardment; cruelty to prisoners; massive relocation of civilians; destruction of crops; and so forth. An absolutist position opposes to this the view that certain acts cannot be justified no matter what the consequences. Among those acts is murder—the deliberate killing of the harmless: civilians, prisoners of war, and medical personnel.

In the present war such measures are sometimes said to be regrettable, but they are generally defended by reference to military necessity and the importance of the long-term consequences of success or failure in the war. I shall pass over the inadequacy of this consequentialist defense in its own terms. (That is the dominant form of moral criticism of the war, for it is part of what people mean when they ask, "Is it worth it?") I am concerned rather to account for the inappropriateness of offering any defense of that kind for such actions.

Many people feel, without being able to say much more about it, that something has gone seriously wrong when certain measures are admitted into consideration in the first place. The fundamental mistake is made there, rather than at the point where the overall benefit of some monstrous measure is judged to outweigh its disadvantages, and it is adopted. An account of absolutism might help us to understand this. If it is not allowable to *do* certain things, such as killing unarmed prisoners or civilians, then no argument about what will happen if one doesn't do them can show that doing them would be all right.

Absolutism does not, of course, require one to ignore the consequences of one's acts. It operates as a limitation on utilitarian reasoning, not as a substitute for it. An absolutist can be expected to try to maximize good and minimize evil, so long as this does not require him to transgress an absolute prohibition like that against murder. But when such a conflict occurs, the prohibition takes complete precedence over any consideration of consequences. Some of the results of this view are clear enough. It requires us to forgo certain potentially useful military measures, such as the slaughter of hostages and prisoners or indiscriminate attempts to reduce the enemy civilian population by starvation, epidemic infectious diseases like anthrax and bubonic plague, or mass incineration. It means that we cannot deliberate on whether such measures are justified by the fact that they will avert still greater evils, for as intentional measures they cannot be justified in terms of any consequences whatever. . . .

Once the door is opened to calculations of utility and national interest, the usual speculations about the future of freedom, peace, and economic prosperity can be brought to bear to ease the consciences of those responsible for a certain number of charred babies.

For this reason alone it is important to decide what is wrong with the frame of mind which allows such arguments to begin. But it is also important to understand absolutism in the cases where it genuinely conflicts with utility. Despite its appeal, it is a paradoxical position, for it can require that one refrain from choosing the lesser of two evils when that is the only choice one has. And it is additionally paradoxical because, unlike pacifism, it permits one to do horrible things to people in some circumstances but not in others.

IV

. . . First, it is important to specify as clearly as possible the kind of thing to which absolutist prohibitions can apply. We must take seriously the proviso that they concern what we deliberately do to people. There could not, for example, without incoherence, be an absolute prohibition against *bringing about* the death of an innocent person. For one may find oneself in a situation in which, no matter what one does, some innocent people will die as a result. . . . I have in mind a case in which someone is bound to die, but who it is will depend on what one does. Sometimes these situations have natural causes, as when too few resources (medicine, lifeboats) are available to rescue everyone threatened with a certain catastrophe. . . . Whatever one does in cases such as these, some innocent people will die as a result. If the absolutist prohibition forbade doing what would result in the deaths of innocent people, it would have the consequence that in such cases nothing one could do would be morally permissible.

This problem is avoided, however, because what absolutism forbids is *doing* certain things to people, rather than bringing about certain *results*. Not everything that happens to others as a result of what one does is something that one has *done* to them. Catholic moral theology seeks to make this distinction precise in a doctrine known as the *law of double effect*, which asserts that there is a morally relevant distinction between bringing about the death of an innocent person deliberately, either as an end in itself or as a means, and bringing it about as a side effect of something else one does deliberately. In the latter case, even if the outcome is foreseen, it is not murder, and does not fall under the absolute prohibition, though of course it may still be wrong for other reasons (reasons of utility, for example). Briefly, the principle states that one is sometimes permitted knowingly to bring about as a side effect of one's actions something which it would be absolutely impermissible to bring about deliberately as an end or as a means. In application to war or revolution, the law of double effect permits a certain amount of civilian carnage as a side effect of bombing munitions plants or attacking enemy soldiers. And even this is permissible only if the cost is not too great to be justified by one's objectives. . . .

It might be thought easy to dismiss this as sophistry: if one bombs, burns, or strafes a village containing a hundred people, twenty of whom one believes to be guerrillas, so that by killing most of them one will be statistically likely to kill most of the guerrillas, then isn't one's attack on the group of one hundred a *means* of destroying the guerrillas, pure and simple? If one makes no attempt to discriminate between guerrillas and civilians, as is impossible in a aerial attack on a small village, then one cannot regard as a mere side effect the deaths of those in the group that one would not have bothered to kill if more selective means had been available.

The difficulty is that this argument depends on one particular description of the act, and the reply might be that the means used against the guerrillas is not killing everybody in the village but rather obliteration bombing of the *area* in which the twenty guerrillas are known to be located. If there are civilians in the area as well, they will be killed as a side effect of such action.[1] . . .

The second technical point to take up concerns a possible misinterpretation of this feature of the position. The absolutist focus on actions rather than outcomes does not merely introduce a new, outstanding item into the catalogue of evils. That is, it does not say that the worst thing in the world is the deliberate murder of an innocent person. For if that were all, then one could presumably justify one such murder on the ground that it would prevent several others, or ten thousand on the ground that they would prevent a hundred thousand more. That is a familiar argument. But if this is allowable, then there is no absolute prohibition against murder after all. Absolutism requires that we *avoid* murder at all costs, not that we *prevent* it at all costs.[2]

Finally, let me remark on a frequent criticism of absolutism that depends on a misunderstanding. It is sometimes suggested that such prohibitions depend on a kind of moral self-interest, a primary obligation to preserve one's own moral purity, to keep one's hands clean no matter what happens to the rest of the world. If this were the position, it might be exposed to the charge of self-indulgence. After all, what gives one man a right to put the purity of his soul or the cleanness of his hands above the lives or welfare of large numbers of other people? It might be argued that a public servant like Truman has no right to put himself first in that way; therefore if he is convinced that the alternatives would be worse, he must give the order to drop the bombs, and take the burden of those deaths on himself, as he must do other distasteful things for the general good.

But there are two confusions behind the view that moral self-interest underlies moral absolutism. First, it is a confusion to suggest that the need to preserve one's moral purity might be the *source* of an obligation. For if by committing murder one sacrifices one's moral purity or integrity, that can only be because there is *already* something wrong with murder. The general reason against committing murder cannot therefore be merely that it makes one an immoral person. Secondly, the notion that one might sacrifice one's moral integrity justifiably, in the service of a sufficiently worthy end, is an incoherent notion. For if one were justified in making such a sacrifice (or even morally required to make it), then one would not be sacrificing one's moral integrity by adopting that course: one would be preserving it.

Moral absolutism is not unique among moral theories in requiring each person to do what will preserve his own moral purity in all circumstances. This is equally true of utilitarianism, or of any other theory which distinguishes between right and wrong. Any theory which defines the right course of action in various circumstances and asserts that one should adopt that course, *ipso facto* asserts that one should do what will preserve one's moral purity, simply because the right course of action *is* what will preserve one's moral purity in those circumstances. Of course utilitarianism does not assert that this is *why* one should adopt that course, but we have seen that the same is true of absolutism.

V

. . . Absolutist restrictions in warfare appear to be of two types: restrictions on the class of persons at whom aggression or violence may be directed and restrictions on the manner of attack, given that the object falls within that class. These can be combined, however, under the principle that hostile treatment of any person must be justified in terms of something *about that person* which makes the treatment appropriate. . . .

A coherent view of this type will hold that extremely hostile behavior toward another is compatible with treating him as a person—even perhaps as an end in himself. This is possible only if one has not automatically stopped treating him as a person as soon as one starts to fight with him. If hostile, aggressive, or combative treatment of others always violated the condition that they be treated as human beings, it would be difficult to make further distinctions on that score *within* the class of hostile actions. That point of view, on the level of international relations, leads to the position that if complete pacifism is not accepted, no holds need be barred at all, and we may slaughter and massacre to our hearts' content, if it seems advisable. Such a position is often expressed in discussions of war crimes.

But the fact is that ordinary people do not believe this about conflicts, physical or otherwise, between individuals, and there is no more reason why it should be true of conflicts between nations. There seems to be a perfectly natural conception of the distinction between fighting clean and fighting dirty. To fight dirty is to direct one's hostility or aggression not at its proper object, but at a peripheral target which may be more vulnerable, and through which the proper object can be attacked indirectly. This applies in a fist fight, an election campaign, a duel, or a philosophical argument. If the concept is general enough to apply to all these matters, it should apply to war—both to the conduct of individual soldiers and to the conduct of nations. . . .

The importance of such restrictions may vary with the seriousness of the case; and what is unjustifiable in one case may be justified in a more extreme one. But they all derive from a single principle: that hostility or aggression should be directed at its true object. This means both that it should be directed at the person or persons who provoke it and that it should aim more specifically at what is provocative about them. The second condition will determine what form the hostility may appropriately take. . . .

If absolutism is to defend its claim to priority over considerations of utility, it must hold that the maintenance of a direct interpersonal response to the people one deals with is a requirement which no advantages can justify one in abandoning. The requirement is absolute only if it rules out any calculation of what would justify its violation. I have said earlier that there may be circumstances so extreme that they render an absolutist position untenable. One may find then that one has no choice but to do something terrible. Nevertheless, even in such cases absolutism retains its force in that one cannot claim *justification* for the violation. It does not become *all right*. . . .

Absolutism is associated with a view of oneself as a small being interacting with others in a large world. The justifications it requires are primarily interpersonal. Utilitarianism is associated with a view of oneself as a benevolent bureaucrat distributing such benefits as one can control to countless other beings, with whom one may have various relations or none. The justifications it requires are primarily administrative. The argument between the two moral attitudes may depend on the relative priority of these two conceptions.[3]

VI

Some of the restrictions on methods of warfare which have been adhered to from time to time are to be explained by the mutual interests of the involved parties: restrictions on weaponry, treatment of prisoners, etc. But that is not all there is to it. The conditions of directness and relevance which I have argued apply to relations of conflict and aggression apply to war as well. I have said that there are two types of absolutist restrictions on the conduct of war: those that limit the legitimate targets of hostility and those that limit its character, even when the target is acceptable. I shall say something about each of these. As will become clear, the principle I have sketched does not yield an unambiguous answer in every case.

First let us see how it implies that attacks on some people are allowed, but not attacks on others. It may seem paradoxical to assert that to fire a machine gun at someone who is throwing hand grenades at your emplacement is to treat him as a human being. Yet the relation with him is direct and straightforward.[4] The attack is aimed specifically against the threat presented by a dangerous adversary, and not against a peripheral target through which he happens to be vulnerable but which has nothing to do with that threat. For example, you might stop him by machine-gunning his wife and children, who are standing nearby, thus distracting him from his aim of blowing you up and enabling you to capture him. But if his wife and children are not threatening your life, that would be to treat them as means with a vengeance.

This, however, is just Hiroshima on a smaller scale. One objection to weapons of mass annihilation—nuclear, thermonuclear, biological, or chemical—is that their indiscriminateness disqualifies them as direct instruments for the expression of hostile relations. In attacking the civilian population, one treats neither the military enemy nor the civilians with that minimal respect which is owed to them as human beings. This is clearly true of the direct attack on people who present no threat at all. But it is also true of the character of the attack on those who *are* threatening you, viz., the government and military forces of the enemy. Your aggression is directed against an area of vulnerability quite distinct from any threat presented by them which you may be justified in meeting. You are taking aim at them through the mundane life and survival of their countrymen, instead of aiming at the destruction of their military capacity. And of course it does not require hydrogen bombs to commit such crimes.

This way of looking at the matter also helps us to understand the importance of the distinction between combatants and noncombatants, and the irrelevance of much of the criticism offered against its intelligibility and moral significance. According to an absolutist position, deliberate killing of the innocent is murder, and in warfare the role of the innocent is filled by noncombatants. This has been thought to raise two sorts of problems: first, the widely imagined difficulty of making a division, in modern warfare, between combatants and noncombatants; second, problems deriving from the connotation of the word "innocence."

Let me take up the latter question first.[5] In the absolutist position, the operative notion of innocence is not moral innocence, and it is not opposed to moral guilt. If it were, then we would be justified in killing a wicked but noncombatant hairdresser in an enemy city who supported the evil policies of his government, and unjustified in killing a morally pure conscript who was driving a tank toward us with the profoundest regrets and nothing but love in his heart. But moral innocence has very little to do with it, for in the definition of murder "innocent" means "currently harmless," and it is opposed not to "guilty" but to "doing harm." It should be noted that such an analysis has the consequence that in war we may often be justified in killing people who do not deserve to die, and unjustified in killing people who do deserve to die, if anyone does.

So we must distinguish combatants from noncombatants on the basis of their immediate threat or harmfulness. I do not claim that the line is a sharp one, but it is not so difficult as is often supposed to place individuals on one side of it or the other. . . . The threat presented by an army and its members does not consist merely in the fact that they are men, but in the fact that they are armed and are using their arms in the pursuit of certain objectives. Contributions to their arms and logistics are contributions to this threat; contributions to their mere existence as men are not. It is therefore wrong to direct an attack against those who merely serve the combatants' needs as human beings, such as farmers and food suppliers, even though survival as a human being is a necessary condition of efficient functioning as a soldier.

This brings us to the second group of restrictions: those that limit what may be done even to combatants. These limits are harder to explain clearly. Some of them may be arbitrary or conventional, and some may have to be derived from other sources; but I believe that the condition of directness and relevance in hostile relations accounts for them to a considerable extent. . . .

By extending the application of this idea, one can justify prohibitions against certain particularly cruel weapons: starvation, poisoning, infectious diseases (supposing they could be inflicted on combatants only), weapons designed to maim or disfigure or torture the opponent rather than merely to stop him. . . . That this well-known fact plays no (inhibiting) part in the determination of U.S. weapons policy suggests that moral sensitivity among public officials has not increased markedly since the Spanish Inquisition.

Finally, the same condition of appropriateness to the true object of hostility should limit the scope of attacks on an enemy country: its economy, agriculture, transportation system, and so forth. Even if the parties to a military conflict are considered to be not armies or governments but entire nations (which is usually a grave error), that does not justify one nation in warring against every aspect or element of another nation. That is not justified in a conflict between individuals, and nations are even more complex than individuals, so the same reasons apply. Like a human being, a nation is engaged in countless other pursuits while waging war, and it is not in those respects that it is an enemy.

The burden of the argument has been that absolutism about murder has a foundation in principles governing all one's relations to other persons, whether aggressive or amiable, and that these principles, and that absolutism, apply to warfare as well, with the result that certain measures are impermissible no matter what the consequences.[6] I do not mean to romanticize war. It is sufficiently utopian to suggest that when nations conflict they might rise to the level of limited barbarity that typically characterizes violent conflict between individuals, rather than wallowing in the moral pit where they appear to have settled, surrounded by enormous arsenals. . . .

Notes

1. This counterargument was suggested by Rogers Albritton.

2. Someone might of course acknowledge the *moral relevance* of the distinction between deliberate and nondeliberate killing, without being an absolutist. That is, he might believe simply that it was *worse* to bring about a death deliberately than as a secondary effect. But that would be merely a special assignment of value, and not an absolute prohibition.

3. Finally, I should mention a different possibility, suggested by Robert Nozick: that there is a strong general presumption against benefiting from the calamity of another, whether or not it has been deliberately inflicted for that or any other reason. This broader principle may well lend its force to the absolutist position.

4. It has been remarked that according to my view, shooting at someone establishes an I-thou relationship.

5. What I say on this subject derives from Anscombe.

6. It is possible to draw a more radical conclusion, which I shall not pursue here. Perhaps the technology and organization of modern war are such as to make it impossible to wage as an acceptable form of interpersonal or even international hostility. Perhaps it is too impersonal and large-scale for that. If so, then absolutism would in practice imply pacifism, given the present state of things. On the other hand, I am skeptical about the unstated assumption that a technology dictates its own use.

18.2

The Moral Duties of Statesmen

John Rawls

"Fifty Years after Hiroshima"[1]

The fiftieth year since the bombing of Hiroshima is a time to reflect about what one should think of it. Is it really a great wrong, as many now think, and many also thought then, or is it perhaps justified after all? I believe that both the firebombing of Japanese cities beginning in the spring of 1945 and the later atomic bombing of Hiroshima on August 6 were very great wrongs, and rightly seen as such. In order to support this opinion, I set out what I think to be the principles governing the conduct of war—*jus in bello*—of democratic peoples. These peoples[2] have different ends of war than non-democratic, especially totalitarian, states, such as Germany and Japan, which sought the domination and exploitation of subjected peoples, and in Germany's case, their enslavement if not extermination.

Although I cannot properly justify them here, I begin by setting out six principles and assumptions in support of these judgments. I hope they seem not unreasonable; and certainly they are familiar, as they are closely related to much traditional thought on this subject.

1. The aim of a just war waged by a decent democratic society is a just and lasting peace between peoples, especially with its present enemy.

2. A decent democratic society is fighting against a state that is not democratic. This follows from the fact that democratic peoples do not wage war against each other;[3] and since we are concerned with the rules of war as they apply to such peoples, we assume the society fought against is nondemocratic and that its expansionist aims threatened the security and free institutions of democratic regimes and caused the war.[4]

3. In the conduct of war, a democratic society must carefully distinguish three groups: the state's leaders and officials, its soldiers, and its civilian population. The reason for these distinctions rests on the principle of responsibility: since the state fought against is not democratic, the civilian members of the society cannot be those who organized and brought on the war. This was done by its leaders and officials assisted by other elites who control and staff the state apparatus. They are responsible, they willed the war, and for doing that, they are criminals. But civilians, often kept in ignorance and swayed by state propaganda, are not.[5] And this is so even if some civilians knew better and were enthusiastic for the war. In a nation's conduct of war many such marginal cases may exist, but they are irrelevant. As for soldiers, they, just as civilians, and leaving aside the upper ranks of an officer class, are not responsible for the war, but are conscripted or in other ways forced into it, their patriotism often cruelly and cynically exploited. The grounds on which they may be attacked directly are not that they are responsible for the war but that a democratic people cannot defend itself in any other way, and defend itself it must do. About this there is no choice.

4. A decent democratic society must respect the human rights of the members of the other side, both civilians and soldiers, for two reasons. One is because they simply have the rights by the law of peoples. The other reason is to teach enemy soldiers and civilians the content of those rights by the example of how they hold in their own case. In this way their significance is best brought home to them. They are assigned a certain status, the status of the members of some human society who possess rights as human persons.[6] In the case of human rights in war the aspect of status as applied to civilians is given a strict interpretation. This means, as I understand it here, that they can never be attacked directly except in times of extreme crisis, the nature of which I discuss below.

5. Continuing with the thought of teaching the content of human rights, the next principle is that just peoples by their actions and proclamations are to foreshadow during war the kind of peace they aim for and

Source: "Fifty Years after Hiroshima," reprinted by permission of the publisher from *John Rawls: Collected Papers*, edited by Samuel Freeman, pp. 565–572, Cambridge, MA: Harvard University Press. Originally published in *Dissent* (Summer 1995): 323–327.

the kind of relations they seek between nations. By doing so, they show in an open and public way the nature of their aims and the kind of people they are. These last duties fall largely on the leaders and officials of the governments of democratic peoples, since they are in the best position to speak for the whole people and to act as the principle applies. Although all the preceding principles also specify duties of statesmanship, this is especially true of 4 and 5. The way a war is fought and the actions ending it endure in the historical memory of peoples and may set the stage for future war. This duty of statesmanship must always be held in view.

6. Finally, we note the place of practical means-end reasoning in judging the appropriateness of an action or policy for achieving the aim of war or for not causing more harm than good. This mode of thought—whether carried on by (classical) utilitarian reasoning, or by cost-benefit analysis, or by weighing national interests, or in other ways—must always be framed within and strictly limited by the preceding principles. The norms of the conduct of war set up certain lines that bound just action. War plans and strategies, and the conduct of battles, must lie within their limits. (The only exception, I repeat, is in times of extreme crisis.)

In connection with the fourth and fifth principles of the conduct of war, I have said that they are binding especially on the leaders of nations. They are in the most effective position to represent their people's aims and obligations, and sometimes they become statesmen. But who is a statesman? There is no office of statesman, as there is of president, or chancellor, or prime minister. The statesman is an ideal, like the ideal of the truthful or virtuous individual. Statesmen are presidents or prime ministers who become statesmen through their exemplary performance and leadership in their office in difficult and trying times and manifest strength, wisdom, and courage. They guide their people through turbulent and dangerous periods for which they are esteemed always, as one of their great statesmen.

The ideal of the statesman is suggested by the saying: the politician looks to the next election, the statesman to the next generation. It is the task of the student of philosophy to look to the permanent conditions and the real interests of a just and good democratic society. It is the task of the statesman, however, to discern these conditions and interests in practice; the statesman sees deeper and further than most others and grasps what needs to be done. The statesman must get it right, or nearly so, and hold fast to it. Washington and Lincoln were statesmen. Bismarck was not. He did not see Germany's real interests far enough into the future, and his judgment and motives were often distorted by his class interests and his wanting himself alone to be chancellor of Germany. Statesmen need not be selfless and may have their own interests when they hold office, yet they must be selfless in their judgments and assessments of society's interests and not be swayed, especially in war and crisis, by passions of revenge and retaliation against the enemy.

Above all, they are to hold fast to the aim of gaining a just peace, and avoid the things that make achieving such a peace more difficult. Here the proclamations of a nation should make clear (the statesman must see to this) that the enemy people are to be granted an autonomous regime of their own and a decent and full life once peace is securely reestablished. Whatever they may be told by their leaders, whatever reprisals they may reasonably fear, they are not to be held as slaves or serfs after surrender,[7] or denied in due course their full liberties; and they may well achieve freedoms they did not enjoy before, as the Germans and the Japanese eventually did. The statesman knows, if others do not, that all descriptions of the enemy people (not their rulers) inconsistent with this are impulsive and false.

Turning now to Hiroshima and the firebombing of Tokyo, we find that neither falls under the exemption of extreme crisis. One aspect of this is that since (let's suppose) there are no absolute rights—rights that must be respected in all circumstances—there are occasions when civilians can be attacked directly by aerial bombing. Were there times during the war when Britain could properly have bombed Hamburg and Berlin? Yes, when Britain was alone and desperately facing Germany's superior might; moreover, this period would extend until Russia had clearly beat off the first German assault in the summer and fall of 1941, and would be able to fight Germany until the end. Here the cutoff point might be placed differently, say the summer of 1942, and certainly by Stalingrad.[8] I shall not dwell on this, as the crucial matter is that under no conditions could Germany be allowed to win the war, and this for two basic reasons; first, the nature and history of constitutional democracy and its place in European culture; and second, the peculiar evil of Nazism and the enormous and uncalculable moral and political evil it represented for civilized society.

The peculiar evil of Nazism needs to be understood, since in some circumstances a democratic people might better accept defeat if the terms of peace offered by the adversary were reasonable and moderate, did not subject them to humiliation, and looked forward to a workable and decent political relationship. Yet characteristic of Hitler was that he accepted no possibility at all of a political relationship with his enemies. They were always to be cowed by terror and brutality, and ruled by force. From the beginning the campaign against Russia, for example, was a war of destruction against Slavic peoples, with the original inhabitants remaining, if at all, only as serfs. When Goebbels and others protested that the war could not be won that way, Hitler refused to listen.[9]

Yet it is clear that while the extreme crisis exemption held for Britain in the early stages of the war, it never held at any time for the United States in its war with Japan. The principles of the conduct of war were always applicable to it. Indeed, in the case of Hiroshima many involved in higher reaches of the government recognized the questionable character of the bombing and that limits were being crossed. Yet during the discussions among allied leaders in June and July 1945, the weight of the practical means-end reasoning carried the day. Under the continuing pressure of war, such moral doubts as there were failed to gain an express and articulated view. As the war progressed, the heavy fire-bombing of civilians in the capitals of Berlin and Tokyo and elsewhere was increasingly accepted on the allied side. Although after the outbreak of war Roosevelt had urged both sides not to commit the inhuman barbarism of bombing civilians, by 1945 allied leaders came to assume that Roosevelt would have used the bomb on Hiroshima.[10] The bombing grew out of what had happened before.

The practical means-end reasons to justify using the atomic bomb on Hiroshima were the following:

The bomb was dropped to hasten the end of the war. It is clear that Truman and most other allied leaders thought it would do that. Another reason was that it would save lives where the lives counted are the lives of American soldiers. The lives of Japanese, military or civilian, presumably counted for less. Here the calculations of least time and most lives saved were mutually supporting. Moreover, dropping the bomb would give the Emperor and the Japanese leaders a way to save face, an important matter given Japanese samurai culture. Indeed, at the end a few top Japanese leaders wanted to make a last sacrificial stand but were overruled by others supported by the Emperor, who ordered surrender on August 12, having received word from Washington that the Emperor could stay provided it was understood that he had to comply with the orders of the American military commander. The last reason I mention is that the bomb was dropped to impress the Russians with American power and make them more agreeable with our demands. This reason is highly disputed but is urged by some critics and scholars as important.

The failure of these reasons to reflect the limits on the conduct of war is evident, so I focus on a different matter: the failure of statesmanship on the part of allied leaders and why it might have occurred. Truman once described the Japanese as beasts and to be treated as such; yet how foolish it sounds now to call the Germans or the Japanese barbarians and beasts![11] Of the Nazis and Tojo militarists, yes, but they are not the German and the Japanese people. Churchill later granted that he carried the bombing too far, led by passion and the intensity of the conflict.[12] A duty of statesmanship is not to allow such feelings, natural and inevitable as they may be, to alter the course a democratic people should best follow in striving for peace. The statesman understands that relations with the present enemy have special importance: for as I have said, war must be openly and publicly conducted in ways that make a lasting and amicable peace possible with a defeated enemy, and prepares its people for how they may be expected to be treated. Their present fears of being subjected to acts of revenge and retaliation must be put to rest; present enemies must be seen as associates in a shared and just future peace.

These remarks make it clear that, in my judgment, both Hiroshima and the firebombing of Japanese cities were great evils that the duties of statesmanship require political leaders to avoid in the absence of the crisis exemption. I also believe this could have been done at little cost in further casualties. An invasion was unnecessary at that date, as the war was effectively over. However, whether that is true or not makes no difference. Without the crisis exemption, those bombings are great evils. Yet it is clear that an articulate expression of the principles of just war introduced at that time would not have altered the outcome. It was simply too late. A president or prime minister must have carefully considered these questions, preferably long before, or at least when they had the time and leisure to think things out. Reflections on just war cannot be heard in the daily round of the pressure of events near the end of the hostilities; too many are anxious and impatient, and simply worn out.

Similarly, the justification of constitutional democracy and the basis of the rights and duties it must respect should be part of the public political culture and discussed in the many associations of civic society as part of one's education. It is not clearly heard in day-to-day ordinary politics, but must be presupposed as the background, not the daily subject of politics, except in special circumstances. In the same way, there was not sufficient prior grasp of the fundamental importance of the principles of just war for the expression of them to have blocked the appeal of practical means-end reasoning in terms of a calculus of lives, or of the least time to end the war, or of some other balancing of costs and benefits. This practical reasoning justifies too much, too easily, and provides a way for a dominant power to quiet any moral worries that may arise. If the principles of war are put forward at that time, they easily become so many more considerations to be balanced in the scales.

Another failure of statesmanship was not to try to enter into negotiations with the Japanese before any drastic steps such as the firebombing of cities or the bombing of Hiroshima were taken. A conscientious attempt to do so was morally necessary. As a democratic people, we owed that to the Japanese people—whether to their government is another matter. There had been discussions in Japan for some time about finding a way to end the war, and on June 26 the government had been instructed by the Emperor to do so.[13] It must surely have realized that with the navy destroyed and the outer islands taken, the war was lost. True, the Japanese were deluded by the hope that the Russians might prove to be their allies,[14] but negotiations are precisely to disabuse the other side of delusions of that kind. A statesman is not free to consider that such negotiations may lessen the desired shock value of subsequent attacks.

Truman was in many ways a good, at times a very good president. But the way he ended the war showed he failed as a statesman. For him it was an opportunity missed, and a loss to the country and its armed forces as well. It is sometimes said the questioning the bombing of Hiroshima is an insult to the American troops who fought the war. This is hard to understand. We should be able to look back and consider our faults after fifty years. We expect the Germans and the Japanese to do that—*"Vergangenheitsverarbeitung,"* as the Germans say. Why shouldn't we? It can't be that we think we waged the war without moral error!

None of this alters Germany's and Japan's responsibility for the war nor their behavior in conducting it. Emphatically to be repudiated are two nihilist doctrines. One is expressed by Sherman's remark, "War is hell," so anything goes to get it over with as soon as one can. The other says that we are all guilty so we stand on a level and no one can blame anyone else. These are both superficial and deny all reasonable distinctions; they are invoked falsely to try to excuse our misconduct or to plead that we cannot be condemned.

The moral emptiness of these nihilisms is manifest in the fact that just and decent civilized societies—their institutions and laws, their civil life and background culture and mores—all depend absolutely on making significant moral and political distinctions in all situations. Certainly war is a kind of hell, but why should that mean that all moral distinctions cease to hold? And granted also that sometimes all or nearly all may be to some degree guilty, that does not mean that all are equally so. There is never a time when we are free from all moral and political principles and restraints. These nihilisms are pretenses to be free of those principles and restraints that always apply to us fully.

Notes

1. From John Rawls, *Collected Papers*, ed. Samuel Freeman (Cambridge, MA: Harvard University Press, 1999), pp. 565–72. The essay is reproduced here in its entirety. It was originally published in the Summer 1995 issue of *Dissent*, pp. 323–7. Rawls acknowledges Burton Dreben, Thomas Nagel, and T. M. Scanlon for discussing the essay with him.

2. [*All the notes that follow are reproduced from Rawls's text:*] I sometimes use the term "peoples" to mean the same as nations, especially when I want to contrast peoples with states and a state's apparatus.

3. I assume that democratic peoples do not go to war against each other. There is considerable evidence of this important idea. See Michael Doyle's two-part article, "Kant, Liberal Legacies, and Foreign Affairs," *Philosophy and Public Affairs*, 12 (Summer/Fall 1983), pp. 205–35, 323–53. See especially his summary of the evidence in the first part, pp. 206–32.

4. Responsibility for war rarely falls on only one side, and this must be granted. Yet some dirty hands are dirtier than others, and sometimes even with dirty hands a democratic people would still have the right and even the duty to defend itself from the other side. This is clear in World War II.

5. Here I follow Michael Walzer's *Just and Unjust Wars* (New York: Basic Books, 1977).

6. For the idea of status, I am indebted to discussion of Frances Kamm and Thomas Nagel.

7. See Churchill's remarks explaining the meaning of "unconditional surrender" in *The Hinge of Fate* (Boston: Houghton Mifflin, 1950), pp. 685–8.

8. I might add here that a balancing of interests is not involved. Rather, we have a matter of judgment as to whether certain objective circumstances are present which constitute the extreme crisis exemption. As with any other complex concept, that of such an exemption is to some degree vague. Whether or not the concept applies rests on judgment.

9. On Goebbels's and others' protests, see Alan Bullock, *Hitler: A Study in Tyranny* (London: Oldham's Press, 1952), chap. 12, section 5, pp. 633–44.

10. For an account of events, see David M. McCullough, *Truman* (New York: Simon and Schuster, 1992), chap. 9, section IV, and chap. 10, pp. 390–464; and Barton Bernstein, "The Atomic Bombings Reconsidered," *Foreign Affairs*, 74 (Jan.–Feb. 1995), p. 1.

11. See McCullough, *Truman,* p. 458, [for] the exchange between Truman and Senator Russell of Georgia in August 1945.

12. See Martin Gilbert, *Winston Churchill: Never Despair,* vol. VIII (Boston: Houghton Mifflin, 1988), p. 259, reflecting later on Dresden.

13. See Gerhard Weinberg, *A World at Arms* (Cambridge: Cambridge University Press, 1994), pp. 886–9.

14. See ibid., p. 886.

18.3

Morality, Reduced to Arithmetic

Jim Holt

Can the deliberate massacre of innocent people ever be condoned? The atomic bombs dropped on Hiroshima and Nagasaki on Aug. 6 and 9, 1945, resulted in the deaths of 120,000 to 250,000 Japanese by incineration and radiation poisoning. Although a small fraction of the victims were soldiers, the great majority were noncombatants—women, children, the aged.

Among the justifications that have been put forward for President Harry Truman's decision to use the bomb, only one is worth taking seriously—that it saved lives. The alternative, the reasoning goes, was to launch an invasion. Truman claimed in his memoirs that this would have cost another half a million American lives. Winston Churchill put the figure at a million.

Revisionist historians have cast doubt on such numbers. Wartime documents suggest that military planners expected around 50,000 American combat deaths in an invasion. Still, when Japanese casualties, military and civilian, are taken into account, the overall invasion death toll on both sides would surely have ended up surpassing that from Hiroshima and Nagasaki.

Scholars will continue to argue over whether there were other, less catastrophic ways to force Tokyo to surrender. But given the fierce obstinacy of the Japanese militarists, Truman and his advisers had some grounds for believing that nothing short of a full-scale invasion or the annihilation of a big city with an apocalyptic new weapon would have succeeded.

Suppose they were right. Would this prospect have justified the intentional mass killing of the people of Hiroshima and Nagasaki?

In the debate over the question, participants on both sides have been playing the numbers game. Estimate the hypothetical number of lives saved by the bombings, then add up the actual lives lost. If the first number exceeds the second, then Truman did the right thing; if the reverse, it was wrong to have dropped the bombs.

That is one approach to the matter—the utilitarian approach. According to utilitarianism, a form of moral reasoning that arose in the 19th century, the goodness or evil of an action is determined solely by its consequences. If somehow you can save 10 lives by boiling a baby, go ahead and boil that baby.

There is, however, an older ethical tradition, one rooted in Judeo-Christian theology that takes a quite different view. The gist of it is expressed by St. Paul's condemnation of those who say, "Let us do evil, that good may come." Some actions, this tradition holds, can never be justified by their consequences; they are absolutely forbidden. It is always wrong to boil a baby even if lives are saved thereby.

Applying this absolutist morality to war can be tricky. When enemy soldiers are trying to enslave or kill us, the principle of self-defense permits us to kill them (though not to slaughter them once they are taken prisoner).

But what of those who back them? During World War II, propagandists made much of the "indivisibility" of modern warfare: the idea was that since the enemy nation's entire economic and social strength was deployed behind its military forces, the whole population was a legitimate target for obliteration.

"There are no civilians in Japan," declared an intelligence officer of the Fifth Air Force shortly before the Hiroshima bombing, a time when the Japanese were popularly depicted as vermin worthy of extermination.

The boundary between combatant and noncombatant can be fuzzy, but the distinction is not meaningless, as the case of small children makes clear. Yet is wartime killing of those who are not trying to harm us always tantamount to murder?

When naval dockyards, munitions factories and supply lines are bombed, civilian carnage is inevitable. The absolutist moral tradition acknowledges this by a principle known as double effect: although it is always wrong to kill innocents deliberately, it is sometimes

Source: Jim Holt, "Morality, Reduced to Arithmetic," *The New York Times*, August 5, 1995.

permissible to attack a military target knowing some noncombatants will die as a side effect. The doctrine of double effect might even justify bombing a hospital where Hitler is lying ill.

It does not, however, apply to Hiroshima and Nagasaki. Transformed into hostages by the technology of aerial bombardment, the people of those cities were intentionally executed en masse to send a message of terror to the rulers of Japan.

The practice of ordering the massacre of civilians to bring the enemy to heel scarcely began with Truman. Nor did the bomb result in casualties of a new order of magnitude. The earlier bombing of Tokyo by incendiary weapons killed some 100,000 people.

What Hiroshima and Nagasaki did mark, by the unprecedented need for rationalization they presented, was the triumph of utilitarian thinking in the conduct of war. The conventional code of noncombatant immunity—a product of several centuries of ethical progress among nations, which had been formalized by an international commission in the 1920's in the Hague—was swept away. A simpler axiom took its place: since war is hell, any means necessary may be used to end, in Churchill's words, "the vast indefinite butchery."

It is a moral calculus that, for all its logical consistency, offends our deep-seated intuitions about the sanctity of life—our conviction that a person is always to be treated as an end, never as a means.

Left up to the warmakers, moreover, utilitarian calculations are susceptible to bad-faith reasoning: tinker with the numbers enough and virtually any atrocity can be excused in the national interest.

In January, the world commemorated the 50th anniversary of the liberation of Auschwitz, where mass slaughter was committed as an end in itself—the ultimate evil. The moral nature of Hiroshima is ambiguous by contrast. Yet in the post-war era, when governments do not hesitate to treat the massacre of civilians as just another strategic option, the bomb's sinister legacy is plain: it has inured us to the idea of reducing innocents to instruments and morality to arithmetic.

Part III

International Political Economy

The other major subdiscipline within international relations is **international political economy (IPE)**. IPE studies the interaction of politics and economics in relations among states. Politics and economics are mutually interactive, meaning that each affects the other. Economics studies the allocation of scarce resources, while politics impacts the distribution of those resources. Policy choices also affect the level of scarcity of some resources. Part III focuses on understanding the questions, "Why do states do what they do?" and "What causes conflict and cooperation in the international system?" largely by examining conflict as **protectionism** and cooperation as **free trade**—although one can also see conflict and cooperation in IPE related to exchange rate decisions, foreign lending and investment opportunities, and institutional choices of public or private ownership. As in Part II: War and Peace, the reader will need to draw on the concepts and theories discussed in Part I: Theoretical Traditions in International Relations. Additionally, the reader should also think through and recognize that while the definitions of some independent and dependent variables may have changed, some of the theories presented in Part III share the same or similar underlying causal logic with theories or concepts presented in Part II. You will once again see the value of intellectual pluralism in this section's selected readings.

Introduction to International Political Economy

Political scientists Jeffrey Frieden, David Lake, and Lawrence Broz provide an overview of the field of IPE. They explain the interaction of international politics and international economics. The purpose of this section is to provide a general introduction to this field that will help put the remaining sections in Part III into context. Frieden, Lake, and Broz describe different perspectives on IPE and describe the principal schools of thought that explain why conflict and cooperation occur between states based on political-economic interaction. They also describe the general liberal, realist, and constructivist perspectives of IPE and introduce an additional international relations theoretical tradition, **Marxism**. Readers should take the time here to reflect on what they have learned to this point—from Part I and Part II—about the different traditions and theories within those traditions to start framing expectations about how the different traditions will explain state behavior in this section.

International Trade

International trade, the exchange of goods and services between countries, is the central activity of IPE. The purpose of foreign exchange, debt issuance, and foreign investment is to facilitate trade, which is why

Part III focuses largely on trade. Based on the economic principle of **comparative advantage**, when one has a lower opportunity cost to produce a good compared with the opportunity cost of another producer, individuals can increase their welfare by exchanging goods. Opportunity cost is how much you have to give up of one thing to obtain something else. On a larger scale, societies within states can increase their welfare through trade with other states based on the same principle of comparative advantage. Through trade, however, there are winners and losers—the industry that has comparative advantage wins, and the industry that does not loses; hence, trade is a highly political issue.

Nobel laureate economist Paul R. Krugman describes some common misperceptions about international trade and tries to correct them so students better understand the true role and importance of trade. The reading selections by economists Arvind Panagariya and Dani Rodrik are framed as a debate about free trade. The term *free trade* is a misnomer, because no state maintains completely open trade without any trade barriers. Additionally, **autarky**, or complete self-reliance and closure to trade, is virtually nonexistent. The debate about free trade is really about the relative openness of the international trading order, bilaterally and multilaterally. Panagariya argues that the benefits of open trade outweigh the costs, while Rodrik argues that developing countries should not move too quickly toward **trade liberalization**.

Writer and columnist Moisés Naím raises the fact that while freer trade has expanded, **international trade agreements**, such as the latest round of **World Trade Organization (WTO)** negotiations, have stalled. He is concerned that this will erode the rule of law and increase the chance of trade conflicts. Readers should engage the arguments made and the evidence presented by the authors, using social scientific and theoretical analysis to determine which argument they find more compelling and where they can find some common ground between the positions.

Hegemony and Trade

This section explores the role of a hegemon in shaping the structure of international trade by looking at theoretical arguments from three international relations traditions. Political scientist Stephen D. Krasner explains the logic of **hegemonic stability theory** from a realist perspective, focused on the distribution of state power and how that shapes preferences toward the level of openness in the international trading order. After developing his hypotheses, Krasner tests the argument against empirical evidence and then amends his theory based on the findings. This is an outstanding example of the social scientific process.

Political scientist Robert O. Keohane (recall his reading from the "Liberalism II" section in Part I) provides a neoliberal critique of Krasner's argument that a hegemon is required to create and maintain an open international trading order. He argues that the institutions that promote and support open trade will endure after the decline of a hegemon. Readers should understand the function of institutions (or regimes) in order to understand the causal logic of Keohane's argument.

While economist and former Chilean finance minister Andrés Velasco ultimately critiques **dependency theory**, he first explains the basic concept of this Marxist-derived theory that views the underdevelopment of the world's poor countries as the result of exploitation by the world's rich countries. Even though economists, such as Velasco, find theoretical and empirical flaws in dependency theory, the underlying logic has found new voice in the reemergent populist language found in presidential palaces in Latin America since the rise of Hugo Chávez in Venezuela.

Domestic Politics and Trade

In addition to international politics, due to the creation of different winners and losers, trade is also heavily influenced by domestic politics. Political scientist Robert D. Putnam provides a theoretical approach to understanding how domestic politics can influence international relations and how international relations can shape domestic politics. One should think about how it is possible to apply his **two-level game** model not just to issues in IPE but to any other international relations issue that requires negotiations or bargaining between states.

Political scientist Ronald Rogowski develops a theoretical framework to understand what **political cleavages** will emerge domestically in response to a policy or event that affects a state's international trade. Based on the level of relative abundance of a state's **factors of production** and the stage of economic development, Rogowski explains when different domestic groups favor protectionism or freer trade.

Witold J. Henisz and Edward D. Mansfield develop and test an argument explaining that a state's level of openness results from the interaction of both domestic interest groups and domestic institutions rather than from societal pressures or regime-type constraints alone. Readers should consider the theoretical evolution of these explanations about the influence of domestic politics on international trade, and how newly available data and social scientific methods have enabled the further development of knowledge.

International Monetary Affairs

Money is necessary in order to facilitate trade between states. Historically, states have maintained sovereign control over the creation, valuation, and control of their own legal tender. **Monetary policy** can have a major impact on trade and investment between countries. Political scientist Beth A. Simmons describes the evolution of international institutions, culminating in the **International Monetary Fund (IMF)**, that have helped create legal obligations to promote **exchange-rate** stability, nondiscriminatory economic arrangements, and open markets. In the wake of the current global economic struggles, exchange rates and **debt** have become almost daily news, and charges about the weakness of the IMF structure, currency undervaluation by China, and the failure of the euro experiment are rampant.

Economist N. Gregory Mankiw describes the **international finance trilemma**, which explains how states have three financial goals but are able to achieve only two at a time, and so must choose which one to forgo. Each possible choice has different consequences that can impact the possibilities for conflict and cooperation between states. The creation of a common currency, the **euro**, between 17 member states of the European Union has limited the ability of euro members to make their own choices about which financial goal to forgo.

Political scientist Andrew Moravcsik argues that the creditor countries within the eurozone, such as Germany, bear as much responsibility as the debtor countries, such as Greece, for the current crisis. He also explains that eurozone members have done a good job of short-term crisis management but that the common currency faces greater long-term challenges unless members take the necessary political steps toward greater convergence of monetary and **fiscal policy**.

Ethics and International Political Economy

With the focus on distribution of scarce resources in IPE and the political implications of creating winners and losers through the policies that impact that distribution, it is important to consider some of the ethical arguments about international trade. Accounting and business ethicist Robert W. McGee argues that free trade is ethical, but he makes the case that the conventional utilitarian argument that supports free trade comes to the right conclusion but for the wrong reason. Instead, he explains the logic of a rights-based approach to argue why free trade is ethical and protectionism is unethical.

Drawing from a **distributive justice** perspective (refer back to the reading by John Rawls in "The Ethics of War" section in Part II), economist and political scientist Ethan B. Kapstein argues that the ethics of trade should be judged on the impact it has on individuals and on their life chances rather than on overall wealth creation. The reader should recognize how both McGee and Kapstein drew from the deontological ethical tradition (refer back to the readings in the "Ethical Traditions in International Relations" section in Part I), yet came to different conclusions about the ethics of fair trade. Journalists Nicholas D. Kristof and Sheryl WuDunn provocatively argue that sweatshops help the poor and that Western efforts to boycott sweatshops only hurt the people Westerners think they are helping.

Discussion Questions for Part III: International Political Economy

1. Discuss the role of domestic and international competition in the debate about free trade. Apply the general arguments to specific examples in the current headlines about the latest international trade dispute (e.g., the case against China over rare earth metals, brought before the WTO by the United States, the European Union, and Japan; the WTO ruling against China over duties on U.S. steel; etc.) or the latest negotiations of a bilateral or multilateral trade agreement (e.g., the Doha round of WTO negotiations, the U.S.-South Korea Free Trade Agreement, etc.).

2. Explain why a backlash toward the policies of trade liberalization promoted by the United States, the IMF, and the **World Bank** has occurred in Latin America during the 2000s. What are the arguments that the promoters of trade liberalization would likely make? What are the counterarguments that the detractors of free trade would likely make? Which argument do you find more persuasive and why?

3. Evaluate the manner in which domestic institutions and international imperatives work in tandem to influence the outcome of interstate trade negotiations. Describe the political cleavages that exist today in America between the owners of the different factors of production. Which domestic industries or groups would you expect to promote protectionism and why? Which industries or groups would you expect to promote freer trade and why?

4. Describe why understanding the trilemma of international finance matters for understanding conflict and cooperation between states. Assuming the United States chooses to forgo capital mobility in favor of the other two remaining financial goals, what effects would you anticipate on the U.S. economy? Assuming the United States chooses to forgo an independent monetary policy in favor of the other two remaining financial goals, what effects would you anticipate on the U.S. economy? Assuming the United States chooses to forgo a stable currency exchange rate in favor of the other two remaining financial goals, what effects would you anticipate on the U.S. economy? Explain your answer to each question.

5. Apply arguments made from the different ethical traditions discussed in this book to the issue of sweatshop labor. Which arguments do you find most persuasive and why?

Key Concepts

autarky
comparative advantage
debt
dependency theory
distributive justice
euro
exchange rate
factors of production
fiscal policy
free trade
hegemonic stability theory
international finance trilemma
International Monetary Fund (IMF)
international political economy (IPE)
international trade agreements
Marxism
monetary policy
political cleavages
protectionism
trade liberalization
two-level game
World Bank
World Trade Organization (WTO)

19 Introduction to International Political Economy

19.1

International Politics and International Economics

Jeffrey Frieden, David Lake, and Lawrence Broz

During the past forty years, the study of international political economy has undergone a remarkable resurgence. Virtually nonexistent as a field of study before 1970, it is now a popular area of specialization for both undergraduates and graduate students, as well as the source of much innovative and influential scholarship. The revival of international political economy after nearly forty years of dormancy has enriched both social science and public debate, and promises to continue to do so.

International political economy is the study of the interplay of economics and politics in the world arena. In the most general sense, the economy can be defined as the system of producing, distributing, and using wealth; politics is the set of institutions and rules by which social and economic interactions are governed. *Political economy* has a variety of meanings. For some, it refers primarily to the study of the political basis of economic actions—the ways that government policies affect market operations. For others, the principal preoccupation is the economic basis of political action—the ways that economic forces mold government policies. The two focuses are, in a sense, complementary, for politics and markets are in a constant state of mutual interaction.

Most markets are governed by certain fundamental laws that operate more or less independently of the will of firms and individuals. Any shopkeeper knows that an attempt to raise the price of a readily available and standardized product—a pencil, for example—above that charged by nearby and competing shopkeepers will rapidly cause customers to stop buying pencils at the higher price. Unless the shopkeeper wants to be left with piles of unsold pencils, he or she will have to bring the price back into line with "what the market will bear." The shopkeeper will have learned a microcosmic lesson in what economists call *market-clearing equilibrium,* the price at which the number of goods supplied equals the number demanded—the point at which supply and demand curves intersect.

At the base of all modern economics is the general assertion that, within certain carefully specified parameters, markets operate in and of themselves to maintain balance between supply and demand. Other things being equal, if the supply of a good increases far beyond the demand for it, the good's price will be driven down until demand rises to meet supply, supply falls to meet demand, and market-clearing equilibrium is restored. By the same token, if demand exceeds supply, the good's price will rise, thus causing demand to decline and supply to increase until the two are in balance.

If the international and domestic economies functioned as perfectly competitive markets, they would be relatively easy to describe and comprehend. But such

Source: "Introduction: International Politics and International Economics" by Jeffrey Frieden, David Lake, and Lawrence Broz, from *International Political Economy: Perspectives on Global Power and Wealth,* Fifth Edition, edited by Jeffrey A. Frieden, David A. Lake, and Lawrence J. Broz.

markets are only highly stylized or abstract models, which are rarely reproduced in the real world. A variety of factors influence the workings of domestic and international markets in ways that a focus on perfectly competitive and unchanging market forces does not fully capture. Consumer tastes can change—how large is the American market for spats or sarsaparilla today?—as can the technology needed to make products more cheaply, or even to make entirely new goods that displace others (stick shifts for horsewhips, computers for slide rules). Producers, sellers, or buyers of goods can band together to try to raise or lower prices unilaterally, as the Organization of Petroleum Exporting Countries (OPEC) has done with petroleum since 1973. And governments can act, consciously or inadvertently, to alter patterns of consumption, supply, demand, prices, and virtually all other economic variables.

This last fact—the impact of policy and politics on economic trends—is the most visible, and probably the most important, reason to look beyond market-based, purely economic explanations of social behavior. Indeed, many market-oriented economists are continually surprised by the ability of governments or of powerful groups pressuring governments to contravene economic tendencies. When OPEC first raised oil prices in December 1973, some market-minded pundits, and even a few naive economists, predicted that such naked manipulation of the forces of supply and demand could last only a matter of months. However, what has emerged from more than forty years' experience with oil prices is the recognition that they are a function of both market forces and the ability of OPEC's member states to organize concerted intervention in the oil market.

Somewhat less dramatic are the everyday operations of local and national governments, which affect prices, production, profits, wages, and almost every other aspect of the economy. Wage, price, and rent controls; taxation; incentives and subsidies; tariffs and other barriers to trade; and government spending all serve to mold modern economies and the functioning of markets themselves. Who could understand the suburbanization of the United States after World War II without taking into account government tax incentives to home mortgage holders, government-financed highway construction, and politically driven patterns of local educational expenditures? How many American (or Japanese or European) farmers would be left if agricultural subsidies were eliminated? How many Americans would have college educations were it not for public universities, government scholarships and publicly subsidized student loans, and tax exemptions for private universities? Who could explain the proliferation of nonprofit groups in the United States without knowing the tax incentives given to charitable donations?

In these instances and many more, political pressure groups, politicians, and government bureaucrats have at least as much effect on economic outcomes as do the laws of the marketplace. Social scientists, especially political scientists, have spent decades trying to understand how these political pressures interact to produce government policy. Many of the results provide as elegant and stylized a view of politics as the economics profession has developed of markets. As in economics, however, social science models of political behavior are little more than didactic devices whose accuracy depends on a wide variety of unpredictable factors, including underlying economic trends. If an economist would be equally foolish to dismiss the possibilities of inter-governmental producers' cartels (such as OPEC) out of hand, a political scientist would be foolish not to realize that the economic realities of modern international commodity markets ensure that successful producers' cartels will be few and far between.

It is thus no surprise that political economy is far from new. Indeed, until a century ago, virtually all thinkers concerned with understanding human society wrote about political economy. For individuals as diverse as Adam Smith, John Stuart Mill, and Karl Marx, the economy was eminently political and politics was obviously tied to economic phenomena. Few scholars before 1900 would have taken seriously any attempt to describe and analyze politics and economics independently of each other.

Around the turn of the century, however, professional studies of economics and politics became increasingly divorced from one another. Economic investigation began to focus on understanding more fully the operation of specific markets and their interaction; the development of new mathematical techniques permitted the formalization of, for example, laws of supply and demand. By the time of World War I, an economics profession per se was in existence, and its attention was focused on understanding the operation of economic activities in and of themselves. At the same time, other scholars were looking increasingly at the political realm in isolation from the economy. The rise of modern representative political institutions, mass political parties, more politically informed populations, and modern bureaucracies all seemed to justify the study of politics as an activity that had a logic of its own.

With the exception of a few isolated individuals and an upsurge of interest during the politically and economically troubled Depression years, the twentieth century saw an increasing separation of the study of economics from that of politics. Economists developed ever more elaborate and sophisticated models of how economies work, and similarly, political scientists spun out ever more complex theories of political development and activity.

The resurgence of political economy after 1970 had two interrelated sources. The first was dissatisfaction among academics with the gap between abstract models of political and economic behavior, on the one hand, and the actual behavior of polities and economies, on the other. Theory had become more ethereal and seemed less realistic. Many scholars therefore questioned the intellectual justifications for a strict analytic division between politics and economics. Second, as the stability and prosperity of the first twenty-five post-war years started to disintegrate in the early 1970s, economic issues became politicized while political systems became increasingly preoccupied with ecomonic affairs. In August 1971, President Richard Nixon ended the gold-dollar standard, which had formed the basis for postwar monetary relations; two and a half years later, OPEC, a previously little-known group, succeeded in substantially raising the price of oil. In 1974 and 1975, the industrial nations of Western Europe, North America, and Japan fell into the first worldwide economic recession since the 1930s; unemployment and inflation were soon widespread realities and explosive political issues. In the world arena, the underdeveloped countries—most of them recently independent—burst onto center stage as the third world and demanded a fairer division of global wealth and power. If in the 1950s and 1960s, economic growth was taken for granted and politics occupied itself with other matters, in the 1970s and 1980s, economic stagnation fed political strife while political conflict exacerbated economic uncertainty.

For both intellectual and practical reasons, then, social scientists once again began seeking to understand how politics and economics interact in modern society. As interest in political economy grew, a series of fundamental questions was posed and a broad variety of contending approaches arose.

To be sure, today's political economists have not simply reproduced the studies of earlier (and perhaps neglected) generations of scholars in the discipline. The professionalization of both economics and political science led to major advances in both fields, and scholars now understand both economic and political phenomenona far better than they did a generation ago. It is on this improved basis that the new political economy has been constructed, albeit with some long-standing issues in mind.

Just as in the real world, where politicians pay close attention to economic trends and economic actors keep track of political tendencies, those who would understand the political process must take the economy into account, and vice versa. A much richer picture of social processes emerges from an integrated understanding of both political and economic affairs than from the isolated study of politics and economics as separate realms. This much is, by now, hardly controversial; it is in application that disagreements arise. Government actions may influence economic trends, but these actions themselves may simply reflect the pressures of economic interest groups. Economic interest groups may be central in determining government policy, yet the political system—democratic or totalitarian, two-party or multiparty, parliamentary or presidential—may crucially color the outlooks and influence of economic interests. In the attempt to arrive at an integrated view of how politics and economics interact, we must disentangle economic and political causes from effects. In this effort, different scholars have different approaches, with different implications for the resulting views of the world.

Perspectives on the International Political Economy

Analysts of the international political economy must understand the interaction of many disparate forces. It is possible to simplify many such factors so that they can be arrayed on two dimensions. These two dimensions also capture many of the theoretical approaches that characterize scholarship on the politics of international economic relations. While the dimensions are not necessarily mutually exclusive, they do often reflect the fact that scholars can disagree about the relative weights to be placed on explanatory factors that all agree play some role. One set of disagreements has to do with the relationship between the international and domestic political economies; another set concerns the relationship between the state and social forces.

The first dimension of interest concerns the degree to which the causes of international political and economic trends are to be found at the domestic or international level. All observers agree that in a complex world, both global and national forces are important. But different analysts place different emphases on the importance of one or the other. Some focus on how international forces tend to overpower domestic interests; others emphasize the degree to which national concerns override global considerations.

It should surprise no one that, for example, American trade policy, Japan's financial goals, and South Korean development strategies are important in the world's political economy. Scholars may differ, however, over how best to explain the sources of the foreign economic policies of individual nations, or of nations-states in general. At one end of the spectrum, some scholars believe that nations' foreign economic policies are primarily determined by the global environment. The actual room for national maneuver of even the most powerful of states, these scholars believe, is limited by characteristics inherent in the international system. At the other end of the spectrum are scholars who see foreign economic policies primarily as the outgrowth of nations' domestic-level political and economic processes. For them, the international system exists only as a jumble of independent nation-states, each with its own political and economic pecularities.

The international-domestic distinction is at the base of many debates within international political economy, as in the world at large. While some argue, for example, that the cause of third world poverty is in the unequal global economic order, others blame domestic politics and economics in developing nations. Similarly, many scholars see multinational corporations as a powerful independent force in the world—whether working for good or for evil—while others see international firms as extensions of their home countries. Moreover, for some analysts, global geopolitical relations among nations dominate the impulses that arise from their domestic social orders.

The difference between the two approaches can be seen quite clearly, for example, in explanations of trade policy. To take a specific instance, starting in the early 1980s, the United States and many European governments imposed restrictions on the import of Japanese automobiles. The form of the controls varied widely: The U.S. and Japanese governments negotiated "voluntary" export restraints, with which Japanese producers agreed to comply, while in some European countries, quantitative quotas were imposed unilaterally. Concerned about stiff Japanese competition, which was reducing profits and employment, European and North American automakers and the trade unions that represent their employees provided key support for these policies.

From this example, one clear analytic conclusion would be that domestic political and economic pressures—the electoral importance of the regions where auto industries are concentrated; the economic centrality of that sector to the European and North American economies; government concern about the broad, national ramifications of the auto industry; the political clout of the autoworkers' unions—led to important foreign economic measures involving the restriction of Japanese automobile imports. Indeed, many scholars saw the restrictions as confirmation of the primacy of domestic concerns in the making of foreign economic policy.

Yet, analysts who search for the causes of national foreign economic policies in the international rather than the domestic arena could also find support in the auto import restrictions. After all, the policies were responsive to the rise of Japan as a major manufacturer and exporter of automobiles, a fact that had little to do with the domestic scene in the United States or Europe. Many North American and European industries had lost competitive ground to rapidly growing overseas manufacturers, a process that is complex in origin but clearly one of worldwide proportions. Some have argued that trade policies are a function of realities inherent in the international system, such as the existence of a leading, hegemonic power and the eventual decline of that state . . . In this view, the decline of American power set the stage for a proliferation of barriers to trade.

The internationally minded scholar might also argue that it is important to understand why the European and American measures took the relatively mild form they did in simply limiting the Japanese to established (and, often, very appreciable) shares of the markets. If the measures had been adopted solely to respond to the distress of local auto industries, the logical step would have been to exclude foreign cars from the markets in question. Yet the positions of Europe and the United States in the global economic and political system—including everything from world finance to international military alliances—dictated that European and North American policy makers not pursue overly hostile policies toward the Japanese.

More generally, scholars have explained long-term changes in trade policy in very different ways. During the period between World Wars I and II, and especially in the 1930s, almost all European nations and the

United States were highly protectionist. After World War II, on the other hand, the North American and Western European markets were opened gradually to one another and to the rest of the world, a phenomenon that eventually spread to much of the developing world as well.

Scholars whose theoretical bent is international point out that domestic politics in Europe and the United States did not change enough to explain such a radical shift. But the postwar role of the United States and Western Europe in the international political and economic system has indeed been different from what it was during the 1930s: after 1945, North American and Western European countries were united in an American-led military and economic alliance against the Soviet Union. Some internationally oriented analysts argue that the causes of postwar foreign economic policies in North America and Western Europe can be found in international geopolitical positions of these regions—the increase in American power, the decline of Europe, the Soviet challenge, and the rise of the Atlantic Alliance. Others point to broad technological and economic developments such as dramatic improvements in telecommunications and transportation that have altered governments' incentives to either protect or open their economies.

Scholars who favor domestic-level explanations take the opposite tack. For them, the postwar system was itself largely a creation of the United States and the major Western European powers. To cite the modern international political economy as a source of American or British foreign economic policy, these scholars argue, is to put the cart before the horse in that the United States and its allies had created the institutions—the Marshall Plan, the Bretton Woods agreement, the European Union—of today's international political economy. We must therefore search within these nations for the true roots of the shift in trade policy in North America and Western Europe.

The example of trade policy illustrates that serious scholars can arrive at strikingly different analytic conclusions on the basis of the same information. For some, domestic political and economic pressures caused the adoption of auto import restrictions, whereas for others, geopolitical, economic, or technological trends in the international environment explain the same action.

The second dimension along which analysts differ in their interpretation of trends in the international political economy has to do with the relative importance of politicians and political institutions, on the one hand, and private social actors, on the other. The interaction between state and society—between national governments and the social forces they, variously, represent, rule, or ignore—is indeed another dividing line within the field of international political economy. In studying the politics of the world economy, questions continually arise about the relative importance of independent government action and institutions versus a variety of societal pressures on the policy-making process.

The role of the state is at the center of all political science; international political economy is no exception. Foreign economic policy is made, of course, by foreign economic policy makers; this much is trivial. But just as scholars debate the relative importance of overseas and domestic determinants of foreign economic policies, so too they disagree over whether policy makers represent a logic of their own or instead reflect domestic socioeconomic interest groups or classes. According to one view, the state is relatively insulated or autonomous from the multitude of social, political, and economic pressures that emanate from society. The most that pluralistic interest groups can produce is a confused cacophony of complaints and demands; coherent national policy comes from the conscious actions of national leaders and those who occupy positions of political power and from the institutions in which they operate. The state, in this view, molds society, and foreign economic policy is one part of this larger mold.

The opposing school of thought asserts that policy makers are little more than the transmitters of underlying societal demands. At best, the political system can organize and regularize these demands, but the state is essentially a tool in the hands of socioeconomic and political interests. Foreign economic policy, like other state actions, evolves in response to social demands; it is society that molds the state, and not the other way around.

We can illustrate the difference in focus with the previously discussed example of trade policy in North America and Western Europe before and after World War II. Many of those who look first and foremost at state actors would emphasize the dramatic change in the overall foreign policy of these governments after World War II, starting with the Atlantic Alliance, which was formed to meet the demands of European reconstruction, and the cold war, which required that the American market be opened to foreign goods in order to stimulate the economies of the country's allies. Eventually, the European Union arose as a further effort to cement the Atlantic Alliance and bolster it against the Soviet Union.

According to this view, trade liberalization arose out of national security concerns, as understood and articulated by a very small number of individuals in the American and Western European governments, who then went about "selling" the policies to their publics. Alternatively, it might be argued that the traumas of the Great Depression taught the managers of nation-states that a descent into protectionism could lead to intolerable social tensions. In this context, political leaders may have developed a strong belief in the desirability of trade relations that are generally open. In this view of the world, explanatory precedence goes to the opinions, beliefs, and desires of national political leaders—in short, to the state.

Other scholars, for whom society is determinant, emphasize the major socio-economic and political changes that had been gaining force within the industrial capitalist nations after World War I. Corporations became more international and thus came to fear overseas competition less. For important groups, trade protection was counterproductive because it limited access to the rest of the world economy; however, freer trade and investment opened broad and profitable new horizons for major economic actors in North America and Western Europe.

By the same token, socioeconomic trends at a global level were also pushing toward international trade liberalization. The rise of internationally integrated financial markets and global corporations, for example, created private interests that oppose interference with the free movement of goods and capital across national borders. This new group of social forces has, in the opinion of some analysts . . . , fundamentally transformed the very nature of economic policy making in all nations.

When combined, these two dimensions give rise to four different perspectives in international political economy. An *international political* view emphasizes the constraints imposed on national states by the global geostrategic and diplomatic environment within which they operate. It focuses on the inherent conflict among states in a hostile world, within which cooperation, although often desirable and feasible, can be difficult to achieve.

The *international economic* perspective similarly emphasizes the importance of constraints external to individual nations, but it highlights global socioeconomic factors rather than political ones. Accordingly, international developments in technology, telecommunications, finance, and production fundamentally affect the setting within which national governments make policy. Indeed, these developments can matter to the point of making some choices practically impossible to implement and others so attractive as to be impossible to resist.

Domestic approaches look inside nation-states for explanations of the international political economy. The *domestic institutional* view turns its attention to states, as does the international political perspective, but it emphasizes the role and institutions of the state in a domestic setting rather than in the global system. This view, which at times is called simply *institutionalism*, tends to downplay the impact of constraints emanating both from the international system and from domestic societies. National policy makers, and the political institutions within which they operate, are thus seen as the predominant actors in determining national priorities and implementing policies to carry out these goals. Some variants of institutionalism emphasize the autonomy of states from societal actors, while others focus on how state institutions mediate and alter social forces.

The *domestic societal* perspective shares with domestic institutionalism an emphasis on developments within national borders but looks first and foremost at economic and sociopolitical actors rather than political leaders. This view, which at times is known simply as *societal,* tends to minimize international constraints and to emphasize socioeconomic pressures that originate at home. Accordingly, the determinants of national policy are the demands made by individuals, firms, and groups rather than independent action by policy makers.

These diverse perspectives can once again be illustrated by recalling their approaches to the example of trade policy tendencies: International political interpretations would rely on geopolitical trends among states at the global level to explain changing patterns of trade relations. An international economic view would emphasize trends in market forces, technologies, and the like that alter the environment in which governments make trade policy. The domestic institutional approach focuses on the goals and actions of the government within the national political system, for which foreign trade can represent ways to help politicians stay in power. Finally, a domestic societal perspective looks primarily at the pressures brought to bear on policy by various socioeconomic groups, some desirous of trade liberalization and others interested in protection from imports.

It should be noted that these simplistic categories hardly describe the nuance and complexity of actual theoretical approaches; all scholars recognize that the foreign economic policies of all countries are constrained by both international and domestic—and by both political and economic—factors. It may indeed be the case that one set of forces matters more or less in some issue areas than others, in some times than others, and in some countries than others. In particular, international geopolitical concerns will presumably have more impact on a small, weak country surrounded by enemies than a large, powerful nation far from any threat. Similarly, domestic concerns, whether institutional or societal, may have more effect on policy in times of great social and political conflict than in less turbulent times.

Nonetheless, analysts of the international political economy do differ in their interpretations. Rather than being absolute, the disagreements concern relative weights to be assigned to each set of causes. Some scholars assign primacy to social forces, others to autonomous state action: some to global factors, others to domestic ones.

These perspectives can lead to widely different explanations of specific events and general processes within the international political economy. Their differences have generated numerous debates in the field. . . .

Four Alternative Views of International Political Economy

In addition to the perspectives already mentioned, some scholars attempt to classify interpretations of global political and economic developments in a somewhat different manner. Many theories of international political economy can also be categorized into one of four perspectives: Liberalism, Marxism, Realism, and Constructivism. Note that in international political economy, advocates of free trade and free markets are still referred to as Liberals. In twentieth-century American domestic politics, however, the term has come to mean something different. In the United States today, whereas "conservatives" generally support free markets and less government intervention, "liberals" advocate greater governmental intervention in the market to stimulate growth and mitigate inequalities. These contradictory usages of the term *Liberal* may seem confusing, but the context will usually make an author's meaning clear.

The Liberal argument emphasizes how both the market and politics are environments in which all parties can benefit by entering into voluntary exchanges with others. If there are no impediments to trade among individuals. Liberals reason, everyone can be made as well-off as possible, given the existing stocks of goods and services. All participants in the market, in other words, will be at their highest possible level of utility. Neoclassical economists, who are generally Liberals, believe firmly in the superiority of the market as a mechanism for allocating scarce resources. Liberals therefore reason that the economic role of government should be quite limited. Many forms of government intervention in the economy, they argue, intentionally or unintentionally restrict the market and thereby prevent potentially rewarding trades from occurring.

Liberals do generally support the provision by government of certain "public goods"—goods and services that benefit society and that would not be provided by private markets.[1] The government, for example, plays an important role in supplying the conditions necessary for the maintenance of a free and competitive market. Governments must provide for the defense of the country, protect rights, and prevent any unfair collusion or concentration of power within the market. The government should also, according to most Liberals, educate its citizens, build infrastructure, and provide and regulate a common currency. The proper role of government, in other words, is to provide the necessary foundation for the market.

At the level of the international economy, Liberals assert that a fundamental harmony of interests exists between, as well as within, countries. They argue that all countries are best off when goods and services move freely across national borders in mutually rewarding exchanges. If universal free trade were to exist, all countries would enjoy the highest level of utility and there would be no economic basis for international conflict or war. Liberals also believe that governments should manage the international economy in much the same way as they manage their domestic economics. They should establish rules and regulations, often referred to as "international regimes," to govern exchanges between different national currencies and ensure that no country or domestic group is damaged by "unfair" international competition.

Marxism originated with the writings of Karl Marx, a nineteenth-century political economist and perhaps the severest critic of capitalism and its Liberal supporters. Marx saw capitalism and the market as creating extremes of wealth for capitalists and poverty for workers. While the entire populace may have been better-off than before, the capitalists were clearly expanding their wealth more rapidly than everyone else. Marx rejected the assertion that exchange between individuals necessarily maximizes the welfare of the whole society. Accordingly, he perceived capitalism as an inherently conflictual system that both should, and will, be inevitably overthrown and replaced by socialism.

Marxists believe that classes are the dominant actors in the political economy. Specifically, they identify as central two economically determined aggregations of individuals or classes: capital, or the owners of the means of production, and labor, or the workers. Marxists assume that classes act in their economic interests, that is, to maximize the economic well-being of the class as a whole. Accordingly, the basis of the capitalist economy is the exploitation of labor by capital: capitalism, by its very nature, denies labor the full return for its efforts.

Marxists see the political economy as necessarily conflictual, since the relationship between capitalists and workers is essentially antagonistic. Because the means of production are controlled by a minority within society—the capitalists—labor does not receive its full return; conflict between the classes is inevitably caused by this exploitation. Marxists also believe that capitalism is inherently prone to periodic economic crises, which will, they believe, ultimately lead to the overthrow of capitalism by labor and the erection of a socialist society in which the means of production will be owned jointly by all members of society and exploitation will cease.

V. I. Lenin, the Russian revolutionary who founded the Soviet Union, extended Marx's ideas to the international political economy to explain imperialism and war. Imperialism, Lenin argued, was endemic to modern capitalism. As capitalism decayed in the most developed nations capitalists would attempt to solve their problems by exporting capital abroad. As this capital required protection from both local and foreign challengers, governments would colonize regions to safeguard the interests of their foreign investors. Eventually, capitalist countries would compete for control over these areas and intracapitalist wars would follow.

Today, Marxists who study the international political economy are primarily concerned with two issues. The first is the fate of labor in a world of increasingly internationalized capital. The growth of multinational corporations and the rise of globally integrated financial markets appear to have weakened labor's economic and political power. If workers in a particular country demand higher wages or improved health and safety measures, for example, the multinational capitalist can simply shift production to another country where labor is more compliant. As a result, many Marxists fear that labor's ability to negotiate with capital for a more equitable division of wealth has been significantly undermined.

Second, Marxists are concerned with the poverty and continued underdevelopment of the third world. Some Marxists argue that development is blocked by domestic ruling classes, which pursue their own narrow interests at the expense of national economic progress. Others, known as "dependency" theorists, extend class analysis to the level of the international economy. According to these Marxists, the global system is stratified into a wealthy area (the "core," or first world) and a region of oppression and poverty (the "periphery," or third world). International capitalism, in this view, exploits the periphery and benefits the core, just as capitalists exploit workers within a single country. The principal questions here focus on the mechanisms of exploitation—whether they be multinational corporations, international financial markets and organizations, or trade—and the appropriate strategies for stimulating autonomous growth and development in the periphery.

Realism traces its intellectual roots back to Thucydides' writings in 400 B.C.E., as well as those of Niccolo Machiavelli, Thomas Hobbes, and the mercantilists Jean-Baptiste Colbert and Friedrich List. Realists believe that nation-states pursue power and shape the economy to this end. Moreover, they are the dominant actors within the international political economy. According to Realists, the international system is anarchical, a condition under which nation-states are sovereign, the sole judges of their own behaviors, and subject to no higher authority. If no authority is higher than the nation-state, Realists believe, then all actors must be subordinate to it. While private citizens can interact with their counterparts in other countries, Realists assert that the basis for this interaction is legislated by the nation-state. Thus, where Liberals focus on individuals and Marxists on classes, Realists concentrate on nation-states.

Realists also argue that nation-states are fundamentally concerned about international power relations. Because the international system is based on anarchy, the use of force or coercion by other nation-states is always a possibility and no higher authority is obligated to come to the aid of a nation-state under attack. Nation-states are thus ultimately dependent on their own resources for protection. For Realists, then, each nation-state must always be prepared to defend itself to the best of its ability. For Realists, politics is largely a zero-sum game and by necessity conflictual. In other words, if one nation-state is to win, another must lose.

Realists also believe that nation-states can be thought of as rational actors in the same sense that other theorists assume individuals to be rational. Nation-states are assumed to operate according to cost-benefit analyses and choose the option that yields the greatest value, especially regarding the nation's international geopolitical and power positions.

The emphasis on power is what gives Realism its distinctive approach to international political economy. While economic considerations may often complement power concerns, the former are, in the Realist view, subordinate to the latter. Realists allow for circumstances in which nation-states sacrifice economic gain to weaken their opponents or strengthen themselves in military or diplomatic terms. Thus, trade protection, which might reduce a country's overall income by restricting the market, may nonetheless be adopted for reasons of national political power.

Realist political economy is primarily concerned with how changes in the distribution of international power affect the form and type of international economy. The best known Realist approach to this question is the *theory of hegemonic stability*, which holds that an open international economy—that is, one characterized by the free exchange of goods, capital, and services—is most likely to exist when a single dominant or hegemonic power is present to stabilize the system and construct a strong regime . . . For Realists, then, the pursuit of power by nation-states shapes the international economy.

Each of these first three perspectives features different assumptions and assertions. Liberals assume that individuals are the proper unit of analysis, while Marxists and Realists make similar assumptions for classes and nation-states, respectively. The three perspectives also differ on the inevitability of conflict within the political economy. Liberals believe economics and politics are largely autonomous spheres, Marxists maintain that economics determines politics, and Realists argue that politics determines economics.

Constructivism, a fourth and relatively new approach to international political economy, has roots in critical theory and sociology. Unlike the first three approaches, Constructivism is more of a method of analysis than a set of alternative assumptions and assertions. Constructivists believe that actors in the international political economy and their interests are not innate but are produced or constructed through social interactions. Sectors, factors of production, classes, and especially nation-states are not fixed and immutable in this view, but are themselves produced by their social environments. Rather than pursuing wealth over power, or vice versa, individuals, classes, and states vary in their interests and contain the potential for both conflict and cooperation in different social settings.

Constructivists also believe that norms play an important role in international political economy. The other approaches all assume implicitly that actors are purposive and select among possible courses of action by their anticipated effects. This is sometimes referred to as a "logic of consequences." Constructivists assume that actors select roles and actions by what is right, just, or socially expected. In other words, actors choose according to a "logic of appropriateness." In this view, countries may open themselves to trade or international investment not because, as Liberals assert, this improves their welfare in any instrumental sense, but because this is what responsible or "developed" states understand as appropriate in the modern international political economy.

In addition, Constructivists assert that actors and their interactions can be transformed through the introduction of new norms or understandings of their interests or identities. The rough-and-tumble international political economy described by Realists, for example, is not, according to Constructivists, foreordained by the condition of anarchy. If actors come to understand the world differently, the conception of appropriate behavior could also change dramatically. As the "Washington Consensus" took hold internationally during the 1990s, for instance, countries liberalized their economies and held to this policy long after its promised effects failed to materialize.

This fourfold division of international political economy is useful in many ways, especially as it highlights differing evaluations of the importance of economic efficiency, class conflict, and geostrategic and normative considerations. However, the lines between these views are easily blurred. Some Marxists agree with the Realist focus on interstate conflict, while others concur with the Liberal emphasis on economic interests, while still others agree with Constructivists on the role of norms. Likewise, there are many Liberals who use neoclassical tools to analyze interstate strategic interaction in much the same way Realists do or to investigate the clash of classes as do the Marxists. Nearly all Liberals, Marxists, and Realists have come to a deeper understanding of the role of norms, emphasized by Constructivists. Such substantial overlap, in our view, helps clarify the two-dimensional categorization outlined above. We also believe that these two dimensions—international-domestic and state-society—most accurately characterize analytical differences among scholars and observers of the international political economy.

The Contemporary International Political Economy: An Overview

. . . The contemporary international political economy is characterized by unprecedented levels of multinational production, cross-border financial flows, and international trade. It is also plagued by increasing political conflict as individuals, groups, classes, and countries clash over the meaning and implications of these economic transactions. The contradiction between increasing economic integration and the wealth it produces, on the one hand, and the desire for political control and national autonomy, on the other, defines much of what happens in the global political economy.

For the first thirty years after World War II, the general pattern of relations among noncommunist nations was set by American leadership, and this pattern continues to influence the international political economy today. In the political arena, formal and informal alliances tied virtually every major noncommunist nation into an American-led network of mutual support and defense. In the economic arena, a wide-ranging set of international economic organizations—including the International Monetary Fund (IMF), the General Agreement on Tariffs and Trade (GATT), and the International Bank for Reconstruction and Development (World Bank)—grew up under a protective American "umbrella," and often as a direct American initiative. The world economy itself was heavily influenced by the rise of modern multinational corporations and banks, whose contemporary form is largely of U.S. origin.

American plans for a reordered world economy go back to the mid-1930s. After World War I, the United States retreated into relative economic insularity, for reasons explored in Part II, "Historical Perspectives." When the Great Depression hit, American political leaders virtually ignored the possibility of international economic cooperation in their attempts to stabilize the domestic economy. Yet, even as the Franklin Roosevelt administration looked inward for recovery, by 1934 new American initiatives were signaling a shift in America's traditional isolation. Roosevelt's secretary of state, Cordell Hull, was a militant free trader, and in 1934 he convinced Congress to pass the Reciprocal Trade Agreements Act, which allowed the executive to negotiate tariff reductions with foreign nations. This important step toward trade liberalization and international economic cooperation was deepened as war threatened in Europe and the United States drew closer to Great Britain and France.

The seeds of the new international order, which had been planted in the 1930s, began to grow even as World War II came to an end. The Bretton Woods agreement, reached among the Allied powers in 1944, established a new series of international economic organizations that became the foundation for the postwar American-led system. As the wartime American-Soviet alliance began to shatter a new economic order emerged in the noncommunist world. At its center were the three pillars of the Bretton Woods system: international monetary cooperation under the auspices of the IMF, international trade liberalization negotiated within the GATT, and investment in the developing countries stimulated by the World Bank. All three pillars were essentially designed by the United States and dependent on its support.

As it developed, the postwar capitalist world reflected American foreign policy in many of its details. One principal concern of the United States was to build a bulwark of anti-Soviet allies; this was done with a massive inflow of American aid under the Marshall Plan and the encouragement of Western European cooperation within a new Common Market. At the same time, the United States dramatically lowered its barriers to foreign goods and American corporations began to invest heavily in foreign nations. Of course, the United States was not acting altruistically: European recovery, trade liberalization, and booming international investment helped ensure great prosperity within its own borders as well.

American policies, whatever their motivation, had an undeniable impact on the international political economy. Trade liberalization opened the huge American market to foreign producers. American overseas investment provided capital, technology, and expertise for both Europe and the developing world. American governmental economic aid, whether direct or channeled through such institutions as the World Bank, helped finance economic growth abroad. In addition, the American military umbrella allowed anti-Soviet governments in Europe, Japan, and the developing world to rely on the United States for security and to turn their attentions to encouraging economic growth.

All in all, the noncommunist world's unprecedented access to American markets and American capital provided a major stimulus to world economic growth, not to mention the profits of American businesses and general prosperity within the United States. For more than twenty-five years after World War II, the capitalist world experienced impressive levels of economic growth and development, all within a general context of international cooperation under American political, economic, and military tutelage.

This period is often referred to as the *Pax Americana* because of its broad similarity to the British-led international economic system that operated from about 1820 until World War I, which was known as the *Pax Britannica*. In both instances, general political and economic peace prevailed under the leadership of an overwhelming world power—the United Kingdom in one case, the United States in the other. There were, nonetheless, major differences between the two eras . . .

Just as the Pax Britannica eventually ended, however, the Pax Americana gradually eroded. By the early 1970s, strains were developing in the postwar system. Between 1971 and 1975, the postwar international monetary system, which had been based on a gold-backed U.S. dollar, fell apart and was replaced by a new, improvised pattern of floating exchange rates in which the dollar's role was still strong but no longer quite so central. At the same time, pressures for trade protection from uncompetitive industries in North America and Western Europe began to mount; and although tariff levels remained low, a variety of nontariff barriers to world trade, such as import quotas, soon proliferated. In the political arena, détente between the United States and the Soviet Union seemed to make the American security umbrella less relevant for the Japanese and Western Europeans; in the less-developed countries, North-South conflict appeared more important than East-West strife. In short, during the 1970s, as American economic strength declined, the Bretton Woods institutions weakened, and the Cold War thawed, the Pax Americana drew to a close.

The quickening pace of change in the Soviet Union and its allies eventually culminated in the collapse of former Soviet bloc nations in the late 1980s and early 1990s, and ultimately in the disintegration of the former Soviet Union. The end of the Cold War did not, of course, mean an end to international conflict, but it did put an end to the East-West divide that had dominated global politics for so long.

As the Cold War wound down, international economic issues grew in importance, along with a greater willingness on the part of many nations to integrate with the rest of the world economy. Over the course of the 1980s, a wave of trade liberalization and privatization swept many countries in the developing world, so that by the early 1990s they were clearly committed to global economic integration. Then came the most striking development, the collapse of the centrally planned economies and their startling change in direction toward domestic and world markets. The process started in China and Vietnam, but when the Soviet Union disintegrated and the countries of Eastern and Central Europe joined the European Union, the resurgence of an integrated global economy seemed complete.

Since the mid-1990s, the world economy has continued on the general path of globalization. All of the indicators of integration have trended upward—some of them, such as international financial flows, at a very rapid pace. Yet, concern has grown about globalization in many quarters, and the generalized enthusiasm of the early 1990s is now less general, and less enthusiastic.

The principal issue facing analysts of the international political economy today has to do with the future of this era of globalization. Despite continued conflict over the international economy, most people—especially in the industrialized nations—appear to accept that an international system in which goods and capital can move quite freely among countries has become the normal state of affairs, and is likely to continue for the foreseeable future. Nonetheless there is widespread unease about the current state of international economic relations. Activists worry that footloose corporations may undermine attempts to protect the environment, labor, and human rights. Beleaguered businesses are troubled by foreign competitors.

Nationalists and religious traditionalists fear that globalization will undermine cultural and other norms.

All of these apprehensions were heightened by the global economic crisis that began in 2008. Difficulties in the American financial system were quickly transmitted around the world, and within months the entire international economy was in recession. There were even fears that the recession might deepen into depression. The economic downturn raised the spectre of economic conflicts among the world's major powers, as each nation focused its efforts on defending itself and its citizens from the fallout of the economic collapse. National governments and international economic institutions were confronted with problems of unprecedented breadth and scope. In this uncertain and rapidly changing environment, the United States remains the most important country within the international political economy, but it is no longer dominant. The era of American hegemony has been replaced by a new, multilateral order based on the joint leadership of Western Europe, Japan, and the United States. So far, these countries have successfully managed—or, some would say, muddled through—the "oil shocks" of the 1970s, the debt crisis of the early 1980s, the transition to the market of the former centrally planned economies after 1989, the currency crises and other financial volatility of the 1990s, and the macroeconomic imbalances of the new millennium.

Despite greater success than many thought possible, multilateral leadership and the liberal international order remain fragile. Conflicts of interest and economic tensions remain muted, but they could erupt at any time. The politics of international economic relations are made more complex by the new involvement of such countries as China, India, and Russia. These nations played virtually no role in international economic affairs for fifty years after World War II, but they are now actors to be reckoned with on the world economic scene. It is unclear whether, and how, the developed nations will work together with these newly resurgent developing countries in confronting the economic and political problems of the twenty-first century. . . .

NOTE

1. More specifically, a public good is one that, in its purest form, is *nonrival in consumption* and *nonexcludable*. The first characteristic means that consumption of the good by one person does not reduce the opportunities for others to consume that good; for example, clean air can be breathed by one individual without reducing its availability to others. The second characteristic means that nobody can be prevented from consuming the good. Those who do not contribute to pollution control are still able to breathe clean air. These two conditions are fully met only rarely, but goods whose characteristics come close to meeting them are generally considered public goods.

20 International Trade

20.1

What Do Undergrads Need to Know About Trade?

Paul R. Krugman

Few of the undergraduates who take an introductory course in economics will go on to graduate study in the field, and indeed most will not even take any higher-level economics courses. So what they learn about economics will be what they get in that first course. It is now more important than ever before that their basic training include a solid grounding in the principles of international trade.

I could justify this assertion by pointing out that international trade is now more important to the U.S. economy than it used to be. But there is another reason, which I think is even more important: the increased *perception* among the general public that international trade is a vital subject. We live in a time in which Americans are obsessed with international competition, in which Lester Thurow's *Head to Head* is the nonfiction best-seller and Michael Crichton's *Rising Sun* tops the fiction list. The news media and the business literature are saturated with discussions of America's role in the world economy.

The problem is that most of what a student is likely to read or hear about international economics is nonsense. What I want to argue in this paper is that the most important thing to teach our undergrads about trade is how to detect that nonsense. That is, our primary mission should be to vaccinate the minds of our undergraduates against the misconceptions that are so predominant in what passes for educated discussion about international trade.

The Rhetoric of Pop Internationalism

As a starting point, I would like to quote a typical statement about international economics. (Please ignore the numbers for a moment.) Here it is: "We need a new economic paradigm, because today America is part of a truly global economy (1). To maintain its standard of living, America now has to learn to compete in an ever tougher world marketplace (2). That's why high productivity and product quality have become essential (3). We need to move the American economy into the high-value sectors (4) that will generate jobs (5) for the future. And the only way we can be competitive in the new global economy is if we forge a new partnership between government and business (6)."

Ok, I confess: it's not a real quotation. I made it up as a sort of compendium of popular misconceptions about international trade. But it certainly sounds like the sort of thing one reads or hears all the time—it is very close in content and style to the still-influential manifesto by Ira Magaziner and Robert Reich (1982), or for that matter to the presentation made by Apple Computer's John Sculley at President-elect Clinton's Economic Conference last December. People who say things like this believe themselves to be smart, sophisticated, and forward-looking. They do not know that they are repeating a set of misleading clichés that I will dub "pop internationalism."

Source: Paul R. Krugman (1993), "What Do Undergrads Need to Know About Trade?" *The American Economic Review* 83(2): 23–26. Reprinted by permission of The American Economic Association and the author.

It is fairly easy to understand why pop internationalism has so much popular appeal. In effect, it portrays America as being like a corporation that used to have a lot of monopoly power, and could therefore earn comfortable profits in spite of sloppy business practices, but is now facing an onslaught from new competitors. A lot of companies are in that position these days (though the new competitors are not necessarily foreign), and so the image rings true.

Unfortunately, it's a grossly misleading image, because a national economy bears very little resemblance to a corporation. And the ground-level view of businessmen is deeply uninformative about the inherently general-equilibrium issues of international economics.

So what do undergrads need to know about trade? They need to know that pop internationalism is nonsense—and they need to know *why* it is nonsense.

Common Misconceptions

I inserted numbers into my imaginary quotation to mark six currently popular misconceptions that can and should be dispelled in an introductory economics course.

1. "We need a new paradigm . . ." Pop internationalism proclaims that everything is different now that the United States is an open economy. Probably the most important single insight that an introductory course can convey about international economics is that it does *not* change the basics: trade is just another economic activity, subject to the same principles as anything else.

   James Ingram's (1983) textbook on international trade contains a lovely parable. He imagines that an entrepreneur starts a new business that uses a secret technology to convert U.S. wheat, lumber, and so on into cheap high-quality consumer goods. The entrepreneur is hailed as an industrial hero; although some of his domestic competitors are hurt, everyone accepts that occasional dislocations are the price of a free-market economy. But then an investigative reporter discovers that what he is really doing is shipping the wheat and lumber to Asia and using the proceeds to buy manufactured goods—whereupon he is denounced as a fraud who is destroying American jobs. The point, of course, is that international trade is an economic activity like any other and can indeed usefully be thought of as a kind of production process that transforms exports into imports.

   It might, incidentally, also be a good thing if undergrads got a more realistic quantitative sense than the pop internationalists seem to have of the limited extent to which the United States actually has become a part of a global economy. The fact is that imports and exports are still only about one-eighth of output, and at least two-thirds of our value-added consists of nontradable goods and services. Moreover, one should have some historical perspective with which to counter the silly claims that our current situation is completely unprecedented: the United States is not now and may never be as open to trade as the United Kingdom has been since the reign of Queen Victoria.

2. "Competing in the world marketplace": One of the most popular, enduring misconceptions of practical men is that countries are in competition with each other in the same way that companies in the same business are in competition. Ricardo already knew better in 1817. An introductory economics course should drive home to students the point that international trade is not about competition, it is about mutually beneficial exchange. Even more fundamentally, we should be able to teach students that imports, not exports, are the purpose of trade. That is, what a country gains from trade is the ability to import things it wants. Exports are not an objective in and of themselves: the need to export is a burden that a country must bear because its import suppliers are crass enough to demand payment.

   One of the distressing things about the tyranny of pop internationalism is that there has been a kind of Gresham's Law in which bad concepts drive out good. Lester Thurow is a trained economist who understands comparative advantage. Yet his recent book has been a best-seller largely because it vigorously propounds concepts that unintentionally (one hopes) pander to the clichés of pop internationalism: "Niche competition is win-win. Everyone has a place where he or she can excel; no one is going to be driven out of business. Head-to-head competition is win-lose." (Thurow, 1992 p. 30). We should try to instill in undergrads a visceral negative reaction to statements like this.

3. "Productivity": Students should learn that high productivity is beneficial, not because it helps a country to compete with other countries, but because it lets a country produce and therefore consume more. This would be true in a closed economy; it is no more and no less true in an open economy; but that is not what pop internationalists believe. I have found it useful to offer students the following thought experiment. First, imagine a world in which productivity rises by 1 percent annually in all countries. What will be the trend in the U.S. standard of living? Students have no trouble agreeing that it will rise by 1 percent per year. Now, however, suppose that while the United States continues to raise its productivity by only 1 percent per year, the rest of the world manages to achieve 3-percent productivity growth. What is the trend in our living standard? The correct answer is that the trend is still 1 percent, except possibly for some subtle effects via our terms of trade; and as an empirical matter changes in the U.S. terms of trade have had virtually no impact on the trend in our living standards over the past few decades. But very few students reach that conclusion—which is not surprising, since virtually everything they read or hear outside of class conveys the image of international trade as a competitive sport.

   An anecdote: when I published an op-ed piece in the *New York Times* last year, I emphasized the importance of rising productivity. The editorial assistant I dealt with insisted that I should "explain" that we need to be productive "to compete in the global economy." He was reluctant to publish the piece unless I added the phrase—he said it was necessary so that readers could understand why productivity is important. We need to try to turn out a generation of students who not only don't need that kind of explanation, but understand why it's wrong.

4. "High-value sectors": Pop internationalists believe that international competition is a struggle over who gets the "high-value" sectors. "Our country's real income can rise only if (1) its labor and capital increasingly flow toward businesses that add greater value per employee and (2) we maintain a position in these businesses that is superior to that of our international competitors" (Magaziner and Reich, 1982 p. 4).

   I think it should be possible to teach students why this is a silly concept. Take, for example, a simple two-good Ricardian model in which one country is more productive in both industries than the other. (I have in mind the one used in Krugman and Maurice Obstfeld,1991 pp. 20–1). The more productive country will, of course, have a higher wage rate, and therefore whatever sector that country specializes in will be "high value," that is, will have higher value-added per worker. Does this mean that the country's high living standard is the result of being in the right sector, or that the poorer country would be richer if it tried to emulate the other's pattern of specialization? Of course not.

5. "Jobs": One thing that both friends and foes of free trade seem to agree on is that the central issue is employment. George Bush declared the objective of his ill-starred trip to Japan to be "jobs, jobs, jobs"; both sides in the debate over the North American Free Trade Agreement try to make their case in terms of job creation. And an astonishing number of free-traders think that the reason protectionism is bad is that it causes depressions.

   It should be possible to emphasize to students that the level of employment is a macroeconomic issue, depending in the short run on aggregate demand and depending in the long run on the natural rate of unemployment, with microeconomic policies like tariffs having little net effect. Trade policy should be debated in terms of its impact on efficiency, not in terms of phony numbers about jobs created or lost.

6. "A new partnership": The bottom line for many pop internationalists is that since U.S. firms are competing with foreigners instead of each other, the U.S. government should turn from its alleged adversarial position to one of supporting our firms against their foreign rivals. A more sophisticated pop internationalist like Robert Reich (1991) realizes that the interests of U.S. *firms* are not the same as those of U.S. *workers* (you may find it hard to believe that anyone needed to point this out, but among pop internationalists this was viewed as a deep and controversial insight), but still accepts the basic premise that the U.S. government should help our industries compete. What we should be able to teach our students is

that the main competition going on is one of U.S. industries against *each other*, over which sector is going to get the scarce resources of capital, skill, and, yes, labor. Government support of an industry may help that industry compete against foreigners, but it also draws resources away from other domestic industries. That is, the increased importance of international trade does not change the fact the government cannot favor one domestic industry except at the expense of others.

Now there are reasons, such as external economies, why a preference for some industries over others may be justified. But this would be true in a closed economy, too. Students need to understand that the growth of world trade provides no additional support for the proposition that our government should become an active friend to domestic industry.

What We Should Teach

By now the thrust of my discussion should be clear. For the bulk of our economics students, our objective should be to equip them to respond intelligently to popular discussion of economic issues. A lot of that discussion will be about international trade, so international trade should be an important part of the curriculum.

What is crucial, however, is to understand that the level of public discussion is extremely primitive. Indeed, it has sunk so low that people who repeat silly clichés often imagine themselves to be sophisticated. That means that our courses need to drive home as clearly as possible the basics. Offer curves and Rybczinski effects are lovely things. What most students need to be prepared for, however, is a world in which TV "experts," best-selling authors, and $30,000-a-day consultants do not understand budget constraints, let alone comparative advantage.

The last 15 years have been a golden age of innovation in international economics. I must somewhat depressingly conclude, however, that this innovative stuff is not a priority for today's undergraduates. In the last decade of the 20th century, the essential things to teach students are still the insights of Hume and Ricardo. That is, we need to teach them that trade deficits are self-correcting and that the benefits of trade do not depend on a country having an absolute advantage over its rivals. If we can teach undergrads to wince when they hear someone talk about "competitiveness," we will have done our nation a great service.

20.2

International Trade

Think Again

Arvind Panagariya

Why have disagreements between rich and poor nations stalled the global trading system? Because vapid debates over "fair trade" obscure some inconvenient facts: First, notwithstanding their demands for equity, poor countries are more protectionist than advanced economies. Second, if rich nations cut their self-defeating agricultural subsidies, their own publics would benefit, but consumers in many poor countries would not. Finally, despite criticisms to the contrary, the WTO can help promote economic development in low-income countries—but only if rich nations let the global body do its job.

"Economies That Are Open to Trade Grow Faster"

True. In low-income countries, openness to international trade is indispensable for rapid economic growth. Indeed, few developing nations have grown rapidly over time without simultaneous increases in both exports and imports, and virtually all developing countries that have grown rapidly have done so under open trade policies or declining trade protection. India and China are the best recent examples of countries that started with relatively closed trade policy regimes in the 1980s but subsequently achieved accelerating growth while opening up their economies. From the mid-1950s through the mid-1970s, industrial countries also enjoyed rapid growth while dismantling their high post-World War II trade barriers and embracing new technologies. Japan offers the most dramatic example, but countries such as Denmark, France, Greece, Italy, the Netherlands, Norway, and Portugal exhibited similar patterns.

Openness to trade promotes growth in a variety of ways. Entrepreneurs are forced to become increasingly efficient since they must compete against the best in the world to survive. Openness also affords access to the best technology and allows countries to specialize in what they do best rather than produce everything on their own. The fall of the Soviet Union was in no small measure due to its failure to access cutting-edge technologies, compete against world-class producers, and specialize in production. Even as large an economy as the United States today specializes heavily in services, which account for 80 percent of total U.S. output.

Of course, openness to trade is not by itself sufficient to promote growth—macroeconomic and political stability and other policies are needed as well—so some countries have opened up their markets and still not seen commensurate increases in economic growth. That has been particularly true of African countries such as the Ivory Coast during the 1980s and 1990s. But such instances hardly disprove the benefits of openness. Economists do not understand the process of growth well enough to predict precisely when the opportunity will knock on a country's door. But when it does knock, an open economy is more likely to seize it, whereas a closed one will miss it. Even globalization skeptics such as economists Dani Rodrik and Joseph Stiglitz recognize this point; neither chooses trade protection over freer trade.

"Rich Countries Are More Protectionist Than Poor Ones"

Not even close. On average, poor countries have higher tariff barriers than high-income countries. For instance, rich nations' tariffs on industrial products average about 3 percent, compared to 13 percent for poor countries. Even in the textiles and clothing sectors, tariffs in developing nations (21 percent) are more than double those in rich countries (8 percent, on average). And while textiles and clothing are subject to import quotas in rich economies, such restrictions are due to be dismantled entirely by January 1, 2005, under existing World Trade Organization (WTO) agreements.

Of course, not all poor countries are equally protectionist; some are even more open to trade than rich nations. For many years now, Singapore and Hong Kong have been textbook cases of free-trading nations. Likewise, middle-income economies such as South Korea and Taiwan are not significantly more protectionist than developed countries. But overall, the countries that stand to benefit most from greater competition and openness are those nations that display the highest protection, including most countries in South Asia and some in Africa.

The highest tariffs—or "tariff peaks"—in rich countries apply with particular strength to labor intensive products exported by developing countries.

In Canada, the United States, the European Union (EU), and Japan, product categories with especially high tariff rates include textiles and clothing as well as leather, rubber, footwear, and travel goods. But developing countries themselves are often quite zealous in protecting their markets from goods exported by other poor nations. Labor-intensive products such as textiles, clothing, leather, and footwear, which developing countries also export to each other, attract high duties in countries such as Brazil, Mexico, China, India, Malaysia, and Thailand.

Traditionally, rich economies such as the United States and the EU have been quick to engage in antidumping initiatives—erecting trade barriers against countries that allegedly export goods (or "dump" them) at a price below their own cost of production, however difficult it may be to quantify such a charge. But developing countries have been learning the same tricks and initiating antidumping measures of their own, and now the number of such actions has converged between advanced and poor economies. For example, according to the "WTO Annual Report 2003," India now ranks first in the world in initiating new antidumping actions, and third (behind the United States and the EU) in the number of such actions currently in force.

"Freer Trade Increases Poverty in the Third World"

Not true. Historically, countries that have achieved large reductions in poverty are generally those that have experienced rapid economic growth spurred in significant measure by openness to international trade. Newly industrialized economies such as Hong Kong, Singapore, South Korea, and Taiwan have all been open to trade during the past four decades and have been entirely free of poverty, according to the dollar-a-day poverty line, for more than a decade. By contrast, during the 1960s and 1970s, India remained closed to trade, grew approximately 1 percent annually (in per capita terms), and experienced no reduction in poverty during that period.

Trade helps produce rapid growth, and rapid growth helps the poor through three channels. First, it leads to what Columbia University economist Jagdish Bhagwati calls the active "pull-up" rather than the passive "trickle-down" effect—sustained growth rapidly absorbs the poor into gainful employment. Second, rapidly growing economies can generate vast fiscal resources that can be used for targeted anti-poverty programs. And finally, growth that helps raise incomes of poor families improves their ability to access public services such as education and health.

The current impression that the freeing of trade has failed the world's poor is partially rooted in disputable "official" World Bank poverty figures. The bank reports that though the proportion of the poor in developing countries declined from 28.3 percent in 1987 to 23.2 percent in 1999, increased population has left the absolute number of poor unchanged at 1.2 billion. And since that period also witnessed further freeing of trade, some conclude that trade has failed the poor. Yet, independent research by economists Surjit Bhalla in New Delhi and Xavier Sala-i-Martin at Columbia University has persuasively shown that the absolute number of poor declined during 1987–99 by at least 50 million and possibly by much more.

"Agricultural Protectionism in Rich Nations Worsens Global Poverty"

Not necessarily. If developed countries eliminate all forms of agricultural protection, including subsidies to domestic producers and quotas on foreign imports, their agricultural production will decline and the worldwide price of agricultural products will increase. Therefore, poor countries that are efficient agricultural producers will benefit from higher prices and access to new export markets. But consider the flip side: Poor countries that import agricultural products will suffer from higher prices. In 1999, as many as 45 of the 49 least developed countries imported more food than they exported. In 2001, for example, Senegal spent as much as $450 million on food imports, equivalent to about 10 percent of its gross domestic product and one third of its annual export earnings. Certainly, if agricultural trade is liberalized and prices rise, some poor countries will become net agricultural exporters, but many will not.

Some may argue that even if the poor countries pay higher prices for agricultural imports, their poor farmers will still benefit from those increased prices. But, in fact, high domestic prices do not require high world prices. Even under current world trading rules, the least developed countries can offer higher than world prices to their own farmers. In India, for example, the government buys food grains from farmers at prices higher than (and unrelated to) world agricultural prices.

Ironically, the major beneficiaries of widespread agricultural liberalization would be rich countries themselves, which bear the bulk of the cost of the subsidies and protection, and their domestic consumers. Other potential beneficiaries include nations such as those belonging to the Cairns Group—a coalition of 17 agriculture-exporting countries (9 of them from Latin America but also including advanced economies such as Canada and Australia) that enjoy efficient agricultural sectors and lobby for more open trade in agriculture.

Ultimately, even if some poor countries did suffer from more open agricultural trade, the case for liberalizing global agricultural markets remains unimpeachable. The current trading system in agriculture grossly distorts prices and production patterns and results in an inefficient global agricultural market.

"Poor Countries Should Not Open their Markets if Rich Countries Maintain High Trade Barriers"

Big mistake. As the late British economist Joan Robinson once remarked, "if your trading partner throws rocks into his harbor, that is no reason to throw rocks into your own." Responding to protectionism with more protectionism may seem "fair," but it is downright silly. Many Western advocacy organizations and religious groups that make this argument fail to understand that such talk hardly helps poor nations. It is hard enough for leaders in these countries to convince domestic producers that opening national markets is a worthy objective; loose talk of "hypocrisy" and "unfairness" only makes it harder. Even people who should know better fall into this trap. "It is surely hypocritical of rich countries to encourage poor nations to liberalize trade," former World Bank chief economist Nicholas Stern reportedly stated in a March 2001 speech in New Delhi, "whilst at the same time succumbing to powerful groups in their own countries that seek to perpetuate narrow self-interest."

Certainly, trade protectionism by rich nations merits opposition. But whether or not rich nations lower their barriers, poor countries should unilaterally dismantle their own protectionist policies in order to increase trade and stimulate economic growth. Trade barriers are often porous rather than absolute, so that countries with outward-oriented policies often succeed in expanding exports even when markets in partner nations are not fully open. Trade-oriented East Asian economies such as Hong Kong, Singapore, South Korea, and Taiwan have registered excellent export performance since the early 1960s. By contrast, relatively protectionist countries such as India, China, Argentina, and Egypt have hurt their own export growth and, as a result, stifled their overall economic performance in those years. Yet all these countries faced virtually the same trade protectionism abroad. Economic history since the end of World War II confirms that export pessimism is self-fulfilling, whereas nations that adopt export-oriented trade policies manage to exploit international markets despite foreign protectionism.

"There Is No 'Development' in the Doha Development Agenda"

False. Judging by the anger many poor nations displayed at the recent WTO talks in Cancún, it would seem that the current round of WTO trade negotiations—ambitiously dubbed the "development round" when the talks were launched in Doha, Qatar, in late 2001—have nothing to offer the cause of development. But such a conclusion would be mistaken. Insofar as the WTO negotiations aim to liberalize trade in nations both rich and poor, development cannot and will not be missing from the agenda.

For more than four decades, developing countries have demanded that rich economies remove their tariff peaks, which apply in particular to labor-intensive goods (such as textiles, apparel, and footwear) from developing countries. The Doha declaration explicitly addressed this objective. The declaration also addressed the substantial relaxation of agricultural protection in rich nations, including the removal of farm subsidies, which developing nations consider crucial. Brinkmanship by both rich and poor countries produced the failure in Cancún, but the negotiations are far from buried. When they eventually conclude, development concerns will be central to the agreement.

However, even well-intentioned advocates can go too far in linking trade policy with development. Former WTO Director-General Michael Moore has argued that investment and competition policy, transparency in government procurement, and trade facilitation (i.e., less red tape when goods enter a country and adequate information on import and export regulations) are also development issues. The EU has placed these issues on the Doha agenda, even though a large number of developing countries oppose their inclusion.

The expansion of the WTO into these areas contributed in no small measure to the breakdown of talks in Cancún. Agreement in these areas would require developing countries to adopt existing developed-country practices and regulations; this action would therefore impose "asymmetric" obligations on developing countries. Many poor countries lack even the resources necessary to implement these obligations. Finally, differences in local conditions require local solutions rather than an externally imposed and globally uniform regime in these areas. "One size fits all" is the wrong answer.

"The World Trade Organization Harms Poor Countries"

No. Contrary to popular belief among many Western nongovernmental organizations and politicians in developing countries, the WTO is the best friend available to exporters in poor nations. The General Agreement on Tariffs and Trade (GATT), signed in 1947 and incorporated into the WTO at the latter's inception in 1995, substantially opened markets in rich countries during the first 40 years of the GATT's existence. Under its "most favored nation" provision, GATT required that such markets be open to all GATT members, including developing countries. Therefore, even without undertaking any trade liberalization of their own, developing nations became the beneficiaries of the market opening in the developed world.

The GATT's Uruguay Round of trade negotiations, which began in 1986 and culminated in the establishment of the WTO, marked the first time rich nations insisted that developing countries fully participate in the negotiations. Developing countries felt shortchanged in this round on three counts: Their expectations of opening agricultural markets in rich countries were not realized; developing countries committed themselves to cutting industrial tariffs more deeply than developed economies; and developed countries successfully enacted a global intellectual property rights regime that undermined poor countries' access to cheap medicines.

Although the Uruguay Round benefited developed countries more than developing ones, poor nations still gained. First, developing countries liberalized more because they had higher trade barriers to begin with (and remember, in economic terms, greater liberalization is a benefit, not a cost). Second, after years of complaining, developing countries convinced developed nations to commit to dismantling quotas on imports of textiles and clothing. Third, while the Uruguay Round did not enhance developing countries' access to global agricultural markets, it opened the way for future liberalization in this important arena.

Despite the dominance of developed countries and skewed distribution of the bargaining power within the WTO, the global body offers low- and middle-income countries a rules-based forum in which to defend their trading interests and rights. For example, the strength of the WTO has helped developing nations deflect pressures from rich nations to link further trade opening to the creation of stronger labor standards in poor nations. Without the WTO, developed countries simply could have resorted to unilateral trade sanctions to enforce their desired standards. Moreover, at the September 2003 trade talks in Cancún, this rules-based bargaining allowed developing countries to delay negotiations on investment and competition policy.

"Free Trade Is Bad for the Environment"

No. Certainly, trade forces can hurt the global environment. For instance, the rapid expansion of coastal shrimp farming in several countries in Asia and Latin America in the 1980s, driven principally by the demand for exports, led to the contamination of water supplies and destruction of surrounding mangrove forests. But trade opening can bring environmental benefits as well. For example, the agricultural liberalization proposed in the WTO's Doha negotiations would not only bring economic and efficiency benefits by shifting production from high-cost to low-cost producers, but it would also yield environmental benefits by replacing Europe's pesticide-intensive agriculture with natural manure-intensive agriculture in developing countries.

Activists who decry the environmental impact of trade should realize that trade protectionism often brings environmental costs as well. During the 1980s, the United States imposed quotas on Japanese small-car imports; the policy not only hurt U.S. consumers but also harmed the environment by reducing access to lower-pollution vehicles. More broadly, closed-door policies in pre-1989 Eastern Europe were accompanied by an extremely poor environmental record.

When trade produces adverse environmental effects, the solution is not to ban or restrict trade. Instead, governments should adopt appropriate environmental policies to achieve environmental objectives and allow trade policy to target economic objectives. In the shrimp farming case, shrimp producers should be taxed for the pollution they create but then left to trade freely. Such a policy normally will reduce exports and economic output, but that result would be offset by reduced pollution. Reliance on a single instrument (trade policy) to target both economic and environmental objectives is like trying to kill two birds with one stone—a strategy successful hunters would not recommend. Just as governments should not subsidize trade to help the environment, neither should they restrict it to avoid harming the environment.

20.3

Trading in Illusions

Dani Rodrik

A senior U.S. Treasury official recently urged Mexico's government to work harder to reduce violent crime because "such high levels of crime and violence may drive away foreign investors." This admonition nicely illustrates how foreign trade and investment have become the ultimate yardstick for evaluating the social and economic policies of governments in developing countries. Forget the slum dwellers or *campesinos* who live amidst crime and poverty throughout the developing world. Just mention "investor sentiment" or "competitiveness in world markets" and policymakers will come to attention in a hurry.

Underlying this perversion of priorities is a remarkable consensus on the imperative of global economic integration. Openness to trade and investment flows is no longer viewed simply as a component of a country's development strategy; it has mutated into the most potent catalyst for economic growth known to humanity. Predictably, senior officials of the World Trade Organization (WTO), International Monetary Fund (IMF), and other international financial agencies incessantly repeat the openness mantra. In recent years, however, faith in integration has spread quickly to political leaders and policymakers around the world.

Joining the world economy is no longer a matter simply of dismantling barriers to trade and investment. Countries now must also comply with a long list of admission requirements, from new patent rules to more rigorous banking standards. The apostles of economic integration prescribe comprehensive institutional reforms that took today's advanced countries generations to accomplish, so that developing countries can, as the cliché goes, maximize the gains and minimize the risks of participation in the world economy. Global integration has become, for all practical purposes, a substitute for a development strategy.

This trend is bad news for the world's poor. The new agenda of global integration rests on shaky empirical ground and seriously distorts policymakers' priorities. By focusing on international integration, governments in poor nations divert human resources, administrative capabilities, and political capital away from more urgent development priorities such as education, public health, industrial capacity, and social cohesion. This emphasis also undermines nascent democratic institutions by removing the choice of development strategy from public debate.

World markets are a source of technology and capital; it would be silly for the developing world not to exploit these opportunities. But globalization is not a shortcut to development. Successful economic growth strategies have always required a judicious blend of imported practices with domestic institutional innovations. Policymakers need to forge a domestic growth strategy by relying on domestic investors and domestic institutions. The costliest downside of the integrationist faith is that it crowds out serious thinking and efforts along such lines.

Excuses, Excuses

Countries that have bought wholeheartedly into the integration orthodoxy are discovering that openness does not deliver on its promise. Despite sharply lowering their barriers to trade and investment since the 1980s, scores of countries in Latin America and Africa are stagnating or growing less rapidly than in the heyday of import substitution during the 1960s and 1970s. By contrast, the fastest growing countries are China, India, and others in East and Southeast Asia. Policymakers in these countries have also espoused trade and investment liberalization, but they have done so in an unorthodox manner—gradually, sequentially, and only after an initial period of high growth—and as part of a broader policy package with many unconventional features.

The disappointing outcomes with deep liberalization have been absorbed into the faith with remarkable

Source: Dani Rodrik, "Trading in Illusions," *Foreign Policy*, March/April, 2001.

aplomb. Those who view global integration as the prerequisite for economic development now simply add the caveat that opening borders is insufficient. Reaping the gains from openness, they argue, also requires a full complement of institutional reforms.

Consider trade liberalization. Asking any World Bank economist what a successful trade-liberalization program requires will likely elicit a laundry list of measures beyond the simple reduction of tariff and nontariff barriers: tax reform to make up for lost tariff revenues; social safety nets to compensate displaced workers; administrative reform to bring trade practices into compliance with WTO rules; labor market reform to enhance worker mobility across industries; technological assistance to upgrade firms hurt by import competition; and training programs to ensure that export-oriented firms and investors have access to skilled workers. As the promise of trade liberalization fails to materialize, the prerequisites keep expanding. For example, Clare Short, Great Britain's secretary of state for international development, recently added universal provision of health and education to the list.

In the financial arena, integrationists have pushed complementary reforms with even greater fanfare and urgency. The prevailing view in Washington and other Group of Seven (G-7) capitals is that weaknesses in banking systems, prudential regulation, and corporate governance were at the heart of the Asian financial crisis of the late 1990s. Hence the ambitious efforts by the G-7 to establish international codes and standards covering fiscal transparency, monetary and financial policy, banking supervision, data dissemination, corporate governance, and accounting standards. The Financial Stability Forum (FSF)—a G-7 organization with minimal representation from developing nations—has designated 12 of these standards as essential for creating sound financial systems in developing countries. The full FSF compendium includes an additional 59 standards the agency considers "relevant for sound financial systems," bringing the total number of codes to 71. To fend off speculative capital movements, the IMF and the G-7 also typically urge developing countries to accumulate foreign reserves and avoid exchange-rate regimes that differ from a "hard peg" (tying the value of one's currency to that of a more stable currency, such as the U.S. dollar) or a "pure float" (letting the market determine the appropriate exchange rate).

A cynic might wonder whether the point of all these prerequisites is merely to provide easy cover for eventual failure. Integrationists can conveniently blame disappointing growth performance or a financial crisis on "slippage" in the implementation of complementary reforms rather than on a poorly designed liberalization. So if Bangladesh's freer trade policy does not produce a large enough spurt in growth, the World Bank concludes that the problem must involve lagging reforms in public administration or continued "political uncertainty" (always a favorite). And if Argentina gets caught up in a confidence crisis despite significant trade and financial liberalization, the IMF reasons that structural reforms have been inadequate and must be deepened.

Free Trade-Offs

Most (but certainly not all) of the institutional reforms on the integrationist agenda are perfectly sensible, and in a world without financial, administrative, or political constraints, there would be little argument about the need to adopt them. But in the real world, governments face difficult choices over how to deploy their fiscal resources, administrative capabilities, and political capital. Setting institutional priorities to maximize integration into the global economy has real opportunity costs.

Consider some illustrative trade-offs. World Bank trade economist Michael Finger has estimated that a typical developing country must spend $150 million to implement requirements under just three WTO agreements (those on customs valuation, sanitary and phytosanitary measures, and trade-related intellectual property rights). As Finger notes, this sum equals a year's development budget for many least-developed countries. And while the budgetary burden of implementing financial codes and standards has never been fully estimated, it undoubtedly entails a substantial diversion of fiscal and human resources as well. Should governments in developing countries train more bank auditors and accountants, even if those investments mean fewer secondary-school teachers or reduced spending on primary education for girls?

In the area of legal reform, should governments focus their energies on "importing" legal codes and standards or on improving existing domestic legal institutions? In Turkey, a weak coalition government spent several months during 1999 gathering political support for a bill providing foreign investors the protection of international arbitration. But wouldn't a better long-run strategy have involved reforming the existing legal regime for the benefit of foreign and domestic investors alike?

In public health, should governments promote the reverse engineering of patented basic medicines and the importation of low-cost generic drugs from "unauthorized" suppliers, even if doing so means violating WTO rules against such practices? When South Africa passed legislation in 1997 allowing imports of patented AIDS drugs from cheaper sources, the country came under severe pressure from Western governments, which argued that the South African policy conflicted with WTO rules on intellectual property.

How much should politicians spend on social protection policies in view of the fiscal constraints imposed by market "discipline"? Peru's central bank holds foreign reserves equal to 15 months of imports as an insurance policy against the sudden capital outflows that financially open economies often experience. The opportunity cost of this policy amounts to almost 1 percent of gross domestic product annually—more than enough to fund a generous antipoverty program.

How should governments choose their exchange-rate regimes? During the last four decades, virtually every growth boom in the developing world has been accompanied by a controlled depreciation of the domestic currency. Yet financial openness makes it all but impossible to manage the exchange rate.

How should policymakers focus their anticorruption strategies? Should they target the high-level corruption that foreign investors often decry or the petty corruption that affects the poor the most? Perhaps, as the proponents of permanent normal trade relations with China argued in the recent U.S. debate, a government that is forced to protect the rights of foreign investors will become more inclined to protect the rights of its own citizens as well. But this is, at best, a trickledown strategy of institutional reform. Shouldn't reforms target the desired ends directly—whether those ends are the rule of law, improved observance of human rights, or reduced corruption?

The rules for admission into the world economy not only reflect little awareness of development priorities, they are often completely unrelated to sensible economic principles. For instance, WTO agreements on anti-dumping, subsidies and countervailing measures, agriculture, textiles, and trade-related intellectual property rights lack any economic rationale beyond the mercantilist interests of a narrow set of powerful groups in advanced industrial countries. Bilateral and regional trade agreements are typically far worse, as they impose even tighter prerequisites on developing countries in return for crumbs of enhanced "market access." For example, the African Growth and Opportunity Act signed by U.S. President Clinton in May 2000 provides increased access to the U.S. market only if African apparel manufacturers use U.S.-produced fabric and yarns. This restriction severely limits the potential economic spillovers in African countries.

There are similar questions about the appropriateness of financial codes and standards. These codes rely heavily on an Anglo-American style of corporate governance and an arm's-length model of financial development. They close off alternative paths to financial development of the sort that have been followed by many of today's rich countries (for example, Germany, Japan, or South Korea).

In each of these areas, a strategy of "globalization above all" crowds out alternatives that are potentially more development-friendly. Many of the institutional reforms needed for insertion into the world economy can be independently desirable or produce broader economic benefits. But these priorities do not necessarily coincide with the priorities of a comprehensive development agenda.

Asian Myths

Even if the institutional reforms needed to join the international economic community are expensive and preclude investments in other crucial areas, pro-globalization advocates argue that the vast increases in economic growth that invariably result from insertion into the global marketplace will more than compensate for those costs. Take the East Asian tigers or China, the advocates say. Where would they be without international trade and foreign capital flows?

That these countries reaped enormous benefits from their progressive integration into the world economy is undeniable. But look closely at what policies produced those results, and you will find little that resembles today's rule book.

Countries like South Korea and Taiwan had to abide by few international constraints and pay few of the modern costs of integration during their formative growth experience in the 1960s and 1970s. At that time, global trade rules were sparse and economies faced almost none of today's common pressures to open their borders to capital flows. So these countries combined their outward orientation with unorthodox policies: high levels of tariff and non-tariff barriers, public ownership of large segments of banking and industry, export subsidies, domestic-content requirements, patent and copyright infringements, and restrictions on capital flows (including on foreign direct investment). Such policies are either precluded by today's trade rules or are highly frowned upon by organizations like the IMF and the World Bank.

China also followed a highly unorthodox two-track strategy, violating practically every rule in the guidebook (including, most notably, the requirement of private property rights). India, which significantly raised its economic growth rate in the early 1980s, remains one of the world's most highly protected economies.

All of these countries liberalized trade gradually, over a period of decades, not years. Significant import liberalization did not occur until after a transition to high economic growth had taken place. And far from wiping the institutional slate clean, all of these nations managed to eke growth out of their existing institutions, imperfect as they may have been. Indeed, when some of the more successful Asian economies gave in to Western pressure to liberalize capital flows rapidly, they were rewarded with the Asian financial crisis.

That is why these countries can hardly be considered poster children for today's global rules. South Korea, China, India, and the other Asian success cases had the freedom to do their own thing, and they used that freedom abundantly. Today's globalizers would be unable to replicate these experiences without running afoul of the IMF or the WTO.

The Asian experience highlights a deeper point: A sound overall development strategy that produces high economic growth is far more effective in achieving integration with the world economy than a purely integrationist strategy that relies on openness to work its magic. In other words, the globalizers have it exactly backwards. Integration is the result, not the cause, of economic and social development. A relatively protected economy like Vietnam is integrating with the world economy much more rapidly than an open economy like Haiti because Vietnam, unlike Haiti, has a reasonably functional economy and polity.

Integration into the global economy, unlike tariff rates or capital-account regulations, is not something that policymakers control directly. Telling finance ministers in developing nations that they should increase their "participation in world trade" is as meaningful as telling them that they need to improve technological capabilities—and just as helpful. Policymakers need to know which strategies will produce these results, and whether the specific prescriptions that the current orthodoxy offers are up to the task.

Too Good To Be True

Do lower trade barriers spur greater economic progress? The available studies reveal no systematic relationship between a country's average level of tariff and nontariff barriers and its subsequent economic growth rate. If anything, the evidence for the 1990s indicates a positive relationship between import tariffs and economic growth. The only clear pattern is that countries dismantle their trade restrictions as they grow richer. This finding explains why today's rich countries, with few exceptions, embarked on modern economic growth behind protective barriers but now display low trade barriers.

The absence of a strong negative relationship between trade restrictions and economic growth may seem surprising in view of the ubiquitous claim that trade liberalization promotes higher growth. Indeed, the economics literature is replete with cross-national studies concluding that growth and economic dynamism are strongly linked to more open trade policies. A particularly influential study finds that economies that are "open," by the study's own definition, grew 2.45 percentage points faster annually than closed ones—an enormous difference.

Upon closer look, however, such studies turn out to be unreliable. In a detailed review of the empirical literature, University of Maryland economist Francisco Rodriguez and I have found a major gap between the results that economists have actually obtained and the policy conclusions they have typically drawn. For example, in many cases economists blame poor growth on the government's failure to liberalize trade policies, when the true culprits are ineffective institutions, geographic determinants (such as location in a tropical region), or inappropriate macroeconomic policies (such as an overvalued exchange rate). Once these misdiagnoses are corrected, any meaningful relationship across countries between the level of trade barriers and economic growth evaporates.

The evidence on the benefits of liberalizing capital flows is even weaker. In theory, the appeal of capital mobility seems obvious: If capital is free to enter (and leave) markets based on the potential return on investment, the result will be an efficient allocation of global resources. But in reality, financial markets are inherently unstable, subject to bubbles (rational or otherwise), panics, short-sightedness, and self-fulfilling prophecies. There is plenty of evidence that financial liberalization is often followed by financial crash—just ask Mexico, Thailand, or Turkey—while there is little convincing evidence to suggest that higher rates of economic growth follow capital-account liberalization.

Perhaps the most disingenuous argument in favor of liberalizing international financial flows is that the threat of massive and sudden capital movements serves to discipline policymakers in developing nations who might otherwise manage their economies irresponsibly. In other words, governments might be less inclined to squander their societies' resources if such actions would spook foreign lenders. In practice, however, the discipline argument falls apart. Behavior in international capital markets is dominated by mood swings unrelated to fundamentals. In good times, a government with a chronic fiscal deficit has an easier time financing its spending when it can borrow funds from investors abroad; witness Russia prior to 1998 or Argentina in the 1990s. And in bad times, governments may be forced to adopt inappropriate policies in order to conform to the biases of foreign investors; witness the excessively restrictive monetary and fiscal policies in much of East Asia in the immediate aftermath of the Asian financial crisis. A key reason why Malaysia was able to recover so quickly after the imposition of capital controls in September 1998 was that Prime Minister Mahathir Mohamad resisted the high interest rates and tight fiscal policies that South Korea, Thailand, and Indonesia adopted at the behest of the International Monetary Fund.

Growth Begins At Home

Well-trained economists are justifiably proud of the textbook case in favor of free trade. For all the theory's simplicity, it is one of our profession's most significant achievements. However, in their zeal to promote the virtues of trade, the most ardent proponents are peddling a cartoon version of the argument, vastly overstating the effectiveness of economic openness as a tool for fostering development. Such claims only endanger broad public acceptance of the real article because they unleash unrealistic expectations about the benefits of free trade. Neither economic theory nor empirical evidence guarantees that deep trade liberalization will deliver higher economic growth. Economic openness and all its accoutrements do not deserve the priority they typically receive in the development strategies pushed by leading multilateral organizations.

Countries that have achieved long-term economic growth have usually combined the opportunities offered by world markets with a growth strategy that mobilizes the capabilities of domestic institutions and investors. Designing such a growth strategy is both harder and easier than implementing typical integration policies. It is harder because the binding constraints on growth are usually country specific and do not respond well to standardized recipes. But it is easier because once those constraints are targeted, relatively simple policy changes can yield enormous economic payoffs and start a virtuous cycle of growth and additional reform.

Unorthodox innovations that depart from the integration rulebook are typically part and parcel of such strategies. Public enterprises during the Meiji restoration in Japan; township and village enterprises in China; an export processing zone in Mauritius; generous tax incentives for priority investments in Taiwan; extensive credit subsidies in South Korea; infant-industry protection in Brazil during the 1960s and 1970s—these are some of the innovations that have been instrumental in kick-starting investment and growth in the past. None came out of a Washington economist's tool kit.

Few of these experiments have worked as well when transplanted to other settings, only underscoring the decisive importance of local conditions. To be effective, development strategies need to be tailored to prevailing domestic institutional strengths. There is simply no alternative to a homegrown business plan. Policymakers who look to Washington and financial markets for the answers are condemning themselves to mimicking the conventional wisdom du jour, and to eventual disillusionment.

20.4

The Free-Trade Paradox

Why is Trade Booming While Trade Talks are Crashing?

Moisés Naím

One of the most perplexing trends of our time is that free-trade negotiations are crashing while free trade itself is booming. For more than a decade, attempts by governments to get a global agreement to lower trade barriers have gone nowhere. These trade talks are routinely described as "acrimonious," "gridlocked," and "stagnant." In contrast, international trade is commonly described as "thriving" or "surging," and almost every year, its growth is lauded as "record breaking." It's no surprise that trade negotiators feel as despondent as international traders are cheerful.

The last time official trade negotiators had reason to celebrate was in 1994, when 125 nations agreed to a significant drop in trade barriers and the creation of a new institution charged with supervising and liberalizing international trade, the World Trade Organization (WTO). Since then, efforts to liberalize global trade through negotiations have stalled. In many countries, free trade agreements are now politically radioactive, with imports routinely blamed for job losses, lower salaries, heightened inequality, and more recently, even poisoned toothpaste and deadly medicines. The domestic politics of trade reforms are inherently skewed against trade deals. While the benefits of freer trade exist as future promises, the costs can be real, tangible, and immediate.

And while the benefits of trade liberalization are widely distributed throughout the entire population, the costs are borne by highly concentrated groups. Cutting agricultural tariffs, for example, may benefit society at large by reducing what we pay for the food we eat. But it will immediately reduce the income of farmers, who will therefore have a strong incentive to organize to derail trade deals. The same is true of workers in factories forced to compete against far cheaper imports. These social and political realities go a long way in explaining why enthusiasm for reaching trade agreements has dried up in many countries.

It started in 1999, when the attempt to launch a new round of trade negotiations crashed in Seattle. Those botched meetings are now remembered more for the violent clashes between the police and anti-trade activists than for the fact that negotiators went home without even agreeing to start the negotiations. Ironically, the activists were protesting against a deal that wouldn't have happened anyway. Two years later, the trade ministers met again in Doha, Qatar, and decided to initiate a new round that, they agreed, would be concluded in four years. It was not to be. That deadline—and others—came and went. This past June, after six years of talks, negotiators left the meetings on the Doha Round and denounced each other as uncooperative.

Meanwhile, world trade continued to grow at its usual breakneck pace. In 2006, the volume of global merchandise exports grew 15 percent, while the world economy grew roughly 4 percent. In 2007, the growth in world trade is again expected to outstrip the growth rate of the global economy. This sustained, rapid pace of trade growth has led to a more than fivefold increase in world merchandise exports between 1980 and 2005. An unprecedented number of countries, rich and poor alike, are seeing their overall economic performance boosted by strong export growth.

So, what explains the paradox of gridlocked trade agreements and surging trade flows? The short answer is technology and politics. In the past quarter century, technological innovations—from the Internet to cargo containers—lowered the costs of trading. And, in the same period, an international political environment more tolerant of openness created opportunities to lower barriers to imports and exports. China, India, the former Soviet Union, and many other countries launched major reforms that deepened their integration into the world's economy. In developing countries alone, import tariffs dropped from an average of around 30 percent in the 1980s to less than 10 percent today. Indeed, one of the surprises of the past 20 or so years is how much governments have lowered obstacles to trade—unilaterally. Between 1983 and 2003, 66 percent of tariff reductions in the world took place because governments decided it was in their own interests to lower their import duties, 25 percent as a result of agreements reached in multilateral trade negotiations, and 10 percent through regional trade agreements with neighboring countries.

So, who needs free trade agreements if international trade is doing just fine without them?

We all do. Although trade may be booming, giving up on lowering the substantial trade barriers that still exist—in agriculture, in services, or in manufactured goods traded among poor countries—would be a historic mistake. Even the more pessimistic projections show that the adoption of reforms like those included in the Doha Round would yield substantial economic gains, anywhere from $50 billion to several hundred billion. Moreover, according to the World Bank, by 2015 as many as 32 million people could be lifted out of poverty if the Doha Round were successful.

But it isn't just the money. As the volume of trade continues to grow, the need for clearer and more effective rules becomes more critical. In this century, the quality of what is traded will be as important as the need to lower tariffs was in the last. The recent cases of deadly dog food and toxic toothpaste coming out of China prove as much. No country acting alone stands as good a chance of monitoring and curtailing such lethal goods as does the WTO working in concert with governments across the globe.

Moreover, a rules-based system accepted by a majority of nations can protect smaller countries and companies from the abusive practices of bigger nations or large conglomerates. The rule of law is always better than the law of the jungle, even in resolving trade conflicts.

But perhaps what is most important to keep in mind is that, despite all the misgivings about international trade, the fact remains that countries in which the share of economic activity related to exports is rising grow 1.5 times faster than those with more stagnant exports. And though we know that economic growth alone may not be sufficient to alleviate poverty, we have also learned that without growth, all other efforts will fall short. That argument alone should be enough to make us root for the trade negotiators, and not just the trade.

21 HEGEMONY AND TRADE

21.1

State Power and the Structure of International Trade

Stephen D. Krasner

INTRODUCTION

In recent years, students of international relations have multinationalized, transnationalized, bureaucratized, and transgovernmentalized the state until it has virtually ceased to exist as an analytic construct. Nowhere is that trend more apparent than in the study of the politics of international economic relations. The basic conventional assumptions have been undermined by assertions that the state is trapped by a transnational society created not by sovereigns, but by nonstate actors. Interdependence is not seen as a reflection of state policies and state choices (the perspective of balance-of-power theory), but as the result of elements beyond the control of any state or a system created by states.

This perspective is at best profoundly misleading. It may explain developments within a particular international economic structure, but it cannot explain the structure itself. That structure has many institutional and behavioral manifestations. The central continuum along which it can be described is openness. International economic structures may range from complete autarky (if all states prevent movements across their borders), to complete openness (if no restrictions exist). In this paper I will present an analysis of one aspect of the international economy—the structure of international trade; that is, the degree of openness for the movement of goods as opposed to capital, labor, technology, or other factors of production.

Since the beginning of the nineteenth century, this structure has gone through several changes. These can be explained, albeit imperfectly, by a state-power theory: an approach that begins with the assumption that the structure of international trade is determined by the interests and power of states acting to maximize national goals. The first step in this argument is to relate four basic state interests—aggregate national income, social stability, political power, and economic growth—to the degree of openness for the movement of goods. The relationship between these interests and openness depends upon the potential economic power of any given state. Potential economic power is operationalized in terms of the relative size and level of economic development of the state. The second step in the argument is to relate different distributions of potential power, such as multipolar and hegemonic, to different international trading structures. The most important conclusion of this theoretical analysis is that a hegemonic distribution of potential economic power is likely to result in an open trading structure. That argument is largely, although not completely, substantiated by empirical data. For a fully adequate analysis it is necessary to amend a state-power argument to take account of the impact of past state decisions on domestic social structures as well as on international economic ones. The two major organizers of the structure of trade since the beginning of the nineteenth century, Great Britain and the United States, have both been

Source: Stephen D. Krasner. "State Power and the Structure of International Trade," in *World Politics* 28(3): 317–323 and 335–343.

prevented from making policy amendments in line with state interests by particular societal groups whose power had been enhanced by earlier state policies.

The Causal Argument: State Interests, State Power, and International Trading Structures

Neoclassical trade theory is based upon the assumption that states act to maximize their aggregate economic utility. This leads to the conclusion that maximum global welfare and Pareto optimality are achieved under free trade. While particular countries might better their situations through protectionism, economic theory has generally looked askance at such policies. In his seminal article on the optimal tariff, Harry Johnson was at pains to point out that the imposition of successive optimal tariffs could lead both trading partners to a situation in which they were worse off than under competitive conditions.[1] Neoclassical theory recognizes that trade regulations can also be used to correct domestic distortions and to promote infant industries,[2] but these are exceptions or temporary departures from policy conclusions that lead logically to the support of free trade.

State Preferences

Historical experience suggests that policy makers are dense, or that the assumptions of the conventional argument are wrong. Free trade has hardly been the norm. Stupidity is not a very interesting analytic category. An alternative approach to explaining international trading structures is to assume that states seek a broad range of goals. At least four major state interests affected by the structure of international trade can be identified. They are: political power, aggregate national income, economic growth, and social stability. The way in which each of these goals is affected by the degree of openness depends upon the potential economic power of the state as defined by its relative size and level of development.

Let us begin with aggregate national income because it is most straightforward. Given the exceptions noted above, conventional neoclassical theory demonstrates that the greater the degree of openness in the international trading system, the greater the level of aggregate economic income. This conclusion applies to all states regardless of their size or relative level of development. The static economic benefits of openness are, however, generally inversely related to size. Trade gives small states relatively more welfare benefits than it gives large ones. Empirically, small states have higher ratios of trade to national product. They do not have the generous factor endowments or potential for national economies of scale that are enjoyed by larger—particularly continental—states.

The impact of openness on social stability runs in the opposite direction. Greater openness exposes the domestic economy to the exigencies of the world market. That implies a higher level of factor movements than in a closed economy, because domestic production patterns must adjust to changes in international prices. Social instability is thereby increased, since there is friction in moving factors, particularly labor, from one sector to another. The impact will be stronger in small states than in large, and in relatively less developed than in more developed ones. Large states are less involved in the international economy: a smaller percentage of their total factor endowment is affected by the international market at any given level of openness. More developed states are better able to adjust factors: skilled workers can more easily be moved from one kind of production to another than can unskilled laborers or peasants. Hence social stability is, *ceteris paribus*, inversely related to openness, but the deleterious consequences of exposure to the international trading system are mitigated by larger size and greater economic development.

The relationship between political power and the international trading structure can be analyzed in terms of the relative opportunity costs of closure for trading partners.[3] The higher the relative cost of closure, the weaker the political position of the state. Hirschman has argued that this cost can be measured in terms of direct income losses and the adjustment costs of reallocating factors.[4] These will be smaller for large states and for relatively more developed states. Other things being equal, utility costs will be less for large states because they generally have a smaller proportion of their economy engaged in the international economic system. Reallocation costs will be less for more advanced states because their factors are more mobile. Hence a state that is relatively large and more developed will find its political power enhanced by an open system because its opportunity costs of closure are less. The large state can use the threat to alter the system to secure economic or noneconomic objectives. Historically, there is one important exception to this generalization—the oil-exporting states. The level of reserves for some of these states, particularly Saudi Arabia, has reduced the economic opportunity costs of closure to a very low level despite their lack of development.

The relationship between international economic structure and economic growth is elusive. For small states, economic growth has generally been empirically associated with openness.[5] Exposure to the international system makes possible a much more efficient allocation of resources. Openness also probably furthers the rate of growth of large countries with relatively advanced technologies because they do not need to protect infant industries and can take advantage of expanded world markets. In the long term, however, openness for capital and technology, as well as goods, may hamper the growth of large, developed countries by diverting resources from the domestic economy, and by providing potential competitors with the knowledge needed to develop their own industries. Only by maintaining its technological lead and continually developing new industries can even a very large state escape the undesired consequences of an entirely open economic system. For medium-size states, the relationship between international trading structure and growth is impossible to specify definitively, either theoretically or empirically. On the one hand, writers from the mercantilists through the American protectionists and the German historical school, and more recently analysts of *dependencia*, have argued that an entirely open system can undermine a state's effort to develop, and even lead to underdevelopment.[6] On the other hand, adherents of more conventional neoclassical positions have maintained that exposure to international competition spurs economic transformation.[7] The evidence is not yet in. All that can confidently be said is that openness furthers the economic growth of small states and of large ones so long as they maintain their technological edge.

From State Preferences to International Trading Structures

The next step in this argument is to relate particular distributions of potential economic power, defined by the size and level of development of individual states, to the structure of the international trading system, defined in terms of openness.

Let us consider a system composed of a large number of small, highly developed states. Such a system is likely to lead to an open international trading structure. The aggregate income and economic growth of each state are increased by an open system. The social instability produced by exposure to international competition is mitigated by the factor mobility made possible by higher levels of development. There is no loss of political power from openness because the costs of closure are symmetrical for all members of the system.

Now let us consider a system composed of a few very large, but unequally developed states. Such a distribution of potential economic power is likely to lead to a closed structure. Each state could increase its income through a more open system, but the gains would be modest. Openness would create more social instability in the less developed countries. The rate of growth for more backward areas might be frustrated, while that of the more advanced ones would be enhanced. A more open structure would leave the less developed states in a politically more vulnerable position, because their greater factor rigidity would mean a higher relative cost of closure. Because of these disadvantages, large but relatively less developed states are unlikely to accept an open trading structure. More advanced states cannot, unless they are militarily much more powerful, force large backward countries to accept openness.

Finally, let us consider a hegemonic system—one in which there is a single state that is much larger and relatively more advanced than its trading partners. The costs and benefits of openness are not symmetrical for all members of the system. The hegemonic state will have a preference for an open structure. Such a structure increases its aggregate national income. It also increases its rate of growth during its ascendency—that is, when its relative size and technological lead are increasing. Further, an open structure increases its political power, since the opportunity costs of closure are least for a large and developed state. The social instability resulting from exposure to the international system is mitigated by the hegemonic power's relatively low level of involvement in the international economy, and the mobility of its factors.

What of the other members of a hegemonic system? Small states are likely to opt for openness because the advantages in terms of aggregate income and growth are so great, and their political power is bound to be restricted regardless of what they do. The reaction of medium-size states is hard to predict; it depends at least in part on the way in which the hegemonic power utilizes its resources. The potentially dominant state has symbolic, economic, and military capabilities that can be used to entice or compel others to accept an open trading structure.

At the symbolic level, the hegemonic state stands as an example of how economic development can be achieved. Its policies may be emulated, even if they are inappropriate for other states. Where there are very dramatic asymmetries, military power can be used to coerce weaker states into an open structure. Force is not, however, a very efficient means for changing economic policies, and it is unlikely to be employed against medium-size states.

Most importantly, the hegemonic state can use its economic resources to create an open structure. In terms of positive incentives, it can offer access to its large domestic market and to its relatively cheap exports. In terms of negative ones, it can withhold foreign grants and engage in competition, potentially ruinous for the weaker state, in third-country markets. The size and economic robustness of the hegemonic state also enable it to provide the confidence necessary for a stable international monetary system, and its currency can offer the liquidity needed for an increasingly open system.

In sum, openness is most likely to occur during periods when a hegemonic state is in its ascendency. Such a state has the interest and the resources to create a structure characterized by lower tariffs, rising trade proportions, and less regionalism. There are other distributions of potential power where openness is likely, such as a system composed of many small, highly developed states. But even here, that potential might not be realized because of the problems of creating confidence in a monetary system where adequate liquidity would have to be provided by a negotiated international reserve asset or a group of national currencies. Finally, it is unlikely that very large states, particularly at unequal levels of development, would accept open trading relations. . . .

Testing the Argument

The contention that hegemony leads to a more open trading structure is fairly well, but not perfectly, confirmed by the empirical evidence . . . The argument explains the periods 1820 to 1879, 1880 to 1900, and 1945 to 1960. It does not fully explain those from 1900 to 1913, 1919 to 1939, or 1960 to the present.

1820–1879

The period from 1820 to 1879 was one of increasing openness in the structure of international trade. It was also one of rising hegemony. Great Britain was the instigator and supporter of the new structure. She began lowering her trade barriers in the 1820's, before any other state. The signing of the Cobden-Chevalier Tariff Treaty with France in 1860 initiated a series of bilateral tariff reductions. It is, however, important to note that the United States was hardly involved in these developments, and that America's ratio of trade to aggregate economic activity did not increase during the nineteenth century.

Britain put to use her internal flexibility and external power in securing a more open structure. At the domestic level, openness was favored by the rising industrialists. The opposition of the agrarian sector was mitigated by its capacity for adjustment: the rate of capital investment and technological innovation was high enough to prevent British agricultural incomes from falling until some thirty years after the abolition of the Corn Laws. Symbolically, the Manchester School led by Cobden and Bright provided the ideological justification for free trade. Its influence was felt throughout Europe where Britain stood as an example to at least some members of the elite.

Britain used her military strength to open many backward areas: British interventions were frequent in Latin America during the nineteenth century, and formal and informal colonial expansion opened the interior of Africa. Most importantly, Britain forced India into the international economic system.[8] British military power was also a factor in concluding the Cobden-Chevalier Treaty, for Louis Napoleon was more concerned with cementing his relations with Britain than he was in the economic consequences of greater openness. Once this pact was signed, however, it became a catalyst for the many other treaties that followed.[9]

Britain also put economic instruments to good use in creating an open system. The abolition of the Corn Laws offered continental grain producers the incentive of continued access to the growing British market. Britain was at the heart of the nineteenth-century international monetary system which functioned exceptionally well, at least for the core of the more developed states and the areas closely associated with them. Exchange rates were stable, and countries did not have to impose trade barriers to rectify cyclical payments difficulties. Both confidence and liquidity were, to a critical degree, provided by Britain. The use of sterling balances as opposed to specie became increasingly widespread, alleviating the liquidity problems presented by the erratic production of gold and silver. Foreign private and central banks increasingly placed their cash reserves in London, and accounts were cleared through changing bank balances rather than gold flows. Great Britain's extremely sophisticated financial institutions, centered in the City of London, provided the short-term financing necessary to facilitate the international flow of goods. Her early and somewhat fortuitous adherence to the gold—as opposed to the silver or bimetallic—standard proved to be an important source of confidence as all countries adopted at least a *de facto* gold standard after 1870 because of the declining relative value of silver. In times of monetary emergency, the confidence placed in the pound because of the strength of the British economy allowed the Bank of England to be a lender of last resort.[10]

Hence, for the first three-quarters of the nineteenth century, British policy favored an open international trading structure, and British power helped to create it. But this was not a global regime. British resources were not sufficient to entice or compel the United States (a country whose economy was larger than Britain's by 1860 and whose technology was developing very rapidly) to abandon its protectionist commercial policy. As a state-power argument suggests, openness was only established within the geographical area where the rising economic hegemony was able to exercise its influence.

1880–1900

The last two decades of the nineteenth century were a period of modest closure which corresponds to a relative decline in British per capita income, size, and share of world trade. The event that precipitated higher tariff levels was the availability of inexpensive grain from the American Midwest, made possible by the construction of continental railways. National responses varied. Britain let her agricultural sector decline, a not unexpected development given her still dominant economic position. Denmark, a small and relatively well-developed state, also refrained from imposing tariffs and transformed its farming sector from agriculture to animal husbandry. Several other small states also followed open policies. Germany, France, Russia, and Italy imposed higher tariffs, however. Britain did not have the military or economic power to forestall these policies. Still, the institutional structure of the international monetary system, with the City of London at its center, did not crumble. The decline in trade proportions was modest despite higher tariffs.

1945–1960

The third period that is neatly explained by the argument that hegemony leads to an open trading structure is the decade-and-a-half after the Second World War, characterized by the ascendancy of the United States. During these years the structure of the international trading system became increasingly open. Tariffs were lowered; trade proportions were restored well above interwar levels. Asymmetrical regional trading patterns did begin to decline, although not until the late 1950's. America's bilateral rival, the Soviet Union, remained—as the theory would predict—encapsulated within its own regional sphere of influence.

Unlike Britain in the nineteenth century, the United States after World War II operated in a bipolar political structure. Free trade was preferred, but departures such as the Common Market and Japanese import restrictions were accepted to make sure that these areas remained within the general American sphere of influence.[11] Domestically the Reciprocal Trade Agreements Act, first passed in 1934, was extended several times after the war. Internationally the United States supported the framework for tariff reductions provided by the General Agreement on Tariffs and Trade. American policy makers used their economic leverage over Great Britain to force an end to the imperial preference system.[12] The monetary system established at Bretton Woods was basically an American creation. In practice, liquidity was provided by the American deficit; confidence by the size of the American economy. Behind the economic veil stood American military protection for other industrialized market economies—an overwhelming incentive for them to accept an open system, particularly one which was in fact relatively beneficial.

The argument about the relationship between hegemony and openness is not as satisfactory for the years 1900 to 1913, 1919 to 1939, and 1960 to the present.

1900–1913

During the years immediately preceding the First World War, the structure of international trade became more open in terms of trade proportions and regional patterns. Britain remained the largest international economic entity, but her relative position continued a decline that had begun two decades earlier. Still, Britain maintained her commitment to free trade and to the financial institutions of the City of London. A state-power argument would suggest some reconsideration of these policies.

Perhaps the simplest explanation for the increase in trade proportions was the burst of loans that flowed out of Europe in the years before the First World War, loans that financed the increasing sale of goods. Germany and France as well as Britain participated in this development. Despite the higher tariff levels imposed after 1879, institutional structures—particularly the monetary system—allowed these capital flows to generate increasing trade flows. Had Britain reconsidered her policies, this might not have been the case.

1919–1939

The United States emerged from the First World War as the world's most powerful economic state. Whether America was large enough to have put an open system in place is a moot question. America's share of world trade and investment was only 26 and 55 percent greater than that of any other state, while comparable figures for Great Britain during the last part of the nineteenth century are 100 percent. What is apparent, though, is that American policy makers made little effort to open the structure of international trade. The call for an open door was a shibboleth, not a policy. It was really the British who attempted to continue a hegemonic role.

In the area of trade, the U.S. Fordney-McCumber Tariff of 1922 increased protection. That tendency was greatly reinforced by the Smoot-Hawley Tariff of 1930 which touched off a wave of protective legislation. Instead of leading the way to openness, the United States led the way to closure.

In the monetary area, the American government made little effort to alter a situation that was confused and often chaotic. During the first half of the 1920's, exchange rates fluctuated widely among major currencies as countries were forced, by the inflationary pressures of the war, to abandon the gold standard. Convertibility was restored in the mid-twenties at values incompatible with long-term equilibrium. The British pound was overvalued, and the French franc undervalued. Britain was forced off the gold standard in September 1931, accelerating a trend that had begun with Uruguay in April 1929. The United States went off gold in 1933. France's decision to end convertibility in 1936 completed the pattern. During the 1930's the monetary system collapsed.[13]

Constructing a stable monetary order would have been no easy task in the political environment of the 1920's and 1930's. The United States made no effort. It refused to recognize a connection between war debts and reparations, although much of the postwar flow of funds took the form of American loans to Germany, German reparations payments to France and Britain, and French and British war-debt payments to the United States. The great depression was in no small measure touched off by the contraction of American credit in the late 1920's. In the deflationary collapse that followed, the British were too weak to act as a lender of last resort, and the Americans actually undercut efforts to reconstruct the Western economy when, before the London Monetary Conference of 1933, President Roosevelt changed the basic assumptions of the meeting by taking the United States off gold. American concern was wholly with restoring the domestic economy.[14]

That is not to say that American behavior was entirely obstreperous; but cooperation was erratic and often private. The Federal Reserve Bank of New York did try, during the late 1920's, to maintain New York interest rates below those in London to protect the value of the pound.[15] Two Americans, Dawes and Young, lent their names to the renegotiations of German reparations payments, but most of the actual work was carried out by British experts.[16] At the official level, the first manifestation of American leadership was President Hoover's call for a moratorium on war debts and reparations in June 1931; but in 1932 the United States refused to participate in the Lausanne Conference that in effect ended reparations.[17]

It was not until the mid-thirties that the United States asserted any real leadership. The Reciprocal Trade Agreements Act of 1934 led to bilateral treaties with twenty-seven countries before 1945. American concessions covered 64 percent of dutiable items, and reduced rates by an average of 44 percent. However, tariffs were so high to begin with that the actual impact of these agreements was limited.[18] There were also some modest steps toward tariff liberalization in Britain and France. In the monetary field, the United States, Britain, and France pledged to maintain exchange-rate stability in the Tripartite Declaration of September 1936. These actions were not adequate to create an open international economic structure. American policy during the interwar period, and particularly before the mid-thirties, fails to accord with the predictions made by a state-power explanation of the behavior of a rising hegemonic power.

1960–present

The final period not adequately dealt with by a state-power explanation is the last decade or so. In recent years, the relative size and level of development of the U.S. economy has fallen. This decline has not, however, been accompanied by a clear turn toward protectionism. The Trade Expansion Act of 1962 was extremely liberal and led to the very successful Kennedy Round of multilateral tariff cuts during the mid-sixties. The protectionist Burke-Hartke Bill did not pass. The 1974 Trade Act does include new protectionist aspects, particularly in its requirements for review of the removal of non-tariff barriers by Congress and for stiffer requirements for the imposition of countervailing duties, but it still maintains the mechanism of presidential discretion on tariff cuts that has been the keystone of postwar reductions. While the Voluntary Steel Agreement, the August 1971 economic policy, and restrictions on agricultural exports all show a tendency toward protectionism, there is as yet no evidence of a basic turn away from a commitment to openness.

In terms of behavior in the international trading system, the decade of the 1960's was clearly one of greater openness. Trade proportions increased, and traditional regional trade patterns became weaker. A state-power argument would predict a downturn or at least a faltering in these indicators as American power declined.

In sum, although the general pattern of the structure of international trade conforms with the predictions of a state-power argument—two periods of openness separated by one of closure—corresponding to periods of rising British and American hegemony and an interregnum, the whole pattern is out of phase. British commitment to openness continued long after Britain's position had declined. American commitment to openness did not begin until well after the United States had become the world's leading economic power and has continued during a period of relative American decline. The state-power argument needs to be amended to take these delayed reactions into account.

Amending the Argument

The structure of the international trading system does not move in lockstep with changes in the distribution of potential power among states. Systems are initiated and ended, not as a state-power theory would predict, by close assessments of the interests of the state at every given moment, but by external events—usually cataclysmic ones. The closure that began in 1879 coincided with the Great Depression of the last part of the nineteenth century. The final dismantling of the nineteenth-century international economic system was not precipitated by a change in British trade or monetary policy, but by the First World War and the Depression. The potato famine of the 1840's prompted abolition of the Corn Laws; and the United States did not assume the mantle of world leadership until the world had been laid bare by six years of total war. Some catalytic external event seems necessary to move states to dramatic policy initiatives in line with state interests.

Once policies have been adopted, they are pursued until a new crisis demonstrates that they are no longer feasible. States become locked in by the impact of prior choices on their domestic political structures. The British decision to opt for openness in 1846 corresponded with state interests. It also strengthened the position of industrial and financial groups over time, because they had the opportunity to operate in an international system that furthered their objectives. . . .

Institutions created during periods of rising ascendancy remained in operation when they were no longer appropriate. The British state was unable to free itself from the domestic structures that its earlier policy decisions had created, and continued to follow policies appropriate for a rising hegemony long after Britain's star had begun to fall.

Similarly, earlier policies in the United States begat social structures and institutional arrangements that trammeled state policy. After protecting import-competing industries for a century, the United States was unable in the 1920's to opt for more open policies, even though state interests would have been furthered thereby. . . .

The structure of international trade changes in fits and starts; it does not flow smoothly with the redistribution of potential state power. Nevertheless, it is the power and the policies of states that create order where there would otherwise be chaos or at best a Lockian state of nature. The existence of various transnational, multinational, transgovernmental, and other nonstate actors that have riveted scholarly attention in recent years can only be understood within the context of a broader structure that ultimately rests upon the power and interests of states, shackled though they may be by the societal consequences of their own past decisions.

Notes

1. Johnson, "Optimum Tariffs and Retaliation," in Harry Johnson, *International Trade and Economic Growth* (Cambridge: Harvard University Press 1967), 31–61.

2. See, for instance, Everett Hagen, "An Economic Justification of Protectionism," *Quarterly Journal of Economics*, Vol. 72 (November 1958), 496–514; Harry Johnson, "Optimal Trade Intervention in the Presence of Domestic Distortions," in Robert Baldwin and others, *Trade, Growth and the Balance of Payments: Essays in Honor of Gottfried Haberler* (Chicago: Rand McNally 1965), 3–34; and Jagdish Bhagwati, *Trade, Tariffs, and Growth* (Cambridge: MIT Press 1969), 295–308.

3. This notion is reflected in Albert O. Hirschman, *National Power and the Structure of Foreign Trade* (Berkeley: University of California Press 1945); Robert W. Tucker, *The*

New Isolationism: Threat or Promise? (Washington: Potomac Associates 1972); and Kenneth Waltz, "The Myth of Interdependence," in Charles P. Kindleberger, ed., *The International Corporation* (Cambridge: MIT Press 1970), 205–23.

4. Hirschman (fn.3), 13–34.

5. Simon Kuznets, *Modern Economic Growth: Rate, Structure, and Spread* (New Haven: Yale University Press 1966), 302.

6. See David P. Calico and Benjamin Rowland, *America and the World Political Economy* (Bloomington: Indiana University Press 1973), Part II, for a discussion of American thought; Eli Heckscher, *Mercantilism* (New York: Macmillan 1955); and D. C. Coleman, ed., *Revisions in Mercantilism* (London: Methuen 1969), for the classic discussion and a collection of recent articles on mercantilism; Andre Gunder Frank, *Latin America: Underdevelopment or Revolution* (New York: Monthly Review 1969); Arghiri Emmanuel, *Unequal Exchange: A Study of the Imperialism of Trade* (New York: Monthly Review 1972); and Johan Galtung, "A Structural Theory of Imperialism," *Journal of Peace Research*, VIII, No. 2 (1971), 81–117, for some representative arguments about the deleterious effects of free trade.

7. See Gottfried Haberler, *International Trade and Economic Development* (Cairo: National Bank of Egypt 1959); and Carlos F. Diaz-Alejandro, "Latin America: Toward 2000 A.D.," in Jagdish Bhagwati, ed., *Economics and World Order from the 1970s to the 1990s* (New York: Macmillan 1972), 223–55, for some arguments concerning the benefits of trade.

8. John Gallagher and Ronald Robinson, "The Imperialism of Free Trade," *Economic History Review*, 2nd Series, VI (August 1953), 1–15.

9. Kindleberger (fn. 9), 41.

10. Robert Triffin, *The Evolution of the International Monetary System* (Princeton: Princeton Studies in International Finance, No. 12, 1964), 2–20; R. G. Hawtrey, *The Gold Standard in Theory and Practice* (London: Longmans, Green 1947), 69–80; Leland Yeager, *International Monetary Relations* (New York: Harper and Row 1966), 251–61; Sidney E. Rolfe and James Burtle, *The Great Wheel: The World Monetary System, a Reinterpretation* (New York: Quadrangle 1973), 10–11; Condliffe (fn. 9), 343–80.

11. Raymond Aron, *The Imperial Republic* (Englewood Cliffs, N.J.: Prentice-Hall 1973), 191; Gilpin (fn. 12), 409–12; Calico and Rowland (fn. 6), chap. 3.

12. Lloyd Gardner, *Economic Aspects of New Deal Diplomacy* (Madison: University of Wisconsin Press 1964), 389; Gilpin (fn. 12), 409.

13. Triffin (fn. 19), 22–28; Rolfe and Burtle (fn. 19), 13–55; Yeager (fn. 19), 278–317; Kindleberger (fn. 11), 270–71.

14. Kindleberger (fn. 11), 199–224; Yeager (fn. 19), 314; Condliffe (fn. 9), 499.

15. Triffin (fn. 19), 22.

16. Kindleberger (fn. 11), 296.

17. Condliffe (fn. 9), 494–97.

18. Evans (fn. 13), 7.

Bibliography

Brown, Seyom, 1983. *The Faces of Power: Constancy and Change in United States Foreign Policy from Truman to Reagan* (New York: Columbia University Press).

De Cecco, Marcello, 1975. *Money and Empire: The International Gold Standard, 1890–1914* (Totowa, N.J.: Rowman and Littlefield).

Feis, Herbert, 1930. *Europe, The World's Banker* (New Haven, Yale University Press).

Ford, A. G., 1962. *The Gold Standard, 1880–1914* (Oxford: The Clarendon Press).

Gilpin, Robert, 1981. *War and Change in World Politics* (Cambridge: Cambridge University Press).

Hobsbawm, E. J., 1968. *Industry and Empire* (New York: Pantheon Books).

Keohane, Robert O., 1980. "The theory of hegemonic stability and changes in international economic regimes, 1967–1977." In Ole Holsti et al., *Change in the International System* (Boulder: Westview Press), pp. 131–62.

Keohane, Robert O., and Joseph S. Nye, 1977. *Power and Interdependence: World Politics in Transition* (Boston: Little, Brown).

Kindleberger, Charles P., 1973. *The World in Depression, 1929–1939* (Berkeley: University of California Press).

Kindleberger, Charles P., 1978b. *Economic Response: Comparative Studies in Trade, Finance and Growth* (Cambridge: Harvard University Press).

Kindleberger, Charles P., 1978c. *Manias, Panics and Crashes* (New York: Basic Books).

Kindleberger, Charles P., 1981. "Dominance and leadership in the international economy." *International Studies Quarterly*, vol. 25, no. 3 (June), pp. 242–54.

Krasner, Stephen D., 1978b. "United States commercial and monetary policy: unravelling the paradox of external strength and internal weakness." In Katzenstein, 1978, pp. 51–88.

Lewis, W. Arthur, 1978. *Growth and Fluctuation, 1870–1913* (London: George Allen & Unwin).

Lindert, Peter H., 1969. *Key Currencies and Gold, 1900–1913*. Princeton Studies in International Finance no. 24 (Princeton: Princeton University Finance Section).

McKeown, Timothy J., 1983a. "Hegemonic stability theory and 19th century tariff levels in Europe." *International Organizations*, vol. 37, no. 1 (Winter), pp. 73–92.

Olson, Mancur, 1965. *The Logic of Collective Action* (Cambridge: Harvard University Press).

Schroeder, Paul W., 1958. *The Axis Alliance and Japanese-American Relations* (Ithaca: Cornell University Press).

Wallerstein, Immanuel, 1980. *The Modern World-System II: Mercantilism and the Consolidation of the European World-Economy, 1600–1750* (New York: Academic Press).

21.2

Hegemony in the World Political Economy

Robert O. Keohane

It is common today for troubled supporters of liberal capitalism to look back with nostalgia on British preponderance in the nineteenth century and American dominance after World War II. Those eras are imagined to be simpler ones in which a single power, possessing superiority of economic and military resources, implemented a plan for international order based on its interests and its vision of the world. As Robert Gilpin has expressed it, "the *Pax Britannica* and *Pax Americana*, like the *Pax Romana*, ensured an international system of relative peace and security. Great Britain and the United States created and enforced the rules of a liberal international economic order" (1981, p. 144).

Underlying this statement is one of the two central propositions of the theory of hegemonic stability (Keohane, 1980): that order in world politics is typically created by a single dominant power. Since regimes constitute elements of an international order, this implies that the formation of international regimes normally depends on hegemony. The other major tenet of the theory of hegemonic stability is that the maintenance of order requires continued hegemony. As Charles P. Kindleberger has said, "for the world economy to be stabilized, there has to be a stabilizer, one stabilizer" (1973, p. 305). This implies that cooperation also depends on the perpetuation of hegemony.

I discuss hegemony before elaborating my definitions of cooperation and regimes because my emphasis on how international institutions such as regimes facilitate cooperation only makes sense if cooperation and discord are not determined simply by interests and power. In this [reading] I argue that a deterministic version of the theory of hegemonic stability, relying only on the Realist concepts of interests and power, is indeed incorrect. There is some validity in a modest version of the first proposition of the theory of hegemonic stability—that hegemony can facilitate a certain type of cooperation—but there is little reason to believe that hegemony is either a necessary or a sufficient condition for the emergence of cooperative relationships. Furthermore, and even more important for the argument presented here, the second major proposition of the theory is erroneous: cooperation does not necessarily require the existence of a hegemonic leader after international regimes have been established. Post-hegemonic cooperation is also possible. . . .

The task of the present [reading] is to explore in a preliminary way the value and limitations of the concept of hegemony for the study of cooperation. The first section analyzes the claims of the theory of hegemonic stability; the second section briefly addresses the relationship between military power and hegemony in the world political economy. . . .

Evaluating the Theory of Hegemonic Stability

The theory of hegemonic stability, as applied to the world political economy, defines hegemony as preponderance of material resources. Four sets of resources are especially important. Hegemonic powers must have control over raw materials, control over sources of capital, control over markets, and competitive advantages in the production of highly valued goods.

The importance of controlling sources of raw materials has provided a traditional justification for territorial expansion and imperialism, as well as for the extension of informal influence. Guaranteed access to capital, though less obvious as a source of power, may be equally important. Countries with well-functioning capital markets can borrow cheaply and may be able to provide credit to friends or even deny it to adversaries. Holland derived political and economic power from the quality of its capital markets in the seventeenth century; Britain did so in the eighteenth and nineteenth centuries; and the United States has similarly benefited during the last fifty years (De Cecco, 1975; Feis, 1930; Ford, 1962; Kindleberger, 1978c; Lindert, 1969; Wallerstein, 1980).

Potential power may also be derived from the size of one's market for imports. The threat to cut off a particular state's access to one's own market, while allowing other countries continued access, is a "potent and historically relevant weapon of economic 'power'" (McKeown, 1983a, p. 78). Conversely, the offer to open up one's own huge market to other exporters, in return for concessions or deference, can be an effective means of influence. The bigger one's own market, and the greater the government's discretion in opening it up or closing it off, the greater one's potential economic power.[1]

The final dimension of economic preponderance is competitive superiority in the production of goods. Immanuel Wallerstein has defined hegemony in economic terms as "a situation wherein the products of a given core state are produced so efficiently that they are by and large competitive even in other core states, and therefore the given core state will be the primary beneficiary of a maximally free world market" (1980, p. 38). As a definition of economic preponderance this is interesting but poorly worked out, since under conditions of overall balance of payments equilibrium each unit—even the poorest and least developed—will have some comparative advantage. The fact that in 1960 the United States had a trade deficit in textiles and apparel and in basic manufactured goods (established products not, on the whole, involving the use of complex or new technology) did not indicate that it had lost predominant economic status (Krasner, 1978b, pp. 68–69). Indeed, one should expect the economically preponderant state to import products that are labor-intensive or that are produced with well-known production techniques. Competitive advantage does not mean that the leading economy exports *everything*, but that it produces and exports the most profitable products and those that will provide the basis for producing even more advanced goods and services in the future. In general, this ability will be based on the technological superiority of the leading country, although it may also rest on its political control over valuable resources yielding significant rents.

To be considered hegemonic in the world political economy, therefore, a country must have access to crucial raw materials, control major sources of capital, maintain a large market for imports, and hold comparative advantages in goods with high value added, yielding relatively high wages and profits. It must also be stronger, on these dimensions taken as a whole, than any other country. The theory of hegemonic stability predicts that the more one such power dominates the world political economy, the more cooperative will interstate relations be.

Yet, like many such basic force models, this crude theory of hegemonic stability makes imperfect predictions. In the twentieth century it correctly anticipates the relative cooperativeness of the twenty years after World War II. It is at least partially mistaken, however, about trends of cooperation when hegemony erodes. Between 1900 and 1913 a decline in British power coincided with a decrease rather than an increase in conflict over commercial issues.[2] How to interpret the prevalence of discord in the interwar years is difficult, since it is not clear whether any country was hegemonic in material terms during those two decades. The United States, though considerably ahead in productivity, did not replace Britain as the most important financial center and lagged behind in volume of trade. Although American domestic oil production was more than sufficient for domestic needs during these years, Britain still controlled the bulk of major Middle Eastern oil fields. Nevertheless, what prevented American leadership of a cooperative world political economy in these years was less lack of economic resources than an absence of political willingness to make and enforce rules for the system. Britain, despite its efforts, was too weak to do so effectively (Kindleberger, 1973). The crucial factor in producing discord lay in American politics, not in the material factors to which the theory points.

Unlike the crude basic force model, a refined version of hegemonic stability theory does not assert an automatic link between power and leadership. Hegemony is defined as a situation in which "one state is powerful enough to maintain the essential rules governing interstate relations, and willing to do so" (Keohane and Nye, 1977, p. 44). This interpretive framework retains an emphasis on power but looks more seriously than the crude power theory at the internal characteristics of the strong state. It does not assume that strength automatically creates incentives to project one's power abroad. Domestic attitudes, political structures, and decision-making processes are also important.

This argument's reliance on state decisions as well as power capabilities puts it into the category of what March calls "force activation models." Decisions to exercise leadership are necessary to "activate" the posited relationship between power capabilities and outcomes. Force activation models are essentially *post hoc* rather than *a priori*, since one can always "save" such a theory after the fact by thinking of reasons why an actor would not have wanted to use all of its available potential power. In effect, this modification of the theory declares that states with preponderant resources will be hegemonic except when they decide not to commit the necessary effort to the tasks of leadership, yet it does not tell us what will determine the latter decision. As a causal theory this is not very helpful, since whether a given configuration of power will lead the potential hegemon to maintain a set of rules remains indeterminate unless we know a great deal about its domestic politics.[3]

Only the cruder theory generates predictions. When I refer without qualification to the theory of hegemonic stability, therefore, I will be referring to this basic force model. We have seen that the most striking contention of this theory—that hegemony is both a necessary and a sufficient condition for cooperation—is not strongly supported by the experience of this century. Taking a longer period of about 150 years, the record remains ambiguous.[4] International economic relations were relatively cooperative both in the era of British hegemony during the mid-to-late nineteenth century and in the two decades of American dominance after World War II. But only in the second of these periods was there a trend toward the predicted disruption of established rules and increased discord. And a closer examination of the British experience casts doubt on the causal role of British hegemony in producing cooperation in the nineteenth century.

Both Britain in the nineteenth century and the United States in the twentieth met the material prerequisites for hegemony better than any other states since the Industrial Revolution. In 1880, Britain was the financial center of the world, and it controlled extensive raw materials, both in its formal empire and through investments in areas not part of the Imperial domain. It had the highest per capita income in the world and approximately double the share of world trade and investment of its nearest competitor, France. Only in the aggregate size of its economy had it already fallen behind the United States (Krasner, 1976, p. 333). Britain's share of world trade gradually declined during the next sixty years, but in 1938 it was still the world's largest trader, with 14 percent of the world total. In the nineteenth century Britain's relative labor productivity was the highest in the world, although it declined rather precipitously thereafter. . . .

Yet, despite Britain's material strength, it did not always enforce its preferred rules. Britain certainly did maintain freedom of the seas. But it did not induce major continental powers, after the 1870s, to retain liberal trade policies. A recent investigation of the subject has concluded that British efforts to make and enforce rules were less extensive and less successful than hegemonic stability theory would lead us to believe they were (McKeown, 1983a, especially p. 88).[5]

Attempts by the United States after World War II to make and enforce rules for the world political economy were much more effective than Britain's had ever been. America after 1945 did not merely replicate earlier British experience; on the contrary, the differences between Britain's "hegemony" in the nineteenth century and America's after World War II were profound. As we have seen, Britain had never been as superior in productivity to the rest of the world as the United States was after 1945. Nor was the United States ever as dependent on foreign trade and investment as Britain. Equally important, America's economic partners—over whom its hegemony was exercised, since America's ability to make the rules hardly extended to the socialist camp—were also its military allies; but Britain's chief trading partners had been its major military and political rivals. In addition, one reason for Britain's relative ineffectiveness in maintaining a free trade regime is that it had never made extensive use of the principle of reciprocity in trade (McKeown, 1983a). It thus had sacrificed potential leverage over other countries that preferred to retain their own restrictions while Britain practiced free trade. The policies of these states might well have been altered had they been confronted with a choice between a closed British market for their exports on the one hand and mutual lowering of barriers on the other. Finally, Britain had an empire to which it could retreat, by selling less advanced goods to its colonies rather than competing in more open markets (De Cecco, 1975; Hobsbawm, 1968; Kindleberger, 1978b; Lewis, 1978). American hegemony, rather than being one more instance of a general phenomenon, was essentially unique in the scope and efficacy of the instruments at the disposal of a hegemonic state and in the degree of success attained.

That the theory of hegemonic stability is supported by only one or at most two cases casts doubt on its general validity. Even major proponents of the theory refrain from making such claims. In an article published in 1981, Kindleberger seemed to entertain the possibility that two or more countries might "take on the task of providing leadership together, thus adding to legitimacy, sharing the burdens, and reducing the danger that leadership is regarded cynically as a cloak for domination and exploitation" (p. 252). In *War and Change in World Politics* (1981), Gilpin promulgated what appeared to be a highly deterministic conception of hegemonic cycles: "the conclusion of one hegemonic war is the beginning of another cycle of growth, expansion, and eventual decline" (p. 210). Yet he denied that his view was deterministic, and he asserted that "states can learn to be more enlightened in their definitions of their interests and can learn to be more cooperative in their behavior" (p. 227). Despite the erosion of hegemony, "there are reasons for believing that the present disequilibrium in the international system can be resolved without resort to hegemonic war" (p. 234).

The empirical evidence for the general validity of hegemonic stability theory is weak, and even its chief adherents have doubts about it. In addition, the logical underpinnings of the theory are suspect. Kindleberger's strong claim for the necessity of a single leader rested on the theory of collective goods. He argued that "the danger we face is not too much power in the international economy, but too little, not an excess of domination, but a superfluity of would-be free riders, unwilling to mind the store, and waiting for a storekeeper to appear" (1981, p. 253). . . . [S]ome of the "goods" produced by hegemonic leadership are not genuinely collective in character, although the implications of this fact are not necessarily as damaging to the theory as might be imagined at first. More critical is the fact that in international economic systems a few actors typically control a preponderance of resources. This point is especially telling, since the theory of collective goods does not properly imply that cooperation among a few countries should be impossible. Indeed, one of the original purposes of Olson's use of the theory was to show that in systems with only a few participants these actors "can provide themselves with collective goods without relying on any positive inducements apart from the good itself" (Olson, 1965, p. 33; quoted in McKeown, 1983a, p. 79). Logically, hegemony should not be a necessary condition for the emergence of cooperation in an oligopolistic system.

The theory of hegemonic stability is thus suggestive but by no means definitive. Concentrated power alone is not sufficient to create a stable international economic order in which cooperation flourishes, and the argument that hegemony is necessary for cooperation is both theoretically and empirically weak. If hegemony is redefined as the ability and willingness of a single state to make and enforce rules, furthermore, the claim that hegemony is sufficient for cooperation becomes virtually tautological.

The crude theory of hegemonic stability establishes a useful, if somewhat simplistic, starting-point for an analysis of changes in international cooperation and discord. Its refined version raises a looser but suggestive set of interpretive questions for the analysis of some eras in the history of the international political economy. Such an interpretive framework does not constitute an explanatory systemic theory, but it can help us think of hegemony in another way—less as a concept that helps to explain outcomes in terms of power than as a way of describing an international system in which leadership is exercised by a single state. Rather than being a component of a scientific generalization—that power is a necessary or sufficient condition for cooperation—the concept of hegemony, defined in terms of willingness as well as ability to lead, helps us think about the incentives facing the potential hegemon. Under what conditions, domestic and international, will such a country decide to invest in the construction of rules and institutions?

Concern for the incentives facing the hegemon should also alert us to the frequently neglected incentives facing other countries in the system. What calculus do they confront in considering whether to challenge or defer to a would-be leader? Thinking about the calculations of secondary powers raises the question of deference. Theories of hegemony should seek not only to analyze dominant powers' decisions to engage in rule-making and rule-enforcement, but also to explore why secondary states defer to the leadership of the hegemon. That is, they need to account for the legitimacy of hegemonic regimes and for the coexistence of cooperation with hegemony. . . .

Military Power and Hegemony in the World Political Economy

Before taking up these themes, we need to clarify the relationship between this analysis of hegemony in the world political economy and the question of military power. A hegemonic state must possess enough military power to be able to protect the international political economy that it dominates from incursions by hostile adversaries. This is essential because economic issues, if they are crucial enough to basic national values, may become military-security issues as well. For instance, Japan attacked the United States in 1941 partly in response to the freezing of Japanese assets in the United States, which denied Japan "access to all the vitally needed supplies outside her own control, in particular her most crucial need, oil" (Schroeder, 1958, p. 53). During and after World War II the United States used its military power to assure itself access to the petroleum of the Middle East; and at the end of 1974 Secretary of Stare Henry A. Kissinger warned that the United States might resort to military action if oil-exporting countries threatened "some actual strangulation of the industrialized world" (Brown, 1983, p. 428).

Yet the hegemonic power need not be militarily dominant worldwide.... The military conditions for economic hegemony are met if the economically preponderant country has sufficient military capabilities to prevent incursions by others that would deny it access to major areas of its economic activity.

The sources of hegemony therefore include sufficient military power to deter or rebuff attempts to capture and close off important areas of the world political economy. But in the contemporary world, at any rate, it is difficult for a hegemon to use military power directly to attain its economic policy objectives with its military partners and allies. Allies cannot be threatened with force without beginning to question the alliance; nor are threats to cease defending them unless they conform to the hegemon's economic rules very credible except in extraordinary circumstances. Many of the relationships within the hegemonic international political economy dominated by the United States after World War II approximated more closely the ideal type of "complex interdependence"—with multiple issues, multiple channels of contact among societies, and inefficacy of military force for most policy objectives—than the converse ideal type of Realist theory (Keohane and Nye, 1977, ch. 2).

Notes

1. The classic statement of this point is by Hirschman (1945/1980). For a recent discussion of the same issue with reference to textiles, see Aggarwal, 1983, p. 622. Aggarwal notes that a large importer of goods may exercise influence not merely over sellers but also over other buyers, who fear diversion of imports into their markets if a large market is closed.

2. See Krasner, 1976. Krasner's analysis focuses on liberalism, or openness, as the dependent variable rather than on order or cooperation. Cooperation and liberalism are conceptually distinct, and as we will see in Keohane, 1984, chapter 9, in recent years they can also be distinguished empirically. In Krasner's highly aggregated analysis of the last 150 years, however, the distinction does not make a significant difference, since open systems have on the whole also been more predictable and less characterized by conflict—hence more orderly—than the protectionist ones.

3. It should also be evident, in view of our discussion in Keohane, 1984, chapter 2, that the refined version of hegemonic stability theory is not systemic, since it depends for its explanatory power on variations in the internal characteristics of actors.

4. See footnote 2 above.

5. The question of whether Britain was always consistent in its espousal of liberalism is analytically a separate issue from that of its ability to make and enforce rules, since liberalism should not be equated with cooperation. For the nineteenth century, however, as footnote 2 indicates, the order that Britain sought was a liberal one. For discussions of cases outside of Europe in which the rise of British hegemony may have led to restrictions on trade, see Laitin, 1982, and Lawson, 1983.

21.3

Dependency Theory

Andrés Velasco

The scene is fresh in my mind. It was the early 1980s, and the Reagan administration's antics in Central America and Grenada were reviving the campus left. The crowd filling a Yale University common room sat in anticipation, fingering through dog-eared copies of *Dependency and Development in Latin America*, the magnum opus of dependency theory. One of its authors, Brazilian sociologist Fernando Henrique Cardoso (later president of his country), was about to arrive. His attire was the first shock. Cardoso, then a senator from São Paulo, showed up wearing an impeccable blue suit, not the fatigues half the attendees were expecting. After he gave a short speech on Brazilian political tactics, not the ills of imperialism, a woman in a poncho fired the first question: Did democracy mean anything in Brazil without socialism? Yes it did, replied Cardoso. And building socialism was no longer the issue; perfecting capitalism was. Students sitting at his feet stared in disbelief and soon began milling out.

Dependency was a theory of underdevelopment: Poor countries exiled to the periphery of the world economy could not develop as long as they remained enslaved by the rich nations of the center. Dependency was also a religion that shaped the cosmology of a generation of Latin American leftists in the 1960s and 1970s and of leaders from Chilean President Salvador Allende to the Nicaraguan Sandinistas. As would happen again with other half-digested foreign theories—deconstruction is the best example—U.S. college campuses embraced dependency with evangelical fervor. Mixed with Vietnam-era rhetoric, dependency theory became a potent brew, which placed all blame for Third World problems on the hegemonic center, particularly the United States. Cardoso himself worried about this tendency. In a 1977 article published in the *Latin American Research Review* titled "The Consumption of Dependency Theory in the United States," he warned against oversimplifications and against assuming that all of Latin America's problems were foreign made.

Dependency came in two flavors: The radical one, cooked up by economists André Gunder Frank and Amir Samin, claimed that the center grew at the expense of the periphery. The only solution was to delink completely from the world economy. From the start, however, radical dependency faced its share of troubles. Armies of graduate students tried to find a positive correlation between expansion in the North and recession in the South, but failed. (Then, as now, a boom in the United States and Europe often meant growth for developing countries.) Much less did they manage to prove a causal relationship between Northern wealth and Southern poverty. Only Albania and North Korea tried the practical prescription of completely breaking away from the world economy, with predictable consequences. Gunder Frank himself, now a senior fellow at the World History Center at Northeastern University, recently admitted delinking "has not been a very viable or fruitful policy."

The milder version of dependency, pioneered by Cardoso and his coauthor Enzo Faletto, and by others like Chile's Osvaldo Sunkel and Mexico's Pedro Paz, was more useful. It maintained that under capitalism both rich and poor could grow but would not benefit equally. The practical incarnation of this view fell far short of revolution. As preached from the U.N. Economic Commission for Latin America (ECLAC), it was a mixture of protectionism and Keynesianism that became known as import-substituting industrialization. Behind a tariff wall, with generous state subsidies, an active fiscal policy, and a drop of central planning here and there, poor countries could hope to lessen their dependency on the center and develop autonomously.

Why was the global economy considered such a threat? Because, as Argentine economist Raul Prebisch had earlier taught, the price of primary commodities tends to fall relative to the price of manufactures. If a

Source: Andres Velasco, "Dependency Theory," *Foreign Policy,* November 2002. Copyright 2002 by *Foreign Policy;* Carnegie Endowment for International Peace; National Affairs, Inc. Reprinted with permission.

country is stuck producing copper or cotton, then the purchasing power of its exports will fall (or at least stagnate), and so will its ability to import, invest, and grow. Producers of primary commodities will become relatively poorer over time.

This view shaped development thinking for half a century at least. It also turned out to be wrong. Harvard economic historian Jeff Williamson has recently argued that between 1870 and World War I (the period Prebisch had studied) the terms of trade (the prices of exports relative to that of imports) did not deteriorate for producers of commodities. A number of other studies have looked at the evidence for the 20th century and likewise concluded that primary products did not systematically become cheaper relative to manufactures.

If dependency theory had its failings, so too did the policies it engendered. Turning away from the world economy was a good idea during the Great Depression, when the world was truly hostile. Latin American countries that abandoned the gold standard, devalued their currencies, and granted their local industries some degree of protection did better, as the eminent Cuban economist Carlos Díaz-Alejandro showed long ago. But protection made less sense as world trade expanded after World War II. It also led to inefficiency and stifled technological progress. There were some periods of fast growth in countries such as Mexico and Brazil. But over time even the most ardent advocates of import-substituting industrialization came to recognize the policy was not the panacea they had claimed it to be.

The rest of the story is well known. Latin America embarked on a course of drastic trade liberalization and opened itself to the world. Some sectors (such as Mexican *maquiladoras* and Chilean fruit and wine) boomed; others lagged behind. For every growth miracle like Chile's (and more recently the Dominican Republic's), there have been two growth disasters. Integration is no panacea either—no policy is.

Yet Latin American governments are persevering with integration, as they cut tariffs and sign regional agreements in spite of the global recession. Those policies are not simply born out of the conviction that open economies have fared better than those that have remained closed. Liberalization of trade and investment is also here to stay by popular demand: No Latin American politicians would want to deny their constituents the imported consumer goods they have become accustomed to, or the much-improved phone service provided by privatized (and often foreign-owned) telecom companies.

So popularly elected Latin American presidents attend World Trade Organization meetings calling for more globalization, not less. They line up for a free trade agreement with the United States as they duck the stones thrown by U.S. and European college students who claim to be acting on behalf of the world's poor. Those Latin American politicians are not naive: They understand that globalization needs safeguards and regulations if it is to benefit the poor. Their position is pragmatic. The evangelical fervor, this time against globalization, once again comes from the North. Little has changed since the early 1980s.

22 Domestic Politics and Trade

22.1

Diplomacy and Domestic Politics

The Logic of Two-Level Games

Robert D. Putnam

Introduction: The Entanglements of Domestic and International Politics

Domestic politics and international relations are often somehow entangled, but our theories have not yet sorted out the puzzling tangle. It is fruitless to debate whether domestic politics really determine international relations, or the reverse. The answer to that question is clearly "Both, sometimes." The more interesting questions are "When?" and "How?" This article offers a theoretical approach to this issue, but I begin with a story that illustrates the puzzle.

One illuminating example of how diplomacy and domestic politics can become entangled culminated at the Bonn summit conference of 1978.[1] In the mid-1970s, a coordinated program of global reflation, led by the "locomotive" economies of the United States, Germany, and Japan, had been proposed to foster Western recovery from the first oil shock.[2] This proposal had received a powerful boost from the incoming Carter administration and was warmly supported by the weaker countries, as well as the Organization for Economic Cooperation and Development (OECD) and many private economists, who argued that it would overcome international payments imbalances and speed growth all around. On the other hand, the Germans and the Japanese protested that prudent and successful economic managers should not be asked to bail out spendthrifts. Meanwhile, Jimmy Carter's ambitious National Energy Program remained deadlocked in Congress, while Helmut Schmidt led a chorus of complaints about the Americans' uncontrolled appetite for imported oil and their apparent unconcern about the falling dollar. All sides conceded that the world economy was in serious trouble, but it was not clear which was more to blame, tight-fisted German and Japanese fiscal policies or slack-jawed U.S. energy and monetary policies.

At the Bonn summit, however, a comprehensive package deal was approved, the clearest case yet of a summit that left all participants happier than when they arrived. Helmut Schmidt agreed to additional fiscal stimulus, amounting to 1 percent of GNP, Jimmy Carter committed himself to decontrol domestic oil prices by the end of 1980, and Takeo Fukuda pledged new efforts to reach a 7 percent growth rate. Secondary elements in the Bonn accord included French and British acquiescence in the Tokyo Round trade negotiations; Japanese undertakings to foster import growth and restrain exports; and a generic American promise

Source: Robert D. Putnam "Diplomacy and Domestic Politics: The Logic of Two-Level Games," *International Organization* 42:3 (Summer 1988), pp. 427–430, 433–442, 445–448, 450, 452, and 456–460.

to fight inflation. All in all, the Bonn summit produced a balanced agreement of unparalleled breadth and specificity. More remarkably, virtually all parts of the package were actually implemented.

Most observers at the time welcomed the policies agreed to at Bonn, although in retrospect there has been much debate about the economic wisdom of this package deal. However, my concern here is not whether the deal was wise economically, but how it became possible politically. My research suggests, first, that the key governments at Bonn adopted policies different from those that they would have pursued in the absence of international negotiations, but second, that agreement was possible only because a powerful minority within each government actually favored on domestic grounds the policy being demanded internationally.

Within Germany, a political process catalyzed by foreign pressures was surreptitiously orchestrated by expansionists inside the Schmidt government. Contrary to the public mythology, the Bonn deal was not forced on a reluctant or "altruistic" Germany. In fact, officials in the Chancellor's Office and the Economics Ministry, as well as in the Social Democratic party and the trade unions, had argued privately in early 1978 that further stimulus was domestically desirable, particularly in view of the approaching 1980 elections. However, they had little hope of overcoming the opposition of the Finance Ministry, the Free Democratic party (part of the government coalition), and the business and banking community, especially the leadership of the *Bundesbank*. Publicly, Helmut Schmidt posed as reluctant to the end. Only his closest advisors suspected the truth: that the chancellor "let himself be pushed" into a policy that he privately favored, but would have found costly and perhaps impossible to enact without the summit's package deal.

Analogously, in Japan a coalition of business interests, the Ministry of Trade and Industry (MITI), the Economic Planning Agency, and some expansion-minded politicians within the Liberal Democratic Party pushed for additional domestic stimulus, using U.S. pressure as one of their prime arguments against the stubborn resistance of the Ministry of Finance (MOF). Without internal divisions in Tokyo, it is unlikely that the foreign demands would have been met, but without the external pressure, it is even more unlikely that the expansionists could have overridden the powerful MOF. "Seventy percent foreign pressure, 30 percent internal politics," was the disgruntled judgment of one MOF insider. "Fifty-fifty," guessed an official from MITI.[3]

In the American case, too, internal politicking reinforced, and was reinforced by, the international pressure. During the summit preparations American negotiators occasionally invited their foreign counterparts to put more pressure on the Americans to reduce oil imports. Key economic officials within the administration favored a tougher energy policy, but they were opposed by the president's closest political aides, even after the summit. Moreover, congressional opponents continued to stymie oil price decontrol, as they had under both Nixon and Ford. Finally, in April 1979, the president decided on gradual administrative decontrol, bringing U.S. prices up to world levels by October 1981. His domestic advisors thus won a postponement of this politically costly move until after the 1980 presidential election, but in the end, virtually every one of the pledges made at Bonn was fulfilled. Both proponents and opponents of decontrol agree that the summit commitment was at the center of the administration's heated intramural debate during the winter of 1978–79 and instrumental in the final decision.[4]

In short, the Bonn accord represented genuine international policy coordination. Significant policy changes were pledged and implemented by the key participants. Moreover—although this counterfactual claim is necessarily harder to establish—those policy changes would very probably not have been pursued (certainly not the same scale and within the same time frame) in the absence of the international agreement. Within each country, one faction supported the policy shift being demanded of its country internationally, but that faction was initially outnumbered. Thus, international pressure was a necessary condition for these policy shifts. On the other hand, without domestic resonance, international forces would not have sufficed to produce the accord, no matter how balanced and intellectually persuasive the overall package. In the end, each leader believed that what he was doing was in his nation's interest—and probably in his own political interest, too, even though not all his aides agreed.[5] Yet without the summit accord he probably would not (or could not) have changed policies so easily.

In that sense, the Bonn deal successfully meshed domestic and international pressures.

Neither a purely domestic nor a purely international analysis could account for this episode. Interpretations cast in terms either of domestic causes and international effects ("Second Image"[6]) or of international causes and domestic effects ("Second Image Reversed"[7]) would represent merely "partial equilibrium" analyses and would miss an important part of the story, namely, how the domestic politics of several countries became entangled via an international negotiation. The events of 1978 illustrate that we must aim instead for "general equilibrium" theories that account simultaneously for the interaction of domestic and international factors. This article suggests a conceptual framework for understanding how diplomacy and domestic politics interact. . . .

Two-Level Games: A Metaphor for Domestic-International Interactions

The politics of many international negotiations can usefully be conceived as a two-level game. At the national level, domestic groups pursue their interests by pressuring the government to adopt favorable policies, and politicians seek power by constructing coalitions among those groups. At the international level, national governments seek to maximize their own ability to satisfy domestic pressures, while minimizing the adverse consequences of foreign developments. Neither of the two games can be ignored by central decision-makers, so long as their countries remain interdependent, yet sovereign.

Each national political leader appears at both game boards. Across the international table sit his foreign counterparts, and at his elbows sit diplomats and other international advisors. Around the domestic table behind him sit party and parliamentary figures, spokespersons for domestic agencies, representatives of key interest groups, and the leader's own political advisors. The unusual complexity of this two-level game is that moves that are rational for a player at one board (such as raising energy prices, conceding territory, or limiting auto imports) may be impolitic for that same player at the other board.

Nevertheless, there are powerful incentives for consistency between the two games. Players (and kibitzers) will tolerate some differences in rhetoric between the two games, but in the end either energy prices rise or they don't.

The political complexities for the players in this two-level game are staggering. Any key player at the international table who is dissatisfied with the outcome may upset the game board, and conversely, any leader who fails to satisfy his fellow players at the domestic table risks being evicted from his seat. On occasion, however, clever players will spot a move on one board that will trigger realignments on other boards, enabling them to achieve otherwise unattainable objectives. This "two-table" metaphor captures the dynamics of the 1978 negotiations better than any model based on unitary national actors. . . .

Towards a Theory of Ratification: The Importance of "Win-Sets"

Consider the following stylized scenario that might apply to any two-level game. Negotiators representing two organizations meet to reach an agreement between them, subject to the constraint that any tentative agreement must be ratified by their respective organizations. The negotiators might be heads of government representing nations, for example, or labor and management representatives, or party leaders in a multiparty coalition, or a finance minister negotiating with an IMF team, or leaders of a House–Senate conference committee, or ethnic-group leaders in a consociational democracy. For the moment, we shall presume that each side is represented by a single leader or "chief negotiator," and that this individual has no independent policy preferences, but seeks simply to achieve an agreement that will be attractive to his constituents.[8]

It is convenient analytically to decompose the process into two stages:

1. bargaining between the negotiators, leading to a tentative agreement; call that Level I.
2. separate discussions within each group of constituents about whether to ratify the agreement; call that Level II.

This sequential decomposition into a negotiation phase and a ratification phase is useful for purposes of exposition, although it is not descriptively accurate. In practice, expectational effects will be quite important. There are likely to be prior consultations and bargaining at Level II to hammer out an initial position for the Level I negotiations. Conversely, the need for Level II ratification is certain to affect the Level I bargaining. In fact, expectations of rejection at Level II may abort negotiations at Level I without any formal action at Level II. In many negotiations, the two-level process may be iterative, as the negotiators try out possible agreements and probe their constituents' views. Nevertheless, the requirement that any Level I agreement must, in the end, be ratified at Level II imposes a crucial theoretical link between the two levels.

"Ratification" may entail a formal voting procedure at Level II, such as the constitutionally required two-thirds vote of the U.S. Senate for ratifying treaties, but I use the term generically to refer to any decision-process at Level II that is required to endorse or implement a Level I agreement, whether formally or informally. It is sometimes convenient to think of ratification as a parliamentary function, but that is not essential. The actors at Level II may represent bureaucratic agencies, interest groups, social classes, or even "public opinion." For example, if labor unions in a debtor country withhold necessary cooperation from an austerity program that the government has negotiated with the IMF, Level II ratification of the agreement may be said to have failed; *ex ante* expectations about that prospect will surely influence the Level I negotiations between the government and the IMF. . . .

Given this set of arrangements, we may define the "win-set" for a given Level II constituency as the set of all possible Level I agreements that would "win"—that is, gain the necessary majority among the constituents—when simply voted up or down.[9] For two quite different reasons, the contours of the Level II win-sets are very important for understanding Level I agreements.

First, **larger win-sets make Level I agreement more likely**, *ceteris paribus*.[10] By definition, any successful agreement must fall within the Level II win-sets of each of the parties to the accord. Thus, agreement is possible only if those win-sets overlap, and the larger each win-set, the more likely they are to overlap. Conversely, the smaller the win-sets, the greater the risk that the negotiations will break down. . . .

The prospects for international cooperation in an anarchic, "self-help" world are often said to be poor because "unfortunately, policy makers generally have an incentive to cheat."[11] However, as Axelrod, Keohane, and others have pointed out, the temptation to defect can be dramatically reduced among players who expect to meet again.[12] If policymakers in an anarchic world were in fact constantly tempted to cheat, certain features of the 1978 story would be very anomalous. For example, even though the Bonn agreement was negotiated with exquisite care, it contained no provisions for temporal balance, sequencing, or partial conditionality that might have protected the parties from unexpected defection. Moreover, the Germans and the Japanese irretrievably enacted their parts of the bargain more than six months before the president's action on oil price decontrol and nearly two years before that decision was implemented. Once they had done so, the temptation to the president to renege should have been overpowering, but in fact virtually no one on either side of the decontrol debate within the administration dismissed the Bonn pledge as irrelevant. In short, the Bonn "promise" had political weight, because reneging would have had high political and diplomatic costs. . . .

Unlike concerns about voluntary defection, concern about "deliverability" was a prominent element in the Bonn negotiations. In the post-summit press conference, President Carter stressed that "each of us has been careful not to promise more than he can deliver." A major issue throughout the negotiations was Carter's own ability to deliver on his energy commitments. The Americans worked hard to convince the others, first, that the president was under severe domestic political constraints on energy issues, which limited what he could promise, but second, that he could deliver what he was prepared to promise. The negotiators in 1978 seemed to follow this presumption about one another: "He will do what he has promised, so long as what he has promised is clear and within his power." . . .

Involuntary defection can only be understood within the framework of a two-level game. Thus, to return to the issue of win-sets, the smaller the win-sets, the greater the risk of involuntary defection, and hence the more applicable the literature about dilemmas of collective action.[13]

The second reason why win-set size is important is that the relative size of the respective Level II win-sets will affect the distribution of the joint gains from the international bargain. The larger the perceived win-set of a negotiator, the more he can be "pushed around" by the other Level I negotiators. Conversely, a small domestic win-set can be a bargaining advantage: "I'd like to accept your proposal, but I could never get it accepted at home." Lamenting the domestic constraints under which one must operate is (in the words of one experienced British diplomat) "the natural thing to say at the beginning of a tough negotiation."[14]

Determinants of the Win-Set

It is important to understand what circumstances affect win-set size. Three sets of factors are especially important:

- Level II preferences and coalitions
- Level II institutions
- Level I negotiators' strategies

Let us consider each in turn.

1. The size of the win-set depends on the distribution of power, preferences, and possible coalitions among Level II constituents

Any testable two-level theory of international negotiation must be rooted in a theory of domestic politics, that is, a theory about the power and preferences of the major actors at Level II. . . .

Thus far we have implicitly assumed that all eligible constituents will participate in the ratification process. In fact, however, participation rates vary across groups and across issues, and this variation often has implications for the size of the win-set. For example, when the costs and/or benefits of a proposed agreement are relatively concentrated, it is reasonable to expect that those constituents whose interests are most affected will exert special influence on the ratification process.[15] One reason why Level II games are more important for trade negotiations than in monetary matters is that the "abstention rate" is higher on international monetary issues than on trade issues.[16] . . .

Another important restriction of our discussion thus far has been the assumption that the negotiations involve only one issue. Relaxing this assumption has powerful consequences for the play at both levels.[17] Various groups at Level II are likely to have quite different preferences on the several issues involved in a multi-issue negotiation. As a general rule, the group with the greatest interest in a specific issue is also likely to hold the most extreme position on that issue.

Thus, the chief negotiator is faced with tradeoffs across different issues: how much to yield on mining rights in order to get sea-lane protection, how much to yield on citrus exports to get a better deal on beef, and so on. . . .

One kind of issue linkage is absolutely crucial to understanding how domestic and international politics can become entangled.[18] Suppose that a majority of constituents at Level II oppose a given policy (say, oil price decontrol), but that some members of that majority would be willing to switch their vote on that issue in return for more jobs (say, in export industries). If bargaining is limited to Level II, that tradeoff is not technically feasible, but if the chief negotiator can broker an international deal that delivers more jobs (say, via faster growth abroad), he can, in effect, overturn the initial outcome at the domestic table. Such a transnational issue linkage was a crucial element in the 1978 Bonn accord.

Note that this strategy works not by changing the preferences of any domestic constituents, but rather by creating a policy option (such as faster export growth) that was previously beyond domestic control. Hence, I refer to this type of issue linkage at Level I that alters the feasible outcomes at Level II as *synergistic linkage*. For example, "in the Tokyo Round . . . nations used negotiation to achieve internal reform in situations where constituency pressures would otherwise prevent action without the pressure (and tradeoff benefits) that an external partner could provide."[19] Economic interdependence multiplies the opportunities for altering domestic coalitions (and thus policy outcomes) by expanding the set of feasible alternatives in this way—in effect, creating political entanglements across national boundaries. Thus, we should expect synergistic linkage (which is, by definition, explicable only in terms of two-level analysis) to become more frequent as interdependence grows.

2. The size of the win-set depends on the Level II political institutions

Ratification procedures clearly affect the size of the win-set. For example, if a two-thirds vote is required for ratification, the win-set will almost certainly be smaller than if only a simple majority is required. As one experienced observer has written: "Under the Constitution, thirty-four of the one hundred senators can block ratification of any treaty. This is an unhappy and unique feature of our democracy. Because of the effective veto power of a small group, many worthy agreements have been rejected, and many treaties are never considered for ratification."[20] As noted earlier, the U.S. separation of powers imposes a tighter constraint on the American win-set than is true in many other countries. This increases the bargaining power of American negotiators, but it also reduces the scope for international cooperation. It raises the odds for involuntary defection and makes potential partners warier about dealing with the Americans.

The Trade Expansion Act of 1974 modified U.S. ratification procedures in an effort to reduce the likelihood of congressional tampering with the final deal and hence to reassure America's negotiating partners. After the American Selling Price fiasco, it was widely recognized that piecemeal congressional ratification of any new agreement would inhibit international negotiation. Hence, the 1974 Act guaranteed a straight up-or-down vote in Congress. However, to satisfy congressional sensitivities, an elaborate system of private-sector committees was established to improve communication between the Level I negotiators and their Level II constituents, in effect co-opting the interest groups by exposing them directly to the implications of their demands.[21] . . .

3. The size of the win-set depends on the strategies of the Level I negotiators

Each Level I negotiator has an unequivocal interest in maximizing the other side's win-set, but with respect to his own win-set, his motives are mixed. The larger his win-set, the more easily he can conclude an agreement, but also the weaker his bargaining position vis-à-vis the other negotiator. This fact often poses a tactical dilemma. For example, one effective way to demonstrate commitment to a given position in Level I bargaining is to rally support from one's constituents (for example, holding a strike vote, talking about a "missile gap," or denouncing "unfair trading practices" abroad). On the other hand, such tactics may have irreversible effects on constituents' attitudes, hampering subsequent ratification of a compromise agreement.[22] Conversely, preliminary consultations at home, aimed at "softening up" one's constituents in anticipation of a ratification struggle, can undercut a negotiator's ability to project an implacable image abroad. . . .

Uncertainty and Bargaining Tactics

Level I negotiators are often badly misinformed about Level II politics, particularly on the opposing side. In 1978, the Bonn negotiators were usually wrong in their assessments of domestic politics abroad; for example, most American officials did not appreciate the complex domestic game that Chancellor Schmidt was playing over the issue of German reflation. Similarly, Snyder and Diesing report that "decision makers in our cases only occasionally attempted such assessments, and when they tried they did pretty miserably. . . . Governments generally do not do well in analyzing each other's internal politics in crises [and, I would add, in normal times], and indeed it is inherently difficult."[23] . . .

The Role of the Chief Negotiator

In the stylized model of two-level negotiations outlined here, the chief negotiator is the only formal link between Level I and Level II. Thus far, I have assumed that the chief negotiator has no independent policy views, but acts merely as an honest broker, or rather as an agent on behalf of his constituents. That assumption powerfully simplifies the analysis of two-level games. However, as principal-agent theory reminds us, this assumption is unrealistic.[24] Empirically, the preferences of the chief negotiator may well diverge from those of his constituents. Two-level negotiations are costly and risky for the chief negotiator, and they often interfere with his other priorities, so it is reasonable to ask what is in it for him.

The motives of the chief negotiator include:

1. Enhancing his standing in the Level II game by increasing his political resources or by minimizing potential losses. For example, a head of government may seek the popularity that he expects to accrue to him if he concludes a successful international agreement, or he may anticipate that the results of the agreement (for example, faster growth or lower defense spending) will be politically rewarding.

2. Shifting the balance of power at Level II in favor of domestic policies that he prefers for exogenous reasons. International negotiations sometimes enable government leaders to do what they privately wish to do, but are powerless to do domestically. Beyond the now-familiar 1978 case, this pattern characterizes many stabilization programs that are (misleadingly) said to be "imposed" by the IMF. For example, in the 1974 and 1977 negotiations between Italy and the IMF, domestic conservative forces exploited IMF pressure to facilitate policy moves that were otherwise infeasible internally.[25]

3. To pursue his own conception of the national interest in the international context. This seems the best explanation of Jimmy Carter's prodigious efforts on behalf of the Panama Canal Treaty, as well as of Woodrow Wilson's ultimately fatal commitment to the Versailles Treaty.

It is reasonable to presume, at least in the international case of two-level bargaining, that the chief negotiator will normally give primacy to his domestic calculus, if a choice must be made, not least because his own incumbency often depends on his standing at Level II. Hence, he is more likely to present an international agreement for ratification, the less of his own political capital he expects to have to invest to win approval, and the greater the likely political returns from a ratified agreement.

This expanded conception of the role of the chief negotiator implies that he has, in effect, a veto over possible agreements. Even if a proposed deal lies within his Level II win-set, that deal is unlikely to be struck if he opposes it.[26] Since this proviso applies on both sides of the Level I table, the actual international bargaining set may be narrower—perhaps much narrower—than the overlap between the Level II win-sets. . . .

Relaxing the assumption that the chief negotiator is merely an honest broker, negotiating on behalf of his constituents, opens the possibility that the constituents may be more eager for an agreement (or more worried about "no-agreement") than he is. . . . However, if the negotiator's own domestic standing (or indeed, his incumbency) would be threatened if he were to reject an agreement that falls within his Level II win-set, and if this is known to all parties, then the other side at Level I gains considerable leverage. Domestic U.S. discontent about the Vietnam War clearly affected the agreement reached at the Paris talks.[27] Conversely, if the constituents are (believed to be) hard-line, then a leader's domestic weakness becomes a diplomatic asset. In 1977, for example, the Americans calculated that "a delay in negotiating a treaty . . . endangered [Panamanian President Omar] Torrijos' position; and Panama without Torrijos most likely would have been an impossible negotiating partner."[28] . . .

My emphasis on the special responsibility of central executives is a point of affinity between the two-level game model and the "state-centric" literature, even though the underlying logic is different. In this "Janus" model of domestic-international interactions, transnational politics are less prominent than in some theories of interdependence.[29] However, to disregard "cross-table" alliances at Level II is a considerable simplification, and it is more misleading, the lower the political visibility of the issue, and the more frequent the negotiations between the governments involved.[30] . . .

Conclusion

The most portentous development in the fields of comparative politics and international relations in recent years is the dawning recognition among practitioners in each field of the need to take into account entanglements between the two. Empirical illustrations of reciprocal influence between domestic and international affairs abound. What we need now are concepts and theories that will help us organize and extend our empirical observations.

Analysis in terms of two-level games offers a promising response to this challenge. Unlike state-centric theories, the two-level approach recognizes the inevitability of domestic conflict about what the "national interest" requires. Unlike the "Second Image" or the "Second Image Reversed," the two-level approach recognizes that central decision-makers strive to reconcile domestic and international imperatives simultaneously. As we have seen, statesmen in this predicament face distinctive strategic opportunities and strategic dilemmas.

This theoretical approach highlights several significant features of the links between diplomacy and domestic politics, including:

- the important distinction between voluntary and involuntary defection from international agreements;
- the contrast between issues on which domestic interests are homogeneous, simply pitting hawks against doves, and issues on which domestic interests are more heterogeneous, so that domestic cleavage may actually foster international cooperation;
- the possibility of synergistic issue linkage, in which strategic moves at one game-table facilitate unexpected coalitions at the second table;
- the paradoxical fact that institutional arrangements which strengthen decision-makers at home may weaken their international bargaining position, and vice versa;
- the importance of targeting international threats, offers, and side-payments with an eye towards their domestic incidence at home and abroad;
- the strategic uses of uncertainty about domestic politics, and the special utility of "kinky win-sets";
- the potential reverberation of international pressures within the domestic arena;
- the divergences of interest between a national leader and those on whose behalf he is negotiating, and in particular, the international implications of his fixed investments in domestic politics.

Two-level games seem a ubiquitous feature of social life, from Western economic summitry to diplomacy in the Balkans and from coalition politics in

Sri Lanka to legislative maneuvering on Capitol Hill. Far-ranging empirical research is needed now to test and deepen our understanding of how such games are played.

Notes

1. The following account is drawn from Robert D. Putnam and C. Randall Henning, "The Bonn Summit of 1978: How Does International Economic Policy Coordination Actually Work?" *Brookings Discussion Papers in International Economics*, no. 53 (Washington, D.C.: Brookings Institution, October 1986), and Robert D. Putnam and Nicholas Bayne, *Hanging Together: Cooperation and Conflict in the Seven-Power Summits*, rev. ed. (Cambridge, Mass.: Harvard University Press, 1987), pp. 62–94.

2. Among interdependent economies, most economists believe, policies can often be more effective if they are internationally coordinated. For relevant citations, see Putnam and Bayne, *Hanging Together*, p. 24.

3. For a comprehensive account of the Japanese story, see I. M. Destler and Hisao Mitsuyu, "Locomotives on Different Tracks: Macroeconomic Diplomacy, 1977–1979," in I. M. Destler and Hideo Sato, eds., *Coping with U.S.—Japanese Economic Conflicts* (Lexington, Mass.: Heath, 1982).

4. For an excellent account of U.S. energy policy during this period, see G. John Ikenberry, "Market Solutions for State Problems: The International and Domestic Politics of American Oil Decontrol," *International Organization* 42 (Winter 1988).

5. It is not clear whether Jimmy Carter fully understood the domestic implications of his Bonn pledge at the time. See Putnam and Henning, "The Bonn Summit," and Ikenberry, "Market Solutions for State Problems."

6. Kenneth N. Waltz, *Man, the State, and War: A Theoretical Analysis* (New York: Columbia University Press, 1959).

7. Peter Gourevitch, "The Second Image Reversed: The International Sources of Domestic Politics," *International Organization* 32 (Autumn 1978), pp. 881–911.

8. To avoid unnecessary complexity, my argument throughout is phrased in terms of a single chief negotiator, although in many cases some of his responsibilities may be delegated to aides. Later in this article I relax the assumption that the negotiator has no independent preferences.

9. For the conception of win-set, see Kenneth A. Shepsle and Barry R. Weingast, "The Institutional Foundations of Committee Power," *American Political Science Review* 81 (March 1987), pp. 85–104. I am indebted to Professor Shepsle for much help on this topic.

10. To avoid tedium, I do not repeat the "other things being equal" proviso in each of the propositions that follow. Under some circumstances an expanded win-set might actually make practicable some outcome that could trigger a dilemma of collective action. See Vincent P. Crawford, "A Theory of Disagreement in Bargaining," *Econometrica* 50 (May 1982), pp. 607–37.

11. Matthew E. Canzoneri and Jo Anna Gray, "Two Essays on Monetary Policy in an Interdependent World," International Finance Discussion Paper 219 (Board of Governors of the Federal Reserve System, February 1983).

12. Robert Axelrod, *The Evolution of Cooperation* (New York: Basic Books, 1984); Robert O. Keohane, *After Hegemony: Cooperation and Discord in the World Political Economy* (Princeton: Princeton University Press, 1984), esp. p. 116; and the special issue of *World Politics*, "Cooperation Under Anarchy," Kenneth A. Oye, ed., vol. 38 (October 1985).

13. This discussion implicitly assumes uncertainty about the contours of the win-sets on the part of the Level I negotiators, for if the win-sets were known with certainty, the negotiators would never propose for ratification an agreement that would be rejected.

14. Geoffrey W. Harrison, in John C. Campbell, ed., *Successful Negotiation: Trieste 1954* (Princeton: Princeton University Press, 1976), p. 62.

15. See James Q. Wilson, *Political Organization* (New York: Basic Books, 1975) on how the politics of an issue are affected by whether the costs and the benefits are concentrated or diffuse.

16. Another factor fostering abstention is the greater complexity and opacity of monetary issues; as Gilbert R. Winham ("Complexity in International Negotiation," in Daniel Druckman, ed., *Negotiations: A Social-Psychological Perspective* [Beverly Hills: Sage, 1977], p. 363) observes, "complexity can strengthen the hand of a negotiator vis-à-vis the organization he represents."

17. I am grateful to Ernst B. Haas and Robert O. Keohane for helpful advice on this point.

18. I am grateful to Henry Brady for clarifying this point for me.

19. Gilbert R. Winham, "The Relevance of Clausewitz to a Theory of International Negotiation," prepared for delivery at the 1987 annual meeting of the American Political Science Association.

20. Jimmy Carter, *Keeping Faith: Memoirs of a President* (New York: Bantam Books, 1982), p. 225.

21. Winham (see note 37); Twiggs, *The Tokyo Round.*

22. Walton and McKersie, Behavioral Theory of Labor Organizations, p. 345.

23. Snyder and Diesing, *Conflict Among Nations*, pp. 516, 522–23. Analogous misperceptions in Anglo-American diplomacy are the focus of Richard E. Neustadt, *Alliance Politics* (New York: Columbia University Press, 1970).

24. For overviews of this literature, see Terry M. Moe, "The New Economics of Organization," *American Journal of Political Science* 28 (November 1984), pp. 739–77; John W. Pratt

and Richard J. Zeckhauser, eds., *Principals and Agents: The Structure of Business* (Boston, Mass.: Harvard Business School Press, 1985); and Barry M. Mitnick, "The Theory of Agency and Organizational Analysis," prepared for delivery at the 1986 annual meeting of the American Political Science Association. This literature is only indirectly relevant to our concerns here, for it has not yet adequately addressed the problems posed by multiple principals (or constituents, in our terms). For one highly formal approach to the problem of multiple principals, see R. Douglas Bernheim and Michael D. Whinston, "Common Agency," *Econometrica* 54 (July 1986), pp. 923–42.

25. Hillman, "Mutual Influence," and Spaventa, "Two Letters of Intent."

26. This power of the chief negotiator is analogous to what Shepsle and Weingast term the "penultimate" or "ex post veto" power of the members of a Senate-House conference committee. (Shepsle and Weingast, "Institutional Foundations of Committee Power.")

27. William Zartman, "Reality, Image, and Detail: The Paris Negotiations, 1969–1973," in Zartman, *50% Solution*, pp. 372–98.

28. Zbigniew Brzezinski, *Power and Principle* (New York: Farrar, Straus and Giroux, 1983), p. 136, as quoted in Habeeb and Zartman, *Panama Canal Negotiations*, pp. 39–40.

29. Samuel P. Huntington, "Transnational Organizations in World Politics," *World Politics* 25 (April 1973), pp. 333–68; Keohane and Nye, *Power and Interdependence*; Neustadt, *Alliance Politics*.

30. Barbara Crane, "Policy Coordination by Major Western Powers in Bargaining with the Third World: Debt Relief and the Common Fund," *International Organization* 38 (Summer 1984), pp. 399–428.

22.2

Why Changing Exposure to Trade Should Affect Political Cleavages

Ronald Rogowski

The Stolper-Samuelson Theorem

In 1941, Wolfgang Stolper and Paul Samuelson solved conclusively the old riddle of gains and losses from protection (or, for that matter, from free trade).[1] In almost[2] any society, they showed, protection benefits (and liberalization of trade harms) owners of factors in which, relative to the rest of the world, that society is *poorly* endowed, as well as producers who use that scarce factor intensively.[3] Conversely, protection harms (and liberalization benefits) those factors that—again, relative to the rest of the world—the given society holds *abundantly*, and the producers who use those locally abundant factors intensively.[4] Thus, in a society rich in labor but poor in capital, protection benefits capital and harms labor; and liberalization of trade benefits labor and harms capital.[5]

So far, the theorem is what it is usually perceived to be, merely a statement, albeit an important and sweeping one,[6] about the effects of tariff policy. The picture is altered, however, when one realizes that *exogenous* changes can have exactly the same effects as increases or decreases in protection. A cheapening of transport costs, for example, is indistinguishable in its impact from an across-the-board decrease in every affected state's tariffs;[7] so is any change in the international regime that decreases the risks or the transaction costs of trade. The converse is of course equally true: when a nation's external transport becomes dearer or its trade less secure, it is affected exactly as if it had imposed a higher tariff.

The point is of more than academic interest because we know, historically, that major changes in the risks and costs of international trade have occurred: notoriously, the railroads and steamships of the nineteenth century brought drastically cheaper transportation; so, in their day, did the improvements in shipbuilding and navigation of the fifteenth and sixteenth centuries; and so, in our own generation, have supertankers, cheap oil, and containerization.[8] . . .

Global changes of these kinds, it follows, should have had global consequences. The "transportation revolutions" of the sixteenth, the nineteenth, and scarcely less of the mid-twentieth century must have benefited in each affected country owners and intensive employers of locally abundant factors and must have harmed owners and intensive employers of locally scarce factors. The events of the 1930s should have had exactly the opposite effect. What, however, will have been the *political* consequences of those shifts of wealth and income? To answer that question, we require a rudimentary model of the political process and a somewhat more definite one of the economy.

Simple Models of the Polity and the Economy

Concerning domestic political processes, I shall make only three assumptions: that the beneficiaries of a change will try to continue and accelerate it, while the victims of the same change will endeavor to retard or halt it; that those who enjoy a sudden increase in wealth and income will thereby be enabled to expand their political influence as well (cf. Becker 1983); and that, as the desire and the means for a particular political preference increase, the likelihood grows that political entrepreneurs will devise mechanisms that can surmount the obstacles to collective action.[9]

For our present concerns, the first assumption implies that the beneficiaries of safer or cheaper trade will support yet greater openness, while gainers from dearer or riskier trade will pursue even greater self-sufficiency. Conversely, those who are harmed by easier trade will demand protection or imperialism;[10] and the victims of exogenously induced constrictions of trade will seek offsetting reductions in barriers. More important, the second assumption implies that the beneficiaries, potential or actual, of any such

Figure 22.1 Four Main Types of Factor Endowments

	Land-Labor Ratio: High	Land-Labor Ratio: Low
Economy Advanced	ABUNDANT: Capital, Land SCARCE: Labor	ABUNDANT: Capital, Labor SCARCE: Land
Economy Backward	ABUNDANT: Land SCARCE: Capital, Labor	ABUNDANT: Labor SCARCE: Capital, Land

exogenous change will be strengthened politically (although they may still lose); the economic losers will be weakened politically as well. The third assumption gives us reason to think that the resultant pressures will not remain invisible but will actually be brought to bear in the political arena.

The issue of potential benefits is an important one, and a familiar example may help to illuminate it. In both great wars of this century, belligerent governments have faced an intensified demand for industrial labor and, because of the military's need for manpower, a reduced supply. That situation has positioned workers—and, in the U.S. case, such traditionally disadvantaged workers as blacks and women—to demand greatly increased compensation: these groups, in short, have had large *potential* gains. Naturally, governments and employers have endeavored to deny them those gains; but in many cases—Germany in World War I, the United States in World War II, Britain in both world wars—the lure of sharing in the potential gains has induced trade union leaders, and workers themselves, to organize and demand more.[11] Similarly, when transportation costs fall, governments may at first partially offset the effect by imposing protection. Owners of abundant factors nonetheless still have substantial *potential* gains from trade, which they may mortgage, or on which others may speculate, to pressure policy toward lower levels of protection.

So much for politics. As regards the economic aspect, I propose to adopt with minor refinements the traditional three-factor model—land, labor, and capital—and to assume, for now, that the land-labor ratio informs us fully about any country's endowment of those two factors. (I shall presently relax this assumption, but it is useful at this stage of the exposition.) No country, in other words, can be rich in both land and labor: a high land-labor ratio implies abundance of land and scarcity of labor; a low ratio signifies the opposite. Finally, I shall simply define an *advanced* economy as one in which capital[12] is abundant.

This model of factor endowments inevitably oversimplifies reality and will require amendment. Its present starkness, however, permits us in theory to place any country's economy into one of four cells (see Figure 22.1), according to whether it is advanced or backward and whether its land-labor ratio is high or low. We recognize, in other words, only economies that are: (1) capital rich, land rich, and labor poor; (2) capital rich, land poor, and labor rich; (3) capital poor, land rich, and labor poor; or (4) capital poor, land poor, and labor rich.

Political Effects of Expanding Trade

The Stolper-Samuelson theorem, applied to our simple model, implies that increasing exposure to trade must result in *urban-rural conflict* in two kinds of economies, and in *class conflict* in the two others. Consider first the upper right-hand cell of Figure 22.1: the advanced (therefore capital-rich) economy endowed abundantly in labor but poorly in land. Expanding trade must benefit both capitalists and workers; it harms only landowners and the pastoral and agricultural enterprises that use land intensively. Both capitalists and workers—which is to say, almost the entire urban sector—should favor free trade; agriculture should on the whole be protectionist.[13] Moreover, we expect the capitalists and the workers to try, very likely in concert, to expand their political influence. Depending on preexisting circumstances, they may seek concretely an extension of the franchise, a reapportionment of seats, a diminution in the powers of an upper house or of a gentry-based political elite, or a violent "bourgeois" revolution.

Urban-rural conflict should also arise in backward, land-rich economies (the lower left-hand cell of Figure 22.1) when trade expands, albeit with a complete reversal of fronts. In such "frontier" societies, both capital and labor are scarce; hence both are harmed by expanding trade and, normally, will seek protection. Only land is abundant, and therefore only agriculture will gain from free trade. Farmers and pastoralists will try to expand their influence in some movement of a "populist" and antiurban stripe.

Conversely, in backward economics with low land-labor ratios (the lower right-hand cell of Figure 22.1), land and capital are scarce and labor is abundant. The model therefore predicts *class conflict*: labor will pursue free trade and expanded political power (including, in some circumstances, a workers' revolution);[14] landowners, capitalists, and capital-intensive industrialists will unite to support protection, imperialism, and a politics of continued exclusion.[15]

The reverse form of class conflict is expected to arise in the final case, that of the advanced but land-rich economy (the upper left-hand cell of Figure 22.1) under increasing exposure to trade. Because both capital and land are abundant, capitalists, capital-intensive industries, and agriculture will all benefit from, and will endorse, free trade; labor being scarce, workers and labor-intensive industries will resist, normally embracing protection and (if need be) imperialism. The benefited sectors will seek to expand their political power, if not by disfranchisement then by curtailment of workers' economic prerogatives and suppression of their organizations.

These implications of the theory of international trade (summarized in Figure 22.2) seem clear, but do they in any way describe reality? For now it is worth observing how closely the experience of three major countries—Germany, Britain, and the United States[16]—conforms to this analysis in the period of rapidly expanding trade in the last third of the nineteenth century; and how far it can go to explain otherwise puzzling disparities in those states' patterns of political evolution.

Germany and the United States were both relatively backward (i.e., capital-poor) societies: both imported considerable amounts of capital in this period, and neither had until late in the century anything like the per capita industrial capacity of the United Kingdom or Belgium.[17] Germany, however, was rich in labor and poor in land; the United States, of course, was in exactly the opposite position. (Again, we observe that the United States imported, and Germany exported—not least to the United States—workers, which is not surprising since, at mid-century, Prussia's labor-land ratio was fifteen times that of the United States.)[18]

The theory predicts class conflict in Germany, with labor the "revolutionary" and free-trading element, and with land and capital united in support of protection and imperialism. Surely this description will not ring false to any student of German socialism or of Germany's infamous "marriage of iron and rye."[19] For the United States, conversely, the theory predicts—quite accurately, I submit—urban-rural conflict, with the agrarians now assuming the "revolutionary" and free-trading role; capital and labor unite in a protectionist and imperialist coalition. Neither E. E. Schattschneider nor Walter Dean Burnham could have described more succinctly the history of the Populist movement or of the election of 1896.[20]

Figure 22.2 Predicted Effects of Expanding Exposure to Trade

	Land-Labor Ratio: High	Land-Labor Ratio: Low
Economy Advanced	CLASS CLEAVAGE: Land and Capital free-trading, assertive, Labor defensive, protectionist	URBAN-RURAL CLEAVAGE: Capital and Labor free-trading, assertive; Land defensive, protectionist Radicalism
Economy Backward	URBAN-RURAL CLEAVAGE: Land free-trading, assertive; Labor and Capital defensive, protectionist U.S. Populism	CLASS CLEAVAGE: Labor free-trading, assertive; Land and Capital defensive, protectionist Socialism

Britain, on the other hand, was already an advanced economy in the nineteenth century. Its per capita industrial output far exceeded that of any other nation, and it exported capital in vast quantities.[21] That it was also rich in labor is suggested by its extensive exports of that factor to the United States, Canada, Australia, New Zealand, and Africa; in fact, Britain's labor-land ratio then exceeded Japan's by 50 percent and was over thirty times that of the United States.[22] Britain therefore falls into the upper right-hand quadrant of Figure 22.1 and is predicted to exhibit a rural-urban cleavage whose fronts are opposite those found in the United States capitalists and labor unite in support of free trade and in demands for expanded political power, while landowners and agriculture support protection and imperialism.

Although this picture surely obscures important nuances, it illuminates crucial differences between, for example, British and German political development in this period. In Britain, capitalists and labor united in the Liberal party and forced an expanded suffrage and curtailment of (still principally land-owning) aristocratic power. In Germany, liberalism shattered,[23] the suffrage at the crucial level of the individual states was actually contracted, and—far from eroding aristocratic power—the bourgeoisie grew more and more *verjunkert* in style and aspirations.

Political Effects of Declining Trade

When rising costs or declining security substantially increases the risks or costs of external trade, the gainers and losers in each situation are simply the reverse of those under increasing exposure to trade. Let us first consider the situation of the highly developed (and therefore by definition capital-rich) economies.

In an advanced economy with a high land-labor ratio (the upper left-hand cell of Figure 22.1), we should expect intense *class conflict* precipitated by a newly aggressive working class. Land and capital are both abundant in such an economy; hence, under declining trade owners of both factors (and producers who use either factor intensively) lose. Moreover, they can resort to no such simple remedy as protection or imperialism. Labor being the only scarce resource, workers and labor-intensive industries are well positioned to reap a significant windfall from the "protection" that dearer or riskier trade affords; and, according to our earlier assumption, like any other benefited class they will soon endeavor to parlay their greater economic power into greater political power. Capitalists and landowners, even if they were previously at odds, will unite to oppose labor's demands.

Quite to the contrary, declining trade in an advanced economy that is labor rich and land poor (the upper right-hand cell of Figure 22.1) will entail renewed *urban-rural* conflict. Capital and labor are both abundant, and both are harmed by the contraction of external trade. Agriculture, as the intense exploiter of the only scarce factor, gains significantly and quickly tries to translate its gain into greater political control.

Urban-rural conflict is also predicted for backward, land-rich countries under declining trade; but here agriculture is on the defensive. Labor and capital being both scarce, both benefit from the contraction of trade; land, as the only locally abundant factor, is threatened.

Figure 22.3 Predicted Effects of Declining Exposure to Trade

	Land-Labor Ratio: High	Land-Labor Ratio: Low
Economy Advanced	CLASS CLEAVAGE: Labor assertive, Land and Capital defensive U.S. New Deal	URBAN-RURAL CLEAVAGE: Land assertive, Labor and Capital defensive W. European Fascism
Economy Backward	URBAN-RURAL CLEAVAGE: Labor and Capital assertive, Land defensive South American Populism	CLASS CLEAVAGE: Land and Capital assertive, Labor defensive Asian & East European Fascism

The urban sectors unite, in a parallel to the "radical" coalition of labor-rich developed countries under expanding trade discussed previously, to demand an increased voice in the state.

Finally, in backward economies rich in labor rather than land, class conflict resumes, with labor this time on the defensive. Capital and land, as the locally scarce factors, gain from declining trade; labor, locally abundant, suffers economic reverses and is soon threatened politically.

Observe again, as a first test of the plausibility of these results—summarized in Figure 22.3—how they appear to account for some prominent disparities of political response to the last precipitous decline of international trade, the depression of the 1930s.[24] The U.S. New Deal represented a sharp turn to the left and occasioned a significant increase in organized labor's political power. In Germany, a depression of similar depth (gauged by unemployment rates and declines in industrial production)[25] brought to power first Hindenburg's and then Hitler's dictatorship. Landowners exercised markedly greater influence than they had under Weimar;[26] and indeed a credible case can be made that the rural sector was the principal early beneficiary of the early Nazi regime.[27] Yet this is exactly the broad difference that the model would lead us to anticipate, if we accept that by 1930 both countries were economically advanced—although Germany, after physical reparations and cessions of industrial regions, was surely less rich in capital than the United

States—but the United States held land abundantly, which in Germany was scarce (respectively, the left- and right-hand cells of the upper half of Figure 22.3). Only an obtuse observer would claim that such factors as cultural inheritance and recent defeat in war played no role; but surely it is also important to recognize the sectoral impact of declining trade in the two societies.[28]

As regards the less developed economies of the time, it may be profitable to contrast the depression's impact on such South American cases as Argentina and Brazil with its effects in the leading Asian country, Japan. In Argentina and Brazil, it is usually asserted, the depression gave rise to, or at the least strengthened, "populist" coalitions that united labor and the urban middle classes in opposition to traditional, landowning elites.[29] In Japan, growing military influence suppressed representative institutions and nascent workers' organizations, ruling in the immediate interest—if hardly under the domination—of landowners and capitalists.[30] (Similar suppressions of labor occurred in China and Vietnam.)[31] In considering these contrasting responses, should we not take into account that Argentina and Brazil were rich in land and poor in labor, while in Japan (and, with local exceptions, in Asia generally) labor was abundant and land was scarce? . . .

Conclusion

It is essential to recall what I am *not* claiming to do in this volume. I do not contend that changes in countries' exposure to trade explain all, or even most, of their varying patterns of political cleavage. It would be foolish to ignore the importance of ancient cultural and religious loyalties, of wars and migrations, or of such historical memories as the French Revolution and the *Kulturkampf.* Other cleavages antedate, and persist through, the ones I discuss here, shaping, crosscutting, complicating, and indeed sometimes dominating their political resolution. . . .

In the main, I am presenting here a theoretical puzzle, a kind of social-scientific "thought experiment" . . . : a teasing out of unexpected, and sometimes counter-intuitive, implications of theories already widely accepted. For the Stolper-Samuelson theorem *is* generally, indeed almost universally, embraced; yet, coupled with a stark and unexceptionable model of the political realm, it plainly implies that changes in exposure to trade must profoundly affect nations' internal political cleavages. Do they do so? If they do not, what conclusions shall we draw, either about our theories of international trade, or about our understanding of politics?

Notes

1. I briefly discuss two partially dissenting perspectives, conventionally labeled the "specific-factors model" and the "Leontieff paradox," later in this chapter.

2. The principal exceptions are economies that specialize to the extent of abandoning, instead of merely reducing, production of goods in which they lack comparative advantage (Stolper and Samuelson 1941, 70–71). An example would be a society that ceased all agricultural production.

3. In fact, the effect flows backward from products and is an extension of the Heckscher-Ohlin theorem: under free trade, countries export those products whose manufacture uses intensively their abundant factors, and import ones that employ intensively factors in which they are poorly endowed. Stolper and Samuelson 1941, 65–66; cf. Leamer 1984, esp. 8–10.

4. Admittedly, these results depend on simplifying assumptions that are never achieved in the real world, among them perfect mobility of factors within national boundaries and a world of only two factors (Stolper and Samuelson 1941, 72). Still, as an approximation to reality, they remain highly serviceable. On the specific issue of extension of the theorem to cases of more than two factors—where, in essence, it continues to hold as a correlation rather than a certainty—see Ethier 1984, esp. 63–64 and 181.

5. To dispel a misunderstanding that occasionally arises: these effects befall both the country that imposes protection *and* its trading partners—i.e., they flow simply from the constriction of trade. Hence any retaliatory tariffs from other countries will only magnify the benefit to scare, and the harm to abundant, factors. Cf. Magee 1978, 149.

6. Especially for those of us who may have received from our textbooks a more restrictive impression of the theorem's import, it is essential to emphasize how sweeping the original statement was—and, indeed, to reread the original essay. It does not describe only the effect of particular kinds of protection (e.g., of industrial goods), but of blanket protection of precisely the kind that is analogous to a shift in the costs or risks of trade.

7. See, e.g., Mundell 1957, 330.

8. Landes 1969, 153–54, 196, and 201–2; Hobsbawm 1975, chap. 3; Cipolla 1965; Rosecrance 1986, 142.

9. Olson 1968; Frohlich, Oppenheimer, and Young 1971.

10. Countries that lack essential resources can only beggar themselves by protection. Ultimately, those threatened by trade in such a society must advocate conquest of the missing resources, as indeed occurred in Japan and Germany in the 1930s. It should be self-evident, however, that not all imperialisms originate in this way: those of ancient Rome, and of nineteenth-century Britain, aimed to expand trade. Doyle 1986, chaps. 4 and 11.

11. In the United States and Britain, union membership as a share of total work force increased dramatically in wartime; in Germany, unions simply asserted and won a larger share in the formulation of policy. In general, strike rates rose after an initial decline. Bain and Price 1980, 37–88; Stein 1980, 47–51; Feldman 1966, esp. 116–35.

12. The capital may be either human or physical, but—as political scientists must sometimes be reminded—it must be distinguished from mere wealth. Capital is productive investment, not cash. For example, Kuwait has the per capita income and wealth but not the endowments of physical or human capital of European or North American economies.

13. Trade may, however, not emerge as the dominant issue, or even as an explicit one. To take only two examples: in small states, protection may seem so suicidal, and imperialism so ludicrous, that neither gains serious advocates (Katzenstein, 1985); or the parasitism of traditional elites may appear as the immediate obstacle, even while expanding trade has made rebellion desirable and possible.

14. In such an economy, much of the labor may well be rural; and its aims will often include a land reform—i.e., a change of ownership structure—that can institute a more efficient (more labor-intensive) mix of factors and a more export-oriented production. The case of land reform and olive cultivation in ancient Greece ([Rogowski, 1990,] chapter 5) is startlingly instructive. The larger issues of ownership and property rights are discussed later in the present chapter.

15. Lest the picture of a popular rising in support of freer markets seem too improbable a priori, I observe at once its general conformity with Popkin's (1979) astute interpretation of the Vietnamese revolution.

16. A fuller treatment of these cases is presented in chapter two.

17. Feis 1965, 24–25 and chap. 3. Nowadays, of course, governments' fiscal and monetary policies can drastically affect flows of capital: the United States' massive imports of capital under Reagan do not imply—not yet, at least—that capital has become scarce in America. In the nineteenth century, when almost all governments adhered to the gold standard, these flows tended much more to reflect real disparities of endowment. For evidence on per capita levels of industrialization, see chapter 2.

18. Between 1871 and 1890, just under two million Germans emigrated to points outside Europe; over the same period, some seven million immigrants entered the United States. For labor-land ratios at midcentury, see Table 2.4. Migration may of course occur for reasons quite other than local scarcity or abundance, notably to escape political persecution; yet in these years the economic motive seems to have predominated. See for example Hobsbawm 1979, chap. 11.

19. The Stolper-Samuelson analysis also helps to clear up what had seemed even to the perspicacious Gerschenkron (1943, 26–27) an insoluble riddle: why the *smallholding* German peasants had quickly become as protectionist as the *Junker*. Not only landowners, we now see, but all enterprises that *used land intensively*, will have been harmed by free trade. On the other hand—and later the distinction will become crucial—agricultural *wage-labor* should have been free-trading. See further discussion in [Rogowski 1990,] chapter 2.

20. Schattschneider 1960, 78–85; Burnham 1970, esp. 53–54. That the farmers of the Great Plains were hardly prospering is no refutation of the analysis advanced here. Their *potential* gains were great (as noted previously), and their suffering could plausibly be attributed not to expanded trade but to the obstacles or exploitation laid upon that trade by other sectors. As in Marxist analysis, the older relations of production and of rule could be seen as "fetters."

21. Feis 1965, chap. 1; and my discussion in [Rogowski 1990,] chapter 2.

22. Emigrants from the United Kingdom to areas outside Europe totaled 5.1 million between 1871 and 1890 (Mitchell 1978, table A-5). For labor-land ratios, see [Rogowski 1990,] Table 2.4.

23. Sheehan 1978.

24. This discussion prefigures the more complete one of [Rogowski 1990,] chapter 3.

25. Landes 1969, 391.

26. Gessner 1977; Abraham 1981, 85–115 and chap. 4.

27. See, inter alia, Holt 1936, 173–74 and 194ff.; Gerschenkron 1943, 154–63; Schoenbaum 1967, 156–63; and Gies 1968. Certainly peasants and landowners had been among National Socialism's earliest and strongest supporters: virtually every study of late Weimar voting patterns (e.g., Lipset 1960, 138–48, and sources there cited; Brown 1982; Childers 1983) has found a large rural-urban difference, controlling for such other variables as religion and class, in support for National Socialism.

28. Some historians have recognized the sectoral impact of declining trade in Weimar's final convulsions; the controversial essay of Abraham (1981) is only the best-known example. They may, however, have exaggerated agriculture's woes: see Holt 1936 and Rogowski 1982.

29. Skidmore and Smith 1984, 59–60; Sunkel with Paz, 1973, 352–54; Cardoso and Faletto 1979, 124–26 and chap. 5. In Argentina, of course, the populist regime of Perón did not assume full power until 1946; but the cleavage (and the growing strength of the labor-bourgeois forces) was evident from the early 1930s.

30. Reischauer 1974, 186–87 and 195–99; Kato 1974.

31. Clubb 1972, 135–40; Popkin 1979, xix and 215.

22.3

Votes and Vetoes

The Political Determinants of Commercial Openness

Witold J. Henisz and Edward D. Mansfield

. . . In this article, we analyze the domestic determinants of commercial openness for democracies and non-democracies at all stages of economic development. Our core argument is that while interest group demands and institutions are often regarded as having independent and competing effects, it is more fruitful to view the influence of each type of factor as conditional on the other. More specifically, as explanations emphasizing societal interests contend, deteriorating macroeconomic conditions are a potent source of protectionist sentiment. The extent to which such conditions reduce commercial openness, however, depends centrally on the domestic political institutions through which interest group pressures must filter to influence policy.

Two institutional features stand out in this regard. First, countries vary substantially in the degree to which authority is concentrated within the government. In states marked by greater fragmentation of authority and more "veto points," it is harder to change existing policies because any number of actors can block such a change. Consequently, we expect the effects of macroeconomic conditions on trade policy to be weaker in fragmented states (i.e., those with more veto points) than in those characterized by a highly centralized government (i.e., those with fewer veto points).[1] Second, we expect both fragmentation and interest group pressures stemming from the economy to have a more potent impact on commercial openness in democracies than in other regimes. The electoral constraints facing democratic leaders force them to respond to demands made by key segments of society. While autocrats can more easily change policy than democratic leaders, regardless of how concentrated authority is in a democracy, autocrats depend on a narrower set of groups for political power than their democratic counterparts. This set of groups is less likely to base their political support on broad macroeconomic conditions than on whether they benefit from the government's economic policy, regardless of the economy's overall performance.

Taken as a whole, we therefore expect deteriorating macroeconomic conditions to impede commercial openness, but the effect of these conditions is likely to hinge on the extent of institutional fragmentation. Equally, we expect macroeconomic factors to have a more pronounced influence on trade policy in democracies than in other countries. The results of our statistical tests—covering almost 60 countries during the period from 1980 to 2000—strongly support these arguments.

Societal Interests and Trade Policy

Various studies emphasize how interest groups affect trade policy by exerting political pressure on public officials.[2] These studies generally view domestic institutions and policy makers as passive actors that supply the trade policies demanded by the most influential groups in society (Ikenberry, Lake, and Mastanduno 1988). Societal demands for protection are frequently inferred from macroeconomic conditions. . . .

Central to this literature is the argument that public officials must respond to demands made by broad segments of the populace in order to ensure their political survival. There is considerable evidence that voters pay attention to overall macroeconomic conditions as well as their own economic circumstances when casting ballots (Kinder and Kiewiet 1981; Lewis Beck 1988; Colton 2000). Furthermore, survey research indicates that public support for protectionism rises as domestic economic conditions degrade (Shapiro and Page 1994). Government officials therefore have reason to raise trade barriers when these conditions worsen in an effort to bolster their prospects of retaining office.

It is widely argued that, among the macroeconomic determinants of trade policy, unemployment is crucial. In fact, as Bergsten and Cline (1983:77) point out,

Source: Witold J. Henisz and Edward D. Mansfield. "Votes and Vetoes: The Political Determinants of Commercial Openness," in *International Studies Quarterly* 50: 189–193 and 208–209.

"conventional wisdom suggests that high levels of unemployment are the single most important source of protectionist pressures." . . .

High levels of unemployment are expected to generate calls for protectionism by making it more difficult for workers to adjust to increases in imports. . . . (Bradford 2003). So do firms that depend on consumption by these workers. High levels of unemployment stimulate workers, investors, and other interest groups adversely affected by open trade to overcome collective action problems and mobilize to press for policies that reduce openness (Olson 1983). . . .

Veto Points and Trade Policy

Approaches that stress the importance of interest groups in shaping trade policy usually give short shrift to the domestic political institutions that filter demands made by these groups and set policy. Crucial in this regard are the extent of fragmentation within a country's government and its regime type (Garrett and Lange 1996).

The fragmentation of power within a government depends on the number of independent partisan and institutional actors whose agreement is necessary to make policy. These actors include competing branches of government and coalitions within a given branch. As the number of independent actors with such veto power—or veto points—increases, groups in society have greater difficulty pressing for a change in policy (Henisz 2000; Tsebelis 2003).

In the trade policy arena, any actor with the authority to set policy understands that the final outcome must lie within a range of policies that satisfies all veto points. To the extent that the preferences of actors with veto power differ, institutional structures with more veto points limit the range of feasible trade policy choices. As a result, "the potential for policy change decreases with the number of veto players, the lack of congruence (dissimilarity of policy positions among veto players), and the cohesion (similarity of policy positions among the constituent units of each veto player) of these players" (Tsebelis 1995:289). . . .

In a similar vein, we argue that governments will be less responsive to societal pressures as the number of veto points rises in policy making structures (Frieden and Rogowski 1996:43; Garrett and Lange 1996:66). More specifically, we expect that a high level of unemployment will stimulate interest group demands for policies to decrease unemployment at the cost of more expensive imports, including reductions in commercial openness. However, we also expect that more fragmented policy making structures will reduce the sensitivity of government actors to such societal pressures. When a large number of veto points exists, there is more likely to be an actor in control of a veto point who is hostile to raising trade barriers and who can use this control to frustrate societal demands for protection. As the number of veto points declines, it becomes easier to change the existing trade regime as the actors controlling veto points are more likely to have relatively homogeneous interests (Henisz 2000). We therefore anticipate that adverse macroeconomic conditions will stimulate a larger decline in external trade linkages as countries become more institutionally centralized. . . .

Regime Type and Trade Policy

Our analysis adds to the burgeoning literature on the political economy of foreign trade by addressing the combined effects of interest group pressures generated by macroeconomic conditions and institutional fragmentation on political actors' incentives and ability to change trade policy. Of course, the need for leaders to respond to such pressures differs markedly depending on whether the populace is able to monitor their behavior and penalize them for being unresponsive. In democracies, the populace is able to do so. Indeed, the hallmark of democracy is the existence of regular, open, and fair elections involving candidates who compete for the votes of a large portion of the adult population (e.g., Schumpeter 1942; Huntington 1991:5 13; Przeworski et al. 2000). Furthermore, a free press and the relatively free flow of information about governmental activities keep constituents apprised of changes in foreign economic policy and leaders' behavior. If democratic leaders do not take overt steps to cushion the effects of macroeconomic downturns—by increasing trade barriers among other measures—they face audience costs, including the prospect of being turned out of office by voters.

Non-democratic governments, by contrast, are less susceptible to broad based societal demands. The absence of electoral pressures and checks on their power by an independent and representative legislature give non-democratic leaders less incentive to respond to demands for protection arising from higher levels of unemployment than their democratic counterparts. Like democratic leaders, autocrats rely on the support of various interest groups to maintain power. However, the segment of society to which an autocrat must appeal to retain office is typically much narrower and therefore less motivated by aggregate macroeconomic conditions than in a democracy. Instead, an autocrat's key constituents tend to focus greater attention on how resources are distributed within society and their share of these resources than on national economic performance. Autocrats, therefore, should be relatively insensitive to the societal pressures generated by adverse macroeconomic conditions (Frieden and Rogowski 1996; Garrett and Lange 1996; Wintrobe 1998; Brooker 2000; Acemoglu and Robinson 2005).

In sum, then, we expect commercial openness to dip as the level of unemployment rises, and we anticipate that the influence of unemployment will grow larger as the number of veto points declines. In addition, while democracies are generally marked by a higher number of veto points than non-democracies, we expect the impact of unemployment and veto points to be more pronounced in democratic regimes.[3]

Conclusions

The remarkable expansion of global trade since World War II has stimulated a large and important literature, much of which stresses the effects of domestic politics on trade policy. This literature, however, has miscast certain aspects of the domestic determinants of trade policy. Whereas interest groups and political institutions are usually viewed as having independent and competing influences, these factors actually have an interactive effect on trade policy. Deteriorating macroeconomic conditions give rise to societal demands for protectionism. But the extent to which these demands are met and barriers to trade are put in place depends on the domestic institutions through which interest group pressures are filtered.

Various studies have raised the possibility that the interaction between societal demands and institutions is central to shaping trade policy, but remarkably little empirical research has directly confronted this possibility (Mansfield and Busch 1995; Garrett and Lange 1996; Gilligan 1997; Milner 1997; Grossman and Help man 2002). Our findings indicate that the effects of unemployment depend heavily on the number of veto points that constrain decision makers and whether a country is democratic or not. High unemployment leads to protectionist trade policies in stable democracies marked by few veto points. As expected, however, the magnitude of this relationship becomes attenuated as the number of veto points rises, making it more difficult to change the existing trade regime and increasing the heterogeneity of the points' interests. Equally, macroeconomic fluctuations have a much more pronounced influence on the trade regime in stable democracies than other countries, reflecting the need for democratic leaders to be more responsive to demands made by the general population than in other countries.

Our results also bear heavily on recent debates about the relationship between regime type and economic reform. Virtually all of the literature on this topic ignores the effects of institutional variations within both democracies and non-democracies alike. Such variations, however, are crucial to explaining changes in trade policy, especially in democracies. Holding macroeconomic conditions constant, the trade regime changes less within democracies as the number of veto points increases. Furthermore, societal calls for protectionism precipitated by adverse macroeconomic conditions are increasingly likely to be met as the number of veto points declines. Equally, a thriving economy—marked by very low levels of unemployment—creates a substantial constituency for expanding commercial openness. Such an expansion is most likely to occur in countries with few veto points. Not only do these results indicate that regime type is just one of the institutional influences on trade policy, they also point to the importance of veto points, a factor that has been underemphasized in existing studies of trade policy.

Similarly, we find that within democracies, changes in import penetration are more likely to occur as the number of veto points declines. However, whether such changes lead to greater protection or liberalization hinges on the demands being issued by interest groups. When the economy is faltering, giving rise to calls for protection, a small number of veto points tends to promote greater closure; when the economy is flourishing, a small number of these points foster greater openness. Our results offer important qualifications to studies of foreign economic policy that make unconditional comparisons between either domestic political concentration and fragmentation or democracy and autocracy (Haggard 1990; Wade 1990; Haggard and Kaufman 1995). Just as the effects of societal forces depend on domestic institutions, the effects of institutions are contingent on societal forces. Our findings also suggest that whether spreading democracy throughout the world will promote prosperity and free trade—as many observers have argued—depends on institutional factors within democracies, global and local macroeconomic conditions, and the patterns of domestic interest group competition. A better understanding of these factors and how they operate is crucial to improving our understanding of the political economy of trade policy.

Notes

1. As long as the policy preferences by political actors across "veto points" are not perfectly correlated and they encounter some positive decision costs in reaching a consensus, the response to a given shock or change in environmental circumstance will, on average, be muted for a country with multiple veto points as compared with one characterized by a single veto point.

2. The classic statement is Schattschneider (1935).

3. It is important to recognize that regime type and veto points tap different, although somewhat related, aspects of domestic politics. The extent of veto points varies considerably among democracies and non-democracies alike . . . Furthermore, while democracies tend to have more veto points than other countries, the correlation between regime type and veto points is not overwhelmingly high . . .

References

Acemoglu, Daron, and James Robinson. (2005) *The Economic Origins of Dictatorship and Democracy: Economic and Political Origins*. New York: Cambridge University Press.

Bergsten, C. Fred, and William R. Cline. (1983) "Trade Policy in the 1980s: An Overview." In *Trade Policy in the 1980s*, edited by William R. Cline.Washington: Institute for International Economics.

Bradford, Scott. (2003) *Protection and Unemployment*. Available from http://www.nottingham.ac.uk/economics/leverhulme/conferences/june_2003/Bradford.pdf

Brooker, Paul. (2000) *Non-Democratic Regimes: Theory, Government and Politics*. New York: Palgrave Macmillan.

Colton, Timothy. (2000) *Transitional Citizens: Voters and What Influences Them in the New Russia*. Cambridge, MA: Harvard University Press.

Frieden, Jeffry A., and Ronald Rogowski. (1996) "The Impact of the International Economy on National Policies: An Overview." In *Internationalization and Domestic Politics*, edited by Robert O. Keohane and Helen V. Milner. New York: Cambridge University Press.

Garrett, Geoffrey, and Peter Lange. (1996) "Internationalization, Institutions, and Political Change." In *Internationalization and Domestic Politics*, edited by Robert O. Keohane and Helen V. Milner. New York: Cambridge University Press.

Gilligan, Michael J. (1997) "Lobbying as a Private Good with Intra Industry Trade." *International Studies Quarterly* 41:455–474.

Grossman, Gene M., and Elhanan Helpman. (2002) *Interest Groups and Trade Policy*. Princeton: Princeton University Press.

Haggard, Stephan. (1990) *Pathways from the Periphery: The Politics of Growth in the Newly Industrializing Countries*. Ithaca: Cornell University Press.

Haggard, Stephan, and Robert Kaufman. (1995) *The Political Economy of Democratic Transitions*. Princeton: Princeton University Press.

Henisz, Witold Jerzy. (2000) "The Institutional Environment for Economic Growth." *Economics and Politics* 12:1–31.

Henisz, Witold Jerzy. (2004) "Political Institutions and Policy Volatility." *Economics and Politics* 16:1–27.

Huntington, Samuel P. (1991) *The Third Wave: Democratization in the Late Twentieth Century*. Norman: University of Oklahoma Press.

Ikenberry, G. John, David A. Lake, and Michael Mastanduno. (1988) "Introduction: Approaches to Explaining American Foreign Policy." *International Organization* 42:59–90.

Kinder, Donald R., and D. Roderick Kiewiet. (1981) "Sociotropic Politics: The American Case." *British Journal of Political Science* 11:129–161.

Lewis Beck, Michael S. (1988) *Economics and Elections: The Major Western Democracies*. Ann Arbor: University of Michigan Press.

Mansfield, Edward D., and Marc L. Busch. (1995) "The Political Economy of Nontariff Barriers: A Cross National Analysis." *International Organization* 49:723–749.

Milner, Helen V. (1997) *Interests, Institutions, and Information: Domestic Politics and International Relations*. Princeton: Princeton University Press.

Olson, Mancur. (1983) "The Political Economy of Comparative Growth Rates." In *The Political Economy of Growth*, edited by Dennis Mueller. New Haven: Yale University Press.

Przeworski, Adam, Michael E. Alvarez. José Cheibub, and Fernando Limongi. (2000) *Democracy and Development: Political Institutions and Well-Being in the World, 1950–1990*. Cambridge: Cambridge University Press.

Schumpeter, Joseph. (1942) *Capitalism, Socialism and Democracy*. London: G. Allen & Unwin Ltd.

Shapiro, Robert Y. and Benjamin I. Pace. (1994) "Foreign Policy and Public Opinion." In *The New Politics of American Foreign Policy*, edited by David A. Deese. New York: St. Martin's Press.

Tsebelis, George. (1995) Decision Making in Political Systems: Veto Players in Presidentialism, Parliamentarism, Multicameralism and Multipartyism. *British Journal of Political Science* 25:289–325.

Tsebelis, George (2003) *Veto Players: How Political Institutions Work*. Princeton: Princeton University Press.

Wade, Robert. (1990) *Governing the Market: Economic Theory and the Role of the Government in East Asian Industrialization*. Princeton: Princeton University Press.

Wintrobe, Ronald. (1998) *The Political Economy of Dictatorship*. New York: Cambridge University Press.

23 International Monetary Affairs

23.1

The Legalization of International Monetary Affairs

Beth A. Simmons

Sovereign control over money is one of the most closely guarded national prerogatives.[1] Creating, valuating, and controlling the distribution of national legal tender is viewed as an inherent right of a nation-state in the modern period. Yet over the course of the twentieth century, international rules of good monetary conduct have become "legalized" in the sense developed in this [reading]. This historic shift took place after World War II in an effort to bolster the confidence that had been shattered by the interwar monetary experience.[2] If the interwar years taught monetary policymakers anything, it was that economic prosperity required credible exchange-rate commitments, open markets, and nondiscriminatory economic arrangements. International legalization of monetary affairs was a way to inspire private actors to once again trade and invest across national borders.

Sensitivity to sovereignty costs continues to preclude dense hard law in this area. This is especially obvious when compared to other areas of economic relations, such as trade in goods and services. The Bretton Woods institutions involved only three international legal obligations regarding the conduct of monetary policy. The best known of these was to establish and maintain a par value, an obligation that was formally eliminated by the Second Amendment to the International Monetary Fund's (IMF) Articles of Agreement in 1977. But two other obligations remain: to keep one's current account free from restrictions, and to maintain a unified exchange-rate system. The first requires that if a bill comes due for imports or an external interest payment, national monetary authorities must make foreign exchange available to pay it. The second proscribes exchange-rate systems that favor certain transactions or trade partners over others. IMF members can voluntarily declare themselves bound by these rules (Article VIII status) or they can choose to maintain, though not augment, the restrictions that were in place when they joined the IMF (a form of grandfathering under Article XIV).

My premise is that legalization of international monetary relations helps governments make credible policy commitments to market actors. As I will argue, the central mechanism encouraging compliance is the desire to avoid reputational costs associated with reneging on a legal obligation. The hard commitments encoded at Bretton Woods were thought to be necessary because the soft arrangements of the interwar years had proved useless. Governments have used commitment to the rules contained in the Articles of Agreement as a costly commitment to stable, liberal external monetary policies. This does not mean that compliance is perfect, but it is enhanced when other countries comply and when governments have a strong reputation for respecting the rule of law. When these conditions obtain, rule violation entails disproportionate reputational costs, as I shall argue. . . .

Source: Beth A. Simmons, "The Legalization of International Monetary Affairs," *International Organization* 54:3 (Summer, 2000), pp. 573–581 and 598–599.

The International Monetary System Before 1945: National Laws and International "Understandings"

The Nineteenth-Century Gold Standard

The stability of the international monetary system in the nineteenth century owed nothing to international legal agreements. Not a single international treaty addressed obligations of countries under the gold standard. Rather, the international system was anchored in national rules, often in the form of statutes, that specified the rights of private parties to import and export gold. In Britain, at the center of the system, the Peel Act of 1819[3] gave individuals the right to convert bank notes to gold by presenting them to the Bank of England. The Bank Charter Act (1844) extended to individuals the right to acquire notes for gold, and created a legal obligation on the part of the Bank of England to maintain gold backing pound for pound, for all outstanding Bank of England notes beyond the "fiduciary issue" of 14 million pounds.[4]

Although the gold standard certainly had a clear legal basis, there was nothing international about the legal structure on which it rested. It was, at most, a decentralized system of regulatory harmonization.[5] To access international capital and trade, other countries had an incentive to follow Britain onto gold. . . . In 1900 the United States declared gold as the "standard unit of value," which put the country officially on the gold standard (though silver coins still circulated). None of these national decisions involved the international community in their making. . . .

Nor was this system managed through international legal arrangements. . . . As long as investors were confident that the system would be maintained,[6] there was little reason to design an elaborate international legal structure for its maintenance.

The Interwar Years

World War I disrupted not only the economic relationships but also the domestic political and social stability that underlay the confidence in the gold standard.[7] As a result, the interwar years were a "largely unsuccessful groping toward some form of organizational regulation of monetary affairs."[8] . . . In 1922, the governments of the major European countries met in Genoa to agree informally to the principles of a gold exchange standard, which would economize on gold by encouraging smaller financial centers to hold a portion of their reserves in foreign exchange rather than gold. . . . When the Bank for International Settlements was created in 1930, governments were careful to limit their mutual obligations while solidifying the bank as their agent in the collection of reparations from Germany.[9] As the Permanent Court of International Arbitration noted, the international community had quite clearly "accepted [the] principle that a State is entitled to regulate its own currency."[10]

Virtually every important exchange-rate decision made in the interwar years was made unilaterally. On 21 September, the British government implemented the Gold Standard (Amendment) Act of 1931, suspending payments of gold against legal tender and officially leaving the gold standard. Even as multilateral negotiations were in progress, the Roosevelt administration unilaterally imposed exchange controls and an export embargo.[11] Even when governments tried to coordinate their actions, diplomatic declarations were chosen over legal commitments. . . .

That governments tried at all to coordinate their monetary choices during this period had much to do with the growing incentives governments faced after World War I to externalize their problems of economic adjustment. The international monetary system was still dependent on national law, but the nature of the national rules had changed. Certainly governments could no longer passively accept internal adjustments in the face of mounting political demands to manage the economy. In contrast to the nineteenth century, during the 1930s a number of countries claimed to be on a "gold standard" even though gold had little to do with the money supply and hence held no implications for internal adjustment.[12] Once the national rules no longer commanded respect for internal adjustments, governments were increasingly faced with the need for international rules to put limits on external adjustments. Efforts to formalize international monetary relations arose from the need for credible limits on external adjustment.

The IMF and International Monetary Law: Toward the Formalization of "Rules of Good Conduct"

The legalization of international monetary relations burgeoned after World War II.[13] In rejecting the less formalized arrangements of the past century and establishing for the first time a public international law of money,[14] negotiators from the United States and the United Kingdom were consciously choosing an international legal framework to enhance the system's credibility. Moreover, the IMF was to be, among other things, a fund, the purpose of which was to extend loans to members in balance-of-payments trouble. This alone led to a huge increase in legal detail, since these rules are analogous to banking law or at least to banking practice, where terms of loans and their repayment are spelled out in contracts and often limited by statutes and regulations. The IMF was created by a multilateral treaty arrangement, by which signatories agree to pay in subscriptions in exchange for voting and drawing rights. Of course, the decision to create an intergovernmental organization and to codify basic rules required domestic ratification of all signatories. In the United States, this meant that the Articles of Agreement had to be ratified by two-thirds of the Senate and, because of the need for implementing legislation, a simple majority of both houses of Congress. With the entry into force of the IMF's Articles of Agreement, money—like activity on the seas and diplomatic relations among states—was drawn under the system of public international law and became newly subject to its broader norms and principles.[15]

Fixed Exchange Rates: The Rise and Fall of Legalization

The Articles of Agreement set forth two primary regulatory goals that reflected lessons drawn from the interwar years: governments should be obligated to peg exchange rates and to remove exchange controls and discriminatory practices that affected current transactions. . . . According to Article IV of the Articles of Agreement, "The essential purpose of the international monetary system is to provide a framework that facilitates the exchange of goods, services, and capital among countries, and . . . a principle objective is the continuing development of the underlying conditions that are necessary for financial and economic stability."[16] . . . In short, in the postwar monetary system, public international law was to be used as it had been for decades in trade relations: to help facilitate the international exchange of goods and services by providing for currency convertibility in open, free, and legal markets.

The international community thus explicitly recognized for the first time that exchange rates were properly a matter of international concern. To become a member of the IMF, a country had to communicate a "par value" for its currency by direct or indirect reference to gold. Members then had an obligation to maintain that par value within the margins prescribed in the articles.[17]

Not all members complied with the obligation to peg. Some were able to do so only by maintaining other undesirable (or illegal) practices, such as multiple currency arrangements or restrictions on current accounts. The most spectacular instance of noncompliance—that of the United States in 1971—ultimately reversed the trend begun in the 1940s to harden exchange rate obligations. Rules for generalized floating were then negotiated by the "Group of 20"—again, outside of the legal framework of the IMF—and were adopted by the executive board as nonmandatory guidelines.[18] The heyday of multilateral legalized exchange-rate relations were effectively over. It was only left for the IMF membership to officially acknowledge the reassertion of national sovereignty in exchange-rate relations by composing the Second Amendment to the Articles of Agreement, which took effect in 1977.

Remaining Monetary Obligations: Article VIII

Despite the softening of legal obligations with respect to the system of par values, governments who are members of the IMF do retain two important obligations in the conduct of their external monetary policy. Both of these are contained in Article VIII of the Articles of Agreement, which spells out the general obligations of members. . . . Article VIII section 2(a) provides that governments must make foreign exchange available for goods, services, and invisibles.[19] By agreeing to this standard, governments obligate themselves to make available to their citizens' foreign exchange to settle all legal international transactions (it remains up to the government to determine which are legal).[20] . . .

Multiple currency practices that establish different rates of exchange have always been prohibited by the Articles of Agreement. Article VIII section 3 creates a hard legal obligation to avoid such practices,[21] which were viewed as a threat to the original parity rule, potentially discriminatory, and always distortionary. As with the restrictions in section 2, the IMF could, however, approve temporarily such practices, which can serve to soften the proscription in the short run. Multiple currency practices were rampant after World

War II: about a third of all the countries involved in the Bretton Woods negotiations had multiple currency systems in place. . . .

Why were rules forbidding these practices considered necessary? For two general reasons: Governments may want to support developmental objectives that favor certain kinds of imports over others based on established state priorities.[22] More often, however, governments use exchange controls and multiple currency practices as one among a variety of methods to deal with balance-of-payments problems.[23] For either purpose, they may require exporters to surrender foreign currencies received in export sales to government authorities, at governmentally determined rates.[24] In turn, importers are required to obtain foreign currency from the governmental authority or authorized bank. Such systems allow for foreign currency rationing or import discrimination in which foreign currency is made available (or available at favorable rates) for some goods or some transactions but not others.[25] . . .

Conclusions

The legalization of some central aspects of the international monetary regime after World War II allows us to examine the conditions under which law can influence the behavior of governments in the choice of their international monetary policies. Historically, this policy area has been devoid of international legal rules. The classical gold standard did not depend on international legal commitments for its reputed stability. "Soft" international legal commitments began to develop only in the interwar years, largely in response to markets' shattered confidence in the ability of governments to maintain the commitments they had made unilaterally in the previous period. Driven by the need to limit the externalization of macroeconomic adjustment costs, some governments sought international commitments as a way to enhance certainty and reassure markets. However, these commitments were in the softest possible form and did little to constrain behavior or encourage the confidence of economic agents.

The Bretton Woods agreements brought to an end the unbridled national legal sovereignty over monetary affairs. They hardly represent the triumph of legalization over market forces, however, as attested to by the breakdown of the original legal obligation to defend a par value system. Legal obligations cannot stifle market forces: capital mobility has made fixed rates very nearly unmanageable, treaty arrangements to the contrary notwithstanding. The end of the legal obligation to defend pegged rates is a clear reminder that legalization cannot be viewed in teleological terms. Obligations that increasingly frustrate major players as market conditions change are not likely to remain obligations for long.

Members of the IMF still have legal obligations regarding the conduct of their monetary policy. In fact, a growing number of members voluntarily assume these obligations every year. Article VIII Section 2(a) obligates members to keep their current accounts free from restrictions and proscribes the use of multiple exchange rate systems.

Notes

1. Cohen 1998.
2. See Eichengreen 1992; and Simmons 1994.
3. Amended in 1921.
4. Dam 1982, 23–25.
5. See, for example, the description by the MacMillan Committee on Finance and Industry, Cmd. 3897, HMSO 1931, as reprinted in Eichengreen 1985, 185–99.
6. Eichengreen writes extensively about the confidence that investors had in the prewar gold standard. Eichengreen 1992.
7. Simmons 1994.
8. Dam 1982, 50.
9. Simmons 1993.
10. *Case of Serbian Loans*, Permanent Court of International Justice, ser. A, nos. 20/21, 44, 1929, cited in Gold 1984b, 1533. Thus, researchers often speak of the "norms" of the gold standard (for example, Simmons 1994), but these were never codified in international agreements.
11. Presidential Proclamations 2039 (6 March 1933) and 2040 (9 March 1933); Executive orders 6111 (20 April 1933) and 6260 (28August 1933). Cited in Dam 1982, 47, 55.
12. In the United States it was illegal after 1933 (Exec. order 6260) for a resident to hold gold coins or bullion. Sterilization funds in both the United States and Great Britain further severed the relationship between gold flows and international monetary policy.
13. The expression "rules of good conduct" is used by Gold 1965, passim.
14. Gold 1984a, 801. A French plan was offered at the beginning of the postwar monetary negotiations. Although it played no direct role, it did indicate the French preference for agreement among the "principal nations" somewhat analogous to the Tripartite Agreement. The French plan saw an international institution as optional. Dam 1982, 76.
15. Gold 1980, 5. Nonetheless, legal treatments of these obligations are surprisingly few. See generally Denters 1996, 16–20.

16. Art. IV, sec. 1.

17. Art. IV, sec. 4. Furthermore, Art. IV, sec. 2 provided that "no member shall buy gold at a price above par value plus the prescribed margin, or sell gold at a price below par value minus the prescribed margin." A central bank could not enter into any gold transaction with another central bank other than at par without one or the other violating the articles.

18. The executive board decision called on members to "use their best endeavors to observe the guidelines." Decision of 13 June 1974 (IMF 1974, 112). The guidelines said that a member "should" intervene "to prevent or moderate sharp and disruptive fluctuations from day to day and from week to week, . . . should not normally act aggressively with respect to the exchange value of its currency," should adopt a "target zone of rates," and should consult with the IMF.

19. The restriction applies only to payments and transfers for current international transactions. The IMF articles explicitly permit the regulation of international capital movements (Art. VI, sec. 3).

20. See Executive Board Decision 1034 (60/27), 1 June 1960, para. 1, *Selected Decisions of the International Monetary Fund and Selected Documents*, 11:259 (Washington, D.C.: IMF). See also Horse field and de Vries 1969, 3:260.

21. Art. VIII, sec. 3 says: "No member shall engage in, or permit any of its fiscal agencies referred to in Article V, Section 1 to engage in, discriminatory currency arrangements or multiple currency practices . . . except as authorized under this agreement or approved by the Fund."

22. See, for example, India and Article VIII, 11 July 1955, S424, Transitional Arrangements, Article VIII Country Studies (Washington, D.C.: IMF Archives).

23. See Edwards 1985, 381–82; and Gold 1988, 255.

24. Edwards 1985, 391. Surrender requirements are not prohibited, because surrender in itself is not considered to be an impediment to the making of payments. Gold 1984a, 813.

25. Edwards 1985, 382. Avery comprehensive system of exchange controls might prohibit residents to transfer the state's currency to nonresidents except with the state's permission on a case-by-case basis, or prohibit residents to hold foreign currencies except with the state's permission.

23.2

The Trilemma of International Finance

N. Gregory Mankiw

As the world economy struggles to recover from its various ailments, the international financial order is coming under increased scrutiny. Currencies and exchange rates, in particular, are getting a hard look.

Various pundits and politicians, including President Obama himself, have complained that the Chinese *renminbi* is undervalued and impeding a global recovery. The problems in Greece have caused many people to wonder whether the euro is a failed experiment and whether Europe's nations would have been better off maintaining their own currencies.

In thinking about these issues, the place to start is what economists call the fundamental trilemma of international finance. Yes, trilemma really is a word. It has been a term of art for logicians since the 17th century, according to the Oxford English Dictionary, and it describes a situation in which someone faces a choice among three options, each of which comes with some inevitable problems.

What is the trilemma in international finance? It stems from the fact that, in most nations, economic policy makers would like to achieve these three goals:

- *Make the country's economy open to international flows of capital.* Capital mobility lets a nation's citizens diversify their holdings by investing abroad. It also encourages foreign investors to bring their resources and expertise into the country.

- *Use monetary policy as a tool to help stabilize the economy.* The central bank can then increase the money supply and reduce interest rates when the economy is depressed, and reduce money growth and raise interest rates when it is overheated.

- *Maintain stability in the currency exchange rate.* A volatile exchange rate, at times driven by speculation, can be a source of broader economic volatility. Moreover, a stable rate makes it easier for households and businesses to engage in the world economy and plan for the future.

But here's the rub: You can't get all three. If you pick two of these goals, the inexorable logic of economics forces you to forgo the third.

In the United States, we have picked the first two. Any American can easily invest abroad, simply by sending cash to an international mutual fund, and foreigners are free to buy stocks and bonds on domestic exchanges. Moreover, the Federal Reserve sets monetary policy to try to maintain full employment and price stability. But a result of this decision is volatility in the value of the dollar in foreign exchange markets.

By contrast, China has chosen a different response to the trilemma. Its central bank conducts monetary policy and maintains tight control over the exchange value of its currency. But to accomplish these two goals, it has to restrict the international flow of capital, including the ability of Chinese citizens to move their wealth abroad. Without such restrictions, money would flow into and out of the country, forcing the domestic interest rate to match those set by foreign central banks.

Most of Europe's nations have chosen the third way. By using the euro to replace the French *franc*, the German *mark*, the Italian *lira*, the Greek *drachma* and other currencies, these countries have eliminated all exchange-rate movements within their zone. In addition, capital is free to move among nations. Yet the cost of making these choices has been to give up the possibility of national monetary policy.

The European Central Bank sets interest rates for Europe as a whole. But if the situation in one country—Greece, for example—differs from that in the rest of Europe, that country no longer has its own monetary policy to address national problems.

Is there a best way to deal with this trilemma? Perhaps not surprisingly, many American economists argue for the American system of floating exchange rates determined by market forces. This preference underlies much of the criticism of China's financial

---

Source: N. Gregory Mankiw, "The Trilemma of International Finance," in *The New York Times,* July 10, 2010.

policy. It also led to skepticism when Europe started down the path toward a common currency in the early 1990s. Today, those euro skeptics feel vindicated by the problems in Greece.

But economists should be cautious when recommending exchange-rate policy, because it is far from obvious what is best. In fact, Americans' embrace of floating exchange rates is relatively recent. From World War II to the early 1970s, the United States participated in the Bretton Woods system, which fixed exchange rates among the major currencies. Moreover, in 1998, as much of Asia was engulfed in a financial crisis, Robert E. Rubin, then the Treasury secretary, praised China's exchange-rate policy as an "island of stability" in a turbulent world.

Even the euro experiment is based in part on an American model. Anyone taking a trip across the United States doesn't need to change money with every crossing of a state border. A common currency among the 50 states has served Americans well. Europeans were aspiring for similar benefits.

To be sure, Europe is different from the United States, which has a large central government that can redistribute resources among regions as needed. More important, our common language and heritage allow labor to move freely among regions in a way that will always be harder in Europe. The United States of Europe may have been too much to hope for.

Without doubt, the world financial system presents policy makers with difficult tradeoffs. Americans shouldn't be too harsh when other nations facing the trilemma reach conclusions different from ours. In this area of economic policy, as well as many others, there is room for reasonable nations to disagree.

23.3

Europe After the Crisis

How to Sustain a Common Currency

Andrew Moravcsik

From the start, the euro has rested on a gamble. When European leaders opted for monetary union in 1992, they wagered that European economies would converge toward one another: the deficit-prone countries of southern Europe would adopt German economic standards—lower price inflation and wage growth, more saving, and less spending—and Germany would become a little more like them, by accepting more government and private spending and higher wage and price inflation. This did not occur. Now, with the euro in crisis, the true implications of this gamble are becoming clear.

Over the past two years, the eurozone members have done a remarkable job managing the short-term symptoms of the crisis, although the costs have been great. Yet the long-term challenge remains; making European economies converge, that is, assuring that their domestic macroeconomic behaviors are sufficiently similar to one another to permit a single monetary policy at a reasonable cost. For this to happen, both creditor countries, such as Germany, and the deficit countries in southern Europe must align their trends in public spending, competitiveness, inflation, and other areas.

Aligning the continent's economies will first require Europe to reject the common misdiagnoses of today's crisis. The problem is not primarily one of profligate public sectors or broken private sectors in debtor countries. It is rather the result of a fundamental disequilibrium within the single currency zone, which applies a single monetary policy and a single exchange rate to a diverse group of countries. Policy proposals for budgetary austerity, the micromanagement of national budgets, fiscal federalism, bailouts, or large funds to stave off speculators are insufficient to solve this problem alone. Instead, Europeans should trust in the essentially democratic nature of the EU, which will encourage them to distribute the costs of convergence more fairly within and among countries. The burden must be shifted from Europe's public sectors and deficit countries to its private sectors and surplus countries. If this does not occur, the survival of the euro will be called into question and Europe will face a long-term economic catastrophe that could drain its wealth and power for the rest of this decade and beyond.

A Risky Bet

Since Europe began cooperating on monetary issues in the 1970s, nearly every agreement has been negotiated on terms set primarily by Germany. The 1992 Maastricht Treaty, which committed Europeans to the euro, was no exception. Germany's main motivation for a single currency, contrary to popular belief, was neither to aid its reunification nor to realize an idealistic federalist scheme for European political union. It was rather to promote is own economic welfare through open markets, a competitive exchange rate, and anti-inflationary monetary policy. Most German business and government leaders believed then and believe now that the European economy would be best supported by independent central banks that are like their own *Bundesbank*, which almost always prioritizes low inflation over growth or employment.

In France, Italy, Spain, and other countries that have traditionally had weaker currencies, politicians viewed monetary union in part as a means to emulate Germany's success by committing themselves to low inflation and low interest rates, reforming the structures of their economies, and encouraging cross-border investment. Yet they also saw the euro as an instrument to bring Germany closer to their own economic models, thereby relaxing external constraints and competitive pressures on their economies. These weak-currency countries had suffered many debt and exchange-rate crises in the 1970s and 1980s that were driven by the gaps in prices, spending, and wages between themselves and Germany. To avoid repeating this, they hoped to encourage Germany to accept a European structure that would allow for higher domestic spending, wage increases, and inflation. The two approaches would meet somewhere in the middle.

It didn't work. . . .

From the start, then, the single currency imposed high risks on some European governments. If deficit countries, such as Greece and Italy, could not persuade Germany to change its behavior, then they were betting their future prosperity on their own abilities to adopt German standards of wage discipline, government spending, and international competitiveness. These were ambitious goals, because such standards are deeply embedded in national social compromises and political histories. The eurozone had to become more of what economists call on "optimal currency area," in which economic behavior is similar enough to justify a single monetary policy.

In practice, getting there would be very difficult, because the euro system required governments to surrender the tools that they had traditionally used to offset their gap with Germany. These had included unilateral control over interest rates and the money supply, restrictions on capital flows, and the manipulation of exchange rates. Faced with a debt or competitiveness crisis, a country would have to act directly to push down economic activity through wages, private consumption, business investment, and government spending. This is a risky course for any government, because it imposes immediate and visible costs across the entire society. Yet the creators of the euro apparently thought other European countries would be able to converge on something resembling the German model, or that Germany itself would relent, because they made few provisions to address bank collapses, sovereign debt crises, or other potential consequences of failure.

Growing Apart

At first, other European economies seemed to bring their policies in line with Germany's, as optimists had expected. Weak-currency governments restrained wages, government spending, and consumption—or presented statistics that made it seem as if they had done so. Adopting the euro reduced interest rates for these countries and encouraged northern European lending to their economies, stimulating growth.

Yet underneath the surface, the eurozone was a ticking time bomb. Europe's economies once again grew apart, the consequences of which were made clear after the U.S. and British financial collapses in 2008. Deficit governments immediately came under pressure from international markets: speculative domestic markets crashed, interest rates rose, external debts ballooned, and growth plummeted. By contrast, Germany, after a short hiccup, has enjoyed an unprecedented economic boom. These disparate trajectories have called into question the viability of the euro.

According to conventional wisdom and the official rhetoric in Germany and elsewhere, the crisis was caused primarily by excessive public spending in a few extravagant eurozone countries. Solving the crisis, and preventing future ones, would therefore simply require imposing tight restraints on government budgets in deficit countries. To this end, the so-called fiscal compact recently negotiated by EU members would, if ratified, enforce budgetary austerity across the continent. Some economists, including Mario Draghi, who now heads the European Central Bank, also believe that cutting budgets is good for growth.

Yet this is a misleading diagnosis. Although some southern European countries, like many Western democracies, might do well to cut government deficits, public profligacy was not the main cause of the crisis. . . . Far more important in causing the crisis was shortsightedness in and lax regulation of the private sector, which bred imprudent banking policies in Ireland, insufficient competition in markets in Italy, and a housing boom gone bad in Spain. . . .

Although big deficits and broken private sectors may have been part of the problem, the deeper cause of today's crisis lies in contradictions within the euro system itself. Ten years after adopting a common currency, Europe is still not an optimal currency area. Instead, the single currency exaggerates existing differences and eliminated the policy instruments required to overcome them. Bankruptcy in southern Europe and prosperity in Germany are two sides of the same coin.

Greece, Italy, Portugal, and Spain have spent the last decade accumulating large and increasing current account deficits, and so they are accused of inefficiency and overspending. But German policies are equally to blame for the deficits. At the founding of the euro in 1999, the European Central Bank set a continent-wide two percent target for inflation, based on trends in Germany's labor market. Yet Germany subsequently moved the goalposts by dampening its price and wage growth below that level. To see how this helped cause the crisis, consider the most important component in measuring an economy's external competitiveness: the cost of labor per unit produced, also called unit labor costs, which should ideally rise at the same rate as inflation. Between 1999 and 2008, the average unit labor costs in Greece, Italy, Portugal, and Spain rose by one percent per year over the target, slowly rendering their economies uncompetitive and signaling the need for reform. During the same period in Germany, by contrast, sluggish wage growth, weak domestic consumption, labor-market reforms, and cuts in government spending meant that unit labor costs rose by an average of less than one percent per year, well below the European target. Over a decade, this combination of excessive rises in unit labor costs in some places and wage suppression elsewhere generated a 25 percent overall gap in competitiveness between Germany and its European partners. This chiefly benefited Germany's export sector—the only part of its economy to enjoy net growth over the decade—at the expense not just of foreigners but also of German workers and taxpayers, whose wages were not keeping pace with inflation.

Many observers, and not just in Germany, view Germany's competitiveness as the well-deserved fruit of a decade of domestic reform and restraint, during which the government and unions worked together to deregulate labor markets and dampen wages. Southern European countries, they maintain, should simply emulate Germany's success. There is some truth to this view, but it misses the fact that Germany's wage suppression was excessive, fueling both trade imbalances and imprudent international lending. Because Germany is in the eurozone, its external competitiveness was not offset by a rising currency. Germany's real exchange rate today, under the single currency, is roughly 40 percent below where it would be if the *deutschemark* still existed. The result: Germany's trade surplus, at $200 billion a year, is the world's largest, even greater than China's. Forty percent of the surplus comes from Germany's trade within the eurozone—a total roughly equal to the combined deficits of the crisis countries.

Accumulating export surpluses and suppressing domestic consumption, moreover, generated a surplus of capital. German banks and investors lent their extra cash to southern Europe at historically low interest rates, ignoring the longer-term risk. So southern Europe's deficits are as much the fault of northern European lenders as they are the fault of southern European borrowers. In using an undervalued currency to accumulate trade surpluses, Germany is acting like the China of Europe. Yet its eurozone membership spares it from the kind of criticism that China regularly suffers.

This euro-induced disequilibrium helps explain why Germany's export-driven economy has recently been growing at three to four percent per year, while neighboring economies remain mired in crisis. Such large imbalances have historically been more than enough to trigger severe crises in debtor economies. Yet in trying to catch up to Germany, southern European governments are further hampered by the euro system, which stripped them of the main tool they had traditionally employed to keep up with their economically competitive neighbors: currency devaluation. Devaluation reduces the price of exports and increases the price of imports, shifting some of the burden of adjusting to deficits to foreigners whose products have become relatively less competitive. The euro has also forced southern European governments to surrender unilateral control over interest rates and inflation as instruments to tweak prices or reduce their debt burdens. The only remaining policy option deficit countries have to make up for the 25 percent competitiveness gap is to drastically cut wages, private economic activity, and government spending, leading to a reduced level of aggregate consumption. In any country, such direct cuts tend to be controversial, politically costly, and difficult to carry out. Germany, meanwhile, although it bears a large part of the blame for the gap, faces no immediate market pressure to share the cost of adjustment.

Money in the Bank

In the face of these tensions, keeping the eurozone together requires European governments first to address the crisis of liquidity by stabilizing debt-ridden countries and shoring up European banks and then, in the long term, to bring about the fundamental convergence of European economies. The eurozone countries appear to have successfully, if perhaps only temporarily, addressed the first challenge. After two years, bank balance sheets have stabilized, stock and bond markets have rebounded, and the immediate pressure on debtor countries has been relieved. To achieve these goals, the EU, reputed to be slow and cautious, has acted with remarkable flexibility. . . .

It is less clear whether the euro serves the long-term interests of the deficit countries. In these countries, the strongest argument for staying in the eurozone has been that the costs of pulling out would be prohibitive. Were Greece to abandon the euro, for example, the costs imposed by the rapid outward flow of capital, the mass bankruptcy of banks and businesses, and the adjustment to a national currency would likely total one trillion euros. And the risks of a Greek collapse pale in comparison to those of the contagion reaching Italy or Spain.

The American and European media have criticized Merkel for her indecisive leadership, which they say has produced a slow European response focused more on imposing austerity than on rekindling growth. It is true that facing unrealistic expectations for recovery, Germany initially opposed bailouts and debt restructuring and then organized loans at punishing interest rates. Only in October 2011, and largely at the insistence of the IMF, did Europe begin to trim Greek sovereign debt. The best technocratic solution might instead have been for Germany to back a swifter and more generous restructuring of Greek debt, with private bondholders in northern Europe taking their share of the losses, and for the EU to provide more generous funding to pull distressed economies through the recession. This might have prevented those economies from accumulating debt, leaving better prospects for tighter budgets and structural reforms in the long term.

Yet expectations for that kind of outcome underestimate the inherent political difficulty of debt negotiations, which involve bargaining with deficit and creditor governments while worrying about the responses of financial markets and taxpayers. Had Greek debt been forgiven sooner, or had a larger "firewall" been created to protect Italy and Spain from collapse, the incentives for the debtor countries to reform would have diminished. Germany is rightly committed to squeezing significant domestic change out of the process, particularly given its willingness to risk funding other countries without a firm guarantee of repayment. In coping with the short-term consequences of the debt crisis, and in saving a system from which they benefit, German leaders have displayed bolder political leadership than at any other time in the history of European monetary integration.

When in Rome, Do as the Germans Do

Unfortunately, managing the short-term symptoms of the crisis is not enough. Resolving the immediate liquidity crisis has bought European governments several years to address the deeper challenge: how to encourage fundamental economic convergence. For as long as the eurozone countries to take such radically different trajectories regarding labor costs, government spending, private-sector behavior, and competitiveness, Europe will remain no more of an optimal currency area than it was when the euro entered circulation. . . .

These issues will be resolved not in Brussels or Frankfurt but in national capitals. Preserving the euro in its current form depends on crafting a politically sustainable compromise on which countries and which groups within those countries will shoulder the burden of getting Europe's disparate economies to converge.

The German view—that the future of the euro rests on countries making tough reforms and cutting public spending—is partially correct. It would be foolhardy for Germany to assume liabilities for deficit countries without such reforms. That is why Berlin has insisted that the EU fiscal compact require governments to incorporate balanced-budget provisions into their national constitutions. Yet this still leaves unresolved two crucial questions about how to distribute the costs of Europe's adjustment, both within countries and among them.

First, how will Europe's private sectors be reformed? Different private-sector wage and business practices are a greater obstacle to economic convergence than different public-sector spending. Yet it is often unclear exactly how national governments can encourage reforms of wage and business practices or how the EU can assure that such reforms are actually implemented. It is often easier for governments to slash public spending than to impose solutions on powerful banks, corporations, or unions. As a result, even if a crisis originates in the private sector, the cost of stabilization often falls disproportionately on public-sector beneficiaries.

Second, which countries will need to chart new economic paths? Germany benefits greatly from the current system, in which deficit countries must do nearly all the adjusting by cutting spending and Germany provides the funding to assure that they repay their loans, which also serves to bail out northern European banks and bondholders. The new fiscal compact would institutionalize this. Yet imposing the primary cost of recovery on deficit countries in the form of austerity is likely to fail both pragmatically and politically. Economies without growth cannot support or sustain debt reduction or structural reform. . . .

The economist Paul Krugman and others argue that such a burden could come in the form of a more centralized European fiscal federalism. If only Europe possessed a common political identity that supported fiscal transfers among governments—not unlike the transfers among U.S. states carried out through the federal government—the eurozone countries could bring their economies into alignment. This analogy is not entirely persuasive; Europe is not America. Washington allows U.S. states to function under a single currency not through fiscal federalism and orderly bailouts but through local balanced-budget rules backed by the often brutal departure of firms, capital, and people to more economically buoyant regions. When traditional manufacturing collapsed in Michigan, federal intervention did not save the state from suffering a decade of a shrinking population and shrinking incomes; Michiganders and their money simply moved south. . . .

Since austerity and fiscal federalism cannot bear the entire burden of adjustment, particularly for large debtors, Europe's convergence will also require a shift in the domestic policies of Germany and other surplus countries. Berlin must move to increase its public spending, wages, and consumption at a faster rate. This would help bridge the competitiveness gap between surplus and deficit countries, encourage the deficit countries to grow and export more, and reduce current account deficits across southern Europe. . . .

There is some evidence that Germany is moving in this direction, despite what its politicians and diplomats sometimes say; the costs of inaction in the short term are too high. But absent a deeper convergence, the eurozone's long-term economic fundamentals are stacked against success. Whether or not Germany will ultimately make the tough political decisions required to save the euro will likely depend on the contours of the next financial crisis. . . .

The End of the Affair?

The euro crisis will shape not just the fate of the single currency but also the future of the whole continent. The recent turmoil has made clear that the alignment of European domestic policies is a prerequisite for mutually beneficial cooperation. This is typical of the EU. Where basic national interests and regulatory styles have converged, as in the area of trade, governments have developed strong rules to coordinate their policies, and these policies have remained stable through the crisis. In the areas where countries have not brought their policies in line, regulation remains voluntary and largely national. So the outcome to the euro crisis will depend on how well northern and southern Europe can close the gaps in their macroeconomic behavior. But the difficulties in getting European countries to adopt similar monetary policies suggest that the EU's leaders may have pushed integration as far as it will go.

In this regard, the euro crisis is only the latest development in a two-decade-long trend toward the leveling off of European integration. At the time the Maastricht Treaty was ratified, many observers expected the EU to start regulating more and more policies, including those on social welfare, health care, pensions, criminal justice, education, issues of culture and language, local infrastructure, national politics, and, above all, taxation and fiscal priorities. Little of this has occurred, and Europe now puts forward few policies that open up new areas to centralized regulation. Today, European states retain far more control than Brussels over justice and home affairs, immigration, intellectual property, and social policy. And when the EU does launch a new centralized policy, it is rare for every government to sign on or implement it entirely. Not every EU member uses the euro, just as not every EU member adheres to the Schengen agreement, which eliminated border controls, or participates in all EU foreign policy and defense actions.

Yet none of this vindicates the Euro-pessimists. No country has issued a serious challenge to any of the EU's core activities. Nor has a single prominent European politician advocated withdrawal from the EU, as that would amount to economic suicide. Brussels continues to manage about ten percent of national policies, from business regulation to European migration, under a unified legal system. The union has recently expanded, from 12 members at the time of the Maastricht Treaty to 27 today, leaving lasting movement toward open markets, democracy, and the rule of law in its wake. Countries have not responded to the euro crisis by turning to protectionism or refusing to enforce EU policies, because cooperation in these areas is firmly grounded in common interests. The euro crisis itself has even allowed European policy to intensify in existing areas, such as monetary and banking regulation. And even a collapse of the euro would not jeopardize the existence of the EU, despite what such commentators as Walter Laqueur and Wolfgang Münchau have at times suggested. Whatever the outcome of the crisis, the EU will remain without rival the most ambitious and successful example of voluntary international cooperation in world history.

Still, the crisis does signal that the process of European integration is reaching a natural plateau, at least for the foreseeable future, based on a pragmatic division between national policy and supranational policy. The movement toward the "ever-closer union" of which the EU's founding fathers dreamed when they signed the Treaty of Rome in 1957 will have to stop at some point; there will never be an all-encompassing European federal state. But within the increasingly clear mandate of a stable constitutional settlement, Europe will continue to respond to the challenges of an increasingly interdependent world.

24 Ethics and International Political Economy

24.1

Minimal Ethical and Legal Absolutes in Foreign Trade

Robert W. McGee

Foreign trade is an area about which much has been written. The majority of economists, going back to Adam Smith (1776), have generally concluded that trade is good and that it should be free and unhampered, at least most of the time. The reasoning behind their conclusion is almost always utilitarian based. Free and unrestricted trade is good because the majority benefits or because the gains from trade exceed the losses. In economic terms, one would say that trade is a positive-sum game. Economists—or, more likely, politicians—who say that trade should be restricted generally try to make a case for some special interest that has come to the legislature seeking protection.

The approach in this [reading] is distinctively different from what one would find in a standard economics textbook. Although utilitarian approaches will be used to illustrate various points, the flaws inherent in any utilitarian approach are many. In fact, utilitarian arguments will be shown to be fatally flawed. Thus ethical arguments based on utilitarian approaches will be shown to be inferior to a rights approach. I show that trade protectionism, in any form, must necessarily violate individual rights. I also attempt to fill a gap in the trade literature that, until now, has almost always failed to view trade from the perspective of individual rights.

The Utilitarian Approach to Trade Policy

Whereas the utilitarian approach to trade policy is, as we shall see, fatally flawed, such an approach often leads to the same conclusion that a rights approach would reach, only for the wrong reason. Before we criticize the utilitarian approach, let us spend a few minutes reviewing how the utilitarian approach is commonly applied to trade policy. We will then be better able to contrast the utilitarian approach with the rights approach.

Efficiency

The main economic argument for unrestricted trade is efficiency. It is easier to buy oranges and bananas if you live in Maine than to grow them yourself. David Ricardo's *Law of Comparative Advantage* (1817) points out that everyone is better off if they specialize in what they do best and trade for everything else. (Adam Smith said the same thing in 1776.) Productivity is enhanced by producing only the things you are best at producing and allowing others to do the same. Everyone can have more of everything if they concentrate their efforts on what they do best and trade for everything else.

The key to maximizing a society's total wealth is free trade. It makes no sense to specialize in what you

Source: Robert W. McGee. "Minimal Ethical and Legal Absolutes in Foreign Trade," in *Business Ethics in the Global Market*, ed. Tabor R. Machan, 63–86.

do best if you are not able to trade what you have for what you want. So a necessary corollary of specialization is the ability to trade freely. That is why economists generally conclude that free trade is the best policy.

Tariffs and Quotas: The Standard Tools of Protectionists

If economists generally agree that free trade is the best policy, why is it that practically no country on earth, including the United States, has free trade? . . . Although most economists can see the benefits of free trade, politicians generally cannot. One reason for their blindness is their constituencies. Special interests constantly bombard politicians with requests for protection from foreign (or even domestic) competition. Consumers seldom, if ever, provide a countervailing argument for free trade. Political systems have a structural bias in favor of special interests and against the general public. . . .

Domestic textile and apparel manufacturers have a great deal at stake in trade policy, so it is worth their time and effort to go to the legislature to lobby for laws that will benefit them, even if it is at the expense of the general public. Public choice economists call this activity rent seeking (Buchanan, Tollison, and Tullock 1980). This kind of activity exists whenever the benefits of a policy are concentrated and the costs are disbursed or spread among a significant portion of the general public. . . .

Tariffs and quotas have traditionally been the tools of preference for protectionists. Although the techniques are different, the effect is the same. Quotas and tariffs both protect some special interest at the expense of the general public. Thus, they both fail the utilitarian test because the majority is harmed. Nearly every study that has ever been made has concluded that the cost of protecting a particular item exceeds the benefits to be received. . . .

Deadweight losses can also be measured by the cost of every job saved or the net number of jobs that are destroyed by some protectionist policy. One study found that a particular protectionist policy would save thirty-six thousand apparel manufacturing jobs but would destroy fifty-eight thousand jobs in the retailing end of the apparel industry, for a loss/gain ratio of more than 1.6 to 1.0 (Baughman and Emrich 1987). A study of voluntary restraints in the steel industry estimated that the agreement saved 16,900 jobs in the steel industry but destroyed 52,400 jobs in the industries that use steel, for a loss/gain ratio of 3.1 to 1.0 (Denzau 1987). Various studies have estimated that the cost to consumers for each job saved in the benzenoid chemical industry to be more than $1 million; $200,000 in glassware; $30,000 in rubber footwear; $135,000 in ceramic tiles; $240,000 in orange juice; $76,000 in canned tuna; $750,000 in carbon steel; and $1 million in specialty steel (McGee 1994b, 79).

Antidumping Laws

Antidumping laws, while less visible to the average consumer, may become the protectionist tool of choice since the conclusion of the Uruguay Round and the creation of the World Trade Organization supposedly will result in the reduction or elimination of tariffs and quotas sometime in the distant future. Briefly stated, antidumping laws protect consumers from low prices. Of course, what antidumping laws actually do is protect domestic producers from foreign competition.

Here is how it works. If a domestic producer feels threatened by a foreign competitor, all it has to do is complain to Washington (or London, Rome, or whatever) that the foreign producer is dumping its product on the market. According to the antidumping laws in most countries, and according to the antidumping provisions that are part of the World Trade Organization (WTO), the foreign producer will be found guilty of dumping if it either sells its product on some domestic market for a lower price than the price it charges in its home market or if it sells for less than the cost of production, whatever that means. . . .

If a foreign producer is found guilty of dumping, there are several possible remedies. It can either be forced to raise its prices, or it can be prevented from selling its products in the domestic market for a certain number of years. Either way, consumers lose and domestic producers gain. . . .

The antidumping laws invite abuse. Indeed, they have become among the most abused laws on the books. Subject to certain minor restraints, all a domestic producer need do is complain to the Commerce Department that some foreign competitor is dumping and the Commerce Department will take it from there. The foreign producer will have to spend perhaps millions of dollars defending itself in various administrative courts. The odds are stacked against winning because of the way the cost of production is defined. Also, if the accused foreigner is not able to produce

100 percent of the data the Commerce Department wants, when it wants it, and in the form it demands, the Commerce Department is free to totally ignore all the evidence the foreigner has submitted and use unreliable estimates that the domestic producer has submitted instead. It is an abuse of the legal system that such a procedure exists. Yet, because antidumping laws have been incorporated into the WTO, it is likely that such abuses will not only continue but become more widespread. . . .

One weakness of the utilitarian approach to economics is its failure to consider questions of basic fairness. Utilitarianism seldom, if ever, goes beyond discussions of deadweight gains and losses. Interestingly enough, a study by the U.S. International Trade Commission, which jointly administers the antidumping laws with the Commerce Department, published a study (1995) that provides empirical evidence that the antidumping laws result in deadweight losses. This study, which estimated the gains and losses for only a fraction of the antidumping and countervailing duty orders that were outstanding in 1991, found that the net deadweight loss involving just the directly affected parties was $1.85 billion. The gains to the rest of the economy that would have occurred if the antidumping and countervailing duty orders then in force were removed were estimated to be between $2.17 billion and $2.94 billion. . . .

What's Wrong with Utilitarianism?

Utilitarian approaches generally lead to the conclusion that free trade is the best policy because the results are generally beneficial. Gains from trade exceed losses. Free trade results in lower prices or a wider selection of goods or both. If free trade destroys jobs, it also creates more jobs than it destroys.

Although utilitarian approaches usually lead to the correct conclusion—that free trade is good and beneficial—they do so for the wrong reason. At its core, the utilitarian philosophy is rabidly majoritarian. Utilitarians would conclude that free trade is good because the majority benefits. . . .

One major problem with any utilitarian analysis is that it does not provide a way to measure gains and losses (Rothbard 1970, 260–68). Gains and losses may only be estimated. The numerous studies that *have* attempted to measure the gains and losses of various trade or other policies are just that: attempts. Because there is no way of knowing precisely how many jobs are saved or lost as a result of a particular trade policy, assumptions and estimates have to be made. Likewise, because there are so many economic variables that interact with one another and no one knows precisely how they should fit into the equation, there is no way to know precisely how much more consumers must pay for a shirt as a result of some piece of trade legislation. Human action determines values and prices, and there is no way to input that data into a computer.

Another flaw inherent in any utilitarian analysis is that consumer choices are in terms of rank, not dollars or percentages. If a particular consumer prefers the hamburgers made at restaurant A rather than restaurant B, all one can say is that he prefers A's hamburgers to B's. . . .

Another insoluble problem with any utilitarian analysis is that not all individuals stand to gain or lose the same amount as a result of this policy or that. Thus it is impossible to measure total gains and total losses when the amount of the gain or loss differs between and among individuals. For example, millions of consumers stand to lose a little if a piece of protectionist trade legislation is passed that causes the price of shirts to rise. But domestic manufacturers of shirts, as well as their down-line suppliers, stand to gain much if restrictive trade legislation is passed. How can one determine whether the few who stand to gain much benefit more than the many who lose just a little, especially if some of the people who work for the domestic producers wear shirts?

These workers will benefit because their jobs are protected, but they will lose because they must also pay more for the shirts they buy. . . .

Not everyone who loses a job is worse off. Some people actually are better off, in terms of either dollars or intangibles. Some people who lose jobs find other jobs that pay more or have better working conditions. . . .

There is no way to accurately measure the total gains and losses that result from a particular protectionist measure because it is impossible to predict where the money will flow in the absence of protectionism. But it can be concluded, a priori, that total satisfaction will decrease if consumers have to settle for their second or third choice because some protectionist measure prevents them from buying their first choice.

Inherent in the utilitarian approach is the underlying view that governments have some inherent right to regulate trade. The U.S. Constitution states that "the Congress shall have Power to regulate Commerce with foreign Nations"; however, having the authority is not the same as having the right. . . . Governments have the authority to regulate trade, but they do not have the right. Any government action that prevents consenting adults from entering into contracts and trading the property they have for the property they want goes beyond the legitimate functions of government. That some constitution grants government the authority does not change this basic fact. . . .

A long-established rule of common law is that no one can make a contract that someone else may be bound to without that person's consent. Another long-established principle of common law is that no one may enter into a contract that binds people who are not yet born. Thus, the U.S. Constitution cannot bind anyone who was not born at the date of its signing.

We are all bound by it, in any case, because the government punishes us if we violate this supreme law of the land. The Constitution is, however, utilitarian based since some majority, at some time in the past, made rules that supposedly bind all of us. The problem is that some people may have their rights violated by certain terms in the Constitution, such as giving the government the power to regulate trade, when all trade should be between consenting adults and free from government restraints.

The Rights Approach

The rights approach is superior to the utilitarian approach because of the utilitarian approach's inability to measure gains and losses or interpersonal utility. Under the rights approach, which does not require us to make any such calculations, one may determine whether a policy is minimally ethical merely by determining whether anyone's rights have been violated. If rights have been violated, then the policy fails to pass the test of minimal ethical acceptability. If no one's rights are violated, then the policy passes the test.

The rights I am talking about here are negative rights, which must be distinguished from positive rights. Also, different levels of ethics must be distinguished. For example, if a specific trade policy does not result in the violation of anyone's negative rights, then such trade should not be prohibited because the minimal level of ethical conduct has been achieved. It would be unethical for some individual or group of individuals to prevent such exchanges from taking place. But it does not follow that the individuals who engage in all such trades are acting ethically. Take prostitution. Neither the prostitute nor the client violates anyone's rights, which means that it is unethical for anyone to prevent the transaction from taking place. But it does not follow that the prostitute or the client is acting ethically, for prostitution may be considered unethical by some people. The same argument could be made for drug dealers, pimps, sellers of pornography, coffee, red meat, ham and cheese sandwiches, and so on. Unethical acts should be prohibited only if they violate someone's negative rights.

Negative and Positive Rights

Since it is my position that only acts that violate negative rights should be prohibited, I need to say a few words about the distinction between negative and positive rights, which is that negative rights can never conflict, whereas positive rights must necessarily conflict with negative rights. Another distinction is that negative rights are inherent, whereas positive rights are granted by governments.

Negative rights, then, are preexisting rights. They come before government. Indeed, one of the main reasons for the creation of governments is to protect negative rights. Negative rights include the rights to life, liberty, and property. Stated negatively, they are the rights not to have your life, liberty, or property taken from you without your consent. Positive rights, in contrast, are granted by governments to some individuals or groups at the expense of other individuals or groups. . . .

Many laws are based on the theory of positive rights. Anti-discrimination laws, for example, prevent landlords, restaurant owners, and others from refusing to enter into contracts with the people of their choosing. Thus, a black person's right to eat anywhere he wants is gained only at the expense of any restaurant owners who would otherwise refuse service. Any law that awards rights to one person or group at the expense of some other person or group is illegitimate and goes beyond the proper scope of government. . . .

Tariffs, quotas, and antidumping laws are the result of some special interest going to the appropriate legislature and asking for protection. To purchase the foreign product, consumers must part with more of their money than would be the case under a free trade regime. The domestic producer, who has done nothing to earn the higher price, benefits. Protectionism necessarily violates individual rights (McGee and Block 1997b).

An Overlooked Ethical Issue

Now let's turn the tables a bit and take a perspective that has been almost totally absent from both the business and the ethics literature. Is it unethical for someone to go to the government and ask for protection, whether it be in the form of a tariff, quota, or antidumping action? W. M. Curtiss has an interesting reply:

> Through the years, some men have discovered how to satisfy their wants at the expense of others without being accused of theft: they ask their government to do the stealing for them. (Curtiss 1953, 19)

A well-established principle of agency law is that the principal is responsible for the acts of his agent. Thus, if John hires Jill to kill someone, both John and Jill are guilty of murder. John cannot escape liability for the crime by arguing that it was actually Jill who did the killing. Likewise, if an individual representing a special interest, let's say the steel industry, goes to Congress and asks for a higher tariff on the importation of foreign steel or a limitation on the amount of foreign steel that can enter the country, is it any different than if individuals or a group cause the price of foreign steel to go up or stop foreign steel shipments at the border? The effect is exactly the same. Consumers either have to pay higher prices or do without some product that some of them would otherwise buy.

Initiating an antidumping action also presents an interesting ethical question that has gone practically unasked in the literature (McGee and Block 1997a). Is it unethical for someone to initiate an antidumping action? The answer is yes, whether one takes a utilitarian or rights approach. Let's see why.

It is wrong to take property that does not belong to you. Likewise, it is wrong to destroy property that belongs to someone else. Initiating an antidumping action, in essence, amounts to stealing the property of consumers. . . .

When individuals from a domestic producer go to the Commerce Department to launch an antidumping investigation, it is with the intent of either forcing the targeted foreign competitor out of the domestic market altogether or forcing it to raise its prices. Either way, consumers lose. . . .

Thus, consumers have the choice of either paying a higher price for a domestic product or doing without it. The difference between the price they would have paid in a competitive market and the price they now have to pay because of less foreign competition goes into the pocket of the domestic producer(s) who initiated the antidumping action. Those producers thus used the force of government to feather their nests at the expense of the general public, for if they receive an extra $20 a unit because of the antidumping action, the effect is exactly the same as if they stole $20 at gunpoint from every consumer who bought their product. The only difference is that it is the government's gun that was pointed at the head of the foreign producer rather than the head of the consumer. But since the government (Commerce Department) was acting as the agent of the domestic producers, in effect the theft was committed by the domestic producers. It makes no difference whether the agent or the principal does the stealing; either way the consumer is getting fleeced. . . .

It is true that, in the absence of antidumping laws, some domestic competitors would go out of business. Antidumping laws allow weak domestic competitors to stay in business since consumers are not free to vote with their dollars to buy the products of foreign producers that cannot enter the country or that can enter the country only at prohibitively high prices. It should be kept in mind, however, that going out of business because of market forces does not violate anyone's rights.

To use a simple analogy, let's say that a large supermarket opens up across the street from a mom-and-pop grocery store. The supermarket is open twenty-four hours a day and offers a wide selection of products at low prices. Mom and pop will almost surely be harmed by the competition and may even be driven out of business. But their rights have not been violated. They still have inventory; they still have the right to sell it to willing consumers. Mom and pop have no right to force unwilling consumers to pay higher prices for their products when the products are available across the street for lower prices.

The same is true of any other products made or sold in the domestic market. General Motors, Ford, and Chrysler have no right to force consumers to buy their products. Consumers have the right to vote with their dollars to purchase the products of foreign automakers. When that right is taken from them, whether because of antidumping laws, tariffs, or quotas, consumers have their rights violated by the individuals at the domestic auto companies who used the force of government to insulate their companies from foreign competition. . . .

Individual Rights: The Minimal Legal and Ethical Absolute

Economists and most philosophers have used utilitarian-based theories to determine the dividing line between good and bad trade policy. But utilitarian approaches, as we have seen, have several fatal flaws. For one thing, there is no way to measure gains and losses, so one can never be sure whether the gains exceed the losses. A small minority might gain much while the vast majority lose little individually. The analysis thus tends to break down into untrammeled majoritarianism. But even the slide into majoritarianism will not solve the gain/loss question because it is not possible to precisely measure whether a small loss by a large majority can be offset by a large gain by a small special interest, resulting in a net positive benefit.

But an even worse flaw in the majoritarianism approach is the total disregard of individual rights. A utilitarian would approve a trade policy even if someone's rights were violated as long as total utility was deemed to be increased by adoption of the policy. When one breaks down trade policy to its essentials, however, one finds nothing more than individual contracts—individuals trading what they have for what they want. Thus trade policy is nothing more than an application of contract property, and association rights. Governments were formed to protect these rights, and any government that disparages these rights loses its legitimacy. The measure of whether a trade policy meets minimum legal and ethical standards is whether it violates anyone's property, contract or association rights. If it does, then it fails to meet the minimal ethical standard.

Bibliography

Bartlett, Bruce. "What's Wrong with Trade Sanctions?" *Policy Analysis* (Cato Institute), no. 64 (1985).

Bastiat, Frederic. *The Law*. Irvington-on-Hudson, N.Y.: Foundation for Economic Education, 1968.

Baughman, Laura Megna, and Thomas Emrich. "Analysis of the Impact of the Textile and Apparel Trade Enforcement Act of 1985." International Business and Economic Research Corporation, 1985. Cited in I. M. Destler and John S. Odell. *Anti-Protection: Changing Forces in United States Trade Politics*. Washington, D.C.: Institute for International Economics, 1987, pp. 54, 56.

Bovard, James. *The Fair Trade Fraud*. New York: St. Martin's Press, 1991.

Buchanan, James, Robert Tollison, and Gordon Tullock, eds. *Towards a Theory of the Rent Seeking Society*. College Station: Texas A&M University Press, 1980.

Clifford Winston and Associates. *Blind Intersection? Policy and the Automobile Industry*. Washington, D.C.: Brookings Institution, 1987. This study is summarized in Thomas D. Hopkins, *Cost of Regulation*. Rochester, N.Y.: Rochester Institute of Technology, 1991, pp. B8–9.

Cline, William R. *The Future of World Trade in Textiles and Apparel*. Washington, D.C.: Institute for International Economics, 1990.

Curtiss, W. M. *The Tariff Idea*. Irvington-on-Hudson, N.Y.: Foundation for Economic Education, 1953.

Denzau, Arthur T. *How Import Restraints Reduce Employment*. Saint Louis: Washington University, Center for the Study of American Business, 1987.

Gardner, Bruce L. "The United States." In Fred H. Sanderson, ed., *Agricultural Protectionism in the Industrialized World*. Washington, D.C.: Resources for the Future, 1990.

Hufbauer, Gary Clyde, Diane T. Berliner, and Kimberly Ann Elliott. *Trade Protection in the United States: 31 Case Studies*. Washington, D.C.: Institute for International Economics, 1986.

Hufbauer, Gary Clyde, Jeffrey J. Schott, and Kimberly Ann Elliott. *Economic Sanctions Reconsidered: History and Current Policy*. 2d ed. Washington, D.C.: Institute for International Economics, 1990.

———. *Economic Sanctions Reconsidered: Supplemental Case Histories*. 2d ed. Washington, D.C.: Institute for International Economics, 1990.

Knoll, M. S. "United States Antidumping Law: The Case for Reconsideration." *Texas International Law Journal* 22 (1987): 265–90.

Koller, R., Jr. "The Myth of Predatory Pricing: An Empirical Study." *Antitrust Law & Economics Review* 4 (1971): 105–23.

Martin, James J. "Pearl Harbor: Antecedents, Background and Consequences." In James J. Martin, *The Saga of Hog Island*. Colorado Springs, Colo.: Ralph Myles Publisher, 1977, pp. 114–31.

McGee, Robert W. "Trade Embargoes, Sanctions and Blockades: Some Overlooked Human Rights Issues." *Journal of World Trade* 32, no. 4 (August 1998): 139–44.

———. "The Case to Repeal the Antidumping Laws." *Northwestern Journal of International Law & Business 13* (spring 1993): 491–562.

———. "The Fatal Flaw in NAFTA, GATT and All Other Trade Agreements." *Northwestern Journal of International Law & Business 14* (spring 1994a): 549–65.

———. *A Trade Policy for Free Societies: The Case against Protectionism*. Westport, Conn.: Quorum Books, 1994b.

McGee, Robert W., and Walter Block. "Ethical Aspects of Initiating Antidumping Actions." *International Journal of Social Economics* 24 (1997a): 599–608.

———. "Must Protectionism Always Violate Rights?" *International Journal of Social Economics* 24 (1997b): 393–407.

Palmeter, N. David. "Torquemada and the Tariff Act: The Inquisitor Rides Again." *International Lawyer* 20 (1986): 641.

Pareto, Vilfredo. *Manual of Political Economy*. Various publishers, 1927.

Ricardo, David. *Principles of Political Economy and Taxation*. 1817.

Rothbard, Murray N. *Man, Economy and State*. Los Angeles: Nash Publishing, 1970.

Smith, Adam. *An Inquiry into the Causes and Nature of the Wealth of Nations*, 1776.

Spooner, Lysander. *No Treason: The Constitution of No Authority*. Colorado Springs, Colo.: Ralph Myles Publisher, 1973.

Taylor, A. J. P. *The Origins of the Second World War*. New York: Atheneum, 1983.

Turner, I. C. F. *Origins of the First World War*. New York: W. W. Norton, 1970.

United States International Trade Commission. "The Economic Effects of Antidumping and Counter vailing Duty Orders and Suspension Agreements." Investigation No. 332–344. Publication 2900. Washington, D.C.: U.S. International Trade Commission, June 1995.

Willett, Thomas D., and Mehrdad Jalalighajar. "U.S. Trade Policy and National Security." *Cato Journal* 3 (Winter 1983/84): 717–27.

24.2

Does Globalization Have an Ethical Problem?

Ethan B. Kapstein

International economic theory demonstrates that the freeing of trade and capital flows leads to a more efficient allocation of the world's scarce resources, generating greater output and consumption than would be possible if countries adopted policies of self-sufficiency. As a quintessentially utilitarian doctrine, it also claims that openness makes for good policy, since more output and consumption is held to be better than less. This body of theory, however, is relatively silent on the question of how this wealth ought to be distributed both within and between countries.[1] It is the issue of how the gains from globalization are distributed within countries that is discussed in this [reading].

The argument that will be made is that, from a moral or ethical perspective, economic opening must be judged not only in terms of its contribution to national output, but also in terms of how it affects individuals and their life chances. If it can be shown, for example, that globalization or trade opening creates groups of uncompensated "losers," then its alleged contribution to social welfare may be challenged on normative grounds. . . .

Examining the moral order underlying the free trade regime may prove illuminating to those who seek an understanding of why popular movements against globalization have taken root in many countries in recent years. . . .

On Distributive Justice

Economic theory tells us that opening a country to foreign trade may have distributive consequences for the domestic factors of production. But in what way does that constitute a moral problem, a problem of distributive justice?

As a body of theory, distributive justice concerns itself with the manner in which societies allocate scarce resources. That allocation is always a matter of policy choice. We could imagine some countries choosing an egalitarian principle of resource distribution, others adopting a market-based system, and still others following a proportionate scheme, as expressed by Marx's dictum, "to each according to his needs." As John Stuart Mill taught, the distribution of wealth and resources "is a matter of human institution only. The things once there, mankind, individually or collectively, can do with them as they like. They can place them at the disposal of whomsoever they please, on whatever terms. *The distribution of wealth, therefore, depends on the laws and customs of society*" (emphasis added).[2]

It has already been noted that international trade theory is a quintessentially utilitarian doctrine. Utilitarians advance the seemingly commonsense proposition that public policies should be guided by the simple rule of advancing the greatest good for the greatest number. This calculation, still widely used today in "cost-benefit analysis," (for example, the decision to build a new road or offer a tax credit), suggests that Policy 2 should be preferred over Policy 1 if Policy 2 produces the most overall "utility" or "happiness" for a given population (often defined in terms of wealth). Utilitarianism is thus a "consequentialist" philosophy; it argues that public policies should be chosen on the basis of their observable consequences for society, and not on the basis of any abstract "first principles" that must locate their ultimate source in God's will, natural law, or human intuition.

Unfortunately, utilitarianism is also perfectly compatible with wide-scale violations of individual rights in the interests of achieving the greatest good, a point noted by philosophers ranging from the liberal John Rawls to the libertarian Robert Nozick.[3] Take a simple example. Imagine that A, B, and C each earn $5 under

---

Source: Excerpts from Ethan B. Kapstein (2001), "Does Globalization Have an Ethical Problem?" in *Ethics and International Affairs: Extent & Limits*, ed. Jean-Marc Coicaud and Daniel Warner (New York: United Nations University Press): 248–254 and 261–263. Reprinted by permission of United Nations University Press.

Policy 1, for a total of $15. Under Policy 2 (let's call it a shift to free trade), A and B earn $3, but C now earns $12, for a total of $18. A utilitarian would urge us to adopt this policy change no matter the distributive consequences. (A more nuanced argument, such as that made famously by Nicholas Kaldor, would claim that since C *could* compensate A and B for their loss—say giving each of them $4 and keeping $10, so nobody is worse off but C is better off—it is the Pareto-superior policy.[4])

There are several reasons for attacking this utilitarian logic. One could argue, for example, that since A and B had legitimate property rights in their labour, policies which deprive them of the rents that normally accrued to them are unjust in the absence of compensation. But the contrary position could also be adopted: namely, that A and B were in fact "rent-seekers" who benefited from protection under Policy 1, and that the shift to Policy 2 is simply stripping them of that monopoly gain.

An alternative and powerful challenge to utilitarianism was developed by John Rawls in his monumental work, *A Theory of Justice*. The "justice as fairness" framework developed by Rawls has, it will be argued, tremendous relevance for debates over the distributive consequences of economic policy change, including the move towards a more open economy. Rawls's emphasis on the "least advantaged" among us is a powerful reminder that, were we on the losing end of change, we would probably want compensation of some sort to assist us in the adjustment process. It is this sort of argument that will be adopted here.

In making the case against utilitarianism, Rawls asserts that:

> Offhand it hardly seems likely that persons who view themselves as equals, entitled to press their claims upon one another, would agree to a principle which may require lesser life prospects for some simply for the sake of a greater sum of advantages enjoyed by others. Since each desires to protect his interests . . . no one has a reason to acquiesce in an enduring loss for himself in order to bring about a greater net balance of satisfaction . . . a rational man would not accept a basic structure merely because it maximized the algebraic sum of advantages irrespective of his own basic rights and interests.[5]

One of the great strengths of the Rawlsian approach is its reliance on the economic framework, grounded on the assumption of rational, self-interested actors. The question at stake is the sort of institutions such actors would build, and whether such institutions conform to some reasonable notion of justice. For Rawls, the "primary subject of justice is the basic structure of society, or more exactly, the way in which the major social institutions distribute fundamental rights and duties and determine the division of advantages from social cooperation." These institutions, which include the political constitution and the principal social and economic institutions, "define men's rights and duties and influence their life prospects, what they can expect to be and how well they can hope to do." Rawls focuses on these deep structures because their effects on life chances "are so profound and present from the start."[6]

Thus, a societal structure that institutionalizes discrimination against certain individuals—that makes it more difficult or even impossible for certain people (perhaps because of race, creed, colour, or gender) to achieve the same goals as those who are in the favoured group—must be considered unjust. We should evaluate institutions in terms of the inequalities they engender—of income, of life chances, of expectations for holding office or achieving one's goals.

Now in choosing rules and institutions, it is likely that rational individuals, coming together as equals, would seek to establish a "level playing field" for their interaction. That is, they would wish to write rules and build institutions that do not favour one person over another, so that nobody would be unfairly advantaged at the start. In order to succeed at the task of social cooperation, the individuals would have to sit down together and put their own personalities, preferences, and interests aside. They must behave as if they were "representative" members of their community, making choices that they believe any rational individual would also adopt if he or she was in their place.

It is in this context that Rawls posits his famous "original position" in which individuals choose constitutional principles for the society in which they live behind a "veil of ignorance," in which they know nothing about their particular backgrounds or talents and act instead as if they were "representative" individuals. This setting "prevents anyone from being advantaged or disadvantaged by the contingencies of social class and fortune; and hence the bargaining problems which arise in everyday life from the possession of this knowledge do not affect the choice of principles."[7]

What principles of justice would one write from behind this veil of ignorance? Rawls posits two:

> first, each person engaged in an institution or affected by it has an equal right to the most extensive basic liberty compatible with a similar liberty for others; and second, social and economic inequalities are to be arranged so that they are both (a) reasonably expected to be to everyone's advantage, and (b) attached to positions and offices (equally) open to all.[8]

The first principle is fairly straightforward; the second may be less obvious. Further, given its importance to this discussion of distributive justice, it warrants clarification and discussion.

Rawls's second principle, which he calls the "difference principle," is founded upon the idea that the problem of distributive justice concerns the "differences in (an individual's) life prospects" that arise owing to institutional and societal factors. Discrimination against women or minorities in hiring for certain jobs, or the decrease in life chances that may result because one is the child of a plumber rather than of a surgeon, would be examples of structural influences that place certain individuals in a disadvantaged position. For Rawls, these differences are just if "the advantages of the more fortunate promote the well-being of the least fortunate, that is, when a decrease in their advantages would make the least fortunate even worse off than they are. *The basic structure is perfectly just when the prospects of the least fortunate are as great as they can be*" (emphasis added).[9]

Now let us apply the Rawlsian framework to the issue at hand: the distributive consequences of economic policy change. Imagine, as suggested in the earlier example, that the shift from a policy of protection to a policy of openness results in a change in the distribution of income. Imagine further that unskilled workers find their incomes decline, while owners of capital find their incomes rise. As a result of free trade, income inequality has increased and new patterns of winners and losers have emerged.

What is wrong with that outcome? The Rawlsian view leads us to ask whether we, as self-interested actors, would approve such a policy if we were unskilled workers. The reason we would ask ourselves this rhetorical question, even if we were among the winners, is because economic policy change of a different kind could ultimately turn us or our children into losers, and so we have an interest in structuring institutions—buying insurance—in such a way as to account for that eventuality. We would thus probably adopt some compensatory scheme as the "price" we pay for economic opening; and indeed, many scholars have identified a strong relationship between economic openness and the adoption of welfare state policies, with such countries as Germany and Sweden providing notable examples.

Yet there are other types of institutions that are equally important in assisting losers, chiefly financial and economic institutions. These institutions are fundamental to promoting labour and social mobility. To the extent that a loser in Period 1 can get the financing and education needed to become a winner in Period 2, then s/he is more likely to accept economic change. The building of domestic institutions that help potential losers adjust to economic change should thus be seen as a fundamental complement to policies of greater openness. . . .

Conclusions

The latest economic research on the relationship between economic openness and labour outcomes demonstrates that the growth of the 1990s' tide has failed to "lift all boats." Unskilled workers are struggling in the face of unemployment, job insecurity, and rising income inequality. Of all these developments, rising income inequality is of special concern to many scholars, due not only to its political implications for the free trade agenda, but also its possible economic consequence in terms of lower growth rates in future.

What are the implications of these findings for students working at the interface of philosophy and political economy? The literature reveals several important gaps that could usefully be filled by careful theoretical and empirical work. These contributions would help refine our understanding of the issues at stake in the globalization-labour debate.

First, as we have seen, there are important analytical gaps in social welfare analysis. Bridging the utilitarian and liberal perspectives remains a major challenge for political economy scholarship, with important implications for policy analysis as well. We have still not found a way to reconcile the view that economic openness is "good" for society with the design of adequate compensation schemes for losers and their families.

Second, the empirical finding of increasing income inequality in the USA and persistent unemployment in Western Europe raises important questions concerning the making of economic policy. Whose interests are reflected in public policy, and how has that constellation changed in recent decades? Are exporter interests trumping those of organized labour? What explains the differences in national labour adjustment strategies in the face of increasing economic integration? . . .

Third, the openness-labour relationship reminds us of the role of political and economic institutions in influencing the life chances of all citizens, but especially the least advantaged. A just economy would be one in which all members of society can benefit from economic change as their talents permit. This means that change and opportunity must go together, via the capital markets and educational establishments. In countries that simply permit economic change to occur without the creation of such enabling institutions, resentment and backlash may be expected.

In sum, the ethics of globalization are a function of how its effects are channelled through social organizations, mainly nation-states and their associated institutions, to the individuals who constitute the ultimate moral unit. The author has argued that a Rawlsian approach, with its emphasis on the fate of the least advantaged, provides a useful analytical tool for examining questions of distributive justice within the context of economic openness. It reminds us that globalization can only be welfare enhancing when it promotes the life chances of *all* members of the international community. In this respect, we still have a long way to go.

Notes

1. For a classic statement of the utilitarian position with respect to trade theory, see Meade, J., 1955, *The Theory of International Economic Policy, Trade and Welfare*. Oxford: Oxford University Press, p. 5.
2. Mill, J. S., 1970, *Principles of Political Economy*, New York: Penguin, orig. 1848, book II, chap. 1, p. 350.
3. Nozick, R., 1974, *Anarchy, State, and Utopia*. New York: Basic Books.
4. For a useful review of the utilitarian literature see Acocella, N., 1998, *The Foundations of Economic Policy*. New York: Cambridge University Press, p. 34.
5. Rawls, J., 1971, *A Theory of Justice*. Cambridge, MA: Belknap Press, p. 14.
6. *Ibid.*, p. 7.
7. *Ibid.*, p. 321.
8. *Ibid.*, p. 60.
9. *Ibid.*, p. 328.

24.3

Two Cheers for Sweatshops

Nicholas D. Kristof and Sheryl WuDunn

It was breakfast time, and the food stand in the village in northeastern Thailand was crowded. Maesubin Sisoipha, the middle-aged woman cooking the food, was friendly, her portions large and the price right. For the equivalent of about 5 cents, she offered a huge green mango leaf filled with rice, fish paste and fried beetles. It was a hearty breakfast, if one didn't mind the odd antenna left sticking in one's teeth.

One of the half-dozen men and women sitting on a bench eating was a sinewy, bare-chested laborer in his late 30's named Mongkol Latlakorn. It was a hot, lazy day, and so we started chatting idly about the food and, eventually, our families. Mongkol mentioned that his daughter, Darin, was 15, and his voice softened as he spoke of her. She was beautiful and smart, and her father's hopes rested on her.

"Is she in school?" we asked.

"Oh, no," Mongkol said, his eyes sparkling with amusement. "She's working in a factory in Bangkok. She's making clothing for export to America." He explained that she was paid $2 a day for a nine-hour shift, six days a week.

"It's dangerous work," Mongkol added. "Twice the needles went right through her hands. But the managers bandaged up her hands, and both times she got better again and went back to work."

"How terrible," we murmured sympathetically.

Mongkol looked up, puzzled. "It's good pay," he said. "I hope she can keep that job. There's all this talk about factories closing now, and she said there are rumors that her factory might close. I hope that doesn't happen. I don't know what she would do then."

He was not, of course, indifferent to his daughter's suffering; he simply had a different perspective from ours—not only when it came to food but also when it came to what constituted desirable work.

Nothing captures the difference in mind-set between East and West more than attitudes toward sweatshops. Nike and other American companies have been hammered in the Western press over the last decade for producing shoes, toys and other products in grim little factories with dismal conditions. Protests against sweatshops and the dark forces of globalization that they seem to represent have become common at meetings of the World Bank and the World Trade Organization and, this month, at a World Economic Forum in Australia, livening up the scene for Olympic athletes arriving for the competition. Yet sweatshops that seem brutal from the vantage point of an American sitting in his living room can appear tantalizing to a Thai laborer getting by on beetles.

Fourteen years ago, we moved to Asia and began reporting there. Like most Westerners, we arrived in the region outraged at sweatshops. In time, though, we came to accept the view supported by most Asians: that the campaign against sweatshops risks harming the very people it is intended to help. For beneath their grime, sweatshops are a clear sign of the industrial revolution that is beginning to reshape Asia.

This is not to praise sweatshops. Some managers are brutal in the way they house workers in firetraps, expose children to dangerous chemicals, deny bathroom breaks, demand sexual favors, force people to work double shifts or dismiss anyone who tries to organize a union. Agitation for improved safety conditions can be helpful, just as it was in 19th-century Europe. But Asian workers would be aghast at the idea of American consumers boycotting certain toys or clothing in protest. The simplest way to help the poorest Asians would be to buy more from sweatshops, not less.

On our first extended trip to China, in 1987, we traveled to the Pearl River Delta in the south of the country. There we visited several factories, including one in the boomtown of Dongguan, where about 100 female workers sat at workbenches stitching together bits of leather to make purses for a Hong Kong company. We chatted with several women as their fingers flew over their work and asked about their hours.

Source: Nicholas D. Kristof and Sheryl WuDunn, "Two Cheers for Sweatshops," *The New York Times*, September 24, 2000.

"I start at about 6:30, after breakfast, and go until about 7 p.m.," explained one shy teenage girl. "We break for lunch, and I take half an hour off then."

"You do this six days a week?"

"Oh, no. Every day."

"Seven days a week?"

"Yes." She laughed at our surprise. "But then I take a week or two off at Chinese New Year to go back to my village."

The others we talked to all seemed to regard it as a plus that the factory allowed them to work long hours. Indeed, some had sought out this factory precisely because it offered them the chance to earn more.

"It's actually pretty annoying how hard they want to work," said the factory manager, a Hong Kong man. "It means we have to worry about security and have a supervisor around almost constantly."

It sounded pretty dreadful, and it was. We and other journalists wrote about the problems of child labor and oppressive conditions in both China and South Korea. But, looking back, our worries were excessive. Those sweatshops tended to generate the wealth to solve the problems they created. If Americans had reacted to the horror stories in the 1980's by curbing imports of those sweatshop products, then neither southern China nor South Korea would have registered as much progress as they have today.

The truth is, those grim factories in Dongguan and the rest of southern China contributed to a remarkable explosion of wealth. In the years since our first conversations there, we've returned many times to Dongguan and the surrounding towns and seen the transformation. Wages have risen from about $50 a month to $250 a month or more today. Factory conditions have improved as businesses have scrambled to attract and keep the best laborers. A private housing market has emerged, and video arcades and computer schools have opened to cater to workers with rising incomes. A hint of a middle class has appeared—as has China's closest thing to a Western-style independent newspaper, *Southern Weekend*.

Partly because of these tens of thousands of sweatshops, China's economy has become one of the hottest in the world. Indeed, if China's 30 provinces were counted as individual countries, then the 20 fastest-growing countries in the world between 1978 and 1995 would all have been Chinese. When Britain launched the Industrial Revolution in the late 18th century, it took 58 years for per capita output to double. In China, per capita output has been doubling every 10 years.

In fact, the most vibrant parts of Asia are nearly all in what might be called the Sweatshop Belt, from China and South Korea to Malaysia, Indonesia and even Bangladesh and India. Today these sweatshop countries control about one-quarter of the global economy. As the industrial revolution spreads through China and India, there are good reasons to think that Asia will continue to pick up speed. Some World Bank forecasts show Asia's share of global gross domestic product rising to 55 to 60 percent by about 2025—roughly the West's share at its peak half a century ago. The sweatshops have helped lay the groundwork for a historic economic realignment that is putting Asia back on its feet. Countries are rebounding from the economic crisis of 1997-98 and the sweatshops—seen by Westerners as evidence of moribund economies—actually reflect an industrial revolution that is raising living standards in the East.

Of course, it may sound silly to say that sweatshops offer a route to prosperity, when wages in the poorest countries are sometimes less than $1 a day. Still, for an impoverished Indonesian or Bangladeshi woman with a handful of kids who would otherwise drop out of school and risk dying of mundane diseases like diarrhea, $1 or $2 a day can be a life-transforming wage.

This was made abundantly clear in Cambodia, when we met a 40-year-old woman named Nhem Yen, who told us why she moved to an area with particularly lethal malaria. "We needed to eat," she said. "And here there is wood, so we thought we could cut it and sell it."

But then Nhem Yen's daughter and son-in-law both died of malaria, leaving her with two grandchildren and five children of her own. With just one mosquito net, she had to choose which children would sleep protected and which would sleep exposed.

In Cambodia, a large mosquito net costs $5. If there had been a sweatshop in the area, however harsh or dangerous, Nhem Yen would have leapt at the chance to work in it, to earn enough to buy a net big enough to cover all her children.

For all the misery they can engender, sweatshops at least offer a precarious escape from the poverty that is the developing world's greatest problem. Over the past 50 years, countries like India resisted foreign exploitation, while countries that started at a similar economic level—like Taiwan and South Korea—accepted sweatshops as the price of development. Today there can be no doubt about which approach worked better. Taiwan and South Korea are modern countries with low rates of infant mortality and high levels of education; in contrast, every year 3.1 million Indian children die before the age of 5, mostly from diseases of poverty like diarrhea.

The effect of American pressure on sweatshops is complicated. While it clearly improves conditions at factories that produce branded merchandise for companies like Nike, it also raises labor costs across the board. That encourages less well-established companies to mechanize and to reduce the number of employees needed. The upshot is to help people who currently have jobs in Nike plants but to risk jobs for others. The only thing a country like Cambodia has to offer is terribly cheap wages; if companies are scolded for paying those wages, they will shift their manufacturing to marginally richer areas like Malaysia or Mexico.

Sweatshop monitors do have a useful role. They can compel factories to improve safety. They can also call attention to the impact of sweatshops on the environment. The greatest downside of industrialization is not exploitation of workers but toxic air and water. In Asia each year, three million people die from the effects of pollution. The factories springing up throughout the region are far more likely to kill people through the chemicals they expel than through terrible working conditions.

By focusing on these issues, by working closely with organizations and news media in foreign countries, sweatshops can be improved. But refusing to buy sweatshop products risks making Americans feel good while harming those we are trying to help. As a Chinese proverb goes, "First comes the bitterness, then there is sweetness and wealth and honor for 10,000 years."

Part IV

Emerging Issues in International Relations

The purpose of Part IV is to introduce readers to some of the emerging issues in international relations, allowing the reader to see the breadth of the field and current questions that scholars seek to answer. The first three parts of the book focused primarily on topics that fall clearly under the domain of international relations, but this part also draws on and introduces related theories and concepts from the discipline of comparative politics.

Comparative politics generally focuses on the study of the domestic political systems within foreign countries and the identification or explanation of differences and similarities among countries. While international relations and comparative politics overlap in this part of the book, they are two separate fields within political science. However, the two fields are converging more and more as states take on greater roles in the domestic politics of other countries (e.g., Iraq and Afghanistan) and as scholars and policy practitioners have recognized that internal political challenges (e.g., 9/11, immigration patterns, the Arab Spring, etc.) may impact external state behavior.

Some political scientists are now looking at both the interaction among states and how states operate domestically. Further, due to its heavy focus on the role of institutions in enabling cooperation, some international political economy scholars have moved beyond the traditional focus on trade, monetary policy, debt, and foreign investment to also study issues such as poverty, foreign aid, the environment, immigration, criminal networks, etc. Part IV focuses on understanding "Why do states do what they do?" and "What causes conflict and cooperation in the international system?" by examining the challenges that states face due to poverty and uneven wealth distribution, weak internal governance, emerging international legal structures, and pollution. This part of the book allows the reader to draw on Parts I through III in order to apply, using intellectual pluralism, the previous theories and concepts to major existing and emerging challenges in the international system.

Poverty and Inequality

Going back to the section on civil conflict in Part II, there is a popular belief that **poverty** contributes to intrastate conflict, and others argue that poverty causes terrorism. The previous readings explained that, while there is no direct correlation between poverty and conflict, relative deprivation, or **inequality**, can contribute to the preconditions for conflict. The **World Bank** defines poverty "as whether households or individuals have enough resources or abilities today to meet their needs."[1] Inequality is defined by the World Bank as relative deprivation in terms of "the way individuals or households perceive their position in society"[2] related to "the distribution of income, consumption or other attributes across the population."[3]

Political scientist Terry Lynn Karl argues that despite Latin America's embrace of **neoliberal reforms** (e.g., privatization of state-owned enterprises, deregulation of markets, expansion of free trade, promotion of the private sector, etc.) to their economies, those policies further exacerbated the problem of inequality. She argues that these externally driven, one-size-fits-all reforms failed to account for the political context and structures, originating during the colonial period, which set Latin American on a vicious cycle of inequality. Readers should think about the implications of Karl's discussion about the distribution of wealth equaling power and derive the underlying theoretical tradition that she draws on to make her argument.

In addressing the challenges of poverty, economist Paul Collier narrows the definition of poor countries to separate the world's **developing countries** that may be poor relative to wealthy **developed countries** from nations mired in abject poverty. He explains that the **least developed countries** have shown little to no signs of growth or the ability to break out of four different traps that inhibit development. Collier then discusses three aspects of globalization—trade, capital flows, and migration—and the impact of each on the prospects for the "Bottom Billion" (the world's population living in abject poverty) escaping from the **development traps**.

Political scientist Bruce Bueno de Mesquita and political economist Hilton L. Root demonstrate the difficulty of escaping the poor governance trap through their argument that, contrary to popular belief, autocratic "leaders who produce poverty and misery through systemic corruption . . . keep their jobs longer than do [democratic leaders] who enrich their countries."[4]

State-Building

Since the end of the Cold War, foreign interventions, some legitimized by the United Nations and others not, have typically taken the form of peace-building, nation-building, or **state-building** in response to civil conflict. The terms *nation-building* and *state-building* are often used interchangeably, although they do have distinct definitions. Most contemporary foreign interventions of this type, such as those in El Salvador, Mozambique, Haiti, Bosnia, Sierra Leone, East Timor, Kosovo, Afghanistan, and Iraq, are technically state-building efforts—that is, developing the domestic authority structures, political institutions, and economic development within a state that lacks these features. In order to put modern efforts at state-building into context, it is necessary to understand some of the foundational, theoretical arguments about state formation.

Economist Paul Collier describes the historical process, first explained by social scientist Charles Tilly, that explains how violence has shaped **state formation** over centuries. This historical sketch of state formation, however, is based on the development of the European states. Readers should consider how well this model applies in the contemporary international system (Robert H. Jackson and Carl G. Rosberg address this issue in the following section on failed states).

Nobel laureate economist Douglass C. North, economic historian John Joseph Wallis, and political scientist Barry R. Weingast also explore the role of violence in the development of **social order**. They introduce the conceptual categorization of societal organization as social order, which they classify as either **limited-access orders (LAOs)** or **open-access orders (OAOs)**. These orders refer to how much access members of society have to institutions of human organization—using the definition of regimes (or institutions) from Part I: Theoretical Traditions in International Relations—and how those organizations limit and control violence. States may transition from LAOs—authoritarian or pseudo-democratic regimes—to OAOs—liberal democracies—if they can move through three doorstep conditions.

While Collier and North, Wallis, and Weingast describe the internal process of state formation, political scientist Francis Fukuyama discusses the role of other states or international actors in helping build other states. He distinguishes reconstruction from development and argues that despite continued nation-building efforts over many years, there has been little institutional memory and learning, which has led recently to poorly planned and poorly executed state-building efforts.

Failed States

What are **failed states**, and why should other states care about them? The answer to this question directly demonstrates why international relations and comparative politics are converging in certain issue areas. As

9/11 demonstrated, "weak and failed states pose an acute risk to U.S. and global security. . . . When chaos prevails, terrorism, narcotics trade, weapons proliferation, and other forms of organized crime can flourish."[5]

Before addressing the implications of failed and **weak states**, political scientists Robert H. Jackson and Carl G. Rosberg define the concept of statehood, differentiating the **empirical (*de facto*) state** from the **juridical (*de jure*) state**. They further explain that following decolonization after World Wars I and II, the emphasis on the juridical state has halted the state formation process described by Paul Collier (refer back to the section on state-building) and has contributed to the persistence of weak and failed states.

Where Jackson and Rosberg analyze how external actors keep states alive that cannot govern themselves, political scientist Tanisha M. Fazal analyzes the conditions under which external states lead to the deaths of other states. She argues that until the end of World War II, buffer states—those caught between two competing powers—were the most likely candidates for state death, and she provides three reasons, drawn from different theoretical traditions in Part I as well as from Jackson and Rosberg, for why externally driven, violent state death has nearly disappeared.

Political scientist Stephen D. Krasner and diplomat Carlos Pascual describe a policy effort by the U.S. government to create an office within the State Department to address state failure, and the reader should focus on understanding their argument about the four phases of post-conflict transition. Additionally, the reader should recognize the theoretical basis for Krasner and Pascual's argument and which components they derive from other readings in this section.

Foreign Aid

Another form of intervention to help developing or weak states—in an effort to address poverty, promote state development, or prevent state failure—is **foreign aid**. In the United States, foreign aid is often a heated topic during the election cycle, with some believing the United States gives too much aid abroad and others thinking the United States does not give enough. That debate will endure, which is why it is important to try to understand the actual intents and purposes behind foreign aid as well what foreign aid actually is.

While many people lump together **military aid**, **geopolitical aid**, and **official development assistance (ODA)**, they are not the same. Military aid supports the security institutions of a country, and geopolitical aid, also known as Economic Support Funds, supports strategic allies. ODA is the form of foreign aid that is supposed to help promote the general welfare and economic development of developing countries. In 2000, the United Nations established the **Millennium Development Goals (MDGs)** to cut the number of people living in extreme poverty—defined by the World Bank as those living on less than $1.25 per day—in half by 2015. To achieve these goals, aid proponents, such as economist Jeffrey D. Sachs have argued that wealthy nations must contribute more ODA. Sachs further argues that achieving the MDGs is possible based on technocratic solutions, and all that is needed to implement those solutions is a big increase in foreign aid.

The enduring debate about the appropriate level of foreign aid has been captured between Sachs and fellow economist William Easterly. Easterly argues that Sach's top-down, big-bang, foreign-aid–driven theoretical approach to ending poverty is misguided and paternalistic—a new incarnation of the "White Man's Burden." Easterly instead argues that efforts to use aid to reduce poverty require a bottom-up approach. Easterly is not opposed to aid but finds that rather than imposing democratic capitalism on developing states, donors must allow for the natural evolution of state institutions to progress. By just "doing something," large amounts of external aid may exacerbate the internal problems by determining winners and losers, with those already in power usually the winners, and preventing institutional evolution.

Traditionally, foreign aid is given based on ***ex-post* conditionality**, meaning that donors give money with the expectation that the recipient will make certain changes after the money is given. Economist Steven Radelet explains how aid can be used as a form of **"soft" power** to help secure the world. He also describes an evolution in foreign-aid giving by the United States called the **Millennium Challenge Account (MCA)**, not to be confused with the U.N.'s MDGs. The MCA has changed, in part, how the United States gives foreign aid by establishing objective measures, based on political, economic, and social development, to determine which countries should receive aid from the MCA and by switching to a model of ***ex-ante* conditionality**, meaning that recipients have to make the desired changes before receiving the aid money.

INTERNATIONAL LAW

Since the end of World War II, the number of rule-based international organizations established through treaties—such as the General Agreement on Tariffs and Trade/World Trade Organization, the European Economic Community, the **International Criminal Court**, etc.—has expanded. The first two readings argue that with this expansion and evolution of institutions and dispute resolution mechanisms, **international law** has grown in relevance for international politics in terms of international rules impacting domestic laws and state behavior. The reader should return to the concept of anarchy introduced in Part I—the international system lacks an authority higher than the state that can impose known rules and laws, indifferently judge violation of those laws, and impartially enforce punishments for violations—when assessing this argument.

Recognizing the lack of a higher authority in the international system, political scientists and legal scholars Kenneth W. Abbott, Robert O. Keohane, Andrew Moravcsik, Anne-Marie Slaughter, and Duncan Snidal develop a typology to determine the strength of legalization in the international environment. They describe legalization as a set of characteristics, defined along three dimensions (**obligation**, **precision**, and **delegation**), that institutions may (or may not) possess. Institutions then fall on a continuum from hard to soft law based on the level of legalization under each of those dimensions.

Legal scholar Steven R. Ratner provides an overview of the evolution of international law and explains how international law seeks to enhance international stability, protect human rights, and reduce abuses of power, but due to the condition of anarchy, international law has relied on states to develop and accept norms of behavior. Traditionally, international law has focused on regulating relations between states but has begun to address issues traditionally viewed as domestic concerns—human rights, the environment, labor standards, etc. To address these new challenges, Ratner argues that international law must embrace new forms, topics, technologies, and actors.

Legal scholar Jack Goldsmith and political scientist Stephen D. Krasner, however, argue that modern international law, as epitomized by the rise of universal jurisdiction, the International Criminal Court, and demands for humanitarian intervention, is just a return to the **idealism** of the interwar period that damaged international peace and stability, ultimately leading to World War II. They describe four fundamental flaws with the new idealism found in international law. Readers should be able to identify the international relations and ethical traditions introduced in Part I that provide the underlying arguments for the readings in this section.

THE ENVIRONMENT AND CLIMATE CHANGE

How to address **environmental management** and **climate change** are emerging and contentious issues in the field of international policy because of the interaction of politics and economics based on the policy choices related to the distribution of scarcity—**pollution** and costs of policy implementation. To understand the international relations concerns about how environmental management and climate change can lead to conflict or cooperation, one does not need to debate the validity of climate science findings. Rather, one should seek to understand how to reconcile the domestic political and economic policies of different states, aiming to maximize their individual state interests, to achieve international collaboration on policies for managing pollution and the costs of implementing those policies.

The two readings from the British business magazine *The Economist* relate to a memorandum written by economist Lawrence Summers. This provocative memo argued that outsourcing polluting industries to the least developed countries would be good for their economic growth. *The Economist,* in the follow-up article, gave qualified support to Summers's claims based on purely economic principles, ignoring the interaction of politics and economics that takes place in international relations.

To better understand why states choose to support or not support international environmental agreements, political scientists Detlef Sprinz and Tapani Vaahtoranta develop a unit-based (second-image) model (emphasizing domestic causes; refer back to Kenneth Waltz's reading in the "Social Scientific and Theoretical Analysis" section in Part I). This approach explains how state interests shape their position in international negotiations (refer back to the "Bargaining and War" section in Part II and the "Domestic Politics and Trade" section in Part III to better understand the theoretical underpinnings of this argument).

Sprinz and Vaahtoranta develop their model and expectations of state behavior based on a state's levels of **ecological vulnerability** and **abatement costs**. Readers should be able to use the logic of the model to apply other international relations challenges by changing the independent variables.

Policy scholar Ruth Greenspan Bell argues that to address climate change, a one-size-fits-all policy strategy will not work. Instead, policies must be customized to meet the specific needs of each country that will have to implement them. She further argues that current proposals to institute a global **cap-and-trade** regime, based on market economy principles, ultimately will not reduce pollution.

A New International Order?

While the readings in this section are older and responded to the events taking place at the end of the Cold War, they are classic works that people reference to this day, whether or not they agree with them. Political scientist Francis Fukuyama wrote his piece as the Soviet Union was collapsing. Since 9/11, many critics have claimed that Fukuyama was wrong in his claim of "the End of History" because of the rise of radical Islam; however, Fukuyama did argue that alternative ideologies, particularly **religious fundamentalism** and **nationalism**, and conflict would still persist but that, ultimately, political and economic liberalism would become the final form of government of all states in the foreseeable future. Political scientist Benjamin R. Barber responded by arguing that **globalism**—the commercial homogenization of the world—and **tribalism**—divisive nationalism focused on subgroups—are both threats to democracy.

Additionally, political scientist Samuel P. Huntington responded to Fukuyama and Barber by arguing that both described what was taking place in the world but that both missed what the future of global politics would look like. Huntington argued that future conflicts would expand beyond the state and encompass **civilizations**. The major civilizations would likely end up in conflict over different views about the relationship between the form of government and those it governed. Readers should recognize the use of intellectual pluralism in these readings. Fukuyama draws from liberalism and constructivism, while Huntington comes from a realist perspective but makes significant use of identity in his argument.

Ethics and Development Assistance

As discussed earlier, debates about the political implications of foreign aid have become quite fervent. Ethical debates about the provision of **development assistance** are equally passionate. Philosopher Peter Singer argues that individuals and states have a moral obligation to give assistance to those who are suffering. In Singer's view, this giving is not charity or a choice but a responsibility, and the affluent should sacrifice their accustomed standards and give to the point of comparable moral importance.

Conversely, ecologist and bioethicist Garret Hardin argues that the world contains scarce resources and has a limited carrying capacity, similar to that of a lifeboat. As such, it is not possible to redistribute the world's wealth, and any effort to do so is a perversion of the concept of justice. Hardin further states that while his argument may sound harsh, ensuring the survival of future generations is more important than helping the poor of today survive.

Discussion Questions for Part IV: Emerging Issues in International Relations

1. Discuss the potential impact of inequality on conflict and cooperation within and between states.

2. Evaluate the process and challenges for state formation in today's developing world. What impact have weak, failing, and failed states had on recent U.S. foreign policy decisions?

3. Analyze the political-economic arguments for and against foreign aid. Which do you find more persuasive and why? Explain what role and impact, positive and negative, foreign aid can have on state development.

4. Explain how it is possible, if it is, to enforce international law under the condition of international

anarchy. What theoretical traditions did you draw on to explain your argument? What would be a counter-argument from another theoretical tradition?

5. Describe why cooperation among international actors over environmental issues, particularly climate change, is elusive, and how these obstacles may lead to conflict. What are the implications of climate change for international security, based on theories from this book, if the Arctic continues to melt and becomes like the Great Lakes?

6. Does society have a moral obligation to provide foreign aid or development assistance? Will such behavior alleviate poverty? Which of the ethical arguments do you find most persuasive and why?

Key Concepts

abatement costs
cap-and-trade
civilizations
climate change
delegation
developed countries
developing countries
development assistance
development traps
ecological vulnerability
empirical (*de facto*) state
environmental management
***ex-ante* conditionality**
***ex-post* conditionality**
failed states
foreign aid
geopolitical aid
globalism
idealism
inequality
International Criminal Court
international law
juridical (*de jure*) state
least developed countries
limited-access orders (LAOs)
military aid
Millennium Challenge Account (MCA)
Millennium Development Goals (MDGs)
nationalism
neoliberal reforms
obligation
official development assistance (ODA)
open-access orders (OAOs)
pollution
poverty
precision
religious fundamentalism
social order
"soft" power
state-building
state formation
tribalism
weak states
World Bank

Notes

1. The World Bank. 2011. "Measuring Poverty." http://go.worldbank.org/0C60K5UK40 (accessed June 27, 2012).
2. The World Bank. 2011. "Measuring Inequality." http://go.worldbank.org/W2TRRD1PP0 (accessed June 27, 2012).
3. "Measuring Poverty."
4. Bueno de Mesquita and Root, "The Political Roots of Poverty: The Economic Logic of Autocracy", p. 435.
5. Stephen D. Krasner and Carlos Pascual, "Addressing State Failure", p. 466.

25 Poverty and Inequality

25.1

The Vicious Cycle of Inequality in Latin America

Terry Lynn Karl

Latin America is the region in the world with the greatest inequities. The acute disparities, affecting virtually all aspects of economic, social, and political life, are fundamental to understanding why the results of the past two decades of development have been so disappointing there. Economic growth has been surprisingly low despite the region having embraced neoliberal restructuring, which cut inflation to single-digit levels, reduced budget deficits, and generally lowered country public external debt. As of the early years of the new century the quality of services remained poor, unemployment high, and widespread crime and violence threatened daily life. Moreover, more than a third of the people in the region lived in poverty, nearly eighty million in extreme poverty, with incomes of less than one (U.S.) dollar a day. When asked their opinions about social issues, Latin Americans consistently stated that poverty seemed higher than ever before, their quality of life lower, and their political institutions unsatisfactory. They also expressed anxiety about the future. Not surprisingly, in a region characterized by the most unequal distribution of income and assets in the world, most continued to believe their societies to be fundamentally unjust (Lora 2000). . . .

Neoliberals ignored the political context of their reforms in areas where their prescriptions were bound to have adverse consequences for inequality. Thus, while it may be the case that Latin American countries would have had even greater poverty without the macroeconomic adjustments that tamed inflation, there is accumulating evidence that the accentuation of inequality and the failure to reduce poverty is partially the consequence of the types of reforms enacted, and not merely the result of an economic crisis that plagued the region in the 1980s. For example, in their enthusiasm to liberalize financial markets very rapidly, there was little attempt to ensure that regulatory mechanisms aimed at minimizing the risk of financial crises were in place prior to liberalization—even though any resulting economic downturn would disproportionately affect the poor. Nor did they heed constant warnings that privatizations—when implemented in the context of huge wealth disparities, weak judiciaries, and rent-seeking politicians—were very likely to further concentrate wealth, often through the very corruption they sought to correct. Nor were policies designed to stave off the consequences of dismantling labor institutions or to address the growing discontent of the middle strata (civil servants, unionized workers, pensioners, etc.), whose proximity to blatant increases in wealth helped to create an especially corrosive sense of injustice. To the contrary, in a number of cases specific policies unnecessarily increased poverty and further skewed the distribution of income. Subsidies given to Chilean banks in 1983, for example, amounted to ten

Source: Terry Karl. "The Vicious Cycle of Inequality in Latin America," in *What Justice? Whose Justice?*, ed. Susan Eva Eckstein and Timothy P. Wickham-Crowley, 133–137; 139–144.

times the annual cost of the Pinochet regime's emergency employment program.

But such positions are becoming increasingly difficult to sustain in the face of Latin America's record in the struggle against poverty and inequality. A combination of factors—the end of the Cold War, with the demise of the egalitarianism that had long been associated with socialism; growing concerns about globalization's impact on volatility and wages; and sharp critiques coming from Latin Americans themselves, sometimes in the form of armed movements—has contributed to a mounting consensus: that more egalitarian development is both economically and morally desirable in the Americas.[1] Economists now argue that Latin America's highly unequal access to land, education, and other assets are not merely untouched by the benefits of growth; they directly contribute to low growth rates and therefore the perpetuation of poverty (Birdsall and Londoño 1997, 1998; Deininger and Olinto 1999). In effect, a vicious cycle exists in which poverty and high levels of inequality impede growth, and growth rates are subsequently too low to adequately address the problems of poverty and inequality.[2] Thus, if Latin American countries are to reach the more impressive development records of their Asian counterparts, tackling inequality is essential. . . .

This [reading] argues the following: if inequality is based on differences in initial endowments of wealth or family connections, as is surely the case in Latin America, these inequalities will not only affect the prospects for growth, but they will also shape social and political life. High inequalities bias the political rules of the game and mold polities in favor of the wealthy and privileged, and they do so (to different degrees) whether regimes are authoritarian or democratic. Exceptionally high inequalities of wealth and income are the basis for exceptionally inequitable distributions of political power and representation, even in the continent's young democracies, and these power arrangements are subsequently unlikely to address the basic problem of high inequality. . . .

Transforming this vicious cycle into a virtuous cycle will not be easy because, as we shall see, this inevitably involves both asset redistribution and the reordering of political priorities—no easy task in Latin America.

The Origins Of The Vicious Cycle

Why is Latin America so different from other regions? Elsewhere (Karl 1997), I have argued that Latin America's poverty and inequality is linked paradoxically to the asset distribution of its natural wealth, especially its mineral riches. Most certainly a key explanation for the difference between East Asian and U.S. patterns of development, on the one hand, and Latin America, on the other, lies in the difference in the nature of their "natural capital" or assets and the manner in which these assets were initially divided. In Latin America, from the very beginning mineral and agricultural riches were a mixed blessing; in the context of a specific form of colonial rule they produced concentrated rents that centralized economic and political power and established the region's patterns of inequality. This initial asset inequality not only had a significant negative impact on long-term growth, but it also established stable patterns of skewed distributions of political and economic power that persist to this day.

The concentration of political and economic power in Latin America is a legacy of colonialism. The colonizers who arrived from Spain and Portugal encountered highly developed and complex indigenous societies: the population of the Americas in 1492 was probably greater than that of all of Europe. The goal of these colonizers was ownership of Latin America's rich endowment of natural resources, and conquest was the means to that end. Granted control over huge tracts of land and huge concentrations of minerals, these settlers superimposed themselves by force at the top of existing social structures. Initially through the *encomicuda* system, which "granted" huge number of Indians to the conquerors as laborers, and later through the slave trade, which aimed at guaranteeing a labor supply after the indigenous communities had been decimated. Colonizers were able to cultivate vast expanses of land and work the mines. In contrast to the northern United States—where colonizers sought to expel natives from their lands, rather than using their labor—this labor-intensive mode gave rise to a very unequal distribution of income and assets.

This is the past that has its claws in the present. Colonizers captured concentrated rents by establishing hierarchical political structures based on arbitrary executive dominance, an extremely weak rule of law, and excessive militarism—patterns that persist to this day. In order to guarantee its rents, the Crown built an elaborate bureaucracy and military structure, overseen by viceroys who had broad authority to collect taxes, administer justice, and defend property. Thus, from the beginning, the colonial state was highly centralized and intricately tied to the extraction of rents. Both the mining and the *hacienda* or plantation system, reinforced by laws of descent founded on the right of primogeniture, were closely linked to the state, whose very *raison d'être* was the redirection or tribute into the colonizers hands. This fortified the link between family, centralized power, and wealth that has formed the basis for aristocracy everywhere. . . .

Contrast this centralization of political and economic power with events in the north.[3] In the United States, an exceptionally egalitarian social and economic structure, based on small landholdings, established certain patterns of material equality, producing egalitarian sentiments, which in turn formed the basis for the principle of equal citizenship—the mutually recognized right of individuals to participate equally in the making of binding political decisions. Since people's economic circumstances, educational backgrounds, and everyday experiences were so similar they were able to reach and sustain collective choices through majority rule. Politics in the United States became the province of the "common man" rather than the stronghold of an aristocracy deriving its position from superior education, status, or wealth. Furthermore, because all men (though not women or slaves) were created equal, they were equally eligible to hold government positions. Thus the institutional bulwarks of elitism could be removed. Property restrictions on suffrage were lifted, terms of office were limited, and many qualifications for office were removed.

The structure of property was the principal factor that made these developments possible. Because cheap labor was available rather belatedly and then only in the less dominant South, and because production was insufficient to support both owners and tenant farmers, land was broken up into small parcels, thereby destroying the basis for a new landed elite that *haciendas* provided in Latin America. The colonizers of New England, who initially sought religious freedom rather than riches, were exceptionally well educated, and thus were given the unique right to form themselves into a political society and to govern themselves under the protection of England. They established schools in every township and taxed inhabitants to support them, so primary instruction was accessible to everyone at a very early stage. The replacement of primogeniture with new laws of inheritance, the last major step in this egalitarian progression, brought about a virtual revolution in notions of property. By destroying the intimate connection between families and the preservation of landed estates, such laws helped to "divide, distribute and disperse both property and power" (Tocqueville 1990: 1:48), while creating the basis for the subsequent growth of democratic manners and customs.

The difference is striking. In most of Latin America, the historical dispersal of economic resources that is the precursor to a plurality of political power never occurred. Thus there was no institutional balance of power from the start and there was no conception of the state (or any branch of it) as an independent adjudicator of interests. If democracy advances as asset ownership expands, as Tocqueville claims, then Latin America's point of departure did not bode well for its inclusiveness. Only Costa Rica, Uruguay, and to some extent Chile, where indigenous labor was so scarce that land was divided more evenly, initially managed to escape this hyperconcentrated pattern. Not surprisingly, two of these countries, Costa Rica and Uruguay, still have the strongest nonpresidential political institutions and the least inequality today.

The Persistence of the Vicious Cycle

Patterns persist, especially if designers of economies and polities do not choose or are not forced to change them. Independence may have rearranged property ownership and the terms of trade, but it did not change the emphasis on commodity exports or the distribution of property. Throughout the nineteenth century, the great agrarian transformations brought about by the export of cacao and, later, coffee, sugar, cotton, and other products, as well as the modes of development fostered by mineral exports, perpetuated the marked concentration of political and economic power. Wherever landed aristocracies were in command, they set up labor-repressive agriculture as the dominant mode of production and established authoritarian regimes to control the workers—a reality best exemplified by the difference between the development trajectories of Guatemala, El Salvador, and Nicaragua, on the one hand, and yeoman-farmer-based Costa Rica, on the other. Where the dominant class arose primarily from mining and its associated commercial and industrial interests, its need for considerable physical capital and relatively few workers left the majority of people in a difficult situation by lowering real wages and worsening the distribution of income. The confiscation of more lands and the tightening of coercive labor systems in turn reinforced the bias toward exports because the number of beneficiaries was far too few to develop stronger domestic markets. Because the region's exports were subject to strong external shocks, which contributed to a highly volatile macroeconomic environment, the rate of long-term growth was contained and the distribution of income worsened. . . .

By the beginning of the twentieth century, all Latin American states had "hitched their economic star to a dominant commodity," but the fruits of these commodities were not widely shared. Economic development models, especially the free-trade experiments of the 1920s, perpetuated the concentration of income among elites and sustained these patterns of social exclusion. Designed in the interests of ruling families, who were concentrated in export activities and who therefore benefited from economic openness, these models did manage to achieve a growth in exports as a response to increasing demand, especially from Europe and the Americas (Bulmer-Thomas 1994). But they also were the economic basis for an exclusionary political alliance between export elites, foreign investors, and the state, best exemplified by Juan Vicente Gomez in Venezuela, Gerardo Machado in Cuba, and Porfirio Diaz in Mexico. Such regimes were kept in place largely by force, and by the 1920s military institutions became fundamental political actors, possessing the capacity to topple governments and create new ones (Rouquie and Suffern 1994). Not surprisingly, political regimes with this social base never challenged the concentration of asset distribution—except its distribution among themselves—and they never questioned the overall benefits of free trade in a highly oligopolistic setting. Indeed, they used its benefits to strengthen both the political and economic concentration of power. . . .

Notes

A portion of this chapter appeared previously in Terry Lynn Karl, "Economic Inequality and Democratic Instability," *Journal of Democracy* 2, no. 1 (January 2000): 149–56.

1. Evidence for this newly emerging consensus can be seen in the decision of the World Bank and the Inter-American Development Bank to make poverty reduction the overriding objective of their corporate mission, the move towards debt relief for the world's poorest countries, and the awarding of the Nobel Prize to Amartya Sen in 1998, the statements of heads of state of the Americas in the 1998 summit.
2. As far as I can tell, this term was first used by economists in Birdsall, Pinckney and Sabot (1996).
3. The rest of this section is taken from Karl (2000).

References

Amy, Richard M. 1998. "Resource Abundance and Economic Development: Improving the Performance of Resource-Rich Countries." UNU (United Nations University)-WIDER Working paper, Helsinki.

Arack, Jeremy, and Peter Passell. 1994. *A New Economic View of American History.* New York: W. W. Norton.

Bakewell, Peter. 1997. *A History of Latin America*. Oxford: Blackwell Publishers.

Birdsall, Nancy, and Augusto de la Torre, with Rachel Menezes. 2001. *Washington Contentious: Economic Policies for Social Equity in Latin America.* Washington, D.C.: Carnegie Endowment for International Peace and the InterAmerican Dialogue.

Birdsall, N., and J. L. Londoño. 1997. "Asset Inequality Matters: An Assessment of the World Bank's Approach to Poverty Reduction." *American Economic Review* 87, no. 2 (May): 32–37.

———. 1998. "No Tradeoff: Efficient Growth via More Equal Human Capital in Latin America." In *Beyond Tradeoffs: Market Reforms and Equitable Growth in Latin America,* ed. Nancy Birdsall, Carol Graham, and Richard Sabot. Washington, D.C.: Brookings Institution Press and Inter-American Development Bank.

Birdsall. Nancy, Thomas Pinckney, and Richard Sabot. 1996. "Why Low Inequality Spurs Growth." Inter-American Development Bank Working Paper. Washington, D.C.

Bruno. Michael, Martin Ravallion, and Lyn Squire. 2000. "Equity and Growth in Developing Countries." In *Distributive Justice and Economic Development: The Case of Chile and Developing Countries,* ed. Andres Solimano, Eduardo Aninat, and Nancy Birdsall, pp. 37–65. Ann Arbor: University of Michigan Press.

Bulmer-Thomas, Victor. 1994. *The Economic History of Latin America since Independence.* Cambridge: Cambridge University Press.

Cardoso, Fernando Henrique, and Enzo Faletto. 1969. *Dependencia y desarrollo en America Latina.* Mexico City: Siglo XXI Editores.

Cavarozzi, Marcelo J., and James F. Petras. 1974. "Chile." In *Latin America: The Struggle with Dependency and Beyond,* ed. Ronald Chilcote and Joel Edelstein, pp. 495–578. Cambridge: Schenkman.

Collier, David. 1976. *Squatters and Oligarchs: Authoritarian Rule and Policy Change in Peru.* Baltimore: Johns Hopkins University Press.

Deininger, K. [Klaus], and P. Olinto. 1999. "Is Broad Asset Growth Good for Growth: Panel Evidence from 62 Countries." Washington, D.C.: World Bank.

Deininger, Klaus, and Lyn Squire. 1996. "A New Data Set Measuring Income Inequality." *World Bank Economic Review* 10(3): 565–91.

de Mello e Souza. Andre. 2001. "The Perils of Exclusion: Politics and Violence in the Shantytowns of Rio de Janeiro." Field paper, Stanford University Department of Political Science, Stanford, Calif.

Evans, Peter. 1979. *Dependent Development: The Alliance of Multinational, State, and Local Capital in Brazil.* Princeton, N.J.: Princeton University Press.

———. 1995. *Embedded Autonomy: States and Industrial Transformation*. Princeton, N.J.: Princeton University Press.

Graham, Richard. 1990. *Patronage and Politics in Nineteenth-Century Brazil.* Stanford, Calif.: Stanford University Press.

Handelman, Howard. 1979. "Economic Policy and Elire Pressures in Uruguay." American Universities Field Staff Reports, South America Series 27. Hanover, N.H.

Hirschman, Albert. 1971. "The Political Economy of Import-Substituting Industrialization in Latin America." Chap. 4 in *A Bias for Hope: Essays on Development in Latin America,* by Albert Hirschman. New Haven, Conn.: Yale University Press.

Kaldor, N. 1957. "A Model of Economic Growth." *Economic Journal* 67 (December): 591–624.

Karl, Terry Lynn. 1997. *The Paradox of Plenty: Oil Booms and Petro-States.* Berkeley: University of California Press.

———. 2000. "Economic Inequality and Democratic Instability." *Journal of Democracy* II, no. 1 (January): 149–56.

Karst, Kenneth, and Keith Rosenn. 1975. *Law and Development: A Case Book*. Berkeley: University of California Press.

Kuznets, Simon. 1955. "Economic Growth and Income Inequality." *American Economic Review* 45. no.1 (March): 1–28.

Lagos. Marta. 1997. "Latin America's Smiling Mask." *Journal of Democracy* 8, no. 3 (July): 125–38.

———. 2001. "Between Stability and Crisis in Latin America." *Journal of Democracy* 12, no. 1 (January): 137–45.

Leff, Nathaniel. 1968. *Economic Policy Making and Development in Brazil, 1947-1964*. New York: John Wiley and Sons.

Londono, J. L. and M. Szekely. 1997. "Distributional Surprises after a Decade of Reforms: Latin America in the Nineties." In *Latin America after a Decade of Reforms: What Comes Next?* ed. R. Hausman and E. Lora. Washington, D.C: Inter-American Development Bank.

Lora, E. 2000. "Development Challenges for Latin America in the 21st Century." Photocopy, Washington, D.C.: Inter-American Development Bank.

Majon, James E. 1997. "Tax Reform and Its Determinants in Latin America. 1977–1994." Paper presented at the Twentieth International Congress of the Latin American Studies Association, Guadalajara, Mexico, April 17–19.

MORI Internacional. 1998. "Vision Latinoamericana de la Democracia: Encuestas de Opinión Pública en Mèxico, Chile y Costa Rica." Hewlett Foundation.

Muller, E. 1988. "Democracy, Economic Development and Income Inequality." *American Sociological Review* 53-no. 1 (February): 50–68.

Narayan, Deepa, Robert Chambers, Meera K. Shah, and Patti Peresch. 2000. *Voices of the Poor: Crying Out for Change.* New York: Oxford University Press.

Nino, Carlos Santiago. 1996. "Hyperpresidentialism and Constitutional Reform in Argentina." In *Institutional Design in New Democracies: Eastern Europe and Latin America.* ed. Arend Lijphart and Carlos H. Waisman, pp. 161–74. Roulder, Colo.: Westview Press.

O'Donnell, Guillermo. 1994. "Delegative Democracy." *Journal of Democracy* 5. no. 1 (January): 55–69.

Persson, Torsten. and Guido Tabellini. 1994. "Is Inequality Harmful for Growth?" *American Economic Review* 84. no. 3 (June): 600–21.

Przeworski, Adam, Michael Alvarez, José Anronio Cheibub, and Fernando Limongi. 1996. "What Makes Democracies Endure?" *Journal of Democracy* 7.no. 1 (January): 39–55.

Ravallion, Martin, and Gaurav Datt. 1999. "When Is Growth Pro-Poor? Evidence from the Diverse Experience of India's States." Working paper. World Bank, Washington, D.C.

Rawls, John. 1971. A *Theory of Justice.* Cambridge, Mass.: Harvard University Press.

Rosenn, Keith. 1990. "The Success of Constitutionalism in the United States and Its Failure in Latin America: An Explanation." *University of Miami Inter-American Law Review* 22, no. 1.

Rouquie, Alain, and Stephen Suffern. 1994. "The Military in Latin American Politics since 1930." Chap. 4 in *The Cambridge History of Latin America*, vol. 6, *Latin America since 1930*, pt. 2, "Politics and Society," ed. Leslie Bethell, Cambridge: Cambridge University Press.

Snyder, Richard, and David Samuels. 2001. "Devaluing the Vote in Latin America." *Journal of Democracy* 12, no. 1 (January): 146–59.

Solimano, Andres, Eduardo Aninat, and Nancy Birdsall, eds. 2000. *Distributive Justice and Economic Development: The Case of Chile and Developing Countries.* Ann Arbor: University of Michigan Press.

Stallings, Barbara, Nancy Birdsall, and Julie Clugage. 2000. "Growth and Inequality: Do Regional Patterns Redeem Kuzners?" In *Distributive Justice and Economic Development: The Case of Chile and Developing Countries,* ed. Andres Solimano. Eduardo Aninat, and Nancy Birdsall, pp. 98–118. Ann Arbor: University of Michigan Press.

Tocqueville, Alexis de. 1990. *Democracy in America.* New York: Vintage Classics.

Transparency International. 2000. *Annual Report* 2000. Berlin: Transparency International.

Weyland, Kurt G. 1996. *Democracy without Equity: Failures of Reform in Brazil.* Pittsburgh: University of Pittsburgh Press.

Williamson, John. 1990. "What Washington Means by Policy Reform." In *Latin American Adjustment: How Much Has Happened?* ed. John Williamson, pp. 5–20. Washington, D.C.: Institute for International Economics.

———. 1997. "The Washington Consensus Revisited." In *Economic and Social Development into the XXI Century,* ed. Louis Emmerji, pp. 48–69. Washington, D.C.: Inter-American Development Bank.

World Bank. 1999. *World Development Report.* 1998–1999. Oxford and Washington, D.C.: Oxford University Press.

———. 2000. *The Quality of Growth.* Oxford and New York: Oxford University Press.

25.2

What's the Issue? and On Missing the Boat

The Marginalization of the Bottom Billion in the World Economy

Paul Collier

WHAT'S THE ISSUE?

The Third World has shrunk. For forty years the development challenge has been a rich world of one billion people facing a poor world of five billion people. The Millennium Development Goals established by the United Nations, which are designed to track development progress through 2015, encapsulate this thinking. By 2015, however, it will be apparent that this way of conceptualizing development has become outdated. Most of the five billion, about 80 percent, live in countries that are indeed developing, often at amazing speed. The real challenge of development is that there is a group of countries at the bottom that are falling behind, and often falling apart.

The countries at the bottom coexist with the twenty-first century, but their reality is the fourteenth century: civil war, plague, ignorance. They are concentrated in Africa and Central Asia, with a scattering elsewhere. Even during the 1990s, in retrospect the golden decade between the end of the Cold War and 9/11, incomes in this group declined by 5 percent. We must learn to turn the familiar numbers upside down: a total of five billion people who are already prosperous, or at least are on track to be so, and one billion who are stuck at the bottom.

This problem matters, and not just to the billion people who are living and dying in fourteenth-century conditions. It matters to us. The twenty-first-century world of material comfort, global travel, and economic interdependence will become increasingly vulnerable to these large islands of chaos. And it matters now. As the bottom billion diverges from an increasingly sophisticated world economy, integration will become harder, not easier.

And yet it is a problem denied, both by development *biz* and by development *buzz*. Development biz is run by the aid agencies and the companies that get the contracts for their projects. They will fight this thesis with the tenacity of bureaucracies endangered, because they like things the way they are. A definition of development that encompasses five billion people gives them license to be everywhere, or more honestly, everywhere but the bottom billion. At the bottom, conditions are rather rough. Every development agency has difficulty getting its staff to serve in Chad and Laos; the glamour postings are for countries such as Brazil and China. The World Bank has large offices in every middle-income country but not a single person resident in the Central African Republic. So don't expect the development biz to refocus voluntarily.

Development buzz is generated by rock stars, celebrities, and NGOs. To its credit, it does focus on the plight of the bottom billion. It is thanks to development buzz that Africa gets on the agenda of the G8. But inevitably, development buzz has to keep its messages simple, driven by the need for slogans, images, and anger. Unfortunately, although the plight of the bottom billion lends itself to simple moralizing, the answers do not. It is a problem that needs to be hit with several policies at the same time, some of them counterintuitive. Don't look to development buzz to formulate such an agenda: it is at times a headless heart.

What of the governments of the countries at the bottom? The prevailing conditions bring out extremes. Leaders are sometimes psychopaths who have shot their way to power, sometimes crooks who have bought it, and sometimes brave people who, against the odds, are trying to build a better future. Even the appearance of modern government in these states is sometimes a facade, as if the leaders are reading from a script. They sit at the international negotiating tables, such as the World Trade Organization, but they have nothing to negotiate. The seats stay occupied even in

Source: Paul Collier. "What's the Issue?" and "On Missing the Boat: The Marginalization of the Bottom Billion in the World Economy," in *The Bottom Billion: Why the Poorest Countries are Failing and What Can Be Done About It* (2007) pp. 3–12 and 79–96.

the face of meltdown in their societies: the government of Somalia continued to be officially "represented" in the international arena for years after Somalia ceased to have a functioning government in the country itself. So don't expect the governments of the bottom billion to unite in formulating a practical agenda: they are fractured between villains and heroes, and some of them are barely there. For our future world to be liveable the heroes must win their struggle. But the villains have the guns and the money, and to date they have usually prevailed. That will continue unless we radically change our approach.

All societies used to be poor. Most are now lifting out of it; why are others stuck? The answer is traps. Poverty is not intrinsically a trap, otherwise we would all still be poor. Think, for a moment, of development as chutes and ladders. In the modern world of globalization there are some fabulous ladders; most societies are using them. But there are also some chutes, and some societies have hit them. The countries at the bottom are an unlucky minority, but they are stuck.

Traps, and the Countries Caught in Them

Suppose your country is dirt poor, almost stagnant economically, and that few people are educated. You don't have to try that hard to imagine this condition—our ancestors lived this way. With hard work, thrift, and intelligence, a society can gradually climb out of poverty unless it gets trapped. Development traps have become a fashionable area of academic dispute, with a fairly predictable right-left divide. The right tends to deny the existence of development traps, asserting that any country adopting good policies will escape poverty. The left tends to see global capitalism as inherently generating a poverty trap.

The concept of a development trap has been around for a long time and is most recently associated with the work of the economist Jeffrey Sachs, who has focused on the consequences of malaria and other health problems. Malaria keeps countries poor, and because they are poor the potential market for a vaccine is not sufficiently valuable to warrant drug companies making the huge investment in research that is necessary. This book is about four traps that have received less attention: the conflict trap, the natural resources trap, the trap of being landlocked with bad neighbors, and the trap of bad governance in a small country. Like many developing countries that are now succeeding, all the countries that are the focus of this book are poor. Their distinctive feature is that they got caught in one or another of the traps. These traps are not inescapable, however, and over the years some countries have broken free of them and then started to catch up. Unfortunately, that process of catching up has itself recently stalled. Those countries that have only broken clear of the traps during the last decade have faced a new problem: the global market is now far more hostile to new entrants than it was in the 1980s. The countries newly escaped from the traps may have missed the boat, finding themselves in a limbo-like world in which growth is constrained by external factors; this will be the theme in my discussion of globalization. When Mauritius escaped the traps in the 1980s it rocketed to middle-income levels; when neighboring Madagascar finally escaped the traps two decades later, there was no rocket.

Most countries have stayed clear of any of the traps that are the subject of this book. But countries with a combined population of around one billion people have got caught in them. Underlying that statement are some definitions. For example, one of the traps involves being landlocked—although being landlocked is not sufficient to constitute the trap. But when is a country landlocked? You might think that such a matter is clear enough from an atlas. But what about Zaire, which after the ruinous reign of President Mobutu understandably rebranded itself as the Democratic Republic of the Congo? It is *virtually* landlocked but has a tiny sliver of coast. And Sudan has some coast, but most of its people live far away from it.

In defining these traps I have had to draw lines somewhat arbitrarily, and this creates gray areas. Most developing countries are clearly heading toward success, and others are just as clearly heading toward what might be described as a black hole. For some, however, we really cannot tell. Perhaps Papua New Guinea is heading for success; I hope so, and that is how I have classified it. But there are some experts on Papua New Guinea who would shake their heads in disbelief at that. The judgment calls are inevitably going to be open to challenge. But such challenges do not discredit the underlying thesis: that there is a black hole, and that many countries are indisputably heading into it, rather than being drawn toward success. . . .

Given the way I have drawn the lines, as of 2006 there are around 980 million people living in these trapped countries. Since their populations are growing, by the time you read this the figure will be hovering around the one billion mark. Seventy percent of these people are in Africa, and most Africans are living in countries that have been in one or another of the traps. Africa is therefore the core of the problem. In reality, however, Africa and the third world are not coterminous. South Africa, for example, is not among the bottom billion—it is manifestly not in the same desperate situation as Chad. Conversely, much of landlocked Central Asia is disturbingly like Chad. So the countries of the bottom billion do not form a group with a convenient geographic label. When I want to use a geographic label for them I describe them as "Africa +," with the + being places such as Haiti, Bolivia, the Central Asian countries, Laos, Cambodia, Yemen, Burma, and North Korea. They all either are still in one of the traps or escaped too late.

I have identified fifty-eight countries that fall into this group, which highlights one typical feature—they are small. Combined, they have fewer people than either India or China. And since their per capita income is also very low, the income of the typical country is negligible, less than that of most rich-world cities. . . .

So, how have the countries of the bottom billion been doing? First, consider how people live, or rather die. In the bottom billion average life expectancy is fifty years, whereas in the other developing countries it is sixty-seven years. Infant mortality—the proportion of children who die before their fifth birthday—is 14 percent in the bottom billion, whereas in the other developing countries it is 4 percent. The proportion of children with symptoms of long-term malnutrition is 36 percent in the bottom billion as against 20 percent for the other developing countries.

The Role of Growth in Development

Has this gap between the bottom billion and the rest of the developing world always been there, or has it come about because the bottom billion have been trapped? To find out, we have to disaggregate the statistics that have been used in the past to describe all the countries that we label as "developing." Here's a hypothetical example. Prosperia has a big economy that is growing at 10 percent, but the country has only a small population. Catastrophia is a small economy declining at 10 percent, but it has a large population. The usual approach—employed, for example, by the International Monetary Fund (IMF) in its flagship publication *World Economic Outlook*—is to average figures that relate to the size of a country's economy. On this approach, Prosperia's large, growing economy skews the average upward, and so in aggregate the two countries are described as growing. The problem is that this describes what is going on from the perspective of the typical unit of income, not from the perspective of the typical person. Most units of income are in Prosperia, but most people are in Catastrophia. If we want to describe what the typical person experiences in the countries of the bottom billion, we need to work with figures based not on a country's income but on its population. Does it matter? Well, it does if the poorest countries are diverging from the rest, which is the thesis of this [reading], because averaging by income dismisses the poorest countries as unimportant. The experience of their people does not count for much precisely because they are poor—their income is negligible.

When we get the data appropriately averaged, what do we find? Those developing countries that are not part of the bottom billion—the middle four billion—have experienced rapid and accelerating growth in per capita income. Let's take it decade by decade. During the 1970s they grew at 2.5 percent a year, hopeful but not remarkable. During the 1980s and 1990s their growth rate accelerated to 4 percent a year. During the first few years of the twenty-first century it accelerated again to over 4.5 percent. These growth rates may not sound sensational, but they are without precedent in history. They imply that children in these countries will grow up to have lives dramatically different from those of their parents. Even where people are still poor, these societies can be suffused with hope: time is on their side.

But how about the bottom billion? Let's again take it decade by decade. During the 1970s their per capita income rose at 0.5 percent a year, so they were becoming slightly better off in absolute terms but at a rate that was likely to be barely perceptible. Given the high degree of volatility of individual incomes in these societies, the slight overall tendency to improvement is likely to have been drowned by these individual risks. The overall tenor of the society will have been dominated by individual fears of falling rather than hope coming from society-wide progress. But in the 1980s the performance of the bottom billion got much worse, *declining* at 0.4 percent a year. In absolute terms, by the end of the 1980s they were back to where they had been in 1970. If you had been living in these societies over that full sweep of twenty years, the only economic experience was of individual volatility: some people went up and some went down. There was no society-wide reason for hope. And then came the 1990s. This is now seen as the golden decade, between the end of the Cold War and 9/11—the decade of the cloudless sky and booming markets. It wasn't so golden for the bottom billion: their rate of absolute decline accelerated to 0.5 percent a year. By the turn of the millennium they were therefore poorer than they had been in 1970.

Is this dismal performance just an artifact of the data? I think that, on the contrary, the genuine problems that afflict the gathering of economic data in the poorest countries are likely overall to have caused an underestimate of their decline. For the countries that have really fallen apart, there are no usable data. For example, the estimated decline among the bottom billion countries during the 1990s does not include whatever might have been happening in Somalia and Afghanistan. But excluding them is equivalent to assuming that their performance was exactly at the average for the group, and I would be surprised, to say the least, if this was true; I would think it was much worse. In the first four years of the present decade the growth of the bottom billion has picked up to around 1.7 percent, still far below that of the rest of the developing world, but markedly better in absolute terms. Unfortunately, however, this current improvement is likely due to the short-term effects of resource discoveries and high world prices for the natural resources that the bottom billion export. For example, the star growth performer among all the economies of the bottom billion has been Equatorial Guinea. This is a small country of coups and corruption where offshore oil was recently discovered and now dominates income. In sum, even if we were to treat these recent figures as hopeful, which I think would be a misinterpretation, the growth of the bottom billion remains much slower at its peak than even the slowest period of growth in the rest of the developing world and brings them about back to where they were in 1970. . . .

Taking the three decades as a whole, the experience of the societies in the bottom billion was thus one of massive and accelerating divergence. Given the power of compound growth rates, these differences between the bottom billion and the rest of the developing world will rapidly cumulate into two different worlds. Indeed, the divergence has indeed already pushed most of the countries of the bottom billion to the lowest spot in the global pile.

It was not always that way. Before globalization gave huge opportunities to China and India, they were poorer than many of the countries that have been caught in the traps. But China and India broke free in time to penetrate global markets, whereas other countries that were initially less poor didn't. For the last two decades this has produced a growth pattern that appears confusing. Some initially poor countries are growing very well, and so it can easily look as if there is not really a problem: the bottom appears to be growing as fast as the rest. Over the next two decades the true nature of the problem is going to become apparent, however, because the countries that are trapped in stagnation or decline are now pretty well the poorest. The average person in the societies of the bottom billion now has an income only around one-fifth that of the typical person in the other developing countries, and the gap will just get worse with time. Picture this as a billion people stuck in a train that is slowly rolling backward downhill. By 2050 the development gulf will no longer be between a rich billion in the most developed countries and five billion in the developing countries; rather, it will be between the trapped billion and the rest of humankind.

So far I have couched the problem of the bottom billion in terms of growth rates: these countries' growth rate has been negative in absolute terms, and in relative terms massively below that of the rest of the developing world. Nowadays, however, the talk is about poverty reduction and the other Millennium Development Goals, not about growth rates. Many of the people who care most about development feel more comfortable talking about goals such as getting girls into school than discussing growth. I share the enthusiasm for getting girls into school, and indeed for all the other goals. But I do not share the discomfort about growth. While I was directing the World Bank's research department, the most controversial paper we produced was one called "Growth Is Good for the Poor." Some NGOs hated it, and it was the only time in five years that Jim Wolfensohn, the Bank's president, phoned me to voice his concern. Yet the central problem of the bottom billion is that they have not grown. The failure of the growth process in these societies simply has to be our core concern, and curing it the core challenge of development. For policies in the rich world to become more supportive of growth in these societies, we will need the full lobbying power of those who care about the world's poor. And so the people who care will need to take another look at growth.

I am definitely not arguing that we should be indifferent to how an economy grows. The growth of Equatorial Guinea, for example, produces benefits for only a handful of its people, but this is exceptional; growth usually does benefit ordinary people. The exaggerated suspicion of growth by those who are concerned about development has manifested itself in the adjectives with which the word *growth* is now routinely encumbered. In strategy documents the word is now generally seen only in the context of the phrase "sustainable, pro-poor growth." Yet overwhelmingly, the problem of the bottom billion has not been that they have had the wrong *type* of growth, it is that they have not had *any* growth. The suspicion of growth has inadvertently undermined genuinely strategic thinking. I remember when one of the world's great experts on banking consulted me because he had been asked to advise one of the countries of the bottom billion. He was struggling to come up with evidence that banking reform would directly help the poorest people in the country, because he sensed that without such evidence his advice would be dismissed. The much stronger evidence that it would help the growth process would not be valued, he felt. Getting growth started in the bottom billion is going to be hard enough even without such hindrances.

We cannot make poverty history unless the countries of the bottom billion start to grow, and they will not grow by turning them into Cuba. Cuba is a stagnant, low-income, egalitarian country with good social services. If the bottom billion emulated Cuba, would this solve their problems? I think that the vast majority of the people living in the bottom billion—and indeed in Cuba—would see it as continued failure. To my mind, development is about giving hope to ordinary people that their children will live in a society that has caught up with the rest of the world. Take that hope away and the smart people will use their energies not to develop their society but to escape from it—as have a million Cubans. Catching up is about radically raising growth in the countries now at the bottom. The fact that stagnation has persisted over such a long period tells us that it is going to be difficult. What can we do beyond caring?. . . .

On Missing the Boat: The Marginalization of the Bottom Billion in the World Economy

All the people living in the countries of the bottom billion have been in one or another of the traps that I have described. Seventy-three percent of them have been through civil war, 29 percent of them are in countries dominated by the politics of natural resource revenues, 30 percent are landlocked, resource-scarce, and in a bad neighborhood, and 76 percent have been through a prolonged period of bad governance and poor economic policies. Adding up these percentages, you will realize that some countries have been in more than one trap, either simultaneously or sequentially.

But when I speak of traps, I am speaking figuratively. These traps are probabilistic; unlike black holes, it is not impossible to escape from them, just difficult. Take as an example the trap of bad governance and poor policies, and remember that the mathematical expectation of being stuck with bad policies is nearly sixty years. That expectation is built up from the very small chance, less than 2 percent, of escaping from the trap in any single year. But of course that small chance implies that periodically countries do escape. This is true of all the traps: a peace holds (as is currently the case in Angola), natural resources get depleted (as is looming in Cameroon, which has nearly exhausted its oil reserves), reformers succeed in transforming governance and policies (as is now under way in Nigeria). And such transformations have implications for the landlocked: as Nigeria turns itself around, Niger, though still landlocked, is now in a better neighborhood. The focus of this is to ask what happens next.

You might think that if a country escapes from a trap, it can then start to catch up—it will begin to grow, and grow pretty fast. The professional term for catch up is "convergence." The best-studied example of convergence is the European Union. The countries that were initially the poorest members, such as Portugal, Ireland, and Spain, have grown the fastest, whereas the country that was initially richest, Germany, has grown slowly, and so the states that make up the European Union have converged. That is partly why relatively poor countries such as Poland and the other countries of Eastern Europe have been keen to join, whereas the countries that are richer than the European Union, Norway and Switzerland, have decided not to do so. Convergence is also working on a global scale: the lower-income countries are, on the whole, growing faster than the developed countries. People in the developed world are starting to get worried that China is converging on us so fast. The fact that the countries of the bottom billion have bucked this trend to convergence is the puzzle with which I started. And so far my explanation has been that they have been stuck in one or another of the four traps.

Will the countries that emerge from the traps follow the path blazed by the successful majority of developing countries? Will they join the rush to convergence? Globalization arouses passions: it is considered either wonderful or terrible. I think the sad reality is that although globalization has powered the majority of developing countries toward prosperity, it is now making things harder for these latecomers. The purpose of this is to explain why the countries of the bottom billion have missed the boat.

What is globalization? Its effects on the economies of developing countries come from three distinct processes. One is trade in goods, the second is flows of capital, and the third is the migration of people. The three aspects of globalization are so distinct that even the idea that economies have become more globalized depends upon which dimensions you take. In terms of both capital movements and migration, the developing countries were more globalized a century ago than they are now. It is only trade in goods that has grown to unprecedented levels. And even that has not been a continuous process. Between 1914 and 1945 world trade collapsed because of wars and protectionism. It is often said that globalization is inevitable, but those interwar years cast doubt on this assertion: for those who hate globalization, the retreat of trade, capital flows, and migration during the period 1914–45 should be interesting because they are a kind of a natural experiment. Unfortunately, they were a ghastly experiment: the reversal of globalization, though feasible, looks massively undesirable based on the one occasion when we did it.

But the consequences of globalization for the bottom billion are different. Let's take the three aspects of globalization in turn, and see how they affect the bottom billion.

Trade and the Bottom Billion

International trade has taken place for several thousand years. However, the most dramatic transformation of the size and composition of trade has been during the past twenty-five years. For the first time in history, developing countries have broken into global markets for goods and services other than just primary commodities. Until around 1980 developing countries' role was to export raw materials. Now, 80 percent of developing countries' exports are manufactures, and service exports are also mushrooming. The production of primary commodities is basically land-using, and exporting them is most likely to benefit the people who own the land. Sometimes the land is owned by peasant farmers, but often the key beneficiaries are mining companies and big landowners. So trade based on primary commodity exporting is likely to generate quite a lot of income inequality. And its scope is inherently limited by the size of the market: as exports grow, prices turn against exporters. By contrast, manufactures and services offer much better prospects of equitable and rapid development. They use labor rather than land. The opportunity to export raises the demand for labor. Since the defining characteristic of developing countries is that they have a lot of unproductive labor, these exports are likely to spread the benefits of development more widely. And because the world market in manufactures and services is huge and was initially dominated by the rich countries, the scope for expansion by developing countries is massive.

However, before getting starry-eyed about this transformation in developing countries' trade, let us ask why it took so long. In the 1960s and 1970s the rich world dominated global manufacturing despite having wages that were around forty times as high as those in the developing world. Why did this massive wage gap not make developing countries competitive? Part of the answer is that the rich world imposed trade restrictions on the poor world. Another part of the answer is that the poor world shot itself in the foot with its own trade restrictions, which made exporting into a competitive world market unprofitable. But trade restrictions are only part of the explanation for the persistence of the wage gap for so long. The more important explanation is that the rich world could get away with a big wage gap because there are spatial economies of scale in manufacturing. That is, if other firms are producing manufactures in the same location, that tends to lower the costs for your firm. For example, with lots of firms doing the same thing, there will be a pool of workers with the skills that your firm needs. And there will be plenty of firms producing the services and inputs that you need to function efficiently. Try moving to someplace where there are no other firms, and these costs are going to be much higher even if raw labor is much cheaper.

The professional term for this is "economies of agglomeration." . . . In effect, in order to break into global markets for manufactures it is necessary to get over a threshold of cost-competitiveness. If only a country can get over the threshold, it enjoys virtually infinite possibilities of expansion: if the first firm is profitable, so are its imitators. This expansion creates jobs, especially for youth. Admittedly, the jobs are far from wonderful, but they are an improvement on the drudgery and boredom of a small farm, or of hanging around on a street corner trying to sell cigarettes. As jobs become plentiful they provide a degree of economic security not just for the people who get them but for the families behind the workers. And gradually, as jobs expand, the labor market tightens and wages start to rise. . . .

In this initial shift out of Europe and America the bottom billion are those low-income countries that for one reason or another did not get chosen by firms as a good place to relocate. How has this affected their chances of convergence? It suggests to me that there was a moment—roughly the decade of the 1980s—when the wage gap was sufficiently wide that any low-wage developing country could break into global markets as long as it was not stuck in one of the traps. During the 1990s this opportunity receded because Asia was building agglomerations of manufactures and services. These agglomerations became fabulously competitive: low wages combined with scale economies. Neither the rich countries nor the bottom billion could compete. The rich countries did not have low wages, and the bottom billion, which surely had low wages, did not have the agglomerations. They had missed the boat. . . .

If there really has been a process of missing the boat, it is pretty depressing. For one thing, it implies that the incentive for governments in the bottom-billion countries to reform, make peace, or do whatever else is needed to break free of the traps is greatly reduced. Courageous people face down the powerful interests lined up against them and implement reform only to find that little happens. The reactions to reforms that do not deliver economic success can be ugly. All the old vested interests have their knives out to kill off reform attempts. Another type of reaction is the quack remedy: people are liable to become victims of populism. The most depressing reaction is for people to see the society as intrinsically flawed. Their prolonged period of economic failure in Africa and the other countries of the bottom billion has deeply eroded the self-confidence of their societies. The expectation of continued failure reinforces the pressures for the brightest people to leave. . . .

This does not mean that development in the bottom billion is impossible, but it does make it much harder. The same automatic processes that drove Asian development will impede the development of the bottom billion.

So the growth of agglomerations in Asia has made the export diversification route more difficult for the bottom billion. Another effect of this growth is that Asians are increasingly desperate to secure supplies of natural resources. The Chinese are all over the countries of the bottom billion, securing natural resource deals. Superficially this is good news: it is certainly raising prices, most obviously of oil, which some countries of the bottom billion export. But you saw, on the trap of poor policy, that high prices for resource exports are likely to chill the impetus for reform. On the conflict trap, you saw that the spread of high natural resource prices increased the risk of conflict. And you saw, on the natural resource trap, that natural resources are not the royal road to growth unless governance is unusually good. In the bottom billion it is already unusually bad, and the Chinese are making it worse, for they are none too sensitive when it comes to matters of governance. When Zimbabwe's Robert Mugabe was looking for money to bail himself out of the ruinous consequences of his political choices, he came up with the "look east" strategy. East did not mean Russia, it meant China. And China has welcomed his overtures with open arms. . . .

So the bottom billion are locked into natural resource exports twice over: by the threshold effects of Asian export agglomerations and by Asia's desperate need for natural resources.

The growth of global trade has been wonderful for Asia. But don't count on trade to help the bottom billion. Based on present trends, it seems more likely to lock yet more of the bottom-billion countries into the natural resource trap than to save them through export diversification.

Capital Flows and the Bottom Billion

The economies of the bottom billion are short of capital. Traditionally, aid has been supposed to supply the capital that the bottom billion lack, but even where this works it supplies only public capital, not private capital. Public capital can supply much of the infrastructure that these societies need, but it cannot begin to supply the equipment that workers need in order to be productive; that can be supplied only by private investors. . . . Africa is the most capital-scarce region, but this becomes dramatically more pronounced when capital is separated into its private and public components.

In a successful region such as East Asia there is more than twice as much private capital as public capital. By contrast, Africa has twice as much public capital as private capital. What it and the other economies of the bottom billion really lack is private investment. This translates into a lack of equipment for the labor force to work with, and this in turn condemns workers to being unproductive and so to having low incomes. The labor force of the bottom billion needs private capital, and in principle globalization can provide it. Basic economic theory would suggest that in the societies that are short of capital, the returns on capital would be high, and this would attract an inflow of private capital.

Private Capital Inflows

Global capitalism does often work like this. China, for example, is attracting huge private capital inflows. Of course, the East Asian crisis of 1998, during which foreign money panicked and fled the region, showed that short-term financial inflows can be a mixed blessing, exposing countries to financial shocks. But longer-term investment is likely to be beneficial all around. Workers in developing countries get jobs and increased wages, and the firms that move capital to developing countries get higher returns on it. Such capital movements, like trade, normally generate mutual gains. Since political contests are usually presented as zero-sum games—your gain is my loss—the people who are most politically engaged have the hardest time believing in mutual gains. Hence, perhaps, the exaggerated suspicions of globalization.

But what about the bottom billion? Again, I think that the effect of globalization—this time through capital flows—is different. The biggest capital flows are not going to the countries that are most short of capital; they are bypassing the bottom billion. . . .

Why are the most capital-scarce countries not attracting a larger capital inflow? Historically, part of the answer has been poor governance and policy. . . .

The answer is that the perceived risk of investment in the economies of the bottom billion remains high. Investor perceptions of risk can be measured—one useful indicator is a survey, done by the magazine *Institutional Investor,* that scores the perceived risk for each country on a scale of 1 to 100. A score of 100 implies the sort of maximum safety appropriate for your grandmother's nest egg, and a score of 1 is only for kamikaze investors. Risk ratings such as this one show up as significant in statistical explanations of private investment; unsurprisingly, high risk discourages investment.

The problem for the reforming countries of the bottom billion is that the risk ratings take a long time to reflect turnarounds. Why does it take so long for investors to revise their views of the bottom billion? There are three reasons for the problem.

Paradoxically, the countries with the strongest reforms are those that started from the worst governance and policies. Often things have to get really bad to provoke incisive change. And so the reforms start from a truly terrible rating, much as happened in Uganda. . . .

The second problem is that the typical economy of the bottom billion is very small. A corollary is that the community of private investors knows virtually nothing about it—absorbing information is costly, if only in time, and these places are simply not sufficiently important enough to bother with. This became evident when the government of Uganda was trying to change the country's image. The last time Uganda had been in the news had been because of Idi Amin, the publicity-obsessed coup leader who, not content with being styled president, had also made himself a field marshal. . . . By the early 1990s Amin had been gone for over a decade, but most potential investors still thought he was president. There are fifty-eight countries in the bottom billion, and investors do not track them individually but think of them collectively as "Africa" and dismiss them. Contrast this with China: every major international company knows that it has to keep abreast of developments in China. . . .

The third reason is that policy improvements are often genuinely fairly fragile: many incipient turnarounds subsequently abort. Reform is always politically difficult. . . . So the genuine reformers have not been able to distinguish themselves from the bogus reformers. Because they cannot distinguish themselves, investors lump them all together and say, "Don't call us, we'll call you." They go to China instead.

Fundamentally, the problem is one of credibility. . . .

Private Capital Outflows

The lack of capital inflows is only half the story of why global capital markets are not working for the bottom billion. The other half is that their own capital flows out of them. Much of this is illegal, and so it is hidden. It is called capital flight. . . .

Suppose you live in a bottom-billion country and want to get your money out. You have to get hold of foreign currency—dollars. It's often illegal; in many cases all foreign currency has to be sold to the central bank at the official exchange rate, so what can you do? There are various tricks, one of which is to falsify the documentation on exports. You find someone who is exporting $1,000 worth of coffee to the United States. That individual bribes a few people in the customs office so that the documentation says $500. This way, the exporter only has to hand over $500 to the central bank. He can then sell the other $500 to you, and you can deposit it in a foreign bank. . . . By comparing export figures with import figures and using other discrepancies, it is possible to tease out capital flight year by year for each country. This allows you to discover, for example, that by the end of military rule in Nigeria in 1998 Nigerians were holding around $100 billion of capital outside the country. . . .

This yielded what rapidly became one of the famous numbers about Africa: By 1990, 38 percent of its private wealth was held abroad. This was a greater proportion than in any other region. . . . Africa integrated into the global financial economy, but in the wrong direction: the most capital-scarce region in the world exported its capital. . . .

So Africans were voting with their wallets, taking their money out of the region. What was driving this massive capital flight? If you ask Africans, they tell you it is corruption. Those in power loot public money and get it safely abroad. This is surely part of the story, but it is not at the heart of what is going on. For example, Indonesia had corruption on a world-class scale. President Suharto took what we might politely term "Asian family values" to extraordinary heights of paternalistic generosity. But most of the money stayed in the country. Africans took their money, whether corruptly acquired or honestly acquired, out of Africa because the opportunities for investment were so poor. One reason why the investment opportunities were so poor was because the countries were stuck in one or another of the traps. Capital flight was a response to the traps. . . .

So, despite being chronically short of private capital, the bottom billion are integrating into the global economy through capital flight rather than capital inflows. They are losing capital partly because the traps involve conditions such as political instability and poor policies, which make countries unsuited for investment. But even when countries succeed in shedding these characteristics they are still perceived as risky, and fears of retrogression keep capital out. So don't count on global capital mobility to develop the bottom billion, capital-scarce as they are. It is more likely to reinforce the traps.

Migration and the Bottom Billion

The bottom billion have not only integrated into the world economy through capital flight. They are increasingly integrating through migration. People vote with their feet as well as with their wallets. Historically, migration has been the great equalizer. In the nineteenth century the vast movement of people from Europe to North America did more to raise and equalize incomes than trade or capital movements. And more recently for some developing countries, migration has been a very good thing. For example, the Indian diaspora in the United States was probably critical in India's breakthrough into the world market for e-services. . . .

Having studied capital flight, we decided to try a similar approach with migration. We distinguished between the educated and the uneducated. With a bit of imagination you can think of education as a form of wealth: in one of the ugliest phrases in economics, educated people are "human capital," so labeled because their skills are valuable. We wondered whether the migration behavior of the educated from developing countries looked more like that of uneducated people or more like the portfolio choices of capital. . . . The migration decisions of educated people looked very like the portfolio decisions that determine where wealth is held, and not much at all like the migration decisions of the uneducated, who are more likely to migrate the wider the differential between their earnings at home and what they can earn abroad.

What does this imply for the bottom billion? It suggests that these countries will hemorrhage their educated people to a far greater extent than their uneducated people. Migration takes time to build up, but it accelerates. There is a simple reason for this: migration becomes easier if other family members have already moved. Our analysis predicts that the exodus of capital from the bottom billion was only phase one of the global integration of the bottom billion. Phase two will be an exodus of educated people. But emigration will be selective: the brightest and the best will have most to gain from moving. They are also the ones most likely to be welcomed in host countries. . . . Those who do get out will not return, and their remittances will dwindle after a generation of separation. Emigration helps those who leave, but it can have perverse effects on those left behind, especially if it selectively removes the educated. Meanwhile, back in the countries of the bottom billion, the financial sectors are run by people whose understanding of financial economics does not equip them to manage much more than a piggy bank. . . .

The flight of the skilled is at its most rapid in precisely those bottom-billion environments where there is most scope for change: postconflict societies. So, whereas migration has generally been helpful as part of the development process, I am skeptical of it as a force for transforming the bottom billion. I think that by draining these countries of their talent, migration is more likely to make it harder for these nations to decisively escape the trap of bad policy and governance.

Life in Limbo: Out of the Frying Pan . . .

This all adds up to a depressing picture of what globalization is doing for the bottom billion. To get a chance to play in the global economy, you need to break free of the traps, and that is not easy. Remember, in order to turn a country around it helps to have a pool of educated people, but the global labor market is draining the bottom billion of their limited pool of such people. Even once they reform, many of these economies find it difficult to attract private investment inflows, and may continue to hemorrhage their own modest private wealth. And they face a high hurdle in trying to break into diversified markets for exports because China, India, and the other successful developing countries have already done so. Even once free of the traps, countries are liable to be stuck in a kind of limbo—no longer falling apart, but not able to replicate the rapid growth of Asia, and so failing to converge.

This indeed seems to describe a lot of bottom-billion countries that have recently come out of the traps. Remember that in the past four years the average country of the bottom billion has at last started to grow. I have interpreted that as a temporary phenomenon linked to the global boom in commodities. But suppose you were to put the most favorable gloss on it—that they have broken free of the traps. Well, although they are growing, it is at a very sedate pace—much more slowly than the other developing countries even during the slow decade of the 1970s. Even if their present growth rate is sustained, they will continue to diverge rapidly. It will take them many decades to reach what we now consider to be the threshold of middle income, and by that time the rest of the world will have moved on.

There is also a yet more depressing variant of the future for these limbo countries: the traps still await them. As long as they have low incomes and slow growth they continue to play Russian roulette. Côte d'Ivoire survived low income and slow growth for a couple of decades but then fell into conflict as the result of a coup. Zimbabwe survived the same and then fell into bad governance. Tanzania, currently among the most hopeful low-income countries, is about to become resource-rich due to new discoveries of gas and gold. Malawi grew remarkably well for the first decade of its independence, considering that is landlocked and resource-scarce, but then its neighbors fell into the conflict trap and, being dependent upon them, it too began to decline. And so a miserable but possible scenario is that countries in the bottom billion oscillate between the traps and limbo, perhaps switching in the process from one trap to another. . . .

25.3

The Political Roots of Poverty

The Economic Logic of Autocracy

Bruce Bueno de Mesquita and Hilton L. Root

The events of September 11, 2001 have led, among many other things, to the revival of an old debate about the relationship between poverty and political extremism. To get at the root of apocalyptic terrorism, many new initiatives to reduce global poverty have been proposed. British International Development Secretary Clare Short advocates a massive international effort to stop poor countries from becoming breeding grounds for terrorism: "The conditions which bred their bitterness and hatred", she has said, "are linked to poverty and injustice." Britain's Chancellor of the Exchequer, Gordon Brown, has called for a fifty-year Marshall Plan that would disperse aid in exchange for an end to bad government, in his words, for "the developing countries pursuing corruption-free policies for stability, opening up trade and encouraging private investment." Some advocates call for spending targets to be directly linked to the GDP of donor nations, overlooking selectivity or effectiveness. Even more ambitious proposals call for an international tax to limit the adverse consequences of globalization by financing global public goods.

The presumed connection between poverty and terrorism raises general fears of global class warfare—but are these fears justified? The argument that poverty directly causes terrorism is simple-minded. A more compelling argument can be made that *rising* levels of material wellbeing, and with them expectations of social and personal empowerment, actually fuel political extremism and violence.[1] It cannot be refuted, however, that most of the countries incubating terrorism tend to be on the low end of the per capita income spectrum, nor that "poverty and injustice"—and these are *not* the same—fuel resentment of the powerful and wealthy to the extent that terrorism can attract admiration and even peripheral support. And it is certainly true that bad government is a problem so serious that no effort at poverty alleviation can succeed without facing it. . . .

Political Tenure and Economic Development

Our standard approach to economic policy reform typically assumes that leaders are rewarded politically if they help their nation improve its economic performance. In reality, politicians succeed by helping their constituents and, in the vast majority of poor countries, politically significant constituencies are not representative of the whole population. It makes perfect political sense for autocrats in poor countries to enrich the clique of supporters around them, even if it means keeping the majority of the population poor. In short, in such situations, political rationality and economic rationality are not in alignment. . . .

[Josesph] Stiglitz does note, almost in passing however, that poor countries are poor because their leaders have only half-heartedly implemented sensible economic ideas. The real question, then, and one that economists alone are powerless to answer, is why that is so. Why have many governments rejected good economic advice that they have been paid to receive? The answer may be found in the economic logic of autocracy.

Just as we naturally consider successful those leaders who foster economic growth and prosperity for their citizens, we expect that leaders who produce famine, poverty and misery will earn a rapid retirement. *But the data show that leaders who produce poverty and misery through the systematic corruption that is characteristic of autocracy keep their jobs much longer than do those who enrich their countries.* Indeed, the eight countries consistently rated the most corrupt in the world—Congo, Iraq, Myanmar, Sudan, Indonesia, Syria, Pakistan

Source: Bruce Bueno de Mesquita and Hilton L. Root (2002), "The Political Roots of Poverty," *National Interest* 68: 27–33. Reprinted by permission of The National Interest.

and Burundi—are those in which political leadership has been most secure, measured by the longevity of its tenure. (Only countries that have experienced a complete breakdown in social order can rival an entrenched autocracy in generating extreme levels of corruption.)

With rare exception, only autocrats—leaders who are unresponsive to the popular will and who exercise power unchecked either by law or other institutions—hold on to power for a long time. Over the past century, the only leaders who have remained in office for forty years or more have been autocrats. By contrast, nearly half of all democratic leaders—leaders who hold power at the pleasure of the voters or an elected legislature—are out of office within about one year of coming to power. Such a short tenure is true of only about one-third of autocrats, a remarkable difference in survivability. Virtually no democrats—but one-quarter of autocrats—stay in office for more than eight years, even though few democratic leaders are subject to term limits.

To elaborate the point, one can divide the leadership structures of poorer countries into two groups: those who depend on a small group of backers, which may be called exclusive regimes, and those who rely on a relatively broad coalition of support, which may be called inclusive regimes. Exclusive regimes tend toward narrow autocracy and oligopoly; inclusive regimes tend toward what we normally think of as democracy. But there are many poorer countries short of reaching mature and genuine democracy that nonetheless exhibit inclusive characteristics—among these a decade or so ago were, for example, the East Asian tigers and Chile. In other words, there is a spectrum of governance structures, and the more inclusive side of it contains democratizing regimes as well as fully democratic ones. One may measure how broadly based a regime is by taking into consideration such factors as constraints on executive authority and the openness and degree of political competition.[2] A comparison of political survival rates between these two groups, based on economic performance, tells a depressing but important story.

Leaders who depend on a broadly inclusive coalition do better at staying in office only if they manage to promote exceptionally high growth rates. They do worse if, instead of growth, they promote rent-seeking opportunities of the sort that typify countries with vibrant black markets, often controlled by the friends and allies of the leadership. Inclusive leaders who promote growth stay in office, on average, 15 percent longer than those who do not.

The *reverse* is true for those who rule at the pleasure of a small, exclusive group. Exclusive leaders who rely on black-market corruption have a better chance of staying in power than those who engender high rates of growth, staying in office, on average, 25 percent longer. Indeed, at all periods during their tenure in office, these leaders do much better at retaining their jobs if they promote black marketeering, corruption and cronyism—distorting the economy—than if they promote economic policies that lead to growth and prosperity. Why does this perverse outcome occur? As suggested above, leaders who would keep their jobs must produce what their supporters want; when those supporters are unrepresentative of the country, autocrats will not pursue policies that encourage the creation of healthy, educated, prosperous citizens.

Autocrats not only retain power by maintaining the loyalty of a relatively small group of supporters—which usually include those who control the military, the civil service, the communications and information infrastructure, as well as key economic levers—but they also have an interest in keeping that core group as small as possible. In a poor country, an autocrat faces personal political risks if he implements policies that dissipate resources away from the few upon whom he relies to those who have little say in ensuring his political survival. It is therefore politically irrational to implement transparent economic policies aimed at protecting and promoting property rights, rule of law, a broadly educated population, low taxes and free trade, if they enable challenges to the incumbent. It is not in an autocrat's interest that people have ways to enrich themselves that he does not control.

This is why autocrats face their highest risk of being deposed in their first year in office; they have not yet identified their most loyal backers and have not yet fully secured their ability to transfer benefits to them. With time and experience, they get better at identifying those on whose support they really rely. They discover that excluding "the many" from sharing in the wealth of the country is the best way to reward a small clique of supporters.

Even worse, such systems tend to perpetuate themselves, which is why a reform-minded leader who manages to come to power in such a system faces excruciating dilemmas. If he is committed to promoting growth and prosperity, he may find that pursuit of such goals can ensure the loss of office. Elections give a mandate to a democratic leader, but in pursuing reform, even a democratic leader may be forced to implement policies that injure the interests of the constituents who brought him to power. Any politician unable to satisfy his core constituents faces a risk of their defection to another politician who shows more promise of improving their lot. After listening to a long list of measures designed to improve his country's economy, President Rafael Caldera of Venezuela told Nobel laureate Douglass North, "If I were to do the things you are recommending, I would not survive in office long enough to enjoy the benefits." . . .

The policy implications of the dichotomy between exclusive and inclusive systems of governance go beyond the matter of leadership tenure. When the political system is dominated by a small coalition of cronies, relatives or military officers, citizens do markedly worse on public welfare or humanitarian indices than do their counterparts who live under more inclusive systems. Across the board, the data show that more inclusive systems generally do a better job at producing safe drinking water, expanding public education, offering access to medical care, encouraging free trade, avoiding corruption and black marketeering, attracting investors and so forth. Moreover, even quite poor inclusive societies usually offer more of these advantages than do autocratic countries lucky enough to possess some important and valuable resource. The reasons are not difficult to fathom: inclusive governance promotes greater government spending on social policy because, in such systems, the longevity of political leaders is directly tied to the welfare of the majority. El Salvador and Jamaica are two excellent examples of relatively poor but inclusive societies with above-average social welfare (as demonstrated by their low infant mortality rates and high-quality drinking water). By contrast, during their non-democratic years, Mexico and Brazil had above-average income levels, but performed poorly on these social indicators.

Notes

1. See Daniel Pipes, "God and Mammon: Does Poverty Cause Militant Islam?", *The National Interest* (Winter 2001/02).

2. Our measure of inclusiveness or exclusiveness is based on four criteria. The first is regime type—military or hereditary leaders are considered less inclusive. Second, a regime improves on its inclusiveness if its executive recruitment process is competitive. Third, regimes are more inclusive when the opportunity to compete for leadership positions is broadly available to all citizens. Finally, inclusiveness is enhanced when there are few or no restrictions on the rights of citizens to organize to compete for political influence at the national level. The more of these criteria that a regime satisfies, the more inclusive its governing system. We consider a regime inclusive if it meets at least three of the four criteria; otherwise we treat it as exclusive. The analysis used here spans all countries, depending on the availability of data, from 1950 through 1992. This analysis is further developed in a forthcoming work: Bruce Bueno de Mesquita, Alastair Smith, Randolph M. Siverson and James D. Morrow, untitled manuscript (Cambridge, MA: MIT Press, expected 2003).

26 State-Building

26.1

State Building and Nation Building

Paul Collier

Famously, President Bush began by deriding state building and ended up attempting it. I am going to suggest why it is so difficult. The now-successful states were built through a painfully slow and circuitous process of formation that turned them into nations with which their citizens identified. This enabled them to undertake the collective action that is vital for the provision of public goods. In the high-income societies we have come to take these features for granted: so much so that we have forgotten that they are essential. Legally, states can be built by the stroke of an international pen: they need only recognition. This is how the states of the bottom billion came into existence. They have not been forged into nations, and so they face an acute lack of public goods.

Most modern states were once ethnically diverse. The boundaries of a modern state generally emerged not out of deepening bonds forged out of a primordial ethnic solidarity but as the solution to the central security issue of what size of territory was best suited to the creation of a monopoly over the means of violence. Often the sense of a common ethnic origin bonded to the national soil was imagined retrospectively: conjured up by the urban, middle-class, romantic nationalists of the nineteenth century.

State formation was driven not by a sense of community but by the unusual economic properties of violence. We now know that violence is not something that emerged as a result of the formation of states: on the contrary, stateless societies are horribly violent. The production of violence depends upon the available technology. Hunter-gatherer societies are inherently extremely violent because the technology does not permit anything else: the winning strategy for a group of hunter-gatherers is the preemptive strike against neighbors through the predawn raid, catching your enemies detached from their weapons. Any group sufficiently quixotic to trust a peace deal gets eliminated before it can change its mind. So violence is intrinsic to such societies: they would more accurately be described as hunters, gatherers, and killers. However, with technological advance the production of violence becomes subject to specialization and economies of scale. Both make violence a paying proposition.

Start from a primitive landscape with no government and many identical households and now introduce a minimal degree of differentiation. Some people are more productive than others and some people are stronger than others. From the resulting four different types of people, ask yourself how one type, the unproductive strong, are going to earn a living? They are going to plunder those who are productive but weak. By abandoning their incompetent efforts to produce and specializing in violence, the unproductive strong get even better at violence. Violence requires skill and hence gives an advantage to professionals.

Onto this scene of specialization now add economies of scale in violence, this being a fancy way of

Source: "State Building and Nation Building" (pp. 169-87) from *Wars, Guns, and Votes: Democracy in Dangerous Places.*

saying that size matters. It is this that makes violence distinctive. Other economic activities had to wait until the industrial revolution before scale became important. A thousand-person farm was no more productive per person than a one-person farm; a thousand-person firm of cobblers was no more productive per person than a solo cobbler. But a thousand-person army could kill, one by one, a thousand solo fighters: large groups of professionals tend to defeat small groups of professionals. Not always and everywhere: small armies can win if they have better technology and better management; there is even room for differential heroism. The race is not always for the swift, but that is where to put your money.

So, by forming or joining a large group of professionals that establishes a monopoly of violence over a territory, you as a member become safer from attack. That is clearly a powerful incentive. But safety is not the only consideration: life can only be sustained with income. People specialized in violence forgo the chance to produce. Where is your income to come from? The answer, as any mafioso knows, is that having established a monopoly of violence, you now have the power to extort from other inhabitants of the territory. Why do the inhabitants not run away? Perhaps your army can enforce penalties for attempting to escape: you are able to turn the inhabitants into serfs. Perhaps the inhabitants have nowhere to run because the neighboring territories are dominated by similar armies, so flight would merely get them out of your frying pan into some other army's fire. Perhaps the protection from other predators that is a consequence of your local monopoly of violence is worth the payments. You, the army, are inadvertently supplying a public good: you have become a state.

Although the public good of security for the locality may be inadvertent, you gradually realize that it is in your own interest to supply a few other public goods. One is to help your inhabitants to trade with one another. If they become richer, then you can become richer by taxing them. So you provide a contract-enforcement service for them; after all, you are good at enforcement. You call it a court, and around it grows a legal system. You might also run to some trade-enhancing infrastructure: roads, bridges, and market-places. You might even, though this takes a certain amount of vision, put a few limits on yourself. By closing off some options, you make your richer subjects less inclined to adopt the infuriating defensive strategy of refusing to invest. We have arrived at a state, but not a modern one: the range of public goods is too limited because the interests of many people are ignored.

The final step from a state that is effective but serves the interests of a minority to one that serves everyone is another long haul. Once hemmed in by neighboring states, these become the primary threat: either you defeat and swallow them or they defeat and swallow you. Arms races develop. This requires high taxation, and the warfare generates a sense of nationalism: people start to sense a common identity. As the effective state facilitates economic growth, even the politically weak become better off, and this, together with an emerging sense of common identity, gradually makes them more powerful. Recall that autocracies become more prone to political violence as income rises. More specifically, they become increasingly beset by riots, demonstrations, and political strikes. The sense of common identity further eases the collective action of protest. Better provision of public goods is gradually prised out of the elite by this pressure. To make these improvements credibly permanent, elites also concede limited extensions of the franchise: the society inches toward modern democracy.

In trying to apply these simple but powerful economics of violence to the actual history of state formation, it is always convenient if we can find a starting point for history. In the process of European state formation, to my mind, the natural starting point is the fall of the Roman Empire during the fifth century. This has some rudimentary analogy to the decolonization of Africa in the mid-twentieth century. Given the suddenness of the decolonization of Africa, which was basically over a decade after it had first been seriously contemplated, the closest analogy is with the decolonization of Roman Britain. . . .

So this is our beginning: post-Roman chaos. It took Britain, and indeed the rest of Europe, centuries before local thugs coalesced into miniature states, each able to keep a degree of order within its own territory but fearful of its neighbors. By 1555 the German-speaking territories still had no fewer than 360 states. Gradually the states became more frightened of one another than of threats from within their own societies. To defend against neighbors they needed a large standing army. Big defense costs money, and the only sources were taxation or borrowing on a scale not seen since the days of the Roman Empire. Taxation has its limits. If people are taxed beyond their willingness to pay, they will take evasive action, conniving with the tax collectors so that they bribe the collector instead of paying the state. Ultimately, if taxes get too onerous, people retreat into activities that cannot be taxed.

Borrowing is even more of a potential minefield for the state. Whereas taxation is basically coercive, borrowing depends upon people actually volunteering to lend the state their money. Even if they are prepared to lend it, they demand interest, and if the interest rate is high the borrowing becomes unsustainable, the military effort collapses, and the state is defeated.

The first European state to discover how to raise money on a sustainable basis through taxation and borrowing was the tiny commercial state of the Netherlands. This tiny society had a territory badly suited to defense: recall that mountains come in handy. The Netherlands is the least mountainous country in the world. Worse, its citizens were disproportionately urban and bourgeois, not groups with a strong fighting tradition. The Netherlands was facing a massive war machine: the Hapsburg Empire. In this David-and-Goliath struggle, David was sufficiently desperate that it had to evolve one advantage: the ability of the state to raise money. Even here it was up against a huge disadvantage: the Hapsburg Empire had the gold and silver mines of Spanish America.

The critical invention of the Dutch was political accountability. People were only prepared to tolerate high taxation if the government of the state became accountable to citizens. Not all citizens, of course, but the rich citizens who were paying the taxation. Further, with an accountable state the government was able to borrow: people were prepared to lend once they saw that the government was being forced to conduct its finances in such a way that it would always be able to pay them back. The Hapsburgs found that gold and silver were not quite enough, and so they too decided to borrow. But nobody had forced them into accountability. And so the battle for the Netherlands turned into a battle of interest rates.

The power of compound interest to gradually gut the finances of a profligate borrower ensured that final victory would go to the state with the better credit rating. The Hapsburgs had a huge empire and the bullion mines of Spanish America as collateral, and the Dutch had a tiny area and political accountability. The power of compound interest takes time, but the Dutch were able to borrow for around 6 percent whereas the Hapsburgs were paying up to 22 percent. That is, when they could borrow at all: before the end of the war they had gone bankrupt and were shut out of the credit market. David beat Goliath.

Gradually, other states learned the Dutch lesson. Those that didn't got swallowed by those that did. Interstate warfare had two consequences. One was the sentiment of nationalism. It was to rationalize these sentiments that the educated, urban romantics of the nineteenth century conjured up the notion of deep ethnic roots that defined the nation. The clash of states became the clash of ethnicities: the myth of a common ethnic identity was forged on the battlefields. The sense of a common enemy and the myth of shared ancestral origins unified the inhabitants of the state into the people of a nation. The result was potent. As a benevolent force it provided the bonds that, via protest, enabled the ample provision of public goods: probably for the first time in history the collective action problem was overcome for the common good. As a malevolent force it generated vilification of the other: for example, in the First World War the British press was routinely describing Germans as Huns.

The other consequence of warfare was the spread of fiscal accountability: governments had to become accountable to the rich, otherwise they could not raise sufficient taxation and debt. But at this stage states still had not reached anything that looked remotely like the modern liberal state. It was not yet democracy and it was certainly not yet the use of taxation for social spending. The states of the mid-nineteenth century were run by the rich, and their priority was national security. The road from there to the present is paved with political protest from the excluded. Gradually, little by little, to avoid worse, the rich expanded the franchise. This enabled them credibly to commit to redistributive reforms that became irreversible without being so drastic that the economy was damaged.

Nations inched toward democracy, and as they did so the priorities of government inched toward the priorities of ordinary citizens—the supply of public goods such as health and education instead of simply defense. Gradually the state became captured by the interests of ordinary citizens: we have arrived at the modern liberal democracy.

The evolution of the modern state was, on this analysis, violence driven. Step by step, the predatory ruler of the mini-state had evolved into the desperate-to-please, service-promising, modern vote-seeking politician. Such have been the crooked byways by which the modern state has evolved into its role of providing public goods. . . .

The age of empires came to an abrupt end for a variety of reasons, but probably the most powerful was the rise of America to primacy and its resolute antipathy to them. The seeds were sown by President Wilson at the Paris Peace Conference after the First World War. Wilson committed himself to the principle of self-determination of peoples, a concept entirely revolutionary to the then-established principles of international relations. Self-determination implied that instead of identity continuing to adjust to political borders, borders would be adjusted to wherever identity formation had been reached: the music had stopped and peoples rushed to sit down on the chairs. Self-determination was put into practice in the Versailles Treaty, most notably in the territorial mosaic that in due course yielded the catastrophe of the Balkans, but it really came into its stride after the political showdown between America on the one side and Britain and France on the other that constituted the Suez crisis of 1956. Following Suez the British rapidly dismantled their empire, creating precedents that forced the French and Portuguese to follow. Ultimately self-determination even dissolved the Russian Empire. As a result, during the second half of the twentieth century the number of independent states increased massively.

This process of state formation was entirely different from state formation Mark I. With rare exceptions, the new states did not emerge as the solutions to struggles to provide security. It is usually said that the boundaries of the new states were arbitrary. This is not entirely fair to the colonial authorities that faced the task of turning a vast multitude of ethnic communities into manageable countries. The fundamental problem was that neither of the two processes that had happened in the formation of modern states had taken place: there had been neither the emergence of territories viable in terms of security, nor the retrospective creation of an imagined community among the inhabitants of these security-defined spaces. In Africa alone there were some two thousand ethno-linguistic groups. Yet if each were made a nation, its territory and population would be far too small to reap adequate scale economies of security: they would be insecure both internally and externally.

Thus, although the instant states that came into being with the dissolution of the colonial empires were ancient societies with a multiplicity of strong ethnic loyalties, usually they lacked national loyalty: people's primary allegiance was to their ethnic group. As I have argued, this severely impeded the provision of public goods. Anything public was simply up for grabs: a common pool resource, the control of which depended upon winning the political struggle between the various ethnic groups. Much the surest way of overcoming this problem would be to follow the earlier model of nation building: gradually erode ethnic identities and replace them with a national identity. . . .

The decolonization of the bottom billion produced a patchwork of little states not utterly different from the situation of post-Roman Europe. But from then on the stories diverge. To a large extent borders of the bottom billion have been frozen: they did not face powerful challenges from their neighbors, at least not to the extent of fearing that they would be absorbed. I can think of only two mergers between countries in the past fifty years, both in 1989: the East German ambassador to North Yemen was uniquely unfortunate in becoming doubly redundant. The general trend has been the opposite, a further splitting of already small nations as rights of self-determination became recognized. And so, despite the arms races in Lilliput, the governments of the bottom billion have not engaged in international wars to anything like the same extent as did the European states of the nineteenth century. The resulting reduced need to tax has been reinforced by aid: in the typical country of the bottom billion the government gets around a third of its expenditure met by aid. The combination of modest military spending and high aid has left the tax burden quite light: often around 12 percent of GDP. This level of taxation has been too low to provoke citizens into demanding accountability. . . .

Corrupt rulers might be wary of explicit taxation because of its capacity to provoke opposition. They do not want to tax so heavily that they provoke irresistible demands for accountability. It is no good having huge tax revenues if they then have to be spent on things that benefit everyone: your supporters will have no reason to stay loyal if they are rewarded no better than anyone else. So you must trade off high taxation against higher accountability. . . .

This sketch of how accountability and a sense of nation evolve provides a rudimentary explanation for the political problems of the bottom billion: they are stuck. The state is ineffective partly because it would not be in the interests of leaders for it to be more effective, and partly because the supply of public goods is impaired by the lack of a sense of common identity. Based on the analogy with the formation of effective states in Europe, the solution would be greater state military rivalry. As states felt less secure against one another they would need to raise more taxation and this would provoke greater accountability. It would also presumably generate a strong sense of national identity.

I am going to argue that this is not an acceptable solution, but before we discard it I will set out a little evidence in its favor. Among the leaders of the bottom billion, President Museveni of Uganda has been unusually effective. When he came to power in 1986 the society was quite literally in ruins: it had taken less than a quarter century of independence to pass from peace and growing prosperity to mass violence and impoverishment. Uganda was, indeed, not a bad approximation to what Britain must have gone through after the Romans pulled out. Kampala, like fifth-century London, was reverting to the bush. President Museveni has achieved a remarkable transformation. Despite being landlocked and resource-scarce, Uganda has been one of the fastest growing of Africa's economies. He has consistently placed the interests of economic recovery above the patronage and populism that have been so common elsewhere on the continent. What was the driving force behind him: what was his ambition as a leader?

I got to know President Museveni and I came to have great admiration and respect for him: I came to realize that he was not only a statesman but he was a military leader with ambitions for changing the political architecture of Eastern and Central Africa. For this he wanted a strong army. The man whom he most despised was his predecessor, President Amin. Amin had not only wrecked the Ugandan economy, he had suffered the ignominy of being deposed through an invasion by Tanzania, whose army had routed his own. One lesson that I believe President Museveni drew from this was that without a strong economy there could be no strong army. I think this was the bedrock that underpinned economic reform.

He not only rebuilt the economy, he conducted Africa's only truly successful campaign against AIDS. His leadership of this campaign, Zero Grazing, was decisive because it persuaded ordinary Ugandans to change their sexual behavior. Helen Epstein brilliantly describes it in her book *The Invisible Cure*. What she doesn't reveal is the key step in convincing Museveni to act. Given that his army was his priority, Museveni arranged with Fidel Castro that his officer corps should be sent to Cuba for training. Once in Cuba his officers were given medical checks. The message came back from Cuba: do you realize your officer corps is overwhelmingly HIV positive, they are going to die of AIDS? I suspect that Uganda's AIDS campaign, like its economic reforms, was in part motivated by President Museveni's military ambitions.

Uganda certainly has not gone all the way to being an accountable polity, but it is nevertheless a genuine example of increased state effectiveness. A similar story is Rwanda since 1994. The government of Paul Kagame, like President Museveni a successful rebel military leader, is currently the leading African example of effective state building. . . .

However, I balk at the notion that the societies of the bottom billion need to go through the same process as Europe. Even if the solution eventually worked, it would be at enormous cost. Europe tore itself apart with wars, and I do not wish to see the bottom billion do the same. War is even bloodier now than it was when Europe was fighting. There simply has to be a better way of building an effective and accountable state because the war route is utterly appalling. But I do not want to be guilty of believing something because it is so much more attractive than the alternative. Self-deluding thinking has bedeviled issues of development for decades. We have to work within the world as it is, rather than the world we would wish. So, while the appalling cost of the historical route is a good reason for *hoping* that there is a better alternative, it is not a good reason for *thinking* that there is one. . . .

So what are the realistic options? Surely the best is the route taken by President Nyerere in Tanzania: political leadership that builds a sense of national identity. Astonishingly, Nyerere achieved this without resorting to the notion of a neighboring enemy: indeed, he emphasized a Pan-African as well as a national identity. In our guilt-ridden enthusiasm for multiculturalism we may have forgotten that the rights of minorities rest on systems that depend upon the prior forging of an overriding sense of common nationality.

In a very few societies the political process of ethnic polarization may have gone so far that separation into independent states is indeed the only answer. However, it is a path that could easily lead to the proliferation of tiny states. . . .

If nation building is not feasible, then perhaps Canada and Belgium offer an alternative. These are both strong states in societies in which the sense of national identity is weak relative to the sense of subgroup identity. There is so little common national feeling that both of these societies periodically teeter upon the brink of breaking apart as states. . . . Their intense subnational identities are made manageable within a single state by robust accountability: checks and balances keep the federal state impartial despite the intergroup contest. Instead of a shared sense of belonging, the state functions because its component groups are suspicious of each other and can use the institutions of accountability to prevent being disadvantaged. Such societies may not be cozy, but they are viable.

But here is the problem: Canada and Belgium work because they each have robust systems of accountability. How did they acquire accountability despite the problems that are usually encountered in generating public goods in divided societies? . . . In effect, they were free-riding on the norms developed in neighboring societies that had forged a stronger sense of nationhood. The societies of the bottom billion are not in neighborhoods that have the norm of accountability. Given their neighborhoods and their internal divisions, they have not been able to generate the robust systems of accountability that would be needed for them to function like Canada and Belgium. The sequence of introducing elections before either accountability or nation building has been fundamentally flawed. In the now-mature democracies the sequence was reversed: critically, accountability was in place well in advance of competitive elections.

In the absence of accountability electoral competition actually impedes its subsequent supply. The society becomes more polarized and incumbents use strategies of power retention that require them to keep accountability at bay. Unless the states of the bottom billion can forge themselves into nations they will need some *deus ex machina* that introduces accountability.

26.2

Violence and the Rise of Open-Access Orders

Douglass C. North, John Joseph Wallis, and Barry R. Weingast

Every explanation of large-scale social change contains a theory of economics, a theory of politics, and a theory of social behavior. Often the theories are implicit, and even more often, the theory of economics and the theory of politics are independent of each other. Despite a great deal of attention and effort, social science has not come to grips with how economic and political development are connected either in history or in the modern world.

The absence of an integrated theory of economics and politics reflects a lack of systematic thinking about the central problem of violence in human societies. How societies deal with the ubiquitous threat of violence shapes human interaction. In our forthcoming book, we develop a conceptual framework that explains how, over the last ten millennia, societies have used institutions to limit and contain violence. These institutions simultaneously give individuals control over resources and social functions, and limit the use of violence by shaping the incentives that individuals and groups face. We call these patterns of social organization *social orders*. Social orders are characterized by the way in which societies craft the institutions that form human organizations, limit or open access to those organizations, and shape incentives to limit and control violence.

Human history has known just three types of social orders. The first was the *foraging order*: small social groups characteristic of hunter-gatherer societies. Our concern is with the two social orders that arose over the last ten millennia. The *limited-access order* (or *natural state*) emerged between five and ten thousand years ago, and was associated with the increasing scale of human societies. Increasing scale is accomplished through a hierarchy of personal relationships among powerful individuals. Personal relationships among the elite form the basis for political organization and constitute the grounds for individual interaction. A natural state is ruled by a dominant coalition; people outside the coalition have only limited access to organizations, privileges, and valuable resources and activities. *Open-access orders* emerged in the nineteenth century, and are associated with the beginnings of sustained economic and political development. Identity, which in natural states is inherently personal, becomes defined in open-access orders by a set of impersonal characteristics. The development of impersonal categories of individuals, often called citizens, allowed people to interact over wide areas of social behavior where no one needed to know the individual identities of their partners. The ability to form organizations that the larger society supports is open to everyone who meets a set of minimal and impersonal criteria. Both limited- and open-access social orders have public and private organizations, but natural states limit access to those organizations. Open-access societies do not.

The emergence of societies with widespread political participation, the use of elections to select governments, constitutional arrangements to limit and define the powers of government, and unbiased application of the rule of law is a product of the transition from limited- to open-access societies. If "democracy" is defined as a social system that creates responsiveness to citizen interests and polices corruption, then experience shows that it requires more than elections; the formal political institutions of democracy do not produce modern societies by themselves.[1] Open access to organizations in both the polity and the economy animates elections, and a democratic society requires open access in both. A free press—representing open access to information—is also essential to democracy. The transition entails a set of changes in the polity that ensures secure, impersonal political rights; legal support for a wide range of organizational forms (including political parties and economic organizations);

Source: Douglass C. North, John Joseph Wallis, and Barry R. Weingast. "Violence and the Rise of Open-Access Orders." *Journal of Democracy* 20:1 (2009), 55–59 and 63–68.

access to those organizations for all citizens; and enforcement of prohibitions against the use of violence. The transition also entails a set of changes in the economy: the ability to create economic organizations at will, open entry and competition in many markets, and the free movement of goods and individuals over space and time. Over the long term, open-access politics cannot be sustained without open-access economics, and vice-versa. Although evidence from the last few decades is mixed, over the last two centuries, political and economic development appear to have gone hand-in-hand.[2]

An underappreciated feature of the codevelopment of political and economic institutions in the two social orders helps to explain why poor countries stay poor. Economic growth occurs when countries are able to sustain positive growth rates in per capita income over the long term. The evidence suggests that until about 1800, the long-run growth rate was close to zero: For every period of increasing per capita income, a corresponding period of decreasing income occurred.[3] Modern developed societies that made the transition to open access and subsequently became wealthier than any others in human history, did so by greatly reducing their episodes of negative growth.[4] The historical pattern of offsetting periods of positive and negative growth episodes is apparent in the modern world where we have comprehensive data. Using data on per capita income for 184 countries between 1950 and 2004, we calculated annual growth rates and then separated the years by whether the economy was growing or shrinking.[5] Surprisingly, the richest countries were not distinguished from poorer ones by higher positive growth rates when they grew. In our dataset, the richest non-oil countries with per capita incomes over US$20,000 grew at an average annual rate of 3.9 percent in years when income was growing and fell at an average annual rate of 2.3 percent when income was shrinking. In contrast, incomes in countries where the per capita share was less than $20,000 grew at an average annual rate of 5.4 percent when income was rising, but shrank at a rate of 4.9 percent when income was falling. Even more strikingly, the rich countries experienced positive growth in 84 percent of all years, while poor countries experienced positive growth in only 66 percent of the years. The poorest countries, with per capita incomes below $2,000 a year, experienced positive growth in only 56 percent of the years. Poor countries are not poor because they grow more slowly; they are poor because they experience more years of negative income growth and more rapid declines during those years.[6]

While economic outcomes do not map directly onto political outcomes, the slow but steady growth of open-access societies suggests that modern development is not the result of faster growth per se, but instead results from new forms of political, economic, and social organization that make a society much better able to handle change. The difference between the respective economic performances of limited-access and open-access societies reflects the differential ability of the two social orders to deal with change, including a wide range of sudden changes or shocks.

Our conceptual framework does not posit a static social equilibrium, but instead offers a way of thinking about societies that face shifting constraints and opportunities. The dynamism of social orders is a dynamic of change, not a dynamic of progress. Most societies, especially natural states, move backwards and forwards with respect to political and economic development.

All societies must face the problem of violence. Controlling violence through repeated personal contacts can only sustain cooperation among small groups of maybe twenty-five to fifty people. In larger groups, few individuals have sufficient personal knowledge of all the members of the group, so personal relationships alone cannot be used to control violence. In larger societies, social institutions must arise to control violence. No society eliminates violence; at best, violence can be contained and managed.

Dealing with violence requires institutions and organizations. Institutions are the "rules of the game," the patterns of interaction that govern and constrain the relationships among individuals.[7] Institutions include formal rules, written laws, informal norms, and shared beliefs about the world, as well as the means of enforcement. The critical question is what types of institutions can survive given the interactions of institutional constraints, people's beliefs, and their behavior.[8]

In contrast to institutions, organizations are made up of individuals pursuing a mix of common and individual goals through partly coordinated behavior. Organizations coordinate their members' actions, so an organization's actions are more than the sum of the actions of the individuals who belong to it.

We distinguish two types of organizations: An *adherent organization* features self-enforcing agreements among its members. Third parties are not involved. Cooperation by adherent organizations' members must be, at all times, "incentive-compatible" for all members. *Contractual organizations*, by contrast, use within themselves not only incentive-compatible agreements but contracts enforced by third parties external to the organization. Third-party enforcement allows individuals to commit to a subset of arrangements that may not otherwise be incentive-compatible. Our framework revolves around the development of institutional forms that can support complicated and sophisticated contractual organizations, both inside and outside the state.

Modern open-access societies often limit violence through institutions. Institutions frame rules that deter violence by changing the payoffs expected from violent behavior—most obviously by establishing credible punishments for those who are violent. People are more likely to obey rules, even at considerable cost to themselves, if they believe that other people will obey the rules as well.[9] An individual has an incentive to shoot first and talk later when he fears that others will fail to follow such rules. In order for a formal institution to constrain violence, some organization must exist in which a set of officials enforces the rules in an impersonal manner. The larger the society, the larger the set of enforcers that must somehow be organized.

Most social scientists abstract from the question of how the enforcers are actually organized, treating them as a single entity in order to focus on the relationship between the enforcement entity and the rest of society. For example, social scientists have modeled the state as a revenue-maximizing monarch, a stationary bandit, or a single-actor "representative agent."[10] As Max Weber famously said, the state is that organization which has a monopoly on the legitimate use of violence. Collapsing the identity of the state into a single actor or ruler greatly simplifies the problem of explaining state behavior.

The single-actor model of the state, however, assumes away the problem of how societies create a monopoly on violence. This approach also overlooks the reality that all states are organizations. We take another path to understanding the state. The process of controlling violence is central to how individuals and groups behave within a society and how a coalition emerges to structure the state and society. Choosing this path requires us to formulate a model of the state as an organization of several actors rather than a single actor. . . .

The Logic of the Transition

Limited-access orders predominated overwhelmingly until just a century or two ago, making them seem the "natural state" of humankind. This prompts the question: How do natural states become open-access societies? In seeking to understand this transition, we confront two obstacles. First, the transition begins in the natural state and must therefore be consistent with the logic of that state. So how does the transition ever get started? An explanation of the transition must show how conditions arise within a natural state that put elites in a position where, consistent with the logic of the natural state, they find it in their interest to transform personal and privileged intraelite arrangements into *impersonal* ones that treat all elite members the same way.

Second, how do impersonal arrangements within the elite translate into open access for those who are not members of any elite? Some scholars frame the question as "Why do elites give up their privileged position in society by allowing nonelites full participation?" This approach is problematic: It carries the implication that elites give something up, but it is not clear that they do.[11] We frame the question differently: "Why do elites transform their unique and personal privileges into impersonal rights?"

When elites create impersonal open access for themselves to political and economic organizations, they may also create incentives to expand access to the nonelite population as well. The transition, as a result, has two stages. First, a natural state must develop institutional arrangements that enable elites to create the possibility of impersonal intraelite relationships. Second, the transition proper begins when members of the dominant coalition find it a matter of self-interest to expand impersonal relationships and to institutionalize open access for all.

We call the conditions in a natural state that foster impersonal relationships among elites the *doorstep conditions*. The doorstep conditions reflect institutional and organizational support for increased impersonal exchange. The three doorstep conditions are: 1) the application of the rule of law to the elites; 2) the creation of perpetually lived elite organizations in both the public and private spheres; and 3) consolidated political control over the military.

In combination, the doorstep conditions create an environment that fosters impersonal elite relations. Applying the rule of law among elites extends the range of the contracts and relationships that can flourish and makes possible mutual dependencies that could not survive without some form of credible legal protection. Perpetually lived organizations can undertake a wider range of economic and political activities. Moreover, political institutions that bind not only today's officials but tomorrow's require creating a perpetually lived state. Most limited-access orders lack such states. Consolidated control over the military removes the need for elites to maintain alliances with military factions.

Once elite relationships become impersonal, new possibilities begin to open up. If a society on the doorstep creates and sustains new incentives for elites to open up one sort of access followed by another within the elite, then a transition proper ensues. Nothing, however, inevitably impels a society on the doorstep to make the transition.

During the transition proper, all elites gain the right to form organizations—be they political, economic, or social. At that point, the logic holding the dominant coalition together has changed from the natural-state logic of rent-creation through privileges to the open-access logic of rent-erosion through entry.

Our approach has significant implications for a wide range of problems, including economic development, the theory of the state, and democracy.[12] In the remaining space, we concentrate on the implications for democracy.

An important conclusion flowing from our conceptual framework is that the same institutions work differently under conditions of limited as opposed to open access. Markets, for example, perform differently in natural states than they do in open-access orders because the former are characterized by extensive privileges, limited access to organizations, and the absence of secure, impersonal property rights.

Implications for Democracy

This lesson has special force with respect to democracy: Elections and party competition work differently in natural states than they do in open-access orders. This view contrasts with the dominant scholarly view, which follows that of Adam Przeworski and his coauthors and includes the lion's share of empirical studies.[13] The dominant view defines democracy in terms of whether a country sustains competitive elections with peaceful partisan turnover. Similarly, the popular press commonly identifies democracy with the existence of elections. This approach to democracy lumps together elections in limited-access orders with those in open-access orders.

We have a different perspective. Although elections are central to democracy, democracy is not solely about elections, as Robert A. Dahl argued in his landmark 1971 work *Polyarchy*. As a set of institutions in an open-access order, democracy gives citizens a degree of control over political officials, thereby generating responsiveness to citizens' interests while helping to limit corruption. For democracy to work, elections must be embedded in an institutional environment that allows political competition to constrain politicians as well as to convey information to them. Elections in natural states typically fulfill these functions either inadequately or not at all. Indeed, a host of important differences distinguish elections in limited-access orders from their counterparts in open-access orders. These differences show that only open-access orders can sustain democracy in the sense of citizen control over governments and officials.

Open-access orders can deliver policies to citizens on an impersonal basis. This allows such orders to provide a wide range of public goods and large-scale social-insurance programs of the type that are missing from natural states. Poverty-reduction programs can be targeted to reach the poor, as measured by impersonal and observable characteristics; driver's licenses can be issued to anyone who meets an age requirement and passes a competency test; unemployment benefits are available to those who contribute to the system and meet the impersonal requirements for being unemployed.

Impersonal delivery of public goods and services prevents political officials from threatening to withhold such goods as a means to manipulate citizens. By contrast, when natural states provide public goods on a personal basis, officials can use the threat of taking them away to force citizens to support the incumbents.[14] The provision of publicly provided goods in natural states combines with elections to provide natural-state governments with a way to keep citizens in line. Under such circumstances, elections do not represent the free exercise of citizen choice.

Impersonal delivery of public goods has another important implication for the success of democracy. Many scholars emphasize democracy as a means of redistribution: If a country includes more low- and middle-income voters than rich ones, then democracy is likely to result in the redistribution of wealth from the richer to poorer voters.[15] This analysis, however, ignores the means for redistribution that exist if the government is able to deliver redistribution impersonally. Impersonal policies allow open-access orders to respond to citizens in ways that complement markets so that these policies become a positive-sum game.[16] Social-insurance programs are not simply means of redistribution; they lower individual risk from market participation.[17] Natural states cannot credibly deliver impersonal public services, so the poor have incentives to use their votes to secure cash transfers. These states are therefore more susceptible both to populist appeals launched by factional leaders who seek to shift wealth and to coups meant to prevent such shifts. This double vulnerability to sudden populist and antipopulist maneuvers is the dark side of democracy, a side often visible in natural states.

Open access typically supports an effective opposition and a competitive electoral process. It supports a rich civil society, fostering a wide range of economic, political, and social groups that can mobilize interests and help to constrain democratic policy making. Schumpeterian competition constantly produces new interests and groups. Widespread access to organizations makes it difficult for public officials to manipulate economic interests in support of the regime. In contrast, most natural states inhibit or compromise electoral competition—for example, by the use of violence to intimidate opposition, by limits on citizens' ability to organize and the opposition's to compete, and by restrictions on freedom of the press.

Taken together, the differences that distinguish limited-access from open-access orders explain why elections in the former do not perform the same functions that they do in the latter. Elections in open-access orders implement the democratic ideals of citizen expression and control over political officials in ways that elections simply cannot accomplish in natural states. Open access limits the stakes of power; creates perpetually lived organizations that survive crises and partisan turnovers; allows a wider range of groups to form and mobilize; allows more effective competition for office; and allows the impersonal provision of public goods and services.

The ability of open-access orders to sustain political competition depends on their parallel ability to sustain open-access economic competition. It is not simply the form of the institutions in open-access societies that makes democracy work; it is the dynamic relationships among political, economic, and other social systems that result when the ability to create organizations is open to all. In order to spread democracy—and not just elections—more widely, we must learn how to induce societies to adopt social arrangements that move them to the doorstep conditions beyond which sustainable impersonal relationships can develop. Then the problem becomes one of fostering the spread of those political and economic institutions to wider shares of the populace. Sustainable democracy requires not only an open-access polity, but an open-access economy too.

Notes

1. The growing literature on authoritarian elections emphasizes this point. See Beatriz Magaloni, "Credible Power-Sharing and the Longevity of Authoritarian Rule," *Comparative Political Studies* 41 (April 2008): 715–41.

2. In *Political Man: The Social Bases of Politics* (Garden City, N.Y.: Anchor, 1959), Seymour Martin Lipset asked why sustainable democracy seemed to require economic development. Whether a causal link exists between democracy and economic development, and if so which way the link runs, remains an open question. See more recent work, including Adam Przeworksi et al., *Democracy and Development: Political Institutions and Well-Being in the World, 1950–1990* (New York: Cambridge University Press, 2000); Robert J. Barro, *Markets and Choices in a Free Society* (Cambridge: MIT Press, 1996); and Daron Acemoglu et al., "Income and Democracy," *American Economic Review* 98 (June 2008): 808–42.

3. For evidence about long-term growth before 1800, see Gregory Clark, *A Farewell to Alms: A Brief Economic History of the World* (Princeton: Princeton University Press, 2007); see also Robert W. Fogel, *The Escape from Hunger and Premature Death, 1700–2100: Europe, America, and the Third World* (New York: Cambridge University Press, 2004), 20–22.

4. Since we have no reliable way of gauging annual per capita income before 1800, the idea that the recent growth in developed countries is due to the elimination of negative-growth episodes remains an assertion, but one that accords with evidence about economic performance in the past.

5. The following discussion summarizes the analysis of Table 1.2 in Douglass C. North, John Joseph Wallis, and Barry R. Weingast, *Violence and Social Orders: A Conceptual Framework for Interpreting Recorded Human History* (Cambridge: Cambridge University Press, 2009), ch. 1.

6. More sophisticated empirical confirmation is provided by Dani Rodrik, *Making Openness Work: The New Global Economy and the Developing Countries* (Washington, D.C.: Overseas Development Council, 1999); Garey Ramey and Valerie A. Ramey, "Cross-Country Evidence on the Link Between Volatility and Growth," *American Economic Review* 85 (December 1995): 1138–51; and Ahmed Mushfiq

Mobarak, "Democracy, Volatility and Development," *Review of Economics and Statistics* 87 (May 2005): 348–61.

7. Douglass C. North, *Institutions, Institutional Change, and Economic Performance* (New York: Cambridge University Press, 1990), 3–4.

8. See Avner Greif, *Institutions and the Path to the Modern Economy* (New York: Cambridge University Press, 2006); and Barry R. Weingast, "Rational Choice Institutionalism," in Ira Katznelson and Helen V. Milner, eds., *Political Science, State of the Discipline: Reconsidering Power, Choice, and the State* (New York: W.W. Norton, 2002).

9. Margaret Levi, *Consent, Dissent, and Patriotism* (New York: Cambridge University Press, 1997).

10. Three well-known examples are Geoffrey Brennan and James M. Buchanan's notion of the state as Leviathan, Douglass C. North's neoclassical theory of the state, and Mancur Olson's idea of the state as a stationary bandit. Other models include Douglass C. North, *Structure and Change in Economic History* (New York: W.W. Norton, 1981); Yoram Barzel, *A Theory of the State: Economic Rights, Legal Rights, and the Scope of the State* (New York: Cambridge University Press, 2002); Robert Bates, Avner Greif, and Smita Singh, "Organizing Violence," *Journal of Conflict Resolution* (October 2002): 1–65; Bruce Bueno de Mesquita et al., *The Logic of Political Survival* (Cambridge: MIT Press, 2003); and Charles Tilly, *European Revolutions, 1492–1992* (Cambridge, Mass.: Blackwell, 1992).

11. For an example of this approach, which stresses how elites, threatened by revolution or civil unrest, grant nonelites concessions such as democracy, see Daron Acemoglu and James A. Robinson, *The Economic Origins of Dictatorship and Democracy* (New York: Cambridge University Press, 2006).

12. We deal with several of these issues in *Violence and Social Orders*, ch. 7.

13. Przeworski, et al., *Democracy and Development.*

14. Alberto Diaz, Beatriz Magaloni, and Barry R. Weingast, "Tragic Brilliance: Equilibrium Party Hegemony in Mexico," Working Paper, Hoover Institution, Stanford University, 2008. The authors analyze this use of elections as a means of exerting control over citizens.

15. The classic work is Allan H. Meltzer and Scott F. Richard, "A Rational Theory of the Size of Government," *Journal of Political Economy* 89 (October 1981): 914–27. See also Acemoglu and Robinson, Economic *Origins of Dictatorship and Democracy.*

16. Geoffrey Garrett, *Partisan Politics in the Global Economy* (Cambridge: Cambridge University Press, 1998), 5, makes a similar point.

17. Moreover, as the term "social-insurance programs" suggests, these policies are more about insurance than about redistribution. See Peter H. Lindert, *Growing Public: Social Spending and Economic Growth Since the Eighteenth Century*, 2 vols. (Cambridge University Press, 2004).

26.3

Nation-Building and the Failure of Institutional Memory

Francis Fukuyama

I don't think our troops ought to be used for what's called nation-building. I think our troops ought to be used to fight and win war. (October 11, 2000)

We meet here during a crucial period in the history of our nation, and of the civilized world. Part of that history was written by others; the rest will be written by us. (February 26, 2003)

I sent American troops to Iraq to make its people free, not to make them American. Iraqis will write their own history, and find their own way. (May 24, 2004)

George W. Bush

George W. Bush has gone through a striking transformation on the subject of nation-building: from opponent of the very concept as candidate for president, to grandiose social engineer on the eve of the Iraq war, to chastened supporter of indigenous Iraqi nation-building a year later. These changes track the profound ambivalence felt by the American public to this activity. Conservatives have always been skeptical about nation-building as a kind of international social welfare, whereas liberals have seen the effort to create a democratic Iraq as an extension of the American empire. Yet both ends of the political spectrum have come to support nation-building efforts at different times—conservatives as part of the "war on terrorism" and liberals for the sake of humanitarian intervention.

The frequency and intensity of U.S. and international nation-building efforts have increased since the end of the Cold War, which, as Michael Ignatieff has pointed out, left a band of weak or failed states stretching from North Africa through the Balkans and the Middle East to South Asia.[1] In addition, parts of sub-Saharan Africa, East Asia, Central America, and the Caribbean have been the loci of state failure in recent decades. These failures have produced refugees, human rights abuses, inter- and intrastate wars, drug and human trafficking, and other problems that crossed international borders. And after September 11, 2001, it became clear that weak or failed states could sponsor terrorism that threatened the core security interests of the world's sole superpower, the United States.

Although conventional military power was sufficient for some purposes, such as expelling Serbian military forces from Kosovo or defeating Saddam Hussein's army, the underlying problems caused by failed states or weak governance could only be solved through long-term efforts by outside powers to rebuild indigenous state institutions. Security problems in earlier times centered around strong states that could maintain a monopoly of force over their own territory, but many post-Cold War crises involved an internal absence of state power that necessitated outside intervention and long-term receivership by the international community. Thus the ability of outside powers to provide governance and control the internal behavior of failed or weak states has become a key component of their national power. . . .

Some Definitions

Europeans often criticize Americans for the use of the term nation-building, reflecting as it does the specifically American experience of constructing a new political order in a land of new settlement without deeply rooted peoples, cultures, and traditions. Nations—that is to say, communities of shared values, traditions, and historical memory—by this argument are never built, particularly by outsiders; rather, they evolve out of an unplanned historical-evolutionary process. What Americans refer to as nation-building is

Source: Francis Fukuyama, ed. *Nation-Building: Beyond Afghanistan and Iraq*. pp. 1–11.

rather state-building—that is, constructing political institutions, or else promoting economic development.

This argument is largely true: what Americans mean by *nation-building* is usually state-building coupled with economic development. However, the flat assertion that foreigners have never succeeded in nation-building is not true. Many imperial powers have sought to build nations within their colonies, and some have succeeded. The most notable case is the British in India. . . .

But the British legacy on the subcontinent is in many ways unique; few colonial powers had such a large and durable effect on their subject peoples. For all practical purposes, what passes for nation-building is a much more limited exercise in political reconstruction or re-legitimation, or else a matter of promoting economic development. Outside powers can succeed at negotiating and enforcing ceasefires between, say, rival ethnic groups; it is seldom that they can make these groups understand that they are part of a larger, nonethnic identity.

Even in the cases of postwar Germany and Japan—often taken as models of successful nation-building—the influence of outside powers on the political development of these countries is exaggerated or misunderstood. The United States and other occupying powers did relatively little state-building in either country: both Germany and Japan possessed powerful state bureaucracies that survived the war weakened but structurally intact. The occupation authorities conducted political purges of both bureaucracies, but the exigencies of the postwar reconstruction forced them to bring back many former Nazis or senior bureaucrats with ties to the prewar regimes. In Japan in particular, General Douglas MacArthur succeeded in purging only the top couple of layers of officials in the powerful economics ministries; as recent Japanese revisionist historians have shown, the postwar economic planning ministries that became known as "Japan, Inc." had their origin in the 1940 credit-allocation and munitions production system.[2]

What did occur in both Germany and Japan was the re-legitimation of the new governments on a democratic basis, with the drafting of democratic constitutions. (In the Japanese case, the political system was democratized without forcing abdication of the Emperor, a decision of MacArthur's that eased the postwar transition but made the break with the prewar past much less clear than in Germany.) And in both countries, the Allied occupations eventually got around to promoting economic reconstruction, once the Soviets had finished stripping their occupation zones of equipment as war reparations. But in both cases, what went on under the rubric of nation-building looked quite different from more recent efforts in such failed states as Somalia, East Timor, or Afghanistan, where the state itself had ceased to exist.

Reconstruction Versus Development

Nation-building encompasses two different types of activities, reconstruction and development. Although the distinction between the two is often blurred, it was always present to nation-builders of earlier generations dealing with post-conflict situations. The official title of the World Bank is, after all, the International Bank for Reconstruction and Development, and most of its early activity fell under the first heading. *Reconstruction* refers to the restoration of war-torn or damaged societies to their preconflict situation. *Development*, however, refers to the creation of new institutions and the promotion of sustained economic growth, events that transform the society open-endedly into something that it has not been previously.

There is a huge conceptual difference between reconstruction and development. Reconstruction is something that outside powers have shown themselves historically able to bring about. . . . Reconstruction is possible when the underlying political and social infrastructure has survived conflict or crisis; the problem is then the relatively simple matter of injecting sufficient resources to jumpstart the process, in the form of supplying food, roads, buildings, infrastructure, and the like.

Development, however, is much more problematic, both conceptually and as a matter of pragmatic policy. . . . The self-confidence of Americans in their ability to help poor countries develop was quite high soon after World War II and then fell sharply during and after the Vietnam War. This early confidence was based in large measure on the experience of domestic state-building in New Deal projects, such as the Tennessee Valley Authority (TVA), which were seen at that time as huge successes in eliminating poverty in the rural South. There was a great deal of enthusiasm for state-led development at this time, with multilateral agencies like the World Bank and private nongovernmental organizations (NGOs) like the Ford Foundation providing technical training to help developing country governments do economic planning—understandably, perhaps, as this was the norm in most developed countries at the time. On the economic side, aid came in the form of large infrastructure projects or poorly thought-out industrialization projects.

The early American self-confidence in its ability to promote development came crashing down under the pressure of a variety of factors in the 1970s and 1980s.

State-building, done without regard for the democratic legitimacy of the governments involved, implicated foreign donors in the human rights abuses of recipients and failed to prevent coups, revolutions, and wars that led to political breakdown. Pakistan, an early target of foreign development efforts, is a prime example. Economic planning fell out of favor intellectually with the Reagan-Thatcher revolution in the late 1980s and was replaced by orthodox economic liberalism as the dominant conceptual framework. But most importantly, none of the approaches popular in any given decade proved adequate to promote sustained long-term growth in countries with weak institutions or where local elites were uninterested or incapable of managing the development process themselves. . . . Where sustained economic growth did occur, particularly in East Asia, it tended to come about under the leadership of domestic elites and not as a result of the efforts of foreign donors, lenders, or allies.[3]

To the extent that there has been intellectual progress in this area, it lies in an appreciation for the complexity and multidimensionality of the development problem. In the 1950s and 1960s, under the influence of the Harrod-Domar and neoclassical growth models, it was common to think about less-developed countries as if they were simply developed countries minus the resources and could be set on a path to self-sustaining growth through the infusion of sufficient investment capital. This approach was followed in later decades by emphases that shifted in turn to education, population control, debt relief, and structural adjustment as panaceas for development. In recent years, a great deal of attention has been paid, appropriately, to institutions and governance as critical factors in development.[4] But any honest appraisal of where the "state of the art" lies in development today would have to conclude that, although institutions may be important, we know relatively little about how to create them; they are, in any case, only one part of a much more complicated set of necessary strategies.

In light of this record, it is tempting to say that nation-builders should stick to reconstruction and eschew the development function. The problem is that this bifurcation is usually not possible in developing countries with weak or absent state sectors. In many cases, conflict has destroyed basic institutions, obliterating the distinction between reconstruction and development. In Somalia, Afghanistan, and Iraq after the United States-led invasion, no state infrastructure existed to provide security or to distribute state services, as it did in postwar Japan or Europe. These societies had fallen into chaos or warlordism, and new central government institutions had to be created virtually from scratch. To get them back to where they were prior to the outbreak of conflict thus required development as well as reconstruction.

The development function is a critical nation-building skill for another reason: it is only the ability to create and maintain self-sustaining indigenous institutions that permits outside powers to formulate an exit strategy. A lack of conceptual clarity on how to promote institutional development makes it extremely difficult to transition out of the reconstruction phase of nation-building. . . .

In certain respects, reconstruction can even become the enemy of development over the long run. Reconstruction requires rapid, massive outside intervention to stabilize conflicts, rebuild infrastructure, and deal with humanitarian issues. The local government is, by definition, unable to provide these functions itself, and it is often completely bypassed as foreign military forces, aid agencies, and NGOs flood into the country. Capacity-building must take a back seat to service delivery; more often than not, what little capacity exists is undermined by the presence of foreigners richly endowed with both resources and capabilities. In Afghanistan, a driver for a foreign media company makes several times the salary of a government minister; who, under these circumstances, would prefer to continue working for a disorganized and feckless local bureaucracy?

The development phase, by contrast, requires the eventual weaning of local actors and institutions from dependence on outside aid. This is conceptually straightforward, but extremely difficult to implement in practice. First, it is seldom the case that local institutions are actually strong enough to do all of the things that they are intended to do. Weaning them from outside support at times means that a particular governmental function simply is not performed. Second, the outside nation-builders get into the habit of ruling and making decisions, and they are reluctant to allow their local protégés to make their own mistakes. . . . And third, nation-builders often lack clarity about their own impact on local populations. They chant the mantra of institution- or capacity-building, and they fail to understand how their continued presence in the country tends to weaken precisely those institutions they are seeking to strengthen.

The Failure of Institutional Memory

None of these problems is new or unfamiliar to anyone who has been in the reconstruction or development business in times past. The United States plunged into its first big nation-building exercise during the reconstruction of the South in the aftermath of the Civil War, and it undertook numerous new projects in the Philippines and Caribbean during the period leading up to World War II.[5]

What is remarkable about this entire experience is how little institutional learning there has been over time; the same lessons about the pitfalls and limitations of nation-building seemingly have to be relearned with each new involvement. This became painfully evident during the American occupation and reconstruction of Iraq after April 2003. . . .

In every previous nation-building exercise in which the United States was involved after General MacArthur in Japan, there were always two lines of authority—one on the civilian side, going through the ambassador and the State Department, and a second through the field commander via the military chain of command; these two lines of authority were generally coordinated through a country team, usually chaired by the ambassador. The Iraq reconstruction was wholly directed by the Pentagon, breaking this precedent. President Bush was apparently persuaded by Defense Secretary Donald Rumsfeld's argument concerning the need for unity of command in the reconstruction. The lesson that Rumsfeld drew from Bosnia was that split authority on the U.S. side tends to tie U.S. forces down, because the civilian side is always good at devising reasons why U.S. troops are politically necessary and thus cannot be withdrawn. . . .

The Afghan reconstruction influenced the nature of the Iraq reconstruction. The former was run in the traditional way, with two lines of authority and a country team headed by an ambassador. The Pentagon argued that the State Department and USAID were handling the job incompetently; President Bush was evidently furious at the lack of progress on the Kabul-to-Kandahar highway that was to be the centerpiece of the U.S. nation-building effort. This interpretation strengthened the Pentagon's case for sole ownership of the Iraq reconstruction.

Unfortunately, this analysis of the Afghan experience was only partly correct. The early problem with the Afghan reconstruction was not the dual lines of authority or State Department involvement, but rather one of personalities. By 2003, when these problems had largely been fixed, the Afghan reconstruction proceeded much more smoothly than its counterpart in Iraq. Civil-military cooperation worked well both at the level of the ambassador and the local military commander as well as in the field, with the development of provincial reconstruction teams (PRTs) that combined security and reconstruction personnel in a single integrated package. . . .

In principle, unity of command is a good idea; Rumsfeld was right in observing that Bosnia had been marked by continuing squabbles between the civilian and military authorities and an overall lack of coordination. The international division of labor in the Balkans did indeed create overlapping and poorly coordinated national teams that wasted time and money. The problem in Iraq, however, was that the Pentagon office put in charge of organizing the reconstruction (the Office of the Undersecretary of Defense for Policy) had no prior experience with this kind of operation and had limited institutional capacity for setting up the kind of organization needed. The interagency coordination necessary for post-conflict reconstruction is among the most complex tasks of any that the U.S. government attempts to undertake. Defense, State, USAID, Justice, Treasury, and a host of other agencies all have roles to play, many of them defined by statute; just knowing how all of these moving parts fit together is a major task. . . .

The administration did plan for a number of contingencies that did not occur, such as a humanitarian/refugee crisis and oil well fires; however, it was completely blindsided by the collapse of state authority in Iraq and the chaos that followed. This omission is a perfect example of institutional memory failure. Almost every postconflict reconstruction during the previous decade and a half, from Panama to East Timor, had been characterized by the collapse of local police authority and the ensuing disorder.

Notes

1. Michael Ignatieff, "The Burden," *New York Times Magazine*, January 5, 2003, 22–27, 50–54.

2. Eisuke Sakakibara, *Beyond Capitalism: The Japanese Model of Market Economics* (Lanham, Md.: University Press of America, 1993).

3. As the chapter by David Ekbladh shows, South Korea is an interesting partial example. The United States regarded the Republic of Korea as a showcase for its Cold War development efforts, both before and particularly after the Korean War, and pumped substantial money and technical advice into the country. But Korea's economic takeoff under Park Chung-hee, although benefiting from U.S. largess, was mostly an indigenous effort.

4. See, for example, Douglass C. North, *Institutions, Institutional Change, and Economic Performance* (New York: Cambridge University Press, 1990); World Bank, *World Bank Development Report 1997: The State in a Changing World* (Oxford: Oxford University Press, 1997); Francis Fukuyama, *State-Building: Governance and World Order in the 21st Century* (Ithaca, N.Y.: Cornell University Press, 2004).

5. See John D. Montgomery and Dennis A. Rondinelli, eds., *Beyond Reconstruction in Afghanistan: Lessons from the Development Experience* (New York: Palgrave Macmillan, 2004).

27 Failed States

27.1

Why Africa's Weak States Persist

The Empirical and the Juridical in Statehood

Robert H. Jackson and Carl G. Rosberg

Introduction

Black Africa's forty-odd states are among the weakest in the world. State institutions and organizations are less developed in the sub-Saharan region than almost anywhere else; political instability (as indicated by coups, plots, internal wars, and similar forms of violence) has been prevalent in the two-and-a-half decades during which the region gained independence from colonial rule. Most of the national governments exercise only tenuous control over the people, organizations, and activities within their territorial jurisdictions. In almost all of these countries, the populations are divided along ethnic lines; in some, there has been a threat of political disorder stemming from such divisions; in a few, disorder has deteriorated into civil warfare. Some governments have periodically ceased to control substantial segments of their country's territory and population. For example, there have been times when Angola, Chad, Ethiopia, Nigeria, Sudan, Uganda, and Zaire have ceased to be "states" in the empirical sense—that is, their central governments lost control of important areas in their jurisdiction during struggles with rival political organizations.

In spite of the weakness of their national governments, none of the Black African states have been destroyed or even significantly changed. No country has disintegrated into smaller jurisdictions or been absorbed into a larger one against the wishes of its legitimate government and as a result of violence or the threat of violence. No territories or people—or even a segment of them—have been taken over by another country. No African state has been divided as a result of internal warfare. In other words, the serious empirical weaknesses and vulnerabilities of some African states have not led to enforced jurisdictional change. Why not? How can the persistence of Africa's weak states be explained? In order to answer the latter question, we must enquire into contemporary African political history as well as into the empirical and juridical components of statehood. An investigation of this question has implications not only for our understanding of African states and perhaps other Third World states, but also of statehood and contemporary international society.

The Concept of Statehood

Many political scientists employ a concept of the state that is influenced by Max Weber's famous definition: a corporate group that has compulsory jurisdiction, exercises continuous organization, and claims a

Source: Robert H. Jackson and Carl G. Rosberg. "Why Africa's Weak States Persist: The Empirical and the Juridical in Statehood," in *World Politics* 35(1): 1–16 and 21–24.

monopoly of force over a territory and its population, including "all action taking place in the area of its jurisdiction."[1] As Weber emphasized, his definition is one of "means" and not "ends," and the distinctive means for him are force.[2] A definition of the state primarily in terms of means rather than ends—particularly the means of force—emphasizes the empirical rather than the juridical, the *de facto* rather than the *de jure*, attributes of statehood. This emphasis is undoubtedly an important element in the appeal of Weber's sociology of the state to political scientists. To be sure, Weber does not overlook the juridical aspects of statehood. However, he does not explore what many students of international law consider to be the true character of territorial jurisdiction: the reality that such jurisdiction is an international legal condition rather than some kind of sociological given.

By Weber's definition, the basic test of the existence of a state is whether or not its national government can lay claim to a monopoly of force in the territory under its jurisdiction. If some external or internal organization can effectively challenge a national government and carve out an area of monopolistic control for itself, it thereby acquires the essential characteristic of statehood. According to Weber's *de facto* terms of statehood, two concurrent monopolies of force cannot exist over one territory and population. In situations where one of several rival groups—that is, claimant states—is unable to establish permanent control over a contested territory, Weber would maintain that it is more appropriate to speak of "statelessness."

By Weber's definition, a few of Africa's governments would not qualify as states—at least not all of the time—because they cannot always effectively claim to have a monopoly of force throughout their territorial jurisdictions. In some countries, rivals to the national government have been able to establish an effective monopoly of force over significant territories and populations for extended periods—for example, Biafra in Nigeria and Katanga in the Congo (now Zaire). In other countries—such as Chad and Uganda—some of the territories have not been under the continuous control of one permanent political organization, and a condition of anarchy has existed. Furthermore, the governments of many Black African countries do not effectively control all of the important public activities within their jurisdictions; in some, government is perilously uncertain, so that important laws and regulations cannot be enforced with confidence and are not always complied with. If the persistence of a state were primarily the result of empirical statehood, some sub-Saharan African countries would clearly not qualify as states some of the time. Yet it is evident that all of them persist as members of the international society of states; it is also evident that none of the claimant governments that have on occasion exercised *de facto* control over large territories and populations within the jurisdictions of existing states have yet succeeded in creating new states in these areas.

Definitions that give priority to the juridical rather than the empirical attributes of statehood are employed by international legal scholars and institutionally oriented international theorists. One such definition—which shares a number of characteristics with Weber's, but gives them a different emphasis—is that of Ian Brownlie, a British legal scholar. Following the *Montevideo Convention on Rights and Duties of States*, Brownlie describes the state as a legal person, recognized by international law, with the following attributes: (a) a defined territory, (b) a permanent population, (c) an effective government, and (d) independence, or the right "to enter into relations with other states."[3]

If the assumption of juridical statehood as a sociological given is a shortcoming of Weber's definition, a limitation of Brownlie's is the tendency to postulate that the empirical attributes of statehood—i.e., a permanent population and effective government—are as definite as the juridical attributes; they are not. . . . Although Brownlie recognizes the need to incorporate empirical criteria into a "working legal definition of statehood,"[4] he acknowledges (as do other scholars) that there is considerable difficulty in employing these criteria without specifying them concretely. Nonetheless, his definition enables us to undertake an analysis of the empirical as well as the juridical aspects of statehood—that is, a sociological-legal analysis.

Political scientists do not need to be convinced of the limitations of an exclusively legalistic approach to the state, which is usually summed up as "legal-formalism": an undue emphasis on abstract rules, leading to the neglect of concrete behavior and the social conditions that support or undermine legal rules.[5] What is more difficult is to convince a generation of political scientists whose theories and models were formulated in reaction to legal, institutional, and philosophical studies of the state, of the limitations of an exclusively sociological conception of statehood. However, if one assumes that the state is essentially an empirical phenomenon—one cannot explain why some states manage to persist when important empirical conditions of statehood are absent, or are present only in a very qualified manner.[6] In sum, one cannot explain the persistence of some "states" by using a concept of the state that does not give sufficient attention to the juridical properties of statehood.

The Empirical State in Black Africa

Weber's and Brownlie's definitons of statehood provide a useful point of departure for examining empirical and juridical statehood in contemporary Black Africa. (Juridical statehood is discussed in the following section.) We shall begin with Brownlie's definition, which is more explicit and current. As we noted above, Brownlie specifies two empirical attributes of the state: "a permanent population [which] is intended to be used in association with that of territory, and connotes a stable community," and an "effective government, with centralized administrative and legislative organs."[7]

Before we can apply Brownlie's empirical attributes to our analysis, we must clarify them. First, what exactly do we understand by "a stable community" and its crucial empirical component, "a permanent population"? . . . If we take "a stable community" to signify an integrated political community resting on a common culture, we must conclude that few contemporary Black African states can be said to possess this attribute. The populations of many Black African countries are divided internally among several—and often many—distinctive ethnic entities by differences of language, religion, race, region of residence, and so forth. Moreover, these ethnic cleavages can reinforce each other, thus aggravating the differences. In Sudan, for example, the racial division between Arabs and Africans is reinforced by geography, religion, and language; it has resulted in bitter conflicts over the control of the state. Furthermore, many ethnic entities are divided by international boundaries, with members residing in two or more countries; however, the social and political boundaries between these ethnic entities may well be more significant in terms of public attitudes and behavior than are the boundaries between the countries. As a result, political tensions and conflicts arising from ethnic divisions can seriously affect national political stability and the capacity of governments to control their territories.

From our discussion, it appears that few African states can qualify as stable communities. Where ethnic divisions have been politicized, the result has been serious civil conflict. Thus, ethnic divisions have been a major factor contributing to extreme disorder or civil war in the following countries: Sudan (1956–1972); Rwanda (1959–1964); Zaire (1960–1965; 1977–1978); Ethiopia (1962–1982); Zanzibar (1964); Burundi (1966–1972); Chad (1966–1982); Uganda (1966; 1978–1982); Nigeria (1967–1970); and Angola (1975–1982). In other countries, ethnic divisions have been sufficiently threatening to prompt governments to control political participation severely out of fear that they would otherwise jeopardize their command of the state.[8] . . . Efforts by African governments to emphasize the "nation" and "nationalism" at the expense of the "ethnos"—efforts that are evident elsewhere in the Third World as well—indicate their concern about the instability of their political communities and the threat posed by that instability not only to individual governments, but to statehood itself.[9]

Second, by "an effective government" Brownlie means exactly what Weber means by "compulsory jurisdiction": centralized administrative and legislative organs.[10] Such a definition is somewhat Eurocentric because it identifies governing not only with administering, but also with legislating. In contemporary Africa, governments do not necessarily govern by legislation; personal rulers often operate in an arbitrary and autocratic manner by means of commands, edicts, decrees, and so forth.[11] To make this empirical attribute more universal, let us redefine it as a centralized government with the capacity to exercise control over a state's territory and the people residing in it. By "exercise control" we mean the ability to pronounce, implement, and enforce commands, laws, policies, and regulations.

The capacity to exercise control raises the question of means. Analytically, the means of government can be considered in terms of the domestic authority or right to govern (legitimacy) on the one hand, and the power or ability to govern on the other. . . . A government may possess legitimacy, but have little in the way of an effective apparatus of power; or it may have an imposing power apparatus, but little legitimacy in the eyes of its citizens. Other combinations are also possible.[12]

In our judgment, the capacity of Africa's governments to exercise control hinges upon three factors: domestic authority, the apparatus of power, and economic circumstances. First, political authority in Africa (and in other parts of the Third World as well) tends to be personal rather than institutional. . . .

Constitutional and institutional offices that are independent of the personal authority of rulers have not taken root in most Black African countries. Instead, the state and state offices are dominated by ambitious individuals. . . . Wherever African governments have exercised substantial control, strong personal rulers have been firmly in the saddle. . . . Where African governments have not exercised control, it has often been because no personal leader has taken firm command; alternatively, it has been as a result of excessively arbitrary and abusive personal rule, as was the case in Uganda under Idi Amin. In the most unstable African regimes, the military has repeatedly intervened in politics—as in Benin from 1960 to 1972 and in Chad from 1975 to 1982.

Related to the problem of institutional weakness in African states is the disaffection of important elites from the government. The frequency of military coups is perhaps the best indication of elite alienation and disloyalty. Between 1958 and the summer of 1981, more than 41 successful coups had taken place in 22 countries of Black Africa; in addition, there had been many unsuccessful ones.[13] . . . It should be noted that, although Africa's military formations are called "armies" and their members wear uniforms and display other symbols of state authority, they cannot be assumed to be loyal to the government. A military career is sometimes a promising avenue for political advancement; soldiers in Black Africa have become not only government officials, but also rulers of their countries.

Second, the apparatus of power in African governments—the agents and agencies that implement and enforce government laws, edicts, decrees, orders, and the like—can in general be considered "underdeveloped" in regard both to their stock of resources and to the deployment of these resources. In proportion to their territories and populations, African governments typically have a smaller stock of finances, personnel, and materiel than Asian or Western governments, and their staffs are less experienced and reliable. As a result, the concept of governmental administration as a policy instrument bears less relation to reality. Governmental incapacity is exacerbated by overly ambitious plans and policies that are prepared on the assumption that underdevelopment is a problem of economy and society, but not of government. In fact, it is also African governments that are underdeveloped, and in most countries they are very far from being an instrument of development.[14] The modern "administrative state" image of government is of questionable applicability in many parts of the world, but Black African governments are even less likely than others to be rational agencies.

Undoubtedly the biggest problem of both civilian and military administrations in Africa is the questionable reliability of staffs. In a famous phrase, Gunnar Myrdal characterized the governments of South Asia as "soft states."[15] The term can be applied equally to many governments in Black Africa which must operate amidst corruption and disorder. . . .

Of course, there is considerable variation in the administrative capacity of African governments, and Tanzania is by no means the country most seriously affected by an inefficient state. . . . Once relatively efficient Ghana and Uganda are examples of marked deterioration, the origins of which are perhaps more political than economic and relate to a failure to establish an effective and responsible ruling class. One of the worst cases of administrative decay is Zaire, where the state's resources have been plundered and regulations abused by government officials at all levels. . . .

So extreme is the corruption that observers have had to invent new phrases to describe it; Zaire has been referred to as "an extortionist culture" in which corruption is a "structural fact" and bribery assumes the form of "economic mugging."[16] It has been estimated that as much as 60 percent of the annual national budget is misappropriated by the governing elite.

As we have noted, the inefficiency of African governments extends to the military as well as the civilian organs of the state. As in the case of civilian maladministration, military ineffectiveness stems from sociopolitical as well as technical-material factors; the size and firepower of the armed forces can also play a role. Typically, military forces in African countries are small in relation to the size or population of a state; however, they are considerably larger than the colonial armies they replaced. Over the past two decades, the size of African armies has increased (primarily for purposes of internal security), and their equipment has been upgraded. . . .

In practice, most African armies are less like military organizations and more like political establishments: they are infected by corruption, factionalism, and patterns of authority based not only on rank, role, or function, but also on personal and ethnic loyalties. The ability of African armies to deal with internal conflicts is dubious. . . . Moreover, the state's apparatus of power may be not only aided and supported by the solicited intervention of a foreign power in the form of troops, military equipment, advisers, and so forth, but such intervention can be essential to the survival of a regime. In a number of French-speaking countries, a French military presence has enhanced the power of the African government; in Angola and Ethiopia, Cuban soldiers and Soviet arms and advisers have made a decisive difference to the power and survival of incumbent African regimes in their conflicts with both internal and external powers. . . .

Third, governmental incapacity in Black Africa is affected by economic circumstances, which are exacerbated by the small size of the skilled work force. African economies are among the poorest and weakest in the world: in 1978, 22 of them had a per capita GNP below $250; throughout the 1970s, the Black African countries had the lowest worldwide rates of growth. Of the world's poorest countries—those with per capita incomes below $330—the 28 that were African had the lowest projected growth rates for the 1980s. In many of these countries, absolute poverty is increasing as birthrates continue to exceed economic growth rates.[17]

Many African countries are highly dependent on a few primary exports for their foreign exchange earnings. They are therefore vulnerable to uncontrollable fluctuations in world commodity prices and, in the case of agricultural commodities, unpredictable changes in weather conditions and harvest returns. The countries without petroleum resources have had to face dramatically increased prices for oil imports, resulting in very severe balance-of-payments problems. In some countries, more than 50 percent of scarce foreign exchange had to be used to pay for imported oil. Moreover, 27 countries had a shortfall in their production of food crops—principally maize—in 1980; they were therefore forced to import food, which resulted in a further drain of scarce foreign exchange. . . . Lacking industrial and manufacturing sectors of any significance and being highly dependent upon imports, most African countries are caught between the certainty of their demand for foreign goods and the uncertainty of their ability to earn the foreign exchange to pay for them. In many (if not most) of these countries, inflated and consumption-oriented government administrations—whose members enjoy a standard of living far in excess of the national average—weigh down the already overburdened and sluggish economies; in many, the economy is simply exploited to support the political class. The hope that intelligent government planning might effect a substantial economic transformation has long since faded.

It is evident that the term "empirical state" can only be used selectively to describe many states in Black Africa today. With some notable exceptions—for example, Kenya and the Ivory Coast—it seems accurate to characterize Africa's states as empirically weak or underdeveloped. If we adopted a narrow empirical criterion of statehood—such as Weber's monopoly of force—we would have to conclude that some African countries were not states, and that statehood in others has periodically been in doubt. In 1981, the governments of Angola, Chad, Ethiopia, and Uganda could not claim a monopoly of force within their jurisdictions. Furthermore, these countries and some others—for example, Nigeria, Sudan, and Zaire—have exhibited *de facto* statelessness in the past, and there are reasons to believe that they might do so again. Yet it is unlikely that any of their jurisdictions will be altered without the consent of their governments. . . .

The Juridical State in Black Africa

Before we investigate the significance of the juridical state in Black Africa, let us emphasize that "juridical statehood" is not only a normative but essentially an international attribute. The juridical state is both a creature and a component of the international society of states, and its properties can only be defined in international terms. At this point, it is important to clarify what is meant by "international society."[18] It is a society composed solely of states and the international organizations formed by states; it excludes not only individuals and private groups, but also political organizations that are not states or are not composed of states. The doctrine of "states' rights"—that is, sovereignty—is the central principle of international society. It often comes into conflict with the doctrine of international human rights, but international society does not promote the welfare of individuals and private groups within a country or transnational groups among countries; nor does it protect individuals or private groups from their governments.[19] Rather, international society provides legal protection for member states from any powers, internal and external, that seek to intervene in, invade, encroach upon, or otherwise assault their sovereignty.[20] A secondary but increasingly important goal—one that is linked to the emergence of Third World states—is to promote the welfare and development of member states.

According to Brownlie, the juridical attributes of statehood are "territory" and "independence" (as recognized by the international community). In international law, a demarcated territory is the equivalent of the "property" of a government—national real estate, including offshore waters and airspace; international boundaries are the mutually acknowledged but entirely artificial lines where one government's property rights end and another's begin. Determinate and recognized frontiers are therefore a basic institution of the state system and an essential legal attribute of any state. A government recognized as having political independence is legally the equal of other independent governments, and is not only the highest authority within its territorial jurisdiction but is under no higher authority.[21] It has the right to enter into relations with other states and to belong to the international society of states.

A political system may possess some or all of the empirical qualifications of statehood, but without the juridical attributes of territory and independence it is not a state. Furthermore, these attributes—which constitute territorial jurisdiction—serve as a test of a government's claim to be a state; there is no empirical test. . . .

The juridical state in Black Africa is a novel and arbitrary political unit; the territorial boundaries, legal identities, and often even the names of states are contrivances of colonial rule. Only rarely did a colonial territory reflect the shape and identity of a preexisting African socio-political boundary. . . . During the European colonization of Africa in the late 19th century, international society was conceived as a "European association, to which non-European states could be admitted only if and when they met a standard of civilization laid down by the Europeans."[22] With the exceptions of Ethiopia and Liberia, which escaped colonialism and were treated as states, Black African political systems did not qualify as states, but were regarded as the objects of a justified colonialism.

At independence (beginning in the late 1950s), there were therefore very few traditional African states to whom sovereignty could revert.[23] Consequently, there was little choice but to establish independence in terms of the colonial entities;[24] in most cases, a colony simply became a state with its territorial frontiers unchanged. Most attempts to create larger political units—usually conceived as federations—failed. . . . Kwame Nkrumah's vision of a United States of Africa received virtually no support from his counterparts in the newly independent states. Instead, the Organization of African Unity (O.A.U.), formed in May 1963, fully acknowledged and legitimated the colonial frontiers and the principle of state sovereignty within them. As President Modibo Keita of Mali put it: although the colonial system divided Africa, "it permitted nations to be born. . . . African unity . . . requires full respect for the frontiers we have inherited from the colonial system."[25]

It is a paradox of African independence that it awakened both national and ethnic political awareness. In almost every Black African country there are ethnic groups that desire to redraw international boundaries in order to form independent states. Self-determination, which accelerated after World War I and reached its peak in the years after World War II with the independence of numerous colonies, came to a halt in Black Africa. . . . The opposition of existing African states and of international society has reinforced the legitimacy of the inherited frontiers and undermined that of the traditional cultural. . . .

African decolonization—like decolonization elsewhere—demonstrated that it is impossible to have rational empirical qualifications for statehood. Many colonies became states although the viability of their economic bases and their developmental potentiality were questionable. Some of the new states had minuscule populations and/or territories: Cape Verde, the Comoros Islands, Djibouti, Equatorial Guinea, Gabon, The Gambia, Sao Tome and Principe, the Seychelles, and Swaziland. Empirically these entities are really microstates, but juridically they are full-fledged states.[26] Their independence reveals the assumption of the contemporary international community that even countries of very questionable viability and capacities can be preserved by a benevolent international society. In other words, international society has become a global "democracy" based on the principle of legal equality of members. Even the most profound socio-economic inadequacies of some countries are not considered to be a barrier to their membership: all former colonies and dependencies have the right to belong if they wish. The existence of a large number of weak states poses one of the foremost international problems of our time: their protection and preservation, not to mention development. The survival of states is not a new issue; indeed, it is the historical problem of international relations, which has served to define traditional international theory as "the theory of survival."[27] What is new is the enlarged scope, added dimensions, and greater complexity and delicacy of the problem in contemporary international society. . . .

Conclusion

We have argued that juridical statehood is more important than empirical statehood in accounting for the persistence of states in Black Africa. International organizations have served as "post-imperial ordering devices" for the new African states,[28] in effect freezing them in their inherited colonial jurisdictions and blocking any post-independence movements toward self-determination. So far, they have successfully outlawed force as a method of producing new states in Africa.

Membership in the international society provides an opportunity—denied to Black Africa under colonialism—to both influence and take advantage of international rules and ideologies concerning what is desirable and undesirable in the relations of states. The impact of Third World states on those rules and ideologies is likely to increase as the new statesmen learn how to take advantage of international democracy. . . .

The global international society whose most important institutions have been established or expanded since the end of World War II has been generally successful in supporting the new state jurisdictions of independent Africa; thus, the survival of Africa's existing states is largely an international achievement. Still, international effects on empirical statehood are ambiguous. International society has legitimated and fostered the transfer of goods, services, technology, skills, and the like from rich to poor countries with the intention of contributing to the development of the latter. But there are definite limits to what international society can contribute to the further development of the capabilities of African states. A society of states that exists chiefly in order to maintain the existing state system and the independence and survival of its members cannot regulate the internal affairs of members without the consent of their governments. It is therefore limited in its ability to determine that the resources transferred to the new states are effectively and properly used. In spite of a strong desire to do so, there is no way to guarantee such transfers against the wishes of a sovereign government without interfering in its internal affairs. Consequently, the enforcement of state jurisdictions may be at odds with the effort to develop the empirical state in Africa and elsewhere in the Third World. By enforcing juridical statehood, international society is in some cases also sustaining and perpetuating incompetent and corrupt governments. Perhaps the best example in sub-Saharan Africa is the international support that has gone into ensuring the survival of the corrupt government of Zaire. If this relationship is not an uncommon one, we must conclude that international society is at least partly responsible for perpetuating the underdevelopment of the empirical state in Africa by providing resources to incompetent or corrupt governments without being permitted to ensure that these resources are effectively and properly used. . . .

Arnold Wolfers pointed out that in the Anglo-American conceptualization of the international system versus the nation-state, the most persistent image has been one of international discord versus internal order and civility.[29] In contemporary Black Africa, an image of international accord and civility and internal disorder and violence would be more accurate. At the level of international society, a framework of rules and conventions governing the relations of the states in the region has been founded and sustained for almost two decades. But far less institutionalization and political order has been evident during this period at the level of national society: many African countries have been experiencing internal political violence and some internal warfare. Insofar as our theoretical images follow rather than precede concrete historical change, it is evident that the recent national and international history of Black Africa challenges more than it supports some of the major postulates of international relations theory.

Notes

1. Weber, *The Theory of Social and Economic Organization*, ed. by Talcott Parsons (New York: Free Press, 1964), 156.
2. Ibid., 155.
3. Brownlie, *Principles of Public International Law*, 3d ed. (Oxford: Clarendon Press, 1979), 73–76.
4. Brownlie (fn. 3), 75.
5. See Harry Eckstein's brilliant critique, "On the 'Science' of the State," in "The State," *Daedalus*, Vol. 108 (Fall 1979), 1–20.
6. Easton avoids the concept of the "state" in favor of that of the "political system"; see *The Political System: An Inquiry into the State of Political Science* (New York: Knopf, 1953), 90–124.
7. Brownlie (fn. 3), 75.
8. See Nelson Kasfir, *The Shrinking Political Arena: Participation and Ethnicity in African Politics*, with a Case

Study of Uganda (Berkeley, Los Angeles, London: University of California Press, 1976).

9. See Clifford Geertz, "The Judging of Nations: Some Comments on the Assessment of Regimes in the New States," *European Journal of Sociology*, xviii (No. 2, 1977), 249–52.

10. Brownlie (fn. 3), 75; Weber (fn. 1), 156.

11. See Robert H. Jackson and Carl G. Rosberg, *Personal Rule in Black Africa: Prince, Autocrat, Prophet, Tyrant* (Berkeley, Los Angeles, London: University of California Press, 1982).

12. The legitimacy of a government in the eyes of its citizens must be distinguished from its legitimacy in the eyes of other states; it is international legitimacy that is significant in the juridical attribute of statehood. A government may be legitimate internationally but illegitimate domestically, or *vice versa*. An instance of the former is Uganda during the last years of Idi Amin's regime; of the latter, the Soviet Union in its early years.

13. There is a wealth of literature on military intervention in Africa. Two outstanding accounts are Samuel Decalo, *Coups and Army Rule in Africa: Studies in Military Style* (New Haven: Yale University Press, 1976), and Claude E. Welch, Jr., ed., *Soldier and State in Africa: A Comparative Analysis of Military Intervention and Political Change* (Evanston, Ill.: Northwestern University Press, 1970). Both have excellent bibliographies.

14. Jon R. Moris, "The Transferability of Western Management Concepts and Programs, An East African Perspective," in Lawrence D. Stifel, James S. Coleman, and Joseph E. Black, eds., *Education and Training for Public Sector Management in Developing Countries* (Special Report from the Rockefeller Foundation, March 1977), 73–83. For Ghana, see Robert M. Price, *Society and Bureaucracy in Contemporary Ghana* (Berkeley and Los Angeles: University of California Press, 1975); for Kenya, Goran Hyden, Robert Jackson, and John Okumu, eds., *Development Administration: The Kenya Experience* (Nairobi: Oxford University Press, 1970).

15. Myrdal, *Asian Drama: An Inquiry into the Poverty of Nations* (New York: Twentieth Century Fund, 1968).

16. See *West Africa*, No. 3255 (December 3, 1979), 2224; and Ghislain C. Kabwit, "Zaire: The Roots of the Continuing Crisis," *Journal of Modern African Studies*, xvii (No. 3, 1979), 397–98.

17. Africa Contemporary Record, 1979–80, p. C 109.

18. The concept of "international society" is explored in Martin Wight, *Power Politics*, ed. by Hedley Bull and Carsten Holbraad (London: Royal Institute of International Affairs, 1978), 105–12. Also see Hedley Bull, *The Anarchical Society: A Study of Order in World Politics* (London: Macmillan, 1977), 24–52; and Alan James, "International Society," *British Journal of International Studies*, iv (July 1978), 91–106.

19. In considering the issue of human rights in Africa, the O. A. U.'s Assembly of Heads of States stressed the equal importance of "peoples' rights," and recently recommended that an "African Charter on Human and Peoples' Rights" be drafted. Peoples' rights are the rights of a sovereign people and can only be claimed and exercised by state governments. See *Africa Contemporary Record, 1979–80*, p. C 21.

20. Bull argues that the primary historical goal of international society has been to preserve the society of states itself; but it is difficult to see how this can be accomplished in the long run without first guaranteeing the sovereignty of member states. See *The Anarchical Society* (fn. 28), 17.

21. This is essentially the Austinian concept of "sovereignty." See John Austin, *The Province of Jurisprudence Determined*, ed. by H. L. A. Hart (London: Weidenfeld and Nicolson, 1954).

22. Bull (fn. 28), 34.

23. For an argument that at least in some cases "independence" was a "reversion" to sovereignty, see Charles H. Alexandrowicz, "New and Original States: The Issue of Reversion to Sovereignty," International Affairs, XLVII (July 1969), 465–80. For an opposing view, see Martin Wight, *Systems of States*, ed. by Hedley Bull (Leicester: Leicester University Press, 1977), 16–28.

24. French West Africa rather than its constituent units—Senegal, Mali, Upper Volta, Ivory Coast, etc.—could have been one state had Africans been able to agree to it; Nigeria could have been more than one.

25. Quoted in Robert C. Good, "Changing Patterns of African International Relations," *American Political Science Review*, Vol. 58 (September 1964), 632.

26. According to the United Nations, in 1978 there were 13 African countries (8 on the continent and 5 island countries) with a population of less than one million. Nine of these had populations of 600,000 or fewer. See *Africa Contemporary Record*, 1979–80, p. C 107.

27. Martin Wight, "Why is there no International Theory?" in Herbert Butterfield and Martin Wight, eds., *Diplomatic Investigations* (London: George Allen & Unwin, 1966), 33.

28. Peter Lyon, "New States and International Order," in Alan James, ed., *The Bases of International Order: Essays in Honour of C.A.W. Manning* (London: Oxford University Press, 1973), 47.

29. "Political Theory and International Relations," in Wolfers, *Discord and Collaboration: Essays on International Politics* (Baltimore and London: The Johns Hopkins University Press, 1965), 239–40.

27.2

State Death in the International System

Tanisha M. Fazal

Under what conditions do states die? This question is central to the study and practice of international relations. State survival is frequently presumed to be a primary goal of states, policymakers, and citizens.[1] Nonetheless, international history is rife with cases of state death. Wars are fought, dynasties are ended, and populations are relocated when states die. Surprisingly, international relations scholars have not previously offered systematic analyses of state death.[2]

This article constitutes a first attempt at examining state death by laying out the historical record of state death and by offering and testing an explanation for why some states die, but not others. I hypothesize that basic geopolitics are most determinative of prospects for survival. Specifically, I argue that buffer states—states caught between two rivals—are particularly vulnerable to conquest, annexation, and occupation.

State death is defined here as the formal loss of foreign policymaking power to another state. Contrary to conventional wisdom, state death has occurred quite frequently over the past two centuries; fifty of 202 (about 25 percent) states have died, and most have died violently. The violence commonly associated with state death in itself makes this an important topic for study. For example, thirteen states were conquered or occupied in the course of World War II. A generation later, the Iraqi invasion of Kuwait prompted the formation of a broad international coalition in response. State death has been an important feature of the international landscape since the rise of the sovereign state. . . .

I make the somewhat counterintuitive argument that states that great powers have an interest in preserving—buffer states—are in fact in a high-risk group for death. Regional or great powers surrounding buffer states face a strategic imperative to take over buffer states: if these powers fail to act against the buffer, they fear that their opponent will take it over in their stead. By contrast, these concerns do not apply to non-buffer states, where powers face no competition for influence or control. . . .

Stuck in the Middle: To Live and Die in a Buffer State

At least two approaches could be taken when studying state death. The first, and perhaps more natural, approach would be to examine characteristics of states that might enhance or diminish their prospects for survival. This kind of "inside-out" perspective suggests that the fates of individual states lie with their attributes and decisions. Logically, however, one problem with this approach is that it starts from the assumption that all states are in the same security environment. Rather than examining the features of states whose survival may or may not be at risk, a more promising approach suggests examining the incentive structures of states that seek to take over other states. This more "outside-in" perspective suggests that geopolitics can overwhelm the potential effects of state attributes or behaviors on survival. Specifically, I argue that regional or great powers engaged in rivalries with each other face strong strategic imperatives to take over the buffer states that lie between them. Buffer states are particularly likely to die.

Almost by definition, buffer states should enjoy a privileged position in terms of their prospects for survival. Neighboring powers have a stake in preserving buffer states that mitigate the effects of rivalry and, potentially, reduce or delay the effects of war.[3] Indeed, scholars of geopolitics have often asserted the greater survivability of buffer states.[4] Contrary to this basic intuition, I argue that buffer states are in a particularly bad position. Although great powers have a clear interest in maintaining the presence of buffer states, powerful states are more often tempted to acquire territory that their competitors desire, even when such behavior places them right next to a rival.

States between two rivals—"buffer states"—face a high risk of death.[5] Gary Goertz and Paul Diehl identify enduring rivalries along three dimensions: competitiveness over scarce goods; extended conflict; and

Source: Tanisha M. Fazal, "State Death and the International System," *International Organization* 58: 2, Spring, 2004, pp. 313–315 and 339–341.

a dyadic relationship between competitors. Specifically, they code "enduring rivalries [as] those conflicts between the same two states that involve at least five militarized disputes in a period lasting at least ten years."[6] Buffer states are particularly vulnerable because they are potential battlegrounds for surrounding rivals; more importantly, they are a source of a potential advantage for one or both rivals.

To illustrate the logic behind this claim, consider a situation where two states engaged in a rivalry surround a third, buffer, state. The nature of the relationship between the two rivals suggests that the probability that they may go to war is relatively high.[7] If one assumes that the two rivals would prefer not to go to war, then it is in their interest to maintain the sovereignty of the buffer state—the buffer will be functional for them, serving as a sort of barrier to war. This outcome, however, is unlikely to occur if the two rivals do not trust each other. Even if each rival knows that its opponent would prefer to avoid war, neither can be certain that this preference will dominate the strategic imperatives facing the rivals. Geographically speaking, the buffer state is at the heart of a security dilemma between the two rivals. Gaining control of the buffer state would translate into a significant strategic advantage, one that cannot be passed up on the chance that one or both rivals will exercise restraint with respect to the buffer. Both rivals know that they would be better off if they could exercise mutual restraint with respect to the buffer area. But they both also want to avoid the worst-case outcome of being "suckered;" neither rival wants to exercise restraint while its opponent takes over the buffer area.[8]

But why is it that buffer states are more likely to die than nonbuffer states? Consider the implications of different geographies for buffer states versus states that have only one great or regional power as a neighbor. The power neighboring the nonbuffer state does not face a strategic imperative to take over the state, because there exists no rival on the other side of the nonbuffer state that might take it over if the powerful state failed to do so. Similarly, consider a situation where potential rival states surround a third (potential buffer) state. If relations between the would-be rivals are friendly rather than acrimonious, then—all else equal—neither potential rival has incentives to take over the state that lies between them. Thus, buffer states are more likely to die than nonbuffer states because surrounding powers do not fear that nonbuffers will be taken over at their expense.

Buffer states will be more likely to die than nonbuffer states

One might argue that, because of their relative importance to surrounding powers, buffer states' status should decrease their vulnerability. As explained above (and shown below), however, the simple fact of a buffer state is insufficient to protect against predation absent a credible enforcement mechanism governing relations between the two rivals. An alternative institutional arrangement to protect buffer states could be the formation of an alliance with one of the rivals. If one rival started to make threatening moves toward the buffer, why would the other rival not step in to protect the buffer state? Once the threat of war is sufficiently high to mean that one of the rivals is seeking the strategic advantage offered by the buffer state, the opposing rival has few incentives to protect the buffer.

Indeed, the opposing rival will want the strategic advantage offered by the buffer for itself at that point. Forming an alliance with the buffer state would not give either rival the level of control necessary to protect itself against its opponent. Thus, again, the buffer state's geography will determine its fate. . . .

Discussion

When and why do states die? This question is fundamental for international relations theory and practice. A first, critical step to comprehending state death is knowing that states may have little control over the probability of their survival. As illustrated by both the quantitative analysis and brief case studies, buffer states are particularly likely to die, especially before 1945. While this article has focused on the logical and empirical relationship between geography and state death, it is worthwhile to discuss briefly the finding that states after 1945 are very unlikely to die.

At least three possible explanations could account for the shift away from (violent) state death in the postwar era. First, neorealists might suggest that the bipolar nature of the post-1945 period predicts fewer wars and, therefore, fewer violent state deaths.[9] A second explanation suggests that the occupation costs of taking over a state are much higher in the post-1945 period than before.[10] Third, a norm protecting states' territorial sovereignty could prevail in the postwar era.[11] While this norm precedes World War II, strong Allied support might account for its power after the war.

It is possible that all three arguments explain the absence of conquest and occupation after World War II. Tests of corollary hypotheses of these arguments shed additional light on the problem. For example, occupation costs have been shown to have little to do with whether a state death is permanent.[12] While both bipolarity and a norm protecting state territorial sovereignty could work to prevent state death after 1945, additional phenomena cannot be accounted for by bipolarity. These include a rise in state resurrections at the turn of the twentieth century and a continued absence of violent state death in particular after the collapse of the Soviet Union.

That both the buffer state and post-1945 variables continue to drive the results when the dependent variable is expanded to all state deaths raises another question: Why do some states die peacefully and others violently? Clearly, there is a continuum of state death, ranging from those that accede or dissolve completely voluntarily, to those that accede under pressure, to those whose conquest is clearly coerced. For the purposes of this analysis, I have dichotomized this continuum; an important next step will be to consider more carefully how similar causes may lead to different types of state death. Another interesting issue is that some rivalries lead to state death while others do not. This difference may be attributable to the fact that many rivalry dyads are contiguous; if there are no buffer states, no buffer states can die as a result of the rivalry. Also unanswered in this article is the question of why, even before 1945, some buffer states survive while others die.

Ultimately, while the effects of variables referring to attributes or behaviors of states are ambiguous, geopolitical variables clearly exert strong effects on the probability of state death. Note that this argument suggests a return to geopolitical analyses of international conflict.[13] At the same time, the relevant variables identified—specifically, buffer state status—fall under a (classical) realist umbrella.

Major theoretical debates aside, it does appear that buffer states may be in such a bad position that changes in behavior or attributes may not materially affect their probability of state death. Why might this be so? The results of the duration analyses presented above can be thought of as identifying those factors that put states into risk groups. In other words, it helps one identify those states that might be targeted. The effect of power on the probability of being targeted is ambiguous; on some level, though, it makes sense that powerful states will be targeted as much as weak states. Although the cost of taking over a more powerful state will always be higher, the benefit may also be greater. Similarly, the effect of alliance is unclear; allied states do not seem particularly likely to be able to avoid being targeted. Indeed, as illustrated by the Polish case, it may be that states in danger are the most likely to seek alliances; it may also be the allies they find are not trustworthy.

Once a state is targeted, the likelihood that it will be killed off is high. This claim concedes the importance of asymmetries of power in dyadic targetor-targetee relationships but maintains that power is not a blanket protection against being targeted. Less analytically clear is the causal relationship between alliance formation and state survival. Contrary to a basic neorealist analysis, alliances may disadvantage states seeking survival—or, states in danger of dying may have a particularly difficult time finding (reliable) allies. A more sophisticated reading of neorealism, however, suggests that states that form balancing alliances are more likely to survive than states that bandwagon. This insight suggests a further refinement of the data to test the proposition that different types of alliances may have opposite effects on state death.

This analysis, while answering some questions, has raised a host of others. Two messages, though, are clear: buffer states enjoy little leeway—they may only be able to affect the mode of their demise, and not its occurrence; and states in the post-1945 period face few if any threats to their survival. Understanding the cause of this latter phenomenon is particularly important given today's international politics. Ultimately, though, these messages suggest that clear selection on behavior does not occur in the international system. Location and timing are more determinative of state survival than is state behavior.

NOTES

1. For a discussion of the survival assumption in international relations, see Howes 2003.

2. For a recent exception, see Adams 2000.

3. See Schroeder 1994; Chay and Ross 1986; Partem 1983; and Spykman 1938.

4. Spykman 1938.

5. For a more extensive discussion of the definition of buffer states, see Partem 1983.

6. Note that Goertz and Diehl's definition of rivalry limits the problems of the potential stochastic properties of enduring rivalries exposed by Erik Gartzke and Michael

Simon. See Diehl and Goertz 2000, 153, 155; and Gartzke and Simon 1999.

7. Goertz and Diehl 1992.

8. Jervis 1978 provides the general intuition governing the dynamics of security dilemmas, and even refers to a particular security dilemma over a buffer zone. Spykman and Rollins 1939 provide an earlier version of this logic with particular reference to buffer states.

9. However, empirical evidence on the effects of multi- and bipolar systems on stability is ambiguous at best. See Hopf 1991; and Copeland 1996. See also Levy 1983.

10. See Brooks 1999; Kaysen 1990; and Posen 1993; for a contrasting view, see Liberman 1996. However, it is unclear why and how a sharp break in occupation costs could arise.

11. See Barkin and Cronin 1994; Zacher 2001; and Wendt 1999.

12. Liberman 1996.

13. See Mackinder 1962; and Spykman 1938.

References

Adams, Karen Ruth. 2000. *State Survival and State Death: International and Technological Contexts*. Ph.D. diss., University of California, Berkeley.

Barkin, J. Samuel, and Bruce Cronin. 1994. "The State and the Nation: Changing Norms and the Rules of Sovereignty in International Relations." *International Organization* 48 (1):107–30.

Brooks, Stephen G. 1999. "The Globalization of Production and the Changing Benefits of Conquest." *Journal of Conflict Resolution* 43 (5):646–70.

Chay, John, and Thomas E. Ross, eds. 1986. *Buffer States in World Politics*. Boulder, Colo.: Westview Press.

Copeland, Dale. 1996. "Neorealism and the Myth of Bipolar Stability: Toward a New Dynamic Realist Theory of Major War." *Security Studies* 5 (3):29–89.

Diehl, Paul, and Gary Goertz. 2000. *War and Peace in International Rivalry*. Ann Arbor: University of Michigan Press.

Fuller, Stephen M., and Graham A. Cosmas. 1974. *Marines in the Dominican Republic, 1916–1924*. Washington, D.C.: History and Museums Division Headquarters U.S. Marine Corps.

Gartzke, Erik, and Michael W. Simon. 1999. "Hot Hand: A Critical Analysis of Enduring Rivalries." *Journal of Politics* 61 (3):777–98.

Goertz, Gary, and Paul F. Diehl. 1992. "The Empirical Importance of Enduring Rivalries." *International Interactions* 18 (1):151–63.

Hopf, Ted. 1991. "Polarity, the Offense-Defense Balance, and War." *American Political Science Review* 85 (2):475–93.

Howes, Dustin Ellis. 2003. "When States Choose to Die: Reassessing Assumptions About What States Want." *International Studies Quarterly* 47 (4):669–92.

Jervis, Robert. 1978. "Cooperation Under the Security Dilemma." *World Politics* 30 (2):167–214.

Kaysen, Carl. 1990. "Is War Obsolete? A Review Essay." *International Security* 14 (4):42–64.

Levy, Jack. 1983. *War in the Modern Great Power System: 1495–1975*. Lexington: University Press of Kentucky.

Liberman, Peter. 1996. *Does Conquest Pay? The Exploitation of Occupied Industrial Societies*. Princeton, N.J.: Princeton University Press.

Mackinder, Halford J. 1962. *Democratic Ideals and Reality*. New York: Norton.

Mitchell, Nancy. 1999. *The Danger of Dreams: German and American Imperialism in Latin America*. Chapel Hill: University of North Carolina Press.

Partem, Michael Greenfield. 1983. "The Buffer System in International Relations." *The Journal of Conflict Resolution* 27 (1):3–26.

Posen, Barry R. 1993. "Nationalism, the Mass Army, and Military Power." *International Security* 18 (2):80–124.

Schroeder, Paul W. 1994. *The Transformation of European Politics 1763–1848*. Oxford: Oxford University Press.

Spykman, Nicholas J. 1938. "Geography and Foreign Policy, II." *The American Political Science Review* 32 (2):213–36.

Spykman, Nicholas J., and Abbie A. Rollins. 1939. "Geographic Objectives in Foreign Policy, I." *The American Political Science Review* 33 (3):391–410.

Wendt, Alexander. 1999. *Social Theory of International Politics*. Cambridge: Cambridge University Press.

Zacher, Mark W. 2001. "The Territorial Integrity Norm: International Boundaries and the Use of Force." *International Organization* 55 (2):215–50.

27.3

Addressing State Failure

Stephen D. Krasner and Carlos Pascual

The Danger of Failed States

In today's increasingly interconnected world, weak and failed states pose an acute risk to U.S. and global security. Indeed, they present one of the most important foreign policy challenges of the contemporary era. States are most vulnerable to collapse in the time immediately before, during, and after conflict. When chaos prevails, terrorism, narcotics trade, weapons proliferation, and other forms of organized crime can flourish. Left in dire straits, subject to depredation, and denied access to basic services, people become susceptible to the exhortations of demagogues and hatemongers. It was in such circumstances that in 2001 one of the poorest countries in the world, Afghanistan, became the base for the deadliest attack ever on the U.S. homeland, graphically and tragically illustrating that the problems of other countries often do not affect them alone.

The international community is not, however, adequately organized to deal with governance failures. The United States and the rest of the world need to develop the tools to both prevent conflict and manage its aftermath when it does occur. Such efforts will entail not just peacekeeping measures, but also influencing the choices that troubled countries make about their economies, their political systems, the rule of law, and their internal security. Weak countries are unable to take advantage of the global economy not just because of a lack of resources, but also because they lack strong, capable institutions. To promote sustainable peace, Washington and its partners must thus commit to making long-term investments of money, energy, and expertise.

The United States is moving in the right direction. Following a decision of the National Security Council in the spring of 2004, the Bush administration created a new office within the State Department: the Office of the Coordinator for Reconstruction and Stabilization. S/CRS will help lead and coordinate joint operations across agencies to respond effectively to evolving crises around the world, in concert with the international community. The White House has requested $124.1 million from Congress to finance the first phase of the new office and the programs it will support. The price for building a rapid-response capability is small. It is miniscule compared to the cost of ignoring the threats posed by failed states.

Conflict prevention must become a routine element of policymaking. Leaders in Congress, the administration, and the nongovernmental community must continue to devote their energies to stabilizing the vulnerable regions of the world. The U.S. government must be able to anticipate potential problems quickly and effectively so that they can be managed before they develop into full conflagrations. There is always the risk that prevention in any given situation may fail, and that must be accepted—both by senior policy-makers and by the entire government. Crises will inevitably occur, but if they are the United States' only impetus for response, there will be less chance of success.

Learning and Acting

The many U.S. agencies and departments devoted to peacekeeping and development have learned important lessons about effective conflict management—in both prevention and reconstruction. It has become a truism that preventing armed conflict is preferable to resolving differences through force: prevention saves both lives and money. Yet the international community often does not fully appreciate the complexity and difficulty of preventing belligerent parties or criminal militias from going to war. Countries involved in simmering conflicts almost universally lack the requirements for successful stabilization: an effective indigenous leadership that puts national interests over its own; state institutions that are capable, legitimate, and credible; and a citizenry that actively participates in its own governance. Moreover, the traditional tools of diplomacy—démarches, treaties, dialogue—often have limited sway over actors unconcerned about their international image or legitimacy.

Further complicating matters, modern conflicts are far more likely to be internal, civil matters than to be clashes between opposing countries. "State death" as a result of external invasion, common before World War II, has almost disappeared since 1945. The lack of good governance in weak states means they often do not have the ability to deal with disaffected or criminal groups within their own borders. Recent scholarship suggests that civil strife is no more likely in ethnically or religiously divided countries than it is in homogeneous ones. Internal discord is more likely to arise in countries suffering from poverty, a highly unequal income distribution, recent decolonization, weak institutions, ineffective police and counterinsurgency forces, and difficult terrain—conditions that allow small guerrilla bands to thrive. Valuable raw materials, such as diamonds or oil, also tend to spark conflict among competitors who want to seize control of the wealth. Warring groups generally have easy access to weapons and may even control territory, giving them a base for launching attacks on the state, its citizens, or its neighbors. Other nonstate actors, including transnational terrorist organizations, can also take root in such environments, posing a threat to global security.

These elements of state weakness constitute structural threats akin to dead leaves that accumulate in a forest. No one knows what spark will ignite them, or when. Over the long run, the only real way to create lasting peace is to promote better governance. The United States and the international community have increasingly made governance a focal point of development. The U.S. Agency for International Development (USAID) now spends about $1 billion a year on governance assistance. In 2002, in Monterrey, Mexico, international leaders agreed that good governance in developing countries should be rewarded with more resources. The Bush administration's Millennium Challenge Account will provide higher levels of aid to countries that have demonstrated political and economic reform. And the World Bank has increasingly introduced governance criteria into its lending decisions. But governance assistance designed to accomplish long-term change may not have much impact on countries where civil strife is imminent. Untargeted resources channeled into tense environments could even wind up making the conflict worse.

Anticipating, averting, and responding to conflict require a greater, more comprehensive level of planning and organization—which is precisely the mission of S/CRS. The coordinator reports directly to the secretary of state and has a staff drawn from functional bureaus in the State Department, as well as from USAID, the CIA, the military's Joint Staff, the Office of the Secretary of Defense, and others. Within the U.S. government, S/CRS is building civilian capacity to plan and coordinate stabilization and reconstruction efforts. S/CRS and its interagency partners also draw on expertise from nongovernmental organizations, think tanks, private firms, and universities. The U.S. government will use these resources to encourage and coordinate activities with other governments and international organizations. To focus attention on conflict prevention, S/CRS is also partnering with other offices, including those of the director of policy planning, the assistant secretary for intelligence and research, and the assistant secretaries of state in the regional and functional bureaus. The undersecretary for political affairs has strongly supported this engagement.

The United States cannot address every potential conflict, but it can determine which ones present the worst threat and which can be best helped by international attention. Every six months, the National Intelligence Council currently produces a list, compiled from classified and unclassified sources, of the countries at the greatest risk of instability. The list allows agencies across the U.S. government to assess state fragility, chart any changes in status, and develop strategies in case conflicts emerge. Regional bureaus use this crucial information to decide where the United States should focus its attention, personnel, and resources. S/CRS is working to incorporate the expertise of other government agencies and, increasingly, international counterparts into these assessments, to make them more comprehensive and reliable.

Each conflict is unique, and the U.S. response must be tailored to specific situations, but better understanding the broader factors that influence conflicts will help the government recognize warning signs and craft appropriate strategies. To this end, S/CRS is sponsoring expert roundtables on specific countries at risk of instability to generate new policy ideas on prevention. The office is also helping civilian organizations incorporate proven military analytic tools for conflict management and prevention: common planning templates, simulated exercises to test new ideas, and checklists of actions that help transform postwar environments by addressing the factors that drive conflict.

The better the U.S. government operates internally, the more effective it will be in forging partnerships with other important international and nongovernmental actors. As the United States develops a single approach to conflict management, it can improve its coordination with organizations such as the UN, the European Union, and NATO, as well as with nongovernmental organizations and key bilateral partners. The United Kingdom, Canada, Germany, and France are all considering or making their own structural changes to anticipate and manage foreign conflicts. UN reforms on "peace building" provide an opportunity to develop a multilateral context within which these nations can cooperate. There is an unprecedented acknowledgment throughout the world of the need to work together to prevent or manage state failure—and that not doing so would threaten international security.

Understanding Transformation

Even with investments in prevention, violence will still erupt and demand attention. To manage post-conflict engagements effectively, the international community must understand the nature of the changes that need to occur to transform the affected states into ones in which further conflict will be unlikely. The international community must also commit the necessary resources. Although real life is more complex than any model of post-conflict transition, dividing the transition into four phases can help guide future responses. These phases are not necessarily sequential—some may proceed concurrently, and they may not progress consistently.

The first phase is stabilization—the stage that generally garners the most international attention. Stabilization requires taking immediate action: enforcing order, feeding people, restarting basic services, initiating a political transition process, generating local employment, and reintegrating returning refugees and internally displaced persons. The international community often plays a dominant role in this phase, directly delivering services rather than building local capabilities, in order to avert chaos. Even if necessary in the short run, such efforts cannot be sustained indefinitely. Hence, outsiders must at some point stop "doing" and begin "enabling" local involvement and ownership. The faster the international community responds initially, the easier it will be to make sure this transition takes place. Stabilization must lead to conditions that help economic, political, and social development—perhaps most crucially by engendering local leadership and providing incentives and means for local parties to take action. This first period is critical to a country's future success.

Second, the conflict's root causes must be addressed. Such factors can include corruption, collapsed economic systems, political exclusion, or the private exploitation of public resources. If left unchecked, these issues will continue to stymie progress and economic growth in a post-conflict setting, particularly in former authoritarian states. Yet the very act of unraveling the evils of the past can be destabilizing. Shutting down bankrupt state enterprises generates unemployment. Opening up the political system challenges vested interests and political elites. Holding former oppressors accountable at the national level can strain barely functioning institutions. The international community must thus make sure that there is political consensus for reform, and that social safety nets, particularly for the unemployed and pensioners, are developed to prevent tensions from undermining the prospects for success.

Next is the creation of the laws and institutions of a market democracy—or fostering the "supply side" of governance. Many of the features of good governance that advanced states take for granted must be built anew or reinvented in countries that have just emerged from war. These elements include markets, tax systems, banks, and regulatory policies to make an economy function; constitutions, political structures, parties, and electoral processes to underpin participatory politics; and laws, courts, police, and penal systems to create the rule of law. Out of all four phases, this one may be the hardest since it entails defining a new polity. In many cases, the shift is as extreme as replacing authoritarianism with openness, freedom, and competition. Such changes are radical, affecting every aspect of life. They must be woven into the fabric of society. As Secretary of State Condoleezza Rice put it in a speech earlier this year, democracy is a process, not an event.

Finally, the "demand side" of politics, essential for accountability, must be established. Only if there is effective demand from the governed can democratic institutions be sustained. To generate this demand, civil society must evolve—communities need to develop as constituencies that call for political attention for their needs. Rebuilding social cohesion and public confidence in the government will, of course, take time: countries coming out of conflict are often deeply divided. Independent media are also crucial to this process—to help educate the population, reflect public opinion, and keep government officials honest. The free flow of information is essential to a flourishing democracy.

Outsiders can assist, advise, and provide incentives for locals. But ultimately, those within a society must define their own future. Even then, the path will not be easy. The example of the Soviet Union is instructive. Its collapse was generally peaceful; it boasted a working infrastructure, significant resources, and high levels of education—yet 14 years later, the future of decent governance and democracy is still in doubt in many of its former constituent states. The challenge will be much greater in countries wracked by poverty, illness, and illiteracy in the aftermath of war.

If the United States and the rest of the international community do not understand and plan for long-term transitions in advance, the chances of success diminish. Elections are generally not an endpoint, but only one of many necessary steps to build local legitimacy. International actors must be able to shift out of crisis-response mode to supply normal support mechanisms without losing attention or commitment. There will inevitably be international disillusionment with slow progress as countries take control of their own reconstruction and struggle to use the aid they are given. At this point, leadership from the White House and Congress will be key. Decision-makers must maintain a long-term perspective and remember that, although the complexity of transition is frustrating, cutting off funding only increases the likelihood that a country may lapse into chaos.

Innovation

If prevention fails, the fundamental challenge of S/CRS is to make sure that the United States is ready and able to manage all four post-conflict stages. No single government office can take on this sizable task alone. But the nation now has a focal point to lead and coordinate rebuilding efforts with other U.S. agencies and with the rest of the world. The Bush administration is using S/CRS to develop a new set of tools for conflict response. These tools fall into six basic categories.

First, the coordinator's office is developing both the framework and the capability to plan for stabilization and reconstruction. The framework will ensure that the government's post-conflict goals are realistic and linked to the resources needed to achieve them. If the goals and resources do not match, senior policymakers will have to make tough choices about committing additional resources or revising expectations. Setting out at the beginning a catalog of essential tasks will force planners to address both immediate needs and the eventual transition from international to indigenous leadership and sustainable development. In short, the framework will require the United States to develop a long-term perspective from the outset.

Second, S/CRS is making sure that the government is ready to move rapidly to help countries in the aftermath of conflicts. The United States must be better able to provide central leadership and management quickly. It must be ready to use diplomacy to diffuse local tensions, even as it deploys civilians and the military to establish order and initiate, manage, and oversee assistance and rebuilding. To create this capability, the coordinator will need a staff of 80 people and an active response corps of 100 diplomats who would spearhead diplomacy or augment local U.S. embassies in an emergency. Advance civilian teams of diplomats and specialists from other agencies would deploy to the field to foster reconciliation, address public safety, coordinate with international groups, and help broker peace agreements and arrangements for political transitions. In addition to these activities, the teams would constantly take stock of on-the-ground realities and use this information for long-term planning.

To support the larger and longer-term program requirements, the coordinator's office is assessing and filling gaps across government agencies in contracts and more informal arrangements with organizations that specialize in various aspects of stabilization and reconstruction: mobilizing international civilian police, training indigenous police, developing systems of justice, providing fiscal and monetary advice, stimulating the private sector, and supporting civil society. S/CRS is also assessing the feasibility of a civilian reserve corps that could tap individuals with key skills. The goal is to organize all of these resources so that they can mobilize quickly and efficiently after a conflict to fill all the needed functions and skills.

Applying these resources will, of course, take funding. The third tool S/CRS requires is a $100 million conflict-response fund and more flexible spending authority. The Bush administration has proposed that Congress create such a fund, and Senators Richard Lugar (R-Ind.) and Joseph Biden (D-Del.) have championed legislation to this effect. An available supply of money would allow the government to respond faster, creating a greater chance to generate positive momentum, reconcile warring parties, and support local populations as they take control of their own future. This level of funding cannot support a comprehensive response in most countries, but it can jump-start key programs when they are needed most, allowing time to seek alternative long-term funding. Furthermore, flexible spending authority would allow resources to be used to maximum effect. Consultation with Congress, backed by robust planning, would ensure accountability.

Fourth, S/CRS has established new management mechanisms that will foster interagency cooperation. At times when reconstruction efforts are judged central to U.S. interests, a senior interagency policy-level group, led by S/CRS and regional counterparts, will be created to make recommendations to the National Security Council, ensure that policy decisions are implemented, and secure quick action for serious problems. Tying all the key agencies into a common process will ensure that decisions lead to action, that military and civilian resources are fully utilized, and that information flows from the field to Washington.

Fifth, during U.S. or other military or peacekeeping operations, the new office will coordinate stabilization and reconstruction activities between civilian agencies and the military. As part of the military's planning effort, interagency civilian teams will deploy to regional combatant commands to develop strategies for stabilization and reconstruction. This type of involvement will help make certain that assumptions about civilian reconstruction capabilities remain realistic. After the planning stage, advance civilian teams will deploy with the military to help direct stabilization and reconstruction.

Finally, by creating a central locus for stabilization and reconstruction, the United States can cooperate more effectively with international partners. S/CRS has become a focal point within the U.S. government for relevant contacts with the UN, the European Union, regional organizations, and bilateral partners. With the Treasury Department and other State Department bureaus, S/CRS is also developing ongoing relationships with international financial institutions. And USAID plays a leading complementary role in coordinating with its development peers. Like the United States, other countries and institutions have recognized the need to build more effective programs to address conflict. Moreover, as the U.S. government becomes more adept at managing post-conflict scenarios itself, it will be better able to coordinate its actions in the field with experts from around the world.

Global Rewards

If approved, the $124.1 million requested by the Bush administration in the 2006 budget would launch the conflict-response fund, initiate the development of a response corps, and provide the resources to train personnel and prepare operations for rapid deployment. Some may question why the United States should invest resources before crises emerge. But consider that a faster and more effective post-conflict response could create better prospects for success and, in the case of U.S. military involvement, an earlier withdrawal of U.S. forces. For example, bringing one U.S. military division home from Iraq just one month early would save about $1.2 billion—and remove soldiers from harm's way.

The broader payoff is security. Today, stability requires more than maintaining a balance of power among strong states. Safety both here and abroad now depends on the ability of the United States and the international community to make sovereignty work—to establish democracies that improve the lives of ordinary individuals rather than of the ruling elite. The first step in this process must be to prevent conflict if possible, or to ensure a meaningful peace when conflict does occur. The world can do more to help those countries at risk of unrest or recovering from war. If successful, then over the longer term the United States will have enabled more people to enjoy the benefits of peace, democracy, and market economies. That can only be in everyone's best interest.

28 Foreign Aid

28.1

The Development Challenge

Jeffrey D. Sachs

Promises, Promises

As a matter of stated policy, there is no doubt that Washington is committed to supporting economic development in impoverished countries. In September 2000, it joined the UN in issuing the Millennium Declaration, in which the world pledged to cut extreme poverty in half and reduce child mortality by two-thirds within the next 15 years (aims later formalized as part of the Millennium Development Goals). In March 2002, the United States and the international community adopted the Monterrey Consensus, which laid out a multifaceted strategy to achieve these objectives by promoting the private sector in developing countries, opening trade with them, and increasing official development assistance (ODA). That year, the U.S. National Security Strategy promised to "secure public health," "emphasize education," and "continue to aid agricultural development" in low-income countries. "The United States and other developed countries," the document asserted, "should set an ambitious and specific target: to double the size of the world's poorest economies within a decade."

Most Americans, and perhaps most senior U.S. government officials, believe that the United States has been following through on such commitments. The U.S. response, public and private, to December's Indian Ocean tsunami has seemed to confirm the nation's generous engagement with those in need. Ironically, though, this outpouring of concern may obscure rather than clarify a deeper truth. Other than in response to disasters—famines, floods, and earthquakes—U.S. assistance for the world's poorest countries is utterly inadequate. It falls far short of meeting the needs of recipient countries, fails to tap into the vast U.S. capacity for providing aid, does not fulfill Washington's many promises to fund development adequately, and is a small fraction of what Americans believe the U.S. actually provides.

Without a new approach, Washington risks undermining the most important international development goals that the world has accepted—and plunging the international community into a maelstrom of recrimination. Without dramatic reform, the United States will increasingly be tarred as a country ready to invest in war, and perhaps in emergency relief, but not in peaceful development. The number of failed states will increase, spreading disorder and threatening global and national security.

Only a new U.S. international development strategy can avoid this outcome by achieving the objectives set forth in the Millennium Declaration, the Monterrey Consensus, and the National Security Strategy. Embarking on a new, practical course of assistance will have short-term costs, but the long-term benefits will far outweigh them. Continued failure, on the other hand, will be far too expensive to bear.

Source: Jeffrey D. Sachs, "The Development Challenge." Reprinted by permission of Foreign Affairs.

The Development Mirage

The Development Assistance Committee (DAC) of the Organization for Economic Cooperation and Development (OECD) defines official development assistance (ODA) as the sum of grants and sub-market-rate loans made to developing countries to promote economic development and welfare. Military aid is not counted, nor is aid to high-income countries such as Israel. Even with these parameters, the DAC definition is too expansive to measure real assistance for economic development, but it nonetheless gives a systematic measure of U.S. foreign assistance.

By the DAC's definition, in 2003 (the most recent year for which comprehensive international data are available), the United States gave $16.3 billion in net ODA. Of that amount, $1.7 billion went to multilateral organizations such as the World Bank, which in turn grant or lend the money to developing countries. Washington distributed the remaining $14.6 billion bilaterally, directly targeting recipient nations. Together, the multilateral and bilateral aid represented 0.15 percent of the $11 trillion gross national income (GNI) of the United States in 2003. In the 2004 U.S. budget—which totaled $2.3 trillion—development assistance represented just 0.7 percent of budgetary expenditures.

These sums are vastly smaller than the American people think they are. In a 2001 survey, the Program on International Policy Attitudes (PIPA) at the University of Maryland found that Americans, on average, believe that foreign aid accounts for 20 percent of the federal budget, around 30 times the actual figure. PIPA surveys in the mid-1990s came up with essentially the same result. . . .

Not only are the figures for official development assistance themselves not nearly as large as most Americans believe, but the DAC's estimate of $16 billion also overstates U.S. official aid for economic development by including a considerable amount of assistance that contributes little or nothing to long-term development. In a recent white paper, USAID makes the point by distinguishing between five operational goals for foreign aid: promoting transformational development, supporting strategic states, strengthening fragile states, providing humanitarian relief, and addressing global challenges such as the HIV/AIDS epidemic and climate change.

All five operational goals make sense from a foreign policy standpoint, but only the first directly targets economic development. Aid intended for transformational development aims to support long-term economic change by helping a country achieve structural transformations that should allow it ultimately to escape dependence on outside aid. Assistance to strategic countries focuses on nations that have geopolitical importance, such as Colombia, Egypt, Iraq, and Afghanistan, and helps fight terrorism, strengthen alliances, or reduce narcotics trafficking. Aid to fragile states is designed to head off conflict or help countries recover from it. Lastly, humanitarian assistance is earmarked for relief following natural disasters and often takes the form of U.S. grain deliveries. A surprisingly small proportion of U.S. bilateral assistance is directed at transformational development, and only a small part of that actually transforms the economies of developing countries.

Washington's own aid accounting (as opposed to the DAC's) makes a key distinction between developmental assistance and geopolitical aid, which is distributed to strategic countries mostly as Economic Support Funds (ESF). In 2004, the ESF program provided $3.3 billion to 42 countries. . . . Many of the strategic states are in fact middle income countries that are not high development priorities. In many cases, ESF supports corruption or allows a government to reduce its own development spending to free up funds for its military.

Meanwhile, according to the DAC database, very little of the $6.1 billion the United States spent on bilateral assistance to "nonstrategic" developing countries in 2003 actually reached the ground as long-term investment in transformational development. For one thing, $2 billion was distributed as emergency assistance or as nonemergency food aid. Emergency assistance, although salutary, merely addresses immediate crises. Food aid for non-emergency purposes, moreover, has enormously high transaction costs and distorts the local economy by depressing the prices local farmers receive for their goods. Amazingly, nearly half of the money spent on U.S. food aid in 2004 went to cover transport costs rather than the food itself.

In 2003, only $4.1 billion in U.S. bilateral aid was not spent on strategic countries, food aid, or other emergency aid. Of that total, moreover, $1.3 billion took the form of "debt forgiveness grants"—the cancellation of old debts, not the granting of new money. . . .

Of the remaining $2.8 billion in 2003 U.S. bilateral aid, very little actually funded investments in transformational development. According to the DAC, the entire sum went toward technical cooperation: payments made primarily to U.S. entities—consultants from government agencies or nongovernmental organizations

(NGOs)—for assignments in recipient nations. These missions may be useful, but the expenditures are not long-term investments in local clinics, schools, power plants, sanitation, or other infrastructure.

Washington gave very little money directly to non-strategic developing countries to support specific investments in transformational development. Poor countries have proposed sound plans to build schools and clinics and pay the salaries of teachers and doctors, but the United States virtually never funds such programs directly, sending its own consultants instead. In doing so, Washington contributes to an unworkable proliferation of donor-country pet projects, rather than to an integrated strategy adopted by the recipient country and supported by the donors. A balanced and judicious aid program would provide both technical cooperation and budgetary support to countries that could use the money effectively. . . .

Two recent U.S. initiatives will modestly improve the picture, but so far their impact remains very limited. Announced in 2002, the new Millennium Challenge Account (MCA) is designed to give grants to low-income countries that demonstrate good governance. For the current fiscal year, $1.5 billion has been appropriated for the MCA, and in 2002 the Bush administration promised to request $5 billion per year in 2006 and beyond. The MCA is a highly meritorious new approach. No funds, however, have yet been disbursed. The President's Emergency Plan for AIDS Relief (PEPFAR) is also budgeted to give an average of $3 billion per year to certain African and Caribbean countries. In 2004, roughly $2.4 billion was disbursed. This important initiative should be increased in scale significantly, with more of the funding disbursed with other donors through the Global Fund to Fight AIDS, Tuberculosis, and Malaria. Such an approach would better leverage U.S. funding and allow recipient countries to pursue a more integrated approach to fighting AIDS.

Flunking

To evaluate and improve the current U.S. foreign aid system, a three-prong test should be used: How much foreign assistance is needed and can be used effectively to achieve transformational development? What is the U.S. capacity to give? And—most important for the United States' international image—how does U.S. aid stack up against Washington's promises to poor countries?

The answer to the first question can be derived from careful studies conducted to determine the amount of worldwide ODA needed to achieve the goals of the Millennium Declaration. Most recently, the UN Millennium Project undertook the most extensive analysis of this question ever performed and determined that the developing world will require an additional $70 billion in aid over current levels by 2006, rising to $130 billion over current levels by 2015 (in constant U.S. dollars at 2003 prices). With these added funds, total projected aid in 2006 would represent 0.44 percent of total projected donor GNI that year, increasing to 0.54 percent in 2015. Assuming that all 22 DAC donor countries contribute an equal percentage of their national income and that the U.S. economy grows at an average of three per cent a year, the $16 billion contributed by Washington in 2003 would have to increase to $51 billion in 2006 and to $74 billion in 2015. Thus, even the full funding currently promised for the MCA and PEPFAR ($5 billion and $3 billion per year, respectively) would leave the United States far short of doing its part to help poor countries meet the Millennium Development Goals. . . .

Of course, since these countries are impoverished, their own financial means are limited; most of their current income must be used simply to stay alive rather than to invest in the future. Thus, the poorest nations are caught in a poverty trap. They are poor because they lack the basic necessities of health, education, and infrastructure, and because they are poor, they cannot invest in these basic necessities on the scale necessary to achieve the Millennium Development Goals.

Development assistance can close this financing gap. . . .

Such an approach is built on the principles of private-sector led, market-based economic growth. After all, private-sector-led growth depends on adequate infrastructure (roads, power, ports, water, and sanitation) and human capital (a healthy population with adequate levels of literacy, education, and job skills). Domestic and foreign investors will shun a developing country without those prerequisites.

The second standard—U.S. capacity to provide foreign assistance—is far from being fully realized. The small sums that Washington gives in ODA are driven by political considerations, not by economic need. To ensure that the Millennium Development Goals are met, the UN Millennium Project calls for ODA from each donor country to rise to at least 0.44 percent of GNI in 2006, and then to continue to increase to 0.54 percent of GNI by 2015. To meet needs beyond these goals—geopolitical and humanitarian needs, for example—the project recommends that each donor country actually reach 0.7 percent of GNI in development assistance by 2015.

These sums are small not only relative to GNI, but also relative to recent changes in the U.S. budget. Since 2001, defense spending has expanded by about 1.7 percent of GNI, and tax revenues have declined by 3.3 percent of GNI, due mainly to tax cuts. In the same period, U.S. official development aid rose by only 0.04 percent of GNI. The United States has, in short, chosen to spend its money on priorities other than development assistance, yet such assistance is just as fundamental to national security as the military. . . .

As for the final test of measuring U.S. development assistance against U.S. commitments, the enormous gap between promise and performance has been weighing heavily on Washington's foreign policy for many years. . . .

Washington's palpable shortfall has become a pervasive source of friction in U.S. relations with low-income countries. The United States regularly asks these nations for help in the war on terrorism, only to plead its own "poverty" when asked for more development aid—even for areas such as health, education, and agriculture, which are focal points of Washington's national security doctrine. In one striking example, the United States contributed a meager $4 million to Ethiopia in 2002 to raise its agricultural output—and then gave $500 million in emergency food aid when famine predictably hit the country a year later. Low-income nations are painfully aware of the truth: the United States can be counted on to respond to emergencies, but not to help them break free of poverty.

28.2

The Utopian Nightmare

William Easterly

"The past has prepared all the materials and means in superabundance to well-feed, clothe, lodge, train, educate, employ, amuse, and govern the human race in perpetual progressive prosperity—without war, conflict, or competition between nations or individuals."

These words were not uttered by a hopeful world leader at the most recent Group of 8 (G-8) summit, or by Bono at a rock concert—but they certainly sound familiar. They were written in 1857, when British reformer Robert Owen called upon rich countries, who could "easily induce all the other governments and people to unite with them in practical measures for the general good all through futurity." Owen was laughed out of town as a utopian.

How comforted Owen would be if he were alive in 2005, when some of the most powerful and influential people seem to believe that utopia is back. American President George W. Bush has dispatched the U.S. military to spread democracy throughout the Middle East, G-8 leaders strive to end poverty and disease sometime soon, the World Bank promises development as the path to world peace, and the International Monetary Fund (IMF) is trying to save the environment. In a world where billions of people still suffer, these are certainly appealing dreams. But is this surprising new fondness for utopia just harmless, inspirational rhetoric? Are utopian ambitions the best way to help the poor-world majority?

Unfortunately, no. In reality, they hurt efforts to help the world's poor. What is utopianism? It is promising more than you can deliver. It is seeing an easy and sudden answer to long-standing, complex problems. It is trying to solve everything at once through an administrative apparatus headed by "world leaders." It places too much faith in altruistic cooperation and underestimates self-seeking behavior and conflict. It is expecting great things from schemes designed at the top, but doing nothing to solve the bigger problems at the bottom.

The Year of Living Utopianly

At the dawn of the new millennium, the United Nations realized Robert Owen's dream of bringing together the "Potentates of the Earth" in what the global organization called a Millennium Assembly. These potentates set Millennium Development Goals for 2015, calling for, among other things, dramatic reductions in poverty, child mortality, illiteracy, environmental degradation, AIDS, tuberculosis, malaria, unsafe drinking water, and discrimination against women.

But it is in 2005 that utopia seems to have made its big breakthrough into mainstream discourse. In March, Columbia University Professor Jeffrey Sachs, celebrity economist and intellectual leader of the utopians, published a book called *The End of Poverty*, in which he called for a big push of increased foreign aid to meet the Millennium Development Goals and end the miseries of the poor. Sachs proposes everything from nitrogen-fixing leguminous trees to replenish soil fertility to AIDS therapy, cell phones that provide up-to-date market information to health planners, rainwater harvesting, and battery charging stations. His U.N. Millennium Project proposed a total of 449 interventions.

British Chancellor of the Exchequer Gordon Brown likewise called in January for a major increase in aid, a "Marshall Plan" for Africa. Brown was so confident he knew how to save the world's poor that he even called for borrowing against future aid commitments to finance massive increases in aid today. At the World Economic Forum in January, British Prime Minister Tony Blair called for a "big, big push" to meet the goals for 2015, and his administration issued a fat report on saving Africa in March. The World Bank and the IMF issued their own weighty document in April about meeting these goals and endorsing the call for a big push, and utopians of the world will reconvene at the U.N. World Summit in September to evaluate progress on the Millennium Development Goals. The G-8 leaders agreed on a plan in June to cancel

$40 billion worth of poor-country debt to help facilitate the "push." The IMF might even tap its gold reserves to bolster the effort.

The least likely utopian is George W. Bush, who has shown less interest in vanquishing poverty, but has sought to portray the Iraq misadventure as a step toward universal democracy and world peace. As he modestly put it in his Second Inaugural Address in January 2005, "America, in this young century, proclaims liberty throughout all the world, and to all the inhabitants thereof."

These leaders frequently talk about how easy it is to help the poor. According to Brown, medicine that would prevent half of all malaria deaths costs only 12 cents per person. A bed net to prevent a child from contracting malaria costs only $4. Preventing 5 million child deaths over the next 10 years would cost just an extra $3 for each new mother, says Brown.

The emphasis on these easy solutions emerged as worry about terrorist havens in poor states intersected with the campaigning on the part of Sachs, Bono, rocker Bob Geldof, and the British Labourites. All these factions didn't seem to realize aid workers had been trying for years to end poverty.

All Talk, No Traction

We have already seen the failure of comprehensive utopian packages in the last two decades: the failure of "shock therapy" to convert the former Soviet Union from communism to capitalism and the failure of IMF/World Bank "structural adjustment" to transform nations in Africa, the Middle East, and Latin America into free-market paragons. All of these regions have suffered from poor economic growth since utopian efforts began. In the new millennium, apparently unchastened, the IMF and World Bank are trying something even more ambitious—social, political, economic, and environmental transformation of the poorest nations through Poverty Reduction Strategy Papers. These reports, which the IMF and World Bank require that governments design in consultation with the poor, are comprehensive plans to make poverty vanish in each nation. It is a little unclear how a bureaucratic document can make often undemocratic governments yield some of their power to the poor, or how it will be more successful than previous comprehensive plans that seem modest by comparison.

Indeed, we have seen the failure of what was already a "big push" of foreign aid to Africa. After 43 years and $568 billion (in 2003 dollars) in foreign aid to the continent, Africa remains trapped in economic stagnation. Moreover, after $568 billion, donor officials apparently still have not gotten around to furnishing those 12-cent medicines to children to prevent half of all malaria deaths.

With all the political and popular support for such ambitious programs, why then do comprehensive packages almost always fail to accomplish much good, much less attain Utopia? They get the political and economic incentives all wrong. The biggest problem is that the rich people paying the bills do not share the same goals as the poor people they are trying to help. The wealthy have weak incentives to get the right amount of the right thing to those who need it; the poor are in no position to complain if they don't. A more subtle problem is that if all of us are collectively responsible for a big world goal, then no single agency or politician is held accountable if the goal is not met. Collective responsibility for world goals works about as well as collective farms in agriculture, and for the same reason.

To make things worse, utopian-driven aid packages have so many different goals that it weakens the accountability and probability of meeting any one goal. The conditional aid loans of the IMF and World Bank (structural adjustment loans) were notorious for their onerous policy and outcome targets, which often numbered in the hundreds. The eight Millennium Development Goals actually have 18 target indicators. The U.N. Millennium Project released a 3,751-page report in January 2005 listing the 449 intermediate steps necessary to meet those 18 final targets. Working for multiple bosses (or goals) doesn't usually work out so well; the bosses each try to get you to work on their goal and not the other boss's goal. Such employees get overworked, overwhelmed, and demoralized—not a bad description of today's working-level staff at the World Bank and other aid agencies.

Top-down strategies such as those envisioned by President Bush, Prime Minister Blair, and Bono also suffer from complex information problems, even when the incentive problems are solved. Planners at the global top simply don't know what, when, and where to give to poor people at the global bottom.

That is not to say that it is impossible to meet multiple goals for multiple customers with multiple agents. The various needs of the rich are met easily enough by a system of decentralized markets and democracy, which utilize feedback from the customers and accountability of the suppliers. Rich, middle-aged men can buy Rogaine to grow hair on their heads, while women can buy Nair to get rid of hair on their legs. No Millennium Development Goal on Body Hair was necessary. The Rogaine and Nair corporations are accountable to their customers for satisfaction. If the customers don't care for the product, the corporations go out of business; if the customers do like the product, corporations have a profit incentive to supply it. Similarly, men and women in wealthy countries can complain to democratically accountable bureaucrats and politicians if garbage collectors do not pick up their discarded Rogaine and Nair bottles. Private markets also specialize; there is no payoff for them to produce a comprehensive product that both removes hair from women's legs and transfers it to men's heads. The irony of the situation is tragically obvious: The cosmetic needs of the rich are met easily, while the much more desperate needs of the poor get lost in centralized, utopian, comprehensive planning.

Poverty Starts At Home

Free markets and democracy are far from an overnight solution to poverty—they require among many other things the bottom-up evolution of the rules of the game, including contract enforcement and fair political competition. Nor can democratic capitalism be imposed by outsiders (as the World Bank, IMF, and U.S. Army should now have learned). The evolution of markets and democracy took many decades in rich countries, and it did not happen through "big pushes" by outsiders, Millennium Development Goals, or Assemblies of World Leaders. Progress in wealthy countries arrived through piecemeal steps, gradual reforms, incremental improvements, and experimental probing, accompanied by gradually accelerating economic growth, rather than through crash programs.

The problems of the poor nations have deep institutional roots at home, where markets don't work well and politicians and civil servants aren't accountable to their citizens. That makes utopian plans even more starry-eyed, as the "big push" must ultimately rely on dysfunctional local institutions. For example, there are many weak links in the chain that leads from Gordon Brown's 12-cent malaria drug to actual health outcomes in poor countries. According to research by Deon Filmer, Jeffrey Hammer, and Lant Pritchett at the World Bank, anywhere from 30 percent to as much as 70 percent of the drugs destined for rural health clinics in several African countries disappear before reaching the clinics. According to one survey in Zimbabwe, pregnant women were reluctant to use public health clinics to give birth because nurses ridiculed them for not having better baby clothes, forced them to wash bed linens soon after delivery, and even hit them to encourage them to push the baby out faster during delivery. And Africa is not alone—nearly all poor countries have problems of corrupt and often unfriendly civil servants, as today's rich countries did earlier in their history. Researchers find that many people in poor countries bypass public health services altogether, in favor of private doctors or folk remedies.

The poor have neither the income nor political power to hold anyone accountable for meeting their needs—they are political and economic orphans. The rich-country public knows little about what is happening to the poor on the ground in struggling countries. The wealthy population mainly just wants to know that "something is being done" about such a tragic problem as world poverty. The utopian plans satisfy the "something-is-being-done" needs of the rich country public, even if they don't serve the needs of the poor. Likewise, the Bush Doctrine soothes the fears of Americans concerned about evil tyrants, without consulting the poor-country publics on whether they wish to be conquered or democratized.

The "something-is-being-done" syndrome also explains the fixation on money spent on world poverty, rather than how to meet the needs of the poor. True, doubling the relatively trivial proportion of their income that rich Westerners give to poor Africans is a worthy enough cause. But let's not kid ourselves that spending more money on foreign aid accomplishes anything by itself. Letting total aid money stand for accomplishment is like the Hollywood producers of *Catwoman*, recently voted the worst movie of 2004, bragging about their impressive accomplishment of spending $100 million on its production.

The Way Out

Certainly not all aid efforts are futile. Instead of setting utopian goals such as ending world poverty, global leaders should simply concentrate on finding particular interventions that work. Anecdotal and some systematic evidence suggests piecemeal approaches to aid can be successful. Routine childhood immunization combined with measles vaccination in seven southern African nations cut reported measles cases from 60,000 in 1996 to 117 in 2000. Another partnership among aid donors contributed to the near eradication of guinea worm in 20 African and Asian countries where it was endemic. Abhijit Banerjee and Ruimin He at the Massachusetts Institute of Technology list examples of successful aid programs that passed rigorous evaluation: subsidies to families for education and health costs for their children, remedial teaching, uniforms and textbooks, school vouchers, deworming drugs and nutritional supplements, vaccination, HIV prevention, indoor spraying for malaria, bed nets, fertilizer, and clean water.

Of course, finding and maintaining piecemeal approaches that work well requires improving incentives for aid agencies. Better incentives might come from placing more emphasis on the independent evaluation of aid projects. Given the vast sums that are being spent, reliable evaluations remain surprisingly rare. Better incentives could also come from devising means to get more feedback from the poor people that the programs are trying to help, and holding aid agencies accountable when the feedback is negative. It seems more productive to focus on such critical problems in foreign aid rather than simply promising the rich-country public the end of world poverty.

If an aid-financed "big push" will not generate society-wide development, are things hopeless for poor countries? Fortunately, poor countries are making progress on their own, without waiting for the West to save them. The steady improvement in health and education in poor countries (except for the AIDS crisis), the market-driven growth of China and India, the movement toward democracy in Latin America and Africa (even amid continued disappointing economic growth), not to mention earlier successes such as Botswana and the East Asian Tiger economies, offer hope for homegrown and gradual development.

The outpouring of donations for last December's tsunami victims shows that Europeans and Americans have genuine compassion for those in need. Can the rich-country public call their politicians' bluff and refuse to let them get away with utopian dreams as a substitute for the hard slogging of delivering benefits to the poor? Will they hold the aid agencies accountable for getting money to those in need? Will they figure out new ways to give voice to the voiceless? If they asked, they would likely find that the poor are unmoved by utopian dreams. They probably just want those 12-cent medicines.

28.3

Bush and Foreign Aid

Steven Radelet

Out of the Blue

One of the greatest surprises of George W. Bush's presidency so far has been his call to dramatically increase U.S. foreign aid. In March 2002, Bush proposed an increase of 50 percent over the next three years through the creation of a Millennium Challenge Account (MCA), a fund that would provide $5 billion per year to a select group of countries that are "ruling justly, investing in their people, and establishing economic freedom." That September, Bush released his National Security Strategy, which gave rare prominence to development and aid alongside defense and diplomacy. Then came his 2003 State of the Union address, in which he called for $10 billion in new funding ($15 billion total) over the next five years to combat HIV/AIDS in Africa and the Caribbean. This proposal was rapidly signed into law in late May, on the eve of the G-8 summit. And Bush's 2004 budget included two smaller initiatives: a $200 million famine fund and a $100 million fund for "complex emergencies." If these programs are funded as proposed, they will increase U.S. foreign aid from approximately $11 billion in 2002 to $18 billion in 2006—the largest increase in decades. Perhaps more important, they will also fundamentally change the way the United States delivers aid by making recipients more involved in setting priorities and by demanding greater accountability for results.

All of these initiatives were quite unexpected from a conservative Republican president whose party has shown a long-standing antagonism toward foreign aid. Why, then, has Bush pushed for the new spending? Part of the answer is simple political expediency: he needed compelling announcements to make at the development summit in Monterrey, Mexico (hence the MCA), and in his State of the Union address (hence the HIV/AIDS proposal). To some extent, the programs are also part of the administration's response to the September 11, 2001, terrorist attacks. Yet, surprisingly, neither of the major initiatives is aimed at failed states that breed terrorism or at frontline states such as Turkey or Pakistan. The aim seems to be broader, perhaps indicating a reluctant acceptance of the fact that poverty and inequality around the world generate hostility and resentment toward the United States and thereby weaken national security. Both programs, and especially the HIV/AIDS proposal, appear to reflect a growing awareness that Washington must start using both "hard" and "soft" power if it is going to make the world a safer and more secure place.

On their own, however, Bush's new initiatives can have only modest success in fighting poverty, spreading prosperity, and combating AIDS. The MCA and HIV/AIDS programs each target only a small number of countries, leaving behind the vast majority of poor nations—especially poorly performing and failed states. To make aid even more effective in the post-September 11 world, therefore, deeper changes are needed. . . .

Aid and Security

Foreign aid first became an important tool of American national security policy under the Truman administration. The first great foreign aid program, the Marshall Plan, was aimed at rebuilding Western Europe after World War II, in part as a bulwark against Soviet expansion. President Kennedy vastly expanded U.S. foreign assistance by establishing the Peace Corps, USAID, and the Alliance for Progress, all three designed in part to stem the spread of communism. In the late 1960s, Vietnam became the largest recipient of U.S. foreign aid (defined as grants and subsidized loans aimed at economic development and humanitarian assistance and excluding military aid). By the early 1980s, the Reagan administration had started funneling the same kind of money into El Salvador, Honduras, Guatemala, the Philippines, Indonesia, and Zaire—none a paragon of democracy, but all fighting leftist threats of one kind or another. In the late 1970s, Washington began using aid to support another important foreign policy goal: Middle East peace. As part of the Camp David accords, Washington significantly increased its support to Israel and Egypt. . . .

With the end of the Cold War, foreign aid lost its original raison d'être and much of its remaining support. . . .

It should hardly be surprising that aid did not always spur development, however, since that was not its principal aim. Some of its basic goals, such as the support of today's strategic allies, flatly contradicted the interest in longer-term development—contributing to the perception that aid is ineffective. Who believed that Zaire's dictator Mobutu Sese Seko would ever use American largesse to vaccinate children or train teachers? Measured against its true objectives, the supposed failure of aid becomes far less apparent. After all, the United States won the Cold War, the threat of communism has essentially disappeared, and Israel and Egypt have remained at peace with one another since Camp David. . . .

Since the end of the Cold War, the U.S. foreign assistance program has groped to find its bearings. . . . Humanitarian arguments have garnered enough support to keep aid programs alive, but only barely: in fights to close the budget deficits during the early 1990s, foreign aid was a key loser. U.S. assistance to poor countries fell by 25 percent in real terms during the 1990s and by 50 percent as a share of U.S. national income (from two-tenths of one percent to one-tenth).

A New Lease on Life

After September 11 foreign aid came to the fore once again. The most immediate calls for aid, not surprisingly, were to rebuild Afghanistan and to support regional frontline states. The administration quickly committed $297 million to Afghanistan, $600 million to Pakistan, and $250 million to Jordan. Then, in March 2002, almost out of the blue, the president proposed the MCA as part of a broader "compact for development" one week before he traveled to Monterrey, Mexico, for the UN International Conference on Financing for Development. In April, the administration pledged to increase U.S. funding for the World Bank by 18 percent over three years, contingent on the organization's meeting certain performance goals. Finally, in January's State of the Union address, the president unveiled the new Emergency Plan for AIDS Relief, and his new budget included $300 million to fight famine and for "complex emergencies."

This agenda points to a new rationale for foreign assistance in the post-September 11 world, resting on four key motives. First, aid can play a direct role in the war on terror by supporting both frontline countries and weak states where terrorism might breed. . . . But, in addition to the frontline states, clear strategies are needed to deal with *failed* states that have no functional governments (such as Somalia), *failing* states that seem dangerously headed for collapse (such as Zimbabwe), and *fragile* states that could easily implode (such as Nigeria, Pakistan, and perhaps Indonesia). Foreign aid can be part, but probably only a relatively small part, of the strategies for these weak states. In failed states, for example, aid probably can do no more than provide humanitarian assistance, and there are circumstances in which the United States should provide no aid at all.

Second, foreign aid allows the United States to project "soft power" to accompany, and sometimes offset, its use of military power. For example, the juxtaposition of the HIV/AIDS initiative and the Iraq strategy in Bush's State of the Union address was striking. The administration clearly wanted to demonstrate to the American people, its European allies, and countries around the world that it was not simply fixated on military action, but was willing to project its power to address some of the world's most vexing humanitarian problems.

Third, there is the growing recognition—so far only partially embraced by the administration—that global poverty and inequality threaten U.S. security and national interests. The gap between the richest and the poorest countries of the world has widened in the last 20 years, breeding resentment and anger among people who believe—rightly or wrongly—that the rich have rigged the international economic system in their favor. The United States needs poor countries to support the values it champions and to believe that they, too, can achieve openness and prosperity. But they need U.S. support to make it happen. President Bush famously demanded in the aftermath of September 11 that countries would have to choose to be either with the United States or with the terrorists. Today Washington similarly must choose whether it is with the poor countries of the world or against them to enable them to make the same choice about the United States.

And finally, poverty and inequality around the world simply run counter to the values of many Americans who believe that the widening income gap and high levels of absolute poverty in poor countries are morally unacceptable. This belief was at the core of the demonstrations against the World Trade Organization, the World Bank, and the IMF in recent years and helps explain calls for greater debt relief and foreign assistance among activists across the political spectrum. Moreover, these messages appear to be filtering through: the administration now regularly meets with church groups, activists (such as the Irish rock star Bono), and nongovernmental organizations (NGOS) to discuss development policies.

In the end, the key to poverty reduction in poor countries is sustained economic growth, which depends far more on a country's own policies and on world trade and financial systems than on foreign aid. Nevertheless, in the right environment aid can play an important role in fighting poverty, and it is in the U.S.'s interest to make it work better. To be effective, aid has to be both hard-headed and generous. The United States should provide significant support to countries with governments that are committed to making tough decisions consistent with open economic and political systems, as is the MCA's intent. Where governments are less committed or capable, aid should be smaller, with more of it channeled through effective nongovernmental organizations. In some countries, no aid should be given at all. Whenever money is disbursed, Washington should hold recipients more accountable, allocating more funds to activities that succeed and withdrawing money from those that fail.

Whither the MCA?

The MCA was Bush's first step toward making aid more effective and represents a sharp break with past U.S. policies. The basic idea behind it is to select a relatively small number of recipient countries based on their demonstrated commitment to sound policies, provide them with larger sums of money, give them more say in designing aid-funded programs, and hold them accountable for achieving results.

A newly created government corporation called the Millennium Challenge Corporation will run the program, with oversight from a board of directors chaired by the secretary of state. The administration will select recipients based on 16 quantitative indicators meant to measure the extent to which countries are "ruling justly, investing in their people, and establishing economic freedom." The indicators include areas such as budget deficits, trade policy, immunization rates, primary-school completion rates, control of corruption, and the protection of civil liberties. To qualify, a country must score above the median on half of the indicators in each of the three categories, and it must score above the median on corruption. This mechanical process will not dictate the ultimate recipients; the administration will have limited flexibility to adjust the list slightly to take account of gaps, lags, and weaknesses in the imperfect data. About a dozen low-income countries will qualify in the first year, with perhaps 18–20 making the cut by 2006. Once countries qualify, the corporation will fund broad programs designed in close consultation with recipient governments, NGOs, and the private sector. The recipients themselves will set priorities, propose specific activities, and establish benchmarks that will be used to measure progress. In return for this flexibility, the administration must demand greater accountability for results and be willing to cut off funding when programs fail.

Two key points about the selection process are worth emphasizing. First, by using a transparent methodology, the administration is attempting to depoliticize the selection process to a remarkable extent. In fact, the selection process limits (although it does not fully eliminate) the administration's ability to use MCA funds for unrelated diplomatic goals and will therefore strengthen the program's focus on growth and poverty reduction. Unfortunately, this focus on the poorest countries will be eroded starting in 2006, when the administration plans to expand eligibility for MCA funds to middle-income countries with less need and greater access to private capital. This group includes several countries of strategic interest to the United States—such as Russia, Colombia, Egypt, Jordan, and Turkey—raising the possibility that MCA funds could be diverted for political purposes. To keep the MCA focused on the poorest countries and avoid the temptation to allocate aid to political favorites, these countries should not be included in the program.

Second, the number of qualifying countries is necessarily small, a design intended to make the program more effective. But the size involves a tradeoff: the greater the focus on a few countries with a strong commitment to good policy, the less impact the program will have on global poverty and inequality. From this perspective, the MCA will be too small: it may do a lot to help the countries that qualify but do little for the dozens that will not make the grade, leaving a gaping hole in the U.S. strategy to promote global prosperity.

From Aid to AIDS

The president's HIV/AIDS proposal will provide $15 billion—$10 billion of it in new funding— over the next five years to fight the pandemic, including $5 billion to continue existing programs; $1 billion for the Global Fund to Fight AIDS, Tuberculosis, and Malaria; and $9 billion for a new program called the Emergency Plan for AIDS Relief focused on 14 countries in Africa and the Caribbean. Almost as astonishing as the level of funding was Bush's embrace of a comprehensive approach to fighting the disease, encompassing prevention, care, and treatment and including the provision of antiretroviral drugs. This was a huge step forward for an administration in which several top officials had publicly questioned whether Africans have the capacity to implement treatment programs effectively. . . .

29 International Law

29.1

The Concept of Legalization

Kenneth W. Abbott, Robert O. Keohane, Andrew Moravcsik,
Anne-Marie Slaughter, and Duncan Snidal

The Elements of Legalization

"Legalization" refers to a particular set of characteristics that institutions may (or may not) possess. These characteristics are defined along three dimensions: obligation, precision, and delegation. *Obligation* means that states or other actors are bound by a rule or commitment or by a set of rules or commitments. Specifically, it means that they are *legally* bound by a rule or commitment in the sense that their behavior thereunder is subject to scrutiny under the general rules, procedures, and discourse of international law, and often of domestic law as well. *Precision* means that rules unambiguously define the conduct they require, authorize, or proscribe. *Delegation* means that third parties have been granted authority to implement, interpret, and apply the rules; to resolve disputes; and (possibly) to make further rules.

Each of these dimensions is a matter of degree and gradation, not a rigid dichotomy, and each can vary independently. Consequently, the concept of legalization encompasses a multidimensional continuum, ranging from the "ideal type" of legalization, where all three properties are maximized; to "hard" legalization, where all three (or at least obligation and delegation) are high; through multiple forms of partial or "soft" legalization involving different combinations of attributes; and finally to the complete absence of legalization, another ideal type. None of these dimensions—far less the full spectrum of legalization—can be fully operationalized. . . .

Statutes or regulations in highly developed national legal systems are generally taken as prototypical of hard legalization. For example, a congressional statute setting a cap on emissions of a particular pollutant is (subject to any special exceptions) legally binding on U.S. residents (obligation), unambiguous in its requirements (precision), and subject to judicial interpretation and application as well as administrative elaboration and enforcement (delegation). But even domestic enactments vary widely in their degree of legalization, both across states—witness the vague "proclamations" and restrictions on judicial review imposed by authoritarian regimes— and across issue areas within states—compare U.S. tax law to "political questions" under the Constitution. Moreover, the degree of obligation, precision, or delegation in formal institutions can be obscured in practice by political pressure, informal norms, and other factors. International legalization exhibits similar variation; on the whole, however,

Source: Kenneth W. Abbott, Robert O. Keohane, Andrew Moravcsik, Anne-Marie Slaughter, and Duncan Snidal, "The Concept of Legalization," *International Organization* 54:3 (Summer, 2000), pp. 401–404; 408–416; and 418–419.

international institutions are less highly legalized than institutions in democratic rule-of-law states. . . .

Our conception of legalization creates common ground for political scientists and lawyers by moving away from a narrow view of law as requiring enforcement by a coercive sovereign. This criterion has underlain much international relations thinking on the topic. Since virtually no international institution passes this standard, it has led to a widespread disregard of the importance of international law. But theoretical work in international relations has increasingly shifted attention away from the need for centralized enforcement toward other institutionalized ways of promoting cooperation.[1] In addition, the forms of legalization we observe at the turn of the millennium are flourishing in the absence of centralized coercion. . . .

The Variability of Legalization

A central feature of our conception of legalization is the variability of each of its three dimensions, and therefore of the overall legalization of international norms, agreements, and regimes. This feature is illustrated in Figure 29.1. In Figure 29.1 each element of the definition appears as a continuum, ranging from the weakest form (the absence of legal obligation, precision, or delegation, except as provided by the background operation of the international legal system) at the left to the strongest or "hardest" form at the right.[2] Figure 29.1 also highlights the independence of these dimensions from each other: conceptually, at least, the authors of a legal instrument can combine any level of obligation, precision, and delegation to produce an institution exactly suited to their specific needs. (In practice, as we shall explain, certain combinations are employed more frequently than others.)

Figure 29.1 The dimensions of legalization

Obligation	Expressly nonlegal norm	⟷	Binding rule (*jus cogens*)
Precision	Value principle	⟷	Precise, highly elaborated rule
Delegation	Diplomacy	⟷	International court, organization; domestic application

It would be inappropriate to equate the right-hand end points of these dimensions with "law" and the left-hand end points with "politics," for politics continues (albeit in different forms) even where there is law. Nor should one equate the left-hand end points with the absence of norms or institutions; as the designations in Figure 29.1 suggest, both norms (such as ethical principles and rules of practice) and institutions (such as diplomacy and balance of power) can exist beyond these dimensions. Figure 29.1 simply represents the components of legal institutions. . . .

The Dimensions of Legalization

Obligation

Legal rules and commitments impose a particular type of binding obligation on states and other subjects (such as international organizations). Legal obligations are different in kind from obligations resulting from coercion, comity, or morality alone. As discussed earlier, legal obligations bring into play the established norms, procedures, and forms of discourse of the international legal system.[3]

The fundamental international legal principle of *pacta sunt servanda* means that the rules and commitments contained in legalized international agreements are regarded as obligatory, subject to various defenses or exceptions, and not to be disregarded as preferences change. They must be performed in good faith regardless of inconsistent provisions of domestic law. International law also provides principles for the interpretation of agreements and a variety of technical rules on such matters as formation, reservation, and amendments. Breach of a legal obligation is understood to create "legal responsibility," which does not require a showing of intent on the part of specific state organs.

The international legal system also contains accepted procedures and remedies for breaches of legal commitments. Only states injured by a breach have standing to complain; and the complaining state or its citizens must exhaust any domestic remedies within the breaching state before making an international claim. States may then pursue their claims diplomatically or through any formal dispute procedure they have accepted. International law also prescribes certain defenses, which include consent, self-defense, and necessity, as well as the broad doctrine called *rebus sic stantibus*: an agreement may lose its binding character if important conditions change materially. These doctrines automatically

Table 29.1 Indicators of obligation

High
Unconditional obligation; language and other indicia of intent to be legally bound/Political treaty: implicit conditions on obligation
National reservations on specific obligations; contingent obligations and escape clauses
Hortatory obligations
Norms adopted without law-making authority; recommendations and guidelines
Explicit negation of intent to be legally bound
Low

inject a degree of flexibility into legal commitments; by defining particular exceptions, though, they reinforce legal obligations in other circumstances.

When breach leads to injury, legal responsibility entails an obligation to make reparation, preferably through restitution. If this is not possible, the alternative in the event of material harm is a monetary indemnity; in the event of psychological harm, "satisfaction" in the form of an apology. Since achieving such remedies is often problematic, international law authorizes self-help measures, including reprisals, reciprocal measures (such as the withdrawal of equivalent concessions in the WTO), and retorsions (such as suspending foreign aid). Self-help is limited, though, by the doctrine of proportionality and other legal conditions, including restrictions on the unilateral use of force.

Finally, establishing a commitment as a legal rule invokes a particular form of discourse. Although actors may disagree about the interpretation or applicability of a set of rules, discussion of issues purely in terms of interests or power is no longer legitimate. Legalization of rules implies a discourse primarily in terms of the text, purpose, and history of the rules, their interpretation, admissible exceptions, applicability to classes of situations, and particular facts. The rhetoric of law is highly developed, and the community of legal experts—whose members normally participate in legal rule-making and dispute settlement—is highly socialized to apply it. Thus the possibilities and limits of this discourse are normally part and parcel of legalized commitments.

Commitments can vary widely along the continuum of obligation, as summarized in Table 29.1. An example of a hard legal rule is Article 24 of the Vienna Convention on Diplomatic Relations, which reads in its entirety: "The archives and documents of the mission shall be inviolable at any time and wherever they may be." As a whole, this treaty reflects the intent of the parties to create legally binding obligations governed by international law. It uses the language of obligation; calls for the traditional legal formalities of signature, ratification, and entry into force; requires that the agreement and national ratification documents be registered with the UN; is styled a "Convention;" and states its relationship to preexisting rules of customary international law.[4] Article 24 itself imposes an unconditional obligation in formal, even "legalistic" terms.

At the other end of the spectrum are instruments that explicitly negate any intent to create legal obligations. The best-known example is the 1975 Helsinki Final Act. By specifying that this accord could not be registered with the UN, the parties signified that it was not an "agreement . . . governed by international law." Other instruments are even more explicit: witness the 1992 "Non-Legally Binding Authoritative Statement of Principles for a Global Consensus" on sustainable management of forests. Many working agreements among national government agencies are explicitly nonbinding.[5] Instruments framed as "recommendations" or "guidelines"—like the OECD Guidelines on Multinational Enterprises—are normally intended not to create legally binding obligations.[6] . . .

Precision

A precise rule specifies clearly and unambiguously what is expected of a state or other actor (in terms of both the intended objective and the means of achieving it) in a particular set of circumstances. In other words,

Table 29.2 Indicators of precision

High
Determinate rules: only narrow issues of interpretation
Substantial but limited issues of interpretation
Broad areas of discretion
"Standards": only meaningful with reference to specific situations
Impossible to determine whether conduct complies
Low

precision narrows the scope for reasonable interpretation.[7] In Thomas Franck's terms, such rules are "determinate."[8] For a set of rules, precision implies not just that each rule in the set is unambiguous, but that the rules are related to one another in a non-contradictory way, creating a framework within which case-by-case interpretation can be coherently carried out.[9] Precise sets of rules are often, though by no means always, highly elaborated or dense, detailing conditions of application, spelling out required or proscribed behavior in numerous situations, and so on. . . .

In highly developed legal systems, normative directives are often formulated as relatively precise "rules" ("do not drive faster than 50 miles per hour"), but many important directives are also formulated as relatively general "standards" ("do not drive recklessly").[10] The more "rule-like" a normative prescription, the more a community decides *ex ante* which categories of behavior are unacceptable; such decisions are typically made by legislative bodies. The more "standard-like" a prescription, the more a community makes this determination *ex post,* in relation to specific sets of facts; such decisions are usually entrusted to courts. Standards allow courts to take into account equitable factors relating to particular actors or situations, albeit at the sacrifice of some *ex ante* clarity.[11] Domestic legal systems are able to use standards like "due care" or the Sherman Act's prohibition on "conspiracies in restraint of trade" because they include well-established courts and agencies able to interpret and apply them (high delegation), developing increasingly precise bodies of precedent. . . .

In most areas of international relations, judicial, quasi-judicial, and administrative authorities are less highly developed and infrequently used. In this thin institutional context, imprecise norms are, in practice, most often interpreted and applied by the very actors whose conduct they are intended to govern. In addition, since most international norms are created through the direct consent or practice of states, there is no centralized legislature to overturn inappropriate, self-serving interpretations. Thus, precision and elaboration are especially significant hallmarks of legalization at the international level.

Much of international law is in fact quite precise, and precision and elaboration appear to be increasing dramatically, as exemplified by the WTO trade agreements, environmental agreements like the Montreal (ozone) and Kyoto (climate change) Protocols, and the arms control treaties produced during the Strategic Arms Limitation Talks (SALT) and subsequent negotiations. Indeed, many modern treaties are explicitly designed to increase determinacy and narrow issues of interpretation through the "codification" and "progressive development" of customary law. Leading examples include the Vienna Conventions on the Law of Treaties and on Diplomatic Relations, and important aspects of the UN Convention on the Law of the Sea. Even many nonbinding instruments, like the Rio Declaration on Environment and Development and Agenda 21, are remarkably precise and dense, presumably because proponents believe that these characteristics enhance their normative and political value.

Still, many treaty commitments are vague and general, in the ways suggested by Table 29.2.[12] The North American Free Trade Agreement side agreement on labor, for example, requires the parties to "provide for high labor standards." Article VI of the Treaty on the Non-proliferation ofNuclear Weapons calls on the parties "to pursue negotiations in good faith on effective measures relating to cessation of the nuclear arms race . . . and to nuclear disarmament." Commercial treaties typically require states to create "favorable conditions" for investment and avoid "unreasonable" regulations. Numerous agreements call on states to "negotiate" or "consult," without specifying particular procedures. All these provisions create broad areas of discretion for the affected actors; indeed, many provisions are so general that one cannot meaningfully assess compliance, casting doubt on their legal force.[13] . . .

Imprecision is not synonymous with state discretion, however, when it occurs within a delegation of authority and therefore grants to an international body wider authority to determine its meaning. The charters of international organizations provide important examples. In these instruments, generality frequently produces a broader delegation of authority, although member states almost always retain many levers of influence. A recent example makes the point clearly. At the 1998 Rome conference that approved a charter for an international criminal court, the United States sought to avoid any broad delegation of authority. Its proposal accordingly emphasized the need for "clear, precise, and specific definitions of each offense" within the jurisdiction of the court.[14]

Delegation

The third dimension of legalization is the extent to which states and other actors delegate authority to designated third parties—including courts, arbitrators, and administrative organizations—to implement agreements. The characteristic forms of legal delegation are third-party dispute settlement mechanisms authorized to interpret rules and apply them to particular facts (and therefore in effect to make new rules, at least interstitially) under established doctrines of international law. Dispute settlement mechanisms are most highly legalized when the parties agree to binding third-party decisions on the basis of clear and generally applicable rules; they are least legalized when the process involves political bargaining between parties who can accept or reject proposals without legal justification.[15]

In practice, as reflected in Table 29.3, dispute-settlement mechanisms cover an extremely broad range: from no delegation (as in traditional political decision making); through institutionalized forms of bargaining, including mechanisms to facilitate agreement, such as mediation (available within the WTO) and conciliation (an option under the Law of the Sea Convention); nonbinding arbitration (essentially the mechanism of the old GATT); binding arbitration (as in the U.S.-Iran Claims Tribunal); and finally to actual adjudication (exemplified by the European Court of Justice and Court of Human Rights, and the international criminal tribunals for Rwanda and the former Yugoslavia).

Table 29.3 Indicators of delegation

a. Dispute resolution
High
Courts: binding third-party decisions; general jurisdiction; direct private access; can interpret and supplement rules; domestic courts have jurisdiction
Courts: jurisdiction, access or normative authority limited or consensual
Binding arbitration
Nonbinding arbitration
Conciliation, mediation
Institutionalized bargaining
Pure political bargaining
Low

b. Rule making and implementation
High
Binding regulations; centralized enforcement
Binding regulations with consent or opt-out
Binding internal policies; legitimation of decentralized enforcement
Coordination standards
Draft conventions; monitoring and publicity
Recommendations; confidential monitoring
Normative statements
Forum for negotiations
Low

Conclusion

Highly legalized institutions are those in which rules are obligatory on parties through links to the established rules and principles of international law, in which rules are precise (or can be made precise through the exercise of delegated authority), and in which authority to interpret and apply the rules has been delegated to third parties acting under the constraint of rules. There is, however, no bright line dividing legalized from non-legalized institutions. Instead, there is an identifiable continuum from hard law through varied forms of soft law, each with its individual mix of characteristics, to situations of negligible legalization.

This continuum presupposes that legalized institutions are to some degree differentiated from other types of international institutions, a differentiation that may have methodological, procedural, cultural, and informational dimensions.[16] Although mediators may, for example, be free to broker a bargain based on the "naked preferences" of the parties,[17] legal processes involve a discourse framed in terms of reason, interpretation, technical knowledge, and argument, often followed by deliberation and judgment by impartial parties. Different actors have access to the process, and they are constrained to make arguments different from those they would make in a nonlegal context. Legal decisions, too, must be based on reasons applicable to all similarly situated litigants, not merely the parties to the immediate dispute.

On the whole, however, our conception of legalization reflects a general theme . . . : the rejection of a rigid dichotomy between "legalization" and "world politics." Law and politics are intertwined at all levels of legalization. One result of this interrelationship . . . is considerable difficulty in identifying the causal effects of legalization. Compliance with rules occurs for many reasons other than their legal status. Concern about reciprocity, reputation, and damage to valuable state institutions, as well as other normative and material considerations, all play a role. Yet it is reasonable to assume that most of the time, legal and political considerations combine to influence behavior.

At one extreme, even "pure" political bargaining is shaped by rules of sovereignty and other background legal norms. At the other extreme, even international adjudication takes place in the "shadow of politics": interested parties help shape the agenda and initiate the proceedings; judges are typically alert to the political implications of possible decisions, seeking to anticipate the reactions of political authorities. Between these extremes, where most international legalization lies, actors combine and invoke varying degrees of obligation, precision, and delegation to create subtle blends of politics and law. In all these settings, to paraphrase Clausewitz, "law is a continuation of political intercourse, with the addition of other means."

Notes

1. See the debate between the "managerial" perspective that emphasizes centralization but not enforcement, Chayes and Chayes 1995, and the "compliance" perspective that emphasizes enforcement but sees it as decentralized, Downs, Rocke, and Barsoom 1996.

2. On the "obligation" dimension, *jus cogens* refers to an international legal rule—generally one of customary law, though perhaps one codified in treaty form—that creates an especially strong legal obligation, such that it cannot be overridden even by explicit agreement among states.

3. In linking obligation to the broader legal system, we are positing the existence of international law as itself imposing a body of accepted and thereby legitimized obligations on states. If the ultimate foundation of a legal system is its acceptance as such by its subjects, through a Kelsenian *Grundnorm* or an ultimate rule of recognition, then we are positing the existence of that acceptance by states with regard to the existing international legal system. The degree of obligation that we seek to measure refers instead to acceptance by subject states of a particular rule as a legal rule or not, that is, as binding or not binding as a matter of international law.

4. Under accepted legal principles, many of which are codified in the Vienna Convention on the Law of Treaties, the intent of the parties to an agreement determines whether that instrument creates obligations that are legally binding, not merely personal or political in effect, and that are governed by international law, rather than the law of some nation. Intent is sometimes explicitly stated; otherwise it must be discerned from the overall context of an agreement, its negotiating history, the nature of its commitments, and its form. As a practical matter, however, legalization is the default position: significant agreements between states are assumed to be legally binding and governed by international law unless the parties indicate otherwise. U.S. practice on this score is summarized in the State Department's *Foreign Relations Manual*, pt. 181.

5. Zaring 1998.

6. Although precise obligations are generally an attribute of hard legalization, these instruments use precise language to avoid legally binding character.

7. A precise rule is not necessarily more constraining than a more general one. Its actual impact on behavior depends on many factors, including subjective interpretation by the subjects of the rule. Thus, a rule saying "drive slowly" might yield slower driving than a rule prescribing a speed limit of 55 miles per hour if the drivers in question would normally drive 50 miles per hour and understand "slowly" to mean 10 miles per hour slower than normal. (We are indebted to Fred Schauer for both the general point and the example.) In addition, precision can be used to define limits, exceptions, and loopholes that reduce the impact of a rule. Nevertheless, for most rules requiring or prohibiting particular conduct—and in the absence of precise delegation—generality is likely to provide an opportunity for deliberate self-interested interpretation, reducing the impact, or at least the potential for enforceable impact, on behavior.

8. Franck 1990.

9. Franck labels this collective property "coherence." We use the singular notion of precision to capture both the precision of a rule in isolation and its precision within a rule system.

10. The standard regime definition encompasses three levels of precision: "principles," "norms," and "rules." Krasner 1983. This formulation reflects the fact that societies typically translate broad normative values into increasingly concrete formulations that decision-makers can apply in specific situations.

11. Kennedy 1976.

12. Operationalizing the relative precision of different formulations is difficult, except in a gross sense. Gamble, for example, purports to apply a four-point scale of "concreteness" but does not characterize these points. Gamble 1985.

13. The State Department's *Foreign Relations Manual* states that undertakings couched in vague or very general

terms with no criteria for performance frequently reflect an intent not to be legally bound.

14. U.S. Releases Proposal on Elements of Crimes at the Rome Conference on the Establishment of an International Criminal Court, statement by James

15. P. Rubin, U.S. State Department spokesperson, 22 June 1998, <secretary.state.gov/www/briefings/statements/1998/ps980622b.html>, accessed 16 February 1999.

16. Law remains relevant even here. The UN Charter makes peaceful resolution of disputes a legal obligation, and general international law requires good faith in the conduct of negotiations. In addition, resolution of disputes by agreement can contribute to the growth of customary international law.

17. Schauer and Wise 1997.

18. Sunstein 1986.

29.2

International Law

The Trials of Global Norms

Steven R. Ratner

The move from describing the world to prescribing for it forms the core of international law. Can those committing human rights atrocities—war criminals from Bosnia or political leaders from Cambodia—be tried in foreign courts or before international tribunals? How can members of the United Nations ensure respect for the decisions of its Security Council? What is the best way to regulate transnational environmental hazards such as greenhouse gas emissions or ocean dumping? Can the United States allow its citizens to sue European companies for their use of land and factories confiscated by the Cuban government from Americans more than a generation ago?

All these questions turn on political decisions by states—but what international lawyers see and seek in such scenarios is a process whose actions are informed and influenced by principles of law, not just raw power. For international lawyers, devising and enforcing universal rules of conduct for states means overcoming two cardinal challenges: how to make such precepts legitimate in a diverse community of nations; and how to make them stick in the absence of any one sovereign authority or supranational enforcement mechanism. The mission of international law, as described in 1950 by Hersch Lauterpacht, perhaps this century's greatest international law scholar, is to lead "to enhancing the stability of international peace, to the protection of the rights of man, and to reducing the evils and abuses of national power."

For much of this century, however, many practitioners and observers in the two fields straddled by international law regarded such pronouncements with skepticism, if not outright scorn. Diplomats and international relations scholars questioned whether norms counted for much in the behavior of states. And domestic lawyers rejected the idea that law could even exist without the same kind of sanctioning system found within sovereign states.

The shape of the international system during the Cold War reinforced this realist perspective. International institutions and judicial bodies such as the United Nations and the International Court of Justice (otherwise known as the World Court) were hobbled by both the bipolar split in world politics and its aggravation of tensions between the developed and developing worlds. Responding to the inability of organizations to exercise their mandates, or of treaties such as the General Agreement on Tariffs and Trade and the UN Convention on the Law of the Sea to garner global endorsement, legal scholars asked what states could do alone, largely accepting as fixed the limits on what they might do together.

Today, the end of the Cold War has loosened many of the blockages to international lawmaking and implementation. Although legal scholars still ask what states can do on their own—pass extraterritorial laws, use force, or prosecute war criminals—they do so assuming that coordinated action is now more feasible than in the past. Global and regional treaties such as the Chemical Weapons Convention, the Convention on the Prohibition of Anti-Personnel Mines, the Maastricht Treaty, and the North American Free Trade Agreement now serve as the starting point for scrutinizing state behavior according to some objective standard.

The ground seems ready then for an acceleration of this century's great trend in international law: the increasing international regulation of more and more issues once typically seen as part of state domestic jurisdiction. But any attempt to create the lofty, supranational legal edifice idealized by some of the field's practitioners and scholars promises to be problematic at best. Once paralyzed by the deadlock between East and West, and between North and South, the international legal system must now contend not just with the challenge of persuading new states such as Belarus or Croatia to comply with established norms but of coping with Somalia and other failed states, whose circumstances make a mockery of international rules. International law must seek to embrace a growing range of forms, topics, and technologies, as well as a host of new actors. And as it moves further away from strictly "foreign" concerns—the treatment of diplomats or ships on the seas—to traditionally domestic areas—environmental or labor standards—its proponents must increasingly confront new obstacles head-on.

New Realities, New Ideas

This new global context surrounding the field has led to at least four fundamental shifts in the kinds of issues that legal scholars now talk about and study:

New Forms, New Players

Traditionally, most rules of international law could be found in one of two places: treaties—binding, written agreements between states; or customary law—uncodified, but equally binding rules based on long-standing behavior that states accept as compulsory. The strategic arms reduction treaties requiring the United States and Russia to cut their nuclear weapons arsenals offer examples of the former; the rule that governments cannot be sued in the courts of another state for most of their public acts provides an example of the latter. Historically, treaties have gradually displaced much customary law, as international rules have become increasingly codified.

But as new domains from the environment to the Internet come to be seen as appropriate for international regulation, states are sometimes reluctant to embrace any sort of binding rule. In the past, many legal scholars and international courts simply accepted the notion that no law governed a particular subject until a new treaty was concluded or states signaled their consent to a new customary-law rule (witness the reluctance with which human rights norms were considered law prior to the UN's two key treaties in 1966) or, alternatively, struggled to find customary law where none existed. However, today all but the most doctrinaire of scholars see a role for so-called soft law—precepts emanating from international bodies that conform in some sense to expectations of required behavior but that are not binding on states.

For example, in 1992 the World Bank completed a set of Guidelines on the Treatment of Foreign Direct Investment. Though these are not binding on any bank member, states and corporations invoke them as the standard for how developing nations should treat foreign capital to encourage investment. This soft law enables states to adjust to the regulation of many new areas of international concern without fearing a violation (and possible legal countermeasures) if they fail to comply. Normative expectations are built more quickly than they would through the evolution of a customary-law rule, and more gently than if a new treaty rule were foisted on states. Soft law principles also represent a starting point for new hard law, which attaches a penalty to non-compliance. In this case, the bank's guidelines have served as the basis for the negotiation of a new treaty—the Multilateral Agreement on Investment (MAI)—by the Organization for Economic Cooperation and Development (OECD). The MAI gives foreign investors the right to take any government to international arbitration for compensation when a law or state practice limits their freedom to invest or divest.

Whether in the case of hard or soft law, new participants are making increased demands for representation in international bodies, conferences, and other legal groupings and processes. They include substate entities, both those recognized in some way by the international community (Chechnya, Hong Kong) and those not (Tibet, Kashmir); nongovernmental organizations (NGOs); and corporations. Claiming that the states to which they belong do not always adequately represent their interests, these nonstate actors demand a say in the content of new norms. Some have faced staunch opposition to their participation in decision making: In 1995, China's government relegated NGOs to a distant venue during the UN's Fourth World Conference on Women in Beijing.

But other groups may succeed even as far as effectively taking over an official delegation. For example, U.S. telecommunications companies such as Motorola have seemed almost to dictate U.S. positions in the International Telecommunication Union (ITU), the UN agency responsible for setting global telecommunications standards. At the ITU's 1992 conference on allocating the radio spectrum for new technologies, Motorola's stake in protecting its plans for new satellites became a paramount U.S. interest, resulting in a sizeable Motorola team attending as part of the U.S. delegation. Other corporations have acted outside government channels entirely by promulgating private codes: in response to public pressure, Nike issued a set of self-imposed rules to protect worker rights in the developing world. It is not that states are no longer the primary makers of international law. But scholars accept that these other actors have independent views—and the resources to push them—that do not fit neatly into traditional theories of how law is made and enforced.

New Enforcement Strategies

Most states comply with much, even most, international law almost continually—whether the law of the sea, diplomatic immunity, or civil aviation rules. But without mechanisms to bring transgressors into line, international law will be "law" in name only. This state of affairs, when it occurs, is ignored by too many lawyers, who delight in large bodies of rules but often discount patterns of noncompliance. For example, Western governments, and many scholars, insisted throughout the 1960s and 1970s that when nationalizing foreign property, developing states were legally bound to compensate former owners for the full economic value, despite those states' repeated refusals to pay such huge sums.

The traditional toolbox to secure compliance with the law of nations consists of negotiations, mediation, countermeasures (reciprocal action against the violator) or, in rare cases, recourse to supranational judicial bodies such as the International Court of Justice. (The last of these was the linchpin of the world of law that Americans such as Andrew Carnegie and Elihu Root sought to bring into being.) For many years, these tools have been supplemented by the work of international institutions, whose reports and resolutions often help "mobilize shame" against violators. But today, states, NGOs, and private entities, aided by their lawyers, have striven for sanctions with more teeth. They have galvanized the UN Security Council to issue economic sanctions against Iraq, Haiti, Libya, Serbia, Sudan, and other nations refusing to comply with UN resolutions.

On the free-trade front, the dispute settlement panels in the World Trade Organization (WTO) now have the legal authority to issue binding rulings that allow the victor in a trade dispute to impose special tariffs on the loser. In September 1997, for example, the WTO's Dispute Settlement Body recommended that the European Union modify its banana import regime following complaints by Ecuador, Guatemala, Honduras, Mexico, and the United States, paving the way for those states to suspend free trade if the EU fails to comply. And the UN's ad hoc criminal tribunals for the former Yugoslavia and Rwanda show that it is at least possible to devise institutions to punish individuals for human rights atrocities.

Nonetheless, as the impunity to date of former Bosnian Serb president Radovan Karadzic and General Ratko Mladic reveals, the success of these enforcement mechanisms depends on the willingness of states to support them: legalism meets realism. When global institutions do not work, regional bodies may offer more promise due to their "club" atmosphere. Organizations such as the EU and the Organization of American States have demonstrated their influence over member conduct in economics, human rights, and other areas.

Increasingly, domestic courts provide an additional venue to enforce international law. In Spain, for example, Judge Manuel García Castellón of the National Court has agreed to hear a controversial human rights case involving charges against Chile's former dictator, General Augusto Pinochet. Meanwhile, Castellón's colleague, Judge Baltasar Garzón, hears testimony against those responsible for the "Dirty War" of the 1970s in Argentina. (Spain is asserting jurisdiction in both cases because its nationals were among the thousands of victims tortured and killed.) And though Karadzic remains at large, he has been sued in U.S. federal court under the Alien Tort Claims Act, which allows foreign nationals recovery against Karadzic for the rape and torture of civilians during his "ethnic cleansing" campaign in the former Yugoslavia. At a minimum, this provides a symbolic measure of solace for his victims.

The Legitimacy Problem

Even as scholars seek to devise better enforcement mechanisms, a serious debate is brewing about the legitimacy of such measures. As international organizations are freed up to take more actions by the end of the East-West conflict and the tempering of North-South tensions, the United States and its like-minded allies seem well positioned to impose their agenda on all. Legal scholars question whether Western dominance of the Organization for Security and Cooperation in Europe, UN, WTO, and other international institutions is not merely raw power asserting its muscle again, albeit through multilateral bodies, to the detriment of a genuine rule of law. That this debate is more than academic can be seen vividly in the ongoing discussion about reforming the Security Council. Many Americans may laud the council's new muscle—during the last five years, it has slapped a debilitating embargo and weapons inspection regime on Iraq, prohibited air traffic with Libya due to its sanctuary for those accused of the Pan Am 103 bombing, and approved a U.S.-led occupation of Haiti. But smaller states feel threatened by a Security Council in which the West is often able to convince enough states to approve such council actions, and only a Chinese veto (which was used only once in the last 25 years) seems to protect them. . . .

Focusing on enforcement and legitimacy also provides a useful lens through which to evaluate U.S. reactions to international norms: Even as the United States seeks to strengthen the enforcement of international law for its own ends, it has often recoiled at the prospect that these norms might be enforced against it. In the WTO, the very dispute resolution panels that the United States hopes to use to force open closed markets could order it to choose between environmental protection laws (such as those banning imports of tuna caught in nets that kill dolphins) and the prospects of retaliatory sanctions if those laws have incidental discriminatory effects on trade. In such a scenario, international law, as interpreted by the WTO, becomes the friend of business and bugaboo of environmentalists. But when the UN seeks to promulgate environmental law, as it has with the proposed greenhouse gas convention just concluded at Kyoto, then the tables are turned.

Similarly, the United States wants to use the Security Council to keep in place a comprehensive sanctions regime on Iraq that has the diplomatic appeal of being "international" rather than "U.S.-imposed," all the while holding back on paying its dues because not all UN programs conform to Washington's wishes. As the world's sole superpower, the United States can defy international standards with little fear of immediate sanction; but other states will begin to question its motives in trying to strengthen important legal regimes such as those covering nuclear and chemical nonproliferation. . . .

Expanding Old Boundaries

Given that international legal academics are changing how they conduct their conversations and their scholarship, in what subject areas should foreign policymakers and observers expect contributions from them? Several intellectual hot spots deserve mention.

First, trade law is becoming the locus of many critical areas of foreign policy and its primary enforcement mechanism—the WTO—the repository of new powers. International lawyers are busy seeking ways to integrate the environment, intellectual property, investment, labor rights, and perhaps other subjects, including antitrust, into a framework thus far dominated by considerations of free trade. If the WTO is to have a powerful enforcement role, those responsible for interpreting trade agreements or drafting new ones will need to take explicit account of these other interests and the treaties that deal with them. For example, when one state alleges that another state's environmental laws impede trade, such accusations should be evaluated against the backdrop of existing treaties on international environmental matters. Arbitrators and negotiators thus need to approach their task with more than a one-sided "free trade at all costs" outlook. If they do not, then cramming more issues into the WTO's mandate will face major obstacles. Developing nations will see it as yet another attempt to force American views of antitrust or labor rights on them. Moreover, groups within the Western states will fear WTO rulings that could eclipse or override the more balanced norms emanating from other international organizations. These pressures may well prevent the WTO from enlarging its agenda too quickly.

Second, the most pressing transboundary issue in which international law will play a decisive role is the environment. The last decade has seen critical treaties concluded on the protection of the ozone layer, movement of hazardous wastes, and protection of fishing stocks. More will follow. Of course, these regimes need to remain flexible enough to accommodate new scientific discoveries and technology. One particularly promising legal avenue has been the so-called framework convention, which allows all parties to a treaty to adjust their commitments over time (e.g., accelerate their reductions in emissions of a toxic substance) without redrafting the treaty and, in some cases, without subjecting the revisions to renewed ratification by domestic organs. International lawyers are also devising schemes to make those treaties work. Among the most exciting developments are liability regimes to shift the costs of pollution from states to private polluters.

Third, the human rights agenda remains a central area of research and advocacy. Fifty years of codification have yielded much law, from the Genocide Convention in 1948 to the Convention on the Rights of the Child in 1989. But in few areas of international relations have legal norms been so fundamental to understanding a problem and yet so terribly slow at rectifying odious practices.

One area of progress in enforcement, although barely known to foreign policy specialists, is that of regional human rights commissions and courts. The European Commission and Court of Human Rights have scrutinized questionable domestic laws for decades and given individuals an avenue of relief from them. In the last three decades, the Inter-American Commission on Human Rights and the Inter-American Court of Human Rights have investigated the killing, torture, and disappearance of thousands across Latin America and, in recent years, have successfully urged those states responsible to change their behavior. The achievements of these institutions in both regions should serve as a model for the nascent regional human rights commission (and likely future court) for Africa. In addition, domestic truth commissions in countries such as South Africa and the UN's criminal tribunals direct global attention to personal criminal liability for abuses. Although some lawyers and scholars have embraced the criminal remedy so readily that they seem to have forgotten the importance of old-fashioned pressure on states to respect rights, the legal field's work in creating new law and mechanisms to hold individuals accountable should be welcomed and watched by policymakers.

Fourth, international legal academics will be forced more and more to grapple with the increasingly extraterritorial reach of domestic laws. The United States has thrown down the gauntlet at Europe through the ambitious reach of its antitrust laws, as well as through the Helms-Burton Act of 1996, which allows victims of the Cuban government's expropriations to sue in U.S. courts the companies using their former property. The U.S. Supreme Court appears to be upholding such initiatives, adopting an extremely loose interpretation of congressional prerogatives in passing laws with extraterritorial effect. The Europeans responded to U.S. actions last year through a threat issued by the European Commission to prohibit the merger of Boeing and McDonnell Douglas because of its potentially adverse effects on the market for Airbus Industries.

American and European businesses are likely to continue to be confused by the requirements of different systems and foreign policymakers annoyed by the consequences for relations with old allies. Academic international lawyers have mostly been ignored in this dispute. It seems that only bilateral (e.g., U.S.–EU) or multilateral treaties (perhaps through the OECD or WTO) will remedy the situation. But no solution is in sight, as politicians and corporations have recognized the advantages of regulating overseas conduct, even when such conduct has only the slightest impact on the domestic economy.

Lastly, though the average foreign policy aficionado may see no immediate contributions to solving global problems, legal scholars—newly informed by the developments of the post-Cold War era—will continue to engage core theoretical issues. One will be the relevance of customary international law in an era where treaties are seen as the primary locus of lawmaking. The UN Convention on the Law of the Sea of 1982, for example, codified or replaced numerous customary-law rules on the oceans. Perhaps the demise of custom is to be welcomed as a sign of maturation in international law. Another issue will be the general problem of diffusion of lawmaking at different levels in the international system. This latter issue resonates in many areas of foreign policy, as demonstrated by the resentment in some quarters in Europe and the United States when the European Court of Human Rights or the WTO strikes down domestic legislation. A promising solution, which some scholars have explored in detail, involves a shift to implementing international norms via domestic courts. Instead of top-down diktats from distant tribunals made up of unknown, mostly foreign judges, litigants will have their cases judged at home but according to international standards. The challenge of this style of law enforcement is not to be underestimated, however, as the average American judge (or legislator for that matter) remains ignorant of most international norms. . . .

At the same time, however, the days are gone when international lawyers could assume that states would eventually come to their senses and agree on the need to regulate their conduct according to rules. Scholars and practitioners are now realizing that as they continue to delve into issues that for so long seemed to be wholly domestic or, as they seek to enforce norms more assertively, the resistance will be sharper. The old talisman of "sovereignty" will surely rear its ugly head—under the banner of non-intervention, Asian values, EU-trashing, or some such term. International lawyers can no longer dismiss these claims, and they have no bold new paradigm to guide them in creating a more comprehensive legal order. Thus, they must accept that the suffusion of norms into decision-making is a long-term process.

29.3

The Limits of Idealism

Jack Goldsmith and Stephen D. Krasner

In 1939 E. H. Carr published what was to become a modern classic on international relations, *The Twenty Years Crisis, 1919–1939*. Carr has usually been seen as a defender of realism and a debunker of idealism, but his thinking was much more subtle. He believed that power and interest—the bread and butter of realism—were the primary determinants of state behavior. But he also believed that peoples and their nations were motivated by normative values and aspirations, not merely by a desire to marshal power and defend material interests. Carr concluded that "Utopia and reality are thus the two facets of political science. Sound political thought and sound political life will be found only where both have their place."

For Carr the problem of the interwar years was not international idealism itself, but rather international idealism run amuck. At the core of the international idealism he criticized was the assumption that right-minded human beings could agree on abstract normative principles to guide national behavior, and that these principles, once understood and embodied in international law, would influence nations to act with greater justice. By his account, international idealism discounted other factors, including the distribution of power and economic and political interests.

Carr famously argued that such idealism was self-defeating. Some nations, such as Germany, failed to comply with the principles of reason embodied by the League of Nations and similar institutions, and appealed instead to competing principles of law and morality to justify their self-interested and rapacious acts. Other nations, such as Britain and France, relied too heavily on the paper guarantees of international law, and not on a clear-eyed analysis of power and interest (both their own and Germany's), to secure international harmony. Carr attributed the growing international crisis in 1939 (his book was sent to the printer in July of that year) to the idealistic international institutions that were supposed to make a second world war impossible.

The kind of idealism that Carr understood to be so damaging to international peace and stability in the interwar years is again informing many aspects of international politics. Three developments in particular—the rise of universal jurisdiction, the creation of a new International Criminal Court, and recurring demands for humanitarian intervention—reflect a renewed commitment to international idealism. Supporters of these institutions and policies tend to believe that justice is best served when it is isolated from politics and power. Only by insulating international institutions and practice from the bargaining and compromise that characterize political decision-making, and from the domestic political pressure to which politicians must always be alert, can justice be fully realized. On this view, institutions and principles that minimize the influence of power better achieve justice than those in which power plays an important role; and decisions made by unaccountable actors, especially judges, are more likely to be just than decisions made by political leaders responsible to their electorates.

We believe the new international idealism suffers from four fundamental flaws:

- First, it assumes the utopian premise that a global consensus can be reached, not just on normative principles, but also on when and how they should be applied.
- Second, it minimizes considerations of power, and assumes that norms of right behavior can substitute for national capabilities and material interests.
- Third, it neglects political prudence: it offers a deontological rather than a consequentialist ethics.
- Fourth, it consistently slights the value of democratic accountability.

Our claim is not that idealism in international politics is irrelevant or inherently harmful. With Carr, we believe that normative ideals can provide a hope for progress, an emotional appeal, and a ground for

Source: Jack Goldsmith and Stephen D. Krasner, "The Limits of Idealism," *Daedalus* 132:1 (Winter, 2003), pp. 47–48, 53–57.

international action. But we also agree with Carr that ideals can be pursued effectively only if decision-makers are alert to the distribution of power, national interests, and the consequences of their policies. The lesson Carr teaches is that when idealism is not tempered by attention to these factors, the best can become the enemy of the good, and aspiration the enemy of progress. . . .

In July of 2002, international idealists realized a long-held dream: the creation of an International Criminal Court (ICC) with jurisdiction over genocide, crimes against humanity, war crimes, and, potentially, the crime of aggression.[1]

In some respects, the ICC is an improvement over a regime of universal jurisdiction by national courts. The ICC is a centralized institution. Its treaty defines the international crimes within its jurisdiction. It also rejects universal jurisdiction, requiring instead a nexus to the territory or persons of a treaty signatory.

And yet the ICC has most of the other characteristics—and flaws—of universal jurisdiction. Its norms are still much too open-ended and contested to permit a consensus on proscribed behavior; it suppresses considerations of power; it lacks democratic accountability; and it cannot reliably balance legal benefits against possible political costs.

The ICC defines the crimes within its jurisdiction. But these definitions rely a great deal on contested international law norms, and they leave the ICC great interpretive flexibility. For example, "crimes against humanity" include "imprisonment or other severe deprivation of physical liberty in violation of fundamental rules of international law." Unfortunately, international law provides little concrete guidance about what these fundamental rules require. After listing other examples of crimes against humanity, the ICC treaty describes as a final one "other inhumane acts of a similar character intentionally causing great suffering, or serious injury to body or to physical or mental health." Such a criminal prohibition would almost certainly be void for vagueness under U.S. law.

To take another example, the ICC includes dozens of prohibitions under the heading of "war crimes," including "willfully causing great suffering, or serious injury to body or health" of civilians, and "destroying or seizing the enemy's property unless . . . imperatively demanded by the necessities of war." The scope of these prohibitions is obviously uncertain, but it is easy to imagine them being applied to NATO actions in Kosovo and U.S. actions in Afghanistan. The ICC treaty is chock-full of many similarly vague and indeterminate criminal prohibitions.

One reason these vague norms are particularly troublesome is that the ICC prosecutor and court are unaccountable to any democratic institution or elected official. The ICC prosecutor is, to be sure, elected by a secret ballot by a majority of the signatory nations, each of which gets a single vote. But such an electoral system is problematic because, among other things, the vast majority of ICC ratifiers are weak nations that are never seriously involved in international police actions and thus have no incentive to consider the costs of zealous prosecutions.[2] Even more importantly, the prosecutor can initiate investigations and prosecutions on his own, or at the suggestion of the UN or any signatory nation—all without review, or the threat of review, by political actors. His prosecutions are subject to legal review by the trial and appellate courts of the ICC, but these courts are similarly unaccountable to any democratic institution.

This lack of accountability means that the ICC presents many of the dangers of universal jurisdiction. Its structure is remarkably similar to the much-maligned U.S. Independent Counsel statute. By guaranteeing independence at the price of political control, it invites questionable and even politically motivated prosecutions. Legal restrictions and definitional limitations are not likely to provide real checks on the ICC's behavior, for the ICC itself is the ultimate interpreter of these norms. Experiences with the more accountable international tribunals in The Hague and Rwanda have shown that international courts will not be bound by the letter of their governing rules when justice as they conceive it requires otherwise. ICC jurisdiction can only be expected to expand.

In addition, the ICC, like a universal jurisdiction court, lacks the institutional capacity to identify and balance properly the consequences of a prosecution on potentially affected groups. The ICC treaty insists that "the most serious crimes of concern to the international community as a whole must not go unpunished and their effective prosecution must be ensured." Here again we see modern international idealism's commitment to individual accountability at the expense of national amnesties and other forms of political reconciliation. The ICC theoretically permits the prosecutor to decline to investigate when there are "substantial reasons to believe that an investigation would not serve the interests of justice." But the final call rests with the prosecutor, who there is no reason to think has the perspective, information, or incentives to make this decision wisely. (When Richard Goldstone, the Yugoslav Tribunal's first prosecutor, was asked if he "worr[ied] about the consequences to the Bosnian peace process of indicting Radovan Karadzic and Ratko Mladic," he responded that the indictment "was really done as, if you like, as an academic exercise. . . . Because our duty was clear."[3])

It is true that the ICC treaty requires the court to dismiss a case if it is already under investigation in national court, "unless the State is unwilling or unable to genuinely carry out the investigation or prosecution." But the ICC has the final word on what counts as a genuine investigation based on its perception of whether the domestic proceedings are "inconsistent with an intent to bring the person concerned to justice," a provision that opens the possibility of double jeopardy if the prosecutor decides that a national conviction or investigation is too lenient and therefore not genuine. It is natural to expect the ICC to interpret its charter in ways that support its jurisdiction.

Perhaps the most troubling element of the ICC is its relationship to the U.N. Security Council. The United States argued that the ICC should prosecute only on the basis of referrals from the Security Council. The ICC drafters rejected the U.S. proposal on the grounds that it would inject international power politics into the decision whether to prosecute, and would give each of the Big Five powers a veto over any prosecution. The drafters viewed power politics, and the opportunistic use of Security Council vetoes, as an obstacle to individual accountability under international human rights law.

The ICC in its final form does permit the Security Council to delay a prosecution for twelve-month renewable terms. But this just means that an ICC case can go forward so long as a single permanent member vetoes a resolution of delay. And even if the Security Council votes to delay an ICC initiative (as it did when it granted UN peacekeepers a twelve-month immunity from prosecution in July of 2002[4]), many commentators believe the ICC has the power to engage in 'judicial review' of the Security Council and possibly to disregard its decision.

There are at least two problems with this attempt to eliminate power politics from the enforcement of international criminal law and to subvert the recognition of national power incorporated in the UN Security Council. The first parallels a problem with universal jurisdiction: the ICC could initiate prosecutions that aggravate bloody political conflicts and prolong political instability in the affected regions. Relatedly, the possibilities for compromise that exist in a political environment guided by prudential calculation are constricted when political deliberation must compete with an independent judicial process. Many believe that the threat of prosecution by the international tribunal in The Hague made it practically impossible for NATO to reach an early deal with Milosevic, thereby lengthening the war and the suffering in the Balkans in the summer of 1999. The best strategy for stability often depends on context and contingent political factors that are not reducible to a rule of law. There is no reason to think that a politically unaccountable prosecutor and court will make such difficult, context-specific calls wisely, even assuming they had the discretion to do so.

The second problem results from what Carr would have described as a chasm between theory and practice. Proponents of the ICC believe that it may, in the words of Human Rights Watch's Kenneth Roth, "save many lives."[5] This is wishful thinking. Even if the ICC turns out not to have the disruptive effects described above, and even if it is somehow able to prosecute low-level human rights abusers, it is hard to see how the ICC can stop, or even affect, persons responsible for large-scale human rights abuses.

The main reason for this conclusion is that the ICC can only prosecute persons it can get custody over. The Milosovics, Mullah Omars, and Pol Pots of the world, however, tend to hide behind national borders, where they are hard to reach. Moreover, the most notorious human rights abusers have been motivated by their own sense of mission and justice. They have seen themselves as saviors, not sinners. They have been determined to cling to power and they believe, as all leaders with a mission do, that they can reshape the world in their own image. If they have not been deterred by the threat of U.S. military intervention, they are unlikely to worry much about an ICC that lacks any real enforcement mechanism of its own and that must depend on its members, whose decisions are uncertain, to arrest and surrender suspects.

This brings us to the U.S. refusal to participate in the ICC. There are many reasons for the U.S. stance, most notably the perception that the United States's disproportionate share of international policing responsibilities exposes it to a disproportionate risk of politically motivated charges being brought before the ICC.

It may seem odd that an institution that will have little effect on rogue human rights abusers could so concern the world's greatest power. But U.S. troops, unlike rogue government officials, do not hide behind national borders. Hundreds of thousands of them are deployed around the globe, making them potentially easy to grab and bring to The Hague. (The United States is trying to counter this danger by signing bilateral agreements in which the signatories agree not to surrender nationals of the other to the ICC.)

Even if no U.S. defendant is brought before the ICC, it can still cause mischief for the United States by being a public forum for official criticism and judgment of U.S. military actions. For all these reasons, the ICC will more likely affect the activities of the generally human-rights-protecting but militarily active United States than rogue state actors who hide behind walls of sovereignty (or in ungoverned areas) and care little about world public opinion and international legitimacy.

Despite his opposition to the ICC treaty, President Clinton signed it in 2001, just before he left office, so that the United States could participate in ongoing negotiations. In May of 2002, however, the Bush administration officially notified the United Nations that "the United States does not intend to become a party to the treaty." In August of 2002, President Bush signed the American Servicemen's Protection Act (ASPA), a statute that enjoyed broad bipartisan support. ASPA is sometimes called the Hague Invasion Act because it authorizes the president to use all necessary means to release U.S. officials from ICC captivity. It also bars military aid to some nations that support the ICC, and it requires the president to certify that U.S. peacekeepers will be immune from ICC prosecution. U.S. opposition to the ICC is important because U.S. military and financial backing have been crucial to the operation of ad hoc international criminal tribunals. Consider how Milosevic wound up in The Hague. It was not the gravitational pull of international norms that brought him there. Rather, the United States wielded enormous diplomatic and military power to oust him from office, and then threatened to withhold some $50 million in aid to the successor regime in Yugoslavia until it turned over Milosevic to the Yugoslav tribunal.

The Milosevic episode teaches a general lesson. The ICC simply cannot, with out U.S. support, fulfill its dream of prosecuting big-time human rights abusers who hide behind national borders. This is why the ICC's alienation of the United States may actually hinder rather than enhance human rights enforcement. We have already seen this effect on peacekeeping and ad hoc international tribunals. And of course the ICC will most likely chill U.S. military action not when central U.S. strategic interests are at stake (as in Afghanistan), but rather in humanitarian situations (like Rwanda and perhaps Kosovo) where the strategic benefits of military action are low, and thus even a low probability of prosecution weighs more heavily. In this way, the ICC may ironically increase rather than decrease impunity for human rights atrocities.

The establishment of an ICC that is unacceptable to the world's most powerful nation (and also to other large and powerful nations, including Russia, China, Indonesia, and India) represents a folly reminiscent of the League of Nations, and portends a similar fate. The international idealists who rejected U.S. demands for Security Council control over ICC prosecutions aimed to decouple the enforcement of international criminal law from international politics. They wanted "equal justice under law"—the equal application of international human rights law to weak and powerful nations alike. Both aims are a fantasy strongly reminiscent of the interwar idealism that Carr so effectively and presciently criticized. In demanding a full loaf of neutral justice rather than a half loaf of justice that accords with the interests of nations that can enforce it, and in creating an institution that relies on legal norms wholly removed from considerations of power, international idealists may diminish rather than enhance the protection of human rights. . . .

Notes

1. The ICC's charter is available at <http://www.un.org/law/icc/statute/romefra.htm>; all subsequent quotes come from this document.

2. As of November 15, 2002, ICC ratifiers were: Andorra, Antigua and Barbuda, Argentina, Australia, Austria, Belgium, Belize, Benin, Bolivia, Bosnia and Herzigovina, Botswana, Brazil, Bulgaria, Cambodia, Canada, Central African Republic, Columbia, Costa Rica, Croatia, Cyprus, Democratic Republic of Congo, Denmark, Djibouti, Dominica, Ecuador, Estonia, Fiji, Finland, France, Gabon, Gambia, Germany, Ghana, Greece, Honduras, Hungary, Iceland, Ireland, Italy, Jordan, Latvia, Lesotho, Liechtenstein, Luxembourg, Macedonia (FYR), Mali, Marshall Islands, Malawi, Mauritius, Mongolia, Namibia, Nauru, New Zealand, Niger, Nigeria, Norway, Panama, Paraguay, Peru, Poland, Portugal, Romania, Samoa, San Marino, Senegal, Sierra Leone, Slovakia, Slovenia, South Africa, Spain, Sweden, Switzerland, Tajikistan, the Netherlands, Timor-Leste, Trinidad and Tobago, Uganda, United Kingdom, United Republic of Tanzania, Uruguay, Venezuela, and Yugoslavia.

3. Gary Bass, *Stay the Hand of Vengeance* (Princeton, N.J.: Princeton University Press, 2000), 6–7.

4. Sec. Coun. Res. 1422.

5. "The Court the US Doesn't Want," *The New York Review of Books*, 19 November 1998.

30 The Environment and Climate Change

30.1

Let Them Eat Pollution

The Economist

Lawrence Summers, chief economist of the World Bank, sent a memorandum to some colleagues on December 12th. *The Economist* has a copy. Some of the memo has caused a fuss within the Bank:

***

Just between you and me, shouldn't the World Bank be encouraging *more* migration of the dirty industries to the [Least Developed Countries] LDCs? I can think of three reasons:

1. The measurement of the costs of health-impairing pollution depends on the forgone earnings from increased morbidity and mortality. From this point of view a given amount of health-impairing pollution should be done in the country with the lowest cost, which will be the country with the lowest wages. I think the economic logic behind dumping a load of toxic waste in the lowest-wage country is impeccable and we should face up to that.
2. The costs of pollution are likely to be nonlinear as the initial increments of pollution probably have very low cost. I've always thought that under-populated countries in Africa are vastly *under*-polluted; their air quality is probably vastly inefficiently low (sic) compared to Los Angeles or Mexico City. Only the lamentable facts that so much pollution is generated by non-tradable industries (transport, electrical generation) and that the unit transport costs of solid waste are so high prevent world-welfare-enhancing trade in air pollution and waste.
3. The demand for a clean environment for aesthetic and health reasons is likely to have very high income-elasticity. The concern over an agent that causes a one-in-a-million change in the odds of prostate cancer is obviously going to be much higher in a country where people survive to get prostate cancer than in a country where under-5 mortality is 200 per thousand. Also, much of the concern over industrial atmospheric discharge is about visibility-impairing particulates. These discharges may have very little direct health impact. Clearly trade in goods that embody aesthetic pollution concerns could be welfare-enhancing.

Source: "Let Them Eat Pollution" (Lawrence Summer's Internal Memo dated December 12, 1991). *The Economist*, February 8, 1992.

While production is mobile the consumption of pretty air is a non-tradable.

***

The problem with the arguments against all of these proposals for more pollution in LDCs (intrinsic rights to certain goods, moral reasons, social concerns, lack of adequate markets, etc.) could be turned around and used more or less effectively against every Bank proposal for liberalization.

The language is crass, even for an internal memo. But look at it another way: Mr. Summers is asking questions that the World Bank would rather ignore—and, on the economics, his points are hard to answer. The Bank should make this debate public.

30.2

Pollution and the Poor

The Economist

Why "Clean Development" at any Price is a Curse on the Third World

Last week we published part of a memo sent by Lawrence Summers, the chief economist of the World Bank, to some colleagues. The memo pondered whether the Bank should "encourage more migration of the dirty industries to the third world" and said that "the economic logic of dumping a load of toxic waste in the lowest-wage country is impeccable." We objected to Mr. Summers's language but said his economics was hard to answer. Many people, it seems, disagree. Mr. Summers, as one commentator put it, views the world through "the distorting prism of market economics;" his ideas are "a recipe for ruin;" and he ignores the real challenge, which is "to find an equitable way of financing clean growth everywhere."

The Bank says that Mr. Summers, one of America's best economists, was merely trying to provoke debate. If so, it is to be hoped that he succeed—and that the Bank does not, instead, go silent on the subject. Much thinking on "clean development" is muddled. It is a confusion that threatens to cause great, if well-intentioned, harm to the world's poorest people.

The Clarifying Lens of Market Economics

Mr. Summers made three main points. First, the costs of pollution depend on earnings forgone through death or injury; these costs are lowest in the poorest countries. Second, costs rise disproportionately as pollution increases; so shifting pollution from dirty places to clean ones reduces costs. Third, people value a clean environment more as their incomes rise; if other things are equal, costs fall if pollution moves from rich places to poor ones. On the face of it, each seems a reason to dump toxic waste in Africa. All three arguments share a distinctive economic premise: environmental policy involves trade-off and should seek a balance between costs and benefits. If Mr. Summers is wrong, why is he wrong? Many greens would say his premise is false. They appear to believe that the only acceptable amount of pollution is zero or—which looks more sensible, but is almost as daft—that all pollution above, some arbitrarily low threshold must be stopped. This cannot be right. Controlling pollution is expensive (and many third world countries can ill afford the expense), and the benefits (especially when levels of pollution are already low) may be small. Greens and eco-skeptics may disagree about these costs and benefits, and thus about where the proper balance should lie. But the notion that such a balance should in principle be struck—and that, as a result, the "right" level of pollution is greater than zero and varies according to circumstances—ought to be uncontroversial. Without that idea, intelligent discussion of environmental policy is impossible.

But then Mr. Summers makes a further, crucial assumption. He supposes that the value of a life, or of years of life-expectancy, can be measured by an objective observer in terms of incomes per head—in other words, that an Englishman's life is worth more than the lives of a hundred Indians. This is naive utilitarianism reduced to an absurdity. It is so outlandish that even a distinguished economist should see that it provides no basis for World Bank policy.

True, many of the decisions that governments make (on health care, roads and so forth) reflect implicit, and sometimes explicit, answers to the question of how much an average life is worth. That is inescapable—but the key word, in a democracy at any rate, is "average." Few governments would care to defend a policy based on differences in valuations among groups—arguing, for instance, that society values an extra year of life for a white-collar worker more highly than that for a blue-collar worker. Yet this is the counterpart,

Source: "Pollution and the Poor," *The Economist*, February 15, 1992.

within a rich country, of what Mr. Summers appeared to be suggesting for the world.

Suppose then that the Bank and the other multilateral institutions regard the life of an African peasant as equal in value to the life of a broker on Wall Street—as they self-evidently should. What remains of Mr. Summers's arguments? The answer still is: more than most environmentalists care to admit.

The greatest cause of misery in the third world is poverty. This must guide the priorities of poor country governments and aid donors alike. If clean growth means slower growth, as it sometimes will, its human cost will be lives blighted by a poverty that would otherwise have been mitigated. That is why it would be wrong for the World Bank or anybody else to insist upon rich-country standards of environmental protection in developing countries. Often, policies that favour growth (such as setting world-market prices for energy and other resources) will lead to a cleaner environment, too; such policies should be vigorously promoted. But when a trade-off between cleaner air and less poverty has to be faced, most poor countries will rightly want to tolerate more pollution than rich countries do in return for more growth.

So the migration of industries, including "dirty" industries, to the third world is indeed desirable. Not because life there is cheap; if anything, for the opposite reason. Those who insist on "clean growth everywhere" must either deny that there is ever a trade-off between growth and pollution control—or else argue that imposing rich-country standards for clean air worldwide matters more than helping millions of people in the third world to escape their poverty.

Environmental policy is immensely complicated. The debate over Mr. Summers's memo is ignoring many issues altogether: global, as opposed to local, pollution; the links between trade policy and the environment; the opportunities to promote growth and a cleaner environment at the same time; and so on. In working through all this, economic method—the weighing of costs and benefits—is indispensable. Mr. Summers's morally careless arguments, intended seriously or otherwise, must not be allowed to discredit it.

30.3

The Interest-Based Explanation of International Environmental Policy

Detlef Sprinz and Tapani Vaahtoranta

Despite growing international environmental interdependence, the international system lacks a central authority to foster environmental protection. As a consequence, countries have adopted different policies to reduce international environmental problems. More specifically, costly regulations are not universally supported. In order to explain the success and failure of international environmental regulation, it is necessary to systematically focus on the factors that shape the environmental foreign policy of sovereign states. Since such an approach is missing from the literature, we develop an interest-based explanation of support for international environmental regulation and postulate what impact it should have on state preferences for international environmental regulation. . . .

After presenting the interest-based approach to international environmental regulation, we will briefly review the relevant literature on the environmental domains chosen. We shall then apply this concept to [one] prominent case of international air pollution regulation and compare our findings. Finally, in the article's last section, we point to some factors that merit attention in future research.

The Interest-Based Explanation

The interest-based explanation of the international politics of environmental management focuses on those domestic factors that shape a country's position in international environmental negotiations. In other words, the interest-based explanation is a unit-level explanation of international relations.[1] Unit-level explanations refer to elements located at the national or subnational levels, whereas systemic explanations suggest that differences at the unit-level produce less variation in outcomes than one would expect in the absence of systemic constraints. While unit-level explanations emphasize the varying characteristics of countries, systemic theories suggest that countries with different internal characteristics tend to behave in the same way if they are similarly positioned in the international system.

The interest-based perspective on international environmental regulation offers a partial but parsimonious view of how a country's preferences for international regulations are shaped. It focuses on a few unit-level factors that shape a country's behavior toward controlling international ecological problems. These preferences may change during international negotiations if the domestic characteristics of a country change. In addition, the bargaining process itself is a potential source of change. However, including a bargaining theory of international negotiations is beyond the scope of this article. The aim of this article is to present a parsimonious explanation by concentrating on two unit-level factors of major importance, namely, a country's ecological vulnerability toward pollution and the economic costs of pollution abatement.[2]

In our analysis we assume that each country is a self-interested actor that rationally seeks wealth and power by comparing the costs and benefits of alternative courses of action. To assert that countries pursue their national interest or seek wealth and power does not tell us what their specific preferences might be in a given situation. Thus, it is assumed for the issue-areas of ozone depletion and transboundary acidification that states are pursuing two main goals with the help of their environmental foreign policies. First, each country seeks to avoid vulnerability to air pollutants.[3] Each state is concerned in the first place with its own territory and pays only lip service to the idea of "spaceship Earth." In particular, countries pursue policies that minimize adverse environmental effects on their own citizens and

---

Source: Detlef Sprinz and Tapani Vaahtoranta, "The Interest-Based Explanation of International Environmental Policy," *International Organization* 48:1 (Winter, 1994), pp. 77–81, 86–95, and 104–105.

ecosystems ("ecological vulnerability"). Second, states are more inclined to participate in environmental protection when the costs of compliance are relatively minor. In addition a country may promote regulations that would benefit it by increasing international demand for its pollution abatement technology and its substitute compounds.

If all states pursue these goals, why do some promote international regulations vigorously while other countries do not? What makes some countries strive for tight international emission controls? Why do other countries try to prevent or slow internationally coordinated action toward environmental protection?

In most cases environmental policy is a reaction to environmental problems. Without actual or anticipated environmental degradation, there would be no need for environmental protection. Conversely, we hypothesize that the worse the state of the environment, the greater the incentives to reduce the ecological vulnerability of a state. National environmental policies, however, do not depend only on the degree of ecological vulnerability. There are several examples of countries that have not taken effective measures to address serious environmental problems in their territories. This holds because environmental policies are also shaped by socioeconomic and institutional capacities to protect the environment.[4] We wish to emphasize the role that economic capacity plays in determining the ability of the state to strive for tight emission controls. We furthermore suggest that different degrees of ecological vulnerability and of economic capacity explain much of the cross-national variance found in support for international environmental regulation (see below).

States are not equally affected by atmospheric pollution. A state can be a source of international pollution, its victim, or both. A victim country A, that is, a country that is ecologically vulnerable to emissions emanating from country B, should try to improve the state of its environment by asking country B to reduce its emissions. Therefore, we expect victim countries to favor international environmental protection. If the environment of a country is affected by domestic emissions, it is expected to favor international harmonization of environmental policies in order to avoid disadvantages in international competitiveness. Thus, there are two major reasons for a vulnerable country to push for international regulations. First, a country's unilateral abatement activities may be insufficient to substantively improve the state of its environment; and second, it would like to avoid putting its polluting industries at a comparative disadvantage in international markets. Conversely, if a country is in a position where foreign or domestic emissions do not much degrade its environment, it should be less eager to promote international environmental regulation.

Our understanding of the role of knowledge in environmental policymaking is somewhat different from that of the proponents of the theory of epistemic community.[5] According to this theory, the role of knowledge-based experts is significant in shaping a country's environmental policy. For example, Peter Haas suggests that those countries where policymakers turn to experts for advice are likely to become "pushers" for stringent international controls: "The pacing of national response [to the ozone threat] can be explained largely in terms of the extent of the epistemic community's influence on various governments and its ability to help them interpret the emerging scientific consensus and articulate appropriate policies."[6]

We do not deny the influence of the knowledge of experts on policy but emphasize the contents of knowledge rather than its mere existence. Since countries are often unequally affected by environmental problems, we expect that epistemic communities in ecologically vulnerable countries will exert stronger effects on governmental elites to seek international regulations as opposed to their impact in less ecologically vulnerable countries.[7]

In addition, a country's capacity to abate pollution influences its propensity to seek international environmental regulation. In general we expect that the greater the abatement costs of emission reductions, the more reluctant a country should be to support international regulations (other factors being equal). If, on the other hand, international environmental protection is relatively inexpensive, a country should be more inclined to subscribe to international environmental regulations. In particular abatement cost functions are influenced by the state of abatement (or prevention) technology, behavior modification (which can lead to price changes), and other factors. New and cost-reducing abatement technologies may reduce the (actual or anticipated) socioeconomic effort needed to support substantive regulations of the environment.

By combining indicators of a country's ecological vulnerability (low and high) with abatement costs (low and high), countries can be classified into four categories: "pushers," "intermediates," "draggers," and "bystanders" (see Figure 30.1). It is hypothesized that countries in cell 2 of Figure 30.1 (i.e., those expected to act as pushers in international negotiations) strive

Figure 30.1 Classification of a country's support for international environmental regulation.

Abatement costs	Ecological vulnerability: Low	Ecological vulnerability: High
Low	(1) Bystanders	(2) Pushers
High	(3) Draggers	(4) Intermediates

for stringent international regulation, while countries in cell 3 (i.e., draggers) oppose international environmental regulation. The countries falling in cell 4, namely, intermediate countries, find themselves in a particularly precarious situation. On the one hand they have ecological incentives to participate in international environmental regulation, while on the other hand they may not be willing to shoulder the substantial costs involved. Finally, countries falling into cell 1 (bystanders) should have little ecological interests in international regulations, but they are likely to take more ambitious positions than draggers because of the low costs associated with their negotiation position.

Besides typifying the anticipated behavior of states, we also suggest an ordinal ordering of intensity of support for substantive (rather than purely declaratory) environmental regulation. We expect that pusher countries take more stringent environmental positions than intermediate countries do, while the latter group is expected to favor environmental protection more often than draggers. The likelihood of bystanders' supporting environmental protection should fall between those for pushers and draggers; however, no direct comparison with the intermediate group seems to be appropriate on theoretical grounds.

The purpose of the remainder of this article is to assess the extent to which state policies toward controlling air pollution conform to the interest-based hypothesis outlined above. The empirical analysis of state policies is based on the negotiations leading to the signing of the 1987 Montreal Protocol on Substances That Deplete the Ozone Layer (control of stratospheric ozone-depleting substances) and the 1985 Helsinki Protocol (control of transboundary acidification), which are the first two major multilateral agreements that oblige national governments to reduce harmful air pollutants. . . .

Policies Toward Stratospheric Ozone

In the case of stratospheric ozone depletion, we hypothesize that a country's preference for international controls is determined by the vulnerability of its population to increased ultraviolet radiation and the economic cost of reducing CFCs.

UNEP played a major role in making ozone protection a top priority by funding research on the issue and sponsoring international meetings. In 1978 a scientific committee established by UNEP issued an assessment of the scientific evidence of ozone depletion and noted "the consistency in model predictions" but also recognized the continued existence of "large uncertainties in both the predicted ozone depletions and the understanding of their consequences."[8] In the mid-1980s, major difficulties concerning processes and observation of ozone depletion were not yet resolved. For example, it was difficult to quantify future ozone depletion: the estimates varied from 3 to 20 percent. This problem notwithstanding, all models predicted that the continued release of CFCs would damage the ozone layer. The general conclusions drawn by observers were incorporated in a report by UNEP in 1985 that summarized the contemporary understanding of stratospheric ozone depletion in the following way: "Nothing has been discovered to disturb the basic premise, identified some two decades ago, that the ozone layer is likely to be depleted if concentrations of trace gases, particularly chlorine containing substances, continue to increase. . . . Refinement of chemical theory points unwaveringly toward the existence of a problem of ozone layer modification and impacts for man and his environment that are universally bad."[9]

By the mid-1980s, sufficient consensus among natural scientists existed to start formal negotiations on the ozone regime, but governments could still point to the lack of hard evidence regarding the theory of stratospheric ozone depletion.

Increased ultraviolet radiation is believed to have several adverse effects, but we concentrate here on a direct human health effect, skin cancer. During the early 1980s more was known about human health effects than other consequences, and state representatives had been predominantly concerned with skin cancer.[10] It was known that ultraviolet light can produce considerable mortality and morbidity through the induction of skin cancer in white populations who live close to the equator and are therefore more exposed to ultraviolet radiation. Dark-skinned populations as well as populations living farther away from the equator were considered to be less affected by ultraviolet radiation. The threat of the effect of evenly spread global ozone depletion would have amplified the occurrence of skin cancer and exposed larger populations to the conditions found in equatorial regions.[11] In order to determine the vulnerability of a country to global ozone depletion, one would ideally combine its latitude and the skin type of its population. Since no data were found for the latter indicator, the ecological vulnerability of states is determined on the basis of the incidence of skin cancer among their populations in the mid-1970s. No assumption was made regarding the relationship between the local variation in the degree of ozone depletion and skin cancer incidence because of lack of adequate data during the early 1980s. The analysis that follows assumes that the division of populations into categories of high and low skin cancer incidence as observed in the mid-1970s remained unchanged until the mid-1980s. During the negotiations the incidence of skin cancer was linked to policies toward ozone depletion. A representative of Australia mentioned the high incidence in his country to explain Australia's interest in having the ozone layer protected.[12] In the words of a delegate from Malaysia, "Skin cancer doesn't seem to occur in tropical countries, which have been by and large bystanders" in the negotiations.[13]

Besides ecological vulnerability, the economic costs of reducing harmful emissions is assumed to shape a country's preferences and to affect its environmental foreign policy. Specifically we hypothesize that the higher the consumption of CFCs is per unit of gross national product (GNP), the higher the abatement costs should be and vice versa.

The incidence of skin cancer as well as the "intensity" of CFC consumption—measured as the amount of CFC consumption in relation to GNP per capita (for those states that attended most of the sessions of the working groups on the ozone regime and played visible roles in the negotiations)—are displayed in Table 30.1.[14]

On the basis of the data, we hypothesize that the ecological vulnerability of Australia, North America, and Northern Europe had been particularly high, and we expect the countries of these regions to favor strict environmental regulations. If the threshold of three cases of skin cancer per 100,000 inhabitants is employed to classify environmental vulnerability, ozone depletion should not have been regarded as a particularly serious problem in the Federal Republic of Germany (FRG), France, Italy, Japan, and the UK. Of the fourteen countries listed in Table 30.1, the former Soviet Union and the United States stand out because of their particularly high CFC intensity. Using a threshold of 3 metric tons per U.S. dollar of CFCs, the costs of reducing CFCs should also be relatively high in France, the FRG, Italy, Japan, and the UK. In the 1980s, these states should have had a strong economic interest in *opposing* significant reductions of CFC production and consumption.

Combining the vulnerability dimension and the abatement cost dimension, Figure 30.2 displays the categorization of individual countries according to the interest-based hypothesis that was displayed in Figure 30.1.

The states in the upper right-hand cell of Figure 30.2 (pushers), namely, Australia, Canada, Denmark, Finland, Norway, Sweden, and Switzerland, should have had both ecological and economic incentives to support significant emission reductions. Their populations are vulnerable to increased ultraviolet radiation, and emission reductions should not impose a great economic burden on them. Ecological and economic constraints should have made France, the FRG, Italy, Japan, the former Soviet Union, and the UK the most visible dragger states in the negotiations. According to our classification, the United States qualifies as an intermediate country.

Evaluation of the Interest-Based Explanation

The negotiations on the protection of the stratospheric ozone layer began when an ad hoc working group established by UNEP met for the first time in Stockholm in 1982. It held four sessions before the conclusion of the Vienna Convention on the Protection of the Ozone Layer three years later. Following this agreement, a new working group for the preparation of a protocol on emission reductions met three times in 1986–87 so that the Montreal Protocol could be signed in 1987. In order to assess the positions taken by countries during the negotiations, we rely mainly on written documentation. A time series of policy positions of all countries is unfortunately not available from accessible documentation. Country positions ranged from "no reductions" to virtual elimination of commercial use of CFCs.

The Nordic countries, namely, Denmark, Finland, Norway, and Sweden, strove for stringent internationally binding regulations from the very beginning of the

Table 30.1 Ecological vulnerability and abatement costs: stratospheric ozone depletion[a]

Country	Rate of skin cancer (number of cases per 100,000 mid-1970s)	Intensity of CFC consumption in 1986 (net atmospheric increase in relation to GNP per capita)[b]
Australia	16.3	1.1
Canada	3.2	1.5
Denmark	5.4	0.3
Federal Republic of Germany	2.1	3.6
Finland	3.9	0.3
France	2.5	3.7
Italy	3.0	4.7
Japan	0.3	4.5
Norway	8.3	0.1
Soviet Union	NA	22.2[c]
Sweden	5.5	0.3
Switzerland	5.2	0.3
United Kingdom	2.6	4.5
United States	7.2[d]	11.3

[a] Only countries that were participating actively in the negotiations are listed. No data were available for the former Soviet Union, but it was considered to be a country with a low incidence of skin cancer (see Thomas B. Stoel, Jr., Alan S. Miller, and Breck Milroy, *Fluorocarbon Regulation: An International Comparison* [Lexington, Mass.: D.C. Health, 1980]).

[b] Calculated in metric tons per U.S. dollar. GNP = gross national product.

[c] GNP per capita in 1980.

[d] White U.S. population only.

Sources. Data on skin cancer incidence are from J. Waterhouse et al., eds., "Cancer Incidence in Five Continents," in *IARC Scientific Publications* 4 (No. 42) (Lyon: International Agency for Research on Cancer), pp. 730–31. Data on CFC consumption are from World Resources Institute, *World Resources 1990–91* (New York: Oxford University Press, 1990), pp. 348–49. Data on GNP are from Tilastokeskus (Statistics Finland), *Suomen tilastollinen vuosikirja* (Statistical yearbook of Finland) (Helsinki: Valtion Painatuskeskus, 1988 and 1989), pp. 514–15 and 512–13, respectively.

negotiation process. Only the Netherlands clearly supported the Nordic initiative at the first session. In addition, Australia, Canada, and Switzerland were believed to be particularly interested in 1982 in bringing about an internationally binding treaty.[15] Before 1983, the United States had regarded further scientific evidence as a prerequisite for international regulations because of the socioeconomic consequences of emission controls.[16] By 1983, U.S. representatives pointed to the potentially serious impact of CFCs on the ozone layer and regarded it as prudent to take specific steps to control CFC emissions. However, while having banned all aerosol uses of CFCs in 1978, the U.S. government considered restrictions put on non-aerosol uses of CFCs as "inappropriate at this point in time."[17]

In 1984, Canada invited the most active states pushing for international regulations to Toronto to add momentum to the diplomatic process. Seven states besides Canada attended the meeting: Austria, Denmark, Finland, Norway, Sweden, Switzerland, and the United States.[18] While the goal of the "Toronto Group" was to offer an agreement on reducing the use

Figure 30.2 Predicted position of countries: stratospheric ozone depletion

Abatement costs	Ecological vulnerability: *Low*	Ecological vulnerability: *High*
Low	—	Australia, Canada, Denmark, Finland, Norway, Sweden, Switzerland
High	France, Federal Republic of Germany, Italy, Japan, former Soviet Union, United Kingdom	United States

of (aerosol) CFCs in spray cans and to sign the Vienna framework convention, besides the Toronto Group, only the Netherlands was willing to support a control protocol in 1984.[19] During the negotiations in 1986-87, the members of the Toronto Group began to demand that virtually all CFC emissions should be stopped. The United States in particular was active in pushing for significant reductions of ozone-depleting emissions. In 1987, it proposed that the production of CFCs and halons first be frozen at 1986 levels and later eliminated step by step except for uses for which substitutes were not commercially available.[20] Furthermore Canada, the Netherlands, and the Nordic countries were also pushing for large reductions in CFC production. The policy of the FRG also had changed by that time. As late as 1984, it had belonged to the group of dragger states. But the FRG acknowledged in 1987 that sufficient proof of CFC involvement in ozone layer modification had been accumulated to "justify immediate and world-wide action to restrict severely all CFC emissions."[21]

France, Italy, Japan, and the UK tried most consistently to prevent the adoption of drastic reductions in CFC production and consumption. Since three of these countries belonged to the EC, the EC views reflected their interests. In the beginning these states were reluctant even to discuss a control protocol, since they either did not regard it as necessary[22] or thought that any regulation concerning CFCs should be decided on after opening the framework convention for signature.[23] A recommendation put forward in 1984 by six countries, including France, the FRG, Italy, and the UK, was typical of the dragger states' attitude. It contained two modest measures. First, it recommended that the effects of potentially harmful substances on the ozone layer be investigated within three or five years before any decisions on regulations were to be taken. Second, the recommendation encouraged the establishment of a code of conduct for enterprises producing CFCs.[24]

The controversy between the actual (versus the predicted) pusher states (Canada, the Nordic countries, and the United States) and some dragger states (the EC and Japan) characterized the negotiations on the Montreal Protocol. During 1985-86, the EC was willing to limit only the production capacity of CFCs. The proposed ceiling was higher than the then-current production levels within the EC.[25] However by 1987, the EC was convinced that more stringent international action was necessary to control emissions. The new policy of the EC included, besides the freeze on the production of CFCs, an automatic reduction in CFC production and imports of 20 percent, based on 1986 levels.[26] In particular, Denmark, the FRG, and the Netherlands were pushing the EC to accept significant reductions in CFC production, while France and the UK still opposed tighter regulations. The Japanese policy also began to change by the end of the decade. In 1987, a representative of Japan considered it "realistic to establish immediate measures such as regulations on CFC-11 and CFC-12 and to consider to control other substances."[27]

The arguments used by the former Soviet Union during the negotiations resembled those of the dragger states, but the overall policy of the Soviet Union was cautious. Although Winfried Lang, who chaired the sessions that prepared the Montreal Protocol, described the Soviet stand in 1986-87 as "friendly to reductions" ("*eine reduktionsfreundliche Haltung*"),[28] and the press reported in 1987 that the Soviet Union favored big reductions, analysts of the negotiations tend to place the Soviet Union together with the EC and Japan as opponents of international regulations.[29]

Building on this summary of the negotiation process, we assess the validity of the impact of ecological vulnerability and abatement costs on a country's position in international environmental negotiations. The states in the upper right-hand cell of Figure 30.2 correspond well with our hypotheses. These states acted as the most consistent pushers in the negotiations. In addition, Austria and the Netherlands (with low CFC production intensities of 0.5 and 1.0, respectively) were supportive of the position of the predicted pushers.[30]

As expected on the basis of ecological and economic constraints, France, Italy, Japan, and the UK were the most visible dragger states in the negotiations. And the behavior of the former Soviet government is not necessarily surprising.

While the policies of the foregoing countries seem to support the interest-based explanation of support for international environmental regulation, the categorization of the FRG as a dragger state and of the United States as an intermediate is more problematic. Despite their domestic characteristics, both states began to support large reductions by the end of the negotiations. The United States unilaterally banned the aerosol use of CFCs as early as 1978, joined the Nordic countries in 1983 by calling for an international ban on the use of CFC-11 and CFC-12 in aerosol cans, and began to demand an end to all uses in 1986-87. The FRG opposed international regulations, though it reduced the use of aerosol CFC in the early 1980s. Its policy changed significantly in 1987 when the German representatives sought large international reductions in all CFC emissions and announced that they would aim to end production and consumption by the end of the century.

The Impact of Technology on Reducing Abatement Costs

Improvements of the state of technology seem to have played a major role in persuading the FRG and the United States to accept deep cuts in the production and consumption of CFCs. It appears that the environmental foreign policy of these countries toward ozone depletion changed as a result of the success of their industries in substituting new compounds for CFCs. In general the ability to produce substitutes reduces abatement costs and allows countries to favor more stringent regulations.

The covariation between the development of alternative compounds and policy is particularly evident in the United States. As mentioned above, the United States unilaterally banned the manufacture and shipment of CFC-propelled aerosols in 1978. The industry's response was muted, since technically feasible and economically acceptable alternatives existed for most propellant uses of CFCs.[31] Another reason for the relatively low cost of the ban was that, from an economic perspective, aerosol use was not as important as were other uses of CFCs, such as for refrigeration and for air-conditioning.

With respect to international controls on CFCs, the United States had concluded by the early 1980s that it would not profit from being the only country to invoke stringent domestic standards on the use of CFCs. Accordingly the U.S. government continued to oppose international regulations with the exception of controls on the aerosol use of CFCs. In 1986-87, however, the U.S. government began to strive for ending all uses for CFCs. It is noteworthy that the first reports about the development of new substitutes for CFCs appeared in the press at this point in time. It was generally believed that the new position of the United States was bolstered by success in developing new forms of chemical compounds.[32]

Industrial representatives originally opposed controls on CFCs, but by 1986 their opposition had softened considerably. In 1986, the Alliance for Responsible CFC Policy, an industry lobby group, announced that its members were prepared to support a global limit on the growth of CFC production. Du Pont, a company based in the United States and the largest single producer of CFCs, took an even stronger position by calling for a worldwide limit on emissions of the chemicals. This new attitude toward CFC regulation was preceded by extensive industry research on substitutes for CFC-11 and CFC-12. Du Pont, for example, initiated a large research effort as early as the mid-1970s. It ceased this line of research in the beginning of the 1980s, but by 1986 the company had reactivated its research program and announced that suitable alternatives could be available within five years.[33] Two years later Du Pont announced plans to build the world's first commercial-scale plant to produce a substitute for CFC-12[34] and supported "an orderly transition to a total phaseout" of the most harmful CFCs.[35] It was later specified that the target was to complete the phaseout by no later than the end of the century.

Availability of substitutes for specific CFCs could also explain why the policy of the FRG toward regulating CFCs changed. Its government asked the chemical industry in 1987 for a near-total elimination of CFC production and consumption by the year 2000. The government announced that the reduction would begin by concentrating on the aerosol industry, and industry was willing to comply with the plan since it had already gone a long way toward the elimination of all but essential aerosol uses of CFCs.[36]

The significance of the change in positions of the FRG and the United States is even more evident if compared with the situation in the main dragger states. Before the policies of the EC and Japan began to change, their representatives expressed concern during the negotiations that U.S. companies, with their successful development of substitutes, might enjoy a significant competitive advantage if drastic international regulations were adopted. Although the aerosol use of CFCs had declined steadily in the EC as a result of increased substitution by less-expensive propellants,[37] EC representatives complained in 1987 that U.S. companies would benefit from a control protocol with drastic regulations, since they were ahead in the search for substitutes.[38] In the words of a Japanese representative to the ozone negotiations, it was "very important that contracting parties to the protocol should have common access to technological information on substitute chemicals." He also proposed that "a system of international cooperation should be established with a view to making technological information available to all contracting states, thus avoiding the monopoly of that information by specific countries."[39]

Given the positive covariation between the development of CFC substitutes and the more pro-regulatory preferences of national governments, two causal chains might be suggested. First, technological advances led to more ambitious preferences for environmental regulation. Second, public policy can force the development of more efficient environmental technologies. The latter causal chain is emphasized by Benedick, who suggests that changing scientific knowledge and public perceptions of environmental problems are needed to persuade industries to prepare themselves for more stringent environmental regulations.[40] Similarly Alan Miller believes that without anticipation of a regulatory intervention, industry has little incentive to search for alternatives for existing products or production methods.[41] These hypotheses are compatible with the interest-based explanation of international environmental regulation: a growing public perception of the severity of adverse ecological effects puts pressure on governments and creates expectations about regulatory policy. As a result, industry starts preparing itself for more stringent environmental controls by improving the state of abatement technology. As a consequence, lowered abatement costs enhance the likelihood of substantive international environmental regulation.

In conclusion, as a result of a growing perception of the vulnerability to ozone depletion in combination with advances in developing substitutes for CFCs, all states began gradually to perceive common interests in protecting the stratospheric ozone layer by phasing out harmful chemicals. . . .

Concluding Remarks and Suggestions for Future Research

We hypothesized that the interest-based approach provides a parsimonious explanation of support for international environmental regulation. Operationalized as the degree of ecological vulnerability and the costs of abatement, we expected that countries could be typified as pushers, intermediates, draggers, and bystanders in international negotiations. In addition, we found that technological factors may lessen actual or anticipated abatement costs and thereby increase the propensity of a country to support international environmental regulation.

While many of the basic propositions have been supported by the national positions during the negotiations on both the Montreal and the Helsinki Protocols, it remains unclear why we have two different types of draggers and more universal support for international regulation in the former case than in the latter case. Therefore, we suggest a few additional domestic factors for future research that could increase explanatory power for both negotiations.

Changes in value preferences, domestic interest representation of mass political attitudes, and industry lobbying efforts could each play an important role. As can be shown for the member countries of the EC, value change, that is, the shift from an emphasis on materialist values to post materialist values,[42] is strongly related to environmental concern and environmental action.[43] In addition, Western government officials stress the role that public attitudes on the environment play in bringing about domestic and international regulation of pollutants. In parallel to the increasing importance of environmental issues to the general public, green or ecological parties have developed in many countries in Western, Central, and Eastern Europe. Furthermore, traditional parties have discovered the importance of the issue in sustaining electoral support. . . .

In addition to these mass political pressures on national governments, a differentiated industry pressure model could be developed. By explicitly linking abatement costs and international trade in environmental technologies, on the one hand, to the interests of major polluting industries and the abatement technology sector, on the other hand, a differentiated model of industry support for international environmental regulation can be developed.[44]

In conclusion, the interest-based approach provides a parsimonious explanation of the positions taken by governments on the protection of the international environment. More detailed modeling of the domestic policy component may enhance our understanding of why countries wish to allocate scarce resources to substantial improvements of the international environment.

Notes

1. See J. David Singer, "The Level-of-Analysis Problem in International Relations," in Klaus Knorr and Sidney Verba, eds., *The International System: Theoretical Essays* (Princeton, N.J.: Princeton University Press, 1961), pp. 77–92.

2. The term "abatement costs," as used in this article, reflects the resource outlays associated with a governmental position. It does not reflect damage costs. For international comparisons, abatement costs are expressed as a share of gross domestic product (GDP) or gross national product (GNP) so as to reflect a country's "relative effort."

3. Robert O. Keohane and Joseph S. Nye, *Power and Interdependence* (New York: Harper Collins, 1989).

4. Volker von Prittwitz, *Das Katastrophenparadox: Elemente einer Theorie der Umweltpolitik* (The catastrophe paradox: Elements of a theory of environmental policy) (Opladen, Germany: Leske and Budrich, 1990), pp. 103–15.

5. The term "epistemic community" refers to a knowledge-based transnational network of specialists whose members share common views about the causes of environmental problems and the policies to control them. See Peter M. Haas, *Saving the Mediterranean: The Politics of International Environmental Cooperation* (New York: Columbia University Press, 1990).

6. Peter M. Haas, "Banning Chlorofluorocarbons: Epistemic Community Efforts to Protect Stratospheric Ozone," *International Organization* 46 (Winter 1992), pp. 189–224 and p. 215 in particular.

7. This possibility is also mentioned by the proponents of the theory of epistemic communities. See p. 30 of Peter Haas, "Introduction: Epistemic Communities and International Policy Coordination," *International Organization* 46 (Winter 1992), pp. 1–35.

8. Thomas B. Stoel, Jr., "Fluorocarbons: Mobilizing Concern and Action," in David A. Kay and Harold K. Jacobson, eds., *Environmental Protection: The International Dimension* (Totowa, N.J.: Allenheld, Osmun, 1983), pp. 45–74. The quotations are drawn from p. 57.

9. UNEP, "Assessment of Risks to the Ozone Layer," 1st Meeting of Steering Committee to Plan Workshops on Chlorofluorocarbons, 17–18 September 1985, mimeograph, p. 6.

10. We refer to the knowledge available to decision makers in the early 1980s rather than since the late 1980s. Only after the conclusion of the Montreal Protocol did it become evident that the thinning of the stratospheric ozone layer disproportionally affects the polar regions.

11. Robin R. Jones, "Consequences for Human Health of Stratospheric Ozone Depletion," in R. Russell Jones and T. Wigley, eds., *Ozone Depletion: Health and Environmental Consequences* (New York: John Wiley & Sons, 1989), pp. 207–27.

12. UNEP, Ad Hoc Working Group of Legal and Technical Experts for the Preparation of a Protocol on Chlorofluorocarbons to the Vienna Convention for the Protection of the Ozone Layer (Vienna Group), "Report of the Ad Hoc Working Group on the Work of Its Second Session," UNEP/WG 167/2, 4 March 1987, p. 7.

13. Quoted from Craig R. Whitney, "EC Official Says Europeans Soon Can shield Ozone Layer," *International Herald Tribune*, 6 March 1989, p. 5.

14. Skin cancer may also be caused by other factors. However, given the small number of cases, a multiple regression analysis of the various causes of skin cancer appears not to be feasible.

15. Harald Heimsoeth, "The Protection of the Ozone Layer," *Environmental Policy and Law* 10 (April 1983), pp. 34–36.

16. Ibid., p. 35.

17. UNEP, Ad Hoc Working Group of Legal and Technical Experts for the Elaboration of a Global Framework Convention for the Protection of the Ozone Layer (hereafter Working Group for Ozone Layer Protection), "Draft Annex Concerning Measures to Control, Limit, and Reduce the Use and Emissions of Fully Halogenated Chlorofluorocar bons (CFCs) for the Protection of the Ozone Layer, Submitted by Finland, Norway, and Sweden," UNEP/WG 94/4 Add. 3, 17 October 1983, pp. 1–2.

18. Australia had also been invited, but it did not participate in the conference.

19. UNEP, Working Group for Ozone Layer Protection, "Article II to the Protocol: Control of Use of CFCs, Proposal by the Expert from the Netherlands," UNEP/WG 110/CRP.5, 23 October 1984.

20. UNEP, Vienna Group, "Report of the Ad Hoc Working Group on the Work of Its Third Session," UNEP/WG 172/2, 8 May 1987, p. 5.

21. Ibid, p. 7.

22. UNEP, Working Group for Ozone Layer Protection, "Report of the Working Group," UNEP/WG 78/13, 17 June 1983, p. 3.

23. UNEP, Working Group for Ozone Layer Protection, "Draft Annex Concerning Measures to Control, Limit, and Reduce the Use and Emissions of Fully Halogenated Chlorofluorocarbons (CFCs) for the Protection of the Ozone

Layer, Submitted by Finland, Norway, and Sweden," UNEP/WG 94/4 Add. 1, 15 September 1983, p. 3.

24. UNEP, Working Group for Ozone Layer Protection, "Recommendation of the Ad Hoc Working Group of Legal and Technical Experts for the Elaboration of a Global Framework Convention for the Protection of the Ozone Layer for a Decision to be Taken by the Governing Council of UNEP," UNEP/WG 94/CRP 34, 19 January 1984.

25. See UNEP, Conference of Plenipotentiaries on the Protection of the Ozone Layer, "Final Report of the Ad Hoc Working Group of Legal and Technical Experts for the Elaboration of a Global Framework Convention for the Protection of the Ozone Layer," UNEP/IG 53/4, Annex II, 28 January 1985, p. 4; and UNEP, Vienna Group, "Draft Report of the Ad Hoc Working Group on the Work of Its First Session," UNEP/WG 151/L.4, 15 January 1987, pp. 6–7.

26. UNEP/WG 172/2, pp. 5–6.

27. UNEP/WG 167/2, p. 6.

28. Winifried Lang, "Diplomatie zwischen Okonomie und Okologie: Das Beispiel des Ozonver-trags von Montreal" (Diplomacy between economics and ecology: The case of the Montreal Protocol), *Europa-Archiv* 43 (25 February 1988), p. 108.

29. See Benedick, *Ozone Diplomacy: New Directions in Safeguarding the Planet*, p. 85: and Haas, "Banning Chlorofluorocarbons," p. 209.

30. Unfortunately, no data are available on the rate of skin cancer in the mid-1970s for Austria or for the Netherlands.

31. Thomas B. Stoel, Jr., Alan S. Miller, and Breck Milroy, *Fluorocarbon Regulation: An International Comparison* (Lexington, Mass.: D.C. Heath, 1980), p. 221.

32. *International Herald Tribune*, 19 December 1986, p. 4.

33. See pp. 357–58 of James K. Sebenius, "Challenging Conventional Explanations of International Cooperation: Negotiation Analysis of the Case of Epistemic Communities," *International Organization* 46 (Winter 1992), pp. 323–65; and Benedick, *Ozone Diplomacy: New Directions in Safeguarding the Planet*, p. 33; and Morrisette, "The Evolution of Policy Responses to Stratospheric Ozone Depletion," pp. 815–16.

34. Glas, "Protecting the Ozone Layer," p. 150.

35. DuPont is quoted in *International Herald Tribune*, 29 March 1988, p. 4.

36. Steven Dickman, "West Germany Strides Towards CFC Elimination by 2000," *Nature* 327 (14 May 1987), p. 93. A similar observation has been made by Benedick. In explaining the differences in 1990 within the EC on the policy toward regulation, Benedick remarks that the FRG announced that it will phase out CFCs in 1995 and other ozone-depleting substances before the end of the century. This took place after the federal government of the FRG had concluded that alternatives to the major harmful chemicals were close to commercial feasibility for nearly all applications. See Benedick, *Ozone Diplomacy: New Directions in Safeguarding the Planet*, pp. 164–65.

37. James K. Hammitt, et al., *Product Uses and Market Trends of Potential Ozone-depleting Substances, 1985–2000* (Santa Monica, Calif.: Rand Corporation, 1986), p. 17.

38. Debora MacKenzie, "Chemical Giants Battle over Ozone Holes," *New Scientist* 114 (23 April 1987), p. 22.

39. UNEP/WG.172/2,p.6.

40. Benedick, *Ozone Diplomacy: New Directions in Safeguarding the Planet*, pp. 30–31.

41. Alan Miller, "The Development of Substitutes for Chlorofluorocarbons: Public-Private Cooperation and Environmental Policy," *Ambio* 19 (October 1990), pp. 338–40.

42. See Ronald Inglehart, *The Silent Revolution: Changing Values and Political Styles Among Western Publics* (Princeton, N.J.: Princeton University Press, 1977); and Ronald Inglehart, *Culture Shift in Advanced Industrial Society* (Princeton, N.J.: Princeton University Press, 1990).

43. See Detlef Sprinz, "Environmental Concern and Environmental Action in Western Europe: Concepts, Measurements and Implications," presented at the 86th annual meeting of the American Political Science Association, 30 August–2 September 1990, San Francisco.

44. See Sprinz, "Why Countries Support International Environmental Agreements," chaps. 5–7.

30.4

What to Do About Climate Change

Ruth Greenspan Bell

The Heat is On

In the years ahead, climate change will have a significant impact on every aspect of the daily lives of all human beings—possibly greater even than war. Shifting precipitation patterns and ocean currents could change where and how food crops grow. If icecaps melt and low-lying areas are flooded, as is predicted, entire populations could be forced to move to higher ground. The tsunami of 2004 and Hurricane Katrina, in 2005, provided vivid examples of what large-scale climactic catastrophes entail.

And yet climate change remains low on the list of most countries' foreign policy concerns and has yet to be treated as a subject for serious, sustained action. Part of the problem is that the threat still feels abstract. Despite accumulating evidence, the full impact of climate change has not yet been felt; for now, it can only be modeled and forecast. Much of the current planning for meeting this challenge has also had a somewhat abstract feeling. The most prominent action plan devised so far is based on a lot of economic theory and only a bit of empirical evidence, derived from U.S. efforts to deal with acid rain.

Mobilizing public attention around problems that have not fully manifested themselves has historically been difficult. This was true of the threat of terrorism before the attacks of September 11, 2001, and it will likely be even truer of climate change. Most climactic models now predict continued deterioration, but the signs that are currently visible, such as the thawing of the permafrost, lack the drama of two airplanes piercing the World Trade Center. Like the frog in the pan of heating water that does not notice the temperature rising until it is too late, human beings have been lulled into believing that they have many years to deal with climate change. When dramatic changes finally do occur, it will be too late for remedial action.

Pessimistic experts who believe the world has already reached the point of no return advise that society adapt to the new conditions rather than try to correct them. Many politicians are more optimistic. In July 2005, leaders of the Group of Eight highly industrialized states (G-8) pledged to put themselves "on a path to slow and, as the science justifies, stop and then reverse the growth of greenhouse gases." Assuming there still is time to act, the question is, how?

Curbing greenhouse gas emissions, a problem that took many years to develop, will be a prolonged and messy process. But two actions are called for now. The first is to revise the assumptions behind currently proposed fixes, namely emissions-trading regimes, which by themselves actually do too little to cap pollution. The second is to devise strategies customized to the needs and means of the governments that must implement them, distinguishing developed countries from developing ones. In the former, where the necessary legal and regulatory structures, if not always the actual laws, are already in place, the enforcement of environmental standards is largely a matter of political will. In the developing world, limiting greenhouse gas emissions is a more complicated job that requires empowering environment ministers, making an economic case for environmental protection, developing regulatory skills that currently do not exist, and enlisting the help of both civil society and the public sector.

The Gas on Emissions

Current proposals for curbing carbon dioxide emissions start with the reasonable assumption that the first step toward fighting climate change is to make the issue a priority. And so over the past three decades, the standard response to global environmental threats has been to draft international agreements. There are now some 900 environmental treaties on the books. Unfortunately, few have achieved any genuine reductions in pollution. Under the UN Framework Convention on Climate Change, which entered into force in 1994, and its controversial Kyoto Protocol,

---

which entered into force after Russia ratified it in 2005, some industrialized nations agreed to reduce greenhouse gas emissions between 2008 and 2012 to levels below those of 1990. . . .

Worse, current policies aimed at stemming climate change may be inadequate. The generally accepted plan takes an approach with essentially two drivers—one based on economic incentives, the other on technological ones. The first driver, now enshrined in the Kyoto Protocol, is a sophisticated global system for trading greenhouse gas emissions modeled on the successful U.S. "cap-and-trade" system designed to control the release of sulfur dioxide (which produces acid rain). Relying on a trading system assumes that the opportunity to profit from reducing greenhouse gas emissions will motivate industrial emitters, wherever they are located, to change the way they operate power plants and factories. Implicit in this assumption is the belief that advanced technology will help emitters change their ways, because technology can always help solve complex problems. The Kyoto Protocol thus created two flexible mechanisms: the Clean Development Mechanism (CDM), which facilitates trading with the developing world, and Joint Implementation, which allows "donor" countries to invest in pollution-abatement measures in "host" countries in return for "credits" they can use to meet their own pollution-abatement targets. . . .

It is highly unlikely that anything approximating the rigor of the U.S. system can be devised to control climate change worldwide. Enforcement has long been the Achilles' heel of international environmental agreements, largely because countries submit to international oversight, which they see as a threat to their sovereignty, only with the greatest reluctance. Although some progress was made on the issue of noncompliance at a recent meeting of the parties to the Kyoto Protocol, the enforcement plan that came out of it assumes that countries will not risk being shut out of participating in the agreement's flexible trading mechanisms. Even if a more rigorous compliance regime could be instituted, obtaining accurate measurements of actual emissions would be difficult.

Much of the discussion, meanwhile, has centered on how to refine the existing trading mechanisms rather than on the most difficult but most important issue: how to set and enforce caps on greenhouse gas emissions. It is the commitment to make steady reductions in harmful emissions that will make or break the overall scheme. Caps have never worked without serious compliance efforts backed up by old-fashioned penalties against laggards and cheaters. . . . Global trading is no magic remedy. Reducing emissions worldwide requires exactly the same attention to conventional regulatory processes as does effective domestic regulation. . . .

So what will motivate industrial plants that are currently free to pollute to clean up their act? This is where technology is supposed to come into play. Under Joint Implementation, outsiders with the economic incentive to control emissions of carbon dioxide are expected to provide the appropriate technology. But even if the lucky manager of a firm being offered, say, free equipment to capture emissions understands that he is being given something of value, he might not have the incentive to pay for running and maintaining the equipment. If anything, experience shows that he is unlikely to turn it on without the watchful eye of disinterested enforcement bodies looking on. Evidence from China demonstrates that even plants equipped with superior pollution equipment do not run those controls when doing so proves inconvenient.

No wonder some observers are now questioning whether trading mechanisms can contribute to a reliable reduction of greenhouse gas emissions. . . .

Starting Small

For the developing world and much of the former Soviet bloc, where Westerners will inevitably look for emissions credits, achieving steady reductions in emissions will require fundamental reform. Trading and technology are great policy tools, but they must be part of a larger program whose core objective is the systematic reduction of greenhouse gas emissions.

The first steps toward the effective enforcement of high environmental standards should be to adjust expectations on all sides and encourage developing countries to set goals they can meet, as a preliminary move toward developing a more rigorous regime. Achievable caps would not be very ambitious at first. But setting them could help mobilize governments and get them moving in the right direction, helping them gain real experience in managing greenhouse gas emissions. With some practice and success under their belts, governments would then be in a position to tighten the caps.

For any such effort to succeed, environmental regulation will have to become a priority in the developing world; that means making a serious commitment to achieving whatever caps on greenhouse gas emissions that are deemed appropriate. In a handful of countries, regulation is working; in too many others, it is not. Effective environmental regulation will require close cooperation between those leaders who are concerned about the perils of greenhouse gases and those governments whose cooperation is needed to reduce emissions. . . .

Environmental officials will have a better chance of finding their way into the inner circle if they can overcome the perception that environmental controls are a luxury. (Echoing many finance ministers throughout the world, Russian President Vladimir Putin has said that the order of business should be "first the economy, then the environment.") In addition to making the case for energy efficiency, clean air, and drinkable water, environment ministers must show that what they offer not only is consistent with growth but also will facilitate it, because pollution from factories and power plants represents lost money. In Poland, higher prices for energy alone have helped reduce carbon dioxide emissions. Environment ministers must also spotlight the contribution of pollution to worsening public health, an issue so acute in some countries that it is causing social instability. In China, villagers increasingly stage demonstrations to voice their unhappiness with the government's failure to control pollution. Whoever can produce a plan to respond to legitimate grievances about, say, poor air quality will contribute to stability and thereby boost the work force's productivity.

Equally important is achieving independent oversight, to make sure that existing laws actually do what they claim to do. . . . Reliable enforcement also makes good business sense, because it signals regularity to investors, who sometimes care less about what the rules are than about whether their enforcement is predictable or arbitrary.

All Aboard

Another important task is to help developing countries gain appropriate regulatory skills by providing them with training and equipment. Countries without strong experience need assistance to build effective monitoring, inspection, and enforcement practices. Sporadic efforts have been made to help some states in the former Soviet bloc develop regulatory capacity. But the help has not been consistent or systematic. Development assistance efforts have often tried, unsuccessfully, to import Western economic practices into the law, traditions, and culture of the developing world.

A better approach would be to devise practices and institute reforms that are customized to each country's particular circumstances. Take the role of law. Western reformers often assume that enacting a law will produce its objective. But in China, for example, where the strength of personal relationships has guided business and other significant interactions for millennia, relying on legal obligations is very new. In addition to helping the Chinese develop a new legal ethic, reformers must also consider enforcing environmental standards in ways more consistent with local culture, such as through the naming and shaming of polluting plants. . . . Enforcement through locally appropriate measures would breed demand for other enforcement tools, and at that point the developing world might turn to North America and Western Europe for additional compliance methods and techniques.

Implicit in the hope for such progress is the importance of public opinion. Where the government fails to act or to enforce laws, the public can be a force for reform. . . . Public participation is also critical in countries with strong enforcement bodies, because no government has the resources to stop all noncompliance. The right to bring a suit is particularly useful when governments are inactive. . . .

Sometimes the private sector will be motivated to take the initiative. A small number of multinational corporations, General Electric and Shell among them, are putting their own environmental best-practices plans into action at plants worldwide—a move that could embolden local regulators and pressure local companies to improve their habits.

Building the capacity to deliver verifiable reductions of greenhouse gases is tedious work. But with persistence, political will, and some help, regulatory skills can be improved. Internal pressure can speed the way and supplement governments' scarce enforcement resources. The overall objective should be to develop a culture of strict environmental compliance that will ensure that promises of emissions reductions will be met. Focusing on capping emissions requires steadiness of purpose, imperviousness to the siren song of short-term interests, and the willingness to commit significant resources. But it is a realistic and effective strategy for fighting a problem that reaches deep into every economy. Harnessing the magic of the market and enlisting technology may become significant tools in combating climate change, but they will not work on their own. And like climate change itself, this sobering truth is best faced sooner rather than later.

31 A New International Order?

31.1

The End of History?

Francis Fukuyama

In watching the flow of events over the past decade or so, it is hard to avoid the feeling that something very fundamental has happened in world history. The past year has seen a flood of articles commemorating the end of the Cold War, and the fact that "peace" seems to be breaking out in many regions of the world. Most of these analyses lack any larger conceptual framework for distinguishing between what is essential and what is contingent or accidental in world history, and are predictably superficial. If Mr. Gorbachev were ousted from the Kremlin or a new Ayatollah proclaimed the millennium from a desolate Middle Eastern capital, these same commentators would scramble to announce the rebirth of a new era of conflict.

And yet, all of these people sense dimly that there is some larger process at work, a process that gives coherence and order to the daily headlines. The twentieth century saw the developed world descend into a paroxysm of ideological violence, as liberalism contended first with the remnants of absolutism, then Bolshevism and fascism, and finally an updated Marxism that threatened to lead to the ultimate apocalypse of nuclear war. But the century that began full of self-confidence in the ultimate triumph of Western liberal democracy seems at its close to be returning full circle to where it started: not to an "end of ideology" or a convergence between capitalism and socialism, as earlier predicted, but to an unabashed victory of economic and political liberalism.

The triumph of the West, of the Western *idea*, is evident first of all in the total exhaustion of viable systematic alternatives to Western liberalism. In the past decade, there have been unmistakable changes in the intellectual climate of the world's two largest communist countries, and the beginnings of significant reform movements in both. But this phenomenon extends beyond high politics and it can be seen also in the ineluctable spread of consumerist Western culture in such diverse contexts as the peasants' markets and color television sets now omnipresent throughout China, the cooperative restaurants and clothing stores opened in the past year in Moscow, the Beethoven piped into Japanese department stores, and the rock music enjoyed alike in Prague, Rangoon, and Tehran.

What we may be witnessing is not just the end of the Cold War, or the passing of a particular period of postwar history, but the end of history as such: that is, the end point of mankind's ideological evolution and the universalization of Western liberal democracy as the final form of human government. This is not to say that there will no longer be events to fill the pages of *Foreign Affairs's* yearly summaries of international relations, for the victory of liberalism has occurred primarily in the realm of ideas or consciousness and is as yet incomplete in the real or material world. But there are powerful reasons for believing that it is the ideal that will govern the material world *in the long run.* To understand how this is so, we must first consider some theoretical issues concerning the nature of historical change. . . .

***

Have we in fact reached the end of history? Are there, in other words, any fundamental "contradictions" in human life that cannot be resolved in the context of modern liberalism, that would be resolvable by an alternative political-economic structure? If we accept the idealist premises laid out above, we must seek an answer to this question in the realm of ideology and consciousness. Our task is not to answer exhaustively the challenges to liberalism promoted by every crackpot messiah around the world, but only those that are embodied in important social or political forces and movements, and which are therefore part of world history. For our purposes, it matters very little what strange thoughts occur to people in Albania or Burkina Faso, for we are interested in what one could in some sense call the common ideological heritage of mankind.

In the past century, there have been two major challenges to liberalism, those of fascism and of communism. The former[1] saw the political weakness, materialism, anomie, and lack of community of the West as fundamental contradictions in liberal societies that could only be resolved by a strong state that forged a new "people" on the basis of national exclusiveness. Fascism was destroyed as a living ideology by World War II. This was a defeat, of course, on a very material level, but it amounted to a defeat of the idea as well. What destroyed fascism as an idea was not universal moral revulsion against it, since plenty of people were willing to endorse the idea as long as it seemed the wave of the future, but its lack of success. After the war, it seemed to most people that German fascism as well as its other European and Asian variants were bound to self-destruct. There was no material reason why new fascist movements could not have sprung up again after the war in other locales, but for the fact that expansionist ultranationalism, with its promise of unending conflict leading to disastrous military defeat, had completely lost its appeal. The ruins of the Reich chancellory as well as the atomic bombs dropped on Hiroshima and Nagasaki killed this ideology on the level of consciousness as well as materially, and all of the proto-fascist movements spawned by the German and Japanese examples like the Peronist movement in Argentina or Subhas Chandra Bose's Indian National Army withered after the war.

The ideological challenge mounted by the other great alternative to liberalism, communism, was far more serious. Marx, speaking Hegel's language, asserted that liberal society contained a fundamental contradiction that could not be resolved within its context, that between capital and labor, and this contradiction has constituted the chief accusation against liberalism ever since. But surely, the class issue has actually been successfully resolved in the West. As Kojève (among others) noted, the egalitarianism of modern America represents the essential achievement of the classless society envisioned by Marx. This is not to say that there are not rich people and poor people in the United States, or that the gap between them has not grown in recent years. But the root causes of economic inequality do not have to do with the underlying legal and social structure of our society, which remains fundamentally egalitarian and moderately redistributionist, so much as with the cultural and social characteristics of the groups that make it up, which are in turn the historical legacy of premodern conditions. Thus black poverty in the United States is not the inherent product of liberalism, but is rather the "legacy of slavery and racism" which persisted long after the formal abolition of slavery.

As a result of the receding of the class issue, the appeal of communism in the developed Western world, it is safe to say, is lower today than any time since the end of the First World War. This can be measured in any number of ways: in the declining membership and electoral pull of the major European communist parties, and their overtly revisionist programs; in the corresponding electoral success of conservative parties from Britain and Germany to the United States and Japan, which are unabashedly pro-market and anti-statist; and in an intellectual climate whose most "advanced" members no longer believe that bourgeois society is something that ultimately needs to be overcome. This is not to say that the opinions of progressive intellectuals in Western countries are not deeply pathological in any number of ways. But those who believe that the future must inevitably be socialist tend to be very old, or very marginal to the real political discourse of their societies.

One may argue that the socialist alternative was never terribly plausible for the North Atlantic world, and was sustained for the last several decades primarily by its success outside of this region. But it is precisely in the non-European world that one is most struck by the occurrence of major ideological transformations.

Surely the most remarkable changes have occurred in Asia. Due to the strength and adaptability of the indigenous cultures there, Asia became a battleground for a variety of imported Western ideologies early in this century. Liberalism in Asia was a very weak reed in the period after World War I; it is easy today to forget how gloomy Asia's political future looked as recently as ten or fifteen years ago. It is easy to forget as well how momentous the outcome of Asian ideological struggles seemed for world political development as a whole.

The first Asian alternative to liberalism to be decisively defeated was the fascist one represented by Imperial Japan. Japanese fascism (like its German version) was defeated by the force of American arms in the Pacific war, and liberal democracy was imposed on Japan by a victorious United States. Western capitalism and political liberalism when transplanted to Japan were adapted and transformed by the Japanese in such a way as to be scarcely recognizable.[2] Many Americans are now aware that Japanese industrial organization is very different from that prevailing in the United States or Europe, and it is questionable what relationship the factional maneuvering that takes place with the governing Liberal Democratic Party bears to democracy. Nonetheless, the very fact that the essential elements of economic and political liberalism have been so successfully grafted onto uniquely Japanese traditions and institutions guarantees their survival in the long run. More important is the contribution that Japan has made in turn to world history by following in the footsteps of the United States to create a truly universal consumer culture that has become both a symbol and an under pinning of the universal homogenous state. . . .

The economic success of the other newly industrializing countries (NICs) in Asia following on the example of Japan is by now a familiar story. What is important from a Hegelian standpoint is that political liberalism has been following economic liberalism, more slowly than many had hoped but with seeming inevitability. Here again we see the victory of the idea of the universal homogenous state. South Korea had developed into a modern, urbanized society with an increasingly large and well-educated middle class that could not possibly be isolated from the larger democratic trends around them. Under these circumstances it seemed intolerable to a large part of this population that it should be ruled by an anachronistic military regime while Japan, only a decade or so ahead in economic terms, had parliamentary institutions for over forty years. . . .

But the power of the liberal idea would seem much less impressive if it had not infected the largest and oldest culture in Asia, China. The simple existence of communist China created an alternative pole of ideological attraction, and as such constituted a threat to liberalism. But the past fifteen years have seen an almost total discrediting of Marxism-Leninism as an economic system. Beginning with the famous third plenum of the Tenth Central Committee in 1978, the Chinese Communist party set about decollectivizing agriculture for the 800 million Chinese who still lived in the countryside. The role of the state in agriculture was reduced to that of a tax collector, while production of consumer goods was sharply increased in order to give peasants a taste of the universal homogenous state and thereby an incentive to work. The reform doubled Chinese grain output in only five years, and in the process created for Deng Xiaoping a solid political base from which he was able to extend the reform to other parts of the economy. Economic statistics do not begin to describe the dynamism, initiative, and openness evident in China since the reform began.

China could not now be described in any way as a liberal democracy. At present, no more than 20 percent of its economy has been marketized, and most importantly it continues to be ruled by a self-appointed Communist party which has given no hint of wanting to devolve power. Deng has made none of Gorbachev's promises regarding democratization of the political system and there is no Chinese equivalent of *glasnost.* The Chinese leadership has in fact been much more circumspect in criticizing Mao and Maoism than Gorbachev with respect to Brezhnev and Stalin, and the regime continues to pay lip service to Marxism-Leninism as its ideological underpinning. But anyone familiar with the outlook and behavior of the new technocratic elite now governing China knows that Marxism and ideological principle have become virtually irrelevant as guides to policy, and that bourgeois consumerism has a real meaning in that country for the first time since the revolution. The various slowdowns in the pace of reform, the campaigns against "spiritual pollution" and crackdowns on political dissent are more properly seen as tactical adjustments made in the process of managing what is an extraordinarily difficult political transition. By ducking the question of political reform while putting the economy on a new footing, Deng has managed to avoid the breakdown of authority that has accompanied Gorbachev's *perestroika.* Yet the pull of the liberal idea continues to be very strong as economic power devolves and the economy becomes more open to the outside world. There are currently over 20,000 Chinese students studying in the U.S. and other Western countries, almost all of them the children of the Chinese elite. It is hard to believe that when they return home to run the country they will be content for China to be the only country in Asia unaffected by the larger democratizing trend. The student demonstrations in Beijing that broke out first in December 1986 and recurred recently on the occasion of Hu Yaobang's death were only the beginning of what will inevitably be mounting pressure for change in the political system as well.

What is important about China from the standpoint of world history is not the present state of the reform or even its future prospects. The central issue is the fact that the People's Republic of China can no longer act as a beacon for illiberal forces around the world, whether they be guerrillas in some Asian jungle or middle class students in Paris. Maoism, rather than being the pattern for Asia's future, became an anachronism, and it was the mainland Chinese who in fact were decisively influenced by the prosperity and dynamism of their overseas co-ethnics—the ironic ultimate victory of Taiwan.

Important as these changes in China have been, however, it is developments in the Soviet Union—the original "homeland of the world proletariat"—that have put the final nail in the coffin of the Marxist-Leninist alternative to liberal democracy. It should be clear that in terms of formal institutions, not much has changed in the four years since Gorbachev has come to power: free markets and the cooperative movement represent only a small part of the Soviet economy, which remains centrally planned; the political system is still dominated by the Communist party, which has only begun to democratize internally and to share power with other groups; the regime continues to assert that it is seeking only to modernize socialism and that its ideological basis remains Marxism-Leninism; and, finally, Gorbachev faces a potentially powerful conservative opposition that could undo many of the changes that have taken place to date. Moreover, it is hard to be too sanguine about the chances for success of Gorbachev's proposed reforms, either in the sphere of economics or politics. But my purpose here is not to analyze events in the short-term, or to make predictions for policy purposes, but to look at underlying trends in the sphere of ideology and consciousness. And in that respect, it is clear that an astounding transformation has occurred.

Émigrés from the Soviet Union have been reporting for at least the last generation now that virtually nobody in that country truly believed in Marxism-Leninism any longer, and that this was nowhere more true than in the Soviet elite, which continued to mouth Marxist slogans out of sheer cynicism. The corruption and decadence of the late Brezhnev-era Soviet state seemed to matter little, however, for as long as the state itself refused to throw into question any of the fundamental principles underlying Soviet society, the system was capable of functioning adequately out of sheer inertia and could even muster some dynamism in the realm of foreign and defense policy. Marxism-Leninism was like a magical incantation which, however absurd and devoid of meaning, was the only common basis on which the elite could agree to rule Soviet society.

What has happened in the four years since Gorbachev's coming to power is a revolutionary assault on the most fundamental institutions and principles of Stalinism, and their replacement by other principles which do not amount to liberalism *per se* but whose only connecting thread is liberalism. This is most evident in the economic sphere, where the reform economists around Gorbachev have become steadily more radical in their support for free markets, to the point where some like Nikolai Shmelev do not mind being compared in public to Milton Friedman. There is a virtual consensus among the currently dominant school of Soviet economists now that central planning and the command system of allocation are the root cause of economic inefficiency, and that if the Soviet system is ever to heal itself, it must permit free and decentralized decision-making with respect to investment, labor, and prices. After a couple of initial years of ideological confusion, these principles have finally been incorporated into policy with the promulgation of new laws on enterprise autonomy, cooperatives, and finally in 1988 on lease arrangements and family farming. There are, of course, a number of fatal flaws in the current implementation of the reform, most notably the absence of a thoroughgoing price reform. But the problem is no longer a *conceptual* one: Gorbachev and his lieutenants seem to understand the economic logic of marketization well enough, but like the leaders of a Third World country facing the IMF, are afraid of the social consequences of ending consumer subsidies and other forms of dependence on the state sector.

In the political sphere, the proposed changes to the Soviet constitution, legal system, and party rules amount to much less than the establishment of a liberal state. Gorbachev has spoken of democratization primarily in the sphere of internal party affairs, and has shown little intention of ending the Communist party's monopoly of power; indeed, the political reform seeks to legitimize and therefore strengthen the CPSU's rule.[3] Nonetheless, the general principles underlying many of the reforms—that the "people" should be truly responsible for their own affairs, that higher political bodies should be answerable to lower ones, and not vice versa, that the rule of law should prevail over arbitrary police actions, with separation of powers and an independent judiciary, that there should be legal protection for property rights, the need for open discussion of public issues and the right of public dissent, the empowering of the Soviets as a forum in which the whole Soviet people can participate, and of a political culture that is more tolerant and pluralistic—come from a source fundamentally alien to the USSR's Marxist-Leninist tradition, even if they are incompletely articulated and poorly implemented in practice. . . .

The Soviet Union could in no way be described as a liberal or democratic country now, nor do I think that it is terribly likely that *perestroika* will succeed such that the label will be thinkable any time in the near future. But at the end of history it is not necessary that all societies become successful liberal societies, merely that they end their ideological pretensions of representing different and higher forms of human society. And in this respect I believe that something very important has happened in the Soviet Union in the past few years: the criticisms of the Soviet system sanctioned by Gorbachev have been so thorough and devastating that there is very little chance of going back to either Stalinism or Brezhnevism in any simple way. Gorbachev has finally permitted people to say what they had privately understood for many years, namely, that the magical incantations of Marxism-Leninism were nonsense, that Soviet socialism was not superior to the West in any respect but was in fact a monumental failure. The conservative opposition in the USSR, consisting both of simple workers afraid of unemployment and inflation and of party officials fearful of losing their jobs and privileges, is outspoken and may be strong enough to force Gorbachev's ouster in the next few years. But what both groups desire is tradition, order, and authority; they manifest no deep commitment to Marxism-Leninism, except insofar as they have invested much of their own lives in it.[4] For authority to be restored in the Soviet Union after Gorbachev's demolition work, it must be on the basis of some new and vigorous ideology which has not yet appeared on the horizon.

If we admit for the moment that the fascist and communist challenges to liberalism are dead, are there any other ideological competitors left? Or put another way, are there contradictions in liberal society beyond that of class that are not resolvable? Two possibilities suggest themselves, those of religion and nationalism.

The rise of religious fundamentalism in recent years within the Christian, Jewish, and Muslim traditions has been widely noted. One is inclined to say that the revival of religion in some way attests to a broad unhappiness with the impersonality and spiritual vacuity of liberal consumerist societies. Yet while the emptiness at the core of liberalism is most certainly a defect in the ideology—indeed, a flaw that one does not need the perspective of religion to recognize[5]—it is not at all clear that it is remediable through politics. Modern liberalism itself was historically a consequence of the weakness of religiously-based societies which, failing to agree on the nature of the good life, could not provide even the minimal preconditions of peace and stability. In the contemporary world only Islam has offered a theocratic state as a political alternative to both liberalism and communism. But the doctrine has little appeal for non-Muslims, and it is hard to believe that the movement will take on any universal significance. Other less organized religious impulses have been successfully satisfied within the sphere of personal life that is permitted in liberal societies.

The other major "contradiction" potentially unresolvable by liberalism is the one posed by nationalism and other forms of racial and ethnic consciousness. It is certainly true that a very large degree of conflict since the Battle of Jena has had its roots in nationalism. Two cataclysmic world wars in this century have been spawned by the nationalism of the developed world in various guises, and if those passions have been muted to a certain extent in postwar Europe, they are still extremely powerful in the Third World. Nationalism has been a threat to liberalism historically in Germany, and continues to be one in isolated parts of "post-historical" Europe like Northern Ireland.

But it is not clear that nationalism represents an irreconcilable contradiction in the heart of liberalism. In the first place, nationalism is not one single phenomenon but several, ranging from mild cultural nostalgia to the highly organized and elaborately articulated doctrine of National Socialism. Only systematic nationalisms of the latter sort can qualify as a formal ideology on the level of liberalism or communism. The vast majority of the world's nationalist movements do not have a political program beyond the negative desire of independence *from* some other group or people, and do not offer anything like a comprehensive agenda for socio-economic organization. As such, they are compatible with doctrines and ideologies that do offer such agendas. While they may constitute a source of conflict for liberal societies, this conflict does not arise from liberalism itself so much as from the fact that the liberalism in question is incomplete. Certainly a great deal of the world's ethnic and nationalist tension can be explained in terms of peoples who are forced to live in unrepresentative political systems that they have not chosen.

While it is impossible to rule out the sudden appearance of new ideologies or previously unrecognized contradictions in liberal societies, then, the present world seems to confirm that the fundamental principles of socio-political organization have not advanced terribly far since 1806. . . .

What are the implications of the end of history for international relations? Clearly, the vast bulk of the Third World remains very much mired in history, and will be a terrain of conflict for many years to come. But let us focus for the time being on the larger and more developed states of the world who after all account for the greater part of world politics. Russia and China are not likely to join the developed nations of the West as liberal societies any time in the foreseeable future, but suppose for a moment that Marxism-Leninism ceases to be a factor driving the foreign policies of these states—a prospect which, if not yet here, the last few years have made a real possibility. How will the overall characteristics of a de-ideologized world differ from those of the one with which we are familiar at such a hypothetical juncture?

The most common answer is—not very much. For there is a very widespread belief among many observers of international relations that underneath the skin of ideology is a hard core of great power national interest that guarantees a fairly high level of competition and conflict between nations. Indeed, according to one academically popular school of international relations theory, conflict inheres in the international system as such, and to understand the prospects for conflict one must look at the shape of the system—for example, whether it is bipolar or multipolar—rather than at the specific character of the nations and regimes that constitute it. This school in effect applies a Hobbesian view of politics to international relations, and assumes that aggression and insecurity are universal characteristics of human societies rather than the product of specific historical circumstances.

Believers in this line of thought take the relations that existed between the participants in the classical nineteenth century European balance of power as a model for what a de-ideologized contemporary world would look like. Charles Krauthammer, for example, recently explained that if as a result of Gorbachev's reforms the USSR is shorn of Marxist-Leninist ideology, its behavior will revert to that of nineteenth century imperial Russia.[6] While he finds this more reassuring than the threat posed by a communist Russia, he implies that there will still be a substantial degree of competition and conflict in the international system, just as there was say between Russia and Britain or Wilhelmine Germany in the last century. This is, of course, a convenient point of view for people who want to admit that something major is changing in the Soviet Union, but do not want to accept responsibility for recommending the radical policy redirection implicit in such a view. But is it true? . . .

The expansionist and competitive behavior of nineteenth-century European states rested on no less ideal a basis; it just so happened that the ideology driving it was less explicit than the doctrines of the twentieth century. For one thing, most "liberal" European societies were illiberal insofar as they believed in the legitimacy of imperialism, that is, the right of one nation to rule over other nations without regard for the wishes of the ruled. The justifications for imperialism varied from nation to nation, from a crude belief in the legitimacy of force, particularly when applied to non-Europeans, to the "White Man's Burden" and Europe's Christianizing mission, to the desire to give people of color access to the culture of Rabelais and Moliére. But whatever the particular ideological basis, every "developed" country believed in the acceptability of higher civilizations ruling lower ones—including, incidentally, the United States with regard to the Philippines.

This led to a drive for pure territorial aggrandizement in the latter half of the century and played no small role in causing the Great War.

The radical and deformed outgrowth of nineteenth-century imperialism was German fascism, an ideology which justified Germany's right not only to rule over non-European peoples, but over *all* non-German ones. But in retrospect it seems that Hitler represented a diseased bypath in the general course of European development, and since his fiery defeat, the legitimacy of any kind of territorial aggrandizement has been thoroughly discredited.[7] Since the Second World War, European nationalism has been defanged and shorn of any real relevance to foreign policy, with the consequence that the nineteenth-century model of great power behavior has become a serious anachronism. . . . International life for the part of the world that has reached the end of history is far more preoccupied with economics than with politics or strategy.

The developed states of the West do maintain defense establishments and in the postwar period have competed vigorously for influence to meet a worldwide communist threat. This behavior has been driven, however, by an external threat from states that possess overtly expansionist ideologies, and would not exist in their absence. To take the "neo-realist" theory seriously, one would have to believe that "natural" competitive behavior would reassert itself among the OECD states were Russia and China to disappear from the face of the earth. That is, West Germany and France would arm themselves against each other as they did in the 1930s, Australia and New Zealand would send military advisers to block each others' advances in Africa, and the U.S.-Canadian border would become fortified. Such a prospect is, of course, ludicrous: minus Marxist-Leninist ideology, we are far more likely to see the "Common Marketization" of world politics than the disintegration of the [European Economic Community] EEC into nineteenth-century competitiveness. . . .

The real question for the future, however, is the degree to which Soviet elites have assimilated the consciousness of the universal homogenous state that is post-Hitler Europe. From their writings and from my own personal contacts with them, there is no question in my mind that the liberal Soviet intelligentsia rallying around Gorbachev have arrived at the end-of-history view in a remarkably short time, due in no small measure to the contacts they have had since the Brezhnev era with the larger European civilization around them. "New political thinking," the general rubric for their views, describes a world dominated by economic concerns, in which there are no ideological grounds for major conflict between nations, and in which, consequently, the use of military force becomes less legitimate. As Foreign Minister Shevardnadze put it in mid-1988:

> The struggle between two opposing systems is no longer a determining tendency of the present-day era. At the modern stage, the ability to build up material wealth at an accelerated rate on the basis of front-ranking science and high-level techniques and technology, and to distribute it fairly, and through joint efforts to restore and protect the resources necessary for mankind's survival acquires decisive importance.[8]

The post-historical consciousness represented by "new thinking" is only one possible future for the Soviet Union, however. There has always been a very strong current of great Russian chauvinism in the Soviet Union, which has found freer expression since the advent of *glastnost.* It may be possible to return to traditional Marxism-Leninism for a while as a simple rallying point for those who want to restore the authority that Gorbachev has dissipated. But as in Poland, Marxism-Leninism is dead as a mobilizing ideology: under its banner people cannot be made to work harder, and its adherents have lost confidence in themselves. Unlike the propagators of traditional Marxism-Leninism, however, ultranationalists in the USSR believe in their Slavophile cause passionately, and one gets the sense that the fascist alternative is not one that has played itself out entirely there.

The Soviet Union, then, is at a fork in the road: it can start down the path that was staked out by Western Europe forty-five years ago, a path that most of Asia has followed, or it can realize its own uniqueness and remain stuck in history. The choice it makes will be highly important for us, given the Soviet Union's size and military strength, for that power will continue to preoccupy us and slow our realization that we have already emerged on the other side of history.

The passing of Marxism-Leninism first from China and then from the Soviet Union will mean its death as a living ideology of world historical significance. For while there may be some isolated true believers left in places like Managua, Pyongyang, or Cambridge, Massachusetts, the fact that there is not a single large state in which it is a going concern undermines completely its pretensions to being in the vanguard of human history. And the death of this ideology means the growing "Common Marketization" of international relations, and the diminution of the likelihood of large-scale conflict between states.

This does not by any means imply the end of international conflict *per se.* For the world at that point would be divided between a part that was historical and a part that was post-historical. Conflict between states still in history, and between those states and those at the end of history, would still be possible. There would still be a high and perhaps rising level of ethnic and nationalist violence, since those are impulses incompletely played out, even in parts of the post-historical world. Palestinians and Kurds, Sikhs and Tamils, Irish Catholics and Walloons, Armenians and Azeris, will continue to have their unresolved grievances. This implies that terrorism and wars of national liberation will continue to be an important item on the international agenda. But large-scale conflict must involve large states still caught in the grip of history, and they are what appear to be passing from the scene.

The end of history will be a very sad time. The struggle for recognition, the willingness to risk one's life for a purely abstract goal, the worldwide ideological struggle that called forth daring, courage, imagination, and idealism, will be replaced by economic calculation, the endless solving of technical problems, environmental concerns, and the satisfaction of sophisticated consumer demands. In the post-historical period there will be neither art nor philosophy, just the perpetual caretaking of the museum of human history. I can feel in myself, and see in others around me, a powerful nostalgia for the time when history existed. Such nostalgia, in fact, will continue to fuel competition and conflict even in the post-historical world for some time to come. Even though I recognize its inevitability, I have the most ambivalent feelings for the civilization that has been created in Europe since 1945, with its north Atlantic and Asian offshoots. Perhaps this very prospect of centuries of boredom at the end of history will serve to get history started once again.

Notes

1. I am not using the term "fascism" here in its most precise sense, fully aware of the frequent misuse of this term to denounce anyone to the right of the user. "Fascism" here denotes any organized ultranationalist movement with universalistic pretensions—not universalistic with regard to its nationalism, of course, since the latter is exclusive by definition, but with regard to the movement's belief in its right to rule other people. Hence Imperial Japan would qualify as fascist while former strongman Stoessner's Paraguay or Pinochet's Chile would not. Obviously fascist ideologies cannot be universalistic in the sense of Marxism or liberalism, but the structure of the doctrine can be transferred from country to country.

2. I use the example of Japan with some caution, since Kojéve late in his life came to conclude that Japan, with its culture based on purely format arts, proved that the universal homogenous state was not victorious and that history had perhaps not ended. See the long note at the end of the second edition of *Introduction a la Lecture de Hegel,* 462–3.

3. This is not true in Poland and Hungary, however, whose Communist parties have taken moves toward true power-sharing and pluralism.

4. This is particularly true of the leading Soviet conservative, former Second Secretary Yegor Ligachev, who has publicly recognized many of the deep defects of the Brezhnev period.

5. I am thinking particularly of Rousseau and the Western philosophical tradition that flows from him that was highly critical of Lockean or Hobbesian liberalism, though one could criticize liberalism from the standpoint of classical political philosophy as well.

6. See his article, "Beyond the Cold War," *New Republic,* December 19, 1988.

7. It took European colonial powers like France several years after the war to admit the illegitimacy of their empires, but decolonialization was an inevitable consequence of the Allied victory which had been based on the promise of a restoration of democratic freedoms.

8. *Vestnik Ministersiva Inostrannikh Dd SSSR* no. 15 (August 1988), 27–46. "New thinking" does of course serve a propagandistic purpose in persuading Western audiences of Soviet good intentions. But the fact that it is good propaganda does not mean that its formulators do not take many of its ideas seriously.

31.2

Jihad vs. McWorld

Benjamin R. Barber

The two axial principles of our age—tribalism and globalism—clash at every point except one: they may both be threaning to democracy.

Just beyond the horizon of current events lie two possible political futures—both bleak, neither democratic. The first is a retribalization of large swaths of humankind by war and bloodshed: a threatened Lebanonization of national states in which culture is pitted against culture, people against people, tribe against tribe—a Jihad in the name of a hundred narrowly conceived faiths against every kind of interdependence, every kind of artificial social cooperation and civic mutuality. The second is being borne in on us by the onrush of economic and ecological forces that demand integration and uniformity and that mesmerize the world with fast music, fast computers, and fast food—with MTV, Macintosh, and McDonald's, pressing nations into one commercially homogenous global network: one McWorld tied together by technology, ecology, communications, and commerce. The planet is falling precipitately apart *AND* coming reluctantly together at the very same moment.

These two tendencies are sometimes visible in the same countries at the same instant: thus Yugoslavia, clamoring just recently to join the New Europe, is exploding into fragments; India is trying to live up to its reputation as the world's largest integral democracy while powerful new fundamentalist parties like the Hindu nationalist Bharatiya Janata Party, along with nationalist assassins, are imperiling its hard-won unity. States are breaking up or joining up: the Soviet Union has disappeared almost overnight, its parts forming new unions with one another or with like-minded nationalities in neighboring states. The old interwar national state based on territory and political sovereignty looks to be a mere transitional development.

The tendencies of what I am here calling the forces of Jihad and the forces of McWorld operate with equal strength in opposite directions, the one driven by parochial hatreds, the other by universalizing markets, the one re-creating ancient subnational and ethnic borders from within, the other making national borders porous from without. They have one thing in common: neither offers much hope to citizens looking for practical ways to govern themselves democratically. If the global future is to pit Jihad's centrifugal whirlwind against McWorld's centripetal black hole, the outcome is unlikely to be democratic—or so I will argue.

McWorld, or the Globalization of Politics

Four imperatives make up the dynamic of McWorld: a market imperative, a resource imperative, an information-technology imperative, and an ecological imperative. By shrinking the world and diminishing the salience of national borders, these imperatives have in combination achieved a considerable victory over factiousness and particularism, and not least of all over their most virulent traditional form—nationalism. It is the realists who are now Europeans, the utopians who dream nostalgically of a resurgent England or Germany, perhaps even a resurgent Wales or Saxony. Yesterday's wishful cry for one world has yielded to the reality of McWorld.

The Market Imperative

Marxist and Leninist theories of imperialism assumed that the quest for ever-expanding markets would in time compel nation-based capitalist economies to push against national boundaries in search of an international economic imperium. Whatever else has happened to the scientific predictions of Marxism, in this domain they have proved farsighted. All national economies are now vulnerable to the inroads of larger, transnational markets within which trade is free, currencies are convertible,

Source: Published originally in *The Atlantic Monthly* in March 1992 as an introduction to *Jihad vs. McWorld* (Ballantine paperback, 1996), a volume that discussed and extends the themes of the original article. Benjamin R. Barber is Senior Research Scholar at the Center on Philanthropy and Civil Society at The Graduate Center, CUNY, Founder of the Interdependence Movement, Walt Whitman Professor Emeritus at Rutgers University, and the author of 19 books, including the classic *Strong Democracy,* the international best-seller *Jihad vs. McWorld,* and, forthcoming from Yale University Press, *If Mayors Ruled the World.*

access to banking is open, and contracts are enforceable under law. In Europe, Asia, Africa, the South Pacific, and the Americas such markets are eroding national sovereignty and giving rise to entities—international banks, trade associations, transnational lobbies like OPEC and Greenpeace, world news services like CNN and the BBC, and multinational corporations that increasingly lack a meaningful national identity—that neither reflect nor respect nationhood as an organizing or regulative principle.

The market imperative has also reinforced the quest for international peace and stability, requisites of an efficient international economy. Markets are enemies of parochialism, isolation, fractiousness, war. Market psychology attenuates the psychology of ideological and religious cleavages and assumes a concord among producers and consumers—categories that ill fit narrowly conceived national or religious cultures. Shopping has little tolerance for blue laws, whether dictated by pub-closing British paternalism, Sabbath-observing Jewish Orthodox fundamentalism, or no-Sunday-liquor-sales Massachusetts puritanism. In the context of common markets, international law ceases to be a vision of justice and becomes a workaday framework for getting things done—enforcing contracts, ensuring that governments abide by deals, regulating trade and currency relations, and so forth.

Common markets demand a common language, as well as a common currency, and they produce common behaviors of the kind bred by cosmopolitan city life everywhere. Commercial pilots, computer programmers, international bankers, media specialists, oil riggers, entertainment celebrities, ecology experts, demographers, accountants, professors, athletes—these compose a new breed of men and women for whom religion, culture, and nationality can seem only marginal elements in a working identity. Although sociologists of everyday life will no doubt continue to distinguish a Japanese from an American mode, shopping has a common signature throughout the world. Cynics might even say that some of the recent revolutions in Eastern Europe have had as their true goal not liberty and the right to vote but well-paying jobs and the right to shop (although the vote is proving easier to acquire than consumer goods). The market imperative is, then, plenty powerful; but, notwithstanding some of the claims made for "democratic capitalism," it is not identical with the democratic imperative.

The Resource Imperative

Democrats once dreamed of societies whose political autonomy rested firmly on economic independence. The Athenians idealized what they called autarky, and tried for a while to create a way of life simple and austere enough to make the polis genuinely self-sufficient. To be free meant to be independent of any other community or polis. Not even the Athenians were able to achieve autarky, however: human nature, it turns out, is dependency. By the time of Pericles, Athenian politics was inextricably bound up with a flowering empire held together by naval power and commerce—an empire that, even as it appeared to enhance Athenian might, ate away at Athenian independence and autarky. Master and slave, it turned out, were bound together by mutual insufficiency.

The dream of autarky briefly engrossed nineteenth-century America as well, for the underpopulated, endlessly bountiful land, the cornucopia of natural resources, and the natural barriers of a continent walled in by two great seas led many to believe that America could be a world unto itself. Given this past, it has been harder for Americans than for most to accept the inevitability of interdependence. But the rapid depletion of resources even in a country like ours, where they once seemed inexhaustible, and the maldistribution of arable soil and mineral resources on the planet, leave even the wealthiest societies ever more resource-dependent and many other nations in permanently desperate straits.

Every nation, it turns out, needs something another nation has; some nations have almost nothing they need.

The Information-Technology Imperative

Enlightenment science and the technologies derived from it are inherently universalizing. They entail a quest for descriptive principles of general application, a search for universal solutions to particular problems, and an unswerving embrace of objectivity and impartiality.

Scientific progress embodies and depends on open communication, a common discourse rooted in rationality, collaboration, and an easy and regular flow and exchange of information. Such ideals can be hypocritical covers for power-mongering by elites, and they may be shown to be wanting in many other ways, but they are entailed by the very idea of science and they make science and globalization practical allies.

Business, banking, and commerce all depend on information flow and are facilitated by new communication technologies. The hardware of these technologies tends to be systemic and integrated—computer, television, cable, satellite, laser, fiber-optic, and microchip technologies combining to create a vast interactive communications and information network that can potentially give every person on earth access to every other person, and make every datum, every byte, available to every set of eyes. If the automobile was, as George Ball once said (when he gave his blessing to a Fiat factory in the Soviet Union during the Cold War), "an ideology on four wheels," then electronic telecommunication and information systems are an ideology at 186,000 miles per second—which makes for a very small planet in a very big hurry. Individual cultures speak particular languages; commerce and science increasingly speak English; the whole world speaks logarithms and binary mathematics.

Moreover, the pursuit of science and technology asks for, even compels, open societies. Satellite footprints do not respect national borders; telephone wires penetrate the most closed societies. With photocopying and then fax machines having infiltrated Soviet universities and *samizdat* literary circles in the eighties, and computer modems having multiplied like rabbits in communism's bureaucratic warrens thereafter, *glasnost* could not be far behind. In their social requisites, secrecy and science are enemies.

The new technology's software is perhaps even more globalizing than its hardware. The information arm of international commerce's sprawling body reaches out and touches distinct nations and parochial cultures, and gives them a common face chiseled in Hollywood, on Madison Avenue, and in Silicon Valley. Throughout the 1980s one of the most-watched television programs in South Africa was *The Cosby Show.* The demise of apartheid was already in production. Exhibitors at the 1991 Cannes film festival expressed growing anxiety over the "homogenization" and "Americanization" of the global film industry when, for the third year running, American films dominated the awards ceremonies. America has dominated the world's popular culture for much longer, and much more decisively. In November of 1991 Switzerland's once insular culture boasted best-seller lists featuring *Terminator 2* as the No. 1 movie, *Scarlett* as the No. 1 book, and Prince's *Diamonds and Pearls* as the No. 1 record album. No wonder the Japanese are buying Hollywood film studios even faster than Americans are buying Japanese television sets. This kind of software supremacy may in the long term be far more important than hardware superiority, because culture has become more potent than armaments. What is the power of the Pentagon compared with Disneyland? Can the Sixth Fleet keep up with CNN? McDonald's in Moscow and Coke in China will do more to create a global culture than military colonization ever could. It is less the goods than the brand names that do the work, for they convey lifestyle images that alter perception and challenge behavior. They make up the seductive software of McWorld's common (at times much too common) soul.

Yet in all this high-tech commercial world there is nothing that looks particularly democratic. It lends itself to surveillance as well as liberty, to new forms of manipulation and covert control as well as new kinds of participation, to skewed, unjust market outcomes as well as greater productivity. The consumer society and the open society are not quite synonymous. Capitalism and democracy have a relationship, but it is something less than a marriage. An efficient free market after all requires that consumers be free to vote their dollars on competing goods, not that citizens be free to vote their values and beliefs on competing political candidates and programs. The free market flourished in junta-run Chile, in military-governed Taiwan and Korea, and, earlier, in a variety of autocratic European empires as well as their colonial possessions.

The Ecological Imperative

The impact of globalization on ecology is a cliché even to world leaders who ignore it. We know well enough that the German forests can be destroyed by Swiss and Italians driving gas-guzzlers fueled by leaded gas. We also know that the planet can be asphyxiated by greenhouse gases because Brazilian farmers want to be part of the twentieth century and are burning down tropical rain forests to clear a little land to plough, and because Indonesians make a living out of converting their lush jungle into toothpicks for fastidious Japanese diners, upsetting the delicate oxygen balance and in effect puncturing our global lungs. Yet this ecological consciousness has meant not only greater awareness but also greater inequality, as modernized nations try to slam the door behind them, saying to developing nations, "The world cannot afford your modernization; ours has wrung it dry!"

Each of the four imperatives just cited is transnational, transideological, and transcultural. Each applies impartially to Catholics, Jews, Muslims, Hindus, and Buddhists; to democrats and totalitarians; to capitalists and socialists. The Enlightenment dream of a universal rational society has to a remarkable degree been realized—but in a form that is commercialized, homogenized, depoliticized, bureaucratized, and, of course, radically incomplete, for the movement toward

McWorld is in competition with forces of global breakdown, national dissolution, and centrifugal corruption. These forces, working in the opposite direction, are the essence of what I call Jihad.

Jihad, or the Lebanonization of the World

OPEC, the World Bank, the United Nations, the International Red Cross, the multinational corporation . . . there are scores of institutions that reflect globalization. But they often appear as ineffective reactors to the world's real actors: national states and, to an ever greater degree, subnational factions in permanent rebellion against uniformity and integration—even the kind represented by universal law and justice. The headlines feature these players regularly: they are cultures, not countries; parts, not wholes; sects, not religions; rebellious factions and dissenting minorities at war not just with globalism but with the traditional nation-state. Kurds, Basques, Puerto Ricans, Ossetians, East Timoreans, Quebecois, the Catholics of Northern Ireland, Abkhasians, Kurile Islander Japanese, the Zulus of Inkatha, Catalonians, Tamils, and, of course, Palestinians—people without countries, inhabiting nations not their own, seeking smaller worlds within borders that will seal them off from modernity.

A powerful irony is at work here. Nationalism was once a force of integration and unification, a movement aimed at bringing together disparate clans, tribes, and cultural fragments under new, assimilationist flags. But as Ortega y Gasset noted more than sixty years ago, having won its victories, nationalism changed its strategy. In the 1920s, and again today, it is more often a reactionary and divisive force, pulverizing the very nations it once helped cement together. The force that creates nations is "inclusive," Ortega wrote in *The Revolt of the Masses*. "In periods of consolidation, nationalism has a positive value, and is a lofty standard. But in Europe everything is more than consolidated, and nationalism is nothing but a mania . . ."

This mania has left the post-Cold War world smoldering with hot wars; the international scene is little more unified than it was at the end of the Great War, in Ortega's own time. There were more than thirty wars in progress last year, most of them ethnic, racial, tribal, or religious in character, and the list of unsafe regions doesn't seem to be getting any shorter. Some new world order!

The aim of many of these small-scale wars is to redraw boundaries, to implode states and resecure parochial identities: to escape McWorld's dully insistent imperatives. The mood is that of Jihad: war not as an instrument of policy but as an emblem of identity, an expression of community, an end in itself. Even where there is no shooting war, there is fractiousness, secession, and the quest for ever smaller communities. Add to the list of dangerous countries those at risk: In Switzerland and Spain, Jurassian and Basque separatists still argue the virtues of ancient identities, sometimes in the language of bombs. Hyperdisintegration in the former Soviet Union may well continue unabated—not just a Ukraine independent from the Soviet Union but a Bessarabian Ukraine independent from the Ukrainian republic; not just Russia severed from the defunct union but Tatarstan severed from Russia. Yugoslavia makes even the disunited, ex-Soviet, nonsocialist republics that were once the Soviet Union look integrated, its sectarian fatherlands springing up within factional motherlands like weeds within weeds within weeds. Kurdish independence would threaten the territorial integrity of four Middle Eastern nations. Well before the current cataclysm, Soviet Georgia made a claim for autonomy from the Soviet Union, only to be faced with its Ossetians (164,000 in a republic of 5.5 million) demanding their own self-determination within Georgia. The Abkhasian minority in Georgia has followed suit. Even the good will established by Canada's once promising Meech Lake protocols is in danger, with Francophone Quebec again threatening the dissolution of the federation. In South Africa, the emergence from apartheid was hardly achieved when friction between Inkatha's Zulus and the African National Congress's tribally identified members threatened to replace Europeans' racism with an indigenous tribal war. After thirty years of attempted integration using the colonial language (English) as a unifier, Nigeria is now playing with the idea of linguistic multiculturalism—which could mean the cultural breakup of the nation into hundreds of tribal fragments. Even Saddam Hussein has benefited from the threat of internal Jihad, having used renewed tribal and religious warfare to turn last season's mortal enemies into reluctant allies of an Iraqi nationhood that he nearly destroyed.

The passing of communism has torn away the thin veneer of internationalism (workers of the world unite!) to reveal ethnic prejudices that are not only ugly and deep-seated but increasingly murderous.

Europe's old scourge, anti-Semitism, is back with a vengeance, but it is only one of many antagonisms. It appears all too easy to throw the historical gears into reverse and pass from a Communist dictatorship back into a tribal state.

Among the tribes, religion is also a battlefield. ("Jihad" is a rich word whose generic meaning is "struggle"—usually the struggle of the soul to avert evil. Strictly applied to religious war, it is used only in reference to battles where the faith is under assault, or battles against a government that denies the practice of Islam. My use here is rhetorical, but does follow both journalistic practice and history.) Remember the Thirty Years War? Whatever forms of Enlightenment universalism might once have come to grace such historically related forms of monotheism as Judaism, Christianity, and Islam, in many of their modern incarnations they are parochial rather than cosmopolitan, angry rather than loving, proselytizing rather than ecumenical, zealous rather than rationalist, sectarian rather than deistic, ethnocentric rather than universalizing. As a result, like the new forms of hypernationalism, the new expressions of religious fundamentalism are fractious and pulverizing, never integrating. This is religion as the Crusaders knew it: a battle to the death for souls that if not saved will be forever lost.

The atmospherics of Jihad have resulted in a breakdown of civility in the name of identity, of comity in the name of community. International relations have sometimes taken on the aspect of gang war—cultural turf battles featuring tribal factions that were supposed to be sublimated as integral parts of large national, economic, postcolonial, and constitutional entities.

The Darkening Future of Democracy

These rather melodramatic tableaux vivants do not tell the whole story, however. For all their defects, Jihad and McWorld have their attractions. Yet, to repeat and insist, the attractions are unrelated to democracy. Neither McWorld nor Jihad is remotely democratic in impulse. Neither needs democracy; neither promotes democracy.

McWorld does manage to look pretty seductive in a world obsessed with Jihad. It delivers peace, prosperity, and relative unity—if at the cost of independence, community, and identity (which is generally based on difference). The primary political values required by the global market are order and tranquillity, and freedom—as in the phrases "free trade," "free press," and "free love." Human rights are needed to a degree, but not citizenship or participation—and no more social justice and equality than are necessary to promote efficient economic production and consumption. Multinational corporations sometimes seem to prefer doing business with local oligarchs, inasmuch as they can take confidence from dealing with the boss on all crucial matters. Despots who slaughter their own populations are no problem, so long as they leave markets in place and refrain from making war on their neighbors (Saddam Hussein's fatal mistake). In trading partners, predictability is of more value than justice.

The Eastern European revolutions that seemed to arise out of concern for global democratic values quickly deteriorated into a stampede in the general direction of free markets and their ubiquitous, television-promoted shopping malls. East Germany's *Neues Forum*, that courageous gathering of intellectuals, students, and workers which overturned the Stalinist regime in Berlin in 1989, lasted only six months in Germany's mini-version of McWorld. Then it gave way to money and markets and monopolies from the West. By the time of the first all-German elections, it could scarcely manage to secure three percent of the vote. Elsewhere there is growing evidence that *glasnost* will go and *perestroika*—defined as privatization and an opening of markets to Western bidders—will stay. So understandably anxious are the new rulers of Eastern Europe and whatever entities are forged from the residues of the Soviet Union to gain access to credit and markets and technology—McWorld's flourishing new currencies—that they have shown themselves willing to trade away democratic prospects in pursuit of them: not just old totalitarian ideologies and command-economy production models but some possible indigenous experiments with a third way between capitalism and socialism, such as economic cooperatives and employee stock-ownership plans, both of which have their ardent supporters in the East.

Jihad delivers a different set of virtues: a vibrant local identity, a sense of community, solidarity among kinsmen, neighbors, and countrymen, narrowly conceived. But it also guarantees parochialism and is grounded in exclusion. Solidarity is secured through war against outsiders. And solidarity often means obedience to a hierarchy in governance, fanaticism in beliefs, and the obliteration of individual selves in the name of the group. Deference to leaders and intolerance toward outsiders (and toward "enemies within") are hallmarks of tribalism—hardly the attitudes required for the cultivation of new democratic women and men capable of governing themselves. Where new democratic experiments have been conducted in retribalizing societies, in both Europe and the Third World, the result has often been anarchy, repression, persecution, and the coming of new, noncommunist forms of very old kinds of despotism. During the past year, Havel's velvet revolution in Czechoslovakia was imperiled by partisans of "Czechland" and of Slovakia as independent entities. India seemed little less rent by Sikh, Hindu, Muslim, and Tamil infighting than it was immediately after the British pulled out, more than forty years ago.

To the extent that either McWorld or Jihad has a *NATURAL* politics, it has turned out to be more of an antipolitics. For McWorld, it is the antipolitics of globalism: bureaucratic, technocratic, and meritocratic, focused (as Marx predicted it would be) on the administration of things—with people, however, among the chief things to be administered. In its politico-economic imperatives McWorld has been guided by laissez-faire market principles that privilege efficiency, productivity, and beneficence at the expense of civic liberty and self-government.

For Jihad, the antipolitics of tribalization has been explicitly antidemocratic: one-party dictatorship, government by military junta, theocratic fundamentalism—often associated with a version of the *Fuhrerprinzip* that empowers an individual to rule on behalf of a people. Even the government of India, struggling for decades to model democracy for a people who will soon number a billion, longs for great leaders; and for every Mahatma Gandhi, Indira Gandhi, or Rajiv Gandhi taken from them by zealous assassins, the Indians appear to seek a replacement who will deliver them from the lengthy travail of their freedom.

The Confederal Option

How can democracy be secured and spread in a world whose primary tendencies are at best indifferent to it (McWorld) and at worst deeply antithetical to it (Jihad)? My guess is that globalization will eventually vanquish retribalization. The ethos of material "civilization" has not yet encountered an obstacle it has been unable to thrust aside. Ortega may have grasped in the 1920s a clue to our own future in the coming millennium.

"Everyone sees the need of a new principle of life. But as always happens in similar crises—some people attempt to save the situation by an artificial intensification of the very principle which has led to decay. This is the meaning of the 'nationalist' outburst of recent years. . . . Things have always gone that way. The last flare, the longest; the last sigh, the deepest. On the very eve of their disappearance there is an intensification of frontiers—military and economic."

Jihad may be a last deep sigh before the eternal yawn of McWorld. On the other hand, Ortega was not exactly prescient; his prophecy of peace and internationalism came just before *blitzkrieg*, world war, and the Holocaust tore the old order to bits. Yet democracy is how we remonstrate with reality, the rebuke our aspirations offer to history. And if retribalization is inhospitable to democracy, there is nonetheless a form of democratic government that can accommodate parochialism and communitarianism, one that can even save them from their defects and make them more tolerant and participatory: decentralized participatory democracy. And if McWorld is indifferent to democracy, there is nonetheless a form of democratic goverment that suits global markets passably well—representative government in its federal or, better still, confederal variation.

With its concern for accountability, the protection of minorities, and the universal rule of law, a confederalized representative system would serve the political needs of McWorld as well as oligarchic bureaucratism or meritocratic elitism is currently doing. As we are already beginning to see, many nations may survive in the long term only as confederations that afford local regions smaller than "nations" extensive jurisdiction. Recommended reading for democrats of the twenty-first century is not the U.S. Constitution or the French Declaration of Rights of Man and Citizen but the Articles of Confederation, that suddenly pertinent document that stitched together the thirteen American colonies into what then seemed a too loose confederation of independent states but now appears a new form of political realism, as veterans of Yeltsin's new Russia and the new Europe created at Maastricht will attest.

By the same token, the participatory and direct form of democracy that engages citizens in civic activity and civic judgment and goes well beyond just voting and accountability—the system I have called "strong democracy"—suits the political needs of decentralized communities as well as theocratic and nationalist party dictatorships have done. Local neighborhoods need not be democratic, but they can be. Real democracy has flourished in diminutive settings: the spirit of liberty, Tocqueville said, is local. Participatory democracy, if not naturally apposite to tribalism, has an undeniable attractiveness under conditions of parochialism.

Democracy in any of these variations will, however, continue to be obstructed by the undemocratic and antidemocratic trends toward uniformitarian globalism and intolerant retribalization which I have portrayed here. For democracy to persist in our brave new McWorld, we will have to commit acts of conscious political will—a possibility, but hardly a probability, under these conditions. Political will requires much more than the quick fix of the transfer of institutions. Like technology transfer, institution transfer rests on foolish assumptions about a uniform world of the kind that once fired the imagination of colonial administrators. Spread English justice to the colonies by exporting wigs. Let an East Indian trading company act as the vanguard to Britain's free parliamentary institutions. Today's well-intentioned quick-fixers in the National Endowment for Democracy and the Kennedy School of Government, in the unions and foundations and universities zealously nurturing contacts in Eastern Europe and the Third World, are hoping to democratize by long distance. Post Bulgaria a parliament by first-class mail. Fed Ex the Bill of Rights to Sri Lanka. Cable Cambodia some common law.

Yet Eastern Europe has already demonstrated that importing free political parties, parliaments, and presses cannot establish a democratic civil society; imposing a free market may even have the opposite effect. Democracy grows from the bottom up and cannot be imposed from the top down. Civil society has to be built from the inside out. The institutional superstructure comes last. Poland may become democratic, but then again it may heed the Pope, and prefer to found its politics on its Catholicism, with uncertain consequences for democracy. Bulgaria may become democratic, but it may prefer tribal war. The former Soviet Union may become a democratic confederation, or it may just grow into an anarchic and weak conglomeration of markets for other nations' goods and services.

Democrats need to seek out indigenous democratic impulses. There is always a desire for self-government, always some expression of participation, accountability, consent, and representation, even in traditional hierarchical societies. These need to be identified, tapped, modified, and incorporated into new democratic practices with an indigenous flavor. The tortoises among the democratizers may ultimately outlive or outpace the hares, for they will have the time and patience to explore conditions along the way, and to adapt their gait to changing circumstances. Tragically, democracy in a hurry often looks something like France in 1794 or China in 1989.

It certainly seems possible that the most attractive democratic ideal in the face of the brutal realities of Jihad and the dull realities of McWorld will be a confederal union of semi-autonomous communities smaller than nation-states, tied together into regional economic associations and markets larger than nation-states—participatory and self-determining in local matters at the bottom, representative and accountable at the top. The nation-state would play a diminished role, and sovereignty would lose some of its political potency. The Green movement adage "Think globally, act locally" would actually come to describe the conduct of politics.

This vision reflects only an ideal, however—one that is not terribly likely to be realized. Freedom, Jean-Jacques Rousseau once wrote, is a food easy to eat but hard to digest. Still, democracy has always played itself out against the odds. And democracy remains both a form of coherence as binding as McWorld and a secular faith potentially as inspiriting as Jihad.

31.3

The Clash of Civilizations?

Samuel P. Huntington

The Next Pattern of Conflict

World politics is entering a new phase, and intellectuals have not hesitated to proliferate visions of what it will be—the end of history, the return of traditional rivalries between nation states, and the decline of the nation state from the conflicting pulls of tribalism and globalism, among others. Each of these visions catches aspects of the emerging reality. Yet they all miss a crucial, indeed a central, aspect of what global politics is likely to be in the coming years.

It is my hypothesis that the fundamental source of conflict in this new world will not be primarily ideological or primarily economic. The great divisions among humankind and the dominating source of conflict will be cultural. Nation-states will remain the most powerful actors in world affairs, but the principal conflicts of global politics will occur between nations and groups of different civilizations. The clash of civilizations will dominate global politics. The fault lines between civilizations will be the battle lines of the future.

Conflict between civilizations will be the latest phase in the evolution of conflict in the modern world. For a century and a half after the emergence of the modern international system with the Peace of Westphalia, the conflicts of the Western world were largely among princes—emperors, absolute monarchs and constitutional monarchs attempting to expand their bureaucracies, their armies, their mercantilist economic strength and, most important, the territory they ruled. In the process they created nation-states, and beginning with the French Revolution the principal lines of conflict were between nations rather than princes. In 1793, as R. R. Palmer put it, "The wars of kings were over; the wars of peoples had begun." This nineteenth-century pattern lasted until the end of World War I. Then, as a result of the Russian Revolution and the reaction against it, the conflict of nations yielded to the conflict of ideologies, first among communism, fascism-Nazism and liberal democracy, and then between communism and liberal democracy. During the Cold War, this latter conflict became embodied in the struggle between the two superpowers, neither of which was a nation-state in the classical European sense and each of which defined its identity in terms of its ideology.

These conflicts between princes, nation-states and ideologies were primarily conflicts within Western civilization, "Western civil wars," as William Lind has labeled them. This was as true of the Cold War as it was of the world wars and the earlier wars of the seventeenth, eighteenth and nineteenth centuries. With the end of the Cold War, international politics moves out of its Western phase, and its centerpiece becomes the interaction between the West and non-Western civilizations and among non-Western civilizations. In the politics of civilizations, the peoples and governments of non-Western civilizations no longer remain the objects of history as targets of Western colonialism but join the West as movers and shapers of history.

The Nature of Civilizations

During the Cold War the world was divided into the First, Second and Third Worlds. Those divisions are no longer relevant. It is far more meaningful now to group countries not in terms of their political or economic systems or in terms of their level of economic development but rather in terms of their culture and civilization.

What do we mean when we talk of a civilization? A civilization is a cultural entity. Villages, regions, ethnic groups, nationalities, religious groups, all have distinct cultures at different levels of cultural heterogeneity. The culture of a village in southern Italy may be different from that of a village in northern Italy, but both will share in a common Italian culture that distinguishes them from German villages. European communities, in turn, will share cultural features that distinguish them from Arab or Chinese communities. Arabs, Chinese and Westerners, however, are not part of any broader cultural entity. They constitute civilizations. A civilization is thus the highest cultural grouping of people and the broadest level of cultural identity people have short of that which distinguishes humans from other species. It is defined both by common objective elements, such as language, history, religion, customs, institutions, and by the subjective self-identification of people. People have levels of identity: a resident of Rome may define himself with varying degrees of intensity as a Roman, an Italian, a Catholic, a Christian, a European, a Westerner. The civilization to which he belongs is the broadest level of identification with which he intensely identifies. People can and do redefine their identities and, as a result, the composition and boundaries of civilizations change.

Civilizations may involve a large number of people, as with China ("a civilization pretending to be a state," as Lucian Pye put it), or a very small number of people, such as the Anglophone Caribbean. A civilization may include several nation states, as is the case with Western, Latin American and Arab civilizations, or only one, as is the case with Japanese civilization. Civilizations obviously blend and overlap, and may include subcivilizations. Western civilization has two major variants, European and North American, and Islam has its Arab, Turkic and Malay subdivisions. Civilizations are nonetheless meaningful entities, and while the lines between them are seldom sharp, they are real. Civilizations are dynamic; they rise and fall; they divide and merge. And, as any student of history knows, civilizations disappear and are buried in the sands of time.

Westerners tend to think of nation states as the principal actors in global affairs. They have been that, however, for only a few centuries. The broader reaches of human history have been the history of civilizations. In *A Study of History*, Arnold Toynbee identified 21 major civilizations; only six of them exist in the contemporary world.

Why Civilizations Will Clash

Civilization identity will be increasingly important in the future, and the world will be shaped in large measure by the interactions among seven or eight major civilizations. These include Western, Confucian, Japanese, Islamic, Hindu, Slavic-Orthodox, Latin American and possibly African civilization. The most important conflicts of the future will occur along the cultural fault lines separating these civilizations from one another.

Why will this be the case?

First, differences among civilizations are not only real; they are basic. Civilizations are differentiated from each other by history, language, culture, tradition and, most important, religion. The people of different civilizations have different views on the relations between God and man, the individual and the group, the citizen and the state, parents and children, husband and wife, as well as differing views of the relative importance of rights and responsibilities, liberty and authority, equality and hierarchy. These differences are the product of centuries. They will not soon disappear. They are far more fundamental than differences among political ideologies and political regimes. Differences do not necessarily mean conflict, and conflict does not necessarily mean violence. Over the centuries, however, differences among civilizations have generated the most prolonged and the most violent conflicts.

Second, the world is becoming a smaller place. The interactions between peoples of different civilizations are increasing; these increasing interactions intensify civilization consciousness and awareness of differences between civilizations and commonalities within civilizations. North African immigration to France generates hostility among Frenchmen and at the same time increased receptivity to immigration by "good" European Catholic Poles. Americans react far more negatively to Japanese investment than to larger investments from Canada and European countries. Similarly, as Donald Horowitz has pointed out, "An Ibo may be . . . an Owerri Ibo or an Onitsha Ibo in what was the Eastern region of Nigeria. In Lagos, he is simply an Ibo. In London, he is a Nigerian. In New York, he is an African." The interactions among peoples of different civilizations enhance the civilization-consciousness of people that, in turn, invigorates differences and animosities stretching or thought to stretch back deep into history.

Third, the processes of economic modernization and social change throughout the world are separating people from longstanding local identities. They also weaken the nation state as a source of identity. In much of the world religion has moved in to fill this gap, often in the form of movements that are labeled "fundamentalist." Such movements are found in Western

Christianity, Judaism, Buddhism and Hinduism, as well as in Islam. In most countries and most religions the people active in fundamentalist movements are young, college-educated, middle-class technicians, professionals and business persons. The "unsecularization of the world," George Weigel has remarked, "is one of the dominant social facts of life in the late twentieth century." The revival of religion, "la revanche de Dieu," as Gilles Kepel labeled it, provides a basis for identity and commitment that transcends national boundaries and unites civilizations.

Fourth, the growth of civilization-consciousness is enhanced by the dual role of the West. On the one hand, the West is at a peak of power. At the same time, however, and perhaps as a result, a return to the roots phenomenon is occurring among non-Western civilizations. Increasingly one hears references to trends toward a turning inward and "Asianization" in Japan, the end of the Nehru legacy and the "Hinduization" of India, the failure of Western ideas of socialism and nationalism and hence "re-Islamization" of the Middle East, and now a debate over Westernization versus Russianization in Boris Yeltsin's country. A West at the peak of its power confronts non-Wests that increasingly have the desire, the will and the resources to shape the world in non-Western ways.

In the past, the elites of non-Western societies were usually the people who were most involved with the West, had been educated at Oxford, the Sorbonne or Sandhurst, and had absorbed Western attitudes and values. At the same time, the populace in non-Western countries often remained deeply imbued with the indigenous culture. Now, however, these relationships are being reversed. A de-Westernization and indigenization of elites is occurring in many non-Western countries at the same time that Western, usually American, cultures, styles and habits become more popular among the mass of the people.

Fifth, cultural characteristics and differences are less mutable and hence less easily compromised and resolved than political and economic ones. In the former Soviet Union, communists can become democrats, the rich can become poor and the poor rich, but Russians cannot become Estonians and Azeris cannot become Armenians. In class and ideological conflicts, the key question was "Which side are you on?" and people could and did choose sides and change sides. In conflicts between civilizations, the question is "What are you?" That is a given that cannot be changed. And as we know, from Bosnia to the Caucasus to the Sudan, the wrong answer to that question can mean a bullet in the head. Even more than ethnicity, religion discriminates sharply and exclusively among people. A person can be half-French and half-Arab and simultaneously even a citizen of two countries. It is more difficult to be half-Catholic and half-Muslim.

Finally, economic regionalism is increasing. The proportions of total trade that were intraregional rose between 1980 and 1989 from 51 percent to 59 percent in Europe, 33 percent to 37 percent in East Asia, and 32 percent to 36 percent in North America. The importance of regional economic blocs is likely to continue to increase in the future. On the one hand, successful economic regionalism will reinforce civilization-consciousness. On the other hand, economic regionalism may succeed only when it is rooted in a common civilization. The European Community rests on the shared foundation of European culture and Western Christianity. The success of the North American Free Trade Area depends on the convergence now underway of Mexican, Canadian and American cultures. Japan, in contrast, faces difficulties in creating a comparable economic entity in East Asia because Japan is a society and civilization unique to itself. However strong the trade and investment links Japan may develop with other East Asian countries, its cultural differences with those countries inhibit and perhaps preclude its promoting regional economic integration like that in Europe and North America.

Common culture, in contrast, is clearly facilitating the rapid expansion of the economic relations between the People's Republic of China and Hong Kong, Taiwan, Singapore and the overseas Chinese communities in other Asian countries. With the Cold War over, cultural commonalities increasingly overcome ideological differences, and mainland China and Taiwan move closer together. If cultural commonality is a prerequisite for economic integration, the principal East Asian economic bloc of the future is likely to be centered on China. This bloc is, in fact, already coming into existence. As Murray Weidenbaum has observed,

> Despite the current Japanese dominance of the region, the Chinese-based economy of Asia is rapidly emerging as a new epicenter for industry, commerce and finance. This strategic area contains substantial amounts of technology and manufacturing capability (Taiwan), outstanding entrepreneurial, marketing and services acumen

(Hong Kong), a fine communications network (Singapore), a tremendous pool of financial capital (all three), and very large endowments of land, resources and labor (mainland China). . . . From Guangzhou to Singapore, from Kuala Lumpur to Manila, this influential network—often based on extensions of the traditional clans—has been described as the backbone of the East Asian economy.[1]

. . .

As people define their identity in ethnic and religious terms, they are likely to see an "us" versus "them" relation existing between themselves and people of different ethnicity or religion. The end of ideologically defined states in Eastern Europe and the former Soviet Union permits traditional ethnic identities and animosities to come to the fore. Differences in culture and religion create differences over policy issues, ranging from human rights to immigration to trade and commerce to the environment. Geographical propinquity gives rise to conflicting territorial claims from Bosnia to Mindanao. Most important, the efforts of the West to promote its values of democracy and liberalism as universal values, to maintain its military predominance and to advance its economic interests engender countering responses from other civilizations. Decreasingly able to mobilize support and form coalitions on the basis of ideology, governments and groups will increasingly attempt to mobilize support by appealing to common religion and civilization identity.

The clash of civilizations thus occurs at two levels. At the micro-level, adjacent groups along the fault lines between civilizations struggle, often violently, over the control of territory and each other. At the macro-level, states from different civilizations compete for relative military and economic power, struggle over the control of international institutions and third parties, and competitively promote their particular political and religious values.

The Fault Lines Between Civilizations

The fault lines between civilizations are replacing the political and ideological boundaries of the Cold War as the flash points for crisis and bloodshed. The Cold War began when the Iron Curtain divided Europe politically and ideologically. The Cold War ended with the end of the Iron Curtain. As the ideological division of Europe has disappeared, the cultural division of Europe between Western Christianity, on the one hand, and Orthodox Christianity and Islam, on the other, has reemerged. The most significant dividing line in Europe, as William Wallace has suggested, may well be the eastern boundary of Western Christianity in the year 1500. This line runs along what are now the boundaries between Finland and Russia and between the Baltic states and Russia, cuts through Belarus and Ukraine separating the more Catholic western Ukraine from Orthodox eastern Ukraine, swings westward separating Transylvania from the rest of Romania, and then goes through Yugoslavia almost exactly along the line now separating Croatia and Slovenia from the rest of Yugoslavia. In the Balkans this line, of course, coincides with the historic boundary between the Hapsburg and Ottoman empires. The peoples to the north and west of this line are Protestant or Catholic; they shared the common experiences of European history—feudalism, the Renaissance, the Reformation, the Enlightenment, the French Revolution, the Industrial Revolution; they are generally economically better off than the peoples to the east; and they may now look forward to increasing involvement in a common European economy and to the consolidation of democratic political systems. The peoples to the east and south of this line are Orthodox or Muslim; they historically belonged to the Ottoman or Tsarist empires and were only lightly touched by the shaping events in the rest of Europe; they are generally less advanced economically; they seem much less likely to develop stable democratic political systems. The Velvet Curtain of culture has replaced the Iron Curtain of ideology as the most significant dividing line in Europe. As the events in Yugoslavia show, it is not only a line of difference; it is also at times a line of bloody conflict.

Conflict along the fault line between Western and Islamic civilizations has been going on for 1,300 years. After the founding of Islam, the Arab and Moorish surge west and north only ended at Tours in 732. From the eleventh to the thirteenth century the Crusaders attempted with temporary success to bring Christianity and Christian rule to the Holy Land. From the fourteenth to the seventeenth century, the Ottoman Turks reversed the balance, extended their sway over the Middle East and the Balkans, captured Constantinople, and twice laid siege to Vienna. In the nineteenth and early twentieth centuries as Ottoman power declined Britain, France, and Italy established Western control over most of North Africa and the Middle East.

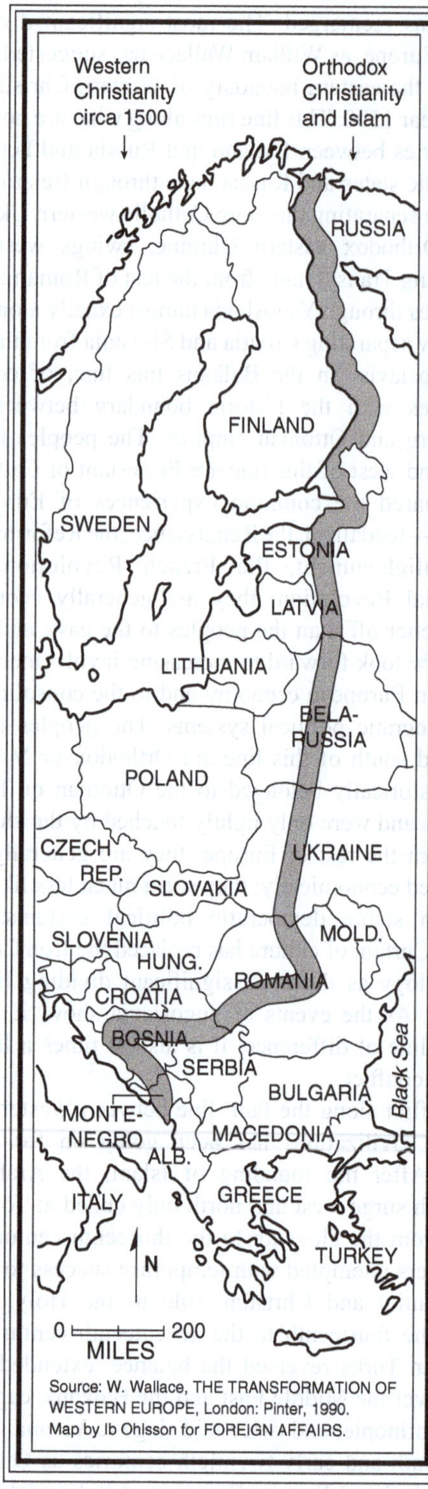

Source: W. Wallace, THE TRANSFORMATION OF WESTERN EUROPE, London: Pinter, 1990. Map by Ib Ohlsson for FOREIGN AFFAIRS.

After World War II, the West, in turn, began to retreat; the colonial empires disappeared; first Arab nationalism and then Islamic fundamentalism manifested themselves; the West became heavily dependent on the Persian Gulf countries for its energy; the oil-rich Muslim countries became money-rich and, when they wished to, weapons-rich. Several wars occurred between Arabs and Israel (created by the West). France fought a bloody and ruthless war in Algeria for most of the 1950s; British and French forces invaded Egypt in 1956; American forces went into Lebanon in 1958; subsequently American forces returned to Lebanon, attacked Libya, and engaged in various military encounters with Iran; Arab and Islamic terrorists, supported by at least three Middle Eastern governments, employed the weapon of the weak and bombed Western planes and installations and seized Western hostages. This warfare between Arabs and the West culminated in 1990, when the United States sent a massive army to the Persian Gulf to defend some Arab countries against aggression by another. In its aftermath NATO planning is increasingly directed to potential threats and instability along its "southern tier."

This centuries-old military interaction between the West and Islam is unlikely to decline. It could become more virulent. The Gulf War left some Arabs feeling proud that Saddam Hussein had attacked Israel and stood up to the West. It also left many feeling humiliated and resentful of the West's military presence in the Persian Gulf, the West's overwhelming military dominance, and their apparent inability to shape their own destiny. Many Arab countries, in addition to the oil exporters, are reaching levels of economic and social development where autocratic forms of government become inappropriate and efforts to introduce democracy become stronger. Some openings in Arab political systems have already occurred. The principal beneficiaries of these openings have been Islamist movements. In the Arab world, in short, Western democracy strengthens anti-Western political forces. This may be a passing phenomenon, but it surely complicates relations between Islamic countries and the West. . . .

On both sides the interaction between Islam and the West is seen as a clash of civilizations. The West's "next confrontation," observes M. J. Akbar, an Indian Muslim author, "is definitely going to come from the Muslim world. It is in the sweep of the Islamic nations from the Maghreb to Pakistan that the struggle for a new world order will begin." Bernard Lewis comes to a similar conclusion:

> We are facing a mood and a movement far transcending the level of issues and policies and the governments that pursue them. This is no less than a clash of civilizations—the perhaps irrational but surely historic reaction of an ancient rival against our Judeo-Christian heritage, our secular present, and the world-wide expansion of both.[2]

Historically, the other great antagonistic interaction of Arab Islamic civilization has been with the pagan, animist, and now increasingly Christian black peoples to the south. In the past, this antagonism was epitomized in the image of Arab slave dealers and black slaves. It has been reflected in the on-going civil war in the Sudan between Arabs and blacks, the fighting in Chad between Libyan-supported insurgents and the government, the tensions between Orthodox Christians and Muslims in the Horn of Africa, and the political conflicts, recurring riots and communal violence between Muslims and Christians in Nigeria. The modernization of Africa and the spread of Christianity are likely to enhance the probability of violence along this fault line. Symptomatic of the intensification of this conflict was the Pope John Paul II's speech in Khartoum in February 1993 attacking the actions of the Sudan's Islamist government against the Christian minority there.

On the northern border of Islam, conflict has increasingly erupted between Orthodox and Muslim peoples, including the carnage of Bosnia and Sarajevo, the simmering violence between Serb and Albanian, the tenuous relations between Bulgarians and their Turkish minority, the violence between Ossetians and Ingush, the unremitting slaughter of each other by Armenians and Azeris, the tense relations between Russians and Muslims in Central Asia, and the deployment of Russian troops to protect Russian interests in the Caucasus and Central Asia. Religion reinforces the revival of ethnic identities and re-stimulates Russian fears about the security of their southern borders. This concern is well captured by Archie Roosevelt:

> Much of Russian history concerns the struggle between the Slavs and the Turkic peoples on their borders, which dates back to the foundation of the Russian state more than a thousand years ago. In the Slavs' millennium-long confrontation with their eastern neighbors lies the key to an understanding not only of Russian history, but Russian character. To understand Russian realities today one has to have a concept of the great Turkic ethnic group that has preoccupied Russians through the centuries.[3]

The conflict of civilizations is deeply rooted elsewhere in Asia. The historic clash between Muslim and Hindu in the subcontinent manifests itself now not only in the rivalry between Pakistan and India but also in intensifying religious strife within India between increasingly militant Hindu groups and India's substantial Muslim minority. . . . In East Asia, China has outstanding territorial disputes with most of its neighbors. It has pursued a ruthless policy toward the Buddhist people of Tibet, and it is pursuing an increasingly ruthless policy toward its Turkic-Muslim minority. With the Cold War over, the underlying differences between China and the United States have reasserted themselves in areas such as human rights, trade and weapons proliferation. These differences are unlikely to moderate. A "new cold war," Deng Xaioping reportedly asserted in 1991, is under way between China and America. . . .

The interactions between civilizations vary greatly in the extent to which they are likely to be characterized by violence. Economic competition clearly predominates between the American and European subcivilizations of the West and between both of them and Japan. On the Eurasian continent, however, the proliferation of ethnic conflict, epitomized at the extreme in "ethnic cleansing," has not been totally random. It has been most frequent and most violent between groups belonging to different civilizations. In Eurasia the great historic fault lines between civilizations are once more aflame. This is particularly true along the boundaries of the crescent-shaped Islamic bloc of nations from the bulge of Africa to central Asia. Violence also occurs between Muslims, on the one hand, and Orthodox Serbs in the Balkans, Jews in Israel, Hindus in India, Buddhists in Burma and Catholics in the Philippines. Islam has bloody borders. . . .

The Confucian-Islamic Connection

The obstacles to non-Western countries joining the West vary considerably. They are least for Latin American and East European countries. They are greater for the Orthodox countries of the former Soviet Union. They are still greater for Muslim, Confucian, Hindu and Buddhist societies. Japan has established a unique position for itself as an associate member of the West: it is in the West in some respects but clearly not of the West in important dimensions. Those countries that for reason of culture and power do not wish to, or cannot, join the West compete with the West by developing their own economic, military and political power. They do this by promoting their internal development and by cooperating with other non-Western countries. The most prominent form of this cooperation is the Confucian-Islamic connection that has emerged to challenge Western interests, values and power.

Almost without exception, Western countries are reducing their military power; under Yeltsin's leadership so also is Russia. China, North Korea and several Middle Eastern states, however, are significantly expanding their military capabilities. They are doing this by the import of arms from Western and non-Western sources and by the development of indigenous arms industries. One result is the emergence of what Charles Krauthammer has called "Weapon States," and the Weapon States are not Western states. Another result is the redefinition of arms control, which is a Western concept and a Western goal. During the Cold War the primary purpose of arms control was to establish a stable military balance between the United States and its allies and the Soviet Union and its allies. In the post-Cold War world the primary objective of arms control is to prevent the development by non-Western societies of military capabilities that could threaten Western interests. The West attempts to do this through international agreements, economic pressure and controls on the transfer of arms and weapons technologies.

The conflict between the West and the Confucian-Islamic states focuses largely, although not exclusively, on nuclear, chemical and biological weapons, ballistic missiles and other sophisticated means for delivering them, and the guidance, intelligence and other electronic capabilities for achieving that goal. The West promotes nonproliferation as a universal norm and nonproliferation treaties and inspections as means of realizing that norm. It also threatens a variety of sanctions against those who promote the spread of sophisticated weapons and proposes some benefits for those who do not. The attention of the West focuses, naturally, on nations that are actually or potentially hostile to the West.

The non-Western nations, on the other hand, assert their right to acquire and to deploy whatever weapons they think necessary for their security. They also have absorbed, to the full, the truth of the response of the Indian defense minister when asked what lesson he learned from the Gulf War: "Don't fight the United States unless you have nuclear weapons." Nuclear weapons, chemical weapons and missiles are viewed, probably erroneously, as the potential equalizer of superior Western conventional power. . . . A top Iranian official has declared that all Muslim states should acquire nuclear weapons, and in 1988 the president of Iran reportedly issued a directive calling for development of "offensive and defensive chemical, biological and radiological weapons."

Centrally important to the development of counter-West military capabilities is the sustained expansion of China's military power and its means to create military power. Buoyed by spectacular economic development, China is rapidly increasing its military spending and vigorously moving forward with the modernization of its armed forces. It is purchasing weapons from the former Soviet states; it is developing long-range missiles; in 1992 it tested a one-megaton nuclear device. It is developing power-projection capabilities, acquiring aerial refueling technology, and trying to purchase an aircraft carrier. Its military buildup and assertion of sovereignty over the South China Sea are provoking a multilateral regional arms race in East Asia. China is also a major exporter of arms and weapons technology. . . . The flow of weapons and weapons technology is generally from East Asia to the Middle East. There is, however, some movement in the reverse direction; China has received Stinger missiles from Pakistan.

A Confucian-Islamic military connection has thus come into being, designed to promote acquisition by its members of the weapons and weapons technologies needed to counter the military power of the West. It may or may not last. At present, however, it is, as Dave McCurdy has said, "a renegades' mutual support pact, run by the proliferators and their backers." A new form of arms competition is thus occurring between Islamic-Confucian states and the West. In an old-fashioned arms race, each side developed its own arms to balance or to achieve superiority against the other side. In this new form of arms competition, one side is developing its arms and the other side is attempting not to balance but to limit and prevent that arms build-up while at the same time reducing its own military capabilities.

Implications for the West

This article does not argue that civilization identities will replace all other identities, that nation-states will disappear, that each civilization will become a single coherent political entity, that groups within a civilization will not conflict with and even fight each other. This paper does set forth the hypotheses that differences between civilizations are real and important; civilization-consciousness is increasing; conflict between civilizations will supplant ideological and other forms of conflict as the dominant global form of conflict; international relations, historically a game played out within Western civilization, will increasingly be de-Westernized and become a game in which non-Western civilizations are actors and not simply objects; successful political, security and economic international institutions are more likely to develop within civilizations than across civilizations; conflicts between groups in different civilizations will be more frequent, more sustained and more violent than conflicts between groups in the same civilization; violent conflicts between groups in different civilizations are the most likely and most dangerous source of escalation that could lead to global wars; the paramount axis of world politics will be the relations between "the West and the Rest"; the elites in some torn non-Western countries will try to make their countries part of the West, but in most cases face major obstacles to accomplishing this; a central focus of conflict for the immediate future will be between the West and several Islamic-Confucian states.

This is not to advocate the desirability of conflicts between civilizations. It is to set forth descriptive hypotheses as to what the future may be like. If these are plausible hypotheses, however, it is necessary to consider their implications for Western policy. These implications should be divided between short-term advantage and long-term accommodation. In the short-term it is clearly in the interest of the West to promote greater cooperation and unity within its own civilization, particularly between its European and North American components; to incorporate into the West societies in Eastern Europe and Latin America whose cultures are close to those of the West; to promote and maintain cooperative relations with Russia and Japan; to prevent escalation of local inter-civilization conflicts into major inter-civilization wars; to limit the expansion of the military strength of Confucian and Islamic states; to moderate the reduction of Western military capabilities and maintain military superiority in East and Southwest Asia; to exploit differences and conflicts among Confucian and Islamic states; to support in other civilizations groups sympathetic to Western values and interests; to strengthen international institutions that reflect and legitimate Western interests and values and to promote the involvement of non-Western states in those institutions.

In the longer term other measures would be called for. Western civilization is both Western and modern. Non-Western civilizations have attempted to become modern without becoming Western. To date only Japan has fully succeeded in this quest. Non-Western civilizations will continue to attempt to acquire the wealth, technology, skills, machines and weapons that are part of being modern. They will also attempt to reconcile this modernity with their traditional culture and values. Their economic and military strength relative to the West will increase. Hence the West will increasingly have to accommodate these non-Western modern civilizations whose power approaches that of the West but whose values and interests differ significantly from those of the West. This will require the West to maintain the economic and military power necessary to protect its interests in relation to these civilizations. It will also, however, require the West to develop a more profound understanding of the basic religious and philosophical assumptions underlying other civilizations and the ways in which people in those civilizations see their interests. It will require an effort to identify elements of commonality between Western and other civilizations. For the relevant future, there will be no universal civilization, but instead a world of different civilizations, each of which will have to learn to coexist with the others.

Notes

1. Murray Weidenbaum, *Greater China: The Next Economic Superpower?,* St. Louis: Washington University Center for the Study of American Business, Contemporary Issues, Series 57, February 1993, pp. 2–3.

2. Bernard Lewis, "The Roots of Muslim Rage," *The Atlantic Monthly*, vol. 266, September 1990, p. 60; *Time*, June 15, 1992, pp. 24–28.

3. Archie Roosevelt, *For Lust of Knowing*, Boston: Little, Brown, 1988, pp. 332–333.

32 Ethics and Development Assistance

32.1

Famine, Affluence, and Morality

Peter Singer

As I write this, in November 1971, people are dying in East Bengal from lack of food, shelter, and medical care. The suffering and death that are occurring there now are not inevitable, not unavoidable in any fatalistic sense of the term. Constant poverty, a cyclone, and a civil war have turned at least nine million people into destitute refugees; nevertheless, it is not beyond the capacity of the richer nations to give enough assistance to reduce any further suffering to very small proportions. The decisions and actions of human beings can prevent this kind of suffering. Unfortunately, human beings have not made the necessary decisions. At the individual level, people have, with very few exceptions, not responded to the situation in any significant way. Generally speaking, people have not given large sums to relief funds; they have not written to their parliamentary representatives demanding increased government assistance; they have not demonstrated in the streets, held symbolic fasts, or done anything else directed toward providing the refugees with the means to satisfy their essential needs. At the government level, no government has given the sort of massive aid that would enable the refugees to survive for more than a few days. Britain, for instance, has given rather more than most countries. It has, to date, given £14,750,000. For comparative purposes, Britain's share of the nonrecoverable development costs of the Anglo-French Concorde project is already in excess of £275,000,000, and on present estimates will reach £440,000,000. The implication is that the British government values a supersonic transport more than thirty times as highly as it values the lives of the nine million refugees. . . .

These are the essential facts about the present situation in Bengal. So far as it concerns us here, there is nothing unique about this situation except its magnitude. The Bengal emergency is just the latest and most acute of a series of major emergencies in various parts of the world, arising both from natural and from man-made causes. There are also many parts of the world in which people die from malnutrition and lack of food independent of any special emergency. I take Bengal as my example only because it is the present concern, and because the size of the problem has ensured that it has been given adequate publicity. Neither individuals nor governments can claim to be unaware of what is happening there.

What are the moral implications of a situation like this? In what follows, I shall argue that the way people in relatively affluent countries react to a situation like that in Bengal cannot be justified; indeed, the whole way we look at moral issues—our moral conceptual

Source: Peter Singer. "Famine, Affluence, and Morality," *Philosophy and Public Affairs* 1(3): 229–236 and 238–243. Copyright 1972. Reproduced with permission of Blackwell Publishing Ltd.

scheme—needs to be altered, and with it, the way of life that has come to be taken for granted in our society.

In arguing for this conclusion I will not, of course, claim to be morally neutral. I shall, however, try to argue for the moral position that I take, so that anyone who accepts certain assumptions, to be made explicit, will, I hope, accept my conclusion.

I begin with the assumption that suffering and death from lack of food, shelter, and medical care are bad. I think most people will agree about this, although one may reach the same view by different routes. . . .

My next point is this: if it is in our power to prevent something bad from happening, without thereby sacrificing anything of comparable moral importance, we ought, morally, to do it. By "without sacrificing anything of comparable moral importance" I mean without causing anything else comparably bad to happen, or doing something that is wrong in itself, or failing to promote some moral good, comparable in significance to the bad thing that we can prevent. This principle seems almost as uncontroversial as the last one. It requires us only to prevent what is bad, and not to promote what is good, and it requires this of us only when we can do it without sacrificing anything that is, from the moral point of view, comparably important. . . . An application of this principle would be as follows: if I am walking past a shallow pond and see a child drowning in it, I ought to wade in and pull the child out. This will mean getting my clothes muddy, but this is insignificant, while the death of the child would presumably be a very bad thing.

The uncontroversial appearance of the principle just stated is deceptive. If it were acted upon, even in its qualified form, our lives, our society, and our world would be fundamentally changed. For the principle takes, firstly, no account of proximity or distance. It makes no moral difference whether the person I can help is a neighbor's child ten yards from me or a Bengali whose name I shall never know, ten thousand miles away. Secondly, the principle makes no distinction between cases in which I am the only person who could possibly do anything and cases in which I am just one among millions in the same position.

I do not think I need to say much in defense of the refusal to take proximity and distance into account. The fact that a person is physically near to us, so that we have personal contact with him, may make it more likely that we *shall* assist him, but this does not show that we *ought* to help him rather than another who happens to be further away. If we accept any principle of impartiality, universalizability, equality, or whatever, we cannot discriminate against someone merely because he is far away from us (or we are far away from him). . . . From the moral point of view, the development of the world into a "global village" has made an important, though still unrecognized, difference to our moral situation. Expert observers and supervisors, sent out by famine relief organizations or permanently stationed in famine-prone areas, can direct our aid to a refugee in Bengal almost as effectively as we could get it to someone in our own block. There would seem, therefore, to be no possible justification for discriminating on geographical grounds.

There may be a greater need to defend the second implication of my principle—that the fact that there are millions of other people in the same position, in respect to the Bengali refugees, as I am, does not make the situation significantly different from a situation in which I am the only person who can prevent something very bad from occurring. Again, of course, I admit that there is a psychological difference between the cases; one feels less guilty about doing nothing if one can point to others, similarly placed, who have also done nothing. Yet this can make no real difference to our moral obligations.[1] Should I consider that I am less obliged to pull the drowning child out of the pond if on looking around I see other people, no further away than I am, who have also noticed the child but are doing nothing? One has only to ask this question to see the absurdity of the view that numbers lessen obligation. It is a view that is an ideal excuse for inactivity; unfortunately most of the major evils—poverty, overpopulation, pollution—are problems in which everyone is almost equally involved. . . .

The result of everyone doing what he really ought to do cannot be worse than the result of everyone doing less than he ought to do, although the result of everyone doing what he reasonably believes he ought to do could be.

If my argument so far has been sound, neither our distance from a preventable evil nor the number of other people who, in respect to that evil, are in the same situation as we are, lessens our obligation to mitigate or prevent that evil. I shall therefore take as established the principle I asserted earlier. As I have already said, I need to assert it only in its qualified form: if it is in our power to prevent something very bad from happening, without thereby sacrificing anything else morally significant, we ought, morally, to do it.

The outcome of this argument is that our traditional moral categories are upset. The traditional distinction between duty and charity cannot be drawn, or at least, not in the place we normally draw it. Giving money to the Bengal Relief Fund is regarded as an act of charity in our society. The bodies which collect money are known as "charities." These organizations see themselves in this way—if you send them a check, you will be thanked for your "generosity." Because giving money is regarded as an act of charity, it is not thought that there is anything wrong with not giving. The charitable man may be praised, but the man who is not charitable is not condemned. People do not feel in any way ashamed or guilty about spending money on new clothes or a new car instead of giving it to famine relief. (Indeed, the alternative does not occur to them.) This way of looking at the matter cannot be justified. When we buy new clothes not to keep ourselves warm but to look "well-dressed" we are not providing for any important need. We would not be sacrificing anything significant if we were to continue to wear our old clothes, and give the money to famine relief. By doing so, we would be preventing another person from starving. It follows from what I have said earlier that we ought to give money away, rather than spend it on clothes which we do not need to keep us warm. To do so is not charitable, or generous. Nor is it the kind of act which philosophers and theologians have called "supererogatory"—an act which it would be good to do, but not wrong not to do. On the contrary, we ought to give the money away, and it is wrong not to do so. . . .

Despite the limited nature of the revision in our moral conceptual scheme which I am proposing, the revision would, given the extent of both affluence and famine in the world today, have radical implications. These implications may lead to further objections, distinct from those I have already considered. I shall discuss two of these.

One objection to the position I have taken might be simply that it is too drastic a revision of our moral scheme. People do not ordinarily judge in the way I have suggested they should. Most people reserve their moral condemnation for those who violate some moral norm, such as the norm against taking another person's property. They do not condemn those who indulge in luxury instead of giving to famine relief. But given that I did not set out to present a morally neutral description of the way people make moral judgments, the way people do in fact judge has nothing to do with the validity of my conclusion. My conclusion follows from the principle which I advanced earlier, and unless that principle is rejected, or the arguments shown to be unsound, I think the conclusion must stand, however strange it appears. . . .

The second objection to my attack on the present distinction between duty and charity is one which has from time to time been made against utilitarianism. It follows from some forms of utilitarian theory that we all ought, morally, to be working full time to increase the balance of happiness over misery. The position I have taken here would not lead to this conclusion in all circumstances, for if there were no bad occurrences that we could prevent without sacrificing something of comparable moral importance, my argument would have no application. Given the present conditions in many parts of the world, however, it does follow from my argument that we ought, morally, to be working full time to relieve great suffering of the sort that occurs as a result of famine or other disasters. . . . This conclusion is one which we may be reluctant to face. I cannot see, though, why it should be regarded as a criticism of the position for which I have argued, rather than a criticism of our ordinary standards of behavior. Since most people are self-interested to some degree, very few of us are likely to do everything that we ought to do. It would, however, hardly be honest to take this as evidence that it is not the case that we ought to do it.

It may still be thought that my conclusions are so wildly out of line with what everyone else thinks and has always thought that there must be something wrong with the argument somewhere. In order to show that my conclusions, while certainly contrary to contemporary Western moral standards, would not have seemed so extraordinary at other times and in other places, I would like to quote a passage from a writer not normally thought of as a way-out radical, Thomas Aquinas.

> Now, according to the natural order instituted by divine providence, material goods are provided for the satisfaction of human needs. Therefore the division and appropriation of property, which proceeds from human law, must not hinder the satisfaction of man's necessity from such goods.
>
> Equally, whatever a man has in superabundance is owed, of natural right, to the poor for their sustenance. So Ambrosius says, and it is also to be found in the *Decretum Gratiani*: "The bread which you withhold belongs to the hungry; the clothing you shut away, to the naked; and the money you bury in the earth is the redemption and freedom of the penniless."[2]

I now want to consider a number of points, more practical than philosophical, which are relevant to the application of the moral conclusion we have reached. These points challenge not the idea that we ought to be doing all we can to prevent starvation, but the idea that giving away a great deal of money is the best means to this end.

It is sometimes said that overseas aid should be a government responsibility, and that therefore one ought not to give to privately run charities. Giving privately, it is said, allows the government and the noncontributing members of society to escape their responsibilities.

This argument seems to assume that the more people there are who give to privately organized famine relief funds, the less likely it is that the government will take over full responsibility for such aid. This assumption is unsupported, and does not strike me as at all plausible. The opposite view—that if no one gives voluntarily, a government will assume that its citizens are uninterested in famine relief and would not wish to be forced into giving aid—seems more plausible. In any case, unless there were a definite probability that by refusing to give one would be helping to bring about massive government assistance, people who do refuse to make voluntary contributions are refusing to prevent a certain amount of suffering without being able to point to any tangible beneficial consequence of their refusal. So the onus of showing how their refusal will bring about government action is on those who refuse to give. . . .

Another, more serious reason for not giving to famine relief funds is that until there is effective population control, relieving famine merely postpones starvation. If we save the Bengal refugees now, others, perhaps the children of these refugees, will face starvation in a few years' time. In support of this, one may cite the now well-known facts about the population explosion and the relatively limited scope for expanded production.

This point, like the previous one, is an argument against relieving suffering that is happening now, because of a belief about what might happen in the future; it is unlike the previous point in that very good evidence can be adduced in support of this belief about the future. I will not go into the evidence here. I accept that the earth cannot support indefinitely a population rising at the present rate. This certainly poses a problem for anyone who thinks it important to prevent famine. Again, however, one could accept the argument without drawing the conclusion that it absolves one from any obligation to do anything to prevent famine. The conclusion that should be drawn is that the best means of preventing famine, in the long run, is population control. It would then follow from the position reached earlier that one ought to be doing all one can to promote population control (unless one held that all forms of population control were wrong in themselves, or would have significantly bad consequences). Since there are organizations working specifically for population control, one would then support them rather than more orthodox methods of preventing famine.

A third point raised by the conclusion reached earlier relates to the question of just how much we all ought to be giving away. One possibility, which has already been mentioned, is that we ought to give until we reach the level of marginal utility—that is, the level at which, by giving more, I would cause as much suffering to myself or my dependents as I would relieve by my gift. This would mean, of course, that one would reduce oneself to very near the material circumstances of a Bengali refugee. It will be recalled that earlier I put forward both a strong and a moderate version of the principle of preventing bad occurrences. The strong version, which required us to prevent bad things from happening unless in doing so we would be sacrificing something of comparable moral significance, does seem to require reducing ourselves to the level of marginal utility. I should also say that the strong version seems to me to be the correct one. I proposed the more moderate version—that we should prevent bad occurrences unless, to do so, we had to sacrifice something morally significant—only in order to show that even on this surely undeniable principle a great change in our way of life is required. On the more moderate principle, it may not follow that we ought to reduce ourselves to the level of marginal utility, for one might hold that to reduce oneself and one's family to this level is to cause something significantly bad to happen. Whether this is so I shall not discuss, since, as I have said, I can see no good reason for holding the moderate version of the principle rather than the strong version. Even if we accepted the principle only in its moderate form, however, it should be clear that we would have to give away enough to ensure that the consumer society, dependent as it is on people spending on trivia rather than giving to famine relief, would slow down and perhaps disappear entirely. . . .

Discussion, though, is not enough. What is the point of relating philosophy to public (and personal) affairs if we do not take our conclusions seriously? In this instance, taking our conclusion seriously means acting upon it. The philosopher will not find it any easier than anyone else to alter his attitudes and way of life to the extent that, if I am right, is involved in doing everything that we ought to be doing. At the very least, though, one can make a start. The philosopher who does so will have to sacrifice some of the benefits of the consumer society, but he can find compensation in the satisfaction of a way of life in which theory and practice, if not yet in harmony, are at least coming together.

NOTES

1. In view of the special sense philosophers often give to the term, I should say that I use "obligation" simply as the abstract noun derived from "ought," so that "I have an obligation to" means no more, and no less, than "I ought to." This usage is in accordance with the definition of "ought" given by the *Shorter Oxford English Dictionary*: "the general verb to express duty or obligation." I do not think any issue of substance hangs on the way the term is used; sentences in which I use "obligation" could all be rewritten, although somewhat clumsily, as sentences in which a clause containing "ought" replaces the term "obligation."

2. *Summa Theologica*, II-II, Question 66, Article 7, in *Aquinas, Selected Political Writings*, ed. A. P. d'Entreves, trans. J. G. Dawson (Oxford, 1948), p. 171.

32.2

Lifeboat Ethics

The Case Against Helping the Poor

Garrett Hardin

Environmentalists use the metaphor of the earth as a "spaceship" in trying to persuade countries, industries and people to stop wasting and polluting our natural resources. Since we all share life on this planet, they argue, no single person or institution has the right to destroy, waste, or use more than a fair share of its resources.

But does everyone on earth have an equal right to an equal share of its resources? The spaceship metaphor can be dangerous when used by misguided idealists to justify suicidal policies for sharing our resources through uncontrolled immigration and foreign aid. In their enthusiastic but unrealistic generosity, they confuse the ethics of a spaceship with those of a lifeboat.

A true spaceship would have to be under the control of a captain, since no ship could possibly survive if its course were determined by committee. Spaceship Earth certainly has no captain; the United Nations is merely a toothless tiger, with little power to enforce any policy upon its bickering members.

If we divide the world crudely into rich nations and poor nations, two thirds of them are desperately poor, and only one third comparatively rich, with the United States the wealthiest of all. Metaphorically each rich nation can be seen as a lifeboat full of comparatively rich people. In the ocean outside each lifeboat swim the poor of the world, who would like to get in, or at least to share some of the wealth. What should the lifeboat passengers do?

First, we must recognize the limited capacity of any lifeboat. For example, a nation's land has a limited capacity to support a population and as the current energy crisis has shown us, in some ways we have already exceeded the carrying capacity of our land.

Adrift in a Moral Sea

So here we sit, say 50 people in our lifeboat. To be generous, let us assume it has room for 10 more, making a total capacity of 60. Suppose the 50 of us in the lifeboat see 100 others swimming in the water outside, begging for admission to our boat or for handouts. We have several options: we may be tempted to try to live by the Christian ideal of being "our brother's keeper," or by the Marxist ideal of "to each according to his needs." Since the needs of all in the water are the same, and since they can all be seen as "our brothers," we could take them all into our boat, making a total of 150 in a boat designed for 60. The boat swamps, everyone drowns. Complete justice, complete catastrophe.

Since the boat has an unused excess capacity of 10 more passengers, we could admit just 10 more to it. But which 10 do we let in? How do we choose? Do we pick the best 10, "first come, first served"? And what do we say to the 90 we exclude? If we do let an extra 10 into our lifeboat, we will have lost our "safety factor," an engineering principle of critical importance. For example, if we don't leave room for excess capacity as a safety factor in our country's agriculture, a new plant disease or a bad change in the weather could have disastrous consequences.

Suppose we decide to preserve our small safety factor and admit no more to the lifeboat. Our survival is then possible although we shall have to be constantly on guard against boarding parties.

While this last solution clearly offers the only means of our survival, it is morally abhorrent to many people. Some say they feel guilty about their good luck. My reply is simple: "Get out and yield your place to others." This may solve the problem of the guilt-ridden person's conscience, but it does not change the ethics of the lifeboat. The needy person to whom the guilt-ridden person yields his place will not himself feel guilty about his good luck. If he did, he would not climb aboard. The net result of conscience-stricken people giving up their unjustly held seats is the elimination of that sort of conscience from the lifeboat.

Source: Garrett Hardin, "Lifeboat Ethics: The Case Against Helping the Poor," *Psychology Today* 8(4): 38–43, 123–124, and 126. Reprinted with permission from *Psychology Today* Magazine,

This is the basic metaphor within which we must work out our solutions. Let us now enrich the image, step by step, with substantive additions from the real world, a world that must solve real and pressing problems of overpopulation and hunger.

The harsh ethics of the lifeboat become even harsher when we consider the reproductive differences between the rich nations and the poor nations. The people inside the lifeboats are doubling in numbers every 87 years; those swimming around outside are doubling, on the average, every 35 years, more than twice as fast as the rich. And since the world's resources are dwindling, the difference in prosperity between the rich and the poor can only increase.

As of 1973, the U.S. had a population of 210 million people, who were increasing by 0.8 percent per year. Outside our lifeboat, let us imagine another 210 million people (say the combined populations of Colombia, Ecuador, Venezuela, Morocco, Pakistan, Thailand and the Philippines) who are increasing at a rate of 3.3 percent per year. Put differently, the doubling time for this aggregate population is 21 years, compared to 87 years for the U.S.

The harsh ethics of the lifeboat become harsher when we consider the reproductive differences between rich and poor.

Multiplying the Rich and the Poor

Now suppose the U.S. agreed to pool its resources with those seven countries, with everyone receiving an equal share. Initially the ratio of Americans to non-Americans in this model would be one-to-one. But consider what the ratio would be after 87 years, by which time the Americans would have doubled to a population of 420 million. By then, doubling every 21 years, the other group would have swollen to 3.54 billion. Each American would have to share the available resources with more than eight people.

But, one could argue, this discussion assumes that current population trends will continue, and they may not. Quite so. Most likely the rate of population increase will decline much faster in the U.S. than it will in the other countries, and there does not seem to be much we can do about it. In sharing with "each according to his needs," we must recognize that needs are determined by population size, which is determined by the rate of reproduction, which at present is regarded as a sovereign right of every nation, poor or not. This being so, the philanthropic load created by the sharing ethic of the spaceship can only increase.

The Tragedy of the Commons

The fundamental error of spaceship ethics, and the sharing it requires, is that it leads to what I call "the tragedy of the commons." Under a system of private property, the men who own property recognize their responsibility to care for it, for if they don't they will eventually suffer. A farmer, for instance, will allow no more cattle in a pasture than its carrying capacity justifies. If he overloads it, erosion sets in, weeds take over, and he loses the use of the pasture.

If a pasture becomes a commons open to all, the right of each to use it may not be matched by a corresponding responsibility to protect it. Asking everyone to use it with discretion will hardly do, for the considerate herdsman who refrains from overloading the commons suffers more than a selfish one who says his needs are greater. If everyone would restrain himself, all would be well; but it takes only one less than everyone to ruin a system of voluntary restraint. In a crowded world of less than perfect human beings, mutual ruin is inevitable if there are no controls. This is the tragedy of the commons.

One of the major tasks of education today should be the creation of such an acute awareness of the dangers of the commons that people will recognize its many varieties. For example, the air and water have become polluted because they are treated as commons. Further growth in the population or per-capita conversion of natural resources into pollutants will only make the problem worse. The same holds true for the fish of the oceans. Fishing fleets have nearly disappeared in many parts of the world, technological improvements in the art of fishing are hastening the day of complete ruin. Only the replacement of the system of the commons with a responsible system of control will save the land, air, water and oceanic fisheries.

The World Food Bank

In recent years there has been a push to create a new commons called a World Food Bank, an international depository of food reserves to which nations would contribute according to their abilities and from which they would draw according to their needs.

This humanitarian proposal has received support from many liberal international groups, and from such prominent citizens as Margaret Mead, U.N. Secretary General Kurt Waldheim, and Senators Edward Kennedy and George McGovern.

A world food bank appeals powerfully to our humanitarian impulses. But before we rush ahead with such a plan, let us recognize where the greatest political push comes from, lest we be disillusioned later. Our experience with the "Food for Peace program," or Public Law 480, gives us the answer. This program moved billions of dollars worth of U.S. surplus grain to food-short, population-long countries during the past two decades. But when P.L. 480 first became law, a headline in the business magazine *Forbes* revealed the real power behind it: "Feeding the World's Hungry Millions: How It Will Mean Billions for U.S. Business."

And indeed it did. In the years 1960 to 1970, U.S. taxpayers spent a total of $7.9 billion on the Food for Peace program. Between 1948 and 1970, they also paid an additional $50 billion for other economic-aid programs, some of which went for food and food-producing machinery and technology. Though all U.S. taxpayers were forced to contribute to the cost of P.L. 480 certain special interest groups gained handsomely under the program. Farmers did not have to contribute the grain; the Government or rather the taxpayers, bought it from them at full market prices. The increased demand raised prices of farm products generally. The manufacturers of farm machinery, fertilizers and pesticides benefited by the farmers' extra efforts to grow more food. Grain elevators profited from storing the surplus until it could be shipped. Railroads made money hauling it to ports, and shipping lines profited from carrying it overseas. The implementation of P.L. 480 required the creation of a vast Government bureaucracy, which then acquired its own vested interest in continuing the program regardless of its merits.

Extracting Dollars

Those who proposed and defended the Food for Peace program in public rarely mentioned its importance to any of these special interests. The public emphasis was always on its humanitarian effects. The combination of silent selfish interests and highly vocal humanitarian apologists made a powerful and successful lobby for extracting money from taxpayers. We can expect the same lobby to push now for the creation of a World Food Bank.

However great the potential benefit to selfish interests, it should not be a decisive argument against a truly humanitarian program. We must ask if such a program would actually do more good than harm, not only momentarily but also in the long run. Those who propose the food bank usually refer to a current "emergency" or "crisis" in terms of world food supply. But what is an emergency? Although they may be infrequent and sudden, everyone knows that emergencies will occur from time to time. A well-run family, company, organization or country prepares for the likelihood of accidents and emergencies. It expects them, it budgets for them, it saves for them.

Learning the Hard Way

What happens if some organizations or countries budget for accidents and others do not? If each country is solely responsible for its own wellbeing, poorly managed ones will suffer. But they can learn from experience. They may mend their ways, and learn to budget for infrequent but certain emergencies. For example, the weather varies from year to year, and periodic crop failures are certain. A wise and competent government saves out of the production of the good years in anticipation of bad years to come. Joseph taught this policy to Pharaoh in Egypt more than 2,000 years ago. Yet the great majority of the governments in the world today do not follow such a policy. They lack either the wisdom or the competence, or both. Should those nations that do manage to put something aside be forced to come to the rescue each time an emergency occurs among the poor nations?

"But it isn't their fault!" Some kind-hearted liberals argue. "How can we blame the poor people who are caught in an emergency? Why must they suffer for the sins of their governments?" The concept of blame is simply not relevant here. The real question is, what are the operational consequences of establishing a world food bank? If it is open to every country every time a need develops, slovenly rulers will not be motivated to take Joseph's advice. Someone will always come to their aid. Some countries will deposit food in the world food bank, and others will withdraw it. There will be almost no overlap. As a result of such solutions to food shortage emergencies, the poor countries will not learn to mend their ways, and will suffer progressively greater emergencies as their populations grow.

Population Control the Crude Way

On the average, poor countries undergo a 2.5 percent increase in population each year; rich countries, about

0.8 percent. Only rich countries have anything in the way of food reserves set aside, and even they do not have as much as they should. Poor countries have none. If poor countries received no food from the outside, the rate of their population growth would be periodically checked by crop failures and famines. But if they can always draw on a world food bank in time of need, their population can continue to grow unchecked, and so will their "need" for aid. In the short run, a world food bank may diminish that need, but in the long run it actually increases the need without limit.

Without some system of worldwide food sharing, the proportion of people in the rich and poor nations might eventually stabilize. The overpopulated poor countries would decrease in numbers, while the rich countries that had room for more people would increase. But with a well-meaning system of sharing, such as a world food bank, the growth differential between the rich and the poor countries will not only persist, it will increase. Because of the higher rate of population growth in the poor countries of the world, 88 percent of today's children are born poor, and only 12 percent rich. Year by year the ratio becomes worse, as the fast-reproducing poor outnumber the slow-reproducing rich.

A world food bank is thus a commons in disguise. People will have more motivation to draw from it than to add to any common store. The less provident and less able will multiply at the expense of the abler and more provident, bringing eventual ruin upon all who share in the commons. Besides, any system of "sharing" that amounts to foreign aid from the rich nations to the poor nations will carry the taint of charity, which will contribute little to the world peace so devoutly desired by those who support the idea of a world food bank.

As past U.S. foreign-aid programs have amply and depressingly demonstrated, international charity frequently inspires mistrust and antagonism rather than gratitude on the part of the recipient nation.

Chinese Fish and Miracle Rice

The modern approach to foreign aid stresses the export of technology and advice, rather than money and food. As an ancient Chinese proverb goes: "Give a man a fish and he will eat for a day; teach him how to fish and he will eat for the rest of his days." Acting on this advice, the Rockefeller and Ford Foundations have financed a number of programs for improving agriculture in the hungry nations. Known as the "Green Revolution," these programs have led to the development of "miracle rice" and "miracle wheat," new strains that offer bigger harvests and greater resistance to crop damage. Norman Borlaug, the Nobel Prize winning agronomist who, supported by the Rockefeller Foundation, developed "miracle wheat," is one of the most prominent advocates of a world food bank.

Whether or not the Green Revolution can increase food production as much as its champions claim is a debatable but possibly irrelevant point. Those who support this well-intended humanitarian effort should first consider some of the fundamentals of human ecology. Ironically, one man who did was the late Alan Gregg, a vice president of the Rockefeller Foundation. Two decades ago he expressed strong doubts about the wisdom of such attempts to increase food production. He likened the growth and spread of humanity over the surface of the earth to the spread of cancer in the human body, remarking that "cancerous growths demand food; but, as far as I know, they have never been cured by getting it."

Overloading the Environment

Every human born constitutes a draft on all aspects of the environment: food, air, water, forests, beaches, wildlife, scenery and solitude. Food can, perhaps, be significantly increased to meet a growing demand. But what about clean beaches, unspoiled forests, and solitude? If we satisfy a growing population's need for food, we necessarily decrease its per capita supply of the other resources needed by men.

India, for example, now has a population of 600 million, which increases by 15 million each year. This population already puts a huge load on a relatively impoverished environment. Thc country's forests are now only a small fraction of what they were three centuries ago and floods and erosion continually destroy the insufficient farmland that remains. Every one of the 15 million new lives added to India's population puts an additional burden on the environment, and increases the economic and social costs of crowding. However humanitarian our intent, every Indian life saved through medical or nutritional assistance from abroad diminishes the quality of life for those who remain, and for subsequent generations. If rich countries make it possible, through foreign aid, for 600 million Indians to swell to 1.2 billion in a mere 28 years, as their current growth rate threatens, will future generations of Indians thank us for hastening the destruction of their environment? Will our good intentions be sufficient excuse for the consequences of our actions?

My final example of a commons in action is one for which the public has the least desire for rational discussion—immigration. Anyone who publicly questions the wisdom of current U.S. immigration policy is promptly charged with bigotry, prejudice, ethnocentrism, chauvinism, isolationism or selfishness. Rather than encounter such accusations, one would rather talk about other matters leaving immigration policy to wallow in the crosscurrents of special interests that take no account of the good of the whole, or the interests of posterity.

Perhaps we still feel guilty about things we said in the past. Two generations ago the popular press frequently referred to Dagos, Wops, Polacks, Chinks and Krauts in articles about how America was being "overrun" by foreigners of supposedly inferior genetic stock. But because the implied inferiority of foreigners was used then as justification for keeping them out, people now assume that restrictive policies could only be based on such misguided notions. There are other grounds.

A Nation of Immigrants

Just consider the numbers involved. Our government acknowledges a net inflow of 400,000 immigrants a year. While we have no hard data on the extent of illegal entries, educated guesses put the figure at about 600,000 a year. Since the natural increase (excess of births over deaths) of the resident population now runs about 1.7 million per year, the yearly gain from immigration amounts to at least 19 percent of the total annual increase, and may be as much as 37 percent if we include the estimate for illegal immigrants. Considering the growing use of birth-control devices, the potential effect of education campaigns by such organizations as Planned Parenthood Federation of America and Zero Population Growth, and the influence of inflation and the housing shortage, the fertility rate of American women may decline so much that immigration could account for all the yearly increase in population. Should we not at least ask if that is what we want?

For the sake of those who worry about whether the "quality" of the average immigrant compares favorably with the quality of the average resident, let us assume that immigrants and native-born citizens are of exactly equal quality, however one defines that term. We will focus here only on quantity; and since our conclusions will depend on nothing else, all charges of bigotry and chauvinism become irrelevant.

Immigration Vs. Food Supply

World food banks move food to the people, hastening the exhaustion of the environment of the poor countries. Unrestricted immigration, on the other hand, moves people to the food, thus speeding up the destruction of the environment of the rich countries. We can easily understand why poor people should want to make this latter transfer, but why should rich hosts encourage it?

As in the case of foreign-aid programs, immigration receives support from selfish interests and humanitarian impulses. The primary selfish interest in unimpeded immigration is the desire of employers for cheap labor, particularly in industries and trades that offer degrading work. In the past, one wave of foreigners after another was brought into the U.S. to work at wretched jobs for wretched wages. In recent years the Cubans, Puerto Ricans and Mexicans have had this dubious honor. The interests of the employers of cheap labor mesh well with the guilty silence of the country's liberal intelligentsia. White Anglo-Saxon Protestants are particularly reluctant to call for a closing of the doors to immigration for fear of being called bigots.

But not all countries have such reluctant leadership. Most educated Hawaiians, for example, are keenly aware of the limits of their environment, particularly in terms of population growth. There is only so much room on the islands, and the islanders know it. To Hawaiians, immigrants from the other 49 states present as great a threat as those from other nations. At a recent meeting of Hawaiian government officials in Honolulu, I had the ironic delight of hearing a speaker who like most of his audience was of Japanese ancestry, ask how the country might practically and constitutionally close its doors to further immigration. One member of the audience countered: "How can we shut the doors now? We have many friends and relatives in Japan that we'd like to bring here some day so that they can enjoy Hawaii too." The Japanese-American speaker smiled sympathetically and answered: "Yes, but we have children now, and someday we'll have grandchildren too. We can bring more people here from Japan only by giving away some of the land that we hope to pass on to our grandchildren some day. What right do we have to do that?"

At this point, I can hear U.S. liberals asking: "How can you justify slamming the door once you're inside? You say that immigrants should be kept out. But aren't we all immigrants, or the descendants of immigrants? If we insist on staying, must we not admit all others?" Our craving for intellectual order leads us to seek and prefer symmetrical rules and morals: a single rule for me and everybody else; the same rule yesterday, today and tomorrow. Justice, we feel, should not change with time and place.

We Americans of non-Indian ancestry can look upon ourselves as the descendants of thieves who are guilty morally, if not legally, of stealing this land from its Indian owners. Should we then give back the land to the now living American descendants of those Indians? However morally or logically sound this proposal may be, I, for one, am unwilling to live by it and I know no one else who is. Besides, the logical consequence would be absurd. Suppose that, intoxicated with a sense of pure justice, we should decide to turn our land over to the Indians. Since all our other wealth has also been derived from the land, wouldn't we be morally obliged to give that back to the Indians too?

Pure Justice Vs. Reality

Clearly, the concept of pure justice produces an infinite regression to absurdity. Centuries ago, wise men invented statutes of limitations to justify the rejection of such pure justice, in the interest of preventing continual disorder. The law zealously defends property rights, but only relatively recent property rights. Drawing a line after an arbitrary time has elapsed may be unjust, but the alternatives are worse.

We are all the descendants of thieves, and the world's resources are inequitably distributed. But we must begin the journey to tomorrow from the point where we are today. We cannot remake the past. We cannot safely divide the wealth equitably among all peoples so long as people reproduce at different rates. To do so would guarantee that our grandchildren and everyone else's grandchildren, would have only a ruined world to inhabit.

To be generous with one's own possessions is quite different from being generous with those of posterity. We should call this point to the attention of those who from a commendable love of justice and equality, would institute a system of the commons, either in the form of a world food bank, or of unrestricted immigration. We must convince them if we wish to save at least some parts of the world from environmental ruin.

Without a true world government to control reproduction and the use of available resources, the sharing ethic of the spaceship is impossible. For the foreseeable future, our survival demands that we govern our actions by the ethics of a lifeboat, harsh though they may be. Posterity will be satisfied with nothing less.